PASCAL
Programming for Music Research

Alexander R. Brinkman

PASCAL Programming for Music Research

The University of Chicago Press Chicago and London

Alexander R. Brinkman is associate professor of music theory at the Eastman School of Music, University of Rochester

THE UNIVERSITY OF CHICAGO PRESS, CHICAGO 60637
THE UNIVERSITY OF CHICAGO PRESS, LTD., LONDON

Printed in the United States of America
00 99 98 97 96 95 94 93 92 91 90 5 4 3 2 1

This book was typeset by the author, on a design supplied by the University of Chicago Press, using the UNIX® text processing program *troff,* with the *tbl* and *eqn* preprocessors for tables and equations. Pages were formatted on a NeXT™ computer and printed on Laseredge® high-resolution paper with a NeXT™ Laser Printer. Music and graphics were prepared on a Macintosh® SE using NoteWriter® with Sonata® font and Superpaint 2.0 and printed on a Varityper VT600 laser printer.

LIBRARY OF CONGRESS CATALOGING-IN-PUBLICATION DATA

Brinkman, Alexander Russell.
Pascal programming for music research / Alexander R. Brinkman.
p. cm.
Includes bibliographical references.
ISBN 0-226-07507-9 (cloth). — ISBN 0-226-07508-7 (pbk.)
1. Music—Data processing. 2. Pascal (Computer program language)
I. Title.
ML74.B74 1990
005.26′2—dc20
89-77168
CIP
MN

The paper used in this publication meets the minimum requirements of the American National Standard for Information Sciences—Permanence of Paper for Printed Library Materials, ANSI Z39.48-1984

For Jane

Contents

Preface

The use of computers in music instruction and in composition, particularly digital music synthesis, has become widely accepted. It is perhaps less well known that much of the important work in music theory, especially the analysis of twentieth-century music, has relied heavily on techniques for modeling music and testing theories with the aid of the computer. This includes the work of Allen Forte, David Lewin, Robert Morris, John Rahn, Bo Alphonce, and Gary Wittlich, to name but a few. Indeed, a number of centers for graduate study in music, such as the Eastman School of Music, Yale University, the University of Michigan, McGill University, and the University of Wisconsin at Madison, include computing courses in their curricula, and the day will come when music researchers are expected as a matter of course to be able to use the computer as a tool in their work.

Because Pascal fosters clarity through use of structured programming techniques, it is an ideal language for learning modern programming concepts. For a number of years it has been the language of choice for teaching students of computer science, and the skills learned in Pascal programming transfer readily to other algorithmic languages, such as C. Pascal has become widely used in industry and business, and is available for virtually every system from microcomputers to mainframes.

Although many books on Pascal programming are available today, none has been designed specifically for use by musicians, and no text has dealt rigorously with the special problems inherent in computer processing of music data for theoretic and musicologic research.

This book was written for those involved in computer-assisted music research and for those who wish to develop the requisite skills to begin work in the field. It can be used as a textbook for the classroom or self-instruction, as a reference manual, or as a "cookbook" of ideas and techniques. I have used the material presented here in an introductory course for graduate students in music and in seminars for Ph.D. candidates in music theory. While the intended audience is professionals and students in music theory, musicology, composition, and education, I have used it successfully with performance majors and undergraduate students with a strong interest in computing.

When I began writing this book in 1985, I had been teaching computing techniques for music research for over ten years, using standard computing textbooks supplemented with materials of my own design. Many of my students urged me to write a book that integrated music and programming—that presented illustrations and exercises relevant to their interests and experience; this is the result. The book addresses several needs: (1) it provides a complete exposition of the Pascal programming language; (2) it integrates algorithm design, language syntax, and music-programming techniques; (3) it contains much information on music encoding, internal representations, and computation techniques; (4) it provides a comprehensive introduction to applied data structures; (5) it provides programming tools and techniques for processing music data that will be valuable to music researchers in many areas of study.

My goal is to teach sound programming techniques that could be applied to many different fields, but with an emphasis on music research. The text uses music problems as a vehicle for teaching programming, and computer programming as a tool for solving music problems. I cover the range from elementary programming through advanced topics such as linked data structures, recursive algorithms, DARMS translation, and score processing. The twenty chapters of the book are grouped into three sections.

Part 1, *Getting Started*, is an introduction to computers, Pascal programming, music encoding, and algorithm design. The first chapter uses an imaginary computer to introduce basic concepts: the parts of a computer, computer instructions, machine code, and assembly-language programming. The purpose is to give the reader some understanding of how a computer works, and to introduce important concepts such as the use of variables to represent data, the nature of computer instructions, basic programming concepts, the distinction between low-level instructions and high-level languages, and the functions of compilers and language interpreters. The second chapter, an overview of the Pascal programming language, serves two purposes. First, it provides a quick introduction so that readers who have programmed in other languages can begin to use Pascal immediately. For the novice, this chapter introduces many new concepts and provides a contextual framework for material in chapters to follow.

Chapters 3 through 5 are a detailed introduction to Pascal: the basic elements of Pascal and simple (unstructured) data types, an introduction to input and output, and the control statements used to structure the program flow. Chapter 6 introduces several methods of encoding music data. The first part of the chapter introduces simple numeric codes for pitch and duration that can be used immediately by novice programmers, and that form the basis of more complex internal representations used later in the book. The latter part of the chapter introduces DARMS, a music encoding language that can represent virtually all aspects of the printed score, and some features of Leland Smith's SCORE code, which has been widely used in computer music synthesis. Chapter 7 is an introduction to algorithms, with an emphasis on top-down methods, stepwise refinement, and other aspects of the design of well-structured programs. These techniques are illustrated by solutions to a series of simple problems that employ numeric music codes introduced in the previous chapter. Chapter 8 gives more detailed information on input and output in Pascal; while chapter 9 introduces functions and procedures, with an emphasis on their use in structured programming.

Part 2, *Structured Types*, introduces Pascal's structured data types. Chapters 10 through 14 detail the use of arrays, set types, record types, and file types. Two chapters are devoted to the use of arrays for processing lists and character strings, implementing stacks and queues, creating lookup tables, representing matrices, etc. These chapters discuss many important topics, including sorting and searching methods and measurement of efficiency in programs, and they present various algorithms that are generally useful in working with arrays. Again, music problems are used to illustrate many principles, and programming techniques are applied to substantial problems, e.g., interpreting DARMS pitch and rhythm codes, and using records to implement fractions for the precise representation of music durations. Chapter 15 is a thorough treatment of recursive algorithms; illustrations include the interpretation of nested grouplets, algorithms for calculating combinations and permutations that can be applied to many fields in addition to music, an algorithm for threading mazes, and a recursive version of the *quicksort* algorithm. Chapter 16, a comprehensive introduction to linked data structures, includes uses of tree structures and an introduction to hashing, which is applied to a thematic catalogue program.

Part 3, *Applications*, consists of four chapters that present larger application programs. Each of these chapters discusses more advanced techniques, which are then used in complete programs along with techniques introduced earlier. Advanced topics include prime-form/normal-order algorithms, searching matrices (with interactive screen graphics), and generating the correct spelling for music structures (intervals, scales, diatonic and chromatic chords, etc.). These chapters also introduce a number of important techniques: using binary numbers for efficient processing of pitch class sets; generating random numbers; and generalizing the calculation of intervals and pitches to include pitch class, octave, and spelling. The final chapter presents a multilinked data structure for representing music scores in the computer memory, and several sample analysis programs using the structure. These programs perform pitch-class set analysis (with various segmentation criteria), tonal harmonic analysis, melodic pattern searches, and graphic representation of scores. The score input to the analysis programs is the output from a DARMS code interpreter, portions of which are used for illustrations throughout the test.

Appendices include the complete listing of the DARMS interpreter, a library of procedures for building and manipulating the linked score structure, and the complete listings of the programs discussed in chapter 20. All of these programs are useful for study, and can be used as the basis for further work in the field. In particular, the DARMS translator and linked data structure will be valuable tools for those working in computer-assisted music research.

The book contains many complete programs, from short illustrations to programs several thousand lines in length. I have tried to make all programs correct in both structure and function. The novice can learn good programming style by studying the programs in the text and using them as models. A great deal can be learned by studying the larger programs in detail, and advanced users will benefit by trying to improve and extend them.

At the end of each chapter I have included a list of references and selected readings. These are not intended to be exhaustive. They include sources that were referenced in the chapter, and a sampling of useful books and articles that are directly related to the topics covered in the chapter. Many chapters also cite a number of suggested readings, representative articles from the field of computer-assisted music research and related fields, that are included to familiarize the reader with the primary literature.

It is difficult to learn a subject as complex as programming just by reading about it, without actively practicing the discipline. The syntax of the language is easy; learning how to think about problems and designing elegant solutions are more difficult. The novice is urged to modify and extend the illustrations in the text, and to write as many programs as time permits. While short programs are beneficial and necessary in the beginning, one can learn more by designing and writing a large application than by writing several shorter ones; hence the student is urged to attempt larger exercises as soon as he or she is ready. Each chapter includes exercises that are designed for independent study as well as for use in a programming course. Although I have not included solutions, many of the exercises use or extend techniques discussed thoroughly in the text, and some programs are partially solved (for example, in some cases the logical division of the problem into separate processes is suggested and some key procedures are provided). As the student becomes more proficient, he or she is encouraged to design programs related directly to specific areas of interest. Since my primary field, and that of many of my students, is music theory, many exercises and illustrations are related to that discipline. But I have included examples and exercises in other areas as well. For example, there are exercises that deal with constructing incipit catalogues, and chapter 19 presents a substantial application in computer-assisted instruction.

This book was prepared and typeset on a personal computer under the UNIX operating system. For the most part, working programs and input/output files were copied directly into the text from external files. Interactive work sessions were recorded with a program called *script*, which records both what the user types and the computer's response. This material was then used in the final typesetting of the book. Thus programs, input and output files, and work sessions were never retyped. While minimal editing was necessary to insert font changes, etc., this method of working has obvious advantages over retyping in terms of accuracy.

All of the programs in this book were written on on a personal computer with a small hard disk and 512K memory. The system ran a version of the UNIX operating system and was limited to 64K per process. While a small system such as this is sufficient for developing and testing algorithms, productive work using the score structure described in chapter 20 really requires a more powerful system, such as current 32-bit personal computers, workstations, or larger systems.

In the past, progress in the field of computer-assisted music analysis has been hindered by a lack of adequate tools. Each researcher has had to begin practically from scratch, inventing or reinventing computational methods before any real analysis could take place. More often than not, published materials reported results but said little about the methods used to get them. Several years ago I came to the conclusion that in order to accomplish the types of projects that interested me, I first had to develop the software tools necessary to do the job right—generalized methods of representing music scores within the computer that could be used as a starting point for many types of analytic work, efficient algorithms, and data structures for manipulating music data. This development effort is a continuing research interest. Nonetheless, while the data structures and methods presented in this book should not be considered a final, finished product, in their present state of development they are sufficient for many research projects. One of my primary goals in writing this book was to make these software tools available to other music scholars.

Acknowledgments

I began writing this book during a sabbatical leave from the Eastman School of Music, University of Rochester, in the autumn of 1985. I am grateful to Robert Freeman, director of the school, for his continuing support of my professional goals.

I also thank all of my students at the Eastman School of Music who tolerated early versions of this material and contributed to this work through discussion and criticism and by testing many ideas in their own work.

I wish to thank Stefan Kostka, who first interested me in computing almost twenty years ago, and who allowed me to use modified versions of some of his exercises in this text; and Chris Brown and Joel Seiferas of the University of Rochester computer science department, who taught me to be more rigorous in my approach.

I am grateful to Allen Forte of Yale University for his friendship and for his interest in my work. Robert Morris, my colleague at Eastman, has been more than generous with his advice on all aspects of my work, serving as an invaluable source of inspiration and information. I am also indebted to the following for their encouragement and helpful suggestions at various times: Bruce Benward, Robert W. Gross, Steven Haflich, John W. Schaffer, Wayne Slawson, James L. Snell, and Gary E. Wittlich. I owe special thanks to Bo Alphonce, who read the entire manuscript with great care and offered innumerable suggestions for improvement of content and style; and to Brian Alegant for his assistance in proofreading the book in its final form.

Bruce Campbell, David Headlam, Edwin Hantz, and Kerala Snyder, all past or present colleagues at Eastman, have audited my course and offered useful suggestions and encouragement.

Several students have contributed directly. The initial work on the DARMS interpreter and score structure was done in a Ph.D. seminar in the spring of 1982. Although these programs have grown and developed a great deal since that time, I wish to acknowledge the considerable contribution made by three members of the seminar—Nola Reed Knouse, Dean Billmeyer, and Jane Sawyer Brinkman. I am also grateful to the following, whose work is presented in modified form in chapter 20: Robert Fink, Jane Sawyer Brinkman, Rhonda Wright, Michael Votta, and Richard Elliott.

I am indebted to superb assistance from the professional staff at the University of Chicago Press.

I wish to thank *Journal of Music Theory* and *Music Theory Spectrum* for permission to include material from published articles in the present volume. I am also grateful to the following publishers for permission to reprint music excerpts under their copyright: Associated Music Publishers; Belmont Publishers; Boosey & Hawkes; Edizioni Suvini Zerboni, Milan; and European American Music Distributors Corporation (representing Universal Edition, Vienna).

I am grateful to my parents, Alix R. Palmer and Robert E. Brinkman, for teaching me that difficult goals can be obtained through perseverance and hard work, and that the rewards for striving toward a goal are as great as those for attaining it.

Finally, I am eternally indebted to my wife, Jane Sawyer Brinkman who read several revisions of much of the material, caught many errors of detail, and made numerous suggestions for improving the manuscript. Without her love, patience, and support, I could not have written this book.

PART I Getting Started

1 | Introduction

The purpose of this chapter is to introduce you to the computer. We will design a simple computer with a small instruction set, write some short programs, and "execute" them by stepping through the programs manually. The purpose is not to teach computer design, or machine-level or assembly-language programming. Rather, it is to introduce a number of important concepts that will help you to understand what is going on inside your computer when you run a program. We want you to realize that the useful results you get when you run a program come from a carefully designed sequence of instructions. We will discuss the nature of a program, the relationship between data and machine instructions, the use of variables to represent values, and input and output from a computer. In addition, we will discuss the differences among machine language, assembly language, and high-level programming languages, and why the last-mentioned are necessary. Finally, we will address various categories of software in a typical computer system.

1.1 Binary Numbers

A computer is an electronic device, and since it is easier and cheaper to build electronic components that recognize two states (on and off) rather than ten, values are stored in binary form within the computer. Binary numbers use only two binary digits or *bits*, 1 and 0. These can be used to represent any condition that has two states, e.g., true and false, the presence or absence of *pixels*[1] in a bit map of the computer screen, or digits in a binary representation of a number. Learning to read binary notation is not difficult. Just as in decimal (base ten) notation, each digit in a binary number has a positional weight. Since the number base or *radix* is two, the positional weight is a power of 2. The rightmost bit has a positional weight of $2^0 = 1$, the next bit has a weight of $2^1 = 2$, the next bit $2^2 = 4$, and so on. The value of a binary number is the sum of each bit times its positional weight. For example, 101011_2 is equal to 43_{10}, as shown in table 1.1.[2] Note that in the table the bits are evaluated from right to left.

1. Pixels, or picture elements, are the dots used to form images on the computer screen.

2. Here we use subscripts to indicate the number base or radix, i.e., 101_2 is the decimal value 5_{10}, while 101_{10} (one hundred one) is equal to 1100101_2.

		101011_2				
$=$		1×2^0	$=$	1×1	$=$	1
	$+$	1×2^1	$=$	1×2	$=$	2
	$+$	0×2^2	$=$	0×4	$=$	0
	$+$	1×2^3	$=$	1×8	$=$	8
	$+$	0×2^4	$=$	0×16	$=$	0
	$+$	1×2^5	$=$	1×32	$=$	32
$=$			43_{10}			

Table 1.1. Converting a Binary Number to Decimal

A decimal number is converted to binary by successive division by 2. After each step the remainder is the next binary digit, and the quotient becomes the new dividend. The process is continued until the quotient is 0. Table 1.2 illustrates the process of converting decimal 13 to binary 1101.

Computer memory is divided into segments called *words*, each of which has the same number of bits. Common word sizes in small computers are 8 bits (a *byte*), 16 bits, and 32 bits. It is obvious that the maximum value of a number is limited by the number of bits used to represent the number. The largest integer that can be stored using n bits is $2^n - 1$. For instance, the largest number that can be stored in 4 bits is $2^4 - 1 = 15$. For reasons that need not concern us here, negative integers are usually stored internally using the one's complement or two's complement. In one's complement the value of each bit is inverted. Thus, with 8 bits, the integer 5 is represented by 00000101, while –5 is represented as 11111010. In two's complement 1 is added to the one's complement representation. In either case, the leftmost bit is 0 in a positive number and 1 in a negative number. Because this bit is used to distinguish between negative and positive, it cannot be used as a significant digit in representing the number. Thus, in a computer that uses n-bit words to store integers, the largest number is $2^{n-1} - 1$.

Internally real numbers, e.g., 4.7891, are stored in a form different from that used for integers. These usually occupy two words, one for the mantissa and one for the exponent.

	Quotient	*Remainder*	
$13 \div 2$	6	1	(the 2^0 bit)
$6 \div 2$	3	0	(the 2^1 bit)
$3 \div 2$	1	1	(the 2^2 bit)
$1 \div 2$	0	1	(the 2^3 bit)
	Thus, $13_{10} = 1101_2$		

Table 1.2. Converting Decimal 13 to Binary

1.2 A Simple Computer

In this section we will describe a simple computer and its instruction set. The system described here is too limited to be of general use and does not represent an actual computer, but it will be helpful for learning something about how a computer works. A computer system consists of hardware and software. The term *hardware* denotes the physical components of the computer, consisting of the computer proper (central processing unit, or CPU, and primary memory) and *peripherals*—input/output devices and secondary storage (hard disks, floppy disk drives, tape drives, etc.). *Software* is a general term that refers to all of the programs that make the computer do useful things.

Hardware. The basic components of a typical computer are shown in figure 1.1. The *input device* may be any hardware device that can be used to enter external data into the computer. This may be a card reader, a keyboard, such as the one on the user's terminal, or a tape or disk drive.

The *output device* is used for getting computed results from the computer. This could be a printer, a tape or disk drive, or the cathode ray tube (CRT) screen on a computer terminal. For our demonstration we will assume that input and output (I/O) take place through a computer terminal, i.e., the keyboard is the input device and the CRT screen is the output device.

The term "memory" has been used in different meanings in recent usage. The *main memory* or *primary memory* consists of memory chips on a memory board and is a primary component of the computer. Computer programs and data are stored in main memory while a program is being executed, and the CPU can interact directly with this memory. The term *secondary memory* is sometimes used for external storage devices, such as hard disks, floppy disks, and tape drives. (The distinction has become somewhat blurred since more sophisticated computers have *virtual memory* capability, that means that they can treat areas on the hard disk as primary memory.) In this chapter we will use the term memory as a synonym for main memory.

The computer's memory is divided into *words* that are numbered from 0 to $n - 1$, where the total number of words is n. Since each storage location can be accessed

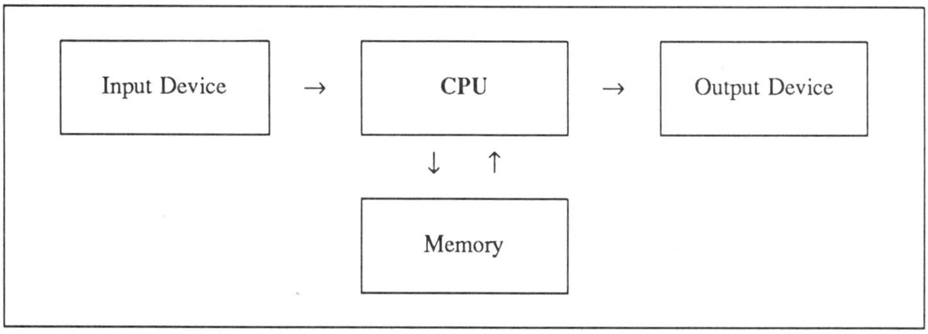

Figure 1.1. A Simple Computer

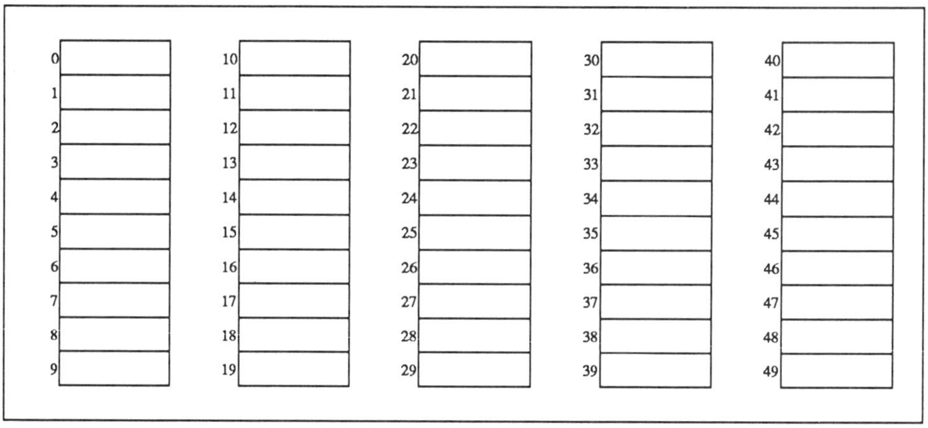

Figure 1.2. Main Memory

directly by its numeric *address*, memory is often referred to as *random access memory*, or RAM. Figure 1.2 illustrates part of our computer's memory. Although the addresses are shown as decimal numbers in the diagram, the words are actually addressed by binary numbers in the computer. In our demonstration machine each word contains 16 bits of information. Each memory location can store binary numbers that may represent instructions or data, which are indistinguishable except from context, as we shall see presently. Memory is characterized by the terms *destructive read-in* and *nondestructive read-out*. This means that the value in a storage location can be examined or copied to another location without changing its value, but when a new value is put into a storage location, it writes over the value stored there, and the old value is lost.

The *central processing unit* (CPU) is the heart of the computer. It controls the execution of program instructions and the interaction of all other parts of the computer. It can cause values to be read from the input device and stored in memory, perform computations using values in memory, and cause values in memory to be printed on the output device.

The CPU—illustrated in figure 1.3—contains a *control unit*, an *arithmetic and logic unit*, and a number of *registers*. Registers are memory locations with special properties and functions. The control unit (CU) contains two registers called the *instruction register* (IR) and *instruction counter* (IC). The IR contains the current

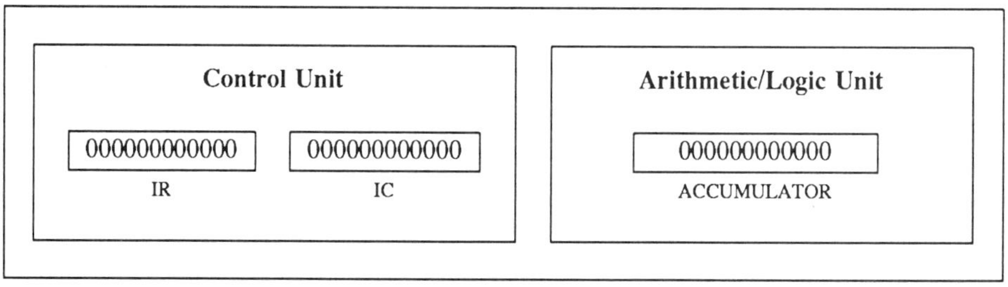

Figure 1.3. The Central Processing Unit

instruction, and the IC the address of the next instruction to be executed. The *arithmetic and logic unit* (ALU) performs arithmetic operations and has simple decision-making capabilities, i.e., it can test values resulting from computations and take specific actions as the result of these values.

The Instruction Set. Every computer has a basic set of operations it can perform based on its set of primitive instructions. The ability to perform these basic instructions is built into the computer. A typical micro- or minicomputer may have well over a hundred instructions in its instruction set. Our simple computer, which has much more limited capabilities, has 15 instructions in its repertoire. These instructions are shown in table 1.3. We will use the decimal and binary form of the instructions to illustrate machine-level programs. The mnemonic form of the instructions is used in assembly language (explained later in this chapter).

Within the computer, instructions are stored in numeric form. Although the computer actually uses binary numbers, we will use decimal numbers for simplicity. Instructions consist of two parts, the instruction number and an address. For our illustration we will use six-digit decimal numbers, in which the first two digits represent the instruction and the last four the address. For example, the instruction 050030 causes the computer to read (instruction 05) a value from the input device and store it in memory location 30. The instruction 060030 means to print (06) the value in memory location 30 on the output device.

All arithmetic operations are performed in the ALU. The instruction 070031 means clear the *accumulator* (place the value 0 in the register) and add the value stored in storage location 31. This has the effect of putting the number in storage location 31 into the accumulator. Now we can perform additional arithmetic operations on this number. For example, the instruction 080032 means add (08) the value

Decimal	*Binary*	*Mnemonic*	*Meaning*	*Argument*
00	0000	HLT	Halt	none (0)
01	0001	NEG	Negate	none (0)
02	0010	INC	Increment	none (0)
03	0011	DCR	Decrement	none (0)
04	0100	LDA	Load Accumulator	number
05	0101	RST	Read and Store	address
06	0110	PRT	Print	address
07	0111	CLA	Clear and Add	address
08	1000	ADD	Add	address
09	1001	SUB	Subtract	address
10	1010	MUL	Multiply	address
11	1011	DIV	Divide	address
12	1100	STO	Store	address
13	1101	JMP	Jump	address
14	1110	JPN	Jump on Negative	address

Table 1.3. A Simple Instruction Set

stored in memory location 32 to the value in the accumulator. This action, which results in a new value in the accumulator, might be followed by 100040—multiply (10) the number in the accumulator by the value in storage location 40, and so on. When the desired final or intermediate result has been calculated, it can be stored (12) in memory, say at address 41, by the instruction 120041.

Some of the instructions in the instruction set do not require an address. For these we will use zeros in the address portion of the instruction. One example is *halt* (00), which means to terminate execution of a program. Other instructions in this group affect the value in the accumulator. For example, *negate* (01) changes the sign of the number in the accumulator, and *increment* (02) adds one to the value in the accumulator. Each of these instructions is specified with zeros in the address portion:

```
000000 halt
010000 negate value in accumulator
020000 increment accumulator
030000 decrement accumulator
```

Our simple computer has one additional instruction for a value in the accumulator. For this instruction, the address portion of the instruction is replaced by a literal number. For example, 040010 means clear the accumulator and then load the value 10. This instruction is provided as a means of initializing values in storage locations without reading from the input device. Thus we can insert the integer 1 in storage location 50 by the instructions

```
040001 load accumulator with 1
120050 store result in location 50
```

Storage locations can be initialized with negative numbers by loading a positive value in the accumulator, negating it, and then storing it in memory.[3]

Now that we have a basic vocabulary of instructions, we need to see how the computer executes these instructions. We will write a simple program that reads two numbers and then calculates and prints their product. The necessary steps are:

1. Read two numbers
2. Calculate their product
3. Print the result

In order to solve this problem we will need to choose specific storage locations for storing the program and the values read. (Remember that input values are stored in memory before they are entered into the accumulator.) We will need three storage locations to store values, say memory locations 30, 31, and 32. Using only the operations specified above, the problem can be solved by the following sequence of instructions:

3. I have not allowed for loading values directly into memory to avoid the complication of instructions that require more than one word of memory.

1. Read the 1st number and store it in memory location 30
2. Read the 2d number and store it in memory location 31
3. Clear the accumulator and add the number from location 30
4. Multiply by the value from memory location 31
5. Store the result in memory location 32
6. Print the value in memory location 32 on the output device
7. Halt execution

The numeric form of these instructions appears as follows:

050030 050031 070030 100031 120032 060032 000000

These instructions are entered into consecutive memory locations, beginning at some arbitrary location, say storage location 11. Thus the program is stored as numbers in storage locations 11 through 17. Now we enter the starting address in the instruction counter of the control unit. The current values in the CPU and memory are shown in figure 1.4. Normally instructions are executed sequentially by memory locations. Remember that the instruction counter (IC) always contains the address of the next instruction to be executed, and the instruction register (IR) contains the current instruction. When we press the "start" button, three things occur:

1. The instruction in location 11 is loaded into the IR
2. The IC is set to the next value, 12
3. The instruction in the IR is executed

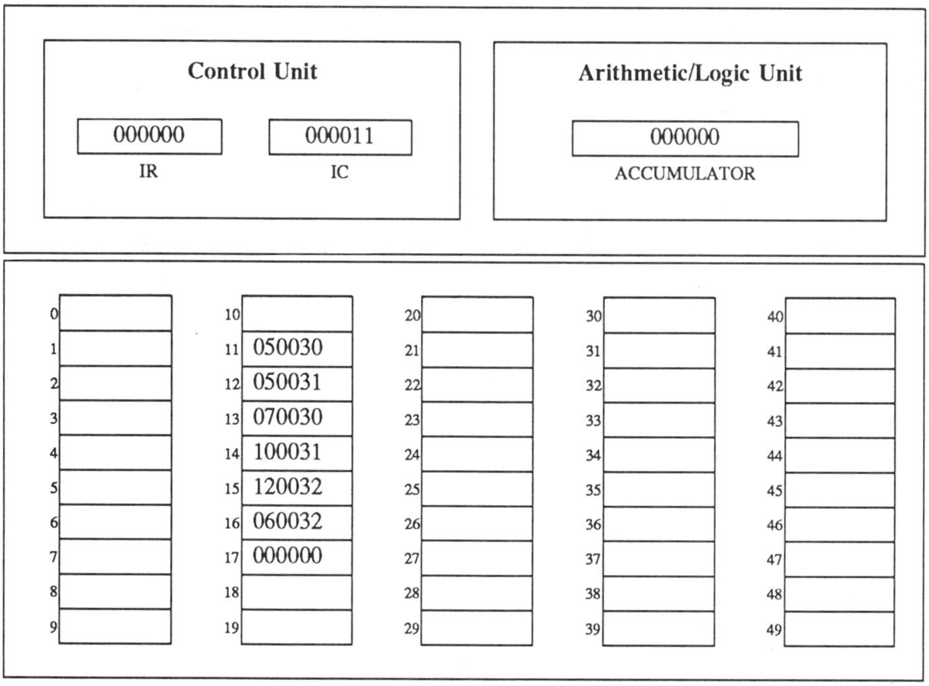

Figure 1.4. The CPU and Main Memory

The current instruction (050030) causes the first number on the input device to be read and stored in memory location 30. Suppose we type the number 17 on the terminal keyboard. This number is read by the computer and stored in memory location 30. Now the three steps listed above are repeated, using the next value in the IC:

1. The instruction in location 12 is loaded into the IR
2. The IC is set to the next value, 13
3. The instruction in the IR is executed

This instruction (050031) causes the computer to read the next number typed on the keyboard, say 5, and to store it in storage location 31. The process is repeated for each additional instruction. The instruction in memory location 13 causes the number 17 in location 30 to be loaded into the accumulator. The next instruction (from location 14) causes the number in the accumulator (17) to be multiplied by the number in storage location 31 (value 5), producing the product 85. The next instruction (from location 15) causes the result in the accumulator to be stored in memory location 32, and the next (from location 16) to print it on the output device (the CRT screen). At this point the IC contains address 17. Now the *halt* instruction (000000) is loaded into the IR, the IC is incremented to 18, and the *halt* instruction is executed. This instruction terminates the execution cycle and the computer stops. Fortunately, this whole process takes place in a few milliseconds—much less time than it takes to read about it.

If this were all the computer could do, programming would not be a worthwhile activity. The power of the computer lies not only in its ability to execute instructions rapidly, but also in its ability to repeat a closed loop of instructions an arbitrary number of times. In a machine-language program a loop is created with the *jump* instruction (13). Suppose we change the final *halt* instruction in memory location 17 to

130011 (jump to memory location 11)

Let's backtrack a bit, to the point where the print instruction in location 16 has just been performed and the IC is set to 17. Now the instruction in location 17 is loaded into the IR, the IC is set to 18, and the jump instruction (130011) is executed. This instruction resets the IC to 11. Now the instruction cycle repeats, starting over at the beginning of the program (memory location 11). This creates a loop that will execute again and again until no more data is supplied. We will assume that the computer is capable of generating a *halt* instruction automatically when the end of data is reached.

Assembly Language. Programming in the numeric language of the computer is not difficult, but it is tedious. Remember that the numbers probably would not be entered as decimal numbers. The program shown above (with the loop) would appear as follows in binary:[4]

4. Here we use the first four bits for the instruction and the next twelve bits for the address. The program is again stored in memory locations 11–17, i.e., 0000000000001011 through 0000000000010001, and locations 30–32 (000000011110 through 000000100000) are used for storing values.

Address	*Instruction*
0000000000001011	0101000000011110
0000000000001100	0101000000011111
0000000000001101	0111000000011110
0000000000001110	1010000000011111
0000000000001111	1100000000100000
0000000000010000	0110000000100000
0000000000010001	1101000000001011

Since these values can be entered into the computer and executed directly, programs in this numeric form are called *machine-language* programs.

Early programmers programmed computers using numeric instructions such as those shown above. Fortunately, it was not long before someone realized that there was an easier way. Instructions could be represented by mnemonic combinations of letters that represented the numeric instruction used within the computer. In order to accomplish this, it was useful to use symbolic names for certain addresses as well. Symbolic names for memory locations containing instructions are called *labels.* Symbolic names for memory locations that contain data are called *variables*, since the values they represent may change. The program shown just above can be represented using symbolic names for instructions, addresses, and variables as follows:

```
START:  RST   A       ; read 1st value
        RST   B       ; read 2d value
        CLA   A       ; place 1st value in accumulator
        MUL   B       ; multiply by 2d value
        STO   C       ; store result
        PRT   C       ; print result
        JMP   START   ; jump to START
```

Note that the statements in this program correlate exactly to the machine-language program shown above. Comments, from ';' to the end of the line, are not part of the program. A language such as this is called an *assembly language*. A special program called an *assembler* translates the symbolic code into machine language, i.e., it assembles the executable code. The assembler finds a set of available contiguous memory locations in which to store the program and data, and builds a *symbol table*, which associates the symbolic names for variables and labels with the appropriate memory locations. If it is assumed that the assembler stores the program and data in the same memory locations used above, the symbol table would contain the following data (here we return to decimal values for the convenience of the reader):

Symbol	*Address*
START	0011
A	0030
B	0031
C	0032

Simple Decisions. The programs shown thus far omit one important capability of the computer—the ability to make decisions based on the value of data or calculations. We will illustrate with a program that reads pairs of numbers representing pitches and calculates the interval between them. For input data we will number the keys on the piano consecutively, with middle C = 48, C-sharp = D-flat = 49, etc.[5] The input data will be pairs of numbers representing pitches. The interval, *I*, between any two pitches *A* and *B* is the difference (*B* – *A*), with the sign indicating direction (negative is down). Now suppose that we wish to calculate this interval and print it, but we also want to print the pitch-class interval. Pitch-class intervals are always positive and in the range between 0 and 11.[6] We define the pitch-class interval based on interval *I* as follows:

> If *I* is negative, add 12 until it becomes positive;
> otherwise, if *I* is greater than 11, subtract 12 until it is not.

The basic steps needed to solve the problem follow:

1. Read integers *A* and *B*
2. Calculate interval *I* as *B* – *A*
3. Print interval *I*
4. Calculate pitch-class interval
5. Print the pitch-class interval
6. Repeat from step 1 for next set of integers

We will work in our pseudo assembly code. Since we will need the values 12 and 11 repeatedly, we will begin by placing these in two storage locations called *T* and *E*, respectively.

```
START:  LDA  12      ; place 12 in accumulator
        STO  T       ; store in variable T
        DCR          ; subtract 1 from value in accumulator
        STO  E       ; store result in variable E
```

Now we read pitches *A* and *B* and store them. We will label this statement because we will need to jump to it to repeat the calculation for successive pairs of numbers.

```
READ:   RST  A       ; read first pitch
        RST  B       ; read second pitch
```

We now calculate interval *I* as the difference *B* – *A* and print the interval.

```
        CLA  B       ; enter B in accumulator
        SUB  A       ; subtract A
        STO  I       ; store result in I
        PRT  I       ; print interval
```

5. Note that the integer representing each C is a multiple of 12, i.e., 0, 12, 24, 36, 48, etc., represent C in each octave.

6. See chapter 6 for more information on music representations.

We now need a new technique. The instruction JPN (jump if negative) provides a conditional branch in the program. If the number in the accumulator is negative, the instruction counter is set to the new location (as in the unconditional jump). If the value in the accumulator is 0 or positive, the instruction counter is incremented so that the next instruction will be executed in sequence. We will use this instruction to branch to another program segment labeled LOW, leaving for the moment the next statements in sequence.

```
        JPN   LOW      ; if negative jump to LOW
                       ; fill this in later
```

At LOW, we add 12 (the value of variable *T*) to the interval in the accumulator. We then test the value again and, if it is still negative, repeat the process. This is accomplished in the following loop:

```
LOW:    ADD   T        ; add 12
        JPN   LOW      ; until number is positive
```

Now the pitch-class interval in the accumulator is stored in variable *I* and printed. Then we loop back to READ to process the next pair of numbers.

```
        STO   I        ; store interval
        PRT   I        ; print interval
        JMP   READ     ; process next set
```

We must now provide the instructions that will be necessary if the original interval is positive. Two possibilities remain: (a) the interval is greater than 11; or (b) the interval is in the range 0–11. We do not have an instruction to test directly whether the number in the accumulator is greater than 11, but we can determine whether $11 - I$ is less than 0, which amounts to the same thing. We can perform this test by placing 11 (variable *E*) in the accumulator and subtracting *I*. If the result is negative, then the value of *I* is too big, otherwise we can print *I* and loop back to the beginning of the program. Since we will need to make this test more than once, we label the instruction.

```
TEST:   CLA   E        ; place 11 in accumulator
        SUB   I        ; subtract interval
        JPN   HIGH     ; interval is greater than 11
                       ; interval in range
        PRT   I        ; print it
        JMP   READ     ; process next set
```

We now complete the program by writing the segment that subtracts 12 from *I*. After this is accomplished, we test to see if the process needs to be repeated:

```
HIGH:   CLA   I        ; place interval in accumulator
        SUB   T        ; subtract 12
        STO   I        ; store result in I
        JMP   TEST     ; test again
```

The entire program is listed as program 1.1. Note that this is not the only sequence of instructions that could solve this problem; many variations are possible.

```
; program reads pairs of integers representing pitches, calculates and prints the interval between
; them, and then calculates the pitch-class interval and prints it
;
START:  LDA  12     ; place 12 in accumulator
        STO  T      ; store in variable T
        DCR         ; subtract 1 from value in accumulator
        STO  E      ; store result in variable E
                    ;
READ:   RST  A      ; read first pitch
        RST  B      ; read second pitch
        CLA  B      ; enter B in accumulator
        SUB  A      ; subtract A
        STO  I      ; store result in I
        PRT  I      ; print interval
        JPN  LOW    ; if negative jump to LOW
                    ;
TEST:   CLA  E      ; place 11 in accumulator
        SUB  I      ; subtract interval
        JPN  HIGH   ; if negative, interval is greater than 11
                    ; interval is in range
        PRT  I      ; print it
        JMP  READ   ; process next set
                    ;
HIGH:   CLA  I      ; place interval in accumulator
        SUB  T      ; subtract 12
        STO  I      ; store result in I
        JMP  TEST   ; test again
                    ;
LOW:    ADD  T      ; add 12
        JPN  LOW    ; until number is positive
        STO  I      ; store interval
        PRT  I      ; print interval
        JMP  READ   ; process next set
```

Program 1.1. Interval Calculation in Assembly Language

Figure 1.5 illustrates this program in memory (using decimal numbers). Assume that the program is stored in memory locations 10 through 34, and that storage locations 40 through 44 are used for variables *T*, *E*, *A*, *B*, and *I* respectively. Table 1.4 represents the symbol table showing the correspondence between variable names and labels and their corresponding addresses in memory.

As an exercise, draw boxes representing the instruction register (IR), instruction counter (IC), accumulator, and variable locations *T*, *E*, *A*, *B*, and *I*. Then place the address 10 in the IC, make up some sample values, and "execute" the program carefully, step by step. You will find it much easier to use the mnemonic (assembly) version of the program.

0		10	040012	20	140030	30	080040	40	(T)
1		11	120040	21	070041	31	140030	41	(E)
2		12	030000	22	090044	32	120044	42	(A)
3		13	120041	23	140026	33	060044	43	(B)
4		14	050042	24	060044	34	130014	44	(I)
5		15	050043	25	130014	35		45	
6		16	070043	26	070044	36		46	
7		17	090042	27	090040	37		47	
8		18	120044	28	120044	38		48	
9		19	060044	29	130021	39		49	

Figure 1.5. Interval Program in Main Memory

Symbol	*Address*
A	0042
B	0043
E	0041
HIGH	0026
I	0044
LOW	0030
READ	0014
START	0010
T	0040
TEST	0021

Table 1.4. Location of Variables and Labels in Interval Program

1.3 High-Level Languages

While early programmers routinely wrote programs in machine language or assembly language, and some programs are still written in these languages when the programmer wants total control over the manner in which his program is implemented, there are drawbacks. The most important of these is that the machine instructions and assembly language for each computer are different. Another is that this level of abstraction is pretty far removed from the types of ideas that we usually wish to express in a program. Both of these problems are solved by high-level languages such as Pascal. High-level languages allow program statements that would require many separate instructions in machine or assembly code, and provide more sophisticated means for controlling the order in which statements are executed. Program 1.2 is a Pascal version of the interval calculation program from the previous section. Comments are enclosed in braces and are not actually part of the program. The Pascal program is much easier to read and understand than the machine- and assembly-language versions, and it could be run without change on any computer that supports the Pascal programming language.

```
program interval(input, output);
  var
    firstnote  : integer;                 { continuous pitch code       }
    secondnote : integer;                 { continuous pitch code       }
    interval   : integer;                 { interval between them       }

  begin { main }
    while not eof do                      { until end of input file     }
      begin { process interval }
        readln(firstnote, secondnote);    { read two pitches            }
        interval := secondnote - firstnote; { calculate real interval   }
        writeln(interval);                { print it                    }
        writeln(interval mod 12)          { calc and print pc int       }
      end  { process interval }
  end.  { main }
```

Program 1.2. Pascal Version of Interval Calculation Program

A *compiler* is a program that generates an executable program, called an *object* program, from a *source* program written in a high-level language. Typically, the translation takes place in two steps. The program is parsed into logical tokens (symbols, identifiers, operators, etc.) and checked for syntax errors. If there are errors, the user is notified and compilation is terminated. Errors of this type are called *compile-time errors.* If no errors are detected, the program is translated into the native machine language for the computer. Frequently the program is first translated into assembly language and then an assembler generates the machine code. Remember that a compiler generates a complete executable program in machine code and that once this code has been created it can be executed any number of times without recompiling unless the programmer wishes to make a change in the program. The compiling process is diagrammed in figure 1.6.

The object program is executed, using external data provided by the user if required. The program performs its designated task and produces output that is

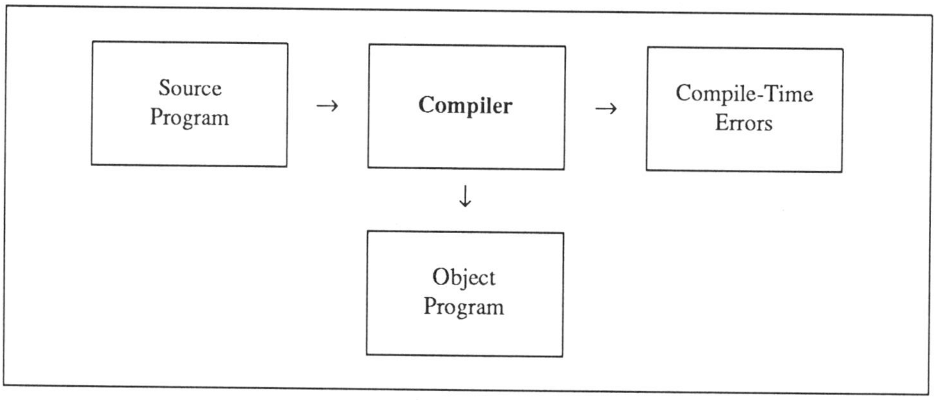

Figure 1.6. Compiling a Pascal Program

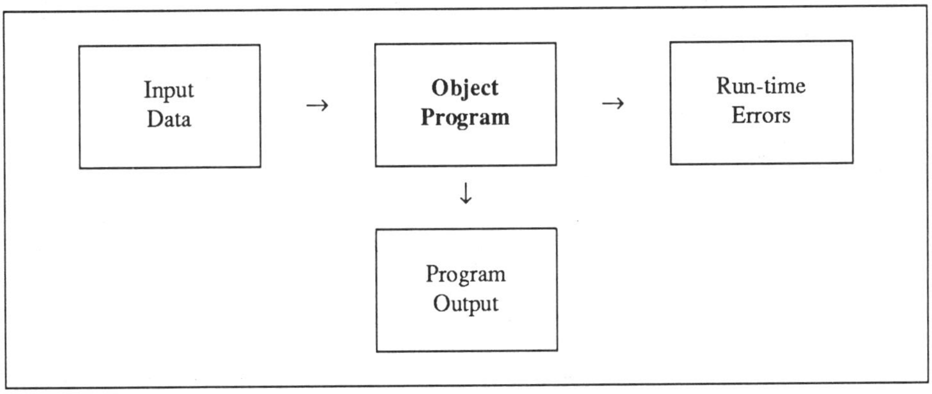

Figure 1.7. Running the Program

printed on one of the computer's output devices. Due to errors in the program or data, it is possible for errors to occur while the program is executing. These errors, called *run-time errors*, usually cause abnormal termination of the program run. The running of a program is shown symbolically in figure 1.7.

There is an alternate means of generating executable code. An *interpreter* processes the program one statement at a time, generating and executing the machine instructions for each statement. Usually the interpreter does some preprocessing, compiling an intermediate nonexecutable code that can be processed more quickly than the original source code. Because less processing is required before the program begins to run, the interpreter usually begins generating results sooner than a compiler. A compiler takes longer to generate executable code, but since the resulting code needs little or no processing, it runs much faster. On the other hand, interpreters usually do more checking while the program is running, detecting errors such as integer overflow and underflow[7] and undefined variables. Some Pascal systems provide a choice of interpreting or compiling the source code. In this case, the programmer can use the interpreter while writing and testing the program and then compile an object program for fast execution.

A good interpreter or compiler with clear error messages can be a great help in *debugging* a program, i.e., removing errors. However, no compiler can find logic errors—these are entirely the responsibility of the programmer.

1.4 Other Software

Computer software can be categorized as *operating systems* and *applications*. An operating system is a program that manages the resources of the computer and serves as an interface between the user and the hardware. Some common operating systems on small computers are MS-DOS, UNIX, and OS/2.[8] Some computers, such as the

7. Overflow means that a computation results in a number too big to be represented in the computer; underflow results when a number is too small.

8. MS-DOS is a registered trademark of Microsoft; UNIX is a registered trademark of AT&T; OS/2 is a trademark of IBM.

Apple Macintosh, have proprietary operating systems that are not available on other computer systems.

The operating system has a command interpreter, or *shell*, which interprets instructions entered by the user. A programmer might use a text editor to enter a Pascal program, a compiler to make an executable version, and a system command to run it. The manner in which the user requests these activities depends on the operating system used and is beyond the scope of this book; you will have to learn the appropriate commands for your system by reading the documentation provided with your computer and software.

Operating systems vary in complexity. On many smaller computers the operating system can only execute one program at a time. A *multitasking* system can run several programs simultaneously. A *multiuser* system is a multitasking system that permits more than one user to work at the same time. MS-DOS and the Macintosh OS are single-user systems. OS/2 permits multitasking. UNIX is a multiuser system.

Multitasking and multiuser operating systems are more complex because they must allocate memory and computing cycles to more than one task and make sure that the various processes do not interfere with each other. These systems perform *time sharing*. Since the CPU can only execute one program at a time, the operating system runs each program for a short time and then gives the next program a turn. Thus each active process gets a series of nonconsecutive *time slices*. If the system is fast enough, each user appears to have an independent system. If the system becomes overloaded, as when too many users are working simultaneously or too many programs are running, the delays become noticeable as sluggish response to commands.

Programs that perform specific tasks are called *application* programs. Examples are text editors and formatting programs, compilers and interpreters, programs that sort data files, computer games, and any other special-purpose programs. In this text you will learn to write application programs in Pascal, with an emphasis on music applications. You will need to become familiar with the utility programs for your particular computer system, so that you have some knowledge of how to create a file using a text editor, how to save and modify this file, how to run your Pascal compiler or interpreter, and how to print files on the printer. A text editor is a program that allows the user to enter text, which may be a letter, class notes, a computer program, a book, or anything that the user wants to write. The editor also has provisions for making changes or corrections in the text, moving blocks of text around in the file, and saving the text on some storage device, such as the computer's hard disk or a floppy disk.

In some systems, particularly on microcomputers, the Pascal system is integrated with its own text editor, which may do some syntax checking and automatic formatting of the program. In these systems, if any errors are detected when the program is run, the user is put back in the editing mode at the point where the error occurred. In other systems, error messages include the line number and perhaps a listing of the line in which the error was found, and the user must invoke the text editor explicitly to make corrections in the program.

1.5 Conclusion

Remember that all programs, whether operating systems or applications, no matter what computer language they are written in, must ultimately be translated into the numeric machine language of the computer before they can be run. High-level languages like Pascal provide a convenient means of expressing programs that are closer to the way we like to solve problems, and that are portable from one computer system to another.

A program is a sequence of instructions that performs a specific task. In general the instructions are executed sequentially, one after the other, but provisions are made for changing the execution order based on simple decisions, and for making loops of statements that are repeated an arbitrary number of times. Programs operate on data that may be supplied by the program itself or be provided externally by the user, and they usually provide some form of output indicating the results of the calculations. All data, whether text, numbers, or computer instructions, is stored in the computer memory as binary numbers, and the type of data is indistinguishable except from context. Compilers and interpreters are programs that translate programs in high-level languages into sequences of numeric instructions that the computer can execute using a more limited set of built-in instructions.

In this text, we will be concerned with a method of writing programs called *structured programming*. The method includes top-down design, stepwise refinement, and writing programs in carefully defined modules, each of which performs a specific task and has only one entry and exit point. We have tried to anticipate this process in the simple programs in this chapter. Note that we were careful to specify the problem to be solved, as well as input data required and output expected from the program. We then described the steps necessary to solve the problem in English and were concerned at first with the general actions that needed to be performed, and only later with the details of implementation.

After this chapter you will not need to be concerned with assembly or machine-language instructions and specific memory locations used to store instructions and data, because the Pascal system takes care of these details for us. The next few chapters will introduce the basic elements of Pascal and methods of representing music data in the computer. Algorithm design will be treated more thoroughly in chapter 7 and later chapters.

References and Selected Readings

The following sources are two of many that contain information on assembly-language programming on small computers. The first reference is intended for use with the Digital Equipment Corporation's PDP-11 minicomputers. Although the second text uses the Computer Automation's Alpha Series minicomputers for an example machine, the material covered applies in a general way to a wide range of minicomputers.

Gill, Arthur. *Machine and Assembly Language Programming of the PDP-11*. Englewood Cliffs, N.J.: Prentice-Hall, 1978.

Weller, Walter J. *Assembly Level Programming for Small Computers.* Lexington Mass.: D.C. Heath and Co., 1975.

The author's initial introduction to computing was through the following text, the first chapter of which contains an overview of digital computers and how they work. The convenient device of using decimal numbers to represent machine code was used in this text:

Organick, Elliott I. *A Fortran IV Primer.* Reading, Mass.: Addison-Wesley, 1966.

The following source is referenced in the exercises:

Jensen, Kathleen, and Niklaus Wirth. *Pascal User Manual and Report*, 3rd ed. Revised by Andrew B. Mickel and James F. Miner. New York: Springer-Verlag, 1985.

You might find it interesting to locate a book on assembly-language programming for your particular computer.

If you are new to the field, you should begin to become familiar with the literature dealing with computer applications in music. The following contains an overview and bibliographic sources:

The New Grove Dictionary of Music and Musicians. 6th ed. S.v. "Computers and Music."

The following source is highly recommended for computer work in musicologic and theoretic research. Besides completed studies, the *Directory* includes lists of dissertations and other works in progress, and names and addresses of scholars working in the field. Each issue includes a report on a special topic (music encoding, music printing, etc.).

Hewlett, Walter B., and Eleanor Selfridge-Field. *Directory of Computer Assisted Research in Musicology.* Menlo Park, Calif.: Center for Computer Assisted Research in the Humanities, 1985–. Annual issues beginning in 1985.

Several professional journals deal with the field. The *Computer Music Journal* (MIT Press) has emphasized work in computer music synthesis, although articles covering other subjects are included as well. The following summarize the contents of the first nine volumes:

Bernardini, Nicola. "Author Index of *Computer Music Journal* Volumes 1–9, 1977–1985." *Computer Music Journal* 10, no. 1 (1986): 37–39.

———. "Contents of *Computer Music Journal* Volumes 1–9, 1977–1985." *Computer Music Journal* 10, no. 1 (1986): 17–36.

———. "Subject Index of *Computer Music Journal* Volumes 1–9, 1977–1985." *Computer Music Journal* 10, no. 2 (1986): 51–55.

The following bibliography contains 4,585 entries through the year 1985, organized by subject and listed alphabetically by author. There are over five hundred entries under the heading "Musicological and Analytic Applications."

Davis, Deta S. *Computer Applications in Music: A Bibliography.* Madison, Wis.: A-R Editions, 1988.

Volume 11, no. 1 of *Music Theory Spectrum*, the journal of the Society for Music Theory, contains papers and bibliographies on the current state of research in music theory, presented at the plenary session of the annual meeting in Rochester, New York in October 1987. While all of the articles are relevant to the subject of this book, two are of particular interest:

Alphonce, Bo H. "Computer Applications: Analysis and Modeling." *Music Theory Spectrum* 11, no. 1 (1989): 49–59.

Wittlich, Gary E. "Computer Applications: Pedagogy." *Music Theory Spectrum* 11, no. 1 (1989): 60–65.

Exercises

1. Express each of the following decimal numbers as binary numbers:

(a) 189	(b) 18	(c) 7	(d) 29	(e) 56	(f) 4095	(g) 0	(h) 37	(i) 1
(j) 2	(k) 4	(l) 8	(m) 16	(n) 32	(o) 64	(p) 128	(q) 256	(r) 512

2. Express each of the following binary numbers as a decimal number:

(a) 10110111	(b) 00011011	(c) 10101011	(d) 111111111111	(e) 00010110
(f) 0000001	(g) 00000010	(h) 00000100	(i) 00001000	(j) 00010000

3. Write the integers from 0 to 65 as binary numbers.

4. Define the following terms. (You can check your answers in the glossary at the end of the book.)

address	CPU	interpreter	OS/2	software
ALU	debugging	machine language	output device	source program
application program	hardware	main memory	peripheral	statement label
assembly language	high-level language	MS-DOS	program	symbol table
compile-time error	input device	object program	register	UNIX
compiler	instruction set	operating system	run-time error	variable

5. Explain the difference between the following:

a) *compiler* and *interpreter*
b) *multitasking* and *multiuser* operating systems
c) *variables* and *statement labels*
d) *machine language* and *assembly language*
e) *syntax* errors and *logic* errors
f) *main* and *secondary* memory
g) *machine instructions* and *data* in memory
h) *hardware* and *software*
i) *compile-time* and *run-time* errors

6. Assume that x / y can be calculated by the instructions

```
CLA X
DIV Y
```

Using the imaginary computer and instructions discussed in this chapter, write a sequence of assembly-language instructions and corresponding machine instructions that will compute the following and print the results:

$$r = \frac{a + b}{a - b}$$

Draw a diagram of main memory, showing the location of all instructions, as well as locations for storing values. Then draw the CPU, including the instruction register, instruction counter, and arithmetic and logic unit, and step though the execution of the program with sample input data. You will need to store an intermediate result.

For each of the following, write the instructions only in assembly language. Draw boxes representing variables and the accumulator, and step through the program with sample data.

7. Write a formula that computes the duration (D) in seconds of a composition, given the meter (M) expressed as the number of beats per measure, the number of measures (N), and the tempo (T) in beats per minute. Assume a constant tempo.

   D =

   Now write a sequence of instructions in assembly language that performs this calculation repeatedly for any number of compositions. Assume a terminal read condition, i.e., that the program will halt when the data is exhausted.

8. Assume that pitches are encoded as integers with middle C equal to 48, C-sharp = D-flat = 49, etc., and that intervals can be represented as signed integers, e.g., M3↑ = 4, P5↓ = –7, etc. Write a sequence of instructions in assembly language that reads an interval and then reads a sequence of pitches, transposes each by the specified interval, and prints out the transposed series.

9. Using the same encoding scheme as in exercise 8, write a sequence of instructions that reads a series of encoded pitches and prints the pitch-class integer representing each pitch. In pitch-class notation, all C-naturals are notated as 0, all C-sharps and D-flats as 1, . . ., all B-naturals as 11. Thus the pc integer is the pitch modulo 12. In other words, any pitch will map into one of the integers between 0 and 11. Try two different algorithms: (a) if the pitch is greater than 11, subtract 12 until the desired result is obtained; (b) use the following algorithm:[9]

   To calculate A mod B:

   let *remainder* = $A - (A \text{ div } B) \times B$;
   if *remainder* < 0 then A mod B = *remainder* + B
   otherwise A mod B = *remainder*

10. Modify the program from exercise 7 so that it prints the results in minutes and seconds. Assume that the divide instruction results in an integer with the fractional part dropped.

11. Write a sequence of assembly instructions that reads two integers x and y and calculates and prints the absolute value of their difference, $|x - y|$. The absolute value is always positive, e.g., $|5 - 1| = |1 - 5| = 4$. Do this two ways, with and without the negation operator. Then modify each sequence so that it can be used for any number of integer pairs.

9. From Kathleen Jensen and Niklaus Wirth, *Pascal User Manual and Report*, 3rd ed. (New York: Springer-Verlag, 1985), 17.

2| A Tutorial Introduction to Pascal

In keeping with the top-down programming methods recommended in this book, we will begin our study of Pascal with an overview of the language. The chapter will introduce program structure, the syntax of statements, basic control constructs, some of the data types used in the language, and the basics of input and output. We will introduce the essential elements of Pascal without excessive attention to details and formalization. Some techniques will be illustrated with simple programs dealing with music data. This chapter is not meant to be complete or precise; all of the concepts introduced in this chapter, and many more, will be covered in more detail in later chapters.

The beginning programmer should not be concerned if he does not understand everything in this chapter, and is not expected to learn programming from this introduction. The overview will help place the next few chapters in a larger context. For those who have used other programming languages, this chapter will serve as an introduction to the primary features of Pascal so that they can begin programming in Pascal immediately.

2.1 Historical Perspective

The first widely available high-level programming language, FORTRAN (**FOR**mula **TRAN**slation), was designed in the mid 1950s and became commercially available in 1957. FORTRAN, which was authored by John Backus at IBM, was designed to simplify the programming of algebraic formulas and has been widely used for scientific applications. The facilities for controlling program flow are similar to those in assembly-language or machine-language programming. Although mechanisms were provided for automating the writing of program loops, the primary control statement was the GOTO, which is functionally equivalent to the *jump* statement in assembly language. The author of the language was more concerned with the speed of its compiler than with the design of the language itself:

> We simply made up the language as we went along. We did not regard language design as a difficult problem, merely a simple prelude to the real problem: designing a compiler which could produce efficient programs.[1]

1. Quoted in Naomi S. Baron, *Computer Languages* (Garden City, N.Y.: Anchor Press/Doubleday, 1986), 207.

In contrast to FORTRAN, the programming language ALGOL (**ALGO**rithmic **L**anguage) was designed in Europe with an emphasis on elegance in the language design itself. Developed between 1958 and 1968, ALGOL provided block-structured design and a rich set of control structures and data types. The language, which is popular in Europe, required rather extensive computer resources and was largely restricted to large *mainframe* computers in the United States. Because the program structures were exceptionally clear, ALGOL became a popular language for expressing algorithms in computer-science publications. The development of ALGOL was closely related to the inception of a new method of designing programs that came to be known as *structured programming*.

The first computer language designed principally for teaching programming to beginners was BASIC (**B**eginner's **A**ll-Purpose **S**ymbolic **I**nstruction **C**ode). BASIC was authored by John Kemeny and Thomas Kurtz at Dartmouth College in 1964. Structurally, the original language is similar to FORTRAN, with many simplifications and the addition of English-like program statements. The language, which predates structured programming, emphasizes ease of use over formulating elegant solutions to problems. BASIC is usually implemented as an interpreter, and since it was the first (and for a long time, only) language available on microcomputers, it is still widely used.

Unlike the languages mentioned above, Pascal is not an acronym; it was named after Blaise Pascal (1623–62), a French mathematician who devised an early calculating machine. Pascal was designed between 1968 and 1971 in Switzerland by Niklaus Wirth, who had also worked on ALGOL and became one of the principal proponents of structured programming techniques. In his original definition of the language he wrote that one of his motivations in designing the language was to "make available a language suitable to teach programming as a schematic discipline based on certain fundamentals of concepts clearly and naturally reflected by the language."[2]

In designing Pascal, Wirth sought to remove the complexity that had become common in many computer languages, while preserving all of the constructs necessary for logical program design. While these criteria kept the language relatively small, Pascal has the tools required for building complex data types and extending the language through user-written subroutines.

As we saw in chapter 1, most compilers translate high-level languages directly into the assembly or machine language for the host computer, a fairly difficult task. In order to facilitate implementation of Pascal on different computer systems, Wirth designed a low-level code called *p-code*, which served as the instruction set for an imaginary computer called the *p-machine*. He then wrote a compiler, mostly in Pascal, to translate Pascal into p-code. Since this intermediate code translates fairly easily into the machine instructions for various computers, this scheme makes it much easier to port Pascal to different computer systems.

Because Pascal is an excellent vehicle for teaching programming and because it is relatively easy to implement on different systems, it disseminated quickly, and by the

2. Niklaus Wirth, "The Programming Language Pascal," *Acta Informatica* 1 (1971): 35–63.

early 1980s it had become the language of choice for teaching programming to computer science students in the United States. It is available for virtually every microcomputer and on all mainframes and workstations, and has become popular in commercial environments as well. In addition, it has had a profound influence on the development of other languages, and new structured versions of both FORTRAN and BASIC have adapted many of the control structures used in Pascal.

I have mentioned only a few of the many high-level programming languages available today. In addition to these, you may have heard of some of the following: COBOL, SNOBOL4, SPITBOL, LISP, PROLOG, PL/I, Modula-2, and C.[3]

2.2 Program Structure

One of the premises of structured programming is to subdivide a problem into well-defined smaller problems until each subproblem is small enough to be solved relatively easily. Large problems are broken down into a series of related smaller problems that make up the whole. Pascal is designed to model and to facilitate this problem-solving mechanism. Pascal programs of more than a few lines are usually subdivided into subprograms, called *functions* and *procedures*, each of which performs a well-defined task.

The basic structural unit in Pascal is the *program block*. Each main program or subprogram unit consists of a *heading* and a *block*. The heading consists of the program name followed by a list of *parameters*. In a main program, these parameters are the names of *files* that will be used to communicate with the program. Consider the following simple program:

```
program exaltation(output);
  begin
    writeln('Ah, Bach!!')
  end.
```

The first line is the program heading. Every Pascal program begins with the reserved word **program**. Reserved words—words that have a special meaning in Pascal—are printed in bold type in this text. The reserved word **program** is followed by the program name, in this case *exaltation*. The name is an *identifier*, which must begin with a letter of the alphabet and may contain any combination of letters and digits. Identifiers are important since they are used to name many things in Pascal, including programs, subprograms, variables, constants, and user-defined types. The program name is followed by the identifier *output* in parentheses. This is the name of the standard output file in Pascal, and tells the compiler that the program will communicate information to the outside world by printing on the computer's standard output device—usually the CRT screen on the user's terminal. The program heading is terminated by a semicolon.

3. Short descriptions are included in the glossary at the end of this book.

In this simple program the heading is followed directly by the *statement* part of the program. This section is demarcated by the reserved words **begin** and **end** with any number of instructions, called *program statements*, between them. The program is terminated by a period '.' marking the end of the program.

In this case the statement part of the program contains a single statement, which calls the standard procedure *writeln* (read "write line"). This procedure causes its argument, here a string of characters between single quotes, to be printed on the CRT screen. When this program is compiled and run, it will print the message:

```
Ah, Bach!!
```

Note that the single quotes that delimit the string are not printed. The *writeln* procedure prints the values represented by its arguments, followed by "control" characters that terminate the output line.[4] Thus the next *write* statement will print on the next line. Alternately, we could use the procedure *write*, which does not end the current line. Thus the above program could be rewritten as follows and produce the same output:

```
program exaltation(output);
  begin
    write('Ah, ');
    writeln('Bach!!')
  end.
```

or

```
program exaltation(output);
  begin
    write('Ah, ');
    write('Bach!!');
    writeln
  end.
```

A program can be made to write several lines of text by including several *writeln* statements. For example, the program

```
program linetest(output);
  begin
    writeln('It is not true that life is one damn thing');
    writeln('after another--It''s one damn thing over');
    writeln('and over.');
    writeln;
    writeln('                Edna St. Vincent Millay')
  end.
```

prints

```
It is not true that life is one damn thing
after another--It's one damn thing over
and over.

                Edna St. Vincent Millay
```
[5]

4. The pair of control characters, carriage return and line feed, terminate the current line.

5. Quoted in Walter J. Savitch, *Pascal* (Menlo Park, Calif.: Benjamin/Cummings, 1984), at the beginning of the chapter on program loops.

Note that statements are separated by semicolons. The line before the reserved word **end** does not need this separator, since it is not followed by a statement. Statements in Pascal may be simple statements, such as the procedure calls shown above and assignment statements; or they may be structured *control statements*, which will be discussed presently.

The program block may contain the following parts, although all but the last are optional:

1. Label declarations
2. Constant declarations
3. Type declarations
4. Variable declarations
5. Procedure and function declarations
6. Statements

If present, these parts must be in the order shown above. The syntax of each part is defined in chapter 3. Most of these parts will be seen in passing in this chapter.

2.3 Constants, Variables, and Arithmetic Operators

Our next program is somewhat more complex. The program performs a conversion from the pitch representation introduced in the previous chapter to two pitch representations used in computer music synthesis programs: octave pitch-class (*oct.pc*) and octave decimal (*oct.dec*) notation. In the original form, called *continuous pitch code* (cpc), the pitches are numbered consecutively from 0, which represents the C below the lowest note on the piano. Since there are twelve notes in the octave, our pitch system is a modulo 12 system, and the octave and pitch class can be extracted from the pitch number by the following Pascal statements:[6]

```
octave := pitch div 12;
pc     := pitch mod 12;
```

The first divides the pitch number by 12, dropping the fractional part, and assigns the result to the variable *octave*. The second uses the **mod** operator, which returns the remainder after division, to calculate the pitch class. Both are examples of *assignment statements*. In each case, the expression on the right is evaluated and the result is assigned to the variable on the left. Now *octave* and *pc* are used to calculate the new pitch numbers. Each of these uses a real number (including a fractional part), with the octave to the left of the decimal point. In *oct.pc* notation, the fractional part (after the decimal point) is the pitch class. This is calculated by dividing the pc integer by 100 and adding the result to the octave:

```
octpc := octave + pc / 100;
```

6. The octaves are numbered consecutively from 0; the pc integers 0 through 11 represent the pitches C through B in any octave. The compound symbol ':=' is the assignment operator in Pascal.

In *oct.dec* notation, the decimal part is the fraction of the octave. This form is calculated as

```
octdec := octave + pc / 12;
```

For example, the pitch code 51 represents the D-sharp or E-flat above middle C. Thus the octave is 51 **div** 12 = 4, and the pitch class is 51 **mod** 12 = 3. In *oct.pc* representation, this is 4.03. Since E-flat is a quarter of the way from C_4 to C_5, the *oct.dec* notation is 4.25.

Program 2.1, *pitchrep*, illustrates a number of new Pascal features. The *constant declaration* part of the program block is introduced by the reserved word **const**. This section defines *constants*, symbolic names for values that will not change in the program. Here we define the modulus of the pitch system, the lowest and highest notes that we wish to calculate, and a character string that will be used as a border in the table that will be printed by the program.

```
(***********************     Program Pitchrep     ***********************)
(* Converts continuous pitch code to oct.pc and oct.dec representation.  *)
(*************************************************************************)
program pitchrep(output);
  const
    modulus  = 12;                              { modulus of pitch system }
    lownote  =  0;                              { lowest note in table    }
    highnote = 96;                              { highest note in table   }
    border   = '======================';        { top and bottom of table }

  var
    pitch  : integer;                           { pitch in cpc code       }
    pc     : integer;                           { pitch class of note     }
    octave : integer;                           { octave of note          }
    octpc  : real;                              { oct.pc notation         }
    octdec : real;                              { oct.dec notation        }

  begin { main }
    writeln(border);                            { print heading           }
    writeln('pitch  oct.pc  oct.dec');
    writeln(border);

    pitch := lownote;                           { set starting pitch      }
    while pitch <= highnote do
      begin { process pitch }
        pc := pitch mod modulus;                { calc. the pitch class   }
        octave := pitch div modulus;            { calc. the octave number }
        octpc := octave + pc / 100;             { oct.pc representation   }
        octdec := octave + pc / 12;             { oct.dec representation  }
        writeln(pitch:4, octpc:9:2, octdec:9:3);
        pitch := pitch + 1                      { get next pitch          }
      end; { process pitch }

    writeln(border)                             { bottom border of table  }
  end. { main }
```

Program 2.1. *Pitchrep*

```
======================
pitch  oct.pc  oct.dec
======================
  0     0.00    0.000
  1     0.01    0.083
  2     0.02    0.167
  3     0.03    0.250
  4     0.04    0.333
  5     0.05    0.417
  6     0.06    0.500
  7     0.07    0.583
  8     0.08    0.667
  9     0.09    0.750
 10     0.10    0.833
 11     0.11    0.917
 12     1.00    1.000
 13     1.01    1.083
 14     1.02    1.167
 15     1.03    1.250
  .
  .     [ part of table omitted here ]
  .
 45     3.09    3.750
 46     3.10    3.833
 47     3.11    3.917
 48     4.00    4.000     [ middle C ]
 49     4.01    4.083
 50     4.02    4.167
 51     4.03    4.250
 52     4.04    4.333
 53     4.05    4.417
 54     4.06    4.500
 55     4.07    4.583
 56     4.08    4.667
 57     4.09    4.750
 58     4.10    4.833
 59     4.11    4.917
 60     5.00    5.000
 61     5.01    5.083
 62     5.02    5.167
  .
  .     [ part of table omitted here ]
  .
 91     7.07    7.583
 92     7.08    7.667
 93     7.09    7.750
 94     7.10    7.833
 95     7.11    7.917
 96     8.00    8.000
======================
```

Program 2.1. Output

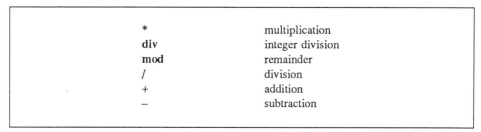

*	multiplication
div	integer division
mod	remainder
/	division
+	addition
–	subtraction

Table 2.1. Arithmetic Operators Used with Integers

The variable declaration part, headed by the reserved word **var**, contains declarations for variables that will be used in the program.[7] Program *pitchrep* will require three *integer* variables that will be used to store whole numbers, and two *real* variables that will store values with a fractional part.

The computation for each pitch takes place within a program loop constructed using a **while** statement, which causes the compound statement, **begin...end**, just after the **while**, to execute for each pitch from 0 to 96. Part of the table printed by program *pitchrep* is shown below. Note that the *write* and *writeln* statements can take more than one argument (or value), separated by commas. Optionally, each argument may be followed by a colon and an integer value representing the *field width*, i.e., the number of spaces the value is to occupy in the printed output. For real numbers, the programmer may also supply the *precision*, i.e., the number of decimal places to be printed.

The arithmetic operators that can be used with integers are shown in table 2.1. The '/' operator can be used with integers but the result is always *real*, i.e., 5 / 2 equals 2.5. All other arithmetic operators produce an integer result when applied to two integer values. The operator **div** performs integer division, i.e., the fractional part of the result is dropped, and **mod** returns the remainder after division. For example, 15 **div** 12 is 1, while 15 **mod** 12 is 3. Multiplication, division, and remaindering are performed before addition and subtraction, and the order of evaluation can be changed by parentheses, i.e., the expression *a* + *b* / c is equivalent to *a* + (*b* / c).

All of the operators except for **div** and **mod** can be used with real operands producing a real result. When an arithmetic operator is applied to a real and an integer operand, the result is real, so all *mixed mode* expressions evaluate to real values.

Pascal is a *strongly typed* language, i.e., it performs strict type checking when evaluating expressions and generates error messages when *type clashes* are detected. It does not perform automatic type conversion with the abandon of languages like SNOBOL4. While an integer value can be assigned to a real variable, the reverse is not allowed. Two standard functions can be used to convert real values to integer:

```
i := trunc(2.6);        { assigns the integer 2 to i }
i := round(2.6);        { assigns the integer 3 to i }
```

7. Recall that variables are symbolic names for memory locations that will be used by the program to store variable data.

Pascal does not provide an operator for performing exponentiation (the process of raising a number to a power); however, this and many other operations can be performed using the *natural log* function *ln* and its inverse *exp*.[8] Recall that

$$\log x^n = n \log x$$

Thus, in Pascal the value x^n can be assigned to variable *a* by the following:

```
a := exp(ln(x) * n)
```

so long as *x* is greater than 0. The result is real but can be converted to integer through the use of *trunc* or *round*. Pascal also provides trigonometric functions and other functions such as *sqrt*, which returns the square root of its argument.

Pascal's predefined types are shown in table 2.2. These types will be covered in more detail in chapter 3.

integer	–	whole numbers
real	–	floating-point numbers
boolean	–	*true* and *false* values
char	–	character data, e.g., 'a', '9', '!'
subrange types	–	e.g., the subrange of integers 0 .. 11
enumerated types	–	user-defined ordinal types, e.g., (*violin, viola, cello, contrabass*)

Table 2.2. Predefined Types in Pascal

2.4 Control Statements

Pascal provides the fundamental flow-control constructs necessary for writing well-structured programs: statement grouping, loops with the test at the top, loops with the test at the bottom, and selecting one of a set of possible cases.

The Compound Statement. We have already seen this program structure, since the statement part of a program block is a compound statement. The compound statement consists of any number of program statements, separated by semicolons, enclosed between the reserved words **begin** and **end**. This structure forms a group of statements that is treated structurally as a single statement. The following is an example from program *pitchrep* (above):

```
begin
  pc := pitch mod modulus;
  octave := pitch div modulus;
  octpc := octave + pc / 100;
  octdec := octave + pc / 12;
  writeln(pitch:4, octpc:9:2, octdec:9:3);
  pitch := pitch + 1
end
```

8. *Ln*(*x*) represents the natural logarithm (log to the base *e*) of its argument *x*, which may be *integer* or *real*. *Exp*(*x*) represents *e* raised to the power *x*, i.e., e^x.

Program Loops. Pascal provides three mechanisms for writing program loops. The most general is the **while** statement, which has the general format:

while <expression> **do**
<statement>

The **while** evaluates a *boolean* expression (which evaluates to *true* or *false*). If the value of the expression is *true*, the statement part of the **while** is executed and the expression is again evaluated. This continues until the expression evaluates to *false*. The statement may be a simple statement, a compound statement, or another structured control statement. In *pitchrep* we used a **while** to calculate values for each pitch. The variable *pitch* was assigned the value of *lownote*. The boolean expression *pitch* <= *highnote* evaluates to *true* so long as the value of *pitch* is less than or equal to that of *highnote*. In this case, the *statement* part of the **while** is a compound statement containing a number of assignment statements that calculate the desired values, and a *writeln* statement that prints out one line of the table. Note that the compound statement also contains the assignment statement

```
pitch := pitch + 1
```

which adds one to the value of *pitch*, so the loop will eventually terminate. Since the **while** tests its condition *before* executing the statement, the statement part is executed zero or more times, i.e., it may not be executed at all.

The **repeat...until** checks its condition at the bottom of the loop, so it always executes its statement at least once. The **while** loop in program *pitchrep* could be replaced by the following loop:

```
pitch := lownote;
repeat
  pc := pitch mod modulus;
  octave := pitch div modulus;
  octpc := octave + pc / 100;
  octdec := octave + pc / 12;
  writeln(pitch:4, octpc:9:2, octdec:9:3);
  pitch := pitch + 1
until pitch > highnote
```

Pascal also provides a **for** loop, which sets a control variable and increments it automatically after each repetition of the statement. Like the **while**, the **for** checks its implied condition before executing its statement, so the statement may not execute at all under some conditions. The loop in program *pitchrep* could have been written using a **for**:

```
for pitch := lownote to highnote do
  begin
    pc := pitch mod modulus;
    octave := pitch div modulus;
    octpc := octave + pc / 100;
    octdec := octave + pc / 12;
    writeln(pitch:4, octpc:9:2, octdec:9:3)
  end;
```

The **for** can be made to count backwards by replacing the keyword **to** with **downto**. Changing the above to

```
for pitch := highnote downto lownote do
  begin
    . . .

  end;
```

would print out the table in reverse order.

Decision Statements. The primary decision statement in Pascal is the **if** statement, which can take several forms including:

if <condition>
  then <statement>;

if <condition>
  then <statement$_1$>
  else <statement$_2$>

In the first type, if the boolean expression evaluates to *true*, the statement is executed, otherwise it is not. The second type chooses between two statements: if the boolean condition is *true*, then the first statement is executed, otherwise the second statement is executed. The statement parts may be simple or compound statements, or another control statement (loop or **if**). Since either statement in the **if...then...else** may be another **if**, **if** statements may be chained:

if <condition$_1$>
  then <statement$_1$>
else if <condition$_2$>
  then <statement$_2$>
else . . .

Consider the following procedure, which skips blank characters in the program's input up to the next nonblank character:

```
procedure skipblanks;
  var
    done : boolean;
  begin
    done := false;
    repeat
      if eof
        then done := true
      else if input↑ = ' '
        then get(input)
      else done := true
    until done
  end; { skipblanks }
```

A *procedure* is a program block that can be called by name when needed in a program. This procedure again uses some new features. The boolean function *eof* (end-of-file) returns *true* when there is no more data in the input file. The variable *input*↑ is a *buffer variable* that provides a window into the input file. Its value is the next character (the one that is about to be read) in the input file. Calling the procedure *get(input)* advances *input*↑ to the next character in the file, i.e., it skips the current character. When procedure *skipblanks* is invoked, the boolean variable *done* is assigned the value *false*. The chained **if** statement performs the following operation:

if at end of input data
  then assign *done* the value *true*,
else if the next character is a blank
  then skip the blank,
else set *done* to *true* {the next character is not a blank}

Since this statement is enclosed in a loop that terminates when *done* is *true*, the result is to skip blanks until the next nonblank character is found, or until there is no more data to be read.

Program 2.2, *pitchclass*, illustrates the use of procedure *skipblanks* along with some other aspects of Pascal programming. The program reads data representing pitch classes. The data is entered using a single character to represent each integer, e.g., the integers 0 through 9 are represented by the characters '0' through '9'. Pitch classes 10 and 11 are represented by the characters 'a' and 'b' or 'A' and 'B'. While it would be possible to read integers directly, this scheme is useful because it enables the user to use one keystroke for each pitch class entered, and it eliminates the need for blanks between the numbers. For example, the twelve-tone row

1 0 4 5 9 8 10 6 7 2 3 11

could be entered into a program as

104598a6723b

using 13 keystrokes instead of 26. Note that it would be simple to modify the program so that it would accept other characters, e.g., 't' and 'e' for ten and eleven.

The program heading includes the *input* file as well as *output*. This signals the compiler that the program will read data from the standard input device. The program block includes a variable declaration part and one procedure declaration (procedure *skipblanks*). The statement part of the main program begins at

```
begin { main }
```

The program first calls *skipblanks*, then for each nonblank character the following steps are taken:

1. The character is read
2. It is converted to a pitch-class integer
3. The pc integer is printed
4. *Skipblanks* is called to find the next nonblank character

```
(***********************  Program Pitchclass   ***********************)
(* Converts char representation of hexadecimal digits to pc integers.   *)
(**********************************************************************)
program pitchclass(input, output);
  var
    c  : char;                           { for reading a character      }
    pc : integer;                        { pc represented by the character }

  procedure skipblanks;                  { skips blank chars in input   }
    var
      done : boolean;
    begin
      done := false;
      repeat
        if eof
          then done := true
        else if input↑ = ' '
          then get(input)
        else done := true
      until done
    end;  { skipblanks }

  begin { main }
    skipblanks;                                  { skip blanks         }
    while not eof do                             { until end of data   }
      begin { process next character }
        read(c);                                 { read a character    }

        if c in ['0' .. '9']                     { convert to integer  }
          then pc := ord(c) - ord('0')
        else if (c = 'a') or (c = 'A')
          then pc := 10
        else if (c = 'b') or (c = 'B')
          then pc := 11
        else pc := -1;                           { signal error        }

        if pc = -1                               { print pitch class   }
          then writeln('bad character')
          else writeln(pc);
        skipblanks                               { skip blanks         }
      end  { process next character }
  end.  { main }
```

Program 2.2. *Pitchclass*

The **while not** *eof* loop causes this sequence to be repeated for each nonblank character in the input file.

Input to the program is accomplished by calling the standard procedure *read*. This procedure is called with one or more variables in its *parameter list*. For each variable in the input list, an appropriate value is read from the standard input device and stored in the memory location referenced by the variable. For example, calling

```
read(c)
```

Input:

```
01a b x 34 5
6 7 AB. 2
```

Output:

```
     0
     1
    10
    11
bad character
     3
     4
     5
     6
     7
    10
    11
bad character
     2
```

Program 2.2. Sample Input and Output

where *c* is a character variable, causes the next character in the input file to be read and stored in variable *c*. This character will now be converted to an integer. The method depends on whether it is a digit or an alphabetic character. First we test to see if it is a digit. This is accomplished by the test

```
if c in ['0' .. '9']
```

which evaluates to *true* if character *c* is a digit. This is roughly equivalent to the following:

```
if (c = '0') or (c = '1') or (c = '2') or
   (c = '3') or (c = '4') or (c = '5') or
   (c = '6') or (c = '7') or (c = '8') or (c = '9')
```

If *c* is a digit, it is converted to an integer using the ordinal position of the character in the character set, obtained by calling the function *ord(c)*.[9] Since the digits '0' through '9' are contiguous characters, the numeric value of each digit can be obtained by subtracting the ordinal position of character '0' from the ordinal position of the character in variable *c*:

```
pc := ord(c) - ord('0')
```

The first **else if** clause assigns variable *pc* the integer 10 if character *c* is an upper- or lowercase *A*; the second assigns the value 11 for upper- or lowercase *B*; and the final **else** assigns the integer –1 to signal that the character is not one of those we are using to represent pitch classes. A final **if...then...else** controls printing of the results. If the value of variable *pc* is –1 we print an error message; otherwise the integer value

9. The ordinal position of characters will be explained in chapter 3.

of *pc* is printed. Finally, *skipblanks* is called again to obtain the next nonblank character or the end of the file.

Sample input data and the output produced by program *pitchclass* are shown on the previous page. Note that the input data tests all aspects of the program, including error messages and skipping optional blanks.

2.5 User-Written Functions and Procedures

We have seen a number of standard functions and procedures, and one procedure, *skipblanks*, that was designed by the programmer. Functions and procedures are two kinds of program blocks that can be predefined and then called when needed in the program. The primary difference is that functions return a value and are used in expressions such as

```
x := sqrt(y)
```

while procedures cause some task to be performed, as in

```
skipblanks
```

or

```
read(x, y, z)
```

Procedures and functions are heavily used in Pascal to divide a program into logical subdivisions. Program *pitchclass2* performs exactly the same task as the program shown above, except that it is divided into more subprograms. We will use this model to introduce a number of features of functions and procedures, and to illustrate some aspects of *top-down* program design, another principle of structured programming. The programmer begins by carefully defining the problem: Exactly what is the program supposed to do, and what form will the input and output data take? Typically the programmer begins with a general description of the whole program, first thinking in terms of processes that need to be performed, and only later settling on details of implementation. Each process is approached top-down and broken into smaller parts if necessary. The processes are described in English or in pseudo code, a combination of English and Pascal control structures. Since we have already defined the problem, we will begin with the overview of the program, corresponding to the main procedure:

```
while not finished with data do
  begin
    obtain a pitch class;
    print it;
    skip blanks
  end;
```

Each process may be implemented as a separate procedure or as a program segment within the current procedure. We have already seen procedure *skipblanks*. "Obtain a pitch class'' represents a separate process that might well be written as a separate procedure. The steps necessary to solve this part of the problem are:

1. Skip blanks
2. Read nonblank character
3. Convert character to integer
4. Return value

Now we examine these steps more carefully. Converting the character to an integer is a separate subtask that might be implemented as a function. Problem solving evolves from the general to the specific through a process called *stepwise refinement*. Once the solution has been sufficiently ''refined,'' it is relatively easy to encode the program in Pascal. After checking the solution, the programmer makes final decisions about program structure and writes the actual program code. The final version, *pitchclass2*, is shown as program 2.3. Although the program is longer than the original version, the structure is clear. Each separate subprogram performs a well-defined task and is easy to check for correctness or to modify later. Once written and checked, the procedure can be called without concern for the details of implementation. Note that the definition of each procedure or function occurs in the program before it is called.[10] Function *toint* is a good example of a Pascal function. The function heading consists of the reserved word **function**, the function name, a *parameter list*, and the type of value that will be returned by the function. The heading

```
function toint(c : char) : integer;
```

tells the compiler that function *toint* will be passed a character, known to the function as *c*, and will return an integer value. The value *returned* by the function is the last value assigned to the function name. The **if** statement checks the value of *c*. If the value is appropriate, the corresponding integer value is assigned to *toint*. In the function, *c* is a *formal parameter*, i.e., a symbolic name that represents the value of the *actual parameter* passed to the function when the function is called. The value of the actual parameter is copied to the formal parameter when the function is called.

Procedure *getpc* takes care of reading a character and converting it to an integer. The procedure heading tells the compiler that *getpc* will use one formal parameter called *pc*, which represents an integer value.

```
procedure getpc(var pc : integer);
```

The reserved word **var** before *pc* in the parameter list signifies that the procedure can change the value of *pc*. This is another way to return a value from a subprogram. When a formal parameter is declared in this way, the actual parameter passed to the procedure must be a variable. Although the procedure can ''return'' a value through this mechanism, the procedure does not have a value in the same sense that the function does. Procedure *getpc* has a *local* variable, *c*, which is known only in this procedure.

10. This rule can be circumvented by using a *forward* directive.

```
(**********************   Program Pitchclass2   **********************)
(* Rewrite of program 2.1 with functions and procedures.              *)
(**********************************************************************)
program pitchclass2(input, output);
  var
    pc : integer;                              { a pitch class integer }

  procedure skipblanks;
    var
      done : boolean;
    begin
      done := false;
      repeat
        if eof
          then done := true
        else if input↑ = ' '
          then get(input)
        else done := true
      until done
    end;

  function toint(c : char) : integer;         { convert char to integer }
    begin
      if c in ['0' .. '9']
        then toint := ord(c) - ord('0')
      else if (c = 'a') or (c = 'A')
        then toint := 10
      else if (c = 'b') or (c = 'B')
        then toint := 11
      else toint := -1                         { signal error          }
    end; { toint }

  procedure getpc(var pc : integer);           { get a pitch class     }
    var
      c : char;
    begin
      skipblanks;                              { skip blanks           }
      read(c);                                 { read a character      }
      pc := toint(c)                           { convert to integer    }
    end; { getpc }

  begin { main }
    while not eof do
      begin { process next character }
        getpc(pc);                             { get a pitch class     }
        if pc = -1                             { print results         }
          then writeln('bad character')
          else writeln(pc);
        skipblanks                             { skip blanks           }
      end { process next character }
  end. { main }
```

Program 2.3. *Pitchclass2*

The extent to which a programmer divides a program into subprograms is an element of programming style; the decision is made by the programmer. Generally, it is considered good programming style to write each logical process as a separate program unit. It is always a good idea if the process will need to be called from different places in the program, or may be useful in many different programs, as in the case of *skipblanks.* As an extension to standard Pascal, many Pascal systems include facilities for compiling procedures separately and storing them in a program library.

Functions can be used to implement processes that have not been implemented as standard functions in Pascal. For example, the following function uses natural logarithms to implement exponentiation (raising to a power):

```
{ returns x to the yth power }
function power(x, y : real) : real;
  begin
    if x = 0
      then power := 0
      else power := exp(ln(x) * y)
  end;  { power }
```

This function is used in program 2.4, which calculates the frequency in cycles per second for the pitches in the tempered scale. If your algebra is a bit rusty, you may want to skip the details of the computation and concentrate on the program structure used to solve the problem. The program uses nested **for** loops to print the table with all frequencies for octave-related pitches on the same line. Pitches are represented by pitch class (the note name) and octave. The basic structure of the main program is:

```
print table heading;

for pc := 0 to 11 do
  begin
    print note name;
    for octave := 0 to 8 do
      calculate and print frequency of note;
    terminate line
  end;

print bottom border;
```

The program takes advantage of the basic premises of the equal-tempered scale:

a) The octave is pure, i.e., the ratio is 2:1
b) The octave is divided into 12 equal semitones

From (a) it is obvious the octave above any frequency x is $2x$, two octaves above x is $4x$, three octaves above x is $8x$, etc. Note that the multipliers for successive octaves are powers of 2:

$$2^0 = 1$$
$$2^1 = 2$$
$$2^2 = 4$$
$$2^3 = 8$$
$$2^4 = 16$$
etc.

Therefore the frequency of the *n*th octave above x, $n \geq 0$, is

$$x \times 2^n$$

Since the octave is divided into 12 equal parts, we can replace n by a real number in the form *oct.dec*. The decimal part is calculated as $m \,/\, 12$, $0 \leq m \leq 11$, where m is the number of semitones above pitch x. The frequency of the note o octaves plus m semitones above pitch x is

$$x \times 2^{(o+m/12)}$$

The lowest pitch in the table will be C_0. It will be more convenient to calculate all other pitches from this frequency than from A_4 (440 cps), so we will use the frequency of C_0 as the base pitch x. Since C_0 is 4 octaves plus 9 semitones below A_4, its frequency can be calculated as follows:

$$C_0 = 440 \times 2^{-(4+9/12)} = 440 \times 2^{-4.75} = 16.35159375$$

Since the fractional part of the frequency is more critical in low notes, where the difference between the frequencies of adjacent notes is smaller, we will arrange to use five digits in all numbers, with more digits after the decimal point at lower frequencies. This could have been accomplished by a chained **if**:

```
if cps < 100
  then precision := 3
else if cps < 1000
  then precision := 2
else precision := 1
```

Instead, I used logarithms to calculate the number of decimal places:

```
precision := 4 - trunc(ln(cps) / ln(10));
```

Procedure *writenote* uses yet another structured control statement. The **case** statement is an efficient means of choosing one action out of a set of possible actions based on the value of a variable.

The complete program listing and program output follow.

```
(*********************** Program Frequency ***********************)
(* Calculates frequency table for the tempered scale.              *)
(*****************************************************************)
program frequency(output);
  const
    C0 = 16.35159;                          { frequency of C0 in cps      }

  var
    pc, octave : integer;                   { pitch class and octave      }
    hertz      : real;                      { freq of note in cps         }

  { returns x ** y }
  function power(x, y : real) : real;
    begin
      if x = 0
        then power := 0
        else power := exp(ln(x) * y)
    end; { power }

  { calculates frequency based on C0 }
  function cps(pc, octave : integer) : real;
    var
      decimal : real;      { part of octave as decimal number }
    begin
      decimal := pc / 12;
      cps := C0 * power(2, octave + decimal)
    end;

  { prints note name for natural notes, blanks for others }
  procedure writenote(pc : integer);
    begin
      case pc of
              0 : write('C |');  { natural pitches   }
              2 : write('D |');
              4 : write('E |');
              5 : write('F |');
              7 : write('G |');
              9 : write('A |');
             11 : write('B |');
     1,3,6,8,10 : write('  |')   { sharps and flats }
      end { case }
    end; { writenote }

  { prints border for table }
  procedure printborder;
    var
      i : integer;
    begin
      for i := 1 to 76 do
        write('=');
      writeln
    end; { printborder }

  { prints heading for table }
  procedure printheading;
    var
      i : integer;
```

```
    begin
      writeln(' ':18, 'Frequency in Hertz for the Tempered Scale');
      printborder;
      write('Octave   0');                              { print heading      }
      for i := 1 to 8 do
        write(i:8);
      writeln;
      printborder
    end;  { printheading }

  { calculates number of decimal places based on cps }
  function precision(cps : real) : integer;
    begin
      precision := 4 - trunc(ln(cps) / ln(10))
    end;

  begin { main }
    printheading;

    for pc := 0 to 11 do
      begin { calc values for pc }
        writenote(pc);
        for octave := 0 to 8 do
          begin { in each octave }
            hertz := cps(pc, octave);
            write(hertz:8:precision(hertz))
          end;  { in each octave }
        writeln
      end;  { calc values for pc }

    printborder
  end.  { main }
```

Program 2.4. *Frequencies*

```
                 Frequency in Hertz for the Tempered Scale
==========================================================================
Octave  0       1       2       3       4       5       6       7       8
==========================================================================
C |  16.352  32.703  65.406  130.81  261.63  523.25  1046.5  2093.0  4186.0
  |  17.324  34.648  69.296  138.59  277.18  554.37  1108.7  2217.5  4434.9
D |  18.354  36.708  73.416  146.83  293.66  587.33  1174.7  2349.3  4698.6
  |  19.445  38.891  77.782  155.56  311.13  622.25  1244.5  2489.0  4978.0
E |  20.602  41.203  82.407  164.81  329.63  659.25  1318.5  2637.0  5274.0
F |  21.827  43.654  87.307  174.61  349.23  698.46  1396.9  2793.8  5587.6
  |  23.125  46.249  92.499  185.00  369.99  739.99  1480.0  2960.0  5919.9
G |  24.500  48.999  97.999  196.00  392.00  783.99  1568.0  3136.0  6271.9
  |  25.957  51.913  103.83  207.65  415.30  830.61  1661.2  3322.4  6644.9
A |  27.500  55.000  110.00  220.00  440.00  880.00  1760.0  3520.0  7040.0
  |  29.135  58.270  116.54  233.08  466.16  932.33  1864.7  3729.3  7458.6
B |  30.868  61.735  123.47  246.94  493.88  987.77  1975.5  3951.1  7902.1
==========================================================================
```

Program 2.4. Output

2.6 Arrays and Other Structured Types

Pascal also has facilities for creating structured data types, i.e., data objects that store more than one value. The types used for structuring data in Pascal shown in table 2.3. These types can be used to construct a practically infinite variety of data structures. For example, the component type of an array may be a set, a record, a pointer, or even another array type, and arrays can have any number of dimensions. A record can contain components of any type, other structured types, or other records. For the sake of brevity, only the array will be illustrated in this overview. Structured types are dealt with in detail in chapters 10 through 20.

The program shown below reads notes in continuous pitch code (cpc), converts each to a pitch class, and uses an array to count the number of occurrences of each pitch class. The elements of the array *count* are referenced by the integers 0 through 11, and are initialized by placing a 0 in each location:

count

0	1	2	3	4	5	6	7	8	9	10	11
0	0	0	0	0	0	0	0	0	0	0	0

As each pitch code is read, it is converted into an integer, *pc*, and 1 is added to the element of the array corresponding to the pitch class, *count*[*pc*].

As before, the program is divided into subprograms. Procedure *readdata* reads the data and tabulates the pitch classes, and procedure *printtable* prints the output table. Procedure *incr* adds 1 to the value of its argument. In this program it is used to increment the pitch-class counts stored in the array:

```
incr(count[pc]);
```

The program listing follows, with sample input and output. The input data is the music from figure 1.1, encoded in continuous pitch code (cpc).

Array types	–	Ordered collections of like items
Set types	–	Unordered sets of similar elements
Record types	–	Data items that may contain components of different types
File types	–	Collections of data of any type that may be accessed via *read* and *write* statements
Pointers	–	Addresses of other data objects, used to construct linked data structures

Table 2.3. Structured Types in Pascal

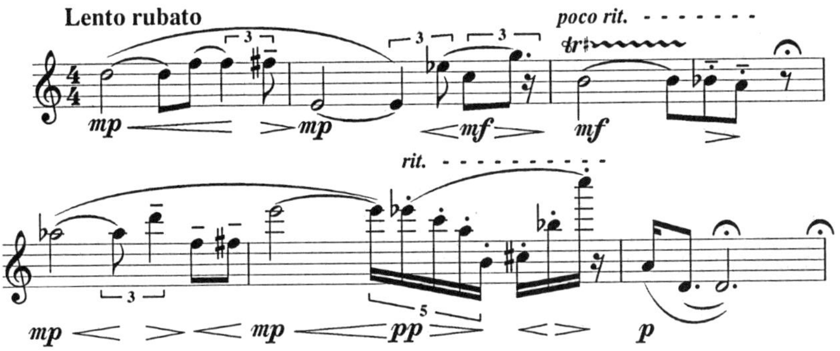

Kazuo Fukushima, *Requiem per flauto solo*, mm. 1–6.

Figure 2.1. Fukushima *Requiem* Excerpt

Input:

```
62 65 66 52 63 60 67 59 61 58 57
68 74 65 66 76 75 72 67 59 61 70 81 56 50
```

Output:

```
pc  frequency
=============
 0     2
 1     2
 2     3
 3     2
 4     2
 5     2
 6     2
 7     2
 8     2
 9     2
10     2
11     2
=============
```

Program 2.5. Input and Output

```
(***********************    Program Countpcs    ***********************)
(* Counts pitch classes in cpc encoded music.                          *)
(**********************************************************************)
program countpcs(input, output);
  type
    pclist = array[0 .. 11] of integer;
  var
    count : pclist;

  { finds next nonblank character in input }
  procedure skipblanks;
    var
      done : boolean;
    begin
      done := false;
      repeat
        if eof
          then done := true
        else if input↑ = ' '
          then get(input)
        else done := true
      until done
    end;

  { adds one to argument }
  procedure incr(var x : integer);
    begin
      x := x + 1
    end;

  { reads pitches and count pitch classes }
  procedure readdata(var count : pclist);
    var
      pc   : integer;
      note : integer;
    begin
      for pc := 0 to 11 do                        { initialize array        }
        count[pc] := 0;

      while not eof do
        begin
          read(note);                             { read note               }
          incr(count[note mod 12]);               { calc pc and incr table  }
          skipblanks                              { skip blanks             }
        end
    end;

  { prints table of pcs and the frequency }
  procedure printtable(var count : pclist);
    var
      pc : integer;
    begin
      writeln;                                    { heading                 }
      writeln('pc  frequency');
      writeln('=============');                  { border                  }
```

```
      for pc := 0 to 11 do                      { data                }
        writeln(pc:2, count[pc]:7);
      writeln('============')                  { border              }
    end;  { printtable }

  begin { main }
    readdata(count);                           { read and tabulate data }
    printtable(count)                          { print the table     }
  end.  { main }
```

Program 2.5. *Countpcs*

References and Selected Readings

The following source is an excellent summary of computer languages, including their basic features, the design philosophy behind them, and their history. The book is clearly written and accessible to readers without an extensive background in computing.

Baron, Naomi S. *Computer Languages.* Garden City, N.Y.: Anchor Press/Doubleday, 1986.

The following dissertation contains a good summary of both computer languages and computer-aided music research up to the mid-1960s.

Kostka, Stefan M. "The Hindemith String Quartets: A Computer-Assisted Study of Selected Aspects of Style." Ph.D. diss., University of Wisconsin, 1969.

The program in this chapter that generates frequencies in Hertz for the tempered scale prints a table that is similar to that one on page 153 of the following source. Backus describes a slightly different method of generating these frequencies on pages 146–48.

Backus, John. *The Acoustical Foundations of Music.* 2d ed. New York: W.W. Norton, 1977.

The following source contains the first published description of Pascal:

Wirth, Niklaus. "The Programming Language Pascal." *Acta Informatica* 1 (1971): 35–63.

The following source details implementation of compilers for Pascal:

Barron, D. W. *Pascal—The Language and its Implementation.* Chichester, U.K.: John Wiley & Sons, 1981.

The Edna St. Vincent Millay quote in section 2.2 was used in the chapter on program loops in the following Pascal text:

Savitch, Walter J. *Pascal, An Introduction to the Art and Science of Programming.* Menlo Park, Calif.: Benjamin/Cummings, 1984.

The following text contains an extensive bibliography of works dealing with Pascal and structured programming techniques:

Grogono, Peter. *Programming in Pascal,* 2d ed. Reading, Mass.: Addison-Wesley, 1984.

If you have not studied any math in some time, it would be a good idea to review. You can find good review books in most bookstores. In addition, the following text is an excellent introduction to group theory and other concepts of modern algebra:

Adler, Irving. *The New Mathematics.* New York: Mentor (New American Library of World Literature), 1960.

The Computer Music Association (P.O. Box 1634, San Francisco, Calif. 94101-1634) is an international association of individuals and institutions involved in the technical, creative, and performance aspects of music. Write to the above address for information regarding memberships or publications. The CMA publishes the *Proceedings of the International Computer Music Conference* for all conferences since 1975, and other materials. Their newsletter, *Array*, is an excellent source of current information. The following source contains invaluable information on institutions and individuals working in the field, lists of compositions and publications, and programs of previous International Computer Music Conferences.

Harris, Craig R., and Stephen T. Pope, eds. *The CMA Source Book: Activities and Resources in Computer Music.* San Francisco: The Computer Music Association, 1987.

As this book goes to press, a new journal devoted to the dissemination of scholarly work in all aspects of computer-related music research has been announced. For more information, write to *Journal of Computers in Music Research*, Wisconsin Center for Music Technology, School of Music, University of Wisconsin, Madison, Wis. 53562.

Exercises

The exercises in this chapter are intended to get you started working with the text editor and Pascal compiler on your computer system. In the process you will begin to become familiar with the syntax of Pascal, and you will also develop a feel for the structured approach to problem solving.

1. Study the programs in this chapter carefully, and get as much out of them as your proficiency level allows.

2. Find out how to use the text editor and compiler/interpreter on your system and enter and run some of the programs in this chapter.

3. If you feel that you are ready, you might experiment with making changes in the programs in the text or writing a few short programs that are similar. You can begin by experimenting with small changes, e.g., omitting parentheses, changing or omitting punctuation, etc., so that you can start to become familiar with the error messages generated by your Pascal system.

3| Pascal Basics and Simple Types

In the last chapter we had an overview of the structure of a Pascal program and saw examples of simple Pascal programs. This chapter introduces the basic elements of Pascal in a more thorough and formal way, starting with symbols, identifiers, and reserved words, and ending with an examination of Pascal's simple data types. By simple types we mean data items that are generally treated as single, indivisible items, such as a number, a character, or a boolean value *true* or *false*. The predefined simple types in Pascal are the ordinal types—*integer*, *boolean*, and *char*—plus the type *real*. Pascal also provides for user-defined ordinal types called *enumerated types*, *subrange types*, and *pointer types* used to construct linked data structures. This chapter covers the simple types, the general structure of a Pascal program, the assignment statement, and the evaluation of expressions.

In addition to the simple types presented here, Pascal provides a number of structured types—arrays, sets, records, files, and linked structures—that can represent collections of related data items and relationships between them. Structured types are the topic of chapters 10 through 16.

3.1 The Basic Elements of Pascal

A Pascal program is made up of symbols and of delimiters that separate the symbols. Pascal symbols consist of special symbols, word symbols, identifiers, numbers, character strings, labels, and directives. Symbols are separated by blanks, newline characters, and comments.

Special Symbols. The special symbols used in Pascal are shown in table 3.1. Note that some special symbols consist of a single special character, and some of two. The characters in the compound symbols are never separated by blanks or other delimiters. Alternate symbols are provided to accommodate computers with less complete character sets.[1]

Reserved Words. Reserved words (or word symbols) are words that have special meaning, and may not be used in any context other than that defined explicitly in Pascal. These words may not be used as identifiers (see below). Reserved words are set in bold font in this text, and are often underlined in handwritten programs. You

1. In this text we will use '↑' instead of '^', since it shows up better in type.

Arithmetic Symbols	+	–	*	/		
Boolean Symbols	=	<>	<	<=	>=	>
Paired Symbols	( )	[ ]	' '	{ }		
Other Symbols	:=	.	,	;	:	^	..
Alternate Special Symbols	(.		for	[		
	).		for	]		
	(*		for	{		
	*)		for	}		
	@ or ↑		for	^		

Table 3.1. Special Symbols used in Pascal

do not need to take any special action in programs typed for submission to the computer. Pascal's reserved words are shown in table 3.2.

Comments. Comments can be inserted in a program anywhere blanks can be used, i.e., between identifiers, numbers, or special symbols, although they are usually placed at the ends of lines or set off by themselves. Comments are one means of providing documentation for human readers. Their inclusion or removal has no effect on the program as far as the computer is concerned. Comments are delimited by braces or, alternately, by parentheses and asterisks, which mark the beginning and end of the comment. Block comments are often set off from the program graphically as follows:

```
(*****************************************************************)
(* This block comment might be used to describe various aspects of  *)
(* a program or subprogram.  Note that each line is begun and ter-  *)
(* minated by a comment delimiter.  This is not really necessary,   *)
(* although it looks nice.  What IS important is that comments are  *)
(* clearly set off from the actual program.  Although some program- *)
(* mers use the form shown below, the writer prefers this form.     *)
(*****************************************************************)
```

and	**downto**	**if**	**or**	**then**
array	**else**	**in**	**packed**	**to**
begin	**end**	**label**	**procedure**	**type**
case	**file**	**mod**	**program**	**until**
const	**for**	**nil**	**record**	**var**
div	**function**	**not**	**repeat**	**while**
do	**goto**	**of**	**set**	**with**

Table 3.2. Reserved Words in Pascal

```
{
  **  This shows an alternate format for block comments.  The border
  **  at the left helps to set off the comment.  The actual comment
  **  delimiters occur only at the beginning and end.
}
```

Line comments are short comments that are added between lines or at the ends of lines to clarify actions of the program:

```
qnum := random(low, high);  { choose question number }
```

It is helpful to the reader to leave at least one space between comment delimiters and the enclosed comments.

```
{ this is easy to read }     {this is a bit more difficult}
```

Identifiers. Identifiers are names that denote constants, types, variables, procedures, and functions. They consist of alphabetic and numeric characters (no special characters, blanks, or punctuation marks). The first character must be alphabetic. The standard endorsed by the International Standards Organization (ISO) states that identifiers may be of any length and all characters are significant. However, Wirth's original Pascal definition stated that only the first eight characters are significant, and many compilers still follow this convention. Thus it is a good idea to make the first eight characters distinct. You may use upper- and lowercase characters, but the computer treats them as equivalent. In this text identifiers are printed in italic type. Table 3.3 illustrates erroneous identifiers with possible corrections. Note that identifiers such as the following are legal, although they may be treated as equivalent by your compiler; i.e., each except the last may be interpreted by the compiler as *lengthof*:

```
lengthofmovement
LengthOfPiece
lengthofmeasure
lengthOfpiece
lengthOfMovement
TheBirthDateOfLudwigVanBeethoven
```

Illegal Identifiers	*Error*	*Correction*
3rdMovement	begins with digit	*mvt3*
end of piece	contains blanks	*fine*
first.part	contains special character	*part1*
A-one-and-a-two	contains special character	*countoff*
1forTheRoad	begins with digit	*nightcap*
22skidoo	begins with digit	*slogan*
set	reserved word	*pcset*
$amount	contains special character	*dollars*
&^$(!!*	contains special characters	*curses*

Table 3.3. Examples of Illegal Identifiers

Overly long identifiers, such as the last one in the previous list, do not really help readability of a program, even though the identifiers may be descriptive. It is better to use identifiers such as the following, which are distinct and reasonably short:

```
barlength
totallength
mvtlength
```

Identifiers should be chosen carefully for their mnemonic value. This is as important as comments are for good documentation. The following statements may accomplish the same task, but the statement on the right tells the human reader a lot more about what is going on in the program:

Poor Identifiers	Mnemonic Identifiers
x := *y* * *z* / *a*;	*duration* := *barlength* * *measures* / *tempo*;
c := *f*(*x*);	*pitchclass* := *pitch*(*nameclass*);
xnarf(*flidget*);	*printheading*(*pagenumber*);

That is not to say that all identifiers must be mnemonic. Programmers frequently use single-letter identifiers for loop variables. While nobody will complain if you invent more interesting identifiers, the following are fine in context, especially with a few comments as shown below:

```
for i := 1 to n do                { print tune    }
   write(tune[i])

for i := 1 to n do                { print matrix }
  begin { print row i }
    for j := 1 to m do
      write(M[i, j]);
    writeln
  end;  { print row i }
```

Standard Identifiers. Pascal includes a number of predefined identifiers, which are used to name standard functions and procedures, data types, and predefined constants and variables. The use of these identifiers is not restricted, i.e., you may redefine them if you wish. However, by so doing you will override the standard meaning in

abs	*eoln*	*new*	*read*	*sqrt*
arctan	*exp*	*odd*	*readln*	*succ*
boolean	*false*	*ord*	*real*	*text*
char	*get*	*output*	*reset*	*true*
chr	*input*	*pack*	*rewrite*	*trunc*
cos	*integer*	*page*	*round*	*unpack*
dispose	*ln*	*pred*	*sin*	*write*
eof	*maxint*	*put*	*sqr*	*writeln*

Table 3.4. Pascal's Standard Identifiers

the program block in which the identifier is defined. The standard predefined identifiers are shown in table 3.4.

Values that are stated explicitly are sometimes called *literals*. These may be numeric, boolean, or character.

Numeric Literals. Numbers are represented in decimal notation, which may represent integers or real numbers. The numbers on the first line below represent integers, and those on the second line real numbers. Numbers may be preceded by a plus or minus sign. Note that all numeric literals begin and end with digits, and that commas are not used. Numeric literals may be preceded by a sign, which is optional with positive numbers.

```
1          56          -13          10065      0
0.5        45.78129    -6.2123e+17  0.0        0.000001
```

Boolean Literals. Boolean values are represented by the standard identifiers *true* and *false*.

Strings. Sequences of characters enclosed in single quotes[2] are called character literals or strings. The single quotation mark may be included in a string by writing it twice. This convention enables the computer system to distinguish between the quotation mark and the end of the string. Examples of character literals:

```
'a'
':'
'This is a string'
'Please don''t talk during the prelude'
' This literal contains 39 characters.   '
'1988'
```

Note that the final example is a character literal, and has no numeric value. Strings consisting of a single character are equivalent to the type *char*.

Delimiters. The blank character, the newline character marking the end of a line, and comments are delimiters that separate other symbols. An arbitrary number of these delimiters may be used to separate reserved words, identifiers, operators, and literals in the program. We will establish more concrete format guidelines later.

3.2 The Parts of a Program

A program consists of two parts—the *heading* and the *body*. The heading gives the name of the program and lists its parameters. Program parameters are file variables, which indicate the files from which the program will receive data and into which it will write the results of its computation. The standard files in Pascal are called *input* and *output*. File *output* is mandatory unless an external file is used, since every program must report the result of its computation. File *input* may be omitted if the program needs no external data to complete its task. The use of additional files besides

2. The single right quotation mark, or apostrophe, is used at the beginning and end of the string when typing a Pascal program. In this text we use the prime (′) to represent this symbol in setting programs.

program <program name> (<file$_1$>, <file$_2$>, . . . , <file$_n$>);

where	**program**	is a Pascal reserved word,
	<program name>	is an identifier,
	( )	are Pascal special symbols, and
	<file$_i$>	$(1 \le i \le n)$ is a file variable

Figure 3.1. SYNTAX: The Program Heading

input and *output* is discussed in chapter 14. The syntax of the program heading is shown in figure 3.1. The program heading below indicates that program *test* will require files *input* and *output*:

```
program test(input, output);
```

The body of the program, called the *program block*, consists of six parts: *label declarations*, *constant declarations*, *type declarations*, *variable declarations*, *procedure* and *function definitions*, and *program statements*. These sections must occur in the order shown in figure 3.2; however, any but the last may be omitted. In this chapter we will define constant, type, and variable declarations and the program statement part. Label declarations are described, along with the **goto**, at the end of chapter 5. All procedures and functions must be declared before they are called. The syntax of these declarations is essentially the same as that for a program, except that the program heading is replaced by a procedure or function heading, and each subprogram block is terminated by a semicolon instead of a period. Functions and procedures are discussed in chapter 9.

< label declarations >
< constant declarations >
< type declarations >
< variable declarations >
< procedure and function definitions >
< program statements >

Figure 3.2. SYNTAX: The Program Block

A *constant* is an identifier with a fixed value that is assigned at the beginning of the program and cannot be changed elsewhere in the program. Careful use of constants helps program readability and makes it easier to modify a program, since the value is changed once rather than every time it occurs. The type of a constant is not declared; it is determined from the syntax. The constant declaration part of a program follows the reserved word **const**, which serves as a heading for the section (see figure 3.3). Some examples of constant declarations are shown below:

```
const
  sharp       = '#';                 { symbol for sharp       }
  flat        = '-';                 { symbol for flat        }
  tuningnote  = 440;                 { A4                     }
  epsilon     = 0.0000001;           { a small value          }
  equaltemp   = true;                { equal-tempered scale   }
  heading     = 'Set Analysis';      { page heading           }
```

The type declaration part is headed by the reserved word **type** (figure 3.4). Type declarations define new type identifiers to represent data types, which may be simple, structured, or pointer types. User-defined simple types are described later in this chapter. Structured types and pointer types are covered in chapters 12 through 16. Each declaration consists of an identifier, which will be used to denote the type, and a type specification, which may be a previously defined type identifier or a new type specification.

const
<identifier$_1$> = <value$_1$>;
<identifier$_2$> = <value$_2$>;
. . .
<identifier$_n$> = <value$_n$>;

where	**const**	is a reserved word heading the section
	<identifier$_i$>	$(1 \le i \le n)$ is an identifier,
	=	is a special symbol, and
	<value$_i$>	$(1 \le i \le n)$ is a literal of one of the standard types (integer, real, boolean, character) or a previously defined constant

Figure 3.3. SYNTAX: The Constant Declaration Part

type
<identifier$_1$> = <type$_1$>;
<identifier$_2$> = <type$_1$>;
. . .
<identifier$_n$> = <type$_n$>;

where	**type**	is a reserved word heading the section,
	<identifier$_i$>	$(1 \le i \le n)$ is an identifier denoting the type,
	=	is a special symbol, and
	<type$_i$>	$(1 \le i \le n)$ is a simple type, a structured type, or a pointer type

Figure 3.4. SYNTAX: The Type Declaration Part

var
<identifier$_1$> : <type$_1$>;
. . .
<identifier$_n$> : <type$_n$>;
[or]
<identifier$_1$>, . . . , <identifier$_n$> : <type>;

where	**var**	is a reserved word heading the section,
	<identifier$_i$>	($1 \le i \le n$) is an identifier,
	:	is a Pascal special symbol, and
	<type$_i$>	($1 \le i \le n$) is one of the standard types (integer, real, boolean, char), or a user-defined type

Figure 3.5. SYNTAX: The Variable Declaration Part

The syntax for type declarations is shown in figure 3.5. In Pascal, all variables and their types must be declared explicitly, as shown in the examples below:

```
var
  i, j, k  : integer;   { loop variables               }
  duration : real;      { decimal value of a duration  }
  symbol   : char;      { whatever                     }
  analyze  : boolean;   { true until analysis is done  }
```

The above example shows variables declared using predefined simple types. The types may be any previously defined type identifier or a new type description. Examples of declarations using enumerated and subrange types will be shown in sections 3.5.4 and 3.5.5.

begin
<statements>
end.

where	**begin** and **end**	are reserved words, and
	<statements>	represents any number of Pascal statements separated by semicolons

Figure 3.6. SYNTAX: The Statement Part

The statement part of the program is a compound statement (see chapter 5). Note that every Pascal program is terminated by a period. It is good practice to affix the comment { main } to the **begin** and **end** delimiters of the main block to distinguish it from other compound statements, as shown in the following example:

```
begin { main }
  writeln('Bach Lives!');
  writeln('So does Beethoven!');
  writeln('Don''t forget Mozart!');
  writeln('And Palestrina, and Stravinsky, and ... ')
end.  { main }
```

3.3 The Assignment Statement and Expressions

The syntax of the assignment statement is shown in figure 3.7. The assignment operator must not be confused with the relational symbol '=' (equals). If the expression type is incompatible with the variable type, a program error results (see appendix B).

An expression can be a simple variable, literal value, or function, the type of which is compatible with the variable, or it can be more complex, including any number of values and operators. Some examples are shown below:

```
i := 7;
x := abs(y) + z;
j := i + 1;
negative := input↑ = '-';
pitchclass := (pitchclass + n) mod 12;
```

When the assignment statement is executed, the expression on the right of the assignment operator is evaluated first, and the result is assigned to the variable. The statement

```
i := i + 1;
```

adds one to the current value of variable *i*, and then assigns the result to *i*, thus incrementing the value of *i* by 1. The operators applicable to various data types and rules for evaluating expressions are covered in the following sections.

<variable> := <expression>

where	<variable>	is a declared variable,
	:=	is the assignment operator, and
	<expression>	is an expression that evaluates to a type compatible with <variable>

Figure 3.7. SYNTAX: The Assignment Statement

3.4 Standard Functions

A function is a subroutine that returns a value. For example, the statement

```
x := sqrt(341)
```

assigns to *x* the square root of 341. Table 3.5 summarizes standard functions in Pas-

Function Type	Argument Type: integer	real	boolean	char	file
integer	*abs* *ord* *pred* *sqr* *succ*	*round* *trunc*	*ord*	*ord*	
real	*arctan* *cos* *exp* *ln* *sin* *sqrt*	*abs* *arctan* *cos* *exp* *ln* *sin* *sqr* *sqrt*			
boolean	*odd*		*pred* *succ*		*eof* *eoln*
char	*chr*			*pred* *succ*	

Table 3.5. Pascal Standard Functions

cal. The function type is the type of value returned by the function. The argument type is the type of the value (literal, constant, variable, or expression) passed to the function. These functions will be described further in forthcoming sections on individual data types.

3.5 Ordinal Types

An ordinal type consists of a finite number of ordered elements. The ordinal types in Pascal are *integer*, *boolean*, and *char*, plus enumerated types. Functions *succ*, *pred*, and *ord* are defined for all ordinal types. For any element x, *succ*(x) is the successor of x in the ordinal type, and *pred*(x) is its predecessor. The predecessor of the first element and the successor of the last element in the type are undefined. Function *ord*(x) returns the ordinal position of x in its ordinal type, beginning with 0 for the first element.

3.5.1 The Type *Integer*

Integers are whole numbers (with no fractional part). A computer uses a subset of whole numbers that is implementation dependent. The predefined constant *maxint* contains the largest integer allowed in a Pascal implementation. Common sizes are

32,767 ($2^{15} - 1$), and 2,147,483,647 ($2^{31} - 1$). The smallest integer that may occur in a program is *–maxint.*

Arithmetic Operators. The arithmetic operators defined for integers are shown in table 3.6. Each of the operators shown above except the last is dyadic, i.e., it takes two arguments. The unary minus sign negates its argument, e.g., –123. Note that in integer division (**div**) the result is truncated, i.e., (5 **div** 2) is equal to 2. The slash (/) may be used with integers, but the result is a real number, e.g., (5 / 2) is equal to approximately 2.50.

*	multiply
div	divide and truncate
/	divide (real result)
mod	remainder[3]
+	add
–	subtract
–	(unary) negation

Table 3.6. Integer Operators in Pascal

Integer Functions. The standard functions yielding integer results are shown in table 3.7. The absolute value of a number is the positive value, e.g., |5| = |–5| = 5. *Trunc* and *round* convert real numbers to integers. *Trunc* drops the fractional part, and *round* converts to the nearest integer. With integers, *succ*(*i*) is equivalent to *i* + 1 and *pred*(*i*) is equivalent to *i* – 1.

abs(*i*)	absolute value of *i*
sqr(*i*)	*i* * *i*
round(*x*)	where *x* is real, rounds to the nearest whole integer.
trunc(*x*)	where *x* is real, returns the whole part, i.e, truncates *x* (discards fractional part)
ord(*i*)	*i*
pred(*i*)	*i* – 1
succ(*i*)	*i* + 1

Table 3.7. Integer Functions in Pascal

3. The formula for calculating **mod** was shown in exercise 9 of chapter 1.

Integer Expressions. Integer expressions consist of *integer literals, variables, constants, function calls,* and *operators.* Expressions are evaluated from left to right but with the following order of precedence:

1. Function evaluation
2. Multiplication and division
3. Addition and subtraction

Example: where x is an integer variable, the statement

```
x := 3 + 5 div 2 - abs(3 - 7) * 2
```

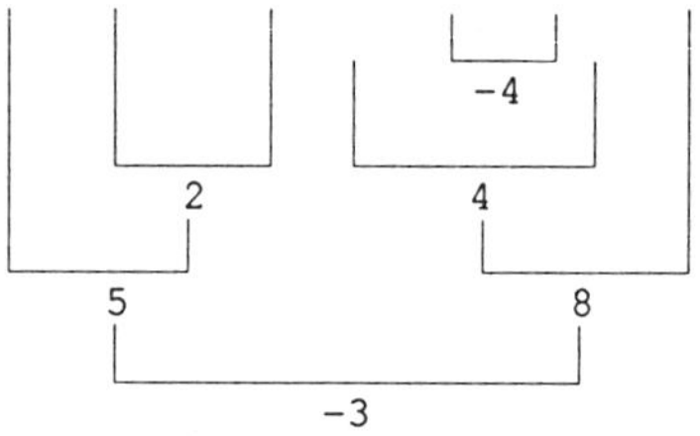

assigns –3 to x.

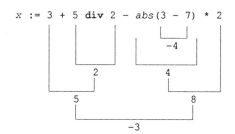

Parentheses can be used to change the order of evaluation. Subexpressions inside parentheses are evaluated first, and parentheses can be nested to any level. The assignment statement

```
i := ((b + 2) * (c - 3)) div ((a + 7) * (d - 4))
```

is equivalent to the formula[4]

$$i = \left\lfloor \frac{(b + 2)(c - 3)}{(a + 7)(d - 4)} \right\rfloor$$

Integer expressions can be used wherever an integer literal or constant can be used, except in constant definitions, which can only use literals and previously defined constants.

Style Note: Always leave one blank space on either side of each arithmetic operator, as shown above. The computer won't care, but any person reading your program will appreciate the increased readability. Compare the statement shown below to the one above.

```
i:=((b+2)*(c-3))div((a+7)*(d-4))
```

4. The floor brackets indicate that the result is rounded down, or truncated.

3.5.2 The Type *Boolean*

A boolean value is one of the two values denoted by the standard identifiers *true* and *false*. The type is implicitly defined in Pascal as an ordinal type of two elements

```
type
  boolean = (false, true);
```

with *false* < *true*. Boolean expressions are composed of *relational operators*, *boolean operators*, and their *operands*. Boolean values are used in control structures such as the following (explained in chapter 5):

```
[ const
    doublebar = 100;

  var
    response     : char;
    n, x, code   : integer;
    affirmative  : boolean;    ]

    if n mod 10 = 0      { if 10 divides n, begin new line }
      then writeln(x)
      else write(x);

    read(code);          { print each code to double bar    }
    while code <> doublebar do
      begin
        write(code);
        read(code)
      end;

    write('Do you need instructions? (yes/no): ');
    repeat               { get user's response to question }
      readln(response);
      if not (response in ['y', 'Y', 'n', 'N'])
        then write('You must answer "yes" or "no": ');
    until response in ['y', 'Y', 'n', 'N'];
    affirmative := response in ['y', 'Y'];

    if affirmative
      then instruct;     { call instruct procedure          }
```

Relational Operators. The relational operators are shown in table 3.5. Relational operators are dyadic, i.e., they compare two operands of compatible types. They can

=	equal
<>	not equal
<=	less than or equal
<	less than
>=	greater than or equal
>	greater than

Table 3.8. Relational Operators

be applied to any type on which an ordering has been defined, i.e., any ordinal type, including enumerated types (section 3.5.4). A few examples are shown below:

Relational Expression	Value
9 = 9	*true*
7 > 9	*false*
7 < 21	*true*
123.3 > 0.0	*true*
4 <= 101	*true*

Obviously, variables or constants of the appropriate types could be used in the place of literals. Using relational operators with incompatible types results in a program error. An expression such as (10 < *true*) or (8 > 'a') is not permitted, although (5.9 > 10) is, since integers are a subset of real numbers.

One should not test real numbers for equality directly, due to the round-off errors inherent in real arithmetic (see section 3.6). Never assume that two calculated real values are equal, i.e., that the expression

```
x = y
```

ought to be true if *x* and *y* are real variables. Instead, we consider them to be equal if they are close enough. "Close enough" depends on many factors, including the precision of reals in your computer and the type of computation that was performed to arrive at the values of *x* and *y*. We test this tolerance by comparing the difference between the values to a small predefined quantity.

```
if abs(x - y) < epsilon
  then <x and y are considered equal>
```

Boolean Operators. There are three boolean operators: **and**, **or**, and **not**. **And** and **or** are dyadic operators, that is, they take left and right arguments, which must be boolean. If B_1 and B_2 are boolean expressions, B_1 **and** B_2 evaluates to *true* only if B_1 and B_2 are both *true*. If either argument is *false*, the **and** operator returns *false*. The boolean operator **or** returns *true* if either or both operands are *true*, and *false* only if neither is *true*. These relationships are shown in table 3.9.

and	*true*	*false*
true	*true*	*false*
false	*false*	*false*

or	*true*	*false*
true	*true*	*true*
false	*true*	*false*

Table 3.9. Truth Tables for **and** and **or**

The operator **not** is unary (it takes one argument). It reverses the truth value of its operand, i.e., **not** *true* evaluates to *false* and **not** *false* to *true*.

The **not** operator is applied first, and **and** is applied before **or**. Parentheses may be used to change the order of evaluation. Thus if B_1, B_2, B_3, and B_4 are boolean expressions, then the expression on the left is equivalent to the one on the right:

not B_1 **or** B_2;	(**not** B_1) **or** B_2;
B_1 **and** B_2 **or** B_3;	(B_1 **and** B_2) **or** B_3;
B_1 **or** B_2 **and** B_3 **or not** B_4;	B_1 **or** (B_2 **and** B_3) **or** (**not** B_4);

The boolean values B_1, B_2 . . . can be derived from the boolean identifiers (*true* or *false*), boolean variables, relational operators, or boolean functions. When relational operators are used in conjunction with boolean operators, parentheses *must* be used around the relational part. This is because the order of precedence is higher for boolean operators. Thus the expression

```
x > y and j = 10
```

is erroneous, since it evaluates as

```
x > (y and j) = 10
```

resulting in type incompatibilities.

Boolean Functions. There are three standard functions that return boolean values. *Eof* and *eoln* will be explained in detail in chapter 8.

eof	*true* at the end of the input file
eoln	*true* at end of an input line
odd(*i*)	*true* if integer *i* is odd

Table 3.10. Boolean Functions

Boolean Assignment. The value of boolean expressions can be assigned directly to boolean variables. For example, if *done* is a boolean variable, *doublebar* is a defined constant, and *code* is a variable of the same type as *doublebar*, we can write

```
done := code = doublebar
```

The inexperienced programmer often writes this as

```
if code = doublebar
  then done := true
  else done := false;
```

While this accomplishes the same thing, it is not as efficient, nor is it good programming practice. A similar inefficiency can occur when the value of a boolean variable is tested:

Wrong	Correct
`if test = true` `  then ...`	`if test` `  then ...`

A boolean variable already has the value *true* or *false*. The first construction forces the compiler to waste time determining that (*true* = *true*) is *true* or that (*false* = *true*) is *false*. Master the correct idiom from the start.

The **in** *Operator.* One other boolean construction should be discussed in this section, because we will want to use it many times before it is explained formally in chapter 12. The reserved word **in** tests for set membership. The first operand is any ordinal value, and the second is a set of elements of the same type. The expression

x **in** [<set>]

returns *true* if *x* is in the set of values in brackets. The values in the set can be separated by commas or can be specified as subrange types (e.g., 0 . . 11 means 0, 1, 2, 3, 4, 5, 6, 7, 8, 9, 10, 11). As an example consider the following:

i **in** [0 . . 11]	is *true* if *i* is a pitch-class integer
c **in** ['a' . . 'z']	is *true* if *c* is a lowercase character
c **in** ['A' . . 'Z', 'a' . . 'z']	is *true* if *c* is an alphabetic character
x **in** ['a' . . 'g']	is *true* if *x* is a note name
ch **in** ['0' . . '9']	is *true* if *ch* is a digit
c **in** [*sharp*, *flat*]	is *true* if *c* is one of the defined character constants representing the sharp and flat.[5]

One final observation: Since the order of precedence of **not** is higher than that of **in**, the **in** construction must be parenthesized if it is negated:

```
if not (input↑ in ['+', '-'])
  then ...
```

The same statement without the parentheses will result in a compiler error.

3.5.3 The Type *Char*

Members of the ordinal type *char* are elements of an implementation-defined set of characters used by the computer system. Unfortunately, there is no universally accepted character set.

Typically, the character set includes alphabetic characters, special characters, and control characters. Character literals are represented by a single character within single quotes. The single quote (prime) is represented by typing it twice. The literals

```
'a'    '!'    'Z'    '0'    ' '    ''''
```

represent the following characters: lowercase a, exclamation point, uppercase Z, the character zero, the blank character, and the single quote ('). Some characters (the control characters) may not have a literal representation. According to Jensen and Wirth (1985), the following assumptions can be made for the type *char*:

5. Assume that *sharp* and *flat* are previously defined character constants.

1. The decimal digits '0' through '9' are in numeric order and consecutive, i.e., *ord*('0') < *ord*('1'), and *succ*('0') = '1'.
2. If uppercase letters 'A' through 'Z' exist, they are in alphabetic order, but they are not necessarily contiguous, i.e., *ord*('A') < *ord*('B'), but it may not be true that *succ*('A') = 'B'.
3. If lowercase letters 'a' through 'z' exist, they are in alphabetic order, but not necessarily contiguous, i.e., *ord*('a') < *ord*('b'), but it may not be true that *succ*('a') = 'b'.

The ASCII character set, which is commonly used in small computers, contains 128 characters.[6] The ordinal position of some of these is shown in table 3.11. The printing characters are in positions 32 through 126. Note that in this character set the uppercase characters are contiguous, and each uppercase character is a fixed distance from the corresponding lowercase character. This is convenient for mapping lower case to upper case or vice versa.

Ordinal Position	*Character Classification*
0– 31	control characters
32	space character
33– 47	punctuation
48– 57	decimal digits '0' through '9'
58– 64	punctuation
65– 90	uppercase alphabet 'A' through 'Z'
91– 96	punctuation
97–122	lowercase alphabet 'a' through 'z'
123–126	punctuation
127	control character

Table 3.11. Location of Characters in the ASCII Character Set

Character Functions. The functions shown in table 3.12 operate on character data. Functions *ord* and *chr* are inverse functions, i.e.,

$$chr(ord('x')) = 'x'$$

and

$$ord(chr(n)) = n$$

These functions are useful for converting character data into numeric data or into different portions of the character set. For example, any character *c*, representing a decimal digit, can be mapped into its integer value *n* by the following:

```
n := ord(c) - ord('0');
```

6. ASCII is an acronym for American Standard Code for Information Interchange. The entire ASCII character set is shown in appendix A.

ord(*c*)	Maps character *c* into its ordinal position
chr(*i*)	Maps integer *i* into the *i*th character in the character set
pred(*c*)	Returns the predecessor of character *c* in the character set
succ(*c*)	Returns the successor of character *c* in the character set

Table 3.12. Character Functions

Conversely, an integer n, $0 \le n \le 9$, can be converted to its corresponding character c by

```
c := chr(ord('0') + n);
```

Since in the ASCII character set the corresponding characters of the upper- and lowercase alphabets are equidistant, the functions *ord* and *chr* can be used to map any uppercase character *UC* into the corresponding lowercase character *LC*:

```
LC := chr(ord(UC) - ord('A') + ord('a'))
```

The expression *ord*(*UC*) – *ord*('*A*') calculates the offset of *UC* from 'A', e.g., 'A' into 0, 'B' into 1, . . . , 'Z' into 25. Adding *ord*('a') maps this offset into the ordinal position of the equivalent character in the lowercase alphabet, and *chr*( ) converts this position to a character. The conversion does not depend on alphabetic characters being contiguous, but rather on a constant distance between 'A' and 'a', 'B' and 'b', 'C' and 'c', etc. Lower case is mapped into upper case by:

```
UC := chr(ord(LC) - ord('a') + ord('A'));
```

The *chr* function is also used to generate the nonprinting control characters, which cannot be represented as literals. For example, in the ASCII character set the tab character (TAB) is *chr*(9), the escape character (ESC) is *chr*(12), and the null character (NUL) is *chr*(0).[7]

When functions *pred* and *succ* are applied to characters, the result depends on the ordering of characters in the character set. In general, for any character c

$$succ(c) = chr(ord(c) + 1)$$

and

$$pred(c) = chr(ord(c) - 1)$$

However, the successor of the last character and the predecessor of the first character in the character set are undefined.

7. We will use the null character to mark the end of variable length character strings (section 11.1). The escape character is commonly used in control sequences for external devices such as CRT terminals (chapter 18).

Comparing Character Data. As with the other ordinal types, characters can be compared using the boolean relational operators. The result depends on the ordering of characters in the character set. In general, for any two characters *x* and *y*,

x <op> *y*

is *true* if and only if

(*ord*(*x*) <op> *ord*(*y*))

where <op> is any of the relational operators:

< <= = >= >

Consider, for example, the characters '3' and '5', ASCII characters 51 and 53. The boolean expression ('3' < '5') is *true* because *ord*('3') < *ord*('5').

The logical operators can also be applied to character literals (strings) of the same length. Here, the first non-equal character is used for the comparison. For example, in the ASCII character set,

Expression	Value
`'abcde'   <  'abdef'`	*true*
`'String'  =  'string'`	*false*
`'Mozart ' <  'stamitz'`	*true*
`'Mozart ' >= 'Stamitz'`	*false*

Note that strings that are not the same length are not type compatible. The expression

```
'Mozart' > 'Stamitz'
```

is no more permissible than

```
'z' >= 124
```

Both expressions apply relational operators to incompatible types.

3.5.4 Enumerated Types

Pascal provides for user-defined ordinal types called *enumerated types*. Enumerated types are declared in the type declaration part of a program. Type declarations are placed in a program just after constant declarations and before variable declarations (see section 3.2). The syntax for declaring enumerated types is shown in figure 3.8. The declaration results in an ordinal type called <type name>, in which the first element has the ordinal value 0. Elements of an enumerated type cannot be members of any other ordinal type; thus integers, characters, and elements of a previously defined enumerated type cannot be included in the definition of a new enumerated type. After declaration, the type can be used to declare variables that can represent elements of the type. Some examples are shown below:

```
type
  dyntype   = (ppppp, pppp, ppp, pp, p, mp, mf, f, ff, fff,
                                                  ffff, fffff);

  formtype  = (binary, ternary, roundedbinary, sonata, rondo,
                                            sonatarondo, unique);

  ptype     = (Forte, Rahn);

  comp20    = (Schoenberg, Webern, Berg, Stravinsky, Babbitt);

var
    dynamic   : dyntype;
    form      : formtype;
    primetype : ptype;
    composer  : comp20;
```

Variables of enumerated types can be assigned values of their designated type:

```
dynamic := mf;
primetype := Forte;
composer := Stravinsky;
form := sonata;
```

<typename> = (E_1, E_2, . . . , E_n);

where	<typename>	is an identifier,
	= ( )	are Pascal special symbols, and
	E_1, E_2, . . . , E_n	are constant identifiers denoting elements of the enumerated type.

Figure 3.8. SYNTAX: Enumerated Type Definition

Functions with Enumerated Types. Functions defined for other ordinal types (except for *chr*), can also be used with enumerated types. Permissible functions are shown in table 3.13. The predecessor of the first element and the successor of the last element in the type are not defined.

ord(*e*)	Returns the ordinal position of element *e* in the type
pred(*e*)	Returns the predecessor of element *e*
succ(*e*)	Returns the successor of element *e*

Table 3.13. Functions used with Enumerated Types

Relational Operators and Enumerated Types. The standard relational operators can be used with user-defined ordinal types. As with character data, the comparison is based on the ordinal position of the elements in the ordinal type. Considering the types defined above, statements such as the following are permissible:

```
if dynamic > f
  then write('That''s loud');

if dynamic > ppppp
  then dynamic := pred(dynamic);

soft := dynamic <= p;       { assign value to boolean variable soft}

if composer = Stravinsky
  then writeln('Stravinsky');

for composer := Schoenberg to Babbitt do
  begin
                    { insert statements here }
  end;
```

It is important to remember that elements of enumerated types must be unique. Thus the following are not permitted:

```
type              { Incorrect Enumerated Types }

  notename  = ('a', 'b', 'c', 'd', 'e', 'f', 'g');

  pcint     = (0, 1, 2, 3, 4, 5, 6, 7, 8, 9, 10, 11);

  composers = (Dufay, Palestrina, Bach, Mozart, Beethoven,
                                                  Stravinsky);

  baroque   = (Buxtehude, Pergolesi, Purcell, Couperin, Handel,
                                                  Bach);

  genre     = (symphony, stringquartet, opera, symphony);
```

The definitions of *notename* and *pcint* are not permitted because their elements are members of types *char* and *integer*. Similarly, type *baroque* contains the constant identifier *Bach*, which is also an element of type *composers*, and is thus not permitted. The element *symphony* occurs twice in type *genre*, thus its ordinal position is ambiguous.

In standard Pascal, values of enumerated types cannot be input or output directly using procedures *read* and *write*, although some implementations include these options as an extension. In most cases the user must write procedures to perform these functions. Examples can be found in chapters 12 and 13. Enumerated types are particularly useful in defining *set* types (chapter 12).

3.5.5 Subrange Types

It is possible to define a type as a *subrange* of any previously defined ordinal type, called the *host type*. The syntax of a subrange type definition is shown in figure 3.9. In defining the subrange, the lower bound of the subrange must not be greater than

$\langle constant_1 \rangle$ .. $\langle constant_2 \rangle$

where $\langle constant_1 \rangle$ and $\langle constant_2 \rangle$ are elements of the host type, and
.. is a special symbol

Figure 3.9. SYNTAX: Subrange Type

the upper bound, i.e., the following condition must be true:

$$ord(\text{constant}_1) <= ord(\text{constant}_2)$$

The subrange definition defines the least and greatest values in the subrange. Any operation defined for the host type may be applied to the subrange type, with the restriction that the result of any evaluated expression must lie within the limits specified in the subrange.

Some examples of subrange type definitions are shown below. Note that one can define subranges of enumerated types as well as of predefined ordinal types.

```
type
  pcint = 0 .. 11;                        { pitch-class integers    }
  ncint = 0 .. 6;                         { name-class integers     }
  notename = 'A' .. 'G';                  { note letter names       }

  instrtype = (violin, viola, cello, contrabass, trumpet,

              frenchhorn, trombone, tuba, flute, oboe,
              clarinet, bassoon);  { an enumerated type      }

  strings = violin .. contrabass;
  brass   = trumpet .. tuba;
  woodwind = flute .. bassoon;            { subranges of the above }
```

Subrange types serve two purposes. First, they allow the programmer to specify explicitly the range of values that a specific variable should be allowed to assume. Thus they are an aid to clarity, since the programmer's intent is explicit. Because many Pascal systems provide automatic checks that values are within range, the programmer may be relieved of the responsibility for some value checking. Second, it is possible to save memory space in programs, since the Pascal implementation can use less memory to implement subrange variables. For example, a subrange of integers might be implemented using 8 bits per integer instead of 16 or 32. Thus you are urged to use subrange types whenever the range of values can be clearly predicted.

3.5.6 Named and Anonymous Types

Any user-defined type (enumerated types, subrange types, and structured types) can be declared in either of two ways. First, it can be named, as in most of the examples in this chapter. The named type is then used to declare variables, as in the following examples:

```
type
  pcint  = 0 .. 11;                          { a subrange type      }
  ensemb = (quartet, quintet, trio, duo);  { an enumerated type }

var
  pc        : pcint;
  ensemble : ensemb;
```

Alternately, the type can be used directly in the variable declaration. We will refer to these types as anonymous types, since they are unnamed. Thus the variables shown above could be declared as follows:

```
var
  pc        : 0 .. 11;
  ensemble : (quartet, quintet, trio, duo);
```

Why bother to name types at all, when the direct method of declaration is more concise? In simple programs either is acceptable. However, there are restrictions in the use of anonymous types. The most important of these is that they cannot be used in the declaration of parameters to subroutines (see chapter 9). If this is your first programming language and your first reading of this text, it may not seem terribly important at this point. However, you are urged to develop the habit of using named types and choosing mnemonic names for these types. This will pay off as your programs become more complex. The exception to this rule is that anonymous subranges are often used in declaring other named types when the subrange will not be used as an independent type, as in declaring the type of an array (chapter 10):

```
const
  max = 100;

type
  listtype = array [1 .. max] of integer;

var
  list : listtype;
```

3.6 The Type *Real*

Real numbers are numbers that have a fractional part. A few examples are shown below:

```
9.75   34.0   4.5782   0.12845 1256.821
```

Computers use a subset of real numbers that is implementation dependent. Although the magnitude of real numbers is not nearly so limited as that of integers, the number of significant digits is limited. The significant digits begin with the first nonzero digit. Each of the following numbers has seven significant digits:

```
1.234567    0.00000000000000000009345167    21470360000000000000.0
```

Real numbers can be written in either of two forms. The first is the decimal notation shown above. In disciplines in which very large or very small numbers are common, scientific notation is frequently used. For example, the second and third numbers shown above could be expressed as 9.345167×10^{-18} and 2.147036×10^{20}. The first part of the number, called the mantissa, specifies the significant digits; the second part, or exponent, places the decimal point. In Pascal these numbers are represented with a decimal number followed by either 'e' or 'E', an optional sign, and an integer value representing the power of 10. The two numbers shown above are expressed in this format as

```
9.345167e-18     and     2.147036e+20
```

Exponential notation is a close approximation of the internal representation, since within the computer the mantissa and exponent are stored in separate memory locations. The sign may be omitted if the exponent is positive; thus the second number could be written 2.147036e20. If you are not used to this notation, think of a positive exponent *n* as moving the decimal point *n* places to the right, or *n* places to the left if *n* is negative.

Exponential Notation	Decimal Notation
3.981360e+0	3.981360
1.234817e+3	1234.817
1.234567e-9	0.000000001234567

The decimal point and decimal digits may also be omitted. In this case the decimal point is assumed to be just to the right of the last digit of the mantissa. Thus all of the following are legal representations of real numbers in Pascal:

```
9   1.2345e7   69e-2   2.982791   46e-12.
```

Remember that numeric values always begin with a digit in Pascal, and that commas are not permitted. Also, the decimal point must be followed by at least one digit, i.e., the decimal point is omitted if no decimal digits are to be shown. Each of the following would result in an error message if they were used in a program or in data to be read by a program:

```
3,567,823     .3123    E7    8.     3.e-20
```

Arithmetic Operators. The arithmetic operators used with real numbers or with integers are shown in table 3.14.

*	multiply
/	divide
+	add
–	subtract
–	(unary) negation

Table 3.14. Arithmetic Operators used with Real Numbers

Real Functions. Table 3.15 lists functions that can be used with real numbers. The standard functions *abs* and *sqr* return a real value when their argument is *real*, or an integer value if their argument is *integer*. The standard functions *sin*, *cos*, *arctan*, *ln*, *exp*, and *sqrt* can be used with real or integer arguments, but always return a real value. Note that *ln* and *exp* are inverse functions, i.e., for any nonzero integer x,

$$exp(ln(x)) \cong x$$

If you have worked in other programming languages, you have probably noticed the omission of an operator for calculating values such as x^3, or in general x^y. In many languages this quantity can be expressed as

```
X ** Y    { not valid in Pascal }
```

In Pascal, we can use the *ln* and *exp* to calculate this value. Since x^y is equal to $log(x) \times y$, we can calculate powers by the Pascal expression

```
power := exp(ln(x) * y)
```

so long as x is greater than 0. Thus the correct calculation is

```
if x = 0
  then power := 0
  else power := exp(ln(x) * y)
```

If an integer result is required, the expression is rounded:

```
if x = 0
  then power := 0
  else power := round(exp(ln(x) * y))
```

In chapter 9 we will learn to write a function to calculate this value; then we can write

```
r := power(x, y)
```

or

```
i := round(power(x, y))
```

abs(*x*)		absolute value
sqr(*x*)		$x * x$
sin(*x*)	}	trigonometric functions
cos(*x*)	}	
arctan(*x*)	}	
ln(*x*)		natural logarithm
exp(*x*)		exponential function
sqrt(*x*)		square root

Table 3.15. Functions used with Real Numbers

Real Expressions. The order of precedence for evaluating real expressions is the same as that for integer expressions, i.e., multiplication and division are performed before addition and subtraction.[8] When two integer values are evaluated in an expression, the rules for integer expressions are used. When part of an expression involves "mixed mode," i.e., a combination of integer and real values, the integer value is converted to real before evaluation. Thus mixed-mode expressions always yield a real result.

Example: where *x* is a variable of type *real*:

```
x := 2 + 5 / 2 * 3 + sqr(25 div 6)
```

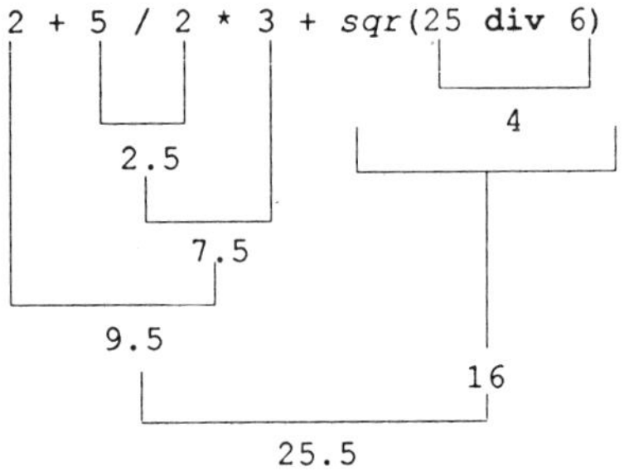

If an integer value is assigned to a real variable, the value is converted to real. Thus

```
r := 123
```

where *r* is a real variable, assigns the real number 123.0 as the value of *r*. The inverse operation is not permitted, i.e., if *i* is an integer variable, then

```
i := 27.5
```

will result in a program error. This assignment is possible if the *trunc* or *round* function is used to convert the real number to an integer.

Remember that the type *real* is not an ordinal type, since it has an infinite number of elements. Thus the functions *succ*(*x*) and *pred*(*x*) are not defined for real values of *x*. Values of type *real* cannot be used to index arrays, control **for** statements, or define the base type of a set.

Precision in Real Numbers. It is important to realize that real numbers are often only approximate in their computer implementation. The precision of real numbers is implementation dependent. Frequently seven significant digits are stored. Larger numbers can be entered, but the result is rounded. For example, if your system uses seven significant digits for real numbers, then the numbers in the left column below would be stored in the form shown at the right:

Value	Stored as
1.8498273649596	1.849827e+00
1.8498276349596	1.849828e+00
19827365127000000.0	1.982737e+16
0.00000012345858482	1.234586e–07

8. Precedence is discussed more thoroughly in appendix B.

Some rational numbers (fractions) cannot be represented precisely in decimal form. Examples are 1 / 3 and 2 / 3:

$$1 / 3 = 0.3333333333333333333\ldots$$
$$2 / 3 = 0.6666666666666666666\ldots$$

Since the computer uses limited precision, these would be stored as 0.3333333 and 0.6666667, respectively.

Because of the approximate nature of real numbers, care must be taken when one is working with real values. A small error can be compounded very quickly in a high-speed computer. Methods for dealing with rational numbers (fractions) will be explained in chapter 13. These methods are more complex, but computations can be made with ultimate precision.

References and Selected Readings

The definitive reference on the Pascal programming language was written by the author of the language with Kathleen Jensen. This source is noted for its conciseness and clarity.

Jensen, Kathleen, and Niklaus Wirth. *Pascal User Manual and Report.* 2d ed. New York: Springer-Verlag, 1974.

The above work has been revised by Mickel and Miner to correspond with the ISO Pascal standard. The new edition has been substantially reworked and is highly recommended to anyone interested in the language.

Jensen, Kathleen and Niklaus Wirth. *Pascal User Manual and Report.* 3d ed. Revised by Andrew B. Mickel and James F. Miner. New York: Springer-Verlag, 1985.

In the present text, "standard Pascal" refers to compilers that conform to the International Standards Organization (ISO) draft distributed by the American National Standards Institute (ANSI):

"DP 7185.1. Specification for the Computer Programming Language Pascal: Second Draft." *Pascal News* 20 (1980): 1–83.

The following source, which presents the Pascal standard in a more accessible form, is highly recommended:

Cooper, Doug. *Standard Pascal: User Reference Manual.* New York: W.W. Norton, 1983.

The notion of literals is borrowed from the following source:

Grogono, Peter. *Programming in Pascal.* 2d ed. Reading, Mass: Addison-Wesley, 1980.

The following describes a number of early experiments in the use of computers in music:

Hiller, L. A., Jr., and L. M. Isaacson. *Experimental Music.* New York: McGraw-Hill, 1959.

Other suggested readings:

Babbitt, Milton. "The Use of Computers in Musicological Research." *Perspectives of New Music* 3, no. 2 (1965): 74–83.

Blombach, Ann K. "A Conceptual Framework for the Use of the Computer in Music Analysis." Ph.D. diss., Ohio State University, 1976.

Brook, Barry S. "Some New Paths for Music Bibliography." In *Computers in the Humanistic Research*, edited by Edmond A. Bowles, 204–11. Englewood Cliffs, N.J.: Prentice-Hall, 1967.

LaRue, Jan. "Two Problems in Musical Analysis: The Computer Lends a Hand." In *Computers in the Humanistic Research*, edited by Edmond A. Bowles, 194–203. Englewood Cliffs, N.J.: Prentice-Hall, 1967.

Exercises

1. Evaluate the following expressions, and indicate the value and type of the result, or specify the reason the expression cannot be evaluated and would cause an error.

   a) 3 + 4 – 7 + 2.0 + 9

   b) 3 **div** 2

   c) 5.0 **div** 2

   d) 3 / 2

   e) *ord*(0)

   f) *ord*('0')

   g) *chr*(*ord*('D') – *ord*('A') + *ord*('a'));

   h) *true* **or** *false* **and not** *false* **or** *false*

   i) 7 < 9 **or** 3 = 1

   j) *odd*(7.5)

   k) *round*(6.5) / 3

   l) *trunc*(7.9999) **div** 4

   m) *sqr*(5);

   n) *sqr*(5.0);

   o) *abs*(6 – 10);

   p) *abs*(5.2 – 3);

2. Translate the following into Pascal statements:

$$v = \frac{a + b}{x - y}$$

$$v = \frac{(a - b)(c - 2)^2}{e(f + 9)}$$

3. Assume that the following declarations and assignments have been made:

   var
   l, m, i, j : *integer*;
   a, b, c : *real*;

   a := 5.0; *b* := 2.5; *i* := 4; *j* := 5; { assignments }

Show the value that will be assigned to the variable in each of the following assignment statements:

a) *c* := *a* / *b*;

b) *l* := *round*((*i* – 1) * *b*);

c) *m* := *j* **div** *i*;

d) *c* := *i* **div** *j* + *sqr*(*a*) * (*i* – 2);

e) *l* := *trunc*(*sqrt*(10 * *b*) – b);

4. Each of the following problems involves mapping of arithmetic values into other arithmetic values. For each problem, find an arithmetic expression that will map each of the values in the left hand column into the values in the right hand column. For simplicity, real numbers are always represented with a decimal point, integers without. Each solution should be formulated as a valid Pascal assignment statement. The first problem is done for you.

a)

x	?	*y*
4.2	→	4.2
5.7	→	5.7
–7.2	→	–7.2

solution: *y* := *x*;

b)

x	?	*y*
4.2	→	4
5.7	→	5
19.999	→	19
–7.2	→	7

c)

x	?	*m*
4.2	→	4
5.7	→	6
19.999	→	20
7.2	→	7

d)

x	?	*m*
–5	→	5
4	→	4
–99	→	99
0	→	0

e)

x	?	*y*
45.2	→	45.2
–12.75	→	12.75
4.5	→	4.5
–12.0	→	12.0

f)

i	?	*x*
1	→	1.0
2	→	0.5
4	→	0.25
5	→	0.20

g)

i	?	*j*
0	→	0
1	→	1
2	→	0
3	→	1
4	→	0

h)

i	?	*k*
0	→	0
4	→	0
5	→	1
6	→	1
9	→	1
10	→	2
15	→	3

i)

i	?	*j*
0	→	4
1	→	5
2	→	6
3	→	7
4	→	8

j)

i	?	*k*
0	→	1
1	→	0
2	→	1
3	→	0
4	→	1

k)

i	?	*k*
0	→	1
1	→	2
2	→	1
3	→	2

l)

l	?	*m*
1	→	1
3	→	0
4	→	1
5	→	2
6	→	0
10	→	1

m)

i	?	*j*
0	→	2
1	→	0
2	→	1
3	→	2
4	→	0

n)

i	?	*k*
1	→	1
2	→	4
3	→	9
5	→	25
9	→	81

o)

x	?	*y*
2.0	→	4.0
1.2	→	1.44
0.3	→	0.9
2.5	→	6.25

p)

x	?	*y*
4.0	→	2.0
25.0	→	5.0
0.25	→	0.5
100.0	→	10.0

q)

i	?	*k*
0	→	1
1	→	2
2	→	4
3	→	8
4	→	16
5	→	32
6	→	64

r)

i	?	*j*
1	→	0
2	→	1
4	→	2
8	→	3
16	→	4
32	→	5

s)

i	?	*x*
1	→	4.0
2	→	2.0
4	→	1.0
8	→	0.5
16	→	0.25

t)

i	?	*x*
1	→	2.0
2	→	1.0
4	→	0.5
8	→	0.25
16	→	0.125

u)

beatnote	*code*	?	*duration*
4	8	→	0.5
2	4	→	0.5
8	8	→	1.0
1	4	→	0.25
4	2	→	2.0
2	1	→	2.0
16	32	→	0.5

v)

nc	?	*pc*
0	→	0
1	→	2
2	→	4
3	→	5
4	→	7
5	→	9
6	→	11

5. The following problems are similar to the previous set, but the mapping is from *char* to *integer*, from *char* to *char*, or from *integer* to *char*.

a)

c	?	*i*
'a'	→	0
'b'	→	1
'c'	→	2
'x'	→	23
'y'	→	24
'z'	→	25

e)

n	?	*nc*
'c'	→	0
'd'	→	1
'e'	→	2
'f'	→	3
'g'	→	4
'a'	→	5
'b'	→	6

b)

c	?	*i*
'A'	→	0
'B'	→	1
'C'	→	2
'X'	→	23
'Y'	→	24
'Z'	→	25

f)

n	?	*nc*
'C'	→	0
'D'	→	1
'E'	→	2
'F'	→	3
'G'	→	4
'A'	→	5
'B'	→	6

c)

c	?	*i*
'a'	→	'A'
'b'	→	'B'
'c'	→	'C'
'x'	→	'X'
'y'	→	'Y'
'z'	→	'Z'

g)

n	?	*pc*
'c'	→	0
'd'	→	2
'e'	→	4
'f'	→	5
'g'	→	7
'a'	→	9
'b'	→	11

d)

c	?	*i*
'A'	→	'a'
'B'	→	'b'
'C'	→	'c'
'X'	→	'x'
'Y'	→	'y'
'Z'	→	'z'

h)

nc	?	*c*
0	→	'C'
1	→	'D'
2	→	'E'
3	→	'F'
4	→	'G'
5	→	'A'
6	→	'B'

4| Input and Output

Input and output, known in computer jargon as I/O (pronounced "eye-oh"), involve transferring values from an external file or device to memory locations available to the program, or from memory to some external file or device. These operations are absolutely essential. Without input, a program could not process data that was external to the program; without output, results could not be communicated from the program to the outside world. Pascal simplifies the I/O process by supplying two standard files for this purpose. These files, called *input* and *output*, are logically connected to specific I/O devices, depending on the operating system or system configuration. In UNIX systems, the standard input device, associated with the file *input*, is the keyboard on the user's terminal, and the standard output device is the CRT display on the user's terminal. This arrangement facilitates writing interactive programs in which the user communicates with the program as it is executing. In other systems files *input* and *output* may be associated with different devices. For example, the standard input device might be a card reader and the standard output device the line printer. In the following discussion, when we refer to writing to file *output*, the values written would actually print on the output device associated with the file called *output*. Reading from file *input* implies reading data from the physical input device associated with this file.

The format used for storing data (numeric data in particular) within the computer's memory is usually different from that used by external devices (such as computer terminals or files stored on computer disks). For example, an integer value is stored as a binary number within the computer's memory, but before it can be printed on the screen of your computer terminal, it must be converted to a series of ASCII characters representing the individual digits in the number.[1] Reading data involves converting from an external representation to an internal form and then storing the value in a memory location identified by a variable name. Likewise, when a value is written to an output device, it is usually converted to an external form. In a computer that uses sixteen-bit binary numbers to store integers, 25 is stored as 0000000000011001. Since most people prefer not to read binary data, this is converted to the ASCII characters '25' before printing on the CRT screen. Pascal programs can also read and write binary data without conversion; this will be discussed chapter 14.

1. ASCII is an acronym for American Standard Code for Information Interchange. See appendix A for a table of ASCII values. Another encoding system used on some computer systems is EBCDIC (Extended Binary Coded Decimal Information Code).

4.1 Program Output: *write* and *writeln*

Most output from Pascal programs is accomplished by calling the standard procedure *write*. This call has the general form:

```
write(<file>, <output list>)
```

where <file> is the name of the file to which values are to be written and <output list> contains the values to be transferred. Parameter <file> must have appeared in the list of file parameters in the program heading. If the file parameter is omitted in the *write* statement, the default value *output* is supplied. Thus

```
write(output, 'Bach lives!')
```

is equivalent to

```
write('Bach lives!')
```

and either statement writes

```
Bach lives!
```

on the standard output device. Since you will not be writing to files other than *output* for some time, you will be quite safe in omitting the file parameter for the present. Note that, although the character literal 'Bach lives!' was enclosed in single quotes in the *write* statement, the quotes are not printed.

The output list specifies the values that are to be written to the output file, separated by commas. These values may be variable names, constants, expressions, or literals (predefined values such as strings, integers, real numbers, etc.). The value printed is the value of the constant, literal, or variable. If a boolean variable, constant, or expression is included in the output list, its value is printed as the standard identifier *true* or *false*. The statement

```
write('values for a and b:', a, b, ';  sum =', a + b)
```

specifies that five items are to be written to the standard output device. These are:

1. The character literal 'values for a and b:'
2. The value of variable *a*
3. The value of variable *b*
4. The character literal '; sum ='
5. The result obtained from evaluating the arithmetic expression *a* + *b*

If variables *a* and *b* are type *integer* and have been assigned the values 9 and 22, respectively, the above *write* statement will print

```
values for a and b:     9    22;    sum =    31
```

The exact format in which items will be printed can be specified by the programmer or left up to Pascal. The *field width* (number of spaces occupied by the value on the output line) is specified by appending :*w* to an item in the output list, where *w* is the desired field width specified as an integer value. Field width may be specified by a constant, variable, literal, or expression. The number to be printed is right-justified within the specified field width, i.e., padded on the left with blanks. The table below illustrates the use of field-width specification in *write* statements. In the second column the blank character is shown as '▯'. Assume that the variable *v* is type *integer* and has been assigned the value 135.

The statement	prints
`write(v:10);`	`▯▯▯▯▯▯▯135`
`write(v:4);`	`▯135`
`write(v:3);`	`135`
`write(v:1);`	`135`
`write('string');`	`string`
`write('string':10);`	`▯▯▯▯string`
`write('string':3);`	`str`
`write(true:6);`	`▯▯true`
`write(true:2);`	`tr`
`write(' ':6);`	`▯▯▯▯▯▯`

All digits of an integer value are printed; if the number of digits is greater than the specified field width, the field width is ignored. Note, however, that strings and the external representation of boolean values can be truncated. If the field-width specification is omitted, an implementation-dependent default value is supplied by Pascal. The default width for characters is 1; for character literals it is the length of the string; for integers it depends on the Pascal compiler you are using and the size of the largest integer available in your Pascal system.

When real numbers are printed, both field width and precision (the number of decimal places) can be specified in the form *:w:d*, where *w* is the field width and *d* is the number of digits to be printed after the decimal point. The following examples illustrate the use of field width and precision in writing real values. Assume that the variable *v* is type *real* and that its current value is 33.7135.

The statement	prints
`write(v:10:2);`	`▯▯▯▯▯33.71`
`write(v:8:3);`	`▯▯33.714`
`write(v:10:5);`	`▯▯33.71350`
`write(v:2:1);`	`33.7`
`write(v:5:0);`	`▯▯▯34`
`write(v);`	`3.371350E+01`

Note that the field width includes the decimal point and that real numbers are rounded to the desired precision when printed. The output value is constructed according to the specified precision, and then padded on the left if necessary by the addition of blanks. If no field width and precision are specified, the value is printed in exponential form with one digit to the left of the decimal point. The number of digits in the mantissa is the number of significant digits available in real numbers in your version of Pascal. If field width is specified without precision, it affects the number of digits printed in the mantissa. The default field width is implementation dependent. In the following examples, assume that *x* is a real variable that has been assigned the value 7.258281.

The statement	prints
writeln(*x*);	□7.258281e+00
writeln(*x*:12);	□7.25828e+00
writeln(*x*:11);	□7.2583e+00
writeln(*x*:10);	□7.258e+00
writeln(*x*:9);	□7.26e+00
writeln(*x*:8);	□7.3e+00
writeln(*x*:7);	□7.3e+00

It is poor practice to specify more decimal digits than the number of significant digits, since this implies greater precision than was actually calculated. Precision may not be specified when integer variables or literals are printed.

Items to be printed may be combined in the output list of a single *write* statement, or divided among several *write* statements. In either case, all values will occur on the same line of the output device. In general,

```
write(a);
write(b);
write(c)
```

is equivalent to

```
write(a, b, c)
```

If the output list is long, it is permissible to split the *write* statement over several lines. The list may be interrupted by a newline <return> at any point where a blank space could occur, but the statement will be easier for the human reader to interpret if it is subdivided only after commas separating items in the list:

```
write(a, b, c,
      d, e, f, g)
```

Character literals cannot be divided between lines. However, long strings can be written as two or more shorter strings:

```
write('This string is too long to fit on the current line')
```

produces exactly the same output as

```
write('This string is too long ',
      'to fit on the current line')
```

This is convenient for formatting a Pascal program when the source code is entered with an editor. It has no effect on the printed output resulting from the *write* statement.

An output line is terminated by invoking the procedure *writeln* (pronounced "write line"). The generalized form is

```
writeln(<file>)
```

If no file is specified, *output* is assumed. Thus

```
writeln(output)
```

and

```
writeln
```

are equivalent. The statement places a single character (called a newline character) into the output file. This end-of-line marker is expanded, either by the operating system or by the output device, to a carriage-return and a line-feed character. Thus the next item written will be placed at the beginning of the next line.

Writeln can also take an output list, in which case the statement is equivalent to a *write* statement followed by a *writeln*. Thus

```
writeln(a, b, c, d)
```

is equivalent to

```
write(a, b, c, d);
writeln
```

Several *writeln* statements, separated by semicolons, can be used to enter blank lines into the program's output. The statements

```
writeln('line of text');
writeln;
writeln('another line of text')
```

produce the output

```
line of text

another line of text
```

4.2 Program Input: *read* and *readln*

The most common method of reading data into a program is to invoke the standard procedure *read*. The generalized form of this statement is

```
read(<file>, <input list>)
```

where <file> is the name of the file from which values are to be read, and <input list> is a list of variable names that are to receive values from this file. Parameter <file> must have occurred in the list of file arguments in the program heading. As with the *write* statement, the standard file is supplied by default:

```
read(input, code)
```

is equivalent to

```
read(code)
```

The input list consists of one or more declared variable names, separated by commas. When reading from *text* files such as *input*, the variables in the input list must be one of the standard types *integer*, *real*, or *char*.[2] Please note that the present discussion concerns only numeric types. The *read* procedure attempts to read a value for each variable in the input list. Reading consists of the following steps:

1. The next data item is found by skipping over any blank characters (and newline characters) preceding it in the file.
2. The ASCII character representation of the number is converted into the internal binary representation. Reading is terminated just before the next character that cannot be converted to the correct data type. If the data cannot be converted to the correct type (e.g., it is not possible to obtain any value due to incorrect

2. Properties of text files will be discussed in chapter 8.

format), an error message is printed and program execution is terminated.

3. The converted value of the data item is stored in the storage location associated with the variable from the input list.

From the above it should be apparent that for each numeric variable in the input list, Pascal expects to find one data item of the same type in the input file. Furthermore, (1) the data items in the input file are unformatted, in the sense that they do not have to occur in specific positions on the input line; (2) numeric data items in the input file are separated by one or more blank and/or newline characters; and (3) the values are assigned to variables in the order in which the variables occur in the input list.

As an example, consider the *read* statement below. Assume that variables *a*, *b*, and *c* have been declared *integer* variables, and that *x*, *y*, and *z* have been declared type *real*. The statement

```
read(a, b, x, y, z, c)
```

requests that six values be read from the standard input file and stored in the variables listed in the input list (*a*, *b*, *x*, *y*, *z*, *c*). This list could be satisfied by the following data in the input file:

```
20  52   3.14  25.7   76 29
```

resulting in the following assignments:

```
a ← 20
b ← 52
x ← 3.14
y ← 25.7
z ← 76.0
c ← 29
```

Note that the number 76 satisfies the *real* variable *z* in the input list, since whole numbers are a subset of real numbers. However, the value is stored in an internal form different from that used for integers. For now, think of it as the real number 76.0 rather than the integer 76. Since the *read* procedure skips over blanks and newline characters when seeking a new numeric value, the above input list could be satisfied by the data

```
20 52 3.14
25.7
76.0
29
```

or

```
20
52
3.14 25.7
76

29
```

or any other arrangement of input values, so long as the first two data items are compatible with type *integer*, the next three type *real*, and the last *integer*. The input values

```
10, 77, 17.345, 0.45, 32.0, 0
```

would cause an error. The first value (10) would be read successfully. Pascal would then skip to the next nonblank character and try, unsuccessfully, to convert the comma to a numeric value.

Similarly, if the variable *code* is type *integer*, the statement

```
read(code)
```

matched with the input value 7.41 would read the integer 7. The next attempt to read an integer would begin at the decimal point, causing a "fatal" execution error. (The error would be fatal only to the program, not to the programmer.) Unfortunately, an attempt to read .99 as a real value would also fail on most processors, since the Pascal standard states that numbers must begin with a digit (0.99 is permissible).

As in *write* statements, the input list can be distributed among several *read* statements. Thus

```
read(a, b, c, d, e)
```

is equivalent to

```
read(a);
read(b);
read(c, d);
read(e)
```

The procedure *readln*(<file>) causes all input data up to and including the next newline character to be skipped over (discarded). As in *read* statements, the file parameter may be omitted when the procedure is applied to the standard input file. The statements

```
read(x, y);
readln
```

when applied to the input line

```
72.3 89 20 14.5 <cr>
```

cause 72.3 to be read into variable *x*, 89.0 to be read into variable *y*, and the rest of the values on the line (including the blank characters and the newline character <cr> to be discarded.

Readln can take an input list, in which case it is equivalent to a *read* statement followed by a *readln*. Thus

```
readln(a, b, c);
```

produces exactly the same results as

```
read(a, b, c);
readln
```

When a variable of type *char* occurs in an input list, the binary representation of a single character is stored in the memory location identified by the variable. Blanks are not skipped, since the blank is a valid character. If the newline character is the next input value, it is treated as a blank. Reading character strings will be fully discussed in chapter 11. Strings cannot be read directly by the *read* procedure in standard Pascal, although a number of processors include procedures to do this as an extension.

Boolean values cannot be read using the *read* procedure. They can be simulated by interpreting either character or integer values in the input stream. For example, if the variable *affirmative* has been declared type *boolean*, and *c* type *char*, the value could be set as follows:

```
write('Type "yes" or "no":  ');
readln(c);
affirmative := (c = 'y');
```

This assumes that the system is ready to read the correct answer (see discussion of *input*↑ in chapter 8). An alternate solution is to read integer values 1 or 0, representing *true* and *false*. Where variable *x* is type *integer* and *answer* is type *boolean*, the following program segment sets *answer* to *true* if the user types "1."

```
write('Type 0 or 1: ');
readln(x);
answer := (x > 0);
```

The above examples do not attempt to ensure that a proper response has been given by the user. A recursive solution to this problem will be presented in chapter 15.

Later we will learn to examine the contents of the input buffer without actually reading a value.

4.3 The *page* Function

The procedure call *page(f)* terminates the current line (as with writeln), but causes any additional text to be printed on a new physical page if the textfile is being printed on a suitable output device. If the file parameter is omitted *output* is supplied, i.e., *page* is equivalent to *page(output)*. The exact effect of this function is implementation dependent.

References and Selected Readings

Read the sections on input and output in the manuals that pertain to your Pascal compiler and/or operating system. In particular, you will want to know if anything in your system is different from that described in this chapter. The documentation should also indicate the maximum and minimum sizes of integers and the precision of real numbers.

The following book summarizes a number of computer-assisted music research projects in the late 1960s. Read critically; you may find that you do not agree with the results or music preconceptions of some of the authors.

Lincoln, Harry B., ed. *The Computer and Music.* Ithaca, N.Y.: Cornell University Press, 1970.

Other suggested readings:

Balzano, Gerald J. "The Group-Theoretic Description of 12-Fold and Microtonal Pitch Systems." *Computer Music Journal* 4, no. 4 (1980): 66–84.

Gross, Dorothy S. "Computer Applications to Music Theory: A Retrospective." *Computer Music Journal* 8, no. 4 (1984): 35–42.

Rothgeb, John E. "Simulating Musical Skills by Digital Computer." *Computer Music Journal* 4, no. 2 (1980): 36–40.

———. "Some Uses of Mathematical Concepts in Theories of Music." *Journal of Music Theory* 10 (1966): 200–215.

Exercises

1. Write short test programs that recreate the I/O statements in this chapter and run the programs on your system. Does everything work as expected? Make note of any differences and try to explain them.

2. Considering the following declarations and assignments:

```
const
  heading = 'Bog dirt up a side track carted is a putrid gob';
  pi      = 3.141593;
  e       = 2.718284;

var
  maxi : integer;

      . . .

  maxi := 32767;
```

Exactly what will be printed by each of the following statements (indicate blanks in the output line)?

a) *writeln(pi* : 8 : 4);

b) *writeln(pi* : 6 : 2);

c) *writeln(*'maxi = ', *maxi* : 1);

d) *writeln(*'e = ' : 9, *e* : 10);

e) *writeln(*'pi = ' : 4, *pi*);

f) *writeln(heading)*;

g) *writeln(heading* : 8);

h) *writeln(pi* < *e* : 10);

3. Considering the following declarations:

```
var
  a, b, c : integer;
  x, y, z : real;
  ch      : char;
```

What assignments and/or errors will result from the following read statement and input data? (Use a decimal point to distinguish between real and integer values, i.e., 16 vs. 16.0.)

	Statement	Data
a)	*readln(x, y);*	0.1234 3.5681 28.1469;
b)	*readln(a, ch, b, z, c);*	123.572 56 359.24
c)	*readln(x, y, z);*	891 42 29.6 281.3 57 0.192
d)	*readln(a, b, c);*	45 29.781 458

4. Considering the declarations shown above, identify errors in the *write* statements shown below:

   a) *writeln(a*: 10 : 3);

   b) *writeln(ch*: 10 : 2);

   c) *writeln(x*: 4 : 8);

   d) *writeln(x*: 20 : 15);

5. Again, using the above declarations, consider the following *read* statement:

   readln(a, x, b, y, c, z);

   Of the sets of input values shown below, which would satisfy this statement in the sense that no errors would result? For incorrect input, give reasons why an error would result.

   a) 17 125.2 0 29.324 59 234.19

   b) 17 125.2 0 29.324
   59 234.19

   c) 123 458 901 1892 891 189

   d) 19.4 15.7 589.12 198.2 44.3 238.9

   e) 28 851 1588 25.32 6

   f) 28 851.00 4123 89.613 356 821 8913

   g) 28 851.00 4123 89.613 356 821 8,913

   h) 28 851.00 4,123 89.613 356 821 8913

6. Run the following program on your system to determine the approximate precision of real numbers. Then experiment with field width and precision. Does your system round real numbers on output? (Some older compilers do not.) What does your system do if you specify more precision than is actually available? If you specify field width without precision?

```
program realtest(input, output);
  var
    pi : real;
  begin
    pi := 3.14159265;
    writeln(pi)
  end.
```

7. If the standard input and output files on your system are not the user's keyboard and terminal display, find out how to print to the screen and accept input from your terminal.

8. If the standard I/O files on your system are the keyboard and display of the user's terminal, find out how to read from and and write to disk files. On many systems this can be accomplished by simple redirection of input and output, e.g.,

obj < inputfile > outputfile

where *obj* is an executable file. Write some simple programs to practice writing to and reading from files.

9. Use your text editor to enter the program shown below and then try to run it. When you get everything working correctly, introduce intentional errors to see what error messages your system gives you. Find out what happens under the following conditions: (a) leave off the quotation marks that delimit a character literal; try omitting the opening quote, the closing quote, and both; (b) specify precision when printing an integer variable or literal. What error messages do you get if you enter a real number beginning or ending with a decimal point (e.g., .5 or 6.) or use commas in numbers. What happens if you use an undeclared variable? If you print a real or integer variable that has not been assigned a value? Make a list of the error messages and the conditions that caused them.

```
program errors(input, output);
  var
    x, y : real;
  begin { main }
    writeln('Hello, I''m your friendly computer');
    write('Please type two real numbers: ');
    readln(x, y);
    writeln('Thanks, I needed that!');
    writeln;
    write('The sum of those numbers is ', x + y)
  end.  { main }
```

10. The following program reads pairs of real numbers and prints them out in exponential form:

```
program format(input, output);
  var
    x, y : real;
  begin { main }
    while not eof do
      begin
        readln(x, y);
        writeln(x, y)
      end
  end.  { main }
```

Modify the program so that it prints its output in a table of the following form:

```
==================
     x        y
==================
  331.89    45.89
 1023.23   123.34
    5.70    41.10
 9384.11     5.00
==================
```

Test the program with numeric data redirected from a file.

5| Control Statements

The normal flow in a Pascal program is sequential, that is, statements are executed one after another. After each statement is executed, the flow of control passes to the statement just after it in the program. Pascal provides a number of devices for changing this sequence of actions. These control structures fall into five groups:

1. *Compound statements* allow a number of statements to be treated as a single unit.
2. *Conditional statements* allow the processor to select one of several different courses of action. The **if** statement in its various manifestations and the **case** statement fall into this group.
3. *Program loops* allow a statement or group of statements to be reiterated until some objective is achieved. Pascal provides three control structures for looping: the **while** statement, the **repeat** statement, and the **for** statement.
4. *Subprograms* (functions and procedures) are program units that can be invoked by a single statement from any point in the program. The procedures *write* and *read*, discussed in the previous chapter, are examples of procedures built into the language. In chapter 9 you will learn to write functions and procedures of your own design.
5. The **goto** statement causes direct transfer of control to another part of a program. This statement is rarely used in structured programming, and many programmers do not use it at all.

While each of these structures except subprograms will be described in this chapter, the novice is not advised to try to master them all at once. Any program can be structured with only **while** and **if** statements (with compound statements). The **repeat...until** construction is more natural than the **while** loop in some instances, and it sometimes simplifies program structure. Master these constructs first, and return to the **for** statement and **case** statement after you become more proficient and the need arises.

In the following discussion each control structure is illustrated by a format diagram and by a flow diagram that clarifies the dynamic behavior of the statement. In the diagrams S, S_1, S_2, etc., represent statements that may be simple (including procedure calls) or compound. B, B_1, B_2, etc., represent arbitrarily complex boolean expressions (which evaluate to *true* or *false*). The diagrams show program branching depending on the truth value of the boolean expression. Statements are diagrammed in square boxes or rectangles, boolean expressions in diamond-shaped boxes with branches for true (T) or false (F), as shown in figure 5.1.

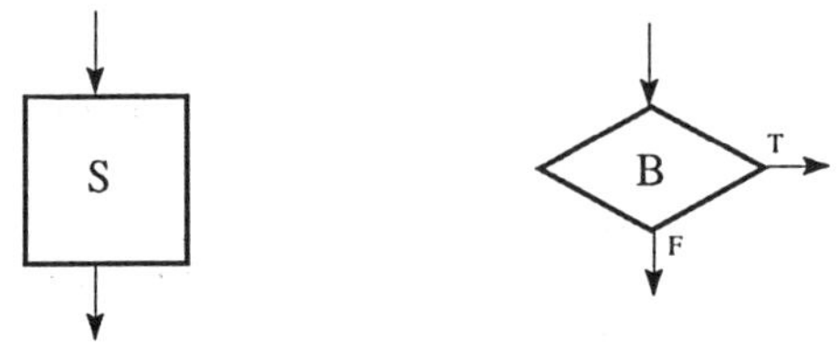

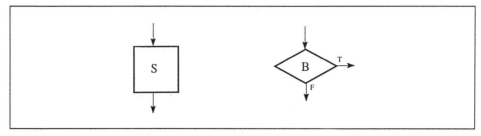

Figure 5.1. Flow Diagrams for Statements and Boolean Expressions

5.1 The Compound Statement: begin...end

The compound statement makes it possible to treat a group of statements as a single statement, and is therefore a principal component in structured programming. Although the syntax is relatively simple, this construct enhances the usefulness of all other control statements. The compound statement is a group of statements enclosed on either side by the word symbols **begin** and **end**, as shown in figure 5.2. Note that **begin** and **end** are not statements, but serve as delimiters to mark the beginning and end of a block of statements. Statements within the compound statement are indented to set off the delimiters. Each statement is terminated by a semicolon except the last statement (since the last is not followed by another statement). The reserved word **begin** never takes a semicolon; **end** is followed by a semicolon if it is followed by another statement. The semicolon is not used if the compound statement is the first part of a more complex statement, e.g., **if...then...else** (section 5.2.2), or if it is followed by another **end** (since **end** is not a statement). The main block of a program is essentially a compound statement. In this case, **end** is terminated by a period, signifying the end of the program.

```
program hello(output);
  begin { main }
    writeln('Hello, world!')
  end.  { main }
```

begin { compound statement }
<statement$_1$>;
<statement$_2$>;
. . .
<statement$_n$>
end { compound statement }

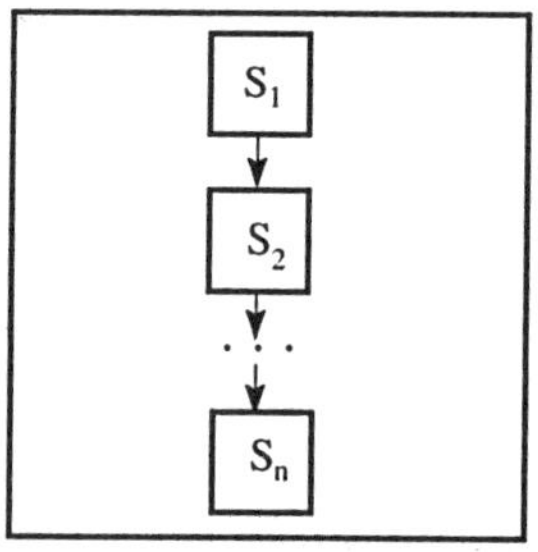

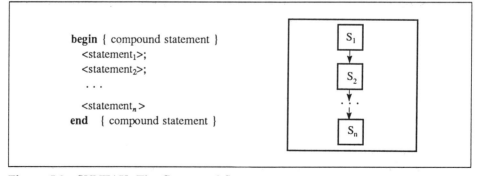

Figure 5.2. SYNTAX: The Compound Statement

Style Note: Matching pairs of **begin-end** delimiters are aligned vertically and should have identical comments, as shown above. Alignment and comments are particularly helpful when compound statements are nested, since they help the programmer to match visually **begin-end** pairs that may be separated by some distance. Nesting means that one compound statement occurs within another. Consistent use of indentation, alignment, and matching comments clarifies the program structure and lessens the chance of mismatched **begin-end** delimiters (a common encoding error). Comments may be omitted from the innermost pair of **begin-end** delimiters.[1] The dummy program below illustrates this principle. (In a real program "comment A," etc., would be replaced by more meaningful comments.)

```
begin { main }
  ...
  while not eof do
    begin { comment A }
      ...
      for i := ... do
        begin { comment B }
          ...
          if ...
            then
              begin { comment C }
                ...
              end;  { comment C }
          ...
        end;  { comment B }
      ...
    end;  { comment A }
  ...
end.  { main }
```

When the general form of statements is given in the following discussion, compound statements will be shortened to

```
begin
  <statements>
end
```

where <statements> stands for

```
<statement1>;
<statement2>;
. . .
<statementn>
```

1. Some programmers prefer to use other styles of indentation; however, the style described here is very common in Pascal programming, and will be used consistently in this text.

5.2 The if Statement

The **if** statement is the primary decision statement in Pascal. The keyword **if** is used in much the same way as in English, that is, if some condition is true, then take some specified action. The condition is specified as a boolean expression, and the action as a simple or compound statement. The **if** statement takes a number of different forms.

5.2.1 Conditional Execution: if...then

The simple **if** statement is shown in figure 5.3. The boolean expression <condition> is evaluated. If its value is *true*, then <statement> is executed. If the expression evaluates to *false*, <statement> is not executed. In either case the next statement to be executed is the one following the **if** statement. The **then** clause is indented to show that it is subordinate to the **if**. Consider the following:

```
if i < 10
  then i := i + 1;
```

If the current value of variable *i* is less than 10, then the value is incremented; otherwise it remains unchanged.

```
if code = barline
  then
    begin { new bar }
      measure := measure + 1;
      writeln('m. ', measure:3, ':')
    end   { new bar }
```

If *code* is equal to the value used to represent a bar line, then the current measure number is incremented and printed; otherwise no action is taken.

if <condition>
  then <statement>

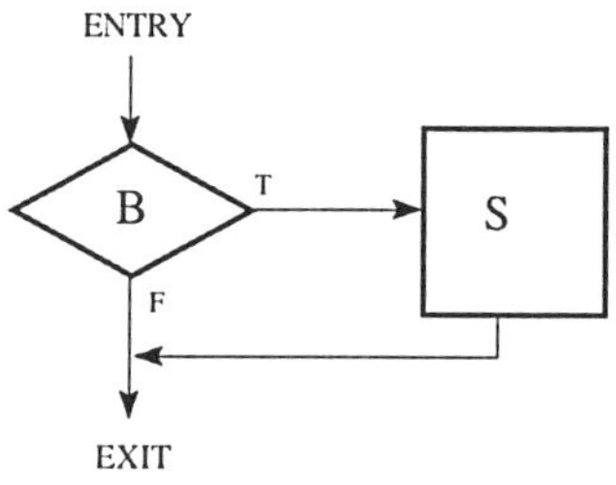

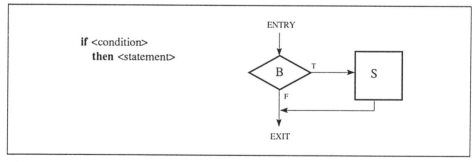

Figure 5.3. SYNTAX: The **if...then** Statement

5.2.2 Compound if Statement: if...then...else

The second form of the **if** statement, shown in figure 5.4, gives a choice of two actions. If the boolean expression evaluates to *true*, <statement$_1$> is executed; otherwise (if the expression is *false*) <statement$_2$> is executed. Note that there is no semi-

if <condition>
  then <statement$_1$>
  else <statement$_2$>

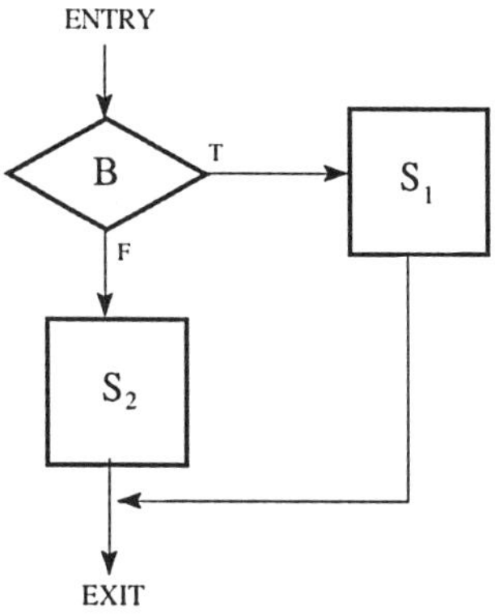

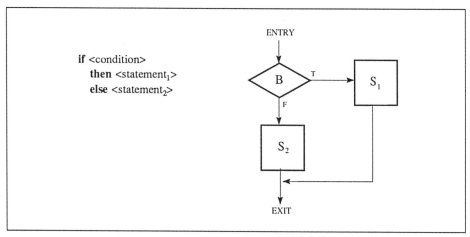

Figure 5.4. SYNTAX: The **if...then...else** Statement

colon before the **else** clause. **Then** and **else** are indented under **if**, but aligned vertically to indicate their equivalent status. In each case, <statement> may be a compound statement. In this case, **begin** is usually placed on the next line, indented:

```
if <condition>
  then
    begin
      <statements>
    end
  else
    begin
      <statements>
    end
```

Alternately, **begin** may be placed on the same line as **then** or **else**, but the normal alignment for the compound statement still applies:

```
if <condition>
  then begin
         <statements>
       end
  else begin
         <statements>
       end
```

Consider the following examples:

```
if code = barline
  then writeln(code)
  else write(code)
```

The value of *code* is written on the current line, but if *code* is equal to *barline*, the current line is terminated by a newline character.

```
if code <> barline
  then write(code)
  else
    begin
      writeln(code);
      measure := measure + 1;
      write(measure:3,':')
    end;
```

The value of *code* is printed on the current line. If the value is not equal to *barline*, no other action is taken. However, if *code* is equal to *barline*, then the line is terminated by a newline character, and the measure number is incremented and printed on the beginning of the next line.

5.2.3 Chained **if** Statements

Type One: **if...then...else if.** Other forms of the **if** statement are variations of those discussed above. As with compound statements, **if** statements can be nested (or chained). This occurs when the statement part of the **then** or **else** clause is another **if**.

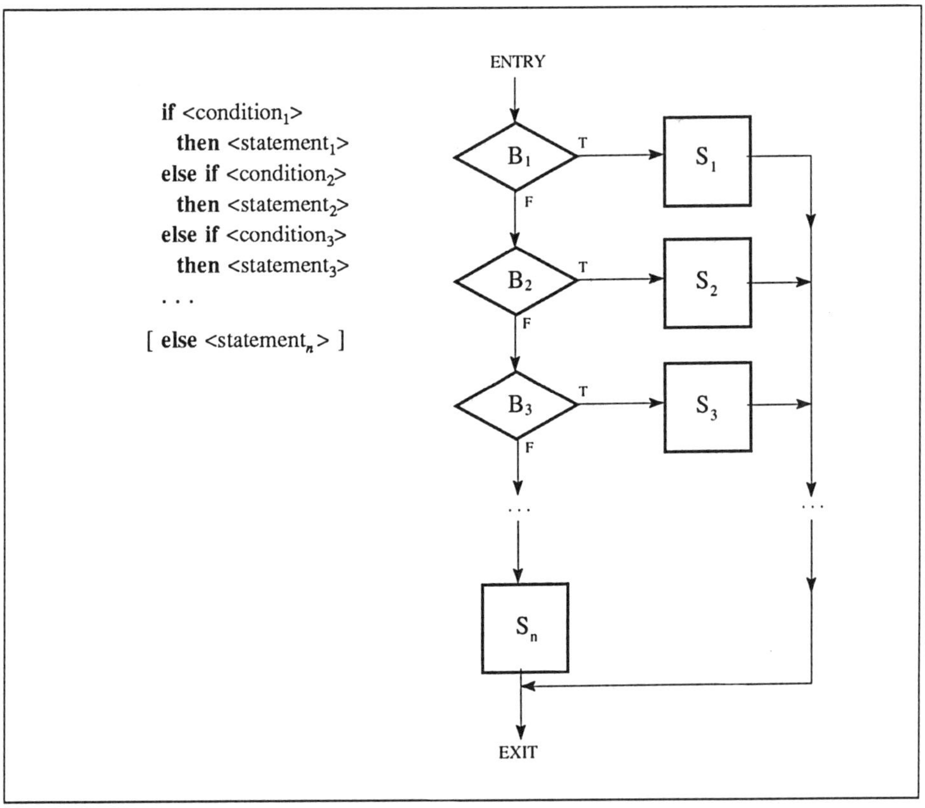

Figure 5.5. SYNTAX: The **if...then...else if** Statement

In the more common form, the **else** clause is another **if** statement, as shown in figure 5.5. This statement is used for choosing one of several alternatives. The style of indentation shown below prevents the program code from wandering across the page to the right. It should be apparent that the efficiency of this construction can be maximized by placing the most common conditions early in the chain, since fewer tests will have to be made. The final **else** is optional. If it is included, it specifies the alternative to be taken by default if none of the other conditions has been met. If it is omitted, no action is taken under these circumstances. Example:

```
read(frequency);

if frequency > 20000
  then writeln(frequency:6, 'is above audible range')
else if frequency < 20
  then writeln(frequency:6, 'is below audible range')
else writeln(frequency:6, 'is audible')
```

If the final **else** clause were omitted, no action would be taken if *frequency* were in the range between 20 and 20,000 Hz.

Type Two: **if...then if**. Alternately, the **then** clause may be another **if** statement. This construction looks like the following:

```
if <condition1>
  then
    if <condition2>
      then <statement1>
      else <statement2>
```

This is not nearly so common as the first type of chained **if**, since it can frequently be reformulated as a simple **if** statement with a more complex <condition>:

```
if (<condition1>) and (<condition2>)
  then <statement1>
  else <statement2>
```

The **if...then if** construction is often more efficient than a simple **if** with a complex boolean expression, since it ensures that only the first part of the test is performed in many cases. This is vital when the failure of one condition may result in an error condition in the other, i.e., when <condition$_2$> should not be evaluated if <condition$_1$> is *false*. Many Pascal processors evaluate the entire boolean expression in order to determine its value. The construction

```
if (x > 0) and ((y / x) > 2)
  then . . .
```

may result in an execution error, since if x is equal to 0, evaluation of the second relational expression requires division by 0. The error can be avoided by using chained **if** statements:

```
if x > 0
   then
      if (y / x) > 2
         then . . .
```

An **else** clause is always matched with the closest unmatched **then**. In the statement below, **else** will be matched with the **then** just above it, not with the first **then**, as indicated by the indentation on the left.

(a) Wrong

```
if <condition1>
  then
    if <condition2>
      then <statement1>
  else <statement2>
```

(b) Correct

```
if <condition1>
  then
    if <condition2>
      then <statement1>
      else <statement2>
```

If the intent is to match the **else** with the first **then**, the desired result can be obtained by using a compound statement:

```
if <condition1>
  then
    begin
      if <condition2>
        then <statement1>
    end
  else <statement2>
```

Remember that the Pascal compiler/interpreter pays no attention to the physical layout of the code on the page! However, for readability, the programmer should take care that the indentation reflects the logical structure of the program.

5.3 The case Statement: [Optional on first reading]

The syntax of the **case** statement is shown in figure 5.6. <Expression> is a variable or expression that evaluates to a standard or user-defined ordinal type; <case label list> is a list of constants or identifiers, separated by commas, of the same type as <expression>; and <statement> is a simple or compound statement. Case labels must be exclusive, i.e., they may not occur in more than one case label list.

```
case <expression> of
  <case label list1>: <statement1>;
  <case label list2>: <statement2>;
  <case label list3>: <statement3>;
  . . .
  <case label listn>: <statementn>
end { case }
```

Figure 5.6. SYNTAX: The **case** Statement

The **case** statement provides a means of branching many different ways, depending on the value of <expression>. If <expression> is equal to one of the values in <case label list$_1$>, then <statement$_1$> is executed; if <expression> is equal to a value in <case label list$_2$>, then <statement$_2$> is executed, and so on. Note that **case** is terminated by **end**, and that the use of semicolons is similar to that in the compound statement. **End** is usually supplied with the comment {case} to avoid confusion with **begin-end** pairs. The **case** statement is similar in effect to the chained **if...then...else if** statement without the optional **else** clause. However, in the **case** statement, <expression> *must* be equal to one of the case labels, or an execution error will result. It is the programmer's responsibility to ensure that <expression> has an appropriate value. This is usually done by combining the **case** statement with an **if** statement, as in the example below. Assume that *errno* has been declared type *integer*, and that it has been assigned a value:

```
if (errno >= 1) and (error <= 7)
  then
    case errno of
      1: writeln('error 1: illegal clef constant');
      2: writeln('error 2: illegal key signature');
      3: writeln('error 3: illegal meter signature');
      4: writeln('error 4: illegal pitch code');
      5: writeln('error 5: illegal duration code');
      6: writeln('error 6: illegal articulation code');
      7: writeln('error 7: illegal dynamic code')
    end { case }
  else writeln('illegal error number: ', errno:2)
```

The **case** statement below illustrates the use of multiple values in the <case label list>.

```
write('type a number between 1 and 10: ');
readln(number);

if number in [1..10]                { good number }
  then
    case number of
         1,3,5,7: writeln(number:3, ' is prime');
      2,4,6,8,10: writeln(number:3, ' is even');
               9: writeln(number:3, ' is nonprime & odd')
    end { case }
  else writeln('error: (number < 1) or (number > 10)')
```

In general, the **case** statement should be used to choose among several statements with a similar probability of selection. Use the chained **if** when certain choices are most likely to occur, and place the more common choices first.

5.4 Program Loops

One of the most powerful features of a computer language is the ability to create program loops, that is, to repeat a group of statements over and over again. In the real world, there are few problems that are worth solving on a computer in order to calculate only a single value. More often we wish to repeat a calculation many times for different values, whether they are supplied externally (via *read* statements) or internally by the program. We wish to read and interpret each encoded value in an encoded composition until the end is reached; calculate the frequency in Hertz for each note in the equal-tempered scale; or generate questions and appropriate answers for a fixed or variable number of problems in a program in computer-assisted instruction (CAI). Each of these problems involves repeating a number of carefully specified steps over and over again (we will begin to develop a methodology for designing these steps in the next chapter).

Pascal provides three mechanisms for designing program loops: the **while** statement, the **repeat** statement, and the **for** statement. (Loops can be created with the **goto** as in unstructured programming languages, but the other looping mechanisms in Pascal make the program clearer, and this use of **goto** should be avoided.) Looping statements are sometimes called *iterative statements*, and programs that use them use *iterative algorithms.*

5.4.1 Testing at the Top of the Loop: while...do

Although there are other types of iterative statements in Pascal, the **while** statement is most generally useful, since it is often appropriate to test a condition before executing the loop. The syntax of the **while** statement is shown in figure 5.7, where <condition> is a boolean expression and <statement> is a simple or compound statement. When a **while** statement is encountered, the boolean expression is evaluated. If the expression has the value *true*, then <statement> (the body of the loop) is executed, and then the expression is evaluated again. This process is repeated so long as <condition> evaluates to *true*. When the boolean expression becomes *false*, control passes to the next statement in the program. The boolean expression is always evaluated before <statement> is executed, so if the initial value is *false*, the <statement> part is not executed, and control passes immediately to the next statement. If <statement> is compound, all statements between **begin** and **end** are executed each time the

while <condition> **do**
<statement>

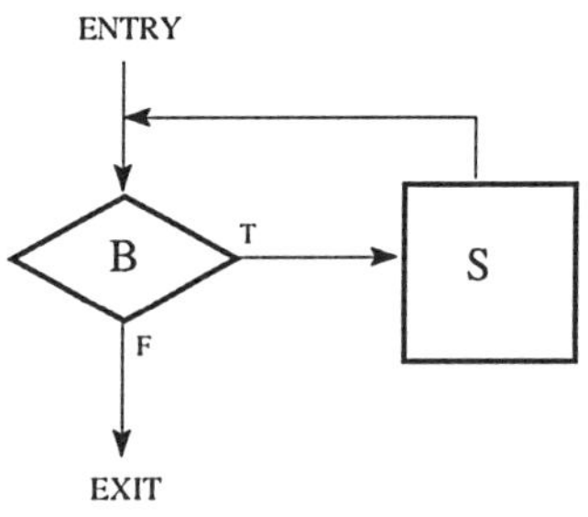

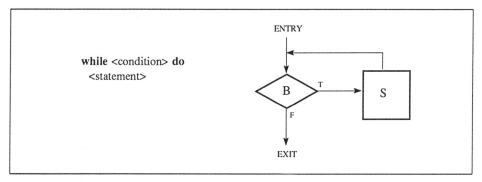

Figure 5.7. SYNTAX: The **while** Statement

condition tests *true*, i.e., <condition> is not tested again until after the entire statement block has been executed:

```
while <condition> do
  begin
    <statements>
  end
```

The statement part of a **while** must be capable of changing the value of the boolean expression, or an endless loop will be created. For example,

```
i := 5;
while i < 100 do
  writeln(i)
```

will write 5 (the value of *i*) over and over again until the program is forcibly terminated by typing a break or interrupt signal, or until some predetermined maximum number of statements has been executed. This is so because the value of *i* never increases and will thus always be less than 100!

Obviously, it must be possible to evaluate the boolean expression when the **while** statement is executed. A construction like

```
while code <> done do
  begin
    <statements>
  end
```

is fine so long as *code* and *done* are defined before <condition> is tested. Failure to assign values before the **while** statement is executed may or may not result in an execution-error message, depending on your Pascal processor. In any case, it is poor programming practice.

Necessary conditions for using the **while** statement are as follows:

1. All values necessary to evaluate the boolean statement <condition> must be defined before the **while** statement is executed.
2. The <statement> part must be capable of altering the values used in the boolean statement so that <condition> will eventually have the value *false*; otherwise an endless loop is created. Optionally, the programmer may provide other means of leaving the loop (this use of **goto** will be discussed later in this chapter).

Consider the following examples:

```
i := 1;
while i <= 10 do
  begin
    write(i:3);
    i := i + 1
  end;
writeln
```

This example prints the numbers from 1 to 10 on a single line of the output file. Note that the loop is constructed so that the initial and terminal values of *i* are explicit. The loop could be written with the boolean expression ($i < 11$), implying a terminal value of 10, but the solution given in the prior example is preferable.

```
read(code);
while code <> 0 do
  begin
    writeln(code);
    read(code)
  end;
```

This second example reads and prints each integer in the input file until a 0 is encountered. The first *read* statement ensures that code will be defined when the boolean expression is evaluated. The *read* statement within the compound statement reads another value for code, making it possible for the loop to terminate. If the initial value of code is 0, the loop is not executed at all. The use of *writeln* in the above loop causes each value for code to be written on a separate line. A simple *write(code)* would be inappropriate, since we cannot predict whether all of the values before 0 will fit on a single line. We could control the number of items per line by adding another variable to count the number of values printed:

```
n := 1;
read(code);
while code <> 0 do
  begin
    write(code:4);
    if n mod 10 = 0
      then writeln;
    n := n + 1;
    read(code)
  end;
```

In the above solution, *n* is used to count the number of values before the first 0 in the input file. After each value is printed, its ordinal position in the list (*n*) is tested to see if it is evenly divisible by 10, and if it is, a newline marker is written into the file. Thus ten values are printed on each line. The variables *code* and *n* are initialized before the **while**, and both change within the loop. If the second *read(code)* were omitted, the loop could not terminate, and if *n* were not incremented within the loop, all values would be printed on the same output line.

5.4.2 Testing at the End of the Loop: repeat...until

The syntax of the **repeat** statement is shown in figure 5.8. The **repeat** construct is not unlike the **while** statement, except that <condition> is tested at the bottom of the loop, after <statement> has been executed. Thus **repeat** always executes its <statement> at least one time. The body of the loop (<statement>) may be a simple statement or a number of statements. Since **repeat** and **until** mark the extent of the block, the delimiters **begin** and **end** are *not* required.

repeat
<statement>
until <condition>

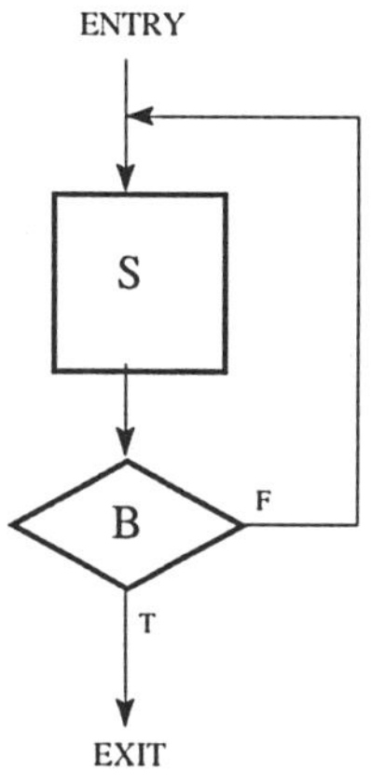

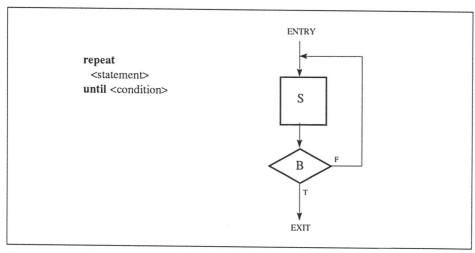

Figure 5.8. SYNTAX: The **repeat** Statement

For the sake of comparison, we will illustrate the same problems that we used to illustrate the **while** statement. The statements

```
i := 1;
repeat
  write(i);
  i := i + 1
until i > 10
```

print the values from 1 to 10. Note again that the solution is formulated such that it states explicitly the initial and terminal values to be printed.

The **repeat** statement has the same prerequisites as the **while** statement, i.e., the necessary values must be defined when the boolean condition is tested, and the body of the loop must be capable of changing the value of the boolean expression in order to terminate the loop. The first requirement is met more easily with the **repeat... until**; since the condition is not tested until the bottom of the loop, the test value may be initialized within the loop (by a *read* statement only). Thus the problem of printing each value preceding the first 0 in the input file is simplified by the following program segment:

```
repeat
  read(code);
  writeln(code)
until code = 0
```

This is not exactly equivalent to the solution given earlier, since the terminal value (0) is printed. This could be avoided by testing the value of *code* before writing:

```
if code <> 0
  then writeln(code)
```

However, this introduces an extra test for every value read. Provided that we wish to eliminate the final 0 from the printout, a more efficient solution is as follows:

```
read(code);
repeat
  writeln(code);
  read(code)
until code = 0
```

Here the addition of an extra *read* statement (executed one time) helps us to avoid an extra test for each value in the input file, thus making for a more efficient program. However, this solution still does not work correctly if the first value read is 0. If there is *any* possibility that the body of the loop should not be executed, the **while** statement is a better choice.

5.4.3 Ordinal Iteration: for...do [Optional on first reading]

The **for** statement is used to repeat a statement a specific number of times. The general form of the statement is shown in figure 5.9. Note that <control variable>, <initial value>, and <final value> must be of the same ordinal type; *real* values may not be used. The initial and final values, which may be constants or expressions, are evaluated only once, at the beginning of the loop. When the **for** statement is executed, the control variable is assigned the initial value. If this value is less than or equal to the final value, then the body of the loop (<statement>) is executed, and then the control variable is assigned the next (higher) value of its scalar type. This sequence of events is repeated until the value of the control variable is greater than that of the final value. Statements within the body of the loop must not explicitly change the value of the control variable, and, by definition, the control variable is undefined after the loop terminates. Note that the terminal condition ($i > t$) is

for <control variable> := <initial value> **to** <final value> **do**
<statement>

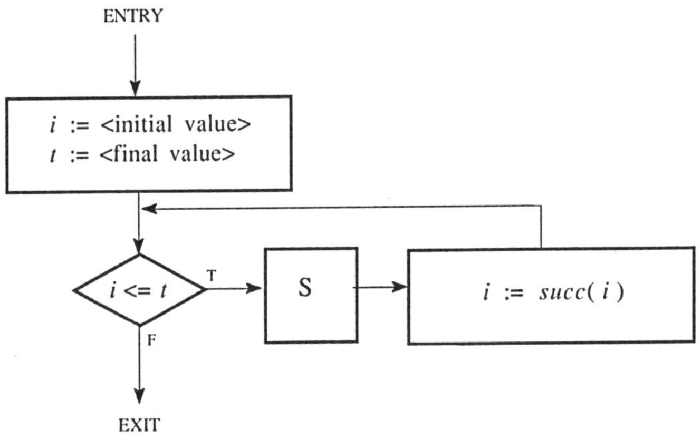

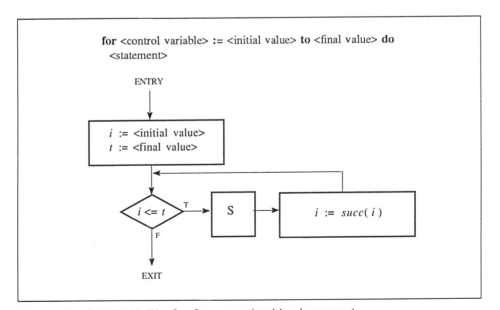

Figure 5.9. SYNTAX: The **for** Statement (positive increment)

for <control variable> := <initial value> **downto** <final value> **do**
<statement>

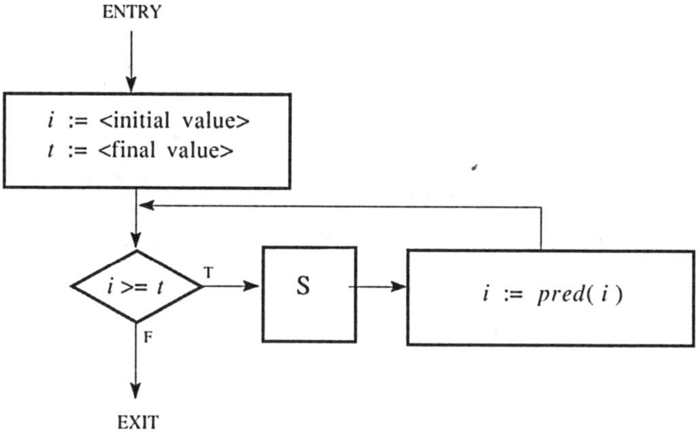

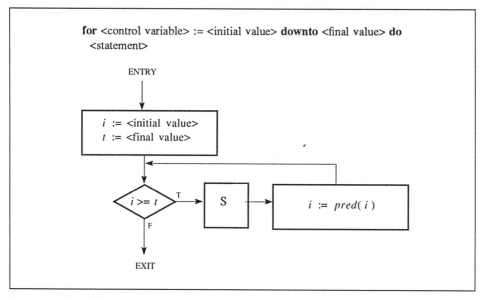

Figure 5.10. SYNTAX: The **for** Statement (negative increment)

evaluated *before* the body of the loop is executed, so if the initial value of the control variable exceeds the final value, the body is not executed and the loop terminates. In the flow diagram, t is a temporary storage location (allocated by the system and not accessible to the programmer) that is used to store the evaluated <final value>. Thus the construct

```
for i := 1 to 10 do
  write(i)
```

is equivalent to

```
i := 1;
while i <= 10 do
  begin
    write(i);
    i := i + 1
  end
```

except that i is undefined after the **for** loop, but has the value 11 after the **while.**[2]

An alternate form of the **for** loop, shown below, works in an analogous manner, except that it counts down instead of up. The body of the loop is executed only if <control variable> is greater than or equal to <final value>, and after the body of the loop is executed, the control variable is decremented before retesting for the terminal condition. Here <initial value> is usually greater than or equal to <final value> (otherwise the body of the loop will not be executed). The two loops shown below are equivalent, except that i is undefined after the **for**:

2. In fact, the value of the control variable after a **for** loop terminates is usually the successor to <final value> just as it is in the **while**, but it is poor programming practice to count on this since, according to the language definition, it is undefined. When the loop is used with enumerated or subrange types, the terminal value is undefined when <final value> in the **for** loop is the last value in the defined type.

```
for i := 10 downto 1 do      |    i := 10;
  write(i);                  |    while i >= 1 do
                             |      begin
                             |        write(i);
                             |        i := i - 1
                             |      end
```

The example below illustrates the use of a compound statement as the body of the **for** loop. The numbers between 1 and *n* are printed, 10 per line:

```
for j := 1 to n do
  begin
    write(j);
    if j mod 10 = 0
      then writeln
  end
```

It is not necessary for the body of the loop to reference the control variable at all. It may simply control the number of iterations of a statement or group of statements:

```
for i := 1 to n do
  write('*')
```

prints *n* asterisks, if *n* is greater than 0.

Although the **for** loop is most commonly used with integer values to control the number of iterations of some process, it may be used with other ordinal types. If it is assumed that *ch* has been declared type *char*, the following loop prints out the uppercase alphabet:

```
for ch := 'A' to 'Z' do
  write(ch);
```

This example assumes the ASCII character set, in which alphabetic characters of the same case are contiguous.

Although some languages permit more flexibility, **for** loops in Pascal always increment or decrement by one, resulting in the immediate successor or predecessor value in the scalar type. One can use simple programming tricks to simulate other incremental values, although in these cases a **while** loop is frequently clearer and/or more efficient. Each of the loops below prints the odd numbers between 1 and 79:

```
          (a)             |          (b)             |        (c)
                          |                          |
for i := 1 to 40 do       | for i := 1 to 79 do      |  i := 1;
  writeln(2 * i - 1)      |   if odd(i)              |  while i <= 79 do
                          |      then writeln(i)     |    begin
                          |                          |      writeln(i);
                          |                          |      i := i + 2
                          |                          |    end;
```

Solution (a) is shortest, but probably least clear in its intent. Solution (b) is easy to read but is inefficient when compared to the **while** loop, since for each iteration it requires the evaluation of an extra boolean expression, and the body of the loop is executed twice as many times.

While fractional increments cannot be specified explicitly in the **for** loop in Pascal, the same effect can be obtained by using the **for** to control the number of iterations of statements that calculate the value of a *real* variable within the body of the loop. This technique is illustrated in program 5.1. The program prints a specified number of values within the period of the sine function. The period of the sine function (the point at which it begins to repeat) is from 0 to 2π radians. If we wish to divide this space into n equal steps, the value of x must be incremented by $2\pi / n$ before each new value for $sin(x)$ is calculated. The values generated by this program form discrete points along a sine curve. A graphic representation of the curve is shown below the program output. The output could also be used to generate a sine tone in a music-synthesis system.

```
(***********************       Program Gen        ***********************)
(* Program gen generates values for sin(x) over one period of the sine   *)
(* function.  The sine function begins to repeat at 2*pi and produces    *)
(* values between 1 and -1:                                              *)
(*                                                                       *)
(*                   1|         ***                                      *)
(*                    | *             *                                  *)
(*          sin(x)   0*-----------------*------------------*             *)
(*                    |                    *             *               *)
(*                  -1|                         ***                      *)
(*                 x: 0       .5pi        pi        1.5pi     2pi        *)
(*                                                                       *)
(* The program generates values on this curve at equidistant points. The *)
(* number of steps in the cycle is specified as the constant n. Output   *)
(* from the program could be used to produce graphic representation of   *)
(* the sine curve on a plotter or to generate a sine tone in a music-    *)
(* synthesis system.                                                     *)
(*************************************************************************)
 program gen(output);
   const
     pi = 3.141593;                         { pi                       }
     n  = 100;                              { the number of steps      }

   var
     i         : integer;                   { control var for looping  }
     x         : real;                      { value of point on x axis }
     increment : real;                      { size of step on x axis   }

   begin { main }
     increment := (2 * pi) / n;
     for i := 0 to n do
       begin
         x := i * increment;
         write(sin(x):10:6);                { print values for sin(x)  }
         if (i + 1) mod 5 = 0               {   5 per line             }
           then writeln
       end
   end. { main }
```

Program 5.1. *Gen*

```
 0.000000  0.062791  0.125333  0.187381  0.248690
 0.309017  0.368125  0.425779  0.481754  0.535827
 0.587785  0.637424  0.684547  0.728969  0.770513
 0.809017  0.844328  0.876307  0.904827  0.929776
 0.951057  0.968583  0.982287  0.992115  0.998027
 1.000000  0.998027  0.992115  0.982287  0.968583
 0.951057  0.929776  0.904827  0.876307  0.844328
 0.809017  0.770513  0.728968  0.684547  0.637424
 0.587785  0.535827  0.481754  0.425779  0.368125
 0.309017  0.248690  0.187381  0.125333  0.062791
 0.000000 -0.062790 -0.125333 -0.187381 -0.248690
-0.309017 -0.368125 -0.425779 -0.481754 -0.535827
-0.587785 -0.637424 -0.684547 -0.728969 -0.770513
-0.809017 -0.844328 -0.876307 -0.904827 -0.929776
-0.951057 -0.968583 -0.982287 -0.992115 -0.998027
-1.000000 -0.998027 -0.992115 -0.982287 -0.968583
-0.951056 -0.929776 -0.904827 -0.876307 -0.844328
-0.809017 -0.770513 -0.728969 -0.684547 -0.637424
-0.587785 -0.535827 -0.481754 -0.425779 -0.368124
-0.309017 -0.248690 -0.187381 -0.125333 -0.062790
 0.000000
```

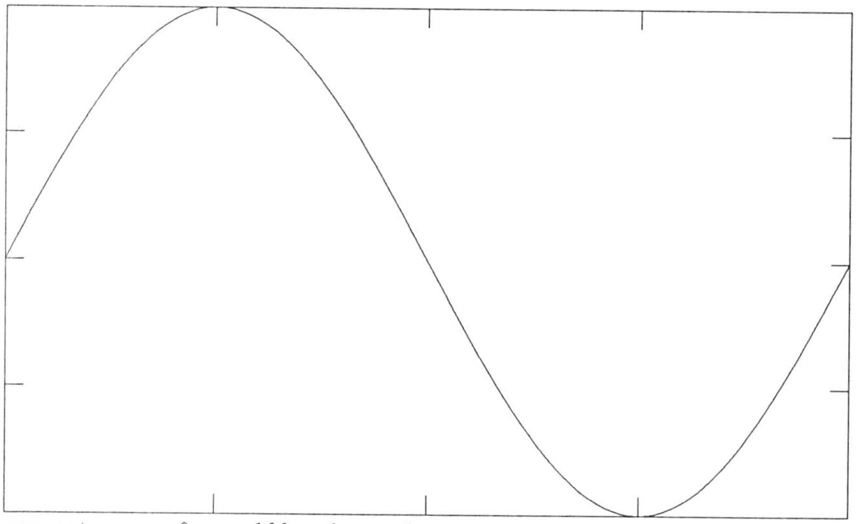

gen.out   0 -x- 100   -1 -y- 1

Program 5.1. Output

Style Note: As you have probably noticed, single-letter identifiers (such as *i*, *j*, *k*, *l*) are frequently used for the control variable. The reason is historical (from FORTRAN usage), but the practice is so pervasive that your programs will be easier for other programmers to read if you follow it. Since these variables simply control the number of repetitions of a loop, mnemonic names will not generally improve readability appreciatively. If you find situations where mnemonic identifiers are useful for control variables, use them—nobody will object.

5.4.4 Which Loop to Use

With three different looping constructs, how does one decide which is best in a particular application? Often a problem can be solved in a number of different ways, and the best choice depends on a number of factors. Program loops can be characterized by the manner in which they terminate. When we know beforehand how many times a loop should be reiterated, the loop is *determinate*. The examples below illustrate determinate loops:

```
(a)
i := 10;
while i <= 50 do
  begin
    writeln(i);
    i := i + 1
  end
```

```
(b)
j := 100;
repeat
  writeln(j);
  j := j - 1
until j <= 39
```

```
(c)
sum := 0;
for i := 1 to n do
  sum := sum + i
```

In each case we know (or can easily calculate) from the initial and terminal conditions of the loop how many times the loop will be executed. Note that the number may be variable and still be determinate. In (c) the loop will execute n times, if n is greater than 0. Determinate loops can be constructed with **while**, **repeat**, or **for** loops. As you become more experienced, you will find that you can most easily construct this type of loop using the **for**, although you will be asked to implement the same loop using different constructs in the exercises at the end of this chapter.

Now consider the following loops:

```
(d)
sum := 0;
read(x);
while x <> 0 do
  begin
    sum := sum + x;
    read(x)
  end;
writeln(sum)
```

```
(e)
repeat
  read(code);
  if code = barline
    then writeln(code)
    else write(code)
until code = doublebar
```

```
(f)
while not eof do
  begin
    readln(a,b);
    writeln(a + b)
  end
```

These loops are *indeterminate*, since the terminal condition depends upon factors outside of the loop's definition. Loop (d) will execute until a 0 is read from the input file; (e) until *code* = *doublebar*; and (f) until the *end-of-file* is reached in the input file. In each case the number of iterations of the body of the loop depends on data that is external to the loop, and thus cannot be predetermined. Indeterminate loops cannot use **for**; they must use **while** or **repeat**.

The second factor to decide is: Is there any possibility that the loop should not execute even one time? If this is the case, then either **while** or **for** should be used, since both of these check their boolean condition before the loop is executed. **Repeat** checks its conditional at the end of the loop, and thus *always* executes its body at least one time.

The preceding discussion is summarized in table 5.1. Note that **while** is the only type of loop that can be used in any situation, thus it is most generally useful. **For** is more compact, and is frequently used instead of **while** for determinate loops, especially when the required increment is 1 or –1. **Repeat** is sometimes more natural, particularly for indeterminate loops, but may be used only if the loop should execute at least one time. Since it is usually desirable to check for the possibility that the loop should not execute even once, **while** and **for** are used much more commonly than **repeat**. General guidelines: If the loop is determinate and the increment is 1 or –1, use **for**, otherwise use **while**; if it is indeterminate and will always execute at least one time, use **while** or **repeat**, but if it may not execute even once, use **while**. When in doubt, use **while**.

TYPE	*Iterations ≥ 0*	*Iterations > 0*
Determinate	**for** **while**	**for** **while** **repeat**
Indeterminate	**while**	**while** **repeat**

Table 5.1. Which Loop to Use

5.4.5 Debugging Loops

Looping errors are common and tend to be fairly predictable. Frequently loops execute one too many or one too few times, due to incorrectly initialized values or improper formulation of the condition that will terminate the loop. Another common problem is the loop's failure to change a test value, so that the loop cannot terminate at all. Check for the following:

1. Make sure that the looping variable is properly initialized, whether by assignment or by a *read* statement, before the condition is tested.
2. Check the terminal condition. Make sure that the boolean expression tests for the proper condition. Common errors are confusing '=' with '>=' or with '<=', or '<' with '>'.
3. Be sure that there is a statement within the body of the loop that can change the test value, and that the manner in which the value changes can eventually satisfy the terminal condition.

4. If the body of the loop is a compound statement, did you remember to use **begin** and **end**? If these delimiters are missing, the only statement that will be executed is the one just after **while** or **for**, no matter how careful you have been about indentation.
5. If the loop depends on a particular input value for termination, be sure that the data contains that value.
6. If the test value is type *real*, never test for equality or inequality directly. Below, loop (a) may not terminate at all, since the sum of an arbitrary number of increments may never exactly equal the real number 100.0. The solution at (b) is better, since the loop must terminate when the value of *x* becomes greater than 100.0. Loop (c) terminates when the difference between *x* and 100.0 is small enough for the values to be considered equal. This is a good solution, but the value of *epsilon* must be chosen carefully: *epsilon* must be smaller than *increment*, or the loop may not terminate, as in (a).

(a) Wrong

```
x := 0.0;
while x <> 100.0 do
  begin
    . . .
    x := x + increment
  end
```

(b) Possible

```
x :=  0.0;
while x <= 100.0 do
  begin
    . . .
    x := x + increment
  end
```

(c) Good

```
x := 0.0;
while abs(x - 100) > epsilon do
  begin
    . . .
    x := x + increment
  end
```

If you can't figure out logically why the loop is not working properly, add some extra *writeln* statements to print the values that control iteration. Place one *write* statement before the loop to print the initial value of the control variable, and one within the loop just after the statement that should change the value. This technique, called *tracing* a variable, is illustrated below:[3]

```
read(code);
writeln('code: ', code);                    { trace code   }
writeln('barline = ', barline);             { check value  }
while code <> barline do
  begin
    . . .
    read(code);
    writeln('code = ', code)                { trace code   }
  end;
```

3. Some compilers have facilities for automatic tracing of specified variables. If yours is one of these, use automatic tracing.

5.5 The goto Statement [Optional on first reading]

The unconditional transfer of control has been associated with programming since its inception. It is a vital part of machine-language and assembly-language programming, and was the primary control structure in early multipurpose languages like FORTRAN. Unfortunately, many students' first language is an unstructured BASIC that does not provide control structures equivalent to compound statements, **if...then...else**, and **while**. The student who has programmed in a language such as these often has some bad habits to break.

A great deal has been written about the use and avoidance of the **goto** statement. While the use of the **goto** is not inherently evil, it is usually avoided in structured programming. The reason is that program structure is clearer if we use control structures with only one entrance and one exit point. The use of unconditional transfer often results in what is sometimes called "spaghetti code," since the flow of control is unruly and difficult to follow. The first program segment below accomplishes the same task as the second, using only **goto** and **if** statements to control the program flow. The second uses structured control statements described earlier in this chapter.

(a) Poor Program Structure

```
        i := 1;
10:     j := 2 * i;
        if j mod 6 <> 0 then goto 20;
        writeln(j);
        jcount := jcount + 1;
        goto 30;
20:     writeln(i);
        icount := icount + 1;
30:     i := i + 1;
        if i <= 20 then goto 10;
        writeln(icount, jcount);
```

(b) Good Program Structure

```
i := 1;
while i <= 20 do
  begin
    j := 2 * i;
    if j mod 6 = 0
      then
        begin
          writeln(j);
          jcount := jcount + 1
        end
      else
        begin
          writeln(i);
          icount := icount + 1
        end;
    i := i + 1
  end;

writeln(icount, jcount);
```

In the second example the flow is linear. We can think of the loop as a series of fixed actions that will be executed so long as the boolean condition is *true*. The **if...then...else** construction with compound statements makes clear the result of either possible evaluation of its conditional. By contrast, the program structure in the first example is obscure. One must step through the program statement by statement, evaluating the implications of each action, in order to understand the program. Code such as this is more difficult to write, understand, correct, or modify.

The author does not recommend use of the **goto** in Pascal, especially by novice programmers. In Pascal it is always possible to avoid its use, and code such as that shown above is never justified in a language with modern control structures. However, in the interest of completeness, this statement will be described on the following pages, with a few examples in which its use may be justified.

The label declaration is the first part of a program block, i.e., it occurs just after the program or procedure heading, and before **const**ant, **type**, **var**iable, and subroutine declarations. The label declaration takes the form of the reserved word **label**, followed by a list of unsigned integer labels separated by commas and terminated by a semicolon:

```
label
  10, 20, 30, 99;
```

The scope of a label (the area in which it is recognized) is the entire program block in which it is declared. After the label is declared, it is prefixed to a single statement in the block, e.g.,

```
10:     <statement>
```

Any other statement within the block can transfer the flow of control to that statement via the statement

```
goto 10
```

The **goto** may not transfer control into a structured statement from outside that statement: for example, do not jump into the body of a loop, into a compound statement, or into a procedure or function. It is possible to use the **goto** to jump out of these structures under abnormal circumstances.

Use of the **goto** should be avoided if at all possible. It should be used only where the natural structure of the program must be broken. In implementations that do not

> **goto** <label>
>
> where <label> is an unsigned integer of no more than four digits, declared in a label declaration prior to its use and used to prefix a single statement.

Figure 5.11. SYNTAX: The **goto** Statement

include a statement such as *halt* or *stop* to cause termination of a program, the **goto** can be used to simulate this action by transferring control to a point just before the final **end** statement of the program:

```
          program demo(input, output);
            label
              999;
            . . .
            begin
              . . .
              if <disaster condition>
                then
                  begin { abort program }
                    writeln('fatal error: ... ');
                    writeln('program run terminated');
                    goto 999                              { halt }
                  end; { abort program }
              . . .
999:
            end.
```

This should be an unusual event, and the conditions that make it necessary should be made clear in program comments.

Some programmers also use the **goto** to exit a loop or procedure abnormally. For example, the program segment below searches for the location of the value *x* in an array:

```
     [ var
         found : boolean; ]

            found := false;
            for i := 1 to n do
              if list[i] = x
                then
                  begin
                    found := true;
                    goto 10;
                  end;

     10:    <next statement>
```

Situations like this are best avoided by careful use of **while** statements and additional checks. After the following loop terminates, if *found* is *true*, then *i* is the location of *x* in *list*:

```
i := 1;
found := false;
while (i <= n) and not found do
  if list[i] = x
    then found := true
    else i := i + 1
```

Blocks of statements that should not be executed under certain conditions can also be circumvented without the use of the **goto**. Instead of

```
          if <error condition>
            then goto 100
            else
              begin
                <statements>
                goto 200
              end;

100:      writeln('error: ... ')
200:      <next statement>
```

use the following:

```
if <error condition>
  then writeln('error: ... ')
  else
    begin
      <statements>
    end
```

Additionally, the program can set boolean variables that will flag certain conditions elsewhere in a program:

```
error := <boolean expression>;
. . .
if not error
  then
    begin
      <statements>
    end
```

If you are used to using the **goto** you may find the habit hard to break, but the end result will be worth the effort. If this is your first programming language, don't form the habit. Niklaus Wirth, the author of Pascal, wrote: "The presence of goto's in a Pascal program is often an indication that the programmer has not yet learned 'to think' in Pascal (as this is a necessary construct in other programming languages)."[4]

References and Selected Readings

The following source contains many helpful suggestions for effective programming. At this point, we suggest that you read the first two chapters, paying particular attention to comments on the use of the **goto**. You will find it helpful to read sections of this and other programming books along with the current text.

Ledgard, Henry F., John F. Hueras, and Paul A. Nagin. *Pascal with Style: Programming Proverbs*. Rochelle Park, N.J.: Hayden, 1979.

4. Kathleen Jensen and Niklaus Wirth, *Pascal User Manual and Report*, 2d ed., (New York: Springer-Verlag, 1974), 33.

A concise discussion of the same topic (**goto**) can be found in chapter 7, "A Purist's View of Structured Programming," of the following:

Ledgard, Henry F. *Professional Pascal: Essays on the Practice of Programming*. Reading, Mass: Addison-Wesley, 1986.

Also cited in this chapter:

Jensen, Kathleen, and Niklaus Wirth. *Pascal User Manual and Report*. 2d ed. New York: Springer-Verlag, 1974.

Other suggested readings:

Brook, Barry S. "Music Bibliography and the Computer." In *Papers from the West Virginia Conference on Computer Applications in Music*, edited by Gerald Lefkoff, 9–28. Morgantown, W.Va.: West Virginia University Library, 1967.

Erickson, Raymond F. "Rhythmic Problems and Melodic Structure in Organum Purum: A Computer-Assisted Study." Ph.D. diss., Yale University, 1970.

Hofstetter, Fred T. *Computer Literacy for Musicians*. Englewood Cliffs, N.J.: Prentice-Hall, 1988.

Lewin, David. "Intervallic Relations Between Two Collections of Notes." *Journal of Music Theory* 3, no. 2 (1959): 298–301.

Morris, Robert, and Daniel Starr. "The Structure of All-Interval Series." *Journal of Music Theory* 18 no. 2 (1974): 364–89.

Exercises

The only control structures to be used in the first ten problems are **while** loops and **if** statements. Each problem should be solved as a short but complete program, and then run on the computer. Each solution will require input and/or output statements and the use of integer variables. You will need to create an input file for exercises 6–10.

1. Print the numbers from 1 to 10 on one line.

2. Print the numbers from 77 to 52, one per line.

3. Print the odd numbers from 1 to 99.

4. Print the even numbers from 200 to 150.

5. Print the numbers from 1 to 200, with ten on each line.

6. Print the first number after the integer 99 in the input file.

7. Count the numbers before the first 0 in the input file. Print the results.

8. Print each positive integer in the input file. Terminate the data with 0.

9. Print each negative integer that is also odd in the input file. Terminate the data with 0.

10. Read an input file and count separately the number of positive integers and the number of negative integers. Terminate the data with 0, and print the results.

Repeat each of the above programs using **repeat...until** for the main loop.

Use appropriate control structures for each of the following:

11. Write a program to print the odd numbers from 49 to 1, five per line.

12. Create a data file containing positive integers and at least one –1 in the file. The file should end with a 0. Example: 14 99 67 –1 48 0. Write a program to print the numbers before the first –1 in the file. Print the numbers three per line, and give the final total showing how many numbers there were before the –1. Do several versions of this program using **repeat** and **while** statements. Which is most appropriate? Why?

13. Write a program that computes the sum of all integers from 1 to 100.

14. Write a program that computes the sum of the even integers from 0 to 100.

15. Write a program that computes the sum of the odd integers from 1 to 100.

16. Write a program that finds each integer from 1 to 100 that is evenly divisible by 7 and 3.

17. Write a program that calculates the sum of the real numbers in the input file. Terminate the data with any negative number.

18. Write a program that calculates the average value of the real numbers in the input file. Terminate the data with a negative number.

19. Write a program that prints each number in the input file that is divisible by 7. Terminate the data with 0.

20. Write a program that prints each number in the input file that is *not* divisible by 7. Terminate the data with 0. If no numbers meet the required condition, print an appropriate message.

21. Write a program for converting points to percentage (for use in grading exams, for example). The program should read the total number of points and then print a table showing, for each whole number of points, the number wrong, the number right, and the percentage.

6| Encoding Music

A thorough consideration of representations of music for computer processing must encompass three separate topics:

1. The encoding of music for input to the computer
2. Internal representation, i.e., how the data is to be stored and manipulated within the computer
3. The data structures that will contain the internal representation and represent the relationship between individual data items

This chapter explores the first two topics. Efficient computer processing of complex music data requires mastering the third, which will be treated in later chapters.

The first portion of the chapter deals with numeric models of pitch and rhythm. Music theorists have demonstrated that number systems serve remarkably well for modeling many styles and processes in twentieth-century music. The most common paradigm is the use of integers within a modulo 12 universe to represent pitch classes in atonal and serial music. Since the concept of pitch class is well established and forms the basis for much contemporary music theory, we will take it as a starting point. We will then use extensions of this concept to develop systems that model diatonic operations accommodating register and spelling as well as pitch, and that are thus applicable to a broad range of applications. Each of these representations constitutes a *number system* in which all defined operations on elements result in other elements in the system. Since they are based on integers, they can be manipulated easily through the use of primitive arithmetic operators in any computer language; thus they are easy to program, and since they can be used directly to input simple music information, the novice programmer need not be concerned with the process of translating one representation to another.[1] As an input code, integers are sufficient for encoding simple music, especially if only one parameter (pitch, rhythm, etc.) is to be represented at a time. They also serve admirably for utility programs, e.g., programs to identify sets or calculate twelve-tone matrices. For more complex analytic tasks, such as score analysis or other applications that require more complete music information, the numeric paradigms are inadequate for external data representation, i.e., for input to computer programs. However, they will still be useful for internal representation when stored in appropriate data structures.

1. Of course, the Pascal system must convert ASCII characters to the binary form of integers used internally, but this process is automated and need not concern the reader for the moment.

The latter part of this chapter introduces two more complete encoding schemes: DARMS and SCORE. Each of these defines a syntax using alphabetic, numeric, and special characters to represent many aspects of a music score. DARMS is treated most thoroughly—although we will use only a subset of the complete language—since it is used extensively in later chapters of this text. Although SCORE is more often used for computer music synthesis than for analysis, it has many interesting features, and we will use certain aspects of the language in some programs and exercises.

These varied music representations are grouped together in one chapter for ease of reference. The student reading this chapter for the first time should concentrate on mastering the concepts in the beginning of the chapter, since these will be put to use immediately in chapter 7 and will form the basis of internal representations used throughout this text. Although DARMS code will not be used extensively until later chapters, it is not too early to become familiar with its basic features; familiarity with the code now will facilitate understanding algorithms that manipulate the code later.

6.1 Numeric Pitch Representation

For the present we will limit ourselves to music representations that consist entirely of integer data. In the beginning we will use these codes (with extensions for bar lines and meter signatures) as the means of encoding pitch and/or rhythm in music. This approach simplifies early exercises, since we will not have to convert from one representation to another. Later, when we have learned more sophisticated programming techniques, the numeric models will form the basis of internal representations that will be derived from more mnemonic and complete external encoding languages.

6.1.1 Pitch Class (pc)

The notions of *pitch class* and *pitch-class set* are fundamental to twelve-tone and atonal theory.[2] The use of the term pitch class to denote pitch as an abstraction, divorced from register, notation, and compositional realization, is usually attributed to Milton Babbitt, who wrote:

> If the elements of the twelve-tone pitch system are, indeed, "traditional" ones, both insofar as they are pitch classes with class membership defined by octave equivalence, and as there are twelve such pitch classes—corresponding to the chromatically equal-tempered quantization of the frequency continuum—even here essential deviations must be noted. In the twelve-tone system there is a one-to-one correlation between pitch notation and presented pitch, as opposed to the many-to-one correlation of triadic-tonal music; there can be no such distinctions as those between explicit and functional "dissonance," or between enharmonically identical "consonance" and "dissonance."[3]

2. Pitch-class sets will be discussed in later chapters.

3. Milton Babbitt, "Twelve-Tone Invariants as Compositional Determinants," *The Musical Quarterly* 46 (1960): 247.

A pitch class (pc) includes all representatives of a pitch, regardless of spelling or octave. In music-theoretic literature, pcs are usually represented by the twelve integers between 0 and 11, with 0 = C, as shown in figure 6.1. When applied to serial composition, the system is sometimes transposed so that 0 represents some other pc, typically the first pitch of the reference form of the tone row.

Integer notation avoids the biases of specific spelling and register that are inherent in notated music. In addition, it simplifies music operations such as interval calculation, transposition, and inversion by reducing them to arithmetic operations.

Pitch-class integers are also used to represent intervals, as shown in table 6.1. The table lists the traditional name for each interval and its size in semitones. Note that the listed name is only one possibility; any enharmonically equivalent interval is represented by the same pc integer, e.g., the integer 1 represents the augmented prime as well as the minor second. Intervals larger than 11 semitones are reduced to simple intervals, thus the octave is equivalent to the prime. The pc system is a modulo 12 system, i.e., all operations on pcs result in one of the twelve pc integers 0 through 11. The interval between any two pcs A and B is calculated by subtracting the first from the second. If the result is negative, twelve is added to the result:

$$pcint = (B - A) \bmod 12$$

where A and B are pcs, and
$pcint$ is the interval between the pcs

Each interval A has an inverse A', such that $A + A' = 0$. Another way of saying this is that the inverse of any pc interval A is $(12 - A) \bmod 12$:

$$A' = (12 - A) \bmod 12$$

where A is a pcint, and
A' is its inverse

Table 6.1 lists the inverse-related pairs of pc intervals. Note that two intervals, 0 and 6, are their own inverse.

In some applications it is useful to consider an interval and its inverse to be equivalent. In this case each *interval class* is represented by the smaller of the two integers; thus all intervals in the pc system belong to one of the interval classes 0, 1, 2, 3, 4, 5, 6. The interval class for any pc interval A is calculated as follows:

if $A \leq 6$
then $pic = A$,
otherwise $pic = 12 - A$

where A is a pc interval, and
pic is its interval class

Figure 6.2 shows pitches encoded as pcs. Below the pcs are shown the pc intervals (pcint) and interval classes (pic) between each pair of pcs.

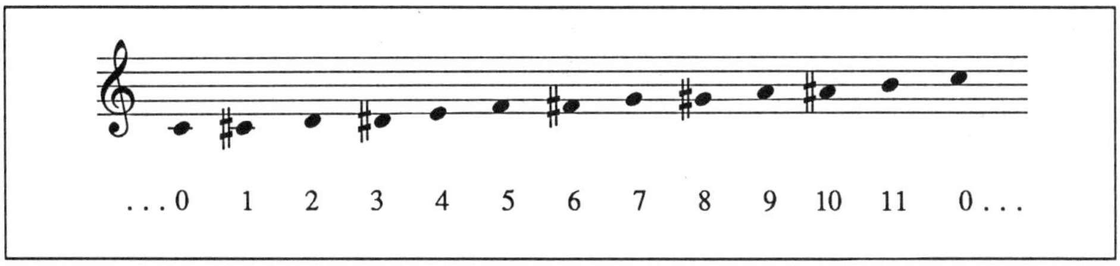

Figure 6.1. Pitch-Class Integers

Name	*pcint*	*pcint*	*Name*
perfect prime	0	0	perfect octave
minor second	1	11	major seventh
major second	2	10	minor seventh
minor third	3	9	major sixth
major third	4	8	minor sixth
perfect fourth	5	7	perfect fifth
augmented fourth	6	6	diminished fifth

Table 6.1. Intervals in the Pitch-Class System

Transposition in the pc system consists of adding a pc interval to each pc element of a pitch collection:

$$T_n(A, B, C, \ldots) = ((A + n) \bmod 12, (B + n) \bmod 12, (C + n) \bmod 12, \ldots)$$

where $A, B, C, \ldots$ are pitch classes, and
n is a pitch-class interval

Example: Transpose a pitch-class collection by interval 4:

$$T_4(0, 7, 3, 2, 5, 10, 8, 11) = (4, 11, 7, 6, 9, 2, 0, 3)$$

When transposition is combined with inversion, the inverse operator is applied first, i.e., $TnI(x) = ((12 - x) + n) \bmod 12$. Since addition is commutative and 12 is

Figure 6.2. Examples of Pitch-Class Integers, Intervals, and Interval Classes

equal to 0 in a modulo 12 system, inversion followed by transposition can be shortened to the following:

$$T_nI(A, B, C, \ldots) = ((n - A) \bmod 12, (n - B) \bmod 12, (n - C) \bmod 12, \ldots)$$

where $A, B, C, \ldots$ are pitch classes, and
n is a pitch-class interval

Example: Inversion followed by transposition of a pc set:

$$T_4I(0, 7, 3, 2, 5, 10, 8, 11) = (4, 9, 1, 2, 11, 6, 8, 5)$$

Sometimes single characters are used to represent pcs 10 and 11. We prefer 'a' and 'b', since they are commonly used in computing,[4] although some music theorists have used other symbols such as 't' and 'e' or 'x' and 'y'. The primary advantage of these substitutions is that each pc is represented by a single character, obviating the use of spaces between pcs in input and output. Although this saves many keystrokes on input and makes the printout more compact, the conversion routines must be written by the programmer. Thus this form of input and output will not be used until later chapters.

Although we will not usually use pc integers as a means of encoding music compositions, a number of larger programs discussed later in this text rely strongly on this concept, and pc integers suggest a theoretic basis for other representations discussed below.

6.1.2 Continuous Pitch Code (cpc)

While the pitch-class system is useful for modeling certain types of pitch relations, we often need a representation that indicates register as well as pitch. Although a number of octave-designation systems are in common use, the most viable for our purpose is that proposed by the Acoustical Society of America and accepted by the U.S.A. Standards Association. This system, shown in figure 6.3, uses an integer subscript indicating the exact octave placement. The octave number refers to notes from C through the B notated a seventh above it. In print, pitches are identified by the note name followed by the octave number as a subscript: C_4 (middle C), F_5, $F\sharp_3$, etc.

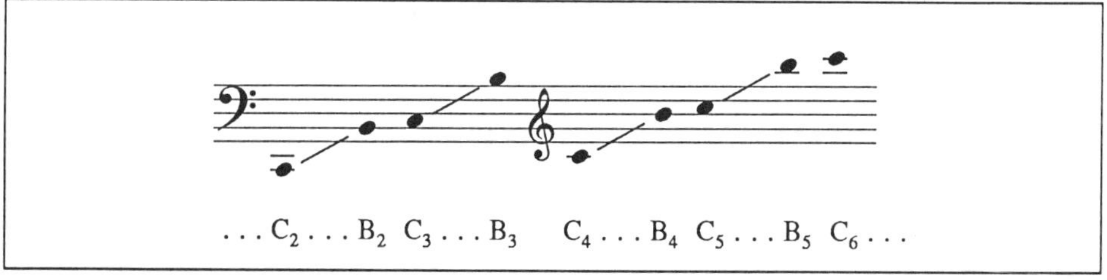

Figure 6.3. Standard Octave Numbers

4. The hexadecimal (base 16) system uses digits $0 \ldots 9$, $A \ldots F$ to represent the integers $0 \ldots 15$ (decimal). Lower case can be used for $a \ldots f$.

Pitch classes can be mapped onto a continuous integer scale by multiplying the octave by 12 and adding the pc integer. Thus pitches in octave 0 are numbered from 0 to 11, in octave 1 from 12 to 23, etc. Pitches in the octave beginning with middle C are numbered from 48 to 59. We will call this pitch representation *continuous pitch code* (cpc). The cpc representing any pitch can be calculated from the pc integer and octave number:

$$cpc = (oct \times 12) + pc$$

where cpc is a continuous pitch code,
oct is a standard octave number, and
pc is a pitch-class integer

The cpc can also be decoded into its component parts through arithmetic operations:

$$oct = cpc \text{ div } 12 \qquad \{\text{ integer division }\}$$
$$pc = cpc \text{ mod } 12$$

Thus the cpc is an integer that specifies the pitch and register, i.e., it places a pitch in the pitch continuum. Figure 6.4 shows a portion of the cpc scale.

Figure 6.4. The Continuous Pitch Code Scale

Intervals in this system are calculated by simple subtraction. The interval between any two cpc encoded pitches A and B is calculated as $B - A$:

$$cpint = B - A$$

where A and B are cpc encoded pitches, and
$cpint$ is the signed cpc interval

The interval is the distance in semitones between the pitches; ascending intervals are positive and descending intervals negative. Note also that intervals can be compound (greater than an octave). Figure 6.5 shows the intervals between some pitches in this system.

Transposition in the cpc system consists of adding a directed cpint to each cpc encoded pitch in a pitch collection. If the interval is negative, the transposition is downward; if the interval is positive, the transposition is upward:

$$T_n(A, B, C, \ldots) = (A + n, B + n, C + n, \ldots)$$

where $A, B, C, \ldots$ are cpc encoded pitches, and
n is a signed cpc interval

Example: Transpose a pitch collection up a major tenth:

$$T_{16}(60, 55, 63, 38, 29, 46, 68, 47) = (76, 71, 79, 54, 45, 62, 84, 63)$$

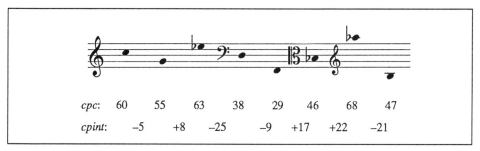

cpc: 60 55 63 38 29 46 68 47

cpint: −5 +8 −25 −9 +17 +22 −21

Figure 6.5. Examples of Continuous Pitch Codes and Continuous Pitch Intervals

6.1.3 Name Class (nc)

The letter names commonly used to represent staff position in music notation are cyclic just as pitch classes are; however, the name series repeats after seven notes. Each letter name can be considered a *name class* (nc), which represents all instances of a given note name regardless of register or chromatic inflection. In this system D, D-sharp, and D-flat are equivalent, but C-sharp and D-flat are not, since they are spelled using different letter names and occupy different staff positions in the same octave.

Just as the twelve pitch classes can be represented by the integers 0 through 11 within a modulo 12 system, the elements of the letter-name scale can be represented by the integers 0 through 6 within a modulo 7 system. With a fixed correspondence between integers and note names, 0 can represent any C, 1 any D, 4 any G, and so forth.[5] The name-class integers are shown in figure 6.6.

Intervals in this system are analogous to intervals in the pitch-class system, i.e., they can be calculated as the modulo 7 difference between the name-class integers. For any two ncs A and B, the interval is calculated by subtracting the first from the second. If the result is negative, add 7 to the difference.

$$ncint = (B - A) \bmod 7$$

where A and B are nc integers, and
$ncint$ is an nc interval

5. As a mnemonic device, name-class integers are easy to remember if related to scale steps in D, e.g., D = 1, E = 2, etc. Name-class intervals are always one less than the standard name: prime = 0, second = 1, third = 2, etc.

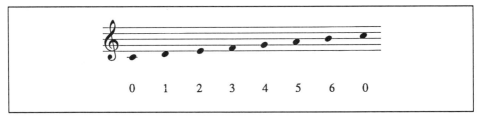

Figure 6.6. Name-Class Integers

Name-class intervals are generic rather than specific. All thirds, whether major, minor, augmented, or diminished, are represented by a difference of 2; all fourths by a difference of 3. Each interval A has an inverse A', such that $A + A' = 0$:

$$A' = (7 - A) \bmod 7$$

where A is an nc interval, and
A' is its inverse

Table 6.2 shows the intervals in the nc system, with inversionally related intervals adjacent. Because of inversional equivalence, there are only four interval classes in the nc system; these are represented by the integers 0–3. The interval class of any ncint A is calculated as follows:

if $A \leq 3$
then $nic = A$,
otherwise $nic = 7 - A$

where A is any nc interval, and
nic is its interval class

Figure 6.7 shows examples of nc encoded pitches, intervals, and interval classes.

Transposition in the nc system consists of adding an nc interval (modulo 7) to each element of a collection of nc encoded pitches:

$$T_n(A, B, C, \ldots) = ((A + n) \bmod 7, (B + n) \bmod 7, (C + n) \bmod 7, \ldots)$$

where $A, B, C, \ldots$ are nc encoded pitches, and
n is an nc interval

Name	*ncint*	*ncint*	*Name*
prime	0	0	octave
second	1	6	seventh
third	2	5	sixth
fourth	3	4	fifth

Table 6.2. Intervals in the Name-Class System

nc:	0		4		2		1		3		6		5		6
ncint:		4		5		6		2		3		6		1	
nic:		3		2		1		2		3		1		1	

Figure 6.7. Examples of Name-Class Integers, Intervals, and Interval Classes

Example: Transpose (C, G, E, D, F, B, A, B) a third
Result: (E, B, G, F, A, D, C, D)

$$T_2(0, 4, 2, 1, 3, 6, 5, 6) = (2, 6, 4, 3, 5, 1, 0, 1)$$

Transposition followed by inversion of an nc integer x is obtained by:

$$T_n I(x) = ((7 - x) + n) \bmod 7$$

Thus a collection of nc encoded pitches can be inverted and transposed by the following:

$$T_n I(A, B, C, \ldots) = ((n - A) \bmod 7, (n - B) \bmod 7, (n - C) \bmod 7, \ldots)$$

where $A, B, C, \ldots$ are nc encoded pitches, and
n is an nc interval

Example: Invert (C, F, E, A, D, G, B) and transpose by a fifth
Result: (G, D, E, B, F, C, G)

$$T_4 I(0, 3, 2, 5, 1, 4, 6) = (4, 1, 2, 6, 3, 0, 5)$$

Each operation or procedure that is possible in the pitch-class system has an analogue in the name-class system. We can create name-class sets, transpose them, calculate inversions, represent their generic interval content by interval vectors, and reduce them to prime forms.

6.1.4 Continuous Name Code (cnc)

The name-class system can also be mapped onto a continuous scale of integers. The *continuous name code* (cnc) of a note is calculated as follows:

$$cnc = (oct \times 7) + nc$$

where oct is a standard octave number,
nc is a name class integer, and
cnc is a continuous name code

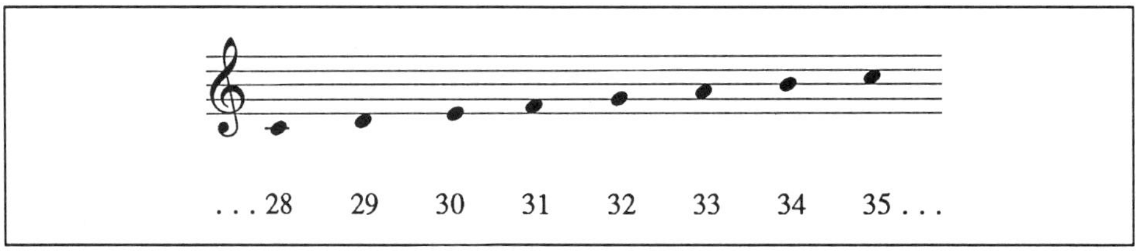

Figure 6.8. The Continuous Name Code Scale

This formula maps the notes in octave 0 into the integers 0–6, the notes in octave 1 into 7–13, etc. The octave beginning with middle C (C_4) is numbered from 28 to 34, as shown in figure 6.8.

Directed nc intervals for any two cncs *A* and *B* are calculated by subtracting *A* from *B*. A negative result indicates a descending interval. Remember that the result is the number of diatonic (nc) steps, not the number of semitones, i.e., the result is the generic interval size.

$$cnint = B - A$$

where *A* and *B* are cnc encoded pitches, and
cnint is a directed nc interval

Figure 6.9 shows some pitches and intervals in the cnc system.

Transposition in this system consists of adding a signed nc interval to a cnc encoded pitch:

$$T_n(A, B, C, \ldots) = (A + n, B + n, C + n, \ldots)$$

where *A*, *B*, *C*, . . . are cpc encoded pitches, and
n is a signed cnc interval

Example: Transpose (C_5, G_4, E_5, D_3, F_2, B_3, A_5, B_3) down a fifth

Result: (F_4, C_4, A_4, G_2, B_1, E_3, D_5, F)

T_{-4}(35, 32, 37, 22, 17, 27, 40, 27) = (31, 28, 33, 18, 13, 23, 36, 23)

The cnc system will enable us to perform diatonic operations on encoded music.

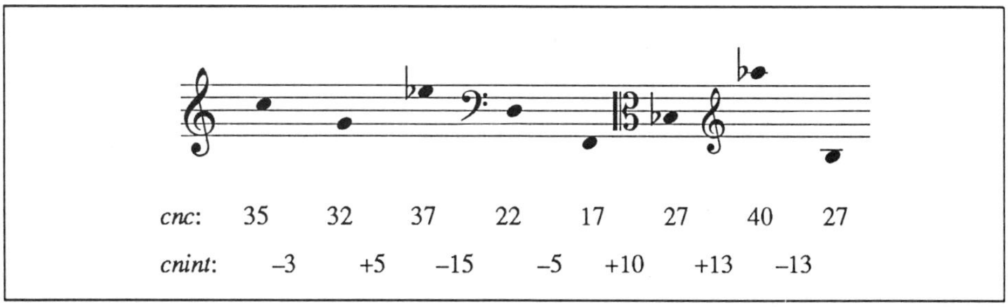

Figure 6.9. Examples of Directed Intervals in the Continuous Name Code System

binomial representation = <pc,nc>

pc equivalence: C♯ = <1,0>; D♭ = <1,1>; E♭♭♭ = < 1,2>

nc equivalence: C = <0,0>; C♯ = <1,0>; C♭ = <11,0>

Figure 6.10. Binomial Representation of Pitch

6.2 Binomial Representation (br)

The pc and nc systems are complementary, with each making up for deficiencies of the other. The pitch class designates the exact pitch, while the name class indicates the spelling. The advantages of both systems can be realized concurrently if pitches are represented by integer couples in the form <pc,nc> with a common point of origin <0,0> representing C. Enharmonic spellings of the same note have the same pitch class but different name classes; chromatic alterations of the same note name share the same name class but have a different pitch-class component, as shown in figure 6.10.

There are 84 (12 × 7) binomial pitch classes in the system. Of these, 35 are in common use, representing notes up to and including double accidentals. Table 6.3 shows the binomial representation of these 35 notes. Enharmonic spellings (those with the same pitch class) occur in the same row, while notes spelled with the same letter name occur in the same column. The system is extensible within reasonable limits. Triple, quadruple, and even quintuple accidentals are theoretically possible, though unlikely to be used. Ambiguities result for more than five accidentals,

Pitch Class	*Name Class* 0	1	2	3	4	5	6
0	C	D♭♭					B♯
1	C♯	D♭					B𝄪
2	C𝄪	D	E♭♭				
3		D♯	E♭	F♭♭			
4		D𝄪	E	F♭			
5			E♯	F	G♭♭		
6			E𝄪	F♯	G♭		
7				F𝄪	G	A♭♭	
8					G♯	A♭	
9					G𝄪	A	B♭♭
10	C♭♭					A♯	B♭
11	C♭					A𝄪	B

Table 6.3. Binomial Representation of Common Notes

although they could be resolved contextually. (Is <6,0> C-sextuple-sharp or C-sextuple-flat?)

The binomial system can also represent intervals. The pitch-class integer specifies the interval size in semitones, and the name-class integer designates the generic interval size. Thus a minor third is represented by the couple <3,2>, a major third by <4,2>, an augmented third by <5,2>, and a diminished third by <2,2>. The system is unambiguous through quintuply augmented or diminished intervals. Table 6.4 shows the binomial representation of intervals through augmented and diminished intervals. The modifiers 'A', 'P', 'M', 'm', and 'd' represent augmented, perfect, major, minor, and diminished, respectively. Intervals of the same generic size occur in the same column, while enharmonically equivalent intervals occur in the same row.

Pitch				*Name Class*			
Class	0	1	2	3	4	5	6
0	P1	d2					A7
1	A1	m2					
2		M2	d3				
3		A2	m3				
4			M3	d4			
5			A3	P4			
6				A4	d5		
7					P5	d6	
8					A5	m6	
9						M6	d7
10						A6	m7
11	d1						M7

Table 6.4. Binomial Representation of Common Intervals

6.2.1 Music Operations

All operations that are possible on pitch classes and name classes are also possible in the binomial system. The operations are performed separately on the ncs in modulo 7 and on the pcs in modulo 12, as follows:

1. Transposition is addition. To transpose a note $<a,b>$ by interval $<c,d>$, do the following:

$$<a,b> + <c,d> = <(a + c) \bmod 12, (b + d) \bmod 7>$$

Example: Transpose D up a major third:

$$<2,1> + <4,2> = <6,3>$$
$$(\text{D} + \text{M3} = \text{F}\sharp)$$

Note: The transposition interval may be negative; e.g., to transpose down by a M3, add $<-4,-2>$. This is equivalent to adding the inverse (see rule 3 below).

2. Interval calculation is subtraction. To find the interval between two notes, subtract the first note from the second note:

$$<a,b> - <c,d> = <(a - c) \bmod 12, (b - d) \bmod 7)$$

Example: The interval between E-flat and A:

$$<9,5> - <3,2> = <6,3>$$
(A − E♭ = aug 4)

or

$$<3,2> - <9,5> = <6,4>$$
(E♭ − A = dim 5)

3. The inverse (inversion) of the interval $<a,b>$ is

$$<12,7> - <a,b> = <(12 - a) \bmod 12, (7 - b) \bmod 7>$$

Example: The inversion of a perfect fourth:

$$<12,7> - <5,3> = <7,4>$$
(P4 P5)

4. Melodic inversion is subtraction of each note from a constant. If the constant is two times the first note, the inversion will begin on the same note as the prime. Example: The melodic inversion of D E F♯ A C:

(D E F♯ A C)
$<2,1>$ $<4,2>$ $<6,3>$ $<9,5>$ $<0,0>$

constant = $2 \times <2,1> = <4,2>$

$$\begin{array}{ccccc} <4,2> & <4,2> & <4,2> & <4,2> & <4,2> \\ -<2,1> & -<4,2> & -<6,3> & -<9,5> & -<0,0> \\ \hline <2,1> & <0,0> & <10,6> & <7,4> & <4,2> \end{array}$$
(D C B♭ G E)

Note: Inversion can also be obtained by multiplying each binomial couple by $<11,6>$ and transposing the result as desired.

5. Diatonic operations (within a specific scale) are obtained by doing the normal operation on the name class (modulo 7) and referencing a table for the correct pitch class. The table (S) is an array indexed by the name classes, with the corresponding pc as the content of each element.

Example: A diatonic sequence in G major:

S	0	1	2	3	4	5	6	ncs
	0	2	4	6	7	9	11	pcs for G major

Sequence G A B G F♯ a second higher:

	(G	A	B	G	F♯)
	<7,4>	<9,5>	<11,6>	<7,4>	<6,3>
	+<*,1>	+<*,1>	+< *,1>	+<*,1>	+<*,1>
=	<*S*[5],5>	<*S*[6],6>	<*S*[0],0>	<*S*[5],5>	<*S*[4],4>
=	<9,5>	<11,6>	<0,0>	<9,5>	<7,4>
	(A	B	C	A	G)

In the above illustration the asterisk is a place holder, indicating that the pitch class cannot be found until the name class has been determined. For example, the first note in the sequence is found by adding nc 1 to the second term of the binomial pc <7,4>, resulting in <*,5>. Now the pitch class can be found in the table: pc = *S*[5] = 9. Thus the new binomial pc is <9,5>.

6.2.2 Properties of the Binomial System

The universal set U consists of 84 binomial pitch classes, such that

$$binomial\ pitch\ class = \langle pc,nc \rangle$$

where $pc \in \{0, 1, 2, 3, 4, 5, 6, 7, 8, 9, 10, 11\}$, and
$nc \in \{0, 1, 2, 3, 4, 5, 6\}$

We define binary operations as follows:

$$+ : \langle a,b \rangle + \langle c,d \rangle = \langle (a + c) \bmod 12, (b + d) \bmod 7 \rangle$$
$$\times : \langle a,b \rangle \times \langle c,d \rangle = \langle (a \times c) \bmod 12, (b \times d) \bmod 7 \rangle$$

The following properties obtain:

1. For any two binomial pcs A and B

$$(A + B) \in U \quad \text{and} \quad (A \times B) \in U$$

2. Both addition and multiplication are commutative on the binomial system since, for any two binomial pcs A and B,

$$A + B = B + A \quad \text{and} \quad A \times B = B \times A$$

3. Both addition and multiplication are associative on the binomial system since, for any three binomial pcs A, B, and C,

$$(A + B) + C = A + (B + C)$$
and
$$(A \times B) \times C = A \times (B \times C)$$

4. Multiplication is distributive over addition on the binomial system since, for any three binomial pcs A, B, and C,

$$A \times (B + C) = (A \times B) + (A \times C)$$
and
$$(A + B) \times C = (A \times C) + (B \times C)$$

5. There exists an identity element for addition that equals $<0,0>$ such that, for any binomial pc A,

$$A + <0,0> = A$$

6. There exists an inverse A′ for every binomial pc A such that

$$A' + A = <0,0>$$

The inverse of $<a,b> \; = \; < (12 - a) \bmod 12, (7 - b) \bmod 7>$

7. There exists an identity element for multiplication that equals $<1,1>$ such that, for any binomial pc A,

$$A \times <1,1> = A$$

8. We define scalar multiplication such that, for any positive integer n and any binomial pc $<a,b>$,

$$n \times <a,b> = <(n \times a) \bmod 12, (n \times b) \bmod 7>$$

Properties one through seven are sufficient to show that the binomial system is a *commutative ring with unity.*

6.2.3 A Single Number Binomial Representation (br)

There are many possible methods of packing the nc and pc into a single integer. We will use the simple method shown below. The single-number representation (br) of a binomial couple $<pc,nc>$ can be obtained as follows:

$$br = (pc \times 10) + nc$$

where pc is the pitch class, and
nc is the name class

The number can be decoded just as simply:

$$nc = br \bmod 10$$
$$pc = br \text{ div } 10 \qquad \{ \text{ integer division, i.e., truncate } \}$$

This encoding system has several desirable qualities. First, it is easy to read, so it need not be decoded before the analyst can understand it: the last digit always indicates the spelling (nc) and the preceding digits give the pc:

br	*pc*	*nc*	*note name*
116	11	6	B
31	3	1	D-sharp
32	3	2	E-flat
1	0	1	D-double-flat
10	1	0	C-sharp

A second advantage of the single-number br is that it is compact. The largest number required is 116. Even with the octave number (discussed below), 9116 or 10116 would be more than sufficient for the top range. Thus the encoded pc, nc, and octave number easily fit into a single 16-bit computer word. A final advantage is that the single-number representation greatly simplifies the problem of defining normal order, prime forms, interval vectors, and so on.[6]

Mathematic operations on br encoded intervals and notes must take into account the decoding and recoding of the brs. We define the following operations on any two brs A and B:[7]

1. Addition (transposition):

$$\begin{aligned} A + B = {} & 10 \times ((A \text{ div } 10 + B \text{ div } 10) \text{ mod } 12) && \{\text{ pc part }\} \\ & + ((A \text{ mod } 10 + B \text{ mod } 10) \text{ mod } 7) && \{\text{ nc part }\} \end{aligned}$$

2. Subtraction (interval calculation or downward transposition):

$$\begin{aligned} A - B = {} & 10 \times ((A \text{ div } 10 - B \text{ div } 10) \text{ mod } 12) && \{\text{ pc part }\} \\ & + ((A \text{ mod } 10 - B \text{ mod } 10) \text{ mod } 7) && \{\text{ nc part }\} \end{aligned}$$

3. Inverse (interval inversion):

$$\begin{aligned} A' = {} & 10 \times ((12 - (A \text{ div } 10)) \text{ mod } 12) && \{\text{ pc part }\} \\ & + ((7 - (A \text{ mod } 10)) \text{ mod } 7) && \{\text{ nc part }\} \end{aligned}$$

4. Multiplication (e.g., inversion through multiplication by 116):

$$\begin{aligned} A \times B = {} & 10 \times (((A \text{ div } 10) \times (B \text{ div } 10)) \text{ mod } 12) && \{\text{ pc part }\} \\ & + (((A \text{ mod } 10) \times (B \text{ mod } 10)) \text{ mod } 7) && \{\text{ nc part }\} \end{aligned}$$

5. Multiplication of a br encoded interval A by some positive integer n (interval projection):

$$\begin{aligned} n \times A = {} & 10 \times (n \times (A \text{ div } 10) \text{ mod } 12) && \{\text{ pc part }\} \\ & + (n \times (A \text{ mod } 10) \text{ mod } 7) && \{\text{ nc part }\} \end{aligned}$$

6.2.4 Continuous Binomial Representation (cbr)

We now examine a method of adding registral information to the binomial representation. Octave designations can be added to the binomial representation by replacing the <pc,nc> couple with the couple <cpc,cnc>, mapping the octave onto the pitch and name parameters as described earlier in this chapter. The integer couple in the con-

6. These are discussed in Alexander R. Brinkman, "A Binomial Representation of Pitch for Computer Processing of Musical Data," *Music Theory Spectrum* 8 (1986): 44–57.

7. The formulas given here assume that the mod function operates properly on *negative* integers, i.e., (−3 mod 12) = 9. This is frequently *not* the case since many computer installations define the mod function thus: a mod $b = a - ((a \text{ div } b) \times a)$. To be safe the user is advised to write a Pascal function that works properly. Function *imod*(x, y) is defined elsewhere in this text.

tinuous scale combines the continuous pitch code and the continuous name code:

$$<cpc,cnc> = <(poct \times 12) + pc, (noct \times 7) + nc>$$

where pc is a pitch class,
nc is a name class, and
$poct$ and $noct$ are octave designators

Separate octave designators make it possible to represent notes with any number of accidentals, since the system can then accommodate any combination of cpc and cnc, even those in which the notated pitch (cnc) is in a different octave from the sounding pitch (cpc).

In practice this is not really necessary, so long as we are willing to accept the limitation of quintuple accidentals and quintuple augmentation and diminution for intervals, as described earlier. Thus we can use a single octave number, that in which the pitch is notated, and calculate the correct pitch level with minimal computation.

The octave number can be added to the single number br described above as follows:

$$cbr = oct \times 1000 + br$$

where cbr is an integer representing oct, pc, and nc,
br is the binomial representation, and
oct is the octave number of the notated pitch

The above can be decoded with the following formulas:

$$oct = cbr \text{ div } 1000$$
$$br = cbr \text{ mod } 1000$$
$$pc = br \text{ div } 10$$
$$nc = br \text{ mod } 10$$

where oct is the standard octave number,
br is the single number representation of pc and nc,
pc is the pitch class, and
nc is the name class

If we allow the cbr to be signed (figure 6.11), and provide operations to manipulate these numbers, we have a registral generalization of the binomial system. For pitches, the cbr designates octave, pitch class, and name class (spelling). When the

$$cbr = \pm opcn$$

where $\pm$ is an optional sign
o is the standard octave number (0 or more digits),
pc is the pitch class (two digits: 00–11), and
n is the name class (one digit: 0–6)

Figure 6.11. Signed Continuous Binomial Representation

cbr represents an interval, the high-order digit allows for compound intervals, and the sign indicates direction. In chapter 19 we will introduce function *add*(x, y), which adds two signed cbrs and returns the result in the same form. Translations to and from standard pitch and interval designations are presented elsewhere in this text and in exercises.

6.3 Reciprocal Duration Code (rdc)

Reciprocal duration code is a simple numeric representation of durations. The name rdc is derived from the fact that each duration is encoded as the reciprocal of its fractional value, e.g., an eighth note (1/8) is encoded as 8, a quarter note (1/4) as 4, a whole note (1/1) as 1, etc. Thus each simple duration can be encoded as a single integer. In its simplest form, using only integers, the code is somewhat limited, since it does not provide for dotted notes, ties, or some grouplets. Although grouplets (triplets, quintuplets, etc.) are not encoded explicitly, they can still be encoded using this system. You may have noticed that each duration code is the number of equal subdivisions of the whole note, represented by the duration code 1. In a whole note (unity), there are two half notes (encoded 2), four quarter notes (4), eight eighth notes (8), etc. Although these subdivisions are common, there is no reason we cannot use the system to represent any durational value that is an even division of the whole note. Thus the duration equal to 1/5 of a whole note is encoded as 5. The code for any subdivision of a duration is the duration code times the number of subdivisions of that duration. Thus the code for one member of a quarter-note triplet is 12 (4×3); one member of a quarter-note quintuplet is 20 (4×5); and one member of a half-note triplet is 6 (2×3).

We can extend the system to rests by using negative numbers: –4 = quarter rest, –8 = eighth rest, etc. The sign is used to detect the presence of a rest rather than a note; the absolute value of the number is used in calculating duration. Thus we can represent any duration that can be represented by a simple, undotted value, or any even subdivision of these values.

This system has several advantages. First, it is mnemonic and easy to use, at least for common duration types. Second, since it is based on rational values used in music notation, it can be manipulated mathematically, i.e, a duration code can be reconverted to a fraction through the use of its reciprocal.[8] Thus it is easy to convert each code to the number of beats it represents, to calculate the total number of beats in a measure, etc.

Before encoded durations are manipulated arithmetically, they are reconverted back to the fractional values they represent. This is accomplished by taking the reciprocal of the duration code, e.g., 4 (quarter note) becomes 1/4 or 0.25. Initially we will use real numbers to store these values. In chapter 13 we will learn to use

8. The reciprocal of a number x is $1/x$. This encoding scheme converts a fraction, say 1/4, to an integer by this formula: $1/(1/4) = 4$. The reciprocal of the duration code is the original fraction (1/4).

records to represent fractions. This will enable us to perform complex operations on rhythmic data without the inherent inaccuracy of real arithmetic.

Later we will allow dots and ties as follows: dots are encoded as the character '.' and ties as ','. Thus we can represent a dotted quarter (4.), a double-dotted sixteenth (16..), a quarter tied to a double-dotted eighth (4,8..), etc. Processing these configurations requires interpreting character data, and would overcomplicate the exercises in early chapters of this text. In chapter 15 we will introduce an extension to the code that can accommodate grouplets and nested grouplets of any complexity.

Mozart, Symphony No. 40 in G Minor, K. 550, 4th movement

Continuous Pitch Code (cpc):
50 0 55 58 62 67 0 70 69 61 64 0 62 66 64 61 62 66 64 61 0 62 99 62 0 63 66 69 72 0 75 74 66 69 0 67 70 69 66 67 70 69 66 0 67 99 100

Continuous Name Code (cnc):
29 0 32 34 36 39 0 41 40 35 37 0 36 38 37 35 36 38 37 35 0 36 99 36 0 37 38 40 42 0 44 43 38 40 0 39 41 40 38 39 41 40 38 0 39 99 100

Continuous Binomial Representation (cbr):
4021 / 4074 4106 5021 5074 / 5106 5095 5010 5042 / 5021 5063 5042 5010 5021 5063 5042 5010 / 5021 r 5021 / 5032 5063 5095 6000 / 6032 6021 5063 5095 / 5074 5106 5095 5063 5074 5106 5095 5063 / 5074 r //

Reciprocal Duration Code (rdc):
4 0 4 4 4 4 0 2 4 8 8 0 8 8 8 8 8 8 8 8 0 2 -4 4 0 4 4 4 4 0 2 4 8 8 0 8 8 8 8 8 8 8 8 0 2 -4 100

DARMS Code:
!G !K2- !M$ 20QL,VP / 3 5' 7' 30' / 32HL 31Q (6#,VF 8*) / (7L 9# 8* 6) (7L 9 8 6) / 7H RQ 7QL,VP / 8- 9#' 31' 33' / 35HL 34Q (9#,VF 31) / (30L 32 31 9#) (30L 32 31 9#) / 30H RQ //

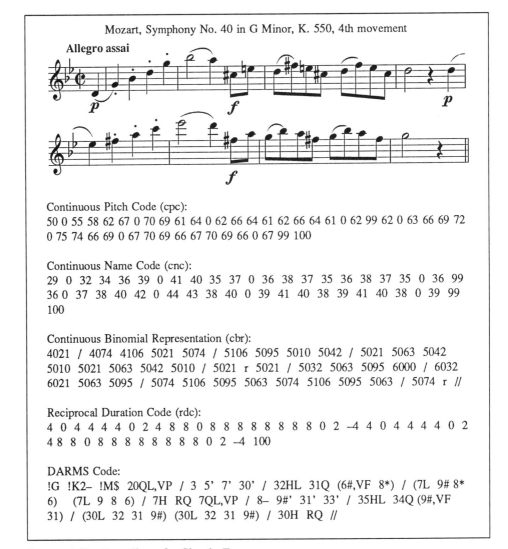

Figure 6.12. Encoding of a Simple Excerpt

6.4 Delimiters

When we deal with numeric codes, desired special features in the code, such as bar lines and rests, can be represented by mnemonic characters ('/', 'r', etc.) or by carefully chosen integer values. Initially we will use integers, since character data would make early problems more difficult than they need be. These special values serve as delimiters that subdivide the code into smaller units and mark the end of the data. For the present, we will encode bar lines as the integer 0 and the final double bar at the end of the piece (or excerpt) as 100. As in standard music notation, the final measure will be terminated by a "double bar" rather than by a bar line. If there is an anacrusis, the code will begin with a note (pitch or duration), otherwise it must begin with an encoded bar line. When using numeric pitch codes, we will encode rests as the integer 99; in reciprocal duration code the duration code will be negative.

The codes for bar lines and double bars are arbitrary and are not part of the number systems. We choose as delimiters numbers that are unlikely to occur otherwise in the code. If we use the integers 0, 99, and 100 as delimiters, we cannot use them for durations; therefore we cannot represent the value of a note with no duration (0 could be used to encode the duration of a grace note), a 99th note, or a 100th note (1/100 of a whole note). Likewise, the use of these delimiters in numeric pitch encoding systems eliminates three pitch codes that otherwise might have represented notes; however, these pitches are in registral extremes and are unlikely to be used in any case.

Figure 6.12 illustrates an excerpt from the last movement of Mozart's Symphony No. 40 in G Minor, encoded in several numeric systems, using 0, 100, and 99 to encode bar lines and rests. In the cbr code '/' is used for bar lines, and 'r' for rests. The rdc version uses negative numbers for rests. The final line renders the same example in DARMS code, which will be discussed in the next section. This version efficiently encodes more information than the other three combined, but it is considerably more difficult to decode.

6.5 DARMS Code

DARMS, a music encoding language developed by Stefan Bauer-Mengelberg in the early 1960s, is an acronym for Digital Alternate Representation of Musical Scores. The encoding scheme was designed as part of an early attempt at computer music printing, using a photon printer. The printing project was eventually abandoned, but the music encoding scheme remains and has been used in many music analysis projects.[9] Because the DARMS project was originally funded jointly by the Ford Foundation and Columbia University, it is sometimes called Ford-Columbia Code.

While this code is efficient and easy to use as a means of encoding music, it cannot be used for music analysis without a fair amount of interpretation. DARMS code

9. A-R Editions, of Madison, Wisconsin, is now doing engraving-quality music printing using DARMS and a photo-typesetting system. Examples of their work can be seen in those volumes of their *Recent Researches* series published after 1979.

is characterized by the same context dependency as the music notation it represents. For example, it is impossible to determine the meaning of a space code (representing a note) without knowing the clef, key signature, and previous accidentals in the current measure. In chapters 11 and 13 we will examine algorithms that translate DARMS pitch and rhythm codes into the numeric isomorphisms discussed earlier in this chapter. Chapter 20 presents a score representation that is built from data derived from DARMS encoded scores.

DARMS is capable of representing virtually every aspect of a printed score. This chapter presents a subset of the language sufficient for encoding those features of a score that are generally relevant to analysis. This same DARMS subset is supported by the programs discussed in the final chapter of this text.

6.5.1 Encoding Pitch

Since DARMS was originally designed for music printing, it encodes music symbols, rather than their meaning. Unlike many other music-encoding languages, DARMS does not name pitches but instead encodes the location of notes on the staff. The lines and spaces on the staff, as well as ledger lines, are assigned integer numbers called *space codes*. The staff lines are numbered from 21 to 29, as shown in figure 6.13. Space codes are used to represent pitches or to specify the position of other symbols relative to the staff. The space codes between 20 and 29 may be encoded with only the last digit. This shorthand notation, called *two suppression*, is one of many shortcuts designed to minimize the number of keystrokes necessary to enter the code. To distinguish between space codes with the first digit suppressed and the space codes 1–9, the latter must be preceded by a 0, i.e., 01, 02, 03, . . ., 09. Another shortcut is that either the space code or the rhythm code may be omitted if it is identical to the previous note.

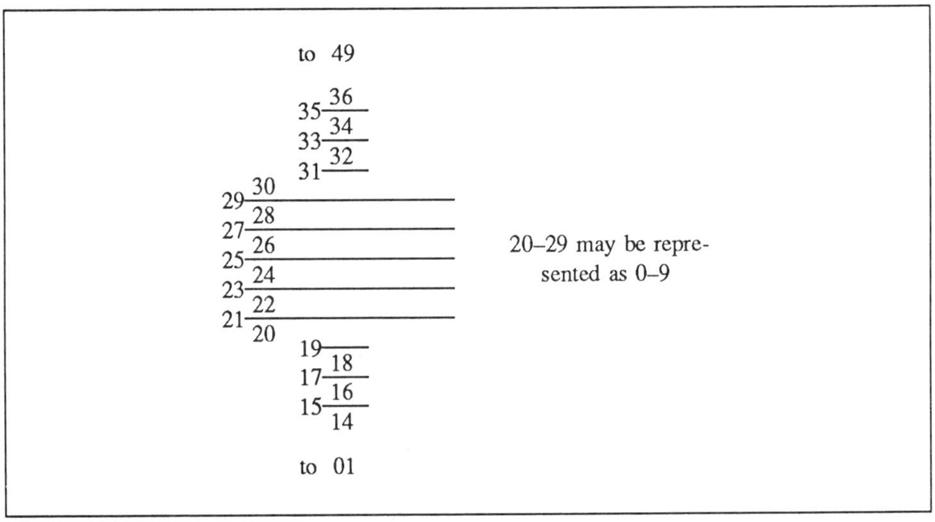

Figure 6.13. DARMS Space Codes

Other aspects of pitch encoding are shown in figure 6.14. Accidentals, which optionally follow space codes, are encoded by the symbols '#', '–', and '*' representing respectively sharps, flats, and naturals. Double sharps and flats are encoded by repeating the appropriate symbol. Clefs are encoded as an exclamation point followed by 'G', 'F', or 'C' indicating the type of clef.[10] Space codes are used to place clefs in less common positions on the staff. Key signatures are encoded as !K*ns*, where *n* is the number of sharps or flats, and *s* is the symbol '#' or '–' representing sharps and flats. Nonstandard key signatures are encoded as pairs of values <sharp or flat sign><space code> indicating the position of sharps or flats on the staff.

Accidentals:

#	sharp
##	double sharp
–	flat
––	double flat
*	natural

Key Signatures:

Standard: !K2# = key of two sharps
!K4– = key of four flats

Nonstandard key signatures use accidental code followed by space code: !K–25#22 (flat on 3d line and sharp on 1st space)

Clefs:

Treble	Alto	Bass	Treble Tenor	French Violin	Tenor	Baritone

!G	!C	!F	!G-8	1!G	7!C	5!F

Normal position (!G, !C, !F, !G-8)

Space code is specified for other positions (1!G, 7!C, 5!F)

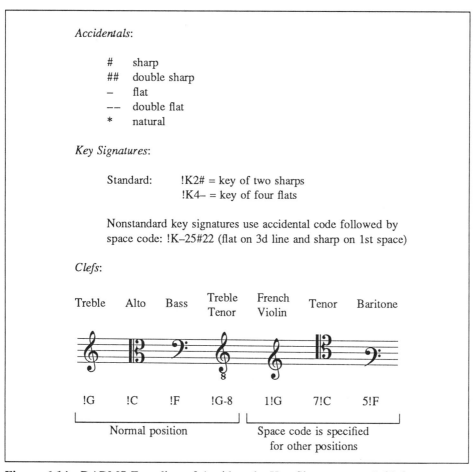

Figure 6.14. DARMS Encoding of Accidentals, Key Signatures, and Clefs

10. Since DARMS was designed for use with a keypunch machine, the original code used all capital letters. The software described in this book treats upper and lower case as equivalent except in a few special instances, e.g., transposition indicators in section 6.5.5. Upper case is used in the examples to aid in distinguishing between the letter L and the digit 1.

6.5.2 Rhythm, Meter, and Bar lines

For unbeamed notes, duration is specified by *duration codes*, which are for the most part mnemonic: 'W' for whole note, 'Q' for quarter note, and so forth (table 6.5). The duration code generally follows a note's space code and accidental code if any, or 'R' for a rest. If the duration is the same as the previous note, the duration code may be omitted. Dots following duration codes have the same meaning as in conventional music notation. Rests may be concatenated:

RHQE. = 

Other features of rhythm are illustrated below. Beamed notes (fig. 6.15) are encoded with parentheses, which indicate the number of beams on the note; a left parenthesis indicates the beginning of a beam, a right parenthesis the end. Beamed notes do not use duration codes, except in grouplets. Obviously the parentheses should be balanced. This scheme provides extreme economy of code and shows in addition the notational groupings used by the composer.

Meter signatures are encoded as !M*xxx*, where *xxx* is the meter signature. The meter may be a simple fraction or ratio, !M3/4 or !M5:8, or it may show more

WWW	Longa
WW	Breve
W	Whole
H	Half
Q	Quarter
E	Eighth
S	Sixteenth
T	Thirty-second
X	Sixty-fourth
Y	One hundred twenty-eighth
Z	Two hundred fifty-sixth
ZZ	Five hundred twelfth
ZZZ	One thousand twenty-fourth
.	(dot)
G	Grace note

Table 6.5. DARMS Duration Codes

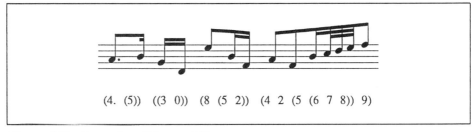

(4. (5)) ((3 0)) (8 (5 2)) (4 2 (5 (6 7 8)) 9)

Figure 6.15. Examples of Beamed Notes

complex groupings. It is even possible to indicate contemporary meter signatures using note heads. Some examples are shown in table 6.6.

Grouplets are defined before they are used, as shown in figure 6.16. The grouplet definer specifies a ratio and a numeric grouplet identifier. For example,

!3H7:2H

specifies that three half notes will occupy the time span that two half notes normally would. The integer 7 is the grouplet identifier. After a grouplet has been defined, it is used by appending the grouplet identifier number after the duration code. For example, after the grouplet definer !5Q3:4 (5 quarters in the time of 4) is defined, the grouplet

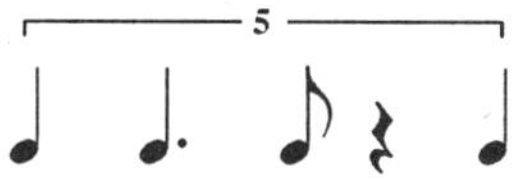

is encoded Q3 Q.3 E3 RQ3 Q3

Since the duration codes within parentheses override the default durations, we can show beaming within grouplets. After the grouplet !3E4:Q (3 eighths in the time of a quarter) is defined, the grouplet

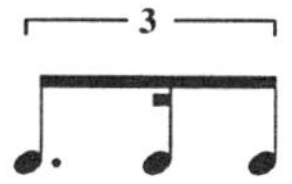

is encoded (E.4 (S4) E4)

!M3/4	3 4
!M6:8	6 8
!C	C
!M2+3+2:8	2+3+2 8
!M3/q.	3 ♩.
!M3+2/4+1+6/8	$\frac{3+2}{4} + \frac{1+6}{8}$

Table 6.6. Examples of DARMS Meter Signatures

$$!n_1 dur_1 id_1 : n_2 dur_2 id_2$$

where

	n_1 and n_2	are repetition counts,
	dur_1 and dur_2	are duration codes, and
	id_1 and id_2	are grouplet identifier numbers

n_2 may be suppressed if $n_2 = 1$
dur_2 may be suppressed if $dur_2 = dur_1$

id_2 is used only for nested grouplet, where id_2 is the identifier number for a previously defined grouplet

Examples:

!3E1:Q	(3 eighths in the time of a quarter)
!7E3:2Q	(7 eighths in the time of 2 quarters)
!5Q4:4	(5 quarters in the time of 4)

Figure 6.16. DARMS Grouplet Definers

Once defined, a grouplet identifier number is in effect until it is redefined, or until the program run terminates.

The symbols used to encode bar lines in DARMS are close approximations of the graphic symbols used in music printing. In general the slash '/' represents a bar line. Double bars are represented by two slashes; heavy bar lines by a slash preceded by an exclamation point. Repeat signs are indicated by the colon. Examples are shown in figure 6.17.

/ // //: :// !//: :/!/ /!/

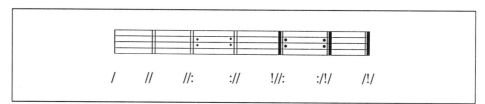

Figure 6.17. DARMS Encoding of Bar Lines

6.5.3 Other Note Attributes

DARMS syntax specifies that note attributes must be encoded in the order shown in table 6.7.[11] Only attributes that occur in the score are encoded. Furthermore, either the space code or the duration code (but not both) may be omitted if it is the same as that of the previous note. As of this writing, the parenthesized attributes have not

11. Raymond F. Erickson, *DARMS: A Reference Manual*, (New York: Queens College, CUNY, 1976), pp. D1–D1.2.

Open beams, short form [( ]
Space code
Accidentals
(Note-head type)
Duration code
Tie
Stem direction
(Tremolo)
(Beam codes, long form)

Articulation codes Dynamics and other dictionary codes Ornaments Slur (Fingering)	} ordered by relative proximity to note head

(Figured bass)
Close beams, short form [ )]

Table 6.7 DARMS Encoding Order for Notes

been implemented in the software described later in this text. Beams, space codes, accidentals, and duration codes were discussed above. In this section we will introduce the encoding of ties, articulations, slurs, ornaments, and dynamics.

A tie is encoded by the letter 'J', just after a note's duration code, or after the space code if the duration code has been suppressed. This indicates that the note is tied to the next note in the same part. A longer form shows the beginning and end of the tie. Here 'J' is followed by an integer. The beginning of the tie is indicated by any odd integer n, and the end of the tie by the next even integer $n + 1$. The encoding of ties is shown in figure 6.18. Note that either the space code or the duration code may be suppressed if it is the same as the previous note. The first encoding

4WJ / 4J / 4J / 4J / 4 //

or

24WJ1 / 24WJ2J3 / 24WJ4J5 / 24WJ6J7 / 24WJ8 //

or

4WJ1 / WJ2J1 / WJ2J1 / WJ2J1 / WJ2 //

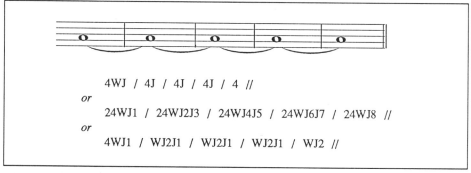

Figure 6.18. DARMS Encoding of Ties

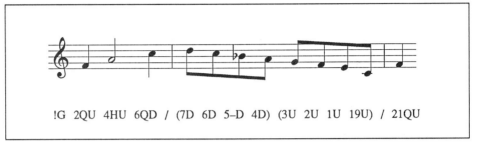

!G 2QU 4HU 6QD / (7D 6D 5–D 4D) (3U 2U 1U 19U) / 21QU

Figure 6.19. DARMS Encoding of Stem Direction

illustrates the short form of ties, two suppression, and delta suppression (omitted duration codes). Alternately, the repeated notes could have been represented by their duration codes with the space code omitted (sigma suppression). The second encoding uses no shortcuts, i.e., two suppression, delta or sigma suppression, or short form of ties. The third encoding illustrates the reuse of integers in the long form of ties.

Stem direction is encoded as 'U' (up) or 'D' (down). Frequently it is omitted, since it defaults to the norm, i.e., notes on the middle line and below default to the downward direction. However, music printing applications require either explicit encoding of stem direction or much more sophisticated stem-direction algorithms (for beamed notes, multiple parts per staff, etc.). Figure 6.19 illustrates DARMS encoding of stem direction. The encoding order of the next items (articulation, dynamics, dictionary codes, ornaments, and slurs) depends on the proximity to the note head in the printed score.

Articulation marks are encoded by special characters that are close to the graphic symbols they represent. Any number of these symbols may be concatenated, with the ones closest to the note head first. Common articulation codes are shown in table 6.8. DARMS dictionary codes extend the vocabulary of articulation marks. These consist of a special character following a question mark '?'. There are many of these symbols in DARMS. Those implemented in the software described in chapter 20 are shown in table 6.9. Note that I have used the unassigned dictionary symbols 'R' and 'Z' to represent arco and pizzicato. For analytic purposes, this is easier than interpreting encoded literals above the staff.

Graphic Symbol	*DARMS Code*	*Name*
•	'	staccato mark
▼ or ▲	"	wedge accent
–	_	tenuto mark
>	>	accent
V or Λ	<	vertical accent
𝄐	;	fermata

Table 6.8. DARMS Encoding of Articulation

Graphic Symbol	*DARMS Code*	*Name*
⊓	?D	downbow
V	?V	upbow
⏀	?Q	snap pizzicato
arco	?R	arco
pizz.	?Z	pizzicato
∘	?O	open (horn, etc.) or harmonic (string)
+	?+	stopped (horn, etc.)
H⌐	?H	Hauptstimme
N⌐	?N	Nebenstimme
⅂	?¯	terminates ?H or ?N

Table 6.9. Implemented Dictionary Codes

Slurs and phrase marks are encoded just like ties, except that the letter 'L' (mnemonic, legato or linked) is used instead of 'J'. Here the long form, using odd-even integer pairs, is more useful, since slurs may be nested and often there are many notes between the beginning and end of a slur. Slur encoding is also used for bowing. (See figure 6.20).

DARMS encoding of ornaments is shown in table 6.10. Ornaments are encoded by the letter 'O' followed by any of the following: 'T' = trill, ';' = trill with wavy line, 'M' = mordent, '?' = turn.[12] An accidental associated with an ornament is encoded as an *attached symbol* following the ornament. The attached symbol is

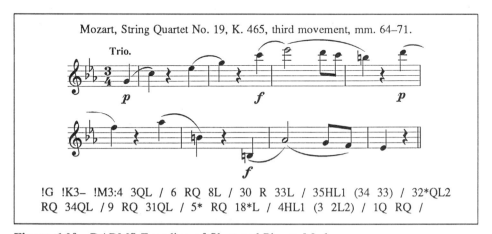

Mozart, String Quartet No. 19, K. 465, third movement, mm. 64–71.

!G !K3– !M3:4 3QL / 6 RQ 8L / 30 R 33L / 35HL1 (34 33) / 32*QL2 RQ 34QL / 9 RQ 31QL / 5* RQ 18*L / 4HL1 (3 2L2) / 1Q RQ /

Figure 6.20. DARMS Encoding of Slurs and Phrase Marks

12. This is a small subset of the ornaments available in full DARMS.

Graphic Symbol	*DARMS Code*	*Meaning*
tr	OT	trill
tr~~~~~~	O;	trill with wavy line
~~	OM	mordent
∽	O?	turn
tr♯~~~~~~	O;AE#	trill with sharp on right
(♮) tr~~~~~~	O;AN(*)	trill with parenthetic natural above
♭ ∽ ♮	O?AS*AN–	turn with natural below and flat above

Table 6.10. DARMS Encoding of Ornaments

encoded as A*ds*, where *d* is the direction encoded as a point of the compass (N, S, E, W, SE, etc.), and *s* is the DARMS symbol representing an accidental.

Simple dynamic markings are encoded as a comma, the letter 'V', and the dynamic:

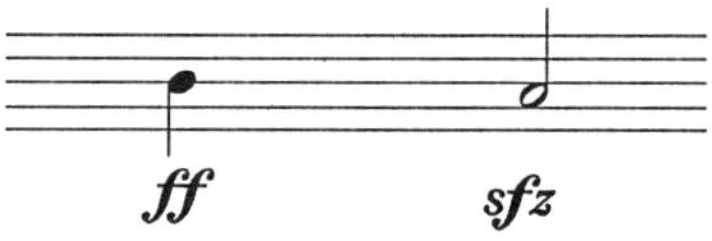

5Q,VFF 4H,VSFZ

The crescendo and diminuendo take several forms in music, which are similarly reflected in the DARMS code. When the crescendo or diminuendo occurs over a single note, the symbol '<' or '>' is used, with or without dynamic markings:

5Q,V< 6H,V<FF 4H.,V<> 5W,V>MP<

When the crescendo or diminuendo spans several notes, the symbols '<' or '>' are paired with identifier numbers similar to those used with ties and slurs, i.e., an odd integer *n* marks the beginning of the event and *n* + 1 the end. When a dynamic level is used, the encoding order is the same as in the graphic symbol, i.e., it is shown before the beginning of the crescendo/diminuendo and after the end.

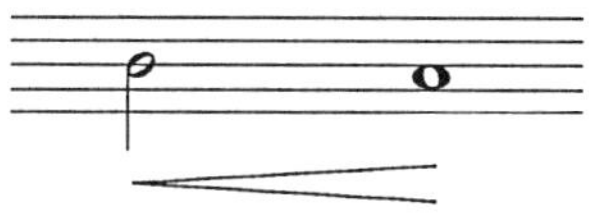

```
5H,V<1  4W,V<2
```

```
5H,VP<3  6Q  8Q,V<4F
```

It is also possible to encode the end of one crescendo or diminuendo and the beginning of another on the same note:

```
3H,VMP<1  4Q  5Q  /  6H,V<2FF>3  5H,V>4P  /
```

Figure 6.21 shows multiple examples of dynamic encoding. We have omitted the tempo changes from the encoding.

Kazuo Fukushima, *Requiem per flauto solo*, mm. 1–6.

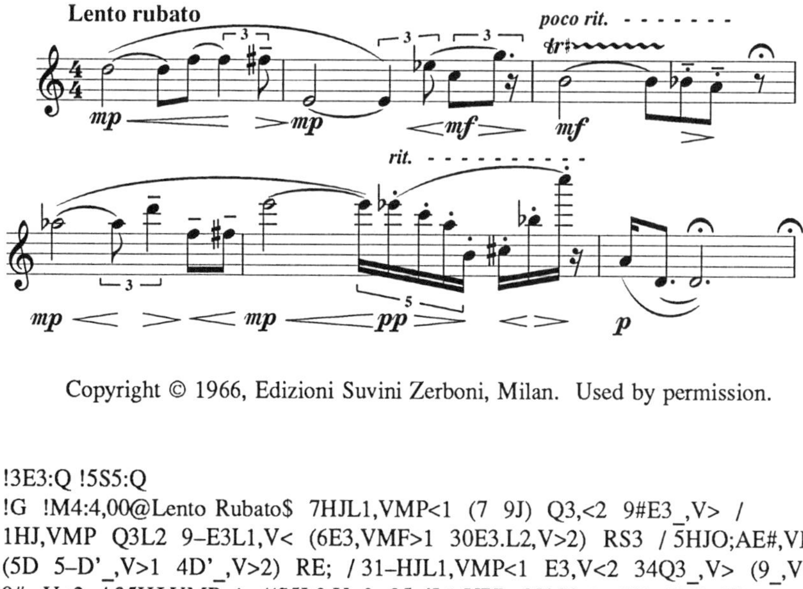


```
!3E3:Q !5S5:Q
!G  !M4:4,00@Lento Rubato$  7HJL1,VMP<1  (7  9J)  Q3,<2  9#E3_,V>  /
1HJ,VMP  Q3L2  9–E3L1,V<  (6E3,VMF>1  30E3.L2,V>2)  RS3  / 5HJO;AE#,VMF
(5D  5–D'_,V>1  4D'_,V>2)  RE;  / 31–HJL1,VMP<1  E3,V<2  34Q3_,V>  (9_,V<1
9#_,V<2  / 35HJ,VMP<1  ((S5L2,V<2  35–'L1,VPP  33',V>1  30'  5',V<2))
((6#',V<1  32–',V<2>1  38'L2,V>2))  RS  /  ((4–L1,VP)  0.J)  H.L2;  /,;
```

Figure 6.21. Examples of DARMS Encoding of Dynamics

Béla Bartók, String Quartet No. 4, first movement, mm. 1–6.

```
I0  00@Allegro, |QU| = 110$
I1  !G  !M4:4  RQ  RE  9E_?V,VF  9#Q._  7#E_  /
I2  !G  !M4:4  1HJ,VF  E  1–E_  2QJ  /
I3  !C  !M4:4  RW  /  RW  /
I4  !F  !M4:4  RQ  17H_,VF  2Q_  /
I1  (8_  7*L  6)  (3L  1–)  REQ  /
I2  (2  1–_)  20–QL  18–E  REQ  /
I4  7#Q_  27!C  8Q_  33E_  REQ  /
I1  19Q._  18–E_  19#H  /  (19*L5,V<1  20  21–L6,V<2)  REH  /
    RH  ((2#L3  1#))  20#Q.J  /  EL4  1Q_  20#E_  1Q._  20E_  /
I2  RE  17E_  18*HJ  E  (18–JL5  /  18–,V<1)  18*QL6,V<2  REH  /
    RQE  ((2L1  1))  20HJ  /  EL2  Q.  19#E_  20Q.J  /
I3  RHE  3–E_,VF  (4–_  3*JL7,V<3)  /  3Q  18EL8,V<4  REH  /
    RE  (7*L1  6#  5#J)  HJ  /  EL2  5*EJ  H  6–E_  5EJ  /
I4  RW  /  RHQE  (9–L1  /  8  7J)  H.J  /  EL2  6–Q.J  E  7–_  6QJ  /
```

Figure 6.22. DARMS Code for a Bartók Excerpt

6.5.4 Parts, Chords, Layers, and Multiple Staves

When more than one instrument is being encoded, the current instrument is identified by an 'I' followed by a numeric identifier. A new instrument code is specified whenever there is a change of instrument. This gives a good deal of freedom to the person encoding the music. The music can be encoded instrumental part by part, measure by measure, system by system, or in any other arrangement desired, so long as each individual part proceeds in chronological order. Figure 6.22 shows the opening measures of Bartók's String Quartet No. 4 and one possible DARMS encoding of the same passage. Instrument '0' is used for the tempo marking that appears above the score, to indicate that this applies to all parts. Note that the special space code '00' indicates the placement of this marking above the staff. This example also illustrates DARMS encoding of literals. The string is delimited by the characters '@' and '$'. Although there are no restrictions, it is generally good practice to place instrument numbers on the beginnings of lines, and to place each measure on a separate line. This aids in checking the code for errors.

DARMS provides three methods of encoding simultaneous notes (chords) in a single part. The first is to use the comma, which generally indicates the absence of temporal motion, between the notes in question. With this method, called *full encoding*, it is possible for notes within the chord to have different attributes, such as dynamics, articulation, stem directions, etc. Examples are shown below:

!G 2QD,4U,6U

!F 1QD_,4QU,6QU'

The second method of encoding chords is called *space-pattern* format. This method may be used only when all notes in the chord are attached to the same stem. Notes in the chord are encoded in a series of cells that are bounded by vertical bars on both left and right. The minimum information in a cell is the space code and relevant accidental codes. In addition, all information that applies to a specific note but not to the entire chord is placed within the cell. Encoding order is the same as for single notes, as shown above. Information common to the whole chord is encoded after the final cell, following the established encoding order. Thus short-form beam openings precede the cell complex, while all other attributes that apply to the whole chord follow it:

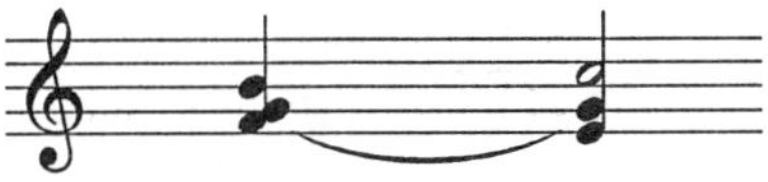

!G|2|3J|5|Q |1|3|6H|Q

The simplest means of encoding chords is called *base increment* mode. Here the space code of the lowest note is shown explicitly, and the other notes are implied by the intervals between successively higher notes. The space code and intervals may be followed by accidental codes if appropriate. Other attributes follow, and apply to all notes of the chord. This is the most efficient and most common method of encoding chordal structures:

3+2#+2#Q

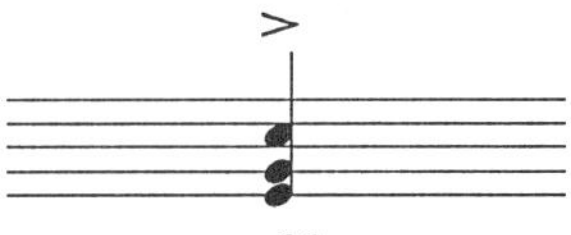

1+2+3Q>,VFF

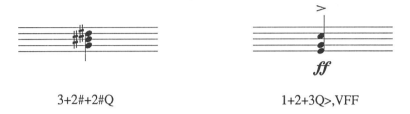

At times it is desirable to encode more than one "layer" within a single part. This is made possible by use of *linear decomposition.*[13] The compound symbol '!&' signals the beginning of a passage in linear decomposition mode, and marks the temporal position of the beginning of this section. The symbol '&' marks the end of each layer (except the last) and the beginning of the next, and indicates that the temporal position in the score is again that marked by the last '!&'. The end of the last layer is marked by the symbol '&$'. This indicates that the temporal position in the score is at the end of the longest layer in the section. An example is shown in figure 6.23. There are restrictions to the use of this technique: (a) no layer can begin earlier than the previous layer, although the end of a subsequent layer need not coincide with the end of any previous layer; (b) notes on the same stem may not be assigned to different layers; (c) ties, beams, and slurs may not begin in one layer and end in another.

When rests do not fill out all beats in a layer, the *skip code* can be used to place notes correctly. The skip code takes the form

~*d*

where *d* is a duration code or concatenation of duration codes. The use of skip codes with linear decomposition is shown in figure 6.24. If the lower part had been written

!G !M3:4 !& (3U 5U 4U 6U 5U 7U) / 6QU
& 3QD 2#D 2*D / 1D &$

Figure 6.23. Linear Decomposition Mode

13. In full DARMS, linear decomposition has many uses besides those described here, e.g., separate encoding of notes and dynamics, notes and text in a single part, or bar lines and notes.

```
!G !& 6H.U 5QU / 6HU & ˉH 0QD (3D 2D) / 1HD &$
```

Figure 6.24. Linear Decomposition with Skip Codes

with a rest, the skip code would not be necessary.

When multiple-staff instruments, such as the piano or organ, are encoded, linear decomposition is used in conjunction with special space-code conventions. Notes (and other symbols) are positioned on subsequent (lower) staves within the same system of the same instrument by adding 50 to the space codes for each staff below the first (topmost) staff. Thus in an organ score the lines of the topmost staff are numbered 21, 23, 25, 27, and 29; those on the middle staff 71, 73, 75, 77, and 79, and those on the pedal staff 121, 123,125,127, and 129.

J. S. Bach, *Nun komm' der Heiden Heiland*, BWV 599, mm. 1–2.

```
!& !G !MC 4HU RS (4U 5U 2#U) 3QU / 6U (5U 4U) 5HU /
& RS ((0D) 1JD) (1D 0#JD) 0QD RSD ((0D) 1JD) /
    (1D 3#D 4D 0#D) 1QJD ((1D 1D) 2*JD) ((2D 0*D 1D 18D)) /
& !+50 !F !MC RES 30SU 31QJU QU
& RQS ((8#D) 9JD) 9QD (30.D (30D)) /
    29QD RS ((30D 31D 7#D)) (8#D 9JD) (9D 8D)
& !+100 !F !MC RQES 2S (6. (5#)) 6Q / 7#Q (8# 9) (6. (5*))
    (6 19) / &$ !+0
```

Figure 6.25 Encoding Multiple-Staff Music

DARMS code supplies special *staff transposition codes* that allow the encoder to use normal space codes on staves other than the first. The symbol

!+*n*

where *n* is an integer, specifies that *n* is to be added to all subsequent space codes. The value of *n* may be changed by a new staff transposition specification, or canceled by the symbol

!+0.

These devices, used in conjunction with linear decomposition, allow for the encoding of multiple-staff music. Figure 6.25 illustrates the encoding of the first two measures of J. S. Bach's chorale prelude *Nun komm' der Heiden Heiland*, from *Das Orgelbüchlein.*

6.5.5 Comments

Comment delimiters are 'K' and '$', signifying the beginning and end of a comment. Comments may not include the comment terminator '$' or include newline characters, although multiple-line comments can be formed by repeating the delimiters on each line. Comments may be placed anywhere within a line, although the code will be easier to read if you separate them from the code proper. Examples:

```
K This is a comment $

I2 !G !M2/2 ...                       K 2d violin part $

K****************************************$
K* Block comments can be set off from the  *$
K* rest of the code in any manner desired. *$
K****************************************$
```

The DARMS manual specifies that comments may be attached to notes and other graphic objects and may occur anywhere in the code, e.g.,

```
4#Knatural in the 1935 edition$Q
```

The software described in the present volume does not support comments embedded within note codes. In fact, our software takes no action for comments other than to skip them.

6.5.6 Extensions

The DARMS software described in this text includes three extensions to standard DARMS that are useful for score analysis. The first is a transposition indicator, which causes encoded parts for a transposed score to be converted to sounding pitch; the second allows one to encode large scores in sections.

The transposition indicator specifies the transposition interval that will convert the current part to concert pitch. The form is shown in figure 6.26. The interval is

!T±<mod><int>

where	!T	indicates a transposition directive,
	±	is the direction of transposition,
	<mod>	is the interval modifier, and
	<int>	is the standard interval name

Figure 6.26. Transposition Directives

specified as a modifier followed by a numeric interval. The modifiers are 'M' = major, 'm' = minor, 'A' or 'a' = augmented, 'D' or 'd' = diminished, and 'P' or 'p' = perfect.[14] These may be followed by any standard interval, which may be simple or compound (greater than an octave). The software checks for illegal interval names, such as 'P3' or 'm5'. Some examples follow:

Code	*Meaning*
I1 !T–M2	transpose part 1 down a major second
I3 !T–P5	transpose part 3 down a perfect fifth
I4 !T–m3	transpose part 4 down a minor third
I5 !T+P8	transpose part 5 up a perfect octave

These codes can change as often as necessary, and they are more meaningful for an analysis program than verbal descriptions such as "trumpet in D," "horn in F," "clarinet in A," and "piccolo," although this method does put more responsibility on the person doing the encoding.

The second extension sets the measure counter for all parts to some arbitrary position in the score. This allows the user to encode music that begins with an anacrusis, or to encode segments that do not begin at the beginning of the score. The format of this directive is shown in figure 6.27. If the brackets and fraction are omitted, the

!A<meter>,<measure>[±<dur>][<fraction>]

where	!A	indicates an anacrusis directive,
	<meter>	is a DARMS encoded meter signature,
	<measure>	is a measure number,
	±	is a plus or minus sign,
	<dur>	is a duration code or concatenation of duration codes, and
	<fraction>	is the starting fractional time (optional)

Figure 6.27. An Anacrusis Directive

14. Here, software does distinguish cases.

starting time is set to 0/1.[15] The sign and duration codes are used to show a starting time that does not coincide with the bar line. This directive is inserted only once, at the very beginning of an excerpt, and applies to all parts. It does *not* replace the meter signatures for each part. If the excerpt is not the beginning of the score, the user must repeat any clefs, key signatures, meter signatures, and transposition codes that apply to each part. The meter specification in the anacrusis directive applies to the anacrusis measure, and is not necessarily the same as that in the first complete measure of the excerpt. Some examples follow:

Code	*Meaning*
!A4/4,1–Q	1 quarter before measure 1, meter = 4/4
!A5/8,29+Q.E	a dotted quarter + an eighth after measure 29, meter = 5/8.
!A3:4,52	start at measure 52, meter = 3/4
!3E5:Q !A3/4,104–E5[97/110]	a triplet-eighth before measure 104, meter = 3/4. Starting fraction is set to 97/110.

6.6 Leland Smith's SCORE Code

Leland Smith of Stanford University designed the SCORE encoding language as a method of encoding music scores for computer music synthesis.[16] His parameter list preprocessor, called SCORE, was written as a front-end program for the Stanford University computer music system. He has used a similar music representation, with extensions, for computer music printing of excellent quality. The primary conceptual differences between this encoding scheme and DARMS are that each music parameter is entered separately, and the code more directly represents the meaning of music symbols rather than graphic information. Our purpose is not to detail the complete language, only to introduce a sampling of input techniques that will be used in programs and exercises elsewhere in this text.[17]

The language is parameter-oriented, with each attribute—instrument name, starting time for the note, duration, dynamic level, etc.—numbered. Some parameters are fixed:

15. The time is calculated with fractional durations, and is tracked as absolute time and as measures. These techniques are discussed in section 13.3.

16. Leland Smith, "SCORE—A Musician's Approach to Computer Music," *Journal of the Audio Engineering Society* 20 (1972): 7–14.

17. This author has written a Pascal program called SCORE-11 that serves as a preprocessor for Music-11 (written by Barry Vercoe at MIT) and other music synthesis systems. This program uses Smith's input language with some extensions. For convenience, the examples in this text are taken from SCORE-11 rather than from Smith's SCORE program. The primary difference in encoding is that Smith's program names instruments rather than numbering them.

p1	instrument name
p2	starting time
p3	duration
p4	pitch

Other parameters depend on the instrument definition, which takes the form of a procedure written in an instrument specification language. The actual meaning of each parameter is defined by the way in which its value is used in the instrument definition procedure.[18] The purpose of the preprocessor program is to translate the encoded score into a note list in the form required by the music-synthesis program. For each note or event, the program calculates the starting time and duration, which may be modified by changes in tempo. It also calculates values that change over time, such as the dynamics during a crescendo or diminuendo, and converts the mnemonic code used in the input language to the numeric representations required by the synthesis program.

Figure 6.28 shows a simple Mozart melody encoded with this system. The example assumes that parameter 5 of instrument 1 represents the dynamic level (specified as integers). The first line indicates a tempo of 60 beats/minute; the second, that instrument 1 will begin at time 0 (beginning) and will play for 12 beats. Figure 6.29 is the output generated by the SCORE-11 program from the input in figure 6.28. This output would be used, with appropriate instrument definition files, as input to the Music-11 synthesis program. Each line is a list of values for each parameter needed by the instrument. They represent, from left to right, the instrument number, the starting time and duration in seconds, the pitch in *oct.pc* format, and the dynamic level.[19]

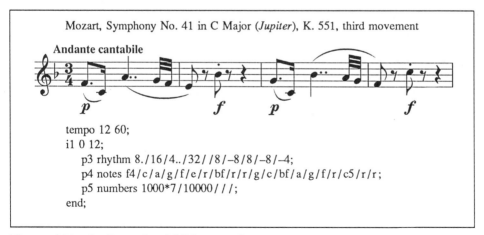

Mozart, Symphony No. 41 in C Major (*Jupiter*), K. 551, third movement

```
tempo 12 60;
i1 0 12;
   p3 rhythm 8./16/4../32/ /8/-8/8/-8/-4;
   p4 notes f4/c/a/g/f/e/r/bf/r/r/g/c/bf/a/g/f/r/c5/r/r;
   p5 numbers 1000*7/10000/ / /;
end;
```

Figure 6.28. An Example of SCORE-11 Code

18. More information can be found in the references at the end of the chapter.

19. Since Music-11 uses a different system of octave numbers, 4 is added to each octave number on output. Note that rests are not printed in the output.

```
i1 0.000 0.750 8.05 1000
i1 0.750 0.250 8.00 1000
i1 1.000 1.750 8.09 1000
i1 2.750 0.125 8.07 1000
i1 2.875 0.125 8.05 1000
i1 3.000 0.500 8.04 1000
i1 4.000 0.500 8.10 10000
i1 6.000 0.750 8.07 1000
i1 6.750 0.250 8.00 1000
i1 7.000 1.750 8.10 1000
i1 8.750 0.125 8.09 1000
i1 8.875 0.125 8.07 1000
i1 9.000 0.500 8.05 1000
i1 10.000 0.500 9.00 10000
end of score
```

Figure 6.29. SCORE-11 Output for Figure 6.28 Data

The essential features of the SCORE input language are as follows:

1. Each parameter is encoded separately, either as a single value or as a list of values.
2. When a list is used, it is preceded by a keyword that specifies the type of values in the list (notes, numbers, rhythm, etc.). The list is terminated by a semicolon.
3. Each element in a list is terminated by a slash '/'. An element can be repeated by repeating the slash. The slash at the end of the list may be omitted. Alternately, a value can be followed by a repetition factor, e.g., "4 * 10" means 10 fours.
4. The primary list keywords are 'rhythm', 'notes', and 'numbers', which can be abbreviated 'rh', 'no', and 'nu'.
5. If the list (or single value) is exhausted before the end of the specified segment, it is repeated as many times as necessary. This is why only half of the durations and dynamic values need be defined in the score segment shown above.

Number lists can be used for many purposes, and can contain integers or real numbers. The numbers might represent values for dynamic level, frequency (Hz), function numbers (for timbre or attack/decay characteristics), pitches in *oct.pc* or *oct.dec* notation, etc.[20]

Note lists contain note names in the form

<name><accidentals><octave>

The note name is the letter name (a, b, c, d, e, f, or g).[21] An 'r' is placed in the note list when a rest is required. Accidentals are represented by 's' and 'f', for sharp and

20. In *oct.pc* notation the pitch is specified as a real number. The part before the decimal point is the octave number; the decimal part is the pitch class. In *oct.dec* notation the decimal part is the fraction of the octave. Thus $F\sharp_4$ can be specified as 4.06 (*oct.pc*) or 4.5 (*oct.dec*).

21. In the input code, lowercase letters may be used for ease of typing.

flat. Multiple accidentals are represented by repeating the appropriate accidental code. The accidental codes are mnemonic, and easier to type than symbols such as '#' and '–', which require a shift to upper case and a change of hand position on the keyboard. The octave is specified by standard octave numbers (middle octave equals 4). Once specified, the octave number is in effect until it is changed. In order to facilitate encoding notes that frequently cross the octave boundary (B to C), notes can be encoded in *proximity mode*. In proximity mode the octave is automatically supplied to place the note as close as possible to the previous note. Proximity mode can be turned on or off at any time by placing the letters 'p' (proximity) or 'o' (off) in the note list. When in effect, this mode can be overridden by specifying the octave explicitly. Thus the note list

```
p4 notes c5/d/ef/c/b4/a/b/c5/c4;
```

can be entered as

```
p4 notes p c5/d/ef/c/b/a/b/c/c4;
```

Chords within a single part are specified by separating pitches by colons. Thus the note list

```
p4 notes c4:e:g/d:fs:a/ef:g:bf;
```

would produce major chords in the rhythm indicated by parameter 3.

The "rhythm" keyword specifies that the list contains durations encoded in reciprocal duration code (see section 6.4). The durations are specified as the reciprocal of the duration type (quarter note = 4, eighth note = 8, etc.). A tie is represented by a comma (','), a dot by a period ('.'), and a rest by a minus sign preceding the duration code. SCORE-11 has a convenient extension for encoding grouplets, which is presented in section 15.4.

Parameters that change over time are encoded with the keywords "move" ("mo") or "movex" ("mx"), which specify linear or exponential change over time. These items may also be placed in lists. The score statement

```
p5 move 10 1000 10000/10 10000 1000;
```

specifies that the value of parameter 5 will change over ten beats from 1000 to 10000, and over the next ten beats from 10000 to 1000. If parameter 5 controls dynamic level, this would be equivalent to a crescendo followed by a diminuendo. The initial and terminal values for each move may be numbers or note names. The actual value at the time of each note is calculated by interpolation along a linear or exponential curve.

A second form of the "move" statement interpolates between two ranges of numbers rather than between two fixed numbers. This form takes five arguments for each segment: the time span, the initial and terminal values of the first range, and the initial and terminal values of the second range. The result at each time point is a value chosen at random between the interpolated points on two curves. For example,

```
p4 move 20 c4 c5 b5 b5;
```

specifies that, over a period of 20 beats, notes are to be chosen at random between two curves. At the beginning of the time span, the range is the octave between C_4 and C_5. At the end of the time span, both curves converge on B_5.

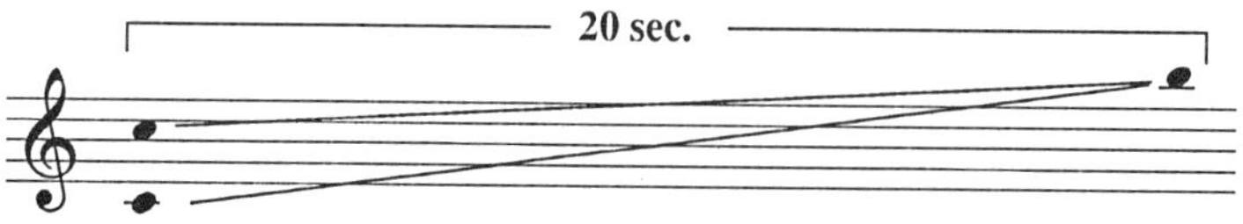

The result is a randomly fluctuating ascending line, with the amount of pitch deviation from note to note decreasing over the time period. Rhythm is controlled by the values in parameter 3. Facilities such as this aid the composer in generating graphic gestures when he or she is not interested in the specific pitch content.

SCORE and SCORE-11 provide many other features, such as random selection of values, articulation, specification of tempo curves, selection of values from sets of values, etc. Because the basic features represent music information in a rather direct way, it is fairly easy to program. In particular, we will use Smith's encoding scheme to enter pitch information as the next step past numeric encoding.

References and Selected Readings

The concepts of pitch class and pitch-class set were introduced by Milton Babbitt. Four important early articles by Babbitt are:

Babbitt, Milton. "Set Structure as a Compositional Determinant." *Journal of Music Theory* 5, no. 2 (1961) : 72–94. Reprinted in Benjamin Boretz and Edward T. Cone, eds. *Perspectives on Contemporary Music Theory.* New York: W.W. Norton, 1972.

———. "Some Aspects of Twelve-Tone Composition." *The Score and IMA Magazine* 12 (1955): 53–61.

———. "Twelve-Tone Invariants as Compositional Determinants." *The Musical Quarterly* 46 (1960): 246–59. Reprinted in Paul Henry Lang, ed. *Problems of Modern Music.* New York: W.W. Norton, 1962.

———. "Twelve-Tone Rhythmic Structure and the Electronic Medium." *Perspectives of New Music* 1, no. 1 (1962): 49–94. Reprinted in Benjamin Boretz and Edward T. Cone, eds. *Perspectives on Contemporary Music Theory.* New York: W.W. Norton, 1972.

The pitch-class system and its applications have been formalized in the following sources, as well as in many articles in the literature. Rahn contains an extensive bibliography. Morris's bibliography is less extensive but more current.

Forte, Allen. *The Structure of Atonal Music.* New Haven: Yale University Press, 1973.

Morris, Robert D. *Composition With Pitch-Classes: A Theory of Compositional Design.* New Haven: Yale University Press, 1987.

Rahn, John. *Basic Atonal Theory.* New York: Longman, 1980.

Much of the discussion of numeric pitch representations was based on the following, and is used with permission of the publisher.

Brinkman, Alexander R. "A Binomial Representation of Pitch for Computer Processing of Musical Data." *Music Theory Spectrum* 8 (1986): 44–57.

Two other methods of representing pitch for computer processing are described in the following publications. The first includes a representation devised by Walter Hewlett of the Center for Computer Assisted Research in the Humanities in Palo Alto, Cal.

Blombach, Ann K. "Tools for Macintosh Music Courseware Development: Hewlett's Representation System and Structured Programming." *Journal of Computer-Based Instruction* 16, no. 2 (1989): 50–58.

Kolosick, J. Timothy. "A Machine Independent Data Structure for the Representation of Musical Pitch Relationships: Computer-Generated Musical Examples for CBI." *Journal of Computer-Based Instruction* 13, no. 1 (1986): 9–13.

For a more comprehensive discussion of diatonic sets and their analytic applications, see:

Clough, John. "Aspects of Diatonic Sets." *Journal of Music Theory* 23, no. 1 (1979): 45–60.

———. "Diatonic Interval Sets and Transformational Structures." *Perspectives of New Music* 18, no. 2 (1980): 461–82.

Clough, John and Gerald Myerson. "Variety and Multiplicity in Diatonic Systems." *Journal of Music Theory* 29, no. 2 (1985): 249–70.

Zimmerman, Thomas. "A Theory of Diatonic Sets and its Application to Selected Works of Ludwig von Beethoven." Ph.D. diss., University of Michigan, 1983.

The following source contains articles on several high-level music encoding languages in addition to the ones discussed in this chapter.

Brook, Barry S., ed. *Musicology and the Computer: Three Symposia.* New York: City University of New York Press, 1970.

More information on DARMS can be found in:

Bauer-Mengelberg, Stefan. "The Ford-Columbia Input Language." In *Musicology and the Computer*, edited by Barry S. Brook, 48–52. New York: City University of New York Press, 1970.

Erickson, Raymond F. *DARMS: A Reference Manual.* New York: DARMS Project, Dept. of Music, Queens College, CUNY, 1976.

———. "'The DARMS Project': A Status Report." *Computers and the Humanities* 9 (1975): 291–98.

———. "A General-Purpose System for Computer Aided Musical Studies." *Journal of Music Theory* 13, no. 2 (1969): 276–94.

———. "Musicomp 76 and the State of DARMS." *College Music Symposium* 17 no. 1 (1977): 90–101.

Erickson, Raymond F. and Anthony B. Wolff. "The DARMS Project: Implementation of an Artificial Language for the Representation of Music." In *Computers and Language Research,* edited by Walter A. Sedelow, Jr. and Sally Yeates Sedelow. New York: Mouton Publishers, 1983.

Another encoding language that has been used widely is Jerome Wenker's MUSTRAN. If you would like to compare this language to those discussed here, see the following two articles:

Wenker, Jerome. "A Computer-Oriented Music Notation Including Ethnomusicological Symbols." In *Musicology and the Computer,* edited by Barry S. Brook. New York: City University of New York Press, 1970.

———. "MUSTRAN II: A Foundation for Computational Musicology." In *Computers in the Humanities*, edited by J. L. Mitchell. Edinburgh: University of Edinburgh Press, 1974.

An introduction to Leland Smith's SCORE code can be found in:

Smith, Leland. "SCORE—A Musician's Approach to Computer Music." *Journal of the Audio Engineering Society* 20 (1972): 7–14.

———. "The 'SCORE' Program for Musical Input to Computers." In *Proceedings of the 1980 International Computer Music Conference.* San Francisco: Computer Music Association, 1980.

The following sources give a good general introduction to computer music synthesis:

Dodge, Charles, and Thomas A. Jerse. *Computer Music—Synthesis, Composition, and Performance.* New York: Schirmer Books (Macmillan), 1985.

Mathews, Max, Joan E. Miller, F. Richard Moore, John R. Pierce, and Jean-Claude Risset. *The Technology of Computer Music.* Cambridge, Mass.: MIT Press, 1969.

Roads, Curtis, and John Strawn, eds. *Foundations of Computer Music.* Cambridge Mass.: MIT Press, 1985.

Exercises

1. Encode the following example using (a) pitch classes, (b) continuous pitch code, (c) name classes, (d) continuous name code, (e) reciprocal duration code. Choose an appropriate delimiter for bar lines and double bar (end of data) for each case.

   Brahms, Symphony No. 1 in C Major, fourth movement, mm. 61-69

2. Calculate the pitch class (pc) and octave (oct) for each of the following cpc encoded pitches, and write them on the staff:

   (a) 48 (b) 87 (c) 34 (d) 29 (e) 56 (f) 75 (g) 13 (h) 68 (i) 6 (j) 51

3. Map each <oct,pc> pair into a cpc.

   (a) 4,0 (b) 2,6 (c) 6,11 (d) 6,6 (e) 7,4 (f) 3,8 (g) 1,2 (h) 5,3 (i) 3,5 (j) 4,7

4. Calculate the name class (nc) and octave number (oct) for each of the following cnc encoded pitches:

   (a) 28 (b) 12 (c) 7 (d) 42 (e) 35 (f) 19 (g) 47 (h) 31 (i) 25 (j) 41

5. Map each <oct,nc> pair into a cnc.

   (a) 4,0 (b) 3,6 (c) 6,2 (d) 5,4 (e) 7,1 (f) 2,6 (g) 4,4 (h) 5,3 (i) 3,5 (j) 3,2

6. Specify the octave, pitch class, and name class for each of the following notes:

   (a) C_4 (b) $D\sharp_3$ (c) $F\flat_5$ (d) $B\times_3$ (e) $E\flat\flat_2$ (f) A_6 (g) $G\sharp_7$ (h) $E\sharp_4$ (i) D_5 (j) $B\flat\flat_6$

7. Name the pitch (standard name and octave) for each of the following pitches encoded in continuous binomial representation (cbr).

   (a) 5042 (b) 6063 (c) 4110 (d) 7084 (e) 6085 (f) 4022 (g) 5006 (h) 2031
   (i) 2032 (j) 2030 (k) 2034 (l) 6106

Even if you are not ready to deal with the complexities of programs that deal with DARMS code, it is not too early to begin learning the code itself.

8. Encode the following in DARMS:

   Beethoven, Piano Sonata in F Minor, Op. 2, No. 1, first movement

9. Decode the following DARMS code on staff paper. Check your answer in figure 13.5.

```
K*****************************************************************$
K Carter, String Quartet No. 2, m. 582-85.                        $
K*****************************************************************$
!A3/4,581                     K* set measure no. with anacrusis   *$
!3E1:Q !3S2:E !7E3:H. !5E4:H  K* grouplet definers                *$
                                                        K m. 581-82 $
```

(continued on next page)

```
I1 !G !M3/4 2QJ ((2) 30-.J) Q / 5-Q. 31*EJ (31. (36J)) //
I2 !G !M3/4 6QJ ((6) 3*.) Q / 7-QJ ((7) 8-.J) (8 32-J) //
I3 !C !M3/4 7-Q 33* 7* / (30 5) (1E1 6 33-) (29*E1 34 RE1 ) //
I4 7!C !M3/4 33*Q 31# 32 / 29 33 34 !G //
I1 !M2/4 (36 38-) (32* 34) /                             K m. 583   $
I2 !M2/4 (32 31J) ((31) 8.J) /
I3 !M2/4 ((RS2 18S2 5-) (9-S2 4- 8)) ((33*S2 30- 36*)) RE /
I4 !M2/4 (20- 7-) (8- 5-) 7!C /
                                                        K m. 584-85 $
I1 !M3/4 (34#E3 36# 37 35 37- 33 39*) / !M2/4 (4E4 33# 37# 36# 34*)
I2 !M3/4 (8E1 32* 7) (6#E1 8# 5*) (7#E1 4* 30#) / !M2/4 (35*E1 30* RE1)
        (RE1 6#E1 1) /
I3 !M3/4 RQ ((R 4* 19* 5*)) ((9* 35# 32# 6#)) / !M2/4 ((R 30# 6*
        35*J)) QJ /
I4 !M3/4 (32 30) (4# 8* 7# 9*) !F / !M2/4 (7# 31*) (8* 3) /
```

7 | Program Design

In this chapter we begin to develop a methodology for writing programs. This methodology includes designing an algorithm, stepwise refinement of the algorithm, and rendering the algorithm in Pascal, as well as suggestions for verifying, testing, and documenting the code. The latter part of the chapter and problems illustrate and exercise the techniques discussed.

7.1 Algorithm Defined

An *algorithm* is a detailed, unambiguous set of instructions for accomplishing a particular task. It must satisfy the following conditions:

1. *Input.* An algorithm has zero or more quantities that are supplied to it before the algorithm begins.
2. *Output.* An algorithm must produce at least one output value. The quantities that are produced by an algorithm have a specified relation to the inputs. A process that accomplishes wonderful things but does not communicate them to the outside world is not an algorithm by definition.
3. *Definiteness.* Each instruction must be clear and unambiguous; i.e., it must be precisely defined for each possible case.
4. *Finiteness.* An algorithm must terminate after a finite number of steps; i.e., if each instruction in the algorithm is performed, then it must be possible to obtain the desired result.
5. *Effectiveness.* In order to be effective, each operation to be performed must be sufficiently basic that it is feasible. One test of feasibility of an operation is that it could in principle be performed by a person using a pencil and paper in a finite amount of time.

A procedure that has all of these attributes of an algorithm, except that of finiteness under some conditions, is called a *computational method.* A computer program is an algorithm or computational method specified in a language that can be processed by a computer.

Algorithms may be expressed in several ways. It is possible to specify an algorithm in English (or some other natural language). The danger is that language is often imprecise, and the steps in an algorithm must be precise. Sometimes flow diagrams are used to specify algorithms. These combine natural language with a graphic representation of the program's "flow of control." Each step is placed in a

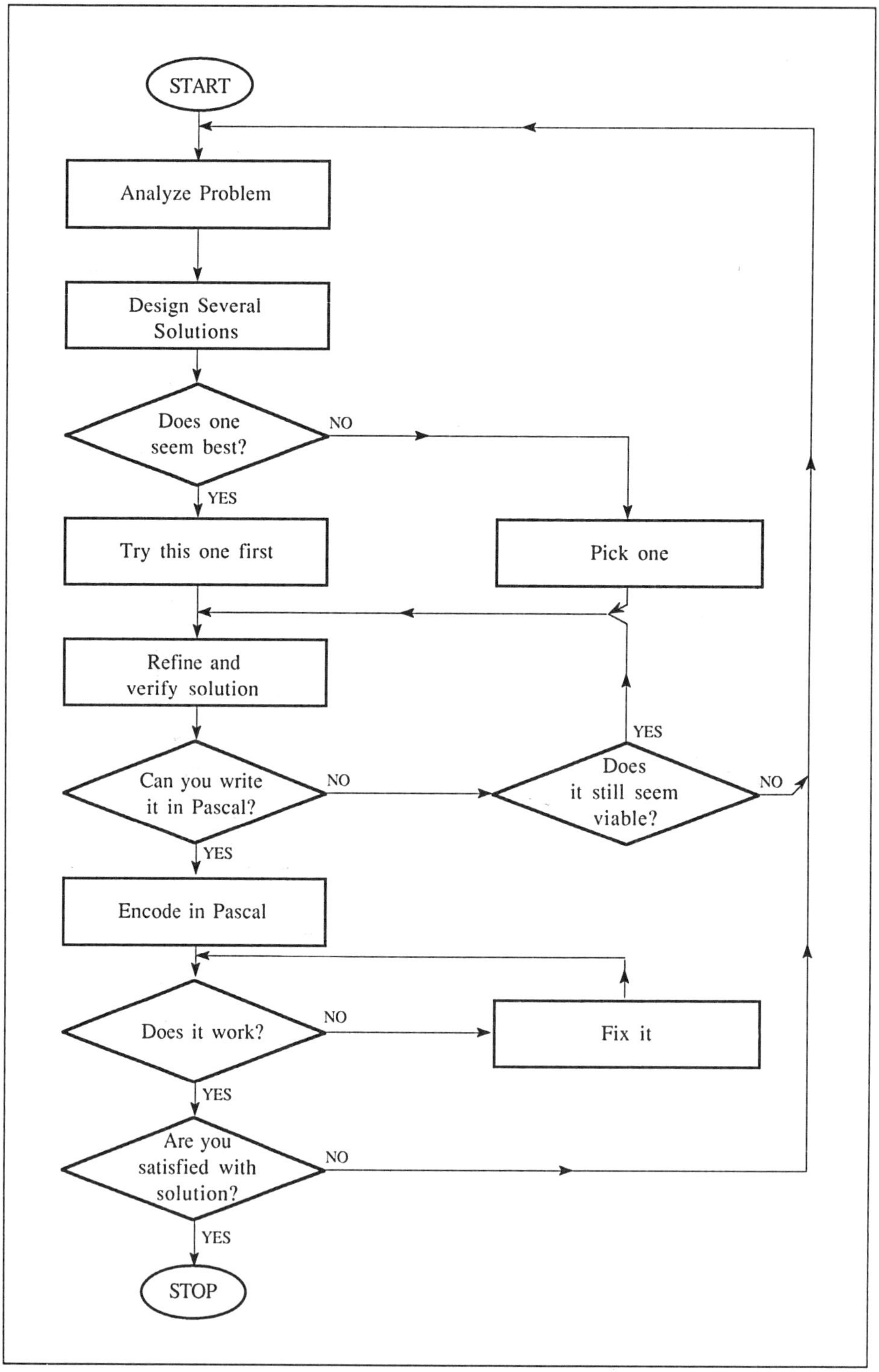

Figure 7.1. Flow Diagram of the Algorithm Design Process

```
repeat

  while you don't have a good algorithm do
    begin { design stage }

      analyze problem;
      design several possible solutions;
      choose the best one;

      verify solution;

      while solution is workable but lacks detail do
        begin { stepwise refinement }
          refine solution;
          verify solution
        end; { stepwise refinement }

    end; { design stage }

  if code is ready to translate
    then
      begin { encode and test }

        encode algorithm in Pascal;

        while you don't have desired results do
          begin { debug code }
            edit program;
            test program
          end { debug code }

      end { encode and test }

until satisfied with the result
```

Figure 7.2. Pseudo Code of Algorithm Design Process

box, the shape of which indicates whether the step represents a decision or some action. The boxes are connected by arrows indicating the order in which the steps are to be executed. In the previous chapter simple flow diagrams were used to show the action of Pascal control structures. More complicated diagrams can show the dynamics of any process. The flow diagram in figure 7.1 summarizes the steps in program design. In this diagram each box represents a procedure or process that could be diagrammed in more detail. Except at the highest level of structure, flow diagrams are perhaps less useful in designing programs intended for structured languages, since the branches represented by decision statements are encoded most directly with **goto** statements. Algorithms can also be expressed in *pseudo code*, a combination of English and control constructs that are available in the computer language in which you are working. Figure 7.2 outlines the program design process in pseudo code. An algorithm in this format is much easier to translate into Pascal, since the pseudo code uses control structures native to the language. It is often helpful to use several different representations when one writes a program. Typically, the algorithm is stated first in English, then in pseudo code. When the algorithm has been sufficiently refined, it can be translated easily to Pascal.

7.2 Algorithm Development

Good algorithms are not designed haphazardly, and they usually don't happen accidentally. Discipline is required to write good programs, even simple ones. One must resist the temptation to sit down at the computer terminal and begin typing in program code. Often beginners (and even more experienced programmers) are too eager to get a program on the computer. The code is entered, errors caught by the compiler are corrected, and the program is run. When it doesn't function as intended, the programmer sits back and says, "Well, maybe if I change this or that statement, it will work." Usually it does not. Even when the program seems to work with one set of data, it may fail with another. When a faulty case is found, the programmer attempts to alter the code by adding conditional statements, etc. This "seat of the pants" approach, sometimes called "kludging," is not the way to develop reliable programs, and ultimately results in a great deal of wasted time.

The best place to write programs is in a quiet spot with few distractions, as far from the computer terminal as possible. The first step is to develop a good algorithm. This is tested, even before it is translated into a computer language. The specific steps used in developing and testing an algorithm are discussed below. While the process described may seem overly complex for simple programs, it is never too early to begin developing good programming habits. If you consistently follow these recommendations, there is no reason that many of your programs should not perform correctly the first time they are run. Even if they do not, you will save a great deal of time correcting logic errors and debugging the code.

Problem Analysis. The first step in developing an algorithm is careful analysis of the problem. Make sure that you thoroughly understand the objectives of the algorithm. What is the algorithm supposed to accomplish? Are there any special cases that will have to be considered? Exactly what is the output to be, and in what form should it be expressed? Carefully study the data that will be used to calculate that result. In what manner is the desired information represented? If you are designing the problem (as opposed to solving an exercise proposed for your solution), this question should be restated: What information is required to solve the problem, and what is the best way to represent that information?

Design. Design at least one method for solving the problem. It is helpful initially to ignore the fact that the algorithm will ultimately be a computer program. Formulate the steps in solving the problem, and write them in English. The initial solution should deal with process and method, rather than detail. Do not worry at this point about what type of loop to use, or exactly what data structures will be most advantageous (e.g., whether a list should be stored in an array or a linked data structure).[1] If

1. If you are a beginner, ignore the comments on data structures for now. Our purpose is to outline a method that can be applied to complex problems as well as simple ones.

you can think of more than one method of solution, write down each in general terms. Then compare each proposed solution to the others. Is one clearer and easier to understand? Is one more extensible? Does one take better advantage of the structure of the data provided? Will one be more efficient? You may be able to decide at this point that one solution is superior to the others. If so, try this one first. Otherwise, choose one and begin to work out the details.

Refinement. Take a proposed solution and refine it. Break larger processes down into smaller steps until the steps are small enough to be easily rendered in a computer language. In the beginning it may seem difficult to determine exactly when this point has been reached, but the process will become easier with practice, and you should already have a fair grasp of the basic constructs in Pascal. This method of refining an algorithm is called *stepwise refinement.* Later we will learn to use separate procedures and functions to represent each larger process in more complex programs, and these steps will be applied to each procedure. During the refinement stage you may find that the basic algorithm is not working out well. Don't be afraid to return to the initial design stage and try a different approach. Sometimes, especially in your first attempts, it will be useful to work through several designs before you make a final choice. As you become more adept, you will learn to see the implications of your choices earlier, and you will make better decisions from the outset.

Encoding. At this point you must decide on the control structures and data structures that will be used in the program. Use all of your accumulated knowledge in making these decisions. If you need a loop, which type is most appropriate? (Review section 5.4, and for now remember that the **while** statement should often be used in preference to the **repeat** statement.) Now express your algorithm in pseudo code. After double-checking the logic of your solution (see below), you are ready to begin encoding the algorithm as a computer program. Decide on clear mnemonic names for identifiers (variable and constant names), and go to work. The refined, step-by-step algorithm should now be fairly easy to translate into Pascal or any other computer language. Carefully check the syntax and layout of your program *as you write the code.* If you are not sure of syntax, look it up. Do not waste computing and editing time fixing errors that should not occur in your code in the first place. Develop the habit of writing accurate code the first time. And remember, neatness counts! Use indentation and spacing to make the program structure clear from the start. This is less time-consuming than fixing it later, and it will help you to get the program structure right.

Verification. Program verification includes (a) proving that the solution works, (b) debugging, and (c) testing. Although we discuss verification separately here, you should have already begun the process during the initial stages of algorithm design. While formal proofs of the correctness of algorithms are perhaps not appropriate for a novice programmer, some effort should be made to show that the algorithm accomplishes its objectives. At the very least, you should check the crucial values that will affect control decisions (exiting loops, **if** statements, etc). Be certain that the logic is correct for the prescribed input data. Also make sure that you have taken care of any special cases that are expected to occur. Does the algorithm terminate correctly under all possible cases? Does it function properly for minimal cases (e.g., an empty file as input, or a file with only the terminal delimiter)? Once you have tested the logic, you should make up some sample data and step through the program manually (some guidelines for doing this will be given later in the chapter). Your sample input file does not have to be long, but it should exercise each part of the program. For example, each branch of an **if...then...else** statement should be executed at least once. Manual checking will help you to find malformed conditionals (e.g., using '>' for '>=' or '<' for '>'), loops that do not terminate, and similar problems.

Once you have checked the program manually and are convinced that your solution is correct, use a text editor to enter the program into your computer system, check it one more time, and then compile the program.[2] If there are syntax errors—they should be few if you are careful about syntax when writing the program—fix them, and recompile the program. Since many compilers stop checking after they find the first error on a line, you may have to repeat this process several times before the program compiles successfully.

Finally, the program should be tested. This consists of running the program and ensuring that the expected output is obtained. If the program requires input data, make up sample data that tests all possible conditions that the program is expected to handle. Design the data so that you can predict the expected output, and check the actual output against the expected results.

The process of getting all errors out of a program is called *debugging* the program. *Bugs* consist of syntax errors and the more insidious logic errors that can occur in a program. Remember that the compiler will catch syntax errors, but it is oblivious to logic errors that may cause a program to give erroneous results. You must find the latter yourself.

While the procedure outlined above will help you to produce correct programs and to demonstrate their correctness, it does not constitute a formal proof that the algorithm works under all possible cases. Formal proofs are beyond the scope of this book; however, the topic of program verification has received much attention in the literature, and several references are listed at the end of this chapter.

Documentation. Documentation is an important part of every program you write. Provide a block comment that lists the programmer and date and describes the program. Include a precise definition of the input data expected by the program and the output produced. The former is vital, since programs generally do not give the expected results for nonconformant data.[3] Finally, give a short description of the method used to solve the problem. This should be easy if you have followed the recommended steps in developing your algorithm. Careful choice of identifiers for variables and constants should make the intention of your code clear. These are

2. On some interpreted systems compiling and running are done in one step. In any case, the system will notify you if it finds syntax errors in your program.

3. Programmers sometimes quote the truism, "Garbage in, garbage out." The meaning should be obvious; if it is not, it will be after the first time you attempt to draw conclusions based on erroneous data. Later we will learn to write programs that check the syntax of the data.

supplemented by brief comments, at the end of lines or between lines of program code, which add information where necessary. Avoid redundant comments such as

```
i := i + 1;     { add one to i }
```

These just clutter the program. Effective commenting is not particularly easy, but it is vital in the real world where programs are sometimes altered or extended, often by a programmer who did not write the original code. You will also find that good documentation is helpful to you if you pick up a program after some time has elapsed.

Although the documentation step is listed separately here, it should not be left for last. Your notes from earlier stages of algorithm design and the choice of identifiers will form the basis of much of the documentation needed by the program. Many experienced programmers write beautiful documentation *before* writing the program.

The programming method described above is called *top-down design* or stepwise refinement. The idea is to define the large processes first, and then to refine them into smaller and smaller steps until a complete solution results. Additional goals of structured programming are verification of the program at each stage of refinement, and segregation of code into modules, each of which performs a well-defined task and has a single entry and exit.[4] These principles help the programmer to write code that is easy to understand, maintain, and extend.

Programmers sometimes begin by solving small parts of a problem that can be encoded directly in a computer language, and work toward a total solution. This technique is called *bottom-up design*. Sometimes a combination of these approaches is used. You are strongly advised to follow the top-down method.

This general methodology, with the addition of procedures to represent larger processes and the inclusion of more complex data structures, will be equally applicable to the development of large programs, and even extended software systems. In fact, the larger the project, the more vital it is to develop the big picture first—to gain an overview of the entire task before proceeding. The top-down approach will help you to do this.

7.3 Examples of Algorithm Development

We will now demonstrate techniques for writing programs using exercises from the first set at the end of this chapter. The exercises are arranged roughly in order of increasing difficulty and increasing program complexity, and each builds on techniques learned in previous problems. In the beginning the problems will seem somewhat trivial, but the skills you will learn are not. The first set of exercises deals with reciprocal duration code (see section 6.3), with the addition of the integer 0 to represent bar lines and 100 to represent the double bar at the end of the excerpt.[5]

We begin by carefully specifying the input code. The code specification is given in the form of a block comment (suitable to be included as part of a program):

4. This is why **goto**s are avoided in structured programming.

5. For these exercises we will use 100 to terminate the input data.

```
(*************  Input Specification for Exercise Set 7.1   *************)
(*                                                                     *)
(*                    Reciprocal Duration Code                         *)
(*                                                                     *)
(* Each of the programs in exercise set 7.1 deals with a partially en- *)
(* coded excerpt.  Durations are encoded as the reciprocal of the dura- *)
(* tion, i.e., 1 = whole note, 2 = half note, 4 = quarter note, etc.,  *)
(* with negative numbers representing rests.  The present form of the  *)
(* code does not allow for dotted notes and ties.  Bar lines are encoded *)
(* as the integer 0, and the double bar at the end of the excerpt as 100.*)
(* The 100 is not preceded by a 0.  If there is an anacrusis, the code  *)
(* will begin with an encoded duration, otherwise it must begin with an *)
(* encoded bar line.                                                   *)
(***********************************************************************)
```

For the first few problems we will use an excerpt from Beethoven's Symphony No. 7, encoded in reciprocal duration code (figure 7.3).

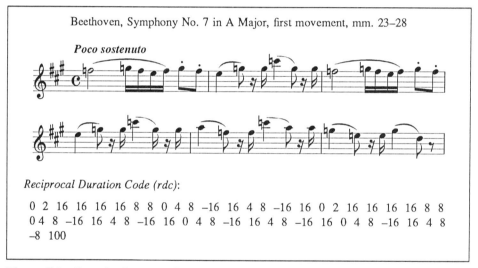

Beethoven, Symphony No. 7 in A Major, first movement, mm. 23–28

Reciprocal Duration Code (rdc):

0 2 16 16 16 16 8 8 0 4 8 –16 16 4 8 –16 16 0 2 16 16 16 16 8 8
0 4 8 –16 16 4 8 –16 16 0 4 8 –16 16 4 8 –16 16 0 4 8 –16 16 4 8
–8 100

Figure 7.3. Data for Program Group One

7.3.1 Program Group One

Exercise 7.1.1. Write a program that counts the number of measures in an excerpt encoded in rdc.

Problem Analysis. The output from the program will be the number of measures in an encoded composition. If you have carefully read section 6.3 (Reciprocal Duration Code), the nature of the input should be clear. From the code specification, we can deduce that the number of encoded bar lines (0) will be equal to the number of measures, since each measure begins with a bar line. This will be true even if there is an anacrusis, since the final (incomplete) measure will begin with a bar line but the anacrusis will not. If the excerpt is correctly notated, the durations in the anacrusis plus those in the final measure should be equal to one complete measure. We could count measure terminators (bar lines and double bars) if we remember that the anacrusis and the final measure are equal to one full measure, so the count will be high by one. (Verify this analysis by making up some simple excerpts and encoding them.)

Design (solution 1). One solution is simply to count the number of bar lines (0) in the code. If the excerpt is short, a person could scan the code visually and quickly count the number of encoded bar lines. The computer cannot read the data in quite the same manner, since it can only examine one value at a time. A reasonable simulation of the way a program reads data is to write each number on a separate slip of paper, and to stack them up so that the first code is on top. You could then read only one encoded symbol (representing a duration or bar line) at a time. If the code were a bar line, you would count it; if it were an encoded duration, you would ignore it. You would know that you were done when you had read the 100 signifying the final double bar.

Refinement. First we state the algorithm in English: Examine each encoded value; if it is a bar line, count it. The process is so simple that very little refinement is possible. However, the algorithm as stated lacks the required quality of definiteness. Exactly how shall we examine each encoded value? A more specific statement of the solution is:

> Read each code until the double bar is encountered.
> If the code is a bar line, count it.
> Print the results.

"Read each code" implies a loop, which could be a **while** or a **repeat** statement. We know that the terminal value is the double bar, encoded as 100. The above can be expressed more precisely in pseudo code. We illustrate both forms of the loop:

```
read a code;
while not end of excerpt do
  begin
    if code is a bar line
      then count it;
    read the next code
  end;
print the number of bar lines counted
```

or, using **repeat**:

```
repeat
  read an encoded value;
  if code is a bar line
    then count it;
until end of excerpt;
print the number of bar lines counted
```

The choice of loop is arbitrary here, since either terminates correctly if the first code is the double bar (the minimal required code). However, note that the **while** avoids testing the double bar to see if it is a bar line, since the body of the loop does not execute after the terminal value has been read.

The translation into Pascal is straightforward. The only statement that does not translate directly is ''count it'' (the bar line). ''Count it'' means *add one to the number of measures*. This implies the use of a variable, which must be initialized (preset) to 0 before code processing begins. The assertion ''end of excerpt'' is the boolean expression *code* = *doublebar*, since the code will be equal to the double bar when all codes have been read. In the **while** loop, ''not end of excerpt'' is **not** (*code* = *doublebar*) or more simply *code* <> *doublebar*.

Encoding. The program requires constant definitions for the values representing the bar line and the double bar, and two variables—one to store the current encoded symbol and one to count the number of measures. Careful choice of identifiers improves program readability and minimizes the number of comments required to document the program. The use of constants makes the program easier to read and facilitates changing the values used to represent bar lines and double bars, should this become necessary.

Two versions of the complete program are shown. Program 7.1 implements the program with a **while** loop, and program 7.2 with a **repeat...until**.

Verification. Verification should begin before you type the program into the computer. We demonstrate using the first solution. First we check the logic. The algorithm specifies that each code will be examined. We have implemented this operation using a **while** loop. The initial *read* statement (just before the **while** loop) defines *code* so the boolean expression in the **while** can be evaluated. The expression *code* <> *doublebar* evaluates to *true* until the terminal value has been read, and becomes *false* when *code* is equal to *doublebar*. The *read* statement within the loop gets the next encoded value, so the loop can terminate. Within the loop, the **if** statement tests the assertion *code* = *barline*, the correct test (see discussion under *Design*). If this assertion is *true*, indicating that the current value of code is a bar line, *measures* is incremented. This variable is initialized to 0 outside of the loop so the expression (*measures* + 1) can be evaluated. Since the measure counter is incremented each time a bar line is encountered, it will contain the number of measures after the loop terminates. The result is printed, so all of this work is not wasted. The minimal input for the program is the single value 100 (double bar). In this case the statement part of the **while** does not execute, *measures* is not incremented, and the program reports that there are 0 measures in the excerpt.

Next we check the program manually. This consists of stepping through the code, statement by statement, with a sample input file. First make up some test data, and write it down. Then make a list of all declared constants and their values, and list each variable and boolean expression. Now start at the beginning of the program and very carefully ''execute'' each step in order. When an assignment is made, write down the value under the variable to which it is assigned. When a value is read, draw a line through the next value in the input data, and write that value under the variable to which it would be assigned. When a boolean expression is evaluated, work out its value, write it down, and follow the flow of control based on this value. Set aside an area on your paper to represent the output device, and when you encounter a *write* statement, write down the printed values. If you really want to make a careful record, you can also record the line number in the program where each change takes place. Figure 7.4 illustrates this process using program 7.1 and a short sample data set. Manual checking locates logic errors before the program is typed into the computer. It is also an excellent way to find errors in a program that does not work as intended.

After the program has been entered into a computer file and compiled without error messages, run the compiled program on several samples of data for which you can predict the output and check the actual results against those you expect. You may need several sets of input data to thoroughly test all aspects of the program. Do not assume that a program that compiles without errors will run correctly. Even if you have checked the logic, you may have introduced typographic errors while editing the program. Each of the programs in this chapter (and in the rest of the book) include sample data and the output produced by the program using this data.

PROGRAM: *countbars1*
SAMPLE DATA: 4 0 2 4 4 0 2 -1 100
CONSTANTS: *barline* = 0; *doublebar* = 100
CONDITIONALS AND VARIABLES:

measure	*code*	*code* <> *doublebar*	*code* = *barline*	(action)
0				
	4			
		true		execute loop
			false	
	0			
		true		execute loop
			true	incr measure
1				
	2			
		true		execute loop
			false	
	4			
		true		execute loop
			false	
	4			
		true		execute loop
			false	
	0			
		true		execute loop
			true	incr. measure
2				
	2			
		true		
			false	
	-1			
		true		execute loop
			false	
	100			
		false		loop terminates

OUTPUT: The piece contains 2 measures.

Figure 7.4. Checking Program 7.1 Manually

```
(***********************    Program Countbars1    ***********************)
(* Exercise 7.1.1 solution 1 (using while loop)                          *)
(*                                                                       *)
(* Synopsis: Counts the number of measures in encoded excerpt.           *)
(*                                                                       *)
(* Input:    Excerpt encoded in reciprocal duration code (see code       *)
(*                   specification for exercise set 7.1).                *)
(*                                                                       *)
(* Output:   The number of measures counted.                             *)
(*                                                                       *)
(* Method:   Each code is examined until the final double bar (100) is   *)
(*           encountered.  If the code is a bar line, it is counted;     *)
(*           otherwise no action is taken.                               *)
(*************************************************************************)

program countbars1(input, output);
  const
    barline   = 0;                          { code for bar line          }
    doublebar = 100;                        { code for end of excerpt    }

  var
    measures : integer;                     { number of measures         }
    code     : integer;                     { duration, or bar line      }

  begin { main }
    measures := 0;                          { init measure counter       }

    read(code);
    while code <> doublebar do
      begin
        if code = barline
          then measures := measures + 1;
        read(code)
      end;

    writeln('The excerpt contains', measures:3, ' measures.')
  end. { main }
```

Program 7.1. *Countbars1*

Input:

```
0 2 16 16 16 16 8 8 0 4 8 -16 16 4 8 -16 16 0 2 16 16 16 16 8 8 0
4 8 -16 16 4 8 -16 16 0 4 8 -16 16 4 8 -16 16 0 4 8 -16 16 4 8 -8 100
```

Output:

```
The excerpt contains  6 measures.
```

Program 7.1. Sample Input and Output

```
(**********************      Program Countbars2      **********************)
(* Exercise 7.1.1 solution 2 (using repeat loop)                           *)
(*                                                                         *)
(* Synopsis: Counts the number of measures in encoded excerpt.             *)
(*                                                                         *)
(* Input:    Excerpt encoded in reciprocal duration code (see code         *)
(*                  specification for exercise set 7.1).                   *)
(*                                                                         *)
(* Output:   The number of measures counted.                               *)
(*                                                                         *)
(* Method:   Each code is examined until the final double bar (100) is     *)
(*           encountered.  If the code is a bar line, it is counted;       *)
(*           otherwise no action is taken.                                 *)
(***************************************************************************)

program countbars2(input, output);
  const
    barline    = 0;                           { code for bar line       }
    doublebar  = 100;                         { code for end of excerpt }

  var
    measures : integer;                       { number of measures      }
    code     : integer;                       { duration, or bar line   }

  begin { main }
    measures := 0;                            { init measure counter    }

    repeat
      read(code);
      if code = barline
        then measures := measures + 1
    until code = doublebar;                   { end of excerpt          }

    writeln('The excerpt contains', measures:3, ' measures.')
  end. { main }
```

Program 7.2. *Countbars2*

Input:

```
0 2 16 16 16 16 8 8 0 4 8 -16 16 4 8 -16 16 0 2 16 16 16 16 8 8 0
4 8 -16 16 4 8 -16 16 0 4 8 -16 16 4 8 -16 16 0 4 8 -16 16 4 8 -8 100
```

Output:

```
The excerpt contains  6 measures.
```

Program 7.2. Sample Input and Output

An Alternate Design. We could have taken a different approach. Suppose that instead of examining each code with an **if** statement, we take advantage of the fact that the excerpt consists of a sequence of measures. The code is processed one measure at a time, and the measure counter is incremented at the end of each measure.

```
initialize measure counter;
repeat
  read a code;
  while not end of measure do
    read a code;
  increment measure counter
until end of excerpt;
print number of measures
```

The test for end-of-measure must take into account the fact that a measure may be terminated by a bar line or a double bar. Thus the **while** loop translates

```
read(code);
while (code <> barline) and (code <> doublebar) do
  read(code);
```

or

```
while not ((code = barline) or (code = doublebar)) do
  read(code);
```

The loop finds the end of each measure by reading encoded values until a measure terminator is found. Since this solution counts the ends of measures (including the anacrusis), the final count will be one too high. This is adjusted in the *write* statement.

Bracketing the statements that process one measure with **repeat...until** cause these statements to be reexecuted for each measure in the excerpt. There is a reason for using the **repeat** for the outer loop. When the inner **while** loop terminates the last time the value of *code* is *doublebar* (i.e., the final encoded value has been read). If a **while** were used for the outer loop, it would be necessary to check for this condition before reading the next value, in order to prevent an attempt to read past the end of the data. This is more cumbersome than using **repeat...until** for the outer loop.

```
read(code);
while code <> doublebar do
  begin
    while (code <> barline) and (code <> doublebar) do
      read(code);
    measures := measures + 1;
    if code <> doublebar                    { <-- extra test }
      then read(code)
  end
```

The new solution to the first exercise is shown in program 7.3. While this solution is slightly more complex than the first two, it makes better use of the structure of the data and will prove to be more extensible; it is therefore a better model for more complex problems to come.

```
(***********************    Program Countbars3    ***********************)
(* Exercise 7.1.1  algorithm 2                                             *)
(*                                                                         *)
(* Synopsis: Counts the number of measures in encoded excerpt.             *)
(*                                                                         *)
(* Input:    Excerpt encoded in reciprocal duration code (see code         *)
(*                  specification for exercise set 7.1).                   *)
(*                                                                         *)
(* Output:   The number of measures counted.                               *)
(*                                                                         *)
(* Method:   The excerpt is processed measure by measure.  After the      *)
(*           values in each measure have been processed, the measure      *)
(*           counter is incremented.  This process continues until the    *)
(*           double bar has been read.  Since the program counts ends of *)
(*           measures, including the anacrusis, the count is decremented.*)
(**************************************************************************)
program countbars3(input, output);
  const
    barline   =   0;                          { code for bar line        }
    doublebar = 100;                          { code for end of excerpt }

  var
    code     : integer;                       { for reading data         }
    measures : integer;                       { measure count            }

  begin { main }
    measures := 0;                            { initialize counter       }

    repeat                                    { process measure          }
      read(code);
      while (code <> barline) and (code <> doublebar) do
        read(code);

      measures := measures + 1
    until code = doublebar;

    writeln('The excerpt contains', measures - 1: 3, ' measures.')
  end. { main }
```

Program 7.3. *Countbars3*

Input:

```
0 2 16 16 16 16 8 8 0 4 8 -16 16 4 8 -16 16 0 2 16 16 16 16 8 8 0
4 8 -16 16 4 8 -16 16 0 4 8 -16 16 4 8 -16 16 0 4 8 -16 16 4 8 -8 100
```

Output:

```
The excerpt contains  6 measures.
```

Program 7.3. Sample Input and Output

Exercise 7.1.2. Write a program that counts the number of rests in an excerpt encoded in rdc.

Problem Analysis. The required output is the number of rests in the encoded excerpt. Recall that rests are indicated by negative integers.

Design. This problem is really easier than the first. Since the same condition indicates all rests, the basic algorithm is: Examine each code, and count the number of negative numbers.

Refinement. Again, we must use a loop that will terminate when the terminal value *doublebar* is encountered. We will use a **while** loop:

```
initialize rest count to 0;
read a value for code;
while not end of excerpt do
  begin
    if code is negative
      then increment rest count;
     read another code
  end;

print the number of rests counted.
```

Encoding. Translation into Pascal is easy. We will need a constant for the double bar, and two variables, say, *code* for reading encoded values and *restcount* for counting rests. The **while** statement translates to

```
while code <> doublebar do
```

and the **if** statement as

```
if code < 0
   then restcount := restcount + 1;
```

The completed solution is shown in program 7.4.

Verification. The initial *read* statement defines the variable used in the conditional in the **while**, and the loop contains another *read*(*code*), so the loop will terminate when the double bar has been read. The **if** statement makes the correct test for rests (*code* < 0), and the **then** clause increments the counter. The counter is initialized before it is used, so the increment will work properly. We leave manual checking and alternate solutions as an exercise for the reader.

```
(***********************     Program Countrests      ***********************)
(* Exercise 7.1.2                                                          *)
(*                                                                         *)
(* Synopsis: Counts the number of rests in encoded excerpt.                *)
(*                                                                         *)
(* Input:    Excerpt encoded in reciprocal duration code (see code         *)
(*           specification for exercise set 7.1).                          *)
(*                                                                         *)
(* Output:   The number of rests counted.                                  *)
(*                                                                         *)
(* Method:   Each encoded value is examined, and if it is negative         *)
(*           (indicating a rest), it is counted.  Processing terminates    *)
(*           when the double bar is read.                                  *)
(***************************************************************************)

program countrests(input, output);
  const
    doublebar = 100;

  var
    code      : integer;                         { for reading data     }
    restcount : integer;                         { number of rests      }

  begin { main }
    restcount := 0;                              { initialize counter }

    read(code);
    while code <> doublebar do
      begin
        if code < 0
          then restcount := restcount + 1;
        read(code)
      end;

    writeln('Rest count =', restcount:4, '.')
  end.  { main }
```

Program 7.4. *Countrests*

Input:

```
0 2 16 16 16 16 8 8 0 4 8 -16 16 4 8 -16 16 0 2 16 16 16 16 8 8 0
4 8 -16 16 4 8 -16 16 0 4 8 -16 16 4 8 -16 16 0 4 8 -16 16 4 8 -8 100
```

Output:

```
Rest count =   8.
```

Program 7.4. Sample Input and Output

Exercise 7.1.3. Count the number of sixteenth notes and the number of eighth notes, giving a separate total for each. Do not count rests.

Problem Analysis. The object is to count the number of sixteenth notes and, separately, the number of eighth notes. These are encoded as the integers 8 and 16, respectively. The input code is terminated by the double bar (100). The required output is the number of eighths and sixteenths counted.

Design. It will be necessary to examine each encoded value until the double bar signifying the end of the code is encountered. If the code is an 8 or a 16, an appropriate counter will be incremented.

Refinement. A loop is required to read each value in the encoded excerpt. Either a **while** or a **repeat** statement will do. It will be necessary to test each code to see if it is one of the desired values. Since these values are mutually exclusive (if code is a sixteenth, it can't be an eighth, and vice versa), the test can be made most efficiently with an **if...then...else if** construction. Thus the basic structure will be:

```
initialize counters for eighths and sixteenths;
read an encoded value;
while not end of excerpt do
  begin
    if code is a sixteenth note
      then add 1 to number of sixteenths
    else if code is an eighth note
      then add 1 to number of eighths;
    read another code
  end;

print results;
```

Encoding. The program will require three variables: one for reading encoded values and two for counting eighth and sixteenth notes. We will use a constant to declare the terminal value (double bar), but the values 8 and 16 are sufficiently mnemonic (and unlikely to change), so constant definitions are not required. The complete listing is shown as program 7.5.

Verification. The main loop examines each value in the encoded composition. The read statement ensures that the **while** can test its initial condition, and *read*(*code*) at the bottom of the loop gets the next value. The chained **if** statement checks for the pertinent values, and ensures that the second test is not made if the first succeeds. The expressions incrementing the counters are valid, since *sixteenths* and *eighthnotes* were initialized before the **while** loop. The *write* statements just before **end** { main } report the number of sixteenths and eighths counted. If no sixteenths or eighths occurred in the excerpt, 0 will be printed as the note counts.

```
(*********************** Program Countdurs1 ***********************)
(* Exercise 7.1.3 *)
(* *)
(* Synopsis: Counts the number of 8th notes and 16th notes. *)
(* *)
(* Input: See code specification for exercise set 7.1. *)
(* *)
(* Output: The number of 8th notes and 16th notes counted. *)
(* *)
(* Method: Each code is examined until the final double bar is *)
(* encountered. If the number is equal to 8 or 16, it is *)
(* counted, otherwise it is ignored. *)
(*******************************************************************)
program countdurs1(input, output);
  const
    doublebar    = 100;              { code for end of excerpt         }

  var
    sixteenths  : integer;           { number of 16th notes in excerpt }
    eighthnotes : integer;           { number of 8th notes in excerpt  }
    code        : integer;           { encoded duration, bar line or   }
                                     {    double bar                   }
  begin { main }
    sixteenths := 0;                 { initialize note counters        }
    eighthnotes  := 0;

    read(code);
    while code <> doublebar do
      begin { process excerpt }
        if code = 16
          then sixteenths := sixteenths + 1
        else if code = 8
          then eighthnotes := eighthnotes + 1;
        read(code)
      end; { process excerpt }

    writeln('The excerpt contains', sixteenths:4, ' 16th notes');
    writeln('                  and', eighthnotes:4, '  8th notes.')
  end. { main }
```

Program 7.5. *Countdurs1*

Input:

```
0 2 16 16 16 16 8 8 0 4 8 -16 16 4 8 -16 16 0 2 16 16 16 16 8 8 0
4 8 -16 16 4 8 -16 16 0 4 8 -16 16 4 8 -16 16 0 4 8 -16 16 4 8 -8 100
```

Output:

```
The excerpt contains  15 16th notes
                 and  12  8th notes.
```

Program 7.5. Sample Input and Output

The next two programs are extensions or elaborations of the previous exercise.

Exercise 7.1.4. Count the occurrences of each of the following durations: whole note, half note, quarter note, eighth note, sixteenth note, and thirty-second note. Include rests in the counting. Print the results in tabular form.

Problem Analysis. This is an extension of the previous exercise. The primary differences are: (1) more different types of duration are to be counted; (2) rests will be included in the duration counts; and (3) the results will be printed in a table.

Design/Encoding. We will use essentially the same design as in the previous exercise, with the addition of new variables to count the added durations. Since rests (encoded as negative numbers) are to be included, it will be necessary to obtain the absolute value of each encoded duration. The **if...then...else if** chain could be extended to accommodate the additional durations. However, with this many choices a **case** statement is more appropriate, more efficient, and easier to read.

Verification. Most of the logic is identical to that in program 7.5, so we will not repeat the discussion here. In addition, note that the program uses an **in** construction to ensure that the **case** statement is not given an undefined case.

```
(************************   Program Countdurs2    ************************)
(* Exercise 7.1.4                                                        *)
(* Synopsis: Counts occurrences of each of the following durations:      *)
(*           whole note, half note, quarter note, eighth, sixteenth,     *)
(*           and thirty-second, INCLUDING rests.                         *)
(* Input:    See code specification for exercise set 7.1.                *)
(* Output:   Table listing number of occurrences of specified durations. *)
(* Method:   Each code in the excerpt is checked.  If it is one of the   *)
(*           specified durations, it is counted.                         *)
(************************************************************************)

program countdurs2(input, output);
  const
    fine    = 100;                      { code for end of excerpt   }

  var
    wcount : integer;                   { number of whole notes     }
    hcount : integer;                   { number of half notes      }
    qcount : integer;                   { number of quarter notes   }
    ecount : integer;                   { number of 8th notes       }
    scount : integer;                   { number of 16th notes      }
    tcount : integer;                   { number of 32d notes       }
    code   : integer;                   { encoded duration, bar     }
                                        {    line, or double bar    }
  begin { main }
    wcount := 0;                        { initialize note counters  }
    hcount := 0;
    qcount := 0;
    ecount := 0;
    scount := 0;
    tcount := 0;
```

```
    read(code);
    while code <> fine do
      begin { count durations }
        code := abs(code);                          { convert rests }

        if code in [1, 2, 4, 8, 16, 32]
          then
            case code of
               1: wcount := wcount + 1;             { whole note     }
               2: hcount := hcount + 1;             { half note      }
               4: qcount := qcount + 1;             { quarter note   }
               8: ecount := ecount + 1;             { 8th note       }
              16: scount := scount + 1;             { 16th note      }
              32: tcount := tcount + 1              { 32d note       }
            end; { case }

        read(code)
      end; { count durations }
                                                    { print table    }
    writeln('======================');
    writeln('Duration', 'Occurrences':14);          { heading        }
    writeln('======================');
    writeln('whole   ', wcount:14);                 { note counts    }
    writeln('half    ', hcount:14);
    writeln('quarter ', qcount:14);
    writeln('8th     ', ecount:14);
    writeln('16th    ', scount:14);
    writeln('32d     ', tcount:14);
    writeln('======================')
  end. { main }
```

Program 7.6. *Countdurs2*

Input:

```
0 2 16 16 16 16 8 8 0 4 8 -16 16 4 8 -16 16 0 2 16 16 16 16 8 8 0
4 8 -16 16 4 8 -16 16 0 4 8 -16 16 4 8 -16 16 0 4 8 -16 16 4 8 -8 100
```

Output:

```
======================
Duration   Occurrences
======================
whole                0
half                 2
quarter              8
8th                 13
16th                22
32d                  0
======================
```

Program 7.6. Sample Input and Output

Exercise 7.1.5. This exercise is identical to exercise 7.1.4, except that the total number of durations is to be counted, and the table is to show the percentage of total durations as well as the number of occurrences.

Problem Analysis. Since this program is so close to the previous exercises, we can concentrate on the new aspects. Although it was not stated in the problem, the total and percentages should probably reflect all durations in the excerpt, including those that are not among the durations specified. We can deduce from the code specification that only durations (including rests), bar lines, and the final double bar are encoded. Thus any code that is not one of the specified durations or a bar line must be some other duration.

Refinement. We will use a new variable called *other* to count unspecified durations. This variable will be incremented if an encoded value is not one of the specified durations, and if it is not an encoded bar line (the only other possibility). After the encoded excerpt has been processed, the total number of durations can be obtained by adding the counters for all durations. This is more efficient than adding one to the total each time a duration code is encountered, since it requires seven additions rather than *n*, where *n* is the total number of durations. The difference becomes more critical if the total number of durations is large. Percentage is calculated as

```
(x / total) * 100.0
```

Since this calculation must be done for each duration type, this would be an excellent place to use a function, but for now we will calculate this value in the *writeln* statements when printing the table. Program 7.7 lists the complete solution.

```
(************************   Program Countdurs3    ************************)
(* Exercise 7.1.5                                                          *)
(* Synopsis: Counts various durations (as in countdurs2) but also calcu-  *)
(*           lates the percentage of the total for each duration.  For    *)
(*           accuracy, durations other than those specified are also      *)
(*           counted.  The variable total is used to sum all durations.  *)
(*           Percentage is calculated by expression in write statements. *)
(* Input:    See code specification for exercise set 7.1.                 *)
(* Output:   Table listing number of occurrences and percentage of total *)
(*           for each duration counted.                                   *)
(* Method:   Each code in the excerpt is checked.  If it is one of the    *)
(*           specified durations it is counted.  Other durations are      *)
(*           also counted. Total is calculated as the sum of all dura-    *)
(*           tions.                                                       *)
(**************************************************************************)

program countdurs3(input, output);
  const
    barline    = 0;                          { code for bar line          }
    doublebar  = 100;                        { code for end of excerpt    }

  var
    wcount : integer;                        { number of whole notes      }
    hcount : integer;                        { number of half notes       }
```

```
    qcount : integer;                    { number of quarter notes  }
    ecount : integer;                    { number of 8th notes      }
    scount : integer;                    { number of 16th notes     }
    tcount : integer;                    { number of 32nd notes     }
    other  : integer;                    { number of other durations}
    total  : integer;                    { total number of durations}
    code   : integer;                    { coded duration, bar line,}
                                         {    or double bar         }

begin { main }
    wcount := 0;                         { initialize note counters }
    hcount := 0;
    qcount := 0;
    ecount := 0;
    scount := 0;
    tcount := 0;
    other  := 0;

    read(code);
    while code <> doublebar do
      begin { count durations }
        code := abs(code);                          { convert rests }

        if code in [1, 2, 4, 8, 16, 32]
          then
            case code of
               1: wcount := wcount + 1;             { whole note    }
               2: hcount := hcount + 1;             { half note     }
               4: qcount := qcount + 1;             { quarter note  }
               8: ecount := ecount + 1;             { 8th note      }
              16: scount := scount + 1;             { 16th note     }
              32: tcount := tcount + 1              { 32d note      }
            end { case }
        else if code <> barline
          then other := other + 1;

        read(code)
      end; { count durations }

    total := wcount + hcount + qcount + ecount + scount + tcount
             + other;
                                                    { print table   }
    writeln('===================================');
    writeln('Duration', 'Occurrences':14, 'Percent':12);
    writeln('===================================');
    writeln('whole   ', wcount:14, wcount / total * 100:12:2);
    writeln('half    ', hcount:14, hcount / total * 100:12:2);
    writeln('quarter ', qcount:14, qcount / total * 100:12:2);
    writeln('8th     ', ecount:14, ecount / total * 100:12:2);
    writeln('16th    ', scount:14, scount / total * 100:12:2);
    writeln('32d     ', tcount:14, tcount / total * 100:12:2);
    writeln('other   ', other:14, other  / total * 100:12:2);
    writeln('===================================');
    writeln('total:  ', total:14, 100.0:12:2)
  end. { main }
```

Program 7.7. *Countdurs3*

Input:

```
0 2 16 16 16 16 8 8 0 4 8 -16 16 4 8 -16 16 0 2 16 16 16 16 8 8 0
4 8 -16 16 4 8 -16 16 0 4 8 -16 16 4 8 -16 16 0 4 8 -16 16 4 8 -8 100
```

Output:

```
==================================
Duration   Occurrences    Percent
==================================
whole                0       0.00
half                 2       4.44
quarter              8      17.78
8th                 13      28.89
16th                22      48.89
32d                  0       0.00
other                0       0.00
==================================
total:              45     100.00
```

Program 7.7. Sample Input and Output

Beethoven, Symphony No. 1 in C Major, first movement, mm. 6–20

Reciprocal Duration Code (rdc):

–16 16 16 16 0 16 16 16 16 8 8 0 4 8 8 0 8 8 16 16 16 16 0 4 16
16 16 16 0 16 16 16 16 8 8 0 8 8 16 16 16 16 0 8 8 16 16 16 16 0
4 –8 8 0 8 8 8 8 0 4 8 8 0 8 8 8 8 0 4 8 8 0 8 8 8 8 0 8 –8 8
–8 0 8 –8 8 –8 0 4 100

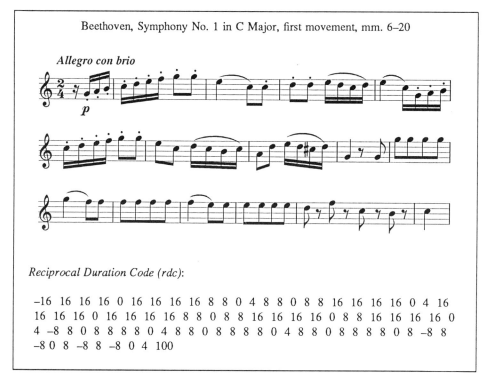

Figure 7.5. Sample Data for Program Group Two

7.3.2 Program Group Two

The next three exercises again represent a progressive series, with each program building on the previous ones. For these exercises we will encode an excerpt from Beethoven's Symphony No. 1 (figure 7.5).

Exercise 7.1.6. Calculate the number of measures that contain at least one sixteenth note.

Problem Analysis: The objective is to find and count the number of measures that contain sixteenth notes, and to print this number. The sixteenth note is encoded as the integer 16, and each measure is terminated with a bar line (0) except the last, which is terminated by a double bar (100). The double bar also signals the end of the excerpt. We will examine two different algorithms for solving this problem.

Design (solution 1). As a first attempt at developing an algorithm, consider the following: Examine each encoded value in the excerpt. When a sixteenth note is found, count the measure and skip to the end of the measure:

```
repeat
  read a code;
  if it is a sixteenth note
    then
      begin
        count the measure;
        skip to the end of the measure
      end;
until the end of the excerpt is found;

print the results;
```

Refinement. Before the **repeat** loop is entered, it will be necessary to initialize the variable used to count measures with sixteenth notes. ''Count the measure'' means add one to this variable. ''Skip to the end of the measure'' implies another loop. It will be necessary to check for either a bar line or a double bar, since the final measure is terminated by the latter. We will know that the end of the excerpt has been reached when a double bar has been read.

```
count := 0;
repeat
  read(code);
  if code = 16
    then
      begin { found it }
        count := count + 1;
        while (code <> barline) and (code <> doublebar) do
          read(code)
      end { found it }
until code = doublebar;
```

Verification. The **repeat** loop ensures that the entire excerpt will be examined. If no sixteenth notes occur, the compound statement in the **if** will never be executed, and the program will report that 0 measures contained sixteenth notes. If a sixteenth note is found, the inner loop (''skip to the end of the measure'') will process all codes up to and including the measure terminator for that measure, so long as it checks for either a bar line or a double bar. If this is not the last measure, the **repeat** loop continues processing until the end of the excerpt, or until another sixteenth note is found. If a sixteenth note is found in the last measure, the inner loop will terminate when the double bar has been read, and this value will also terminate the **repeat** loop.

Encoding. The program will require one variable to read each code, and one to count measures with sixteenth notes. We will use constants for *barline* and *doublebar* to improve readability. This first solution is shown in program 7.8.

```
(**********************  Program Firstattempt  **********************)
(* Exercise 7.1.6 solution 1                                          *)
(* Synopsis: Counts measures containing sixteenth notes.              *)
(*                                                                    *)
(* Input:    See code specification for exercise set 7.1.             *)
(* Output:   The number of measures containing 16th notes.            *)
(*                                                                    *)
(* Method:   1. Each code is examined until the double bar is found.  *)
(*           2. When an encoded 16th note is encountered, the measure is *)
(*              counted, and the rest of the measure is skipped.      *)
(**********************************************************************)
program firstattempt(input, output);
  const
    barline   = 0;                 { code for bar line                 }
    doublebar = 100;               { end of excerpt                    }

  var
    count   : integer;             { number of measures containing 16ths }
    code    : integer;             { duration, bar line, or double bar   }

  begin { main }
    count := 0;                    { initialize measure counter        }

    repeat
      read(code);
      if code = 16
        then
          begin { found it }
            count := count + 1;                    { count measure     }
            while (code <> barline) and (code <> doublebar) do
              read(code)                           { skip to end       }
          end { found it }
    until code = doublebar;

    writeln(count:2, ' measures contain 16th notes.')
  end. { main }
```

Program 7.8. *Firstattempt*

Input:

```
-16 16 16 16 0 16 16 16 16 8 8 0 4 8 8 0 8 8 16 16 16 16 0 4 16
16 16 16 0 16 16 16 16 8 8 0 8 8 16 16 16 16 0 8 8 16 16 16 16 0
4 -8 8 0 8 8 8 8 0 4 8 8 0 8 8 8 8 0 4 8 8 0 8 8 8 8 0 8 -8 8 -8
0 8 -8 8 -8 0 4 100
```

Output:

```
 7 measures contain 16th notes.
```

Program 7.8. Sample Input and Output

Now consider the following alternate algorithm:

Design (solution 2). Until the end of the excerpt: Count the number of sixteenth notes in each measure; if the number is greater than 0, count this measure.

> **repeat**
> read a code;
> count sixteenths in measure;
> **if** number of sixteenths is greater than 0
> **then** count measure
> **until** end of excerpt;
>
> print the results

Refinement. "Count sixteenths in measure" implies another loop and an extra variable to count with. This variable should be reset before the nested loop is entered, so that it will start at 0 for each new measure. Thus counting the sixteenth notes in the measure becomes:

> *num16* := 0;
> **while** not at end of measure **do**
> **begin**
> **if** code is a sixteenth note
> **then** increment *num16*;
> read another code
> **end**

When this loop has terminated, *num16* will contain the number of sixteenths in the measure.

Verification. This algorithm is easier to check than the previous one. The inner loop calculates the number of sixteenth notes in the measure. The initial code is read before the loop is entered, so the test for end-of-measure at the beginning of the **while** is valid. The **if** statement increments the sixteenth-note counter if the current code is a sixteenth note. Since another code is read within the loop, the **while** can terminate properly when a measure terminator is found.

Encoding. At this point encoding in Pascal should be simple. The complete solution is shown in program 7.9.

```
(************************   Program Measure16a    ************************)
(* Exercise 7.1.6 solution 2                                              *)
(* Synopsis: Counts measures with at least one sixteenth note.            *)
(*                                                                        *)
(* Input:    See code specification for exercise set 7.1.                 *)
(* Output:   The number of measures containing 16th notes.                *)
(*                                                                        *)
(* Method:  1. Until the end of the excerpt is encountered:               *)
(*             a. The 16th notes in each measure are counted.             *)
(*             b. If this number is greater than 0, the measure is        *)
(*                counted.                                                *)
(*          2. When the entire excerpt has been processed, the number of *)
(*             measures containing 16th notes is printed.                 *)
(*                                                                        *)
(* Notes:  When checking for the end of the measure, we must check for a *)
(* bar line and for a double bar, since the final measure will be         *)
(* terminated by the latter.                                              *)
(**************************************************************************)
program measure16a(input, output);
  const
    barline = 0;                       { code for bar line             }
    doublebar = 100;                   { code for end of excerpt       }

  var
    count : integer;         { number of measures containing 16ths       }
    code  : integer;         { encoded duration, bar line, or double bar }
    num16 : integer;         { number of 16th notes in a measure         }

  begin { main }
    count := 0;                        { initialize measure counter    }

    repeat
      num16 := 0;                      { number of 16ths in measure    }

      read(code);
      while (code <> barline) and (code <> doublebar) do
        begin { count 16ths in measure }
          if code = 16
            then num16 := num16 + 1;
          read(code)
        end;  { count 16ths in measure }

      if num16 > 0
        then count := count + 1
    until code = doublebar;

    writeln(count:2,' measures contain 16th notes.')
  end.  { main }
```

Program 7.9. *Measure16a*

Input:

```
-16 16 16 16 0 16 16 16 16 8 8 0 4 8 8 0 8 8 16 16 16 16 0 4 16
16 16 16 0 16 16 16 16 8 8 0 8 8 16 16 16 16 0 8 8 16 16 16 16 0
4 -8 8 0 8 8 8 8 0 4 8 8 0 8 8 8 8 0 4 8 8 0 8 8 8 8 0 8 -8 8 -8
0 8 -8 8 -8 0 4 100
```

Output:

```
 7 measures contain 16th notes.
```

Program 7.9. Sample Input and Output

Which algorithm is preferable? Both accomplish the same task in about the same number of statements, and both produce identical output for the same input. Before we attempt to answer the question, consider the extensions to the problem suggested in exercises 7.1.7 and 7.1.8. These extensions include printing the measure number and the number of sixteenth notes in each measure that contains them.

It should be obvious that the second algorithm is a better choice. This is because it takes advantage of the structure of the data, i.e., the fact that an encoded excerpt consists of a series of encoded measures. Since the second algorithm processes the data one measure at a time, it will be relatively simple to add a counter that keeps track of the current measure number. Also, since this solution already accounts for the number of sixteenths in each measure, some of the extensions are included in the simple solution. The second algorithm takes better advantage of the structure of the data, it is easier to verify, and it is more extensible. We will base the next two solutions on this algorithm. As an exercise, you may wish to formulate your own solutions to the next two exercises based on the first design, and compare these solutions to those that follow. You will find that the program structure and logic are much less transparent than the solutions shown here.

Exercise 7.1.7. As in the previous exercise, but print out the measure number for each measure that contains a sixteenth note. Control the number of measure numbers printed per line.

Problem Analysis. The previous solution needs very little modification. All that is required is an extra variable to keep track of the current measure. Recall that we specified that the code would begin with a bar line unless there is an anacrusis. Thus any durations before the first bar line are in measure 0.

Design. We modify the earlier design by adding a measure counter. This should be set to 0 at the beginning of the program and should be incremented after each measure is processed and the measure number has been printed (if there were sixteenth notes):

```
set measure counter to 0;
set counter for measures with sixteenths to 0;
repeat
  set sixteenth-note counter to 0;
  read a code;
  count sixteenth notes in measure;
  if the number of sixteenths is greater than 0
    then
      begin
        count the measure;
        print current measure number
      end;
  increment measure number
until end of excerpt;
print the number of measures with sixteenth notes
```

Refinement. The loop that processes a measure (counting sixteenth notes) remains unchanged. We can use the number of measures that contain sixteenth notes to control the number of items printed on a line. Thus the compound statement in the **if** statement shown above becomes

```
begin
  count := count + 1;
  write(measure);
  if count mod numperline = 0
    then writeln
end;
```

where *count* is the number of measures containing sixteenth notes, *measure* is the current measure number, and *numperline* is number of numbers printed on a line.

Encoding. We will use constants to define *barline*, *doublebar*, and *numperline* (the number of numbers printed on a line). Other required variables have already been discussed. The encoding is straightforward, as can be seen in program 7.10.

Input:

```
-16 16 16 16 0 16 16 16 16 8 8 0 4 8 8 0 8 8 16 16 16 16 0 4 16
16 16 16 0 16 16 16 16 8 8 0 8 8 16 16 16 16 0 8 8 16 16 16 16 0
4 -8 8 0 8 8 8 8 0 4 8 8 0 8 8 8 8 0 4 8 8 0 8 8 8 8 0 8 -8 8 -8
0 8 -8 8 -8 0 4 100
```

Output:

```
measures containing 16th notes:
  0  1  3  4  5  6  7

total:  7 measures contain 16th notes.
```

Program 7.10. Sample Input and Output

```
(*********************** Program Measure16b ***********************)
(* Exercise 7.1.7                                                    *)
(* Synopsis: Prints the measure number for each measure that contains *)
(*           16th notes, and count these measures.                   *)
(* Input:    See code specification for exercise set 7.1.            *)
(* Output:   The number of measures containing 16th notes.           *)
(* Method:   Until the end of the excerpt:                           *)
(*           a) Count the number of 16th notes in each measure.      *)
(*           b) If this number is greater than 0, count the measure and *)
(*              print the measure number.                            *)
(*           Print the total number of measures with 16th notes.     *)
(*********************************************************************)
program measure16b(input, output);
  const
    barline = 0;             { code for bar line                    }
    doublebar = 100;         { code for end of excerpt              }
    numperline = 10;         { numbers printed per line             }

  var
    count  : integer;        { number of measures containing 16ths  }
    code   : integer;        { encoded duration, bar line, or double bar }
    num16  : integer;        { number of sixteenths in a measure    }
    measno : integer;        { the current measure number           }

  begin { main }
    count := 0;              { initialize measure counter and       }
    measno := 0;             {     measure number                   }

    writeln('measures containing 16th notes:');
    repeat
      num16 := 0;            { number of 16th notes in measure      }

      read(code);
      while (code <> barline) and (code <> doublebar) do
        begin { count 16ths in measure }
          if code = 16
            then num16 := num16 + 1;
          read(code)
        end; { count 16ths in measure }

      if num16 > 0                    { if measure contained 16th notes }
        then
          begin
            count := count + 1;             { count measure          }
            write(measno : 3);              { write measure number   }
            if count mod numperline = 0     {    10 per line         }
              then writeln
          end;

      measno := measno + 1                  { incr measure number    }
    until code = doublebar;

    writeln;
    writeln;
    writeln('total: ', count:2, ' measures contain 16th notes.')
  end. { main }
```

Program 7.10. *Measure16b*

```
(***********************   Program Measure16c   ***********************)
(* Exercise 7.1.8                                                      *)
(* Synopsis: For each measure containing 16th notes, prints the measure *)
(*           number and the number of 16th notes.                       *)
(* Input:    See code specification for exercise set 7.1.              *)
(* Output:   A table showing measure number and number of 16th notes for *)
(*           measures containing 16ths.                                 *)
(* Method:   Until the end of the excerpt is encountered:               *)
(*           1. Count the number of 16th notes in each measure.         *)
(*           2. If the number is greater than 0, count the measure and  *)
(*              print the measure number and number of 16ths in measure. *)
(*           Print the total number of measures containing 16ths.       *)
(**********************************************************************)
program measure16c(input, output);
  const
    barline = 0;              { code for bar line                       }
    doublebar = 100;          { code for end of excerpt                 }

  var
    count  : integer;         { number of measures containing 16ths     }
    code   : integer;         { encoded duration, bar line, or double bar }
    num16  : integer;         { number of 16ths in a measure            }
    measno : integer;         { current measure number                  }

  begin { main }
    count := 0;               { initialize measure counter and          }
    measno := 0;              { measure number                          }

    writeln('measures containing 16th notes');               { heading }
    writeln('==============================');
    writeln(' ':2, 'measure':10, '16ths':10);
    writeln('==============================');

    repeat
      num16 := 0;
      read(code);
      while (code <> barline) and (code <> doublebar) do
        begin { count 16ths }
          if code = 16
            then num16 := num16 + 1;
          read(code)
        end; { count 16ths }

      if num16 > 0                      { if measure contained 16th notes }
        then
          begin
            count := count + 1;                   { count measure        }
            writeln(measno:10, num16:10)          { write measure number }
          end;

      measno := measno + 1                        { incr measure number  }
    until code = doublebar;                       { until end of excerpt }

    writeln('==============================');
    writeln('total: ', count:2, ' measures contain 16th notes.')
  end. { main }
```

Program 7.11. *Measure16c*

Input:

```
-16 16 16 16 0 16 16 16 16 8 8 0 4 8 8 0 8 8 16 16 16 16 0 4 16
16 16 16 0 16 16 16 16 8 8 0 8 8 16 16 16 16 0 8 8 16 16 16 16 0
4 -8 8 0 8 8 8 8 0 4 8 8 0 8 8 8 8 0 4 8 8 0 8 8 8 8 0 8 -8 8 -8
0 8 -8 8 -8 0 4 100
```

Output:

```
measures containing 16th notes
==============================
     measure     16ths
==============================
        0          3
        1          4
        3          4
        4          4
        5          4
        6          4
        7          4
==============================
total:  7 measures contain 16th notes.
```

Program 7.11. Sample Input and Output

Exercise 7.1.8. As in exercise 7.1.7, but for each measure containing sixteenth notes, print the measure number and the number of sixteenth notes in the measure. Format the output in a table.

Problem Analysis. Using the present algorithm, we already have the required information. All that is required is to format the output in a table.

Refinement. The table heading must be printed before processing of the data begins. After a measure is processed, if the number of sixteenths in the measure is greater than 0, the table entry, consisting of the measure number and number of sixteenths, is printed. The solution is shown in program 7.11.

7.4 Application: Calculating Fibonacci Numbers

Fibonacci numbers will be familiar to the reader who is acquainted with Lendvai's theories of the music of Béla Bartók. The Fibonacci series is the series of numbers such that each term is the sum of the previous two terms:

$$0 \quad 1 \quad 1 \quad 2 \quad 3 \quad 5 \quad 8 \quad 13 \quad 21 \ldots$$

Devising an algorithm to compute this series is interesting in itself, but techniques used in this algorithm will suggest solutions to other problems in computing.

Problem Analysis. Obviously, the first two terms must be assigned. From there on, the solution would be simple with an infinite number of variables and an infinite number of program statements:

```
f1 := 0;
writeln(f1);
f2 := 1;
writeln(f2);
f3 := f1 + f2;
writeln(f3);
f4 := f3 + f4;
writeln(f4);
f5 := f3 + f4;
etc. . . .
```

This approach is not viable for more than a very few numbers. What is needed is an algorithm that recycles a few variables while calculating the series.

Design. Note that after the first two assignments the task is repetitive. Each successive number is calculated as the sum of the previous two. We can calculate the series using only three variables, say *first*, *second*, and *next*. The series is begun by assigning 0 to *first* and 1 to *second*. Now the next number, *next*, is calculated as the sum of *first* and *second*. In order to continue, we need to shift, assigning *first* the value of *second*, and *second* the value of *next*. Now the new *next* can be calculated and the process can be continued:

```
first := 0;
second := 1;
repeat
  next := first + second;
  first := second;              { shift }
  second := next
until you have gone as far as you wish
```

or using **while**:

```
first := 0;
second := 1;
while you have not gone as far as you wish do
  begin
    next := first + second;
    first := second;            { shift }
    second := next
  end;
```

Refinement. The solution shown above is not an algorithm by definition, since it has no outputs. It does us no good to calculate the series unless we print the results. Thus, to print the whole series, the initial values of *first* and *second* must be printed, and each new value for *next* must be printed.

As an additional refinement, we use another variable to calculate the ordinal position of each number in the series. This is initialized to 0 before the loop, and incremented within the loop to reflect the current position in the series.

It will be possible to calculate only part of the series, since the numbers get large rather quickly, causing an integer overflow error.[6] We can use the ordinal position in the list to terminate execution. A computer that uses 16-bit integers can calculate the first 24 numbers (beginning with 0); if your system uses 32 bits for integers you can calculate the first 47 Fibonacci numbers. If you are not sure of the integer size in your system, or how your system deals with overflow errors, you may find it interesting to experiment with a ''loop forever'' construct such as **while** *true* **do**, or **repeat...until** *false*. (Be sure you know how to terminate the program on your system.) The program is shown below.

```
(***********************    Program Fibonacci     ***********************)
(* The Fibonacci series is an arithmetic series in which each number is  *)
(* the sum of the previous two numbers.  The series begins with 0 1 :    *)
(*          0 1 1 2 3 5 8 13 21 34 55 ...                                *)
(* An algorithm for calculating the beginning of this series is given    *)
(* below.  The first two numbers are initialized.  The while loop calcu- *)
(* lates the next number in the series, and then "shifts" the numbers so *)
(* that the second number becomes the first, and the sum becomes the     *)
(* second number.  Thus the new sum can be calculated.  Integer overflow *)
(* occurs rather rapidly, so the number of terms that will be calculated *)
(* must be limited.  A computer that uses 16 bits for integers can calcu-*)
(* late the first 24 numbers, one that uses 32 bits can calculate 47.    *)
(************************************************************************)
program fibonacci(output);
  const
    max = 47;                                  { use 24 for 16-bit integers}

  var
    first, second : integer;                   { first two Fib. numbers    }
    next          : integer;                   { sum of two previous nos   }
    position      : integer;                   { ordinal position in series}

  begin { main }
    first := 0;                                { prime the pump            }
    writeln(1,':', first);
    second := 1;
    writeln(2,':', second);
    position := 3;                             { next position in series   }
    while position <= max do                   { calculate next in series  }
      begin
        next := first + second;                { next number in series     }
        writeln(position, ':', next);
        first := second;                       { shift: 2d no. becomes 1st }
        second := next;                        {    and next becomes 2d    }
        position := position + 1               { ord. pos. of next number  }
      end
  end.  { main }
```

Program 7.12. *Fibonacci*

6. If your compiler or interpreter does not check for integer overflow, the program will continue to execute with erroneous output. Usually this can be recognized because the numbers will not continue to get larger and some will appear as negative numbers.

```
 1:          0           25:      46368
 2:          1           26:      75025
 3:          1           27:     121393
 4:          2           28:     196418
 5:          3           29:     317811
 6:          5           30:     514229
 7:          8           31:     832040
 8:         13           32:    1346269
 9:         21           33:    2178309
10:         34           34:    3524578
11:         55           35:    5702887
12:         89           36:    9227465
13:        144           37:   14930352
14:        233           38:   24157817
15:        377           39:   39088169
16:        610           40:   63245986
17:        987           41:  102334155
18:       1597           42:  165580141
19:       2584           43:  267914296
20:       4181           44:  433494437
21:       6765           45:  701408733
22:      10946           46: 1134903170
23:      17711           47: 1836311903
24:      28657
```

Program 7.12. Output[7]

References and Selected Readings

A brief but cogent introduction to algorithms can be found in chapter 1 of the first reference. The remainder of this volume presents many useful algorithms and formal proofs of their accuracy and scope. Although the book does not deal with music per se, much of the information can be applied in any field of enquiry.

Knuth, Donald E. *The Art of Computer Programming*. Vol. 1, *Fundamental Algorithms*. 2d ed. Reading, Mass.: Addison-Wesley, 1973.

Many other sources deal with the design, testing, and verification of algorithms. The sources listed here will serve as a starting point.

Aho, Alfred V., John E. Hopcroft, and Jeffrey D. Ullman. *Data Structures and Algorithms*. Reading, Mass.: Addison-Wesley, 1983.

———. *The Design and Analysis of Algorithms*. Reading, Mass.: Addison-Wesley, 1975.

Bently, J. L. *Programming Pearls*. Reading, Mass.: Addison-Wesley, 1985.

Gonnet, G. H. *Handbook of Algorithms and Data Structures*. Reading, Mass.: Addison-Wesley, 1988.

Horowitz, Ellis, and Sartaj Sahni. *Fundamentals of Computer Algorithms*. Rockville, Md.: Computer Science Press, 1978.

7. Program output is reformatted into two columns.

Sedgewick, Robert. *Algorithms*. 2d ed. Reading, Mass.: Addison-Wesley, 1988.

The following includes a less-formal treatment of the same topic:

Schneider, G. Michael, and Steven C. Bruell. *Advanced Programming and Problem Solving with Pascal*. 2d ed. New York: John Wiley & Sons, 1987.

The discussions of top-down design and documentation in the following reference are less formal, but informative.

Ledgard, Henry F., John F. Hueras, and Paul A. Nagin. *Pascal with Style: Programming Proverbs*. Rochelle Park, N.J.: Hayden, 1979.

The following book is a collection of essays on the practice of programming. Of particular interest at this point are essays on naming identifiers, effective commenting, and structured programming.

Ledgard, Henry F. *Professional Pascal*. Reading, Mass: Addison-Wesley, 1986.

The following text on Pascal programming contains many useful suggestions for developing algorithms. It is written in an enjoyable, informal style, without sacrificing accuracy.

Cooper, Doug, and Michael Clancy. *Oh! Pascal!* 2d ed. New York: W.W. Norton, 1985.

For more information on Lendvai's theories on Bartók, see the following:

Lendvai, Ernö. *Béla Bartók: An Analysis of his Music*. London: Kahn & Averill, 1971.

Other suggested readings (the *Spectrum* article summarizes the findings of the dissertation):

Brinkman, Alexander R. "Johann Sebastian Bach's *Orgelbüchlein*: A Computer-Assisted Analysis of the Influence of the Cantus Firmus on the Contrapuntal Voices." Ph.D. diss., University of Rochester, Eastman School of Music, 1978.

———. "The Melodic Process in Johann Sebastian Bach's *Orgelbüchlein*." *Music Theory Spectrum* 2 (1980): 46–73.

Forte, Allen. "Computer-Implemented Analysis of Musical Structure." In *Papers from the West Virginia Conference on Computer Applications in Music*, edited by Gerald Lefkoff, 29–42. Morgantown, W.Va.: West Virginia University Library, 1967.

Lewin, David. "The Intervallic Content of a Collection of Notes." *Journal of Music Theory* 4, no. 1 (1960): 98–101.

Morris, Robert. "On the Generation of Multiple Order-Function Twelve-Tone Rows." *Journal of Music Theory* 21, no. 2 (1977): 238-63.

Exercises

7.1. The data for each of the exercises in this set is any excerpt encoded in reciprocal duration code (section 6.3), with the integer 0 representing bar lines and 100 representing the double bar at the end of the excerpt. The code will begin with a bar line unless there is an anacrusis, and the final double bar is not preceded directly by a bar line. These problems were used for illustration in section 7.3. (a) As an exercise, you may wish to write solutions to these problems without referring to those shown above. Then compare your solutions to the ones in the chapter. (Write a Pascal program to do each of the exercises listed below, following the procedure described in this chapter. Make up some test data and run each program.) (b) Make up a short sample data set and step through some of the solutions given in this chapter.

1. Count the number of measures in the composition.

2. Count the number of rests.

3. Count the number of sixteenth notes and the number of eighth notes. Give a separate total for each. Do not count rests.

4. Count the number of times any simple duration (whole note through 32d note) occurs. Include notes and rests in each total. Print the results in a table.

5. As above, but count the total number of notes and calculate the percentage of the total for each duration, i.e., 23.2% are eighth notes, etc. Print the results in a table.

6. Calculate the number of measures that contain at least one sixteenth note.

7. As above, but print out the measure number for each measure that contains a sixteenth note. Do not print measure numbers for measures that do not contain sixteenth notes, or print any measure number more than one time. Control the number of measure numbers printed per line.

8. As above, but for each measure containing sixteenth notes, print the measure number and the number of sixteenth notes in the measure. Format the output in a table.

7.2. The data for this set of problems is any music excerpt encoded in continuous pitch code (see section 6.1.2). A bar line is encoded as the integer 0, the double bar at the end of the excerpt as 100, and a rest as 99. As in exercise 7.1, the code should begin with a bar line unless there is an anacrusis (you don't need to check, just treat everything up to the first bar line as measure 0). Design an algorithm, and then write a Pascal program that performs each of the following tasks. Test each program with sample input data.

1. Read an encoded composition in free format, and print it out with one measure per line. The bar line should be printed at the end of the line. This program simply reformats the data.

2. As above, but precede each printed line with the measure number and a colon. Example:

   1: 40 42 44 40 0 . . .

   An anacrusis will be considered measure 0.

3. Write a "filter" that prints the input data *without* bar lines and double bar. Print values for each measure on a separate line.

4. Write a program that translates each pitch code to a pitch class. Filter out rests and bar lines, but print the data for each measure on a separate line.

5. As above, but print only the standard octave number.

6. Print the octave and pitch class for each note on a separate line.

7. The excerpt is preceded (on a separate line) by a number indicating how the part is to be transposed. This transposition interval indicates the number of semitones and the direction of transposition:

   2 means transpose up a major second
   –3 means transpose down a minor third
   7 means transpose up a perfect fifth
   –1 means transpose down a minor second
   0 means transpose a perfect prime
   etc.

   Write a program that reads the transposition interval and then transposes and prints the part in the format used in exercise 1 above. Make sure that only notes are transposed, not bar lines or rests!

8. Print out the sequence of intervals in the part. Negative numbers indicate descending intervals, and positive numbers indicate ascending intervals. Example: The sequence of notes 48 50 52 48 represents the melodic intervals 2 2 –4. Print the intervals for each measure on a separate line. Make sure that you account for intervals across bar lines and rests. Do not print bar lines and double bars (0 indicates the interval between repeated notes). Program Fibonacci should suggest a useful technique for solving this problem.

9. Run the above program using an excerpt encoded in continuous name code (section 6.1.4). Are the generic intervals correct according to the explanation given in section 6.1.4?

10. Redesign exercise 8 explicitly for continuous name code. Adjust the output so that the intervals printed are mnemonic (1 for primes, 2 for seconds, 3 for thirds, etc.). Print a plus sign '+' before each ascending interval and minus '–' before each descending interval (primes will be considered ascending). Take care that you make the proper adjustment for descending intervals; i.e., for the input 28 29 27 28 25 the printed contour should be +2 –3 +2 –4.

7.3. Interpreting Duration Codes. This exercise uses reciprocal duration code (section 6.3) with bar lines encoded as 0, the end of the excerpt as 100, and rests as negative numbers. In addition, meter signatures will be encoded as two integers placed on the line preceding the first line of encoded music. The first integer will indicate the number of beats in the measure, and the second the type of note that gets one beat. Example: 4 4 means that there are four quarter-note beats in a measure; 3 2 means that there are three half-note beats in a measure; 6 8 means that there are six eighth-note beats in the measure. Note that this corresponds exactly to simple meter signatures.

Each exercise involves interpreting reciprocal duration code, i.e., mapping each duration code into the number of beats it represents considering the meter signature, and then calculating the total number of beats in each measure. You will have to find an arithmetic means of mapping each code into the number of beats it represents (remember that this will depend on the meter signature: a quarter note does not represent the same number of beats in 4/4 meter as it does in 3/8 or 4/2). An alternate approach depends on the observation that, with each duration treated as its fractional value, the sum of the fractional values in a measure must be equal to the fractional value of the meter signature. This should be obvious if you think of the numeric "meaning" of meter signatures: 4/4 means there are 4 quarter notes in a measure (4 × 1/4); 6/8 means that there are 6 eighths (6 × 1/8) or 2 dotted quarters (2 × 3/8); etc.

Warm-up: Find an arithmetic mapping for the following, assuming that you have read the meter signature as two separate numbers (*beats* and *beatnote*), as specified above:

a) Convert duration codes to beats directly, using the code representing the beat note.

b) Convert duration codes to real numbers representing their fractional value (4 = 1/4 = 0.25).

c) How can this fractional value be converted to beats? Assume that *beatnote* represents the reciprocal duration code for the note getting a full beat.

Write a Pascal program that accomplishes each of the following tasks. Be sure that you understand the encoding scheme before you begin work. Then carefully define the problem, and develop and refine an algorithm before encoding in Pascal. Write your program on paper away from the terminal, and step through it to prove that it works before you enter your Pascal code and data and run the program. Do the problems in order and make each one run successfully before doing the next. Devise several sets of input data that test all possible conditions in your programs. Make sure that your program works with different meter signatures.

1. Using the code specified above, write a Pascal program that does the following: (a) reads the meter signature, storing the number of beats and the beat note in appropriately named variables; (b) prints a table showing the meter (number of beats per measure and code for *beatnote*) and, for each measure, the measure number and number of beats (use precision of three decimal places). Hints: (1) Your solution should be sufficiently general that it will work correctly with any undotted code as the beat note. (2) You will have to calculate the total number of beats in each measure. Note that the calculated number of beats in a measure and the durations in beats will be *real* numbers. (What would be the problems in using integer values for this calculation?)

2. Write a program that checks the number of beats in each measure and prints out the measure number for each measure that does not contain the correct number of beats. For this program assume that the composition will not have an anacrusis (so the code must begin with the encoded bar line). Thus if the first code after the meter signature is not a bar line, an appropriate message should be printed (however, you should still be able to continue processing the rest of the piece). Hint: You will have to compare the actual number of beats in each measure to the correct number of beats. Recall that it is poor programming to compare two real numbers for equality directly. Instead, consider the numbers equal if they are "close enough," that is, within some predefined tolerance:

   if *abs*(*r1* – *r2*) <= *epsilon*
   then <the numbers are considered equal>

   or, conversely:

   if *abs*(*r1* – *r2*) > *epsilon*
   then <the values are not considered equal>

   where epsilon is a predefined program constant (say 0.00001).

3. Write another (definitive) version of the above program that allows an anacrusis. Remember that if there is an anacrusis, then the durations in the first and last measures should add up to a complete measure. Your program should work correctly with any simple meter signature (consider that a signature like 6/8 represents 6 eighth-note beats to the measure).

8| Eof, Eoln, and Input↑

In most of the programs that we have seen so far, the data has been terminated by some special value such as 0 or 100. This is not always convenient, and it is certainly not desirable for all types of programs and input data sets. For example, the programs that we have designed to deal with simple music encoding schemes depend on the programmer-defined constant *doublebar* to terminate the data. What if we wish to process more than one piece or several instrumental parts of one composition in one set of input data? We could invent yet another delimiter, say 1000, to terminate the data, and still use *doublebar* to terminate individual parts within that data. Fortunately that is not necessary, since the input file already has delimiters that we have not been using—end-of-line and end-of-file—and Pascal provides boolean functions to test for these. We did not introduce these functions earlier because using them effectively requires a thorough understanding of the structure of the input and output files and the use of techniques that would have complicated relatively simple programs. This chapter explains the structure of a *textfile* and the use of *eof*, *eoln*, and *input*↑.

8.1 The Structure of a Textfile

The standard files *input* and *output* are members of a type called *textfile*; they are implicitly declared as follows:

```
var
  input, output : text;
```

Textfiles consist of character data, i.e, the only unit that can be read or written directly is a single character.[1] The data is sequential, that is, the characters can only be accessed (read or written) in order. Thus we can think of a textfile as a continuous stream of characters. These characters are grouped into units called lines, each of which is terminated by a special character called the *newline* character (or end-of-line mark).

This structure is not difficult to envision, although you cannot see the special characters when a file is printed. The space character can only be seen as the absence of some other printing character: it is not printed, but rather causes the output device to

1. As we saw in chapter 4, procedures *read* and *write* convert data from this external form to other internal formats. In chapter 9 we will write a procedure to simulate the *read* procedure for integers.

skip one space to the right. In a similar manner, the newline character is expanded by the operating system or output device to the combination of a line-feed character and a carriage return, which cause the next character to be printed on the beginning of the next line of the output device. A file that when printed appears thus:

```
Line one
Line two
Line three
```

actually contains the sequence of characters

```
Line▯one₦Line▯two₦Line▯three₦Ɇ
```

So that we can see exactly which control characters are present, we use '▯' to represent the blank character and '₦' to represent the newline character. The symbol 'Ɇ' represents the end of the file, i.e., the position just past the last character in the file. The end-of-file mark is never typed into a disk file; it is supplied by the operating system when the file is written to the disk. When typing data directly to a program from your computer terminal, you signal end-of-file by typing <control-D>. (The end-of-file signal may vary from system to system.)

8.2 How Pascal Deals with Textfiles

For each input file *f*, Pascal provides a special *buffer variable* called *f*↑. The value of this variable is the next character to be read from the file *f*. Thus the buffer variable provides us with a "window" into the input buffer. The buffer variable for file *input* is called *input*↑. When the file is opened for reading, *input*↑ has as its value the first character in the input file. Data can be read directly by assigning the value of *input*↑ to a character variable. The buffer variable is advanced to the next character in the buffer by calling the primitive function *get(f)*, where *f* is the name of the file. A character can be read and assigned to the character variable *c* by the two statements:

```
c := input↑;          { assign character from buffer to c }
get(input);           { advance buffer variable           }
```

These statements are equivalent to the procedure call

```
read(c)
```

In either case, we can envision the input buffer before and after the first character is read, as shown in figure 8.1. The important thing to remember is that after each character is read, *input*↑ is advanced to the next character in the input file; thus it always points to the character after the last one that was processed.

Before reading a number, *read* skips over any blanks in the buffer. The equivalent operation in Pascal is:[2]

```
while input↑ = ' ' do
    get(input);
```

The effect is to leave *input*↑ where it is if its value is not a blank, otherwise to

2. This loop is simplified for the present discussion; more details will be given presently.

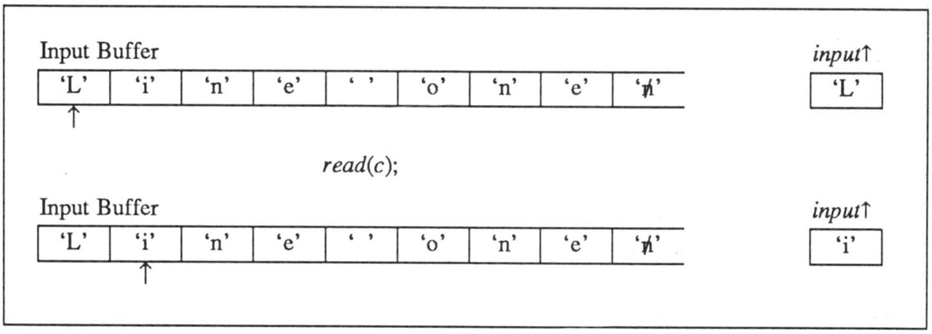

Figure 8.1. The Input Buffer Before and After Reading the First Character

advance *input*↑ to the next nonblank character. This skips newline characters as well, since Pascal treats the newline character as a blank except when explicitly testing for end-of-line using function *eoln*.

Figure 8.2 illustrates the input buffer while reading integers. The statement

```
read(i)
```

where *i* is an integer variable, causes *input*↑ to be moved to '2', the first nonblank character. Then the numeric values are read and converted to the integer 25, which is stored in the memory location referenced by *i*. *Input*↑ is left at the first nonnumeric character, in this case the blank character (' '). The statement

```
read(x)
```

where *x* is real, moves *input*↑ past the blank characters, interprets the next three characters '1.7' as the real number 1.7, stores this number in variable *x*, and leaves *input*↑ at the newline character following the number. Note that the value of *input*↑ is the blank character when the buffer variable is positioned at a newline character.

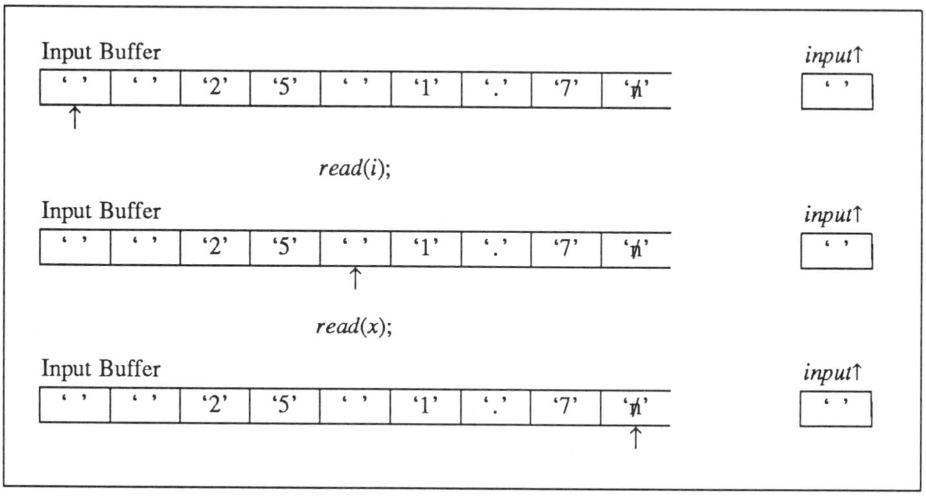

Figure 8.2. The Input Buffer While Reading Numbers

In practice, the buffer length is finite and the buffer is refilled at some point. When reading input from the terminal, the operating system sends one line at a time to Pascal's input buffer. This is why it is possible to backspace to correct an input error until you type <return>. However, we don't really have to be concerned with this, since *input*↑ will always be positioned after the last character read.

The value of *input*↑ is not always assigned to another variable, since it can be used directly: *input*↑ can appear in an expression just like any other character variable, literal, or constant. For example, after skipping past blanks, we could test for a '/', perhaps symbolizing a bar line, by the statement:

```
if input↑ = '/'
  then ...
```

or, better,

```
if input↑ = barline
  then ...
```

where *barline* has been assigned the value '/' in a constant declaration.

8.3 End-of-File and End-of-Line

Pascal provides boolean functions to test for the end-of-line and end-of-file. These functions are called *eoln* and *eof*. Either can take a file name as an argument, but if this is omitted, file *input* is assumed. Thus *eof* means *eof(input)*, and *eoln* means *eoln(input)*. Although these functions often cause difficulties for newcomers to Pascal, they are not difficult once a few details are understood. The function *eoln* returns *true* if *input*↑ is positioned at a newline character in the buffer. Conceptually, *eof* is *true* when *input*↑ is positioned just after the last character in the file; however, it is important to remember that, according to the International Standards Organization (ISO) Pascal standard, *input*↑ is undefined at the end-of-file. In the first diagram in figure 8.3 *eoln* is *true*, the value of *input*↑ is the blank character, and *eof* is *false*. After advancing *input*↑ one more time [via *get*(*input*) or *read*(*c*)], *eoln* is *false*, *input*↑ is undefined, and *eof* is *true*. Thus *eoln* and *eof* cannot be true at the same time:

1. When *eoln* is *true*, *eof* is *false*, and the value of *input*↑ is ' '
2. When *eof* is *true*, *eoln* is *false*, and *input*↑ is undefined

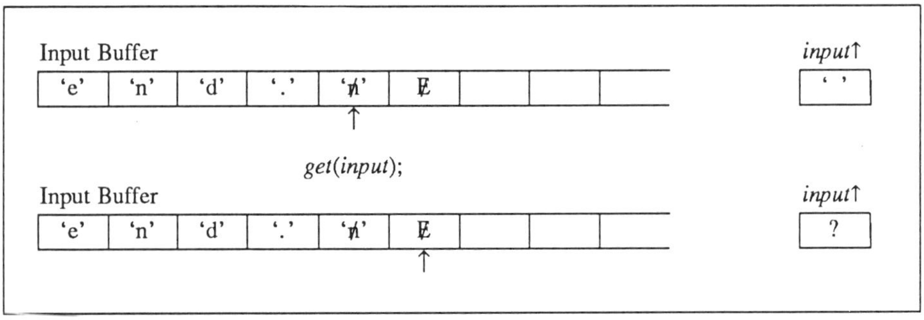

Figure 8.3. The Input Buffer at End-of-Line and End-of-File

Eoln and *eof* are quite easy to use when character data is read, since every character in the input file is examined explicitly. Consider a program that makes a copy of a file. The program reads an input file and copies it exactly to its standard output file. The basic algorithm is shown below:

```
while not at end of input file do
  begin { copy line }
    while not at end of input line do
      begin
        copy a character from input to output file
      end;
    skip the newline character in input file;
    write a newline character into output file
  end  { copy line }
```

It is necessary to check for, read, and write the newline characters explicitly because Pascal treats the newline character as a blank; without this special treatment the entire file would be copied to a single line. Programs 8.1 and 8.2 both implement this algorithm. *Copy1* actually reads each input character and then writes it to the output file. *Copy2* doesn't store the character, it just writes its value (obtained from *input*↑). *Copy2* must explicitly advance *input*↑ after each character is read; otherwise the program would loop, writing the first character again and again. Both programs must use *readln* or *get*(*input*) to move *input*↑ past the newline mark; otherwise, after the end of the first line the program would loop endlessly, since the boolean expression at the top of the *eoln* loop would always return *false*, and the expression at the top of the *eof* loop always *true*. Note that the values of *eof* and *eoln* are defined before reading begins—thus one must *not* read prior to the **while**. In this sense, testing for end-of-file is different from testing for a numeric terminal value.

```
program copy1(input, output);
  var
    c : char;                         { for reading characters     }
  begin { main }
    while not eof do
      begin { copy a line }
        while not eoln do
          begin { copy a character }
            read(c);
            write(c)
          end;  { copy a character }
        readln;                       { skip newline char in input }
        writeln                       { put newline char in output }
      end   { copy a line }
  end. { main }
```

Program 8.1. *Copy1*

```
program copy2(input, output);
  begin { main }
    while not eof do
      begin { copy a line }
        while not eoln do
          begin { copy a character }
            write(input↑);
            get(input)                    { advance input↑          }
          end;  { copy a character }
        readln;                           { skip newline in input  }
        writeln                           { put newline in output  }
      end   { copy a line }
  end.  { main }
```

Program 8.2. *Copy2*

8.3.1 Testing for End-of-File (*eof*)

By now you should be beginning to understand why using *eof* can be tricky. *Eof* is not necessarily true when you have read the last numeric value. The function only determines whether or not there are any more characters in the file before the end-of-file.

The program shown below is intended to sum the values in the input file. On most systems it will result in a run-time error:

```
program add(input, output);             { WRONG }
  var
    x, sum : real;
  begin { main }
    sum := 0.0;
    while not eof do
      begin
        read(x);
        sum := sum + x
      end;
    writeln('sum = ', sum:4)
  end.  { main }
```

The reason is that the final value for *x* is followed by a newline character, and therefore the end-of-file is not detected in time (figure 8.4). After the last number is read, *eof* is *false* (since *input*↑ is positioned at the newline character), so the body of the

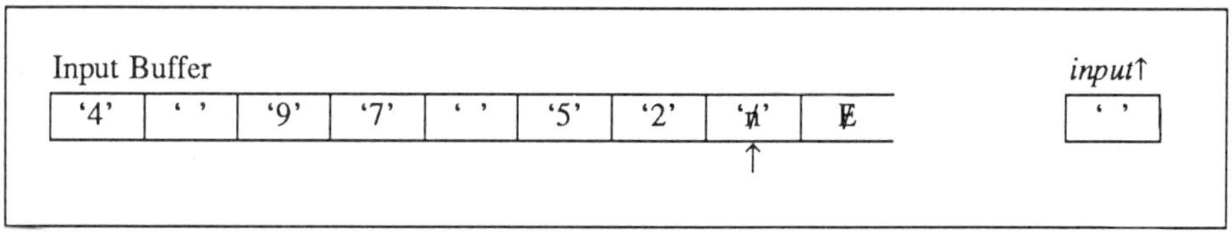

Figure 8.4. End-of-File is *false* at End-of-Line

loop is executed again. This time *read*(*x*) skips over blanks (including the newline character) and encounters the end-of-file. At this point the usual error message is something like "attempt to read past end-of-file on integer read."

A solution that works in most cases is to use *readln*, as in the following program:

```
program testchr(input, output);
  var
    n : integer;
  begin { main }
    while not eof do
      begin
        readln(n);                      { read integer n       }
        writeln(chr(n))                 { nth char in char set }
      end
  end.  { main }
```

This is tolerable for simple programs like the one above, which tests a function. However, this solution severely limits the format of the input data (above, all numbers after the first on a line are lost), and the solution is still not general enough: the program will fail if there are blank lines after the final input value, since *readln* positions *input*↑ directly after the first newline character and *eof* is *false* (figure 8.5).

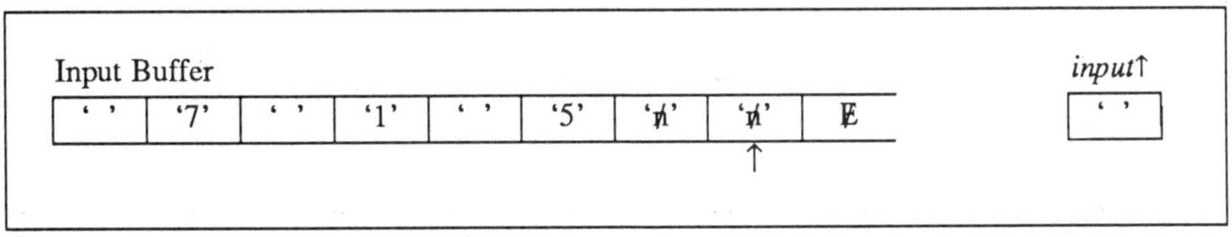

Figure 8.5. The Input Buffer after one *readln*

Why wasn't Pascal designed so that it skips over blanks before checking for the end-of-file? The reason, presumably, is that blanks are legal as character data and may have significance in some instances. The best solution, for systems that conform to the ISO standard, is to explicitly skip over blanks and newline characters. This is accomplished by the loop shown below. The boolean variable *done* ensures that *input*↑ is not referenced after the end-of-file is reached. The loop terminates if the end-of-file has been reached, or if the current character in the buffer is not a blank; otherwise the blank is skipped:

```
done := false;
repeat
  if eof
    then done := true
  else if input↑ = ' '
    then get(input)
  else done := true
until done
```

This loop should be placed within the *eof* loop, after the value has been read. A useful convention is to include it just before the **end**, thus ensuring that blanks and newline characters will be skipped before the **while** rechecks for end-of-file:

```
program addfile(input, output);          { correct version }
  var
    x, sum : integer;
  begin { main }
    sum := 0;
    while not eof do
      begin
        read(x);
        sum := sum + x;

        done := false;
        repeat
          if eof
            then done := true
          else if input↑ = ' '
            then get(input)
          else done := true
        until done
      end;

    writeln('sum = ', sum)
  end.  { main }
```

The program shown above is impervious to variations in input format: any number of values may occur on each input line, so long as they are all of the appropriate type and they are separated by blank and/or newline characters. This technique is useful in any program that needs to check for end-of-file, and whenever it is necessary to find the next nonblank character. A large program may use it many times. For these reasons, and because it will be used in many different programs, the loop is often implemented as a procedure as shown in program 8.3. The procedure, which is called *skipblanks*, executes the **repeat** loop shown above. It is invoked by simply using its name in a Pascal statement. Thus the statement

```
skipblanks
```

in the main block is equivalent to the loop

```
done := false;
repeat
  if eof
    then done := true
  else if input↑ = ' '
    then get(input)
  else done := true
until done
```

You will probably want to make a file called *skipblanks* that contains this procedure, and to learn how to copy it into any program that needs to call the procedure. Note that making *skipblanks* into a separate procedure does not make the program shorter. However, it does segregate this operation, and it simplifies the *eof* loop. We can now think in terms of process; the details of implementation have already been worked out. (Procedures and functions will be introduced formally in the next chapter.)

```
(**********************       Program Average       **********************)
(* This version of program average uses eof to terminate the data.  The  *)
(* program illustrates the use of procedure skipblanks to ensure detec-  *)
(* tion of the end-of-file condition.                                    *)
(*************************************************************************)
program average(input, output);
  var
    n   : integer;                          { the number of values read }
    x   : real;                             { for reading each value    }
    sum : real;                             { sum of values read        }
(**********************        skipblanks        *************************)
(* Skips over blanks and newline characters in the input file.           *)
(*************************************************************************)
  procedure skipblanks;
    var
      done : boolean;
    begin
      done := false;
      repeat
        if eof
          then done := true
        else if input↑ = ' '
          then get(input)
        else done := true
      until done
    end;

  begin { main }
    sum := 0.0;                             { initialize sum and n      }
    n := 0;

    while not eof do
      begin { count and add input values }
        n := n + 1;
        read(x);
        sum := sum + x;
        skipblanks
      end; { count and add input values }

    writeln('average = ', sum / n:6:2)
  end. { main }
```

Program 8.3. *Average*

Input:

```
87.5 89.1 99.0 88.4 56.5 67.2 55.7
100.0 99.3 87.3 93.5
```

Output:

```
average =  83.95
```

Program 8.3. Sample Input and Output

Again, you may wonder, if *skipblanks* is so useful, why isn't it included as a standard (built-in) procedure like *read* and *write*? To do so would be to cast it in concrete, as it were. Programs often require different varieties of skips, which can be implemented easily by modifying the procedure shown above. As an example, the version shown below moves *input*↑ past blanks (and newline characters), tabs, and commas:

```
procedure skipblanks;
  var
    done : boolean;
  begin
    done := false;
    repeat
      if eof
        then done := true
      else if input↑ in [' ', chr(9), ',']
        then get(input)
      else done := true
    until done
  end;
```

8.3.2 Testing for End-of-Line (*eoln*)

Testing for end-of-line is not as common as testing for end-of-file, but it is often useful, especially when each set of input values can conveniently fit on a single line. In this case the newline character can be an extremely useful delimiter. The program listed below is intended to sum the values on each line; however, it does not work. Can you figure out why?

```
program addlines(input, output);          { WRONG }
  var
    m : integer;                 { input value              }
    sum : integer;               { sum of values on a line  }
  begin { main }
    while not eof do
      begin { process file }
        sum := 0;
        while not eoln do
          begin { add integers on line }
            read(m);
            sum := sum + m
          end;  { add integers on line }
        writeln('sum =', sum:4)
      end   { process file }
  end.  { main }
```

The first problem with the above program is that we cannot guarantee that the newline character will immediately follow the last number on the line. The most frequent offenders are trailing blanks, i.e., blanks after the last useful data on a line. In figure 8.6, the last value on the line has been read, leaving *input*↑ to the right of the last numeric value. If one or more blank characters precede the end-of-line mark, *eoln* will return *false*. The solution is similar to that for testing for end-of-file: we

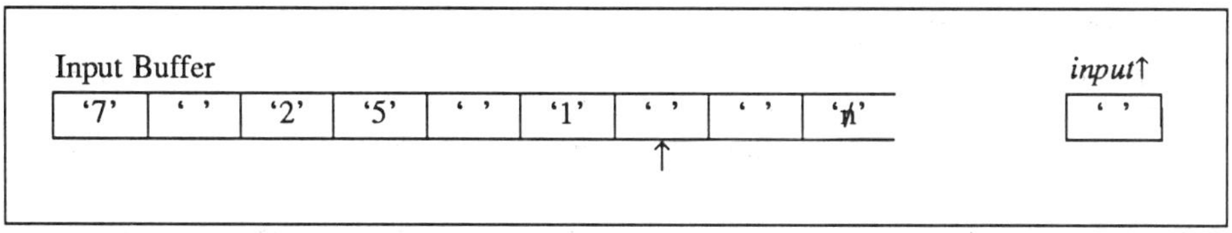

Figure 8.6. Trailing Blanks May Cause *eoln* to Fail

need to skip over any blanks between the last data item and the newline character. The following loop, inserted just before the **end** in the *eoln* loop, will correct this problem:

```
while (input↑ = ' ') and not eoln do
  get(input)
```

This will position *input↑* at the newline character (figure 8.7). However, the "corrected" version of the program still won't work as advertised. Can you find the second error?

```
program addln2(input, output);                    { STILL WRONG!}
  var
    m : integer;                                  { input value }
    sum : integer;                                { sum of line }
  begin { main }
    while not eof do
      begin { process file }
        sum := 0;
        while not eoln do
          begin { add values on line }
            read(m);
            sum := sum + m;
            while (input↑ = ' ') and not eoln do
              get(input)                          { skip blanks }
          end; { add values on line }
        writeln('sum =', sum:4)
      end   { process file }
  end. { main }
```

After each number is read, the innermost **while** loop skips over any blanks, so after processing the last value on the line, *eoln* is *true*, the *eoln* loop terminates, and the value of *sum* is printed. Now the boolean expression in the **while not** *eof* loop is tested again. Since *input↑* is still positioned at the newline character, *eof* is *false*, and

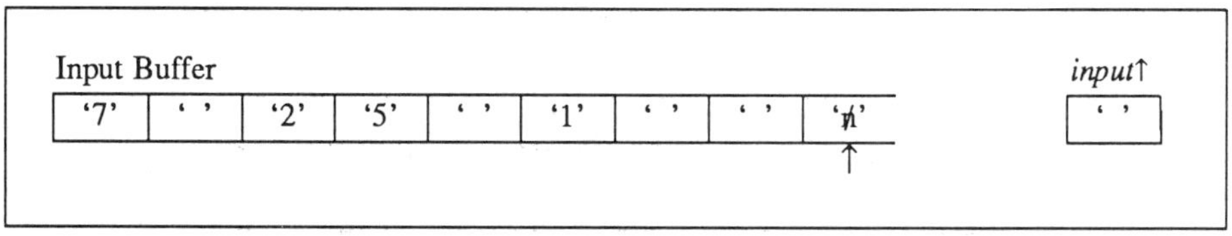

Figure 8.7. The Input Buffer After Skipping Trailing Blanks

not *eof* is *true*, so the outer loop executes again. *Sum* is reinitialized to 0, but *input*↑ is still positioned at the newline character; i.e., **not** *eoln* is *false*, so the inner loop will not execute. The program is in an endless loop, and will print 'sum = 0' over and over until terminated forcibly.[3] As in programs *copy1* and *copy2* shown earlier, the program requires a *readln* to get past the newline character at the end of the line. The correct solution:

```
program addln3(input, output);              { CORRECT VERSION    }
  var
    m : integer;                            { input value        }
    sum : integer;                          { line sum           }
  begin { main }
    while not eof do
      begin { process file }
        sum := 0;
        while not eoln do
          begin { add line }
            read(m);
            sum := sum + m;
            while (input↑ = ' ') and not eoln do
              get(input)                    { skip blanks        }
          end; { add line }
        readln;                             { skip newline char  }
        writeln('sum =', sum:4)
      end   { process file }
  end.  { main }
```

Step through the above programs until you are sure that you understand both the errors and the solutions.

Note that the above solution could *still* fail if extra newline characters and/or blanks followed by newline characters follow the last real data line. To be absolutely safe, we can use both blank-skipping procedures, as in program 8.4, which averages the values on each input line. Here procedure *skipln* skips blanks up to a newline character, and *skipf* skips blank and newline characters up to the end-of-file.

Note that procedure *skipln* can use a simple **while** loop:

```
procedure skipln;
  begin
    while (input↑ = ' ') and not eoln do
      get(input)
  end;
```

This is possible because the test for *eoln* and (*input*↑ = ' ') are compatible, i.e., *input*↑ is defined at the end of the line. A similar loop should not be used for skipping blanks to the end-of-file, since *input*↑ is undefined when *eof* is *true*. Although some Pascal systems permit this construction, it is technically wrong and does cause problems with some compilers. Thus the best course is to use the slightly more complex form of *skipblanks* shown earlier for skipping blanks to the end-of-file.

3. On many systems a looping program can be terminated by typing the interrupt signal <control-C>.

```
(***********************      Program Average2      ***********************)
(* Averages numbers on each line of the input file.  Procedures skipln   *)
(* and skipf move input↑ past blanks to eoln and eof respectively.        *)
(*************************************************************************)
program average2(input, output);                      { correct version }
  var
    x   : real;                                    { input value            }
    sum : real;                                    { sum of values on a line }
    n   : integer;                                 { number of values on line }

(***********************          skipln          ***********************)
(* Skips blanks to first nonblank character or end-of-line.              *)
(*************************************************************************)
  procedure skipln;
    begin
      while (input↑ = ' ') and not eoln do
        get(input)
    end;

(***********************          skipf           ***********************)
(* Skips blanks to first nonblank character or end-of-file.              *)
(*************************************************************************)
  procedure skipf;
    var
      done : boolean;
    begin
      done := false;
      repeat
        if eof
          then done := true
        else if input↑ = ' '
          then get(input)
        else done := true
      until done
    end;  { skipf }

  begin { main }
    while not eof do
      begin { process file }
        n   := 0;                                  { init counter and sum }
        sum := 0.0;
        while not eoln do
          begin { add line }
            n := n + 1;
            read(x);                               { read nth value       }
            sum := sum + x;                        { add to sum           }
            skipln                                 { skip blanks to eoln  }
          end;  { add line }
        readln;                                    { skip newline char    }
        writeln(sum / n:9:2);                      { print average        }
        skipf                                      { skip blanks to eof   }
      end   { process file }
  end.  { main }
```

Program 8.4. *Average2*

Input:

```
84.4 89.0 93.2 86.3 92.0 89.3 87.1 89 94
92.1 94.6 90.4 91.9 89.6 96.2 91.4 96.3
77.1 76 82 73.2 80.5 75 80 83 50.5
```

Output

```
89.37
92.81
75.26
```

Program 8.4. Sample Input and Output

8.3.3 *Eof* and Prompting

Interactive programs (those that take input directly from the user's terminal) frequently prompt users when input data is expected. For example, in the above program, the prompt might be

```
Type data:
```

This line could be generated by the statement

```
write('Type data: ')
```

appropriately placed in the program. The problem is that appropriate placement of the prompt is not intuitive when using *eof* to structure loops. The novice programmer usually first tries placing the prompt inside the *eof* loop, as in the following program that exercises the *ord* function:

```
{ Incorrect Placement of Prompt }

program testord1(input, output);
  var
    c : char;                           { for reading       }
  begin { main }
    while not eof do
      begin
        write('Type a char:  ');        { prompt            }
        readln(c);                      { read character    }
        writeln(ord(c))                 { print its ordinal }
      end                               {   position        }
  end. { main }
```

The expectation is that, while not at end-of-file, the program will write a prompt, read a character, and print the ordinal position of that character in the character set. Unfortunately, the program cannot evaluate the function *eof* until the input buffer is initialized with a line of input data. This will not occur until the user types <return>. The user is waiting for a prompt, and the program is waiting for data so it can determine whether or not it should prompt the user. This would work if the program were reading from a disk file instead of from the user's terminal, but then, of course, the prompt would not be necessary. The solution is simple once you understand the problem. The user must be told to type data *before* the program tests for end-of-file.

The prompt is placed before the *eof* loop (for the first iteration) and at the bottom of the loop (for each successive iteration):

```
            { Correct Placement of Prompt }

program testord2(input, output);
  var
    c : char;                              { for reading         }
  begin { main }
    write('Type a char: ');                { prompt              }
    while not eof do
      begin
        readln(c);                         { read character      }
        writeln(ord(c));                   { print ord(char)     }
        write('Type a char: ')             { prompt              }
      end
  end. { main }
```

Now the user is prompted before the program tests for end-of-file. If any character is typed followed by <return>, the program executes the body of the loop. If the user types the end-of-file signal, the loop terminates normally.

8.4 Some Final Observations on *eof* and *eoln*

You will note that all of the examples in this chapter have used *eof* and *eoln* in **while** loops, rather than in **repeat** loops. There is a good reason for this. Recall that **repeat** always executes its body at least one time. It is usually (one is tempted to say always here) appropriate to take into account the possibility that *eof* loops should not execute even once, since if *input↑* is at the end-of-file, any attempt to read will cause a run-time error. A well-written program should not terminate abnormally if presented with an empty input file. Compare the two short programs listed below:

```
program sum1(input, output);
  var
    m, sum : integer;
  begin { main }
    sum := 0;
    while not eof do
      begin
        readln(m);
        sum := sum + m
      end;
    writeln('sum = ', sum)
  end.  { main }
```

```
program sum2(input, output);
  var
    m, sum : integer;
  begin { main }
    sum := 0;
    repeat
      readln(m);
      sum := sum + m
    until eof
    writeln('sum = ', sum)
  end.  { main }
```

Each program calculates the sum of the values in the input file (typed one number per line). However, if the file is empty (or the interactive user types the end-of-file signal before any data), then the program on the left prints the sum as 0, while on many systems the program on the right terminates abnormally with a run-time error when it attempts to read.[4] Therefore the solution on the left is a better solution.

4. Some Pascal compilers (Berkeley Pascal is an example) are designed so that the first attempt to read at the end-of-file returns 0, and the next attempt causes an error. You cannot count on this.

Remember that it is usually inappropriate to read before testing for end-of-file, which accounts for the difference in usage when compared to the loops we studied in chapter 5 that used a numeric terminal value:

```
{ loop with eof }                  { loop with numeric terminator }

  while not eof do           |      read(n);
    begin                    |      while n <> endvalue do
      read(n);               |        begin
      sum := sum + n;        |          sum := sum + n;
      skipblanks             |          read(n)
    end;                     |        end;
  writeln(sum)               |      writeln(sum)
```

Although the outward form appears different, the usage is totally consistent. In each case the conditions necessary to evaluate the boolean expression are defined before the expression is tested, and in each case the body of the loop ensures that the terminal condition can eventually become *true*. Learn to use both idioms correctly.

Actually, this seeming inconsistency in format can be a real advantage when one is expanding a simple program to handle multiple sets of data. Consider the program below, which reformats a piece encoded in reciprocal duration code (see section 6.3) with one measure per line, printed with measure numbers and without bar lines:

```
program format1(input, output);
  const
    barline = 0;                          { code for bar line    }
    doublebar = 100;                      { code for double bar  }
  var
    code    : integer;                    { duration, bar line,  }
                                          { or double bar        }
    measure : integer;                    { measure number       }
  begin { main }
    measure := 0;                                                  |
    repeat                                                         |
      write(measure:2, ':  ');                                     |
      read(code);                                                  |
      while (code <> barline) and (code <> doublebar) do           |
        begin { process measure }                                  |
          write(code:4);                                           |
          read(code)                                               |
        end;  { process measure }                                  |
      writeln;        { newline char at end of measure }           |
      measure := measure + 1                                       |
    until code = doublebar                                         |
  end.  { main }
```

If we wish to rewrite this program so that it will work correctly with many encoded instrumental parts, each terminated by a double bar, the body of the main procedure can be nested within an *eof* loop. Program 8.5 shows this expanded version, with the addition of a counter to keep track of the part number and *skipblanks* to ensure detection of the end-of-file. The portion marked '|' is taken without change from the simpler version of the program shown above.

```
(***********************        Program Format2       ***********************)
(* Expansion of program format1.  Program processes any number of parts, *)
(* each headed by ordinal number of part.                                   *)
(***************************************************************************)
program format2(input, output);
  const
    barline = 0;                          { code for bar line              }
    doublebar = 100;                      { code for double bar            }

  var
    code       : integer;                 { duration, bar line or dbl bar  }
    partnumber : integer;                 { ordinal number of part         }
    measure    : integer;                 { measure number                 }

  procedure skipblanks;
    var
      done : boolean;
    begin
      done := false;
      repeat
        if eof
          then done := true
        else if input↑ = ' '
          then get(input)
        else done := true
      until done
    end;

  begin { main }
    partnumber := 0;     { init part number }
    while not eof do
      begin { process file }
        partnumber := partnumber + 1;
        writeln;
        writeln('part ', partnumber:1);

        measure := 0;                                             |
        repeat                                                    |
          write(measure:2, ':  ');                                |
          read(code);                                             |
          while (code <> barline) and (code <> doublebar) do     |
            begin { process measure }                             |
              write(code:4);                                      |
              read(code)                                          |
            end;  { process measure }                             |
          writeln;       { newline char at end of measure }       |
          measure := measure + 1                                  |
        until code = doublebar                                    |

        skipblanks
      end  { process file }
  end.  { main }
```

Program 8.5. *Format2*

Input:

```
4 0 4 4 4 4 0 4 4 8 8 4 0 4 4 4 8
8 0 2 4 4 0 4 4 4 8 8 0 4 4 4 4 0
2 4 4 0 2 -4 100
4 0 8 8 4 4 4 0 4 4 4 4 0 8 8 4 4
4 0 4 4 4 8 8 0 8 8 4 4 4 0 8 8 4
8 8 8 8 0 8 16 16 4 4 4 0 2 -4 100
-4 0 2 4 4 0 2 2 0 2 -2 0 4 4 4 4
0 2 2 0 2 -2 0 2 2 0 2 -4 100
```

Output:

```
part 1
0:       4
1:       4   4   4   4
2:       4   4   8   8   4
3:       4   4   4   8   8
4:       2   4   4
5:       4   4   4   8   8
6:       4   4   4   4
7:       2   4   4
8:       2  -4

part 2
0:       4
1:       8   8   4   4   4
2:       4   4   4   4
3:       8   8   4   4   4
4:       4   4   4   8   8
5:       8   8   4   4   4
6:       8   8   4   8   8   8   8
7:       8  16  16   4   4   4
8:       2  -4

part 3
0:      -4
1:       2   4   4
2:       2   2
3:       2  -2
4:       4   4   4   4
5:       2   2
6:       2  -2
7:       2   2
8:       2  -4
```

Program 8.5. Sample Input and Output

8.5 Using *input↑*

We have already seen that the buffer variable, *input↑*, allows us to examine the "current" character in the buffer, and that we can advance the buffer variable to the next character by invoking *get(input)*. The first step in interpreting any type of code, whether a computer program, English text, or a music code, is to parse the code into logical units called *tokens*. The tokens in a Pascal program are identifiers, keywords, and combinations of special characters representing separators (e.g., ':=' '+' '–' '*' '/'); the tokens in a natural language are words and punctuation.

Program 8.6 uses these devices to parse a DARMS[5] file into individual tokens representing notes, bar lines, key signatures, meter signatures, etc. This simple version of the parser treats blanks and parentheses as token delimiters.[6] Each token consists of a string of nonblank characters terminated by a space or a parenthesis (beginning or end of beam). Each token is printed on a separate line; in addition, if the current delimiter is a left or right parenthesis, it is printed on a separate line. Comments, beginning with 'k' and ending with '$', are skipped. The algorithm in pseudo code follows:

```
skip blanks;

while not eof do
  begin
    if current character is start of comment
      then skip to end of comment
    else if current character is a parenthesis
      then print it
    else
      while current character is not blank or parenthesis do
        begin
          print current character;
          get next character
        end;

    skipblanks
  end.
```

The program is shown on the following page.

5. DARMS code is summarized in section 6.5.

6. Note that this version will not correctly parse tokens that include parentheses, such as parenthesized dynamic marks.

```
(***********************   Program DARMSparser   ***********************)
(* Parses DARMS code into key and meter signatures, bar lines, etc.     *)
(**********************************************************************)
program DARMSparser (input, output);
  const
    blankchar    = ' ';
    leftparen    = '(';
    rightparen   = ')';
    startcomment = 'k';
    endcomment   = '$';

  procedure skipblanks;           { skips blanks to nonblank char or eof }
    var
      done : boolean;
    begin
      done := false;
      repeat
        if eof
          then done := true
        else if input↑ = ' '
          then get(input)
        else done := true
      until done
    end;

  begin { main }
    skipblanks;
    while not eof do
      begin
       if input↑ = startcomment                   { skip comment        }
         then
           begin
             while input↑ <> endcomment do
               get(input);
             get(input)                            { discard end comment }
           end
        else if input↑ in [leftparen, rightparen]  { parentheses         }
          then
            begin
              writeln(input↑);
              get(input)
            end
        else                                       { any other token     }
          begin
            while not (input↑ in [blankchar, leftparen, rightparen]) do
              begin
                write(input↑);
                get(input)
              end;
            writeln
          end;
        skipblanks
      end
  end. { main }
```

Program 8.6. *DARMSparser*

Input:

```
k************************************$
k* Bartok 4th Quartet, mm 1-13      *$
k************************************$

i1 !g !m4:4 rq re 9e_<,vf 9#q._ 7#e_ /
i2 !g !m4:4 1hj,vf e 1-e_ 2qj /
i3 !m4:4 !c rw / rw /
i4 !m4:4 !f rq 17h_,vf 2q_ /
i1 (8_ 7*1 6) (31 1-) req /
i2 (2 1-_) 20-ql 18-e req /
i4 7#q_ 27!c 8q_ 33e_ req /
i1 19q._ 18-e_ 19#h / (19*15,v<1 20 21-16,v<2) reh /
   rh ((2#13 1#)) 20#q.j / el4 1q_ 20#e_ 1q._ 20e_ /
i2 re 17e_ 18*hj e (18-jl5 / 18-,v<1) 18*ql6,v<2 reh /
   rqe ((2l1 1)) 20hj / el2 q. 19#e_ 20q.j /
i3 rhe 3-e_,vf (4-_ 3*jl7,v<3) / 3q 18el8,v<4 reh /
   re (7*l1 6# 5#j) hj / el2 5*ej h 6-e_ 5ej /
i4 rw / rhqe (9-l1 / 8 7j) h.j / el2 6-q.j e 7-_ 6qj /
i1 1hj e s',vsf rse 1#e / 2#h.. 19#s 20j / h 20#s,vmf 1q. 20s /
   1q,v<1 ((20#) 21.j) e re ((19*l,v<2f 1)) re /
   re 18-e'_ ((21-l 18)) (19#<'_,vff 20'_ 1-'_)
   ((20l3 20-) 19'l4) / re (8-'_ 7'_ 6#'_)
   ((7l5 8) 8*'l6) ((34l1 34#) 8',35l2') / rq 19,1e,vsff reh /
i2 hj e s',vsf rsq / re 1s 2sj 2h. /
   19s 20-q..j e 20-s,vmf 20*j qj /
   e,v<1 ((19# 20j)) (20. (1-)) 20e re ((19#l3,v<2f 20l4)) re /
   r 19*e'_ ((20 19)) ree (20-<'_,vff 19'_ 18'_) /
   ((17#l1 18) 19'l2) (18'_ 19'_ 20-'_) ((19l3 18) 18-'l4)
   ((6l1 6#) / 20',7'l2) re 19#e,20,vsff reh /
i3 hj e s',vsf rsq / rq 6#e 7j hj / e 4s 5j h 6-s,vmf 5e. /
   ((6-,v<1) 5.j) (5 (6 5j)) e re ((6*l,v<2f 5)) re /
   re 6e'_ ((5#l 6)) (18#>'_,vff 19'_ 20-'_) ((19l1 19-) 18*l2) /
   re (7-'_ 6'_ 5#'_) ((6l3 7) 7*'l4) rq / ((4-l1 4*) 18+7'l2)
   4+2#,vsff reh /
i4 6-e (6*'_,vff 7'_ 8-'_) ((7l1,v<1 6) (6-l2,v<2)) rsq /
   rh !f 32s,vf 33-q..j / q 30-s 31-e.j q. 31s,vmf 30j /
   ((30-,v<1 31-) 30-j) ((30 31) 30j) e re ((33-l,v<2f 30)) re /
   r 33*e'_ ((31l 33)) ree (5->'_,vff 5'_ 3'_) /
   ((2#l1 3) 4'l2) (3'_ 4'_ 5'_) ((4l1 3) 3-'l2) re /
   r ((2-l1,v<1 2*) 3-+3l2,v<2ff) reh /
```

Output (partial):

```
i1          7#e_        1-e_                    rq          7*1
!g          /           2qj         /           17h_,vf     6
!m4:4       i2          /           rw          2q_         )
rq          !g          i3          /           /           (
re          !m4:4       !m4:4       i4          i1          31
9e_<,vf     1hj,vf      !c          !m4:4       (           1-
9#q._       e           rw          !f          8_          )
```

Program 8.6. Sample Input and Output[7]

7. Output edited for multiple-column printing.

Program 8.7 duplicates the function of program 8.6 without using *input*↑ and *skipblanks.* Instead it reads each character as a character variable and examines it. This version of the parser could be used with Pascal compilers that do not allow access to the buffer variable.[8] The output from this program is identical to that for program 8.6.

```
(***********************     Program Parser2      ***********************)
(* This program performs exactly the same task as program 8.6, but reads *)
(* each character.  It does not use skipblanks or input↑ and would be    *)
(* appropriate for compilers that do not allow access to the buffer      *)
(* variables.                                                             *)
(*************************************************************************)
program parser2(input, output);
  var
    c : char;

  begin { main }
    while not eof do
      begin
        read(c);
        if c = 'k'                                    { skip comment     }
          then
            while c <> '$' do
              read(c)

        else if c in ['(',')']                        { parentheses      }
          then
            writeln(c)

        else if c <> ' '                              { any other token  }
          then
            begin
              while not (c in [' ' , '(' , ')']) do
                begin
                  write(c);
                  read(c)
                end;
              writeln
            end
      end
  end.  { main }
```

Program 8.7. *Parser2*

8.6 The Output Buffer

Now that you understand the structure of the standard input file, the standard output file should be relatively easy. As you would expect, file *output* is a textfile, with the same structure as file *input*; i.e., it is a continuous stream of characters subdivided

8. At least one popular compiler, Borland's Turbo Pascal, does not provide access to buffer variables.

into lines, each of which is terminated by a newline character. When writing to a textfile such as *output*, the standard procedure *write* (see chapter 4) converts data from an internal representation to character data and writes it into the output file. End-of-line characters are placed in the output file by the *writeln* procedure. The end-of-file is not written explicitly; it is supplied automatically when the output file is closed before the program terminates.

Each output file *f* is associated with a buffer variable *f*↑. The buffer variable for file *output* is called *output*↑. *Output*↑ functions both as a variable (a storage location) and a position indicator for the output buffer. When file *output* is opened for writing (this occurs automatically when the program is run), *output*↑ is positioned at the first location in the output buffer and is undefined, as shown in figure 8.8.

The buffer variable is the window through which characters can be put into the output buffer. This is done in two steps: first *output*↑ is assigned a character (literal, variable, function result, etc.), then the value is written into the buffer via the primitive function *put*, which writes the character into the buffer and advances *output*↑ to the next element of the buffer. The pair of statements

```
output↑ := 'x';
put(output);
```

is equivalent to the statement

```
write('x')
```

If *c* has the value 'x', then either of the above leaves the buffer in the condition shown in the lower diagram in figure 8.8. Note that assigning 'x' to *output*↑ changes the value of *output*↑, but has no effect on the output buffer. *Put(output)* writes the value of *output*↑ into the buffer at the position indicated by *output*↑ and advances *output*↑ to the next buffer position, but does not change the value of *output*↑.

The Pascal procedure *writeln* puts a newline character into the buffer at the position indicated by *output*↑ and advances the buffer variable. Thus calling *writeln* has the following effect on the output buffer shown in figure 8.9. In Pascal systems

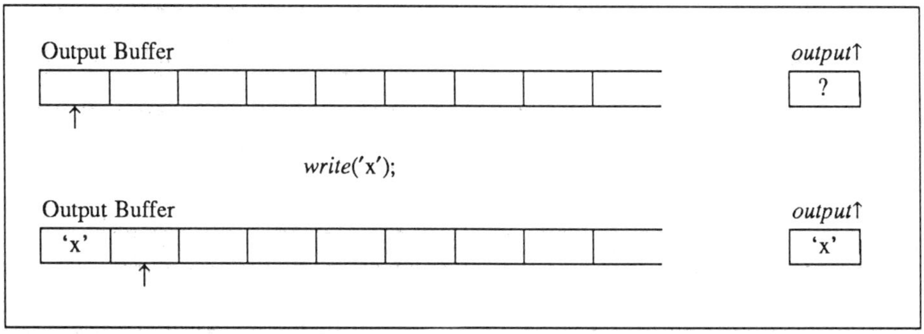

Figure 8.8. The Output Buffer When Opened and After Writing

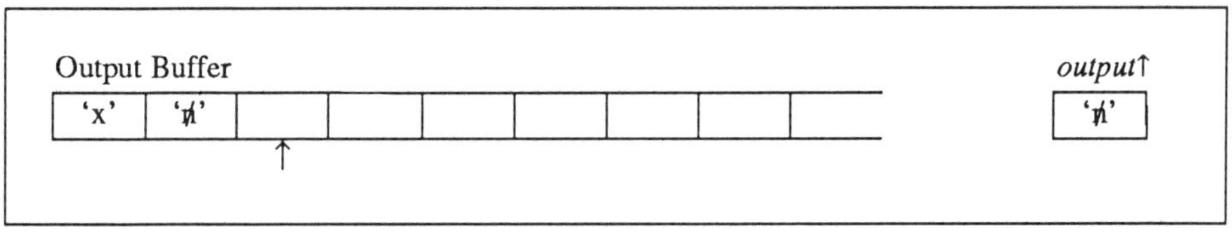

Figure 8.9. The Output Buffer after *writeln*

where the newline character is *chr*(10),[9] the statement

```
writeln
```

is equivalent to

```
write(chr(10))
```

or to the pair of statements

```
output↑ := char(10);
put(output);
```

In some versions of Pascal output is unbuffered, that is, the length of the input buffer is one character, and whenever a value is placed in the buffer, it is transferred directly to the output device associated with the standard output file. Other Pascal versions buffer output, sending the contents of the buffer to the output device only when a *writeln* is received. This improves the efficiency of printing, but can cause problems in interactive programming when one wishes to have the program type a prompt without beginning a new line. Usually it is possible to specify unbuffered output as a compiler option, or to call a special function to empty the buffer. As an example, Berkeley Pascal allows one to specify unbuffered output by including the following as the first line of the source code:

```
{$b0}
```

Optionally the buffer can be explicitly emptied prior to a *writeln* by the procedure *flush.* Thus in this system the pair of statements

```
write('Type a number: ');
flush(output);
```

cause the prompt to be written on the output device without a newline character. Details such as these must be gleaned from the reference manual for your particular version of Pascal. If you are working on a large computer system, there are probably people available to answer questions like these.

Unfortunately, the details of input and output, and particularly testing for end-of-file, are one area in which versions of Pascal sometimes differ. This difference can occur because of problems in interfacing with various operating systems, or because the programmers implementing the system think that they can simplify the I/O process. When this results in local conventions that are different from standard Pascal, it

9. *Chr*(10) is the tenth character in the ASCII character set, the linefeed character. This is the newline character in most UNIX systems.

causes portability problems, rendering more difficult the process of moving programs from one computer system to another. If the techniques in this chapter do not work on your machine, you may have to seek advice from a local expert, become adept at interpreting programming manuals, or see if you can get access to a standard Pascal compiler or interpreter.

The only way to write truly portable Pascal programs is to implement your own buffer, and to write your own procedures and functions to convert data from the external form to the desired internal forms. These techniques will be discussed in chapter 11.

References and Selected Readings

Carefully read the sections on testing for end-of-file and end-of-line in the reference manuals for your Pascal compiler. In some cases you will find that these functions are not treated as described in this chapter. For example, Turbo Pascal does not provide access to I/O buffer variables, but supplies functions such as *seekeoln* and *seekeof*, which combine the action of *eof* and *skipblanks* or of *eoln* and *skipln*. Differences such as these should be clearly understood so that you may avoid confusion in studying and adapting programs later in this book.

Other suggested reading:

Lefkoff, Gerald. "Computers and the Study of Musical Style." In *Papers from the West Virginia Conference on Computer Applications in Music*, edited by Gerald Lefkoff, 43–62. Morgantown, W.Va.: West Virginia University Library, 1967.

Lewin, David. "A Theory of Segmental Association in Twelve-Tone Music." *Perspectives of New Music* 1, no. 1 (1962): 89–116. Reprinted in *Perspectives on Contemporary Music Theory*, edited by Benjamin Boretz and Edward T. Cone. New York: W.W. Norton, 1972.

Logrippo, Luigi, and Bernard Stépien. "Cluster Analysis for the Computer-Assisted Statistical Analysis of Melodies." *Computers and the Humanities* 20 (1986): 19–23.

Morris, Robert. "A Similarity Index for Pitch-Class Sets." *Perspectives of New Music* 18, no. 2 (1974): 445–60.

Rahn, John. "On Some Computational Models of Music Theory." *Computer Music Journal* 4, no. 2 (1980): 66–72.

Roads, Curtis. "Grammers as Representations for Music." *Computer Music Journal* 3, no. 1 (1979): 48–55.

Exercises

1. Rework exercise 7.2.2 from the previous chapter to allow for multiple parts. The original problem was to reformat an excerpt encoded in continuous pitch code so that each measure is printed on a separate line, preceded by the measure number. The new version should do the same for multiple parts, printing the ordinal number of each part above the excerpt. Each part will be terminated with a double bar (100). Use a **while not** *eof* loop and procedure *skipblanks*, to process each part in the input file. Note that the ordinal number will be calculated, not read from the input file, i.e., the first part is numbered 1, the second part is 2, the third part is 3, etc.

```
part 1

     0:        0
     1:        48 50 53 52 0
     2:        99 57 57 57 55 53 52 50 48 0
     3:        53 53 52 52 40   ... 100

part 2

     0:        ... etc.
```

2. Rework exercise 7.2.7 (transposing pitch codes) in a manner similar to that described above, but without part and measure numbers. Note that each part will be preceded by a separate transposition interval. Encode the excerpt shown below, using four parts for the soprano, alto, tenor, and bass parts. Then use your program to transpose the parts for flute, B-flat clarinet, alto flute, and horn in F. Finally, save the output from the program in a file and edit the file to add the transposition numbers needed to transpose the excerpt back to concert pitch, run the program again, and check the results.

J.S. Bach: Chorale, *Es ist genug!*, mm. 1–6

Write a second version that will use a "global" transposition interval to change the key of the entire excerpt. For example, the program should be able to transpose the whole excerpt by some specified interval, say a minor third down (interval –3), while still transposing each individual part correctly for any instrument.

3. Write a program that averages the real numbers on each line of the input file. Use function *eoln* to detect the end-of-line, and *eof* to detect the end-of-file.

4. Redo problem 7.2.1 using '/' for bar lines, '//' for the double bar, and 'r' for rests. Pitches are encoded as continuous pitch code (cpc). The problem is to reformat an excerpt encoded in data in free format, printing one measure per line. The bar lines should be printed at the end of each line. Hint: Before attempting to read each pitch, you will need to skip blanks and use *input*↑ to check for the special characters. Process the code one measure at a time.

5. Write a program that uses *input*↑ to examine an excerpt in DARMS code and counts the number of times each clef (G, F, or C) is used. Don't worry about nonstandard positions of the clefs, e.g., 27!c for tenor clef or 25!f for baritone clef. Recall that clefs are encoded as follows:

!g	treble clef
!f	bass clef
!c	alto clef

6. Write a program that processes an excerpt encoded in DARMS and prints out and identifies each token that begins with an exclamation point, i.e., clefs, meter signatures, and key signatures. Each token should be printed on a separate line and identified with a literal string. You can place a tab character in the output by writing *chr*(9). Your print-out might look something like the following:

```
!g          clef
!k4-        key signature
!m3/4       meter signature
!c          clef
!k2#        meter signature
!m3/4       meter signature
!f          clef
. . . etc.
```

7. Rework program 8.6 (the DARMS parser) so that each token is preceded by the line number and character position in the line. Begin numbering lines and character positions at 1. It will be helpful to process the data file line by line, checking for the end-of-line with function *eoln*. You will need variables for counting lines and characters in each line. Your output for the input data used for program 8.6 should look like the following:

```
5     1   i1
5     4   !g
5     7   !m4:4
5    13   rq
5    16   re
5    19   9e_<,vf
5    27   9#q._
5    33   7#e_
5    38   /
6     1   i2
6     4   !g
6     7   !m4:4
6    13   1hj,vf
6    20   e
6    22   1-e_
6    27   2qj
6    31   /
7     1   i3
7     4   !m4:4
. . .  etc.
```

8. Write a program that averages the real numbers on each line of the input file. This could be used for averaging student grades, etc.

9| Functions and Procedures

Functions and procedures are named program blocks that are defined once in a program, and may be called or *invoked* from different points in the main program or from other subprograms. Since there are no anonymous blocks in Pascal, all blocks other than the main program are implemented as functions and procedures. Functions and procedures differ in the manner in which they are called, and in the way they return values to the calling program. Pascal provides a number of predefined functions and procedures that are a part of the programming language. For example, *read* and *write* statements are actually procedures that transfer data between memory and external I/O devices. *Eof, eoln, sin, sqrt, sqr*, and *trunc* are examples of built-in functions—subprograms that return a single value and are used in expressions of the appropriate type. Since these subprograms are predefined in Pascal, it is not necessary to know the details of their implementation in order to use them; it is sufficient to understand their function and syntax, i.e., we need only know what they will do and how to call them.

There are many reasons for using subprograms in designing programs:

1. Procedures subdivide larger programs into smaller segments or modules, each of which has a clearly defined purpose. Thus their use helps to clarify program structure.
2. Subprograms aid in the top-down program design, since they enable the programmer to think in terms of process rather than detail at each level of program design.
3. For the same reason, the use of subprograms makes it easier to read and understand larger programs.
4. Subprograms can be verified and tested separately, and thus make it easier to design and test correct programs.
5. Since it can be called from many different points in a program and is defined with formal parameters, a code segment that is needed in several different places in a large program or that will operate on different values need only be written once.
6. In large software systems, procedures make it possible to subdivide a very large program into manageable segments, which can be developed, tested, and verified separately, even by different programmers on the development team.

The structure of a function or procedure is similar to that of a program. Each consists of a heading and a block, and may contain **constant** declarations, **type** definitions, variable declarations, and even internal **function** and **procedure** definitions. The body of a function or procedure is a program block delimited by **begin** and **end**. Unlike the main procedure, subprograms are terminated by a semicolon rather than a period. Function and procedure definitions are placed in the main program after constant definitions, type declarations, and variable declarations, and before the main procedure block.

9.1 Functions

The syntax of a function declaration is shown in figure 9.1. The function heading begins with the reserved word **function.** The function name is any valid Pascal identifier, i.e., it is a string of alphanumeric characters, the first of which must be alphabetic. The name may be any length, although only the first eight characters may be significant to the compiler. The identifier should be chosen carefully for its mnemonic value, as this will help readability and clarity in your program.

The formal parameter list declares symbolic names and types of values to be passed to the function. The syntax of the parameter list, which is enclosed in parentheses, is almost identical to variable declarations in the main program. Each segment of the list consists of one or more parameter names (identifiers) separated by commas, and followed by a colon and a standard or programmer-defined type name. When more than one type is used, the segments are separated by semicolons.

Examples of formal parameter lists:

```
(x, y : real)
(i, j, k : integer)
(a, b, c : real; x, y : integer; test : boolean)
(c : char)
(a, b : real; x, y, z : integer)
```

If no formal parameters are used in the function, the parameter list and parentheses are omitted, both in the function definition and when the function is called.

Functions may return standard types—boolean, integer, or real—and pointers.[1] The last part of the function heading specifies this type. In most Pascal systems, functions

```
function <function name> (<formal parameter list>) : <return type>;
  begin
    <statement>;
    <statement>;
    . . .
    <function name> := <return value>
  end;
```

Figure 9.1. SYNTAX: Function Declaration

1. Pointer types will be discussed in chapter 16.

cannot return user-defined types. A function is called by using it in an expression. The simplest case is assigning the function result to a variable of the same type as the function.

As a simple example, consider a function that returns the sum of two integers. The function is trivial; it would not be used in a practical program, since addition can be performed easily without a function and the function does not improve clarity or readability in the program. Our purpose here is to study the syntax and dynamics of using a function. The definition is as follows:

```
function add(x, y : integer) : integer;
  begin
    add := x + y
  end;
```

The function heading specifies that the function name is *add*, that the function will use two formal parameters *x* and *y* of type *integer*, and that the function will return an integer value. The body of the function is delimited by the keywords **begin** and **end**. The function definition is terminated by a semicolon. In this case the body consists of a single statement. The value returned by a function is the last value to be assigned to the function name. Thus in this case function *add* will return the sum of *x* and *y*.

The formal parameters *x* and *y* are assigned the values of the actual parameters, or arguments, passed to the function when it is called. The function is invoked by using the function name with a list of actual parameters in the calling program. Since the function returns an integer value, it can be used anywhere an integer constant, literal, or variable could appear in a program. Thus we could write

```
total := add(10, 5);
writeln(add(a, b));
x := add(x, y) div 3;
```

In the first statement, *total* is assigned the sum of 10 and 5. In the second, the sum of *a* and *b* is printed on the standard output device, assuming that *a* and *b* are integer variables. In the third statement, the sum of *x* and *y* is divided by 3 and the result assigned to *x*. In each case, when the function is invoked there is an implicit assignment of the values of the actual parameters to the formal parameter names used in the function definition. This assignment is position dependent, i.e., the value of the first actual parameter is assigned to the first formal parameter, the value of second actual parameter is assigned to the second formal parameter, etc. The code specified in the

<variable> := <function name>(<actual parameter list>)

Figure 9.2. SYNTAX: Function Call

function definition is then executed, and the last value assigned to the function name replaces the function call in the invoking expression. Executing the statement

```
t := add(14, 29)
```

invokes the function *add* (defined above). Before executing the function, 14 is assigned to *x* and 29 is assigned to *y*. *Sum* is assigned the value 43 (14 + 29). This value is "returned," that is, it replaces the function call in the calling statement and is assigned to the variable *t*.

When the function is called, the number and type of actual parameters must agree with the number and type of formal parameters in the function heading. The following statements are erroneous and would result in compiler errors:

	Statement	*Error*
a)	*t* := *add*(*a*, *b*, *c*);	too many actual parameters
b)	*t* := *add*(*x*);	too few actual parameters
c)	*t* := *add*;	too few actual parameters
d)	*t* := *add*(4.2, 5.7);	type of actual parameters does not agree with type of formal parameters
e)	*add*(4, 5);	cannot store function result

In (a), (b), and (c) the function is called with the wrong number of arguments, i.e., the number of actual parameters is either greater or less than the number of formal parameters in the function definition. At (d) the number of parameters is correct but their type is not compatible with that of the formal parameters in the function definition. Although the number and type of actual parameters are correct at (e), no provision has been made to store the value returned by the function. Since the function returns an integer, it must be used in an arithmetic expression, or in a syntax where an arithmetic expression could be used. Examples of the latter are actual parameters in other function or procedure calls, field-width specifications in *write* statements, or limits in loops:

```
writeln('The sum of a and b is ', add(a, b));
writeln(n:add(fw, 3));
x := add(add(a, b), add(c, d));
for i := 1 to add(j, 1) do
  . . .
```

The function and procedure definitions are placed in a main program after global variable declarations and before the main procedure block. In general, a function or procedure must be defined before it is called.[2] Program 9.1 illustrates the use of function *add*.[3]

2. It is possible to get around this restriction with a *forward* declaration, explained in section 9.8.
3. Note that this program will terminate abnormally if the number of input values is odd.

```
program funcdemo(input, output);
  var
    a, b : integer;

  function add(x, y : integer) : integer;
    begin
      add := x + y
    end;

  begin { main }
    while not eof do
      begin
        readln(a, b);
        writeln('sum =', add(a, b):5)
      end
  end. { main }
```

Program 9.1. *Funcdemo*

9.2 Functions and Top-Down Design

As our first example of program development using functions, we will rewrite a program that appeared as an exercise in chapter 7. The exercise (7.3.3) deals with simple reciprocal duration code (rdc), with bar lines encoded as 0 and the double bar terminating the excerpt encoded as 100. The excerpt is preceded by a meter signature encoded as two integers (the top and bottom numbers of the meter signature). The goal is to check the number of beats in each measure, and to print an error message for each measure with the incorrect number of beats. This program should deal correctly with an excerpt with or without an anacrusis.

For the solution shown here, the algorithm is based on the observation that the sum of the fractional values of the durations in each measure should be equal to the fractional value of the meter signature. For example, in 3/4 meter (fractional value .75) the sum of the fractional values of the durations in a correctly encoded measure will total 3/4 or .75.

Examples:

♩ ♩ ♩	= 1/4 + 1/4 + 1/4	=	3/4
𝅗𝅥 ♩	= 1/2 + 1/4	=	3/4
♫ ♩ ♩	= 1/8 + 1/8 + 1/4 + 1/4	=	3/4

Since the encoding scheme uses the reciprocal of the fractional value of the duration, the fractional value can be calculated by dividing 1 by the duration code. It is impossible to determine whether the duration of the anacrusis is correct until the final measure has been processed. Thus the total of the fractional durations in the anacrusis must be saved before the rest of the excerpt is processed. The last measure is treated as any other measure unless there was an anacrusis; in this case the sum of the last measure and the anacrusis should be equal to a whole measure. If we have saved the number of beats in the anacrusis, this value can be used later to determine whether or not there was an anacrusis at the beginning of the piece. Since we wish to know which measures have the wrong duration, we will use a variable to count measures.

The algorithm in pseudo code looks like this:

```
read meter and store its value;
set measure counter to 0;
calculate total fractional value of anacrusis;

while not at end of excerpt do
  begin
    increment measure counter;
    calculate duration of measure;
    if not at end of excerpt or there was no anacrusis
      then
        if the duration of measure is incorrect
          then print error message
  end;

[Complete excerpt has now been processed]

if there was an anacrusis
  then
    if sum of anacrusis and last measure is incorrect
      then print appropriate message
```

We will need to calculate the fractional total of the durations up to the end of a measure. Since this total represents a single numeric value, implementation as a function is appropriate. The same function can be used to calculate the value of the anacrusis (an incomplete measure), which will be equal to 0.0 if there is no anacrusis. This value can be used later to determine if there was, in fact, an anacrusis. We will also have to know whether the end of the excerpt has been reached. This test could be implemented as a boolean function, or we could simply use a boolean variable as a flag that is initialized as *false* and will be set to *true* when the end of the excerpt is encountered.

We now encode the main procedure in Pascal, using as-yet undefined functions as if they already existed. We will assume the existence of function *measuretotal*, which will return the total fractional duration in a measure, and *readmeter*, which will return the fractional duration of the meter signature.

```
begin { main }
  wholemeasure := readmeter;           { read meter signature    }
  measure := 0;                        { set measure counter     }
  anacrusis := measuretotal;           { beats in anacrusis      }

  while not done do
    begin
      measure := measure + 1;          { incr measure counter    }
      bardur := measuretotal;          { save beats in measure   }
      if (not done) or (anacrusis = 0.0)
        then
          if abs(bardur - wholemeasure) > epsilon
            then writeln('duration error in measure', measure:3)
    end;

  if anacrusis > 0                     { was there an anacrusis? }
    then
      if abs(anacrusis + bardur - wholemeasure) > epsilon
        then writeln('duration error in anacrusis or last measure')

end.  { main }
```

When encoding the main procedure we made certain assumptions about the functions. We must be careful to fulfill these specifications when writing the functions:

1. Function *readmeter* will read the numerator and denominator of the meter signature and return a real number representing the fractional value.
2. Function *measuretotal* will process the encoded durations up to the end of a measure, and return as a real number the sum of the fractional values of all durations in the measure. It will also set a boolean variable *done* to *true* or *false* depending on whether or not the end of the excerpt has been reached. It will have to read all codes up to and including the measure terminator in order to accomplish this.

Verification of the main procedure consists of the following observations:

1. Initialization
   a) The meter signature is read and its fractional value stored in *wholemeasure*.
   b) The measure counter *measure* is initialized to 0, since we are about to process the anacrusis (measure 0).
   c) *Anacrusis* is assigned the total of the fractional values in the anacrusis. This value will be 0.0 if there is no anacrusis.
2. The main loop (**while not** *done*)
   a) Since *measuretotal* sets *done* to *true* when the end of the excerpt is encountered, the loop must terminate after the final measure is processed. If the initial measure terminates with an encoded double bar, the body of the loop will not be executed.
   b) The variable *measure* is incremented to reflect the current measure number. Since measure was initialized to 0 and is incremented before each measure is processed, it will always indicate the correct number.

c) The fractional total of the durations in the measure is assigned to *bardur* by invoking *measuretotal.* The function resets *done* to reflect the location in the excerpt.

d) The test **if** (**not** *done*) **or** (*anacrusis* = 0.0) must evaluate to *true* if the end of the excerpt has not been reached (*done* = *false*). When the end is encountered (*done* = *true*), the first part of the test fails and the total expression evaluates to *true* only if there was no anacrusis. Thus all measures are treated the same unless there was an anacrusis, in which case the following test is not made. In general we should not test real values for equality directly; it is permissible here, since if anacrusis is equal to 0.0 no computation will have taken place, and no arithmetic error is possible.

e) The duration of the measure is checked by testing the difference between the actual and desired values to see if it is within a specified tolerance (*epsilon*). This is the appropriate test for equality in real numbers, provided that we have chosen a reasonable value for *epsilon.*

f) The loop terminates after the last measure has been processed by *measuretotal.* At this point the final measure will have been checked if there is no anacrusis.

3. Post-loop processing

   If there was an anacrusis, then the final measure will not have been checked within the **while** loop, and *bartotal* will still contain the total fractional duration of the final measure. In this case the sum of the anacrusis and the last measure is checked against the correct value.

We now write the functions, taking care that they fulfill the assumptions we made when writing the main procedure. *Readmeter* is rather simple. Since it does not depend on any external values to accomplish its task, it does not need a parameter list. However, it will need two local variables in order to read the numerator and denominator of the meter signature. It returns a real number, which is the quotient of the numerator and denominator:

```
function readmeter : real;
  var
    beats     : integer;           { numerator of meter sig    }
    beatnote  : integer;           { denominator of meter sig  }
  begin
    read(beats, beatnote);
    readmeter := beats / beatnote
  end;
```

Function *measuretotal* is a bit more complex, so we will approach its development top-down. The function will process each encoded value until an end-of-measure symbol is reached. Each encoded duration must be converted to its reciprocal value and added to the total. The boolean variable *done* is then set to *true* or *false* to indicate whether or not the end of the excerpt has been reached. The basic algorithm in pseudo code follows:

initialize *total* to 0;

read a duration code;
while not at end of measure **do**
  begin
    convert duration code to fractional value and add it to *total*;
    read another duration code
  end;

set boolean flag *done*; {*true* if end of excerpt, else *false*}
return total;

We will use a local variable *code* for reading and *total* for calculating the sum of the fractional durations. Since each measure will be terminated by an encoded bar line except the last, which is terminated by an encoded double bar, we must check for either condition: we are at end-of-measure if (*code* = *barline*) **or** (*code* = *doublebar*). The **while** loop could read

```
while not ((code = barline) or (code = doublebar)) do
```

or

```
while (code <> barline) and (code <> doublebar) do
```

Although either is correct, readability can be improved at a small cost in efficiency by writing a boolean function *eom* (end-of-measure), which returns *true* if *code* is a *barline* or a *doublebar*. Since no other function or procedure will need to call this subordinate function, we will make it internal to *measuretotal*:[4]

```
function measuretotal : real;
  var
    total : real;
    code  : integer;

  function eom : boolean;
    begin { end of measure }
      eom := (code = barline) or (code = doublebar)
    end;  { end of measure }

  begin
    total := 0;
    read(code);
    while not eom do
      begin
        total := total + (1 / abs(code));
        read(code)
      end;
    done := (code = doublebar); { set flag }
    measuretotal := total
  end;
```

4. Here, variables *barline*, *doublebar*, and *done* are assumed to be declared outside of this block. "Global" and "local" variables are discussed in section 9.4.

Verification of *measuretotal* consists of the following observations:

1. Initialization

   Total is initialized to 0, and an encoded duration is read, so it will be possible to test the boolean expression in the **while** statement.

2. The **while** loop

   a) The loop tests for either possible measure terminator (*barline* and *doublebar*) through calling *eom.*
   b) Each duration code in the measure is converted to its fractional value by taking its reciprocal value. This value is added to the local variable *total.*
   c) The loop terminates when an end-of-measure symbol has been read.
   d) If the initial code is a *barline* or *doublebar* the loop will not execute, and *total* will remain 0. Thus the function works properly even when no duration codes precede the measure terminator. This will be the case in the beginning of the excerpt if there is no anacrusis.

3. Post-loop processing

   a) The global variable *done* is set to *true* if the end of the excerpt has been reached, or to *false* if it has not.
   b) The value of *total* is assigned to *measuretotal* so that it will be returned to the calling program.

All that remains is the program heading and declaration of constants and global variables. The complete listing is shown as program 9.2.

Input:

```
3 4
4 0 4 4 4 0 2 4 0 2 4 0 2 0 8 8 4 4 0 2 8 8 0 2 4 0 2 -4 0
2 4 0 2 4 0 4 4 4 0 2 0 4 4 4 0 2 4 0 2 -4 100
```

Output:

```
duration error in measure  4
duration error in measure 12
duration error in anacrusis or last measure
```

Program 9.2. Sample Input and Output

```
(***********************    Program Checkbeats    ***********************)
(* Synopsis: Checks the number of beats in each measure of an encoded   *)
(*           excerpt and reports measures with wrong number of beats.   *)
(*           The program treats the anacrusis and final measure as one  *)
(*           complete measure.                                          *)
(* Input:    Reciprocal duration code with bar line = 0 and final double *)
(*           bar = 100.  The excerpt is preceded by two integers repre-  *)
(*           senting the top and bottom numbers of the meter signature.  *)
(* Output:   An error message for each measure with incorrect duration  *)
(*           total.                                                     *)
(* Method:   Each duration code is converted to a decimal fraction by   *)
(*           taking its reciprocal.  The durations in each measure are  *)
(*           summed, and the total is compared to the fractional value of*)
(*           the meter signature.  If there is an anacrusis, it is added *)
(*           to the total for the final measure.  Appropriate messages  *)
(*           are printed for measures with incorrect beat totals.       *)
(*************************************************************************)
program checkbeats(input, output);
  const
    barline    = 0;                      { code for bar line            }
    doublebar  = 100;                    { code for end of excerpt      }
    epsilon    = 0.00001;                { tolerance for testing real nos}

  var
    measure      : integer;              { current measure number       }
    wholemeasure : real;                 { fractional value of measure  }
    anacrusis    : real;                 { fractional value of anacrusis }
    bardur       : real;                 { actual frac value of measure }
    done         : boolean;              { flag: true at end of piece   }

(***********************      measuretotal      ***********************)
(* Returns the sum of the fractional values of durations in a measure   *)
(* and sets the boolean flag done to be true when the final measure     *)
(* has been processed.                                                  *)
(*************************************************************************)
  function measuretotal : real;
    var
      total : real;                          { for calculating total }
      code  : integer;

    function eom : boolean;                  { end of measure        }
      begin
        eom := (code = barline) or (code = doublebar)
      end;

    begin { measuretotal }
      total := 0;
      read(code);
      while not eom do
        begin
          total := total + (1 / abs(code));
          read(code)
        end;
      done := (code = doublebar);
      measuretotal := total
    end; { measuretotal }
```

```
(***********************          readmeter          ***********************)
(* Returns the fractional value of the meter signature.                     *)
(***************************************************************************)
  function readmeter : real;
    var
      beats, beatnote : integer;
    begin
      read(beats, beatnote);
      readmeter := beats / beatnote
    end;

(***********************       main procedure        ***********************)
(* Exercises the above procedures.                                          *)
(***************************************************************************)
  begin { main }
    wholemeasure := readmeter;                     { read meter signature }
    measure := 0;                                  { set measure counter  }
    anacrusis := measuretotal;                     { value of anacrusis   }

    while not done do
      begin
        measure := measure + 1;
        bardur := measuretotal;
        if (not done) or (anacrusis = 0)
          then
            if abs(bardur - wholemeasure) > epsilon
              then writeln('duration error in measure', measure:3)
      end;

    if anacrusis > 0                    { if there was an anacrusis }
      then
        if abs(anacrusis + bardur - wholemeasure) > epsilon
          then writeln('duration error in anacrusis or last measure')

  end.  { main }
```

Program 9.2. *Checkbeats*

9.3 Functions with Side Effects

In one respect, functions *readmeasure* and *measuretotal* are different from simple functions like *add* and *eom* and all built-in functions in Pascal. They do not simply define a relationship between their arguments. They process data from the standard input file while calculating their return value. Thus, each time they are called they have the potential of returning a different value, since their value depends not on arguments passed to them, but on input data processed by them. Each time they are called they process data from the standard input file—data that cannot be retrieved and reprocessed. Functions (or procedures) such as these are said to have *side effects*, since they alter the values they use to do their work. Each time *measuretotal* is called, it processes the data for a different measure. Thus the following would be a serious programming error:

```
if abs(measuretotal - wholemeasure) > epsilon
  then writeln('Error: m. ', measure:3, ' has ', measuretotal, ' beats');
```

The intent is to report the incorrect number of beats in the current measure, but the second call of *measuretotal* calculates the number of beats in the *subsequent* measure. This problem can be avoided by calling *measuretotal* only once per measure, and assigning its value to a variable:

```
bardur := measuretotal;
if abs(bardur - wholemeasure) > epsilon
  then writeln('Error: m. ', measure:3, ' has ', bardur, ' beats');
```

9.4 The Scope of Identifiers: Global versus Local Variables

Functions and procedures are nested within the main program, and may be internal to other functions and procedures. In figure 9.3 subprograms *A* through *E* are internal to the main program. In addition, procedure *D* is internal to procedure *C*, and procedure *E* is internal to *D*. Since variables may be defined within each block, how does one determine which blocks have access to a variable? In general, an identifier is known in the entire block in which it is defined, including other blocks defined within that block. Table 9.1 shows the scope of identifiers in figure 9.3, so long as the identifiers are distinct.

Variables defined in the main program block are available throughout the program, unless they are redefined within another block. These variables are said to be *global.* Variables defined in a procedure or function are known only within that subprogram, and are said to be *local.* Since local variables are reallocated whenever a procedure or function is invoked, they do not retain their values after the procedure or function terminates, i.e., there are no *static* variables in Pascal. A subroutine can redefine a variable that is already in use, but in so doing it loses access to the global variable. This practice does not affect the value of the variable in the external block. Thus variables *i* and *j* in function *A* do not reference the same storage locations as *i* and *j* in the main block. When function *A* is called, it uses two new storage locations called *i* and *j* for its own purposes. When this function terminates, its variables *i* and *j* are no longer available, and identifiers *i* and *j* again refer to the global variables, the

Objects defined in	are accessible in
main	main, *A*, *B*, *C*, *D*, *E*
A	*A*
B	*B*
C	*C*, *D*, *E*
D	*D*, *E*
E	*E*

Table 9.1. Scope of Identifiers in Figure 9.3

```
program main(input, output);
  var  { global variable declarations }
    i, j, k : integer;
    a, b, c : real;

  function A : integer;
    var  { local variables for function A }
      i, j : integer;
    begin { A }
      . . .
    end;  { A }

  function B : integer;
    var  { local variables for procedure B }
      i, j, k : integer;
    begin { B }
      . . .
    end;  { B }

  procedure C;
    var  { local variables for procedure C }
      i, j, k : integer;

    procedure D;
      var  { local variables for procedure D }
        i          : integer;
        a, b, c, d : real;

      function E : real;
        var  { local variables for function E }
          i : integer;
          a : real;
        begin { E }
          . . .
        end;  { E }

      begin { D }
        . . .
      end;  { D }

    begin { C }
      . . .
    end;  { C }

  begin { main }
    . . .
  end.  { main }
```

Figure 9.3. The Scope of Identifiers

Program block	can invoke block
main	*A, B, C*
A	*A*, (*B, C*)
B	*A, B*, (*C*)
C	*A, B, C, D*
D	*A, B, C, D, E*
E	*A, B, C, D, E*

Table 9.2. Subprogram Access in Figure 9.3

values of which are unaffected by invoking function *A*. However, function *A* could still access global variables *k, a, b*, and *c*.

The scope of identifiers also determines which blocks can invoke a subprogram. A program block can call any subprogram that is defined within the same program block, but that is not internal to another block. In most systems there is a further restriction that a subroutine must be defined before it can be called, unless a **forward** declaration is used.[5] Table 9.2 shows subprogram access for figure 9.3. The blocks in parentheses can be invoked only if appropriate **forward** declarations have been used prior to the call. Note that each function or procedure can call itself recursively.[6]

9.5 Procedures

The second type of named program block is the *procedure*. Procedures are designed to perform some task, rather than to return a value directly. Examples of built-in procedures in Pascal are the *read* and *write* statements. Although a procedure may change the value of its arguments, the procedure itself does not have a value. Thus, unlike a function, a procedure cannot be used in an expression or anywhere else where a value is expected. A procedure is invoked by using the procedure name, with its list of actual parameters, as a statement. The syntax of the procedure declaration is shown in figure 9.4.

```
procedure <procedure name> (<formal parameter list>);
  begin
    <statement>;
    <statement>;
    . . .
    <statement>
  end;
```

Figure 9.4. SYNTAX: Procedure Definition

5. This restriction is due to the structure of single-pass compilers.

6. Recursion will be formally introduced in chapter 15.

The procedure heading begins with the reserved word **procedure**. The procedure name is any legal Pascal identifier; program readability is enhanced by choosing mnemonic identifiers for procedure names. The parameter list is a definition of symbolic names and types of values to be passed to the procedure, and takes exactly the same form as in functions. The statements in the procedure are enclosed by the delimiters **begin** and **end**.

9.6 Value and Variable Parameters

The formal arguments for procedures may take two forms, depending on whether the procedure is to have the ability to change the value of the actual parameter passed to it.[7] The first mechanism is called *pass by value*, and is the default, i.e., the way arguments are passed unless the programmer takes special action. All of the formal arguments in the functions shown earlier in this chapter were passed by value. If a parameter is passed by value, the subprogram uses a separate storage location, identified by the name of the formal parameter. When the subprogram is called, the value of the actual parameter is copied into this new storage location. Thus the subprogram can change the value of its formal parameter without affecting the value of the actual parameter passed to it. Because of this, the actual parameter (the value passed) may be a variable, a literal, a constant, or it may be the value returned by a function.

The second mechanism for passing arguments is called *pass by reference*. The programmer specifies that a parameter will be passed by reference by inserting the keyword **var** before a sublist in the parameter list of the procedure declaration. Parameters that are passed by reference are sometimes called *variable parameters*, while those passed by value are referred to as *value parameters*. When a parameter is passed by reference, the procedure does not receive a copy of the value of the actual parameter. Instead, it is passed the address in memory of the variable passed to it. Thus if the procedure changes the value of the parameter, it is actually changing the value of the variable passed to it. By using variable parameters, a procedure can return values to the calling program, but, unlike a function, the procedure has no inherent value and cannot be used in expressions. Because variable parameters are passed by address, *only* variables may be passed to them as actual parameters.

Figure 9.5 illustrates the difference between a value parameter and a variable parameter. Procedure *valdemo* uses a value parameter. When it is invoked by the *calling* procedure, the value of variable a is copied to variable x used by the procedure. Changing x has no effect on a. In procedure *vardemo*, parameter x is passed by reference (**var**), thus x refers to the same storage location as a.[8] Changing x now alters a in the calling program.

7. This discussion applies to functions as well, but it is not considered good form to use variable parameters with functions, which should return a single value by the normal means.

8. Note that the names used for the actual and formal parameters are not significant; they could be identical without changing the result.

Pass by Value:

Calling Program	Subprogram
var *a* : *integer*;	**procedure** *valdemo*(*x* : *integer*);
a := 10;	The calling program assigns a value to memory location *a*.
	The value of *a* is copied to *x* when the procedure is called. Different memory locations are used.
valdemo(*a*); *a* ⟶ [10]	*x* ⟶ [10]
	Changing *x* does not change *a* *x* := *x* + 1;
a ⟶ [10]	*x* ⟶ [11]

Pass by Reference:

Calling Program	Subprogram
var *a* : *integer*;	**procedure** *vardemo*(**var** *x* : *integer*);
a := 10;	The calling program assigns a value to memory location *a*.
	The address of *a* is passed to the procedure, which calls this storage location *x*.
vardemo(*a*); *a* ⟶ [10] ⟵ *x*	
	Changing the value of *x* changes the value of *a* in the calling program *x* := *x* + 1;
a ⟶ [11] ⟵ *x*	

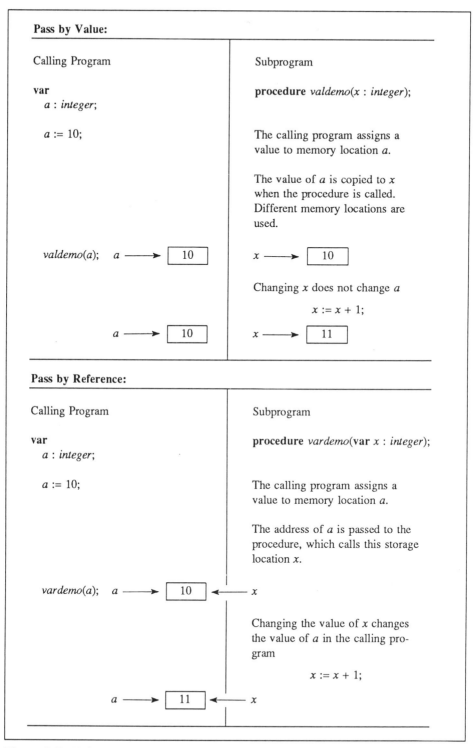

Figure 9.5. Value and Variable Parameters

If the foregoing discussion seems difficult, the following rule should suffice for the present:

> *Use a variable parameter whenever it is intended that the procedure change the value of its argument. Use a value parameter if the procedure will not alter the value passed to it.*[9]

When a parameter is used for both input to and output from a subprogram, it must be declared **var**. Below are examples of procedure headings illustrating the declaration of variable and value parameters. Note that the **var** directive applies only to the following sublist in the parameter list, and that any valid type, including user-defined types, can be passed as a variable or value parameter.

1. **procedure** *calc*(*a*, *b*, *c* : *real*; **var** *result* : *real*); — *calc* has three real parameters (*a*, *b*, *c*) passed by value, and one real parameter (*result*) passed by reference. Presumably *result* will be used to return the result of the calculation. A reasonable alternative to this procedure would be **function** *calc*(*a*, *b*, *c* : *real*) : *real*; the only difference is the manner in which the result is returned and the way the function is called.

2. **procedure** *incr*(**var** *x* : *integer*); — *incr* has one variable parameter of type *integer*. Since its purpose is to add 1 to its argument, it could also be written as **function** *incr*(*x* : *integer*) : *integer*; however, it is more direct to write

   ```
   incr(measure)
   ```

   than

   ```
   measure := incr(measure)
   ```

3. **procedure** *swap*(**var** *x*, *y* : *integer*); — *swap* will interchange the values of its parameters, thus both parameters must be passed by reference.

4. **procedure** *crunch*(*l*, *m*, *n* : *integer*; **var** *t* : *integer*; **var** *x*, *y* *real*); — *crunch* has three integer parameters (*l*, *m*, *n*) passed by value, one integer parameter (*t*) passed by reference, and two real parameters (*x*, *y*) passed by reference. Presumably the procedure will use integer values *l*, *m*, and *n* without changing their values, and will return new values for *t*, *x*, and *y*.

<procedure name> (<actual parameter list>)

Figure 9.6. SYNTAX: Procedure Call

9. We will see exceptions to this in later chapters; for example, arrays are usually passed by reference for efficiency.

When a procedure is called, the number and type of actual parameter must agree with the formal parameters in the procedure heading. If *i, j, k,* and *m* have been declared as *integer* variables, and *q, r, s,* and *t* have been declared type *real*, then the following are legal statements invoking the procedures:

```
calc(q, r, s, t);              { t returns result }
incr(i);
incr(j);
incr(k);
swap(i, j);
swap(j, k);
crunch(i, j, k, m, s, t);
```

The following procedure calls would be erroneous for the reasons stated:

Procedure Call	*Error*
calc(i, j, k, m);	parameter types are incompatible
calc(q, r, s);	too few actual parameters
incr(s);	parameter types are incompatible
incr(i, j);	too many actual parameters
swap(i, t);	parameter types are incompatible
swap(i);	too few actual parameters
crunch(t, s, m, k, j, i);	parameter types are incompatible

As a simple example of a procedure, we will write procedure *incr(x)*, suggested above. The procedure adds 1 to the value of its argument. Since the value of the parameter will be changed, it must be passed by reference.

```
procedure incr(var x : integer);
  begin
    x := x + 1
  end;
```

Once this procedure has been defined, it could be used to add 1 to any integer variable. The following would increment *measure*, *x*, and *total*, if it is presumed that each is a declared integer variable and that each has been assigned a value:

```
incr(measure);
incr(x);
incr(total);
```

The actual parameter must be defined (assigned a value) before the procedure is called, since the procedure uses this argument in its calculation. Note again that the actual parameter passed to the procedure must be a variable of the correct type. In the context of the following declarations and assignments,

```
const
  firstmeasure = 1;
```

```
var
  total   : real;
  measure : integer;

begin
  ...

  total := 0.0;
```

the following procedure calls would be erroneous for the reason stated:

Procedure Call	*Error*
incr(7);	incompatible types (literal)
incr(5.6);	incompatible types (real and literal)
incr(*total*);	incompatible types (real)
incr(*measure*);	measure not defined
incr(*firstmeasure*);	incompatible types (constant)

Frequently procedures do not alter the value of their parameters. Procedure *error*, shown below, uses its formal parameter in a **case** statement to determine which error message to print. The procedure could also take corrective action, and even call other procedures necessary in certain cases. Note that the formal parameter is passed by value, since it will not be altered and will in all probability be passed an integer literal. The procedure should check the value of its argument, because a value that is not in one of the case label lists would result in a **case** error.

```
procedure error(errno : integer);
  begin { error }
    if not (errno in [0 .. 5])
      then writeln('error: argument out of range')
      else
        case errno of
          0 : writeln('improper clef designation');
          1 : writeln('end of measure expected');
          2 : writeln('improper meter signature');
          3 : writeln('erroneous dynamic code');
          4 : writeln('incorrect number of beats in measure');
          5 : writeln('this feature not yet implemented')
         end { case }
  end;  { error }
```

A procedure such as this often begins with a few cases and is expanded as the diagnostic capability of the program is improved. In order to add a new error message, the programmer would modify the **if** statement to include the new number and add another case label. The calling procedures should include a short comment to aid in readability. Appropriate calls of the above procedure would be:

```
error(0);              { clef error              }
error(4);              { incorrect beat total    }
error(5);              { unimplemented feature   }
```

9.7 Procedures and Top-Down Design

Perhaps the greatest benefit of using functions and procedures is their aid in top-down design and modularization of algorithms. Each function or procedure should represent a single process, with a clearly defined task and clearly defined input and output values in the form of parameters and return values. Using subprograms, we can write the higher levels of code first, thinking in terms of process rather than detail. When some task needs to be accomplished, the programmer calls a function or procedure that may not yet have been written. He or she must be careful to note the exact specifications of the unwritten subprogram. At each level of design, beginning with the top, the algorithm is checked and verified for correctness. After each level has been written, the programmer writes the functions and procedures that were called in the higher-level procedure. These subprograms may also call other subprograms that will be written after them. In a large program some of these procedures may represent large subprocesses, each of which may represent another top-down chain of development. These may be written as dummy procedures, with just a program heading and an empty block:

```
procedure addincipit(var incips : incipfile; var n : integer);
  begin { add incipit to file }
  end;  { add incipit to file }
```

With this dummy procedure declaration in the program, the main procedure can call procedure *addincipit*, which will do nothing for the time being. Thus the programmer can encode and debug each primary process separately, while making the higher levels complete.[10]

9.7.1 Application: Directed Intervals in Melody

As our first example of top-down program development using procedures, we will recast a program suggested as an exercise in chapter 6. The program will calculate the directed intervals in a melody encoded in continuous pitch code (cpc). As in the earlier program, we will encode rests as the integer 99, bar lines as 0, and the final double bar as 100. The basic algorithm is to get the first two encoded pitches. The interval between the two, calculated by subtracting the first note from the second, is printed, then the next pair of notes is obtained by assigning the value of the second note to the first and reading a new second note. The biggest problem in writing the earlier exercise was to ensure that the program skipped bar lines and rests and only calculated intervals between codes that actually represented notes. The use of procedures will greatly simplify this problem.

If we posit procedure *getnote*(*x*), which will find and return the next pitch code and take appropriate action for rests and bar lines, the program is much easier to write. The main algorithm in pseudo code follows:

10. This technique will be used in some exercises in later chapters, where incomplete but compilable programs are provided, with dummy subroutines to be completed by the student.

```
get first and second notes;
while not end of piece do
  begin
    print interval;
    second note becomes new first note;
    get new second note
  end;
```

The same algorithm encoded in Pascal:

```
begin { main }
  getnote(first);                       { read first note       }
  getnote(second);                      { read second note      }
  while not done do
    begin
      write(second - first:3);          { write interval        }
      first := second;                  { shift right           }
      getnote(second)
    end;
  writeln                               { terminate last line }
end.  { main }
```

The main program presupposes two subroutines: procedure *getnote*(*x*), which will return the next pitch code, and function *done*, which will return *true* when the end of the excerpt has been reached. We can now write the subroutines.

In analyzing the task to be performed by function *done*, we note that once the variables *first* and *second* have been initialized, *first* always gets its value from *second*, and the value of *second* is obtained from the input file via *getnote*(*second*). If we presume that there is at least one encoded pitch in the excerpt, the program must terminate when *second* contains the value representing a double bar. Function *done* makes this test, using the global variable *second* and the global constant *doublebar*:

```
function done : boolean;
  begin
    done := (second = doublebar)
  end;
```

We will write *getnote* as a procedure with a variable parameter, so that it can return the next pitch code using the actual parameter passed to it (*first* or *second*). The program specification states that pitches, bar lines, double bar lines, and rests will be encoded. Our primary objective is to return the next pitch code. If no pitches are left, the procedure will return the final double bar instead, and this value will signal the end of the excerpt. Thus the procedure should skip rests and bar lines. The procedure will terminate the current output line whenever a bar line is encountered, since the output for any excerpt of reasonable size will not fit on one line. The algorithm in pseudo code follows:

read a code;
while it is a bar line or a rest **do**
  begin
   if the code is a bar line
     then terminate output line;
   read another code
  end;
return next pitch or excerpt terminator

The procedure encoded in Pascal is shown below. Here we use boolean functions to see if *code* represents a bar line or a rest. These tests could have been implemented as boolean expressions; using functions makes the code clearer (and helps us to illustrate top-down design).

```
procedure getnote(var code : integer);
  begin
    read(code);
    while isbar(code) or isrest(code) do
      begin { get next note }
        if isbar(code)
          then writeln;
        read(code)
      end   { get next note }
  end;
```

We now write functions *isbar* and *isrest*:

```
function isbar(x : integer) : boolean;
  begin
    isbar := x = barline
  end;

function isrest(x : integer) : boolean;
  begin
    isrest := x = rest
  end;
```

The complete program and test data follow.

Input:

```
60 60 62 64 0 65 67 65 64 65 67 65 0 64 67 99 67 72 67 99 67 0 65
67 65 64 65 67 65 0 64 67 99 67 72 67 99 67 0 69 65 99 65 72 69 99
69 67 64 99 64 67 62 100
```

Output:

```
 0  2  2
 1  2 -2 -1  1  2 -2
-1  3  0  5 -5  0
-2  2 -2 -1  1  2 -2
-1  3  0  5 -5  0
 2 -4  0  7 -3  0 -2 -3  0  3 -5
```

Program 9.3. Sample Input and Output

```
(***********************      Program Intervals     ***********************)
(* Objective: Prints successive directed intervals in encoded excerpt.    *)
(* Input:  Cpc code with bar line = 0, double bar = 100, and rest = 99.   *)
(* Output: Series of directed intervals in encoded part.                  *)
(* Method:     Get first and second notes                                 *)
(*             while not end of piece do                                  *)
(*               begin                                                    *)
(*                 print interval [second - first]                        *)
(*                 first <-- second                                       *)
(*                 get new second note                                    *)
(*               end                                                      *)
(**************************************************************************)
program intervals(input, output);
  const
    barline    =   0;                        { code for bar line          }
    doublebar  = 100;                        { code for end of excerpt    }
    rest       =  99;                        { code for rest              }

  var
    first, second : integer;                 { first and second           }
                                             { pitches in interval        }

(***********************            done            ***********************)
(* Returns true if second "note" is a double bar, otherwise false.        *)
(**************************************************************************)
  function done : boolean;
    begin
      done := second = doublebar
    end;

(***********************           isbar            ***********************)
(* Returns true if the value passed to it is a bar line.                  *)
(**************************************************************************)
  function isbar(x : integer) : boolean;
    begin
      isbar := x = barline
    end;

(***********************           isrest           ***********************)
(* Returns true if the value of its argument is a rest.                   *)
(**************************************************************************)
  function isrest(x : integer) : boolean;
    begin
      isrest := x = rest
    end;

(***********************          getnote           ***********************)
(* Uses a var parameter to return the next actual note; skips bar lines  *)
(* and rests.  When it reads a bar line it terminates the current line in*)
(* output file.  When no notes are left, the procedure returns the value *)
(* of doublebar, indicating the end of the piece.  This is the key pro-  *)
(* cedure, which really simplifies the logic of the main program.  Note  *)
(* that parameter code stands for the first or second note, depending on *)
(* how the procedure is called.  (See main procedure.)                   *)
(**************************************************************************)
```

```
procedure getnote(var code : integer);
  begin
    read(code);
    while isbar(code) or isrest(code) do
      begin { get next note }
        if isbar(code)
          then writeln;
        read(code)
      end   { get next note }
  end;

(***********************     main procedure      ***********************)
(* Exercises the above procedures.                                     *)
(**********************************************************************)
begin { main }
  getnote(first);                              { read first note   }
  getnote(second);                             { read second note  }
  while not done do
    begin
      write(second - first:3);                 { write interval    }
      first := second;                         { shift right       }
      getnote(second)                          { get next note     }
    end;
  writeln
end.  { main }
```

Program 9.3. *Intervals*

Another advantage of using functions and procedures in a well-designed program is that they modularize processes and make it easier to change the program to meet new requirements. Suppose, for example, that we decide to use more mnemonic symbols, say '/' and '//' for bar lines and double bars, and 'r' for rests in the above program. This complicates the program slightly, since we must determine before reading whether the next symbol is numeric or character. This change could be made easily by substituting both *read(code)* statements in procedure *getnote* with calls to a user-written procedure *getcode(code)*:

```
procedure getnote(var code : integer);
  begin
    getcode(code);                 { read next code }
    while isbar(code) or isrest(code) do
      begin { get next note }
        if isbar(code)
          then writeln;
        getcode(code)              { read next code }
      end   { get next note }
  end;
```

Procedure *getcode* must first determine whether the next code is a character or a numeric pitch code. If it is a bar line, it must determine if it is a single or double bar line, and return the proper numeric code in either case. If the next code is a rest, the numeric value for the rest is returned. If no bar line or rest is present, the procedure can use *read* to read the next pitch code. The basic algorithm in pseudo code is:

skip blanks;
if the next character is '/'
  then
    begin
      skip the '/';
      if there is another '/'
        then return value for double bar
        else return value for bar line
    end
  else if *input*↑ = 'r'
    then
      begin
        skip the 'r';
        return value for rest
      end
  else read a pitch code

The additional Pascal procedures required are shown below. Since the double bar signals the end of the data, procedure *getcode* does not skip the final '/'. This would be necessary if more data were to be processed.

```
procedure skipblanks;
  var
    done : boolean;
  begin
    done := false;
    repeat
      if eof
        then done := true
      else if input↑ = ' '
        then get(input)
      else done := true
    until done
  end;

procedure getcode(var code : integer);
  begin
    skipblanks;
    if input↑ = '/'
      then
        begin { process bar line }
          get(input);                          { skip bar line }
          if input↑ = '/'
            then code := doublebar
            else code := barline
        end  { process bar line }
    else if input↑ = 'r'
      then
        begin { process rest }
          get(input);                          { skip rest     }
          code := rest
        end  { process rest }
    else read(code)
  end;
```

These changes would make it possible for the program to process the following input data:

```
60 60 62 64 / 65 67 65 64 65 67 65 / 64 67 r 67 72 67 r 67 /
65 67 65 64 65 67 65 / 64 67 r 67 72 67 r 67 / 69 65 r 65 72
69 r 69 67 64 r 64 67 62 //
```

This produces exactly the same output as program 9.3. There are two advantages to using nonnumeric values for nonpitch items: the code is easier to read, and we regain the use of the integers 0, 99, and 100 to represent pitch data.

9.7.2 Application: Integer Conversion

Our second example of top-down design using procedures is a program that converts the ASCII character representation of integers to the numeric form used within the computer. The program duplicates the function of the built-in procedure *read* when it is used to read an integer. In addition to providing another example of top-down design, this program will demonstrate the conversion from character to numeric data, which will be adapted for other purposes in later chapters. It also serves as a review of using *input*↑ to examine characters in the input buffer (see chapter 8).

The conversion depends on the fact that the characters in the character set are ordered, and each character occupies a specific position in this order. The set is arranged so that the characters representing the digits between 0 and 9 are contiguous, as are characters in the uppercase and lowercase alphabets. Pascal provides the *ord* function, which returns the ordinal position in the ASCII character set of the character passed as its argument.[11] Since the numeric characters are contiguous (table 9.3), the value of a numeric character can be calculated as the offset from the character '0', i.e., the difference between the position of the character and that of '0'. Thus the integer value *v* of any numeric character *ch* can be calculated as

$$v := ord(ch) - ord('0')$$

Examples:

$$\text{value of character '0'} = ord('0') - ord('0') = 48 - 48 = 0$$

$$\text{value of character '2'} = ord('2') - ord('0') = 50 - 48 = 2$$

11. Each character in the ASCII character set is represented as a binary number. These numbers are contiguous beginning with octal 0 (the null character), and ending with octal 0177 (delete). In some programming languages (such as C or assembler) the position in the character set could be determined by using the numeric value of the ASCII character.

ord(*ch*):	48	49	50	51	52	53	54	55	56	57
ch:	'0'	'1'	'2'	'3'	'4'	'5'	'6'	'7'	'8'	'9'

Table 9.3. Ordinal Position of Numeric Characters in the ASCII Character Set

We begin with the main procedure. Since the program is designed to test procedure *readint*, the main program consists of a simple loop:

```
begin { main }
  while not eof do
    begin { read and print integer }
      readint(n);
      writeln(n);
      skipblanks
    end
end.  { main }
```

Procedure *readint* converts a string of contiguous numeric characters with an optional sign to an integer value. If we assume that we have a function to convert each numeric character to its integer value, the procedure must still calculate the correct positional weight for each digit. In a base 10 number system, moving a digit one position to the left increases its value by a factor of 10, i.e., the digits from right to left indicate the number of ones, tens, hundreds, thousands, etc. Thus the integer 189 represents the value

$$1 \times 10^2 \;+\; 8 \times 10^1 \;+\; 9 \times 10^0$$

$$= \;\; 100 \;\;+\;\; 80 \;\;+\;\; 9$$

It is not necessary to know how many digits there will be. We can begin by assigning x the value 0. As each next digit is found x is multiplied by 10, and the value of the new digit is added to it. Multiplying by 10 shifts all digits to the left, making room for the new digit in the ones place. The procedure must also skip any preceding blanks and take care of an optional sign. A boolean variable is used to indicate the presence of a minus sign; after the string has been converted to its numeric form, the number is negated if there was a minus sign. An error message is printed if no numeric characters are found. The algorithm in pseudo code can be stated thus:

skip blank and newline characters;
set flag to indicate negative number;
if there is a sign
  then skip it;

```
if there is a numeric character
  then
    begin
      set x equal to 0;
      while there is a digit do
        begin
          multiply x by 10 and add the
            value of the current digit;
          skip the numeric character
        end
    end
  else print error message;
if there was a minus sign
  then negate x;
x now contains the numeric value
```

Procedure *readint* will use a variable parameter to return the value of the converted integer, and a local boolean variable *negative* to indicate the presence of a minus sign:

```
procedure readint(var x : integer);
  var
    negative : boolean;

  begin { readint }
    skipblanks;                          { move input↑ past blanks    }
    negative := input↑ = '-';

    if issign(input↑)
      then get(input);                   { skip plus or minus sign    }

    if isdigit(input↑)
      then
        begin { read integer }
          x := 0;                        { initial value              }
          while isdigit(input↑) do
            begin
              x := 10 * x + toint(input↑);
              get(input)                 { move input↑ to next char }
            end
        end   { read integer }
      else writeln('error: digit expected');

    if negative
      then x := -x
  end;
```

We now provide the missing functions. Procedure *skipblanks* was shown in the previous section. Its purpose is to skip over blanks and newline characters in the input buffer. Boolean functions *issign* and *isdigit* return *true* if their parameters represent, respectively, a sign or a digit:

```
function issign(ch : char) : boolean;
  begin
    issign := ch in ['-', '+']
  end;


function isdigit(ch : char) : boolean;
  begin { isdigit }
    isdigit := ch in ['0' .. '9']
  end; { isdigit }
```

Function *toint* returns the integer value of its formal parameter, a numeric character. The method used was discussed above.

```
function toint(ch : char) : integer;
  begin { toint }
    toint := ord(ch) - ord('0')
  end; { toint }
```

An alternate version of this procedure, which does not depend on contiguous numeric characters, is shown below. This version is necessary for computer systems that do not use the ASCII character set, and is more portable. It tests the actual parameter to ensure that it contains an appropriate value. This test was omitted in the previous version, since the calling procedure ensured that the function would not be called with a nonnumeric character as its argument:

```
function toint(ch : char) : integer;
  begin { toint }
    if not (ch in ['0' .. '9'])
      then writeln('toint: error, nonnumeric argument')
      else
        case ch of
          '0' : toint := 0;
          '1' : toint := 1;
          '2' : toint := 2;
          '3' : toint := 3;
          '4' : toint := 4;
          '5' : toint := 5;
          '6' : toint := 6;
          '7' : toint := 7;
          '8' : toint := 8;
          '9' : toint := 9
        end { case }
    end; { toint }
```

The complete program and sample run are shown on the following pages.

```
(***********************           Program Readints          ***********************)
(* Demonstrates a method of converting character representations of in-    *)
(* tegers to integer values.  Calling readint(n) is exactly equivalent      *)
(* in function to calling the Pascal procedure read(n), where n is any      *)
(* integer variable.  That is, the procedure will read the next integer     *)
(* in the input buffer, and store it in variable n.  Procedure readint      *)
(* calls a number of other functions described below.                       *)
(***************************************************************************)
program readints(input, output);
  var
    n  : integer;                                { for reading integers }

(***********************              isdigit              ***********************)
(* Has one parameter (argument) of type char.  Isdigit checks the           *)
(* value of its argument, and returns true if the character is a            *)
(* character representation of a digit (0,1,2,3,4,5,6,7,8,9), or false     *)
(* if it is not.                                                            *)
(***************************************************************************)
  function isdigit(ch : char) : boolean;
    begin { isdigit }
      isdigit := ch in ['0' .. '9']
    end;  { isdigit }

(***********************               issign              ***********************)
(* Returns true if its argument is a + or - sign, else false.               *)
(***************************************************************************)
  function issign(ch : char) : boolean;
    begin
      issign := ch in ['-', '+']
    end;

(***********************               toint               ***********************)
(* Has one argument (type char), which should be a character represent-     *)
(* ing a digit.  The function uses the ord function to calculate the        *)
(* integer value of this character.  This value is returned to the point    *)
(* of call.  Thus toint('1') has the integer value 1, etc.  Since the       *)
(* function does not check the value of its argument, it is the responsi-*)
(* bility of the calling procedure to check for an appropriate value.       *)
(***************************************************************************)
  function toint(ch : char) : integer;
    begin { toint }
      toint := ord(ch) - ord('0')
    end;  { toint }

(***********************            skipblanks             ***********************)
(* Moves input↑ past blanks and <cr>s in the input buffer. It is called     *)
(* by readint before attempting to read an integer, and by the main         *)
(* procedure before checking for the eof condition.                         *)
(***************************************************************************)
  procedure skipblanks;
    var
      done : boolean;
```

```
    begin  { skipblanks }
      done := false;
      repeat
        if eof
          then done := true
        else if input↑ = ' '
          then get(input)
        else done := true
      until done
    end;   { skipblanks }

(**********************         readint         **********************)
(* Has one var parameter (pass by reference) of type integer. The pro- *)
(* cedure skips blanks and then reads the next integer in the input    *)
(* buffer, assigning this value to the variable "passed to" readint.   *)
(* The character representation of the integer is translated one digit *)
(* at a time. The previous value is multiplied by 10, changing its     *)
(* positional weight, and the new digit is added.                      *)
(***********************************************************************)
  procedure readint(var x : integer);
    var
      negative : boolean;
    begin { readint }
      skipblanks;                              { move input↑ past blanks }
      negative := input↑ = '-';
      if issign(input↑)
        then get(input);                       { skip plus or minus sign }
      if isdigit(input↑)
        then
          begin { read integer }
            x := 0;                            { initialize value        }
            while isdigit(input↑) do
              begin { translate digit }
                x := 10 * x + toint(input↑);
                get(input)                     { get next char           }
              end   { translate digit }
          end   { read integer }
        else writeln('error: digit expected');
      if negative
        then x := -x
    end;

(**********************      main procedure      **********************)
(* Exercises the above procedures.                                     *)
(***********************************************************************)
  begin { main }
    skipblanks;
    while not eof do
      begin
        readint(n);                                    { read an integer }
        writeln(n);                                    { and print it    }
        skipblanks
      end
  end.  { main }
```

Program 9.4. *Readints*

```
43 58 -729 125
      43
      58
    -729
     125
0 3482 845 -345
       0
    3482
     845
    -345
^D
```

Program 9.4. Sample Run (Interactive)

9.7.3 Application: Converting Note Names to Pitch Classes

For our final programming example, we will write a program that reads note names and translates them to pitch classes. The input data consists of letter names optionally followed by symbols for sharps or flats. In this case we will use 's' for sharp and 'f' for flat.[12] Double and triple accidentals are specified by repeating the sharp or flat symbol: 'dss' = D-double-sharp; 'efff' = E-triple-flat. Note names are separated by space characters or newline characters. In addition, we will specify that the line format of the program output will reflect that of the input; i.e., whenever a newline character is encountered in the input file, one will be written on the output file.

In writing the main procedure, we will assume a procedure *readnote(pc)* that will translate the input code to a pitch class; it will return –1 if it doesn't find a legal note name. The main procedure will have to process the input file line by line:

```
begin { main }
  while not eof do
    begin { process line }
      while not eoln do
        begin { process note }
          readnote(pc);                 { translate a note           }
          if negative(pc)               { write pc or error          }
            then write('error':6)
            else write(pc:6);
          skipln                        { find note or newline char }
        end; { process note }
      readln;                           { skip input newline char    }
      writeln                           { terminate output line      }
    end   { process line }
end.  { main }
```

12. See section 6.6. Many other symbols could be used for accidentals, e.g., '#' for sharp and '–' for flat. The symbols 's' and 'f' are mnemonic and easy to type, since they do not require a shift or change from the normal typing position. Using a different symbol would not require a change in the program other than changing the constant definitions.

Procedure *readnote(pc)* will process the input data representing one note and return the pitch class representing that note. It will signal an error by returning –1. The procedure will use *input*↑ to look ahead in the input file, so that it can process note names and accidentals properly. The algorithm in pseudo code is shown below:

```
skip blanks;
if the next character is a note name
  then
    begin { process note }
      get pitch class for natural note;
      skip the character;
      while the next character is an accidental do
        begin
          if it is a sharp
            then increment the pitch class
            else decrement the pitch class;
          skip the accidental
        end
    end  { process note }
  else
    begin { error }
      skip past the note;
      set pitch class equal to -1
    end; { error }

return pitch class to calling program;
```

The program with supporting procedures is listed below. The reader is urged to work through the complete program top-down (beginning with the main procedure and working back through the details).

```
(***********************    Program Getpitch     ***********************)
(* Reads note names from standard input and prints the corresponding    *)
(* pitch classes.  The program processes the input file line by line,   *)
(* and begins a new line in the output file whenever an input line is   *)
(* terminated.                                                          *)
(* Input:  Note names followed by any number of sharps or flats.  Notes *)
(*         are separated by blanks or newline characters, e.g.,         *)
(*              c df fss (c d-flat f-double-sharp).                     *)
(* Output: A pc integer for each note, or 'error' for erroneous name.   *)
(************************************************************************)
program getpitch(input, output);
  const
    sharp = 's';                            { symbol for sharp }
    flat  = 'f';                            { symbol for flat  }

  var
    pc : integer;
```

```
(***********************          isnote          ***********************)
(* Returns true if c is a note name.                                      *)
(**************************************************************************)
  function isnote(c : char) : boolean;
    begin
      isnote := c in ['a' .. 'g']
    end;

(***********************       isaccidental       ***********************)
(* Returns true if c is an accidental.                                    *)
(**************************************************************************)
  function isaccidental(c : char) : boolean;
    begin
      isaccidental := c in [sharp, flat]
    end;

(***********************          pitch           ***********************)
(* Returns pc of note in natural scale.                                   *)
(**************************************************************************)
  function pitch(name : char) : integer;
    begin
      case name of
        'c' : pitch := 0;
        'd' : pitch := 2;
        'e' : pitch := 4;
        'f' : pitch := 5;
        'g' : pitch := 7;
        'a' : pitch := 9;
        'b' : pitch := 11
      end  { case }
    end;

(***********************       skiptoblank        ***********************)
(* Finds the next blank or eof.                                           *)
(**************************************************************************)
  procedure skiptoblank;
    begin
      while not (input↑ = ' ') and not eof do
        get(input)
    end;

(***********************        skipblanks        ***********************)
(* Finds next nonblank char or eof.                                       *)
(**************************************************************************)
  procedure skipblanks;
    var
      done : boolean;
    begin
      done := false;
      repeat
        if eof
          then done := true
        else if input↑ = ' '
          then get(input)
        else done := true
      until done
    end;
```

```
(***********************          skipln          ***********************)
(* Finds next nonblank char or newline character.                       *)
(************************************************************************)
  procedure skipln;
    begin
      while (input↑ = ' ') and not eoln do
        get(input)
    end;

(***********************         negative         ***********************)
(* Returns true if argument is negative.                                *)
(************************************************************************)
  function negative(x : integer) : boolean;
    begin
      negative := x < 0
    end;

(***********************           incr           ***********************)
(* Adds one to its argument.                                            *)
(************************************************************************)
  procedure incr(var x : integer);
    begin
      x := x + 1
    end;

(***********************           decr           ***********************)
(* Subtracts one from its argument.                                     *)
(************************************************************************)
  procedure decr(var x : integer);
    begin
      x := x - 1
    end;

(***********************         readnote         ***********************)
(* Reads a note name, adjusts for accidentals, and returns the pc integer*)
(* as a var parameter.  Returns -1 if no legal note name was found.     *)
(************************************************************************)
  procedure readnote(var pc : integer);
    begin {readnote}
      if isnote(input↑)
        then
          begin { good note }
            pc := pitch(input↑);
            get(input);                          { skip note name        }
            while isaccidental(input↑) do
              begin { adjust pc }
                if input↑ = sharp
                  then incr(pc)
                  else decr(pc);
                get(input);                      { skip accidental       }
              end;  { adjust pc }
            pc := (pc + 12) mod 12
          end   { good note }
        else
```

```
        begin { error }
          skiptoblank;                              { skip token          }
          pc := -1                                  { signal error        }
        end   { error }
    end;  { readnote }

(***********************        main procedure        ***********************)
(* Exercises the above procedures.                                          *)
(***************************************************************************)
  begin { main }
    while not eof do
      begin { process line }
        skipblanks;
        while not eoln do
          begin { process note }
            readnote(pc);                         { translate a note        }
            if negative(pc)                       { write pc or error       }
              then write('error':6)
              else write(pc:6);
            skipln                                { find note or newline char }
          end;  { process note }
        readln;                                   { skip input newline char  }
        writeln; writeln                          { terminate output line    }
      end   { process line }
  end.  { main }
```

Program 9.5. *Getpitch*

```
c d e f g a b
     0     2     4     5     7     9    11

cs d ef f gs
     1     2     3     5     8

css d eff f gsss a
     2     2     2     5    10     9

fs g x e bf ff
     6     7 error     4    10     4

e f g e as d e f bff
     4     5     7     4    10     2     4     5     9

q cs f d e r g
 error     1     5     2     4 error     7
```

Program 9.5. Sample Run (Interactive)

9.8 Subprogram Directives

A directive is a predefined identifier that follows a function or procedure heading and replaces the subroutine block. The directive gives the compiler special information about the subroutine. The only directive defined in the Pascal standard is *forward*, but other implementation-dependent directives may be provided for a Pascal compiler.

9.8.1 The *forward* Directive

Normally a procedure or function must be defined in a program before it is called. This is sometimes inconvenient. When writing a large program, the programmer may wish to keep similar definitions together. For example, it is useful to keep all user-defined mathematic functions together, or all procedures that deal with internal buffers, etc. Sometimes it is impossible to define all procedures before they are called. This is the case in mutually recursive procedures, in which each calls the other (see section 15.4). The *forward* directive is also useful if the programmer wishes to list procedures and functions in some specific order. Pascal provides a mechanism for telling the compiler that, although a subprogram has not yet been defined, it will be later. This mechanism is the *forward* reference. If procedure *B* needs to call procedure *A*, which has not yet been defined, the heading for procedure *A* is placed anywhere before the heading of procedure *B*. The form of this heading is exactly as it would normally be, except that it is followed by the directive *forward.*

```
procedure A (x : integer); forward;

function  F (z : integer) : real; forward;
```

Later, when the actual procedure or function definition is placed in the program, the procedure or function name is given *without* the parameter list and, in the case of a function, the return type. This is followed by the body of the function or procedure.

```
procedure A;
  begin
    <statements>
  end;

function F;
  begin
    <statements>
  end;
```

In practice it is helpful to show the parameter list and return type with the procedure or function definition. This is accomplished by following the original form but using comment delimiters instead of standard parentheses. In the case of functions, the parameter list and return type may be enclosed in comment delimiters.

```
procedure A {x : integer};
  begin
    <statements>
  end;
```

```
function F {(z : integer) : integer};
  begin
    <statements>
  end;
```

The use of the *forward* declaration is illustrated in program 15.2, section 15.4.

9.8.2 Other Directives

Some Pascal implementations provide other subprogram directives. Directives for using external subprograms are common, and usually take the form *external* or *extern*. These make possible the development and use of libraries of external procedures and functions that can be called by other programs. Sometimes it is also possible to specify subprograms written in other languages:

```
function  calc(x, y, z : real) : real;      external;

procedure plot(x, y);       fortran;
```

See your programming manual for a list of options available in your version of Pascal, but remember that directives other than *forward* may not be supported by other systems and should not be considered portable.

9.9 Subprograms as Parameters

It is possible to pass functions and procedures as parameters to other functions or procedures. This is useful when most of a procedure can serve in different situations, but part of a calculation requires action that varies for different situations. Thus using procedures and functions as parameters can make some subprograms more flexible. This technique is commonly used in implementing libraries of mathematic subroutines.

The principle is illustrated by program 9.6, which reads notes encoded in continuous pitch code and prints each note in several different formats. Separate procedures calculate and print the pitch as a note name with octave designation, *oct.pc* notation, *oct.dec* notation, and cycles per second or Hz (e.g., 57 = A_4 = 4.09 = 4.75 = 440 Hz). Procedure *writenote* is passed one of these formatting procedures and the note, and calls the formatting procedure, passing the note as an argument. The formal parameter list for procedure *writenote* includes a dummy procedure declaration as an argument, and the dummy procedure is called from *writenote*. (In some installations, the parameter list of the dummy procedure is omitted in the declaration.)

```
procedure writenote(procedure p(x : integer); note : integer);
  begin
    p(note)                           { format and print note  }
  end;
```

When procedure *writenote* is called, an actual procedure name is passed as the argument. Thus when the main program calls

```
writenote(cps, note);
```

the actual procedure *cps* is used in place of procedure *p* in *writenote*. When functions are passed as parameters, the return type is specified as well.

```
procedure calc(function f(x : integer) : real; x : integer);
```

There are some restrictions on the use of functions and procedures as parameters. Obviously, the actual parameter must be a function or procedure identifier, and the number and type of arguments in the actual (passed) procedure or function must agree with those in the formal parameter list. When functions are passed, the return type of the actual function must agree with that in the formal declaration. Many implementations of Pascal do not allow variable parameters to be used in the passed subprogram's parameter list, and some do not allow standard functions or procedures to be passed. The latter restriction can be circumvented easily, with little overhead, by using a user-defined function that calls the standard one:

```
function sine(x : real) : real;
  begin
    sine := sin(x)
  end;
```

```
(***********************    Program Passproc    ***********************)
(* Illustrates passing procedures as parameters to other procedures.  *)
(* The basic procedure, writenote, is passed a note in cpc notation and *)
(* one of several procedures that print the note in different formats. *)
(* The formatting procedures calculate and print the note using letter *)
(* names, oct.pc, oct.dec, and Hz (cps).                               *)
(**********************************************************************)
program passproc(input, output);
  var
    note : integer;                         { a note in cpc notation }

(***********************       writenote       ***********************)
(* Is passed two parameters, a formatting procedure and a note in con- *)
(* tinuous pitch code.  The note is used as an argument to the procedure *)
(* that will format it.                                                *)
(**********************************************************************)
  procedure writenote(procedure p(x : integer); note : integer);
    begin
      p(note)                               { format and print note  }
    end;

(***********************         octpc         ***********************)
(* Extracts the octave and pc components of the note and prints them in *)
(* the format oct.pc.                                                  *)
(**********************************************************************)
  procedure octpc(note : integer);
    begin
      writeln('oct.pc    = ', note div 12 + (note mod 12) / 100 :4:2)
    end;
```

```
(***********************           octdec          ***********************)
(* Prints the note in oct.dec form.  The decimal part is the fraction of *)
(* the octave, with each pc equal to 1/12 of an octave.                  *)
(*************************************************************************)
 procedure octdec(note : integer);
   var
     oct : integer;                               { octave part of note }
     dec : real;                                  { decimal part of note}

   begin
     oct := note div 12;
     dec := (note mod 12) / 12;
     writeln('oct.dec    = ', oct + dec :4:2)
   end;


(***********************          stdname          ***********************)
(* Prints the note name followed by the standard octave number.  Since   *)
(* cpc does not convey the actual spelling of the note, sharps are used  *)
(* for all chromatic pitches.                                            *)
(*************************************************************************)
 procedure stdname(note : integer);
   var
     oct, pc : integer;                         { octave and pc of note  }

   begin
     oct := note div 12;
     pc  := note mod 12;
     write('note name = ');

     case pc of                                 { print note name        }
       0 : write('C');
       1 : write('C#');
       2 : write('D');
       3 : write('D#');
       4 : write('E');
       5 : write('F');
       6 : write('F#');
       7 : write('G');
       8 : write('G#');
       9 : write('A');
      10 : write('A#');
      11 : write('B')
     end; { case }
     writeln(oct:1)                             { and octave number      }
   end;


(***********************            cps            ***********************)
(* Cycles per second are calculated using as a bass pitch the frequency  *)
(* for C0, 16.352 Hz.  This number is multiplied by 2 raised to the      *)
(* power represented by oct.dec of note.  Thus C1 is 16.352 * 2, C2 is   *)
(* 16.352 * 4, etc.  The decimal part of the exponent gives twelve equal *)
(* divisions of the octave.  The ln and exp functions are use to cal-    *)
(* culate the powers of 2.                                               *)
(*************************************************************************)
```

```
  procedure cps(note : integer);
    var
      oct      : integer;                        { octave part of note }
      dec, cps : real;                           { decimal part and Hz }
    begin
      oct := note div 12;
      dec := (note mod 12) / 12;
      cps := 16.352 * exp(ln(2) * (oct + dec));
      writeln('Hz         =', cps:6:2)
    end;

(***********************     main procedure     ***********************)
(* Loops until the user types the eof char.  Procedure writenote is    *)
(* passed each formatting function to print a different notation of the *)
(* pitch.                                                              *)
(**********************************************************************)
  begin { main }
    write('enter cpc:  ');
    while not eof do
      begin
        readln(note);
        writenote(stdname, note);
        writenote(octpc, note);
        writenote(octdec, note);
        writenote(cps, note);
        writeln; writeln;
        write('enter cpc:  ')
      end
  end.  { main }
```

Program 9.6. *Passproc*

```
enter cpc:  0          enter cpc:  49         enter cpc:  59
note name = C0         note name = C#4        note name = B4
oct.pc    = 0.00       oct.pc    = 4.01       oct.pc    = 4.11
oct.dec   = 0.00       oct.dec   = 4.08       oct.dec   = 4.92
Hz        = 16.35      Hz        =277.19      Hz        =493.90

enter cpc:  12         enter cpc:  50         enter cpc:  60
note name = C1         note name = D4         note name = C5
oct.pc    = 1.00       oct.pc    = 4.02       oct.pc    = 5.00
oct.dec   = 1.00       oct.dec   = 4.17       oct.dec   = 5.00
Hz        = 32.70      Hz        =293.67      Hz        =523.26

enter cpc:  48         enter cpc:  58         enter cpc:  ^D
note name = C4         note name = A#4
oct.pc    = 4.00       oct.pc    = 4.10
oct.dec   = 4.00       oct.dec   = 4.83
Hz        =261.63      Hz        =466.18
```

Program 9.6. Sample Run (Interactive)[13]

13. Edited for three-column printing.

References and Selected Readings

Read chapters 2 and 3 of the following:

Ledgard, Henry F., John F. Hueras, and Paul A. Nagin. *Pascal With Style.* Rochelle Park, N.Y.: Hayden, 1979.

Other suggested reading:

Forte, Allen. "The Structure of Atonal Music: Practical Aspects of a Computer-Oriented Research Project." In *Musicology and the Computer*, edited by Barry S. Brook, 10–18. New York: City University of New York Press, 1970.

Hiller, Lejaren A. "Programming a Computer for Music Composition." In *Papers from the West Virginia Conference on Computer Applications in Music*, edited by Gerald Lefkoff, 63–88. Morgantown, W.Va.: West Virginia University Library, 1967.

Lewin, David. "On Certain Techniques of Re-Ordering in Serial Music." *Journal of Music Theory* 10, no. 2 (1966): 276–87.

Smoliar, Stephen W. "Music Programs: An Approach to Music Theory Through Computational Linguistics." *Journal of Music Theory* 20, no. 1 (1976): 105–31.

———. "Process Structuring and Music Theory." *Journal of Music Theory* 18, no. 2 (1974): 308–36.

Exercises

Each of the following functions and procedures should be used in a short program that illustrates its use.

Functions: Remember that functions return values directly so that you may use them in expressions or write their values without storing them first. Example:

```
while not eof do
  begin
    readln(note);
    writeln('pitch class =', pc(note), ' octave =', oct(note))
  end;
```

Pitch Class and Continuous Pitch Code

1. Write function *pc(note)*, which returns the pitch-class equivalent of a note encoded in continuous pitch code (cpc).

2. Write function *oct(note)*, which returns the octave of a cpc encoded note.

3. Write function *cpc(pc, oct)*, which returns the cpc representation of a note, given the pitch class and octave.

Name Class and Continuous Name Code

4. Write function *nc(note)*, which returns the name-class equivalent of a note encoded in continuous name code (cnc).

5. Write function *oct(note)*, which returns the octave of a cnc encoded note.

6. Write function *cnc(nc, oct)*, which returns the cnc representation of a note, given the name class and octave.

Rhythm

7. Write function *beats(dur, beatnote)*, which converts durations encoded in reciprocal duration code (rdc) to the number of beats. *Dur* and *beatnote* are encoded as described in exercise set 7.3.

Character Testing and Manipulation

8. Write a boolean procedure to test its character argument for each of the following:

Function		*Action*
islower(c)	—	returns *true* if *c* is a lowercase letter
isupper(c)	—	returns *true* if *c* is an uppercase letter
isalpha(c)	—	returns *true* if *c* is an upper- or lowercase letter
isdigit(c)	—	returns *true* if *c* is a digit
isalnum(c)	—	returns *true* if *c* is alphabetic or numeric
iscntrl(c)	—	returns *true* if *ord(c)* <= 31
isspace(c)	—	returns *true* if *c* is a space, or any of the following: horizontal tab [*chr*(9)], newline character [*chr*(10)], vertical tab [*chr*(11)], formfeed [*chr*(12)], or carriage return [*chr*(13)]
ispunct(c)	—	returns *true* if *c* is not a control character, space character, or an alphanumeric character
isname(c)	—	returns *true* if *c* is a note name ['a' . . 'g', 'A' . . 'G']
isacc(c)	—	returns *true* if *c* is a sharp or flat (define with constants in main program)
isbar(c)	—	returns *true* if *c* is a bar line (defined as a constant)
ispc(c)	—	returns *true* if *c* is a digit or any of the following: 'a', 'A', 'b', 'B'

Expand the program below to exercise these functions and test the value of each character typed. The program should print out a message identifying each applicable attribute.

```
program ctest(input, output);
  const
    sharp = 's';                              { sharp    }
    flat  = 'f';                              { flat     }
    bar   = '/';                              { bar line }

  { your function definitions go here }

  begin { main }
    write('type any character followed by <cr>: ')
    while not eof do
      begin { character test }
        if isdigit(input↑)
          then writeln('digit');
        if ispc(input↑)
          then writeln('pitch class');
        . . .
        readln;                               { finish line }
        write('type any character followed by <cr>: ')
      end   { character test }
  end.  { main }
```

9. Write function *tolower(c)*, which returns the lower case of *c* if *c* is an uppercase alphabetic character, otherwise returns *c*. Use arithmetic mapping for the translation.

10. Write function *toupper(c)*, which returns the upper case of *c* if *c* is a lowercase alphabetic character, otherwise returns *c*. Use arithmetic mapping for the translation.

11. Use each of the above (*toupper* and *tolower*) in a separate program that copies the standard input file to the standard output file, translating upper case to lower case or vice versa. (Modify program *copy1* or *copy2*, section 8.2.)

12. Modify the programs from 11 above, so that lower- and uppercase conversion does not affect characters within strings delimited by ′ and ′, or ″ and ″.

13. Write function *pc(c)*, which returns the pitch class (0 . . . 11) for any letter name: 'c' = 0; 'd' = 2, 'e' = 4, 'f' = 5, . . ., 'b' = 11.

Procedures: Each of the following procedures changes the value of its argument(s). Thus you must arrange things so that new values can be returned by using **var** parameters (call by reference). Example:

```
procedure incr(var x : integer);
```

Remember that procedures do not return values directly, so it is not possible to use the procedure in an expression, i.e, *write(incr(x))* is not legal. Instead, your program should call the procedure to change the value of a variable, and then write the new value. Example:

```
while not eof do
  begin
    readln(n);
    incr(n);
    writeln(n)
  end;
```

14. Write procedure *incr(x)*, which adds one to the value of its integer argument.

15. Write procedure *decr(x)*, which subtracts one from the value of its argument.

16. Write procedure *swap(x, y)*, which exchanges the values of integer arguments *x* and *y*. The procedure should use a local variable *t* as a temporary storage location for making the exchange.

17. Write procedure *rswap(x, y)*, which exchanges the values of two real variables.

18. Write procedure *getpc(pc)*, which reads a pitch class expressed as a single character. It may be a digit ('0' . . . '9') or upper- or lowercase 'a' or 'b' representing pc integers 10 and 11. The procedure should return the pc integer using a **var** parameter. Use the procedure in a program that reads pcs on each line of input and prints their numeric equivalent on a line of output. Note that with this encoding scheme it is not necessary to separate characters by blanks. Sample input and output are shown below:

Input	*Output*
124ab	1 2 4 10 11
673113	6 7 3 1 1 3
b 2 4 a b 8 9	11 2 4 10 11 8 9

19. *In Search of Tritones.* The data for this problem consists of encoded harmonic intervals derived from a two-voiced composition. The intervals are encoded as the number of semitones between the two notes, i.e., P1 = 0, M3 = 4, m2 = 1, M10 = 16. Bar lines are encoded as the integer 100, and there is no special code for the end of the excerpt (use *eof* for this). The piece may have an anacrusis, in which case the first encoded value will be an interval, or it may begin with a bar line. Intervals before the first bar line are in measure 0.

a) Write a program that examines each encoded interval. For each measure that contains one or more harmonic tritones, print the measure number and the number of tritones in the measure. When the entire composition has been processed, print the total number of tritones. Print no message for measures that do not contain tritones. Your program should use the following functions and procedures:

procedure *skipblanks* — finds the next nonblank character in the input buffer, skipping blanks and newline characters.

procedure *increment*(*x*) — adds one to the value of its argument.

function or procedure *reduce*(*int*) — reduces compound intervals to simple ones. It should not change simple intervals or bar lines.

function or procedure *count6* — returns the number of tritones in the current measure.

Decide whether a function or procedure is more appropriate for each of the above tasks.

b) Write a program that finds each tritone (interval class 6), and prints out the number of the measure in which the tritone occurs, the interval to which the tritone resolves, and the measure in which the resolution occurs. Example:

```
                    Tritones
================================================
Measure  Resolution interval  Resolution measure
=======  ===================  ==================
   5              4                   6
  10              8                  10
  12              6                  13
  13              9                  13
================================================
```

If a vertical tritone is followed by another, show both as in the last two entries in the above table. Remember that a bar line may occur between the tritone and its resolution.

You may decide how to proceed with functions or procedures in this problem. Use functions and procedures to modularize the program, and design your algorithm top-down. In addition to the procedures for part (a) above, you may find the following helpful:

procedure *getint*(*x*) — returns the next interval (reduced) in the input file. The procedure should skip over bar lines to find the next real interval. If no more intervals occur in the file, it should return the final bar line (100).

Hint: Before designing your algorithm for (b), you may find it helpful to review the algorithm for generating Fibonacci numbers (section 7.4) and program 9.3 (*intervals*) in this chapter.

c) If the input data represents common-practice tonal music, a program should be able to deduce whether a tritone (interval class 6) represents a diminished fifth or an augmented fourth. How would this determination be made?

PART II Structured Types

10| The Array and List Processing

Thus far we have used only simple, unstructured types. Scalar and subrange types are unstructured, in the sense that each data item is an indivisible unit. Even though we can write functions that decompose a simple type, e.g., return the fractional part of a real number or the ones digit of an integer, conceptually they are treated as a single item, and are accessed as such by Pascal.

Pascal, like most other languages, also provides structured data types that allow us to group simple data items in meaningful ways, depending on relationships between the data items. Structured types are characterized by the types of their components and the method used to structure the data. The array is the most basic structured type; in fact, it is the only structured type offered in some computer languages. In this chapter and the next we will consider the structure and uses of arrays. Later, we will study Pascal's other structured types—sets, records, and linked data structures.

10.1 Properties of Arrays

The *array* enables us to give a single name to a group of related data items. An array is a set of variables (called *components* or *elements* of the array) that are all the same type and are known by the same name. The value of an element is accessed by the name of the array and an index, or subscript, which indicates a position in the array. We can conceptualize the array as a series of storage locations with a single name and an index that distinguishes each location in the array. For example, if the array *list* has been declared to have storage locations indexed by the integers 1 to max, we can picture the structure shown in figure 10.1.

The elements of *list* are accessed by using the array name and an index, enclosed in brackets. Thus we can refer to *list*[1], *list*[2], *list*[9], or *list*[*i*], where *i* is a variable having the value of a legal subscript of *list*. The fact that we can use variables and

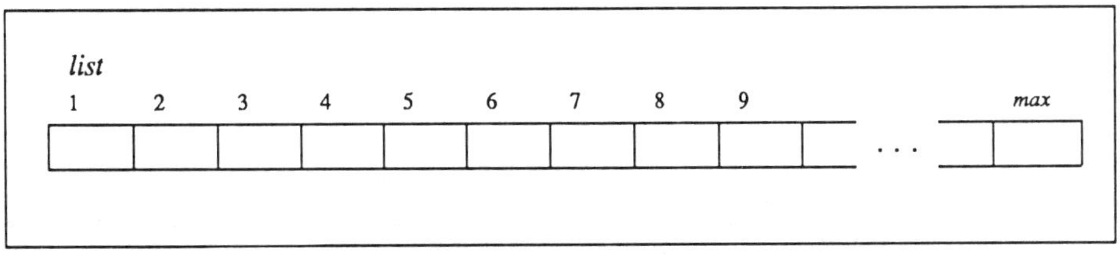

Figure 10.1. An Array Indexed from 1 to *max*

expressions to index arrays is one of the real advantages of using arrays for processing data. Because of this, we can use a loop to perform the same operation on each element of an array. For example, the following loop prints the value of each element in the *list* array:

```
for i := 1 to n do
  write(list[i])
```

Internally, arrays are implemented with contiguous storage locations in memory. The actual address of each element in memory is calculated as the offset of the element from the address of the first element in the array (the base address). For example, if the first element of the array *list* is stored at memory location x, and the array indexes are numbered from 0, then the actual address of any element *list*[i] is memory location $x + i$.[1] Thus any element in the array can be accessed in a fixed amount of time. Because of this property, arrays are termed *random-access* data structures.

Space for arrays is allocated when the program is compiled, and cannot be changed while the program is running. It is the responsibility of the programmer to reserve enough space for each array and to incorporate in the program tests to ensure that this space is not exceeded. Data structures that use dynamic storage allocation will be discussed in chapter 16. Table 10.1 summarizes properties of arrays.

- All elements are of the same type, which may be simple or structured.
- Since space for arrays is allocated when the program is compiled, the size of the array cannot be changed while the program is running.
- Array elements are referenced by the array name and an index indicating the desired element in the array.
- Since the actual address of each element is calculated arithmetically, any element can be accessed in a fixed amount of time, which does not depend on the value of the index. This property is called random access.

Table 10.1. Properties of Arrays

10.2 Using Arrays

Before an array can be used, it must be declared. The syntax of the array declaration is shown in figure 10.2.

1. This simple example assumes that each array element uses only one storage location, and that the indexes are numbered beginning at 0. The algorithm for calculating the address for other cases is slightly more complex, but still takes a fixed amount of time.

```
type
  <array type> = array[<index type>] of <component type>;

var
  <array name> : <array type>;
```

Figure 10.2. SYNTAX: Array Declaration

The declaration is in two parts. The first part defines the array type, and the second declares a variable of that type. Type declarations are placed after any constant declarations and before variable declarations. The type declaration for arrays specifies both the type of value used as an index and the type of value that will be stored in the array. <Array type> is any valid Pascal identifier that will be used to identify the array type. <Index type> is a scalar or subrange type. It may be a subrange of integers, but the type *real* is not allowed for indices. <Component type> is the type of value that will be stored in each array element. The component type may be any simple type or another structured type such as a record, or even another array.[2] The actual array is declared with other variables in the variable declaration part of the program. It is specified as <array name>, a valid Pascal identifier, declared to be type <array type>, which must have been declared previously in a type declaration. In practice, subrange types used as the index type frequently use constants declared in the constant declaration part of the program. This practice simplifies changing the size of arrays, should this become necessary.

The program segment shown below illustrates many of these points. The first type declaration is a subrange of integers, and specifies that *pcints* (pitch-class integers) will be integers between 0 and 11 inclusive. The type *string* is declared as a **packed array** that will contain *maxstring* characters.[3] The identifier *listtype* specifies an array that will contain at most *max pcints*. *Counttype* specifies an array indexed by *pcints* 0 through 11 that will contain integers. Type *check* is an array indexed by the subrange of integers 0 through 11 that will contain boolean values *true* or *false*; and *pitchtype* is an array of *pcints* indexed by the characters 'a' through 'g'.

```
program demo(input, output);
  const
    max       = 100;        { max length of note list    }
    maxstring =  80;        { max length of char strings }

  type
    pcints    = 0 .. 11;
    string    = packed array[1 .. maxstring] of char;
    listtype  = array [1 .. max] of pcints;
    counttype = array[pcints] of integer;
    check     = array[0 .. 11] of boolean;
    pitchtype = array['a' .. 'g'] of integer;
```

2. These possibilities will be addressed in chapters 11 and 13.

3. The directive **packed** used in declaring strings will be explained in chapter 11.

```
var
  S1, S2      : string;       { character strings            }
  notelist    : listtype;     { array to store pcs           }
  n           : integer;      { actual number of pcs         }
  count       : counttype;    { number of each specific pc   }
  have        : check;        { check for duplicates         }
  pitch       : pitchtype;    { converts letter names to pcs }
  i, j, pc    : integer;
```

Once the above declarations have been made, any of the following are legal Pascal statements, so long as the values used in calculating the subscripts are defined and the resulting values are within the range specified in the array declarations:

```
S1[i + 1] := chr(0);
notelist[j] := 9;
t := notelist[1];
count[pc] := count[pc] + 1;
have[pc] := false;
if have[pc]
  then . . . ;
pitch['a'] := 9;
pc := pitch[input↑];
```

Arrays can be declared directly, without prior declaration of an array type. This is seldom done except for local variables in procedures, since arrays declared in this manner cannot be passed as arguments to subroutines. The type declaration occurs in place of the type name in the variable declaration itself; otherwise the form is exactly as shown above.

```
var
  have : array[0..11] of boolean;
```

There are many uses for arrays in computing. On the following pages we will demonstrate their use for storing and processing linear lists. The next chapter explores other uses for arrays—implementing other data structures such as stacks and queues, manipulating character strings, implementing data buffers, and building lookup tables for fast conversion of data, as well as arrays in two or more dimensions. Music applications are explored further in the exercises at the end of each chapter.

10.3 List Defined

It is important to make a distinction between a data object and the data structure used to implement that object. In this chapter we will use arrays to store lists; later we will learn how to represent lists in linked data structures.

An ordered or linear list is a collection of related items arranged in some specific order. Some examples are the notes in the C major scale:

(C, D, E, F, G, A, B, C)

or the notes in the main theme of the fourth movement of Brahms's Symphony No. 1:

(G, C, B, C, A, G, C, D, E, D, E, C, D, D, G, C, B, C, A, G, C, D, E, F, E, C, D, C)

or composers:

(Palestrina, Monteverdi, Bach, Mozart, Beethoven, Schubert, Brahms, Wagner, Debussy, Schoenberg, Webern, Berg, Stravinsky, Ligeti)

or Fibonacci numbers:

(0, 1, 1, 2, 3, 5, 8, 13, 21, 34, 55, 89, 144)

The specific order of the elements in the list is not important—the fact that they are ordered is. The list of composers shown above could be ordered chronologically, alphabetically, by some criteria of greatness or personal preference, or even randomly. Whatever the ordering, each member has a specific position in the list. It is also not necessary that a list be complete. If your favorite composer is not in the list, he or she can be added.

Formally, either a list is empty or we can write it in the form

$$(e_1, e_2, e_3, \ldots, e_n)$$

where each e_i is an element in the list. Useful operations that can be performed on the list include finding its length, finding the value of the ith value, reading the list (forward or backward), adding a new element either at the end or at some arbitrary position in the list, changing the value of any element, deleting an element, copying the list, joining two lists, reordering the list, searching the list for some specific value, etc.

The most common way to represent lists in arrays is to associate element e_i with index i of the array. This simplifies most of the operations listed above, since we can directly access any element of an array.

We will use procedures for processing arrays. Arrays should almost always be passed as variable parameters (through use of the **var** declaration in the procedure heading when the array parameter is declared). This saves space and computing time, especially if arrays are large. The reason for this has to do with the way values are passed to subprograms (you may wish to review chapter 9.6 on value and variable parameters). When an array is passed by value (the default), Pascal allocates space for a new array of the desired type for use by the procedure, and each element of the actual parameter is passed on the stack and copied into the new array represented by the formal parameter name. If an array is passed by reference (as a **var** parameter), only the base address of the array (a single value) is passed, and the procedure uses the same storage locations as the calling program without moving any data. Obviously this saves time as well as space. Remember:

Arrays should be passed by reference even if the procedure will not change the contents of the array. The only exceptions are rare cases in which the procedure will change values in the array, but the calling procedure must retain the original values.

10.4 Reading and Writing Lists

It is not always possible to know how many elements will be in a list, and a single array is sometimes used to store a succession of lists of different lengths. When this is the case, arrays are declared with some reasonable maximum number of elements, and only part of the array is actually used to store the list. The program must keep track of both the maximum number of elements in the array and the actual number of elements in the list stored in the array. The procedures shown below assume that the following declarations have been made in the main program:

```
program main(input, output);
  const
    max = 100;            { maximum length of list              }

  type
    listtype = array[1 .. max] of integer;

  var
    list : listtype;      { array for storing list of integers }
    n    : integer;       { actual number of elements in list  }
```

For our demonstration, *list* will contain at most *max* values of type *integer*. The program should ensure that *n* <= *max*, since an attempt to reference an array element that is not within the declared bounds will result in an error message ("array bound error") and abnormal termination of the program.

The actual number of elements can be obtained in one of two ways. The simpler scheme is to precede the list with an integer specifying the length of the list. Thus the input values might look like the following:

```
4 3 5 8 12                                  { 4-element list }
3 89 21 7                                   { 3-element list }
9 98 12 73 94 122 74 84 18 199              { 9-element list }
```

The procedure first reads the number of elements and then uses a loop to read the list. The first version of procedure *readlist* uses a **for** loop and does not check to make sure that the array bounds are not exceeded. The procedure uses **var** parameters to return the array containing the list and the length of the list. The *readln* at the end of the procedure is optional. It assumes that no data will follow the end of the list on the same line, and makes it possible to place the procedure call in a loop that terminates at the end-of-file.

```
procedure readlist(var list : listtype; var n : integer);
  var
    i : integer;
  begin
    read(n);                                  { length of list }
    for i := 1 to n do
      read(list[i]);
    readln
  end;
```

The version of *readlist* shown below tests *n* against *max*. If the list is too long, it discards the list by reading each value and returning 0 as the length of the list. This makes it possible to process other input lists after the one that is too long. The global constant *max* is used without being passed as a parameter.

```
procedure readlist(var list : listtype; var n : integer);
  var
    i : integer;
  begin
    read(n);
    if n <= max
      then
        for i := 1 to n do
          read(list[i])
      else
        begin { overlength list }
          writeln('error: list longer than', max);
          for i := 1 to n do        { discard list }
            read(list[1]);
          n := 0
        end;  { overlength list }
    readln
  end;
```

It is often more convenient to have the program count the number of items in the list as it reads them. Thus the list need not be preceded in the input file by its cardinality. In order to do this, some special value must terminate the list. Our third version of *readlist* reads all of the integers on a single line of the input file. This is a good strategy for programs that will process short sets of data entered interactively by the user. In other applications, a list might be read from an external data file and be terminated by the end-of-file. The procedure uses parameter *n* to count each element before it is read. If no integers are typed on the line, the procedure returns an empty list ($n = 0$). The *readln* at the end of the procedure is necessary; without it the next invocation of the procedure would return an empty list. This procedure does not check *n* against *max*, since *max* is large enough that the user is unlikely to enter too many elements on a single line.

```
procedure readlist(var list : listtype; var n : integer);
  begin
    n := 0;
```

```
    while not eoln do
      begin
        incr(n);
        read(list[n]);
        skipln  { skip blanks to next nonblank char or eoln }
      end;
    readln { skip newline character }
  end;  { readlist }
```

A procedure to print the list is even simpler. Because the length of the list is already known, the task can be accomplished with a **for** loop. Note that the array is passed as a variable parameter, even though its values will not change. The *writeln* statement could be omitted from the procedure, leaving open the option to terminate the line after the list is printed.

```
procedure printlist(var list : listtype; n : integer);
  var
    i : integer;
  begin
    for i := 1 to n do
      write(list[i]);
    writeln                                   { terminate line }
  end;
```

We can add a few bells and whistles for finer control over the printing process. The version of *printlist* shown below adds two extra parameters that specify the number of elements to print on each line and the field width to use. Thus calling

```
printlist(list, n, 10, 4);
```

would print the first *n* elements of *list*, ten per line, using a field width of 4. This kind of control is important if lists are too long to fit on a single line of the output device.

```
procedure printlist(var list : listtype; n, length, fw : integer);
  var
    i : integer;
  begin
    for i := 1 to n do
      begin
        write(list[i]:fw);
        if i mod length = 0
          then writeln
      end;
    writeln
  end;
```

10.5 Simple Operations with Lists

As in printing a list, most operations with lists involve doing the same thing to each element. When the list is stored in an array, and we know the length of the list, this can always be done with a **for** loop. The loop sets the value of a variable used to index the array. The initial and final values of the control variable are the first and last subscripts of the list. Thus each element is referenced. Suppose that we wish to calculate the sum of all of the elements of a list stored in $A[i]$, $1 \le i \le n$:[4]

```
sum := 0;
for i := 1 to n do
  sum := sum + A[i];
writeln('sum = ', sum);
```

If we want to find the smallest value in the list, we can do so by arbitrarily choosing one element and saving its value. We then compare each other element to the one saved, and if the new element is less than the smallest found so far, we save the new value. Again the loop examines each value in the list:

```
small := A[1];
for i := 2 to n do
  if A[i] < small
    then small := A[i];
writeln('the least value is ', small:5);
```

An alternate approach is to find the *location* of the smallest value in the list. Since we can randomly access any value in the array, we can get the value from the location. This is an important technique, since it is used in sorting lists. The version shown below uses the first location if two values are equal. Changing '<' to '<=' would use the last.

```
loc := 1;                      { assume that 1st location        }
                               {    contains the largest number  }
for i := 2 to n do             { compare the others to it        }
  if A[i] < A[loc]             {    and save location of new     }
    then loc := i;             {    largest number               }
writeln('the smallest number is: ', A[loc]);
```

As we have seen, the random-access property of arrays makes them easy to process with a loop that sets the value of the index. Another property of arrays—that they use contiguous storage locations—complicates insertion and deletion of arbitrary elements in a list. Each of these operations involves moving a portion of the list. Suppose, for example, that $A[i]$, $1 \le i \le n$ contains the list (1, 7, 18, 32, 52, 92), as shown in figure 10.3. Now suppose that we want to insert a new element, say the

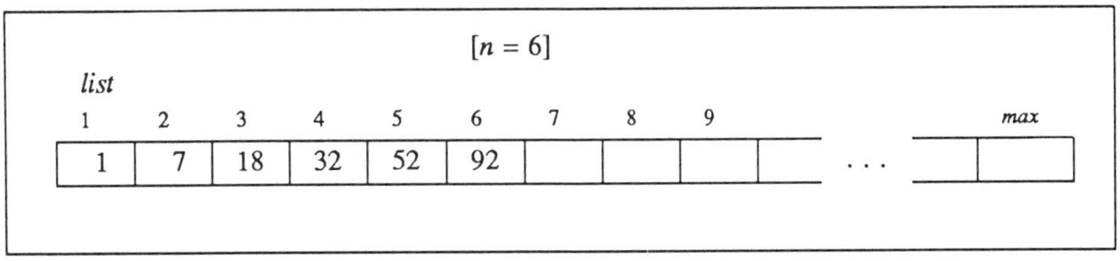

Figure 10.3. A List of Integers in an Array

4. This notation means all $A[i]$ for which i is greater than or equal to 1 and i is less than or equal to n. An alternate notation, $A[1] \ldots A[n]$, is sometimes used. Either refers to elements 1 through n of A.

integer 25, into the list after the 18 (insert at element 4). Each of the elements from element 4 to element *n* must be shifted to the right to make space for the new element. We must work backward from the end of the list so that we don't write over other elements in the list. Element 6 is moved to position 7, element 5 is moved to position 6, and element 4 to position 5. Now that the end of the list has been shifted to the right, the new value can be inserted. Finally, we increment the cardinality of the list so that it reflects the new length. The following pseudo-code sequence accomplishes the task:

```
for i := 6 downto 4 do                    { make room }
   copy A[i] to A[i + 1];
insert 25 in position 4;
set the length of the list equal to 7;
```

The algorithm above is too specific to be generally useful, but it can be generalized for any list. Procedure *insert*, shown below, inserts *x* into the array *A* of *n* elements at position *m*. The value of *m* cannot be greater than $n + 1$, or the list would have empty spaces, and the procedure must make sure that there is room in the array to insert another element, i.e, that $n < max$. Note that *n* must be a variable parameter, since its value will change.

```
procedure insert(var A : listtype; var n : integer; x, m : integer);
  var
    i : integer;
  begin
    if n = max
      then writeln('insert: out of space')
    else if m > n + 1
      then writeln('insert: that would leave holes in array')
    else if m < 1
      then writeln('insert: cannot insert before beginning')
    else
      begin { insert x at location m }
        for i := n downto m do
          A[i + 1] := A[i];                   { make room         }
        A[m] := x;                            { insert new value  }
        incr(n)                               { increment length  }
      end   { insert x at location m }
  end;
```

The process of deleting an item from an array is similar. Here each element past the one to be deleted must be shifted to the left, such that the deleted element is written over and the list is shortened. Procedure *delete* removes element *m* from list *A*, which contains *n* elements.

```
procedure delete(var A : listtype; var n : integer; m : integer);
  var
    i : integer;
  begin { delete }
```

```
    if (m < 1) or (m > n)
      then writeln('delete: element', m:3, ' not in list')
      else
        begin { remove element m }
          for i := m to n - 1 do                  { shift left         }
            A[i] := A[i + 1];
          decr(n)                                 { decrement length }
        end   { remove element m }
  end;  { delete }
```

An alternate solution is to delete elements by inserting a special value to mark "empty" elements. The marker must be a value that would not otherwise occur in the list, but it must be of the correct type. For example, if the list will contain only positive integers greater than 0, then 0 can be used to mark deleted elements. At some point it may be necessary to remove the "empty" elements from the array. This can be done efficiently, without moving any element more than once, by using a variable, say *p*, to indicate the next place to be filled. Initially *p* is set to 1. A **for** loop is used to reference each element in the list, and if the element is not empty, its value is copied to position *p*, and *p* is incremented. Since *p* always "points" to the next available location, when the process is finished the cardinality of the list must be $p - 1$. The basic algorithm is

```
p := 1;                              { next available position    }
for i := 1 to n do
  if not empty(A[i])
    then
      begin { fill in the hole }
        A[p] := A[i];
        incr[p]
      end;  { fill in the hole }
n := p - 1;                          { reset cardinality of list }
```

where *empty* is a boolean function that returns *true* if its argument matches the "empty" marker. The algorithm shown above copies each element over itself until the first empty position is found. Efficiency can be improved by letting *p* point to the first empty location, and making the initial value of *i* the position after *p*. Procedure *compact* incorporates these refinements. Note that if there are no empty elements, then the value of *p* after the **while** loop is $n + 1$, the **for** loop does not execute, and the final statement sets $n = (p - 1) = n$, thus no substantive action is taken.

```
procedure compact(var A : listtype; var n : integer);
  var
    p, i : integer;

  begin { compact }
    p := 1;                           { find first empty element    }
    while not empty(A[p]) and (p <= n) do
      incr(p);
```

```
   for i := p + 1 to n do              { check rest of list         }
     if not empty(A[i])
       then
         begin { fill hole }
           A[p] := A[i];
           incr(p)
         end; { fill hole }
   n := p - 1                          { reset cardinality of list }
 end; { compact }
```

The reader is urged to step through this algorithm with some sample data to make sure he or she understands it thoroughly. The general technique suggested can simplify many programming problems.

Lists can be copied with a loop, but if the array types are compatible, Pascal allows us to simply assign one array to the other. Thus

```
for i := 1 to n do                    { copy list A to B }
  B[i] := A[i];
```

is accomplished more efficiently by

```
B := A                                { copy list A to B }
```

Concatenation, joining two lists into one, is done by copying one list to the end of the other. The following statements append the array in $B[1] \ldots B[m]$ to the end of the list in $A[1] \ldots A[n]$.

```
for i := 1 to m do                { concatenate lists A and B }
  A[n + i] := B[i];
n := n + m;                       { length of new list        }
```

Alternately, we can use a variable to indicate the next position in A, as in compacting (see above). This technique is easier to use if the second list does not begin at $B[1]$, since it simplifies calculating the appropriate index in A. If $j = 1$, the following segment performs exactly the same operation as the one above. As an exercise, modify the above loop so that it does exactly what this one does when $j \neq 0$.

```
p := n + 1;                           { next position in A }
for i := j to m do
  begin
    A[p] := B[i];
    incr(p)
  end;
n := p - 1;                           { length of new list }
```

We will show a general procedure for concatenating arrays in section 11.1.1.

10.6 Using Arrays to Count or Check List Elements

When it is necessary to count the number of occurrences of many different related items, it is inconvenient to use a simple variable for each item. The problem with this approach is the amount of code needed to deal with the separate variables. Consider the problem of reading pitch data encoded in continuous pitch code (cpc), and counting the number of times each pitch class occurs. It would be possible to use twelve separate variables, say *pc0*, *pc1*, *pc2*, *pc3*, *pc4*, . . . , *pc11*. Before these could be used to count pcs, each would have to be initialized in a separate assignment statement:

```
pc0  := 0;
pc1  := 0;
pc2  := 0;
 . . .

pc11 := 0;
```

As each pitch code was then converted to a pitch class, the appropriate variable would have to be incremented. This could be done with a chained **if** statement or a **case** statement:

```
pc := note mod 10;
case pc of
  0 : incr(pc0);
  1 : incr(pc1);
  2 : incr(pc2);
  . . .

 11 : incr(pc11)
end { case }
```

Our problems are not over yet. Each value must be printed separately, and so on—the code keeps expanding. Now imagine that we wish to count something more numerous, say the number of occurrences of each different pitch code. Obviously a different solution is needed.

Random access, the property of arrays that helps us to process lists efficiently, can aid us in this related task. If we arrange to use the items we wish to count as indices of an array, the problem is greatly simplified and processing is made more efficient. In order to count the pcs as suggested above, we can use an array declared as follows:

```
type
  pccount  = array[0 .. 11] of integer;

var
  pc : pccount;       { array to count pcs }
```

We will use *pc*[*i*], $0 \le i \le 11$, to count the number of occurrences of each pitch class *i*. First the array must be initialized by setting each element to 0:

```
for i := 0 to 11 do
  pc[i] := 0;
```

pc

0	1	2	3	4	5	6	7	8	9	10	11
0	0	0	0	0	0	0	0	0	0	0	0

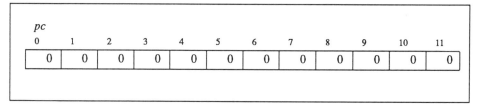

Figure 10.4. An Array Indexed by the Pitch Class Integers 0 . . . 11

We now have an array indexed by pitch-class integers, where each element contains the number of occurrences of its index (figure 10.4). Now a single statement can be used to count any pitch class. For each pitch class *x* we increment the appropriate element by the statement

```
pc[x] := pc[x] + 1;
```

or better,

```
incr(pc[x]);
```

where *incr* has been defined as a procedure.

When we have performed this operation for each *x* that we wish to count, each element *pc*[*x*] contains the number of times pitch class *x* occurred. Program 10.1 illustrates this technique. The program processes continuous pitch code, with bar lines represented by '/' and rests by 'r'. Since we are interested only in the pitch codes, a modified version of *skip* is used to discard the nonnumeric codes along with blanks. The program is subdivided into logical subprocesses, which are implemented as procedures. Note that the only global variable used is the *pc* array. The main procedure passes this array to each of the other procedures, which initialize it, use it to count the pcs, and print the results of the tabulation. These procedures call other procedures and functions to perform clearly defined subtasks. Thus the top-down structure of the program is clear. The Mozart excerpt in figure 10.5 is encoded as sample input to the program.

Mozart, Symphony No. 41 in C Major (*Jupiter*), K. 551, third movement, mm. 1–11

Figure 10.5. Data for Program *Countpcs*

```
(***********************     Program Countpcs      ***********************)
(* Reads an excerpt encoded as cpcs, and prints a table showing how many *)
(* times each pitch class occurred.  The program demonstrates the use of *)
(* arrays to count multiple related items.                                *)
(* Input:  Numeric pitch code; each pitch is encoded as 12 * octave + pc.*)
(*         Bar lines are encoded as '/' and rests as 'r'.                *)
(* Output: A table showing the number of occurrences of each pc.         *)
(*************************************************************************)
program countpcs(input, output);
  const
    barline = '/';                              { code for a bar line }
    rest    = 'r';                              { code for a rest     }
  type
    pccount = array[0 .. 11] of integer;
  var
    pc : pccount;                               { array to count pcs  }


(***********************           skip          ***********************)
(* Skips rest and bar line codes as well as blanks.                      *)
(*************************************************************************)
  procedure skip;
    var
      done : boolean;
    begin
      done := false;
      repeat
        if eof
          then done := true
        else if (input↑ in [' ', barline, rest])
          then get(input)
        else done := true
      until done
    end;


(***********************           topc          ***********************)
(* Converts its parameter, cpc encoded pitch, to a pitch class.          *)
(*************************************************************************)
  function topc(pitch : integer) : integer;
    begin
      topc := pitch mod 12
    end;


(***********************           init          ***********************)
(* Initializes pc array, setting each element to 0.                      *)
(*************************************************************************)
  procedure init(var pc : pccount);
    var
      i : integer;
    begin
      for i :=  0 to 11 do
        pc[i] := 0
    end;
```

```
(***********************          incr          ***********************)
(* Adds one to the value of its argument.                              *)
(***********************************************************************)
  procedure incr(var x : integer);
    begin
      x := x + 1
    end;

(***********************        readdata        ***********************)
(* Reads the input file, skipping over rests and bar lines. As each pitch*)
(* code is read, it is converted to a pitch class, and pc[pitch class]  *)
(* is incremented.  Thus the procedure counts the occurrences of each   *)
(* pitch class in the excerpt.                                          *)
(***********************************************************************)
  procedure readdata(var pc : pccount);
    var
      pitch : integer;
    begin
      skip;
      while not eof do
        begin
          read(pitch);
          incr(pc[topc(pitch)]);
          skip
        end
    end;

(***********************          sum           ***********************)
(* Returns the total number of pitch classes.                          *)
(***********************************************************************)
  function sum(var pc : pccount) : integer;
    var
      i, t : integer;
    begin
      t := 0;    { total }
      for i := 0 to 11 do
        t := t + pc[i];
      sum := t
    end;

(***********************       maketable        ***********************)
(* Prints the results in a table with headings.                        *)
(***********************************************************************)
  procedure maketable(var pc : pccount);
    var
      i : integer;
    begin
      writeln(' Pitch Class Occurrences');
      writeln('========================');
      writeln('pc':6, 'occurrences':16);
      writeln('========================');
      for i := 0 to 11 do
        writeln(i:6, pc[i]:12);
      writeln('========================');
      writeln('        total:', sum(pc):4)
    end;
```

```
(***********************        main procedure        ***********************)
(* Calls procedures to initialize the pc array, process data, and print    *)
(* the results.                                                             *)
(***************************************************************************)

  begin { main }
    init(pc);                                     { initialize pc array }
    readdata(pc);                                 { count pitch classes }
    maketable(pc)                                 { print table         }
  end. { main }
```

Program 10.1. *Countpcs*

Input:

```
53 48 57 55 53 / 52 r 58 r r / 55 48 58
57 55/ 53 r 60 r r / 65 60 69 67 65 64
/ 60 59 58 57 / 62 64 62 61 62 64 67 65
64 63 / 62 60 60 61 62 58 / 57 58 57
56 57 56 57 60 58 57 55 / 60 57 53 55 57
57 55 53 52 / 53 r r //
```

Output:

```
 Pitch Class Occurrences
=========================
   pc      occurrences
=========================
    0           9
    1           2
    2           5
    3           1
    4           6
    5           9
    6           0
    7           8
    8           2
    9          12
   10           6
   11           1
=========================
        total:  61
```

Program 10.1. Sample Input and Output

This technique can be used whenever the indices can be expressed as a subrange type; for example, the following statements could be used to count the number of occurrences of each lowercase letter in an input file:

```
type
  letter        = 'a' .. 'z';
  lettercounter = array[letter] of integer;

var
  lcount : lettercounter;
  c      : letter;
  ch     : char;
  . . .

 for c := 'a' to 'z' do          { initialize lcount            }
   lcount[c] := 0;

 while not eof do                { count lcase letters in file }
   begin
     read(ch);
     if ch in letter
       then incr(lcount[ch]);
     skipblanks
   end;
```

Or an array declared

```
type
  countint = array[-max .. max] of integer;

var
  interval : countint;
```

where *max* is greater than the largest interval size expected, could be used to count the occurrences of each directed interval generated by program 9.3.

A similar technique can be used to mark which elements of a list have been found. The element type of the array is boolean rather than integer. Consider the following procedure designed to read pitch-class sets from a single line of the input file. A boolean array *have*, referenced by the pc integers, is used to remove duplicate pcs from the input list. The procedure uses variable parameters to return the pc set and its cardinality, and illustrates the declaration of an array as a local variable without first declaring its type.

```
        { global declarations }
[  type
     list = array[1..12] of integer;

   var
     pcset : list;
     n     : integer;          { cardinality of pcset }    ]
```

```
procedure readset(var pcset : list; var n : integer);
  var
    pc   : integer;
    have : array[0 .. 11] of boolean;
  begin { readset }
    for pc := 0 to 11 do               { initialize have         }
       have[pc] := false;

    n := 0;                            { initialize cardinality }
    while not eoln do
      begin { process a pc }
        read(pc);
        if not have[pc]
          then
            begin
              incr(n);
              pcset[n] := pc;
              have[pc] := true
            end;
        skipln
      end; { process a pc }
    readln                             { skip newline character }
  end; { readset }
```

Each element of *have* is initialized to *false*. Now the expression **not** *have*[*pc*] is *true* if *pc* has not already been placed in *pcset*. If this is the case, cardinality *n* is incremented, *pc* is placed in *pcset*[*n*], and *have*[*pc*] is set to *true* so that this pitch class cannot be used again. If a duplicate pitch class is read, **not** *have*[*pc*] evaluates to *false*, and the duplicate is discarded. When a boolean array is used in this manner, its function is much the same as a **set** type. The use of sets is a more efficient way to deal with this problem and will be discussed in chapter 12.

10.7 Specialized Lists

Two common data structures with many uses in programming are *stacks* and *queues*. Stacks and queues are best understood in terms of their properties and functions; the data structures used to implement them are secondary. Stacks and queues are special types of ordered lists. In both, data objects are inserted and deleted one at a time by special predefined operators. They differ in the relationship between their inputs and outputs. In the stack, items are entered and removed from one end, called the *top* of the stack. In the queue, items are entered at one end, called the *rear*, and removed from the other end, called the *front*. Thus items are removed from a queue in the same order in which they are entered, while in the stack the order is reversed. In this section we will implement stacks and queues using arrays. Later we will design linked data structures that have the same function.

10.7.1 Stacks

A stack is a special kind of data structure known as a last-in-first-out or LIFO data structure. A good analogy for a stack is a spring-loaded plate dispenser in a cafeteria. Plates can only be put on or taken off the top of the stack. The only plate that can be removed is the one on top, and only if there is a plate on the stack. The bottom-most plate on the stack cannot be removed until each of the other plates on the stack has been removed.

In computing, the stack data structure works in much the same way. Generally, only a few operations are defined for stacks; these are shown in table 10.2. *Push*(x) places x on top of the stack. *Pop*(x) takes the top value off the stack and assigns it to x. *Stackfull* tests the stack and returns *true* if it is full, i.e., there is no more room to add values; *stackempty* returns *true* if the stack is empty, i.e., no more values can be taken off the stack.

The last two operations are optional. The test for a full stack is needed only for certain implementations of a stack (such as arrays). Testing the top value can always be done by taking an item off the stack, testing its value, and returning it to the stack again; however, when a stack is implemented with an array, we can always access the top value directly.

There are many uses for stacks in programming. The computer system uses a stack whenever a procedure is called. The value of each argument is pushed on the stack, as is the "return address," the address of the next statement to be executed after the procedure "returns." The called procedure removes the value of each parameter in reverse order, performs its task, and then transfers control to the address indicated by the "return address." This is why a procedure can be called from many different points in a program. Some computer languages are designed almost entirely around stack operations and stack arithmetic. For example, the *add* operator might remove the top two items from the stack, add them together, and push the result back on the stack.[5]

The simplest way to implement a stack is to use an array, say S, indexed from 1 to *max*. Associated with the stack is a variable, called *top* or *sp* (for stack pointer),

$sp := 0$	initialize stack pointer
push(x)	place an item on the stack
pop(x)	take an item off of the stack
stackempty	test to see if stack is empty
stackfull	test to see if the stack is full
$S[sp]$	return the value on the top of the stack (without removing it)

Table 10.2. Operations on Stacks

5. The programming language FORTH is one example, as is POSTSCRIPT, a language designed to control graphic printing devices, including the Apple LaserWriter and Linotronic photo-typesetters. Some brands of pocket calculators are also designed as stack machines.

which indicates the index of the top of the stack. *Sp* is initialized to 0, indicating that no values are on the stack, and the boolean expression *sp* = 0 will always return *true* when the stack is empty.

We create a stack by the following declarations:

```
const
   max = 30;

type                                  { component type could differ }
   stack = array[1 .. max] of integer;

var
   S  : stack;                        { stack implemented as array   }
   sp : integer;                      { index of top of the stack    }
```

The stack must be initialized (once in the beginning of the main program) by setting *sp* = 0. In all of these procedures we will treat *sp* and *S* as global variables. It would be necessary to pass them to procedures if more than one stack were used in a program or if the procedures were external to the main program (an extension to standard Pascal). Figure 10.6 shows a stack containing the integers 23, 56, 9, and 14, with 14 on the top of the stack.

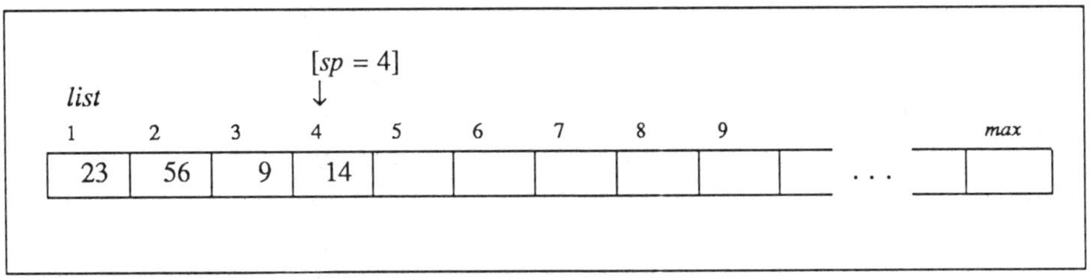

Figure 10.6. A Stack Containing Four Integers

Procedure *push*(*x*) places a value on the stack by incrementing *sp* and then assigning *S*[*sp*] the value of *x*. It is a good idea for *push* to make sure that there is room on the stack, although this step may be eliminated if the program is designed so that the stack can never overflow.

```
procedure push(x : integer);  { push x onto stack         }
  begin { push }
    if stackfull
      then writeln('push: error, stack is full')
      else
        begin                 { place x on top of stack }
          incr(sp);
          S[sp] := x
        end
  end;  { push }
```

Stackfull is a boolean function that returns *true* if the stack is full, i.e., if *sp* = *max*:

```
function stackfull : boolean;
  begin
    stackfull := sp = max
  end;
```

Elements are taken from the stack by procedure *pop*(*x*). Obviously *x* must be a variable parameter. Again, it is a good idea for *pop* to make sure there is something on the stack, although this should be taken care of by the calling program:

```
procedure pop(var x : integer);
  begin
    if stackempty
      then writeln('pop: error, stack is empty')
      else
        begin
          x := S[sp];
          decr(sp)
        end
  end;
```

Function *stackempty* simply tests to see if $sp = 0$:

```
function stackempty : boolean;
  begin
    stackempty := sp = 0
  end;
```

We will not write a procedure to return the top of the stack, as it is readily available as *S*[*sp*], so long as there is something on the stack.

Program 10.2 illustrates the use of these procedures. It simply reads a list of integers, storing them on a stack, and then prints the values as they are removed from the stack (in reverse order).

```
Type list: 1 2 3 4 5
   5   4   3   2   1

Type list: 78 32 5 1
   1   5  32  78

Type list: 1
   1

Type list: 3 4 89 1 96 8
   8  96   1  89   4   3

Type list: 0 1 2 4 8 16 32 64 128 256 512 1024
1024 512 256 128  64  32  16   8   4   2   1   0

Type list: ^D
```

Program 10.2. Sample Run (Interactive)

```
(***********************     Program Stackdemo     ***********************)
(* A stack is a last-in-first-out (LIFO) data structure used for storage *)
(* in computer programs.  Basic operations on a stack are: (1) push -    *)
(* put a number on the stack, and (2) pop - take a number off the stack. *)
(* We should also be able to test the stack to see if it is empty or     *)
(* full.  Stacks can be implemented in different ways:  here we use an   *)
(* array numbered from 1 to max, and a variable sp (stack pointer) that  *)
(* points to the top of the stack.  Sp is initialized to 0, indicating   *)
(* that the stack is empty. Note that any type of value could be stored  *)
(* in the stack by changing the type of the array.  This program exer-   *)
(* cises a stack.  As each number is read, it is pushed onto the stack.  *)
(* Then each value on the stack is popped and printed.  Output order is  *)
(* the reverse of input order.                                           *)
(*************************************************************************)
program stackdemo (input, output);
  const
    max = 20;                            { max number of items on stack }

  type
    stack = array[1 .. max] of integer;

  var
    sp : integer;                        { stack pointer                }
    S  : stack;                          { stack implemented as array   }

(***********************            incr           ***********************)
(* Adds one to value of its argument.                                    *)
(*************************************************************************)
  procedure incr(var x : integer);
    begin
      x := x + 1
    end;

(***********************            decr           ***********************)
(* Subtracts one from value of its argument.                             *)
(*************************************************************************)
  procedure decr(var x : integer);
    begin
      x := x - 1
    end;

(***********************         stackfull         ***********************)
(* Returns true if sp = max, i.e., no more space.                        *)
(*************************************************************************)
  function stackfull : boolean;
    begin
      stackfull := sp = max
    end;

(***********************         stackempty        ***********************)
(* Returns true if sp = 0, i.e., no items on stack.                      *)
(*************************************************************************)
  function stackempty : boolean;
    begin
      stackempty := sp = 0
    end;
```

```
(***********************          error          ***********************)
(* Here procedure error prints an error message.  In some programs it   *)
(* might take more drastic action.                                       *)
(***********************************************************************)
  procedure error(n : integer);
    begin
      case n of
        1 : writeln('error: stack full');
        2 : writeln('error: stack empty')
      end { case }
    end;

(***********************          push           ***********************)
(* Puts x on the stack by incrementing sp and then assigning S[sp] the  *)
(* value of x.  Prints message if stack is full.                         *)
(***********************************************************************)
  procedure push(x : integer);
    begin
      if stackfull
        then error(1)
        else
          begin
            incr(sp);
            S[sp] := x
          end
    end;

(***********************           pop           ***********************)
(* Returns the top value on the stack by assigning x the value of S[sp]  *)
(* and then decrementing sp.  If the stack is empty, an error message is *)
(* printed.                                                              *)
(***********************************************************************)
  procedure pop(var x : integer);
    begin
      if stackempty
        then error(2)
        else
          begin
            x := S[sp];
            decr(sp)
          end
    end;

(***********************         skipln          ***********************)
(* Skips blanks to next nonblank character or newline character.        *)
(***********************************************************************)
  procedure skipln;
    begin
       while (input↑ = ' ') and not eoln do
        get(input)
    end;

(***********************        readdata         ***********************)
(* Reads each value on a single line of the input file, pushing each    *)
(* onto the stack.                                                       *)
(***********************************************************************)
```

```
procedure readdata;
  var
    x : integer;
  begin
    while not eoln do
      begin
        read(x);
        push(x);
        skipln
      end;
    readln
  end;

(***********************          printdata          ***********************)
(* Pops each value off the stack and prints it.                             *)
(***************************************************************************)
procedure printdata;
  var
    x : integer;
  begin
    while not stackempty do
      begin
        pop(x);
        write(x : 4)
      end;
    writeln
  end;

(***********************        main procedure       ***********************)
(* Exercises stack implemented as an array of integers.                     *)
(***************************************************************************)
begin { main }
  sp := 0;                                          { initialize stack       }
  write('Type list: ');
  while not eof do
    begin
      readdata;                                     { read values            }
      printdata;                                    { print in reverse order }
      writeln;
      write('Type list: ')
    end
end. { main }
```

Program 10.2. *Stackdemo*

10.7.2 Queues

A queue is a first-in-first-out (FIFO) data structure. Think of a queue as a line, say at the bank. People get in the line at the rear, and get out at the front. The line length may vary and may be nil, i.e., there is nobody in line. Typical uses of queues in computing systems include scheduling jobs in a batch system, or allotting time slices in a timesharing system. Operations generally defined for queues are listed in table 10.3. The queue is implemented with two variables, *front* and *rear*, that point to the

front, rear := 0	initialize queue
insertq(*x*)	place an item in the queue
removeq(*x*)	take item out of queue
Qempty	test to see if the queue is empty
Qfull	test to see if the queue is full
Q[*front*]	return the value at the front of the queue (without removing it)

Table 10.3. Operations on Queues

beginning and end of the queue. After the queue is initialized, *insertq*(*x*) will place *x* in the queue at the rear, and *removeq*(*x*) will take the item from the front of the queue and assign it to *x*. *Qempty* and *Qfull* return boolean values that are *true* if the queue is empty and full respectively. In the array implementation, *Q*[*front*] accesses directly the value at the front of the queue.

We will implement a queue with an array numbered from 0 to *max*, where *max* is the maximum number of items that may be placed in the queue. The variables *front* and *rear* index the beginning and end of the queue. These are initially set to the same value, arbitrarily chosen as 0, indicating that the queue is empty. Whenever a value is placed in the queue, *rear* is set one position, in a clockwise direction, from the last value in the queue. The array is treated as if it were circular, through use of modular arithmetic, so that the position *Q*[*maxque* + 1] is *Q*[0]. The queue must be considered full when *rear* is one position counterclockwise from *front*, otherwise it is impossible to distinguish between a full queue and an empty one. Figure 10.7. shows a queue with four numbers in it.

The queue is set up by the following declarations:

```
const
  max = 20;                 { maximum length of queue            }

type
  queue = array[0 .. max] of integer;

var
  Q : queue;                { a queue                            }
  front, rear: integer;     { index of front and rear of queue   }
```

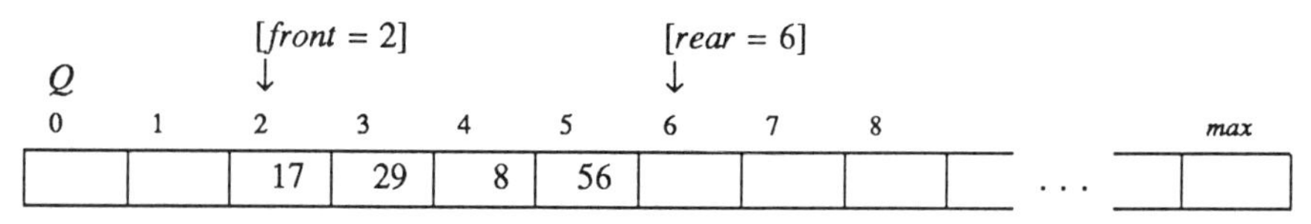

Figure 10.7. A Queue Implemented with an Array

The queue is initialized by setting front and rear equal to 0. This value is arbitrary, and could be any value between 0 and *max* – 1. The important thing is that front and rear are equal.

```
procedure initq(var front, rear : integer);
  begin
    front := 0;
    rear  := 0                                    { empty queue }
  end;
```

An item is entered into the queue by procedure *insertq*. If the queue is full, error is called. Our error routine will simply print an error message. It would be possible to take more drastic action, such as terminating the program or attempting to take corrective action. The value *x* is inserted in the array at position *rear*, and then *rear* is incremented, using circular arithmetic, so that *Q*[*max* + 1] becomes *Q*[0]. Note that after insertion, *rear* is always one position clockwise from the last value inserted.

```
procedure insertq(x : integer);
  begin
    if Qfull
      then error(1)
      else
        begin
          Q[rear] := x;
          rear := (rear + 1) mod (max + 1)
        end
  end;
```

In this scheme the queue is full when *rear* is one position counterclockwise from *front*, while it is empty when *front* = *rear*.

```
function Qfull : boolean;
  begin
    Qfull := (rear + 1) mod (max + 1) = front
  end;

function Qempty : boolean;
  begin
    Qempty := front = rear
  end;
```

Procedure *removeq* returns the value of *Q*[*front*] and increments *front*, using our circular algorithm. If the queue is empty, an error message is printed.

```
procedure removeq(var x : integer);
  begin
    if Qempty
      then error(2)
      else
        begin
          x := Q[front];
          front := (front + 1) mod (max + 1)
        end
  end;
```

Note that in this implementation of a queue, *front* and *rear* move clockwise around a conceptually circular array. *Front* follows *rear*, and when it catches up, the queue is empty. If *rear* laps *front*, coming up from behind, the queue is full. The reader is urged to draw a representation of the array, and to exercise these procedures manually until the principle is understood. Program 10.3 is a simple demonstration of this queue implementation. A real application using the queue can be seen in program 10.5, which implements the *mergesort* algorithm.

```
(***********************    Program  Queuedemo     ***********************)
(* A queue is a first-in-first-out (FIFO) data structure.  The primary   *)
(* operations on queues are (1) insert an item in queue, and (2) remove  *)
(* an item from the queue.  It is also necessary to test for an empty or *)
(* full condition of the queue.  Program queuedemo demonstrates a method *)
(* of implementing a queue using an array. Details are contained in text.*)
(*************************************************************************)
program queuedemo(input, output);
  const
    max = 20;                                 { maximum length of queue }

  type
    queue    = array[0 .. max] of integer;

  var
    Q : queue;                                { a queue                 }
    front, rear: integer; { index of front and rear of queue }

(***********************          initq          ***********************)
(* Initializes front and rear of queue.                                  *)
(*************************************************************************)
  procedure initq(var front, rear : integer);
    begin
      front := 0;
      rear  := 0                                          { empty queue }
    end;

(***********************         Qempty          ***********************)
(* Returns true if queue is empty.                                       *)
(*************************************************************************)
  function Qempty : boolean;
    begin
      Qempty := front = rear
    end;

(***********************          Qfull          ***********************)
(* Returns true if queue is full.                                        *)
(*************************************************************************)
  function Qfull : boolean;
    begin
      Qfull := (rear + 1) mod (max + 1) = front
    end;
```

```
(***********************          error          ***********************)
(* Prints an error message, but could take more drastic action.        *)
(***********************************************************************)
 procedure error(err : integer);
   begin
     case err of
       1 : writeln('error: queue is full');
       2 : writeln('error: queue is empty')
     end { case }
   end;

(***********************         insertq         ***********************)
(* Places integer x at rear of queue.                                   *)
(***********************************************************************)
 procedure insertq(x : integer);
   begin
     if Qfull
       then error(1)
       else
         begin
           Q[rear] := x;
           rear := (rear + 1) mod (max + 1)
         end
   end;

(***********************         removeq         ***********************)
(* Returns as x the integer at the front of queue.                      *)
(***********************************************************************)
 procedure removeq(var x : integer);
   begin
     if Qempty
       then error(2)
       else
         begin
           x := Q[front];
           front := (front + 1) mod (max + 1)
         end
   end;

(***********************         skipln          ***********************)
(* Finds next nonblank character or end-of-line.                        *)
(***********************************************************************)
 procedure skipln;
   begin
     while (input↑ = ' ') and not eoln do
       get(input)
   end;

(***********************        readdata         ***********************)
(* Reads list on integers and stores in queue.                          *)
(***********************************************************************)
 procedure readdata;
   var
     x : integer;
   begin
```

```
      while not eoln do
        begin
          read(x);                               { read a value         }
          insertq(x);                            { place it in queue    }
          skipln
        end;
      readln                                     { skip newline character }
    end; { readdata}

(***********************          printdata          ***********************)
(* Prints list of integers stored in queue.                                *)
(***************************************************************************)
  procedure printdata;
    var
      x : integer;
    begin
      while not Qempty do
        begin
          removeq(x);                            { take value from queue }
          write(x:3)                             {   and print it        }
        end;
      writeln
    end;

(***********************        main procedure       ***********************)
(* Exercises the queue procedures.                                         *)
(***************************************************************************)
  begin { main }
    initq(front, rear);                          { initialize queue      }
    write('Type list: ');
    while not eof do
      begin
        readdata;
        printdata;
        writeln
        write('Type list: ')
      end
  end. { main }
```

Program 10.3. *Queuedemo*

```
Type list: 2 4 6 8 10
  2  4  6  8 10

Type list: 1 2 3 4 5 7 8 43 12 90 1
  1  2  3  4  5  7  8 43 12 90  1

Type list: 6 5 4 3 2 1
  6  5  4  3  2  1

Type list: 1 2 3 4 5 6 7 8 9 10
  1  2  3  4  5  6  7  8  9 10
```

```
Type list: 1 2 3 4 5 6 7 8 9 10 11 12 13 14 15 16 17 18 19 20 21 22
error: queue is full
error: queue is full
  1  2  3  4  5  6  7  8  9 10 11 12 13 14 15 16 17 18 19 20

Type list: 4 2 5 7 1
  4  2  5  7  1

Type list: ^D
```

Program 10.3. Sample Run (Interactive)

10.8 Searching Lists

In this section and the next we will examine methods of searching and sorting lists. Searching means finding the location of a specific element within a list; sorting means ordering a list (numerically, alphabetically, etc.). Finding efficient methods for doing these tasks has been the subject of a great deal of research in computer science.

The efficiency of algorithms is sometimes described in terms of *O-notation*. $O(1)$ means an algorithm takes constant time, and is not dependent on a variable quantity. If an algorithm has worst-case behavior of $O(n)$, this means that its computation time is at most n multiplied by some constant, and is said to be linear. This is obviously better than $O(n^2)$, much better than $O(2^n)$, and considerably worse than $O(\log_2 n)$.[6] The variable n denotes the number of inputs to or outputs from an algorithm; for sorting and searching it is the length of the list. The constant depends on the number of statements in one iteration and the length of time it takes to execute these statements, which depends in turn on the number of statements, their complexity, and the characteristics of the compiler and computer used. Since the constant may vary widely, a less efficient algorithm with a low constant may actually be better for a small value of n; for a sufficiently large n, a more efficient algorithm is always desirable. Table 10.4 compares values for some common computing-time functions for a small set of values.

$\log_2 n$	n	$n \log_2 n$	n^2	n^3	2^n
0	1	0	1	1	2
1	2	2	4	8	4
2	4	8	16	64	16
3	8	24	64	512	256
4	16	64	256	4096	65536
5	32	160	1024	32768	2147483648

Table 10.4. Common Computing-Time Functions

6. $\text{Log}_2\ n$ is the power to which 2 must be raised to obtain n.

10.8.1 Linear Search

The simplest method of searching a list is to examine each element of the list until the desired one is located, or until the entire list has been searched unsuccessfully. In the worse case—when the item does not occur in the list or when we need to find each occurrence of the item—this requires examining each element in the list. Thus the efficiency is $O(n)$, where n is the length of the list, and the algorithm is called *linear search.*

In the first case, we wish to find the first occurrence of a specific element in the list. We need a looping construct that will examine each element and fall out of the loop when the desired element is found. This can be accomplished by using a **while** loop and a variable, say *answer*, to determine when the desired element has been located. The loop terminates when an answer has been found or when all elements have been examined. Function *linear1* searches a list of n elements in array A for value x. It returns the location of x in the list, or 0 if the element does not occur in the list.

```
function linear1(var A : listtype; n, x : integer) : integer;
  var
    i : integer;
    answer : integer;

  begin { linear1 }
    answer := 0;                    { indicates not found }
    i := 1;
    while (i <= n) and (answer = 0) do
      begin
        if A[i] = x
          then answer := i
          else incr(i)
      end;
    linear1 := answer
  end;  { linear1 }
```

The procedure is called in a sequence such as the following:

```
location := linear1(list, n, x);
if location > 0
  then writeln(' ':8, x:3, ' occurs in position', location:3)
  else writeln(' ':8, x:3, ' not found');
```

If the list may contain duplicate entries and we wish to find all of them, the above algorithm is not sufficient. The version shown below prints the subscript of each element that contains x, and returns *true* if the search succeeded. A boolean variable match is initialized to *false.* When a match is found, the location is printed and *match* is set to *true*. If no matches are found, *match* remains *false*. An alternate version might save the locations in another array, perhaps a stack or queue, for further processing by the calling program.

```
function linear2(var A : listtype; n, x : integer) : boolean;
  var
    i : integer;
    match : boolean;
  begin { linear2 }
    match := false;
    for i := 1 to n do
      if A[i] = x
        then
          begin
            writeln(' ':8, x:3, ' occurs in position', i:3);
            match := true
          end;
     linear2 := match
  end; { linear2 }
```

Since this version returns a boolean value, it can be used directly in an **if** statement:

```
if not linear2(list, n, x)
  then writeln(' ':8, x:3, ' not found');
```

Program 10.4 illustrates both of these functions.

```
(*********************** Program Linearsearch ***********************)
(* Illustrates two versions of linear search.                          *)
(*********************************************************************)
program linearsearch(input, output);
 const
   max = 100;                        { maximum length of list        }
   fw  = 3;                          { field width for printing      }

 type
   listtype = array[1 .. max] of integer;

 var
   list : listtype;                  { for storing list of integers  }
   n    : integer;                   { actual number of elements     }
   x, loc: integer;                  { a value & its location in list }

(***********************        skipln        ***********************)
(* Skips blanks to next nonblank character or newline character.      *)
(*********************************************************************)
 procedure skipln;
   begin
     while (input↑ = ' ') and not eoln do
       get(input)
   end;

(***********************         incr         ***********************)
(* Adds one to the value of its argument.                              *)
(*********************************************************************)
 procedure incr(var x : integer);
   begin
     x := x + 1
   end;
```

```
(************************            readlist            ************************)
(* Reads list into array A; returns array and size of list, n.                   *)
(*********************************************************************************)
  procedure readlist(var A : listtype; var n : integer);
    begin
      n := 0;
      while not eoln do
        begin
          incr(n);
          read(A[n]);
          skipln
        end;
      readln                                        { skip newline character }
    end;

(************************            linear1             ************************)
(* Returns location of first occurrence of x in A[1] ... A[n].                   *)
(*********************************************************************************)
  function linear1(var A : listtype; n, x : integer) : integer;
    var
      i : integer;
      answer : integer;
    begin
      answer := 0;                                     { indicates not found }
      i := 1;
      while (i <= n) and (answer = 0) do
        begin
          if A[i] = x
            then answer := i
            else incr(i)
        end;
      linear1 := answer
    end;

(************************            linear2             ************************)
(* Prints each location of x in A[1] ... A[n].  Returns true if x occurs         *)
(* in list, false if it does not.                                                *)
(*********************************************************************************)
  function linear2(var A : listtype; n, x : integer) : boolean;
    var
      i : integer;
      match : boolean;
    begin
      match := false;
      for i := 1 to n do
        if A[i] = x
          then
            begin
              writeln(' ':8, x:fw, ' occurs in position', i:fw);
              match := true
            end;
       linear2 := match
    end;

(************************              main              ************************)
(* While not eof, reads a list, prompts for a value, and calls linear1           *)
(* and linear2 to search list for the value.                                     *)
(*********************************************************************************)
```

```
begin { main }
  write('Type list: ');
  while not eof do
    begin
      readlist(list, n);
      write('Type x: ');
      readln(x);

      writeln('linear1: ');                              { test linear1 }
      loc := linear1(list, n, x);
      if loc > 0
        then writeln(' ':8, x:fw, ' occurs in position', loc:fw)
        else writeln(' ':8, x:fw, ' not found');
      writeln;

      writeln('linear2: ');                              { test linear2 }
      if not linear2(list, n, x)
        then writeln(' ':8, x:fw, ' not found');
      writeln;
      write('Type list: ')
    end
end.  { main }
```

Program 10.4. *Linearsearch*

```
Type list: 1 3 5 7 9 8 6 4 2
Type x: 5
linear1:
          5 occurs in position  3

linear2:
          5 occurs in position  3

Type list: 2 5 3 7 7 23 9 8 7 43 7 0
Type x: 7
linear1:
          7 occurs in position  4

linear2:
          7 occurs in position  4
          7 occurs in position  5
          7 occurs in position  9
          7 occurs in position 11

Type list: 23 5 7 90 8 77 2 9
Type x: 6
linear1:
          6 not found

linear2:
          6 not found

Type list: ^D
```

Program 10.4. Sample Run (Interactive)

10.8.2 Binary Search

If the list is ordered, and there are no duplicate entries, then it can be searched much faster. Suppose the list is stored *A*[1] . . . *A*[*n*], and we want to find the location of value *x*. We begin by setting two variables, *low* and *high*, equal to 1 and *n* respectively. We now make as our first guess the midpoint of the list *A*[*mid*], where *mid* equals (*low* + *high*) **div** 2. If we are lucky, this is the element we are looking for and we are done. But even if we are not so lucky, we can eliminate half the list: if *x* is greater than *A*[*mid*], we set *low* equal to *mid* + 1; if *x* is less than *A*[*mid*], we set *high* equal to *mid* − 1. Then we recalculate the midpoint and repeat the process. Each time we guess we eliminate half of the remaining list.

Suppose we want to find the location of the number 29 in the list shown in figure 10.8. We set *low* equal to 1 and *high* equal to 8. Our first guess is *mid* = (1 + 8) **div** 2 = 4. Since *A*[4] (22) is less than 29, we set *low* equal to 5. Our second guess is *mid* = (5 + 8) **div** 2 = 6. Since *A*[6] (33) is greater than 29 we set *high* = *mid* − 1 = 5. Our third guess is *mid* = (5 + 5) **div** 2 = 5. Since *A*[5] contains the element we are seeking, we are done. If the value occurs in the array, the algorithm must terminate by finding its location. We know that the number does not occur in the list when *low* > *high*. We will use a technique similar to that used in *linear1* to make the loop terminate as soon as the location is found. The function shown below searches array *A*[*i*], *low* ≤ *i* ≤ *high*, for the value *x*. It returns the location of *x* in the array (the index of *x*), or 0 if *x* does not occur in the array. An appropriate call of the procedure might be

```
m := binsearch(list, 1, n, z);
```

which assigns to *m* the index of *z* in *list*[*i*], 1 ≤ *i* ≤ *n*, or 0 if *z* does not occur in the list.

```
function binsearch(var A : arraytype; low, high, x : integer) : integer;
  var
    mid, answer : integer;
  begin
    answer := 0;                                { location of x in A }
    while (high >= low) and (answer = 0) do
      begin
        mid := (low + high) div 2;              { guess midpoint       }
        if x = A[mid]
          then answer := mid                    { got it               }
        else if x > A[mid]
          then low := mid + 1                   { shorten list         }
        else high := mid - 1
      end;
    binsearch := answer                         { return answer        }
  end;
```

If *x* does not occur in the list, it is sometimes useful to know its proper position in case we wish to insert it. The final value of *low* is always the position where it should be placed. (A proof of this statement is left as an exercise). The function can be modified to return this value using the variable parameter *loc*.

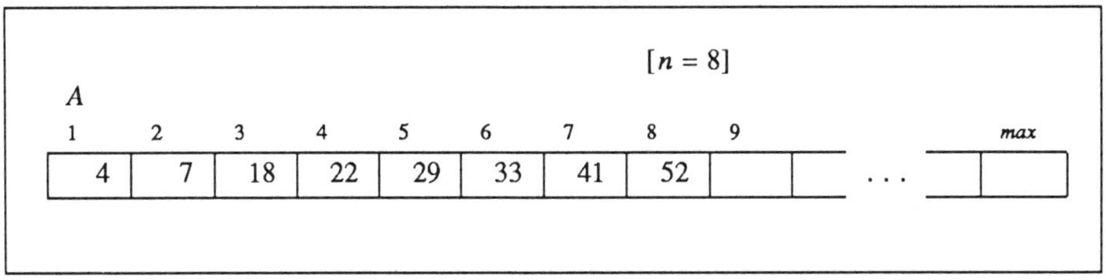

Figure 10.8. A Sorted List in an Array

```
function binsearch(var A : arl; low, high, x : integer;
                              var loc : integer) : integer;
  var
    mid , answer : integer;

  begin
    loc    := 0;                  { where to put x if not in list }
    answer := 0;                  { location of x in list or 0    }

    while (high >= low) and (answer = 0) do
      begin
        mid := (low + high) div 2; { calculate midpoint of list   }
        if x = A[mid]
          then answer := mid       { got it                        }
        else if x > A[mid]
          then low := mid + 1      { shorten list                  }
        else high := mid - 1
      end;

    if answer = 0
      then loc := low;            { return place to insert x      }
    binsearch := answer           { return location of x or 0     }
  end;
```

This modification gives us the option of adding the value to the list if it does not occur:

```
m := binsearch(list, 1, n, z, loc);
if m = 0
  then insert(list, n, z, loc)
  else . . .
```

How efficient is this algorithm? We have seen that each guess eliminates half of the remaining list. In other words, every time we double the length of the list we require at most one more guess to find the location. Thus the computation time of the algorithm is $O(\log_2 n)$. Although the constant is higher than for linear search (division takes longer than addition, and there are more tests to make for each element), this is an excellent algorithm for searching long lists, as we can see by extending the comparison on n and $\log_2 n$ from table 10.4:

n	$\log_2 n$	n	$\log_2 n$
1	0	128	7
2	1	256	8
4	2	512	9
8	3	1024	10
16	4	2048	11
32	5	4096	12
64	6	8192	13

In order to obtain this excellent time, the list must be sorted in ascending order. Sorting is the topic of the next section of this chapter.

10.9 Sorting Lists in Arrays

We frequently want to arrange a list in some specific order (ascending, descending, alphabetic, scale order, etc.). This process is called *sorting*. Any list for which the components have some definable ordering criteria can be sorted. We will use lists of integers for our illustrations.

Generally there is a trade-off between a program's speed and complexity, and required storage space, i.e, faster sorting methods are usually more complex or require more work space in memory. While a thorough discussion of sorting methods and their analysis is beyond the scope of this book, it will be informative to examine two or three different methods of sorting lists in arrays.

We will begin with a simple algorithm, and then look at two more advanced sorting algorithms with better computing times—*shellsort* and *mergesort*. We will see other sorting methods in later chapters: a recursive version of *quicksort* in chapter 15, and a fast method of sorting using binary trees in chapter 16.

10.9.1 A Simple Exchange Sort

We will begin with a simple algorithm that is not terribly efficient, but that is sufficient for fairly short lists and easy to understand. Suppose a list is stored in $A[i]$ . . . $A[n]$, and we wish to sort this list in ascending numeric order in place (without using extra memory as work space). We begin by finding the location of the least value in the list and exchanging this value with the first element of the list. This element is now in place and need not be examined again. We then repeat the process, using the shorter list beginning with the second element, and so on. The final pass must compare $A[n-1]$ with $A[n]$. Thus $n-1$ passes are required. The algorithm in pseudo code is

```
for i := 1 to n - 1 do  { sort the list in A[i] . . . A[n] }
  begin
     find the location (m) of the least value
        in the list beginning with element i;
     exchange A[i] and A[m]
  end;
```

Procedure *exchangesort* implements this algorithm. The elements are exchanged by *swap*(*x*, *y*), which performs *t* := *x*; *x* := *y*; *y* := *t*.

```
procedure exchangesort(var A : listtype; n : integer);
  var
    i, j, m : integer;
  begin
    for i := 1 to n - 1 do
      begin
        m := i;                      { find location of least value    }
        for j := i + 1 to n do
          if A[j] < A[m]
            then m := j;
        swap(A[i], A[m])             { place least value in position }
      end
  end;
```

The algorithm can be made to sort in descending numeric order by changing the comparison to **if** *A*[*j*] > *A*[*m*]. The procedure can be made to sort in either direction, depending on the value of a boolean parameter. The version shown below can be called by

```
sort(A, n, ascending);
```

or

```
sort(A, n, descending);
```

The flags *ascending* and *descending* are boolean constants defined globally in the main program. The formal parameter *ascending* in the procedure takes the value *true* or *false*, depending upon how the procedure is called.

```
[ const
    ascending  = true;
    descending = false; ]

  procedure exchangesort(var A : listtype; n : integer;
                                            ascending : boolean);
    var
      i, j, m : integer;
    begin
      for i := 1 to n - 1 do
        begin
          m := i;                { find loc of least or greatest value   }
          for j := i + 1 to n do
            if (A[j] < A[m]) = ascending
              then m := j;
          swap(A[i], A[m])       { place it in position                  }
        end
    end;
```

If the elements of the list are nonnumeric, containing some other structured type, for example, a user-written boolean function can be used to test which element is "less" or "greater" based on any criteria desired. For example, two character strings could be compared by a function *lexlt*(*A*[*i*], *A*[*m*]) which returns *true* if *A*[*i*] is lexically less than *A*[*m*]. We will see an example of this in the chapter 11.

This algorithm is one of a class of algorithms called *exchange* or *interchange sorts*. Since the number of comparisons made here is

$$\frac{n(n-1)}{2}$$

the efficiency is $O(n^2)$. The number of exchanges is always $n - 1$.

10.9.2 Shell Sort

An interesting variation on the exchange sort was proposed in 1959 by Donald L. Shell. Shell's sorting method uses a varying displacement between the elements compared on each pass. The displacement, or gap between the compared elements, starts out large and gets smaller as the algorithm progresses. Since the gap is big at the beginning, out-of-order elements move large distances at first, leaving less work to do as the sorting process approaches completion. Many variations are possible, so long as the last gap size is 1, thus comparing adjacent elements. The choice of gap size for most efficient computation is a complex problem. This and an analysis of the algorithm's performance are discussed by Knuth.[7] In the simple version shown here,

Pass	Gap	Swap Indices *i*	*j*	Indices: 1	2	3	4	5	6	7	8	9	10	11	12	13
			Original List:	8	2	0	1	5	7	3	4	9	8	6	4	9
1	6	1	7	3	2	0	1	5	7	8	4	9	8	6	4	9
		6	12	3	2	0	1	5	4	8	4	9	8	6	7	9
2	3	1	4	1	2	0	3	5	4	8	4	9	8	6	7	9
		5	8	1	2	0	3	4	4	8	5	9	8	6	7	9
		9	12	1	2	0	3	4	4	8	5	7	8	6	9	9
3	1	2	3	1	0	2	3	4	4	8	5	7	8	6	9	9
		7	8	1	0	2	3	4	4	5	8	7	8	6	9	9
		8	9	1	0	2	3	4	4	5	7	8	8	6	9	9
		10	11	1	0	2	3	4	4	5	7	8	6	8	9	9
		1	2	0	1	2	3	4	4	5	7	8	6	8	9	9
		9	10	0	1	2	3	4	4	5	7	6	8	8	9	9
		8	9	0	1	2	3	4	4	5	6	7	8	8	9	9
			Sorted List:	0	1	2	3	4	4	5	6	7	8	8	9	9

Length (n) = 13; Comparisons = 82; Exchanges = 12

Table 10.5. Demonstration of Shell Sort

7. Donald E. Knuth, *The Art of Computer Programming*, vol. 3, *Searching and Sorting*. (Reading, Mass.: Addison-Wesley, 1973), 84–95.

the initial gap, which is half the length of the list, is halved after each pass.[8] During each pass through the data (the **repeat...until** *done* loop) the **for** loop sets *i*, the index of the first element of each pair. The terminal value of *i* (*n* – *gap*) is the last value that can be used without exceeding the length of the list. Each element *A*[*i*] is compared with element *A*[*i* + *gap*]; if they are out of order they are exchanged and *done* is set to *false*, thus forcing the current pass to repeat. When no more elements, *gap* positions apart, are out of order, *done* remains *true*, the current pass is terminated, and the gap size is halved.

```
procedure shellsort(var A : listtype; n : integer);
  var
    gap, i, j : integer;
    done : boolean;

  begin
    gap := n;
    while gap > 1 do
      begin
        gap := gap div 2;
        repeat      { one pass }
          done := true;
          for i := 1 to n - gap do           { index of 1st element }
            begin
              j := i + gap;                  { index of 2d element   }
              if A[j] < A[i]
                then
                  begin
                    swap(A[i], A[j]);
                    done := false            { keep going            }
                  end
            end
        until done { one pass }
      end
  end;
```

This algorithm, using a *decreasing increment*, is efficient for an exchange sort because in the beginning, when the list is relatively disordered, the number of comparisons is small (since the length of the list is effectively reduced to *n* – *gap*.) As the list gets longer, it also becomes relatively well ordered, and fewer exchanges have to be made. In addition, each pass terminates as soon as no more exchanges can be made; unlike the exchange sort shown above, the algorithm terminates rather quickly for a list that is already in order or only slightly out of order. Table 10.5 shows the sequence of events for a sample input list. The total number of comparisons made in calculating the final order is 82, while the total number of exchanges is 12.[9]

8. This variation is suggested by Peter Grogono, *Programming in Pascal*, 2nd ed. (New York: Addison-Wesley, 1984), 182–87.

9. Compare to 78 and 12 for the first version of *exchangesort* with the same list, but remember that this is a short list. For a much longer list the number of comparisons is dramatically less for *shellsort*, although for this version the number of exchanges is greater.

10.9.3 Merge Sort

We now examine a sorting method with very good average behavior. This sorting method depends on the fact that merging two presorted lists is much faster than sorting. Two lists stored in $A[1] \ldots A[n]$ and $B[1] \ldots B[m]$, and already in ascending numeric order, can be merged into a single list in $C[1] \ldots C[n+m]$ by the following algorithm:

```
while not at end of either list do
  begin
    compare the current value in lists A and B;
    for whichever list has the smaller value,
      place this value in the next position
      in list C, and obtain the next item in the list
  end;

copy the rest of the longer list into C
```

If two elements are equal, either may be chosen. In implementing the algorithm, we use three variables, *i*, *j*, and *p*, to indicate the current positions in arrays *A*, *B* and *C*, respectively.[10] The algorithm as a Pascal procedure:

```
{ Merge A[1]... A[n] and B[1]... B[m]; store result in C[1]... C[p],
  p = n + m.  Lists A and B are already in numeric order. }

procedure merge(var A ,B, C : listtype; n, m : integer; var p : integer);
  var
    i, j : integer;

  begin { merge }
    i := 1;                            { current position in list A }
    j := 1;                            { current position in list B }
    p := 1;                            { current position in list C }

    while (i <= n) and (j <= m) do
      begin
        if A[i] <= B[j]
          then
            begin
              C[p] := A[i];
              incr(i)                  { get next element of A      }
            end
          else
            begin
              C[p] := B[j];
              incr(j)                  { get next element of B      }
            end;
        incr(p)                        { next position element in C }
      end;
```

10. Compare this algorithm to procedure *compact* in section 10.5.

```
    if i > n                          { if list A is done          }
      then                            { copy rest of B to C        }
        for j := j to m do
          begin
            C[p] := B[j];
            incr(p)
          end
      else                            { else copy rest of A to C   }
        for i := i to n do
          begin
            C[p] := A[i];
            incr(p)
          end;
    p := p - 1                        { actual length of C         }
  end;  { merge }
```

How can we sort using this algorithm? *Mergesort* begins with an unordered list, and sorts it by merging successively longer lists. Consider the problem of sorting the list

(8, 7, 6, 5, 4, 3, 2, 1)

At first, each element is treated as a separate list:

(8) (7) (6) (5) (4) (3) (2) (1)

Now we can sort by merging each pair of lists until only one list remains. First each pair of single-element lists is merged:

(7, 8) (6) (5) (4) (3) (2) (1)
(7, 8) (5, 6) (4) (3) (2) (1)
(7, 8) (5, 6) (3, 4) (2) (1)
(7, 8) (5, 6) (3, 4) (1, 2)

The process is repeated, merging the four two-element lists into two four-element lists:

(5, 6, 7, 8) (3, 4) (1, 2)
(5, 6, 7, 8) (1, 2, 3, 4)

Finally, the two halves of the list are merged:

(1, 2, 3, 4, 5, 6, 7, 8)

This illustration worked out perfectly because the number of elements in the list is 2^3. But what if the number of lists is odd? We solve the problem by defining "next" circularly: if there are no more lists, use the first list. We can illustrate by beginning with an odd number of elements, but a similar situation eventually arises for any list in which the number of elements cannot be expressed as 2^i, where i is an integer, e.g., (2, 4, 8, 16, 32, 64, 128, . . .). Note that if we merge elements in place, i.e., only write over values in the portion of the list that is currently being merged, the final merge results in a circular permutation of the desired list.

original list:	(5, 4, 3, 2, 1)
as single element lists:	(5) (4) (3) (2) (1)
merge (5) and (4):	(4, 5) (3) (2) (1)
merge (3) and (2):	(4, 5) (2, 3) (1)
merge (1) and (4 5):	4, 5) (2, 3) (1,
merge (2 3) and (1 4 5):	4, 5) (1, 2, 3,
sorted list:	(1, 2, 3, 4, 5)

Problem Analysis. In general, after each pass through the list, the size of each sublist doubles while the number of sublists is halved. During each pass, n elements must be examined, thus each pass takes $O(n)$. Since each pass halves the number of sublists that must be merged, the number of passes is $O(\log_2 n)$. Thus the algorithm sorts an n-element list in $O(n \log_2 n)$. This excellent time is achieved by a trade-off for space: $4n$ storage locations are needed for the list A, workspace B, and a queue to store locations of the sublists. This is an excellent algorithm for sorting large lists if sufficient space is available.

In order to implement this sorting algorithm, procedure *merge* must be modified so that it merges two adjacent sublists of array A: $A[n1]$ . . . $A[n2]$, and $A[m1]$ . . . $A[m2]$. These are merged into a workspace in array $B[1]$ . . . $B[p]$, and then the ordered list is copied back into $A[n1]$ . . . $A[m2]$. Addressing is circular, so that any element past the end of the list in A wraps back to the beginning of the list. This allows for odd numbers of sublists, as discussed above. The adjustment of indices is managed by function *adjust*, where x is the index and *len* the length of the list:

```
function adjust(index : integer) : integer;
  begin { adjust indices for wrapping back }
    if index <= len
      then adjust := index
      else adjust := index mod len
  end;
```

Procedure *merge* begins by merging the two sublists of A into the array B:

```
  i := n1;            { current position in list A for first list  }
  j := m1;            { current position in list A for second list }
  p := 1;             { current position in list B                 }

  while (i <= n2) and (j <= m2) do
    begin
      ii := adjust(i);
      jj := adjust(j);
      if A[ii] <= A[jj]
        then
          begin
            B[p] := A[ii];
            incr(i)                { get next element in 1st sublist }
          end
```

```
        else
          begin
            B[p] := A[jj];
            incr(j)                  { get next element in 2d sublist    }
          end;
      incr(p)                        { next position element in B        }
    end;
```

The end of the longer list is copied into *B*:

```
  if i > n2                          { if 1st list is done               }
    then                             { copy rest of 2d list to B         }
      for j := j to m2 do
        begin
          B[p] := A[adjust(j)];
          incr(p)
        end
    else                             { else copy rest of 1st list to B }
      for i := i to n2 do
        begin
          B[p] := A[adjust(i)];
          incr(p)
        end;
```

Then the merged sublists are copied back into array *A*, written over the two sublists. If this is the final merge, *A* is copied directly to *B*. Otherwise only the two merged sublists of *A* are overwritten.

```
  if qempty                           { if done                          }
    then A := B                       { copy B to A                      }
    else
      begin                           { copy B to correct portion of A }
        q := n1;
        for i := 1 to p - 1 do        { copy list back into A            }
          begin
            A[adjust(q)] := B[i];
            incr(q)
          end
      end
```

Procedure *mergesort* calls this procedure to merge appropriate sublists. Each sublist is specified by an ordered pair of indices <*i1*, *i2*> representing the starting and ending point of the sublist in *A*. The indices for each sublist are placed in a queue. If the list will initially be treated as a series of one-element lists, each index of *A* is inserted into the queue twice:

```
  for i := 1 to len do
    begin
      insertq(i);  insertq(i)   { loc of short list in A }
    end;
```

However, we can improve efficiency even further by taking into account the portions of the list that are already in order:

```
                                        { place indices of ordered }
                                        {      sublists in queue }
    i := 1;
    while i <= n do
      begin
        insertq(i);                      { start of sublist        }
        while (A[i] <= A[i + 1]) and (i < n) do
          incr(i);
        insertq(i);                      { end of sublist          }

        incr(i)
      end;
```

Now four indices, representing the location of the first two sublists in *A*, are removed from the queue and passed to procedure *merge*, which merges the sublist. Then the pair of values representing the beginning and end of the merged sublist is placed in the queue. The process is repeated until the queue is empty, indicating that the entire list in *A* has been sorted.

```
    removeq(n1); removeq(n2);            { loc of 1st list in A    }
    while not qempty do
      begin
        removeq(m1); removeq(m2);        { loc of 2d list in A     }
        merge(A, n1, n2, m1, m2, len);   { merge 1st and 2d list   }
        m2 := n1 + n2 - n1 + m2 - m1 + 1; { end of new list        }
        insertq(n1); insertq(m2);        { loc of new list in A    }
        removeq(n1); removeq(n2)         { loc of 1st list in A    }
      end
```

Program 10.5 illustrates all of the procedures required to implement this algorithm, as well as procedures *readlist* and *printlist*.

```
Type list: 8 7 6 5 4 3 2 1
    1    2    3    4    5    6    7    8

Type list: 7 6 5 4 3 2 1
    1    2    3    4    5    6    7

Type list: 29 241 17 721 -2 -12
  -12   -2   17   29  241  721

Type list: 13 144 0 8 55 34 1 233 21 2 89 5 1 377 3
    0    1    1    2    3    5    8   13   21   34   55   89  144  233  377

Type list: 12 94 999 -45 90 124 -10 3 44 27 94
  -45  -10    3   12   27   44   90   94   94  124  999

Type list: ^D
```

Program 10.5. Sample Run (Interactive)

```
(***********************     Program Mergesort     ***********************)
(* Demonstrates sorting by merging as described in text.                  *)
(**************************************************************************)

program mergesort(input, output);

  const
    max = 100;                               { maximum length of list       }
    maxq = 199;                              { maximum length of queue - 1  }

  type
    listtype = array [1 .. max] of integer;
    queue    = array [0 .. maxq] of integer;

  var
    A : listtype;                            { for storing list of integers }
    n : integer;                             { number of elements in list   }
    Q : queue;                               { a queue                      }
    front, rear: integer;                    { front and rear of queue      }

(***********************           incr           ***********************)
(* Adds one to the value of its argument.                                 *)
(**************************************************************************)
  procedure incr(var x : integer);
    begin
      x := x + 1
    end;

(***********************           initq          ***********************)
(* Initializes front and rear of queue.                                   *)
(**************************************************************************)
  procedure initq(var front, rear : integer);
    begin
      front := 0;                                          { empty queue }
      rear  := 0
    end;

(***********************          qempty          ***********************)
(* Returns true if queue is empty.                                        *)
(**************************************************************************)
  function qempty : boolean;
    begin
      qempty := front = rear
    end;

(***********************          insertq         ***********************)
(* Places integer x at rear of queue.                                     *)
(**************************************************************************)
  procedure insertq(x : integer);
    begin
      Q[rear] := x;
      rear := (rear + 1) mod maxq
    end;
```

```
(***********************          removeq          ***********************)
(* Returns as x the integer at front of queue.                            *)
(**************************************************************************)
  procedure removeq(var x : integer);
    begin
      x := Q[front];
      front := (front + 1) mod maxq
    end;

(***********************          skipln           ***********************)
(* Finds next nonblank character or end-of-line.                          *)
(**************************************************************************)
  procedure skipln;
    begin
      while (input↑ = ' ') and not eoln do
        get(input)
    end;

(***********************          readlist         ***********************)
(* Reads list on integers and store in array.                             *)
(**************************************************************************)
  procedure readlist(var A : listtype; var n : integer);
    begin
      n := 0;
      while not eoln do
        begin
          incr(n);
          read(A[n]);
          skipln
        end;
      readln    { skip newline character }
    end;

(***********************         printlist         ***********************)
(* Prints list of integers stored in an array.                            *)
(**************************************************************************)
  procedure printlist(var A : listtype; n, linelen, fw : integer);
    var
      i : integer;
    begin
      for i := 1 to n do
        begin
          write(A[i]:fw);
          if i mod linelen = 0
            then writeln
        end;
      writeln
    end;

(***********************           merge           ***********************)
(* Merges A[n1]...A[n2] with A[m1]...[m2], using workspace B[1]...B[p].  *)
(* Then copies the list back over A[n1]...A[m2].                          *)
(**************************************************************************)
  procedure merge(var A : listtype; n1, n2, m1, m2, len : integer);
    var
      B                   : listtype;          { workspace }
      i, j, p, q, ii, jj : integer;
```

```
function adjust(index : integer) : integer;
  begin                                          { for wrap-around }
    if index <= len
      then adjust := index
      else adjust := index mod len
  end;

begin { merge }
  i := n1;                        { current position of 1st list in A }
  j := m1;                        { current position of 2d list in A  }
  p := 1;                         { current position in list B        }

  while (i <= n2) and (j <= m2) do
    begin
      ii := adjust(i);
      jj := adjust(j);
      if A[ii] <= A[jj]
        then
          begin
            B[p] := A[ii];
            incr(i)                       { get next element of A       }
          end
        else
          begin
            B[p] := A[jj];
            incr(j)                       { get next element of A       }
          end;
      incr(p)                             { next position element in B }
    end;

  if i > n2                               { if 1st list is done         }
    then                                  { copy rest of 2d list to B   }
      for j := j to m2 do
        begin
          B[p] := A[adjust(j)];
          incr(p)
        end
    else                                  { copy rest of 1st list to B }
      for i := i to n2 do
        begin
          B[p] := A[adjust(i)];
          incr(p)
        end;

  if qempty                               { if done                     }
    then A := B                           { copy B to A                 }
    else                                  { otherwise                   }
      begin
        q := n1;
        for i := 1 to p - 1 do            { copy list back into A       }
          begin
            A[adjust(q)] := B[i];
            incr(q)
          end
      end
end; { merge }
```

```
(***********************          mergesort          ***********************)
(* Sorts the list in A[1]...A[len] by successive merging.                  *)
(***************************************************************************)
  procedure mergesort(var A : listtype; len : integer);
    var
      n1, n2, m1, m2, i : integer;
    begin
      i := 1;
      while i <= n do            { place indices of each sublist in queue }
        begin
          insertq(i);                              { start of sublist     }
          while (A[i] <= A[i + 1]) and (i < n) do
          incr(i);
          insertq(i);                              { end of sublist       }
          incr(i)
        end;

      removeq(n1); removeq(n2);                    { loc of 1st list in A }
      while not qempty do
        begin
          removeq(m1); removeq(m2);                { loc of 2d list in A  }
          merge(A, n1, n2, m1, m2, len);           { merge lists 1 and 2  }
          m2 := n1 + n2 - n1 + m2 - m1 + 1;        { end of new list      }
          insertq(n1); insertq(m2);                { loc of new list in A }
          removeq(n1); removeq(n2)                 { loc of 1st list in A }
        end
    end;

(***********************            main            ***********************)
(* Processes lists terminated by newline character.                        *)
(***************************************************************************)
  begin { main }
    initq(front, rear);                                   { init queue    }
    write('Type list: ');                                 { prompt        }
    while not eof do
      begin { process list }
        readlist(A, n);                                   { read a list   }
        mergesort(A, n);                                  { sort it       }
        printlist(A, n, 15, 5);                           { and print it  }
        writeln; writeln;
        write('Type list: ')                              { prompt        }
      end   { process list }
  end.  { main }
```

Program 10.5. *Mergesort*

References and Selected Readings

A thorough discussion of algorithms and how to analyze them, including *O* notation, can be found in chapter 1 of the following:

Knuth, Donald E. *The Art of Computer Programming.* Vol. 1, *Fundamental Algorithms.* 2d ed. Reading, Mass.: Addison-Wesley, 1973.

The definitive work on searching and sorting techniques is:

Knuth, Donald E. *The Art of Computer Programming.* Vol. 3, *Sorting and Searching.* Reading, Mass.: Addison-Wesley, 1973.

You will also find the following helpful:

Aho, Alfred V., John E. Hopcroft, and Jeffrey D. Ullman. *Data Structures and Algorithms.* Reading, Mass.: Addison-Wesley, 1983.

Horowitz, Ellis, and Sartaj Sahni. *Fundamentals of Data Structures.* Potomac, Md.: Computer Science Press, 1976.

Rich, Robert P. *Internal Sorting Methods Illustrated with PL/1 Programs.* Englewood Cliffs, N.J.: Prentice-Hall, 1972.

Rivest, R. L., and Donald E. Knuth. "Bibliography 26: Computer Sorting." *Computing Reviews* 13, no. 6 (1972): 283–89.

Sedgewick, Robert. *Algorithms.* 2d ed. Reading, Mass.: Addison-Wesley, 1988.

The version of *shellsort* presented in this chapter was adapted from the following source:

Grogono, Peter. *Programming in Pascal,* 2d ed. New York: Addison-Wesley, 1984.

Other suggested readings:

Lewin, David. *Generalized Musical Intervals and Transformations.* New Haven: Yale University Press, 1987.

Pope, Stephen Travis. "Music Notations and the Representation of Musical Structure and Knowledge." *Perspectives of New Music* 24, no. 2 (1986): 156–89.

Roeder, John. "A Geometric Representation of Pitch-Class Series." *Perspectives of New Music* 25, nos. 1–2 (1987): 362–409.

Exercises

10.1. *Exercise Group One.*

1. What is wrong with each of the following procedures?

```
procedure readlist(A : arraytype; n : integer);
  begin
    n := 0;
    while not eoln do
      begin
        incr(n);
        read(list[n])
      end
  end;

procedure printlist(A : arraytype; n : integer)
  begin
    for i := 1 to n do
      write(A[n])
  end;
```

2. The following function purports to return *true* if *x* occurs in the list, or *false* if it does

not. Explain why it does not work and suggest a method of making it work as advertised.

```
function linear(var A : listtype; n, x : integer) : boolean;
  var
    i : integer;
    match : boolean;
  begin
    for i := 1 to n do
      match := A[i] = x;
    linear := match
  end;
```

3. Prove the assertion in section 10.8.2, that for the modified version of procedure *binsearch*, *low* is always the location where *x* should be placed if it does not occur in the list.

10.2. *Exercise Group Two.* Solve each of these problems using a simple loop. You do not have to write a complete program. Assume that the following declarations have been made and declare additional variables if you need them.

```
const
  max = 10;          { maximum elements in list }

type
  ar1 : array[1 .. max] of integer;
  ar2 : array[0 .. max] of integer;
  ar3 : array[1 .. max] of real;

var
  list1, list2 : ar1;
  jsqr         : ar2;
  twopower     : ar2;
  sqroot       : ar3;
```

1. Set each value of the array *list1* to 0.
2. Assign ones and zeros to alternate locations in *list1* (1 0 1 0 1 . . .).
3. Assign zeros and ones to alternate locations in *list1* (0 1 0 1 0 . . .).
4. Store the numbers 1, 2, 3, . . . , *max* in elements of *list1*.
5. Store the numbers 0, 1, 2, 0, 1, 2, . . . in elements of *list2*.
6. Set *jsqr*[*j*] to j^2 for $j = 0, 1, 2, \ldots, max$.
7. Set each element of the *sqroot* array to the square root of the index.
8. Set *twopower*[*j*] to 2^j, for $j = 0, 1, 2, \ldots, max$.
9. Copy the elements of *list1* to *list2*.
10. Copy the elements of *list1* to *list2* in reverse order.
11. Reverse the order of elements in *list1* without using another array.
12. Print the values stored in *list2*.
13. Print the values in *list2* in reverse order.
14. Compare *list1* and *list2*, printing out the subscripts of equal elements.

15. As in 14, but print indexes of unequal elements and the values stored in them.

16. Compare *list1* with the reverse order of *list2*, i.e., compare the first element of *list1* with the last element of *list2*, etc. Print the indexes and values for unequal values.

10.3. *Exercise Group Three.* These problems deal with an array called *list*, that was declared by the following statements:

```
const
  maxlen = 100;   { maximum number of values in array }

type
  ar1 = array[1 .. maxlen] of integer;
  ar2 = array[1 .. 5] of integer;

var
  list         : ar1;        { an array of integers          }
  n            : integer;    { the number of values in list  }
  i            : integer;    { for looping                   }
  oddn         : boolean;    { boolean flag                  }
  temp         : ar2;        { temporary array               }
  total        : integer;
  small, large : ar2;
```

1. Read the value of *n*, then read *n* integers into the array *list*.

2. Set *oddn* to *true* if the list contains an odd number of elements; otherwise set *oddn* to *false*.

3. Find the largest number in *list*.

4. Find the smallest number in *list*.

5. Find the location of the largest number in *list*.

6. Find the location of the smallest number in *list*.

7. Exchange the largest and smallest numbers in *list*.

8. Store the sum of the values in list in *total*.

9. Store the sum of the values in locations with odd indexes of *list* in *temp*[1] and the sum of the values in locations with even indexes in *temp*[2].

10. Store the sum of the odd integers in *list* in *temp*[3], and the sum of the even integers in list in *temp*[4].

11. Sort list in ascending order.

Assume that *list* is already sorted in order from small to large values:

12. Store the 5 smallest values of *list* in increasing order in the array *small*.

13. Store the 5 largest values of *list* in increasing order in *large*.

14. Store the 5 largest values of *list* in decreasing order in *large*.

15. Store the 5 smallest values of *list* in decreasing order in *small*.

10.4. *Exercise Group 4: Program Assignments*

1. *Tessitura.* The input data for this problem is continuous pitch code (cpc) with '/' representing bar lines, '//' for double bar (end of excerpt), and 'r' for rests. Each

encoded part or excerpt will be preceded by a one-line title terminated by a newline character <return>, and each excerpt will be terminated by the double bar '//'. An input data set may contain any number of encoded excerpts, so long as each is in the format described above. Examples are shown below the following excerpts.

Brahms, Symphony No. 1 in C Major, fourth movement, mm. 61–69

Olivier Messiaen, *Quatuor pour la Fin du Temps*; III. *Abîme des oiseaux*, mm. 1–10.

```
Brahms, Symphony No. 1
43 / 48 47 48 / 45 43 48 / 50 52 50 52 48 / 50 50
43 / 48 47 48 / 45 43 48 / 50 54 55 54 48 / 50 48 //

Messiaen, Abime des oiseaux
52 56 55 58 / 52 53 55 52 53 55 / 52 56 55 58 / 52 53 55 53 55 56 / 52
/ 65 58 / 59 58 55 61 59 50 55 / 58 56 / 47 / 49 50 //
```

Program *Tessitura.* Sample Input Data

The program will deal with tessitura, which for our purposes will be defined as the range of notes in a melody and the number of occurrence of notes within that range. Your program should do the following (the order does not necessarily reflect the best order of computation):

a) Count the number of occurrences of each cpc encoded note in the melody (ignore bar lines and rests). You will find that an array is useful for this task.

b) Find the lowest and highest notes in the melody.

c) Count the total number of notes in the melody (try to find the most efficient method of doing this).

d) Print the title, the number of notes, the highest and lowest notes, and the number of occurrences of each note in that range, expressed as the actual note count and as the percentage of the total number of notes.

e) Print a bar graph showing the distribution of notes in the melody. The bar graph should use the number of occurrences by percentage (rounded to the nearest integer) to determine the length of each measure. The graph should include all pitches between the highest and lowest notes in the range of the piece, listed in descending order from high to low.

f) The program should be able to deal with any number of encoded tunes, each preceded by a title.

Suggestions. Design your program top-down, i.e., think in larger processes first, then refine the steps. Use functions and procedures to modularize each process. On the other hand, it is not necessary to debug the whole program at once. Enter and test the procedures one at a time. Make sure that you can read the data and count the number of occurrences of each encoded note before you try to make a graphic representation. Verify and test each procedure before going on to the next.

Designing the Algorithm. Work top-down; think in terms of larger processes first, and then refine them. A reasonable division of labor for processing each piece or excerpt is:

a) Print the title.

b) Read the tune, counting the frequency of occurrence of each note.

c) Do necessary calculations and print the graphic output.

Thus your main procedure might be something like the following (procedure specifications are given below the program):

```
program tessitura(input, output);
  const
    . . .

  type
    counter = array[0 .. 99] of integer;

  var
    note : counter;             { array for storing note counts    }

{ your functions and procedures go here }

  begin { main }
    while not eof do
      begin { process piece }
        printtitle;             { copy title from input to output }
        readtune(note);         { read tune, counting notes        }
        maketable(note);        { make and print table             }
        skipblanks
      end { process piece }
  end. { main }
```

Suggested Procedures:

a) **procedure** *printtitle*; — copies one line from the input file to the output file. No parameters are needed. (In the next chapter we will learn to store the title so that we can print it whenever we wish.)

b) **procedure** *readtune*(**var** *note* : *counter*); — initializes the *note* array (sets each element to 0), then using a local variable, say *code*, and a procedure that returns the next encoded note, reads each encoded value in the excerpt and for each note increments *note*[*code*]. When the array *note* is returned to the main program, each element *note*[*i*] will contain the number of occurrences of the cpc encoded pitch *i*.

c) **procedure** *getnote*(**var** *x* : *integer*); — returns the next encoded note in the input file, or sets the boolean variable *done* to *true* if the double bar is encountered. *Getnote* will be simplified by calling the following procedure, which finds the next encoded note and processes rests and bar lines:

```
procedure findnote;
  begin { findnote }
    skipblanks;
    while not isdigit(input↑) and not done do
      begin
        if input↑ = barline
          then
            begin
              get(input);                  { skip bar line        }
              if input↑ = barline
                then
                  begin { double bar }
                    done := true;
                    get(input)             { skip bar line        }
                  end   { double bar }
            end
        else if input↑ = rest
          then get(input)                  { skip rest            }
        else
          begin { error }
            writeln('getnote: bad character in code (',
                                                      input↑, ')');
            get(input)                     { skip bad character }
          end;  { error }
        skipblanks
      end
  end;  { findnote }
```

d) **procedure** *maketable*(**var** *note* : *counter*); — calls other functions and procedures to count the total number of notes, find the lowest and highest notes, calculate the percentage of total for each note, etc. It will also print the table. N.B.: Notice that the array *note* is passed as a **var** parameter (for efficiency) even though the procedure will not change its values.

e) **procedure** *skipblanks*; — you already know about this one.

Each of these procedures should in turn be designed top-down, and may call other procedures and/or functions of your own design. Use parameters to pass to each procedure or function all of the values it needs to do its task, and use local variables for values that are needed only in a particular procedure or function. Some functions used in this program may be useful in other programs as well. For example, you will probably want a function to calculate percentage. Be sure to generalize this procedure so that it can be used without change in other programs.

Test your program on a variety of different excerpts, using different scales (major, minor, whole tone, pentatonic, octatonic, etc.). Does this graphic representation help to visualize scale characteristics? What is the advantage of deriving the bar graph from the percentage rather than from raw number of occurrences of each note?

```
Title:  Brahms, Symphony No. 1
note count:        28
highest note:     55
lowest note:      43

tessitura:
===================
note count percent
===================
  55      1      3.6 |****
  54      2      7.1 |*******
  53      0      0.0 |
  52      4     14.3 |**************
  51      0      0.0 |
  50      4     14.3 |**************
  49      0      0.0 |
  48      9     32.1 |********************************
  47      2      7.1 |*******
  46      0      0.0 |
  45      2      7.1 |*******
  44      0      0.0 |
  43      4     14.3 |**************
===================

Title: Messiaen, Abime des oiseaux
note count:      35
highest note:    65
lowest note:     47

tessitura:
===================
note count percent
===================
  65      1      2.9 |***
  64      0      0.0 |
  63      0      0.0 |
  62      0      0.0 |
  61      1      2.9 |***
  60      0      0.0 |
  59      2      5.7 |******
  58      5     14.3 |**************
  57      0      0.0 |
  56      4     11.4 |***********
  55      8     22.9 |***********************
  54      0      0.0 |
  53      4     11.4 |***********
  52      6     17.1 |*****************
  51      0      0.0 |
  50      2      5.7 |******
  49      1      2.9 |***
  48      0      0.0 |
  47      1      2.9 |***
===================
```

Program *Tessitura.* Sample Output

2. *Interval Vectors.* An interval vector is a concise way to represent the interval relations among the pcs in a pitch-class set. Recall that a pc set consists of a set of unique pcs (no duplicates) and that the unordered interval between any two pcs is obtained as the absolute value of the difference between the pcs. An interval vector represents the number of times each interval class (*ic*) occurs between pairs of pcs in a pc set. An ic is the smallest number in the pair of intervals consisting of an interval and its inverse. This is analogous to taking the inversion of an interval in conventional terms. Thus ic 1 represents 1 (minor second) and 11 (12 – 1 or major seventh); ic 2 represents 2 (major second) and 10 (12 – 2, minor seventh); etc. Thus the interval class, *ic*, between any two pcs, *pc1* and *pc2*, can be obtained by the following:

```
ic := abs(pc2 - pc1);          { find unordered interval }
if ic > 6                      { if greater than 6, use  }
  then ic := 12 - ic;          {      its inverse        }
```

An interval vector is an array that shows how many times each interval class (1 through 6) occurs in a pc set. (Ic 0 cannot occur, since a pc set contains no duplicates by definition.)

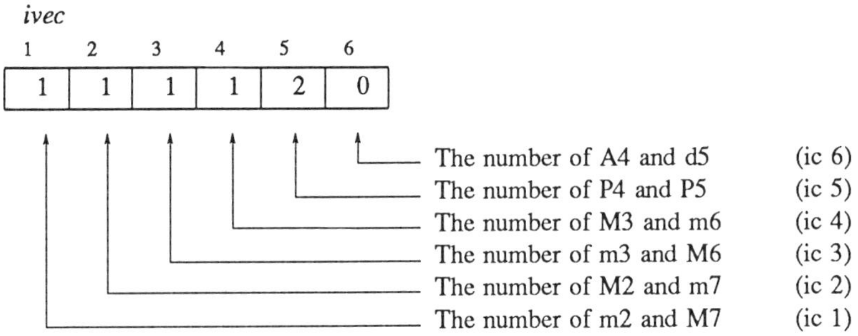

In constructing an interval vector from a set of *n* pcs stored in another array (*pcset*), it is necessary to find the interval class between each pair of pcs and to increment the appropriate element of *ivec* for each interval class. Thus for the four-note set {0,2,3,7} (shown below) the following comparisons are made:

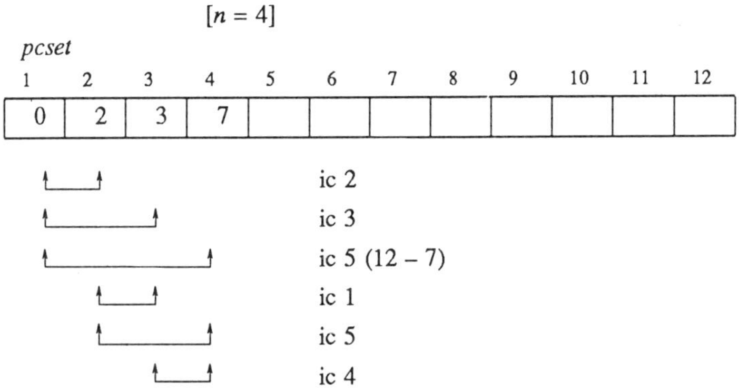

Thus the interval vector for {0,2,3,7} is [111120].

Exercise: You are to write a Pascal program that performs each of the tasks outlined below. Use separate functions and procedures to modularize the program, and design your algorithm top-down.

a) Read a pitch collection from a single line of input, removing all duplicate entries. An array *have* : **array**[0 .. 11] **of** *boolean* will provide an efficient way to check for duplicate pcs. Procedure *readset* should return the pc set and its cardinality.

b) Input and output will use hexadecimal notation, i.e., pcs and interval counts will be represented by the characters 0123456789abc (c = 12 in interval vector). This obviates the use of spaces or other separators in the input and output. Use separate procedures for each operation, e.g., *getpc*(*x*) to read pitch class *x*, *tochar*(*x*) to convert the integer to the character representation, etc.

c) Print out the set without duplicates. Optionally, you may wish to sort the pcs in ascending order.

d) Calculate the interval vector for the pc set, storing the vector in an array.

e) Print the interval vector.

f) Use an *eof* loop to process any number of sets. Use of prompts is optional but desirable.

g) One refinement would be to use one array type (**array** [1 .. 12] **of** *integer*) for the pc set and for the interval vector. Thus the same procedure (*printarray*) could be used to print the set or the interval vector.

N.B.: Please remember that **set** is a Pascal reserved word, i.e., you will avoid many problems by *not* trying to use **set** as an identifier.

3. *Imbrication.* Imbrication is the process of extracting ordered segments of an ordered list, is a common analytic procedure in music analysis. For example, if we represent contours as generic intervals where any second is encoded as '2', any third '3', etc., and the sign indicates direction, then the melodic subsets of the contour class –2 –2 –2 +2 –2 –2, from three notes to the length of the phrase, are shown below:

–2	–2	–2	+2	–2	–2	the contour (six intervals)
–2	–2					two-interval segments
	–2	–2				(three notes)
		–2	+2			
			+2	–2		
				–2	–2	
–2	–2	–2				three-interval segments
	–2	–2	+2			(four notes)
		–2	+2	–2		
			+2	–2	–2	
–2	–2	–2	+2			four-interval segments
	–2	–2	+2	–2		(five notes)
		–2	+2	–2	–2	
–2	–2	–2	+2	–2		five-interval segments
	–2	–2	+2	–2	–2	(six notes)

This can be generalized, since the process is the same no matter what the contents of the original list. For example, the same process could be used to find the ordered subsegments of a collection of pitch classes or notes in any of the numeric representations discussed in chapter 6.

You are to write **procedure** *imbricate*(**var** *A* : *list*; *n* : *integer*; *short*, *long* : *integer*); — that prints the imbricated subsets of a list of integers in $A[1] \ldots A[n]$. The length of the imbricated segments will range from *short* to *long* elements, where $short \geq 1$, $long \leq n$, and $short \leq n$.

Use this procedure in a program that prompts the user for a list of integers, reads the list terminated by a newline character (carriage return), prompts the user for values for *short* and *long*, and prints the list and its imbrications. Use other procedures (*readlist*, *printlist*), to modularize the program.

Hints: Procedure *imbricate* will require nested **for** loops to control (1) the length of segment, (2) the first element in the segment, and (3) selection of each element in the segment. Aligning the elements of the segments with the elements of the original list makes the problem a bit more difficult. If you wish to add this refinement, do so only after you have successfully extracted the ordered segments of the list.

11 | Other Uses for the Array

In chapter 10 we studied algorithms for processing lists with arrays. In this chapter we will see some other possible uses for this versatile data structure: manipulating character strings, maintaining buffers for internal processing of input files, and using arrays as lookup tables for fast conversion of data. This chapter also introduces multidimensional arrays.

11.1 Packed Arrays and Character Strings

Many Pascal compilers provide a string data type and procedures that facilitate string operations. However, there are two good reasons for writing our own string routines. The first is that string operations are extensions to the Pascal standard; string procedures vary from system to system, and are sometimes absent altogether. Thus programs that use their own string-handling procedures tend to be more portable. The second is that string-handling procedures provide an excellent opportunity to exercise arrays and to learn new programming techniques. The choice of whether or not to use extensions to standard Pascal depends to a great extent on whether you plan to run your programs on different computer systems with different Pascal compilers.

In Pascal, strings are usually implemented as packed arrays of characters. The directive **packed** can be used with any array and with other structured data types (such as records). "Packing" means that the memory space used is to be minimized. Packing is not ordinarily used for variables of other types, since numeric values usually use at least one word of computer memory. However, computer systems with larger words can store more than one character per word. The cost of this optimization may be slower execution and larger object code size, due to the code and time necessary to pack and unpack the data structure. The effect is implementation dependent; on some systems it has no effect at all. Packed arrays are used just like other arrays, with the exception that many compilers do not permit a component of a packed array to be passed as a variable parameter.

We declare the type *string* as follows:[1]

1. If your system has a predefined string type, you will probably have to use a different identifier, say *str*, to avoid conflict with the predefined identifier *string*.

```
const
  maxstring =  81;          { maximum string length plus 1       }
  max       = 200;          { maximum no. of strings in strlist  }

type
  string = packed array[1 .. maxstring] of char;
  strlist = array[1 .. max] of string;
```

Now we can use *string* like any other type.

```
var
  title  : string;
  S1, S2 : string;
  line   : strlist;    { an array of strings }
  {etc.}
```

The packed array of *char* is type compatible with a character literal of the same length. The literal can be assigned to the array name with an assignment statement. The two can also be compared through relational operators, and the array can be printed in a simple *write* statement. Thus the following are permitted:

```
[ type
    alpha = packed array[1 .. 10] of char;

  var
    name : alpha;  ]

    . . .

    name := 'Bach      ';

    write(name);

    if name = 'Mozart    '
      then ...
```

Although packed arrays can be written as shown above, in standard Pascal they must be read one character at a time with a loop.

When strings are compared with '<' or '>', the distinction is made according to the ordinal position in the character set of the first nonequal characters. Thus

```
'Bach      ' < 'Back      '
```

is *true* since, *ord*('h') < *ord*('k'). Remember that the lengths of the character literal and of the packed array *must* be identical; statements such as the following result in a type-clash error:

```
{ WRONG }

name := 'Bach';          { incorrect string length }

if name = 'Mozart'
  then ...
```

Fixed-length strings are too limited for many applications. It is often preferable to treat strings as if their length were variable. Although it would be possible to use a separate variable to store the actual number of characters in each string, programs that deal with strings often use many of them, and it will be more convenient to mark the end of the string in an array with a special ''end of string'' character. Since we want a character that is not likely to occur as an element of a string, we will use the *null* character, the first character in the ASCII character set. Although this character usually cannot be entered from a terminal, it can be specified in Pascal as *chr*(0).[2] In the diagrams in this chapter, we will use the symbol '∅' to indicate this character. Thus character strings will be stored as shown in figure 11.1, with one character stored in each element of the array, and the null character in the location just past the end of the string. The null character marks the end of the string but is not part of it.

The procedure shown below reads a single line from the input file and stores it as a string. It ensures that the array bounds are not violated, and prints a warning if the string is truncated. Since the input string is terminated by a newline character, it uses *eoln* to determine if the string is too long. The procedure performs a *readln* to discard the newline character and any truncated characters in the string.

```
procedure readstring(var S : string);
  var
    i : integer;
  begin { readstring }
    i := 1;
    while not eoln and (i < maxstring) do
      begin
        read(S[i]);
        incr(i)
      end;
    S[i] := chr(0);                              { mark end of string    }
    if not eoln                                  { check for truncation  }
      then writeln('warning: string truncated to', maxstring - 1:4,
                                                       ' chars');
    readln                                       { skip newline          }
  end; { readstring }
```

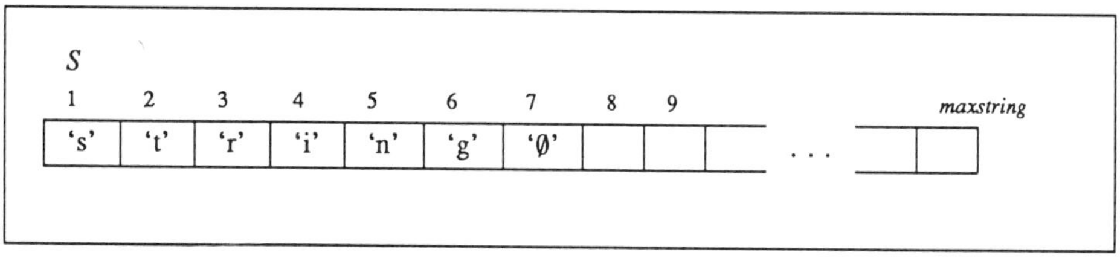

Figure 11.1. A Character String in an Array

2. Even when the null character can be generated by a terminal, e.g., by typing a control character, it is often filtered out by the operating system. In any case, it is a nonprinting character, and is not likely to occur as a legitimate component of a character string.

Procedure *writestring* uses a **while** loop to print each character before the null character in the array. The procedure could do a *writeln*, but we prefer to leave open the option of terminating the line after writing the string.

```
procedure writestring(var S : string);
  var
    i : integer;
  begin
    i := 1;
    while S[i] <> chr(0) do
      begin
        write(S[i]);
        incr(i)
      end
  end;
```

Accessing components of a packed array takes longer than it does in an array that is not packed. Depending on your computer system, it may be advisable to unpack arrays before using them and to repack them when finished. Thus the compiler does not have to perform this operation for each element referenced. Pascal provides procedures for packing and unpacking arrays for this purpose. If *P* is an array of type

```
packed array[a .. b] of <component type>      { packed      }
```

and *N* is an array of type

```
array[c .. d] of <component type>             { not packed }
```

where $(d - c) \geq (b - a)$, then *pack(N, i, P)* packs the components of array *N*, beginning with *N*[*i*], into array *P*, and is thus equivalent to

```
for j := a to b do
  P[j] := N[j - a + i]
```

Procedure *unpack*(*P*, *N*, *i*), which unpacks array *P* into array *N*, beginning with *N*[*i*], is equivalent to

```
for j := a to b do
  N[j - a + i] := P[j]
```

Thus arrays can be packed or unpacked in one operation.[3] In practice these procedures are used in conjunction with a temporary array (which is not packed) in order to avoid the slower process of locating individual components in a packed array. We illustrate by rewriting *readstring* and *writestring*, using *pack* and *unpack*. The new procedure reads the characters into a temporary array *T*, and then packs it into the packed array *S*, which is returned to the calling procedure.

3. Note that the illustration above assumes the indices of arrays *P* and *N* are subranges of the type *integer*. In fact, they may be any ordinal type.

```
procedure readstring(var S : string);
  var
    T : array[1 .. maxstring] of char;
    i : integer;
  begin { readstring }
    i := 1;
    while not eoln and (i < maxstring) do
      begin
        read(T[i]);
        incr(i)
      end;
    T[i] := chr(0);
    if not eoln
      then writeln('warning: string truncated to',
                                        maxstring - 1:4, ' chars');
    readln;
    pack(T, 1, S)                        { pack T into string S }
  end; { readstring }
```

The alternate version of *writestring* unpacks string *S* into temporary array *T* before printing it.

```
procedure writestring(var S : string);
  var
    T : array[1 .. maxstring] of char;
    i : integer;
  begin { writestring }
    unpack(S, T, 1);                     { unpack S into temp array T }
    i := 1;
    while T[i] <> chr(0) do
      begin
        write(T[i]);
        incr(i)
      end
  end; { writestring }
```

Using these procedures, a subprogram that modifies a preexistent string unpacks the string into a temporary array, makes the desired changes, and then repacks it into the original array. On systems where these operations improve performance, they should be used by any subroutine that accesses individual elements of the array, whether or not values are changed. In the rest of this section, procedures will be presented without packing and unpacking so that we can concentrate on the basic algorithms used.

11.1.1 Functions and Procedures for String Handling

We will now examine a few subprograms for manipulating strings in the internal form suggested above. The first is so simple that it could be omitted. However, its use may aid in program readability. Procedure *copy* copies its first argument to its second.

```
procedure copy(var A, B : string);
  begin
    B := A
  end;
```

Function *length* returns the length of its argument string, which is found by locating the null character marking the end of the string.

```
function length(var S : string) : integer;
  var
    i : integer;
  begin
    i := 1;
    while S[i] <> chr(0) do
      incr(i);
    length := i - 1
  end;
```

The next function is suggested by the *strcmp* function in UNIX systems library functions for C programs. *Compare*(*A*, *B*), compares its arguments and returns an integer greater than, equal to, or less than 0, indicating that *A* is lexicographically greater than, equal to, or less than *B*. Thus it can replace three common string functions that would return boolean values—*ident*(*x*, *y*), *lexlt*(*x*, *y*), and *lexgt*(*x*, *y*). If the strings are not identical, our version, *compare*, finds the first nonequal characters, and returns the difference between their ordinal positions in ASCII character set. Thus an uppercase character has a lower value than the corresponding lowercase character. Modification of this procedure to disregard case is suggested as an exercise.

```
function compare(var A, B : string) : integer;
  var
    i : integer;
  begin
    i := 1;
    while (A[i] = B[i]) and (A[i] <> chr(0)) do
      incr(i);
    compare := ord(A[i]) - ord(B[i])
  end;
```

Procedure *lcmap*(*a*, *b*) copies string *a* to string *b*, but with each uppercase character mapped into the corresponding lowercase character.

```
procedure lcmap(var A, B : string);
  var
    i : integer;
  begin
    i := 0;
    repeat
      incr(i);
      B[i] := tolower(A[i])
    until B[i] = chr(0)
  end;
```

The character translation is accomplished by function *tolower(ch)*, which returns *ch* if it is not an uppercase character. If *ch* is upper case, then its offset from the character 'A' is calculated and added to the ordinal position of 'a' to find the position of the corresponding lowercase character. The *chr* function translates this ordinal position into the corresponding character.

```
function tolower(ch : char) : char;
  begin
    if ch in ['A' .. 'Z']
      then tolower := chr(ord('a') + ord(ch) - ord('A'))
      else tolower := ch
  end;
```

Procedure *concatenate(a, b, c)* concatenates strings *a* and *b*, storing the result in *c*. This is accomplished by copying string *a* into *c*, followed by string *b*, which is copied complete with null character. Note that *a* and *b* are passed as value parameters, and thus act as temporary storage locations. This is necessary in order to generalize the procedure so that *a*, *b*, and *c* need not be mutually exclusive. As an exercise, see what would happen if all three parameters were passed by reference and the procedure was called by *concatenate(b, a, a)* or *concatenate(a, b, b)*.

```
procedure concatenate(A, B : string; var C : string);
  var
    i, p               : integer;
    alength, blength : integer;                 { length of a and b     }
  begin { concatenate }
    alength := length(A);
    blength := length(B);
    if alength + blength >= maxstring
      then
        begin
          writeln('Concatenate: strings are too long');
          C[1] := chr(0)                        { return empty string }
        end
      else
        begin
          p := 1;                               { next position in C    }
          for i := 1 to alength do              { copy A into C         }
            begin
              C[p] := A[i];
              incr(p)
            end;
          for i := 1 to blength + 1 do          { copy B into C         }
            begin                               { with chr(0)           }
              C[p] := B[i];
              incr(p)
            end
        end
  end;  { concatenate }
```

The last two subprograms are adapted from the programming language PL/1. Function *index(A, B)* returns the index of string *B* in string *A*, i.e., the position in *A* of the beginning of a substring that matches string *B*. It returns 0 if *B* does not occur in

A. The method: String *B* is compared to string *A* beginning at each position *i* in *A*. When *B*[1] = *A*[*i*], two position indicators (*j* and *k*) are used to step through the strings, comparing each character so long as they are equal. If each character *B*[*k*] matches *A*[*j*], the starting position *i* is returned. The boolean test for (*answer* = 0) in the **while** construct forces continuation of the process until a matching substring is found or until all possibilities have been exhausted.

```
function index(var A, B : string) : integer;
  var
    i, j, k : integer;
    answer  : integer;
  begin { index }
    answer := 0;
    i := 1;                                 { starting position in A }
    while (A[i] <> chr(0)) and (answer = 0) do
      begin
        j := i;                                       { position in A }
        k := 1;                                       { position in B }
        while (A[j] = B[k]) and (B[k] <> chr(0)) do
          begin
            incr(j);            { get next position in both strings }
            incr(k)
          end;
        if B[k] = chr(0)                  { entire substring matched }
          then answer := i
          else incr(i)
      end;
    index := answer                                   { return answer }
  end; { index }
```

Procedure *substr*(*B*, *A*, *p*, *n*) finds the *n*-character substring of *A* beginning in position *p*, and copies it to string *B*. It first checks to see that this is possible.

```
procedure substring(var B, A : string; p, n : integer);
  var
    i : integer;
  begin
    if ((p + n - 1) > length(A)) or (p < 1)
      then
        begin
          writeln('substring: illegal arguments');
          B[1] := chr(0)                      { return empty string }
        end
      else
        begin
          for i := 1 to n do
            begin
              B[i] := A[p];
              incr(p)
            end;
          B[n + 1] := chr(0)
        end
  end;
```

The subprograms shown above are representative of string handling procedures and functions. You may wish to add some of your own as need dictates.

11.1.2 Lexicographic Sorting

Lexicographic sorting means sorting strings in alphabetic order. This can be accomplished by any of the sorting methods we have examined, with only a few modifications. We will modify the simple exchange sort that we saw in chapter 10. Suppose that we have made the following declarations, creating an array *list*, each component of which is a string:

```
const
  strlen = 80;                        { maximum length of strings }
  max    = 100;                       { maximum number of strings }

type
  string   = packed array[1 .. strlen] of char;
  listtype = array[1 .. max] of string;

var
  list    : listtype;                 { an array of strings        }
  n       : integer;                  { actual number of strings   }
```

and that we have already stored *n* strings in *list*. Procedure *swap* is modified so that it exchanges two strings instead of two integers.

```
procedure swap(var x, y : string);
  var
    t : string;
  begin
    t := x; x := y; y := t
  end;
```

The only change in procedure *sort*, other than type changes, is that a special function must be written to compare the strings. Function *lexlt*(*a*, *b*) returns *true* if string *a* is lexicographically less than string *b*. It disregards case by translating all uppercase letters to lower case.

```
function lexlt(var A, B : string) : boolean;
  var
    i : integer;
  begin { lexlt }
    i := 1;
    while (tolower(A[i]) = tolower(B[i])) and (A[i] <> chr(0)) do
      incr(i);
    lexlt := ord(tolower(A[i])) < ord(tolower(B[i]))
  end; { lexlt }
```

Now calling *sort*(*list*, *n*) will arrange the *n* strings in *list* in aphabetic order. Compare this algorithm to *exchangesort* in section 10.9.1.

```
procedure sort(var A : listtype; n : integer);
  var
    i, j : integer;
    m    : integer;
  begin { sort }
    for i := 1 to n - 1 do
      begin
        m := i;
        for j := i + 1 to n do
          if lexlt(A[j], A[m])
            then m := j;
        swap(A[i], A[m])
      end
  end; { sort }
```

Program 11.1 illustrates these procedures, as well as some of those demonstrated earlier.

```
(***********************    Program Alphsort      ***********************)
(* Reads each line of the input file into a packed array of characters.  *)
(* The strings are then sorted in alphabetic order and the sorted list   *)
(* is printed in the standard output file.                               *)
(*************************************************************************)
program alphsort(input, output);
  const
    maxstring = 81;                      { maximum string length + 1 }
    max       = 100;                     { maximum number of strings }

  type
    string   = packed array[1 .. maxstring] of char;
    listtype = array[1 .. max] of string;

  var
    list   : listtype;                   { an array of strings       }
    n      : integer;                    { actual number of strings  }

(***********************          incr          ***********************)
(* Adds one to the value of its argument.                              *)
(***********************************************************************)
  procedure incr(var x : integer);
    begin
      x := x + 1
    end;

(***********************       readstring       ***********************)
(* Reads all characters up to a newline char, and stores them in a     *)
(* packed array of characters.  The end of the string is marked with a *)
(* null character, chr(0).                                             *)
(***********************************************************************)
  procedure readstring(var S : string);
    var
      i : integer;
```

```
  begin { readstring }
    i := 1;
    while not eoln and (i < maxstring) do
      begin
        read(S[i]);
        incr(i)
      end;
    S[i] := chr(0);                                { mark end of string    }
    if not eoln                                    { check for truncation }
      then writeln('warning: string truncated to', maxstring - 1:4,
                                                          ' chars');

    readln                                         { skip newline char     }
  end; { readstring }


(***********************        readdata        ***********************)
(* Stores each line of the input file in an element of list.  The array *)
(* of strings and n, the number of strings, are returned.               *)
(**********************************************************************)
  procedure readdata(var list : listtype; var n : integer);
    begin
      n := 0;                    { init number of strings }
      while not eof do
        begin
          incr(n);
          readstring(list[n])
        end
    end;


(***********************        writestring     ***********************)
(* Prints out the characters stored in string S.                        *)
(**********************************************************************)
  procedure writestring(var S : string);
    var
      i : integer;
    begin
      i := 1;
      while S[i] <> chr(0) do
        begin
          write(S[i]);
          incr(i)
        end;
      writeln
    end;


(***********************        writedata       ***********************)
(* Prints n strings in list into the output file, one string per line.  *)
(**********************************************************************)
  procedure writedata(var list : listtype; n : integer);
    var
      i : integer;
    begin
      for i := 1 to n do
        writestring(list[i])
    end;
```

```
(***********************          swap          ***********************)
(* Exchanges strings x and y, using a temporary string t.               *)
(**********************************************************************)
  procedure swap(var x, y : string);
    var
      t : string;
    begin
      t := x; x := y; y := t
    end;


(***********************          tolower          ***********************)
(* Converts upper case to lower.                                          *)
(**********************************************************************)
  function tolower(c : char) : char;
    begin
      if c in ['A' .. 'Z']
        then tolower := chr(ord('a') + ord(c) - ord('A'))
        else tolower := c
    end;


(***********************          lexlt          ***********************)
(* Returns true if string A is lexicographically less than B.           *)
(**********************************************************************)
  function lexlt(var A, B : string) : boolean;
    var
      i : integer;
    begin
      i := 1;
      while (tolower(A[i]) = tolower(B[i])) and (A[i] <> chr(0)) do
        incr(i);
      lexlt := ord(tolower(A[i])) < ord(tolower(B[i]))
    end;


(***********************          sort          ***********************)
(* Sorts n character strings in array A in alphabetic order.  Upper case *)
(* is converted to lower for comparison.                                 *)
(**********************************************************************)
  procedure sort(var A : listtype; n : integer);
    var
      i, j : integer;
      m    : integer;
    begin
      for i := 1 to n - 1 do
        begin
          m := i;
          for j := i + 1 to n do
            if lexlt(A[j], A[m])
              then m := j;
          if m <> i
            then swap(A[i], A[m])
        end
    end;
```

```
(***********************     main procedure       ***********************)
(* Exercises the above procedures.                                      *)
(************************************************************************)
  begin { main }
    readdata(list, n);                               { read file        }
    sort(list, n);                                   { alphabetize it   }
    writedata(list, n)                               { print the file   }
  end. { main }
```

Program 11.1. *Alphsort*

Input:

```
Dunstable, John (c. 1370-1453)
Binchois, Giles (c. 1400-1460)
Dufay, Guillaume (c. 1400-1474)
Isaac, Heinrich (c. 1450-1517)
Josquin des Prez (c. 1450-1521)
Obrecht, Jacob (1452-1505)
Jannequin, Clement (c. 1475-c. 1560)
Tallis, Thomas (c. 1505-1585)
Palestrina, Giovanni Pierluigi da (c. 1525-1594)
Lassus, Orlandus (1532-1594)
Byrd, William (1543-1623)
Caccini, Giulio (c. 1546-1618)
Victoria, Tomas Luis de (c. 1549-1611)
Morley, Thomas (1557-1602)
Gabrieli, Giovanni (1557-1612)
Monteverdi, Claudio (1567-1643)
```

Output:

```
Binchois, Giles (c. 1400-1460)
Byrd, William (1543-1623)
Caccini, Giulio (c. 1546-1618)
Dufay, Guillaume (c. 1400-1474)
Dunstable, John (c. 1370-1453)
Gabrieli, Giovanni (1557-1612)
Isaac, Heinrich (c. 1450-1517)
Jannequin, Clement (c. 1475-c. 1560)
Josquin des Prez (c. 1450-1521)
Lassus, Orlandus (1532-1594)
Monteverdi, Claudio (1567-1643)
Morley, Thomas (1557-1602)
Obrecht, Jacob (1452-1505)
Palestrina, Giovanni Pierluigi da (c. 1525-1594)
Tallis, Thomas (c. 1505-1585)
Victoria, Tomas Luis de (c. 1549-1611)
```

Program 11.1. Sample Input and Output

11.1.3 Indirect Sorting

Although the above program works perfectly well, the process of moving strings is more time consuming than moving integers, which occupy single storage locations.[4] An alternative to moving all of this data is to create an array of integers, say *index*, that will be used to reference the array of strings indirectly. The *index* array has the same number of elements as *list*.

```
const
  maxstring = 81;                        { maximum string length + 1    }
  max       = 100;                       { maximum number of strings    }

type
  string    = packed array[1 .. maxstring] of char;
  listtype  = array[1 .. max] of string;
  listindex = array[1 .. max] of integer;

var
  list   : listtype;                     { an array of strings          }
  n      : integer;                      { actual number of strings     }
  index  : listindex;                    { array with order of strings  }
```

The *index* array is initialized with the integers from 1 to *n*, where *n* is the number of strings in *list*; thus *index* contains the original ordering of the strings in *list*.

```
procedure init(var index : listindex; n : integer);
  var
    i : integer;
  begin
    for i := 1 to n do
      index[i] := i
  end;
```

Sort is modified so that it references *list* indirectly. Instead of comparing *list*[*i*] with *list*[*j*], it compares *list*[*index*[*i*]] and *list*[*index*[*j*]]. When elements need to be exchanged, the integers in *index* are exchanged rather than the strings in *list*. Note that *swap* exchanges integers rather than strings.

```
procedure swap(var x, y : integer);
  var
    t : integer;
  begin
    t := x; x := y; y := t
  end;

procedure sort(var A : listtype; var index : listindex; n : integer);
  var
    i, j : integer;
    m    : integer;
  begin
    init(index, n);                        { initialize index }
```

4. Even though *swap* exchanges the strings in three statements in Pascal, the compiler must generate code that copies each memory location used by the string.

```
    for i := 1 to n - 1 do
      begin
        m := i;
        for j := i + 1 to n do
          if lexlt(A[index[j]], A[index[m]])
            then m := j;
        if m <> i
          then swap(index[i], index[m])
      end
  end; { sort }
```

After *sort* has done its work, the *index* array contains the correct ordering of the strings in *list*. Procedure *writedata* uses this information to print the list in alphabetic order, i.e, it prints string *list*[*index*[*i*]], $1 \le i \le n$.

```
procedure writedata(var list : listtype; var index : listindex;
                                                   n : integer);
  var
    i : integer;
  begin
    for i := 1 to n do
      writestring(list[index[i]])
  end;
```

The technique is not dependent on this particular sorting algorithm, and could be used with any of the sorting algorithms we studied in chapter 10, or many others. It could also be adapted to sorting matrices, keying on the value of one column or row.

11.2 Internal Buffers

A buffer is an area in memory used to store data temporarily while it is being processed. In Pascal, the input buffer is an array of character data, with one character per array location, that is used to store data being read by a computer program. The value of the buffer variable *input*↑ is the next character to be read.

As we intimated in chapter 8, input buffering and associated functions—*eoln* and *eof*—constitute one area that has been treated in nonstandard ways in many Pascal compilers. Some compilers do not allow the programmer access to *input*↑, denying the limited but useful ability to look ahead in the buffer before reading, a real advantage in standard Pascal. Whether due to misguided attempts to improve Pascal, or to problems in interfacing Pascal with certain operating systems, these differences often make it difficult to move a Pascal program from one environment to another. The only way to write truly portable programs is for us to use an internal buffer and to write our own functions and procedures to deal with it, using only Pascal constructs that are likely to be compatible with any Pascal system, requiring at most minor modification. There are additional advantages to using this approach. We gain the ability to scan the buffer before reading to check for syntactic correctness of its contents, and we can print the contents of the buffer. Thus we can improve the ability of our programs to diagnose errors. We can also overcome some of the annoying foibles in Pascal, such as the requirement that real numbers begin with a digit. If we write our own conversion routines, we can accept .01234 as well as 0.01234.

In writing our own buffer routines, we will keep the useful aspects of buffering in standard Pascal, while maintaining the option of making changes or extensions to suit our programming needs.

We will implement our buffer in much the same manner as strings, except that we will not pack the array because it is short and will need to be accessed frequently. The primary components are an array of characters and a variable *bp* that will indicate the current buffer position.

```
program bufdemo(input, output);
  const
    maxline = 85;

  type
    buftype = array[1 .. maxline] of char;

  var
    buffer     : buftype;                  { a character buffer       }
    bp         : integer;                  { current buffer position  }
    n          : integer;                  { an integer               }
```

The buffer is filled by calling procedure *getline*. The procedure is similar to *readstring*, except that after reading the line it sets *bp* equal to 1 to indicate the current buffer position. Here, *null* is a function that returns the null character.

```
procedure getline(var buffer : buftype; var bp : integer);
  begin
    bp := 1;
    while not eoln and (bp < maxline) do
      begin
        read(buffer[bp]);
        incr(bp)
      end;
    buffer[bp] := null;                              { mark end of line }
    if not eoln
      then writeln('Getline: warning, input line truncated');
    readln;
    bp := 1                    { reset index at beginning of buffer }
  end;
```

Function *eob* (end-of-buffer) returns *true* if *buffer*[*bp*] is the null character. (*Null* is a user-defined function that returns the null character.) This function can be used exactly like *eoln*.

```
function eob(var buffer : buftype; bp : integer) : boolean;
  begin
    eob := buffer[bp] = null
  end;
```

Function *nextchar* returns the current value of *buffer*[*bp*] or the blank character if at end-of-buffer; thus it functions exactly like *input*↑ in standard Pascal.

```
function nextchar(var buffer : buftype; bp : integer) : char;
  begin
    if eob(buffer, bp)
      then nextchar := ' '
      else nextchar := buffer[bp]
  end;
```

Procedure *getchar* returns the current character in the buffer and advances *bp* to the next character. If *bp* is already at the end of the buffer, it returns a blank. Calling *incr(bp)* is equivalent to *get(input)*.

```
procedure getchar(var buffer : buftype; var bp : integer; var c : char);
  begin
    if not eob(buffer, bp)
      then
        begin
          c := buffer[bp];
          incr(bp)
        end
    else c := ' '
  end;
```

Procedure *skipbuf* skips past blank characters until the next nonblank character or the end of the buffer. Thus it functions like procedure *skipln*, which we wrote in chapter 8. Here *tab* is a function that returns the ASCII tab character.

```
procedure skipbuf(var buffer : buftype; var bp : integer);
  begin
    while (nextchar(buffer, bp) in [' ', tab])
                                            and not eob(buffer, bp) do
      incr(bp)
  end;
```

Now we must write input conversion routines to transfer data from the buffer to internal storage locations. The general technique was described in chapter 9. Here we modify procedure *getint* to read from our buffer instead of the standard input buffer, using the functions described above.

```
procedure getint(var buffer : buftype; var bp : integer;
                                                var x : integer);
  var
    negative : boolean;
  begin
    skipbuf(buffer, bp);                              { skip blanks    }
    negative := nextchar(buffer, bp) = '-';           { check for sign }
    if issign(nextchar(buffer, bp))
      then incr(bp);                                  { skip sign      }
    if not isdigit(nextchar(buffer, bp))
      then error(buffer, bp)
      else
        begin { read number }
          x := 0;
```

```
          while isdigit(nextchar(buffer, bp)) do
            begin
              x := 10 * x + toint(nextchar(buffer, bp));
              incr(bp)
            end
        end;  { read number }
    if negative
      then x := -x
  end;
```

Since we are in control, the error procedure could take any action desired. Here we will simply print an error message and terminate the program, but it would be possible to take corrective action, as described in section 15.3.2. If your Pascal does not include a *halt* statement, this would be an appropriate place to use a **goto** to transfer control to the end of the program.

```
procedure error(var buffer : buftype; bp : integer);
  begin
    writeln; writeln;
    writeln('Getint: digit expected');
    writeln;
    printbuffer(buffer, bp);
    halt                                          { terminate execution }
  end;
```

Procedure *printbuffer* prints the contents of the buffer and a pointer to the offending character. This is a luxury we don't have when using the standard input buffer.

```
procedure printbuffer(var buffer : buftype; bp : integer);
  var
    i : integer;
  begin { printbuffer }
    write('Buffer: ');
    i := 1;
    while buffer[i] <> null do
      begin
        write(buffer[i]);
        incr(i)
      end;
    writeln;
    write('Error:  ');
    for i := 1 to bp - 1 do
      write('-');
    writeln('^')
  end;  { printbuffer }
```

We could test our input procedures by printing each integer using *writeln*(*x*). Instead, we will use procedure *putint*(*x*), which reverses the process of reading characters. The last digit is obtained by taking x **mod** 10, and then dropped by dividing x by 10. The process is repeated until $x = 0$. Since the digits are extracted in the wrong order, they are stored in an array and then converted to characters as they are printed in the correct order.

```
procedure putint(x : integer);
  var
    i        : integer;
    n        : integer;                      { number of digits        }
    digit    : array[1 .. 6] of integer;     { to store digits         }
    negative : boolean;                      { true if x is negative   }

  begin
    negative := x < 0;
    x := abs(x);

    n := 0;                                  { extract digits          }
    while x > 0 do
      begin
        incr(n);
        digit[n] := x mod 10;
        x := x div 10
      end;

    if negative                              { print number            }
      then write('-');
    if n = 0
      then write('0')
      else                                   { digit by digit          }
        for i := n downto 1 do
          write(tochar(digit[i]));
    write(' ')
  end;  { putint }
```

Most of these procedures are demonstrated in program 11.2. The program reads integers from the input file and echoes them, line by line, on the standard output file. Each input line is stored in an internal character buffer and processed by the routines described above.

```
(***********************       Program Bufdemo       ***********************)
(* Illustrates the use of an internal buffer and user-written buffer      *)
(* procedures and functions to process integer data.  Other procedures    *)
(* are discussed in text.                                                 *)
(**************************************************************************)

program bufdemo(input, output);
  const
    maxline = 85;

  type
    buftype = array[1 .. maxline] of char;

  var
    buffer    : buftype;                     { a character buffer        }
    bp        : integer;                     { current buffer position }
    n         : integer;                     { an integer                }
```

```
(***********************             incr          ***********************)
(* Adds one to the value of its argument.                                  *)
(**************************************************************************)
  procedure incr(var x : integer);
    begin
      x := x + 1
    end;


(***********************             null          ***********************)
(* Returns the ASCII null character.                                       *)
(**************************************************************************)
  function null : char;
    begin
      null := chr(0)
    end;


(***********************              tab          ***********************)
(* Returns the ASCII tab character.                                        *)
(**************************************************************************)
  function tab : char;
    begin
      tab := chr(9)
    end;


(***********************           getline         ***********************)
(* Reads one line from file f into program buffer.  End of line is marked*)
(* with the null character.                                                *)
(**************************************************************************)
  procedure getline(var buffer : buftype; var bp : integer);
    begin
      bp := 1;
      while not eoln and (bp < maxline) do
        begin
          read(buffer[bp]);
          incr(bp)
        end;
      buffer[bp] := null;                              { mark end of line }
      if not eoln
        then writeln('Getline: warning, input line truncated');
      readln;
      bp := 1                        { reset index at beginning of buffer }
    end;


(***********************              eob          ***********************)
(* Returns true if no more characters remain in buffer.                    *)
(**************************************************************************)
  function eob(var buffer : buftype; bp : integer) : boolean;
    begin
      eob := buffer[bp] = null
    end;


(***********************           nextchar        ***********************)
(* Returns next char in buffer, works like input↑.                         *)
(**************************************************************************)
```

```
  function nextchar(var buffer : buftype; bp : integer) : char;
    begin
      if eob(buffer, bp)
        then nextchar := ' '
        else nextchar := buffer[bp]
    end;


(***********************          skipbuf          **********************)
(* Skips blanks in buffer, equivalent to skipln.                         *)
(************************************************************************)
  procedure skipbuf(var buffer : buftype; var bp : integer);
    begin
      while (nextchar(buffer, bp) in [' ', tab]) and not eob(buffer, bp) do
        incr(bp)
    end;


(***********************          isdigit          **********************)
(* Returns true if its argument is a character digit.                    *)
(************************************************************************)
  function isdigit(c : char) : boolean;
    begin
      isdigit := c in ['0' .. '9']
    end;


(***********************          issign           **********************)
(* Returns true if its argument is a plus or minus sign.                 *)
(************************************************************************)
  function issign(c : char) : boolean;
    begin
      issign := c in ['-', '+']
    end;


(***********************        printbuffer        **********************)
(* Prints contents of buffer and a pointer to the current position of bp.*)
(************************************************************************)
  procedure printbuffer(var buffer : buftype; bp : integer);
    var
      i : integer;
    begin { printbuffer }
      write('Buffer: ');
      i := 1;
      while buffer[i] <> null do
        begin
          write(buffer[i]);
          incr(i)
        end;
      writeln;
      write('Error:  ');
      for i := 1 to bp - 1 do
        write('-');
      writeln('^')
    end;  { printbuffer }
```

```
(***********************          toint          **********************)
(* Converts the character c to its integer representation.            *)
(**********************************************************************)
  function toint(c : char) : integer;
    begin
      toint := ord(c) - ord('0')
    end;


(***********************          error          **********************)
(* Here an error message is printed and the program run is terminated, *)
(* but it would be possible to take corrective action.                *)
(**********************************************************************)
  procedure error(var buffer : buftype; bp : integer);
    begin
      writeln; writeln;
      writeln('Getint: digit expected');
      writeln;
      printbuffer(buffer, bp);
      halt                                  { terminate execution }
    end;


(***********************          getint          *********************)
(* Reads an integer from the buffer.  Calls error procedure if next non- *)
(* blank character is not a digit.                                    *)
(**********************************************************************)
  procedure getint(var buffer : buftype; var bp : integer; var x : integer);
    var
      negative : boolean;
    begin
      skipbuf(buffer, bp);                           { skip blanks     }
      negative := nextchar(buffer, bp) = '-';        { check for sign  }
      if issign(nextchar(buffer, bp))
        then incr(bp);                               { skip sign       }
      if not isdigit(nextchar(buffer, bp))
        then error(buffer, bp)
        else
          begin { read number }
            x := 0;
            while isdigit(nextchar(buffer, bp)) do
              begin
                x := 10 * x + toint(nextchar(buffer, bp));
                incr(bp)
              end
          end; { read number }
      if negative
        then x := -x
    end;


(***********************          tochar          *********************)
(* Converts integer x to character.                                   *)
(**********************************************************************)
  function tochar(x : integer) : char;
    begin
      tochar := chr(ord('0') + x)
    end;
```

```
(***********************                putint          *********************)
(* Translates integer to characters and prints it in standard output.      *)
(***************************************************************************)

  procedure putint(x : integer);
    var
      i        : integer;
      n        : integer;                      { number of digits           }
      digit    : array[1 .. 6] of integer;     { to store digits            }
      negative : boolean;                      { true if x is negative      }

    begin
      negative := x < 0;
      x := abs(x);

      n := 0;                                  { extract digits             }
      while x > 0 do
        begin
          incr(n);
          digit[n] := x mod 10;
          x := x div 10
        end;

      if negative                              { print number               }
        then write('-');
      if n = 0
        then write('0')
        else                                   { digit by digit             }
          for i := n downto 1 do
            write(tochar(digit[i]));
      write(' ')
    end;  { putint }

(***********************             main procedure     *********************)
(* Tests buffer and integer conversion procedures.                         *)
(***************************************************************************)

  begin { main }
    write('Type integers: ');
    while not eof(input) do
      begin { process line }
        getline(buffer, bp);                { read line into buffer         }

        while not eob(buffer, bp) do
          begin                             { while not at end of buffer    }
            getint(buffer, bp, n);          { read an integer from buffer   }
            putint(n);                      { and print it                  }
            skipbuf(buffer, bp)             { skip blanks in buffer         }
          end;

        writeln; writeln;
        write('Type integers: ')
      end   { process line }
  end.  { main }
```

Program 11.2. *Bufdemo*

```
Type integers: 89 3 4 5 23 4 567 1 2 56
  89   3   4   5  23   4 567   1   2  56

Type integers: 1 3 4 5 6 7 89 435 231 9 3 4 5 6 92 1 45 96 12 34 954 \
56 976 4 3 2 3 4 5 6 76 123 456 765 345 678 3 2
Getline: warning, input line truncated
   1   3   4   5   6   7  89 435 231   9   3   4   5   6  92   1  45
  96  12  34 954  56 976   4   3   2   3   4   5   6  76 123  45

Type integers: 1 3 4 5 6 7 89 2 x 23 5 6 7 1
   1   3   4   5   6   7  89   2

Getint: digit expected

Buffer: 1 3 4 5 6 7 89 2 x 23 5 6 7 1
Error:  -----------------^
```

Program 11.2. Sample Run (Interactive)

11.3 Pattern Matching

Pattern matching in strings is the process of seeing if a predefined pattern occurs within the string. Function *index* performs a simple pattern match. We can easily define pattern-matching functions in Pascal using boolean functions that attempt to match some predefined sequence of characters and return *true* or *false*, depending on whether the pattern succeeded or not.

These functions could be used with strings, or by omitting the **packed** directive, with buffers. One use of this technique with buffers is to ensure that the data matches the input expectations of the program before it actually reads the data. Suppose, for example, that we wish to read set names in the form

<cardinal><dash><ordinal>

where <cardinal> is the cardinal number of the set, i.e., the number of elements, and <ordinal> is the position of the set in an ordered list.[5] The following set names match this format: 3-6, 4-29, 8-20.

We need a pattern-matching function that matches a string of digits, followed by a dash, followed by another string of digits. The function checks the sequence of characters in the buffer beginning at *bp*. The position indicator *bp* is used to scan the buffer, but since it is passed by value, its value is not changed outside of the function.

5. This form of set names was first used by Allen Forte. See his *The Structure of Atonal Music* (New Haven and London: Yale University Press, 1973).

```
function setname(var buffer: buftype; bp : integer) : boolean;

  procedure skip;                          { skip optional blanks      }
    begin
      while buffer[bp] = ' ' do
        incr(bp)
    end;

  function digits : boolean;               { match a string of digits }
    begin
      skip;
      digits := isdigit(buffer[bp]);
      while isdigit(buffer[bp]) do
        incr(bp)
    end;

  function dash : boolean;                 { match a dash              }
    begin
      skip;
      if buffer[bp] = '-'
        then
          begin
            dash := true;
            incr(bp)       { skip dash }
          end
        else dash := false
    end;

  begin { setname }
    setname := false;
    if digits
      then if dash
      then setname := digits
  end; { setname }
```

Above, each of the subpatterns is defined internally to function *setname*. An alternate approach would be to define them externally, with *buffer* and *bp* passed to them as variable parameters. This would be desirable if the smaller functions would be used in other larger patterns. The function that matches a string of digits returns *true* if at least one digit is present, and moves *bp* past all of the digits. If there is a dash, function *dash* returns *true* and moves *bp* past it. Function *setname* uses these primitives to test for the larger pattern:

```
setname := false;
if digits
  then if dash
  then setname := digits
```

After these statements have been executed, *setname* is *true* only if the sequence of characters in the buffer beginning at the current position is a string of digits, a dash, and another string of digits. We have defined the functions to allow for optional spaces between the primary elements of the pattern. One is tempted to formulate the assignment

```
setname := digits and dash and digits;
```

In general this is not a good idea, since the order in which dyadic operators are evaluated is implementation dependent, i.e., we cannot guarantee that the boolean expression will be evaluated from left to right. Note that this procedure does not check the values of the digits to make sure that they are valid, only the syntax.

Once the buffer has been tested and found to contain data in the desired format, a procedure is called to read the data from the buffer, using procedures defined earlier.

```
procedure getname(var cardinal, ordinal : integer);
  begin
    getint(cardinal);
    skipbuf;                                  { skip blanks }
    incr(bp);                                 { skip dash   }
    getint(ordinal)
  end;
```

Program 11.3 tests these procedures. Only the main procedure is shown, since most of the program duplicates program 11.2.

```
begin { main }                         { from program patmatch }
  write('Type set name: ');
  while not eof(input) do
    begin
      getline(input, buffer, bp);
      if setname(buffer, bp)
        then
          begin
            getname(cardinal, ordinal);
            writeln(cardinal:1, '-', ordinal:1)
          end
        else writeln('Invalid set name');
      write('Type set name: ')
    end
end.  { main }
```

Program 11.3. *Patmatch* (Partial Listing)

```
Type set name: 3-2
3-2

Type set name: 4-15
4-15

Type set name: 3 - 12
3-12

Type set name: setname
Invalid set name
```

```
Type set name: 4 28
Invalid set name

Type set name: 123-578
123-578

Type set name:^D
```

Program 11.3. Sample Run (Interactive)

11.4 Arrays and Lookup Tables

Thus far we have used functions to convert various types of values, e.g., *toint*('9') to convert the character '9' to the integer 9. This approach works well so long as the values do not vary and the list is not too long. However, if the conversion must be made many times or the relationship between the value and its conversion may change periodically, it is more efficient to use arrays to make the conversion. Suppose we need to convert the character representation of note names to their corresponding pitch classes. We could write a function:

```
function topc(c : char) : integer;
  begin
    case c of
      'c' : topc :=  0;
      'd' : topc :=  2;
      'e' : topc :=  4;
      'f' : topc :=  5;
      'g' : topc :=  7;
      'a' : topc :=  9;
      'b' : topc := 11
    end { case }
  end;
```

Alternately, we can use an array indexed by the characters 'a' through 'g', with each element containing the desired integer value (figure 11.2).

topc

'a'	'b'	'c'	'd'	'e'	'f'	'g'
9	11	0	2	4	5	7

Figure 11.2. A Lookup Table for Converting Note Names to Pitch-Class Integers

This table is set up by an array declaration and statements that initialize the array to the proper values:

```
type
  convert : array['0' .. '9'] of integer;

var
  topc : convert;

. . .

  procedure init(var topc : convert);
    var
      c : char;
    begin
      topc['c'] := 0; topc['d'] := 2; topc['e'] := 4;
      topc['f'] := 5; topc['g'] := 7; topc['a'] := 9;
      topc['b'] := 11
    end;
```

After the table has been initialized, the statement

```
x := topc[c]
```

is functionally equivalent to

```
x := topc(c)
```

where *topc* has been defined as a function as shown above.[6] The array implementation of the table is very fast, since it eliminates the extra time required for a function call. The values are assigned only once, when the array is initialized.

Arrays can be used for creating "lookup tables" whenever the reference values can be expressed as a subrange of a scalar type, so that they can be used to index the array. Common uses are converting characters to integers (or vice versa) and mapping one type of value into another, such as finding the pitch class corresponding to each name class.

11.5 Application: Interpreting DARMS Pitch Codes

In this section we will illustrate an algorithm for translating DARMS pitch codes[7] into pitch classes, name classes, and octave information more useful to analysis programs. These three factors will be mapped into a single four-digit integer (cbr) in the form shown in figure 11.3. (See also section 6.2.4.)

Almost any code can be subdivided, or *parsed*, into separate items called *tokens*. In DARMS a token is an encoded pitch, meter signature, key signature, etc. Our demonstration program will decode each pitch token and print its value. If the token is a note, the pitch will be printed in cbr form and as a conventional note name. If it is a clef or key signature, we will identify it in the program output and store its infor-

6. Obviously, the identifier *topc* could be defined only once in a single program block, i.e., the function *topc* and the array *topc* could not exist concurrently.

7. The reader may wish to review DARMS encoding of pitch in section 6.5.1.

cbr ::= <oct><pc><nc>

where <oct> ∈ (0, 1, 2, 3, 4, 5, 6, 7, 8, 9),
<pc> ∈ (00, 01, 02, . . . , 11), and
<nc> ∈ (0, 1, . . . , 6)

Figure 11.3. SYNTAX: Continuous Binomial Representation (cbr)

mation in a form that can be used to affect consequent note data. The decoding algorithm makes use of a number of formulas and tables shown in figure 11.4.

The system of space codes is a series of integers that parallels the continuous nc scale, except that each note is displaced by some constant, the value of which depends on the current clef. The space code is read (and expanded if two suppression has been used) and converted to cnc by adding the current clef constant. The cnc is decoded into the octave and name class. The pitch class is found by "table lookup," and adjusted for the key signature and previous accidentals in the measure. These adjustments are managed through an array called *adjust*, which contains the value to be added to the pitch class for each note in the cnc scale. The adjustment value is –2 for a double flat, –1 for a flat, 0 for no adjustment, 1 for a sharp, 2 for a double sharp, etc. The values in this array are initially set to correspond to the key signature, and are adjusted whenever an accidental is encountered. At each bar line the array is reset to reflect the current key signature. This is accomplished with a duplicate array, called *keysig*, which stores the adjustments appropriate for the key signature. This array is copied to the *adjust* array at each bar line, and *adjust* is used to calculate notes and is updated for accidentals.

The procedures that process DARMS pitch code, taken from program 11.3, make use of the buffer routines discussed in a previous section of this chapter.[8] The heart of the program is procedure *scan*, which calls the other subroutines depending on the value of the next character in the buffer. The main procedure reads one line at a time into the buffer and passes it to procedure *scan*:

```
procedure scan(var buffer : buftype; var bp : integer);
  begin
    skipbuf(buffer, bp);
    while not eob(buffer, bp) do
      begin
        if goodtoken(nextchar(buffer, bp))
          then
            begin
              if isdigit(nextchar(buffer, bp))          { space code   }
                then setcode(spacecode)
              else if isacc(nextchar(buffer, bp))        { accidental   }
                then setnote(spacecode)
```

8. The routines shown here are adapted from the DARMS interpreter listed in appendix C.

(a) Octave (oct)

(b) Pitch class (pc)

(c) Name class (nc)

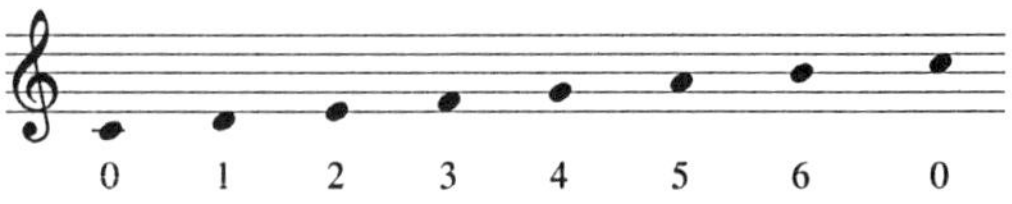

(d) The continuous nc scale (cnc): *cnc* = (*oct* x 7) + *nc*

0 1 2 3 4 5 6 | 7 8 9 10 11 12 13 | 14 15 16 17 18 19 20 | 21 22 23 24 25 26 27 | 28 . . .
octave 0 | octave 1 | octave 2 | octave 3 | . . .

(e) Unpacking the cnc scale:

nc = *cnc* mod 7 { remainder after division }
oct = *cnc* div 7 { integer division, truncates }

(f) Mapping the space code into cnc

space code:	25	25	25
clef constant:	+9	+3	−3
cnc:	34	28	22

(g) Getting pc for natural scale from lookup table

scale

0	1	2	3	4	5	6	← name
0	2	4	5	7	9	11	← pitch class in natural scale

pc = *scale*[*nc*]

(h) Adjusting for key signatures and accidentals

adjust

. . .	28	29	30	31	32	33	34	35	36	37	38	39	. . .	← cnc
	0	0	0	+1	+1	0	−1	0	+2	0	+1	0		← adjustment to pc

pc = (*pc* + *adjust*[*cnc*]) mod 12;

(i) Packing oct, pc, and nc into a cbr:

br = 10 x *pc* + *nc*
cbr = 1000 x *oct* + *br*

(j) Unpacking the cbr:

oct = *cbr* div 1000; *br* = *cbr* mod 1000
pc = *br* div 10; *nc* = *br* mod 10

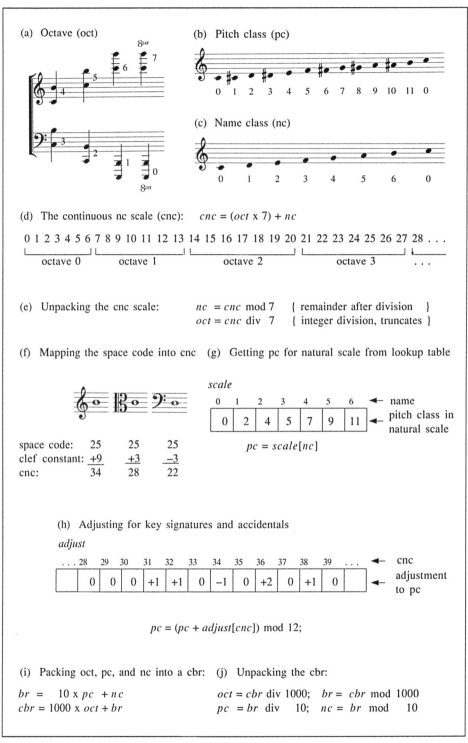

Figure 11.4. Decoding DARMS Pitch Codes

```
            else if isexclamation(nextchar(buffer, bp)) { exclam  pt   }
              then exclamation(0)
            else if isbar(nextchar(buffer, bp))          { bar line     }
              then newmeasure
            else if nextchar(buffer, bp) = 'r'           { rest         }
              then rest;
            if not isspace(nextchar(buffer, bp))       { missing delim }
              then error(buffer, bp, 10);
          end
        else badtoken;                                   { error        }
      skipbuf(buffer, bp)                                { skip blanks  }
    end
  end;  { scan }
```

Recall that space codes do not necessarily represent notes. If the code is followed by an exclamation point, it represents the position of a clef on the staff. If the buffer contains a space code, procedure *setcode* is called to decide the next action. *Setcode* saves the current space code so that it can be restored later if necessary, then calls procedure *getcode* to interpret the space code. If the space code is followed by an exclamation point, procedure *exclamation* is called, otherwise the space code is passed to procedure *setnote*.

```
procedure setcode(var spacecode : integer);
  var
    t        : integer;
  begin
    t := spacecode;                            { save to restore sc   }
    getcode(spacecode);                        { read the space code }
    if nextchar(buffer, bp) = '!'
      then
        begin
          exclamation(spacecode);
          spacecode := t                       { restore sc for note }
        end
      else setnote(spacecode)
  end;   { setcode }
```

Procedure *getcode* uses *nextchar* to look ahead and see if the space code begins with a 0, indicating one of the ledger lines numbered from 00 to 09. If this is not the case and the value of the space code is less than 10, then it is expanded by adding 20.

```
procedure getcode(var spacecode : integer);
  var
    lownote : boolean;
  begin
    lownote := false;
    if nextchar(buffer, bp) = '0'
      then
        begin
          spacecode := 0;
          incr(bp);                                    { skip 0     }
          lownote := isdigit(nextchar(buffer, bp))
        end;
```

```
    if isdigit(nextchar(buffer, bp))
      then getint(buffer, bp, spacecode);
    if (not lownote) and (spacecode < 10)
      then spacecode := spacecode + 20
  end; { getcode }
```

Procedure *setnote* converts the space code to cnc (continuous name code) by adding the current clef constant. If the input character is an accidental, procedure *accidental* is called to update the *adjust* array. Then the cnc is disassembled into its name-class and octave components, and the pitch class is obtained from the *scale* array and adjusted for accidentals and key signatures by adding the adjustment from the *adjust* array. Finally, the octave, pc, and nc are mapped into a single number (cbr), and procedure *writepitch* is called to print the cbr and note name.

```
procedure setnote(spacecode : integer);
  var
    oct, nc, pc, cnc : integer;
  begin
    cnc := spacecode + clef;
    if (cnc < 0) or (cnc > 70)
      then error(buffer, bp, 11)
      else
        begin
          if isacc(nextchar(buffer, bp))
            then accidental(adjust, cnc);
          nc  := cnc mod 7;
          oct := cnc div 7;
          pc  := (scale[nc] + adjust[cnc] + 12) mod 12;
          pitch := cbr(oct, pc, nc);
          writepitch(pitch)
        end
  end;  { setnote }
```

Procedure *accidental* changes the adjustment for the single note affected by the accidental. This adjustment will remain in effect until it is canceled by another accidental or until the next bar line is reached.

```
procedure accidental(var adjust : scalearray; cnc : integer);
  var
    t : integer;
  begin
    if isacc(nextchar(buffer, bp))
      then
        begin
          t := 0;
          while isacc(nextchar(buffer, bp)) do
            begin
              case nextchar(buffer, bp) of
                '#' : t := t + 1;
                '-' : t := t - 1;
                '*' : t := 0
              end;  { case }
              incr(bp)                                   { skip accidental }
            end;
```

```
        adjust[cnc] := t
      end
  end;  { accidental }
```

Procedure *exclamation* may be called by *setcode*, which passes to it a new space code, or by *scan*, which passes the value 0. The exclamation point functions as an escape character in DARMS, and may be followed by a clef name ('g', 'c', or 'f'), a key signature ('k'), a meter signature ('m'), or other possibilities that will not be discussed here. Thus this procedure acts as a switchbox, calling the appropriate procedure depending on the character after the exclamation point. In this program we limit the choices to pitch-related objects. If the token represents a clef and the exclamation point was preceded by a space code, this space code is passed to the clef-processing routine; otherwise the default staff position is used. Since we will ignore possibilities other than clefs and key signatures, an error message is printed if these were not found.

```
procedure exclamation(spacecode : integer);
  begin
    incr(bp);                                         { skip !        }
    if nextchar(buffer, bp) = 'k'                     { key signature }
      then setkey
    else if isclef(nextchar(buffer, bp))              { clef          }
      then
        begin
          if spacecode = 0
            then spacecode := normclef[nextchar(buffer, bp)];
          setclef(spacecode)
        end
    else                                              { error         }
        begin
          incr(bp);
          error(buffer, bp, 9);
          findblank(buffer, bp)                       { skip to blank }
        end
  end;
```

Procedure *setclef* calculates the new clef constant, using the value for the clef modified by the offset of the actual space code from the normal position for the clef. It also checks for the possibility of a treble tenor clef (sounding an octave below the normal treble clef) and makes an appropriate adjustment. It then saves the new clef constant and calls another procedure to print the name of the new clef.

```
procedure setclef(spacecode : integer);
  var
    clefconst : integer;
  begin
    case nextchar(buffer, bp) of                  { set clef constant }
      'c': clefconst :=  3;
      'f': clefconst := -3;
      'g': clefconst :=  9
    end;  { case }
```

```
                                                    { for movable clefs }
    clefconst := clefconst + normclef[nextchar(buffer, bp)] - spacecode;
    incr(bp);                                       { skip clef code     }
    if  nextchar(buffer, bp) = '-'
      then
        begin { treble tenor clef }
          incr(bp);                                 { skip '-'           }
          if nextchar(buffer, bp) = '8'
            then clefconst := clefconst - 7
            else error(buffer, bp, 4);
          incr(bp)           { skip digit }
        end; { treble tenor clef }
    clef := clefconst;                         { assign clef for instrument }
    printclef(clefconst)
  end; { setclef }
```

If procedure *exclamation* finds that the exclamation point is followed by a 'k' indicating a key signature, procedure *setkey* is called to process the key signature. First, the *keysig* array is reinitialized by setting each element to 0. Then the number and type of accidentals are read from the buffer and passed to procedure *standard*, which processes standard key signatures.[9]

```
procedure setkey;
  var
    accidentals : integer;
    sign        : char;
    i           : integer;
  begin { setkey }
    for i := 0 to 70 do
      keysig[i] := 0;                               { initialize array }
    incr(bp);
    if isdigit(nextchar(buffer, bp))
      then
        begin { standard key signature }
          getint(buffer, bp, accidentals);
          if isacc(nextchar(buffer, bp))
            then
              begin
                getchar(buffer, bp, sign);
                standard(accidentals, sign)
              end
            else
              begin
                error(buffer, bp, 6);
                incr(bp);
              end
        end  { standard key signature }
      else if isacc(nextchar(buffer, bp))
        then
          begin
            getchar(buffer, bp, sign);
            standard(1, sign)
          end
```

9. A procedure to process nonstandard key signatures is left as an exercise for the reader.

```
      else error(buffer, bp, 5);
    adjust := keysig
  end;  { setkey }
```

Procedure *standard* sets the *keysig* array to reflect accidentals in the key signature. The adjustments must reflect the fact that key signatures affect notes in all octaves. The algorithm makes use of the order of sharps and flats in normal key signatures. The first sharp is F-sharp, and each successive sharp is the name class a fifth above the previous sharp. Flats begin on B and progress by ascending fourths (or descending fifths). The initial values of *nc* and *inc* (increment) are set to reflect these facts, and the adjustment *acc* is set to 1 or –1, depending on the accidental. The loop

```
for oct := 0 to 9 do
  keysig[oct * 7 + nc] := acc;
```

sets the adjustment for each octave, and the statement

```
nc := (nc + inc) mod 7
```

calculates the next accidental. This process is repeated for the actual number of accidentals.

```
procedure standard(accidentals : integer; sign : char);
  var
    nc, inc, acc, oct : integer;
    i                 : integer;
  begin
    writeln('New key signature =', accidentals:3, ' ', sign);
    case sign of
      sharp :
        begin
          nc := 3;                              { first sharp is F     }
          inc := 4;                             { interval of a fifth  }
          acc := 1                              { adjustment to note   }
        end;
      flat :
        begin
          nc := 6;                              { first flat is B      }
          inc := 3;                             { a fourth             }
          acc := -1                             { adjustment to note   }
        end;
      natural :
        accidentals := 0                        { no accidentals       }
    end;  { case }
    for i := 1 to accidentals do
      begin                                     { set each accidental  }
        for oct := 0 to 9 do                    { in each octave       }
          keysig[oct * 7 + nc] := acc;
        nc := (nc + inc) mod 7                  { next accidental      }
      end
  end;  { standard }
```

Procedure *writepitch* also uses tables to convert data from one form to another. The *cbr* is broken down into its components: octave, pitch class, and name class.

The *name* array maps the *nc* into a letter name, which is printed. Now the number and type of accidentals are calculated as the difference between the actual pitch class and the pitch class of the natural note, again obtained from the *scale* array. This is positive if the note has been modified by sharps, negative if by flats. If the absolute value of the difference is greater than 6, it is adjusted by changing the sign and using the modulo 12 inverse of the difference. This prevents boundary errors, such as B-sharp <00,6> printing as B with eleven flats, or C-flat <11,0> as C with eleven sharps. Finally, a **for** loop is used to print the accidentals, and the octave number is printed.

```
procedure writepitch(pitch : integer);
  var
    nc, pc, oct, br : integer;
    difference      : integer;
    accidental      : char;
    i               : integer;
  begin
    write('pitch: ', pitch:4, ' = ');
    oct  := pitch div 1000;
    br   := pitch mod 1000;
    pc   := br div 10;
    nc   := br mod 10;
    write(name[nc]);

    difference := pc - scale[nc];                  { number of accidentals }
    if difference > 6                              { more than 6 sharps?   }
      then difference := difference - 12
    else if difference < -6                        { more than 6 flats?    }
      then difference := difference + 12;

    if difference > 0
      then accidental := sharp
      else accidental := flat;

    for i := 1 to abs(difference) do
      write(accidental);

    writeln(oct:1)
  end;
```

Program 11.4 uses tables implemented as arrays for each of the following:

1. Finding the pitch class equivalent to a name class
2. Finding the adjustment to the pc for key and accidentals
3. Converting the name class to a letter name
4. Recalculating the number of accidentals on output

Each of these processes except the second could have been implemented with functions instead of tables. Unlike a function, the array can be updated to reflect new key signatures, accidentals, etc. The program also provides an illustration of programming using the buffer procedures discussed earlier. This is the most complex program we have seen so far, and time taken to study it carefully will be well spent.[10] A sample run is shown after the program. It will help to review the summary of DARMS pitch decoding in figure 11.4 before continuing.

```
(*********************** Program Pitch ***********************)
(* This program processes DARMS pitch codes. It is a stripped-down ver- *)
(* sion of the DARMS interpreter shown in appendix C. The program illus-*)
(* trates use of an internal buffer, lookup tables, and processing of *)
(* subset of DARMS music input code (see text). *)
(************************************************************************)
program pitch(input, output);
  const
    maxline = 85;                                { maximum line length }
    sharp   = '#';
    flat    = '-';
    natural = '*';

  type
    buftype      = array[1 .. maxline] of char;
    pcarray      = array[0 .. 6] of integer;
    scalearray   = array[0 .. 70] of integer;
    clefposition = array['c' .. 'g'] of integer;
    namearray    = array[0 .. 6] of char;

(************************************************************************)
(*                        global variables                              *)
(************************************************************************)
  var
    buffer    : buftype;         { a character buffer                  }
    bp        : integer;         { current buffer position             }
    clef      : integer;         { constant for current clef           }
    scale     : pcarray;         { pcs for natural scale               }
    keysig    : scalearray;      { adjustments for key signature       }
    adjust    : scalearray;      { keysig plus accidentals in meas     }
    normclef  : clefposition;    { normal space code for clefs         }
    name      : namearray;       { note name array                     }
    spacecode : integer;         { current space code                  }
    pitch     : integer;         { pitch in cbr notation               }

(*********************** boolean functions ***********************)
(* Function isXXX(ch) returns true if c is an XXX. *)
(************************************************************************)

  function isdigit(c : char) : boolean;
    begin
      isdigit := c in ['0' .. '9']
    end;

  function isacc(c : char) : boolean;
    begin
      isacc := c in ['-', '#', '*']
    end;
```

10. Suggestion: Get an overview of the program structure by reading the program quickly from beginning to end, then start with the main procedure and work through the program top-down, attempting to follow the action of the program for a sample input that exercises all options.

```
function isclef(c : char) : boolean;
  begin
    isclef := c in ['c', 'f', 'g']
  end;

function isbar(c : char) : boolean;
  begin        { bar lines }
    isbar := c in ['/', ':']
  end;

function isrest(c : char) : boolean;
  begin
    isrest := c = 'r'
  end;

function isexclamation(c : char) : boolean;
  begin
    isexclamation := c = '!'
  end;

function isspace(c : char) : boolean;
  begin
    isspace := c = ' '
  end;

function issign(c : char) : boolean;
  begin
    issign := c in ['-', '+']
  end;

function goodtoken(c : char) : boolean;
  begin
    goodtoken := isdigit(c) or isacc(c) or isbar(c) or isrest(c)
                 or isexclamation(c)
  end;

function goodclef(x : integer) : boolean;  { checks clef const }
  begin
    goodclef := (x = -3) or (x = -1) or (x = 1) or (x = 2) or
        (x = 3) or (x = 5) or (x = 7) or (x = 9) or (x = 11)
  end;

(***************************************************************************)
(*                          arithmetic functions                           *)
(***************************************************************************)

function cbr(oct, pc, nc : integer) : integer;
  begin { cont binomial rep }
    cbr := (1000 * oct) + (10 * pc) + nc
  end;  { cont binomial rep }

procedure incr(var x : integer);
  begin
    x := x + 1
  end;
```

```
(**********************************************************************)
(*                        character functions                         *)
(**********************************************************************)

  function null : char;
    begin
      null := chr(0)
    end;

  function tab : char;
    begin
      tab := chr(9)
    end;

(***********************    buffer procedures    ***********************)
(* Procedures listed in section 11.2 are omitted here to save space. The *)
(* external directive indicates that the routines are listed elsewhere.  *)
(**********************************************************************)

  procedure getline(var buffer : buftype; var bp : integer); external;
  function eob(var buffer : buftype; bp : integer) : boolean; external;
  procedure getchar(var buffer : buftype; var bp : integer; var c : char);
                                                               external;
  function nextchar(var buffer : buftype; bp : integer) : char; external;
  procedure skipbuf(var buffer : buftype; var bp : integer); external;
  procedure printbuffer(buffer : buftype; bp : integer); external;

  procedure findblank(var buffer : buftype; var bp : integer);
    begin  { skip to next blank in buffer }
      while nextchar(buffer, bp) <> ' ' do
        incr(bp)
    end;

  procedure error(var buffer : buftype; bp, key : integer);
    begin { error }
      writeln;
      printbuffer(buffer, bp);
      case key of
        1: writeln(nextchar(buffer, bp), ' not recognized by scanner');
        2: writeln(nextchar(buffer, bp), ' cannot follow !');
        3: writeln(nextchar(buffer, bp), ' is not legal accidental');
        4: writeln(nextchar(buffer, bp), ' is not a clef hanger');
        5: writeln(nextchar(buffer, bp), ' accidental or digit expected');
        6: writeln(nextchar(buffer, bp), ' is not an accidental code');
        7: writeln(nextchar(buffer, bp), ' digit expected');
        8: writeln(nextchar(buffer, bp), ' abnormal position of clef');
        9: writeln(nextchar(buffer, bp), ' cannot follow exclamation point');
       10: writeln('Blank character expected');
       11: writeln('Note out of range');
      end; { case }
      writeln
    end;    { error }

  procedure getint(var buffer : buftype; var bp : integer; var x : integer);
                                                                external;
```

```
(***********************          init          ***********************)
(* Initializes arrays and default values.                               *)
(**********************************************************************)
  procedure init;
    var
      i : integer;
    begin { init }
      for i := 0 to 6 do                               { init scale array }
          scale[i] := (2 * i) - (i div 3)  + (i div 6);

      name[0] := 'C';  name[1] := 'D';                 { init name array  }
      name[2] := 'E';  name[3] := 'F';
      name[4] := 'G';  name[5] := 'A';  name[6] := 'B';

      for i := 0 to 70 do
        begin
          adjust[i] := 0;
          keysig[i] := 0
        end;

      normclef['c'] := 25;               { default space codes for clefs}
      normclef['f'] := 27;
      normclef['g'] := 23;

      clef := 9                          { default is treble clef       }
    end;  { init }

(***********************        standard        ***********************)
(* Sets keysig array to reflect standard key signatures.                *)
(**********************************************************************)
  procedure standard(accidentals : integer; sign : char);
    var
      nc, inc, acc, oct  : integer;
      i                  : integer;
    begin
      writeln('New key signature =', accidentals:3, ' ', sign);
      case sign of
        sharp :
          begin
            nc := 3;                              { first sharp is F     }
            inc := 4;                             { interval of a fifth  }
            acc := 1                              { adjustment to note   }
          end;
        flat :
          begin
            nc := 6;                              { first flat is B      }
            inc := 3;                             { a fourth             }
            acc := -1                             { adjustment to note   }
          end;
        natural :
          accidentals := 0                        { no accidentals       }
      end;  { case }
      for i := 1 to accidentals do
        begin                                     { set each accidental  }
          for oct := 0 to 9 do                    { in each octave       }
            keysig[oct * 7 + nc] := acc;
          nc := (nc + inc) mod 7                  { next accidental      }
        end
    end;  { standard }
```

```
(***********************          setkey          ***********************)
(* Sets the keysig array to reflect adjustments to each note in scale for*)
(* key signatures.  This version handles only standard key signatures.   *)
(*************************************************************************)
  procedure setkey;
    var
      accidentals : integer;
      sign        : char;
      i           : integer;
    begin { setkey }
      for i := 0 to 70 do
        keysig[i] := 0;                                  { initialize array }
      incr(bp);
      if isdigit(nextchar(buffer, bp))
        then
          begin { standard key signature }
            getint(buffer, bp, accidentals);
            if isacc(nextchar(buffer, bp))
              then
                begin
                  getchar(buffer, bp, sign);
                  standard(accidentals, sign)
                end
              else
                begin
                  error(buffer, bp, 6);
                  incr(bp)
                end
          end   { standard key signature }
        else if isacc(nextchar(buffer, bp))
          then
            begin
              getchar(buffer, bp, sign);
              standard(1, sign)
            end
        else error(buffer, bp, 5);
      adjust := keysig
    end;  { setkey }

(***********************        accidental        ***********************)
(* Modifies the adjust array to reflect accidental.                      *)
(*************************************************************************)
  procedure accidental(var adjust : scalearray; cnc : integer);
    var
      t : integer;
    begin
      if isacc(nextchar(buffer, bp))
        then
          begin
            t := 0;
            while isacc(nextchar(buffer, bp)) do
              begin
                case nextchar(buffer, bp) of
                 '#' : t := t + 1;
                 '-' : t := t - 1;
                 '*' : t := 0
                end;  { case }
```

```
                incr(bp)                                    { skip accidental }
              end;
            adjust[cnc] := t
          end
    end; { accidental }

(************************         writepitch        ************************)
(* Prints pitch in cbr and note-name notation.                             *)
(**************************************************************************)
  procedure writepitch(pitch : integer);
    var
      nc, pc, oct, br : integer;
      difference      : integer;
      accidental      : char;
      i               : integer;
    begin
      write('pitch: ', pitch:4, ' = ');
      oct := pitch div 1000;
      br  := pitch mod 1000;
      pc  := br div 10;
      nc  := br mod 10;
      write(name[nc]);

      difference := pc - scale[nc];                   { number of accidentals }
      if difference > 6                               { more than 6 sharps?   }
        then difference := difference - 12
      else if difference < -6                         { more than 6 flats?    }
        then difference := difference + 12;

      if difference > 0
        then accidental := sharp
        else accidental := flat;

      for i := 1 to abs(difference) do
        write(accidental);

      writeln(oct:1)
    end;

(************************          setnote          ************************)
(* Setnote is passed a space code, which is used to calculate the name    *)
(* class, pitch class, and octave.  Accidental is called to adjust for    *)
(* accidentals.  Here, the pitch is printed.                              *)
(**************************************************************************)
  procedure setnote(spacecode : integer);
    var
      oct, nc, pc, cnc : integer;
    begin
      cnc := spacecode + clef;
      if (cnc < 0) or (cnc > 70)
        then error(buffer, bp, 11)
        else
          begin
            if isacc(nextchar(buffer, bp))
              then accidental(adjust, cnc);
            nc  := cnc mod 7;
            oct := cnc div 7;
```

```
        pc  := (scale[nc] + adjust[cnc] + 12) mod 12;
        pitch := cbr(oct, pc, nc);
        writepitch(pitch)
      end
  end;  { setnote }

(***********************         printclef        ***********************)
(* Prints name of clef or error message if wrong position.               *)
(*************************************************************************)
  procedure printclef(clefconst : integer);
    begin
      if goodclef(clefconst)
        then
          case clefconst of
            -3 : writeln('Bass clef');
            -1 : writeln('Baritone clef');
             1 : writeln('Tenor clef');
             2 : writeln('Treble tenor clef');
             3 : writeln('Alto clef');
             5 : writeln('Mezzo soprano clef');
             7 : writeln('Soprano clef');
             9 : writeln('Treble clef');
            11 : writeln('French violin clef')
          end { case }
        else error(buffer, bp, 8)          { abnormal position for clef }
    end;

(***********************          setclef         ***********************)
(* Sets the constant 'clef' to reflect the current clef.  This procedure *)
(* is called whenever a new clef code is encountered.                    *)
(*************************************************************************)
  procedure setclef(spacecode : integer);
    var
      clefconst : integer;
    begin

      case nextchar(buffer, bp) of                  { set clef constant }
        'c': clefconst :=  3;
        'f': clefconst := -3;
        'g': clefconst :=  9
      end;  { case }
                                                    { for movable clefs }
      clefconst := clefconst + normclef[nextchar(buffer, bp)] - spacecode;
      incr(bp);                                     { skip clef code     }
      if  nextchar(buffer, bp) = '-'
        then
          begin { treble tenor clef }
            incr(bp);                               { skip '-'           }
            if nextchar(buffer, bp) = '8'
              then clefconst := clefconst - 7
              else error(buffer, bp, 4);
            incr(bp)           { skip digit }
          end;  { treble tenor clef }
      clef := clefconst;                      { assign clef for instrument }
      printclef(clefconst)
    end;  { setclef }
```

```
(***********************       exclamation        ***********************)
(* Called when an exclamation pt is found in input, this procedure      *)
(* checks the next character and calls the appropriate routine (keysig  *)
(* or clef).  There are other possibilities, but this program does not  *)
(* employ them.                                                          *)
(************************************************************************)
  procedure exclamation(spacecode : integer);
    begin
      incr(bp);                                           { skip !         }
      if nextchar(buffer, bp) = 'k'                       { key signature }
        then setkey
      else if isclef(nextchar(buffer, bp))                { clef           }
        then
          begin
            if spacecode = 0
              then spacecode := normclef[nextchar(buffer, bp)];
            setclef(spacecode)
          end
      else                                                { error          }
          begin
            incr(bp);
            error(buffer, bp, 9);
            findblank(buffer, bp)                         { skip to blank }
          end
    end;

(***********************       getcode        ***********************)
(* Reads a space code and expands it if necessary.                      *)
(************************************************************************)
  procedure getcode(var spacecode : integer);
    var
      lownote : boolean;
    begin
      lownote := false;
      if nextchar(buffer, bp) = '0'
        then
          begin
            spacecode := 0;
            incr(bp);                                         { skip 0 }
            lownote := isdigit(nextchar(buffer, bp))
          end;
      if isdigit(nextchar(buffer, bp))
        then getint(buffer, bp, spacecode);
      if (not lownote) and (spacecode < 10)
        then spacecode := spacecode + 20
    end; { getcode }

(***********************       setcode        ***********************)
(* Calls getcode to read a space code.  If space code is followed by an *)
(* exclamation pt, exclamation is called to determine next move.  Other- *)
(* wise the setnote is called to process code.                          *)
(************************************************************************)
  procedure setcode(var spacecode : integer);
    var
      t        : integer;
    begin
      t := spacecode;                                 { save to restore sc  }
```

```
      getcode(spacecode);                       { read the space code }
      if nextchar(buffer, bp) = '!'
        then
          begin
            exclamation(spacecode);
            spacecode := t                      { restore sc for note }
          end
        else setnote(spacecode)
    end;   { setcode }

(***********************         newmeasure         ***********************)
(* Resets the the adjust array to reflect the key signature, thereby     *)
(* canceling accidentals.  Called at each bar line.                      *)
(*************************************************************************)
  procedure newmeasure;
    begin
      writeln('Bar line');
      incr(bp);                               { skip /              }
      adjust := keysig                        { copy keysig to adjust }
    end;

(***********************          badtoken          ***********************)
(* Called when the initial character of next token is not recognized.    *)
(* Reports an error and skips to next blank delimiter.                   *)
(*************************************************************************)
  procedure badtoken;
    begin
      error(buffer, bp, 1);
      findblank(buffer, bp)
    end;

(***********************            rest            ***********************)
(* Here, skips rest symbol and prints message.                           *)
(*************************************************************************)
  procedure rest;
    begin
      incr(bp); { skip rest }
      writeln('rest')
    end;

(***********************            scan            ***********************)
(* Scans input data for pitch information.                               *)
(*************************************************************************)
  procedure scan(var buffer : buftype; var bp : integer);
    begin
      skipbuf(buffer, bp);
      while not eob(buffer, bp) do
        begin
          if goodtoken(nextchar(buffer, bp))
            then
              begin
                if isdigit(nextchar(buffer, bp))            { space code }
                  then setcode(spacecode)
                else if isacc(nextchar(buffer, bp))         { accidental }
                  then setnote(spacecode)
```

```
              else if isexclamation(nextchar(buffer, bp)) { exclam pt     }
                then exclamation(0)
              else if isbar(nextchar(buffer, bp))         { bar line      }
                then newmeasure
              else if nextchar(buffer, bp) = 'r'          { rest          }
                then rest;
              if not isspace(nextchar(buffer, bp)) { missing delimiter }
                then error(buffer, bp, 10)
            end
          else badtoken;                                  { error         }
        skipbuf(buffer, bp)                               { skip blanks}
      end
  end; { scan }

(***********************     main procedure     ***********************)
(* It pays to learn to delegate responsibility!                        *)
(**********************************************************************)
 begin { main }
   init;                       { initialize arrays and set defaults }
   while not eof do
     begin
       getline(buffer, bp);    { read one input line                }
       scan(buffer, bp);       { and interpret code                 }
       writeln
     end
 end. { main }
```

Program 11.4. *Pitch*

Input:

```
!g !k3# 1 2# 3 2 / 2 !f 1 r 3 4 31 /
!c !k2- 1 2 7!c 3- 4* / 1!g 1 1* 20 25 /
```

Output:

```
Treble clef
New key signature =  3 #
pitch: 4042 = E4
pitch: 4063 = F#4
pitch: 4084 = G#4
pitch: 4063 = F#4
Bar line
pitch: 4063 = F#4
Bass clef
pitch: 2084 = G#2
rest
pitch: 2116 = B2
pitch: 3010 = C#3
pitch: 4010 = C#4
Bar line

Alto clef
New key signature =  2 -
```

```
pitch: 3053 = F3
pitch: 3074 = G3
Tenor clef
pitch: 3043 = F-3
pitch: 3074 = G3
Bar line
French violin clef
pitch: 4074 = G4
pitch: 4074 = G4
pitch: 4053 = F4
pitch: 5021 = D5
Bar line
```

Program 11.4. Sample Input and Output

11.6 Matrices

A matrix is a rectangular array in which each component is the same type. In Pascal, we can conceive of a matrix in several ways; the declaration depends on the conception. First, we can treat the matrix as an array in which the component type is another array, i.e., an array of arrays. This structure is declared as follows:

```
type
  matrix = array[a .. b] of array[c .. d] of X;

var
  M : matrix;
```

where X is the component type. In this case

```
M[i][j]
```

denotes the jth component (of type X) of the ith component of M. The subrange types $a .. b$ and $c .. d$ may be predefined and may be the same if the matrix is square.

It is normal practice, and more convenient, to abbreviate the definition:

```
type
  matrix = array[a .. b, c .. d] of X;

var
  M : matrix;
```

In this case an individual element is denoted

```
M[i,j]
```

where $a \leq i \leq b$ and $c \leq j \leq d$. The first subscript is generally treated as the row number and the second subscript as the column. Consider the 4 by 10 matrix shown in figure 11.5. The value of $M[1, 1]$ is 39, the value of $M[3, 8]$ is 293, and the value of $M[4, 5]$ is 0. In general we can refer to $M[i, j]$, where i is the row number and j is the column number.[11]

M

	1	2	3	4	5	6	7	8	9	10
1	39	42	21	14	75	83	77	91	19	70
2	84	33	13	67	62	51	54	82	24	81
3	19	87	56	78	456	81	32	293	77	54
4	97	45	62	73	0	88	45	18	99	23

Figure 11.5. A Four Row by Ten Column Matrix

11.6.1 Reading and Printing Matrices

Matrices are frequently generated by a program. When they are read from the input file and the dimensions are not constant, the dimensions are usually read before the values for the matrix are read. Reading the matrix requires nested **for** loops. The outer loop sets the row number, and the inner loop the column number. The following procedure reads the number of rows (n) and columns (m), followed by the values. Variable parameters are used to return the dimensions and values in the matrix. Modification of this procedure to check the dimensions against predefined constants is suggested as an exercise.

```
procedure readmatrix(var M : matrix; var n, m : integer);
  var
    i, j : integer;
  begin
    readln(n, m);
    for i := 1 to n do
      for j := 1 to m do
        read(M[i, j])
  end;
```

This procedure would be appropriate for any input with rows numbered 1 through n and columns numbered 1 through m, where n and m are within the limits prescribed by the matrix definition:

```
 2  3          { 2 by 3 matrix }
23 45  6
 1  9 32
```

11. There is nothing sacred about i and j. You can use any variables you like, for example, $M[r, c]$, so long as r and c are variables of the appropriate type and within range.

```
 4  4              { 4 by 4 matrix }
 5  7  1  9
99  2  8  9
12 89 74  7
12  5  7  8
```

The procedure to print a matrix is similar, but the newline character must be entered into the output file at the end of each line of the matrix. Spacing can be adjusted by specifying field width and/or more than one *writeln* after each row is printed if desired.

```
procedure printmatrix(var M : matrix; n, m : integer);
  var
    i, j : integer;
  begin
    for i := 1 to n do
      begin { print row i }
        for j := 1 to m do
          write(M[i, j]);
        writeln                     { terminate row }
      end   { print row i }
  end;
```

11.6.2 Processing Matrices

Since the array is a random-access data structure, any element can be referenced at will. If we wish to examine the entire matrix, it is easiest to process it row by row or column by column. In the procedures shown above, the outer loop (**for** *i*) sets the row number, and the nested loop (**for** *j*) sets the column number to each successive element in the row. Thus the matrix is read or printed row by row. This order is called *row-major* order. If the outer loop sets the second subscript and the inner loop the first subscript, then the array is processed in *column-major* order (column by column). The following statements print the matrix in column-major order, i.e., the contents of the first column are printed on the first line of output, the contents of the second column on the second line, and so on. Assume that there are *n* rows and *m* columns.

```
for j := 1 to m do
  begin { print jth column }
    for i := 1 to n do
      write(M[i, j]);
    writeln
  end;  { print jth column }
```

This loop structure prints the matrix

```
 1  2  3  4  5
 6  7  8  9 10
11 12 13 14 15
16 17 18 19 20
```

in the following format:

```
1  6 11 16
2  7 12 17
3  8 13 18
4  9 14 19
5 10 15 20
```

Since computer memory is one-dimensional, matrices and other multidimensional arrays cannot be stored in the format in which we envision them. Instead, they are stored in consecutive storage locations and an addressing algorithm is used to find the referenced element. Thus the matrix shown above could be stored in row-major order:

1 2 3 4 5 6 7 8 9 10 11 12 13 14 15 16 17 18 19 20

or in column-major order:

1 6 11 16 2 7 12 17 3 8 13 18 4 9 14 19 5 10 15 20

In either case, elements are stored in consecutive storage locations and an addressing algorithm is used to calculate the location in the computer's memory of any element $M[i, j]$ from the base address of the array (the address of the first element) and the subscripts. You may wish to try to work out addressing algorithms for each of these storage schemes as an exercise.

11.6.3 Application: Twelve-Tone Matrices

The most familiar application of matrices in music theory is the twelve-tone matrix or "Babbitt Square." This matrix shows in compact form all forty-eight permutations of a twelve-tone row. The matrix is most easily calculated if we begin the row on 0. We leave the calculation for a row that does not begin on 0 as an exercise.

The matrix is formed by placing the twelve-tone row in the first row of the matrix, and the inversion of the row (beginning on the same pitch class) in the first column. The prime form of the row is then transposed to begin on each pitch class of the inversion, filling the matrix. Since we are working with pitch classes, all operations are performed modulo 12. A partially filled matrix is shown below.

```
 0 11  8  1  2  7  6  3  4  5 10  9
 1  0  9  2  3  8  7  4  5  6 11 10
 4  3  0  5  6 11 10  7  8  9  2  1
11 10  7  0  1  6  ...
10  9  6 11  0 ...
 5  4  1  6 ...
 6  5  2  ...
 9  8  5 ...
 8  7  4 ...
 7  6  3 ...
 2  1 10 ...
 3  2 11 ...
```

This matrix shows the twelve transpositions of the row (read rows from left to right), the twelve transpositions of the inversion (read columns from top to bottom), the twelve transpositions of the retrograde (read rows from right to left), and the twelve transpositions of the retrograde inversion (read columns from bottom to top).

Assuming that the matrix has been declared

```
type
  matrix = array[1 .. 12, 1 .. 12] of integer;

var
  M : matrix;
```

the following steps will fill the matrix.

The twelve-tone row is read into the first row of the matrix (we will assume for now that the row begins on 0).

```
for i := 1 to 12 do
  read(M[1, i]);
```

Since the row begins on 0, the inversion can be calculated by subtracting each pitch class from 12. Each pc of the inversion will be the starting pitch of a transposition of the row. We can combine this step with the next by calculating the first pitch of each row form and then adding it to each element of the original row (beginning on 0) to obtain the correct transposition of the series:

```
for i := 2 to 12 do
  begin { calculate the ith row }
    t := 12 - M[1, i];               { transposition level      }
    for j := 1 to 12 do              { transpose row 1 to level t }
      M[i, j] := (M[1, j] + t) mod 12
  end;  { calculate the ith row }
```

The twelve-tone matrix is actually a special case of an addition matrix. The matrix can be constructed from any two ordered sets, say row *X* across the top and row *Y* on the left. In the twelve-tone matrix shown above, *X* is the prime form of the row and *Y* is the inversion transposed to 0. The matrix is filled by assigning to each element *M*[*i*, *j*] the sum of *Y*[*i*] and *X*[*j*], as shown in figure 11.6.

Bo Alphonce has shown that the invariant properties of the row can be read from the relative position of the various pc integers in the matrix.[12] The zeros on the diagonal from upper left to lower right indicate that the row transposed to 0 is completely invariant, i.e., each pc stays in the same order position. The same principle holds for identical values in any adjacent positions on any diagonal. For example, diagonal nines in the last four rows indicate that the corresponding values in row *X* (pcs 1 2 7 6) remain invariant in $T_9(X)$. Since they occur on the diagonal from upper left to lower right, they will occur in the same order. The position of the diagonal nines

12. Bo H. Alphonce, *The Invariance Matrix,* Ph.D. diss., Yale University, 1974 (Ann Arbor: University Microfilms, 1975).

		Set X											
		0	b	8	1	2	7	6	3	4	5	a	9
Set	0	0	b	8	1	2	7	6	3	4	5	a	9
	1	1	0	9	2	3	8	7	4	5	6	b	a
Y	4	4	3	0	5	6	b	a	7	8	**9**	2	1
	b	b	a	7	0	1	6	5	2	3	4	**9**	8
	a	a	9	6	b	0	5	4	1	2	3	8	7
	5	5	4	1	6	7	0	b	8	**9**	a	3	2
	6	6	5	2	7	8	1	0	**9**	a	b	4	3
	9	9	8	5	a	b	4	3	0	1	2	7	6
	8	8	7	4	**9**	a	3	2	b	0	1	6	5
	7	7	6	3	8	**9**	2	1	a	b	0	5	4
	2	2	1	a	3	4	**9**	8	5	6	7	0	b
	3	3	2	b	4	5	a	**9**	6	7	8	1	0

Figure 11.6. An X/Y Addition Matrix

relative to row Y indicates the order positions in which the invariant segment will occur, i.e., the invariant segment will occur as the last four pcs of $T_9(X)$. The matrix shows that two other segments remain invariant in $T_9(X)$. The nines on the diagonal from lower left to upper right indicate that pcs 3–4 will occur in reverse order in $T_9(X)$.

$$T_0(X) = 0\ B\ 8\ \underline{1\ 2\ 7\ 6}\ \underline{3\ 4}\ \underline{5\ A}\ 9$$

$$T_9(X) = 9\ 8\ \underline{5\ A}\ B\ \underline{4\ 3}\ 0\ \underline{1\ 2\ 7\ 6}$$

The same principle holds for any two ordered sets, i.e., set Y does not have to be derived from set X. The matrix constructed from row X and the inversion of Y is called a T-matrix because it shows invariant properties between X and transpositions of Y. By changing the method used to derive the row on the left of the matrix, we can read invariant properties under different twelve-tone operations. The I-matrix, constructed from the prime forms of X and Y, shows invariant properties between X and the inversion of Y. The M-matrix is constructed from X and MI(Y) and shows invariant properties between X and M(Y); the MI-matrix is constructed from X and M(Y) and shows invariant properties between X and MI(Y).[13]

13. The M operator signifies that each element of the set is multiplied by 5, mod 12. In MI, each element is multiplied by 7.

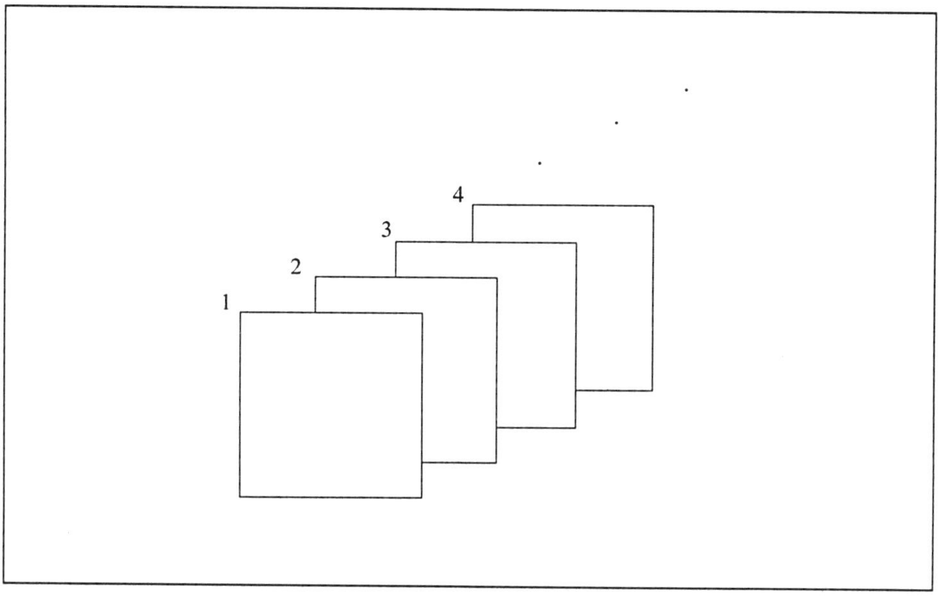

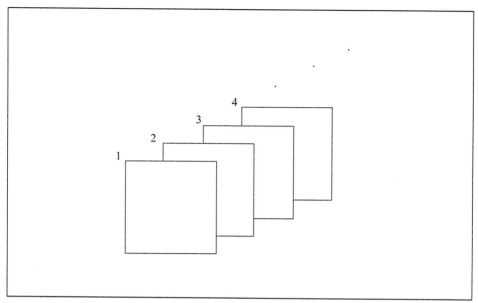

Figure 11.7. An Array in Three Dimensions

11.7 Arrays in More Than Two Dimensions

We can declare arrays in as many dimensions as needed, although it is easy to run out of storage space if you get carried away.[14] The declaration of multidimensional arrays is an extension of that shown for matrices. The subrange type used to index each dimension is separated by commas. For example, we could declare a 12 by 12 by 12 cubic array as:

```
type
  cube = array[1 .. 12, 1 .. 12, 1 .. 12] of integer;

var
  C : cube;
```

The third dimension is the "plane." Think of the structure as twelve matrices, one behind the other, as shown in figure 11.7.

If you wish to use matrix procedures to deal with each individual plane, it would be helpful to declare this structure in the following manner:

```
type
  matrix = array[1 .. 12, 1 .. 12] of integer;
  cube   = array[1 .. 12] of matrix;

var
  C : cube;
```

Now the cube is an array of matrices, and *C*[*i*] refers to the *i*th plane, which is itself

14. The number of elements in a multidimensional array is the product of the size of the dimensions: a 12 by 12 matrix requires 144 storage locations, a 12 by 12 by 10 matrix 1440, etc.

a matrix. An individual component is addressed $C[i][j, k]$, and $C[i]$, could be passed to a procedure that expects a matrix as an actual parameter.

References and Selected Readings

Many applications for the invariance matrix are described in the following:

Alphonce, Bo H. *The Invariance Matrix.* Ph.D. diss., Yale University, 1974. Ann Arbor: University Microfilms, 1975 [#75-15m280].

Additional uses of the matrix are discussed in:

Morris, Robert D. *Composition with Pitch-Classes: A Theory of Compositional Design.* New Haven: Yale University Press, 1987.

Rogers, John E. "Some Properties of Non-Duplicating Rotational Arrays." *Perspectives of New Music* 7, no. 1 (1968): 80–102.

Other suggested readings:

Coombs, David P. "An Analysis of Expectation in Music: A Computer-Aided Study." M.A. thesis, University of Rochester, Eastman School of Music, 1984.

Hessert, Norman D. "The Use of Information Theory in Musical Analysis." Ph.D. dissertation, Indiana University, 1971.

Laske, Otto E. "In Search of a Generative Grammer for Music." *Perspectives of New Music* 12, nos. 1 and 2 (1973–74): 351–78.

Lewin, David. "Some Application of Communication Theory to the Study of Twelve-Tone Music." *Journal of Music Theory* 12, no. 1 (1968): 50–84.

Morris, Robert D. "Sets, Groups, Complementation, and Mappings Among Pitch-Class Sets." *Journal of Music Theory* 26, no. 1: 101–44.

Exercises

11.1. *Exercise Group One.*

1. Write procedure *pad(S)*, which adds a blank character at the end of a string if there is not one already there.
2. Write procedure *center(S, w)*, which prints string *S* centered on a line *w* characters long. The procedure should print the appropriate number of blank characters and then call procedure *writestring* to print the string.
3. Write function *palindrome(S1)*, which returns *true* if string *S1* is a palindrome (a string that reads the same forward and backward). Generalize so that case, punctuation, and spaces do not matter, i.e., each of the following should register as a palindrome:

   Able was I ere I saw Elba.
   A man, a plan, a canal, Panama.
   Doc, note—I dissent. A fast never prevents a fatness. I diet on cod.
   Bog dirt up a side track carted is a putrid gob!

4. Modify program 11.4 (DARMS pitch decoding) by adding function *nonstandard*, which

will process nonstandard DARMS-encoded key signatures. The syntax for DARMS key signatures is described in section 6.5.1.

5. Write a program that uses a procedure to read DARMS strings, one at a time, into a packed array of characters, and another to parse the string into tokens as defined in exercise 7 of chapter 8.

11.2. *Exercise Group Two: Matrix Practice Problems.* The following problems assume a two-dimensional array or matrix, *M*, that has *rows* rows and *cols* columns. All values in *M* are integer. The following declarations define all global variables necessary for the exercises. Develop an algorithm for each exercise, and write a procedure implementing that algorithm.

```
const
  max = 25;

type
  matrix = array[1 .. max, 1 .. max] of integer;
  list   = array[1 .. max] of integer;

var
  M      : matrix;               { a matrix                     }
  rows   : integer;              { actual number of rows in M }
  cols   : integer;              { actual number of cols in M }
  corner : integer;              { largest corner element       }
  rowsum : list;                 { sum of each row              }
  colsum : list;                 { sum of each col              }
  aver   : real;                 { average value                }
  bignum : integer;              { largest number in M          }
```

1. Write procedure *readmat(M, rows, cols)*, which reads the values of *rows* and *cols* and then reads the values to fill the matrix *M*.

2. Write procedure *printmat(M, rows, cols)*, which prints out the values in *M* in an appropriate format. Assume that a row will fit on one line of your output device.

3. Write procedure *bigcorner(M, rows, cols, corner)*, which sets *corner* equal to the largest corner element in *M*.

4. Write procedure *swaprow(M, rows, cols, r1, r2)*, which interchanges the values in rows *r1* and *r2* of *M* using procedure *swap(x, y)*. The procedure should print a message containing the values of *r1* and *r2*. How would you call the procedure to exchange the first and last rows?

5. Write procedure *swapcol(M, rows, cols, c1, c2)*, which interchanges the values in columns *c1* and *c2* of *M*, using procedure *swap(x, y)*. The procedure should print a message containing the values of *c1* and *c2*. How would you call the procedure to exchange the first and last columns?

6. Write procedure *average(M, rows, cols, aver)*, which calculates the average value in *M* as a real number. Use parameter *aver* to return the value.

7. Write procedure *getbig(M, rows, cols, bignum)*, which finds the largest number in *M*, and returns it as parameter *bignum*.

8. Write procedure *littlebigswap(M, rows, cols)*, which interchanges the largest and smallest values in *M*. In case of ties, use the first number.

9. Write procedure *rsum(M, rows, cols, rowsum)*, which calculates the sum of each row. For each row *i*, store the sum in *rowsum*[*i*].

10. Write procedure *csum(M, rows, cols, colsum)*, which calculates the sum of each column. For each column *j*, store the sum in *colsum*[*j*].

11. Write procedure *rcsum(M, rows, cols, rowsum, colsum)*, which combines the previous two exercises in one procedure, making but a single pass through matrix *M*.

11.3. *Exercise Group Three: Larger Programs*

1. The twelve-tone matrix is a useful tool for anyone writing or analyzing serial music, since it shows, in a concise form, all forty-eight permutations of a twelve-tone row. The matrix is formed by placing the prime form of the tone row across the first row of the matrix, and the inversion of the row down the first column. The prime row is then transposed to begin on each note of the inversion.

   Each row of the matrix, read left to right, is one of the twelve transpositions of the prime form of the row, and read from right to left, the retrograde of the same row. Each column, read from top to bottom, is one of the twelve transpositions of the inversion, and from bottom to top, the retrograde of the inversion.

   Although the matrix can be calculated with note names, it is really much easier, even for people, to use pitch-class integers. The calculation is easiest if we use the row beginning on 0 as the prime (or reference) form. Each note of the inversion is calculated by subtracting the corresponding element of the prime form from 12 (mod 12). Thus, if we begin with the row

   0 11 7 8 3 1 2 10 6 5 4 9

   then the second row will begin with 1 (12 – 11), and we can calculate the entire row by adding 1 (mod 12) to each element of the first row, thus transposing the row to 1. The third row of the matrix will begin with 5 (12 – 7), etc. Study the first matrix on page 396 until you are sure that you understand the process.

   Your program should be able to process any number of tone rows on each program run. The input data for this exercise consist of a pair of lines for each row to be processed. The first line of each pair is a title (or other identifying information). The second is a twelve-tone row, in pitch-class integer notation, using the integers 0–11. The specified row may begin on any of the twelve pitch classes. An example is shown below.

```
Schoenberg: String Quartet No. 4, Op. 37
2 1 9 10 5 3 4 0 8 7 6 11
```

Program *Matrix*. Sample Input

The program will read the title string, storing it in an array. Then it will read the row, calculate the matrix, and print the matrix using integer notation and note names. The matrix should be printed first beginning on 0 (C), the form in which the matrix is calculated. Then, if the specified row did not begin on 0, the two matrices should be printed again, transposed to the original pitch level. (Sample output is shown on pages 396–97.)

Suggestion: Do it your way if you prefer.

Your program should have the following declarations (or something like them):

```
const
  numbers = true;       { flags for printing numbers     }
  names = false;        { or note names                  }
```

```
type
  matrix = array[1 .. 12, 1 .. 12] of integer;
  string = packed array[1 .. 100] of char;

var
  M     : matrix;      { the twelve-tone matrix         }
  title : string;      { for storing the title          }
  first : integer;     { the first pc of specified row  }
```

Some possible procedures:

procedure *readstring(title)* — reads the title, storing it in the array title. Place a *chr*(0) after the last character in the title to mark the end of the string.

procedure *writestring(title)* — prints the title, by printing each character before the *chr*(0).

procedure *readrow(M, first)* — reads the twelve pcs of the row into the first row of the matrix, transposes it to begin on 0, and returns the matrix *M* and the original first pc *first*.

procedure *fillmatrix(M)* — fills in the matrix.

procedure *printmatrix(M, first, numbers, title)* — prints matrix *M* transposed to begin on pc *first*. *Numbers* is a boolean parameter, which will have the value ***true*** if the matrix is to be printed with integers, or *false* if it is to be printed with note names. The *title* array is passed so that this procedure can print the title above each matrix (centering optional). The procedure can thus print the four required forms of the matrix by the following calls:

```
printmatrix(M, 0, numbers, title);      { numbers, start on 0     }
printmatrix(M, 0, names, title);        { names,   start on C     }
printmatrix(M, first, numbers, title);  { numbers, start on first }
printmatrix(M, first, names, title);    { names,   start on first }
```

The boolean "flag" can be used to control the format as follows:

```
if numbers
  then write(M[i, j] : 4)
  else writename(M[i, j], 4)
```

Procedure *writename* is shown below:

```
procedure writename(pc, w : integer);
  begin
    case pc of
      0 : write('c ':w);
      1 : write('c#':w);
      2 : write('d ':w);
      3 : write('d#':w);
      4 : write('e ':w);
      5 : write('f ':w);
      6 : write('f#':w);
      7 : write('g ':w);
      8 : write('g#':w);
      9 : write('a ':w);
     10 : write('a#':w);
     11 : write('b ':w)
    end  { case }
  end;
```

A similar procedure can be followed if you wish to print pc integers in hexadecimal notation ('A' = 10, 'B' = 11).

Schoenberg: String Quartet No. 4, Op. 37

0	11	7	8	3	1	2	10	6	5	4	9
1	0	8	9	4	2	3	11	7	6	5	10
5	4	0	1	8	6	7	3	11	10	9	2
4	3	11	0	7	5	6	2	10	9	8	1
9	8	4	5	0	10	11	7	3	2	1	6
11	10	6	7	2	0	1	9	5	4	3	8
10	9	5	6	1	11	0	8	4	3	2	7
2	1	9	10	5	3	4	0	8	7	6	11
6	5	1	2	9	7	8	4	0	11	10	3
7	6	2	3	10	8	9	5	1	0	11	4
8	7	3	4	11	9	10	6	2	1	0	5
3	2	10	11	6	4	5	1	9	8	7	0

Schoenberg: String Quartet No. 4, Op. 37

c	b	g	g#	d#	c#	d	a#	f#	f	e	a
c#	c	g#	a	e	d	d#	b	g	f#	f	a#
f	e	c	c#	g#	f#	g	d#	b	a#	a	d
e	d#	b	c	g	f	f#	d	a#	a	g#	c#
a	g#	e	f	c	a#	b	g	d#	d	c#	f#
b	a#	f#	g	d	c	c#	a	f	e	d#	g#
a#	a	f	f#	c#	b	c	g#	e	d#	d	g
d	c#	a	a#	f	d#	e	c	g#	g	f#	b
f#	f	c#	d	a	g	g#	e	c	b	a#	d#
g	f#	d	d#	a#	g#	a	f	c#	c	b	e
g#	g	d#	e	b	a	a#	f#	d	c#	c	f
d#	d	a#	b	f#	e	f	c#	a	g#	g	c

Schoenberg: String Quartet No. 4, Op. 37

2	1	9	10	5	3	4	0	8	7	6	11
3	2	10	11	6	4	5	1	9	8	7	0
7	6	2	3	10	8	9	5	1	0	11	4
6	5	1	2	9	7	8	4	0	11	10	3
11	10	6	7	2	0	1	9	5	4	3	8
1	0	8	9	4	2	3	11	7	6	5	10
0	11	7	8	3	1	2	10	6	5	4	9
4	3	11	0	7	5	6	2	10	9	8	1
8	7	3	4	11	9	10	6	2	1	0	5
9	8	4	5	0	10	11	7	3	2	1	6
10	9	5	6	1	11	0	8	4	3	2	7
5	4	0	1	8	6	7	3	11	10	9	2

Schoenberg: String Quartet No. 4, Op. 37

d	c#	a	a#	f	d#	e	c	g#	g	f#	b
d#	d	a#	b	f#	e	f	c#	a	g#	g	c
g	f#	d	d#	a#	g#	a	f	c#	c	b	e
f#	f	c#	d	a	g	g#	e	c	b	a#	d#
b	a#	f#	g	d	c	c#	a	f	e	d#	g#
c#	c	g#	a	e	d	d#	b	g	f#	f	a#
c	b	g	g#	d#	c#	d	a#	f#	f	e	a
e	d#	b	c	g	f	f#	d	a#	a	g#	c#
g#	g	d#	e	b	a	a#	f#	d	c#	c	f
a	g#	e	f	c	a#	b	g	d#	d	c#	f#
a#	a	f	f#	c#	b	c	g#	e	d#	d	g
f	e	c	c#	g#	f#	g	d#	b	a#	a	d

Program ***Matrix.*** Sample Output

2. Explore the alternate calculation of matrices using two rows, as described in the discussion of invariance matrices in section 11.6.3. Include code to generate T-matrices, I-matrices, M-matrices, and MI-matrices. The program should be able to operate on any two pitch-class sets, which need not be twelve-tone sets.

3. Although this exercise deals with conversion among various number systems, we will use similar techniques for encoding music data. Program 11.3 employed a buffer and user-written conversion procedures to read and write integers in decimal (base 10) format. The process for other numbering systems is almost identical. The number base of the numbering system is called the radix; i.e., in decimal numbers the radix is 10, in binary numbers the radix is 2, etc. In computing, binary, octal, and hexadecimal (base 16) numbers are frequently used in addition to the more familiar decimal numbers.[15] In each of these systems, the positional weight of each digit is a power of the number base or radix. The weight of the rightmost digit is $radix^0$, the next digit is $radix^1$, etc. We have seen that in base 10 the value of a number, say 104, is calculated as follows:

$$\begin{array}{rcrcr} 4 \times 10^0 & = & 4 \times 1 & = & 4 \\ +\,0 \times 10^1 & = & 0 \times 10 & = & 0 \\ +\,1 \times 10^2 & = & 1 \times 100 & = & \underline{100} \\ & & & & 104 \end{array}$$

Binary numbers follow the same principle, except the radix is 2 and the only digits are 0 and 1. Thus the value of binary 1011 is

$$\begin{array}{rcrcr} 1 \times 2^0 & = & 1 \times 1 & = & 1 \\ +\,1 \times 2^1 & = & 1 \times 2 & = & 2 \\ +\,0 \times 2^2 & = & 0 \times 4 & = & 0 \\ +\,1 \times 2^3 & = & 1 \times 8 & = & \underline{8} \\ & & & & 11 \end{array}$$

Octal numbers use radix 8 and digits 01234567. Thus the value of octal 457 is

$$\begin{array}{rcrcr} 7 \times 8^0 & = & 7 \times 1 & = & 7 \\ +\,5 \times 8^1 & = & 5 \times 8 & = & 40 \\ +\,4 \times 8^2 & = & 4 \times 64 & = & \underline{256} \\ & & & & 303 \end{array}$$

Hexadecimal numbers use radix 16 and digits 0123456789ABCDEF. Thus the value of hexadecimal 32D is

$$\begin{array}{rcrcr} 13 \times 16^0 & = & 13 \times 1 & = & 13 \\ +\;2 \times 16^1 & = & 2 \times 16 & = & 32 \\ +\;3 \times 16^2 & = & 3 \times 256 & = & \underline{768} \\ & & & & 813 \end{array}$$

The individual digits for a positive integer x in any numbering system can be calculated (from right to left) by the following algorithm:

15. Binary numbers are used internally in computers, since it is relatively easy to build electronic devices that have only two states (on or off), which are represented by the binary digits (bits) 1 and 0. Programmers use octal and hexadecimal numbers because they are easier to read than binary but, unlike decimal numbers, represent even partitions of binary numbers. Each octal digit represents 3 bits; each hexadecimal digit equals 4. Thus binary 111001101010 can be easily expressed in octal or hexadecimal notation:

111	001	101	010		1110	0110	1010
7	1	5	2		E	6	A

```
while x > 0 do
  begin
    nextdigit := x mod radix;
    x := x div radix
  end;
```

Thus decimal 189 decoded as a decimal number is 189:

x	*x* mod 10	*x* div 10
189	9	18
18	8	1
1	1	0

The same integer (decimal 189) decoded into octal is 275:

x	*x* mod 8	*x* div 8
189	5	23
23	7	2
2	2	0

Decimal 189 in hexadecimal is BD:

x	*x* mod 16	*x* div 16
189	13 (D)	11
11	11 (B)	0

Your exercise is to modify program 11.2 (*bufdemo*) so that it can read and write integers in binary, octal, decimal, or hexadecimal notation. The modification will require passing the radix as a parameter to several procedures, the headings of which are shown below:

```
procedure getint(var buffer : buftype; var bp, x : integer;
                                                radix : integer);
procedure putint(x, radix : integer);
function isdigit(c : char; radix : integer);
procedure error(var buffer : buftype; bp, radix : integer);
```

The program should read the radix before processing begins, read integers in the specified number system, and print them in each system. The main procedure will look something like that shown below.

```
begin { main }
  write('Type radix (2,8,10,16): ');
  getline(buffer, bp);
  getint(radix, 10);
  if not (radix in [2, 8, 10, 16])
    then writeln('illegal radix')
    else
      begin
        write('Type integers: ');
        while not eof(input) do
          begin { process line }
            getline(buffer, bp);          { read line into buffer }
```

```
            while not eob do
              begin                 { while not at end of buffer  }
                getint(n, radix);          { get int from buffer  }
                write('bin: ');
                putint(n, 2); writeln;     { print it in binary   }
                write('oct: ');
                putint(n, 8); writeln;     { print it in octal    }
                write('dec: ');
                putint(n, 10); writeln;    { print it in decimal  }
                write('hex: ');
                putint(n, 16); writeln;    { print it in hex      }
                writeln;
                skipbuf(buffer, bp)        { skip blanks          }
              end;
            writeln;
            write('Type integers: ')
          end   { process line }
      end
end.  { main }
```

4. In this assignment you will write a program that does diatonic transposition. The input/output code consists of letter names followed optionally by sharps or flats (encoded 's' and 'f'). (See section 6.6.) Thus a C-sharp major chord is 'cs es gs'. Multiple accidentals are encoded by repeating the sharp or flat symbol as many times as required: 'dff' (D-double-flat), 'esss' (E-triple-sharp), etc. The pitches will be stored within the computer as single-number binomial pitch classes (brs), in which the last digit (0–6) is the name class, indicating spelling, and the leading digits (0–11) indicate the pitch class:

c	00
ds	31
b	116
bf	106
fss	73

Your program will prompt the user ('Type tune: ') and then accept as input a line of encoded notes separated by spaces. It will then request an interval of transposition. This will be specified as an optional sign (indicating direction), followed by a single character modifier and an interval name. Possible modifiers are

p or P	perfect
M	major
m	minor
d or D	diminished
a or A	augmented

Intervals will be encoded with integer representation of the standard interval name (1 = prime, 2 = second, 4 = fourth, 8 = octave, 10 = tenth, etc.). If the sign is absent, it will be assumed to be positive. Thus the transposition interval will be input as

P4	{ perfect fourth up }
A2	{ augmented second down }
+M3	{ major third up }
	. . . etc.

You will need to translate the interval into brs. The basic algorithm consists of the following steps:

a) Check for a sign and set a boolean flag indicating direction. Skip the sign if there is one.

b) Read the modifier using a character variable.

c) Read the interval as an integer. Convert the external form into name class.

d) Make sure that the modifier and interval agree, i.e., do not allow m5 or M4.

e) Use a function to determine the pc for the major/perfect form of the interval.

f) Modify the pc if necessary to reflect the modifier.

g) Encode the interval as a br and return.

Your program should not accept an inappropriate interval, e.g., M5, P3. Use either a loop or recursion (see chapter 15) to ensure an acceptable response. The program will then add the interval (binomial addition) to each binomial pc and print out the transposed notes using the input code.

In order to implement this algorithm, you will need several operations:

a) Given a letter name, get the name class.

b) Given the nc, get the corresponding pc in the natural scale. Note that this corresponds exactly to the perfect and major intervals.

c) Given the name class, get the letter name (for decoding binomial representation).

Each of these can be accomplished via function calls (using either case statements or arithmetic calculation).

It will be necessary to look ahead in the buffer while reading. For this program, instead of using *input*↑, use an array to create your own buffer, as explained in section 11.2. Do all input by reading a line at a time into the buffer and then reading from the buffer.

The program should loop, reading and transposing pitch collections until the user types the end-of-file signal. A sample run might look something like the following:

```
Type notes:     c e g
Type interval:  M3
Result:         e gs b

Type notes:     c e g
Type interval:  -M3
Result:         af c ef

Type notes:     (etc.)
```

Program *Diatrans.* Sample Input and Output (Interactive)

12| Set Types

Pascal's set type provides a convenient and efficient method of dealing with *unordered* sets of elements of the same type. Sets may be any ordinal type: integers, characters, enumerated types, and subrange types.[1] The type of values to be represented by the set is called the *base type* of the set. The set type represents all sets, including the empty set, that can be constructed from the base type. The value of a set-type variable is a single set, which either is empty or contains unordered values of its ordinal type. Although the position is defined in the ordinal type, the set is considered to be unordered, and it never contains duplicate elements. The syntax for declaring a set type is shown in figure 12.1. The reserved word **packed** is optional. The result of packing is implementation dependent. Packing may save some space at the cost of computation time on some computer systems, with some implementations of Pascal. We will not use packed sets in the illustrations in this text.

The maximum number of elements of a set is implementation dependent and may be quite small (e.g., equal to the number of bits in a computer word), although better compilers allow more flexibility. The type **set of** *char*, representing the characters in the character set, is a reasonable limit and may be legal; the set of *integer* almost certainly will not be, although you may use a subrange of integers.[2]

Some examples of set-type definitions are shown below. The first uses a subrange of integers, commonly used to represent pitch classes, to declare the type *pset*. The second uses an enumerated type called *strings* to declare the type *ensemble*—a set of strings. The last uses an enumerated type representing articulation marks to declare a set of articulations.[3] After definition, the user-defined types are used to declare the variables *pcset* (a set of pitch-class integers); *quartet*, *trio*, and *duo* (ensembles consisting of a set of strings); and *articulation*, a set of articulation marks:

1. The reader may wish to review sections 3.5.4 and 3.5.5.

2. Some Pascal systems have compiler options to change the maximum size of sets. See the technical manual for your compiler for more information.

3. Note that we cannot declare the enumerated type using elements of type *char*, e.g., ('''', '"', '_', '>', '<', ';'), because values cannot be members of two different ordinal types, in this case *articmark* and *char*.

```
type
  pcint = 0 .. 11;                                    { subrange type    }
  pset  = set of pcint;                               { set type         }

  strings = (violin1, violin2, viola, cello, bass); { enumerated type }
  ensemble = set of strings;                          { set type         }

  articmark = (staccato, wedgeaccent, tenuto, accent, upbow, fermata);
  artictype = set of articmark;

var
  pcset          : pset;                  { set of pitch classes         }
  quartet        : ensemble;              { set of strings               }
  trio, duo      : ensemble;              { sets of strings              }
  articulation   : artictype;             { set of articulation marks    }
```

Alternately, unnamed set types can be defined directly in variable declarations:

```
var
  pcset          : set of 0 .. 11;              { set of pc integers   }

  quartet        : set of (violin1, violin2,
                           viola, cello, bass); { set of strings       }

  articulation : set of (staccato, wedgeaccent, tenuto, accent,
                         upbow, fermata);       { set of articulation }
```

While this may seem simpler at first glance, it is not recommended and should be used only when the sets will be used locally, since variables declared with unnamed types cannot be passed as arguments to subprograms. In either case, the actual contents of variables *pcset*, *articulation*, and *quartet* are undefined until a value has been assigned to them. At this point we have simply designated the types of values that they may contain.

The operations defined on sets are assignment, testing for equality, testing for membership, plus all of the normal operations used with sets (intersection, union, etc.). Sets are built with *set constructors*.

> [**type**]
> <settype> = **set of** <basetype>
>
> or
>
> <settype> = **packed set of** <basetype>
>
> where <settype> is a legal Pascal identifier and <basetype> is a standard ordinal type (e.g. char), an enumerated type, or a subrange of these.

Figure 12.1. SYNTAX: The Set Type

12.1 Set Constructors

The values in a set are specified by a set constructor in the form

$$[\ S_1, S_2, \ldots, S_n\ ]$$

where S_1, S_2, . . ., S_n are elements of the set (and must be in the base ordinal type), subranges of base type in the form

$$S_a \ldots S_b$$

or expressions that evaluate to members of the base type. When subranges are used, if $ord(S_a) > ord(S_b)$, then no element results. Examples of set constructors are shown in table 12.1.

Again, note that although set constructors may contain duplicate elements, the resulting sets do not. The set constructors [*a*, *b*, *c*], [*c*, *b*, *a*], and [*c*, *a*, *a*, *b*, *c*, *b*] all result in the same three-note set. The definition of *strings* given in the last section was sufficient for declaring the instruments in a standard string quartet because we allowed for elements *violin1* and *violin2*. It would not be sufficient to declare the instrumentation of Schubert's Quintet, Op. 163 (2 violins, viola, 2 cellos), since the set constructor [*violin1*, *violin2*, *viola*, *cello*, *cello*] results in the four-element set [*violin1*, *violin2*, *viola*, *cello*].

Expressions may be freely used so long as the result is in the desired set type. The expression in the set constructor

```
[(pc + n) mod 12]
```

must evaluate to an integer between 0 and 11, so the result could be used with the set type *pset* as defined in the previous section.

Since set constructors do not include an indication of whether or not the set is packed, they may be used for either. When the resulting set is assigned to a variable, it is packed if the variable has been defined as a packed set type.

[ ]	A null set of any type
['0' .. '9']	The set of base 10 digits
['a' .. 'z']	The set of characters in the lowercase alphabet
['a' .. 'z', 'A' .. 'Z']	Any alphabetic character
[0 .. 11]	A subrange of integers (in this case the universal set of pc integers)
[*violin1*]	A single element
[*violin2* .. *cello*]	A subrange of an enumerated type
[0, 1, 4]	Specified elements
[(*pc* + *n*) **mod** 12]	An expression that evaluates to an element type

Table 12.1. Examples of Set Constructors

As a simple example of set constructors, we will rewrite procedure *skip* from chapter 8 in a more flexible form. Here we define an argument, *skipset*, which is a set of *char*.[4]

```
[ type
    charset : set of char;   ]

  procedure skip(var f : text; skipset : charset);
   var
     done : boolean;
   begin
     done : false;
     repeat
       if eof(f)
         then done := true
       else if f↑ in skipset
         then get(f)
       else done := true
     until done
   end;
```

This implementation of the procedure allows the programmer to specify the characters to be skipped, as well as the file when the procedure is called. For example,

```
skip(input, [' ', chr(9), ',', ';']);
```

will skip blanks, tab characters, commas, and semicolons in file *input*, while

```
skip(data, ['a' .. 'z', 'A' .. 'Z']);
```

skips to the next nonalphabetic character in file *data*.

12.2 Operations on Sets

The replacement (or assignment) statement with sets takes the form

$$V := E$$

where V is a set-type variable and E is a set expression, each element of E is of the same base type as V, and E and V are either both packed or both unpacked. Where variables A and B are both of the same defined type or B is a compatible set constructor, the assignment may be simple, e.g.,

$$A := B; \quad \text{or} \quad A := [\ ];$$

or the expression on the right may contain set operators for intersection (*), union (+), or difference (–). If A is a set variable and B and C are compatible variables or

4. This example assumes a Pascal compiler that allows the type **set of** *char*. This is not always the case, as indicated above.

Meaning	*Mathematic Symbol*	*Pascal Symbol*	*Value*	*Examples*
Assignment	$\leftarrow$	:=	set	$A := B$
Set constructor	$\{...\}$	[...]	set	$A := [0 .. 11, x, y]$
Null set	$\emptyset$	[ ]	set	$A := [\ ]$
Union	$\cup$	+	set	$C := A + B$; $A := A + [x]$
Intersection	$\cap$	*	set	$C := A * B$
Difference	$-$	−	set	$C := A - B$; $A := A - [y]$
Subset of	$\subset$	<=	boolean	$A <= B$
Superset of	$\supset$	>=	boolean	$A >= B$
Equivalence	$\equiv$	=	boolean	$A = B$
Inequality	$\neq$	<>	boolean	$A <> B$
Inclusion	$\in$	**in**	boolean	x **in** A

(A, B, and C are sets; x and y are compatible elements)

Table 12.2. Operations with Sets

set constructors,[5]

$A := B + C$	assigns to A the union of B and C
$A := B * C$	assigns to A the intersection of B and C
$A := B - C$	assigns to A the difference between B and C

Sets may be compared for equality or inequality by the following:

$A = B$	is *true* if set A is identical to set B
$A <> B$	is *true* if set A is not identical to set B

Subset inclusion is tested as shown below:

$A <= B$	is *true* if A is a proper or an improper subset of B
$A >= B$	is *true* if A is a proper or an improper superset of B

We can test a single element x, which is of the same ordinal type as the base type of A, for membership in A by the following:

x **in** A	is *true* if x is a member of set A

This construction is frequently used in a loop to test for the presence of each possible element in a set:

5. The union of set A and set B is the set of all elements that occur in A or B or both. The intersection of A and B is the set of elements that occur in both A and B. The difference $B - C$ is the set of elements that occur in set B that do not occur in C.

```
[ var
    ins : strings; ]

for ins := violin1 to bass do
  if ins in quartet
    then ...
```

Note that testing for membership is *not* the same as testing for inclusion, since the former tests an element and the latter tests a relationship between two sets. Therefore (x **in** A) tests the same relationship as ($[x] <= A$). In the latter the set constructor is used to form the set consisting of the single element x. The operations on sets are summarized in table 12.2.

Program 12.1 illustrates many of these operations with sets of instruments defined as an enumerated type. Note that in the definition of *instruments*, the members of the same family (woodwinds, strings, brass, etc.) are kept together in order to facilitate set construction using subranges of instruments.

```
(***********************       Program Setdemo      ***********************)
(* Illustrates many operations on sets.                                    *)
(**************************************************************************)

program setdemo(input, output);
  const
    stringlength = 15;

  type
    string = packed array[1 .. stringlength] of char;

    instrument = (violin, viola, cello, bass, harp, guitar, trumpet,
                  cornet, flugelhorn, trombone, basstrombone,
                  frenchhorn, tuba, piccolo, flute, altoflute, clarinet,
                  altoclar, bassclar, soprasax, altosax, tenorsax,
                  barisax, oboe, englishhorn, oboedamore, bassoon,
                  contrabassoon, tympani, snaredrum, bassdrum, cymbals,
                  marimba, vibraphone, piano, celesta, harpsichord, organ);

     instrtype = set of instrument;

  var
    allinstr,                                  { all instruments         }
    strings,                                   { string instruments      }
    brass,                                     { brass instruments       }
    woodwinds,                                 { woodwind instruments    }
    percussion,                                { percussion instruments  }
    keyboard,                                  { keyboard instruments    }
    sopranoinstr,                              { soprano instruments     }
    altoinstr,                                 { alto instruments        }
    bassinstr,                                 { bass instruments        }
    stdorchestra,                              { standard orchestra      }
    temp          : instrtype;
    test          : instrument;                { for reading instrument  }
    error         : boolean;                   { flag for readinstr      }
```

```
(*************************************************************************)
(*                          Output Routines                              *)
(*************************************************************************)


(***********************      writeinstr      ***********************)
(* Writes string representing value in enumerated type.              *)
(*************************************************************************)
  procedure writeinstr(instr : instrument);
    begin
      write('       ');
      case instr of
        violin         : writeln('violin');
        viola          : writeln('viola');
        cello          : writeln('violoncello');
        bass           : writeln('double bass');
        harp           : writeln('harp');
        guitar         : writeln('guitar');
        trumpet        : writeln('trumpet');
        cornet         : writeln('cornet');
        flugelhorn     : writeln('flugelhorn');
        trombone       : writeln('trombone');
        basstrombone   : writeln('bass trombone');
        frenchhorn     : writeln('french horn');
        tuba           : writeln('tuba');
        piccolo        : writeln('piccolo');
        flute          : writeln('flute');
        altoflute      : writeln('alto flute');
        clarinet       : writeln('clarinet');
        altoclar       : writeln('alto clarinet');
        bassclar       : writeln('bass clarinet');
        soprasax       : writeln('soprano sax');
        altosax        : writeln('alto sax');
        tenorsax       : writeln('tenor sax');
        barisax        : writeln('baritone sax');
        oboe           : writeln('oboe');
        englishhorn    : writeln('english horn');
        oboedamore     : writeln('oboe d''amore');
        bassoon        : writeln('bassoon');
        contrabassoon  : writeln('contrabassoon');
        tympani        : writeln('tympani');
        snaredrum      : writeln('snare drum');
        bassdrum       : writeln('bass drum');
        cymbals        : writeln('cymbals');
        marimba        : writeln('marimba');
        vibraphone     : writeln('vibraphone');
        piano          : writeln('piano');
        celesta        : writeln('celesta');
        harpsichord    : writeln('harpsichord');
        organ          : writeln('pipe organ')
      end { case }
    end;  { writeinstr }

(***********************       printset       ***********************)
(* Calls writeinstr to print each value of set S.                    *)
(*************************************************************************)
```

```
  procedure printset(S : instrtype);
    var
      instr : instrument;
    begin
      for instr := violin to organ do
        if instr in S
          then writeinstr(instr);
      writeln
    end;  { printset }


(***********************************************************************)
(*                         Input Routines                              *)
(***********************************************************************)

  procedure skipln;                 { finds next nonblank char or end-of-line }
    begin
      while (input↑ = ' ') and not eoln do
        get(input)
    end;

  procedure incr(var x : integer);                 { adds one to argument }
    begin
      x := x + 1
    end;

  procedure readstring(var S : string);             { reads string into S   }
    var
      i : integer;
    begin
      skipln;
      i := 1;
      while not eoln and (i <= stringlength) do
        begin
          read(S[i]);
          incr(i)
        end;
      while i <= stringlength do
        begin
          S[i] := ' ';
          incr(i)
        end;
      readln
    end;  { readstring }

(***********************         readinstr         *********************)
(* Reads instrument name as string and converts to element of enumerated *)
(* type.  Sets error flag if string does not match any element.          *)
(***********************************************************************)
  procedure readinstr(var I : instrument; var allinstr : instrtype;
                                                var error : boolean);
    var
      instrname : string;
    begin
      readstring(instrname);                       { read instrument name    }
      error := false;
```

```
if instrname = 'violin          '              { assign enumerated type }
  then I := violin
else if instrname = 'viola          '
  then I := viola
else if (instrname = 'cello          ')
     or (instrname = 'violoncello    ')
  then I := cello
else if (instrname = 'double bass    ')
     or (instrname = 'bass           ')
     or (instrname = 'contrabass     ')
     or (instrname = 'string bass    ')
  then I := bass
else if instrname = 'harp           '
  then I := harp
else if instrname = 'guitar         '
  then I := guitar
else if instrname = 'trumpet        '
  then I := trumpet
else if instrname = 'cornet         '
  then I := cornet
else if instrname = 'flugelhorn     '
  then I := flugelhorn
else if instrname = 'trombone       '
  then I := trombone
else if instrname = 'bass trombone  '
  then I := basstrombone
else if (instrname = 'french horn    ')
     or (instrname = 'horn           ')
  then I := frenchhorn
else if instrname = 'tuba           '
  then I := tuba
else if instrname = 'piccolo        '
  then I := piccolo
else if instrname = 'flute          '
  then I := flute
else if instrname = 'alto flute     '
  then I := altoflute
else if instrname = 'clarinet       '
  then I := clarinet
else if instrname = 'alto clarinet  '
  then I := altoclar
else if instrname = 'bass clarinet  '
  then I := bassclar
else if instrname = 'soprano sax    '
  then I := soprasax
else if instrname = 'alto sax       '
  then I := altosax
else if instrname = 'tenor sax      '
  then I := tenorsax
else if instrname = 'baritone sax   '
  then I := barisax
else if instrname = 'oboe           '
  then I := oboe
else if instrname = 'english horn   '
  then I := englishhorn
```

```
      else if instrname = 'oboe d''amore       '
        then I := oboedamore
      else if instrname = 'bassoon             '
        then I := bassoon
      else if instrname = 'contrabassoon       '
        then I := contrabassoon
      else if instrname = 'tympani             '
        then I := tympani
      else if instrname = 'snare drum          '
        then I := snaredrum
      else if instrname = 'bass drum           '
        then I := bassdrum
      else if instrname = 'cymbals             '
        then I := cymbals
      else if instrname = 'marimba             '
        then I := marimba
      else if instrname = 'vibraphone          '
        then I := vibraphone
      else if instrname = 'piano               '
        then I := piano
      else if instrname = 'celesta             '
        then I := celesta
      else if instrname = 'harpsichord         '
        then I := harpsichord
      else if (instrname = 'pipe organ          ')
           or (instrname = 'organ               ')
        then I := organ
      else error := true                                    { signal error }
    end; { readinstr }


(***********************      main procedure       ***********************)
(* The first part exercises Pascal's set operations.  The second reads  *)
(* strings, converts them to sets, and then uses the in operator to list *)
(* each set's main classification.                                      *)
(************************************************************************)
  begin { main }
                        { set constructors }
    allinstr     := [violin .. organ];
    strings      := [violin .. guitar];
    brass        := [trumpet .. tuba];
    woodwinds    := [piccolo .. contrabassoon];
    percussion   := [tympani .. vibraphone];
    keyboard     := [piano .. organ];
    bassinstr    := [cello, bass, basstrombone, tuba,
                                   bassclar, bassoon, contrabassoon];
    sopranoinstr := [violin, trumpet, piccolo .. clarinet, oboe,
                                               soprasax .. altosax];
    altoinstr    := [viola, altoflute, englishhorn, altosax,
                                             altoclar, flugelhorn];
    stdorchestra := allinstr - [cornet, flugelhorn, vibraphone,
                        soprasax .. barisax] - keyboard;

    writeln('strings:');
    printset(strings);
```

```
    writeln('brass:');
    printset(brass);

    writeln('woodwinds:');
    printset(woodwinds);

    writeln('percussion:');
    printset(percussion);

    writeln('keyboard:');
    printset(keyboard);

    writeln('alto instruments:');
    printset(altoinstr);

    writeln('bass instruments:');
    printset(bassinstr);

    writeln('standard orchestral instruments:');
    printset(stdorchestra);

(************************************************************************)
(*             Now demonstrate boolean operators on sets.               *)
(************************************************************************)

                      { subset and superset }

    writeln('brass <= allinstr is ', brass <= allinstr);
    writeln('brass >= [trumpet, tuba] is ', brass >= [trumpet, tuba]);
    writeln('[violin, viola] <= strings is ', [violin, viola] <= strings);

                          { inclusion }

    writeln('tympani in percussion is ', tympani in percussion);
    writeln('violin in percussion is ', violin in percussion);
    writeln('trumpet in strings is ', trumpet in strings);

                    { equality and nonequality }

    writeln('brass = strings is ', brass = strings);
    writeln('brass <> strings is ', brass <> strings);

    writeln;

                        { set difference }

    temp := strings - [bass, violin, harp];
    writeln('middle strings:');
    printset(temp);

                         { intersection }

    writeln('soprano woodwind instruments:');
    printset(woodwinds * sopranoinstr);

                      { union & difference }

    writeln('brass band:');
```

```
   printset(brass + percussion - [marimba, vibraphone,
                              flugelhorn, tympani, basstromb]);

(*************************************************************************)
(*    Demonstrate procedures for reading and classifying instruments.    *)
(*************************************************************************)

   write('Type instrument name: ');
   while not eof do
     begin
       readinstr(test, allinstr, error);
       if not error
         then
           begin
             if test in strings
               then writeln('  strings')
             else if test in woodwinds
               then writeln('  woodwind')
             else if test in brass
               then writeln('  brass')
             else if test in percussion
               then writeln('  percussion')
             else if test in keyboard
               then writeln('  keyboard')
           end
         else writeln('Instrument not known to this program');
       writeln;
       write('Type instrument name: ')
     end
 end. { main }
```

Program 12.1. *Setdemo*

```
            strings:
                    violin
                    viola
                    violoncello
                    double bass
                    harp
                    guitar

            brass:
                    trumpet
                    cornet
                    flugelhorn
                    trombone
                    bass trombone
                    french horn
                    tuba
```

```
woodwinds:
        piccolo
        flute
        alto flute
        clarinet
        alto clarinet
        bass clarinet
        soprano sax
        alto sax
        tenor sax
        baritone sax
        oboe
        english horn
        oboe d'amore
        bassoon
        contrabassoon

percussion:
        tympani
        snare drum
        bass drum
        cymbals
        marimba
        vibraphone

keyboard:
        piano
        celesta
        harpsichord
        pipe organ

alto instruments:
        viola
        flugelhorn
        alto flute
        alto clarinet
        alto sax
        english horn

bass instruments:
        violoncello
        double bass
        bass trombone
        tuba
        bass clarinet
        bassoon
        contrabassoon

standard orchestral instruments:
        violin
        viola
        violoncello
        double bass
        harp
```

```
        trumpet
        trombone
        bass trombone
        french horn
        tuba
        piccolo
        flute
        alto flute
        clarinet
        alto clarinet
        bass clarinet
        oboe
        english horn
        oboe d'amore
        bassoon
        contrabassoon
        tympani
        snare drum
        bass drum
        cymbals
        marimba

brass <= allinstr is  true
brass >= [trumpet, tuba] is  true
[violin, viola] <= strings is  true
tympani in percussion is  true
violin in percussion is false
trumpet in strings is false
brass = strings is false
brass <> strings is  true

middle strings:
        viola
        violoncello
        guitar

soprano woodwind instruments:
        piccolo
        flute
        alto flute
        clarinet
        soprano sax
        alto sax
        oboe

brass band:
        trumpet
        cornet
        trombone
        french horn
        tuba
        snare drum
        bass drum
        cymbals
```

```
Type instrument name: double bass
  strings

Type instrument name: string bass
  strings

Type instrument name: contrabass
  strings

Type instrument name: bass
  strings

Type instrument name: french horn
  brass

Type instrument name: oboe d'amore
  woodwind

Type instrument name: clarinet
  woodwind

Type instrument name: cymbals
  percussion

Type instrument name: flugelhorn
  brass

Type instrument name: pipe organ
  keyboard

Type instrument name: piano
  keyboard

Type instrument name: guitar
  strings

Type instrument name: celesta
  keyboard

Type instrument name: cello
  strings

Type instrument name: violoncello
  strings

Type instrument name: harp
  strings

Type instrument name: alto flute
  woodwind

Type instrument name: mandolin
Instrument not known to this program

Type instrument name: ^D
```

Program 12.1. Sample Run (Interactive)

12.3 Application: Processing Pitch-Class Sets

Pascal's set type is well suited to implementing operations on pitch–class sets, if we first define a set type using the subrange of integers:

```
type
  pcint = 0 .. 11;
  pcset = set of pcint;
```

The following procedures read and write pitch-class sets in hexadecimal notation (using digits 0–9, a, b) to represent the pc integers 0–11. Note that the use of set types makes this version of *readset* more efficient than that shown in chapter 10.

```
{ reads pc set A, and sets error to true to indicate bad read }
procedure readset(var A : pcset; var error : boolean);
  var
    pc     : integer;
  begin
    error := false;
    A := [];                         { begin with null set }
    while not eoln and not error do
      begin
        getpc(pc);                   { return pc integer    }
        if pc in [0 .. 11]
          then A := A + [pc]         { add pc to set        }
          else error := true;
        skipln
      end;
    readln
  end;

{ prints pc set in hexadecimal }
procedure printset(var A : pcset);
  var
    pc : pcint;
  begin
    for pc := 0 to 11 do
      if pc in A
        then write(tochar(pc))
  end;
```

The following procedures perform the standard transformations—transposition, inversion, M5, and M7—on pc sets:[6]

```
{   B <-- Tn(A)      }
procedure transpose(A : pcset; n : integer; var B : pcset);
  var
    pc : pcint;
  begin
    B := [];                    { null set }
    for pc := 0 to 11 do
      if pc in A
        then B := B + [(pc + n) mod 12]
  end;
```

6. The operations on pitch classes were described in chapter 6.

```
{    B <-- TnI(A)       }
procedure invert(A : pcset; n : integer; var B : pcset);
  var
    pc : pcint;
  begin
    B := [];                       { null set }
    for pc := 0 to 11 do
      if pc in A
        then B := B + [(n - pc + 12) mod 12]
  end;

{    B <-- TnM(A)       }
procedure m5(A : pcset; n : integer; var B : pcset);
  var
    pc : pcint;
  begin
    B := [];                       { null set }
    for pc := 0 to 11 do
      if pc in A
        then B := B + [((pc * 5) + n) mod 12]
  end;

{    B <-- TnMI(A)      }
procedure m7(A : pcset; n : integer; var B : pcset);
  var
    pc : pcint;
  begin
    B := [];                       { null set }
    for pc := 0 to 11 do
      if pc in A
        then B := B + [((pc * 7) + n) mod 12]
  end;
```

As an alternative to procedures *transpose*, *invert*, *m5*, and *m7*, we can write a generalized procedure *calc*(*A*, *op*, *n*, *B*) that multiplies each element of *A* by *op*, adds *n* (mod 12), and stores the result in *B*. This is called with $op = 1$ for identity [$B = T_n(A)$], $op = 11$ for inversion [$B = T_n I(A)$], $op = 5$ for M [$B = T_n M(A)$], $op = 7$ for MI [$B = T_n MI(A)$], where $0 \leq n \leq 11$:

```
{    B <-- TnMx(A), where x = 1, 11, 5, or 7     }
procedure calc(A : pcset; op, n : integer; var B : pcset);
  var
    pc : pcint;
  begin
    B := [];                       { null set }
    for pc := 0 to 11 do
      if pc in A
        then B := B + [((pc * op) + n) mod 12]
  end;
```

Testing for simple inclusion relationships is accomplished easily with standard set operations. The following function tests for abstract inclusion: it returns *true* if *B* maps into *A* under any level of transposition or transposition after inversion, i.e., if $T_n(B) \subset A$ or $T_n I(B) \subset A$, where $0 \leq n \leq 11$.

```
{ returns true if B is an abstract subset of A }
function subset(A, B : pcset) : boolean;
  var
    n     : integer;                  { transposition level }
    C, D  : pcset;
    found : boolean;
  begin
    found := false;
    n := 0;
    while (t <= 11) and not found do
      begin
        calc(B, 1, n, C);                   { C = Tn(B)  }
        calc(B, 11, n, D);                  { D = TnI(B) }
        found := (C <= A) or (D <= A);
        n := n + 1
      end;
    subset := found
  end;
```

Procedure *complement(A, B)* assigns to *B* the complement of *A*, using the set difference between the universal set and set *A*:

```
procedure complement(A : pcset; var B : pcset);
  begin
    B := [0 .. 11] - A
  end;
```

Program 12.2 illustrates many of these functions. Procedure *setmap* uses these techniques to calculate and print a table showing all transposition levels *n*, $0 \leq n \leq 11$, for which the operations T_n or T_nI map set *B* into *A*.

```
(***********************       Program Settest      ***********************)
(* Demonstrates procedures and functions for dealing with pitch-class    *)
(* sets using Pascal's set type.                                         *)
(*************************************************************************)
program settest(input, output);
  type
    pcint = 0 .. 11;
    pcset = set of pcint;

  var
    A, B : pcset;
    error : boolean;


(*************************************************************************)
(*                          Input Routines                                *)
(*************************************************************************)

  procedure incr(var x : integer);         { add one to argument          }
    begin
      x := x + 1
    end;
```

```
procedure skipln;                          { skip blanks in input buffer }
  begin
    while (input↑ = ' ') and not eoln do
      get(input)
  end;

function toint(c : char) : integer;        { conv hex char to pc int     }
  begin
    case c of
      '0' : toint := 0;
      '1' : toint := 1;
      '2' : toint := 2;
      '3' : toint := 3;
      '4' : toint := 4;
      '5' : toint := 5;
      '6' : toint := 6;
      '7' : toint := 7;
      '8' : toint := 8;
      '9' : toint := 9;
      'a' : toint := 10;
      'b' : toint := 11
     end { case }
  end;

function ispc(c : char) : boolean;      { true if c represents pc integer }
  begin
    ispc := c in ['0' .. '9', 'a', 'b']
  end;

procedure getpc(var x : integer);       { read pc, return -1 if error     }
  var
    c : char;
  begin
    skipln;
    if ispc(input↑)
      then
        begin
          read(c);
          x := toint(c)
        end
      else x := -1
  end;

{ reads pc set A, and sets error to true to indicate bad read           }
procedure readset(var A : pcset; var error : boolean);
  var
    pc    : integer;
  begin
    error := false;
    A := [];
    while not eoln and not error do
      begin
        getpc(pc);
        if pc in [0 .. 11]
          then A := A + [pc]
          else error := true;
        skipln
      end;
```

```
    readln                                  { discard newline character }
  end; { readset }


(**************************************************************************)
(*                          Output Routines                               *)
(**************************************************************************)

 function tochar(pc : integer) : char;       { converts int to hex char   }
  begin
   case pc of
     0 : tochar := '0';
     1 : tochar := '1';
     2 : tochar := '2';
     3 : tochar := '3';
     4 : tochar := '4';
     5 : tochar := '5';
     6 : tochar := '6';
     7 : tochar := '7';
     8 : tochar := '8';
     9 : tochar := '9';
    10 : tochar := 'a';
    11 : tochar := 'b'
   end { case }
  end;

 procedure writeset(var A : pcset);        { print pc set in hexadecimal }
  var
    pc : pcint;
  begin
    write('{');
    for pc := 0 to 11 do
      if pc in A
        then write(tochar(pc));
    write('}')
  end;

(**************************************************************************)
(*                     Set Manipulation Routines                          *)
(**************************************************************************)

 {  B <-- TnMx(A), where x = 1, 11, 5, or 7, and 0 <= n <= 11          }
 procedure calc(A : pcset; op, n : integer; var B : pcset);
  var
    pc : pcint;
  begin
    B := [];                    { null set }
    for pc := 0 to 11 do
      if pc in A
        then B := B + [((pc * op) + n) mod 12]
  end;

(**********************            setmap            **********************)
(* Prints a table showing transposition levels (n) for which Tn(B) or    *)
(* TnI(B) is a literal subset of A.                                       *)
(**************************************************************************)
```

```
procedure setmap(A, B : pcset);
  var
    n    : integer;
    C, D : pcset;
  begin
    writeln;
    writeln('All n for which Tn(B) or TnI(B) is included in A');
    writeln('================================================');
    writeln(' n      Tn       TnI');
    writeln('================================================');
    for n := 0 to 11 do
      begin
        write(' ', tochar(n));
        calc(B,  1, n, C);      { C = Tn(B)  }
        calc(B, 11, n, D);      { D = TnI(B) }
        if C <= A
          then write('      x        ')
          else write('               ');
        if D <= A
          then write(' x');
        writeln
      end;
    writeln('================================================')
  end;


(***********************          subset          ***********************)
(* Returns true if B is abstract subset of A.                            *)
(*************************************************************************)
function subset(A, B : pcset) : boolean;
  var
    n : integer;                       { transposition level            }
    C, D : pcset;                      { temporary variables for pc sets }
    found : boolean;                   { true when match has been found  }
  begin
    found := false;
    n := 0;
    while (n <= 11) and not found do
      begin
        calc(B,  1, n, C);                      { C = Tn(B)  }
        calc(B, 11, n, D);                      { D = TnI(B) }
        found := (C <= A) or (D <= A);
        n := n + 1
      end;
    subset := found
  end;


(***********************      main procedure      ***********************)
(* Exercises the pc-set manipulation routines above.                     *)
(*************************************************************************)
begin { main }
  write('Type set A: ');                               { prompt user     }
  while not eof do
    begin
      readset(A, error);                               { read pc set A   }
```

```
        while error do                                    { reread if error }
          begin
            writeln('Input error');
            write('Please retype set A: ');
            readset(A, error)
          end;
        write('Type set B: ');                            { read pc set A    }
        readset(B, error);                                { read pc set B    }
        while error do                                    { reread if error }
          begin
            writeln('Input error');
            write('Please retype set B: ');
            readset(B, error)                             { read set A       }
          end;
        writeln;
        write('set A = '); writeset(A); writeln;          { echo sets        }
        write('set B = '); writeset(B); writeln;
        setmap(A, B);                           { find all n for which Tn(B) }
                                                { or TnI(B) is included in A }
        writeln;
        if subset(A, B)
          then writeln('B is a subset of A')
          else writeln('B is not a subset of A');
        writeln;
        write('Type set A: ')                             { prompt user      }
      end
  end. { main }
```

Program 12.2. *Settest*

```
        Type set A: 01478
        Type set B: a12

        set A = {01478}
        set B = {12a}

        All n for which Tn(B) or TnI(B) is included in A
        =================================================
         n      Tn        TnI
        =================================================
         0
         1
         2                 x
         3
         4
         5
         6      x
         7
         8
         9
         a
         b
        =================================================
```

```
B is a subset of A

Type set A: 046a97136
Type set B: 014

set A = {0134679a}
set B = {014}

All n for which Tn(B) or TnI(B) is included in A
================================================
n     Tn        TnI
================================================
0      x
1               x
2
3      x
4               x
5
6      x
7               x
8
9      x
a               x
b
================================================

B is a subset of A

Type set A: ba9876543210
Type set B: 13592

set A = {0123456789ab}
set B = {12359}

All n for which Tn(B) or TnI(B) is included in A
================================================
n     Tn        TnI
================================================
0      x         x
1      x         x
2      x         x
3      x         x
4      x         x
5      x         x
6      x         x
7      x         x
8      x         x
9      x         x
a      x         x
b      x         x
================================================

B is a subset of A

Type set A: 38952xu3
Input error
Please retype set A: wq
```

```
Input error
Please retype set A: 02468a
Type set B: 901f
Input error
Please retype set B: 026

set A = {02468a}
set B = {026}

All n for which Tn(B) or TnI(B) is included in A
================================================
n     Tn       TnI
================================================
0      x        x
1
2      x        x
3
4      x        x
5
6      x        x
7
8      x        x
9
a      x        x
b
================================================

B is a subset of A

Type set A: ^D
```

Program 12.2. Sample Run (Interactive)

References and Selected Readings

If you are working in a language other than Pascal, you probably do not have a set type. You can implement similar operations using binary numbers. The following sources explore binary operations on pc sets in the C programming language:

Harris, Craig R., and Alexander R. Brinkman. "An Integrated Software System for Set-Theoretic and Serial Analysis of Contemporary Music." *Journal of Computer-Based Instruction* 16, no. 2 (1989): 59–70.

Harris, Craig R., and Alexander R. Brinkman. *Contemporary Music Analysis Package (CMAP) Reference Manual.* San Francisco: Craig Harris Consulting, Ltd., 1987.

The following source details several different representations of sets that could be implemented in many different languages:

Aho, Alfred V., John E. Hopcroft, and Jeffrey D. Ullman. *Data Structures and Algorithms.* Reading, Mass.: Addison-Wesley, 1983.

The following contains a description of Forte's K/Kh relations (exercise 12.6):

Forte, Allen. *The Structure of Atonal Music.* New Haven, Conn.: Yale University Press, 1973.

Other suggested readings:

Lewin, David. "On Partial Ordering." *Perspectives of New Music* 14, no. 2 and 15, no. 1 (1976): 252–59.

Lockwood, Lewis. "A Stylistic Investigation of the Masses of Josquin Desprez with the Aid of the Computer: A Progress Report." In *Musicology and the Computer*, edited by Barry S. Brook, 19–27. New York: City University of New York Press, 1970.

Morris, Robert. "Combinatoriality without the Aggregate." *Perspectives of New Music* 21, nos. 1 and 2 (1982/83): 432–86.

———. "Set-Type Saturation among Twelve-Tone Rows." *Perspectives of New Music* 22, nos. 1 and 2 (1983–84): 187–217.

Snell, James L. "Design for a Formal System for Deriving Tonal Music." M.A. thesis, State University of New York, Binghamton, 1979.

Winograd, Terry. "Linguistics and the Computer Analysis of Tonal Harmony." *Journal of Music Theory* 12, no. 1 (1968): 2–49.

Exercises

1. Study program 12.1 carefully until you understand all of the set operators, and then work through the program manually, comparing your calculated output to the output shown.

2. Write a program that reads DARMS articulation codes in the form:

'	=	staccato
"	=	wedge accent
–	=	tenuto
>	=	accent
<	=	vertical accent
;	=	fermata

Your program should read the articulation codes as characters and store all concatenated codes on an input line as a set of articulation marks defined in chapter 12. Each articulation that occurs in the set should then be converted to character data and printed to test your procedures. A skeleton program is provided below. You will need to complete all procedures and functions and test the program.

```
program artictest(input, output);

  type
    articmark = (staccato, wedgeaccent, tenuto, accent, vaccent,
                                                          fermata);
    artictype = set of articmark;

  var
    articulation : artictype;

  procedure skip;
    begin
    end;
```

```
function isartic(c : char) : boolean;
  begin
  end;

procedure readartic(var A : artictype);
  begin
  end;

procedure writemark(x : articmark);
  begin
  end;

procedure writeartic(x : artictype);
  begin
  end;

begin { main }
  write('Type codes: ');
  while not eof do
    begin
      readartic(articulation);
      readln;
      writeartic(articulation);
      writeln;
      write('Type codes: ')
    end
end. { main }
```

3. Study program 12.2 carefully until you thoroughly understand the operations on pc sets. Then work through the program manually, comparing your calculated output to the output shown.

4. Calculating Invariance Vectors. Robert Morris's invariance vector is an array that shows the invariant properties of a set. The first four positions list the number of times the set maps into itself under the operations $T_n(S)$, $T_nI(S)$, $T_nM(S)$, and $T_nMI(S)$, for $0 \le n \le 11$. The next four positions show the number of times the set maps into its complement under the same operations. Your assignment is to use the Pascal set operators to calculate this vector. In addition to procedures *readset*, *writeset*, and *calc*, which we saw in section 12.3, you will need the following (procedure headings shown):

   procedure *invector*(**var** *A* : *pcset*; **var** *V* : *invec*); — calculates the invariance vector for set *A*, storing the result in *V*, where *invec* = **array**[1 .. 8] **of** *integer*.

   procedure *printvector*(**var** *v* : *invector*); — prints the invariance vector.

   Your program should prompt the user for a set, read and echo the set, and print the invariance vector. The sets and vector should be printed in hexadecimal notation. The program should loop so that it can process any number of sets.

5. Study the use of sets to implement articulation in the DARMS interpreter shown in appendix C.

6. Allen Forte's K/KH relation[7] is a model of relations among pc set classes based on

7. Allen Forte, *The Structure of Atonal Music* (New Haven, Conn.: Yale University Press, 1973).

subset/superset relations among complexes of pairs of complementary set classes. The relations are defined for any two sets S and T, of cardinality greater than 2 and less than 10, where the cardinality of S is not equal to the cardinality of T or of $\bar{T}$ (the complement of T).

The K relation is defined as follows: The pair of set classes consisting of S and its complement $\bar{S}$ is a member of the set complex about T and its complement $\bar{T}$ if and only if S can contain or can be contained in T, *or* S can contain or can be contained in $\bar{T}$. This is formalized as follows:

$$S/\bar{S} \in K(T, \bar{T}) \text{ iff } S \supset\subset T \mid S \supset\subset \bar{T}$$

The Kh relation is similar: The pair of set classes consisting of S and its complement $\bar{S}$ is a member of the set complex about T and its complement $\bar{T}$ if and only if S can contain or can be contained in T, *and* S can contain or can be contained in $\bar{T}$:

$$S/\bar{S} \in Kh(T, \bar{T}) \text{ iff } S \supset\subset T \ \& \ S \supset\subset \bar{T}$$

The property "can contain or can be contained in" may be tested with the abstract subset relation implemented by function *subset* in section 12.3. Thus you have the requisite tools to calculate these relations. The table shown below was generated by a program written by the author and included in a commercially available software package.[8] Although the relationship as defined applies to complement pairs, only the specified sets are actually shown in the table, and complements are paired. Thus the table represents a model of the set classes specified as input to the program. As in Forte, the asterisk indicates the K relation with a six-note Z-related set, where only one set from the Z-related pair actually occurs in the composition.

Type set names: **4-8 4-9 4-15 8-15 8-28 5-6 7-6 5-7 5-19 6-6 6-38 6-13**

	4-8	4-9	8-15 4-15	5-6	7-7 5-7	5-19	6-38 6-6	6-13	8-28
4-8				Kh	Kh	K	Kh		
4-9				K	Kh	Kh	Kh	K*	
4-15/8-15				Kh	K	Kh	K	K*	
5-6	Kh	K	Kh				K		
5-7 /7-7	Kh	Kh	K				Kh		
5-19	K	Kh	Kh					K*	K
6-6 /6-38	Kh	Kh	K	K	Kh				
6-13		K*	K*			K*			K*
8-28						K		K*	

Program KH. Sample Run (Interactive)

Accepting set names as input requires devising a method for converting set names to pc sets. The program can be simplified somewhat by entering pc sets rather than set names, and by omitting the check for complementary Z-related sets.

8. Craig R. Harris and Alexander R. Brinkman, *Contemporary Music Analysis Package (CMAP)* (San Francisco: Craig Harris Consulting, Ltd., 1987).

13| Record Types

Thus far we have seen two structured data types: arrays and sets. While arrays are ordered collections, and sets are unordered, each represents a group of elements that must be all the same declared type. Pascal's record type enables us to treat related data as a single complex item, even though specific data elements may be of different simple types or other structured types. Consider, for example, the data required to represent a musical note. If the data is to be used for different purposes (printing, synthesis, analysis, etc.), we might wish to store many types of information about it, e.g., frequency (in cps), starting time, duration (as a fraction), the name class, pitch class, and octave (as integer values), the instrument name (as a character string), the dynamic (as a user-defined ordinal type), etc.

13.1 Fixed Records

A record is a data structure with various elements called *fields*, each of which may have its own type. Records are declared with other user-defined types in the type declaration section of a program or subprogram. The syntax of a record declaration is shown in figure 13.1, where <recordtype> is an identifier that will be used to identify the record type, **record** and **end** are Pascal reserved words marking the beginning and end of the record definition, and <fieldlist> is a list of field declarations. Optionally the reserved word **record** may be preceded by **packed**. This will result in saving memory space at the cost of speed on some systems. The field list takes the form

$$\begin{array}{l} fieldname_1 : fieldtype_1; \\ fieldname_2 : fieldtype_2; \\ \ldots \\ fieldname_n : fieldtype_n \end{array}$$

```
[type]

    <recordtype>    = [packed] record
                                 <fieldlist>
                               end;
```

Figure 13.1. SYNTAX: Record Definition

where $fieldname_1$ $fieldname_2$, . . ., $fieldname_n$ are the names of fields in the record, and $fieldtype_1$, $fieldtype_2$, . . ., $fieldtype_n$ are types for each field. Note that field definitions use exactly the same format as variable definitions, and that the alternate form, in which fields of the same type are listed together, is also permissible:

$$fieldname_1, fieldname_2, \ldots, fieldname_n : fieldtype;$$

Field names are any legal identifier, and field types may be any standard Pascal type (*integer*, *char*, *real*, *boolean*), pointer types, enumerated types, subrange types, or structured types (arrays, sets, other records, etc). Once a record type has been defined, it is used in type declarations just like any other predefined or user-defined type.

Assuming that we had already defined the structured components:

```
type
  string = packed array[1 .. maxstring] of char;
  dyntype = (ppppp, pppp, ppp, pp, p, mp, mf, f, ff, fff, ffff,
                                                          fffff);

  fraction = record
               num : integer;         { numerator    }
               den : integer          { denominator  }
             end;
```

we could then define type *note* as follows:[1]

```
  note = record
           frequency  : real;
           octave     : integer;
           pc         : integer;
           nc         : integer;
           starttime  : fraction;
           duration   : fraction;
           dynamic    : dyntype;
           instrument : string
         end;
```

Type *note* can now be used to declare other types:

```
  tunetype : array[1 .. max] of note;
```

and to declare variables:

```
var
  x, y  : note;
  tune  : tunetype;
```

Two operations are defined for whole records: assignment and field selection. Entire records may be assigned in one assignment statement. For example, if x and y have been defined as shown above, $x := y$ assigns all of the values in record y to

1. This record structure is intended as an illustration, and is not meant to be definitive.

record *x*. Individual fields are referenced by the name of the variable followed by a dot (period) and the field name. We can refer to individual fields as *x.frequency*, *x.duration*, *x.dynamic*, etc. Structured elements may be referred to in whole or in part. *X.instrument* refers to the *instrument* field (a packed array of characters), while *x.instrument*[*i*] refers to the *i*th character in that field; *x.duration* references the duration record (type *fraction*), while the numerator and denominator of the fraction are referenced by *x.duration.num* and *x.duration.den.*

Similarly, if *tune* has been declared as an array of records of type *note*, then *tune*[*i*] references the *i*th element (an entire record of type *note*). Thus *tune*[1] is the first note in the tune, *tune*[1]*.frequency* is its cycles per second, *tune*[1]*.instrument* is the string containing the instrument name, *tune*[1]*.instrument*[*i*] is the *i*th character in the instrument name, etc.

In practice, it is not usually necessary to refer to subelements. It is easier, and better programming style, to write procedures that deal separately with the desired portion of a record. Frequently it is convenient to use a separate procedure for each field that is not a simple type.[2] We might create procedure *readnote*(*N*), which would read a single note. This procedure could call *readstring*(*N.instrument*) to read the instrument name, and might be called by procedure *readtune*(*T*), which would call *readnote*(*tune*[*i*]) for each element of the tune. Program 13.1 illustrates procedures to read and write a tune with the data structures described above. The excerpt in figure 13.2 serves as input data.

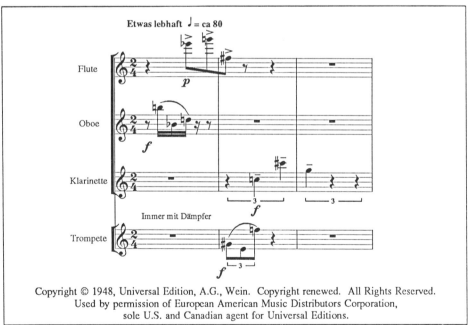

Figure 13.2. Anton Webern: Concerto, Op. 24, first movement, mm. 1–3[3]

2. For this reason I do not recommend using packed records. Many compilers do not allow elements of packed structures to be passed as **var** parameters.

3. The following parts have rests and are not shown: horn, trombone, violin, viola, and piano.

```
(***********************        Program Tuneio      ***********************)
(* Illustrates procedures to read and write a series of notes stored in  *)
(* an array of records.                                                   *)
(*************************************************************************)
program tuneio(input, output);
  const
    max = 100;
    maxstring = 15;

  type
    string = packed array[1 .. maxstring] of char;
    dyntype = (ppppp, pppp, ppp, pp, p, mp, mf, f, ff, fff, ffff, fffff);

    fraction = record
                 num : integer;                              { numerator    }
                 den : integer                               { denominator  }
               end;

    note     = record
                 octave     : integer;
                 pc         : integer;
                 nc         : integer;
                 frequency  : real;
                 starttime  : fraction;
                 duration   : fraction;
                 dynamic    : dyntype;
                 instrument : string
               end;

    tunetype = array[1 .. max] of note;

  var
    tune : tunetype;
    n    : integer;

  procedure incr(var x : integer);                 { increment argument }
    begin
      x := x + 1
    end;

(*************************************************************************)
(*                           Input Routines                              *)
(*************************************************************************)
  procedure skip;                                  { skip blanks in input }
    var
      done : boolean;
    begin
      done := false;
      repeat
        if eof
          then done := true
        else if input↑ = ' '
          then get(input)
        else done := true
      until done
    end;
```

```
procedure readstring(var S : string);              { read string            }

  var
    i : integer;

  begin
    skip;
    i := 1;
    while input↑ <> ' ' do
      begin
        read(S[i]);
        incr(i)
      end;
    S[i] := chr(0)
  end;


procedure readdynamic(var D : dyntype);            { read dynamic           }

  var
    count  : integer;
    symbol : char;

  begin
    skip;
    if input↑ = 'm'
      then
        begin
          get(input);
          if input↑ = 'f'
            then D := mf
            else D := mp;
          get(input)             { skip second char }
        end
    else if (input↑ = 'f') or (input↑ = 'p')
      then
        begin
          read(symbol);
          count := 1;
          while input↑ = symbol do
            begin
              incr(count);
              get(input)
            end;
          if symbol = 'f'
            then
              case count of
                1 : D := f;
                2 : D := ff;
                3 : D := fff;
                4 : D := ffff;
                5 : D := fffff
              end { case }
          else if symbol = 'p'
            then
              case count of
                1 : D := p;
                2 : D := pp;
                3 : D := ppp;
```

```
                4 : D := pppp;
                5 : D := ppppp
              end { case }
         end
   end;  { readdynamic }


  procedure readfrac(var F : fraction);                  { read a fraction        }
    begin
      read(F.num);
      skip;
      if input↑ in ['/', ':']
        then get(input);               { skip / }
      read(F.den)
    end;


  procedure readnote(var N : note);                      { read values for note }
    begin
      read(N.octave, N.pc, N.nc, N.frequency);
      readfrac(N.starttime);
      readfrac(N.duration);
      readdynamic(N.dynamic);
      readstring(N.instrument);
      readln
    end;
                                                         { read and count notes }

  procedure readtune(var tune : tunetype; var n : integer);
    begin
      n := 0;
      while not eof do
        begin
          incr(n);
          readnote(tune[n]);
          skip
        end
    end;



(***********************************************************************)
(*                         Output Routines                             *)
(***********************************************************************)

  procedure writestring(var S : string);                 { write string          }
    var
      i : integer;
    begin
      i := 1;
      while S[i] <> chr(0) do
        begin
          write(S[i]);
          incr(i)
        end
    end;
```

```
procedure writedynamic(var D : dyntype);            { print dynamic level }
  begin
    case D of
      ppppp : write('ppppp');
      pppp  : write('pppp ');
      ppp   : write('ppp  ');
      pp    : write('pp   ');
      p     : write('p    ');
      mp    : write('mp   ');
      mf    : write('mf   ');
      f     : write('f    ');
      ff    : write('ff   ');
      fff   : write('fff  ');
      ffff  : write('ffff ');
      fffff : write('fffff')
    end { case }
  end;

procedure writefrac(var F : fraction);              { print fraction      }
  begin
    write(F.num:4);
    write(' /');
    write(F.den:3)
  end;

procedure writenote(var N : note);                  { print field values  }
  begin
    write(N.octave:5, N.pc:5, N.nc:5, N.frequency:12:3);
    writefrac(N.starttime);
    writefrac(N.duration);
    write('    ');
    writedynamic(N.dynamic);
    write('  ');
    writestring(N.instrument);
    writeln
  end;

                                   { print tune stored in array of records }
procedure writetune(var tune : tunetype; n : integer);
  var
    i : integer;
  begin
    for i := 1 to n do
      writenote(tune[i])
  end;

(***********************        main procedure      ***********************)
(* Exercises the above procedures.                                        *)
(**************************************************************************)
begin { main }
  readtune(tune, n);                                       { read tune  }
  writetune(tune, n)                                       { print tune }
end.  { main }
```

Program 13.1. *Tuneio*

Input:

```
5 11  6     987.77   1/8    1/16  f   oboe
4 10  6     466.16   3/16   1/16  f   oboe
5  2  1     587.33   1/4    1/16  f   oboe
6  3  2    1244.50   1/4    1/8   f   flute
6  7  4    1568.00   3/8    1/8   f   flute
5  6  3     739.99   1/2    1/8   f   flute
4  8  4     415.30   1/2    1/12  f   trumpet
4  4  2     329.63   7/12   1/12  f   trumpet
5  5  4     698.46   2/3    1/12  f   trumpet
5  0  0     523.25   2/3    1/6   f   clarinet
6  1  0    1108.70   5/6    1/6   mp  clarinet
5  9  5     880.00   1/1    1/6   p   clarinet
```

Output:

```
5   11   6     987.770   1 /  8   1 / 16   f      oboe
4   10   6     466.160   3 / 16   1 / 16   f      oboe
5    2   1      73.416   1 /  4   1 / 16   f      oboe
6    3   2    1244.500   1 /  4   1 /  8   f      flute
6    7   4    1568.000   3 /  8   1 /  8   f      flute
5    6   3     739.990   1 /  2   1 /  8   f      flute
4    8   4     415.300   1 /  2   1 / 12   f      trumpet
4    4   2     329.630   7 / 12   1 / 12   f      trumpet
5    5   4     698.460   2 /  3   1 / 12   f      trumpet
5    0   0     523.250   2 /  3   1 /  6   f      clarinet
6    1   0    1108.700   5 /  6   1 /  6   mp     clarinet
5    9   5     880.000   1 /  1   1 /  6   p      clarinet
```

Program 13.1. Sample Input and Output

13.1.1 Anonymous Records

It is possible to declare record types without naming them. This is not recommended except when the record is to be used only in one program block, since unnamed types cannot be passed to procedures and functions as arguments. Anonymous records are declared in the variable declaration part of the program or as part of a record definition. The array of records declared in program 13.1 could be declared

```
var
  tune : array[1 .. max] of
    record
      frequency  : real;
      octave     : integer;
      pc         : integer;
      nc         : integer;

      starttime = record
                    num : integer;
                    den : integer
                  end;
```

```
duration    : record
                num : integer;
                den : integer
              end;

dynamic     : (ppppp, pppp, ppp, pp, p, mp, mf, f, ff, fff, ffff,
                                                            fffff);
instrument  : packed array[1 .. maxstring] of char;
end;
```

Since none of the types are named, it would not be possible to pass fields of each element of the array to separate procedures for processing.

13.1.2 The **with** Statement

When several fields in the same record must be referenced, the repetition of higher levels of the qualified name can be tedious. Pascal provides a means of abbreviation called the **with** statement. The general form of this statement is shown in figure 13.3, where <identifiers> is a single identifier or a list of identifiers in the form

$$identifier_1, identifier_2, \ldots, identifier_n$$

and <statement> is a simple statement or a structured statement (**for**, **repeat**, **case**, compound statement, etc.). The most common form uses the single identifier. For example, in procedure *readnote* in program 13.1, the statements

```
read(N.octave, N.pc, N.nc, N.frequency);
readfrac(N.starttime);
readfrac(N.duration);
readdynamic(N.dynamic);
readstring(N.instrument);
readln
```

could be rewritten as

```
with N do
  begin
    read(octave, pc, nc, frequency);
    readfrac(starttime);
    readfrac(duration);
    readdynamic(dynamic);
    readstring(instrument);
    readln
  end
```

```
with <identifiers> do
  <statement>
```

Figure 13.3. SYNTAX: The **with** Statement

Note that the compound statement is necessary, since the scope of the **with** is a single statement.

With statements can also be nested, as in the following example. Where *tune* is an array of *notes* (as defined in the previous section), the program statements

```
tune[i].octave := 4;
tune[i].pc := 9;
tune[i].nc := 5;
tune[i].frequency := 440;
tune[i].duration.num := 3;
tune[i].duration.den := 8;
tune[i].instrument := 'clarinet  '
```

can be rewritten as

```
with tune[i] do
  begin
    octave := 4;
    pc := 9;
    nc := 5;
    frequency := 440;
    with duration do
      begin
        num := 3;
        den := 8
      end;
    instrument := 'clarinet  '
  end;
```

When multiple levels of qualification are necessary, the form of the **with** statement using a multiidentifier list can be used. The following program segment is equivalent to the one just above. Note that the compiler is capable of determining the level of qualification necessary for each field.

```
with tune[i], duration do
  begin
    octave := 4;
    pc := 9;
    nc := 5;
    frequency := 440;
    num := 3;
    den := 8
    instrument := 'clarinet  '
  end;
```

One must be careful to use unique identifiers within the scope of a **with** statement. It is permissible to assign fields of a record to simple variables with identical names, as in the following segment:

```
[ var
    octave, pc, nc : integer;  ]

octave := N.octave;
pc     := N.pc;
nc     := N.nc;
```

But the short form would be ambiguous:

```
{ WRONG }

with N do
  begin
    octave := octave;
    pc     := pc;
    nc     := nc
  end;
```

Although judicious use of the **with** statement can help to clarify program structure and make programs easier to write and to read, the **with** statement is more than a convenience for the programmer. Its use enables the compiler to generate more efficient code.

13.2 Procedures for Rational Arithmetic

As we have seen in earlier chapters, computers represent real numbers with only limited accuracy. In many applications it is important to know the exact result of calculations. This is particularly true in situations where rounding errors accumulate. Exact results can be obtained by using computation based on fractions rather than floating-point approximations. The methods shown below produce results without any accumulated rounding error. As we implied in the previous section, fractions can be represented with a record defined as follows:

```
fraction =
  record
    num : integer;      { numerator   }
    den : integer       { denominator }
  end;
```

We can represent any fractional value exactly, using this structure, since the numerator and denominator are stored as integers. If *x* has been declared a fraction, then the number 0 is represented by the <*x.num, x.den*> duple <0, 1>; the integer 1 is represented by <1, 1> and any other fraction by <*x.num, x.den*>, where *x.num* and *x.den* are relatively prime. Any nonzero whole number results in a fraction in which *x.num* <> 0 and *x.den* = 1. Negative fractions are represented by a negative numerator.

We only need a few basic procedures to manipulate fractions in this form. The first two, which we saw in the last section of this chapter, read and write fractions:

```
procedure fracread(var x : fraction);
  begin
    read(x.num);
    skip;
    if input↑ in ['/', ':']
      then get(input);
    read(x.den)
  end;
```

```
procedure fracwrite(x : fraction);      { write fraction }
  begin
    write(x.num:4,' /', x.den:4, ' ':4)
  end;
```

If we wish to convert a fraction to its approximate real value, we can use the following function:

```
function toreal(x : fraction) : real;      { convert fraction to real }
  begin
    toreal := x.num / x.den
  end;
```

If real results are required, this function can be used after all computations have been made without loss of accuracy.

Algorithms dealing with fractions often require a procedure to find the greatest common divisor between two numbers. The function shown below is based on a modern rendering of Euclid's algorithm. Since the algorithm requires $x \geq y$, we check for this condition and exchange x and y if necessary:

```
procedure swap(var x, y : integer);      { exchange values of x and y }
  var
    t : integer;
  begin
    t := x; x := y; y := t
  end;

function gcd(x, y : integer) : integer;  { greatest common divisor     }
  var
    t : integer;
  begin
    x := abs(x);
    y := abs(y);
    if y > x
      then swap(x, y);
    while y <> 0 do                     { find greatest common divisor }
      begin
        t := x mod y;
        x := y;
        y := t
      end;
    gcd := x
  end;
```

Although the arithmetic procedures shown below return their results in reduced form, it is sometimes necessary to reduce fractions explicitly. When we wish to ensure that a fraction is in reduced form, i.e., that the numerator and denominator are relatively prime, the following procedure is useful:

```
procedure reduce(var x : fraction);
  var
    t : integer;
```

```
begin { reduce }
  t := gcd(x.num, x.den);
  if t > 1
    then
      begin
        x.num := x.num div t;
        x.den := x.den div t
      end
end;  { reduce }
```

The following procedures perform multiplication, division, addition, and subtraction of fractions. It would be convenient to write these as functions, but most versions of Pascal do not allow functions to return user-defined types. The first procedure multiplies fractions *a* and *b*, returning the result as fraction *c*. The result is in reduced form.

```
{ performs c := a * b , where a, b, and c are fractions }
procedure fracmult(var c : fraction; a : fraction; b : fraction);
  var
    d1, d2 : integer;
  begin
    d1 := gcd(a.num, b.den);       { multiplication procedure        }
    d2 := gcd(a.den, b.num);
    c.num := (a.num div d1) * (b.num div d2);
    c.den := (a.den div d2) * (b.den div d1)
  end;  { fracmult }
```

Division consists of inverting the second fraction, adjusting the signs if necessary, and then multiplying:

```
{ performs c := a / b , where a, b, and c are fractions }
procedure fracdiv(var c : fraction; a : fraction; b : fraction);
  begin
    swap(b.num, b.den);                 { invert second fraction   }
    if b.den < 0                        {    get the signs right   }
      then
        begin { switch signs }
          b.num := -b.num;
          b.den := -b.den
        end;  { switch signs }
    fracmult(c, a, b)                   { and then multiply        }
  end;  { fracdiv }
```

The following procedure adds fractions *a* and *b*, returning the result in *c*. The result is in reduced form:

```
{ performs c := a + b , where a, b, and c are fractions }
procedure fracadd(var c : fraction; a : fraction; b : fraction);
  var
    d1, d2, t : integer;
  begin
    d1 := gcd(a.den, b.den);            { addition procedure        }
```

```
    if d1 = 1
      then
        begin
          c.num := a.num *  b.den + a.den * b.num;
          c.den := a.den * b.den
        end
      else
        begin
          t := a.num * (b.den div d1) + b.num * (a.den div d1);
          d2 := gcd(t, d1);
          c.num := t div d2;
          c.den := (a.den div d1) * (b.den div d2)
        end
  end;  { fracadd }
```

Subtraction consists of negating the second fraction and then adding:

```
{ performs c := a - b , where a, b, and c are fractions }
procedure fracsub(var c : fraction; a : fraction; b : fraction);
  begin
    b.num := -b.num;                         { negate second fraction }
    fracadd(c, a, b)                         { and then add           }
  end;  { fracsub }
```

The following boolean functions compare fractions:

```
function equal(x, y : fraction) : boolean;          { true if x = y }
  begin
    equal := (x.num * y.den) = (y.num * x.den)
  end;

function greater(x, y : fraction) : boolean;        { true if x > y }
  begin
    greater := (x.num * y.den) > (y.num * x.den)
  end;

function lessthan(x, y : fraction) : boolean;       { true if x < y }
  begin
    lessthan := (x.num * y.den) < (y.num * x.den)
  end;
```

13.3 Rational Duration Representation (rdr)

In earlier chapters we used real numbers to approximate the fractional value of music durations, and accommodated round-off errors by checking computed values, e.g., the total of the durations in a measure, by comparing the difference between the actual value and the expected value to a small error tolerance *epsilon*:

```
if abs(measuretotal - barduration) > epsilon
  then <there is an a duration error in measure>
```

The floating-point approximation of fractions is not adequate if we need to track temporal position in a composition with a high degree of accuracy, because real numbers cannot represent many fractions perfectly. (Recall that 1/3 + 1/3 + 1/3 is *not* exactly equal to 1.000 in the floating-point representation.) While the round-off error may be small, it is cumulative and may become intolerable over the course of a large composition, particularly if complex rhythms are used.

By using the techniques described in the previous section, we can do calculations with absolute accuracy. Any notated duration can be represented accurately as a fraction. Consider the example in table 13.1. On close examination, several relationships become apparent. For example, the sum of the fractions in each measure is equal to the fractional value of the meter signature, and the sum of the fractions in each grouplet is equal to the duration it replaces; e.g., the triplet in the second measure is equal to 1/12 + 1/12 + 1/12 = 3/12 = 1/4. Other relationships are described below.

The meter signature M is equal to the number of beats in the measure n times the beat note β:

$$M = n \times \beta$$

The fractional value of M is equal to the sum of the fractional durations, $f_1, f_2, \ldots, f_n$, in each bar:

$$M = \sum_{i=1}^{n} f_i$$

Meter	3/4			1/1	3/4
Fraction	1/4	1/2 1/4	1/4 1/12 1/12 1/12 1/8 1/8	1/4 1/12 1/6 3/8 1/8	1/4 1/4
Raw time	0/1	1/4 3/4	1/1 5/4 4/3 17/12 3/2 13/8	7/4 2/1 25/12 9/4 21/8	11/4 3/1
Fraction sum	1/4	3/4	3/4	1/1	2/4
Part of meas.	1/3	2/3 1/3	1/3 1/9 1/9 1/9 1/6 1/6	1/4 1/12 1/6 3/8 1/8	1/3 1/3
Measure time	2/3	1/1 5/3	2/1 7/3 22/9 23/9 8/3 17/6	3/1 13/1 10/3 7/2 31/8	4/1 13/3
Beats per dur.	1/1	2/1 1/1	1/1 1/3 1/3 1/3 1/2 1/2	1/1 1/3 2/3 3/2 1/2	1/1 1/1
Beats per meas.	1/1	3/1	3/1	4/1	2/1

Table 13.1 Rational Duration Representation (rdr)

The duration in beats (δ) represented by each fractional duration (f) is equal to the duration divided by the beat note (β):

$$\delta = \frac{f}{\beta}$$

The fraction of a measure μ represented by each fractional duration f is equal to the duration divided by the meter M:

$$\mu = \frac{f}{\mathrm{M}}$$

The position in the piece after the nth duration is equal to the sum of durations 1 through n. If we use the fractional value of the notes to make the calculations, we call this *raw time*:

$$raw\ time = \sum_{i=1}^{n} f_i$$

Raw time begins at 0/1 at the beginning of a piece. The time at the beginning of each note or rest is equal to the time at the end of the previous note or rest.

The position can be calculated with the part-of-measure fractions (μ). In this case we call the position *measure time*. The initial starting time is set to 1/1 less the value of the anacrusis, so that the position at the beginning of each measure will be a whole number in the form (m/1), where m is the measure number:

$$measure\ time = initial\ time + \sum_{i=1}^{n} \mu_i$$

An approximation of the current position in a piece can be obtained by converting *measure time* to a real number. For example, 21.250 indicates a position a quarter of the way into measure 21. Alternately, the current position in the measure can be converted to beats by multiplying the fractional part of the measure (in this case .25) by the number of beats in the measure.

13.4 Grouplets in rdr

The fractional value of notes in grouplets is calculated by multiplying the normal fractional duration by the characteristic ratio for the grouplet. This ratio, R, is calculated by dividing the actual duration of the grouplet by the total of the durations that will replace it:

$$R = \frac{D}{T}$$

In the triplet in measure 2 of table 13.1, the normal quarter note (1/4) is replaced by three eighth notes (3/8). Thus the characteristic ratio for this grouplet is

$$R = \frac{1}{4} \div \frac{3}{8} = \frac{1}{4} \times \frac{8}{3} = \frac{2}{3}$$

In other words, each duration in the grouplet will get 2/3 of its normal value. Thus each triplet eighth note has a fractional value of 1/12:

$$\frac{1}{8} \times \frac{2}{3} = \frac{1}{12}$$

When grouplets are nested, e.g., a triplet within a quintuplet, the ratio for the nested grouplet is multiplied by the ratio for the external grouplet. Consider the quintuplet shown below:

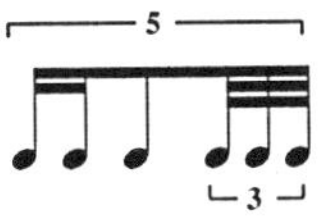

The ratio for the quintuplet is calculated

$$R_1 = \frac{1}{4} \div \frac{5}{16} = \frac{1}{4} \times \frac{16}{5} = \frac{4}{5}$$

and the ratio for the nested triplet is

$$R_2 = \frac{1}{16} \div \frac{3}{32} \times R_1 = \frac{1}{16} \times \frac{32}{3} \times \frac{4}{5} = \frac{8}{15}$$

All of the fractional durations in the quintuplet can be determined as follows:

$$\frac{1}{16} \times R_1 + \frac{1}{16} \times R_1 + \frac{1}{8} \times R_1 + \frac{1}{32} \times R_2 + \frac{1}{32} \times R_2 + \frac{1}{32} \times R_2$$

$$= \frac{1}{16} \times \frac{4}{5} + \frac{1}{16} \times \frac{4}{5} + \frac{1}{8} \times \frac{4}{5} + \frac{1}{32} \times \frac{8}{15} + \frac{1}{32} \times \frac{8}{15} + \frac{1}{32} \times \frac{8}{15}$$

$$= \frac{1}{20} + \frac{1}{20} + \frac{1}{10} + \frac{1}{60} + \frac{1}{60} + \frac{1}{60} = \frac{15}{60} = \frac{1}{4}$$

13.5 Application: Interpreting DARMS Duration Codes

Converting DARMS duration codes into rdr is not difficult.[4] For simple duration codes, the numerator is set to 1 and the denominator is set according to the duration code—8 for *E*, 4 for *Q*, etc. The value of *dot* is assigned half the duration of the note. If the duration code is followed by a dot, the fractional value for *dot* is added to the duration, and the value of *dot* is halved. This process is repeated for any number of dots, as shown in table 13.2.

The decoding of beamed notes is shown in table 13.3. Recall that the beginnings and ends of beams are signified by left and right parentheses. The default fractional value (unbeamed) is set initially to 1/4. This is called level 0 to indicate the absence of parentheses (or beams). Whenever a left parenthesis is encountered, the

4. The reader may wish to review section 6.5.2, which deals with DARMS encoding of rhythm.

	Q.. [♩..]	= 1/4 + 1/8 + 1/16	
Calculation:	*Duration*		*Dot*
duration code:	dur = 1/4		dot = 1/8
add 1st dot:	dur = 1/4 + 1/8 = 3/8		dot = 1/16
add 2d dot:	dur = 3/8 + 1/16 = 7/16		dot = 1/32
final value:	7/16		

Table 13.2. Converting DARMS Duration Codes to RDR

denominator of the default is multiplied by 2 and 1 is added to the level. When a right parenthesis is encountered, the denominator is divided by 2 and the level is decremented by 1. The level is always equal to the number of beams and the default duration is correct. The values of dots are calculated as described above, and the terminal value of the parenthesis level, if it is not 0, indicates unbalanced parentheses (an encoding error).

In DARMS, grouplets must be defined before they occur in the score. The grouplet definition shown at (a) of figure 13.4 indicates that three quarter notes will occur in the time usually taken by one half note. The integer 7 just before the colon is the grouplet identifier number. This grouplet definition specifies the ratio used to scale any duration that occurs as a subdivision of a two-beat triplet. The ratio, which will be stored in an array indexed by the grouplet identifier number, is calculated by dividing the normal duration by the notated duration that will replace it, as shown at (b). The constant ratio for type 7 grouplets is 1/2 divided by 3/4, or 2/3. The actual grouplet is encoded by appending the grouplet identifier number to each encoded duration. The process is illustrated at (c), using the grouplet defined above. The illustration shows the music notation, the DARMS representation, the calculation, and the resulting fractional values. Note that the sum of the fractional durations is equal to 1/2. Nested grouplets are processed as explained in the preceding section of this chapter.

Program 13.2 illustrates the decoding of DARMS duration codes, the use of rational duration representation, and the procedures for rational arithmetic discussed

DARMS code:		(	(	)	(	(	)	)	)
Parenthesis level:	0	1	2	1	2	3	2	1	0
Default duration:	1/4	1/8	1/16	1/8	1/16	1/32	1/16	1/8	1/4

Table 13.3. Processing DARMS Beam Codes (short form)

a) Grouplet identifier: !3Q7:H 

b) Grouplet[7] = 1/2 ÷ 3/4

= 1/2 × 4/3

= **2/3** [grouplet constant 7]

c) Notation: 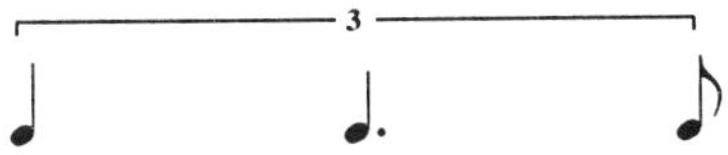

DARMS code:	Q7	Q.7	E7
Calculation:	1/4 × 2/3	3/8 × 2/3	1/8 × 2/3
Duration:	1/6	1/4	1/12

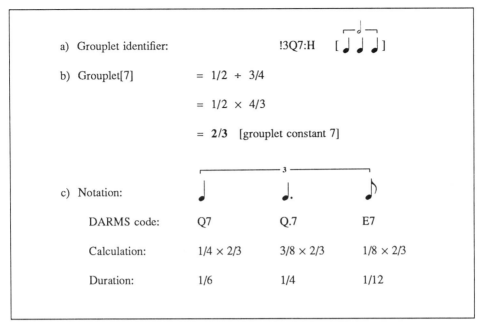

Figure 13.4. Processing DARMS Grouplets

earlier in this chapter. The program is a simplified excerpt from the DARMS interpreter in appendix C. The heart of the program is procedure *scan*, which parses the code and calls appropriate procedures to process various classifications of DARMS tokens. The program has been adjusted so that it accepts only simple meter signatures, e.g., !M3/4 or !M6/8, and simple bar lines (/). Note codes are included (since they are necessary to illustrate beam codes) but are skipped by the program. The program tracks temporal position as both raw time and measure time, and prints an error message for measures that do not have the correct number of beats. In particular, you will want to study procedures *durcode*, *setdot*, and *setgroup*, which process duration codes; procedure *paren*, which processes beam codes; and procedure *grouplet*, which interprets grouplet definitions. To save space, procedures that have been discussed elsewhere in the text are omitted. These procedures are declared with the directive *external*.[5] The external procedures can be seen in the program library listings in appendix D. The excerpt in figure 13.5 was used to exercise the program. This is followed by the DARMS code, output from the program, and the program listing.

5. While the procedure directive *external* is not a feature of standard Pascal, it is used here to save space. The procedures could be included in the program in place of the external declarations.

Figure 13.5. Elliot Carter: Second String Quartet, mm. 581–85

```
k*********************************************************$
k Elliot Carter, String Quartet No. 2, mm. 582-85, dynamics, $
k slurs, articulation, and tempo indications omitted.        $
k  i1 = violin 1;  i2 = violin 2;  i3 = viola;  i4 = cello    $
k*********************************************************$

!a3/4,581       k set measure number using anacrusis directive $

                k grouplet definitions                         $

!3e1:q          k  type 3 = 3 eighths in time of one quarter   $
!3s2:e          k  type 1 = 3 sixteenths in time of one eighth $
!7e3:h.         k  type 2 = 7 eighths in time of dotted half   $
!5e4:h          k  type 4 = 5 eighths in time of one half      $

                                                  k m. 581-82 $
i1 !g !m3/4 2qj ((2) 30-.j) q / 5-q. 31*e (31. (36j)) //
i2 !g !m3/4 6qj ((6) 3*.) q / 7-qj ((7) 8-.) (8 32-j) //
i3 !c !m3/4 7-q 33* 7* / (30 5) (1e1 6 33-) (29*e1 34 re1 ) //
i4 7!c !m3/4 33*q 31# 32 / 29 33 34 !g //

i1 !m2/4 (36 38-) (32* 34) /                      k m. 583     $
i2 !m2/4 (32 31j) ((31) 8.j) /
i3 !m2/4 rs2 18s2 5- 9- 4- 8 33* 30- 36* re /
i4 !m2/4 (20- 7-) (8- 5-) 7!c /

i1 !m3/4 (34#e3 36# 37 35 37 33 39*) /            k m. 584     $
i2 !m3/4 (8e1 32* 7) (6#e1 8# 5*) (7#e1 4* 30#) /
i3 !m3/4 rq ((r 4* 19* 5*)) ((9* 35# 32* 6#)) /
i4 !m3/4 (32 30) (4# 8* 7# 9*) !f /

i1 !m2/4 (4e4 33# 37# 36# 34*)                    k m. 585     $
i2 !m2/4 35*e1 30* re1 r 6# 1. /
i3 !m2/4 ((r 30# 6* 35*j)) qj /
i4 !m2/4 (7# 31*) (8* ) /
```

Program 13.2. Sample Input

```
==============================================================================
Ins |       Raw Time          |            Measure          | Fractional | Other
No. | Start         Note End  |     Start         Note End  |  Duration  | Attrib.
==============================================================================
c anacrusis: meter=     3 /   4
c starting measure reset to  581 /   1
c meter signature instrument 1:     3 /   4
i1    0 /   1       1 /   4     581 /   1     1744 /   3          1 /   4    tie
i1    1 /   4       5 /  16    1744 /   3     6977 /  12          1 /  16
i1    5 /  16       1 /   2    6977 /  12     1745 /   3          3 /  16    tie
i1    1 /   2       3 /   4    1745 /   3      582 /   1          1 /   4
```

```
i1    3 /   4       9 /   8      582 /   1     1165 /   2       3 /   8
i1    9 /   8       5 /   4     1165 /   2     1748 /   3       1 /   8   tie
i1    5 /   4      23 /  16     1748 /   3     6995 /  12       3 /  16
i1   23 /  16       3 /   2     6995 /  12      583 /   1       1 /  16   tie

c Meter signature instrument 2:     3 /   4
i2    0 /   1       1 /   4      581 /   1     1744 /   3       1 /   4   tie
i2    1 /   4       5 /  16     1744 /   3     6977 /  12       1 /  16
i2    5 /  16       1 /   2     6977 /  12     1745 /   3       3 /  16
i2    1 /   2       3 /   4     1745 /   3      582 /   1       1 /   4

i2    3 /   4       1 /   1      582 /   1     1747 /   3       1 /   4   tie
i2    1 /   1      17 /  16     1747 /   3     6989 /  12       1 /  16
i2   17 /  16       5 /   4     6989 /  12     1748 /   3       3 /  16   tie
i2    5 /   4      11 /   8     1748 /   3     3497 /   6       1 /   8
i2   11 /   8       3 /   2     3497 /   6      583 /   1       1 /   8   tie

c Meter signature instrument 3:     3 /   4
i3    0 /   1       1 /   4      581 /   1     1744 /   3       1 /   4
i3    1 /   4       1 /   2     1744 /   3     1745 /   3       1 /   4
i3    1 /   2       3 /   4     1745 /   3      582 /   1       1 /   4

i3    3 /   4       7 /   8      582 /   1     3493 /   6       1 /   8
i3    7 /   8       1 /   1     3493 /   6     1747 /   3       1 /   8
i3    1 /   1      13 /  12     1747 /   3     5242 /   9       1 /  12
i3   13 /  12       7 /   6     5242 /   9     5243 /   9       1 /  12
i3    7 /   6       5 /   4     5243 /   9     1748 /   3       1 /  12
i3    5 /   4       4 /   3     1748 /   3     5245 /   9       1 /  12
i3    4 /   3      17 /  12     5245 /   9     5246 /   9       1 /  12
i3   17 /  12       3 /   2     5246 /   9      583 /   1       1 /  12   rest

c Meter signature instrument 4:     3 /   4
i4    0 /   1       1 /   4      581 /   1     1744 /   3       1 /   4
i4    1 /   4       1 /   2     1744 /   3     1745 /   3       1 /   4
i4    1 /   2       3 /   4     1745 /   3      582 /   1       1 /   4

i4    3 /   4       1 /   1      582 /   1     1747 /   3       1 /   4
i4    1 /   1       5 /   4     1747 /   3     1748 /   3       1 /   4
i4    5 /   4       3 /   2     1748 /   3      583 /   1       1 /   4

c Meter signature instrument 1:     2 /   4
i1    3 /   2      13 /   8      583 /   1     2333 /   4       1 /   8
i1   13 /   8       7 /   4     2333 /   4     1167 /   2       1 /   8
i1    7 /   4      15 /   8     1167 /   2     2335 /   4       1 /   8
i1   15 /   8       2 /   1     2335 /   4      584 /   1       1 /   8

c Meter signature instrument 2:     2 /   4
i2    3 /   2      13 /   8      583 /   1     2333 /   4       1 /   8
i2   13 /   8       7 /   4     2333 /   4     1167 /   2       1 /   8   tie
i2    7 /   4      29 /  16     1167 /   2     4669 /   8       1 /  16
i2   29 /  16       2 /   1     4669 /   8      584 /   1       3 /  16   tie

c Meter signature instrument 3:     2 /   4
i3    3 /   2      37 /  24      583 /   1     6997 /  12       1 /  24   rest
i3   37 /  24      19 /  12     6997 /  12     3499 /   6       1 /  24
```

```
i3   19 /  12      13 /   8     3499 /   6     2333 /   4       1 /  24
i3   13 /   8       5 /   3     2333 /   4     1750 /   3       1 /  24
i3    5 /   3      41 /  24     1750 /   3     7001 /  12       1 /  24
i3   41 /  24       7 /   4     7001 /  12     1167 /   2       1 /  24
i3    7 /   4      43 /  24     1167 /   2     7003 /  12       1 /  24
i3   43 /  24      11 /   6     7003 /  12     1751 /   3       1 /  24
i3   11 /   6      15 /   8     1751 /   3     2335 /   4       1 /  24
i3   15 /   8       2 /   1     2335 /   4      584 /   1       1 /   8    rest

c Meter signature instrument 4:      2 /   4
i4    3 /   2      13 /   8      583 /   1     2333 /   4       1 /   8
i4   13 /   8       7 /   4     2333 /   4     1167 /   2       1 /   8
i4    7 /   4      15 /   8     1167 /   2     2335 /   4       1 /   8
i4   15 /   8       2 /   1     2335 /   4      584 /   1       1 /   8

c Meter signature instrument 1:      3 /   4
i1    2 /   1      59 /  28      584 /   1     4089 /   7       3 /  28
i1   59 /  28      31 /  14     4089 /   7     4090 /   7       3 /  28
i1   31 /  14      65 /  28     4090 /   7     4091 /   7       3 /  28
i1   65 /  28      17 /   7     4091 /   7     4092 /   7       3 /  28
i1   17 /   7      71 /  28     4092 /   7     4093 /   7       3 /  28
i1   71 /  28      37 /  14     4093 /   7     4094 /   7       3 /  28
i1   37 /  14      11 /   4     4094 /   7      585 /   1       3 /  28

c Meter signature instrument 1:      2 /   4
i1   11 /   4      57 /  20      585 /   1     2926 /   5       1 /  10
i1   57 /  20      59 /  20     2926 /   5     2927 /   5       1 /  10
i1   59 /  20      61 /  20     2927 /   5     2928 /   5       1 /  10
i1   61 /  20      63 /  20     2928 /   5     2929 /   5       1 /  10
i1   63 /  20      13 /   4     2929 /   5      586 /   1       1 /  10

c Meter signature instrument 2:      3 /   4
i2    2 /   1      25 /  12      584 /   1     5257 /   9       1 /  12
i2   25 /  12      13 /   6     5257 /   9     5258 /   9       1 /  12
i2   13 /   6       9 /   4     5258 /   9     1753 /   3       1 /  12
i2    9 /   4       7 /   3     1753 /   3     5260 /   9       1 /  12
i2    7 /   3      29 /  12     5260 /   9     5261 /   9       1 /  12
i2   29 /  12       5 /   2     5261 /   9     1754 /   3       1 /  12
i2    5 /   2      31 /  12     1754 /   3     5263 /   9       1 /  12
i2   31 /  12       8 /   3     5263 /   9     5264 /   9       1 /  12
i2    8 /   3      11 /   4     5264 /   9      585 /   1       1 /  12

c Meter signature instrument 2:      2 /   4
i2   11 /   4      17 /   6      585 /   1     3511 /   6       1 /  12
i2   17 /   6      35 /  12     3511 /   6     1756 /   3       1 /  12
i2   35 /  12       3 /   1     1756 /   3     1171 /   2       1 /  12    rest
i2    3 /   1      37 /  12     1171 /   2     1757 /   3       1 /  12    rest
i2   37 /  12      19 /   6     1757 /   3     3515 /   6       1 /  12
i2   19 /   6      53 /  16     3515 /   6     4689 /   8       7 /  48
c Error: instr. 2 m. 585 beatcount off by:    1 /  16

c Meter signature instrument 3:      3 /   4
i3    2 /   1       9 /   4      584 /   1     1753 /   3       1 /   4    rest
i3    9 /   4      37 /  16     1753 /   3     7013 /  12       1 /  16    rest
i3   37 /  16      19 /   8     7013 /  12     1169 /   2       1 /  16
```

```
i3   19 /   8      39 /  16     1169 /   2    7015 /  12       1 /  16
i3   39 /  16       5 /   2     7015 /  12    1754 /   3       1 /  16
i3    5 /   2      41 /  16     1754 /   3    2339 /   4       1 /  16
i3   41 /  16      21 /   8     2339 /   4    3509 /   6       1 /  16
i3   21 /   8      43 /  16     3509 /   6    7019 /  12       1 /  16
i3   43 /  16      11 /   4     7019 /  12     585 /   1       1 /  16

c Meter signature instrument 3:      2 /   4
i3   11 /   4      45 /  16      585 /   1    4681 /   8       1 /  16   rest
i3   45 /  16      23 /   8     4681 /   8    2341 /   4       1 /  16
i3   23 /   8      47 /  16     2341 /   4    4683 /   8       1 /  16
i3   47 /  16       3 /   1     4683 /   8    1171 /   2       1 /  16   tie
i3    3 /   1      13 /   4     1171 /   2     586 /   1       1 /   4   tie

c Meter signature instrument 4:      3 /   4
i4    2 /   1      17 /   8      584 /   1    3505 /   6       1 /   8
i4   17 /   8       9 /   4     3505 /   6    1753 /   3       1 /   8
i4    9 /   4      19 /   8     1753 /   3    1169 /   2       1 /   8
i4   19 /   8       5 /   2     1169 /   2    1754 /   3       1 /   8
i4    5 /   2      21 /   8     1754 /   3    3509 /   6       1 /   8
i4   21 /   8      11 /   4     3509 /   6     585 /   1       1 /   8

c Meter signature instrument 4:      2 /   4
i4   11 /   4      23 /   8      585 /   1    2341 /   4       1 /   8
i4   23 /   8       3 /   1     2341 /   4    1171 /   2       1 /   8
i4    3 /   1      25 /   8     1171 /   2    2343 /   4       1 /   8
c Error: instr. 4 m. 584 beatcount off by:   -1 /   8
```

Program 13.2. Output

```
(***********************       Program Darmsdur       ***********************)
(* This program is a stripped down version of the DARMS interpreter in    *)
(* appendix C, designed to illustrate processing of DARMS duration         *)
(* encoding: duration codes, grouplets, beams, etc.  All time values are *)
(* stored as fractions and are manipulated with rational arithmetic        *)
(* procedures shown above.  Basic pitch encoding (clefs, key signatures, *)
(* space codes, accidentals, etc.) is permitted but ignored by the         *)
(* program.  Output is a table giving, for each note, the raw time and    *)
(* measure at the beginning and end of the note, the fractional duration,*)
(* and an indication of ties or rests. A blank line indicates a bar line.*)
(*************************************************************************)
program darmsdur(input, output);

  const
    maxline  = 80;                     { maximum line length + 1          }
    maxins   = 15;                     { max no. of instruments            }
    maxgroup = 30;                     { max no. of grouplet identifiers  }
    sharp    = '#';                    { DARMS symbol for sharp            }
    flat     = '-';                    { DARMS symbol for flat             }
    natural  = '*';                    { DARMS symbol for natural          }
    isrest   = true;                   { flags to distinguish rest         }
    isnote   = false;                  {   from note                       }
```

```
type
  buftype = record                    { for internal buffer              }
            B  : array[1 .. maxline] of char;
            bp : integer
           end;

  fraction = record
              num : integer;          { numerator   }
              den : integer           { denominator }
             end;

  grouptable = array[1 .. 30] of fraction;   { grouplet constants      }

  note = record
          dur   : fraction;          { fractional value of duration      }
          pitch : integer;           { as cbr (ignored in this program)  }
          tie   : integer            { code for ties                     }
         end;

  pdat = record                      { data for each part                }
          default    : fraction;     { current default dur of note       }
          dot        : fraction;     { current value of dot              }
          time       : fraction;     { current time in part              }
          lastdot    : fraction;     { value of last dot                 }
          restdot    : fraction;     { value of dot for rests            }
          beatnote   : fraction;     { value of beat note                }
          lasttime   : fraction;     { latest time in layer              }
          measno     : fraction;     { measure position                  }
          measure    : fraction;     { measure time for note             }
          meter      : fraction;     { number of beats per measure       }
          lrestdot   : fraction;     { value of dot of last rest         }
          start      : fraction;     { starting time, note or rest       }
          savestart  : fraction;     { starting time for lin decomp      }
          lastbar    : fraction;     { time at last bar line             }

          inum       : integer;      { instrument number                 }
          level      : integer;      { level of parentheses (beams)      }

          current    : note;         { values for current note           }
          restval    : note;         { values for current rest           }
          lastnote   : note;         { for restoring after parens        }
          lastrest   : note          { value of last rest                }
         end;

  pdattab = array[0 .. maxins] of pdat; { info for each instrument       }

(*************************************************************************)
(*                        Global Variables                               *)
(*************************************************************************)

 var
  buffer     : buftype;           { stores one line of input             }
  inum       : integer;           { current instrument number            }
  group      : grouptable;        { grouplet definer constants           }
  partdata   : pdattab;
```

```
(***********************    Boolean Functions    ***********************)
(* Function isXXX(ch) returns true if ch is an XXX                      *)
(***********************************************************************)

  function issign(c : char) : boolean; external;        { plus or minus    }
  function isdigit(ch : char) : boolean; external;      { digit 0-9        }

  function isacc(ch : char) : boolean;             { accidental codes      }
    begin
      isacc := ch in ['-', '#', '*']
    end;

  function isclef(ch : char) : boolean;            { clefs                 }
    begin
      isclef := ch in ['c', 'f', 'g']
    end;

  function isparen(ch : char) :  boolean;          { parentheses           }
    begin
      isparen := ch in ['(', ')']
    end;

  function isdur(ch : char) : boolean;             { duration codes        }
    begin
      isdur := ch in ['w', 'h', 'q', 'e', 's', 't', 'x', 'y', 'z', 'g']
    end;

  function isbar(ch : char) : boolean;             { bar line              }
    begin
      isbar := ch in ['/', ':']
    end;

  function isother(ch : char) : boolean;           { other stuff           }
    begin { other stuff }
      isother := ch in ['!', '.', 'j', '/', ' ',  'm', 'r', 'i', 'n', 'k']
    end;

  function goodtoken(ch : char) : boolean;
    begin
      goodtoken := isdigit(ch) or isdur(ch) or isacc(ch)
                or isparen(ch) or isbar(ch) or isother(ch)
    end;

(***********************    Buffer Procedures    ***********************)
(* The following implement an internal buffer (see section 11.2 ).      *)
(***********************************************************************)

  function tab : char;                                          external;
  function null : char;                                         external;
  function toint(c : char) : integer;                           external;
  procedure getline(var fi, fo : text; var buffer : buftype);   external;
  function eob(var buffer : buftype) : boolean;                 external;
  function tolower(c : char) : char;                            external;
  function nextchar(var buffer : buftype): char;                external;
  procedure skipbuf(var buffer : buftype);                      external;
  procedure getchar(var buffer : buftype; var c : char);        external;
  procedure printbuffer(var f : text; var buffer : buftype);    external;
```

```
  procedure getint(var f : text; var buffer : buftype;
                               var x : integer);                  external;

(**********************************************************************)
(*                 Procedures for Rational Arithmetic                 *)
(**********************************************************************)

  procedure incr(var x : integer);                                external;
  procedure swap(var x, y : integer);                             external;
  function gcd(x, y : integer) : integer;                         external;
  procedure fracadd(var c : fraction; a, b : fraction);           external;
  procedure fracsub(var c : fraction; a, b : fraction);           external;
  procedure fracmult(var c : fraction; a, b : fraction);          external;
  procedure fracdiv(var c : fraction; a, b : fraction);           external;
  function greater(x, y : fraction) : boolean;                    external;
  function lessthan(x, y : fraction) : boolean;                   external;
  function equal(x, y : fraction) : boolean;                      external;
  procedure fracwrite(var f : text; x : fraction);                external;
  procedure fracread(var f : text; var buffer : buftype;
                                     var x : fraction);           external;
  procedure reduce(var x : fraction);                             external;

(**********************        err          ***********************)
(* Prints error messages.                                             *)
(**********************************************************************)
  procedure err(var f : text; var buffer : buftype; errno : integer);
    begin { error }
      printbuffer(f, buffer);
      case errno of
        1: writeln(f, 'Error 1: "', nextchar(buffer),
                                      '" not recognized by scanner.');
        2: writeln(f, 'Error 2: "', nextchar(buffer),
                                               '" Cannot follow !');
        3: writeln(f,'Error 3: "', nextchar(buffer),
                                           '" illegal accidental.');
        7: writeln(f, 'Error 7: unbalanced parentheses');
        9: writeln(f, 'Error 9: "', nextchar(buffer),
                             '" cannot follow other duration codes.');
       12: writeln(f, 'Error 12: " ', nextchar(buffer),
                                            '" is not a rest code.');
       15: writeln(f, 'Error 15: instrument number must be >= 0.');
       16: writeln(f, 'Error 16: ',
                    'Instrument number too big, maxins =', maxins:1);
       24: writeln(f, 'Error 24: token delimiter expected.')
      end  { case }
    end;   { error }

(**********************        init         ***********************)
(* Initializes variables, etc.                                        *)
(**********************************************************************)
  procedure init(var inum : integer; var group : grouptable;
                                        var partdata : pdattab);
    var
      i : integer;
    begin { init }
      inum := 1;                 { instrument number                 }
```

```
    for i := 0 to maxins do
      with partdata[i] do
        begin
          beatnote.num := 1;        { beat note default = 1/4           }
          beatnote.den := 4;
          default.num := 1;         { default is quarter note           }
          default.den := 4;
          dot.num := 1;             { dot = 1/8                         }
          dot.den := 8;
          lastbar.num := 0;         { default measure number 1          }
          lastbar.den := 1;
          measno.num := 1;          { default measure number 1          }
          measno.den := 1;
          measure.num := 1;         { measure at beginning of note      }
          measure.den := 1;
          meter.num := 4;           { meter default is 4/4              }
          meter.den := 4;
          restdot.num := 1;         { dot = 1/8                         }
          restdot.den := 8;
          start.num := 0;           { starting time for note            }
          start.den := 1;
          time.num := 0;            { raw time                          }
          time.den := 1;
          inum := i;
          level := 0;               { no parentheses                    }
          with current do
            begin
              dur.num :=    1;
              dur.den :=    4;
              tie     :=    0
            end;
          with restval do
            begin
              dur.num :=  1;        { default for rest is 1/4           }
              dur.den :=  4;
              tie     :=  0
            end;
          lastrest := restval;
          lastnote := current
        end;

    for i := 1 to maxgroup do       { init grouplet constants to 1/1   }
      begin
        group[i].num := 1;
        group[i].den := 1
      end
  end; { init }


(***********************           paren           ***********************)
(* Sets default durations for beams (parentheses).                         *)
(**************************************************************************)
 procedure paren(var f : text; var buffer : buftype; var partdata : pdat);
   begin
     with partdata do
       begin
```

```
        if nextchar(buffer) = '('                          { start of beam }
          then
            begin { left parenthesis }
              level := level + 1;
              default.den := default.den * 2
            end  { left parenthesis }
          else
            begin { right parenthesis }                    { end of beam   }
              level := level - 1;
              default.den := default.den div 2
            end;  { right parenthesis }

        if level > 0
          then
            begin { reset duration and dot }
              current.dur := default;
              restval.dur := default;
              dot.den := default.den * 2;
              restdot.den := default.den * 2
            end   { reset current duration and dot }
        else if level = 0
          then
            begin { restore last duration and dot }
              dot := lastdot;
              restdot := lrestdot;
              current := lastnote;
              restval := lastrest
            end   { restore last duration and dot }
        else if level < 0
          then err(f, buffer, 7);  { unbalanced parens }
        incr(buffer.bp)
      end   { with partdata }
  end;  { paren }


(***********************           setins          ***********************)
(* Gets new instrument number.                                            *)
(*************************************************************************)
  procedure setins(var f : text; var buffer : buftype; var inum : integer);
    var
      t : integer;
    begin { setins }
      incr(buffer.bp);        { skip I }
      getint(f, buffer, t);
      if t < 0
        then err(f, buffer, 15)
      else if t > maxins
        then err(f, buffer, 16)
      else inum := t
    end;  { setins }


(***********************          savelast         ***********************)
(* Saves last dur and dot for rest or note, when leaving beamed group.   *)
(*************************************************************************)
  procedure savelast(var partdata : pdat; rest : boolean);
```

```
    begin { savelast }
      with partdata do
        begin
          if not rest
            then
              begin                                   { save last note and dot }
                lastdot  := dot;
                lastnote := current
              end
            else
              begin                                   { save last rest and dot }
                lastrest := restval;
                lrestdot := restdot
              end;
          current.tie := 0;
          restval.tie := 0
        end
    end; { savelast }


(************************        writenote       ************************)
(* Prints the current data for the prototypical note.                    *)
(************************************************************************)
  procedure writenote(var f : text; var buffer : buftype;
                                  var partdata : pdat; rest : boolean);

    var
      t : fraction;
      x : note;

    begin
      with partdata do
        begin
          if rest
            then x := restval
            else x := current;
          start := time;                         { start time for note      }
          fracadd(time, start, x.dur);           { terminal time for note   }
          fracdiv(t, x.dur, meter);              { dur as part of measure   }
          measure := measno;                     { current measure number   }
          fracadd(measno, measno, t);            { new measure time         }
          write(f, 'i', inum:1, ' ');            { instrument number        }
          fracwrite(f, start);                   { start time               }
          write(' ':3);
          fracwrite(f, time);                    { terminal time            }
          write(' ':3);
          fracwrite(f, measure);                 { measure position         }
          write(' ':3);
          fracwrite(f, measno);                  { meas no. at end          }
          write(' ':3);
          fracwrite(f, x.dur);                   { duration as fraction     }
          if x.tie = 1
            then write(f, '  tie');              { indicate tie             }
          if rest
            then write(f, '  rest');             { indicate rest            }
          writeln(f);
```

```
        if (not rest) or (rest and not isdur(nextchar(buffer)))
          then                                      { check for token delimiter }
            if not (nextchar(buffer) in [' ',','(',')'])
              then err(f, buffer, 24)
      end;  { with partdata }
    savelast(partdata, rest)                        { save last note and dot     }
  end;  { writenote }

(***********************           settie           ***********************)
(* Sets the tie field of the note, then calls setartic.                    *)
(**************************************************************************)
 procedure settie(var f : text; var buffer : buftype;
           var group : grouptable; var partdata : pdat; rest : boolean);
  begin { settie }
    with partdata do
      begin
        if nextchar(buffer) <> 'j'
          then
            begin { no tie }
              current.tie := 0;
              restval.tie := 0
            end   { no tie }
          else
            begin { simple tie }
              incr(buffer.bp);         { skip j }
              current.tie := 1
            end;  { simple tie }
        writenote(f, buffer, partdata, rest)
      end { with partdata }
  end;   { settie }

(***********************          setgroup          ***********************)
(* Adjusts duration for grouplet constant.                                  *)
(**************************************************************************)
 procedure setgroup(var f : text; var buffer : buftype;
                               var group  : grouptable; var x : note);
  var
    id : integer;                          { grouplet identifier number  }
  begin { setgroup }
    getint(f, buffer, id);                 { read grouplet id number     }
    fracmult(x.dur, x.dur, group[id])      { multiply by grouplet const  }
  end;  { setgroup }

(***********************           setdot           ***********************)
(* Processes dots in duration codes.                                        *)
(**************************************************************************)
 procedure setdot(var buffer : buftype; var x, xdot : fraction);
  begin { setdot }
    while nextchar(buffer) = '.' do
      begin
        fracadd(x, x, xdot);
        xdot.den := xdot.den * 2;
        incr(buffer.bp)
      end
  end;  { setdot }
```

```
(***********************          durcode          ***********************)
(* Sets fractional duration of note.                                      *)
(*************************************************************************)

procedure durcode(var f : text; var buffer : buftype;
                         var x, xdot : fraction; rest : boolean);
  begin { set dur from durcode }
    if isdur(nextchar(buffer))
      then
        begin { set duration }
          x.num := 1;                       { set numerator              }
          xdot.num := 1;
          case nextchar(buffer) of
            'w': x.den :=   1;              { set denominator according }
            'h': x.den :=   2;              {   to duration code         }
            'q': x.den :=   4;
            'e': x.den :=   8;
            's': x.den :=  16;
            't': x.den :=  32;
            'x': x.den :=  64;
            'y': x.den := 128;
            'z': x.den := 256;
            'g': begin { grace note }
                   x.num := 0;
                   x.den := 1
                 end   { grace note }
          end; { case }

          incr(buffer.bp);                    { skip duration code      }
          if nextchar(buffer) = 'w'           { breves,  longas, etc.   }
            then
              while nextchar(buffer) = 'w' do
                begin
                  x.num := x.num * 2;
                  incr(buffer.bp)
                end
          else if nextchar(buffer) = 'z'      { dur shorter than 1/256 }
            then
              while nextchar(buffer) = 'z' do
                begin
                  x.den := x.den * 2;
                  incr(buffer.bp)
                end;
          if isdur(nextchar(buffer)) and (not rest)
            then
              begin
                err(f, buffer, 9);
                incr(buffer.bp)
              end;
          if x.num <> 0   { grace note }
            then xdot.den := x.den * 2
        end;  { set duration }
    setdot(buffer, x, xdot)  { set for dots }
  end;  { durcode }
```

```
(***********************          setdur          ***********************)
(* Calls durcode to set duration and dot values, then calls settie.     *)
(************************************************************************)
 procedure setdur(var f : text; var buffer : buftype;
          var group : grouptable; var partdata : pdat; rest : boolean);
   begin
     with partdata do
       begin
         if rest
           then
             begin { process rest }
               durcode(f, buffer, restval.dur, restdot, rest);
               if isdigit(nextchar(buffer))
                 then setgroup(f, buffer, group, restval)
             end   { process rest }
           else
             begin { process note }
               durcode(f, buffer, current.dur, dot, rest);
               if isdigit(nextchar(buffer))
                 then setgroup(f, buffer, group, current)
             end;  { process note }
         settie(f, buffer, group, partdata, rest)
       end   { with partdata }
   end;

(***********************        grouplet         ***********************)
(* Sets fractional value of constant for specified grouplet definer.    *)
(************************************************************************)
 procedure grouplet(var f : text; var buffer : buftype;
                                         var group : grouptable);

   var
     x, y : fraction;
     dot : fraction;
     num  : integer;
     id1, id2 : integer;                   { grouplet id numbers      }
   begin
     getint(f, buffer, num);
     durcode(f, buffer, x, dot, false);    { calc fractional value    }
     x.num := x.num * num;                 { adjust numerator         }
     getint(f, buffer, id1);               { read identifier number   }
     incr(buffer.bp);                      { skip colon               }
     if isdigit(nextchar(buffer))
       then getint(f, buffer, num)
       else num := 1;                      { default for numerator    }
     if isdur(nextchar(buffer))
       then durcode(f, buffer, y, dot, false)
       else
         begin
           y.den := x.den;                 { default for duration     }
           y.num := 1
         end;
     y.num := y.num * num;
     fracdiv(group[id1], y, x);            { calculate constant       }
     if isdigit(nextchar(buffer))
```

```
        then
          begin                                  { for nested grouplet      }
            getint(f, buffer, id2);
            fracmult(group[id1], group[id1], group[id2])
          end
    end;  { grouplet }

(***********************           setrest          ***********************)
(* Calls setdur with the last parameter (rest) set to true.                 *)
(***************************************************************************)
  procedure setrest(var f : text; var buffer : buftype;
          var group : grouptable; var partdata : pdat; rest    : boolean);
    begin { setrest }
      incr(buffer.bp);
      if nextchar(buffer) in [' ', '.', ')', '(']
        then setdur(f, buffer, group, partdata, rest)
      else if isdur(nextchar(buffer))
        then                            { allow for concatenated rests }
          while isdur(nextchar(buffer)) do
            setdur(f, buffer, group, partdata, rest)
      else err(f, buffer, 12)
    end;  { setrest }

(***********************          setmeter          ***********************)
(* Reads simple meter signature.                                            *)
(***************************************************************************)
  procedure setmeter(var f : text; var buffer : buftype;
                                   var partdata : pdat; print : boolean);
    begin
      with partdata do
        begin
          meter.num := 4;              { set defaults }
          meter.den := 1;
          beatnote.num := 1;
          beatnote.den := 4;
          incr(buffer.bp);             { skip M  }
          if isdigit(nextchar(buffer))
            then
              begin
                fracread(f, buffer, meter);
                beatnote.den := meter.den
              end
          else if nextchar(buffer) = '$'
            then
              begin
                incr(buffer.bp);
                meter.num := 2;
                beatnote.den := 2
              end
          else if nextchar(buffer) = 'c'
            then
              begin
                incr(buffer.bp);
                meter.num := 4;
                beatnote.den := 4
              end;
```

```
        if print
          then
            begin
              write(f, 'c Meter signature instrument ', inum:1, ':  ');
              fracwrite(output, meter); writeln
            end;
        reduce(meter);
        reduce(beatnote)
      end
  end;  { setmeter }

(***********************          anacrusis        ***********************)
(* Sets raw time, measure, and meter for segments that don't begin on    *)
(* beat one, measure one.                                                *)
(************************************************************************)
procedure anacrusis(var f : text; var buffer : buftype;
                                          var partdata : pdattab);

  var
    tempdur, tempdot, xmeasure   : fraction;
    tempbeat, tempmeter, pickup : fraction;
    negative : boolean;
    i   : integer;

  begin
    incr(buffer.bp);                              { skip !         }
    setmeter(f, buffer, partdata[0], false);
    tempbeat := partdata[0].beatnote;
    tempmeter := partdata[0].meter;
    write(f, 'c anacrusis: meter= ');
    fracwrite(f, tempmeter); writeln;
    if nextchar(buffer) = ','
      then incr(buffer.bp);
    xmeasure.num := 1;                            { init measure }
    xmeasure.den := 1;
    getint(f, buffer, xmeasure.num);
    if nextchar(buffer) = ','
      then incr(buffer.bp);
    negative := nextchar(buffer) = '-';
    if issign(nextchar(buffer))
      then incr(buffer.bp);              { skip sign                 }
    skipbuf(buffer);

    pickup.num := 0;                     { calc value of anacrusis   }
    pickup.den := 1;
    while isdur(nextchar(buffer)) do
      begin
        durcode(f, buffer, tempdur, tempdot, true);
        fracadd(pickup, pickup, tempdur)
      end;

    tempdur := pickup;                   { convert to part of measure }
    fracdiv(tempdur, tempdur, tempmeter);

    if negative                          { adjust measure position    }
      then fracsub(xmeasure, xmeasure, tempdur)
      else fracadd(xmeasure, xmeasure, tempdur);
```

```
    { set pickup (offset for anacrusis) }
    if negative                                { init value for last measure}
      then fracsub(pickup, pickup, tempmeter)
      else pickup.num := -pickup.num;

    for i := 0 to maxins do
      with partdata[i] do
        begin
          measno   := xmeasure;                { set measure number         }
          meter    := tempmeter;               { set meter                  }
          beatnote := tempbeat;                { set beat note              }
          lastbar  := pickup                   { fudge last measure         }
        end;

    write(f, 'c starting measure reset to ');
    fracwrite(f, xmeasure); writeln;
    if nextchar(buffer) = '['
      then
        begin
          incr(buffer.bp);
          getint(f, buffer, tempdur.num);
          skipbuf(buffer);
          if nextchar(buffer) = '/'
            then incr(buffer.bp);
          skipbuf(buffer);
          getint(f, buffer, tempdur.den);
          skipbuf(buffer);
          if nextchar(buffer) = ']'
            then incr(buffer.bp);

          for i := 0 to maxins do
            with partdata[i] do
              begin
                time := tempdur;
                fracadd(lastbar, lastbar, tempdur)
              end;

          write(f, 'c starttime set to fraction ');
          fracwrite(f, tempdur); writeln
        end { real time }
  end; { anacrusis }

(**********************          skiptoken          **********************)
(* Skips over unused tokens (pitch, clefs, etc.).                        *)
(*************************************************************************)
 procedure skiptoken(var buffer : buftype);
   begin
     while nextchar(buffer) <> ' ' do
       incr(buffer.bp)
   end;

(**********************         exclamation         **********************)
(* Called when the scanner encounters an exclamation pt.  Checks the     *)
(* character after the exclamation and calls the appropriate routine     *)
(* (keysig, clef, etc.).                                                 *)
(*************************************************************************)
```

```
 procedure exclamation(var f : text; var buffer : buftype;
                                                 var partdata : pdat);
   begin
     incr(buffer.bp);                            { skip !              }
     with partdata do
       if nextchar(buffer) = 'k'                 { key signature       }
         then skiptoken(buffer)                  { skip it             }
       else if isclef(nextchar(buffer))          { clef                }
         then skiptoken(buffer)                  { skip it             }
       else if nextchar(buffer) = 'm'            { meter signature     }
         then setmeter(f, buffer, partdata, true)
       else if isdigit(nextchar(buffer))         { grouplet definer    }
         then grouplet(f, buffer, group)
       else err(f, buffer, 2)
   end;

(***********************          barcode          ***********************)
(* In this version simply skips bar line codes.                         *)
(************************************************************************)
 procedure barcode(var f : text; var buffer : buftype; var code : integer);
   begin
     while isbar(nextchar(buffer)) do
       incr(buffer.bp)  { skip / }
   end;        { barcode }

(***********************        newmeasure         ***********************)
(* Called when a bar line is encountered by scan.                       *)
(************************************************************************)
 procedure newmeasure(var f : text; var buffer : buftype;
                                                 var partdata : pdat);
   var
     code : integer;                      { bar line code              }
     bardur : fraction;                   { frac duration of measure   }
   begin { newmeasure }
     code := 0;                           { set default bar line code  }
     barcode(f, buffer, code);
     with partdata do                     { check duration of measure  }
       begin
         fracsub(bardur, time, lastbar);
         fracsub(bardur, bardur, meter);  { calculate difference       }
         if bardur.num <> 0
           then
             begin                        { report duration error      }
               write(f, 'c error: instr. ', inum:1, ' m. ',
                 (measno.num div measno.den) -1:1, ' beat count off by: ');
               fracwrite(f, bardur);  writeln
             end;
         lastbar := time;                 { save time for next test    }
         writeln                          { leave blank line           }
       end
   end;

(***********************         badtoken          ***********************)
(* Called by scanner if first char of token is not recognized.          *)
(************************************************************************)
```

```
  procedure badtoken(var f : text; var buffer : buftype);
    begin
      err(f, buffer, 1);                                  { report error   }
      incr(buffer.bp);                                    { skip bad char  }
      skiptoken(buffer)                                   { skip token     }
    end;

(***********************     skipaccidentals     ***********************)
(* Skips accidentals in code.                                           *)
(***********************************************************************)
  procedure skipaccidentals(var f : text; var buffer : buftype;
              var group : grouptable; var partdata : pdat; rest : boolean);
    begin
      while isacc(nextchar(buffer)) do
        incr(buffer.bp);                             { skip accidentals     }
      setdur(f, buffer, group, partdata, rest)
    end;

(***********************       spacecode       ***********************)
(* Skips space code in code.                                          *)
(*********************************************************************)
  procedure spacecode(var f : text; var buffer : buftype;
              var group : grouptable; var partdata : pdat; rest : boolean);
    begin
      while isdigit(nextchar(buffer)) do
        incr(buffer.bp);                             { skip accidentals     }
      if nextchar(buffer) = '!'
        then exclamation(f, buffer, partdata)
        else skipaccidentals(f, buffer, group, partdata, rest)
    end;

(***********************        comment        ***********************)
(* Skips over comments.  Comment delimiters are 'k' ... '$'.          *)
(*********************************************************************)
  procedure comment(var buffer : buftype);
    begin
      with buffer do
        begin
          incr(bp);                                       { skip 'k'       }
          while (B[bp] <> '$') and not eob(buffer) do { skip comment }
            incr(bp);
          if B[bp] = '$'
            then incr(bp)                                 { skip '$'       }
        end
    end;  { comment }

(***********************          scan          ***********************)
(* The heart of the program, checks the first character of each token *)
(* and calls the appropriate routines to deal with each case.         *)
(*********************************************************************)
  procedure scan(var f : text; var buffer   : buftype; var inum : integer;
              var group : grouptable; var partdata : pdattab);
    begin
      while not eob(buffer) do
        begin
```

```
        if not goodtoken(nextchar(buffer))
          then badtoken(f, buffer)
          else
            begin
              if isdigit(nextchar(buffer))              { space code      }
                then spacecode(f, buffer, group, partdata[inum], isnote)
              else if isacc(nextchar(buffer))           { accidental      }
                then skipaccidentals(f, buffer, group, partdata[inum],
                                                                  isnote)
              else if isdur(nextchar(buffer))           { duration code   }
                then setdur(f, buffer, group, partdata[inum], isnote)
              else if nextchar(buffer) = '.'            { duration dot    }
                then setdur(f, buffer, group, partdata[inum], isnote)
              else if nextchar(buffer) = 'r'            { rest            }
                then setrest(f, buffer, group, partdata[inum], isrest)
              else if nextchar(buffer) = '!'            { exclamation pt  }
                then
                  if buffer.B[buffer.bp + 1] = 'a'      { anacrusis       }
                    then anacrusis(f, buffer, partdata)
                    else exclamation(f, buffer, partdata[inum])
              else if isbar(nextchar(buffer))           { bar lines       }
                then newmeasure(f, buffer, partdata[inum])
              else if isparen(nextchar(buffer))         { parentheses     }
                then paren(f, buffer, partdata[inum])
              else if nextchar(buffer) = 'i'            { instr. number   }
                then setins(f, buffer, inum)
              else if nextchar(buffer) = 'k'            { comment         }
                then comment(buffer)
              else if nextchar(buffer) = ' '            { blank           }
                then skipbuf(buffer)
            end   { scan code }
      end
  end;  { scan }


(***********************         writeborder        ***********************)
(* For printing output table.                                               *)
(**************************************************************************)
  procedure writeborder;
    var
      i : integer;
    begin
      for i := 1 to 79 do
        write('=');
      writeln
    end;


(***********************         writeheading        ***********************)
(* Prints table heading.                                                     *)
(**************************************************************************)
  procedure writeheading;
    begin
      writeborder;
      writeln('Ins |        Raw Time        |               ',
                          'Measure        | Fractional | Other');
```

```
    writeln('No.  | Start        Note End |     Start',
                   '              Note End |  Duration    | Attrib.');

    writeborder
  end;  { writeheading }

(***********************        main procedure      ***********************)
(* Initializes variables, then passes one line at a time to proc. scan.   *)
(**************************************************************************)
begin { main }
  init(inum, group, partdata);
  writeheading;

  while not eof do
    begin { process line }
      getline(input, output, buffer);           { read one line of code }
                                                 {   and interpret it    }
      scan(output, buffer, inum, group, partdata)
    end; { process line }

  for inum := 1 to maxins do          { check for unbalanced parentheses }
    with partdata[inum] do
    if level <> 0
      then writeln('c error: instrument', inum:3,
                   ' parenthesis level = ', level:2)
end.  { main }
```

Program 13.2. *Darmsdur*

13.6 Variant Records

It is sometimes useful to have records in which some fields are different under certain conditions, depending on the value of another field. For example, we might define the duration and starting time of a note so that they could be stored as fractions or as real numbers, with another field acting as a flag to indicate which type of value is to be used.

Pascal provides for records with a variant part. The syntax of the variant part is shown in figure 13.6, where **case** and **of** are Pascal reserved words; <tag> is a Pascal identifier associated with a field that has already been defined in the fixed part of the record definition; $constant_1$, $constant_2$, . . ., $constant_n$ are case constants (or lists of

> **case** <tag> **of**
> $constant_1$: ($fieldlist_1$);
> $constant_2$: ($fieldlist_2$);
>   . . .
> $constant_n$: ($fieldlist_n$)

Figure 13.6. SYNTAX: Variant Part of Record Definition

constants separated by commas) of the same type as <tag>; and $fieldlist_1$, $fieldlist_2$, . . ., $fieldlist_n$ are declarations of the component fields for each variant. Identifiers in the field lists must be unique, i.e., the same identifier may not occur in more than one field list.

Usually the type of the tag field is a user-defined ordinal type, the elements of which mnemonically describe the variants of the record. The fixed part of the record is always declared first. Note that the case list is not terminated by **end**, as in the normal case statement; it is terminated by the **end** delimiter for the record.

As an example of a variant record definition, we will redefine the *note* record from program 13.1. Here we define three variants in which the starting time and duration will be specified as fractions, real numbers, or arbitrary units of type *integer*. In addition, we will specify that only notes in which the starting time and duration are specified as real numbers will have the frequency specified, and that these will have the dynamic level specified as an integer value. We will define a fourth variant in which the variant part is undefined. The variant will depend on the type of note, a user-defined ordinal type. Other user-defined component types remain unchanged:

```
[type]
  ntype = (fracnote, intnote, realnote, empty);

  fraction = record
                num : integer;   { numerator   }
                den : integer    { denominator }
             end;

  string = packed array[1 .. maxstring] of char;

  dyntype = (ppppp, pppp, ppp, pp, p, mp, mf, f, ff, fff, ffff,
                                                            fffff);
```

Now type *note* is defined with a fixed and a variant part:

```
  note =
    record
      notetype   : ntype;                        { fixed part     }
      octave     : integer;
      pc         : integer;
      nc         : integer;
      instrument : string;
      case ntype of                              { variant part   }
        fracnote : (fdynamic   : dyntype;
                    fstart     : fraction;
                    fduration  : fraction);

        intnote  : (idynamic   : dyntype;
                    istart     : integer;
                    iduration  : integer);

        realnote : (rdynamic   : integer;
                    rstart     : real;
                    rduration  : real;
                    frequency  : real);
        empty    : ( )
    end;                                         { end of record  }
```

This defines three variants of the *note* record, as shown in table 13.4. Note the following:

1. Fields in the variant part must not use the same field names, even when the component type is the same as in the first variant field of *fracnote* and *intnote.*
2. The number of components and the component types may differ in the variants.
3. Each variant is actually the same size, although in some variants some of the space is not used.
4. Although the record contains variants, each of the variant records is the same type.

The choice of variants is specified by assigning a value to the *notetype* field. For example, if *x* has been defined type *note*, then the variant of *x* is set by

```
x.notetype := fracnote;   { or realtype or inttype }
```

Thereafter, the variant fields are referenced by the appropriate name and they have the defined type. In this case *x.fdynamic* references the dynamic field (type *dyntype*), *x.fstart* references the starting time (a *fraction*), etc. At another time the variant of *x* could be reset, e.g.,

```
x.notetype := realnote;
```

Now the variant fields would be accessed as *x.rdynamic* (*integer*), *x.rstart* (*real*), *x.rduration* (*real*), and *x.frequency* (*real*).

Fixed Part					Variant Part			
ntype	*octave*	*pc*	*nc*	*instrument*	*fdynamic*	*fstart*	*fduration*	
fracnote	5	7	4	'trumpet'	*ffff*	7/8	3/8	
ntype	*octave*	*pc*	*nc*	*instrument*	*idynamic*	*istart*	*iduration*	
intnote	3	6	3	'flute'	*mp*	115	16	
ntype	*octave*	*pc*	*nc*	*instrument*	*rdynamic*	*rstart*	*rduration*	*frequency*
realnote	5	9	5	'synthesizer'	2500	7.250	1.500	880
ntype	*octave*	*pc*	*nc*	*instrument*				
empty	-	-	-	''				

Table 13.4. Variants of the *note* Record

Since each of the variants of a variant record is considered to be of the same type, it is not inconsistent to have an array of variant records, e.g,

```
tunetype = array [1 .. max] of note;
```

where *note* has been defined as the variant record specified above.

Records, of both the fixed and variant types, are vital to the definition and use of dynamic data structures. We will see many examples of their use in later chapters.

References and Selected Readings

The procedures for manipulating fractions in this chapter were adapted from algorithms given in the following:

Knuth, Donald E. *The Art of Computer Programming.* Vol. 2, *Seminumerical Algorithms.* Reading, Mass.: Addison-Wesley, 1969.

For a different representation of fractions, based on factorials, see the following:

Wayner, Peter. "Error-Free Fractions." *Byte* 13, no. 6 (1988): 289-98.

Some material on processing DARMS duration codes is based on the following article (used by permission of the publisher):

Brinkman, Alexander R. "Representing Musical Scores for Computer Analysis." *Journal of Music Theory* 30, no. 2 (1986): 225–75.

Other suggested readings:

Brook, Barry S. "Music Documentation of the Future." In *Musicology and the Computer*, edited by Barry S. Brook, 28–36. New York: City University of New York Press, 1970.

Laske, Otto E. *Music, Memory, and Thought: Explorations in Cognitive Musicology.* Ann Arbor: University Microfilms, 1977.

Lewin, David. "A Label-Free Development for 12-Pitch-Class Systems." *Journal of Music Theory* 21, no. 1 (1977): 29–48.

Wolff, Anthony B. "Problems of Representation in Musical Computing." *Computers and the Humanities* 11 (1977): 3–12.

Exercises

1. Study the syntax of records. Then study the examples in the chapter until you understand them thoroughly. We will use them extensively in later chapters.

2. Rewrite program 13.1, using the **with** statement. If your system has facilities for timing program execution, run both versions on the same data. Is there any difference in execution time? (You will need a substantial input file to see any difference.)

3. Review the basic operations on a queue (section 10.7.2), then write the procedures necessary to implement a queue, using a record to define the queue as follows:

```
type
  queuetype = record
                Q     : array[1 .. maxq] of integer;
                front : integer;
                rear  : integer
              end;

var
  queue : queuetype;
```

Headings for the required functions and procedures are shown below. Note that since the queue is a structured type, it is always passed by reference for efficiency.

procedure *init*(**var** *queue* : *queuetype*); — initializes the queue.

function *empty*(**var** *queue* : *queuetype*) : *boolean*; — tests for empty queue.

function *full*(**var** *queue* : *queuetype*) : *boolean*; — tests for full queue.

procedure *insert*(*x* : *integer*; **var** *queue* : *queuetype*); — inserts *x* at the rear of the queue.

procedure *remove*(**var** *x* : *integer*; **var** *queue* : *queuetype*); — removes the value at the front of the queue.

4. Review the procedures used to implement an internal buffer in section 11.2, then implement the buffer using the following record definition:

```
type
  buftype = record
              B  : array[1 .. maxbuf] of char;   { array for buffer }
              bp : integer                       { buffer position  }
            end;

var
  buffer : buftype;
```

Headings for the required functions and procedures are shown below.

procedure *getline*(**var** *buffer* : *buftype*); — reads one line from the standard input file into the buffer, marks the end of the buffer with a null character [*chr*(0)], and sets the position indicator to the beginning of the buffer.

function *eob*(**var** *buffer* : *buftype*) : *boolean*; — tests for the end of the buffer.

function *nextchar*(**var** *buffer* : *buftype*) : *char*; — returns the next character in the buffer (without changing *bp*). The function should return a blank if at the end of the buffer.

procedure *skipbuf*(**var** *buffer* : *buftype*); — skips blank characters in buffer.

procedure *getint*(**var** *buffer* : *buftype*; **var** *x* : *integer*); — reads an integer from the buffer.

procedure *getchar*(**var** *buffer* : *buftype*; **var** *c* : *char*); — reads the next character in the buffer.

5. The primary exercise for this chapter is a program for managing an incipit catalogue. Since the program requires the use of external files, the exercise has been placed at the end of chapter 14.

14 | File Types

In earlier chapters we learned the basics of using text files—reading and writing, using the standard files *input* and *output*, and using *eoln*, *eof*, and *input*↑ effectively. This chapter extends these techniques to text files other than the standard ones, and covers the definition and use of external and internal files, as well as the use of files of types other than *text*. The latter are binary files containing data in a form that can be read and written by a program directly, so no conversion needs to be performed on input and output.

All files in standard Pascal have certain aspects in common, so there is much that will carry over from our previous discussions. Each file consists of a sequence of elements of the component type of the file. A file of type *text*, e.g., *input* or *output*, is a special case in which the component type is *char* and characters are grouped into lines, each of which is terminated by a special nonprinting character (the newline character).

Each file *f* has associated with it a buffer variable *f*↑, which serves as a window into the file. The file is accessed one element at a time, in order from the first element to the last. When the file is opened for reading, the buffer variable *f*↑ is positioned at the beginning of the file and *f*↑ is assigned the value of the first component. When the last element in the file has been read, *eof(f)* becomes *true*. The primitive *get(f)* moves *f*↑ to the next element in the file. In general,

```
read(f, x);
```

is equivalent to

```
x := f↑;
get(f);
```

where *f* is a file of *any* component type and *x* is a variable of the same type.

When a file is opened for output, the file is created (or emptied if it already exists), and *f*↑ is positioned at the beginning of the file. The statement

```
write(f, x);
```

is equivalent to

```
f↑ := x;
put(f)
```

where *f* is a file of any component type and *x* is an expression that evaluates to the appropriate component type.[1]

External files are files that exist apart from the Pascal program that reads and writes them. Data written into an external file is available after the program terminates, i.e., it can be reread by another program or another invocation of the same program. These files must be passed to the program as file parameters. Internal files are allocated locally, i.e., they exist only while the program or procedure that creates them is being executed, after which the space occupied by them is released, and the files are no longer accessible to the program or to other programs.

Except for the standard files *input* and *output*, all files must be declared and opened before they can be accessed.

14.1 External Files

Until now, we have been using the standard files *input* and *output* for communicating with programs. While this is often sufficient for simple programs, it is sometimes necessary or desirable for a program to read from and write to other files or devices while reserving the standard I/O channels for communicating with the program user. In this unit you will learn to use files other than *input* and *output* for communicating with Pascal programs.

In order to use an external file, four steps are necessary:

1. The file name must appear in the program's parameter list (along with or instead of *input* and *output*).
2. The file name must appear in the list of variable declarations. If the file is a textfile, the type is declared as *text*. Files of other data types will be discussed in section 14.3.
3. The file must be *opened*; that is, the operating system must set up communications between the actual file and the program. This is accomplished through calls of *reset(f)* or *rewrite(f)*, where *reset(f)* opens file *f* for reading and *rewrite(f)* opens it for writing. If file *f* already exists, *reset(f)* positions the buffer variable $f\uparrow$ at the beginning of the file, and *rewrite(f)* empties the file and then positions $f\uparrow$ at the beginning, ready to begin writing into the file.
4. The file name must appear as the first argument to each *write* or *read* statement.

Program 14.1 is a simple illustration of the use of external files. The program reads two integers from one external file and writes them into another. The program heading (line 1) lists three formal file parameters, *output*, *infile*, and *outfile*. (Input would also appear here if it were used in the program.) *Infile* and *outfile* are declared on lines 4 and 5. Line 7 writes the message 'Testing . . . ' to the CRT screen. Since the file parameter (first argument) has been omitted, it defaults to *output*. The statement could have listed the file explicitly:

```
write(output, 'Testing . . . ');
```

1. In the special case of text files, *read* and *write* perform the conversion between the internal representation of *integer*, *real*, and *boolean* values and the external character representation.

```
1   program copyint(output, infile, outfile);
2     var
3       a, b    : integer;        { two integers   }
4       infile  : text;           { external files }
5       outfile : text;
6     begin { main }
7       write('Testing . . . ');
8       reset(infile);            { open infile for reading       }
9       rewrite(outfile);         { open outfile for writing      }
10      read(infile, a, b);       { read two integers from infile }
11      writeln(outfile, a, b);   { write them to outfile         }
12      writeln('Done')
13    end. { main }
```

Program 14.1. *Copyint*

Line 8 opens *infile* for reading; line 9 opens *outfile* for writing. Line 10 reads two integers from *infile*, and stores them in variables *a* and *b*. Line 11 writes the values of *a* and *b* into *outfile*. Finally, line 12 writes the message 'Done' to the CRT screen. Thus the only output to the user's terminal is

```
Testing . . . Done
```

Between writing 'Testing . . . ' and 'Done' the numbers are copied from *infile* to *outfile*.

The method of specifying the actual file to be used is installation dependent. In some systems the actual file name is supplied when the program is run. For example, if the above program had been compiled and the binary (executable) code named *copyint*, the program would be run by the following command:

```
copyint testin testout
```

This supplies the actual file names *testin* and *testout*, which will be used in place of the file parameters *infile* and *outfile* in the program heading and elsewhere. This is analogous to passing actual parameters to a procedure or function. The operating system locates files named *testin* and *testout* in the current directory of the file system. If the input file is found, it is used, otherwise an error results. The system creates an output file if the named file does not exist. If it already exists, it is emptied and made ready for writing.

In systems with less sophisticated handling of command-line arguments, it is sometimes necessary to specify the actual file names in the program. This declaration is made in statements like the following:

```
assign(infile, 'testin');
assign(outfile, 'testout');
```

or alternately in the statement that opens the file:

```
reset(infile, 'testin');
rewrite(outfile, 'testout');
```

Normally these statements must be placed in the program after the file is declared, and before (or as) the file is opened for reading or writing. In some systems the actual file names must appear in the program statement. The *assign* statement or its equivalent is not part of standard Pascal, but it is used in many implementations. Details for opening files can be found in the documentation for your compiler or interpreter.

14.1.1 Using *eoln* and *eof* with External Files

Like *read* and *readln*, the standard functions *eoln* and *eof* can be used with files other than *input*. The file parameter must be included with the function call, e.g., *eof(f)* and *eoln(f)*. Remember that without a file parameter, these functions always refer to the standard input file.

As an example, we will rewrite a program that copies one *text* file to another (from chapter 8). The version for copying from the standard *input* file to the standard *output* file is shown in figure 14.1. The version using external files is shown in figure 14.2. Recall that the default file argument for *eof*, *eoln*, *read*, and *readln* is *input*, while the file argument for *write* and *writeln* defaults to *output*. Thus the two versions of *copy1* shown in figure 14.1 are equivalent. Once this is understood, it is easy to see that the only real differences between the programs in figures 14.1 and 14.2 are that the external file arguments must be used with each of these subroutines, and that the external files are declared and opened explicitly. In fact, files *input* and *output* are implicitly declared and opened by the Pascal system when the program is

Using default file parameters:

```
program copy1(input, output);
  var
    c : char;
  begin
    while not eof do
      begin
        while not eoln do
          begin
            read(c);
            write(c)
          end;
        readln;
        writeln
      end
  end.
```

File parameters specified:

```
program copy1(input, output);
  var
    c : char;
  begin
    while not eof(input) do
      begin
        while not eoln(input) do
          begin
            read(input, c);
            write(output, c)
          end;
        readln(input);
        writeln(output)
      end
  end.
```

Figure 14.1. Program *Copy* with standard input and output files

```
program copy2(fin, fout);
  var
    c    : char;                    { for reading a character       }
    fin  : text;                    { external file for input       }
    fout : text;                    { external file for output      }
  begin
    reset(fin);                     { open fin for input            }
    rewrite(fout);                  { open fout for output          }
    while not eof(fin) do
      begin
        while not eoln(fin) do
          begin
            read(fin, c);           { read char from fin            }
            write(fout, c)          { write char to fout            }
          end;
        readln(fin);                { discard newline char in fin   }
        writeln(fout)               { terminate line in fout        }
      end
  end.
```

Figure 14.2. Program *Copy* with External Files

run in a manner that is functionally equivalent to the following statements:

```
var
  input, output : text;

begin { main }

  reset(input);
  rewrite(output);
```

In standard Pascal implementions, explicitly opening files *input* and *output* via *reset(input)* and *rewrite(output)* has no effect, but it is not disallowed. Files other than *input* and *output* must be opened explicitly and may be opened more than once in a program. For example, it is not uncommon to read from a file and later to rewrite the file with updated information. It is also possible to read a file more than once by calling *reset* again. This is not possible using the standard *input* file. Remember that in many operating systems opening a file via *rewrite* first empties the file if it already exists. This is an easy way to delete files accidentally.

14.1.2 Files as Arguments to Subroutines

Files can be passed as arguments to functions and procedures if the subroutine has been declared with a formal file parameter of the appropriate type. The formal parameter *must* be declared **var**. As an example we will rewrite function *skipblanks* (chapter 8) so that it can be used with any text file.

```
procedure skipblanks(var f : text);
  var
    done : boolean;
  begin
    done := false;
    repeat
      if eof(f)
        then done := true
      else if f↑ = ' '
        then get(f)
      else done := true
    until done
  end;
```

Now the procedure can be invoked by *skipblanks(input)* to skip blanks in the standard *input* file, or by *skipblanks(data)* to skip blanks in file *data* (provided that *data* has been declared a text file, and opened for reading). In practice, it is often useful to declare procedures that perform a program's input and output so that the file can be supplied when the procedure is called.

14.2 Internal Files

In Pascal, it is possible to create and use files that will not exist after the program or procedure that creates them has terminated. These files are useful for temporary storage of data in a form that can be read again and processed further by the same program or procedure. The procedure for using internal files is identical to that for external files, except that the file does not appear as a file argument in the program heading. I will illustrate the use of an internal file in a program that adds to the end of a preexisting file. Since standard Pascal does not provide for opening files in an *update* mode (i.e., so that the program can add to the end of the file), an alternative approach is as follows:

1. Open the external file for reading and the internal file for writing
2. Copy the external file to the internal file
3. Add to the end of the internal file
4. Open the external file for writing and the internal file for reading
5. Copy the internal file to the external file

Remember that step (4) empties the external file before it is rewritten. This algorithm is implemented in program 14.2. Text is copied from one file to another by procedure *copy* (compare this procedure to figure 14.2). Here files representing the source and destination files for the copy are opened explicitly before procedure *copy* is called, since *tempfile* must not be opened by *rewrite* before the contents of the standard *input* file are copied into it.

Internal files can be used whenever a program or procedure needs to store data temporarily in a form that allows it to be reread and processed by the same program or procedure. In such a case the internal file is preferable to storing the data in an array, because the size of the file is not fixed at compile time, and because standard *read* and *write* procedures can be used to process the information.

```
(***********************      Program Update      ***********************)
(* Adds new text to the end of a preexistent file using a temporary      *)
(* internal file.                                                         *)
(*************************************************************************)
program update (input, output, data);
  var
    data     : text;
    tempfile : text;

(***********************           copy           ***********************)
(* Copies all text from file fin to file fout.                            *)
(*************************************************************************)
  procedure copy(var fin, fout : text);
    var
      c       : char;
    begin
      while not eof(fin) do
        begin
          while not eoln(fin) do
            begin
              read(fin, c);
              write(fout, c)
            end;
          readln(fin);
          writeln(fout)
        end
    end;

(***********************      main procedure      ***********************)
(* Copies all text from file fin to file fout.                            *)
(*************************************************************************)
  begin { main }
    reset(data);                     { open data for reading             }
    rewrite(tempfile);               { open tempfile for writing         }
    copy(data, tempfile);            { copy data file to tempfile        }

    writeln('Type additional data; terminate with eof signal:');
    copy(input, tempfile);           { copy input file to end of tempfile }

    reset(tempfile);                 { open tempfile for reading         }
    rewrite(data);                   { open data file for writing        }
    copy(tempfile, data)             { copy tempfile to data             }
  end. { main }
```

Program 14.2. *Update*

External file before update:

```
This text represents data stored in an external
text file, which we wish to update by adding
new text to the end.
```

Program run (interactive):

```
Type additional data; terminate with eof signal:
We will add this text to the end of the external
file by using a temporary internal file as a buffer.
The external file is copied to the temporary file,
followed by any text in the standard input.  Finally,
we will update the external file by rewriting it with
the contents of the temporary file.
^D
```

External file after update:

```
This text represents data stored in an external
text file, which we wish to update by adding
new text to the end.
We will add this text to the end of the external
file by using a temporary internal file as a buffer.
The external file is copied to the temporary file,
followed by any text in the standard input.  Finally,
we will update the external file by rewriting it with
the contents of the temporary file.
```

Program 14.2. Sample Input and Output

14.3 Binary Files

Pascal can read and write files of types other than *text*. The data is read or written in the binary format used by Pascal internally to store data. For example, a Pascal program can write or read a file of integers without converting to and from the ASCII character representation. Since no conversion takes place, the I/O operations are much faster than processing text files representing the same data. The penalty is that you cannot create the file using a text editor or examine the file using the ordinary operating system utilities for printing files and displaying them on the CRT screen. Also, the files may not be portable from one operating system or computer to another, and must be recreated for each new system.

Since they can be processed much more quickly, binary files are often used for getting large amounts of data into a program. This format might be used for initializing lookup tables, or for speeding up I/O in programs for which the data file is created and updated by the program and does not need to be read by human beings, who are better adapted to processing text files.

As a simple example of using binary files, consider program 14.3. The program reads a text file, converting the character representation of each number to the internal representation used for integers, and writing it to *binfile* in the binary format. The binary file is then opened for reading, and each number is read and then written to the standard output file. Here *bindata* is an external file declared as **file of** *integer*.

Reading and writing to this file require no conversion to and from character data. Note that *eof* can be used with binary files; *eoln* applies only to text files.

```
(***********************      Program Binary      ***********************)
(* Illustrates writing and reading binary files in Pascal.               *)
(*************************************************************************)
program binary(input, output, bindata);
  var
    x        : integer;
    n        : integer;
    bindata  : file of integer;

  procedure skipblanks(var f : text);               { skip blanks          }
    var
      done : boolean;
    begin
      done := false;
      repeat
        if eof(f)
          then done := true
        else if f↑ = ' '
          then get(f)
        else done := true
      until done
    end;

  procedure incr(var x : integer);                  { increment            }
    begin
      x := x + 1
    end;


(*************************************************************************)
(*                          main procedure                               *)
(*************************************************************************)

  begin { main }
    writeln(output, 'Copying input file to binary file');
    rewrite(bindata);                     { open data file for writing      }
    n := 0;
    while not eof(input) do
      begin
        incr(n);
        read(input, x);                   { read integer from file input    }
        write(bindata, x);                { write in binary to file bindata }
        skipblanks(input)                 { skip blanks in input file       }
      end;
    writeln(output, n, ' integers copied into binary file');
    writeln(output);
    writeln(output, 'Copying binary file to output: ');
    writeln(output);
    reset(bindata);                       { open bindata for reading        }
    n := 0;
```

```
    while not eof(bindata) do
      begin
        incr(n);
        read(bindata, x);                  { read binary integer              }
        write(output, x);                  { write as text in standard output }
        if n mod 10 = 0                    { write ten numbers per line       }
          then writeln(output)
      end;
    writeln(output);
    writeln(output, n, ' integers copied from binary file to output')
  end.  { main }
```

Program 14.3. *Binary*

Textfile Used for Standard Input:

```
15706 20546  6261 26169 29048  6713 21283 32255  8758  1359
19825 30181 32148 22404 17759 25579 20882 30426  6381 32273
 3120 26960 17947  6744 15214 21734 27369 11966  3404 32668
17751 20803 20426 20338 13157 14314 28904 19048 13075 14512
32422  5759 25185 18837  9988 31156 32591   156 14338 23050
26589  5058  8096 15745  6667 22791 27614 18966 13273 18029
19132 17868 29511 29171  2618  5795 13909  4506  6232 17048
31491 31583   790 28590 24401  9542 30836 25572  8511  9548
18034  1339  7885 12658 23312 22960 22011  8120 17486  1863
25801 26141 12332 21500  2359  6820 27818  9683  8517 29513
```

Standard Output File:

```
Copying input file to binary file
   100 integers copied into binary file

Copying binary file to output:

15706 20546  6261 26169 29048  6713 21283 32255  8758  1359
19825 30181 32148 22404 17759 25579 20882 30426  6381 32273
 3120 26960 17947  6744 15214 21734 27369 11966  3404 32668
17751 20803 20426 20338 13157 14314 28904 19048 13075 14512
32422  5759 25185 18837  9988 31156 32591   156 14338 23050
26589  5058  8096 15745  6667 22791 27614 18966 13273 18029
19132 17868 29511 29171  2618  5795 13909  4506  6232 17048
31491 31583   790 28590 24401  9542 30836 25572  8511  9548
18034  1339  7885 12658 23312 22960 22011  8120 17486  1863
25801 26141 12332 21500  2359  6820 27818  9683  8517 29513

   100 integers copied from binary file to output
```

Program 14.3. Sample Input and Output

The component type of files may be complex. It is often useful to declare files of structured types such as records. For example, the program discussed in chapter 17 reads data from an external file into two data tables, declared as follows:

```
program setid(input, output, setdata);

  type
    tabinfo = record
                 start : integer;
                 stop  : integer
              end;

    ar600    = array[1 .. 12] of tabinfo;

    fset     = record
                 z       : integer;
                 mmi     : integer;
                 name    : integer;
                 setnum  : integer
              end;

    ar300    = array[1 .. 229] of fset;

  var
    setdata : text;
    loc     : ar600;
    table   : ar300;
```

The data tables are read by the following procedure:

```
  procedure readtable(var data : text; var loc : ar600;
                                        var table : ar300);
    var
      i : integer;
    begin { read external data in tables }
      reset(data);
      for i := 1 to 12 do           { read loc table }
        with loc[i] do
          readln(data, start, stop);
      for i := 1 to 229 do          { read set table }
        with table[i] do
          readln(data, setnum, name, z, mmi)
    end;  { readtable }
```

This arrangement necessitates converting the data from the external (character) form to the internal binary format every time the program is run. Although this only takes a few seconds, the table-loading time could be made to seem practically instantaneous by converting the data to two binary files, which could then be read without conversion processing. The program that converts the data is shown as program 14.4. The procedure uses three external files: *setdata* (the original textfile), and two binary files, *locdata* and *tabdata*. The program reads the textfile using the original *readtable* procedure (shown above). It then opens and writes the two binary files, declared as **file of** *tabinfo* and **file of** *fset*.

```
(************************      Program Convert      ************************)
(* Reads data from a text file into two arrays of records, and then       *)
(* writes binary files representing this data. The program converts the  *)
(* data table used in program setid (chapter 17).                          *)
(**************************************************************************)
program convert(setdata, locdata, tabdata);
  type
    tabinfo = record
                start : integer;
                stop  : integer
              end;

    ar600   = array[1 .. 12] of tabinfo;

    fset    = record
                z      : integer;
                mmi    : integer;
                name   : integer;
                setnum : integer
              end;

    ar300   = array[1 .. 229] of fset;

    bintab  = file of fset;
    binloc  = file of tabinfo;

  var
    setdata : text;                       { external text file          }
    tabdata : bintab;                     { binary file for table data }
    locdata : binloc;                     { binary file for loc   data }
    loc     : ar600;
    table   : ar300;

(************************        readtable        ************************)
(* Reads data tables from external text file.                             *)
(**************************************************************************)
  procedure readtable(var data : text; var loc : ar600; var table : ar300);
    var
      i : integer;
    begin { read external data in tables }
      reset(data);
      for i := 1 to 12 do                                   { read loc table }
        with loc[i] do
          readln(data, start, stop);
      for i := 1 to 229 do                                  { read set table }
        with table[i] do
          readln(data, setnum, name, z, mmi)
    end;  { readtable }

(************************        writedata        ************************)
(* Writes tables into external binary files.                              *)
(**************************************************************************)
```

```
procedure writedata(var loc : ar600; var table : ar300;
                    var locdata : binloc; var tabdata : bintab);
  var
    i : integer;
  begin
    rewrite(locdata);                    { open locdata for writing    }
    for i := 1 to 12 do                  { and write loc records in    }
      write(locdata, loc[i]);            {     binary format           }

    rewrite(tabdata);                    { open tabdata for writing    }
    for i := 1 to 229 do                 { and write table records     }
      write(tabdata, table[i])           {     in binary format        }
  end;  { writedata }

(**********************      main procedure      **********************)
(* Converts one text file into two binary files.                     *)
(*********************************************************************)
  begin { main }
    readtable(setdata, loc, table);            { read the text data   }
    writedata(loc, table, locdata, tabdata)    { rewrite as bin files }
  end.  { main }
```

Program 14.4. *Convert*

The main procedure of program *setid* would be changed in the following ways:

1. Files *locdata* and *tabdata* would replace *setdata* in the program heading, and file declarations identical to those in program 14.4 would be included.
2. Procedure *readtable* would be replaced with the following:

```
procedure readtable(var loc : ar600 ; var table : ar300;
                    var locdata : binloc ; var tabdata : bintab)
  var
    i : integer;
  begin
    reset(locdata);                  { open locdata for reading }
    for i := 1 to 12 do              { read binary loc table    }
      read(locdata, loc[i]);

    reset(tabdata);                  { open tabdata for reading }
    for i := 1 to 229 do             { read binary set table    }
      read(tabdata, table[i])
  end;  { readtable }
```

In the new version of procedure *readtable*, each *read* statement reads an entire record in its binary format and the tables load more rapidly than in the original version. The modification is worth the extra trouble, since it only has to be done once for each new computer system, and the program will initialize much more quickly each time it is run.

References and Selected Readings

The following thematic index was implemented as a computer program and later published as a book:

Lincoln, Harry B. *The Italian Madrigal and Related Repertories: Indexes to Printed Collections, 1500–1600*. New Haven: Yale University Press, 1988.

The following was used in preparing exercise 14.4:

Wonderlich, Elvira. *Chorale Collection*. 3rd ed. New York: Appleton-Century-Crofts, 1948.

Other suggested readings:

Lincoln, Harry B. "Musicology and the Computer: The Thematic Index." In *Computers in Humanistic Research*, edited by Edmond A. Bowles, 184–93. Englewood Cliffs, N.J.: Prentice Hall, 1967.

———. "The Thematic Index: A Computer Application to Musicology." *Computers and the Humanities* 2 (1967–68): 215–20.

Tenney, James. *Hierarchical Temporal Gestalt Perception in Music: A "Metric Space" Model.* Toronto: York University, 1978.

Wittlich, Gary, Donald Byrd, and Rosalee Nerheim. "A System for Interactive Encoding of Musical Scores Under Computer Control." *Computers and the Humanities* 12 (1978): 309–19.

Exercises

1. Find out how to use external files on your Pascal system, then modify program *copy2* (figure 14.2) and use it to make a copy of a text file on your system.

2. Modify program 14.2 so that the original data file is printed to the user's terminal before the user is asked to add to it.

3. Find a way to get around the restriction that the standard input file can only be read once. Obviously, the solution is only applicable when the standard input is redirected from a file, and will not work in an interactive program where the input comes from the user's terminal.

4. *Incipit Index* (version 1). This exercise is highly recommended, since it combines the use of external files and records in a substantial, structured program. This program and the next will exercise many of the techniques discussed in this chapter and the last.[2] We will see a more sophistocated version of this program, which uses numeric encoding of the incipits and hashing techniques, in chapter 16.

2. This exercise was modeled on a FORTRAN program assigned to the author by Stefan Kostka in an introductory computer course. While the program has been extended in a number of directions, including structured programming techniques, the use of records and external files, and the use of the stack to keep track of empty locations in the table, the basic premise was designed by Professor Kostka and the author wishes to thank him for permission to include this exercise in the present volume.

Program Incips1

Techniques—use of external text file; use of record structures; use of a stack (implemented as an array); interactive programming; menu-driven program; linear search.

The thematic index is a valuable musicologic tool. While many indices are eventually published in book form, a thematic index more typically consists of a card file in which each card contains a representation of an incipit (the beginning of a melody) along with information concerning the source of the melody. Since the file may grow quite large, the researcher may devise a system for ordering incipits to facilitate finding entries. Nevertheless, a large file of hundreds or thousands of incipits will be cumbersome to use.

As the musicologist works with the file, he or she will be engaged in two basic tasks: (1) making out a card for a new incipit and placing it in the file, and (2) finding out whether an incipit has already been entered in the file.

A large thematic index would be much more convenient to use if the musicologist would translate the music to machine-readable symbols. The index could then be stored in some direct-access device such as a disk, and all entries and searches could be made via a remote console. Besides being happier, our musicologist would have more time to devote to really creative work (like browsing through dusty old manuscripts looking for new entries to add to the thematic index).

You are to write a Pascal program that will do the following:

a) Read a file of incipits into the *incips* array. This array simulates the disk on which the file could be stored.
b) Handle any number of requests as specified below.
c) Rewrite the updated file onto disk.

Requests will consist of keywords (only the first letter will be used) indicating:

help	– type this instruction table
add	– add incipit to file
search	– search file for incipit
print	– print out entire file with entry numbers
delete	– delete entries
compact	– compact file

When a user runs the program, it should prompt 'Do you need instructions? (yes/no)'. If the user answers 'yes', it should type the above menu. It should then prompt 'Command?', and wait for a request. In response to a correctly encoded request, the program should call a procedure that will prompt the user for any additional information it needs to perform its task. In response to an incorrect request, the program should respond 'Illegal request. Do you need instructions? (y/n)' and give instructions if needed.

The program should use a stack to keep track of empty spaces in the array. Whenever an incipit is deleted, its position should be pushed onto the stack. All holes should be filled before incipits are added to the end of the array.

Notes on action for commands:

a (add) Prompt the user for incipit and title (which may contain any additional information). Store new incipit and title in record where deletion was made, or in the $n + 1$ position in the *incips* array, or give message 'Out of array space' if $n = max$. A useful procedure is **procedure** *getloc*(**var** *x* : *integer*); which returns an available location, or 0 if the array is full. Confirm that the task is completed by responding: 'c d e f g a b - <title> added as entry no. xx', where *c d e f g a b* represents the encoded incipit, <title> represents the information on the title, and *xx* represents the actual location of the incipit in the array.

s (search) Prompt the user for an incipit. Read the new incipit into a temporary array (*new*). List by number and title every location in which the incipit occurs, or state that the incipit does not occur in the file. You will find the boolean variable *found* useful for the last specification.

p (print) Print the file on the CRT screen with line numbers.

d (delete) Prompt the user for the identification number of the incipit to be deleted. Type out the incipit and title, and then prompt 'Delete? (yes/no)'. This will help prevent erroneous deletions. Delete by replacing the incipit with blanks, marking the end of the title by placing a null character, *chr*(0), in the first position of the title array, and placing the row number on the stack so it can be used again.

c (compact) Compact the array by moving entries up to fill in spaces left by deletion. Don't forget to empty the stack when this is done. Hint: An algorithm similar to this one is given in section 10.5. This procedure should be called in response to the 'compact' command, and before the disk file is rewritten. Procedure *compact* should check the status of the stack, and do nothing if no entries have been deleted. Do not forget to empty the stack and reset the value of *n* (the actual number of entries) after compacting.

When the user types end-of-file (control-D) the array should be compacted if necessary, and the disk file should be rewritten. The program should then say 'End of job. The file now contains *n* entries' (where *n* is the actual number of entries after compacting) and terminate.

Test your program thoroughly, using all possible commands and the test file provided. The file consists of the incipits of the first fifty chorale melodies of the *Wonderlich Chorale Collection.* An incipit is defined as the first seven notes of the soprano, transposed to begin on C, with repeated notes and accidentals ignored. While this method might be ideal for some bodies of music, it has weaknesses in a chorale-melody application. However, it is better to find some incorrect entries (because of the incipit encoding) than to miss entries because the encoding is too specific.

The following pages contain a listing of a sample input file and a skeleton version of the program containing all declarations, complete I/O routines, and the main procedure block. Study the completed procedures carefully, paying particular attention to the manner in which records and fields of records are passed. Then complete the program according to the above specifications. The primary procedure headings are given with empty blocks. You may write any other functions and procedures you need to complete a well-structured, modular program. You will benefit from completing and testing one procedure at a time. N.B.: Use procedures that are already written whenever possible.

A sample input file is listed below. The line numbers are not part of the data.

```
 1. c b a g a b c Ach Gott und Herr, wie gross und schwer (Wonderlich 1)
 2. c b a g a b c Ach Gott und Herr, wie gross und schwer (Wonderlich 2)
 3. c d c b f e d Ach Gott, vom Himmel sieh' darein (Wonderlich 3)
 4. c d c b f e d Ach Gott, vom Himmel sieh' darein (Wonderlich 4)
 5. c a b c d c b Ach Gott, wie manches Herzeleid (Wonderlich 5)
 6. c a b c d c b Ach Gott, wie manches Herzeleid (Wonderlich 6)
 7. c e f g b a g Ach, was soll ich Suender machen (Wonderlich 7)
 8. c d e f g f e Allein Gott in der Hoeh' sei Ehr' (Wonderlich 8)
 9. c g a b c d e Allein zu dir, Herr Jesu Christ (Wonderlich 9)
10. c e c d c b a Als Jesus Christus in der Nacht (Wonderlich 10)
11. c d e f g f e Auf meinen lieben Gott (Wonderlich 11)
12. c g e d c d e Aus meines Herzens Grunde (Wonderlich 12)
13. c f c d c b a Aus tiefer Not schrei' ich zu dir (Wonderlich 13)
14. c d e d e f g Befiehl du deine Wege (Wonderlich 14)
15. c b c d e f e Christ lag in Todesbanden (Wonderlich 15)
16. c b c d e f e Christ lag in Todesbanden (Wonderlich 16)
17. c d e f g f b Christ, unser Herr, zum Jordan kam (Wonderlich 17)
18. c e c b c d e Christe, der du bist Tag und Licht (Wonderlich 18)
19. c d e d g a b Christe, du Beistand deiner Kreuzgemeine (Wonderlich 19)
```

```
20. c e d e f g e Christus, der ist mein Leben (Wonderlich 20)
21. c b a g a b c Christus, der uns selig macht (Wonderlich 21)
22. c g a b c g c Christus ist erstanden, hat ueberwunden (Wonderlich 22)
23. c e d e f g f Danket dem Herren, denn er ist sehr freundlich (W. 23)
24. c b a g c b g Das alte Jahr vergangen ist (Wonderlich 24)
25. c g f e g f e Das neugeborne Kindelein (Wonderlich 25)
26. c b f a b c b Der du bist drei in Einigkeit (Wonderlich 26)
27. c e f g c b a Die Sonn' hat sich mit ihrem Glanz (Wonderlich 27)
28. c d e f g f c Dies sind die heil'gen zehn Gebot' (Wonderlich 28)
29. c f a g a f d Dir, dir, Jehova, will ich singen (Wonderlich 29)
30. c a b c e d c Du Friedefuerst, Herr Jesu Christ (Wonderlich 30)
31. c d e g c d e Du grosser Schmerzensmann (Wonderlich 31)
32. c g c b a g e Du, o schoenes Weltgebaude (Wonderlich 32)
33. c g c d b a g Du, o schoenes Weltgebaude (Wonderlich 33)
34. c b c a g f c Durch Adams Fall ist ganz verderbt (Wonderlich 34)
35. c g a b c b a Ein' feste Burg ist unser Gott (Wonderlich 35)
36. c e f g a g f Erbarm' dich mein, o Herre Gott (Wonderlich 36)
37. c d e d c b c Erhalt' uns, Herr, bei deinem Wort (W 37)
38. c d e f g f g Ermuntre dich, mein schwacher Geist (Wonderlich 38)
39. c d e f g f g Ermuntre dich, mein schwacher Geist (Wonderlich 39)
40. c g a b a g f Erschienen ist der herrlich' Tag (Wonderlich 40)
41. c g a b a g f Erschienen ist der herrlich' Tag (Wonderlich 41)
42. c e d c b c a Es ist das Heil uns kommen her (Wonderlich 42)
43. c d e d c b c Es ist das Heil uns kommen her (Wonderlich 43)
44. c d e d c b c Es ist das heil uns kommen her (Wonderlich 44)
45. c d e f g d f Es ist genug, so nimm, Herr (Wonderlich 45)
46. c d e d c d e Es ist gewisslich an der Zeit (Wonderlich 46)
47. c b a g c d e Es spricht der Unweisen Mund (Wonderlich 47)
48. c e c b c d e Es steh'n vor Gottes Throne (Wonderlich 48)
49. c g a b g e f Es wird schier der letzte Tag herkommen (Wonderlich 49)
50. c d c b c d e Es woll' uns Gott genaedig sein (Wonderlich 50)
```

Program *Incips1*. Sample Data File

```
(****************************************************************************)
(*       Skeleton solution for program incips1 (exercise 14.4)             *)
(****************************************************************************)

program incips1(input, output, data);

  const
    inciplen  = 7;                  { number of notes in incipit            }
    maxstring = 76;                 { maximum string length + 1             }
    max       = 52;                 { maximum number of entries in file     }
    terminal  = true;               { switches to control destination       }
    disk      = false;              {    of printing                        }

  type
    string  = packed array[1 .. maxstring] of char;
    incipit = packed array[1 .. inciplen] of char;
    stack   = array[1 .. max] of integer;
```

```
  entry = record
            incip : incipit;         { array to store encoded incipit     }
            title : string           { array to store title information   }
          end;
                                     { array of records to store file     }
  incipfile = array[1 .. max] of entry;

var                                  { global variables                   }
  data   : text;                     { external data file                 }
  incips : incipfile;                { the storage array                  }
  n      : integer;                  { actual number of entries           }
  S      : stack;                    { array for implementing stack       }
  top    : integer;                  { top of stack indicator             }
  key    : char;                     { stores first char of user requests }

(****************************************************************************)
(*                          Utility Routines                                *)
(****************************************************************************)
procedure skip(var f : text);
  var
    done : boolean;
  begin
    done := false;
    repeat
      if eof(f)
        then done := true
      else if f↑ = ' '
        then get(f)
      else done := true
    until done
  end;

procedure incr(var x : integer);
  begin
    x := x + 1
  end;

function stackempty : boolean;
  begin
    stackempty := top = 0
  end;

function stackfull : boolean;
  begin
    stackfull := top >= max
  end;

procedure push(x : integer);
  begin
    if stackfull
      then writeln('Error : stack is full')
      else
        begin
          top := top + 1;
          S[top] := x
        end
  end;
```

```
procedure pop(var x : integer);
  begin
    if stackempty
      then writeln('Error : stack is empty')
      else
        begin
          x := S[top];
          top := top - 1
        end
  end;

function affirmative : boolean;
  var
    ch : char;
  begin
    skip(input);
    readln(ch);
    if ch = 'y'
      then affirmative := true
    else if ch = 'n'
      then affirmative := false
    else
      begin
        write('You must answer yes or no: ');
        affirmative := affirmative
      end
  end;

function isdigit(c : char) : boolean;
  begin
    isdigit := c in ['0' .. '9']
  end;

procedure getint(var x : integer);
  begin
    skip(input);
    if isdigit(input↑)
      then read(x)
      else
        begin
          readln;     { clear buffer }
          write('Integer required: ');
          getint(x)
        end
  end;

(**************************************************************************)
(*                           Input Routines                               *)
(**************************************************************************)

procedure readincip(var f : text; var incip : incipit);

  var
    i : integer;
  begin { readincip }
```

```
    for i := 1 to inciplen do
      begin
        skip(f);
        read(f, incip[i])
      end
  end;  { readincip }

procedure readstring(var f : text; var S : string);
  var
    i : integer;
  begin
    skip(f);
    i := 1;
    while not eoln(f) do
      begin
        read(f, S[i]);
        incr(i)
      end;
    S[i] := chr(0)
  end;

procedure readfile(var f : text; var incips : incipfile; var n : integer);
  begin
    reset(f); { open file for reading }
    n := 0;
    while not eof(f) do
      begin
        incr(n);
        readincip(f, incips[n].incip);
        readstring(f, incips[n].title);
        readln(f)
      end
  end;

(**************************************************************************)
(*                             Output Routines                            *)
(**************************************************************************)
procedure writeincip(var f : text; var incip : incipit);
  var
    i : integer;
  begin
    for i := 1 to 7 do
      write(f, incip[i], ' ')
  end;

procedure writestring(var f : text; S : string);
  var
    i : integer;
  begin
    i := 1;
    while S[i] <> chr(0) do
      begin
        write(f, S[i]);
        incr(i)
      end;
    writeln(f)
  end;
```

```
procedure writefile(var f : text; var incips : incipfile;
                              n : integer; toterminal :  boolean);
  var
    i : integer;
  begin
    for i := 1 to n do
      begin
        if toterminal
          then write(f, i:3, '.  ');
        writeincip(f, incips[i].incip);
        writestring(f, incips[i].title)
      end
  end;


(**********************************************************************)
(*                Primary Program Routines (your job)                 *)
(**********************************************************************)

procedure instruct;
  begin
    writeln('Procedure not yet implemented')
  end;

procedure getloc(var x, n : integer)          { return location to add }
  begin
  end;

procedure add(var incips : incipfile; var n : integer);
  begin
    writeln('Procedure not yet implemented')
  end;

function empty(var E : entry) : boolean;       { a gift                 }
  begin
    empty := E.incip[1] = ' '
  end;

procedure compact(var incips : incipfile; var n : integer);
  begin
    writeln('Procedure not yet implemented')
  end;

procedure clear(var E : entry);                { clear deleted entry    }
  var
    i : integer;
  begin
    for i := 1 to inciplen do                  { empty incipit          }
      E.incip[i] := ' ';
    E.title[1] := chr(0)                       { empty title string     }
  end;

procedure delete(var incips : incipfile; n : integer);
  begin
    writeln('Procedure not yet implemented')
  end;
```

```
procedure search(var incips : incipfile; n : integer);
  begin
    writeln('Procedure not yet implemented')
  end;

function goodkey(key : char): boolean;
  begin
    goodkey := key in ['a', 'c', 'd', 'h', 'p', 's']
  end;

(**************************************************************************)
(*                          Main Procedure                               *)
(**************************************************************************)

begin { main }
  readfile(data, incips, n);             { read data file into array    }
  top := 0;                              { initialize  stack            }

  write('Do you need instructions? (y/n)  ');
  if affirmative
    then instruct;
  writeln;
  write('Command?  ');
  skip(input);

  while not eof do
    begin { process user requests }
      skip(input);
      readln(key);                       { get first letter of command }
      if goodkey(key)
        then
          case key of
            'a' : add(incips, n);        { add entry to file            }
            'c' : compact(incips, n);    { remove blank entries         }
            'd' : delete(incips, n);     { delete entry from file       }
            'h' : instruct;              { give instructions            }
                                         { print file to terminal       }
            'p' : writefile(output, incips, n, terminal);
            's' : search(incips, n)      { locate incipits in file      }
          end  { case }
        else
          begin
            write('Illegal command.  Do you need instructions? (y,n) ');
            if affirmative
              then instruct              { print instructions           }
          end;
      writeln;
      write('Command?  ')
    end;

  compact(incips, n);
  rewrite(data);                         { open data file for writing }
  writefile(data, incips, n, disk);      { rewrite disk file            }
  writeln('End of job, file contains', n:3, ' entries.')
end.  { main }
```

Program *Incips1* (skeleton)

```
Do you need instructions? (y/n)  yes

*********************************************
Commands are:

    add      - add incipit to file
    compact  - remove blank entries
    delete   - delete entries
    help     - type this table
    print    - print file with line numbers
    search   - search file for incipit
    ^D       - terminate execution

Commands may be abbreviated to first letter
*********************************************

Command?  search
Type incipit: cdefgab
Matching entries:
      c d e f g a b does not occur in file.

Command?  s
Type incipit: cbagabc
Matching entries:
  1.  c b a g a b c Ach Gott und Herr, wie gross und schwer (Wonderlich 1)
  2.  c b a g a b c Ach Gott und Herr, wie gross und schwer (Wonderlich 2)
 21.  c b a g a b c Christus, der uns selig macht (Wonderlich 21)

Command?  delete
Type number of entry to be deleted: wt
Integer required: 25
c g f e g f e Das neugeborne Kindelein (Wonderlich 25)
Delete? (y/n):  n

Command?  remove
Illegal command.  Do you need instructions? no

Command?  d
Type number of entry to be deleted: 2
c b a g a b c Ach Gott und Herr, wie gross und schwer (Wonderlich 2)
Delete? (y/n):  y
Entry  2 deleted.

Command?  d
Type number of entry to be deleted: 4
c d c b f e d Ach Gott, vom Himmel sieh' darein (Wonderlich 4)
Delete? (y/n):  y
Entry  4 deleted.

Command?  add
Type incipit: cbagfcd
Type title: Jesu Meine Freude
c b a g f c d Jesu Meine Freude
  added as entry no.  4
```

```
Command?  add
Type incipit: cdefgab
Type title: scalar tune
c d e f g a b scalar tune
  added as entry no.  2

Command?  a
Type incipit: cdcdcdc
Type title: trill
c d c d c d c trill
  added as entry no. 51

Command?  delete
Type number of entry to be deleted: 5
c a b c d c b Ach Gott, wie manches Herzeleid (Wonderlich 5)
Delete? (y/n):  y
Entry  5 deleted.

Command?  print
  1.  c b a g a b c Ach Gott und Herr, wie gross und schwer (Wonderlich 1)
  2.  c d e f g a b scalar tune
  3.  c d c b f e d Ach Gott, vom Himmel sieh' darein (Wonderlich 3)
  4.  c b a g f c d Jesu Meine Freude
  5.
  6.  c a b c d c b Ach Gott, wie manches Herzeleid (Wonderlich 6)
  7.  c e f g b a g Ach, was soll ich Suender machen (Wonderlich 7)
  8.  c d e f g f e Allein Gott in der Hoeh' sei Ehr' (Wonderlich 8)
  9.  c g a b c d e Allein zu dir, Herr Jesu Christ (Wonderlich 9)
 10. c e c d c b a Als Jesus Christus in der Nacht (Wonderlich 10)
 11. c d e f g f e Auf meinen lieben Gott (Wonderlich 11)
 12. c g e d c d e Aus meines Herzens Grunde (Wonderlich 12)
 13. c f c d c b a Aus tiefer Not schrei' ich zu dir (Wonderlich 13)
 14. c d e d e f g Befiehl du deine Wege (Wonderlich 14)
 15. c b c d e f e Christ lag in Todesbanden (Wonderlich 15)
 16. c b c d e f e Christ lag in Todesbanden (Wonderlich 16)
 17. c d e f g f b Christ, unser Herr, zum Jordan kam (Wonderlich 17)
 18. c e c b c d e Christe, der du bist Tag und Licht (Wonderlich 18)
 19. c d e d g a b Christe, du Beistand deiner Kreuzgemeine (Wonderlich 19)
 20. c e d e f g e Christus, der ist mein Leben (Wonderlich 20)
 21. c b a g a b c Christus, der uns selig macht (Wonderlich 21)
 22. c g a b c g c Christus ist erstanden, hat ueberwunden (Wonderlich 22)

     . . .

 49.  c g a b g e f Es wird schier der letzte Tag herkommen (Wonderlich 49)
 50.  c d c b c d e Es woll' uns Gott genadig sein (Wonderlich 50)
 51.  c d c d c d c trill

Command?  compact
File compacted.  File now contains  50 entries.

Command? ^D
 End of job, file contains 50 entries.
```

Program *Incips1*. Sample Run (Interactive)

5. If you think of any other functions that would be useful in the above program, implement them. One suggestion is a keyword search that attempts to match portions of the title strings. This could be implemented with the *index* function, listed in section 10.5, combined with a function that converts uppercase letters to lower case. In other respects the procedure should operate approximately like the 'search' command.

6. Modify the program from exercise 14.4 so that it stores the incipit file in a binary file (file of entry). You should begin with an empty file, and all data will have to be entered via 'add' commands. Obviously, procedure *readfile* will have to be replaced, and a new procedure (other than *printdata*) will have to be used to rewrite the binary file at the end of the program run.

7. A program to implement a real thematic index would probably need to store more information than we used in the above exercise. Choose a body of literature that interests you and decide on the type of data you would like the program to store. Then design the record structures and an incipit encoding scheme to suite your index. You do not have to implement the actual program at this time.

15 | Recursive Algorithms

A *recursive* algorithm is an algorithm that is defined in terms of itself. Imagine a picture of a person looking at the same picture of himself looking at the picture, and you begin to grasp the concept. Many people find recursion a bit circular and confusing at first, but it is a powerful technique for problem solving, and once you get the hang of it, you will find that recursive solutions to some types of problems are much more natural than nonrecursive ones. We introduce recursion here because it is a useful tool for dealing with linked data structures, the topic of chapter 16.

Direct recursion occurs when a function or procedure calls itself. Recursion is said to be *indirect* when procedure *A* calls procedure *B* which calls procedure *A*, or when *A* calls *B* which calls other routines which eventually call *A*. In this chapter we will also see an example of *mutually recursive* procedures, where procedure *A* calls procedure *B* which calls procedure *A*, and so on.

15.1 Using Recursion

Any procedure that can be written using assignment, **if...then...else**, and a loop (**while**, **repeat**, or **for**) can be recast as a recursive procedure, although this is not always desirable. As a simple example, consider printing out notes 1 to *n* of a tune stored in an array, *tune*. The iterative solution uses a simple **for** loop:

```
procedure printlist(var A : arraytype; n : integer);
  var
    i : integer;
  begin
    for i := 1 to n do
      write(A[i]);
    writeln
  end;
```

The tune is printed by calling *printlist*(*tune*, *n*).

An alternate solution prints the list by printing one element and calling itself recursively to print the list beginning with the next element. Consider the steps necessary to print a list of five elements (*a*, *b*, *c*, *d*, *e*):

To print the list beginning with	print
a	*a* followed by the list beginning with *b*
b	*b* followed by the list beginning with *c*
c	*c* followed by the list beginning with *d*
d	*d* followed by the list beginning with *e*
e	*e* (followed by an empty list)

Note that each step is essentially the same case: in order to print the list beginning with element *i*, print element *i* followed by the list beginning with element *i* + 1. When element *i* is past the end of the list, no action is taken and the algorithm terminates. The recursive version of the procedure is shown below:

```
procedure printlist(var A : arraytype; i, n : integer);
  begin
    if i <= n
      then
        begin
          write(A[i]);
          printlist(A, i + 1, n)
        end
  end;
```

This procedure is called with *i* = 1:

```
printlist(tune, 1, n);
writeln;
```

The new version of procedure *printlist* prints *tune*[1], then calls itself recursively with *i* = 2 to print the second note. This process continues until *i* = *n*. At this point the procedure prints the last note in the tune and makes one last recursive call with *i* = *n* + 1. This time the boolean test *i* <= *n* evaluates to *false*, and the procedure takes no action other than to terminate and return to the previous level of recursion (where *i* = *n*). Since there are no other statements to execute in the procedure, this call of *printlist* terminates, returning to the previous level (where *i* = *n* – 1), and so on until the initial procedure call, shown above, terminates and the following *writeln* statement is executed. If the value of *n* is less than the initial value of *i* (1), the first call of *printlist* terminates without taking any other action.

In the above example, the recursive solution treats the list as if it were defined recursively. Instead of thinking of the list as a succession of elements, we define it thus: Either a list is empty or it consists of an element followed by a list. Processing the list is simplified, since the procedure deals with only one element at a time. To process a tune: If there are no notes in the tune, we are done, otherwise we print the current note and then process the tune beginning with the next note. If there are *n* notes in the tune and *i* is the ordinal position of a note in the tune, then there are no more notes in the tune when *i* > *n*. This test is crucial—without it the recursive plunge would go on until a program error (e.g., array bound or arithmetic overflow) occurs or the memory allocated to the program is exhausted.[1] Remember:

> *Every recursive procedure or function must provide a means for terminating the recursion.*

Problems that can be defined recursively and algorithms dealing with data structures that are recursively defined lend themselves quite naturally to recursive solutions.[2] In many cases the recursive solution is more elegant and clearer than the nonrecursive one. Hence the recursive solution may be preferable, even though there is a cost.

Recursion is possible because Pascal allocates space for local variables and subroutine parameters dynamically whenever a function or procedure is called. Thus each invocation of a recursive routine is allocated its own copy of these variables. For this reason recursive algorithms use more space than iterative ones. This is one cost of recursion. The other is that function and procedure calls themselves involve some overhead, e.g., passing arguments on the stack. Still, the clarity or simplicity of the recursive solution is often worth the cost. The iterative solution to printing a list is so simple that the recursive one is not warranted, although it serves well enough as an initial illustration of recursion.

Factorials provide the classic example of a recursive function. The factorial of a positive integer n (written $n!$) is

$$n \times (n - 1) \times (n - 2) \times \ldots \times 1$$

(Zero factorial is 1 by definition.) For example, 6! is

$$6 \times 5 \times 4 \times 3 \times 2 \times 1 = 720$$

While an iterative solution is possible, the recursive one is natural. Note that we could define 6! as $6 \times 5!$, and 5! as $5 \times 4!$, and so on. In fact, we can define $n!$ as $n \times (n - 1)!$ for any positive n. A recursive definition follows:

if $n = 0$
  then $n! = 1$
  otherwise $n! = n * (n - 1)!$

As a Pascal function, the above is written thus:

```
function fac(n : integer) : integer;
  begin
    if n = 0
      then fac := 1
      else fac := n * fac(n - 1)
  end;
```

1. This would be true even if no arguments were passed, since the return address (the address of the statement following the function call) would have to be saved on the stack in any case).

2. The latter is common with linked data structures; we will see examples in chapter 16.

Again, the definition provides a means of terminating recursion. In this case recursion ends when $n = 0$, provided that n is positive in the first place. The above function will not terminate correctly if called with a negative value for n.[3] The statement $x := fac(4)$ results in several levels of recursion, as shown in figure 15.1. The original call of $fac(4)$ cannot be resolved until $fac(3)$, the first level of recursion, returns a value. Likewise, $fac(3)$ cannot be calculated until $fac(2)$, at level 2, is resolved, and so on. Recursion terminates after $fac(0)$ is called (level 4). This is so because $fac(0)$ is not defined recursively (see the function definition above). $Fac(0)$ returns 1. Now $fac(1)$, at level 3, evaluates to 1×1 or 1; $fac(2)$ can be evaluated as $2 \times 1 = 2$; and $fac(3)$ as $3 \times 2 = 6$. Finally, level 1 evaluates to $4 \times 6 = 24$. This value is returned as the value of $fac(4)$ and is assigned to x.

Function Call	Recursion Level
$x := \underline{fac(4)}$	0
$= 4 * \underline{fac(3)}$	1
$= 3 * \underline{fac(2)}$	2
$= 2 * \underline{fac(1)}$	3
$= 1 * \underline{fac(0)}$	4
$= 1$	

Figure 15.1. Levels of Recursion for a Recursive Function

15.2 Tracing Recursive Algorithms

Stepping through a recursive algorithm manually can be confusing at first. Although this will probably not be necessary after you become more comfortable with recursion, you should try it a few times to make sure that you understand exactly what is going on. While making the trace, you must keep track of the recursion level as well as line numbers and values. The recursion level increases each time the function is called recursively, and decreases each time the function returns from a recursive call. Table 15.1 traces the factorial function discussed above, from its initial call, $x := fac(4)$, to the final value. The function goes through four levels of recursion before $n = 0$ and the recursive plunge is terminated. The double horizontal line marks the end of recursion—the point where the final recursive call is resolved and the program begins to fall back through the previous calls to level 0.

3. The function could be made to terminate correctly for negative numbers by changing the test to **if** $n \leq 0$; however, this is not mathematically correct.

```
1  function fac(n : integer) : integer;
2    begin
3      if n = 0
4        then fac := 1
5        else fac := n * fac(n - 1)
6    end;
```

Initial call: $x := fac(4)$

Level	Line	n	$(n = 0)$	Function Call	*fac*
0	1	4			
	3		*false*		
	5			*fac*(3)	
1	1	3			
	3		*false*		
	5			*fac*(2)	
2	1	2			
	3		*false*		
	5			*fac*(1)	
3	1	1			
	3		*false*		
	5			*fac*(0)	
4	1	0			
	3		*true*		
	4				1
3	5				1
2	5				2
1	5				6
0	5				**24**

24 is assigned to x

Table 15.1. Tracing a Recursive Function

15.3 Examples of Direct Recursion

In this section we will study two simple recursive subroutines that can be used in writing interactive programs. In each case recursion is used when the user gives an invalid response; recursion allows the same code to process another answer.

15.3.1 Function *affirmative*

Recursion is especially appropriate when the number of levels of recursion is limited, since the cost is small compared to the benefits obtained. A useful function in interactive programs returns *true* if the user responds "yes" or *false* if he answers "no." It can be called after the program prompts the user with any question that requires a "yes" or "no" answer:

```
writeln('REALLY delete all of your files? (y/n): ');
if affirmative
  then ...
```

Function *affirmative* checks the first letter of the response, prints an error message if the response is not one of the expected ones, and returns *true* or *false* when an appropriate response is received. The algorithm in pseudo code is

```
get a valid response;
if it is yes
  then return true
  else return false;
```

The hard part is ensuring a valid response. An iterative solution uses a loop and a test for a correct response:

```
function affirmative : boolean;
  var
    response : char;
  begin
    repeat
      skipblanks;
      readln(response);
      if not (response in ['y', 'n'])
        then writeln('You must answer yes or no: ')
    until response in ['y', 'n'];
    affirmative := response = 'y'
  end;
```

In the recursive solution, the loop is replaced by a recursive call of the function itself:

```
function affirmative : boolean;
  var
    response : character;
  begin
    skipblanks;
    readln(response);
    if response in ['y', 'n']
      then affirmative := response = 'y'
      else
        begin { try again }
          write('Please answer yes or no: ');
          affirmative := affirmative
        end   { try again }
  end;
```

15.3.2 Procedure *getint*

The general technique shown above is useful whenever we want to guarantee that the user gives an appropriate response, possibly saving the program from abnormal termination. For example, if the program expects to read an integer and the user's response begins with anything other than a digit, an execution error will result. Under these circumstances, the following sequence could cause abnormal termination of the program with an error something like 'File input: integer expected on source line . . . ':

```
write('How many problems do you want to do? ');
read(n);
```

This error may be acceptable in an exercise designed to test an algorithm, but in the real world users take a dim view of programs that allow a simple error to cause loss of data that may have taken several hours to enter.

One technique to help make programs foolproof is to write procedures that insist on data of the correct type and within prescribed limits; recursion can facilitate this task. For example, procedure *getint*, shown below, is designed to read an integer:[4]

```
procedure getint(var x : integer);
  begin
    skipblanks;
    if isdigit(input↑)
      then read(x)
      else
        begin { try again }
          readln;               { skip bad data }
          write('You must type an integer: ');
          getint(x)
        end   { try again }
  end;
```

Skipblanks moves *input*↑ to the first nonblank character. If the character is a digit, the integer is read, leaving *input*↑ at the first nonnumeric character. If no digits are present, *readln* clears the input buffer, the user is given instructions, and *getint* is called recursively to process the next answer.

In writing recursive procedures and functions such as those above, it is important that no active statements follow the recursive call. The following attempt at procedure *getint* does not return the correct value if an error is made on the first response. The reason is that the value returned by the recursive call is replaced by the undefined value from the present level of recursion after the recursive call returns its value.

```
          { Erroneous Solution }

procedure getint(var x : integer);
  var
    temp : integer;
```

4. The version of *getint* shown here expects positive integers with no sign. A version of the procedure that accepts signed integers is suggested as an exercise at the end of this chapter.

```
begin
  skipblanks;
  if isdigit(input↑)
    then read(temp)
    else
      begin { bad data }
        readln;                   { skip bad data }
        write('You must type an integer: ');
        getint(x)
      end;  { bad data }
  x := temp                       { ← ERROR!! }
end;
```

The same type of error can occur in other instances where the programmer forgets that the recursive call has done some processing that should not be undone after the recursion has terminated. While the problem seems obvious in this example, this type of error is common among students coming to grips with recursion for the first time. You should study this example carefully.

15.3.3 Reciprocal Duration Code Revisited

The reciprocal duration code that we used in earlier chapters has several limitations. The most serious of these is the lack of a representation for dotted notes and ties. We now suggest solutions to both of these problems. The solution to the first requires application of techniques we learned in earlier chapters; the second is solved handily using recursion.[5]

Dotted note values can be encoded by following the duration code with an arbitrary number of dots (periods). Some examples are shown in table 15.2.

Internally, we will represent each duration by its fractional value, e.g., quarter note = 1/4 = .25. Later, the fractional value will be converted to beats by the formula

$$beats = \frac{duration}{beatnote}$$

Notation	*Code*	*Meaning*
♩.	4.	dotted quarter
♩..	4..	double-dotted quarter
𝅗𝅥.	2.	dotted half
𝅘𝅥𝅯...	16...	triple-dotted sixteenth

Table 15.2. Dotted Notes in Reciprocal Duration Code

5. Recursive dot processing is suggested as an exercise at the end of this chapter.

Recall that the value of the first dot is half that of the undotted note, and that the value of each successive dot is half of the previous dot. The value of a triple-dotted quarter note is

$$1/4 + 1/8 + 1/16 + 1/32 = 15/32$$

♩... $= .25 + .125 + .0625 + .03125 = .46875$

Computer processing of this code requires a combination of techniques. First, the integer part of the code is read and converted to a fractional value by taking its reciprocal. After the integer is read, the value of *input*↑ will be either a blank (or newline character) or a dot. If the next character in the input buffer is a dot, an appropriate value is added to the duration, and *input*↑ is advanced to the next character. Since any number of dots may be present, a **while** statement is preferable to an **if** statement. Thus the basic algorithm is:

```
read duration code;
assign duration 1 / code;
assign dot half the value of duration;
while the next character is a dot do
   begin
      add dot to duration;
      skip the dot;
      halve the value of dot
   end;
```

The duration code must be read as an integer; if a real variable is used, the *read* procedure will interpret the dot as a decimal point. This is undesirable for two reasons: our program could not know if the dot were there, and an input error would occur because the dot is not followed by digits.

We can use commas to represent ties in rdc, as shown in table 15.3. The algorithm for processing tied notes is:

```
calculate the value of the first duration; { see above }
if there is a tie (comma)
   then
     begin
        skip the comma;
        calculate the fractional value of the next duration
          and add it to the first duration
     end;
```

If *getdur* is written as a function, then the statement "calculate the value of the next duration and add it to the first" becomes

```
duration := duration + getdur
```

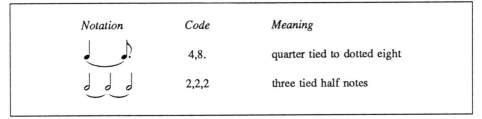

Notation	*Code*	*Meaning*
	4,8.	quarter tied to dotted eight
	2,2,2	three tied half notes

Table 15.3. Tied Notes in Reciprocal Durtion Code

The recursive call of *getdur* processes the tied duration, and since each level of recursion can call another, any number of notes may be tied together.

Program 15.1 exercises function *getdur*, which also processes an optional sign (a minus sign means a rest here) in a manner identical to that used in procedure *readint* (program 8.4). Note that the basic algorithms shown here apply to any encoding convention. The details vary with the specific encoding scheme used.

```
(************************       Program Durtest       ***********************)
(* Exercises a function that reads and interprets reciprocal duration      *)
(* code (rdc).  The program prompts the user for the note representing a *)
(* beat, and then accepts encoded durations.  Input: durations are        *)
(* encoded as the reciprocal of the duration name optionally followed by *)
(* any number of dots (periods).  Ties are encoded as commas; rests are  *)
(* preceded by a minus sign.  Examples: 4,8. (quarter tied to dotted      *)
(* 8th); 16... (triple-dotted 16th); -16. (dotted 16th rest).             *)
(* Output: for each duration, the fractional value of the duration as a  *)
(* decimal number, and the number of beats.                               *)
(**************************************************************************)
program durtest(input, output);
  var
    beatnote : real;
    duration : real;

(************************          skipblanks         ***********************)
(* Skips to first nonblank character or end-of-file.                      *)
(**************************************************************************)
  procedure skipblanks;
    var
      done : boolean;
    begin
      done := false;
      repeat
        if eof
          then done := true
        else if input↑ = ' '
          then get(input)
        else done := true
      until done
    end;
```

```
(***********************          getdur          ***********************)
(* Reads encoded durations and returns the fractional value of the dura- *)
(* tion as a real number, which is negative if the duration was a rest.  *)
(*************************************************************************)
  function getdur : real;
    var
      code     : integer;                  { for reading duration code     }
      dur      : real;                     { fractional value of duration }
      dot      : real;                     { fractional value of dot       }
      negative : boolean;                  { if true indicates a rest      }

    begin { getdur }
      skipblanks;                          { skip spaces                   }
      negative := input↑ = '-';            { check for sign                }
      if input↑ in ['+', '-']
        then get(input);                   { skip sign                     }
      read(code);                          { read duration code            }
      dur := 1 / code;                     { convert to fraction           }
      dot := dur / 2;                      { value for first dot           }

      while input↑ = '.' do                { process dots                  }
        begin { process dots }
          dur := dur + dot;
          get(input);                      { skip dot                      }
          dot := dot / 2                   { halve dot                     }
        end; { process dots }

      if input↑ = ','                      { process tie                   }
        then
          begin { process tied note }
            get(input);                    { skip comma                    }
            dur := dur + getdur            { get tied note recursively     }
          end; { process tied note }

      if negative
        then getdur := -dur                { return duration               }
        else getdur := dur
    end; { getdur }

(*************************************************************************)
(*                           Main Procedure                              *)
(*************************************************************************)
  begin { main }
    write('Type beat note: ');
    beatnote := getdur;                        { get duration of beat }
    writeln(beatnote:10:6,' = one beat');
    writeln('Type duration codes, terminate run with ctrl-D:');
    writeln;
    while not eof do
      begin
        duration := getdur;                { get duration of note or rest }
        writeln('  value: ', duration:10:6,
                '  beats: ', duration / beatnote:10:6);
        skipblanks
      end
  end. { main }
```

Program 15.1. *Durtest*

```
Type beat note: 4
  0.250000 = one beat
Type duration codes, terminate run with ctrl-D:

1 2 4 8 16 32
  value:    1.000000   beats:    4.000000
  value:    0.500000   beats:    2.000000
  value:    0.250000   beats:    1.000000
  value:    0.125000   beats:    0.500000
  value:    0.062500   beats:    0.250000
  value:    0.031250   beats:    0.125000
4.  4,8 2,4...
  value:    0.375000   beats:    1.500000
  value:    0.375000   beats:    1.500000
  value:    0.968750   beats:    3.875000
4. 4.. 4... 4....
  value:    0.375000   beats:    1.500000
  value:    0.437500   beats:    1.750000
  value:    0.468750   beats:    1.875000
  value:    0.484375   beats:    1.937500
2...,4.,8..,16.
  value:    1.625000   beats:    6.500000

                 * * * * *

Type beat note: 4.
  0.375000 = one beat
Type duration codes, terminate run with ctrl-D:

4.
  value:    0.375000   beats:    1.000000
2.
  value:    0.750000   beats:    2.000000
4 8 8.
  value:    0.250000   beats:    0.666667
  value:    0.125000   beats:    0.333333
  value:    0.187500   beats:    0.500000
8 8 8 4 4 4
  value:    0.125000   beats:    0.333333
  value:    0.125000   beats:    0.333333
  value:    0.125000   beats:    0.333333
  value:    0.250000   beats:    0.666667
  value:    0.250000   beats:    0.666667
  value:    0.250000   beats:    0.666667
2,4,8.
  value:    0.937500   beats:    2.500000
```

Program 15.1. Two Sample Runs (Interactive)

15.4 Indirect Recursion: Processing Grouplets in rdc

As we saw in chapter 6, grouplets (triplets, quintuplets, etc.) can be encoded in reciprocal duration code because any note that is an even division of the whole note can be encoded directly as a reciprocal. Combined with dots and ties as presented above, complex rhythms can be represented. For example, the rhythm

could be encoded

6. 12 6

Although most rhythmic patterns can be encoded using this convention, complex patterns, particularly those including nested grouplets (e.g., a triplet within a septuplet) are cumbersome at best.

In this section we will explore a more accessible encoding scheme for complex rhythms. A procedures that process the code demonstrate indirect recursion.[6] The grouplet syntax is shown in figure 15.2. The grouplet is enclosed in parentheses. The left parenthesis is followed by any valid rdc encoded duration, indicating the duration of the grouplet in the current time frame. This is followed by an equal sign and a string of duration codes that will be scaled to fit within the desired duration. Since the duration string may contain other grouplets, the encoding scheme can handle grouplet nesting to any depth. A few examples are shown in figure 15.3. The last two illustrate nested grouplets.

A pair of procedures is used to process duration strings containing grouplets. The first, *rhythm*, interprets a string of durations, storing their values in a list (in this case an array). When *rhythm* encounters a grouplet, it calls another procedure, *grouplet*, which processes the grouplet. In order to do this, it reads the grouplet duration (*groupdur*) and then calls procedure *rhythm* to read the duration string, which is stored in a temporary list. It then calculates the sum of the durations (*total*) in the temporary list, and scales each duration by multiplying it by the ratio (*groupdur/total*). Finally, it concatenates the list of durations in the grouplet to the end of the original duration list. The process involves mutual recursion, since *rhythm* calls *grouplet* which calls *rhythm*. If another grouplet is nested within the duration string for the first grouplet, recursion continues, with the second invocation of procedure *rhythm* recursively calling procedure *grouplet*, which again invokes *rhythm*, and so on.

(<grouplet duration> = <duration string>)

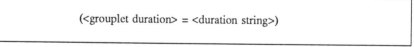

Figure 15.2. SYNTAX: Grouplets in Reciprocal Duration Code

6. The encoding of grouplets described here is used in the author's computer music preprocessor SCORE-11. The encoding and algorithms shown here omit some of the fancier features, such as repetition counts. This simplification makes the algorithms easier to understand, and allows us to concentrate on the use of indirect recursion in solving the programming problem presented. The procedures also differ from their model in that they use arrays instead of linked lists to store durations; thus the length of the duration lists is limited.

Both procedures call procedure *getdur* to read and interpret duration codes. Since a note may be tied to the first note of a grouplet (or the last note of a grouplet may be tied to the next note), *getdur* cannot always process ties recursively as it did in the previous program. Procedure *getdur* has been given a parameter (*key*), which is passed the value 0 or 1. If it is called with *key* = 1, it processes ties recursively, otherwise it reads single duration codes. After each duration is read, a boolean variable *tie* is set to reflect the presence or absence of a tie. If this flag indicates that the current duration is tied to the previous one, the current duration is added to the last duration entered in the list; otherwise it is inserted at the end of the list as a new duration. Note that *tie* must always reflect the presence or absence of a tie *before* the current note. For this reason, procedure *settie* is not called until after the current note has been inserted into the list.

The algorithm for procedure *rhythm* is shown below. The duration list may be terminated by a right parenthesis (in a grouplet) or by a semicolon (the end of the list).

```
set tie to false;
set duration counter to 0;
skip blanks;
while not at the end of the list do
  begin
    if the next character is a left parenthesis
      then call procedure grouplet
      else
        begin
          read a duration;
          insert it into the duration list;
          if there is a tie
            then skip it and set tie = true
            else set tie = false;
          skip blanks
        end
  end;
skip the list terminator: ';' or ')'
```

The following is the algorithm for processing a grouplet:

```
skip the left parenthesis;
read the grouplet duration (groupdur);
skip the '=';
call procedure rhythm to store the duration string;
store the sum of the durations in the string in total;
multiply each duration by (groupdur / total);
concatenate the grouplet durations to the original list;
set tie to reflect the presence or absence of a tie
  after the grouplet;
```

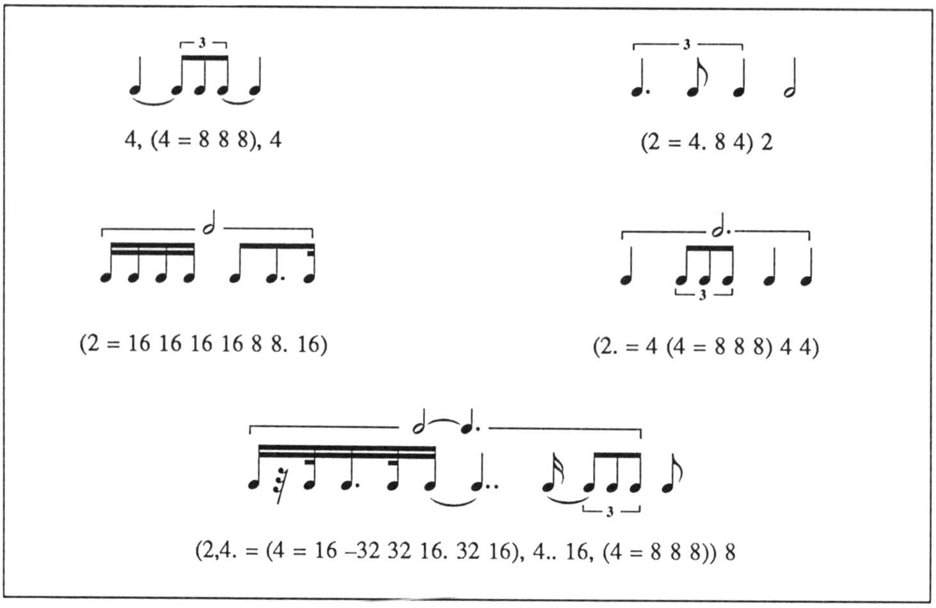

Figure 15.3. Examples of Grouplet Notation in Reciprocal Duration Code

Durations are placed in an array by procedure *insert*. If the duration is tied to the previous duration, it must account for positive or negative durations (representing notes or rests):

```
if there was a tie
  then
    begin
      if the last duration is negative
        then subtract the new duration from the last
        else add the new duration to the previous one
    end
  else
    begin
      increment the duration counter;
      insert the new duration at end of list
    end;
```

Procedure *settie* checks for ties and sets a boolean flag to indicate their presence or absence:

```
skip blanks;
set flag = true if there is a tie, otherwise tie = false;
if there is a tie (',')
  then skip it;
```

Procedure *printlist* prints a table showing, for each duration, the duration's ordinal position in the list, its fractional value, and the number of beats it represents. Program 15.2 demonstrates use of these routines. Note that procedure *grouplet* uses local variables to store the grouplet duration, the temporary list, and the length of the list. Otherwise multiple levels of recursion would not be possible.

```
(***********************   Program Grouplet    ***********************)
(* Demonstrates processing reciprocal duration code including dots, ties,*)
(* and grouplets.  The program processes short (<=200) lists of dura-   *)
(* tions.  The user enters the type of note receiving a beat in rdc     *)
(* notation, followed by a duration string terminated by a semicolon.   *)
(* The program demonstrates the use of indirect recursion, since the    *)
(* rhythm and grouplet procedures call each other recursively.          *)
(*                                                                      *)
(* Input Specification: (Backus-Naur)                                   *)
(*     <input>      ::= <data> [ <data> ... ] <eof>                     *)
(*     <data>       ::= <beatnote> <durations> ;                        *)
(*     <beatnote>   ::= <duration>                                      *)
(*     <duration>   ::= <rdc> [<dots>] [<tie> | <tie> <duration>]       *)
(*     <durations>  ::= <element> [<element> ... ]                      *)
(*     <element>    ::= <duration> | <grouplet>                         *)
(*     <grouplet>   ::= ( <duration> = <durations> )                    *)
(*     <rdc>        ::= integer (even division of whole note)           *)
(*     <dots>       ::= <dot> [<dot> ... ]                              *)
(*     <dot>        ::= .                                               *)
(*     <tie>        ::= ,                                               *)
(*                                                                      *)
(* Output: for each <input>: a table showing for each duration its      *)
(*         ordinal position in the list, its fractional value, and the  *)
(*         number of beats it represents.                               *)
(**********************************************************************)
program grouplet(input, output);
  const
    max = 200;                      { maximum number of durations in list }

  type
    list = array[1 .. max] of real;

  var
    durlist  : list;                { array to store durations         }
    n        : integer;             { number of durations in list      }
    tie      : boolean;             { true if previous note tied       }
    beatnote : real;                { value of note receiving beat     }

(***********************       skipblanks       ***********************)
(* Skips to next nonblank character or eof.                            *)
(**********************************************************************)
  procedure skipblanks;
    var
      done : boolean;
    begin
      done := false;
      repeat
        if eof
          then done := true
```

```
      else if input↑ = ' '
        then get(input)
      else done := true
    until done
  end;

(***********************         settie         ***********************)
(* Finds next nonblank character.  If it is a comma, tie is set to true  *)
(* and the comma is skipped.  If no tie is present, tie is set to false. *)
(*************************************************************************)
procedure settie(var tie : boolean);
  begin
    skipblanks;
    tie := (input↑ = ',');
    if tie
      then get(input);                     { skip tie                    }
  end;

(***********************         getdur         ***********************)
(* Reads rdc encoded durations and returns the fractional value of the   *)
(* duration as a real number, which is negative if the duration was a    *)
(* rest.  If key=1, then getdur calls itself recursively to process ties.*)
(*************************************************************************)
function getdur (key : integer) : real;
  var
    code     : integer;                    { for reading duration code   }
    dur      : real;                       { fractional value of duration }
    dot      : real;                       { fractional value of dot     }
    negative : boolean;                    { if true indicates a rest    }
  begin { getdur }
    skipblanks;                            { skip spaces                 }
    negative := input↑ = '-';              { check for sign              }
    if input↑ in ['+', '-']
      then get(input);                     { skip sign                   }
    read(code);                            { read duration code          }
    dur := 1 / code;                       { convert to fraction         }
    dot := dur / 2;                        { value for first dot         }
    while input↑ = '.' do                  { process dots                }
      begin { process dots }
        dur := dur + dot;
        get(input);                        { skip dot                    }
        dot := dot / 2;                    { halve dot                   }
        skipblanks
      end; { process dots }
    if key = 1                             { process ties                }
      then
        if input↑ = ','
          then
            begin
              get(input);                  { skip comma                  }
              dur := dur + getdur(1)       { add next duration           }
            end;
    if negative
      then getdur := -dur                  { rest                        }
      else getdur :=  dur;                 { note                        }
  end; { getdur }
```

```
(***********************          incr          ***********************)
(* Adds one to the value of its argument.                                *)
(*************************************************************************)
  procedure incr(var x : integer);
    begin
      x := x + 1
    end;


(***********************         insert         ***********************)
(* Inserts dur into list of durations stored in durlist.  If tie is set  *)
(* (true), then dur is added to the last duration, otherwise dur is      *)
(* inserted at the end of the list.                                      *)
(*************************************************************************)
  procedure insert(dur : real; var durlist : list;
                                       var n : integer; tie : boolean);
    begin { insert }
      if tie
        then
          begin { tied duration }
            if durlist[n] >= 0
              then durlist[n] := durlist[n] + dur
              else durlist[n] := durlist[n] - dur
          end   { tied duration }
        else
          begin { new duration }
            incr(n);                             { get next location }
            durlist[n] := dur                    { insert duration   }
          end   { new duration }
    end;  { insert }

(***********************        grouplet        ***********************)
(* See below; this procedure is declared here with a forward directive   *)
(* because rhythm and grouplet call each other recursively.              *)
(*************************************************************************)
  procedure grouplet(var durlist : list; var n : integer;
                                       var tie : boolean); forward;


(***********************         rhythm         ***********************)
(* Processes a list of durations encoded in rdc.  Each duration is       *)
(* inserted into the array durlist.  If a left parenthesis is encoun-    *)
(* tered, procedure grouplet is called to process a grouplet.  After     *)
(* each note is read, tie is set to reflect the presence or absence of a *)
(* tie.                                                                  *)
(*************************************************************************)
  procedure rhythm(var durlist : list; var n : integer; var tie : boolean);
    var
      dur : real;
    begin { rhythm }
      tie := false;                     { no tie at beginning of list }
      n := 0;                           { note count                  }
      skipblanks;
      while not (input↑ in [';' , ')']) do
        begin
          if input↑ = '('
            then grouplet(durlist, n, tie)          { process grouplet    }
```

```
          else
            begin { process duration }
              dur := getdur(0);                           { get duration         }
              insert(dur, durlist, n, tie);               { insert in list       }
              settie(tie);                                { is there a tie?      }
              skipblanks
            end  { process duration }
        end;
      get(input)                                          { skip terminator      }
    end; { rhythm }


(***********************          listsum          ***********************)
(* Returns total of durations in A[1] ... A[n].  Since rests are stored  *)
(* as negative numbers, the absolute value of each value is used in cal- *)
(* culating the total.                                                   *)
(*************************************************************************)
  function listsum(var A : list; n : integer) : real;
    var
      i   : integer;
      sum : real;
    begin
      sum := 0;
      for i := 1 to n do
        sum := sum + abs(A[i]);
      listsum := sum
    end;


(***********************          grouplet          ***********************)
(* Reads the duration of the grouplet, then calls procedure rhythm to     *)
(* store the list of rhythms in templist.  Then a constant is calculated  *)
(* as the ratio of the actual duration of the grouplet to the notated     *)
(* duration.  This ration is used to scale each duration in templist.     *)
(* Finally, the scaled durations in templist are copied to the end of     *)
(* the array durlist.  Tie is true if there was a tie after the last      *)
(* duration in durlist.  Templ and temp2 are used to check for ties       *)
(* before and after the right parenthesis at the end of the grouplet      *)
(* specification.                                                         *)
(**************************************************************************)
  procedure grouplet { var durlist : list; var n : integer;
                                            var tie : boolean };
    var
      templist : list;                 { to store grouplet durations      }
      count    : integer;              { number of durations in grouplet  }
      groupdur : real;                 { actual duration of the grouplet  }
      total    : real;                 { total of durations in grouplet   }
      ratio    : real;                 { scaling ratio: groupdur/total    }
      templ    : boolean;              { T if tie before ')' in grouplet  }
      temp2    : boolean;              { T if tie after ')' in grouplet   }
      i        : integer;              { loop index                       }
    begin { grouplet }
      get(input);                      { skip '('                         }
      groupdur := getdur(1);           { real duration of grouplet        }
      skipblanks;
      get(input);                      { skip '='                         }
```

```
      rhythm(templist, count, temp1);      { read list of durations         }
      settie(temp2);                       { tie after grouplet?            }

      total := listsum(templist, count);   { sum of durations               }

      ratio := groupdur / total;           { scale durations                }
      for i := 1 to count do
        templist[i] := ratio * templist[i];

      for i := 1 to count do               { copy grouplet to durlist       }
        begin
          insert(templist[i], durlist, n, tie);
          tie := false                     { cancel tie after 1st duration }
        end;

      tie := temp1 or temp2                { and reset at end of grouplet   }
    end;  { grouplet }


(************************          printlist          ************************)
(* Prints a table showing the fractional duration and number of beats in *)
(* each duration, and sum of beats in list.                               *)
(**************************************************************************)
  procedure printlist(var durlist : list; n : integer; beat: real);
    var
      i : integer;
    begin
      writeln;
      writeln('==============================');
      writeln('Note/rest':9, 'Duration':10, 'Beats':10);
      writeln('==============================');
      for i := 1 to n do
        writeln(i:2, ' ':7, durlist[i]:10:6, durlist[i]/beat:10:6);
      writeln('==============================');
      writeln('total beats:':19, listsum(durlist, n) / beat:10:6);
      writeln
    end;


(************************       main procedure       ************************)
(* Until eof, reads the beat note, and then processes a list of dura-    *)
(* tions terminated by a semicolon.                                       *)
(**************************************************************************)
  begin { main }
    write('Type beat note in rdc: ');                 { prompt              }
    while not eof do
      begin { process list }
        beatnote := getdur(1);                        { read beat note      }
        rhythm(durlist, n, tie);                      { read duration list  }
        printlist(durlist, n, beatnote);              { print list          }
        write('Type beat note in rdc: ');             { prompt              }
        skipblanks
      end  { process list }
  end.  { main }
```

Program 15.2. *Grouplet*

```
Type beat note in rdc: 4
4 8 8,(4 = 8 8 8) 4;

==============================
Note/rest  Duration      Beats
==============================
 1          0.250000  1.000000
 2          0.125000  0.500000
 3          0.208333  0.833333
 4          0.083333  0.333333
 5          0.083333  0.333333
 6          0.250000  1.000000
==============================
       total beats:  4.000000

Type beat note in rdc: 4
4 4 (2 = 8 8 8. 16 8) 2;

==============================
Note/rest  Duration      Beats
==============================
 1          0.250000  1.000000
 2          0.250000  1.000000
 3          0.100000  0.400000
 4          0.100000  0.400000
 5          0.150000  0.600000
 6          0.050000  0.200000
 7          0.100000  0.400000
 8          0.500000  2.000000
==============================
       total beats:  6.000000

Type beat note in rdc: 4
(1 = 8 (8 = 16 16 16) 8. 16 8);

==============================
Note/rest  Duration      Beats
==============================
 1          0.200000  0.800000
 2          0.066667  0.266667
 3          0.066667  0.266667
 4          0.066667  0.266667
 5          0.300000  1.200000
 6          0.100000  0.400000
 7          0.200000  0.800000
==============================
       total beats:  4.000000
```

```
Type beat note in rdc: 4
(2. = 4,(4 = 8. 16 8) -4 4);

==============================
Note/rest  Duration      Beats
==============================
 1         0.281250   1.125000
 2         0.031250   0.125000
 3         0.062500   0.250000
 4        -0.187500  -0.750000
 5         0.187500   0.750000
==============================
       total beats:   3.000000

Type beat note in rdc: 4.
(4. = 16 8 -8 8 8 16), 4.;

==============================
Note/rest  Duration      Beats
==============================
 1         0.037500   0.100000
 2         0.075000   0.200000
 3        -0.075000  -0.200000
 4         0.075000   0.200000
 5         0.075000   0.200000
 6         0.412500   1.100000
==============================
       total beats:   2.000000

Type beat note in rdc: ^D
```

Program 15.2. Sample Run (Interactive)

15.5 Permutations and Combinations

In computer-aided music research, as in other fields, it is sometimes desirable to find the different possible permutations or combinations of a set of elements. In this section we will use recursion to develop solutions to this class of problems.

15.5.1 A Procedure for Calculating Permutations

Permutations are ordered arrangements of a list of objects. If there are n elements in the list, then any of the n elements can occupy the first position, any of the remaining $n - 1$ elements can occupy the second position, any of $n - 2$ the third position, and so on. Thus it is easy to see that for an n-element list, there are $n!$ different ways of ordering the list. But how can we calculate these permutations?

In developing an algorithm, we begin by examining a short list (a, b, c, d). The possible permutations are:

(*a*, *b*, *c*, *d*) (*a*, *b*, *d*, *c*) (*a*, *c*, *b*, *d*) (*a*, *c*, *d*, *b*) (*a*, *d*, *b*, *c*) (*a*, *d*, *c*, *b*)
(*b*, *a*, *c*, *d*) (*b*, *a*, *d*, *c*) (*b*, *c*, *a*, *d*) (*b*, *c*, *d*, *a*) (*b*, *d*, *a*, *c*) (*b*, *d*, *c*, *a*)
(*c*, *a*, *b*, *d*) (*c*, *a*, *d*, *b*) (*c*, *b*, *a*, *d*) (*c*, *b*, *d*, *a*) (*c*, *d*, *a*, *b*) (*c*, *d*, *b*, *a*)
(*d*, *a*, *b*, *c*) (*d*, *a*, *c*, *b*) (*d*, *b*, *a*, *c*) (*d*, *b*, *c*, *a*) (*d*, *c*, *a*, *b*) (*d*, *c*, *b*, *a*)

Another way of saying this is:

a followed by all permutations of (*b*, *c*, *d*)
b followed by all permutations of (*a*, *c*, *d*)
c followed by all permutations of (*a*, *b*, *d*)
d followed by all permutations of (*a*, *b*, *c*)

Observe that we can obtain all permutations of a list by taking each element followed by all permutations of the remaining elements. The fact that the same can be said of each shorter list consisting of "the remaining elements" suggests a recursive algorithm. The procedure below finds all permutations of elements 1 through *n* stored in array *A*. It is called by invoking *perm*(*A*, 1, *n*).

```
procedure perm(A : list; i, n : integer);
  var
    j : integer;
  begin
    if i = n
      then printlist(A, n)
      else
        for j := i to n do
          begin
            swap(A[i], A[j]);
            perm(A, i + 1, n)
          end
  end;
```

The **for** loop calls procedure *swap* to exchange each element in the list with the first. If the array contains the list (*a*, *b*, *c*, *d*), then the loop makes the following exchanges:

swap elements 1 and 1: (*a*, *b*, *c*, *d*)
swap elements 1 and 2: (*b*, *a*, *c*, *d*)
swap elements 1 and 3: (*c*, *a*, *b*, *d*)
swap elements 1 and 4: (*d*, *a*, *b*, *c*)

Thus each element is placed in the first position, and then *perm*(*A*, *i* + 1, *n*) is invoked to find the permutations of the shorter list beginning with the next element. Whenever the current value of *i* is equal to *n* (the length of the list), the list is printed by invoking procedure *printlist* and the procedure returns to the previous level of recursion. Note that the array is passed as a value parameter, thus all elements in the list are passed, and order inversions taking place at higher levels of recursion are not returned to lower levels; otherwise the algorithm would not work properly. The deepest level of recursion is equal to $n - 1$.[7] Program 15.3 demonstrates the use of this procedure.

7. The initial call from the main program is not recursive.

```
(***********************     Program Testperm      ***********************)
(* Tests permutation algorithm described in text (section 15.5.1).       *)
(* Input:  A string of characters terminated by a newline character.     *)
(*         Any blanks, commas, and parentheses are discarded; other      *)
(*         characters are stored in an array.                            *)
(* Output: All permutations of the list of characters.                   *)
(*************************************************************************)
program testperm(input, output);
  const
    max = 15;                          { maximum number of elements in list }

  type
    list = array[1 .. max] of char;

  var
    A : list;                          { array to store the list            }
    n : integer;                       { the number of elements in the list }

(***********************          skipln           ***********************)
(* Skips blanks, commas, and parentheses to nonblank or newline char.    *)
(*************************************************************************)
  procedure skipln;
    begin
      while (input↑ in [' ', '(', ')', ',']) and not eoln do
        get(input)
    end;

(***********************         readlist          ***********************)
(* Stores each nonblank character on the line in array A.                *)
(*************************************************************************)
  procedure readlist(var A : list; var n : integer);
    begin
      n := 0;                                 { cardinality of list }
      skipln;                                 { skip blanks         }
      while not eoln do
        begin
          n := n + 1;
          read(A[n]);
          skipln
        end;
      readln                                  { skip newline char   }
    end;

(***********************         printlist         ***********************)
(* Prints n characters in the array A in format (a,b,c...).              *)
(*************************************************************************)
  procedure printlist(var A : list; n : integer);
    var
      i : integer;
    begin
      write('          (');                { left parenthesis        }
      for i := 1 to n - 1 do
        write(A[i], ',');
      writeln(A[n], ')')                   { last element and paren }
    end;
```

```
(***********************          swap          ***********************)
(* Exchanges elements x and y using temporary location t.            *)
(**********************************************************************)
  procedure swap(var x, y : char);
    var
      t : char;
    begin
      t := x;   x := y;   y := t
    end;

(***********************          perm          ***********************)
(* Prints all permutations of n elements in list A.  The recursive algo- *)
(* rithm is described in the text.                                      *)
(**********************************************************************)
  procedure perm(A : list; i, n : integer);
    var
      j : integer;
    begin
      if i = n
        then printlist(A, n)            { print current permutation     }
        else
          for j := i to n do
            begin
              swap(A[i], A[j]);         { place each element in 1st pos. }
              perm(A, i + 1, n)         { calc permutations of rest      }
            end
    end;

(**********************************************************************)
(*                         Main Procedure                              *)
(**********************************************************************)
  begin { main }
    write('Type list: ');
    while not eof do
      begin
        readlist(A, n);                 { read list and count elements }
        perm(A, 1, n);                  { calculate permutations       }
        writeln;
        write('Type list: ')
      end
  end. { main }
```

Program 15.3. *Testperm*

```
Type list: 1 2
        (1,2)
        (2,1)

Type list: (a,b,c)
        (a,b,c)
        (a,c,b)
        (b,a,c)
        (b,c,a)
        (c,a,b)
        (c,b,a)
```

```
Type list: (a,b,c,d)
           (a,b,c,d)
           (a,b,d,c)
           (a,c,b,d)
           (a,c,d,b)
           (a,d,b,c)
           (a,d,c,b)
           (b,a,c,d)
           (b,a,d,c)
           (b,c,a,d)
           (b,c,d,a)
           (b,d,a,c)
           (b,d,c,a)
           (c,a,b,d)
           (c,a,d,b)
           (c,b,a,d)
           (c,b,d,a)
           (c,d,a,b)
           (c,d,b,a)
           (d,a,b,c)
           (d,a,c,b)
           (d,b,a,c)
           (d,b,c,a)
           (d,c,a,b)
           (d,c,b,a)

Type list: ^D
```

Program 15.3. Sample Run (Interactive)

15.5.2 Algorithms for Computing Combinations

Combinations, as distinguished from permutations, are unordered sets of objects. The number of combinations of n objects taken r at a time is

$$\frac{n!}{r!(n-r)!}$$

For example, the combinations of elements of the list (1, 2, 3) taken two at a time are (1, 2), (1, 3), and (2, 3).

The permutation algorithm shown earlier used a single loop at different levels of recursion to set the values for each position in the list. We will use a similar technique here; however, we will use a temporary array S to store the solutions as we calculate them. Thus the arrays can be passed as variable parameters, saving memory space during recursion. The procedure shown below calculates combinations of the list in $A[i]$, $1 \le i \le n$, storing each combination of r elements in $S[p]$, $1 \le p \le r$. The procedure is invoked by calling *comb*(A, 1, n, r, 1, S). Note that in the initial call i and p are both 1. The **for** loop inserts each element in array A into the pth position of the solution ($S[p]$). If a solution is complete, $p = r$, it is printed; otherwise *comb* is called recursively to insert each possible element into the next position of the solution ($S[p + 1]$). In order to avoid repetition of elements in the solution, the first element taken from the subject list is $A[j + 1]$, the element following the current element in the list.

```
procedure comb(var A : list; i, n, r, p : integer; var S : list);
  var
    j : integer;
  begin
    for j := i to n do
      begin
        S[p] := A[j];
        if p = r
          then printlist(S, r)
          else comb(A, j + 1, n, r, p + 1, S)
      end
  end;
```

This procedure is easy to modify. Procedure *rcomb*, shown below, is identical to procedure *comb*, except that the current element (j) is passed to the next level of recursion as the first element in the next position. As a result, the procedure allows repetition of elements in the combinations, i.e., the combinations of (1, 2, 3) taken two at a time with repetition are (1, 1), (1, 2), (1, 3), (2, 2), (2, 3), and (3, 3).

```
procedure rcomb(var A : list; i, n, r, p : integer; var S : list);
  var
    j : integer;
  begin
    for j := i to n do
      begin
        S[p] := A[j];
        if p = r
          then printlist(S, r)
          else rcomb(A, j, n, r, p + 1, S)
      end
  end;
```

The number combinations of n objects taken r at a time with repetition is

$$\frac{n(n + 1) \ldots (n + r - 1)}{r(r - 1) \ldots 1}$$

This formula can be implemented easily, through use of a function that recursively calculates the product of the series $x \times (x + 1) \times (x + 2) \ldots \times y$.

```
function ps(x, y : integer) : integer;
  begin
    if x = y
      then ps := y
      else ps := x * ps(x + 1, y)
  end;
```

Another variation of this algorithm provides a different way to calculate permutations. Procedure *perm2*, shown below, calculates all permutations of n objects taken r at a time. For example, the permutations of (1, 2, 3) taken two at a time are (1, 2),

(1, 3), (2, 1), (2, 3), (3, 1), and (3, 2). The procedure is almost identical to those shown above, except that the possible choices for each position in the solution include all elements in list *A*, so long as they are not currently in use in any other position. Thus the value of *i*, the first position in array *A*, does not change during recursion. Instead, a variable of type *set* is used to ensure that no element is used in more than one position at a time. At each level of recursion, the **for** loop tests each element in *A*. If it is not in use, it is placed in the current position of solution *S*[*p*] and added to the the set *use* (by the union operation) so that it cannot be reused in a later position. After the solution is printed, or after the next recursive call of *perm2* returns, the element is removed from *use* so that it is available for later positions of the solution.

```
procedure perm2(var A : list; i, n, r, p : integer; var S : list;
                                                   var use : pcs);

  var
    j : integer;
  begin
    for j := i to n do
      begin
        if not (A[j] in use)
          then
            begin
              S[p] := A[j];
              use := use + [A[j]];          { mark element in use      }
              if p = r
                then printlist(S, r)
                else perm2(A, i, n, r, p + 1, S, use);
              use := use - [A[j]]           { mark element available }
            end
      end
  end;
```

The number of permutations of *n* objects taken *r* at a time is

$$\frac{n!}{(n-r)!}$$

Program 15.4 demonstrates the use of these three variants of the basic combination algorithm. The program does combinations and permutations of pitch-class collections that are entered in hexadecimal notation, i.e, the integers between 0 and 11 are represented by the digits 0–9, a, b. The *readlist* procedure from program 15.3 has been modified (by changing *skipln*) so that it discards all input values other than the characters in the set ['0' . . '9', 'a', 'b']. Although the pitch classes are read and printed as hexadecimal characters, they are stored as integers in the arrays.

The combination and permutation procedures have been modified by the addition of parameter *sn*, which represents the number of each solution. This variable is set to 0 before the initial call of each recursive procedure. The value is incremented by procedure *printlist* just before each solution is printed. Output is in list notation (1, 2, 3, . . .). Since the program skips all input data except the twelve characters representing pitch classes, this format is acceptable as input as well.

```
(**********************    Program Testcomb      **********************)
(* Demonstrates combination and permutation algorithms (section 15.4.2). *)
(* Input:  A string of pitch-class characters (0...9, a, b) terminated by*)
(*         a newline character. Other characters are discarded. The char-*)
(*         acters are converted to pc integers and stored in an array.   *)
(* Output: All combinations, combinations with repetition, and permuta-  *)
(*         tions of the list, printed in list notation.                  *)
(***********************************************************************)
program testcomb(input, output);
  const
    max = 15;                              { maximum length of list      }
  type
    pcint = 0 .. 11;                       { pitch-class integers        }
    pcs = set of pcint;                    { set of pitch-class integers }
    list = array[1 .. max] of pcint;       { stores list of pc integers  }
  var
    A   : list;                            { array to store the list     }
    S   : list;                            { array to store solutions    }
    n   : integer;                         { no. of elements in the list }
    r   : integer;                         { elements per combination    }
    sn  : integer;                         { solution number             }
    use : pcs;                             { for eliminating duplicates  }

(**********************       skipln        **********************)
(* Skips anything except character rep of pcs and newline characters.   *)
(***********************************************************************)
  procedure skipln;
    begin
      while not (input↑ in ['0' .. '9', 'a', 'b']) and not eoln do
        get(input)
    end;

(**********************        getpc        **********************)
(* Reads a single character representing a pc, and returns the corres-  *)
(* ponding pitch-class integer.                                         *)
(***********************************************************************)
  procedure getpc(var x : pcint);
    begin
      case input↑ of
        '0' : x := 0;
        '1' : x := 1;
        '2' : x := 2;
        '3' : x := 3;
        '4' : x := 4;
        '5' : x := 5;
        '6' : x := 6;
        '7' : x := 7;
        '8' : x := 8;
        '9' : x := 9;
        'a' : x := 10;
        'b' : x := 11
      end; { case }
      get(input)                           { skip input char             }
    end;
```

```
(***********************          readlist          ***********************)
(* Stores each pitch-class integer in array A.                             *)
(***************************************************************************)
  procedure readlist(var A : list; var n : integer);
    begin
      n := 0;                                  { n counts elements in list    }
      skipln;
      while not eoln do
        begin
          n := n + 1;
          getpc(A[n]);
          skipln
        end;
      readln                                   { skip newline character       }
    end;

(***********************          tochar          ***********************)
(* Converts pitch-class integers to character representation.             *)
(***************************************************************************)
  function tochar(x : integer) : char;
    begin
      case x of
        0: tochar := '0';
        1: tochar := '1';
        2: tochar := '2';
        3: tochar := '3';
        4: tochar := '4';
        5: tochar := '5';
        6: tochar := '6';
        7: tochar := '7';
        8: tochar := '8';
        9: tochar := '9';
       10: tochar := 'a';
       11: tochar := 'b'
      end  { case }
    end;

(***********************          printlist          ***********************)
(* Prints n characters in the array A in format (a, b, c ...).  Also      *)
(* increments and prints solution number (sn).                            *)
(***************************************************************************)
  procedure printlist(var A : list; n : integer; var sn : integer);
    var
      i : integer;
    begin
      sn := sn + 1;                            { increment solution number }
      write(' ':2, sn:3, '. (');
      for i := 1 to n - 1 do
        write(tochar(A[i]), ',');
      writeln(tochar(A[n]), ')')               { print last element        }
    end;

(***********************          comb          ***********************)
(* Recursive procedure for calculating the combinations of n objects      *)
(* taken r at a time.  The original list is in A[i], 1 <= i <= n; the     *)
(* solution is in S[p], 1 <= p <= r.  Sn is the solution number.          *)
(***************************************************************************)
```

```
procedure comb(var A : list; i, n, r, p : integer;
                                       var S : list; var sn : integer);
  var
    j : integer;
  begin { comb }
    for j := i to n do
      begin
        S[p] := A[j];
        if p = r
          then printlist(S, r, sn)
          else comb(A, j + 1, n, r, p + 1, S, sn)
      end
  end;  { comb }

(***********************          rcomb          ***********************)
(* Calculates the combinations of n objects taken r at a time with repe- *)
(* tition.  The original list is in A[i], 1 <= i <= n; the solution is   *)
(* in S[p], 1 <= p <= r.  Sn is the solution number.                     *)
(*************************************************************************)
procedure rcomb(var A : list; i, n, r, p : integer;
                                       var S : list; var sn : integer);
  var
    j : integer;
  begin
    for j := i to n do
      begin
        S[p] := A[j];
        if p = r
          then printlist(S, r, sn)
          else rcomb(A, j, n, r, p + 1, S, sn)
      end
  end;

(***********************          perm2          ***********************)
(* Calculates the permutations of n objects taken r at a time.  The orig-*)
(* inal list is in A[i]...A[n]; the solution is in S[p]...S[r].  A set   *)
(* type is used to eliminate duplicates; sn is the solution number.      *)
(*************************************************************************)
procedure perm2(var A : list; i, n, r, p : integer;
                          var S : list; var use : pcs; var sn : integer);
  var
    j : integer;
  begin
    for j := 1 to n do
      begin
        if not (A[j] in use)
          then
            begin
              S[p] := A[j];
              use := use + [A[j]];            { mark element in use     }
              if p = r
                then printlist(S, r, sn)
                else perm2(A, i, n, r, p + 1, S, use, sn);
              use := use - [A[j]]             { mark element available  }
            end
      end
  end;
```

```
(***********************           fac(n)           ***********************)
(* Returns n! calculated recursively.                                      *)
(***************************************************************************)
  function fac(n : integer) : integer;
    begin
      if n = 0
        then fac := 1
        else fac := n * fac(n - 1)
    end;

(***********************           c(n,r)           ***********************)
(* The number of combinations of n objects taken r at a time.              *)
(***************************************************************************)
  function c(n, r : integer) : integer;
    begin
      c := fac(n) div (fac(r) * fac(n - r))
    end;

(***********************           ps(x,y)          ***********************)
(* The product of the series x * (x + 1)...y calculated recursively.       *)
(***************************************************************************)
  function ps(x, y : integer) : integer;
    begin
      if x = y
        then ps := y
        else ps := x * ps(x + 1, y)
    end;

(***********************           rc(n,r)          ***********************)
(* The number of combinations of n objects taken r at a time with repe-   *)
(* tition of elements.                                                     *)
(***************************************************************************)
  function rc(x, r : integer) : integer;
    begin
      rc := ps(x, x + r - 1) div ps(2, r)
    end;

(***********************           p(n,r)           ***********************)
(* The number of permutations of n objects taken r at a time.              *)
(***************************************************************************)
  function p(n, r : integer) : integer;
    begin
      p := fac(n) div fac(n - r)
    end;

(***************************************************************************)
(*                             Main Procedure                              *)
(***************************************************************************)
  begin { main }                                 { prompt                   }
    write('Type list: ');
    while not eof do
      begin
        readlist(A, n);                          { read list of pcs         }
        write('Number of elements per combination: ');
        readln(r);                               { card of solutions        }
        writeln('Combinations: (', c(n, r):1, ')');
        sn := 0;                                 { init solution number     }
```

```
        comb(A, 1, n, r, 1, S, sn);
        writeln;
        writeln('Solutions with repetition: (', rc(n, r):1,')');
        sn := 0;                               { init solution number   }
        rcomb(A, 1, n, r, 1, S, sn);
        writeln;
        writeln('Permutations: (', p(n, r):1 ,')');
        use := [];                             { in use = null set      }
        sn := 0;                               { init solution number   }
        perm2(A, 1, n, r, 1, S, use, sn);
        writeln;
        write('Type list: ')                   { prompt                 }
    end
end. { main }
```

Program 15.4. *Testcomb*

```
Type list: (1,2,3)
Number of elements per combination: 2
Combinations: (3)
    1. (1,2)
    2. (1,3)
    3. (2,3)

Solutions with repetition: (6)
    1. (1,1)
    2. (1,2)
    3. (1,3)
    4. (2,2)
    5. (2,3)
    6. (3,3)

Permutations: (6)
    1. (1,2)
    2. (1,3)
    3. (2,1)
    4. (2,3)
    5. (3,1)
    6. (3,2)

Type list: (1,2,a,b)
Number of elements per combination: 3
Combinations: (4)
    1. (1,2,a)
    2. (1,2,b)
    3. (1,a,b)
    4. (2,a,b)

Solutions with repetition: (20)
    1. (1,1,1)
    2. (1,1,2)
    3. (1,1,a)
    4. (1,1,b)
```

```
     5.  (1,2,2)
     6.  (1,2,a)
     7.  (1,2,b)
     8.  (1,a,a)
     9.  (1,a,b)
    10.  (1,b,b)
    11.  (2,2,2)
    12.  (2,2,a)
    13.  (2,2,b)
    14.  (2,a,a)
    15.  (2,a,b)
    16.  (2,b,b)
    17.  (a,a,a)
    18.  (a,a,b)
    19.  (a,b,b)
    20.  (b,b,b)

Permutations: (24)
     1.  (1,2,a)
     2.  (1,2,b)
     3.  (1,a,2)
     4.  (1,a,b)
     5.  (1,b,2)
     6.  (1,b,a)
     7.  (2,1,a)
     8.  (2,1,b)
     9.  (2,a,1)
    10.  (2,a,b)
    11.  (2,b,1)
    12.  (2,b,a)
    13.  (a,1,2)
    14.  (a,1,b)
    15.  (a,2,1)
    16.  (a,2,b)
    17.  (a,b,1)
    18.  (a,b,2)
    19.  (b,1,2)
    20.  (b,1,a)
    21.  (b,2,1)
    22.  (b,2,a)
    23.  (b,a,1)
    24.  (b,a,2)

Type list: ^D
```

Program 15.4. Sample Run (Interactive)

15.6 Threading a Maze

At first glance, finding a path through a maze seems to have little to do with music. However, the problem is a good illustration of recursive programming techniques, and it is an excellent model for a number of music analysis problems.[8]

8. The problem of threading a maze is similar to that of identifying the row forms in a serial composition, suggested as an exercise in chapter 20.

The maze will be entered as the number of rows and and number of columns, m and n, followed by an $m \times n$ element maze with 0 representing a path (unblocked) and 1 representing a wall (blocked). Internally, we will store the maze as a boolean array, with the value *true* signifying a path and *false* signifying a wall. Procedure *readmaze* reads the dimensions of the maze, and if either is greater than *max*, it prints an error message and discards $m \times n$ input values so that the next maze can be processed. While reading the maze, the procedure considers only nonblank characters. Zeros are stored as *true*, any other characters as *false*.

We will allow vertical, horizontal, and diagonal moves. Thus from any position i, j in the maze, there are eight possible moves, which can be characterized as points of the compass: N, NE, E, SE, S, SW, W, and NW, as shown in figure 15.4. Some of these moves are not possible from locations on the periphery of the maze. In order to avoid checking for this condition, we will draw a border of *false* values around the maze before beginning to search for a path. If at any point a wall is encountered, the current path must be abandoned.

If we specify that the maze must be entered at the NW corner and exited from the SE corner, then the recursive solution for threading an m row by n column maze can be stated as follows:

```
start at element 1,1
if we are not through the maze
  then
    if the current element is not a wall
      then
        begin
          if this is element m, n
            then we are through
            else recursively try each possible next move
        end
      else return to the previous location and continue search
```

This algorithm will find a path through the maze if a solution is possible; the max-

NW		N		NE
	i−1, j−1	i−1, j	i−1, j+1	
W	i, j−1	**i, j**	i, j+1	E
	i+1, j−1	i+1, j	i+1, j+1	
SW		S		SE

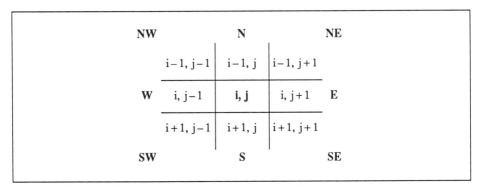

Figure 15.4. Possible moves from $M[i, j]$.

imum depth of recursion is equal to the length of the path. Once a solution has been found, the program must retrace the path in reverse order while returning through the recursive levels. During this process we will push the coordinates of each element on a user-implemented stack. Thus, when the procedure returns to the main program, the stack will contain row-column duples representing the path through the maze.

In order to improve efficiency of the algorithm, we will use a second boolean matrix, C, for checking off visited elements. Matrix C is initialized to *true* values. Each time $M[i, j]$ is visited, $C[i, j]$ is set to *false*. This device is used to prevent retrying false paths approached from new directions. It would be possible to mark these elements in the original maze, M, but this would destroy the maze. The recursive plunge is terminated when a solution has been found or when all paths have failed. With these refinements worked out, the maze-threading procedure can be completed:

```
procedure thread(var M, C : maze; row, col : integer);
  begin
    if not solved
      then
        if M[row, col] and C[row, col]
          then
            begin { good path }
              C[row, col] := false;             { mark it       }
              if (row = rows) and (col = cols)
                then solved := true
                else
                  begin { find next move }
                    thread(M, C, row    , col + 1);    { E  }
                    thread(M, C, row + 1, col + 1);    { SE }
                    thread(M, C, row + 1, col    );    { S  }
                    thread(M, C, row + 1, col - 1);    { SW }
                    thread(M, C, row    , col - 1);    { S  }
                    thread(M, C, row - 1, col - 1);    { NW }
                    thread(M, C, row - 1, col    );    { N  }
                    thread(M, C, row - 1, col + 1)     { NE }
                  end; { find next move }
              if solved
                then
                  begin
                    push(col);                 { save col and }
                    push(row)                  { row on stack }
                  end
            end   { good path }
    end; { thread }
```

We could print the path as a series of <*row*, *col*> duples, popping these values off the stack. However, the solution is easier to visualize in graphic form, so we will print the maze with zeros for paths, ones for walls, and asterisks to show the solved path. Once the maze has been threaded, we can reuse matrix C to store the path. After C is reinitialized to all *true* values, the coordinates of the path are popped off the stack and the corresponding positions in C are set to *false*. Procedure *printmaze* prints the maze with or without the solution:

```
      for i := 1 to rows do
        begin
          for j := 1 to cols do
            if not C[i, j]                    { no effect unless }
              then write('*')                 {   path is marked }
            else if M[i, j]
              then write('0')
            else write('1');
          writeln
        end
```

The entire program is shown below.

```
(***********************       Program Maze        ***********************)
(* Reads a maze, attempts to find a path through it using the recursive  *)
(* algorithm described in the text, and prints the solution if there is  *)
(* one.  The maze is entered in the NW corner and exited in the SE       *)
(* corner.  If these elements are blocked, there is no solution by defi- *)
(* nition.  Input: The number of rows and columns, followed by the maze  *)
(* in zeros and ones, where 0 is a path and 1 a wall.  Since the maze is *)
(* read as character data, blanks are optional.  Output: The maze with   *)
(* the path marked with asterisks.                                       *)
(* Example:                                                              *)
(*                                                                       *)
(*        Input:               | Output:                                 *)
(*              3 3            |       maze     solution                 *)
(*              0 1 0          |       010      *10                      *)
(*              1 0 1          |       101      1*1                      *)
(*              1 0 0          |       100      1**                      *)
(*                             |                                         *)
(* A stack implemented as an array is used to store the coordinates of   *)
(* the path in the maze.  The stack (S), stack pointer (sp), and boolean *)
(* variable (solved) are treated as global variables.                    *)
(*************************************************************************)
program maze(input, output);
  const
    max = 51;                             { maximum dimension of maze + 1 }
    maxstack = 2500;                      { maximum depth of stack        }

  type
    maze  = packed array[0 .. max, 0 .. max] of boolean;
    stack = packed array[1 .. maxstack] of integer;

  var
    M           : maze;                                 { the maze       }
    C           : maze;                                 { for checking   }
    S           : stack;                                { the stack      }
    sp          : integer;                              { stack pointer  }
    rows, cols  : integer;                              { size of maze   }
    solved      : boolean;                              { true when done }

(***********************     utility routines      ***********************)
(* Skipblanks, increment, and decrement.                                 *)
(*************************************************************************)
```

```
procedure skipblanks;
  var
    done : boolean;
  begin
    done := false;
    repeat
      if eof(input)
        then done := true
      else if input↑ = ' '
        then get(input)
      else done := true
    until done
  end;

procedure incr(var x : integer);
  begin
    x := x + 1
  end;

procedure decr(var x : integer);
  begin
    x := x - 1
  end;

(***********************          stack utilities       ***********************)
(* Standard stuff: push, pop; tests for empty or full stack.                   *)
(******************************************************************************)
function stackfull : boolean;
  begin
    stackfull := sp = maxstack
  end;

function stackempty : boolean;
  begin
    stackempty := sp = 0
  end;

procedure push(x : integer);
  begin
    incr(sp);
    S[sp] := x
  end;

procedure pop(var x : integer);
  begin
    x := S[sp];
    decr(sp)
  end;

(***********************            readmaze          ***********************)
(* Reads number rows and columns in maze.  If too big, it throws away the*)
(* matrix values and returns empty matrix.  Otherwise it reads the maze, *)
(* storing paths as true, and walls as false values.  Finally it draws a *)
(* wall around the matrix, so we don't have to check for maze boundaries *)
(* while looking for a path through the maze.                            *)
(******************************************************************************)
```

```
procedure readmaze(var M : maze; var rows, cols : integer);
  var
    i, j : integer;
    c    : char;

  begin
    readln(rows, cols);
    if (rows > max - 1) or (cols > max - 1)
      then
        begin { too big }
          writeln('error: maximum dimension = ', max - 1);
          for i := 1 to rows * cols do
            begin
              skipblanks;
              read(j);                           { throw away value }
              rows := 0;                         { return null maze }
              cols := 0
            end
        end  { too big }
      else
        begin { read matrix }
          for i := 1 to rows do
            for j := 1 to cols do
              begin
                skipblanks;
                read(c);
                M[i, j] := (c = '0')
              end;
                                             { draw wall around matrix }
          for i := 0 to cols + 1 do
            begin
              M[0, i] := false;
              M[rows + 1, i] := false
            end;

          for i := 0 to rows + 1 do
            begin
              M[i, 0] := false;
              M[cols + 1, i] := false
            end
        end   { read matrix }
 end; { readmaze }


(***********************            init            ***********************)
(* Initializes maze C to true values.                                      *)
(**************************************************************************)
  procedure init(var C : maze; rows, cols : integer);
    var
      i, j : integer;
    begin
      for i := 0 to rows + 1 do
        for j := 0 to cols + 1 do
          C[i, j] := true
    end;
```

```
(***********************        markpath        ***********************)
(* After initializing matrix C to all true values, draws the solved path *)
(* through the maze using false values.  Path coordinates are taken off  *)
(* of stack.                                                              *)
(***********************************************************************)
  procedure markpath(var C : maze);
    var
      i, j : integer;
    begin
      init(C, rows, cols);                                  { clear C    }
      while not stackempty do
        begin                                               { mark path }
          pop(i); pop(j);
          C[i, j] := false
        end
    end;

(***********************        printmaze        ***********************)
(* The maze is printed using zeros for the paths and ones for walls.  If *)
(* a path through the maze has been found and saved in matrix C, these   *)
(* positions are marked with asterisks.                                  *)
(***********************************************************************)
  procedure printmaze(var M, C : maze; rows, cols : integer);
    var
      i, j  : integer;
    begin
      for i := 1 to rows do
        begin
          for j := 1 to cols do
            if not C[i, j]                          { no effect unless }
              then write('*')                       {   path is marked }
            else if M[i, j]
              then write('0')
            else write('1');
           writeln
        end
    end; { printpath }

(***********************         thread          ***********************)
(* Recursively finds path through maze.  If the current positon is not a *)
(* wall, the position is marked in maze C so it will not be visited      *)
(* again.  If the final destination has been reached, the boolean flag   *)
(* solved is set to true, otherwise each posible next move is explored   *)
(* recursively.  The recursive plunge is terminated when a solution has  *)
(* been found or when all possible moves have been exhausted.  Once a    *)
(* solution has been found, the coordinates of each element in the path  *)
(* are pushed onto a stack as the program falls back through the succes- *)
(* sive levels of recursion.                                             *)
(***********************************************************************)
  procedure thread(var M, C : maze; row, col : integer);
    begin
      if not solved
        then
          if M[row, col] and C[row, col]
            then
              begin { good path }
                C[row, col] := false;                   { mark it      }
```

```
              if (row = rows) and (col = cols)
                then solved := true
                else
                  begin { find next move }
                    thread(M, C, row    , col + 1);                 { E  }
                    thread(M, C, row + 1, col + 1);                 { SE }
                    thread(M, C, row + 1, col    );                 { S  }
                    thread(M, C, row + 1, col - 1);                 { SW }
                    thread(M, C, row    , col - 1);                 { S  }
                    thread(M, C, row - 1, col - 1);                 { NW }
                    thread(M, C, row - 1, col    );                 { N  }
                    thread(M, C, row - 1, col + 1)                  { NE }
                  end; { find next move
              if solved
                then
                  begin
                    push(col);                              { save row and }
                    push(row)                               { col on stack }
                  end
            end   { good path }
      end; { thread }



(***********************      main procedure       **********************)
(* Each maze is read and printed, then the maze is threaded if possible, *)
(* and a the solution printed.  If there is no solution, a message is    *)
(* printed reporting this fact.                                          *)
(***********************************************************************)
  begin { main }
    while not eof do
      begin { process maze }
        solved := false;                              { done marker      }
        sp := 0;                                      { init stack       }
        readmaze(M ,rows ,cols);                      { read maze        }
        init(C, rows, cols);                          { init checker     }
        writeln; writeln;
        writeln('Maze:'); writeln;
        printmaze(M, C, rows, cols);                  { print maze       }
        writeln; writeln;
        thread(M, C, 1, 1);                           { start NE corner  }
        if solved
          then
            begin
              markpath(C);
              writeln('Solution:');
              printmaze(M, C, rows, cols);
              writeln
            end
          else writeln('No solution');
        skipblanks
      end  { process maze }
  end.  { main }
```

Program 15.5. *Maze*

Input:

```
25 50
01110000000000000000000001000110000000011110100111 1
01101111111111110101111101011101111100111101011000 1
01110000000000001101011110001111011101101110111011 0
01111111111111100010111101111111000111101101111011 0
10000000000000011010111110001111101110110101111101 0
11011111111111111010110011111110111010101011110110
11011111111111001110101100000000111101010101110111 0
11000000001101101101101111111111111101010101111011 0
11110111111011101101110000000000000011010101110110 1
00000110000100101101111111111111111110101011011011
11111101111101101110000000000000000000101011101101
00000001000001101111111111111111111011110101111011 0
01101100101111110000000000000000011011111011111101 0
01110101101111111111111111111111101011111111011011 0
01101101111000000000000000000000011011100000100111 0
01110101110111111111111111111111111111011111111111 0
01101101111000000000000000000000000000011011110011 0
01100110001111111111111111111111111111101011011010
01111111110110100111100101010001111110011100110110
01100000001101011011010101110000000111111111101111
01011111111011110110111111111111111111011000110001
01100000000000001100111100000000000000001001110111 10
01111101110111111111100011111111011111111111110000 1
01111101111100000010111100010001111000000010111111 1
00000000000011111111000011101110000110111010000000
```

Output:

```
Maze:

01110000000000000000000001000110000000011110100111 1
01101111111111110101111101011101111100111101011000 1
01110000000000001101011110001111011101101110111011 0
01111111111111100010111101111111000111101101111011 0
10000000000000011010111110001111101110110101111101 0
11011111111111111010110011111110111010101011110110
11011111111111001110101100000000111101010101110111 0
11000000001101101101101111111111111101010101111011 0
11110111111011101101110000000000000011010101110110 1
00000110000100101101111111111111111110101011011011
11111101111101101110000000000000000000101011101101
00000001000001101111111111111111111011110101111011 0
01101100101111110000000000000000011011111011111101 0
01110101101111111111111111111111101011111111011011 0
01101101111000000000000000000000011011100000100111 0
01110101110111111111111111111111111111011111111111 0
01101101111000000000000000000000000000011011110011 0
01100110001111111111111111111111111111101011011010
01111111110110100111100101010001111110011100110110
01100000001101011011010101110000000111111111101111
01011111111011110110111111111111111111011000110001
01100000000000001100111100000000000000001001110111 10
01111101110111111111100011111111011111111111110000 1
01111101111100000010111100010001111000000010111111 1
00000000000011111111000011101110000110111010000000
```

```
Solution:

*1110000000000*****000001000110000000001111*1**1111
*1101111111111*1*1111101011101111**1111*1*11*001
*111000000000011*1*1111000111101111*11*111*111*1110
*1111111111111***1*11110111111***1111*11*1111*110
1*************1101*11111000111111*111*11*1*11111*10
1101111111111111101*11**11111111*111*1*1*1*1111*110
1101111111111**111*1*11********1111*1*1*1*111*1110
11000000011*11*11*11*1111111111111*1*1*1*1111*110
11110111111*111*11*111*************11*1*1*111*1101
000001100001**1*11*11111111111111111*1*1*11*11011
111111011111*11*111*****************1*1*111*1101
00000001*0***11*111111111111111111101111*1*1111*110
0110110*1*111111****************11011111*111111*10
011101*1101111111111111111111111*1011111111*11*110
011011*1111********************110111*****1**1110
011101*111*111111111111111111111111*11111111110
011011*1111**************************11*1111**110
0110011***1111111111111111111111111111*1*11*11*10
0111111111*11*1**1111**1*1*1***111111**111**11*110
011*******11*1*11*11*11*1*1*111******11111111*1111
01*11111111*1111*11*111111111111111111*11***11***1
011**********0011**1111*********0*****1**111*1111*
011111011101111111111***111111111*1111111111111****1
011111011111000000001*1111***1***1111******1*1111111
00000000000001111111****111*111****110111*1*******
```

Program 15.5. Sample Input and Output

15.7 Quicksort

As our final example of recursive programming, we will examine a sorting algorithm that has excellent average computing time and does not require the extra workspace required by *mergesort* (section 10.9.3).[9]

We will sort a list stored in array $A[i]$, $n \le i \le m$. The idea is to take one element, say $A[i]$, and move it to the position it should occupy in the sorted list. At the same time, the other elements are rearranged so that they are correctly positioned with respect to $A[i]$, i.e., none greater than $A[i]$ occur to the left of it, and none less than $A[i]$ occur to the right of it. Thus the list is divided into two shorter lists, $A[j]$, $m \le j \le (i - 1)$ and $A[k]$, $(i + 1) \le k \le n$, each of which is sorted recursively with the same method. Recursion is terminated when the length of the sublist is 1.

```
procedure quicksort(var A : list; m, n : integer);
  var
    i, j : integer;
    k    : integer;
```

9. Note that space is used for the system stack during recursion.

```
begin { quicksort }
  if m < n
    then
      begin
        i := m;
        j := n + 1;
        k :=A[m];
        repeat
          repeat
            incr(i)
          until A[i] >= k;
          repeat
            decr(j)
          until A[j] <= k;
          if i < j
            then swap(A[i], A[j])
        until i >= j;
        swap(A[m], A[j]);
        quicksort(A, m, j - 1);
        quicksort(A, j + 1, n)
      end
end; { quicksort }
```

Horowitz and Sahni show that the average computing time for this algorithm is $O(\log_2 n)$, where n is the length of the list.[10]

References and Selected Readings

It is possible to implement recursive algorithms without recursive function or procedure calls. The technique, which uses **goto** statements, is discussed on pp. 160–62 of the following:

Horowitz, Ellis, and Sartaj Sahni. *Fundamentals of Data Structures.* Potomac, Md: Computer Science Press, 1976.

The above source also presents an iterative solution to the maze problem (pp. 86–91).

Further discussion and analyses of *quicksort* can be found in Horowitz and Sahni and in the following sources. The second reference includes an excellent chapter on the algorithm.

Knuth, Donald E. *The Art of Computer Programming.* Vol. 3, *Sorting and Searching.* 2d ed. Reading, Mass: Addison-Wesley, 1973.

Sedgewick, Robert. *Algorithms.* 2d ed. Reading, Mass.: Addison-Wesley, 1988.

———. *Quicksort.* New York: Garland, 1978.

The following contains a description of another algorithm designed by Brinkman using mutually recursive procedures. The algorithm is described on p. 77:

Morris, Robert D., and Brian Alegant. "The Even Partitions in Twelve-Tone Music." *Music Theory Spectrum* 10 (1988): 74–101.

10. Ellis Horowitz and Sartaj Sahni, *Fundamentals of Data Structures* (Potomac, Md.: Computer Science Press, 1976), 347–50.

Other suggested reading:

Lewin, David. "An Interesting Global Rule for Species Counterpoint." *In Theory Only* 6, no. 8 (1983): 19–44).

Patrick, P. Howard. "A Computer-Study of a Suspension-Formation in the Masses of Josquin Deprez." *Computers and the Humanities* 8 (1974): 321–31.

Polansky, Larry. "A Hierarchical Gestalt Analysis of Ruggles' *Portals*." *Proceedings of the 1978 International Computer Music Conference*. San Francisco: The Computer Music Association, 790–852.

Exercises

1. Choose several of the recursive procedures and functions shown in this chapter and step through them manually, using a trace table similar to the one shown in table 15.1.

2. Write an iterative version (using a loop rather than recursion) of function *fac*(*n*) (see section 15.1). Compare it to the recursive version. Which is easier to understand? Which is more efficient? Why? Both versions will die fairly quickly due to integer overflow if the initial argument is large. This problem could be corrected by using real arithmetic; however, the accuracy of the result would be limited by the precision of real numbers on your system. Rewrite both versions of *fac*(*n*) using real arithmetic.

3. Modify procedure *getint* (section 15.3.2) so that it will accept an optional sign ('+' or '–') before the first digit.

4. Write procedure *limits*(*low*, *high*, *n*), which reads and returns two integer values, ensuring that these values are between 1 and *n*, and that *low* < *high*. This procedure may call procedure *getint*(*x*) shown in section 15.3.2.

5. Write a recursive version of linear search (see section 10.8.1).

6. Write a recursive version of binary search (see section 10.8.2).

7. Write function *dot*(*dur*), which processes dots (in dotted notes) recursively. It should return 0 if *input*↑ <> '.', otherwise it should return the value of the first dot plus (recursively) the next dot. This procedure should simplify procedure *getdur* in program 15.1, i.e., the lines

```
dot := dur / 2;                  { value for first dot }
while input↑ = '.' do            { process dots        }
  begin { process dots }
    dur := dur + dot;
    get(input);                  { skip dot            }
    dot := dot / 2               { halve dot           }
  end;  { process dots }
```

would be replaced by the single statement

```
dur := dur + dot (dur);
```

8. Modify the maze-threading algorithm in section 15.6 so that it finds *all* possible paths through the maze. Suggestions: (a) You will have to save the current path on a stack as

you go. (b) You will have to allow retracing of paths, but you would do well not to permit backing up to the previous location from any given location.

9. Use the series of integers below to step through the *quicksort* procedure:

9 14 89 –1 27 82 39 71 12 10

Study the procedure until you understand it well enough to write the algorithm in pseudo code similar to that presented for algorithms earlier in the chapter.

10. Use the techniques discussed in this chapter to write a program that reads a pitch-class set and prints all the subsets of the set.

11. The following procedure is a modified version of the one used in program 11.3 (*bufdemo*) to convert the internal form of integers to the external character format. The modifications enable the procedure to print numbers in any radix (or number base).

```
procedure putint(x, radix : integer);

  var
    digits   : array[1 .. 16] of integer;
    i        : integer;
    n        : integer;
    negative : boolean;

  begin
    negative := x < 0;
    if x = 0
      then writeln('0')
      else
        begin
          x := abs(x);
          n := 0;

          while x > 0 do
            begin
              n := n + 1;
              digits[n] := x mod radix;
              x := x div radix
            end;

          if negative
            then write('-');
          for i := n downto 1 do
            write(tochar(digits[i]));
          writeln
        end
  end; { putint }
```

Now that you know about recursion, you can write a more elegant version that does not have to store the characters in an array in order to print them in the correct order. This is so because we can define the process recursively. If we assume that a number is nonzero and positive: *To decode a number, decode the number without the last digit and then print the last digit.* This "algorithm" is not complete because it does not include the exit condition that will terminate the recursive plunge. As with the iteritive version of *putint* shown above, our new version will print a number in any reasonable radix. The following procedure takes care of the special cases, $x = 0$ and $x < 0$, and then calls procedure *decode* to print the digits in the correct order:

```
procedure putint(x, radix : integer);
  begin
    if x = 0
      then write('0')
      else
        begin
          if x < 0
            then write('-');
          decode(abs(x), radix)
        end;
    writeln
  end;
```

You are to write the following (subprogram headings are shown):

procedure *decode(x, radix : integer)* — prints out the digits in the correct order, based on the recursive definition described above. *Decode* should call the following function:

function *tochar(x : integer) : char* — uses arithmetic mapping to return the character representing the integer *x*, $0 \leq x \leq 35$. The value returned is

character '0' through '9' for integer 0 through 9
character 'a' through 'z' for integer 10 through 35

12. In our first incipit program (exercise 14.4), we specified that the incipit should be encoded as seven letters, representing the opening notes, transposed to begin on C, with accidentals and repeated notes omitted. However, the program, as specified, did not ensure that the incipit met these conditions. You are to write a new version of procedure *readincipit* that returns only correctly encoded incipits, i.e., seven characters, beginning on C, with no repeated notes. In addition, it should ensure that only characters representing note names are used. Your solution should assume that the user's response will be terminated by a carriage return (*eoln*), and that the following declarations are in effect:

```
{   const
      inciplen = 7;

    type
      inciptype = packed array[1 .. incipitlen] of char;   }
```

If the incipit is incorrect, the procedure should inform the user of the nature of his or her error and request a new entry. It should not return until a correct incipit has been entered. The procedure heading is shown below:

```
procedure readincipit(var f : text; var incipit : inciptype);
```

13. Write a program that recursively generates all possible first-species counterpoints to a given cantus firmus. You will find David Lewin's "An Interesting Global Rule for Species Counterpoint," in *In Theory Only* 6, no. 8 (1983): 19–44, helpful as a starting point. Add additional rules according to familiar counterpoint texts until you are satisfied with the results.

16| Linked Data Structures

The programming techniques in this chapter are perhaps the most important in the book. Novice programmers sometimes avoid linked structures because they seem different and difficult to comprehend at first. Nothing could be further from the truth. Once a few simple concepts are understood and a few new syntactic constructions are mastered, most students find that linked data structures are not really difficult and are actually rather enjoyable. We will begin by comparing linked structures and arrays, with which we are already familiar. This overview will include a short discussion of the relative strengths of linked and nonlinked structures, and situations where each is appropriate. We will see that, although each type of structure has advantages and disadvantages, the linked representation is more suitable for representing intricate structures and often can better represent complex data and the relationships among different parts of the data.

The overview will be followed by an introduction to the Pascal constructs used to build linked data structures, and a tutorial on visual representations useful for checking programs. The rest of the chapter will present different types of linked structures and algorithms for building, traversing, and erasing them. A number of structures will be illustrated with programs dealing with music data, which will also be the focus of some exercises at the end of the chapter. The use of linked structures for the solution of more complex problems is illustrated in the larger applications in the last section of this book, particularly in chapters 18 and 20.

16.1 Overview

Figure 16.1 illustrates two common methods of allocating storage in the computer memory. Each part of the figure shows a different method of storing an ordered list of items (what these items represent is irrelevent for now). At (a) the list of items is stored in an array called *list*. Each box represents one component of the array, which may occupy more than one memory location depending on the component type. Items in the list are accessed by referring to the name of the array and a subscript giving the position in the array. Here item 1 is stored in *list*[0], item 2 is stored in *list*[1], and so on. Since arrays use contiguous storage locations in memory, this is called *sequential storage allocation*. Each time an array element is referenced, the computer calculates the address of the desired element, i.e., the ordinal position of the storage location in memory. Since the first subscript of the array is 0 here, the

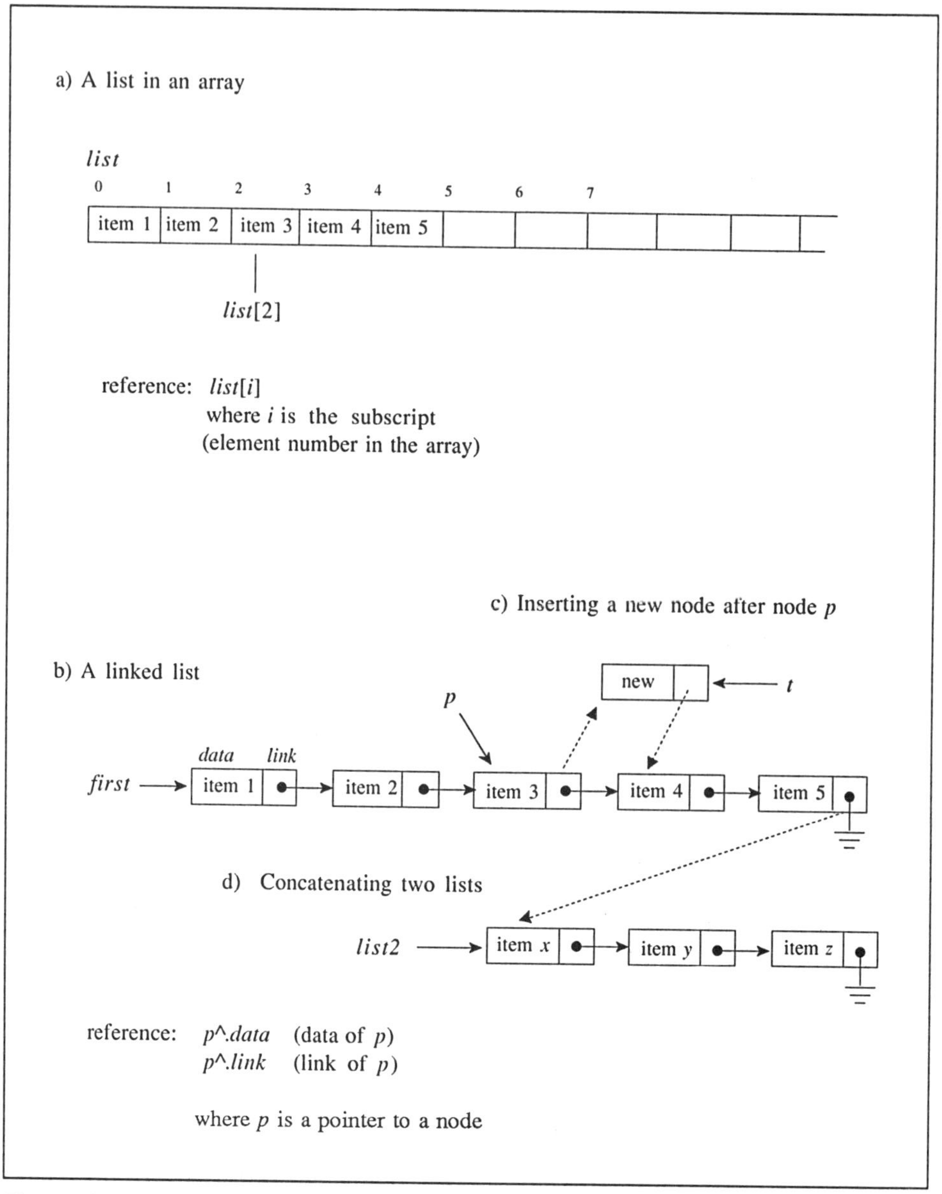

Figure 16.1. Sequential and Linked Storage Allocation

address is found by the formula

$$A = B + I \times W$$

where A is the address, B is the base address of the array (the address of the first element), I is the subscript, and W is the size of each element in words. Because each element of the array can be accessed directly, an array is a *random-access* data structure.

At (b) of figure 16.1, the same list of items is shown stored in a simple linked list. A linked data structure contains data objects called *nodes*, which have various *fields* for storing data and *pointers* (or links) to other nodes. In our simple list, each node has two fields, called *data* and *link*. The data field contains an item and the link field contains the address of the next node in the computer's memory. The links, or pointers, are shown as arrows in the diagram, although they are actually the numeric address of the next node in memory. The pointer variable *first* contains the address of the first node in the list and thus *points* to the beginning of the list; the link field of the last node contains a **nil** pointer, that is, it doesn't point to anything. Values are accessed for any node, say the one pointed to by *p*, by referring to *p*↑*.data* or *p*↑*.link* (read "data of *p*" and "link of *p*"). Because the nodes do not necessarily occupy contiguous storage locations, but rather are linked together by the address fields (pointers), this is called *linked storage allocation.*

Both types of data structures have advantages and disadvantages, and each is suitable in different applications. For a list of items of fixed length, an array requires less memory, since the linked structure needs an extra storage location for each link field. However, the size of an array must be declared before the program is compiled; thus its size cannot be changed while the program is running. Linked data structures are *dynamic*, that is, storage space for nodes can be allocated and released as needed, and the size of the structure can change during program execution. Thus if the number of items to be stored will vary but may be large, the linked list may actually use less memory. Suppose, for example, that the maximum number of items expected in the list is 5000. The array will have to occupy 5000 storage locations even if only a few are actually being used, while we can allocate just as much or as little memory as is needed for the linked structure.

Accessing an arbitrary item is more efficient in the array, since it can be located in a fixed amount of time by calculation; in the linked list the same item can only be reached by entering the list at the beginning and stepping through (or traversing) the list until the desired node is found. However, once we have a pointer to a node in the linked list, that node can be accessed with little or no calculation.

Inserting a new value within a list is more efficient in the linked representation than in the sequential one. Suppose we wish to insert a new item between item 2 and item 3 in figure 16.1. In the array, items 3 through 5 will have to be moved to the right in reverse order, one at a time, to make room. In the linked list, we need only obtain a new node and insert it into the list by resetting two pointers, as in (c) of figure 16.1. Items can also be deleted more efficiently in the linked list, since we only have to reset one pointer, rather than shifting many items.

The linked structure also has a tremendous advantage for the concatenation of two lists. Linked lists can be joined by setting the link field at the end of the first list to point to the first node of the second list, as shown at (d) of figure 16.1. To concatenate two lists stored in arrays, each item from one array must be copied into the other array.

The linked data structure is not limited to simple ordered lists of the type shown above. Nodes may have more than one link field and may be linked together in

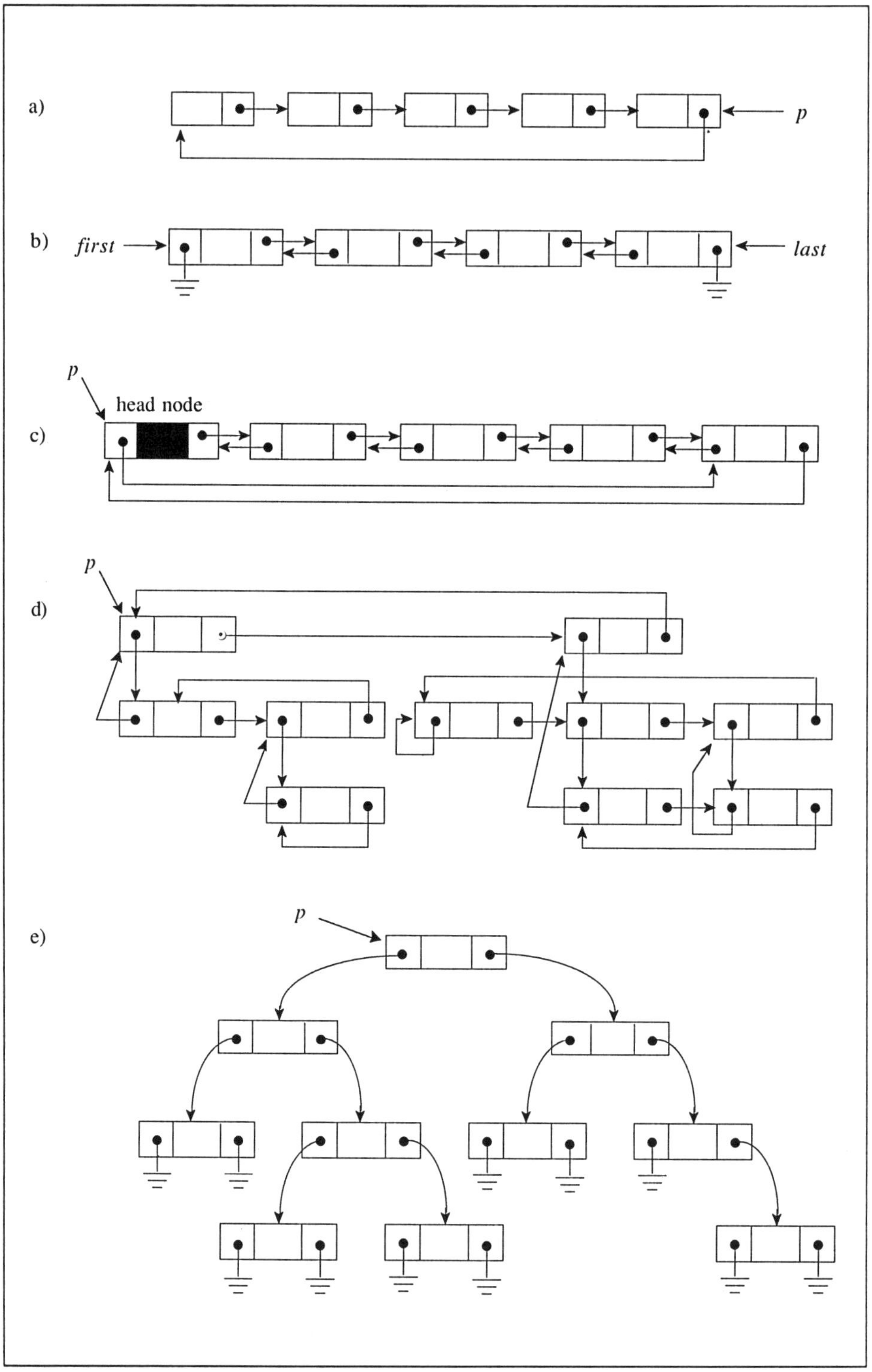

Figure 16.2. Some Linked Data Structures

many different configurations. A few examples are shown in figure 16.2. At (a) we see a circular linked list, or ring, with the last node pointing back to the first. It may be convenient to treat the list as a continuum, with no beginning and no end. However, if we use this list to represent an ordered list of values, it is convenient to keep a pointer to the end, as shown here. Thus we have immediate access to the end of the list through variable *p*, and to the beginning through the link field of the last node. At (b) we see a doubly linked list. Each node has two pointers, one to the next node and one to the previous node in the list. This list can be traversed in either direction. Part (c) shows a doubly linked circular list with a head node, (d) is a more complex ring structure, and (e) is a linked representation of a binary tree.

A node in a list is not limited to one data field. It typically has several fields for different information relating to the data object being represented. For example, a node representing a note may have data fields to represent pitch, duration, dynamic level, articulation, and so on.

The linked data structure can easily be adapted to more intricate structures. It is possible to have a variable number of variable-length lists, any node can be the starting point for another list, and nodes can be linked into several different lists simultaneously. Thus it is possible to design data structures that not only contain values for data, but also represent the structure of the data and relationships among various data items. A note in a score may have a melodic and a harmonic function at the same time; a linked structure can represent both functions.

16.2 Basic Operations

Two reasons why a linked data structure is so flexible are that space is allocated dynamically, and the structure is built and possibly dismantled under control of the program. We will illustrate most of the simple types of lists using a minimum configuration consisting of nodes with two *fields*, called *data* and *link*. The data field will contain an integer, and the link field a pointer.

The basic operations for dealing with simple lists are shown in table 16.1. The node is defined with a pointer type and a record type.

```
type
  ptr = ↑node;                          { pointer to a node }
  node = record
            data : integer;             { the data field     }
            link : ptr                  { the link field     }
         end;

var
  p, q : ptr;                           { pointer variables }
```

Note that the definition is circular, since we must define a pointer to a node and a node that contains a pointer to a node. In Pascal, the pointer type is *always* defined

Operation	*Pascal Implementation*
define node	define pointer type and record
obtain node	*new(p)*
set data field	*p↑.data* := *x*;
read data field	x := *p↑.data*
set link field	*p↑.link* := *q*; *p↑.link* := **nil**
read link field	*q* := *p↑.link*
compare pointers	*q* = *p*; *q* = **nil**
recycle node	*dispose(p)*

Table 16.1. Basic Operations

first. The pointer type is then used in the record defining the node and in variable declarations. The fact that Pascal is a strongly typed language is again apparent in this definition. Note that a pointer is defined so that it points to a specific type of object. Although pointers to two different types of objects are both addresses, they are not assignment compatible, i.e., these values are not interchangeable in expressions, and a pointer value of one type may not be assigned to a pointer variable of another type. There is nothing special about the identifiers *node*, *link*, and *ptr*, but these terms are commonly used in discussing linked structures and will be used consistently in this chapter, except when more mnemonic identifiers are required for special applications. We will also see later that a node can be arbitrarily complex and may contain many different fields for both data and pointers.

Programs using pointers and linked data structures cannot be checked manually in the same way as programs that do not use these devices. First, the actual addresses are not readily available, and even if they were, it is easier to picture linked structures with diagrams. The best way to learn to use and understand linked structures is to draw them on a piece of paper or a blackboard. Stepping through a program involves drawing nodes and arrows representing pointers.

When a node is required, it is obtained by calling the Pascal procedure *new*. If *p* has been defined as above, the Pascal statement *new(p)* allocates memory space of the required size and assigns the address of this space to the variable *p*. We will show this graphically as:

```
new(p);
```

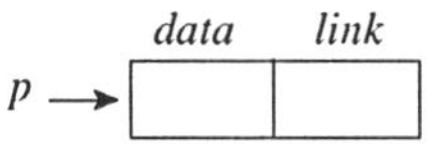

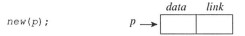

Internally, the address of the node is the address of the beginning of the node; however, it will be helpful, particularly when drawing more complex diagrams, to think of pointers as pointing to the whole node rather than to any one specific field.

Now we can set fields in the node. Recall that the individual fields are referenced by the name of a pointer that points to the node followed by an up arrow (↑), a dot, and the field name. Thus the assignment *p↑.data* := 10 places the integer 10 in the data field of the node pointed to by *p*, i.e., "assign 10 to data of *p*":

```
p↑.data := 10;
```

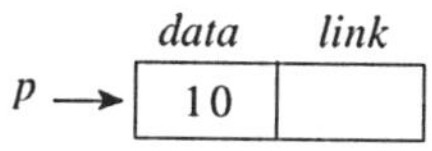

The value of the data field is obtained by referencing the field by name:

```
write(p↑.data);        x := p↑.data
```

Pointer variables, including the *link* field of a node, are set by assignment or by calling the standard procedure *new.* The value may be a previously assigned pointer value of the same type or the value **nil**, which signifies a pointer that does not point at anything. In diagrams, we will use the electrical *ground* symbol to denote a **nil** pointer:

```
p↑.link := nil;
```

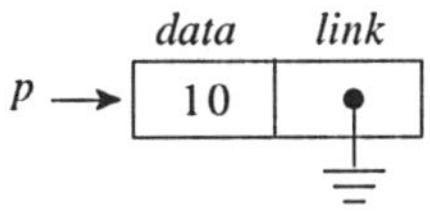

Assigning a value to a pointer variable is diagrammed by showing a second pointer pointing to the same node:

```
q := p;
```

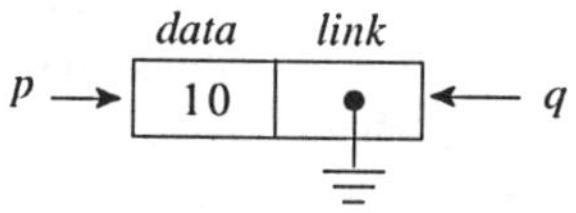

A **nil** value for a variable is symbolized in the same way as for a data field in a node:

```
q := nil;
```

An entire node, say the one pointed to by *p*, can be referred to collectively by the expression *p*↑. Thus if both *p* and *q* point to nodes, the statement

```
q↑ := p↑;
```

assigns the value of the data field of node *p* to the data field of node *q*, and the value of the link field of node *p* to the link field of node *q*. Note that this does not allocate new storage locations in memory; it merely copies all of the values in one node to another. In this regard it is similar to assigning an entire record to another. Nor is it the same as the statement *q* := *p*, which assigns to pointer *q* the address of node *p*, as shown above.

If a pointer variable points to a node in a linked list, it is often possible to access other nodes indirectly. For example, if *p* points to a node and the link field of that node points to another, then *p*↑.*link*↑.*data* and *p*↑.*link*↑.*link* reference the data and link fields of the second node. This chained reference is equivalent to *q* := *p*↑.*link*, followed by references to *q*↑.*data* and *q*↑.*link*:

```
x := p↑.link↑.data;

{ assigns 89 to x }
```

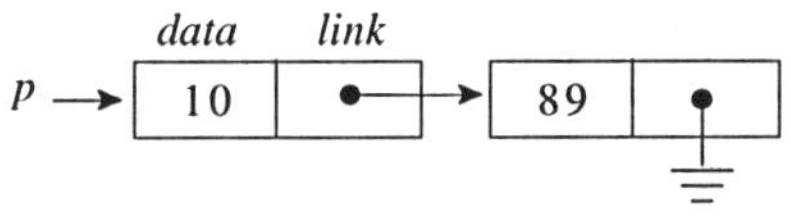

Arithmetic operations involving pointers are not allowed in Pascal, and the only valid comparisons are for equality. The boolean expression ($p = q$) is *true* if p and q both point to the same node or both are **nil**. It is also possible to test a pointer variable directly for a **nil** value:

```
if p = nil          |          while q <> nil do
  then ...          |            ...
```

When a node is no longer needed it can be recycled, i.e., returned to the operating system for reuse at a later time, by calling *dispose*:

```
dispose(q);              { recycle node pointed to by q }
```

The reader is urged to work through the procedures in this chapter with a pencil and paper (or blackboard and chalk). There is no better way to understand linked data structures than to draw them. ''Execute'' each statement by drawing appropriate nodes with arrows representing links. Each time a pointer is assigned, draw the arrow that represents it. If a pointer is changed, erase the old arrow and draw a new one. The same method should be followed when writing procedures, but in the reverse order. Decide what needs to be done, draw the picture, and write the code. Then double-check by stepping through the algorithm with a fresh diagram. Remember that a node that cannot be accessed through a pointer is lost to your program and cannot be recovered. The order in which statements are executed is critical in some cases. Suppose, for example, that we wish to concatenate two lists accessed through pointers p and q. Assume for now that we have already set t to point to the last node in the first list. The lists before and after concatenation are shown below.

Before concatenation:

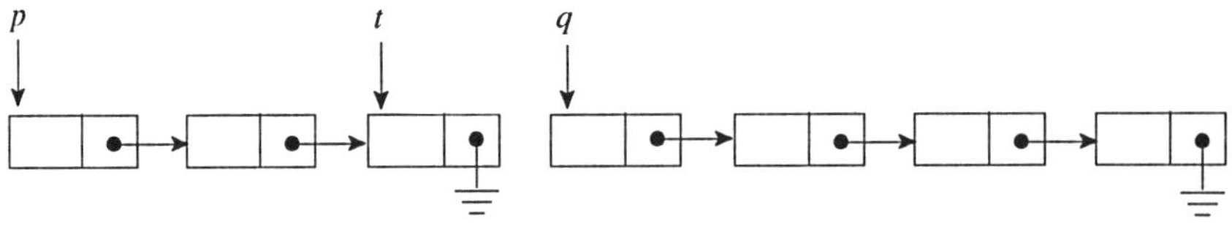

After concatenation:

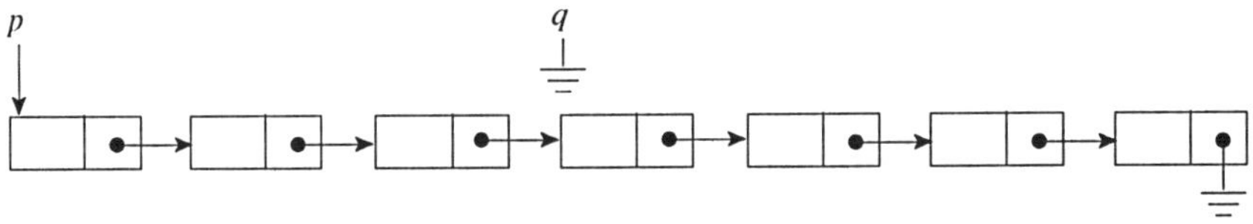

Two steps are necessary to get from the *before* condition to the *after* condition:

```
t↑.link := q;
q := nil;
```

Reversing the order of these statements results in the loss of list q, since as soon as the statement q := **nil** is executed there is no way to access the nodes that had been in list q. This is obvious if you draw the diagram:

```
q := nil;
t↑.link := q;
```

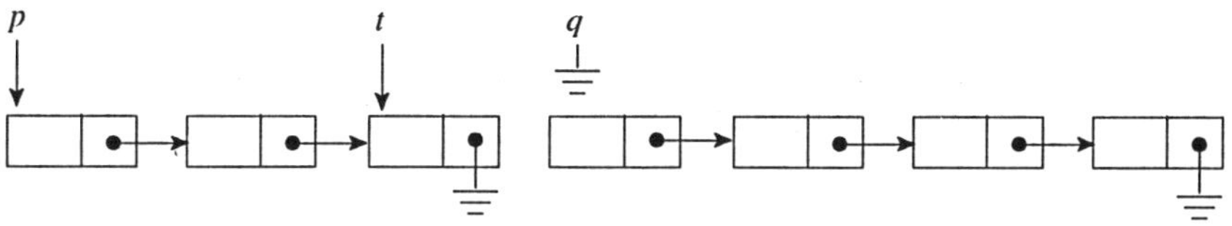

Follow this procedure until you can visualize the operations without the diagrams. Even then, diagrams will be useful in testing algorithms and debugging when things go wrong.

16.3 Linked Stacks

Perhaps the most natural of all linked structures is the linked implementation of the *stack*. We will implement the stack as a pointer variable s, which is initially set to **nil**, indicating an empty stack. Either the stack is empty, or it consists of a pointer to the top node on the stack. The link field of each node points to the next node on the stack, and the link field of the last node is a **nil** pointer.

Empty Stack

Nonempty Stack

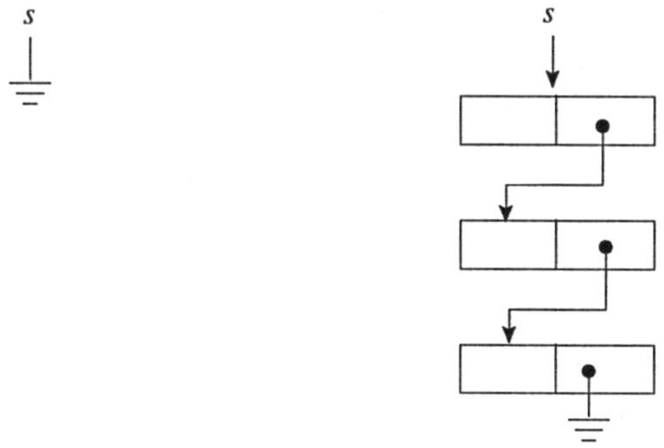

The test for an empty stack is simple:

```
function empty(s : ptr) : boolean;
  begin
    empty := s = nil
  end;
```

Procedure *push*, which places a value on the stack, obtains a node *t*, places the value in it, and then links the value onto the stack by assigning the value of *s* to the link field of the new node, and then pointing *s* to the new node. Note that the first time the procedure is called the stack is empty, i.e., *s* is a **nil** pointer. The statement *t*↑.*link* := *s* assigns a **nil** pointer to the *link* field of *t*, and *s* := *t* points *s* to the new top of the stack. The push operator is shown in figure 16.3. On subsequent calls, *t*↑.*link* := *s* points the link field of the new node to the top node of the stack, and *s* := *t* places node *t* on the top of the stack. The reader is urged to step through these procedures by drawing link diagrams. Unlike the array implementation of stacks (section 10.7.1), the linked stack is never "full," although eventually it is possible to reach a point where the Pascal system cannot allocate any more memory.

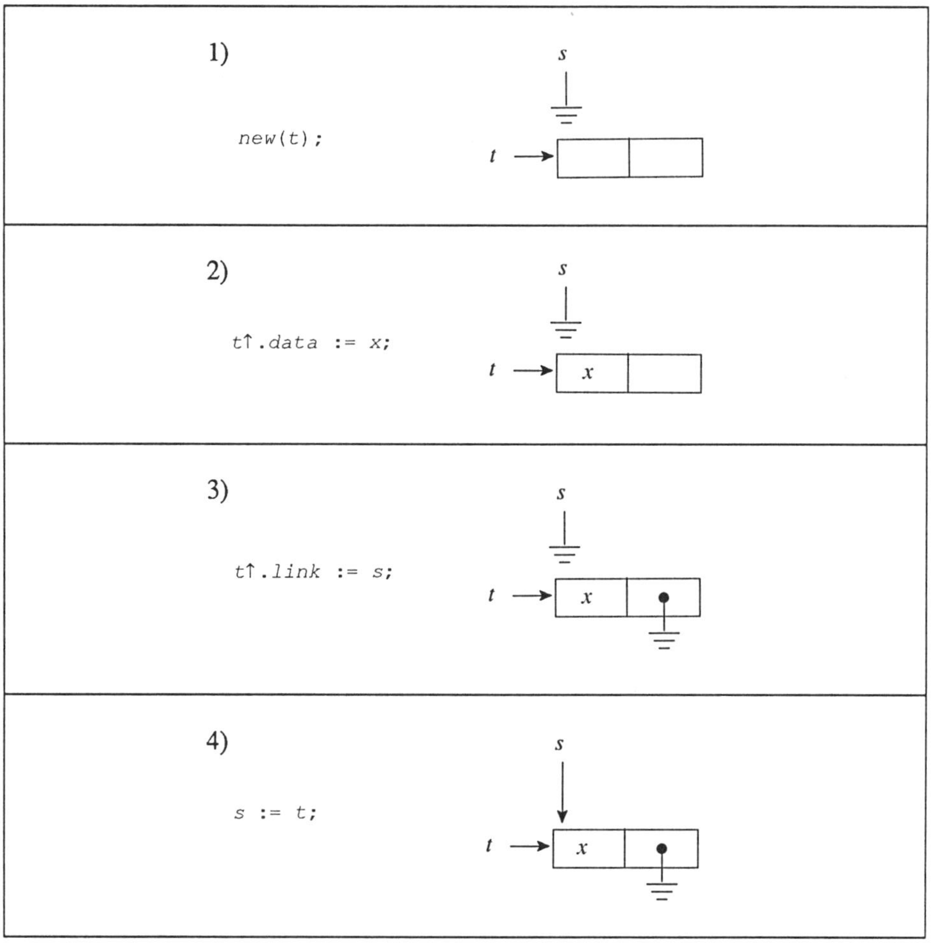

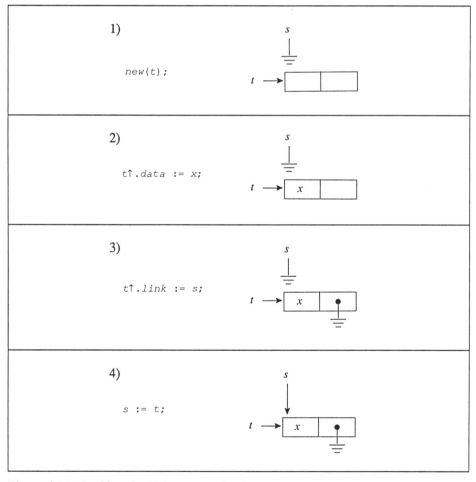

Figure 16.3. Pushing the Value *x* on a Stack.

```
procedure push(x : integer; var s : ptr);
  var
    t : ptr;
  begin
    new(t);                             { get a node        }
    t↑.data := x;                       { assign value      }
    t↑.link := s;                       { link into stack   }
    s := t
  end;
```

Procedure *pop* removes the top value from the stack. First it assigns the value of the top node to a **var** parameter so that it can be returned. Then it points *t* to the top node, and removes this node from the stack by assigning *s* the value of *s*↑*.link*. Finally, it returns node *t* to the operating system via *dispose*(*t*). Note that the temporary pointer *t* is necessary. Calling *dispose*(*s*) would return the top node, but all other nodes would be lost since there would no longer be a pointer to them. Testing for an empty stack is a precaution; this test should really be made before the procedure is called.

```
procedure pop(var x : integer; var s : ptr);
  var
    t : ptr;
  begin
    if not empty(s)
      then
        begin
          x := s↑.data;               { get value from top node }
          t := s;                     { save top node           }
          s := t↑.link;               { remove from stack       }
          dispose(t)                  { return to storage       }
        end
    else writeln('Pop: error stack is empty')
  end;
```

16.4 Storage Management

In an ideal world the procedures *new* and *dispose* would be sufficient for dynamic memory allocation. However, the standard procedure *dispose* has been implemented differently in different systems. In a few Pascal systems, you can only *dispose* of nodes in the reverse order in which they were allocated; i.e., nodes obtained by

```
new(a);          new(b);          new(c);
```

must be returned to storage in the order

```
dispose(c);      dispose(b);      dispose(a);
```

While one can live with this restriction with simple programs, it is totally unacceptable when complex linked structures have been built. In some systems *dispose* does nothing, and in others it actually returns the memory segments in a manner that allows them to be reused at a later time, as intended. Documentation for your Pascal system should detail the implementation of this procedure on your system.

Because of these variations in implementation, it is a good idea to take care of storage management within your programs, especially if your programs will eventually be implemented on different Pascal systems. Fortunately, the technique is not difficult and it is a good exercise in linked stacks. We will maintain a pool of available nodes, managed by two complementary procedures *getnode* and *release*. The storage pool, or free list, is a linked stack pointed to by the pointer variable *free*. *Free* is initialized as a nil pointer. Nodes will be obtained by procedure *getnode*, shown below. *Getnode* checks the free list, and if it is not empty, the procedure returns the top node from the stack. If the stack is empty, *getnode* uses the standard procedure *new* to obtain a node from the Pascal system.

```
procedure getnode(var p : ptr);
  begin { getnode }
    if free = nil
      then new(p)                  { get new node               }
      else
        begin                      { take node from stack       }
          p := free;
          free := free↑.link
        end
  end;  { getnode }
```

Procedure *release* places a node on the stack *free*. Thus once a node has been allocated by calling *new*, it is either in use in a linked data structure or it is kept on the free list until it is needed again. Programs that build a data structure just one time do not need to recycle allocated memory.

```
procedure release(var p : ptr);
  begin { release }
    p↑.link := free;           { link node p into free list }
    free := p;
    p := nil                   { assign p a nil pointer     }
  end;  { release }
```

Program 16.1 illustrates the use of stack and storage management procedures. In addition, I have included a procedure that prints a symbolic representation of a list. For example, if the stack contains the values 10, 43, and 89, *printlist* prints the following:

```
s------> 10---> 43---> 89--->  nil
```

This procedure is used to trace the contents of both the stack *s* and the free list *free*. Thus the program output dynamically traces the contents of both the stack and the free list. Studying the sample run from this program will help you to understand the dynamics of our storage management scheme.[1] Procedure *readdata* reads integers from one line and saves them on a stack. Procedure *printdata* pops each value off of the stack and prints it. Note that variables *s* and *free* must be initialized as nil

1. In the output, overly long lines have been edited to print on two lines.

pointers before they can be used. Failure to initialize these pointers will result in run-time errors.

```
(***********************    Program Linkstack    ***********************)
(* Implements a stack as a linked list.  Pointer s points to the top    *)
(* node on the stack, or is nil if the stack is empty.  The program     *)
(* reads the values from one line of input from the terminal, storing   *)
(* these values on the stack s.  The values are then printed in reverse *)
(* order as they are popped off the stack.  In order that nodes can be  *)
(* reused in subsequent lists, all unused (free) nodes are kept in a    *)
(* storage pool implemented as a stack of nodes pointed to by the       *)
(* pointer free.  Procedures getnode and release manage this storage    *)
(* pool.  Procedure printlist has been provided so that we can examine  *)
(* the contents of each linked list at will.                            *)
(***********************************************************************)
program linkstack(input, output);
  const
    freelist = true;                           { boolean flags used by }
    stack    = false;                          {      printlist        }

  type
    ptr  = ↑node;                              (********  node  *********)
    node = record                              (*       data link       *)
             data : integer;                   (*       _________       *)
             link : ptr                        (*      |____|____|      *)
           end;                                (************************)

  var
    free : ptr;                      { pointer to a stack of free nodes}
    s    : ptr;                      { pointer to the top of a stack   }


(***********************          empty          ***********************)
(*  Tests for empty stack.                                              *)
(***********************************************************************)
  function empty(s : ptr) : boolean;
    begin
      empty := s = nil
    end;


(***********************         getnode         ***********************)
(* Gets node from storage pool.                                         *)
(***********************************************************************)
  procedure getnode(var p : ptr);
    begin { getnode }
      if free = nil
        then new(p)                            { get new node           }
        else
          begin                                { take node from stack  }
            p := free;
            free := free↑.link
          end
    end;  { getnode }
```

```
(***********************          release          ***********************)
(* Returns node to storage pool.                                           *)
(***************************************************************************)
  procedure release(var p : ptr);
    begin { release }
      p↑.link := free;
      free := p;
      p := nil
    end;  { release }

(***********************          push             ***********************)
(* Pushes the value x onto the stack s.                                    *)
(***************************************************************************)
  procedure push(x : integer; var s : ptr);
    var
      t : ptr;
    begin { push }
      getnode(t);                                  { get a node            }
      t↑.data := x;                                { set data field        }
      t↑.link := s;                                { push t onto stack s   }
      s := t
    end;  { push }

(***********************          pop              ***********************)
(* Returns top value on stack s as variable parameter x.                   *)
(***************************************************************************)
  procedure pop(var x : integer; var s : ptr);
    var
      t : ptr;
    begin { pop }
      x := s↑.data;                          { take value off top of stack }
      t := s;                                { temp pointer to top node    }
      s := s↑.link;                          { remove top node from stack  }
      release(t)                             { return node to storage pool }
    end; { pop }

(***********************        printlist          ***********************)
(* Prints a list with arrows and integers representing link and data      *)
(* fields.  This procedure is provided so that we can examine the stack   *)
(* and free list dynamically.                                              *)
(***************************************************************************)
  procedure printlist(p : ptr; freelist : boolean);
    begin { printlist }
      if freelist
        then write('free')
        else write('s---');
      if p = nil
        then writeln('--->  nil')
        else
           begin { traverse list }
             while p <> nil do
               begin
                 write('--->', p↑.data:3);
                 p := p↑.link
               end;
             writeln('--->  nil')
           end  { traverse list }
    end;  { printlist }
```

```
(***********************         skipln          ***********************)
(* Skips blanks to next nonblank or newline character.                 *)
(***********************************************************************)
 procedure skipln;
   begin
     while (input↑ = ' ') and not eoln do
       get(input)
   end;

(***********************        readdata         ***********************)
(* Values on one line are read and stored on stack s.                  *)
(***********************************************************************)
 procedure readdata(var s : ptr);
   var
     x : integer;
   begin
     while not eoln do
       begin
         read(x);
         push(x, s);
         skipln
       end;
     readln
   end;  { readdata }

(***********************        printdata        ***********************)
(* Pops all values off of stack and prints them.                       *)
(***********************************************************************)
 procedure printdata(var s : ptr);
   var
     x : integer;
   begin
     write('values popped from stack: ');
     while not empty(s) do
       begin
         pop(x, s);                                { get value from stack }
         write(x : 4)                              { print it             }
       end;
     writeln
   end;  { printdata }

(***********************************************************************)
(*                            Main Procedure                           *)
(***********************************************************************)
 begin { main }
   free := nil;                              { init free list          }
   s    := nil;                              { init stack pointer      }
   writeln;
   printlist(free, freelist);                { examine storage pool    }
   printlist(s, stack);                      { examine stack s         }
   writeln;
   write('Type list:  ');                    { prompt user             }
   while not eof do
     begin
       readdata(s);                          { read data, store on stack }
       writeln;
       printlist(free, freelist);            { examine storage pool    }
       printlist(s, stack);                  { examine stack           }
```

```
        writeln;
        printdata(s);                       { print values from stack    }
        writeln;
        printlist(free, freelist);          { examine storage pool       }
        printlist(s, stack);                { examine stack              }
        writeln;
        write('Type list:  ')               { prompt user                }
      end
  end.  { main }
```

Program 16.1. *Linkstack*

```
free---> nil
s------> nil

Type list:  1 2 3 4 5

free---> nil
s------> 5---> 4---> 3---> 2---> 1---> nil

values popped from stack:    5   4   3   2   1

free---> 1---> 2---> 3---> 4---> 5---> nil
s------> nil

Type list:  89 43 10

free---> 4---> 5---> nil
s------> 10---> 43---> 89---> nil

values popped from stack:   10  43  89

free---> 89---> 43---> 10---> 4---> 5---> nil
s------> nil

Type list:  99 24 88 199 -1 839 23 89 54 8 1

free---> nil
s------> 1---> 8---> 54---> 89---> 23--->839---> -1--->199--->
         88---> 24---> 99---> nil

values popped from stack:    1   8  54  89  23 839  -1 199  88  24  99

free---> 99---> 24---> 88--->199---> -1--->839---> 23---> 89--->
         54---> 8---> 1---> nil
s------> nil

Type list:  199

free---> 24---> 88--->199---> -1--->839---> 23---> 89---> 54--->
          8---> 1---> nil
s------>199---> nil
```

```
values popped from stack:  199

free--->199---> 24---> 88--->199---> -1--->839---> 23---> 89--->
         54--->  8--->  1--->  nil
s------>  nil

Type list: ^D
```

Program 16.1. Sample Run (Interactive)

16.5 Linked Lists

The tools we have discussed thus far are sufficient for constructing many different types of linked structures. In this section we will examine a number of structures that are useful in dealing with ordered lists. For most of these we will use the same simple node structure as in the previous programs, but keep in mind that the nodes can be arbitrarily complex and may contain data fields of different types to store related data. We will study various lists in increasing order of complexity.

16.5.1 Simple Lists

The simplest type of linked list is structured just like the stack shown above, but the operations defined for the structure are different. The list is accessed through a pointer variable that points to the first node in the list, or is **nil** if the list is empty. The link field of the last node is a **nil** pointer.

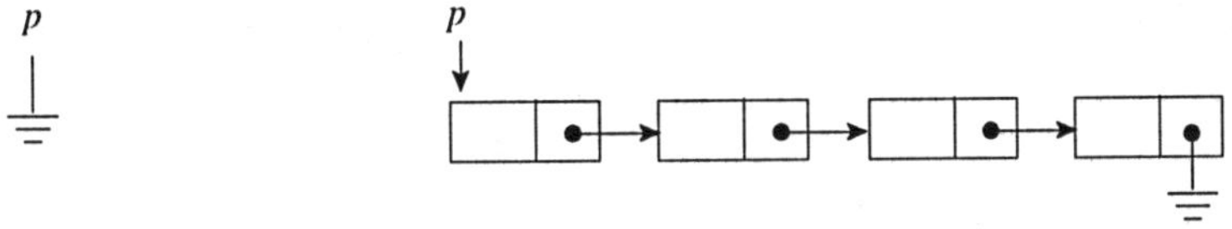

The list is built using procedure *insert*, which inserts the integer x after an arbitrary node q. First, a new node, t, is obtained and the data field is set. If q is a **nil** pointer, the new node is inserted as the first node in the list, otherwise node t is linked into the list after node q. The insertion algorithm works for any node in the list, including the last.

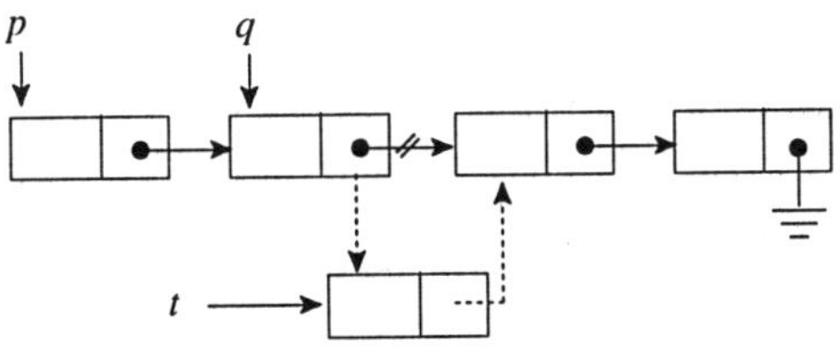

```
{ insert integer x after node q }
procedure insert(x : integer; var q : ptr);
  var
    t : ptr;
  begin
    getnode(t);                        { get a new node             }
    t↑.data := x;                      { and set fields             }
    if empty(q)                        { if list is empty           }
      then
        begin
          q := t;                      { t becomes first node       }
          t↑.link := nil
        end
      else
        begin                          { insert after q             }
          t↑.link := q↑.link;          { point to list after q      }
          q↑.link := t                 { link new node into list    }
        end
  end;
```

If the list is to be built by adding each new value at the end, we must have a way of finding the end of the list. Function *lastnode* returns a pointer to this node. Note that *p* points to the last node when *p*↑.*link* = **nil**; testing for *p* = **nil** would go one step too far:

```
{ find last node in list }
function lastnode(p : ptr) : ptr;
  begin
    while p↑.link <> nil do
      p := p↑.link;
    lastnode := p
  end;
```

Procedure *readdata* reads a list of integers on one input line and stores them in order in a linked list. Function *lastnode* is used to find the last node in the list:

```
procedure readdata(var p : ptr);
  var
    x : integer;                            { for reading a value    }
    q : ptr;                                { the end of the list    }
  begin
    while not eoln(input) do
      begin
        read(x);                            { read value             }
        if empty(p)                         { if list is empty       }
          then insert(x, p)                 {   insert x             }
          else
            begin                           { insert at end of list  }
              q := lastnode(p);             { find last node         }
              insert(x, q)                  { insert after it        }
            end;
        skipln(input)
      end;
    readln
  end;  { readdata }
```

The following procedure deletes an arbitrary node *t* from list *p*. It is necessary to first get a pointer, say *q*, to the node before the one we want to delete. Then *q*↑.*link* is set to *t*↑.*link*, and node *t* is returned to the storage pool. If the node to be deleted is the first in the list, *p* is assigned *p*↑.*link* and node *t* is returned.

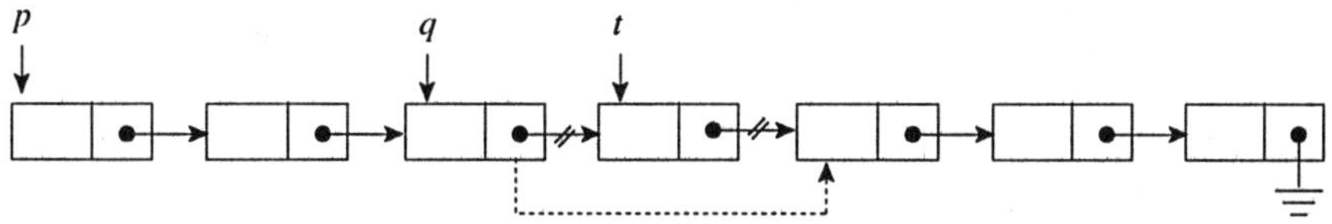


```
{ delete node t from list p }
procedure delete(var t, p : ptr);
  var
    q : ptr;                              { node before t       }
  begin
    if t = p
      then p := p↑.link;                  { remove first node }
      else
        begin                             { get node before t }
          q := p;
          while q↑.link <> t do
              q := q↑.link;
          q↑.link := t↑.link              { remove node t       }
        end;
     release(t)                           { return to storage }
  end;  { delete }
```

Iterative Traversals. To *traverse* a list means to visit each node. Visit could mean many things; for our demonstration we will print the value of the data field of each node. The simplest traversal is iterative. A temporary variable is set to point to the beginning of the list, and then a **while** loop is used to print each value and obtain the next node, until the final **nil** pointer is encountered. Since the **while** tests at the top of the loop, it protects against traversing an empty list.

```
t := p;
while t <> nil do
  begin
    write(t↑.data);
    t := t↑.link
  end
```

After each value is written, the next node is obtained by setting *t* equal to *t*↑.*link*. The algorithm terminates when *t* becomes **nil**. Using temporary variable *t* prevents loss of the list. When the algorithm is written as a procedure, the temporary variable is not needed since the pointer to the first node is passed by value, i.e., it is already a copy of the actual value:

```
procedure traverse1(p : ptr);                  { iterative traversal }
  begin
    while p <> nil do
      begin
        write(p↑.data);                        { write value     }
        p := p↑.link                           { get next node }
      end;
    writeln
  end;  { traverse }
```

This traversal is easily adapted to other tasks. Function *lastnode* (above) is one example. Another is function *length*, which returns the length of the list:

```
function length(p : ptr) : integer;           { count nodes in list }
  var
    n : integer;
  begin
    n := 0;
    while p <> nil do
      begin
        incr(n);
        p := p↑.link
      end;
    length := n
  end;  { length }
```

Copying a list is also essentially a traversal. Procedure *copy* makes a copy of list *p* in list *q*. As each node is visited, its value is copied into a second list. This procedure also uses function *lastnode*:

```
procedure copy(p : ptr; var q : ptr);     { copy list p to list q }
  var
    t : ptr;                                  { end of list     }
  begin
    q := nil;
    while p <> nil do
      begin
        if q = nil
          then insert(p↑.data, q)
          else
            begin
              t := lastnode(q);
              insert(p↑.data, t)
            end;
        p := p↑.link                          { get next node }
      end;
    writeln
  end;
```

The following procedure reverses linked list *p*. As the list is traversed, each node is removed and pushed onto stack *q*. When no nodes are left on list *p*, the traversal terminates and the address of the queue is assigned to *p*. Essentially, this algorithm treats list *p* as if it were a stack. Each element is popped off stack *p* and pushed onto stack *q*, thus reversing the list.

```
procedure reverse(var p : ptr);                    { reverse list }
  var
    q, t : ptr;
  begin
    q := nil;                          { an empty stack              }
    while p <> nil do
      begin
        t := p;                        { take top node from list p }
        p := p↑.link;
        t↑.link := q;                  { and push it on stack q      }
        q := t
      end;
    p := q                             { assign q to p               }
  end;  { reverse }
```

Concatenating Lists. Two lists are concatenated by finding the last node in the first and setting its link field to point to the beginning of the second list. If the first list is empty, the second list becomes the first. Procedure *concatenate* joins lists *p* and *q*. After concatenation, list *p* contains the concatenation of *p* and *q*, and *q* is **nil**. The only special case occurs when list *p* is empty, in which case *q* is assigned to *p*.

Two lists before concatenation:

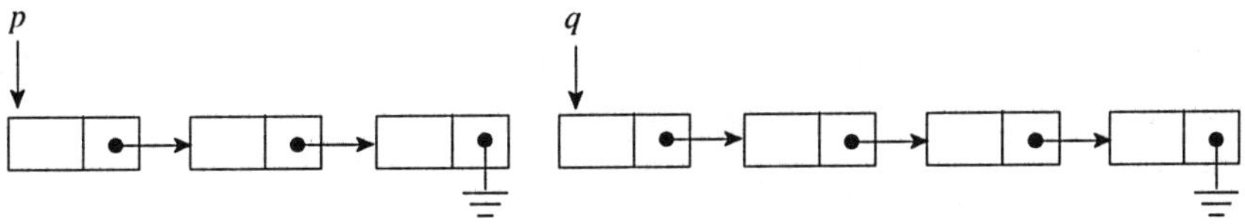

After concatenation:

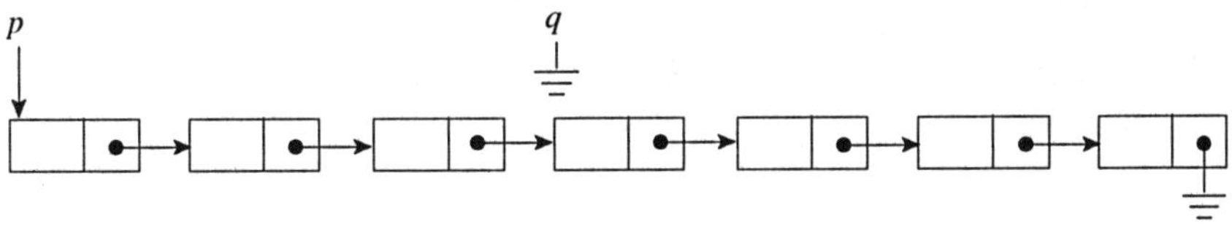


```
procedure concatenate(var p, q : ptr);      { join two lists }
  var
    t : ptr;
  begin
    if p = nil
      then p := q
      else
        begin
          t := lastnode(p);             { get last node in p      }
          t↑.link := q                  { point link field to q }
        end;
    q := nil
  end;
```

Recursive Traversals. You may have noticed that the linked list can be defined recursively:

Either a list is empty or it contains a node with a pointer to another list.

This leads quite naturally to a recursive traversal:

If the list is not empty, visit the current node and then traverse the list pointed to by the link field of the current node.

Again, the value parameter prevents the loss of the list:

```
{ recursive traversal }
procedure traverse2(p : ptr);
  begin
    if p <> nil
      then
        begin
          write(p↑.data);         { write value of current node }
          traverse2(p↑.link)      { traverse sublist              }
        end
  end; { traverse }
```

Note that this traversal does not include a *writeln*, since we do not wish to print each value on a separate line. *Writeln* must be called explicitly after traversing:

```
traverse2(p);
writeln
```

The recursive traversal can be made to print the list in reverse order by exchanging the order of two statements:

If the list is not empty, traverse the list pointed to by the current node and then print the value of the current node.

```
{ recursive traversal in reverse order }
procedure traverse3(p : ptr);
  begin
    if p <> nil
      then
        begin
          traverse3(p↑.link);      { traverse sublist              }
          write(p↑.data)           { write value of current node }
        end
  end;
```

The list can be erased by a variation of the reverse order traversal. As each node is visited, the remainder of the list is erased, and then the current node is returned to the storage pool. A variable parameter must be used so that each pointer can be set to **nil** when the mode to which it points is released:

```
{ erase list recursively }
procedure erase(var p : ptr);
  begin
    if p <> nil
      then
        begin
          erase(p↑.ptr);         { erase sublist                  }
          release(p)             { release current node           }
        end
  end;
```

The list can be returned without the overhead of recursion and repeated calls to procedure *release* by the following procedure, which sets a temporary pointer to the last node in the list and then returns all of the nodes to the free list at once:

```
{ bulk-erase list }
procedure bulkerase(var p : ptr);
  var
    t : ptr;
  begin
    if p <> nil
      then
        begin
          t := lastnode(p);      { t points to end of list         }
          t↑.link := free;       { link of t points to free list   }
          free := p;             { free points to beginning of list }
          p := nil               { p is now empty                  }
        end
  end; { bulkerase }
```

16.5.2 Lists with Pointers to Beginning and End

A number of operations with the previous list configuration are inefficient because the list must be traversed repeatedly to find the last node. Performance can be improved by keeping a pointer to both ends of the list. In the empty list both *p* and *pend* are **nil** pointers.

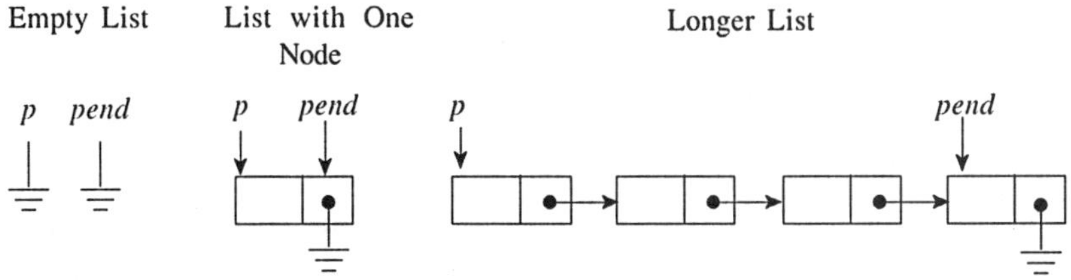

Since all of the benefits of this list can be obtained by using a circular list (section 16.5.4), procedures for implementing this list are left as an exercise. However, the structure shown above is ideal for implementing a queue as a linked list.

16.5.3 Linked Queues

The most natural linked implementation of a *queue* is a simple linked list with two pointers called *front* and *rear*, which point to the beginning and end of the list.

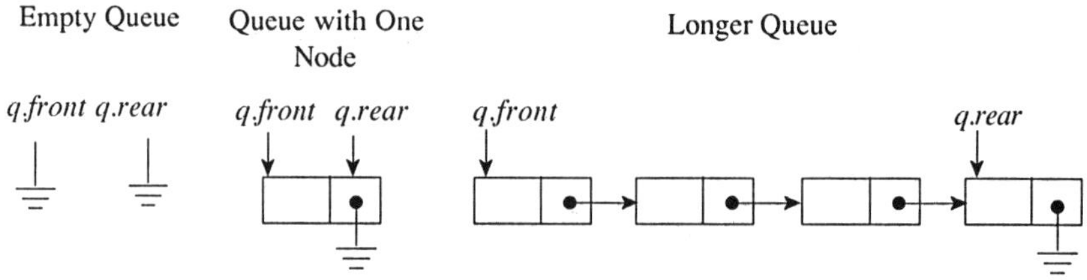

We will implement the queue as a record with two fields, *front* and *rear*.

```
type
  queue = record
            front : ptr;              { points to front of queue }
            rear  : ptr               { points to rear of queue  }
          end;
```

The queue is initialized by a function that sets *q.front* and *q.rear* to **nil**:

```
{ initilize queue }
procedure initialize(var q : queue);
  begin
    q.front := nil;
    q.rear  := nil
  end;
```

Function *empty* tests for the empty queue.

```
{ test for empty queue }
function empty(var q : queue) : boolean;
  begin
    empty := q.front = nil
  end;
```

Values are placed in the queue by procedure *insert*. Inserting in an empty queue is a special case. Otherwise, the new node is linked into the list after the last node, and *rear* is reassigned to point to the new end of the list.

```
{ insert x in linked queue }
procedure insert(x : integer; var q : queue);
  var
    t : ptr;
  begin
    getnode(t);                    { get a new node              }
    t↑.data := x;                  { and set fields              }
    t↑.link := nil;
    if empty(q)
      then q.front := t;           { insert in empty queue       }
      else q.rear↑.link := t;      { rear points to new node     }
    q.rear := t                    { rear points to new end of list }
  end;
```

Values are taken off of the front of the queue by procedure *remove*, which takes the value of the first node and then removes this node from the queue.

```
{ remove x from queue }
procedure remove(var x : integer; var q : queue);
  var
    t : ptr;
  begin
    if empty(q)
      then writeln('Error: queue is empty')
      else
        begin
          x := q.front↑.data;
          t := q.front;
          q.front := q.front↑.link;
          release(t)
        end
  end; { remove }
```

16.5.4 Circular Lists

In a circular list, or *ring*, the link field of the last node points to the first node. If the structure represents an ordered list, the list is accessed through a pointer to the last node in the list. The programmer has immediate access to the last node through a pointer, and to the first node through the link field of the last node: if *p* points to the last node, then *p*↑*.link* points to the first. Thus the circular list has most of the advantages of a list with pointers to the beginning and end, without the bother of maintaining two pointers. An empty list is recognized by a **nil** pointer as before. The list is kept circular, even when only one node is in the list, by pointing the link field of the node to the node. In this case it is important to remember that conceptually it is the link field of the *last* node that points to the first, not the link field of the first node. The only instance of a **nil** pointer in this type of list is the empty list.

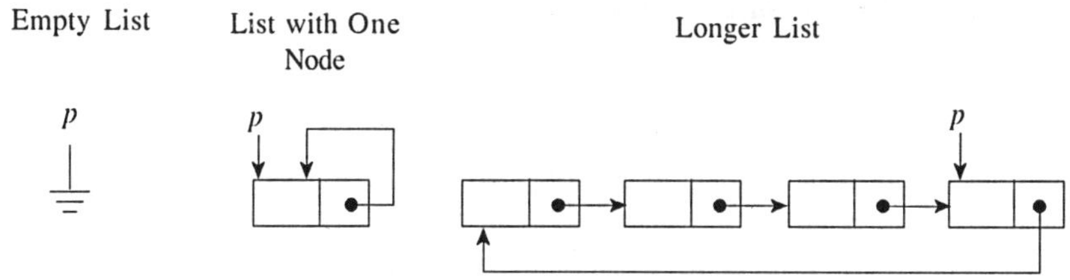

The procedure listed below constructs this list by adding values at the end. The empty list is a special case. All other cases are identical, so long as the above warning is heeded.

```
{ insert at end of circular list }
procedure cinsert(x : integer; var p : ptr);
  var
    t : ptr;
  begin
    getnode(t);                        { get a new node           }
    t↑.data := x;                      { and set fields           }
    if empty(p)                        { if list is empty         }
      then t↑.link := t                { start new list           }
      else
        begin                          { add to end of list       }
          t↑.link := p↑.link;          { point to first node      }
          p↑.link := t                 { link new node into list  }
        end;
      p := t                           { point to new end         }
  end;  { cinsert }
```

The circular list is traversed using a **repeat...until** loop. A temporary pointer is set to the beginning of the list, then the list is traversed until the starting condition is obtained. As an exercise, prove that the loop cannot be traversed with a **while** loop without treating the last node as a special case.

```
{ travese circular list }
procedure ctraverse(p : ptr);
  var
    t : ptr;
  begin
    if p <> nil then
      begin
        t := p↑.link;                  { t points to list beginning  }
        repeat
          write(t↑.data);              { write value of current node }
          t := t↑.link                 { get next node               }
        until t = p↑.link
      end;
    writeln
  end;  { ctraverse }
```

After a pointer is set to the beginning of the list, the circular list can be "bulk-erased" just like the simple list in section 16.5.1.

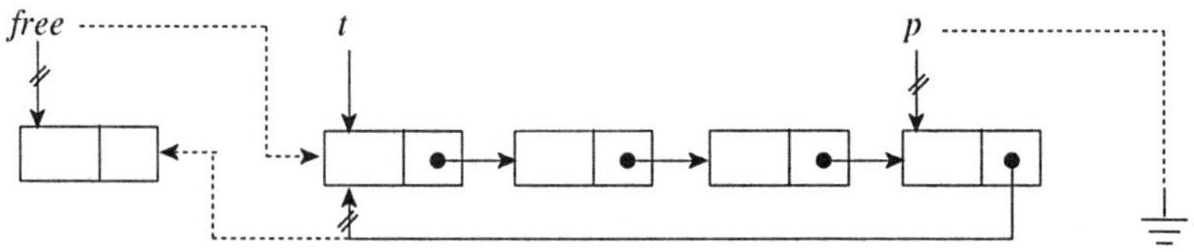


```
{ bulk-erase circular list }
procedure cerase(var p : ptr);
  var
    t : ptr;
```

```
begin { cerase }
  if p <> nil
    then
      begin
        t := p↑.link;           { point t to beginning }
        p↑.link := free;        { bulk-erase list      }
        free := t;
        p := nil
      end
end; { cerase }
```

Although the circular construction has many advantages, some operations require special care. For example, when inserting a new value after an arbitrary node q, one must remember to reassign the pointer to the end of the list if q is the last node in the list:

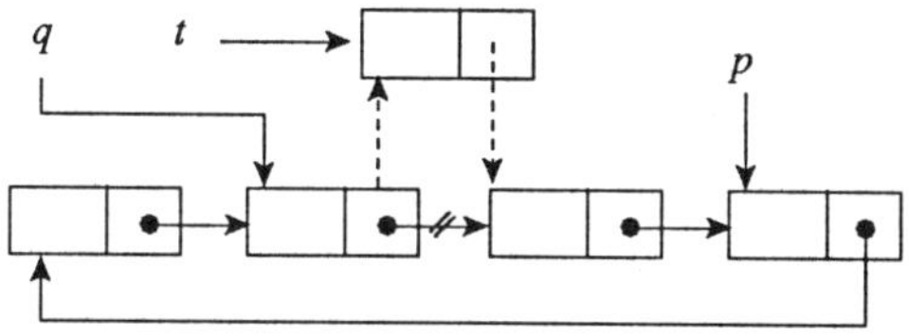


```
{ insert integer x after node q in list p }
procedure arbinsert(x : integer; q : ptr; var p : ptr);
  var
    t : ptr;
  begin
    getnode(t);                 { get new node           }
    t↑.data := x;               { set data field         }
    t↑.link := q↑.link;         { link t into list       }
    q↑.link := t;
    if p = q                    { check for end condition }
      then p := t
  end; { arbinsert }
```

The same problem can occur when deleting an arbitrary node, since if the last node is deleted the list is lost. The following procedure deletes the nth node in the list. As in earlier deletions, we need two temporary pointers. We will point q to the node before the one to be deleted, and t to the node we wish to delete. There are two special cases:

1. If there is only one node in the list, we can release it.
2. If the node to be deleted is the last node in the list, the pointer p must be moved before the node is released.

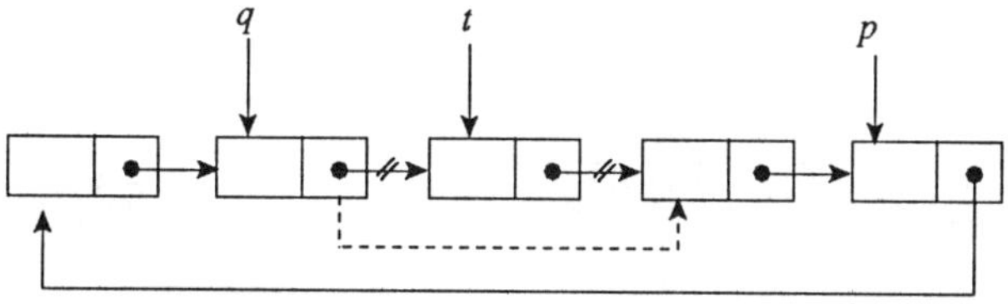

```
{ delete nth node in circular list p }
procedure delete(n : integer; var p : ptr);
  var
    i    : integer;
    q, t : ptr;
  begin
    if p = p↑.link                    { if only one node in list }
      then release(p)                 {     delete it            }
      else
        begin                         { delete arbitrary node    }
          q := p;                     { get node before deletion }
          for i := 1 to n - 1 do
            q := q↑.link;
          t := q↑.link;               { t is the one to delete   }
          if t = p                    { if t is last node,       }
            then p := q;              {    reassign p            }
          q↑.link := t↑.link;         { remove node t            }
          release(t)                  { and return to storage    }
        end
  end;  { delete }
```

16.5.5 Bidirectional Lists

Bidirectional lists have two pointers, say *llink* and *rlink*, which point to the nodes on either side of the node:

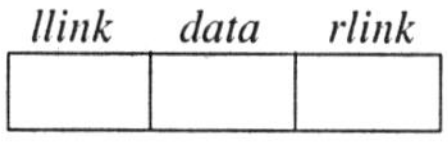

The node is defined in the following type declaration:

```
type
  ptr = ↑node;                    { pointer to a node }
  node = record
           llink : ptr;
           data  : integer;       { the data field    }
           rlink : ptr            { the link field    }
         end;

var
  p, pend : ptr;                  { pointer variables }
```

In the configuration shown here, *llink* of each node points to the node on its left, and *rlink* points to the node on the right. *Llink* of the first node and *rlink* of the last are **nil** pointers. *P* points to the first node in the list and *pend* to the last. As in the list shown in section 16.5.2, *p* and *pend* are **nil** when the list is empty. If there is only one node, both identifiers point to it, and *llink* and *rlink* of the node are **nil** pointers.

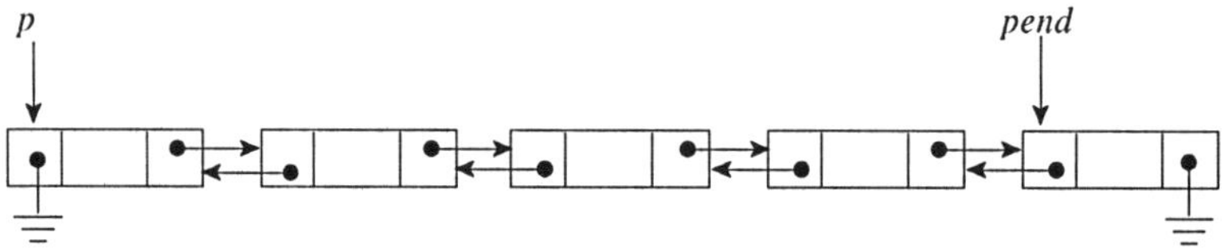

This structure is built by the procedure shown below, which adds each new node at the end of the list. Assume that the free list maintains the list of nodes linked through the *llink* field, and that *getnode* and *release* have been modified accordingly.

```
{ add x to end of list }
procedure addlist(x : integer; var p, pend : ptr);
  var
    t : ptr;
  begin
    getnode(t);
    t↑.data := x;                  { set fields          }
    t↑.llink := nil;
    t↑.rlink := nil;
    if p = nil
      then p := t                  { begin new list      }
      else
        begin                      { add at end of list }
          t↑.llink := pend;
          pend↑.rlink := t
        end
    pend := t
  end; { addlist }
```

The list can be traversed in either direction with iterative or recursive algorithms. The iterative traversals, called by *traverse(p)* or *rtraverse(pend)*, are shown below.

```
{ forward traversal }                |  { reverse traversal }
procedure traverse(p : ptr);         |  procedure rtraverse(p : ptr);
  begin                              |    begin
    while p <> nil do                |      while p <> nil do
      begin                          |        begin
        write(p↑.data);              |          write(p↑.data);
        p := p↑.rlink                |          p := p↑.llink
      end;                           |        end;
    writeln                          |      writeln
  end; { traverse }                  |    end; { rtraverse }
```

Recursive traversals, insertion after an arbitrary node, node deletion, concatenation, and erasure of lists of this type are suggested exercises.

16.5.6 Doubly Linked Circular Lists

The doubly linked circular list combines the advantages of the circular list with those of the doubly linked list from the previous section. The list takes the following form:

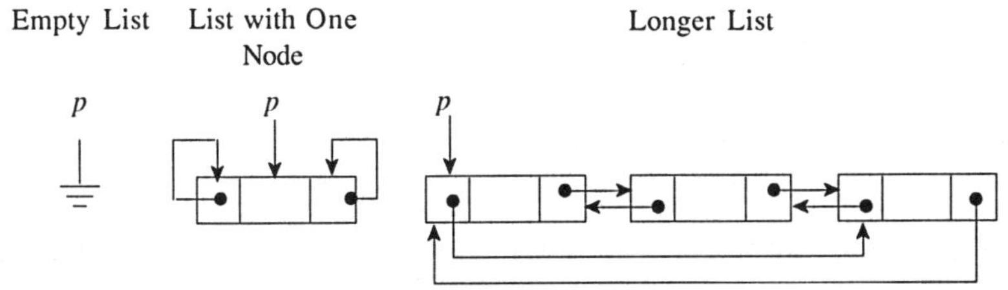

Insertion after an arbitrary node *p* is accomplished by the procedure shown below. Note that the existence of bidirectional links makes it unnecessary to use extra pointers. Because of the multitude of pointers, a number of different sequences of instructions is possible.

```
{ insert x in doubly linked circular list }
procedure insert(x : integer: var p : integer);
  var
    t : ptr;
  begin
    getnode(t);                               { get a node              }
    t↑.data := x;                             { set data field          }
    if p = nil
      then
        begin                                 { insert in empty list    }
          p := t;
          p↑.rlink := p;                      { keeping it circular     }
          p↑.llink := p
        end
      else                                    { insert after node p     }
        begin
          t↑.rlink := p↑.rlink;               { set links from new node }
          t↑.llink := p;
          p↑.rlink := t;                      { set links to new node   }
          t↑.rlink↑.llink := t
        end
  end; { insert }
```

The following procedure removes an arbitrary node *q* from list *p*:

```
{ delete node q from list p }
procedure delete(var q, p : ptr);
  begin
    if q = p
      then p := p↑.rlink;                     { save the list           }
    if q := q↑.rlink                          { only one node in list   }
      then p := nil
      else
        begin                                 { unlink q from list      }
          q↑.llink↑.rlink := q↑.rlink;
          q↑.rlink↑.llink := q↑.llink
        end
    release(q)
  end; { delete }
```

Other procedures for manipulating this list are left as an exercise for the reader. Most are complicated by thė need to check for nil pointers in empty lists.

16.5.7 Doubly Linked Rings with Head Nodes

The doubly linked circular list can be improved by the addition of a special node called a *head node*.[2] The list is linked in the following manner:

2. This variation of the doubly linked list is the basis of the score structure presented in chapter 20.

1. *Rlink* of the head node points to the first node in the list.
2. *Llink* of the head node points to the last node in the list.
3. *Rlink* of the last node node points to the head node.
4. *Llink* of the first node points to the head node.

The list is initialized by setting a pointer, say *p*, to the head node, and pointing both link fields of the head node back to the head node. Thus the list is always doubly linked and circular. The head node is often empty except for pointers, although it may contain data pertinent to the list. The list is empty if it contains no nodes in addition to the head node.

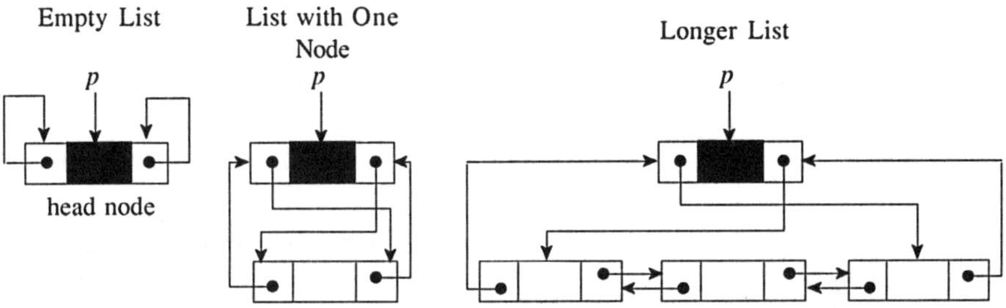

A new list is initialized by the following procedure:

```
{ initialize head node of doubly linked circular list }
procedure initialize(var p : ptr);
  begin
    getnode(p);
    p↑.llink := p;
    p↑.rlink := p
  end;
```

One can test either pointer to see if the list is empty; here we use *rlink*.

```
{ test for empty list }
function empty(p : ptr) : boolean;
  begin
    empty := p↑.rlink = p
  end;
```

A node *q* is inserted into the list after some arbitrary node *t* by the following:[3]

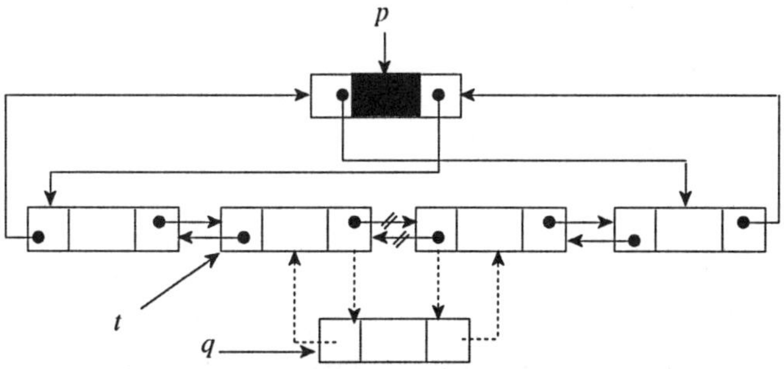

3. Here we assume that the data fields of *q* have been set previously.

```
{ insert node q after node t }
procedure insert(q, t : ptr);
  begin
    q↑.llink := t;                { set pointers from q }
    q↑.rlink := t↑.rlink;
    t↑.rlink↑.llink := q;         { set pointers to q   }
    t↑.rlink := q
  end;  { insert }
```

The use of the head node simplifies algorithms for working with the list because there are no special cases. The same procedure can be used to insert a node at the end, beginning, or middle of the list, and operations on an empty list do not require any special treatment. If *p* points to the head node of the list:

```
insert(q, p);          { inserts node q at beginning of list p     }
insert(q, p↑.llink);   { inserts node q at end of list p           }
insert(q, t);          { q <> p, q <> p↑.llink, inserts in middle  }
```

Use link diagrams to test these assertions, and to show that the statements are true even for the empty list.

Deletion is also simplified; it is only necessary to make sure that the head node is never deleted. The procedure below removes node *q* from list *p*:

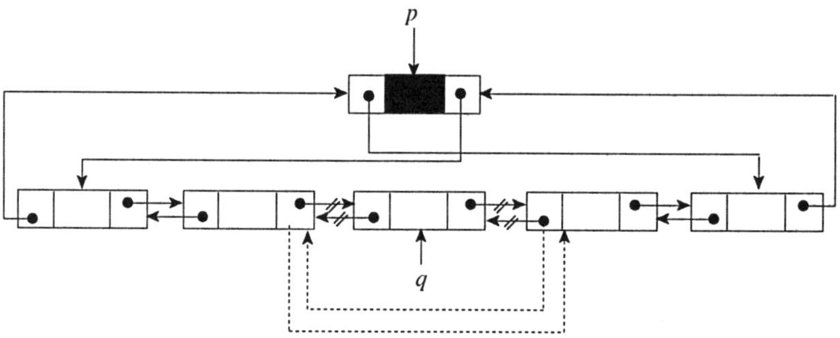


```
{ delete node q from list p }
procedure delete(var q : ptr; p : ptr);
  begin
    if p <> q
      then
        begin
          q↑.llink↑.rlink := q↑.rlink;      { unlink q from list }
          q↑.rlink↑.llink := q↑.llink;
          release(q)
        end
  end;  { delete }
```

Procedure *concatenate* joins lists *p* and *q*. There is only one special case: nothing needs to be done if list *q* is empty.

Before concatenation:

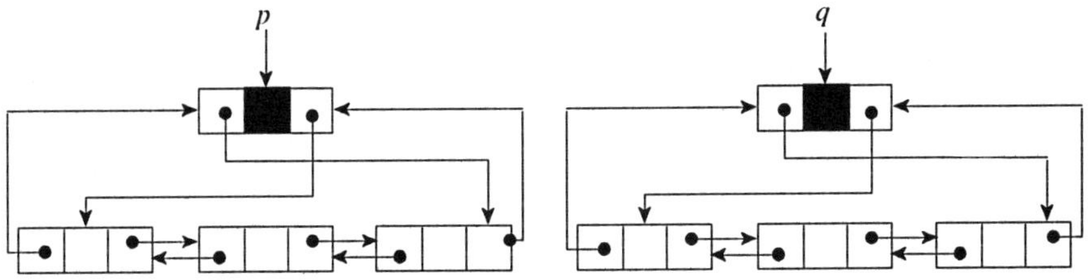

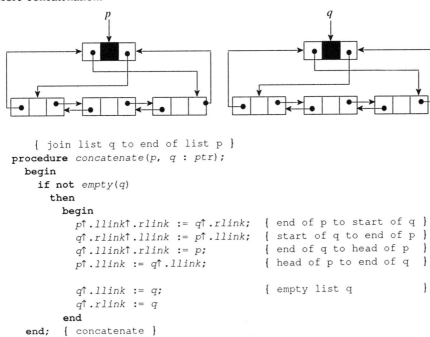

```
  { join list q to end of list p }
procedure concatenate(p, q : ptr);
  begin
    if not empty(q)
      then
        begin
          p↑.llink↑.rlink := q↑.rlink;   { end of p to start of q }
          q↑.rlink↑.llink := p↑.llink;   { start of q to end of p }
          q↑.llink↑.rlink := p;          { end of q to head of p  }
          p↑.llink := q↑.llink;          { head of p to end of q  }

          q↑.llink := q;                 { empty list q           }
          q↑.rlink := q
        end
  end;  { concatenate }
```

After concatenation:

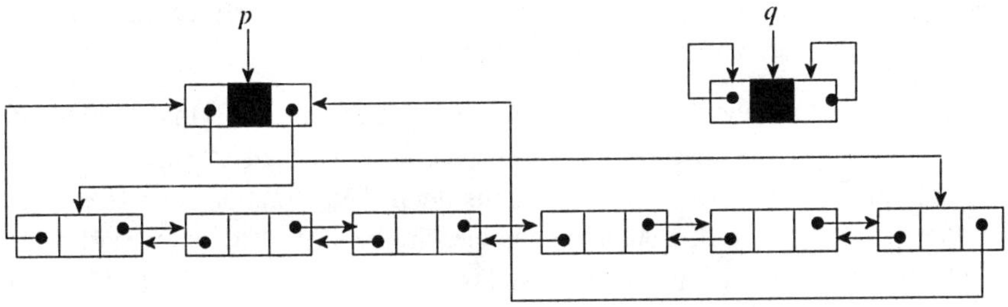

The procedure can be traversed in either direction, with the head node marking the end of the list:

```
{ traverse list p }
procedure traverse(p : ptr);
  var
    t : ptr;
  begin
    t := p↑.rlink;   { first node }
    while t <> p do
      begin
        visit(t);
        t := t↑.rlink
      end
  end;  { traverse }
```

```
{ traverse backwards }
procedure rtraverse(p : ptr);
  var
    t : ptr;
  begin
    t := p↑.llink;   { last node }
    while t <> p do
      begin
        visit(t);
        t := t↑.llink
      end
  end;  { rtraverse }
```

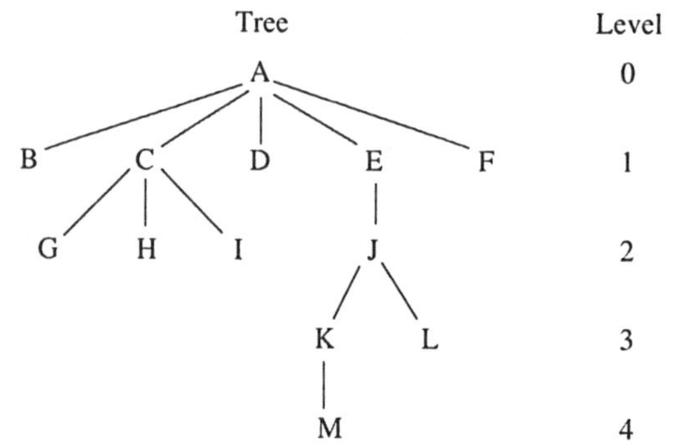

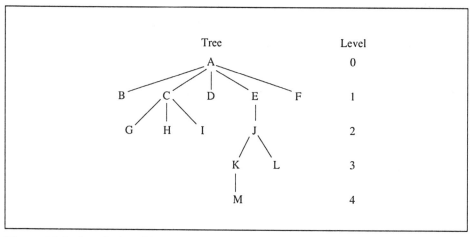

Figure 16.4. Levels in a Tree

16.6 Trees

In contrast to a list, a *tree* is a nonlinear structure with branches. More formally, we define a tree as follows:

> *A tree is a finite set of one or more nodes in which one node is designated as the root of the tree and the remaining nodes are partitioned into zero or more disjunct subtrees. The term "node" refers collectively to an item of information plus branches to other information.*

The definition does not allow for an empty tree. The specification that subtrees must be disjunct means that no two subtrees can ever be connected to each other. Note that this definition is recursive, since the tree is defined in terms of other trees. Every node in the tree is the root of a subtree contained in the tree. The number of subtrees on a node is the *degree* of the node. Nodes with no subtrees are called *terminal nodes* or *leaves*. Nonterminal nodes are called *branches*. In the tree shown in figure 16.4 the degree of A is 5, the degree of C is 3, the degree of J is 2, the degree of K is 1, and the degree of B, D, F, G, H, I, L, and M is 0.

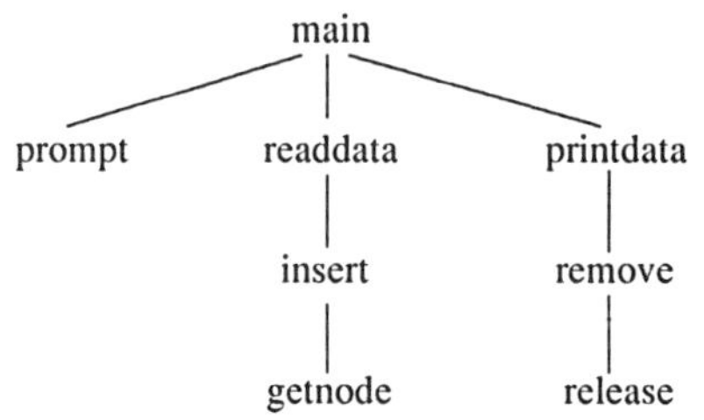

Figure 16.5. The Heirarchical Structure of Program 16.2.

Familial terms are also used to describe the parts of a tree. The roots of the subtrees of a node are called its *children*. Thus *B*, *C*, *D*, *E*, and *F* are children of *A*; *G*, *H*, and *I* are children of *C*; *J* is a child of *E*; etc. Children of the same parent are called *siblings*: *B*, *C*, *D*, *E*, and *F* are siblings, as are *G*, *H*, and *I*.

The *level* of a node is the number of generations from the root of the tree to the node. The children of a node are at level 1 with respect to that node, the grandchildren are level 2, etc. The notations on the diagram show the levels with respect to *A*, the root of the tree. Trees can be grouped into *forests*. A forest is a (usually ordered) set of 0 or more disjunct trees.

Trees can be used to represent any data that is hierarchical. Obviously, they can be used to represent familial relationships, such as ancestry or pedigree. A structured program can be represented as a tree structure, emphasizing the top-down design. The structure of program 16.2 is shown in figure 16.5 as an example. Trees can be used to represent formal hierarchies in music structure. For example, the form of the first movement of a classical symphony might be represented by the tree diagram shown in figure 16.6 (diagram is incomplete).

In computing, trees are represented by nodes with pointers to subtrees. Since the number of subtrees in a tree is variable, it is impractical to represent general trees directly in programming. We will concentrate on a special type of tree called the *binary tree*. Later we will see that binary trees can be used to represent trees of any degree.

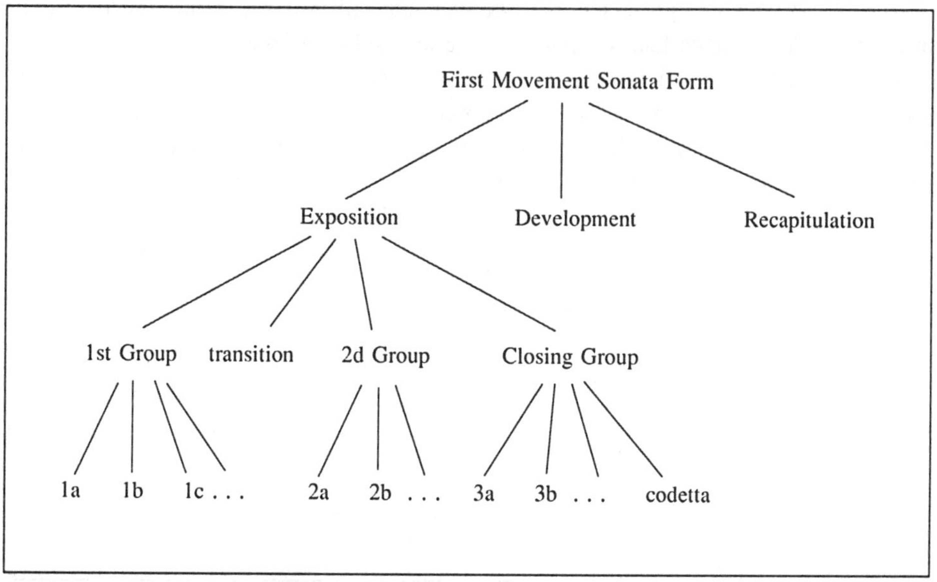

Figure 16.6. A Tree Diagram of Sonata Form

16.6.1 Binary Trees

Nodes in binary trees always have exactly two branches. We can define the binary tree recursively as follows:

> *A binary tree either is empty or consists of a node with branches to two subtrees, known as the left and the right subtree.*

The binary tree differs from the generalized tree in several important aspects. First, the definition allows for an empty tree, which is vital for computer implementation. Second, the number of subtrees of any node is fixed, and the branches are ordered. The two trees at (a) and (b) in figure 16.7 are different. The first has an empty left subtree, and the second has an empty right subtree. Either might be represented as the general tree at (c). Since the binary tree has a fixed number of nodes, it is easy to implement with a node structure containing two links:

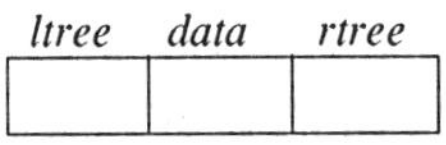


```
type
  ptr  = ↑node;
  node = record
           ltree : ptr;          { pointer to left subtree  }
           data  : integer;      { data field               }
           rtree : ptr           { pointer to right subtree }
         end;

var
  p : ptr;                       { pointer to root of       }
                                 {    binary tree           }
```

The binary tree is represented by a pointer that either is **nil**, signifying an empty tree, or points to a node that has pointers to a left and right subtree.

A binary tree is much more predictable than the general tree. Consider the tree shown in figure 16.8. The binary tree is said to be *full* or *balanced* if there are no empty terminal nodes until the highest level. In a full binary tree, there is one node (the root) at level 0, and the number of nodes on each successive level doubles. Thus there are two nodes on level 1, four on level 2, eight on level 3, sixteen on level 4, etc. Consequently the maximum number of nodes on level n is 2^n and the maximum

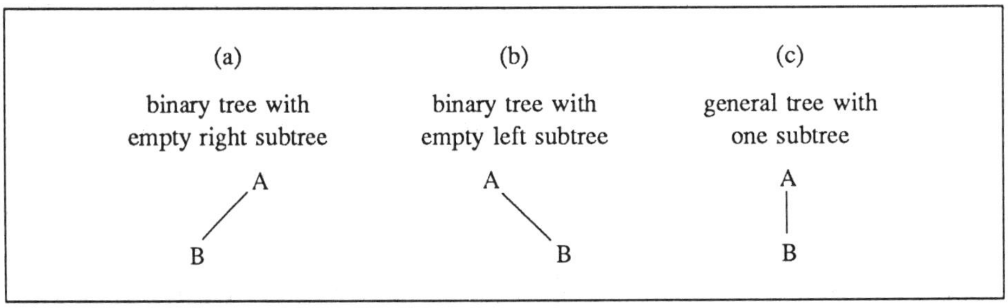

Figure 16.7. Three Distinct Tree Types

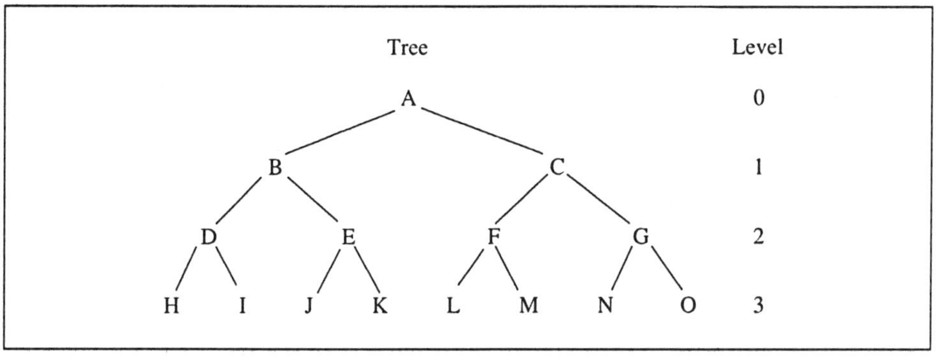

Figure 16.8. A Balanced Binary Tree

number of nodes in a binary tree of n levels is $2^{n+1} - 1$.

The binary tree can be used to represent any data that can be structured with two possible branches from each element. The left and right subtrees could represent any type of binary process, such as the answers to a series of questions that require yes/no or true/false answers or successive results of flipping a coin. By letting the branches represent the relationship between values, where the left branch points to a lesser value and the right a greater value, we can design efficient sorting and searching algorithms. The tree in figure 16.9 represents the prime forms of the twelve three-note pitch-class sets: 012, 013, 014, 015, 016, 024, 025, 026, 027, 036, 037, and 048. See if you can discover the rule used to construct the tree.[4]

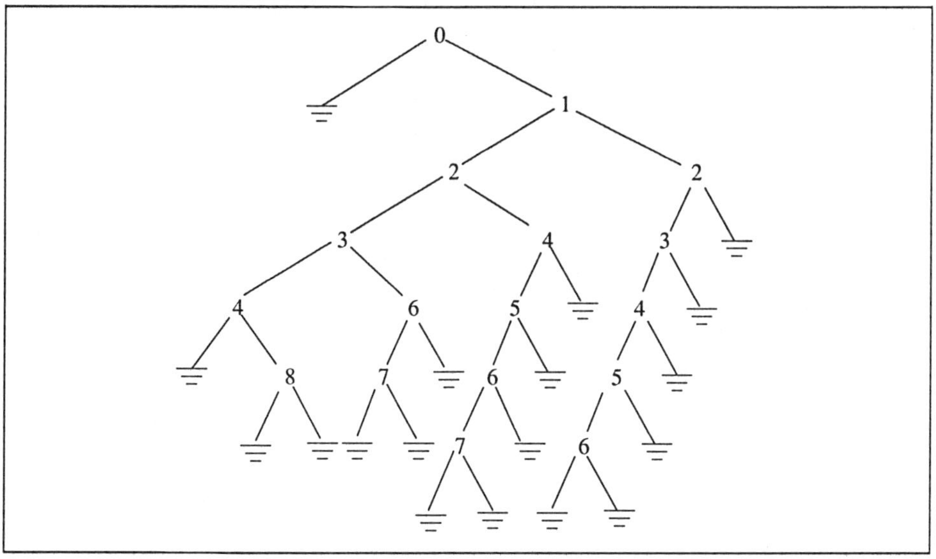

Figure 16.9. A Binary Tree Representing Three-Note Pitch-Class Sets

4. The right branch represents successors, the left alternatives. For example, the branch to the right of 0 represents the set 012. The branch to the left of the 2 represents alternatives to 2 as the third pitch class.

16.6.2 Traversing Binary Trees

There are three standard methods of traversing a binary tree, all of which can be described recursively. As the tree is traversed, three things are done at each node:

1. The node is "visited," i.e., the data is read, the node is counted, etc.
2. The left subtree is traversed.
3. The right subtree is traversed.

The names of traversals derive from the order in which these three actions occur. In the *preorder* traversal, the node is visited before the subtrees are traversed; in the *postorder* traversal, the node is visited after the subtrees are traversed; and in the *inorder* traversal, the left subtree is traversed, the node is visited, and then the right subtree is traversed. In each case we describe what is done if the tree is not empty. If the tree is empty, nothing is done, and control reverts to the previous level of recursion.

Inorder Traversal

```
if the tree is not empty
  then
    begin
      traverse left subtree;
      visit current node;
      traverse right subtree
    end
```

Preorder Traversal

```
if the tree is not empty
  then
    begin
      visit current node;
      traverse left subtree;
      traverse right subtree
    end
```

Postorder Traversal

```
if the tree is not empty
  then
    begin
      traverse left subtree;
      traverse right subtree;
      visit current node
    end
```

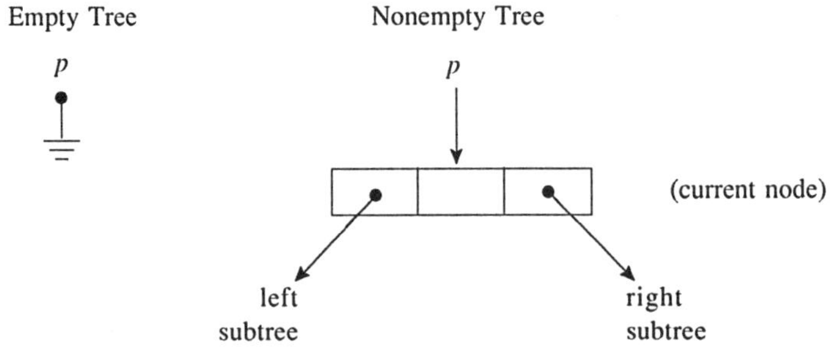

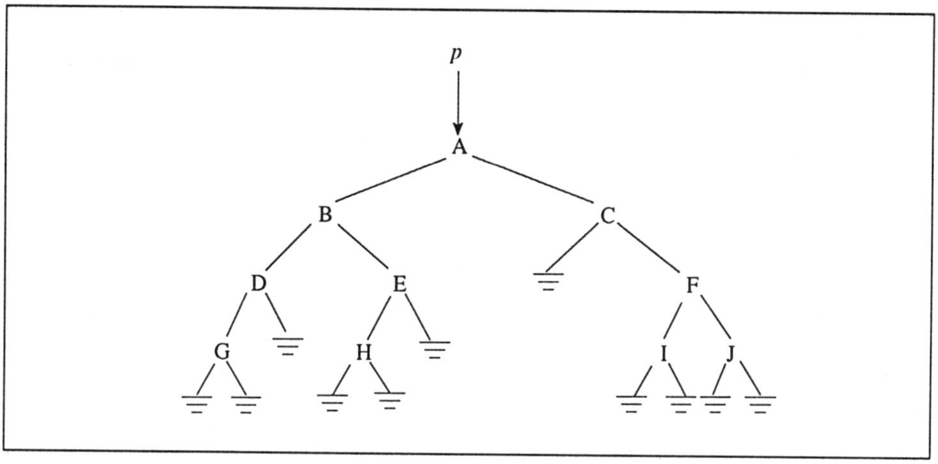

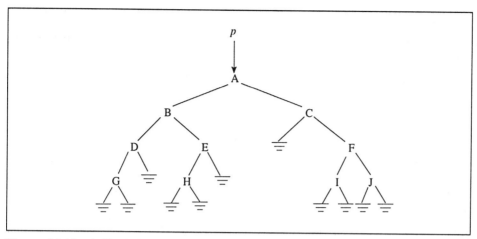

Figure 16.10. A Nonbalanced Binary Tree

The pointer *p* points to the root of a tree, or if the tree is empty it is a **nil** pointer. Since the tree is defined recursively, the same is true of *p*↑*.ltree*, and *p*↑*.rtree*, the pointers to the left and right subtrees. The procedures implementing these traversals are shown in program 16.2.

As the tree is traversed, parameter *p* recursively points to each node in the tree. The recursive plunge is terminated when a **nil** pointer is encountered. Consider the tree in figure 16.10. Each traversal results in a linear ordering of the elements in the tree. In the *inorder* traversal, at each node the left subtree is traversed, the node is visited, and the right subtree is traversed. Thus the tree is traversed recursively all the way down the left side to the left subtree of *G*. Since this tree is empty, no action is taken. Now node *G* is visited, and the *G*'s right subtree, also **nil**, is traversed. At this point *D*'s left subtree has been traversed, so *D* is visited and *D*'s right subtree is traversed. Now *B* is visited and *B*'s right subtree is traversed. Before *E* is visited, its left subtree is traversed, and so on. Thus the nodes are visited in the order:

G D B H E A C I F J

In the *preorder* traversal, each node is visited before its subtrees are traversed, so the order of visitation is:

A B D G E H C F I J

A *postorder* traversal visits both subtrees before the current node, resulting in the order:

G D H E B I J F C A

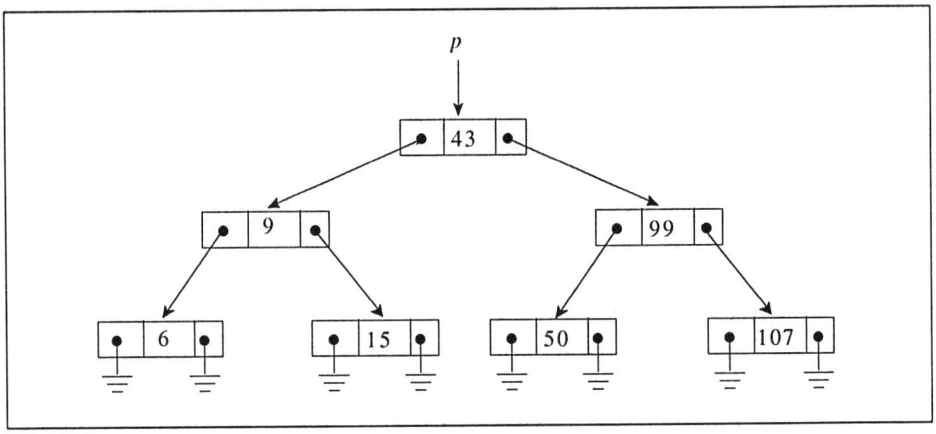

Figure 16.11. An Ordered Tree

16.6.3 Application: *treesort*

A binary tree can be used to sort a list of values. We will place each integer x in the tree using the following recursive algorithm:

> **if** the tree is empty
> **then** insert new value here
> **else if** $x \leq$ *data* of current node
> **then** insert in left subtree
> **else** insert in right subtree

With this algorithm, the integers

43 9 99 50 107 15 6

would result in the tree shown in figure 16.11. Now an *inorder* traversal of the tree produces the following ordered list:

6 9 15 43 50 99 107

How efficient is this sorting method? If the values are inserted in random order the tree remains balanced. At each juncture, the value is inserted into either the left or right subtree. In either case, half of the remaining list is eliminated at each branch until a **nil** pointer is encountered and the value can be inserted. Thus finding the correct position for each value is equivalent to finding a value in an ordered list through the use of a binary search (section 10.8.2), i.e., the efficiency is $O(\log_2 n)$ for each value, or $O(n \log_2 n)$ for a list of n integers.

If the list is already in order or in reverse order, the tree becomes totally skewed and the algorithm turns out to be a rather inefficient approximation of a linear search (figure 16.12). Much of the benefit of the method is realized even if the list only roughly approximates random order, since many branches eliminate a substantial number of the remaining elements.

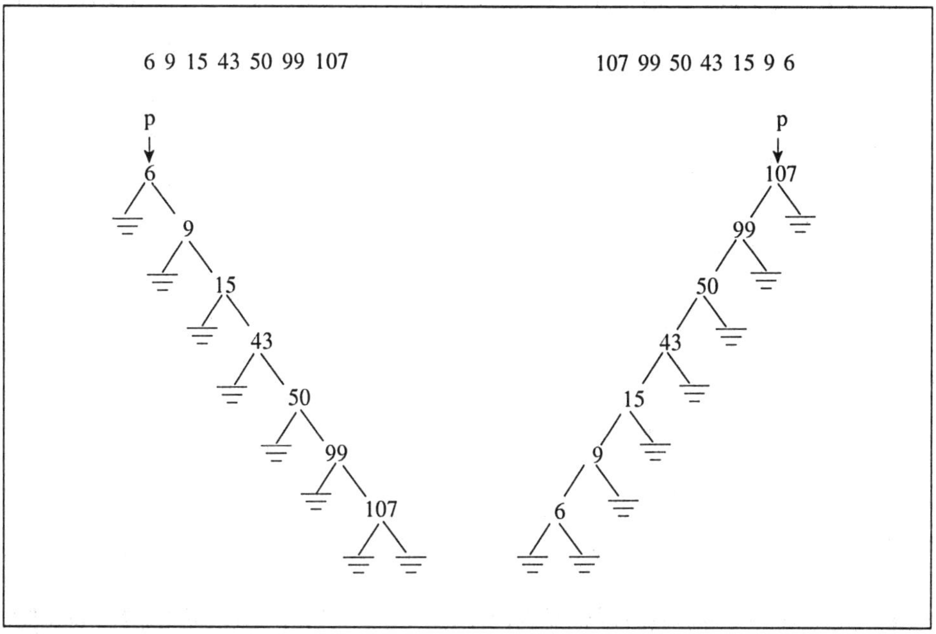

Figure 16.12. Skewed Trees Resulting from Ordered Lists in *Treesort*

Program 16.2 implements this algorithm, and illustrates the three common traversals for each tree built. We will also add a *reverseorder* traversal, which prints the list in descending order:

> **if** the tree is not empty
>   **then**
>   **begin**
>   traverse the right subtree;
>   visit the current node;
>   traverse the left subtree
>   **end**;

Each tree is "erased" by a postorder traversal in which visiting each node consists of returning it to the storage pool. This procedure must use a postorder traversal, since it is necessary to release all nodes linked to a node before releasing the node.

```
(***********************   Program Treesort     ***********************)
(* Illustrates a simple application of binary trees: sorting lists.  The *)
(* tree is built using the rule:  If the tree is empty, insert the value,*)
(* else if the value is less than or equal to the current node, insert    *)
(* in the left subtree, else insert in the right subtree.  The list is    *)
(* printed in ascending order by using an inorder traversal of the tree. *)
(* The program also illustrates other common traversals.  It maintains a *)
(* list of free nodes as a stack linked arbitrarily through the ltree     *)
(* field.                                                                  *)
(************************************************************************)
```

```
program treesort(input, output);

  type                                      (************  tree node **************)
    ptr = ↑treenode;                        (*       ltree     data    rtree        *)
    treenode =                              (*     _______________________          *)
    record                                  (*    |       |         |       |       *)
      ltree : ptr;                          (*    |___|___|_________|___|___|       *)
      data  : integer;                      (*        |                 |           *)
      rtree : ptr                           (*        V                 V           *)
    end;                                    (*************************************)

  var
    free : ptr;                             { pointer to stack of free nodes      }
    p    : ptr;                             { pointer to binary tree              }

(***********************          getnode          ***********************)
(* Obtains a node from the freelist or from the operating system.          *)
(*************************************************************************)
  procedure getnode(var p : ptr);
    begin
      if free = nil
        then new(p)
        else
          begin
            p := free;
            free := free↑.ltree
          end
    end;

(***********************          release          ***********************)
(* Returns node p to freelist so it can be reused.                         *)
(*************************************************************************)
  procedure release(var p : ptr);
    begin
      p↑.ltree := free;
      free := p;
      p := nil
    end;

(***********************         treesort          ***********************)
(* Inserts integer x in binary tree p.                                     *)
(*************************************************************************)
  procedure treesort(x : integer; var p : ptr);
    begin
      if p = nil                                     { if tree is empty     }
        then
          begin
            getnode(p);                              { insert node          }
            p↑.data := x;                            { assign value         }
            p↑.ltree := nil;                         { initialize subtrees  }
            p↑.rtree := nil                          {  to nil pointers     }
          end
      else if x <= p↑.data                           { if less or equal     }
          then treesort(x, p↑.ltree)                 { insert in left tree  }
      else treesort(x, p↑.rtree)                     { else insert in right }
    end; { treesort }
```

```
(***********************          inorder          ***********************)
(* Inorder traversal of binary tree.                                      *)
(*************************************************************************)
 procedure inorder(p : ptr);
   begin
     if p <> nil
       then
         begin
           inorder(p↑.ltree);                  { traverse left subtree  }
           write(p↑.data);                     { visit current node     }
           inorder(p↑.rtree)                   { traverse right subtree }
         end
   end;

(***********************          preorder         ***********************)
(* Preorder traversal of binary tree.                                     *)
(*************************************************************************)
 procedure preorder(p : ptr);
   begin
     if p <> nil
       then
         begin
           write(p↑.data);                     { visit current node     }
           preorder(p↑.ltree);                 { traverse left subtree  }
           preorder(p↑.rtree)                  { traverse right subtree }
         end
   end;

(***********************          postorder        ***********************)
(* Postorder traversal of binary tree.                                    *)
(*************************************************************************)
 procedure postorder(p : ptr);
   begin
     if p <> nil
       then
         begin
           postorder(p↑.ltree);                { traverse left subtree  }
           postorder(p↑.rtree);                { traverse right subtree }
           write(p↑.data)                      { visit current node     }
         end
   end;

(***********************        reverseorder       ***********************)
(* Prints ordered binary tree in reverse order.                           *)
(*************************************************************************)
 procedure reverseorder(p : ptr);
   begin
     if p <> nil
       then
         begin
           reverseorder(p↑.rtree);             { traverse right subtree }
           write(p↑.data);                     { visit current node     }
           reverseorder(p↑.ltree)              { traverse left subtree  }
         end
   end;
```

```
(***********************          skipln          ***********************)
(* Skips to next nonblank character or newline character.                 *)
(***************************************************************************)
  procedure skipln;
    begin
      while (input↑ = ' ') and not eoln do
        get(input)
    end;

(***********************         readdata         ***********************)
(* Reads data on one line, storing values in binary tree.                 *)
(***************************************************************************)
  procedure readdata(var p : ptr);
    var
      x : integer;
    begin { readdata }
      while not eoln do
        begin
          read(x);                              { read value            }
          treesort(x, p);                       { insert in binary tree }
          skipln                                { skip blanks           }
        end;
      readln                                    { discard newline char  }
    end; { readdata }

(***********************          erase           ***********************)
(* Nodes are returned to storage pool through postorder traversal.        *)
(***************************************************************************)
  procedure erase(var p : ptr);
    begin
      if p <> nil
        then
          begin
            erase(p↑.ltree);                    { erase left subtree    }
            erase(p↑.rtree);                    { erase right subtree   }
            release(p)                          { release current node  }
          end
    end; { erase }

(***************************************************************************)
(*                          Main Procedure                                 *)
(***************************************************************************)
  begin { main }
    p    := nil;                        { initialize pointers         }
    free := nil;

    write('Type list: ');               { prompt user                 }
    while not eof do
      begin
        readdata(p);                    { store data in binary tree   }
        writeln;
        write('inorder:     ');
        inorder(p); writeln;            { print values in order       }
        write('preorder:    ');
        preorder(p); writeln;           { print values in order       }
        write('postorder:   ');
        postorder(p); writeln;          { print values in order       }
```

```
        write('reverseorder: ');
        reverseorder(p); writeln;              { print values in order       }
        erase(p);                              { erase tree                  }
        writeln;
        write('Type list: ')                   { prompt user                 }
      end
   end.  { main }
```

Program 16.2. *Treesort*

```
Type list: 34 9 1 3 0 89 7 2 56

inorder:            0    1    2    3    7    9   34   56   89
preorder:          34    9    1    0    3    2    7   89   56
postorder:          0    2    7    3    1    9   56   89   34
reverseorder:      89   56   34    9    7    3    2    1    0

Type list: 1 3 5 7 9 8 6 4 2

inorder:            1    2    3    4    5    6    7    8    9
preorder:           1    3    2    5    4    7    6    9    8
postorder:          2    4    6    8    9    7    5    3    1
reverseorder:       9    8    7    6    5    4    3    2    1

Type list: 1 2 3 4 5 6

inorder:            1    2    3    4    5    6
preorder:           1    2    3    4    5    6
postorder:          6    5    4    3    2    1
reverseorder:       6    5    4    3    2    1

Type list: 6 5 4 3 2

inorder:            2    3    4    5    6
preorder:           6    5    4    3    2
postorder:          2    3    4    5    6
reverseorder:       6    5    4    3    2

Type list: 7 6 8 5 9 4

inorder:            4    5    6    7    8    9
preorder:           7    6    5    4    8    9
postorder:          4    5    6    9    8    7
reverseorder:       9    8    7    6    5    4

Type list: 6 5 7 4 8 3 9 2 0 1

inorder:            0    1    2    3    4    5    6    7    8    9
preorder:           6    5    4    3    2    0    1    7    8    9
postorder:          1    0    2    3    4    5    9    8    7    6
reverseorder:       9    8    7    6    5    4    3    2    1    0

Type list: ^D
```

Program 16.2. Sample Run (Interactive)

16.6.4 Application: *treesearch*

The *treesort* algorithm can be modified for searching lists. In order to eliminate the possiblity that a value occurs more than once in the tree, the node structure is modified by adding a field to count the number of times each value occurs, and the insertion algorithm is modified to count multiple occurrences of the same value:

```
procedure insert(x : integer; var p : ptr);
  begin
    if p = nil                              { if tree is empty     }
      then                                  { insert node          }
        begin
          new(p);                           { get a node           }
          p↑.data                           { assign value         }
          p↑.counter := 1;                  { set counter to 1     }
          p↑.ltree := nil;                  { initialize subtrees  }
          p↑.rtree := nil                   {  to nil pointers     }
        end
     else if x = p↑.data                    { if equal, increment  }
        then incr(p↑.counter)               {    counter           }
     else if x < p↑.data                    { if less, insert in   }
        then insert(x, p↑.ltree)            {    left subtree      }
     else if x > p↑.data                    { if greater, insert   }
        then insert(x, p↑.rtree)            {    in right subtree  }
  end;  { treesort }
```

The tree is searched by a function that returns the number of times the value x occurs in the list or 0 if it does not occur.

```
function treesearch(x : integer; p : ptr) : integer;
  begin
    if p = nil                                          { not found    }
      then treesearch := 0
    else if x = p↑.data                                 { found it     }
      then treesearch := p↑.counter
    else if x < p↑.data                                 { search ltree }
      then treesearch := treesearch(x, p↑.ltree)
    else treesearch := treesearch(x, p↑.rtree)          { search rtree }
  end;
```

This scheme is efficient and enables us to deal with a large range of values in the data structure. The list is sorted as the tree is built, and both the insertion and searching algorithms approach $O(\log_2 n)$ so long as the list is not presorted.

Compare this technique to two possible alternate solutions using arrays. First we could use an array of integers. The list would be inserted into the array and values found by linear search, or $O(n)$. If we first sort the list—$O(n \log_2 n)$ with a good algorithm—values could be found using binary search, $O(\log_2 n)$, with a bit of overhead to look on either side of the located item for duplicates. A second approach would be to use an array, A, indexed by the subrange of integers *low* .. *high* to count the values directly. After the array is initialized to zeros, each value could be counted in constant time by incrementing $A[x]$ for each value x in the list. Each search would then be a table lookup taking fixed time $O(1)$. However, this solution would be practical only for integers within a small range. In the first solution, the length of the list is limited by the declared size of the array. In the second, the difference between the largest and smallest values is limited. By contrast, the *treesearch* algorithm can handle values from *–maxint* to *maxint*, and the list size is variable. The cost is two pointers for each value in the list for constructing the tree. The use of *treesort* in a more complex application is demonstrated in chapter 18.

16.6.5 Application: Contour Counting

We will now implement an algorithm that uses a binary tree to calculate the imbricated subsets of melodic contours.[5] The contours are represented by a succession of signed intervals representing generic intervals. For example, +2 +2 +3 –2 indicates two ascending seconds followed by an ascending third and a descending second. Our goal is to tabulate the contours imbedded in this contour:

+2 +2 +3 –2

Count	Contour
1	+2 +2 +3 –2
2	+2
1	+2 +2
1	+2 +3
1	+2 +2 +3
1	+2 +3 –2
1	+3
1	+3 –2
1	–2

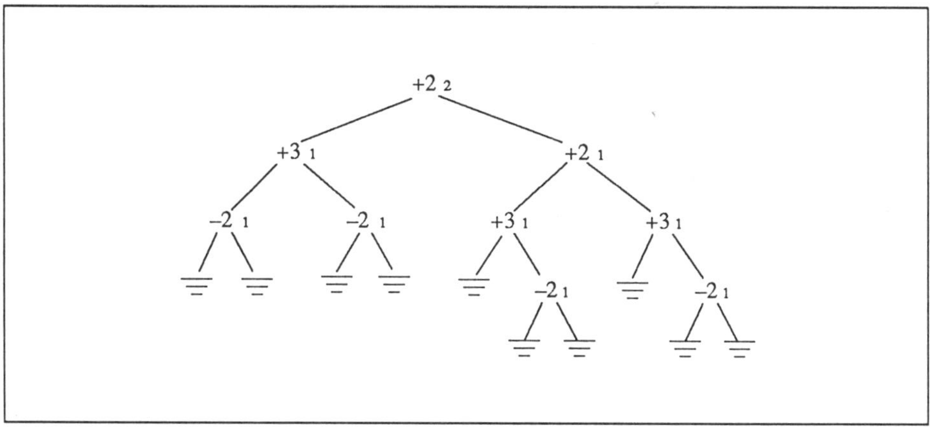

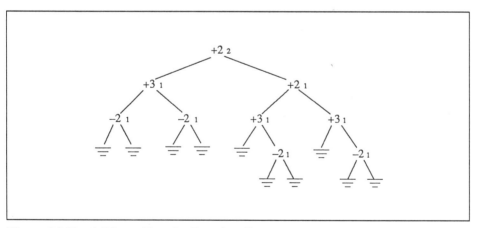

Figure 16.13. A Binary Tree for Counting Contours

5. Imbrications are subsets consisting of ordered contiguous elements of a set.

All of this information is represented in the binary tree shown in figure 16.13. We will store one interval in each node. In the tree, one branch represents successors, and the other alternate intervals in the same ordinal position. In addition, each node will contain a counter for the number of times the node was accessed building the tree was built. This number represents the number of times a particular contour occurs in the subject contour.

As the contour is read, the intervals are stored in a standard linked list:

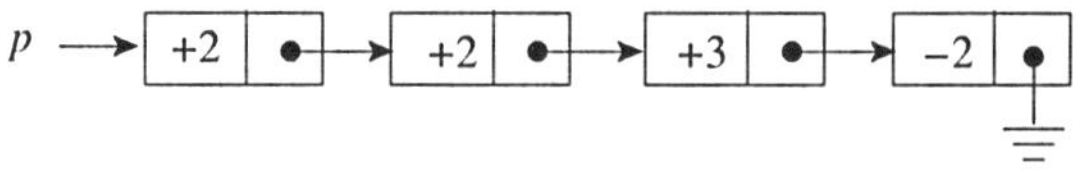

In order to avoid keeping separate free lists for the two types of nodes, we define the nodes as variant records. The variant *avail* represents free (or available) nodes (figure 16.14). The intervals are inserted into the binary tree by procedure *tinsert*. The algorithm in pseudo code is:

```
if there are more intervals in the list
 then
     if the tree is empty
       then
         begin
            insert a node here;
            set the interval field;
            initialize contour counter to 1;
            set successor and alternate fields to nil;
            insert the next interval in the contour in
               the empty tree pointed to by the
               successor field of this node
         end
     else if the interval is equal to the current interval in tree
       then
         begin
           increment contour counter for this node;
           insert the next interval in the contour as
              the successor field of this interval
         end
     else insert interval as alternate interval for this position
```

The pointer p points to the first node in the list of intervals representing the contour. The pointer to the root of the tree, t, is initialized as a **nil** pointer. The process of inserting contours into the tree is essentially a traversal of the list of intervals:

while the interval list is not empty **do**
  begin
    insert list p into tree t;
    set p to next interval in list
  end;

During tree insertion, the next interval in the list is obtained through the link field of the current node in the interval list. The first time the list is inserted into the tree, all contours beginning with the first interval are tabulated: first interval; first and second intervals; first, second, and third intervals; etc. Repeating the process after dropping the first node accounts for all patterns beginning with the second interval. The process is repeated until the list of intervals is empty.

Each subcontour is represented by a path through the tree beginning with the interval in the root of the tree or one of its alternates (on the left branch in the diagram). The process of printing out the various contours is complicated by the fact that each interval in the tree may be part of many different contours. We use an array *list*[i], $1 \leq n \leq m$ to store m intervals in each imbricated contour. The procedure is called with $n = 1$. The tree is traversed recursively in preorder, i.e., each node is visited before its subtrees:

if the tree is not empty
  then
    begin
      place the current interval in *list*[n];
      print the interval counter in the current node;
      print *list*[i], $1 \leq i \leq n$;
      traverse the successor subtree with array position $n + 1$;
      traverse the alternate subtree with array position n
    end;

After the table is printed, the nodes in the linked list representing the coutour and the tree representing the imbricated subcontours are returned to the storage pool for reuse. Program 16.3 implements this algorithm.

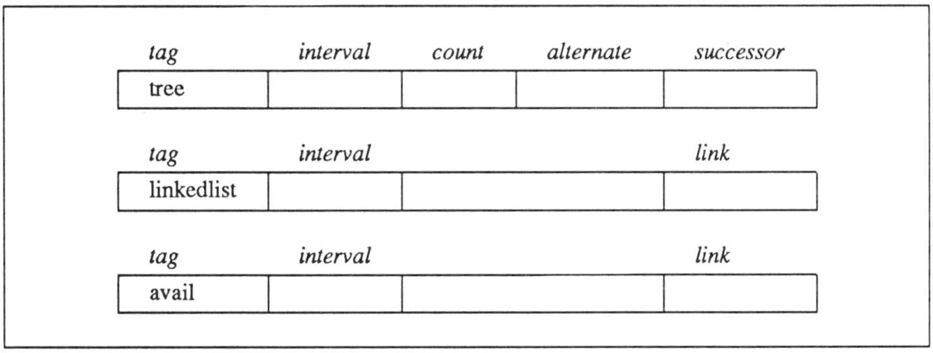

Figure 16.14. Variant Records in Program 16.3.

```
(************************        Program Tree        ************************)
(* Uses a tree structure to tabulate melodic contours.  The tree is        *)
(* binary, with one branch representing successors, and the other alter-  *)
(* nate intervals in the same ordinal position.  In addition to the        *)
(* current interval and pointers to successors and alternates, each tree  *)
(* node contains a counter for the number of times the node was accessed  *)
(* while the tree was built.  In order for us to get all imbricated sub-  *)
(* sets of the contour, the contour is first stored in a linked list, and*)
(* this list is treated as successively shorter lists by dropping off the*)
(* first node.  The tree is traversed recursively, and an array is used  *)
(* to store each solution.  Without this it would be impossible to print *)
(* out the entire contour.                                                 *)
(**************************************************************************)
program tree(input, output);
  const
    max = 20;

  type
    intlist = array[1 .. max] of integer;     { ordered list of intervals }

    kind = (avail, tree, linkedlist);         { kinds of nodes            }

    ptr = ↑node;                              { variant record definition }
    node = record
             tag      : kind;
             interval : integer;

             case kind of                     { variant part              }
               linkedlist,
               avail : (link       : ptr);

               tree  : (count      : integer;
                        successor  : ptr;
                        alternate  : ptr)
           end; { variant record definition }

  var
    contour : ptr;                            { linked list of intervals  }
    free    : ptr;                            { free nodes                }
    table   : ptr;                            { pointer to tree structure }
    list    : intlist;                        { array of intervals        }

(************************          getnode         ************************)
(* Gets node from free list.                                               *)
(**************************************************************************)
  procedure getnode(var p : ptr);
    begin
      if free = nil
        then new(p)
        else
          begin
            p := free;
            free := free↑.link
          end
    end;
```

```
(***********************          release          ***********************)
(* Returns node to free list.                                              *)
(***************************************************************************)
  procedure release(var p : ptr);
    begin
      p↑.tag := avail;
      p↑.link := free;
      free := p;
      p := nil
    end;


(***********************         erasetree         ***********************)
(* Recursively erases tree using postorder traversal.                      *)
(***************************************************************************)
  procedure erasetree(var p : ptr);
    begin
      if p <> nil
        then
          begin
            erasetree(p↑.successor);
            erasetree(p↑.alternate);
            release(p)
          end
    end;


(***********************         eraselist         ***********************)
(* Recursively erases linked list.                                         *)
(***************************************************************************)
  procedure eraselist(var p : ptr);
    begin
      if p <> nil
        then
          begin
            eraselist(p↑.link);
            release(p)
          end
    end;


(***********************           incr            ***********************)
(* Adds one to argument.                                                   *)
(***************************************************************************)
  procedure incr(var x : integer);
    begin
      x := x + 1
    end;


(***********************          insert           ***********************)
(* Adds to end of linked list.                                             *)
(***************************************************************************)
  procedure insert(x : integer; var p : ptr);
    var
      t, q : ptr;
```

```
    begin { insert }
      getnode(t);                                    { get node       }
      t↑.tag := linkedlist;                          { set fields     }
      t↑.interval := x;
      t↑.link := nil;
      if p = nil                                     { start new list }
        then p := t
        else
          begin
            q := p;
            while q↑.link <> nil do
              q := q↑.link;
            q↑.link := t
          end
    end;  { insert }


(***********************          writeint          ***********************)
(* Writes interval with sign.                                              *)
(**************************************************************************)
  procedure writeint(x : integer);
    begin
      if x >= 0
        then write(' +', x:1)
        else write(' -',  x:1)
    end;


(***********************           skipln           ***********************)
(* Skips to next nonblank character or end of line.                        *)
(**************************************************************************)
  procedure skipln;
    begin
      while (input↑ = ' ') and not eoln do
        get(input)
    end;


(***********************        readcontour         ***********************)
(* Reads contour and inserts in linked list.                               *)
(**************************************************************************)
  procedure readcontour(var contour : ptr);
    var
      x : integer;
    begin
      while not eoln do
        begin
          read(x);
          insert(x, contour);
          skipln
        end;
      readln
    end;


(***********************          tinsert           ***********************)
(* Inserts contour into tree structure.                                    *)
(**************************************************************************)
```

```
  procedure tinsert(p : ptr; var t : ptr);
    begin
      if p <> nil
        then
          begin
            if t = nil
              then
                begin
                  getnode(t);                             { get a node    }
                  t↑.tag := tree;                         { set its type }
                  t↑.interval := p↑.interval;             { set fields    }
                  t↑.count := 1;
                  t↑.successor := nil;
                  t↑.alternate := nil;
                  tinsert(p↑.link, t↑.successor)
                end
            else if p↑.interval = t↑.interval
              then
                begin { common node }
                  incr(t↑.count);
                  tinsert(p↑.link, t↑.successor)
                end   { common node }
            else tinsert(p, t↑.alternate)
          end
    end;  { tinsert }

(************************          tabulate           ************************)
(* Gets imbricated subsets by successively dropping first interval.         *)
(****************************************************************************)
  procedure tabulate(p : ptr; var t : ptr);
    begin
      while p <> nil do
        begin
          tinsert(p, t);
          p := p↑.link
        end
    end;

(************************          printlist          ************************)
(* Prints list of intervals.                                                 *)
(****************************************************************************)
  procedure printlist(var list : intlist; n : integer);
    var
      i : integer;
    begin
      for i := 1 to n do
         writeint(list[i]);
      writeln
    end;

(************************          printtable         ************************)
(* Prints table by doing preorder traversal of tree.  An array is used     *)
(* to store contours so that whole contours can be printed.  N is the      *)
(* ordinal position of an interval in the array. The procedure is called *)
(* with n = 1.                                                               *)
(****************************************************************************)
```

```
  procedure printtable(t : ptr; var list : intlist; n : integer);
    begin
      if t <> nil
        then
          begin
            list[n] := t↑.interval;              { place interval in array }
            write(t↑.count:3, '    ');           { print current contour   }
            printlist(list, n);

            printtable(t↑.successor, list, n + 1);    { get next interval }
            printtable(t↑.alternate, list, n)         { and alternate in  }
          end                                         { same position     }
    end;  { printtable }

(**********************************************************************)
(*                         Main Procedure                             *)
(**********************************************************************)
  begin { main }
    free    := nil;                          { initialize pointers    }
    contour := nil;
    table   := nil;

    write('Enter contour: ');
    while not eof do
      begin
        readcontour(contour);                { store contour in list  }
        tabulate(contour, table);            { count coutours in tree }
        printtable(table, list, 1);          { print table            }
        eraselist(contour);                  { erase linked list      }
        erasetree(table);                    { erase tree             }
        writeln;
        write('Enter contour: ')
      end
  end.  { main }
```

Program 16.3. *Tree*

```
Enter contour: +2 +2 -3 +2 +2 +2 -3
  5    +2
  3    +2 +2
  2    +2 +2 -3
  1    +2 +2 -3 +2
  1    +2 +2 -3 +2 +2
  1    +2 +2 -3 +2 +2 +2
  1    +2 +2 -3 +2 +2 +2 -3
  1    +2 +2 +2
  1    +2 +2 +2 -3
  2    +2 -3
  1    +2 -3 +2
  1    +2 -3 +2 +2
  1    +2 -3 +2 +2 +2
  1    +2 -3 +2 +2 +2 -3
  2    -3
  1    -3 +2
```

```
  1     -3 +2 +2
  1     -3 +2 +2 +2
  1     -3 +2 +2 +2 -3

Enter contour: +2 -3 +2 -4 +2 -5 +2 -4 +2
  5     +2
  1     +2 -3
  1     +2 -3 +2
  1     +2 -3 +2 -4
  1     +2 -3 +2 -4 +2
  1     +2 -3 +2 -4 +2 -5
  1     +2 -3 +2 -4 +2 -5 +2
  1     +2 -3 +2 -4 +2 -5 +2 -4
  1     +2 -3 +2 -4 +2 -5 +2 -4 +2
  2     +2 -4
  2     +2 -4 +2
  1     +2 -4 +2 -5
  1     +2 -4 +2 -5 +2
  1     +2 -4 +2 -5 +2 -4
  1     +2 -4 +2 -5 +2 -4 +2
  1     +2 -5
  1     +2 -5 +2
  1     +2 -5 +2 -4
  1     +2 -5 +2 -4 +2
  1     -3
  1     -3 +2
  1     -3 +2 -4
  1     -3 +2 -4 +2
  1     -3 +2 -4 +2 -5
  1     -3 +2 -4 +2 -5 +2
  1     -3 +2 -4 +2 -5 +2 -4
  1     -3 +2 -4 +2 -5 +2 -4 +2
  2     -4
  2     -4 +2
  1     -4 +2 -5
  1     -4 +2 -5 +2
  1     -4 +2 -5 +2 -4
  1     -4 +2 -5 +2 -4 +2
  1     -5
  1     -5 +2
  1     -5 +2 -4
  1     -5 +2 -4 +2

Enter contour: ^D
```

Program 16.3. Sample Run (Interactive)

16.6.6 Using Binary Trees to Represent General Trees

We have seen that general trees are useful for representing many types of hierarchical information, but they cannot be rendered directly in a computer program. However, any tree can be represented as a binary tree if we change our orientation slightly. Consider the tree in figure 16.15. We cannot implement the generalized tree efficiently because it is impossible to predict how many subtrees, or children, each

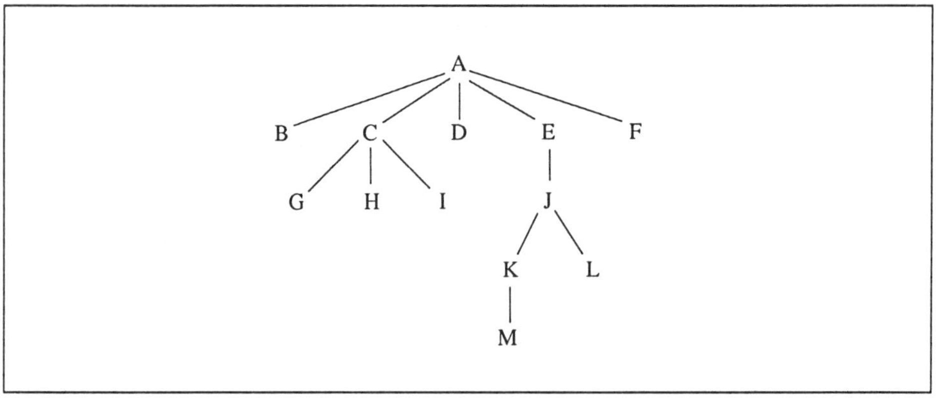

Figure 16.15. A General Tree

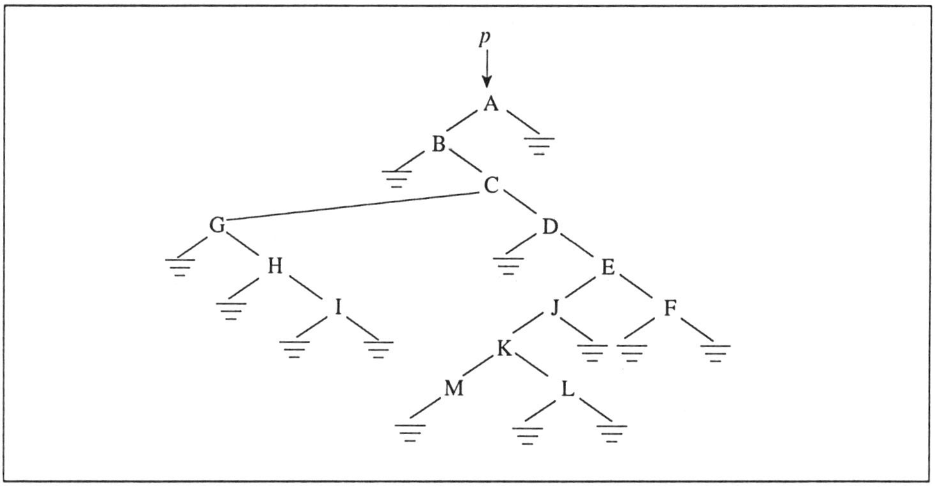

Figure 16.16. Binary Tree Representation of Tree from Figure 16.15.

node will have. However, we have seen that there are several ways to think about each node. For example, node C is a child of A, a sibling of B, D, E, and F, and the parent of G, H, and I. Suppose we represent only the first child of each node directly, and allow for siblings. The generalized tree can now be represented as a binary tree in which each node has a link to a child and a sibling, either of which may be a **nil** pointer. The node structure is as follows:

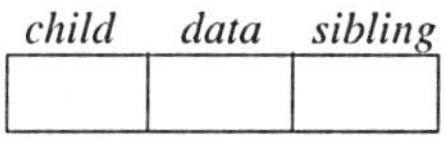

With this scheme, the tree shown in figure 16.15 can be represented as follows: A has no sibling, but it has a child B; B has no children but it has a sibling C; C has a child G and a sibling D; etc. Thus the binary tree in figure 16.16 represents all of the relationships in the general tree.

16.7 Multilinked and Hybrid Structures

We have seen a number of simple linked structures and some applications for them. The programmer is not limited to simple structures. In the introduction to this chapter we saw that nodes can be linked to other nodes in many configurations. Since nodes can have any number of pointers, any node in any type of linked structure can point to another linked structure, and it is possible for one node to be part of a number of linked lists simultaneously. These flexible ***multilinked structures*** are useful for many applications in which simpler data structures are inadequate for representing data. It is also possible to design ***hybrid structures*** that combine arrays with linked structures. For example, one can use an array of pointers to access a forest of ordered binary trees, or a node in any type of list can incorporate an array instead of an unstructured data field.

Two of the applications discussed in the next four chapters rely heavily on hybrid multilinked data structures. In chapter 18 we will see a program that utilizes a forest of binary trees, accessed by an array of pointers, in which each tree node is linked to a circular list containing more specific information. This type of structure makes use of the binary tree for efficient sorting and searching of a list of values, and it allows for a variable amount of information associated with each node. Chapter 20 describes a multilinked structure for representing music scores, in which each node exists simultaneously in four different bidirectional circular lists. These lists partition the notes in the score by part, starting time, and termination time. In this chapter we will examine a hybrid multilinked structure that combines an array for random access with multilinked circular lists for dynamic allocation of data.

Algorithms that deal with more complex data structures need not be much more difficult than those we have seen earlier in this chapter, because structured programming techniques enable us to treat each part of the data structure as a separate problem. For example, we might use a **for** loop to access each element of an array, with each element of the array pointing to a binary tree that can be traversed using a standard method. As one step in visiting each tree node, we might traverse a list of values accessed through an extra pointer in the node, and so on. Each part of the structure is traversed with techniques that we have already learned, plus use of a procedure that traverses another type of list. In many instances multilinked data structures can better represent the values or relationships among them. By combining various simple data structures, we can take advantage of the best features of both linked and dynamic storage allocation. A hash table is a good example of this technique.

16.7.1 Hash Tables

Thus far we have seen two basic methods of searching for an item in a list of values. Linear search can be applied equally well to lists stored in arrays and linked lists, but its efficiency $O(n)$ depends on the length of the list. Binary search is much more efficient, $O(\log_2 n)$, but it requires random access of a presorted list stored in an array or the correct placement of each value in a balanced binary tree. A good hashing algorithm can do even better without the overhead of presorting the list.

In the searching methods we have examined previously, finding the correct value depends upon comparing the desired value to a number of other values in the list until the value is found or until all possibilities are eliminated. Hashing differs from these methods in that a formula is used to calculate the location in the list directly. This formula is called a *hash function*. A hash function $f(x)$ calculates the position of item x in a list of possible values called a *hash table*.

Hashing has many analogies in real life. At the Eastman School of Music, students get notes and messages in communal mailboxes that are arranged alphabetically. A student whose last name begins with B looks in the B box to see if he or she has any messages. While this is not as convenient as having a private mail box, it takes only a few moments to check the appropriate box for messages, even though the messages in each box are in no particular order. It is certainly a better system than throwing all messages into one large box. In this case, each student might take all afternoon to find a message, or worse, to find none. The system works, even though most mail personel and students probably are not aware that their mail system is a close approximation of a hash table.

Since efficient hashing requires the use of contiguous storage locations, hash tables are usually implemented using arrays. The same algorithm is used when placing a value in the table, and again when searching the table to see if a particular value has been placed in it. As in the case of the ESM student mailboxes, it is unlikely that each value will hash into a unique array element, and *collisions* are bound to occur. There are many ways of resolving collisions. Since this chapter deals with linked lists, we will take care of the problem by letting each array element point to a linked list of values. One obvious advantage of this solution, called *chaining*, is that the hash table never becomes full, although efficiency suffers as the number of entries becomes excessive. If our hash function is reasonably good and the length of the table is appropriate, there will be relatively few collisions. As a result, each value can be placed in the correct box very quickly, and added to a short list of other values that hash into the same location. In order to search the list, we locate the correct box using the hash function. Either the location is empty, or it is necessary to search a short list to see if the required value is present. Since the hash function is arithmetic, it locates the correct box in fixed time $O(1)$. And because the list is short, we can use linear search without worrying about the order of elements. Typically, a value can be found by hashing an address and searching a list of perhaps three or four values.

An efficient hash function is fast and distributes values uniformly over the length of the table, thus minimizing collisions. Efficient processing also depends on choosing an appropriate length for the table. If the table is very long, lists are short but a great deal of space is wasted. If the table is too short, searching the lists becomes inefficient. Excellent results can usually be obtained by using a table length one and a half to two times the number of values expected.

16.7.2 Application: A Thematic Index

We will use a hash table to develop a variation on the thematic index program presented as an exercise in chapter 14. The sample data consists of a collection of Bach chorale incipits, encoded by transposing the tune to begin on C, removing accidentals and repeated notes, and using the first seven notes as the key for searching. We will have to deal with two types of "collisions": (a) more than one encoded incipit may hash into the same location in the hash table, and (b) the same encoded incipit may represent several different chorale tunes. We will resolve both of these possibilities using linked lists.

The data structure consists of an array of pointers, each of which points to the end of a circular list of head nodes. Each head node contains an incipit encoded as an integer, a pointer to the next head node, and a pointer to the end of a circular linked list of title nodes. Title nodes include the title of the chorale and where it is found in the sample collection. In a real application program, this node might include a record with diverse information such as the source of the piece, the actual notes used in the incipit of the chorale tune, etc. An encoded incipit occurs only once in the structure but may point to many titles, and several incipits may hash into the same address in the table. Each *tnode* (title node) contains a string—stored as a packed array of characters terminated by the null character, *chr*(0)—and a link field that points to the next node in the list. This data structure is shown in figure 16.17. A hash function is used to map each incipit into an address in the array in fixed time $O(1)$. Collisions (different incipits that map into the same position in the hash table) are resolved by the short list of head nodes that are searched with linear search.

In order to hash the encoded incipit into an address in the table, we must represent the incipit as a number. We will encode each note in the encoded incipit as a digit, with C = 0, D = 1, . . . , A = 6), and then map these digits into an integer, using 7 as a radix. Using a radix of 10 would result in a decimal number in which each digit is the name-class integer representing the note; however, numbers would be larger—and we will decode the number for human consumption in any case. The following procedures translate the incipit from the external to the internal form and vice versa.

```
[ const
    radix   =   7;
    modulus = 100; ]

 { encode incipit from file f into long integer }
 procedure encode(var f : text; var code : long);
   var
     ch : char;
     i  : integer;
   begin
     code := 0;
     for i := 1 to 7 do
       begin
         skip(f);
         read(f, ch);
         code := radix * code + toint(ch)
       end
   end;
```

```
{ decode incipit to output file; call with ordinal = inciplen }
procedure decode(var f : text; code : long; ordinal : integer);
  begin
    if ordinal > 0
       then
         begin
           decode(f, code div radix, ordinal - 1);
           write(f, tochar(code mod radix), ' ')
         end
  end;
```

This numeric incipit will be mapped into the hash table by the simple hash function:

```
{ hash encoded incipit into address for hash table }
function hash(code : long) : integer;
  begin
    hash := code mod modulus
  end;
```

This function maps the integer representation of the incipit into an array location *incips*[*i*], $0 \le i \le (modulus - 1)$. The relationship between the modulus and the radix used for encoding the incipit is important. For example, if we use a radix of 10 and a modulus of 100, only the last two notes in the incipit would influence the location

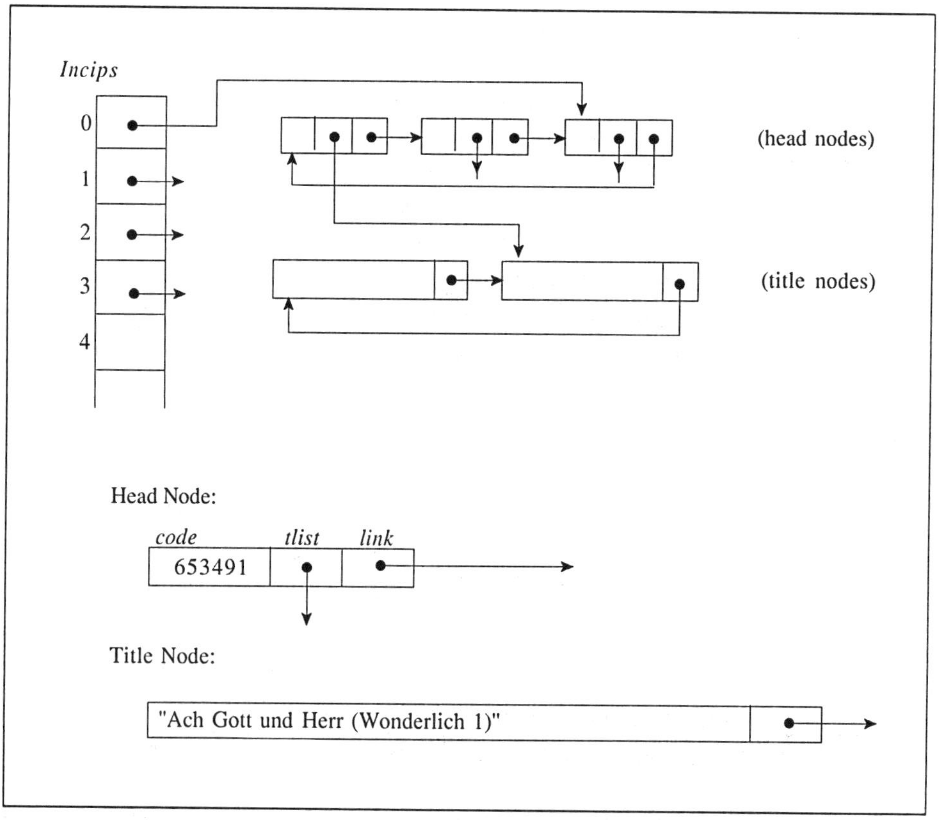

Figure 16.17. Data Structures for Program *Hashincips*

in the table. To minimize collisions in the table, the radix must be prime relative to the modulus.

A program to implement a thematic index using this algorithm is included as an exercise. The program is complete enough to read in the file, build the hash table, and print out the file. Other tasks are suggested as an exercise.

References and Selected Readings

The overview in the first part of this chapter is adapted from material previously published in the following article and used with the permission of the publisher:

Brinkman, Alexander R. "Representing Musical Scores for Computer Analysis," *Journal of Music Theory* 30, no. 2 (1986): 225–75.

The following source details the linked structures used to implement many different functions in a program that processes SCORE code for use in a computer music synthesis system.

Brinkman, Alexander R. "Data Structures for a Note-List Preprocessor." *Computers in Music Research* 1, no. 1 (1989): 75-101.

The reader who wishes to learn more about linked data structures can find information in many texts on applied data structures. I recommend the following sources:

Aho, Alfred V., John E. Hopcroft, and Jeffrey D. Ullman. *Data Structures and Algorithms.* Reading, Mass.: Addison-Wesley, 1983.

Knuth, Donald E. *The Art of Computer Programming.* Vol. 1, *Fundamental Algorithms.* 2d ed. Reading, Mass: Addison-Wesley, 1973.

Horowitz, Ellis, and Sartaj Sahni. *Fundamentals of Data Structures.* Potomac, Md.: Computer Science Press, 1976.

The hashing algorithm used in this chapter is simple, but the design of these algorithms can be rather complex, and a good deal has been written on the subject. This author recommends the following:

Aho, Alfred V., John E. Hopcroft, and Jeffrey D. Ullman. *The Design and Analysis of Algorithms.* Reading, Mass.: Addison-Wesley, 1975.

Horowitz, Ellis, and Sartaj Sahni. *Fundamentals of Data Structures.* Potomac, Md.: Computer Science Press, 1976.

Knuth, Donald E. *The Art of Computer Programming.* Vol. 3, *Sorting and Searching.* Reading, Mass: Addison-Wesley, 1973.

Sedgewick, Robert. *Algorithms.* 2d ed. Reading, Mass.: Addison-Wesley, 1988.

Other suggested reading:

Bennighof, James. "Set-Class Aggregate Structuring, Graph Theory, and Some Compositional Strategies." *Journal of Music Theory* 31, no. 1 (1987): 51–98.

Duisberg, Robert. "On the Role of Affect in Artificial Intelligence and Music." *Perspectives of New Music* 23, no. 1 (1984): 6–35.

Roads, Curtis. "Research in Music and Artificial Intelligence." *ACM Computing Surveys* 17 (1985): 163–90.

Exercises

16.1. The following exercises deal with simple linked lists with a pointer to the beginnning of the list. If this pointer is **nil**, the list is empty. The link field of the last node in the list is **nil**. The nodes and pointers are defined as follows:

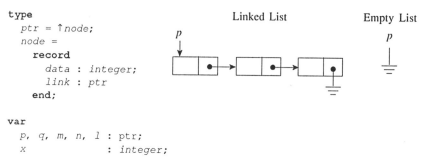

```
type
  ptr = ↑node;
  node =
    record
      data : integer;
      link : ptr
    end;
```

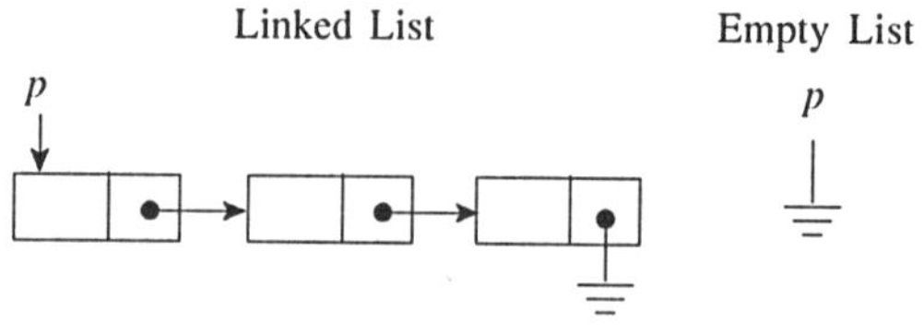


```
var
  p, q, m, n, l : ptr;
  x             : integer;
```

1. For the problems below, assume that variables have been declared as shown above, and that *p* and *q* point to nodes with all fields assigned. The problems are noncumulative. Be brief but explicit; state precisely what each statement does—what type of value is transferred (data field, pointer, copy of all values in node, etc). If the statement is not valid, state the reason:

    a) *p*↑.*link* := *q*;

    b) *p*↑.*link* := *q*↑.*link*;

    c) *q*↑.*data* := *x*;

    d) *p*↑.*data* := *q*↑.*data*;

    e) *p*↑.*data* := *q*↑.*link*;

    f) *incr*(*p*↑.*link*);

    g) *l* := *q*;

    h) *n*↑ := *q*↑;

    i) *q*↑ := *p*;

    j) *new*(*x*);

2. Write a nonrecursive procedure to traverse list *p*.

3. Write a recursive procedure to traverse list *p*.

4. Write **function** *length*(*p* : *ptr*) : *integer*; that will return the length of list *p*.

5. Assume that the data field of each node in the list contains a pitch-class integer. Write a procedure that traverses the list, printing out the interval from each pc to the next. Your procedure should call the following function, which returns the interval between two pitch classes:

```
function int(pc1, pc2 : integer) : integer;
  var
    t : integer;
```

```
begin { int }
  t := pc2 - pc1;
  if t < 0
    then t := t + 12;
  int := t
end; { int }
```

6. Write **procedure** *getnode*(**var** *p* : *ptr*); and **procedure** *release*(**var** *p* : *ptr*); that could be used for maintaining a storage pool of free nodes. The free list should be treated as a stack, pointed to by *free*.

16.2. Shorter Programs with Linked Lists.

1. *List with Pointer to End.* One disadvantage of the simple list is that the user must traverse it to insert a value at the end. This can be overcome by keeping a pointer to the beginning and to the end, with the following record structure:

```
type
  ptr = ↑node;
  node    =    record
                 data : integer;
                 link : ptr
               end;

  listtype = record
                 first : ptr;
                 last  : ptr
               end;

var
  free : ptr;
  p    : listtype;
```

The list is implemented with a pointer to the first and last node. The link field of the last node is a **nil** pointer.

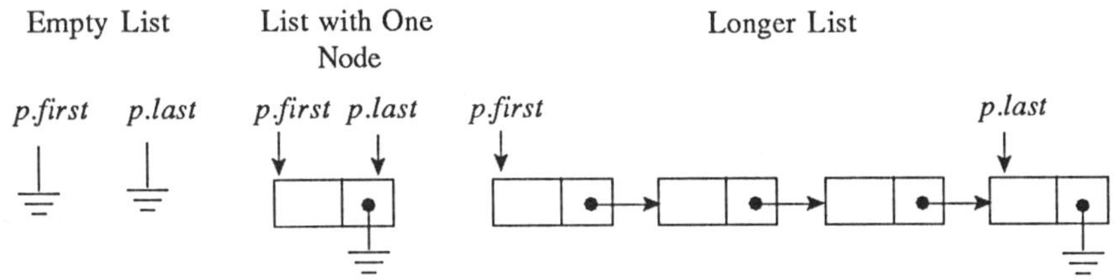

You are to write a program that implements this list type. The main procedure is shown below:

```
begin { main }
  init(p, free);
  write('Type list: ');
  while not eof do
    begin
      readdata(p);
      trav1(p.first); writeln;
      trav2(p.first); writeln;
```

```
        trav3(p.first); writeln;
        erase(p);
        writeln;
        write('Type list: ')
      end
  end.  { main }
```

The headings for the required procedures are listed below:

procedure *init*(**var** *p* : *listtype*; **var** *free* : *ptr*); — initializes *free*, *p.first* and *p.last* to **nil** pointers.

procedure *getnode*(**var** *t* : *ptr*); — gets a node from the free list or from the operating system if necessary.

procedure *readdata*(**var** *p* : *listtype*); — reads the values on one input line, storing them in the linked list.

procedure *trav1*(*t* : *ptr*); — uses a loop to traverse the list pointed to by *t*.

procedure *trav2*(*t* : *ptr*); — traverses list *t* recursively.

procedure *trav3*(*t* : *ptr*); — traverses list *t* recursively, printing list in reverse order.

procedure *erase*(**var** *p* : *listtype*); — "bulk-erases" the list, returning all nodes to the stack of free nodes. (Make this as efficient as possible.)

2. *Linked Queue*. Recall that a queue is a First In First Out (FIFO) data structure, in which values are added at the rear of the queue and taken off of the front. Modify the list from the previous exercise so that it can be used to implement a linked queue. Change the fields *first* and *last* to *front* and *rear* (you decide which end is which, based on required operations).

```
type
  queuetype = record
                 front : ptr;
                 rear  : ptr
              end;

var
  q    : queuetype;
  free : ptr;
```

You will need the following procedures (headings are shown):

procedure *init*(**var** *q* : *queuetype*; **var** *free* : *ptr*); — initializes *free*, *q.front* and *q.rear* to **nil** pointers.

procedure *getnode*(**var** *t* : *ptr*); — gets a node from the free list or from the operating system if necessary.

procedure *release*(**var** *t* : *ptr*); — places node *t* on the stack of free nodes.

function *empty*(*q* : *queuetype*) : *boolean*; — tests for empty queue.

procedure *insert*(*x* : *integer*; **var** *q* : *queuetype*); — inserts integer *x* into the queue.

procedure *remove*(**var** *x* : *integer*; **var** *q* : *queuetype*); — removes integer *x* from the front of the queue and returns the node to the stack of free nodes.

procedure *readdata*(**var** *q* : *queuetype*); — reads the values on one input line, placing them in the queue.

procedure *printdata*(**var** *q* : *queuetype*); — removes values from the queue and prints them until the queue is empty.

3. *Circular Queue.* We have already seen that an ordered list can be stored in a circular list, with a pointer to the last node. Since this structure gives us access to both the first and the last nodes in the list, it is also ideal for implementing a queue. Study the diagrams below, and decide which end of the list should be treated as the front and which the rear of the queue.

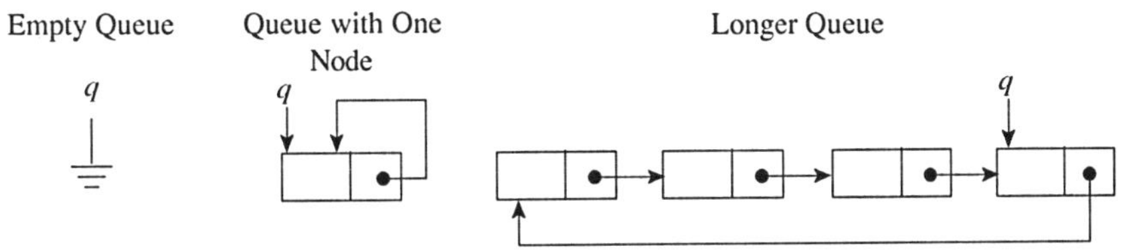

Now write the routines necessary to implement the queue (headings are shown):

function *empty*(*Q* : *ptr*) : *boolean*; — returns *true* if the queue is empty.

procedure *insert*(*x* : *integer*; **var** *Q* : *ptr*); — inserts integer *x* into the queue at the rear. Obviously, you will have to get a new node to do this. Remember to take care of the special case of the empty queue, and to keep the queue circular at all times.

procedure *remove*(**var** *x* : *integer*; **var** *Q* : *ptr*); — returns the integer from the node at the front at the queue and calls *release* to return the node to the stack of free nodes.

You will need the following utilities:

procedure *getnode*(**var** *p* : *ptr*); — points *p* to a node, obtained from the *free* list if possible, or from the storage allocator *new*.

procedure *release*(**var** *p* : *ptr*); — places node *p* on the top of the stack of free nodes.

Test your queue implementation with a program that reads the values from each line of the input file, stores them in the queue, and then prints them out in the original order. Your main program should prompt the user for a list of values, which will be terminated by the newline character. The program should run interactively, and should reconstruct the queue for each line of input. You will need the following:

procedure *readdata*(**var** *q* : *ptr*); — reads values on input line storing them in the queue.

procedure *printdata*(**var** *q* : *ptr*); — removes each value from the queue and prints it, terminating when the queue is empty.

16.3. Review

1. Write procedures to do various operations on each of the following types of lists:

- Simple list with pointer to beginning and **nil** pointer at end
- List with pointer to beginning and end
- Circular list with pointer to end
- Bidirectional list with pointer to first and last node
- Bidirectional circular list
- Bidirectional circular list with head node

Implement each of the following operations:

a) Insert a value after an arbitrary node.

b) Traverse the list.

c) Count the number of nodes in the list.

d) Sum the values in the list.

e) Make a copy of the list.

f) Erase the list (returning nodes to the free list).

g) Compare two lists for equality.

h) Concatenate two lists. In each case, the result of calling *concatenate*(*A*, *B*) should be the concatenation of *A* and *B* in list *A*, and an empty list *B*.

2. *Manual Checking*. Procedure *xnarf*(*x*), shown at (a) below (the name has been changed to confuse the innocent) is designed to manipulate a list of the type shown at (b). Work through the procedure, redrawing the links as you "execute" each statement. (You may find it helpful to redraw the list in pencil before you begin so that you can change the links.) Then describe what the procedure does and draw the list as it would appear after procedure *xnarf* had done its work.

```
(a) procedure xnarf(var x : ptr);
     var
       p, q, r : ptr;
     begin
       p := x; q := nil;
       while p <> nil do
         begin
           r := q;
           q := p;
           p := p↑.link;
           q↑.link := r
         end;
       x := q
     end;
```

(b)

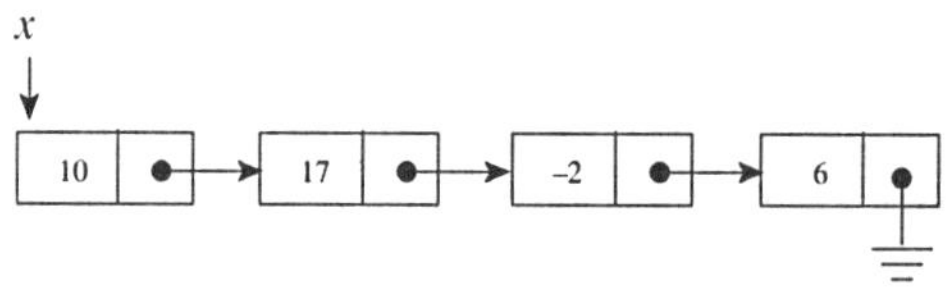

3. *Essay*. A list is an ordered set of values. Compare the merits of arrays and linked lists as data structures to represent lists. Weigh the relative strengths and weaknesses of each representation. Consider (a) inserting or deleting a value, (b) accessing a random value (e.g., the *n*th member), (c) traversing the list (looking at each value in order), (d) concatenating (joining) lists, (e) memory requirements (storage space needed for the list), and (f) other considerations (flexibility and ability to represent complex relationships among data items, etc.). In (e), consider under what circumstances each representation is best. You may wish to cite examples from programs that you have written or studied to support your arguments.

16.4. *Can't see the forest for the !#&*$ Trees.* The binary tree shown below is constructed of nodes with three fields: one for integer data, and two pointers called *ltree* and *rtree.*

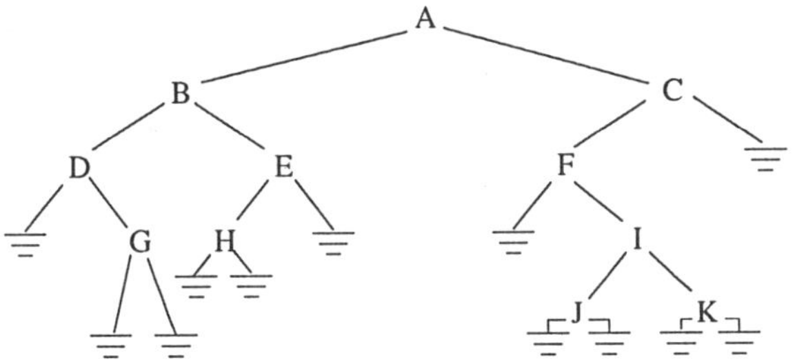

1. Write a recursive version of each of the three standard traversals (inorder, preorder, and postorder), and show the ordering of the values in the tree obtained by each traversal.

2. Recall that a binary tree can be used to represent a generalized tree (a tree with any number of subtrees on each node). The rule is that the left link points to the first child of a node, and the right link points to the node's siblings (brothers or sisters). According to this convention, the generalized tree on the left is equivalent to the binary tree on the right:

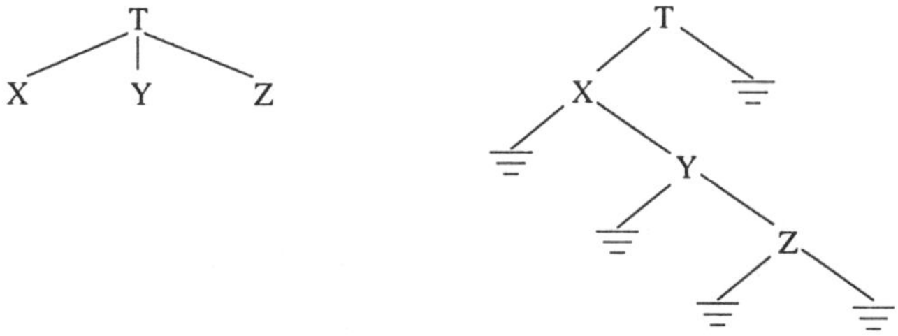

   Using this rule, draw the generalized tree represented by the binary tree at the beginning of this exercise set.

3. In section 16.6.6 we saw a generalized tree representing a sonata form. Draw a binary tree that could represent this tree.

4. Write a program that builds a binary tree representing all 222 prime forms for pitch-class sets (omitting the null set), using the scheme described in section 16.6.1. The program should then accept queries in the form of prime forms, which will be identified by searching the binary tree. The node structure for the tree will be as follows:

```
type
  nameptr  = ↑alpha;                          { pointer to string    }
  alpha    = packed array[1 .. 5] of char;    { to store set name    }

  treeptr  = ↑treenode;                       { pointer to treenode  }
  treenode = record
               alternate : treeptr;
               successor : treeptr;
               setname   : nameptr            { pointer to string    }
             end;
```

We will see a much more efficient way to implement this table in chapters 17 and 18; however, this is an excellent exercise for manipulating trees.

16.5 Return of *Incips*. This program will be a much more efficient version of the incipit-file program from chapter 14, exercise 4. The same data file can be used. The basic algorithm was discussed in section 16.7.1. New features: encoding and decoding incipits as long integers; hashing and hash tables; use of hybrid multilinked data structure (array with pointers to circular linked lists); use of variant records. The data structure consists of an array of pointers, each of which points to the end of a circular list of head nodes. Each head node contains an incipit encoded as an integer, a pointer to the next head node, and a pointer to the end of a circular linked list of title nodes. This incipit is encoded in C-major scale order (C = 0, D = 1, . . ., A = 6) encoded with 7 as a radix. An incipit occurs only once in the structure but may point to many titles, and several incipits may hash into the same address in the table:

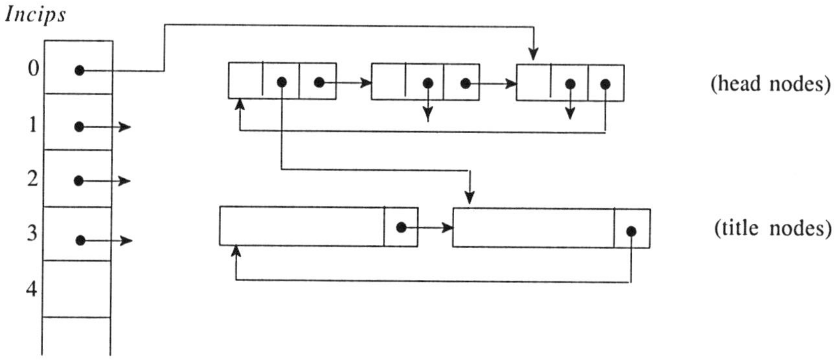

Each *tnode* (title node) contains a string, stored as a packed array of characters terminated by a null character, and a link field that points to the next node in the list:

Head Node:

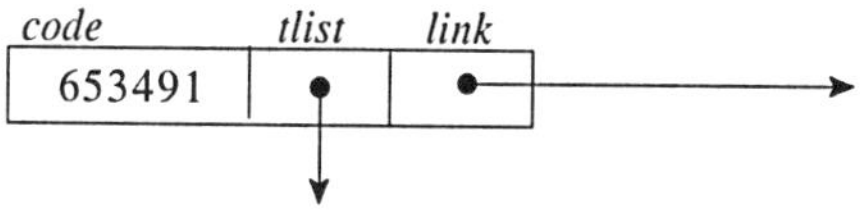

Title Node:

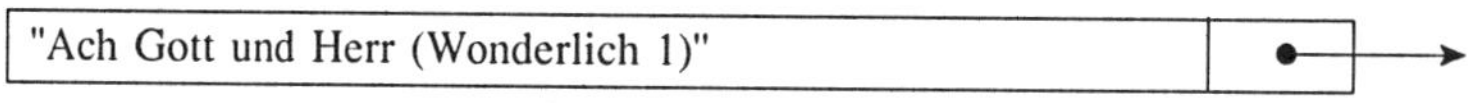

A hash function is used to map each incipit into an address in the array in fixed time $O(1)$. Collisions (different incipits that map into the same position in the hash table) are resolved by the short list of head nodes, which are searched with linear search.

You will need to write procedures *add*, *search*, *delete*, *compact*, and *report*. *Add*, *search*, and *delete* will each prompt for an incipit, and will loop until the user types 'quit' instead of an incipit. Notes on implementation of individual procedures follow:

procedure *search*(**var** *incips* : *hashtable*); — will prompt the user for an incipit, encode the incipit, and call the hash function to locate the correct "bucket" in the hash table. The list of head nodes is then searched for the specified incipit. If the incipit is found, it is printed (via decoding) and the circular list of title nodes is traversed, printing each title with its sequence number:

```
Type incipit: cbagabc

c b a g a b c

    1. Ach Gott und Herr, wie gross und schwer (Wonderlich 1)
    2. Ach Gott und Herr, wie gross und schwer (Wonderlich 2)
    3. Christus, der uns selig macht (Wonderlich 21)
```

If the incipit is not found, or if all title nodes have been deleted, print an appropriate message:

```
c d e f g a b  does not occur in file
```

procedure *add*(**var** *incips* : *hashtable*; **var** *n* : *integer*); — prompts the user for, and reads (encodes), an incipit and a title. The encoded incipit is stored in a local variable, and the title is stored in a *tnode* obtained via *getnode*(*t*). The incipit is hashed to find the location in the table, say *x*, and then the list of head nodes pointed to by *incips*[*x*] is searched. If the incipt already occurs in the list, say at head node *q*, the *tnode* is linked into the end of the circular list pointed to by *q*↑.*tlist*. If the new incipit does not occur in the array, then a node is inserted in the list of head nodes, and the title is linked to it. A message is printed, informing the user that the task has been completed. Note that you will not run out of space until the computer system does, though the list of head nodes may become unmanageably long.

procedure *delete*(**var** *incips* : *hashtable*); — this is the most difficult procedure because there are several special cases. First the user is prompted for an incipit and it is encoded. Hashing is used to find the location in the hash table, and a linear search is used to find the correct head node. If the incipit does not occur or if there are no titles in the *tlist*, an appropriate message is printed. Otherwise the incipit and titles are printed as in *search*. In general, you will ask the user which title he wishes to delete, find that node, and double-check by printing the title and asking 'Delete? (y/n): '. If the response is 'yes', unlink the node and return it to the storage pool. Remember that in order to delete a node, you will have to locate the node before it in the linked list. The following special cases need careful treatment: (a) there is only one node in the list (no need to ask which one to delete, is there?); (b) the node to be deleted is the last one in the list (why is this a problem?); (c) the user responds 'all' instead of typing a number (double-check and then bulk-erase the list). In all cases make sure that, if the last node is deleted, the pointer to the list is **nil**.

procedure *compact*(**var** *incips* : *hashtable*); — removes all head nodes that are no longer linked to title nodes, and returns them to the free list..

procedure *report*(**var** *incips* : *hashtable*); — traverses the data structure and prints a report of the number of incipits (head nodes), the average and maximum number of head nodes in a "bucket," and the total number of titles in the structure. Empty lists are ignored. This procedure helps the user determine when the lists have become too long and the program should be recompiled with a larger table size (*modulus*).

The startup file is listed below. Make sure that you describe the data structure in your initial block comment. Pictures help and are not too difficult with a screen editor. The input file from exercise 4 of chapter 14 can be used with this program. Provide complete documentation for each procedure or function, including the ones you write.

```
(***********************   Program Hashincips    ***********************)
(* Contains incomplete procedures.  N.B. The type 'long' is used to    *)
(* denote 32-bit integers.  If your compiler uses 32 bits for all      *)
(* integers, change 'long' to 'integer' globally.  If your compiler uses *)
(* a special identifier such as 'long', use it.  If you must use 16-bit  *)
(* integers, do the following: (a) change each 'long' to 'integer'; (b)  *)
(* change inciplen to 5; (c) change modulus to 101; (d) edit the input  *)
(* file, truncating the incipits to 5 notes.  Remember that the modulus  *)
(* and inciplen must be relatively prime.                                *)
(************************************************************************)
program hashincips(input, output, data);

  const
    inciplen  =   7;          { number of notes in incipit                }
    maxstring =  71;          { maximum string length + 1                 }
    modulus   = 100;          { modulus for hashing and size of hash table }
    radix     =   7;          { radix used while encoding incipit         }
    terminal  = true;         { switches to control destination of printing }
    disk      = false;

  type
    string  = packed array[1 .. maxstring] of char;
    kind = (avail, tnode, headnode);             { kinds of nodes              }

    ptr = ↑node;                                 { variant record definition  }
    node =
      record
        tag      : kind;                         { common part                 }
        link     : ptr;

        case kind of                             { variant part                }
          avail : ();                            { available on free list      }
                                                 { head node:                  }
          headnode : (code  : long;              { encoded incipit             }
                      tlist : ptr);              { pointer to list of titles   }
                                                 { title node:                 }
          tnode    : (title : string)            { string for information      }

      end; { variant record definition }

    hashtable = array[0 .. modulus] of ptr;      { pointers to head nodes      }

  var
    data   : text;                 { data file                                 }
    incips : hashtable;            { pointers to "buckets"                     }
    key    : char;                 { to store first letter of user requests    }
    free   : ptr;                  { pointer to storage pool of tnodes         }

  procedure skip(var f : text);
    var
      done : boolean;
    begin
      done := false;
      repeat
        if eof(f)
```

```
        then done := true
      else if f↑ in [' ', ',']
        then get(f)
      else done := true
    until done
  end;

procedure incr(var x : integer);
  begin
    x := x + 1
  end;

function isdigit(ch : char) : boolean;
  begin
    isdigit := ch in ['0' .. '9']
  end;

function affirmative : boolean;
  var
    ch : char;
  begin
    skip(input);
    readln(ch);
    if ch = 'y'
      then affirmative := true
    else if ch = 'n'
      then affirmative := false
    else
      begin
        write('You must answer yes or no: ');
        affirmative := affirmative
      end
  end;

procedure getint(var x : integer);
  begin
    skip(input);
    if isdigit(input↑)
      then read(x)
      else
        begin
          readln;
          write('Integer value required: ');
          getint(x)
        end
  end;

procedure getnode(var p : ptr);
  begin { getnode }
    if free = nil
      then new(p)                    { get new node               }
      else
        begin                        { take top node from stack }
          p := free;
          free := free↑.link
        end
  end; { getnode }
```

```
{ insert node t at end of circular list p }
  procedure insert(t : ptr; var p : ptr);
    begin { insert }
      if p = nil          { empty list }
        then
          begin { start new list }
            p := t;
            p↑.link := p
          end   { start new list }
        else
          begin { add to old list }
            t↑.link := p↑.link;
            p↑.link := t;
            p := t
          end   { add to old list }
    end;  { insert }

{ initialize hash table }
  procedure init(var incips : hashtable; var free : ptr);
    var
      i : integer;
    begin
      for i := 0 to modulus do
        incips[i] := nil;
      free := nil
    end;

{ release node }
  procedure release(var p : ptr);
    begin
      p↑.tag := avail;
      p↑.link := free;
      free := p;
      p := nil
    end;

  function toint(ch : char) : integer;
    begin
      toint := (ord(ch) - ord('a') + 5) mod 7
    end;

{ encode incipit into long integer }
  procedure encode(var f : text; var code : long);
    var
      ch : char;
      i  : integer;
    begin
      code := 0;
      for i := 1 to 7 do
        begin
          skip(f);
          read(f, ch);
          code := radix * code + toint(ch)
        end
    end;
```

```
{ convert name-class integer to letter name }
  function tochar(x : integer) : char;
    begin
      tochar := chr(ord('a') + ((x + 2) mod 7))
    end;

{ decode incipit to file f }
  procedure decode(var f : text; code : long; ordinal : integer);
    begin
      if ordinal > 0 then
        begin
          decode(f, code div radix, ordinal - 1);
          write(f, tochar(code mod radix), ' ')
        end
    end;

  procedure readstring(var f : text; var S : string);
    var
      i : integer;
    begin
      skip(f);
      i := 1;
      while (not eoln(f)) and (i < maxstring) do
        begin
          read(f, S[i]);
          incr(i)
        end;
      S[i] := chr(0);
      if not eoln(f)
        then writeln('Warning: string truncated to ',
                                          maxstring - 1:2, ' chars')
    end;

  procedure writestring(var f : text; S : string);
    var
      i : integer;
    begin
      i := 1;
      while S[i] <> chr(0) do
        begin
          write(f, S[i]);
          incr(i)
        end
    end;

{ hashes encoded incipit into address for hash table }
  function hash(code : long) : integer;
    begin
      hash := code mod modulus
    end;

{ returns pointer to head node containing code, or nil pointer }
  function findincip(code : long; p : ptr) : ptr;
    var
      t : ptr;
```

```
    begin { findincip }
      if p = nil
        then findincip := nil
        else
          begin
            t := p↑.link;
            repeat
              if t↑.code <> code
                then t := t↑.link
            until (t↑.code = code) or (t = p↑.link);
            if t↑.code = code
              then findincip := t
              else findincip := nil
          end
    end; { findincip }

  procedure readfile(var f : text; var incips : hashtable);
    var
      t, q  : ptr;                   { pointers to nodes              }
      code : long;                   { coded incipit                  }
      x    : integer;                { location of code in hash table }
    begin { readfile }
      reset(f);                      { open file for reading          }
      while not eof(f) do
        begin
          encode(f, code);           { encode incipit                 }
          x := hash(code);           { find location in array         }
          q := findincip(code, incips[x]);{ point q to head node      }
          if q = nil                 { not found                      }
            then
              begin
                getnode(q);                         { get node        }
                q↑.tag := headnode;                 { set fields      }
                q↑.code := code;
                q↑.tlist := nil;
                insert(q, incips[x])                { insert into list }
              end;              { q now points to incipt head node }
          getnode(t);                               { get a title node }
          t↑.tag := tnode;                          { set fields      }
          readstring(f, t↑.title); readln(f);       { read title      }
          insert(t, q↑.tlist)                       { insert in tlist }
        end
    end; { readfile }

{ traverse list of titles }
  procedure ttraverse(var f : text; p : ptr; code : long;
                                            toterminal : boolean);
    var
      t : ptr;
      i : integer;
    begin { ttraverse }
      if p <> nil
        then
          begin
            t := p↑.link;              { t points to first title node }
            i := 0;                    { title number                 }
```

```
       repeat
         incr(i);
         if toterminal
           then
             begin
               write(i:6, '. ');                             { write number      }
               writestring(f, t↑.title); writeln(f) { and title         }
             end
           else                                              { to file on disk }
             begin
               decode(f, code, inciplen);                    { write incipit     }
               writestring(f, t↑.title); writeln(f) { and title         }
             end;
         t := t↑.link                          { get next title node         }
       until t = p↑.link                       { until back where we started }
     end
 end; { ttraverse }

{ traverse incipit list (head nodes) }
  procedure itraverse(var f : text; p : ptr; toterminal : boolean);
    var
      t : ptr;
    begin
      if p <> nil
        then
          begin
            t := p↑.link;
            repeat
              ttraverse(f, t↑.tlist, t↑.code, toterminal);
              t := t↑.link
            until t = p↑.link
          end
    end;

  procedure swap(var x, y : integer);
    var
      t : integer;
    begin
      t := x; x := y; y := t
    end;

{ how much of the list should we print? }
  procedure limits(var first, last : integer; toterminal : boolean);
    begin
      if not toterminal                                    { if to disk         }
        then
          begin
            first := 0;                                    { write whole file }
            last  := modulus - 1
          end
        else                                     { otherwise get range from user }
          begin
            write('Type range (limits = 0,', modulus - 1:1,'): ');
            getint(first); getint(last); readln;
            if last < first
              then swap(first, last);
```

```
            if (first < 0) or (last > modulus - 1)
              then
                 begin
                   writeln('Illegal range');
                   limits(first, last, toterminal)          { try again }
                 end
          end
    end;

{ print incipit and matching titles }
  procedure printentry(var f : text; var p : ptr; toterminal : boolean);
    begin { printentry }
      if toterminal
        then
          begin
            decode(f, p↑.code, inciplen);              { print incipit  }
            writeln(f); writeln(f)
          end;
      ttraverse(f, p↑.tlist, p↑.code, toterminal)     { and all titles }
    end; { printentry }

{ print all entries in "bucket" }
  procedure dumpbucket(var f : text; p : ptr; toterminal : boolean);
    var
      t : ptr;
    begin
      if p <> nil
        then
          begin { traverse head-node list }
            t := p↑.link;
            repeat
              if toterminal
                then writeln;
              printentry(f, t, toterminal);
              t := t↑.link
            until t = p↑.link
          end  { traverse head-node list }
    end;

{ write info to file f }
  procedure writefile(var f : text; var incips : hashtable;
                                          toterminal : boolean);
    var
      i : integer;
      first, last : integer;
    begin { writefile }
      limits(first, last, toterminal);
      for i := first to last do
        dumpbucket(f, incips[i], toterminal)
    end; { writefile }

{ instruct user }
  procedure instruct;
    begin { instruct }
      writeln('Procedure instruct not implemented')
    end; { instruct }
```

```
{ add incipits to hash table }
  procedure add(var incips : hashtable);
    var
      code : long;
      t, q : ptr;
      x    : integer;
    begin { add }
      writeln('Procedure add not implemented')
    end;  { add }

{ bulk-erase list of title nodes }
  procedure bulkerase(var p : ptr);
    var
      t : ptr;
    begin
    end;

{ delete incipits }
  procedure delete(var incips : hashtable);
    var
      code : long;
      x    : integer;
      q    : ptr;
    begin { delete }
      writeln('Procedure delete not implemented')
    end;  { delete }

{ search for incipits }
  procedure search(var incips : hashtable);
    var
      x    : integer;
      code : long;
      q    : ptr;
    begin { search }
      writeln('Procedure search not implemented')
    end;  { search }

{ test first character of user response }
  function legal(ch : char) : boolean;
    begin
      legal := ch in ['h', '?', 'i', 'a', 'c', 's', 'd', 'p', 'r']
    end;

{ report statistics on hash table }
  procedure report(var incips : hashtable);
    begin
      writeln('Procedure report not implemented')
    end;

{ remove head nodes without titles attached }
  procedure compact(var incips : hashtable);
    begin
      writeln('Procedure compact not implemented')
    end;
```

```
(***********************************************************************)
(*                           Main Procedure                            *)
(***********************************************************************)

 begin { main }
   init(incips, free);
   readfile(data, incips);          { read data file into array       }
   write('Do you need instructions? (y/n)  ');
   if affirmative
     then instruct;
   write('Command?  ');
   skip(input);
   while not eof do
     begin { process user requests }
       skip(input);
       readln(key);                  { get first letter of command     }
       if legal(key)
         then
           case key of
             'a' : add(incips);      { add entry to file               }
             'c' : compact(incips);  { remove empty head nodes         }
             'd' : delete(incips);   { delete entry from file          }
     'h','i','?' : instruct;         { give instructions               }
             'p' : writefile(output, incips, terminal);     { to terminal }
             'r' : report(incips);   { print statistics on hash table  }
             's' : search(incips)    { locate incipits in file         }
           end  { case }
         else
           begin
             write('Illegal command.  Do you need instructions? ');
             if affirmative
               then instruct
           end;
       writeln;
       write('Command?  ')
     end;
   compact(incips);                 { clean up                        }
   report(incips);                  { print table stats               }
   rewrite(data);                   { open data file for writing      }
   writefile(data, incips, disk);   { rewrite disk file               }
   writeln('file written to disk')
 end.  { main }
```

PART III Applications

17| Prime-Form Algorithms

This chapter is the first of four discussing larger programs for more advanced study. Each contains an exposition of new material followed by a complete program illustrating the new techniques and others discussed earlier in this text. The programs are longer and more complex than those discussed previously and will reward careful study.

We will examine several algorithms for finding the *normal order* and *prime form* of pitch-class sets. The prime form of a set represents all members of a class of sets that are equivalent under the operations of transposition or transposition after inversion. We will use the term normal order to denote the specific ordering of a set of pcs that is closest to prime form but maintains the actual pitch classes in the set. This may be a transposition or a transposition of the inversion of the prime form.[1]

In this chapter and the next we will explore a representation of pitch-class sets based on bit patterns in binary integers. Each pc set is stored as a single binary number, which can be used to index tables for implementation of efficient search procedures. Since Pascal does not provide operators that directly manipulate binary numbers at the bit level, we use arithmetic operations that perform the same task.

17.1 Binary Representation of Pitch-Class Sets

In chapter 12 we learned to use Pascal's set type to manipulate pitch-class sets. An alternate scheme utilizes the binary representation of integers within the computer. Binary numbers consist of binary digits, called bits, which can have one of two values: 0 or 1. The value of a binary digit depends on its positional weight. The weight of each position is a power of two with the rightmost bit equal to 2^0, or 1, the second digit from the right 2^1, or 2, and so on.[2] The value of a binary number is calculated as the sum of each bit times its positional weight.[3]

1. The term has been used in various ways. Milton Babbitt, in "Set Structure as a Compositional Determinant," *Journal of Music Theory* 5, no. 1 (1961): 72–94, uses *normal form* to denote the referential form of the pc set. Allen Forte, in *The Structure of Atonal Music* (New Haven: Yale University Press, 1973), uses *normal order* to denote any of the circular permutations of a set that shares the smallest outside interval, and then chooses the "best normal order" by other criteria. Forte's *prime form* is the best normal order transposed to begin on 0 (see section 17.6.1).

2. We will refer to the 2^0 bit as bit 0, the 2^1 bit as bit 1, etc. When it is not clear from the context, we will use subscripts to indicate the radix, e.g., 101_{10} is one hundred one (decimal), while 101_2 is the binary representation of the integer 5_{10}.

3. Binary numbers are discussed in section 1.1.

Binary integers can be used for a compact representation of pc sets. Each pc set is represented as a binary integer, with the 2^i bit representing pc i. Thus bit 0 represents pc 0, bit 1 represents pc 1, and so on. The value of each bit represents the presence (1) or absence (0) of the pitch class. We call this representation a *bit vector*. For example, the set $S = \{0, 1, 4\}$ [C, C♯, E] is represented as the binary number 000000010011:

```
S  =  000000010011
             |  ||
             |  |└──── 0   [C         ]
             |  └───── 1   [C# or Db  ]
             └──────── 4   [E         ]
```

The computer system converts decimal numbers to binary for us, so we can use the more familiar decimal number 19, which has the same value. Each of the 4096 possible pitch-class sets is represented by a unique integer. This figure includes the null set (000000000000 = 0) and the twelve-tone set (111111111111 = 4095).

We will construct the bit vector S for a set of n unique pitch-class integers P_i, $1 \le i \le n$ as the sum of 2^{P_i} for each pitch class P_i:

$$S = \sum_{i=1}^{n} 2^{P_i}$$

In Pascal, this is accomplished by the following:

```
S := 0;
for i := 1 to n do
  S := S + power(pcset[i])
```

where *pcset* is an array containing the pcs in the set and *power*(n) is a user-written function that returns the value 2^n. The bit vector for the inversion of the set (T_0I) is calculated by substituting pitch class $((12 - P_i) \bmod 12)$ for each pitch class P_i:

```
SI := 0;
for i := 1 to n do
  SI := SI + power((12 - pcset[i]) mod 12)
```

The binary representation has many useful properties. First, it can be decoded by algorithm. If the number is odd, then the rightmost bit is 1, indicating that pc 0 is in the set. Dividing by 2 shifts all bits to the right, discarding the rightmost bit. Bit 0 now indicates the presence or absence of pc 1 in the set. The process is repeated until the bit vector is equal to 0, indicating that no pcs remain. Table 17.1 illustrates the decoding the bit vector 19.

```
pc := 0;
while S > 0 do
  begin
    if odd(S)
      then <pc is in the set>;
    S := S div 2;                  { shift right }
    pc := pc + 1
 end;
```

S	*pc*	*S=0*	*odd(S)*	*Result*
19	0	false	true	0 is in set
9	1	false	true	1 is in set
4	2	false	false	2 is not in set
2	3	false	false	3 is not in set
1	4	false	true	4 is in set
0	5	true	–	algorithm terminates

Table 17.1. Decoding Bit Vector 19.

Each twelve-tone operation can be implemented as a combination of bitwise operations, many of which can be simulated by arithmetic operations. For example, the set's complement (all elements that are not in the set) is calculated by changing all zeros to ones and vice versa. The bitwise operation that accomplishes this is called *ones complement*; arithmetically, it is obtained by subtracting the bit vector from 4095 (111111111111):

S = 000000010011 [19]

$\bar{S}$ = ~000000010011 [4095 – 19]
= 111111101100 [4076]

Shifting all bits to the left (with bit 11 rotating to position 0) transposes the set by one. We will refer to this operation as *left rotation.*

$T_1(S)$ = 000000100110 [1, 2, 5]
$T_2(S)$ = 000001001100 [2, 3, 6]
$T_3(S)$ = 000010011000 [3, 4, 7]
. . .
$T_7(S)$ = 100110000000 [7, 8, 11]
$T_8(S)$ = 001100000001 [0, 8, 9]
etc.

Left rotation is analogous to the following arithmetic operation:[4]

```
S := S * 2;
if S > 4095
  then S := S - 4095
```

The boolean expression ($S > 4095$) is *true* if the left shift has set bit 12 (positional weight 4096) to 1. If it has, we subtract 4096 and add 1, thus setting bit 12 to 0 and bit 0 to 1.

4. In an assembly language or in a high-level language such as C that provides for bitwise operations, these operations would be performed by bit shifting, masking, etc.

Inversion is obtained by mapping each bit i into bit $(12 - i) \bmod 12$. Note that under this operation bit 0 maps into itself:

$$S \;=\; 000000010011 \qquad [0, 1, 4]$$

$$S' = T_0I(S) = \; 100100000001 \qquad [0, 8, 11]$$

17.2 Starr's Prime-Form Algorithm

As pointed out by Daniel Starr, these operations can be combined to implement a fast prime-form algorithm. The set is represented as a bit vector S and its inverse S'. Then S and S' are each left-rotated eleven times.[5] The rotation that yields the smallest integer value represents the prime form. The number of rotations required to get this value is the number of semitones by which the set must be transposed to get the prime form, i.e., n in $T_n(S)$ or $T_nI(S)$. As an example, consider finding the prime form of the set [1, 4, 5]. In table 17.2, r is the rotation, the decimal value of the bit vector is shown in parentheses, and the pitch classes in the set are shown in brackets. Since the smallest bit vector is 19, [0, 1, 4] is the prime form. Because this set is obtained after inversion and five left rotations, we know that the operation T_5I maps set S into its prime form. For symmetric sets, the smallest number occurs in more than one position, i.e., the prime form can be generated at more than one level of transposition or transposition after inversion ($T_n(S)$ or $T_nI(S)$). Note also that for each rotation r, the set S = [1, 4, 5] maps into the new set under the operation $T_r(S)$ or $T_rI(S)$.

r	*bit vector*	*pcs*	*bit vector*	*pcs*
0	000000110010 (50)	[145]	100110000000 (2432)	[78b]
1	000001100100 (100)	[256]	001100000001 (769)	[089]
2	000011001000 (200)	[367]	011000000010 (1538)	[19a]
3	000110010000 (400)	[478]	110000000100 (3076)	[2ab]
4	001100100000 (800)	[589]	100000001001 (2057)	[03b]
5	011001000000 (1600)	[69a]	000000010011 (**19**)	[014]
6	110010000000 (3200)	[7ab]	000000100110 (38)	[125]
7	100100000001 (2305)	[08b]	000001001100 (76)	[236]
8	001000000011 (515)	[019]	000010011000 (152)	[347]
9	010000000110 (1030)	[12a]	000100110000 (304)	[458]
a	100000001100 (2060)	[23b]	001001100000 (608)	[569]
b	000000011001 (25)	[034]	010011000000 (1216)	[67a]

Table 17.2. Finding the Prime Form of [145] using Starr's Algorithm

5. Daniel Starr, "Sets, Invariance and Partitions," *Journal of Music Theory* 22, no. 1 (1978): 1–42, indicates in a footnote that Bo Alphonce had independently arrived at the binary representation of sets and their uses in programming. Others have used the technique as well; this author learned of it from Leland Smith (Stanford University) in 1974.

Set Name	Starr/Rahn Prime Form (*bitvec*)		Forte Prime Form (*bitvec*)	
5-20	01568	(355)	01378	(395)
6-29	023679	(717)	013689	(843)
6-31	014579	(691)	013589	(811)
7-18	0145679	(755)	0123589	(815)
7-20	0125679	(743)	0124789	(919)
8-26	0134578a	(1467)	0124579a	(1719)

Table 17.3. Variant Prime Forms Using Starr and Forte Algorithms

This algorithm generates the same prime form as the manual method described by Rahn but yields a different prime form from that described by Forte for the six sets shown in table 17.3.[6] Note that in each case the bit vector representing the prime form for the Starr/Rahn algorithm is less than that for the Forte prime form. This has significance for the program described on the following pages.

17.3 Program *Setid*: Specifications

The program described below was designed to meet the following specifications:

Function. The program will identify pc sets input either as collections of pitch classes or as set names. For each input, it will identify the normal form of the set, the set name, the prime form of the set class, the twelve-tone operator that generates the set from the prime form, the interval-class vector, the Z- and M/MI-related sets, and symmetric sets.[7] The user should be able to specify prime forms a la Forte or Starr/Rahn, and should be able to switch forms at will. The program must have clear on-line instructions and must be robust, i.e., it should be tolerant of user input errors.

Input. Input will consist of pc sets in hexadecimal notation, i.e., the digits 0123456789ab represent the integers 0 through 11. This scheme obviates spaces or commas, thus minimizing keystrokes necessary for input and space required for output. All pcs on a single line will constitute a pitch collection, and the program will

6. John Rahn, (*Basic Atonal Theory* [New York and London: Longman, 1980]) does not use set names, but identifies sets by their prime form. Robert Morris (*Composition with Pitch-Classes* [New Haven: Yale University Press, 1987]) uses Rahn's prime forms with Forte's set names. Implementations of Forte's and Rahn's algorithms are described in detail later in this chapter.

7. Z-related sets are sets that have the same interval-class content (as indicated by the interval vector), but cannot be reduced to the same prime form by transposition or transposition after inversion (see Forte, *Structure of Atonal Music*). The M/MI set is the set class obtained by multiplying each element of the set by 5 or 7, and then finding the prime form of the resulting set. The primary characteristic of this transformation is mapping semitones into fifths and vice versa (see Hubert Howe, "Some Combinational Properties of Pitch Structures," *Perspectives of New Music* 4, no. 1 (1965): 45–61; Rahn, *Basic Atonal Theory*; and Morris, *Composition with Pitch-Classes*). Symmetric sets can be mapped into the prime form by transposition or by transposition after inversion.

remove duplicates. Set names will be entered as the cardinal number of the set, a dash, and the ordinal number of the set, e.g. 3-6, 6-29, or 4-16.[8] In addition, the program will accept substitute characters for 'a' and 'b'. These are initialized to 't' and 'e' (for ten and eleven) but may be reset by the user, who may wish to use 'x' and 'y' or even special characters such as ',' and '.' in order to enter all data from a numeric keypad. The following special characters will be recognized when entered as the first character of an input line:

'?' or 'h' : print instruction summary
'*' : reset substitute characters for 10 and 11
'!' : reset prime-form type

The program, which is designed to run interactively, prompts the user for input and terminates when the user types the end-of-file mark (Control-D) or <rubout>.

Output. For each valid input (pitch collection or set name) the program will identify normal order, the set name, the prime form, the twelve-tone operator that maps the prime form into the input set, and the Z- and M/MI-related sets. It will also flag sets that are inversionally symmetric. For erroneous input, an error message will be printed with an arrow pointing to the offending character in the input line.

17.4 Implementation

The program allows the user to specify which prime form he or she wishes to use. Prime forms are calculated with the bitwise algorithm; then if the Forte form is desired and the set is one of the variant set classes, the bit vector and transposition level are modified to correspond to the Forte representation.

Once the bit vector representing the appropriate prime form has been found, other information is obtained by a table lookup. The table is indexed by bit vectors, sorted in numeric order within each cardinality class. Thus binary search is used on maximally short lists for rapid location of the set. In addition to the bit vector, the table (an array of records), contains the ordinal number of the set class and the ordinal number of the Z- and M/MI-related sets. The interval vector is calculated for each set; this does not take long and saves storage space.

The program uses a simple pattern-matching algorithm to check for set-class names in the input. If the input is a valid set name, a linear-search algorithm is used to locate the set by its ordinal number. Only the sets in the correct cardinality class are searched. When the Forte prime form differs from that generated by the Starr algorithm, the former always occurs after the latter in the table. Thus the sublists are searched in order (by array index) for Starr/Rahn sets, and in reverse order for Forte forms.

To facilitate this table structure we use an ancillary table, called *loc*, which contains the starting and ending position of each cardinality class in the main table.

8. These set names were first proposed by Forte (*Structure of Atonal Music*) and are retained by Morris (*Composition with Pitch-Classes*). Forte uses a Z before the ordinal number of the set to indicate the Z-relation. In this program, sets will be entered without the Z, i.e., 4-Z15 will be entered as 4-15.

These end points are used as the limits for binary search when we are looking for a prime form, and for linear search when looking for set names. Handling of errors and special cases is facilitated by an internal character buffer that holds one line of input.

The data read into the data tables is shown in figure 17.1. The first portion is the data stored in *loc* and the remainder is that stored in *table*. Note that annotations documenting the table are not part of the data and are skipped (via *readln*) by the procedure that reads the table. The first part of the data, labeled [LOC], contains the location of each cardinality class in the larger table. For example, the first line indicates that the one-note set is found in *table*[1], the third line that three-note sets are located in *table*[8] through *table*[19], etc. The second part of the data, labeled [SET TABLE], contains the data for each set class: the bit vector, the ordinal number of the set (from the second part of the set name), and the ordinal number of the Z- and M-related sets. The comments in square brackets indicate the location of set classes and the index of the array. The data is listed in two-column format here to save space; obviously, the actual file is in single-column format.

```
  1   1  [cardinality 1 ] [LOC]
  2   7  [cardinality 2 ]
  8  19  [cardinality 3 ]
 20  48  [cardinality 4 ]
 49  87  [cardinality 5 ]
 88 139  [cardinality 6 ]
140 179  [cardinality 7 ]
180 209  [cardinality 8 ]
210 221  [cardinality 9 ]
222 227  [cardinality 10]
228 228  [cardinality 11]
229 229  [cardinality 12]

   1  1  0  1   [ SET TABLE  ] [  1]

   3  1  0  5   [ 2-note sets] [  2]
   5  2  0  2                  [  3]
   9  3  0  3                  [  4]
  17  4  0  4                  [  5]
  33  5  0  1                  [  6]
  65  6  0  6                  [  7]

   7  1  0  9   [ 3-note sets] [  8]
  11  2  0  7
  19  3  0 11
  21  6  0  6
  35  4  0  4
  37  7  0  2
  67  5  0  5
  69  8  0  8
  73 10  0 10
 133  9  0  1
 137 11  0  3
 273 12  0 12                  [ 19]
```

```
 15  1  0 23   [ 4-note sets] [ 20]
 23  2  0 22
 27  3  0 26
 39  4  0 14
 43 11  0 11
 45 10  0 10
 51  7  0 20
 71  5  0 16
 75 13  0 13
 77 12  0 27
 83 15 29 29
 85 21  0 21
 99  8  0  8
135  6  0  6
139 29 15 15
141 14  0  4
147 18  0 18
149 22  0  2
153 17  0 17
163 16  0  5
165 23  0  1
195  9  0  9
275 19  0 19
277 24  0 24
291 20  0  7
293 27  0 12
297 26  0  3
325 25  0 25
585 28  0 28                  [ 48]

 31  1  0 35   [ 5-note sets] [ 49]
 47  2  0 23
 55  3  0 27
 79  4  0 29
```

```
  87  9  0 24
  91 10  0 25
  93  8  0 34
 103  6  0 20
 107 12 36 12
 143  5  0 14
 151 36 12 36
 155 16  0 32
 157 11  0 11
 167 14  0  5
 171 24  0  9
 173 23  0  2
 179 18 38 38
 199  7  0  7
 203 19  0 19
 279 13  0 30
 283 17 37 37
 295 38 18 18
 299 27  0  3
 301 25  0 10
 307 21  0 21
 309 26  0 26
 313 37 17 17
 327 15  0 15
 331 29  0  4
 333 28  0 28
 339 30  0 13
 341 33  0 33
 355 20  0  6  [Rahn's  5-20]
 395 20  0  6  [Forte's 5-20]
 403 22  0 22
 587 31  0 31
 595 32  0 16
 597 34  0  8
 661 35  0  1                 [ 87]

  63  1  0 32  [ 6-note sets] [ 88]
  95  2  0 33
 111  3 36 25
 119  4 37 26
 159 36  3 47
 175  9  0  9
 183 11 40 40
 187 10 39 46
 189  8  0  8
 207  5  0 18
 215 12 41 12
 219 13 42 50
 231  6 38 38
 287 37  4 48
 303 40 11 11
 311 15  0 31
 315 14  0 14
 317 39 10 24
 335 41 12 41
 343 22  0 22
 347 24 46 39
 349 21  0 34
 359 43 17 43
 363 25 47  3
 365 23 45 23
 371 16  0 16
 399 38  6  6
 407 17 43 17
 411 19 44 44
 423 18  0  5
 427 26 48  4
 455  7  0  7
 591 42 13 29
 599 46 24 10
 603 27  0 27
 605 45 23 45
 615 44 19 19
 619 28 49 28
 663 47 25 36
 667 49 28 49
 679 48 26 37
 683 34  0 21
 685 33  0  2
 691 31  0 15  [Rahn's  6-31]
 693 32  0  1
 715 30  0 30
 717 29 50 42  [Rahn's  6-29]
 723 50 29 13
 811 31  0 15  [Forte's 6-31]
 819 20  0 20
 843 29 50 42  [Forte's 6-29]
1365 35  0 35                 [139]

 127  1  0 35  [ 7-note sets] [140]
 191  2  0 23
 223  4  0 29
 239  5  0 14
 319  3  0 27
 351  9  0 24
 367 36 12 36
 375 13  0 30
 379 11  0 11
 381  8  0 34
 415  6  0 20
 431 14  0  5
 439 38 18 18
 443 37 17 17
 463  7  0  7
 471 15  0 15
 607 10  0 25
 623 16  0 32
 631 17 37 37
 671 12 36 12
 687 24  0  9
 695 27  0  3
 699 26  0 26
 701 23  0  2
 719 19  0 19
```

```
 727 29  0  4
 731 31  0 31
 733 25  0 10
 743 20  0  6  [Rahn's  7-20]
 747 28  0 28
 755 18 38 38  [Rahn's  7-18]
 815 18 38 38  [Forte's 7-18]
 823 21  0 21
 855 30  0 13
 859 32  0 16
 871 22  0 22
 919 20  0  6  [Forte's 7-20]
1367 33  0 33
1371 34  0  8
1387 35  0  1                 [179]

 255  1  0 23  [ 8-note sets] [180]
 383  2  0 22
 447  4  0 14
 479  5  0 16
 495  6  0  6
 639  3  0 26
 703 11  0 11
 735 13  0 13
 751 29 15 15
 759 14  0  4
 763 12  0 27
 765 10  0 10
 831  7  0 20
 863 15 29 29
 879 18  0 18
 887 19  0 19
 891 17  0 17
 927  8  0  8
 943 16  0  5
 951 20  0  7
 975  9  0  9
1375 21  0 21
1391 22  0  2
1399 24  0 24
1455 23  0  1
1463 27  0 12
1467 26  0  3  [Rahn's  8-26]
1495 25  0 25
1719 26  0  3  [Forte's 8-26]
1755 28  0 28                 [209]

 511  1  0  9  [ 9-note sets] [210]
 767  2  0  7
 895  3  0 11
 959  4  0  4
 991  5  0  5
1407  6  0  6
1471  7  0  2
1503  8  0  8
1519  9  0  1
1759 10  0 10
1775 11  0  3
1911 12  0 12                 [221]

1023  1  0  5  [10-note sets] [222]
1535  2  0  2
1791  3  0  3
1919  4  0  4
1983  5  0  1
2015  6  0  6                 [227]

2047  1  0  1  [11-note sets] [228]

4095  1  0  1  [12-note sets] [229]
```

Figure 17.1. Tables Read from External Data File

17.5 The Program

The basic structure of the program, as implemented in the main procedure, is shown below in pseudo code.

```
begin { main }
  initialize substitute characters for 10 and 11 to 'a' and 'b';
  set the desired prime-form type;
  read the data tables from an external file;
  prompt the user for a set;
  while not at end of file do
    begin
      read a pc set and return status code;
      if no errors or special requests are detected
        then
          begin
            calculate the prime form, etc.
            print the results
          end
        else take required action for error or request
      prompt the user for a set
    end
end. { main }
```

Flexibility is incorporated at several points. For example, the procedure that reads the pc set first checks the buffer. If it contains a set name, the prime form of the set is found in the table; if it is a pc set, the set is returned. This procedure also returns a status code. This value is 0 if a set was read successfully, or some nonzero value indicating an error condition or a request for special action, e.g., reset the prime-form type or reset characters to use for 10 and 11 on input.

Details can be found in the program listing and discussion below. The program is discussed "bottom-up" (in the order of the program listing) rather than "top-down" so that it does not need to appear in a separate listing. Note, however, that the program was written using the top-down technique. A sample interactive run appears at the end of the program.

The program uses the standard input and output files to communicate with the user and one external file to read the stored data into tables. The maximum input line length is set to 85 characters.

```
program setid(input, output, setdata);
  const
    maxline = 85;
```

The array type *ar100* is used for storing pc sets. *Pftype* is an enumerated type, which will indicate the desired prime-form type. An internal buffer is declared through use of a record that includes an array, *B*, and a position indicator, *bp*. Type *ar300* will be used for the primary table, an array of records of type *fset*. The contents of each record are documented in the comments. Most of the array types are not named mnemonically since some are used for more than one purpose, but names unlikely to be used by another programmer are used in case this program is incorporated into a larger program that needs access to set information.

```
type
  ar100 = array[1 .. 12] of integer;

  pftype = (Forte, Rahn);          { prime-form type                              }

  buftype = record
              B  : array[1 .. maxline] of char;
              bp : integer
            end;

  fset = record
           z      : integer;     { number of Z-related set, 0 if none     }
           mmi    : integer;     { set resulting from M5 or M7            }
           name   : integer;     { ordinal position in list               }
           bitvec : integer      { summation 2**pc[i] for i = 1 to card   }
         end;

  ar300 = array[1 .. 229] of fset;
```

Type *ar600* will be used to store the beginning and ending positions of each cardinality class in the larger table. This type is an array of records of type *tabinfo*. This will be used for the table *loc*, such that *loc*[*n*].*start* and *loc*[*n*].*stop* contain the limits of the sublist of the primary table containing sets of cardinality *n*.

```
  tabinfo = record
              start : integer;    { loc[n] = loc in table of beginning    }
              stop  : integer     { end of sublist for cardinality n      }
            end;

  ar600 = array[1 .. 12] of tabinfo;
```

Set information will be passed between procedures in a record of type *setinfo*. The record will be passed by reference, so that only the address of the record will actually be placed on the stack. Individual components or substructures of the record can also be passed when necessary.

```
  setinfo = record                        { information record          }
              trans     : integer;        { transposition level         }
              form      : char;           { 'p' or 'i'                  }
              card      : integer;        { cardinality of set          }
              z         : integer;        { Z-related set or 0          }
              name      : integer;        { ordinal number of set       }
              mmi       : integer;        { set obtained by M5 or M7    }
              pcset     : ar100;          { the given pitch-class set   }
              prime     : ar100;          { prime form of set           }
              vector    : ar100;          { interval vector for set     }
              symmetric : boolean         { true if inv = prime         }
            end;
```

The declaration of global variables follows. Their use is described in the comments following each declaration and in the documentation for the rest of the program.

```
var
  primetype    : pftype;          { prime-form type                   }
  buffer       : buftype;         { programs input buffer             }
  setdata      : text;            { data file                         }
  table        : ar300;           { internal table                    }
  loc          : ar600;           { loc of sets in table by card      }
  dat          : setinfo;         { record, returns all pc-set info   }
  code         : integer;         { return code for readset           }
  asub, bsub   : char;            { keyboard substitutes for a and b  }
```

Function *power* returns the powers of 2 from 2^0 to 2^{11}. These will be used in constructing bit vectors for pc sets.

```
function power(x : integer) : integer;                  { powers of 2 }
  begin
    case x of
       0 : power :=    1;
       1 : power :=    2;
       2 : power :=    4;
       3 : power :=    8;
       4 : power :=   16;
       5 : power :=   32;
       6 : power :=   64;
       7 : power :=  128;
       8 : power :=  256;
       9 : power :=  512;
      10 : power := 1024;
      11 : power := 2048
    end { case }
  end;
```

Procedures *incr* and *decr* need no further explanation at this point. These operations are implemented as procedures to aid clarity in the rest of the program.

```
procedure incr(var x : integer);
  begin
    x := x + 1
  end;

procedure decr(var x : integer);
  begin
    x := x - 1
  end;
```

Two character functions are declared, returning the tab and null characters. Function *tab* is used primarily in output routines and by the procedure that skips spaces in the input file. Function *null* is used by the buffer procedures, since in our implementation a null character marks the end of useful information in the buffer.

```
function tab : char;
  begin
    tab := chr(9)
  end;

function null : char;
  begin
    null := chr(0)
  end;
```

A number of boolean functions will be used to test characters in the buffer. In general, *isXXX(ch)* is *true* if *ch* is an *XXX*. The functions test for digits, signs, upper- and lowercase alphabetic characters, command characters, and characters that represent pcs.

```
function isdigit(ch : char): boolean;
  begin
    isdigit := ch in ['0' .. '9']
  end;

function issign(c : char) : boolean;
  begin
    issign := c in ['-', '+']
  end;

function isupper(ch : char) : boolean;
  begin
    isupper := ch in ['A' .. 'B']
  end;

function islower(ch : char) : boolean;
  begin
    islower := ch in ['a' .. 'b']
  end;

function iscommand(ch : char) : boolean;
  begin
    iscommand := ch in ['h', 'H', '?', '*', '!']
  end;

function ispc(ch : char) : boolean;
  begin
    ispc := isdigit(ch) or (ch in ['a', 'b', 'A', 'B', asub, bsub])
  end;
```

The following procedures implement an internal buffer that stores one line of the user's input. These procedures were discussed in section 11.2. They are modified here to use a file parameter and to take advantage of the structured definition of the buffer. *Getline* reads one line into the buffer. Here we do not test the length of the line, since an input line is not likely to approach the declared maximum line length of 84 characters.

```
procedure getline(var f : text; var buffer : buftype);
  begin
    with buffer do
      begin
        bp := 1;
        while not eoln(f) and (bp < maxline) do
          begin
            read(f, B[bp]);
            incr(bp)
          end;
        B[bp] := null;                                  { mark end of line }
        if not eoln(f)
          then writeln('Getline: warning, input line truncated');
        readln;
        bp := 1                        { reset index at beginning of buffer }
      end
  end;
```

Function *eob* returns *true* when the buffer position indicator *bp* is at the end of the buffer. Thus it functions much like Pascal's *eoln* function.

```
function eob(var buffer : buftype) : boolean;
  begin
    with buffer do
      eob := B[bp] = null
  end;
```

Function *nextchar* returns the next character in the buffer without advancing *bp*, thus it functions like Pascal's *input*↑.

```
function nextchar(var buffer : buftype) : char;
  begin
    with buffer do
      if eob(buffer)
        then nextchar := ' '
        else nextchar := B[bp]
  end;
```

Procedure *getchar* returns the next character in the buffer and increments the buffer position indicator.

```
procedure getchar(var buffer : buftype; var c : char);
  begin
    with buffer do
      begin
        c := B[bp];
        if not eob(buffer)
          then incr(bp)
      end
  end;
```

Skipbuf skips over blanks and tab characters in the buffer, finding the next non-blank character or the null character marking the end of the buffer.

```
procedure skipbuf(var buffer : buftype);
  begin
    while (nextchar(buffer) in [' ', tab]) and not eob(buffer) do
      incr(buffer.bp)
  end;
```

Procedure *printbuffer* prints the contents of the buffer with a pointer to the current buffer position. This procedure will be called when an error is encountered.

```
procedure printbuffer(var buffer : buftype);
  var
    i : integer;
  begin { printbuffer }
    with buffer do
      begin
        write('buffer: ');
        i := 1;
        while B[i] <> null do
          begin
            write(B[i]);
            incr(i)
          end;
        writeln;
        write('error:  ');
        for i := 1 to bp - 1 do
          write('-');
        writeln('^')
      end
  end;  { printbuffer }
```

Procedure *getint* reads an integer from the buffer, using function *toint* to convert characters to digits. Procedure *error* is declared *forward*, since it will occur later in the program.

```
function toint(c : char) : integer;
  begin
    toint := ord(c) - ord('0')
  end;

procedure error(var buffer : buftype; key : integer); forward;

procedure getint(var buffer : buftype; var x : integer);
  var
    negative : boolean;
  begin
    with buffer do
      begin
        skipbuf(buffer);                              { skip blanks     }
        negative := nextchar(buffer) = '-';           { check for sign }
        if issign(nextchar(buffer))
          then incr(bp);                              { skip sign       }
        if not isdigit(nextchar(buffer))
          then error(buffer, 7)                       { digit expected }
          else
```

```
            begin { read number }
              x := 0;
              while isdigit(nextchar(buffer)) do
                begin
                  x := 10 * x + toint(nextchar(buffer));
                  incr(bp)
                end
            end; { read number }
        if negative
          then x := -x
      end
  end;
```

Function *affirmative* (section 15.3.1) is modified here to read the user's response into the buffer before testing.

```
function affirmative(var buffer : buftype) : boolean;
  begin
    getline(input, buffer);
    skipbuf(buffer);  { skip blanks }
    if nextchar(buffer) = 'y'
      then affirmative := true
    else if nextchar(buffer) = 'n'
      then affirmative := false
    else
      begin
        write('Please answer yes or no: ');
        affirmative := affirmative(buffer)        { call this procedure }
      end
  end;
```

Procedure *init* assigns initial values to *asub* and *bsub*, the input substitutes for hexadecimal 'a' and 'b'.

```
procedure init(var asub, bsub : char);
  begin
    asub := 't';                                 { ten    }
    bsub := 'e'                                  { eleven }
  end;
```

Readtable reads the set data from an external file into the *loc* and *table* arrays. This is called only once, from the main procedure.

```
procedure readtable(var setdata : text; var loc : ar600;
                                         var table : ar300);
  var
    i : integer;
  begin { read external data into tables }
    reset(setdata);
    for i := 1 to 12 do                          { read loc table }
      with loc[i] do
        readln(setdata, start, stop);
    for i := 1 to 229 do                         { read set table }
      with table[i] do
        readln(setdata, bitvec, name, z, mmi)
  end;
```

The following functions and procedures convert a set stored in an array to a bit vector and vice versa. Function *pencode* makes a direct translation from the array to the bit vector. The set is stored in the *pcset* array, and the cardinality of the set is *n*. The initial value of the bit vector is 0, indicating the null set. For each *pc* in the set, 2^{pc} is added to the bit vector, effectively setting the appropriate bit in the binary number.

```
function pencode(var pcset : ar100; n : integer) : integer;
  var
    t : integer;            { temp variable representing the bit vector }
    i : integer;
  begin
    t := 0;                                               { null set }
    for i := 1 to n do
      t := t + power(pcset[i]);                           { set bit  }
    pencode := t
  end; { pencode }
```

Function *iencode* performs the same function as *pencode*, except that it returns the bit vector representing T_0I of the set stored in *pcset*. The method was explained earlier in this chapter.

```
function iencode(var pcset : ar100; n : integer) : integer;
  var
    t : integer;  { bit vector }
    i : integer;
  begin
    t := 0;                                               { null set }
    for i := 1 to n do
      t := t + power((12 - pcset[i]) mod 12);             { set bit  }
    iencode := t
  end;  { iencode }
```

Procedure *decode* decodes the bit vector *x*, storing the pcs in the array *A* and the cardinality of the set in *n*.

```
procedure decode(x : integer; var A : ar100; var n : integer);
  var
    pc : integer;
  begin
    n := 0;                                     { cardinality      }
    pc := 0;
    while x > 0 do
      begin
        if odd(x)                               { if last bit is 1 }
          then
            begin
              incr(n);
              A[n] := pc
            end;
        incr(pc);
        x := x div 2                            { right shift      }
      end
  end;  { decode }
```

We will now examine the procedures used to implement the prime-form algorithm. Procedure *rotate* left-rotates the the rightmost twelve bits of a binary integer. Multiplication by 2 shifts all bits to the left. If the new number is greater than 4095, indicating that bit 12 has been set to 1, then this bit is set to 0 and bit 0 is set to 1.

```
procedure rotate(var x : integer);
  begin
    x := x * 2;
    if x > 4095
      then x := x - 4095
  end;
```

After the bit vector representing the prime form is found, procedure *adjust* can be used to map the bit vector and transposition level into those appropriate for the Forte prime form. The procedure checks the bit vector against each of the six variant forms and makes the appropriate adjustments.

```
procedure adjust(var bitvec, trans : integer);
  begin
    if bitvec = 355                                        { 5-20 }
      then
        begin
          bitvec := 395;
          trans := trans + 7
        end
    else if bitvec = 691                                   { 6-31 }
      then
        begin
          bitvec := 811;
          trans := trans + 8
        end
    else if bitvec = 717                                   { 6-29 }
      then
        begin
          bitvec := 843;
          trans := trans + 6
        end
    else if bitvec = 743                                   { 7-20 }
      then
        begin
          bitvec := 919;
          trans := trans + 7
        end
    else if bitvec = 755                                   { 7-18 }
      then
        begin
          bitvec := 815;
          trans := trans + 8
        end
    else if bitvec = 1467                                  { 8-26 }
      then
        begin
          bitvec := 1719;
          trans := trans + 9
        end
  end;  { adjust }
```

Function *primeform* returns the bit vector representing the prime form, calculated using Starr's algorithm. It uses variable parameters to return the form of the subject set relative to the prime form (*p* for prime or *i* for inverted), the transposition level to map the prime form into the subject, and a value set to *true* if the set is inversionally symmetric. Functions *pencode* and *iencode* are called to calculate the bit vectors of the set and its inversion. As described in the introductory section of this chapter, the prime form is the rotation of the original bit vector or its inversion that yields the smallest integer value. If the parameter *primetype* is set to *Forte*, procedure *adjust* is called to convert the values to those appropriate for the Forte prime form.

```
function primeform(primetype      : pftype;          { Forte or Rahn    }
                   var pcset      : ar100;           { pc set           }
                   n              : integer;         { cardinality      }
                   var form       : char;            { p or i           }
                   var trans      : integer;         { n in Tn or TnI   }
                   var symmetric  : boolean)         { true if p = i    }
                                  : integer;         { return type      }
 var
   p, i           : integer;         { set numbers for T0 and T0I        }
   plow, ilow     : integer;         { lowest p or i bitvec              }
   ptrans, itrans : integer;         { n for lowest value of tn or tni   }
   j              : integer;         { transposition level               }

 begin { primeform }
   p := pencode(pcset,n);                       { bitvec for prime form     }
   plow := p;
   i := iencode(pcset,n);                       { bitvec for inversion      }
   ilow := i;
   ptrans := 0; itrans := 0;

   for j := 1 to 11 do                          { check other trans levels  }
     begin
       rotate(p);                               { transpose 1 semitone      }
       if p < plow
         then
           begin
              plow := p;
              ptrans := j
           end;
       rotate(i);                               { transpose 1 semitone      }
       if i < ilow
         then
           begin
              ilow := i;
              itrans :=  j
           end
     end;

   symmetric := (plow = ilow);                     { check for symmetry  }
   if plow <= ilow
     then
       begin { Tn(plow) }
         if primetype = Forte
           then adjust(plow,ptrans);               { change prime form   }
         primeform := plow;
```

```
          form := 'P';
          trans := (12 - ptrans) mod 12
        end  { Tn(plow) }
      else
        begin { TnI(plow) }
          if primetype = Forte
            then adjust(ilow, itrans);                { change prime form  }
          primeform := ilow;
          form := 'I';
          trans := itrans mod 12
        end   { TnI(plow) }
  end;  { primeform }
```

Setname is a simple pattern-matching function that checks for a valid set name in the buffer. This function was described in section 11.4.

```
function setname(var buffer : buftype) : boolean;
  var
    t : integer;

  procedure skip;
    begin
      with buffer do
        while B[t] = ' ' do
          incr(t)
    end;

  function digits : boolean;
    begin
      skip;
      with buffer do
        begin
          digits := isdigit(B[t]);
          while isdigit(B[t]) do
            incr(t)
        end
    end;

  function dash : boolean;
    begin
      skip;
      with buffer do
        if B[t] = '-'
          then begin
                 dash := true;
                 incr(t)
               end
          else dash := false
    end;

  begin { setname }
    t := buffer.bp;                       { copy bp so we don't change it }
    setname := false;
    if digits
      then if dash
        then setname := digits
  end;  { setname }
```

Procedure *getname* reads a set name from the buffer. It uses variable parameters to return the cardinal number and ordinal number, and skips the intervening dash and any blanks. This procedure is called only after function *setname* has determined that a name actually occurs in the buffer.

```
procedure getname(var buffer : buftype; var cardinal, ordinal : integer);
  begin
    with buffer do
      begin
        getint(buffer, cardinal);
        skipbuf(buffer);
        incr(bp); { skip dash }
        getint(buffer, ordinal)
      end
  end;
```

Procedure *getpc*, which reads a pitch class from the buffer, returns a pitch-class integer or –1 to signal an input error.

```
procedure getpc(var buffer : buftype; var pc : integer);
  begin
    skipbuf(buffer);
    if ispc(nextchar(buffer))
      then
        begin
          if isdigit(nextchar(buffer))
            then pc := ord(nextchar(buffer)) - ord('0')
          else if islower(nextchar(buffer))
            then pc := ord(nextchar(buffer)) - ord('a') + 10
          else if isupper(nextchar(buffer))
            then pc := ord(nextchar(buffer)) - ord('A') + 10
          else if nextchar(buffer) = asub
            then pc := 10
          else if nextchar(buffer) = bsub
            then pc := 11;
          incr(buffer.bp)                      { advance buffer pointer }
        end
      else pc := -1                            { return error code      }
  end;
```

Three functions are used to search the primary data table. When we wish to search for a bit vector, function *binsearch* is used. This procedure is passed the array *table*, the upper and lower limits of the cardinality class, and *x*, the bit vector that is the object of the search. The function returns the index of *x* in the table, or 0 if *x* is not found. (The latter should not occur in this program.)

```
function binsearch(var A : ar300; lower, upper : integer;
                                              x : integer) : integer;
  var
    mid, answer : integer;
  begin { binary search }
    answer := 0;
```

```
    while (upper >= lower) and (answer = 0) do
      begin
        mid := (lower + upper) div 2;
        if A[mid].bitvec = x
          then answer := mid
        else if x > A[mid].bitvec
          then lower := mid + 1
        else upper := mid - 1
      end;
    binsearch := answer
  end;  { binary search }
```

Lineara and *linearb* perform linear searches of the table. Each searches *A*[*i*], *lower* <= *i* <= *upper*, for *x* (the ordinal number from a set name). *Upper* and *lower* are passed as the limits of the cardinality class in the table. The functions return the index of the set in the table, or 0 if the set name is not found. The latter may occur if an illegal set name is entered by the user. *Lineara* and *linearb* differ in that the former searches the table segment from *lower* to *upper*, and the latter searches the same segment in reverse order from *upper* to *lower*. Thus *lineara* is used for locating Starr/Rahn prime forms, and *linearb* for locating Forte's prime forms.

```
function lineara(var A : ar300; lower, upper : integer; x : integer)
                                                            : integer;
  var
    i : integer;
  begin { forward linear search }
    i := lower;
    while (i < upper) and (A[i].name <> x) do
      incr(i);
    if A[i].name = x
      then lineara := i
      else lineara := 0
  end;  { forward linear search }

function linearb(var A : ar300; lower, upper : integer; x : integer)
                                                            : integer;
  var
    i : integer;
  begin { backward linear search }
    i := upper;
    while (i > lower) and (A[i].name <> x) do
      decr(i);
    if A[i].name = x
      then linearb := i
      else linearb := 0
  end;  { backward linear search }
```

Procedure *lookup* is called when a set name is detected in the buffer. The procedure uses variable parameters to return a pc set (as an array), the cardinality of the set, and a "return code" that indicates all is well (*code* = 0) or the set name was erroneous (*code* = 1). It calls *getname* to read the components of the name from the buffer. If the cardinality is less than 1 or greater than 12, *code* is set to 1. If the cardinality is within range, the appropriate linear search function is called to find the set. The *loc* array is used to find the limits of the cardinality class in the main table. If the search routine does not find the set (the set name is erroneous), *code* is set to 1; otherwise the bit vector is decoded into its pcs, which are stored in an array, and its cardinality. The set and cardinality are returned to the calling procedure (see below).

```
procedure lookup(var buffer : buftype; var pcset : ar100;
                 var n : integer; primetype : pftype; var code : integer);
  var
    c, o : integer;                      { cardinal and ordinal part of name }
    x    : integer;                      { location of set c-o in table      }
  begin  { lookup }
    code := 0;                           { begin with good return code       }
    getname(buffer, c, o);                         { read set name   }
    if (c < 1) or (c > 12)
      then code := 1                               { bad set name    }
      else
        begin { find set in table via linear search }
          if primetype = Forte
            then x := linearb(table, loc[c].start, loc[c].stop, o)
            else x := lineara(table, loc[c].start, loc[c].stop, o);
          if x = 0                                 { didn't find it }
            then code := 1                         { bad set name    }
            else decode(table[x].bitvec, pcset, n)
        end   { find set in table via linear search }
  end;  { lookup }
```

Procedure *readset* attempts to read a pc set. If it succeeds, the set and its cardinality are returned. The parameter *code* is set to 0 to indicate a successful read, or to various integers greater than 0 to indicate errors or requests for special action (resetting the prime-form type or substitute characters for entering pcs 10 and 11, or printing instructions). The procedure first reads an input line into the buffer. If the line contains a set name, procedure *lookup* is called to find the set. Otherwise, we attempt to read a pc set from the buffer. A set type variable *check* is used to weed out duplicates (chapter 13). If the first nonblank character in the buffer is one of those chosen to indicate requests for special action, *code* is set to an appropriate nonzero value. Otherwise the set is stored in *pcset*, and its cardinality in *n*. Finally, if the set is null, this fact is signaled by a return code.

```
procedure readset(var buffer : buftype; var pcset : ar100;
                  var n : integer; primetype : pftype; var code : integer);
  type
    pcs = 0 .. 11;
    pset = set of pcs;
  var
    pc    : integer;
    check : pset;
  begin
    getline(input, buffer);
    if setname(buffer)
      then lookup(buffer, pcset, n, primetype, code) { get from table    }
      else
```

```
      begin
        check := [];                                    { null set            }
        n := 0;                                         { cardinality         }
        code := 0;                                      { signal OK           }
        skipbuf(buffer);
        if iscommand(nextchar(buffer))
          then
            case nextchar(buffer) of
              '?','h','H': code := 4;                   { request for help    }
              '*'        : code := 5;                   { reset asub & bsub   }
              '!'        : code := 6                    { reset prime type    }
            end; { case }
        while not eob(buffer) and (code = 0) do
          begin
            getpc(buffer, pc);
            if pc >= 0
              then
                begin
                  if not (pc in check)
                    then
                      begin
                        incr(n);
                        pcset[n] := pc;
                        check := check + [pc]
                      end;
                  skipbuf(buffer)
                end
              else code := 2                            { illegal character   }
          end;
        if code = 0                                     { normal return code  }
          then if n = 0                                 { but cardinality = 0}
            then code := 3                              { signal null set     }
      end
  end; { readset }
```

We now examine the output routines. Function *convert* converts a pc integer to its character representation. The hexadecimal digit ‘c’ (12) cannot be a pitch class, but it will be used occasionally to represent the integer 12 in interval vectors.

```
function convert(pc : integer) : char;
  begin
    case pc of
      0 : convert := '0';
      1 : convert := '1';
      2 : convert := '2';
      3 : convert := '3';
      4 : convert := '4';
      5 : convert := '5';
      6 : convert := '6';
      7 : convert := '7';
      8 : convert := '8';
      9 : convert := '9';
     10 : convert := 'A';
     11 : convert := 'B';
     12 : convert := 'C'                    { used in ic vector }
    end  { case }
  end;  { convert }
```

Procedure *printlist* will be called by *printdata* to print the contents of an array. The array may contain a pc set, in which case the second argument is the cardinality of the set, or an interval vector, in which case the second argument is 6.

```
procedure printlist(var list : ar100; n : integer);
  var
    i : integer;
  begin
    for i := 1 to n do
      write(convert(list[i]))
  end;
```

Procedure *printdata* prints the normal form of the original pc set, the derivation (e.g., T3I), the set name, the prime form, and the interval vector. If the set was found to be inversionally symmetric, an additional message is printed.

```
procedure printdata(var dat : setinfo);
  begin
    with dat do
      begin
        write('normal form =', tab, ' ');
        printlist(pcset, card);
        write(' ', tab);
        if card < 6
          then write(tab);
        write('Z =', z:3, ';', tab, 'M/MI =', mmi:3, ';');
        if symmetric
          then write('  P/I symmetric');
        writeln;
        write('= T', convert(trans):1, form:1, '(');
        write(card:1, '-');
        if z <> 0
          then write('Z');
        write(name:1, ')', tab, '{');
        printlist(prime, card);
        write('}', tab);
        if card < 6
          then write(tab);
        write('ic vector = [');
        printlist(vector, 6);
        writeln(']');
        writeln
      end { with dat }
  end;  { printdata }
```

Procedure *setsub* is called when the user wants to change the substitute input characters for pcs 10 and 11. After this is done, the new values are printed and the user is asked to confirm or reject the choices. If the settings are rejected, *setsub* is called recursively.

```
procedure setsub(var buffer : buftype; var asub, bsub : char);
  begin
    write('Type sub for 10: ');
    getline(input, buffer);                          { get line in buffer }
```

```
    skipbuf(buffer);                        { skip blanks         }
    getchar(buffer, asub);                  { read sub for 10     }
    write('Type sub for 11: ');
    getline(input, buffer);                 { get line in buffer  }
    skipbuf(buffer);                        { skip blanks         }
    getchar(buffer, bsub);                  { read sub for 11     }
    writeln(asub,' = A; ', bsub, ' = B');   { double check        }
    write('OK? (y/n): ');
    if not affirmative(buffer)
      then setsub(buffer, asub, bsub)
      else writeln
  end; { setsub }
```

Procedure *newtype* allows the user to set or reset the prime-form type used in the program. If an inappropriate response is typed, the procedure is called recursively.

```
procedure newtype(var buffer : buftype; var primetype : pftype);
  begin
    writeln;
    writeln('Setting prime-form type ...');
    write('Type "Forte" or "Rahn": ');
    getline(input, buffer);
    skipbuf(buffer);                    { skip blanks }
    if nextchar(buffer) in ['f','F','r','R']
      then
        begin { good response }
          if nextchar(buffer) in ['f','F']
            then
              begin
                primetype := Forte;
                writeln('type = Forte')
              end
            else
              begin
                primetype := Rahn;
                writeln('type = Rahn/Morris/Starr')
              end;
          writeln
        end   { good response }
      else
        begin { error }
          writeln('Illegal response');
          newtype(buffer, primetype)
        end   { error }
  end;  { newtype }
```

Procedure *instruct* prints a summary of commands and I/O conventions. This procedure is called on demand whenever the user types '?' or 'help' in response to the prompt 'Type set: '.

```
procedure instruct;
  begin { instruct user }
    writeln;
    writeln('Program Setid - Synopsis:');
    writeln;
```

```
      writeln('to run:     setid <cr>');
      writeln('prompt:     Type set:');
      writeln('input:      pc sets in integer notation with a = 10, b = 11,');
      writeln('              blanks optional, terminate set with <return>');
      writeln('              example: 014ab <return> enters 0 1 4 10 11');
      writeln('              program removes duplicate pcs from input set');
      writeln('              subs for A and B: "', asub, '" = A; "', bsub,
                                                          '" = B');
      writeln('            or set names in the form 3-1, 6-17, etc.');
      writeln('output:     - normal order for set');
      writeln('            - TTO to map prime form into normal order');
      writeln('            - set name');
      writeln('            - prime form');
      writeln('            - number of Z-related set (0 if none)');
      writeln('            - number of M/MI-related set');
      writeln('            - interval-class vector (A = 10, B = 11, C = 12)');
      writeln('commands:   ? or h - print this synopsis');
      writeln('            * - reset special characters for 10 and 11');
      writeln('            ! - reset prime-form type (Forte/Rahn)');
      writeln('messages:   error message and reprompt for bad input');
      writeln('quit:       ^D or <rubout>');
      writeln
    end; { instruct user }
```

Procedure *error* is passed *key*, the status code returned by *readset.* If this value indicates an error, an appropriate message is printed; if it is a request for action, *instruct*, *setsub*, or *newtype* is called.

```
  procedure error{var buffer : buftype; key : integer};
    begin
      case key of
        1 : begin
              writeln('Illegal set name'); writeln
            end;
        2 : begin { input error }
              printbuffer(buffer);
              write('Error: pc = 0|1|2|3|4|5|6|7|8|9|a|b,');
              writeln('  blanks optional');
              writeln
            end;  { input error }
        3 : begin
              writeln('null set');
              writeln
            end;
        4 : instruct;                          { give instructions        }
        5 : setsub(buffer, asub, bsub);        { reset subs for 10 and 11 }
        6 : newtype(buffer, primetype);        { reset prime-form  type   }
        7 : begin
              writeln; writeln;
              writeln('Getint: digit expected');
              writeln;
              printbuffer(buffer)
            end
      end { case }
    end;  { error }
```

Procedure *makevector* calculates an interval-class vector, showing the interval content of the *n*-element pc set stored in *pcset*. (Interval vectors are explained in exercise 4.2 in chapter 10).

```
procedure makevector(var pcset : ar100; n : integer; var ivec : ar100);
  var
    i,j : integer;

  function ic(x : integer) : integer;
    begin
      if x > 6
        then ic := 12 - x
        else ic := x
    end;

  begin { calc interval vector }
    for i := 1 to 6 do                              { initialize vector }
      ivec[i] := 0;
    for i := 1 to n - 1 do
      for j := i + 1 to n do
        incr(ivec[ic(abs(pcset[i] - pcset[j]))])
  end;  { calc interval vector }
```

The ultimate purpose of procedure *calc* is to calculate all of the desired information about a set and store this information in the *dat* record. This structure already contains the pc set and its cardinality. In order to double-check the results, *test* is set to the bit vector representing the set as read. Function *prime* calculates the bit vector representing the prime form of the set and assigns it to *x*. It also sets the fields representing the derivation ('P' or 'I'), the transposition level, and the symmetry flag. Then the bit vector *x* is decoded into the *prime* array. Function *binsearch* finds the location of the set in the main lookup table, and data from this table entry are copied into the appropriate locations in the data record. The interval vector is calculated and stored in the data record. Then the calculated data is used to generate the normal form of the set, which is written over the original set in the *pcset* array. Finally, this set is encoded as a bit vector, which is checked against the bit vector representing the original set, and an error message is printed if the sets do not match. This should never occur if the algorithms are correct.

```
procedure calc(var f : text; primetype : pftype; var dat : setinfo;
                              var loc : ar600; var table : ar300);
  var
    i    : integer;
    pos  : integer;                          { position in table        }
    test : integer;                          { for double checking      }
    x    : integer;                          { prime form as set number }

  begin { calc }
    with dat do
      begin
        test := pencode(pcset, card);
        x := primeform(primetype, pcset, card, form, trans, symmetric);
        decode(x, prime, card);            { store prime form in array }
```

```
        with loc[card] do
          pos := binsearch(table,start,stop,x);

        z     := table[pos].z;               { set other data fields }
        mmi   := table[pos].mmi;
        name  := table[pos].name;
        makevector(prime,card,vector);

        if form = 'P'                      { store normal order in array }
          then
            for i := 1 to card do
              pcset[i] := (prime[i] + trans) mod 12
          else
            for i := 1 to card do
              pcset[i] := (trans - prime[card - i + 1] + 12) mod 12;

        if test <> pencode(pcset,card)               { double-check }
          then writeln(f,'Calc: prime-form error')
      end { with dat }
  end;  { calc }
```

Procedure *prompt* prompts the user for a pc set.

```
procedure prompt;
  begin
    write('Type set: ')
  end;
```

The main procedure initializes the substitute input values *asub* and *bsub*, asks the user to specify the prime-form type, allocates a data node, and reads the external data into tables. Then the user is prompted for input, and *readset* is called to process the input line. If *readset* returns the status code 0 (normal read), the required data is calculated and printed, otherwise procedure *error* is called to print a message or take other special action. The process is repeated until the user types the end-of-file signal.

```
begin { main }
  init(asub, bsub);
  newtype(buffer, primetype);                        { set prime type }
  readtable(setdata, loc, table);                    { read table     }
  prompt;
  while not eof do
    begin
      with dat do
        readset(buffer, pcset, card, primetype, code); { read pc set   }
      if code = 0
        then
          begin
            calc(output, primetype, dat, loc, table);  { prime form etc }
            printdata(dat)                             { print set data }
          end
        else error(buffer, code);
      prompt
    end
end.  { main }
```

Since the entire program was shown above, it will not be listed again. A sample interactive run is shown below.

```
Setting prime-form type ...
Type "Forte" or "Rahn": Forte
type = Forte

Type set: help

Program Setid - Synopsis:

to run:     setid <cr>
prompt:     Type set:
input:      pc sets in integer notation with a = 10, b = 11,
              blanks optional, terminate set with <return>
              example: 014ab <return> enters 0 1 4 10 11
              program removes duplicate pcs from input set
              subs for A and B: "t" = A; "e" = B
            or set names in the form 3-1, 6-17, etc.
output:     - normal order for set
            - TTO to map prime form into normal order
            - set name
            - prime form
            - number of Z-related set (0 if none)
            - number of M/MI-related set
            - interval-class vector (A = 10, B = 11, C = 12)
commands:   ? or h - print this synopsis
            * - reset special characters for 10 and 11
            ! - reset prime-form type (Forte/Rahn)
messages:   error message and reprompt for bad input
quit:       ^D or <rubout>

Type set: 014
normal form =   014          Z =  0; M/MI = 11;
= TOP(3-3)     {014}         ic vector = [101100]

Type set: 034
normal form =   034          Z =  0; M/MI = 11;
= T4I(3-3)     {014}         ic vector = [101100]

Type set: 145
normal form =   145          Z =  0; M/MI = 11;
= T5I(3-3)     {014}         ic vector = [101100]

Type set: 541
normal form =   145          Z =  0; M/MI = 11;
= T5I(3-3)     {014}         ic vector = [101100]

Type set: 12348q8845
               -----^
Error: pc = 0|1|2|3|4|5|6|7|8|9|a|b,  blanks optional

Type set: 102938375
normal form =   01235789       Z =  0; M/MI =  5;
= TOP(8-16)    {01235789}      ic vector = [554563]
```

```
Type set: ab0192837465
normal form =   0123456789AB  Z =  0; M/MI =  1;  P/I symmetric
= T0P(12-1)    {0123456789AB} ic vector = [CCCCC6]

Type set: 128te
normal form =   8AB12         Z =  0; M/MI = 25;
= T2I(5-10)    {01346}        ic vector = [223111]

Type set: 128ab
normal form =   8AB12         Z =  0; M/MI = 25;
= T2I(5-10)    {01346}        ic vector = [223111]

Type set: 5-20
normal form =   01378         Z =  0; M/MI =  6;
= T0P(5-20)    {01378}        ic vector = [211231]

Type set: 6-29
normal form =   013689        Z = 50; M/MI = 42;  P/I symmetric
= T0P(6-Z29)   {013689}       ic vector = [224232]

Type set: 7-20
normal form =   0124789       Z =  0; M/MI =  6;
= T0P(7-20)    {0124789}      ic vector = [433452]

Type set: 245789b0
normal form =   789B0245      Z =  0; M/MI =  3;  P/I symmetric
= T7P(8-26)    {0124579A}     ic vector = [456562]

Type set: !

Setting prime-form type ...
Type "Forte" or "Rahn": Rahn
Type = Rahn/Starr/Morris

Type set: 5-20
normal form =   01568         Z =  0; M/MI =  6;
= T0P(5-20)    {01568}        ic vector = [211231]

Type set: 6-29
normal form =   023679        Z = 50; M/MI = 42;  P/I symmetric
= T0P(6-Z29)   {023679}       ic vector = [224232]

Type set: 7-20
normal form =   0125679       Z =  0; M/MI =  6;
= T0P(7-20)    {0125679}      ic vector = [433452]

Type set: 245789b0
normal form =   45789B02      Z =  0; M/MI =  3;  P/I symmetric
= T4P(8-26)    {0134578A}     ic vector = [456562]

Type set: 1456
normal form =   1456          Z =  0; M/MI = 14;
= T6I(4-4)     {0125}         ic vector = [211110]

Type set: 934
normal form =   349           Z =  0; M/MI =  5;
= T3P(3-5)     {016}          ic vector = [100011]
```

```
Type set: !

Setting prime-form type ...
Type "Forte" or "Rahn": Forte
type = Forte

Type set: 1456
normal form =   1456            Z =  0; M/MI = 14;
= T6I(4-4)     {0125}           ic vector = [211110]

Type set: 934
normal form =   349             Z =  0; M/MI =  5;
= T3P(3-5)     {016}            ic vector = [100011]

Type set: *
Type sub for 10: ,
Type sub for 11: .
, = A; . = B
OK? (y/n): y

Type set: 789,
normal form =   789A            Z =  0; M/MI = 23;  P/I symmetric
= T7P(4-1)     {0123}           ic vector = [321000]

Type set: 4566
normal form =   456             Z =  0; M/MI =  9;  P/I symmetric
= T4P(3-1)     {012}            ic vector = [210000]

Type set: ,654.
normal form =   456AB           Z =  0; M/MI =  7;
= T4P(5-7)     {01267}          ic vector = [310132]

Type set: 8-89
Illegal set name

Type set: 0-0
Illegal set name

Type set:
null set

Type set: 3-12
normal form =   048             Z =  0; M/MI = 12;  P/I symmetric
= T0P(3-12)    {048}            ic vector = [000300]

Type set: ^D
```

Program *Setid.* Sample Run (Interactive)

17.6 Other Approaches

Of course, there are other approaches to finding prime forms. We will now examine three of these. The first is to write a program that simulates an algorithm used to perform the task without a computer. This "direct" approach is a useful exercise for two reasons. First, while this method may not be as efficient as an algorithm that makes use of the natural resources of the computer, it will still be much faster than doing it by hand, and it may be the only method available. Second, it is an excellent way to test a manual algorithm to make sure that we have formulated it correctly.

In this section, we will demonstrate direct implementation of Forte's prime-form algorithm. Then we will examine a method used by Bo Alphonce that is very fast, but that requires a large data table. Finally, we will model Rahn's normal-order algorithm with a procedure based on matrix manipulation.

17.6.1 Forte's Prime-Form Algorithm

In *The Structure of Atonal Music*, Allen Forte gives an algorithm for finding the "normal order" and "prime form" of a set.[9] Forte's method in outline form follows. We will explore the steps to find the prime form of the set [1, 2, 6, 10].

1. Arrange the pc integers in ascending normal order.

[1, 2, 6, 10]

2. Calculate the circular permutations of the set by placing the first element in the last position, adding twelve to keep the set in ascending order. The number of circular permutations is equal to the cardinality of the set. For each circular permutation, calculate the difference between the first and last elements by subtracting the first element from the last. The normal order is that permutation that has the least difference. Forte calls this "Requirement 1."

Circular Permutation	Difference
0. [1, 2, 6, 10]	9
1. [2, 6, 10, 13]	11
2. [6, 10, 13, 14]	8
3. [10, 13, 14, 18]	8

3. If two or more circular permutations share the least difference, "Requirement 2" must be invoked to choose the "best normal order." For those circular permutations with the same least difference, choose the permutation with the least difference between the first and second integers. If this is the same, select the one with the least difference between the first and third elements. Continue until one set has a lesser difference than the others or until you have checked the difference between the first and penultimate elements. If the differences are the same, choose one permutation arbitrarily.

Circular Permutation		Difference
2. [6, 10, 13, 14]		8
——	10 − 6 =	4

9. Forte, *The Structure of Atonal Music*, 3–5.

Circular Permutation		Difference
3. [10, 13, 14, 18]		8
——	13 – 10 =	3 (best normal order)

4. Using the best normal order from step 2 or 3, transpose the set to 0 by subtracting the first element from each of the others. Try to find this set in the table of prime forms. If it occurs in the table, this set is the prime form, and the algorithm terminates.

```
 10, 13, 14, 18
-10, 10, 10, 10
---------------
  0,  3,  4,  8  (prime form?)
```

5. If the set does not occur in the table ([0348] does not), invert the original set by subtracting each element from 12, modulo 12, and repeat the process from step 1.

```
  12, 12, 12, 12
-[ 1,  2,  6, 10]
-----------------
  11, 10,  6,  2  (inversion)
```

Step 1: Ascending order:

[2, 6, 10, 11]

Step 2: Find normal order:

Circular Permutation	Difference
0. [2, 6, 10, 11]	9
1. [6, 10, 11, 14]	8
2. [10, 11, 14, 18]	8
3. [11, 14, 18, 22]	11

Step 3: Select best normal order:

1. [6, 10, 11, 14]		8	
——	10 – 6 =	4	
2. [10, 11, 14, 18]		8	
——	11 – 10 =	1	(best normal order)

Step 4: (transpose to zero):

```
  [10, 11, 14, 18]
 - 10, 10, 10, 10
 ----------------
  [ 0,  1,  4,  8]   (PRIME FORM!)
```

We will implement this algorithm top down. Most declarations and support procedures are identical to those in program *setid*, so the complete program will not be listed. The input and output are also identical, except that the user is not given a choice of prime-form types and no special indication is given for symmetric sets. Our primary concern here is the translation of Forte's algorithm into Pascal. Only the necessary procedures will be shown.

The central procedure calculates normal order. We will assume that the input routine has already omitted duplicate pcs. First, the set is sorted in ascending order. Next, we compare each circular permutation to find the one with the smallest outside interval. Two shortcuts make this easier, based upon the observation that the twelve-tone system is circular and can be thought of as a clock face with 12 = 0. (This is another way of saying that pcs are within a modulo 12 system). The first shortcut is this: We can find the smallest outside interval by locating the largest interior interval. Thus we can compare contiguous pcs in the set. Further, the comparisons are more efficient if we don't actually rotate the set in the array. This step can be eliminated if the sorted set is stored twice consecutively. In the second copy, twelve is added to each pitch class. Thus we need not be concerned about wrap-around (mod 12 operations) until the smallest outside interval has been found. For example, consider the set {1, 2, 6, 10}:

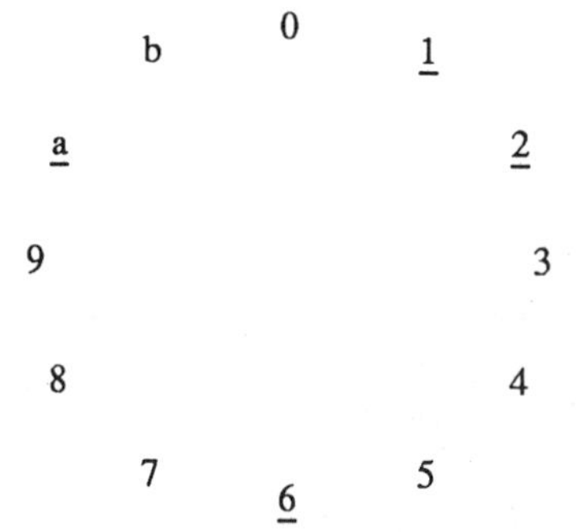

We store this set twice in an array used as workspace (the second time 12 is added to each pc), and then examine each interval between adjacent pcs in order to find the largest interval:

	1		2		6		10		13		14		18		22	
intervals:		1		4		4		3		1		4		4		
				=		=										

Since the largest interval, 4, occurs twice, we can get the smallest span with the rotation beginning with 6 or that beginning with 10. Thus Forte's second criterium must be invoked. This test is also easy in this representation. We compare the numbers following each 4 to find the smallest interval. Since 4 follows the first 4 and 3 follows the second 4, the best normal order is the circular permutation beginning with 10, i.e., (10, 13, 14, 18) = (10, 1, 2, 6). This set is transposed to 0 (by adding 2 to each element mod 12), yielding {0, 3, 4, 8}. Since this set does not occur in Forte's table, we begin over, using the inversion of the original set, $T_0I(1, 2, 6, 10) = (2, 6, 10, 11)$:

	2	6	10	11	14	18	22	23
intervals:	4	4	1	3	4	4	1	
	=	=						

Now the best normal order as defined above is (10, 11, 14, 18), or (10, 11, 2, 6), which transposed to zero is {0, 1, 4, 8}, the prime form of the set. By comparing the intervals in both directions, we could determine if the set requires inversion without looking in the table. However, our binary search method is fast, and we should succeed without inversion better than 50% of the time (since some sets are symmetric), so we will leave the algorithm as is.

Procedure *calc* calculates the prime form, normal order, derivation, etc., and stores them in the *dat* record. The line comments should be sufficient for you to follow the process.

```
procedure calc(var f : text; var loc : ar600; var table : ar300;
                                                  dat : setinfo);
  var
    test   : integer;                        { to double-check results  }
    pos    : integer;                        { location of set in table }
    bitvec : integer;                        { bit vector of prime form }

  begin { calc }
    with dat do
      begin
        prime := pcset;                              { save set           }
        test := encode(prime, card);                 { get bit vector     }
        normalize(prime, card);                      { calc normal order  }
        trans := prime[1];                           { save trans level   }
        transpose(prime, card, 12 - trans);          { transpose to 0     }
        bitvec := encode(prime, card);               { encode set         }
        with loc[card] do                            { find set in table  }
          pos := binsearch(table, start, stop, bitvec);

        if pos > 0                                   { got it             }
          then
            begin                                    { calc normal order  }
              pcset := prime;                        { start with prime   }
              transpose(pcset, card, trans);         { original level     }
              form := 'P'                            { signal p form      }
            end
          else                                       { use inversion      }
            begin { invert set }
              prime := pcset;                        { start over         }
              invert(prime, card, 12);               { invert set         }
              normalize(prime, card);                { calc normal order  }
              trans := (12 - prime[1]) mod 12;       { transposition      }
              transpose(prime, card, trans);         { trans to 0         }
              bitvec := encode(prime, card);         { encode             }
              with loc[card] do                      { find set in table  }
                pos := binsearch(table, start, stop, bitvec);

                                          { calc normal order from prime  }
              pcset := prime;                        { start with p.f.    }
              invert(pcset, card, trans);            { Calc T-trans-I     }
```

```
            reverse(pcset, card);                 { reverse order      }
            form := 'I'                           { signal inversion   }
          end; { use inversion }

      z     := table[pos].z;                      { copy from table    }
      mmi   := table[pos].mmi;
      name  := table[pos].name;
      makevector(prime, card, vector);

      if test <> encode(pcset,card)               { double-check       }
        then writeln(f, 'calc: error in data or program')
    end { with dat }
  end;  { calc }
```

Procedure *normalize* finds the best normal order using the algorithm described above.

```
procedure normalize(var pcset : ar100; n : integer);
  var
    list : array[1 .. 24] of integer;           { for workspace      }
    i, j, dif1, dif2, p, t1, t2 : integer;
  begin { normalize }
    sort(pcset,n);                              { in ascending order }
    for i := 1 to n do                          { copy to workspace  }
      begin
        list[i] := pcset[i];
        list[i + n] := pcset[i] + 12
      end;

                          { find largest interval and its position }
    dif1 := list[n + 1] - list[n];
    p := 1;
    for i := 2 to n do
      begin
        dif2 := list[i] - list[i - 1];
        if dif2 > dif1
          then
            begin
              p := i;
              dif1 := dif2
            end
          else if dif1 = dif2                 { big interval occurs > 1 }
            then                              { invoke second criteria  }
              begin { part 2 }
                j := 0; t1 := 0; t2 := 0;
                while (t1 = t2) and (j < n) do
                  begin
                    j := j + 1;
                    t1 := list[p + j] - list[p];
                    t2 := list[i + j] - list[i]
                  end;
                if t2 < t1
                  then p := i;
              end { part 2 }
      end;
```

```
    for i := 1 to n do                    { copy normal order from workspace }
      begin
        pcset[i] := list[p] mod 12;
        p := p + 1
      end
  end;  { normalize }
```

Since the lists are short, we use the simple exchange sort described in section 10.9.1.

```
procedure swap(var x,y : integer);
  var
    t : integer;
  begin
    t := x;   x := y;   y := t
  end;

procedure sort(var list : ar100; n : integer);
  var
    i,j,m : integer;
  begin
    for i := 1 to n - 1 do
      begin
        m := i;
        for j := i+1 to n do
          if list[j] < list[m]
            then m := j;
        swap(list[i],list[m])
      end
  end;  { sort }
```

Procedure *transpose* performs T_c(*pcset*) by adding the constant *c* to each element modulo 12. We use function *imod* to perform **mod** 12, since many computer implementations of **mod** do not function properly for negative numbers. An alternate method here would be to use (*pcset*[*i*] + *c* + 12) **mod** 12.

```
procedure transpose(var pcset : ar100; n : integer; c : integer);
  var
    i : integer;
  begin
    for i := 1 to n do
      pcset[i] := imod(pcset[i] + c, 12)
  end;
```

Function *imod(x, m)* is equivalent to *x* **mod** *m*, except that it will always work as expected for a negative value of *x*.

```
function imod(x,m : integer) : integer;
  begin
    if x >= 0
      then imod := x mod m
      else imod := (m - abs(x) mod m) mod m
  end;
```

Procedure *invert* inverts a set by subtracting each element from a constant value *c*. This is equivalent to the operation $T_c I(pcset)$.

```
procedure invert(var pcset : ar100; n : integer; c : integer);
  var
    i : integer;
  begin
    for i := 1 to n do
      pcset[i] := imod(c - pcset[i], 12)
  end;  { invert }
```

Procedure *reverse* reverses the order of elements in *pcset*. This is used above to place the pc integers representing the normal order in ascending order if the set was derived by transposition after inversion.

```
procedure reverse(var pcset : ar100; n : integer);
  var
    i : integer;
  begin
    for i := 1 to (n div 2) do
      swap(pcset[i], pcset[n + 1 - i])
  end;
```

You will probably agree that the bitwise prime-form algorithm is more elegant for computer implementation, and it is somewhat faster. While it is usually possible to simulate the manner in which you solve a problem manually, it is often worthwhile to step back and see if an algorithm can be devised that makes better use of computer resources. However, implementation of manual solutions as computer programs can be an important tool in testing a theory or methodology, since the computer algorithm may not work if some steps are not explicit.

17.6.2 Alphonce's Prime-Form Algorithm

The fastest prime-form algorithm I have seen was invented by Bo Alphonce of McGill University in Montreal.[10] Alphonce uses a large table that in Pascal would be declared:

```
  type
    table = array[1 .. 4095] of integer;

  var
    T : table;
```

The array is indexed directly by each of the bit vectors between 1 and 4095, which represent all possible combinations of pitch classes. Each component of the array is an integer that encodes the set name (ordinal part), and the operation that maps prime form into the set. This packing is accomplished by multiplying the ordinal part of the

10. I would like to thank Professor Alphonce for permission to present this previously unpublished algorithm. I reconstructed the procedure from a casual description of the algorithm, not from the actual code.

name by 100, adding the transposition level, and negating the number if the set is an inversion of the prime form.

```
code := 100 * ordinal + transposition;
if inversion
  then code := -code;
```

For example, data for pitch-class set [1, 2, 6, 10], into which the prime form of set 4-19 maps under the twelve-tone operation T_2I, is encoded as –1902, calculated –(100 * 19 + 2). Since [1, 2, 6, 10] maps into the bit vector 1094, this value is stored in *T*[1094]. The data for each bit vector *S* is encoded and stored in *T*[*S*]. The amount of other information that could be packed into the integer depends on the word size of the computer on which the program will be implemented.

As each pc set is read, it is calculated as a bit vector *S*, and the elements are counted to determine the cardinality *C*. Then *S* is used to index table *T*, i.e., the number stored in *T*[S] is decoded to obtain the ordinal number *O* of the set within cardinality class *C* and the information showing its T_nI and/or T_n relation to the prime form.

This algorithm is very fast, since the set read is not sorted or otherwise manipulated. Calculating a bit vector is a simple operation, and other information is obtained by a direct table lookup.

The data for the table is calculated once and stored in an external file, which is read when the program is run. The table used is large, but the amount of program code required to process the data is relatively small.

17.6.3 Rahn's Normal Form

John Rahn defines a canonic order or *normal form* for any set of pitch classes:

> The normal form of a set is that ordering of its members which is increasing within an octave and most packed to the left; if there is more than one such ordering, it is the remaining ordering with the smallest initial pc number.[11]

Rahn's normal form can be calculated by sorting the list of pcs and then examining the adjacency intervals, in a manner similar to the one we used to calculate Forte's prime form. However, the algorithm can be implemented more easily with a matrix to represent the intervals in each circular permutation, as shown in figure 17.2.

First the elements of the set are sorted in numeric order as shown at (a). Then a matrix is constructed as shown at (b). The ordered pitch classes are copied into the first column and into the first row of the matrix. The matrix is filled by placing each successive rotation of the ordered set in a separate row. Finally, each row is transposed to begin on 0 as at (c). The last column of the matrix contains the interval from the first to the last pc in each circular permutation, the antepenultimate row contains the interval from the first to the penultimate pc, etc.

11. Rahn, *Basic Atonal Theory*, 38.

PC SET:		**8**	**2**	**11**	**5**	**1**	**0**
a)		**0**	**1**	**2**	**5**	**8**	**11**
b)	**0**	0	1	2	5	8	11
	1	1	2	5	8	11	0
	2	2	5	8	11	0	1
	5	5	8	11	0	1	2
	8	8	11	0	1	2	5
	11	11	0	1	2	5	8
c)	**0**	0	1	2	5	8	11
	1	0	1	4	7	10	11
	2	0	3	6	9	10	11
	5	0	3	6	7	8	9
	8	0	3	4	5	6	9
	11	0	1	2	3	6	9
d)	**5**	0	3	6	7	8	**9**
	8	0	3	4	5	6	**9**
	11	0	1	2	3	6	**9**
	0	0	1	2	5	8	11
	1	0	1	4	7	10	11
	2	0	3	6	9	10	11
e)	**8**	0	3	4	5	**6**	9
	11	0	1	2	3	**6**	9
	5	0	3	6	7	8	9
	0	0	1	2	5	8	11
	1	0	1	4	7	10	11
	2	0	3	6	9	10	11
f)	**11**	0	1	2	**3**	6	9
	8	0	3	4	5	6	9
	5	0	3	6	7	8	9
	0	0	1	2	5	8	11
	1	0	1	4	7	10	11
	2	0	3	6	9	10	11
RNF:		**11**	**0**	**1**	**2**	**5**	**8**

Figure 17.2. Matrix Calculation of Rahn's Normal Form

Now the rows of the matrix are sorted in ascending order, keying on the values in the last column. Sorting places rows with the smallest outside interval at the top of the matrix, as shown at (d) of figure 17.2. If the smallest outside interval occurs more than once, the rows in which the duplicates occur are sorted on the next column to the left, and so on until no duplicates occur. In this figure the smallest interval (9) occurs in three rows, so the first three rows are sorted on the values in the next column to the left, resulting in the matrix at (e). Again, the smallest interval (6) is duplicated, so the first two rows of the matrix are sorted on the third-to-last column, resulting in the matrix at (f). The smallest interval (3) is not duplicated, so the first row represents the intervals in the normal form. Finally, the pitch class in the first column of the first row is added to each interval in the first column, resulting in the normal order of the original set.

Efficiency is improved by sorting only if the number of duplicates is less than the number of duplicates in the next column to the right. If no column is decisive, i.e., the smallest interval always occurs more than once, the remaining columns are sorted on the first column, which contains the original pitch classes. This ensures that the normal form of symmetric sets always begins with the smallest initial pc integer. In asymmetric sets, the pc in the first column just goes along for the ride, as it were, so that the interval pattern can be transposed to the correct pitch level.

The procedures shown below implement this algorithm, assuming the following type declarations:

```
type
  pcarray = array[ 1 .. 12] of integer;       { an array of pcs          }
  row     = array[-1 .. 12] of integer;       { one row of matrix        }
  matrix  = array[ 0 .. 12] of row;           { matrix for calculations  }
```

The pc set is sorted by placing each pc in a set type variable, and then extracting the pcs in the set and placing them back in the array. This technique, which is a form of hash sorting, is extremely efficient. Since each pc is placed in its correct position in one pass through the array, the efficiency is $O(n)$, where n is the cardinality of the set.[12]

```
{ sort pc set using Pascal's set type }
  procedure setsort(var A : pcarray; n : integer);
    type
      pcset = set of 0 .. 11;
    var
      i, pc : integer;
      x     : pcset;
    begin
      x := [];
      for i := 1 to n do
        x := x + [A[i]];
      n := 0;                      { copy pcs into array in ascending order }
      for pc := 0 to 11 do
        if pc in x
          then
            begin
              incr(n);
              A[n] := pc
            end
    end;  { setsort }
```

12. Hashing is discussed in section 16.7.1.

The matrix will be sorted by the pair of procedures shown below. Procedure *swaparray* exchanges the values in two rows, using a temporary array *t*. Procedure *sortmat* is an adaptation of the exchange sort presented in section 10.9.1. The procedure sorts the first *n* rows of matrix *M*, keying on the values in column *key*.

```
{ exchange two arrays x an y; used by proc sortmat }
  procedure swaparray(var x, y : row);
    var
      t : row;
    begin
      t := x;  x := y;  y := t
    end;

{ sort matrix n rows of matrix M on value in column key }
  procedure sortmat(var M : matrix; n, key : integer);
    var
      i, j, k : integer;
    begin
      for i := 0 to n - 1 do
        begin
          k := i;                            { get loc of smallest value  }
          for j := k + 1 to n do
            if M[j][key] < M[k][key]
              then k := j;
          swaparray(M[i], M[k])              { exchange with element i    }
        end
    end;
```

Procedure *normal* calculates the normal form of the *n* element set in array *A*, using the algorithm described above. The normal order is returned in the same array.

```
{ calculates Rahn's normal order }
  procedure normal(var A : pcarray; n : integer);
    var
      i, j      : integer;          { loop variables                         }
      c         : integer;          { n - 1                                  }
      column    : integer;          { current column                         }
      dups      : integer;          { number of duplicate pcs in column      }
      lastdups  : integer;          { number of dups in last column          }
      M         : matrix;           { matrix                                 }
    begin
      setsort(A, n);                { sort pc set                            }
      c := n - 1;                   { last column, numbered from zero        }
      for i := 0 to c do            { copy set into matrix                   }
        begin
          M[i,-1] := A[i + 1];
          M[0,i]  := A[i + 1]
        end;

      for i := 1 to c do                       { do rotations                }
        for j := 0 to c do
          M[i,j] := M[0, (i + j) mod n];

      for i := 0 to c do                       { calculate intervals         }
        for j := 0 to c do
          M[i,j] := (M[i,j] + 12 - M[i,-1]) mod 12;
```

```
sortmat(m, c, c);                          { sort matrix on last column }
column := c;
lastdups := c;
repeat
  dups := 0;                               { how many duplicates?       }
  while (M[0, column] = M[dups + 1, column]) and (dups < lastdups) do
    incr(dups);
  if dups > 0
    then
      begin
        column := column - 1;
        if (dups < lastdups) or (column = -1)
          then sortmat(m, dups, column);
        lastdups := dups
      end
until dups = 0;

for i := 0 to c do                   { copy normal order back to array A }
  A[i+1] := (M[0,i] + M[0,-1]) mod 12
end; { normal }
```

Rahn calculates the prime form of a set by comparing the normal form of the set and the normal form of its inversion. This algorithm is suggested as an exercise.

References and Selected Readings

The following sources deal with pitch-class sets in detail:

Forte, Allen. *The Structure of Atonal Music.* New Haven: Yale University Press, 1973.

Howe, Hubert S., Jr. "Some Combinational Properties of Pitch Structures." *Perspectives of New Music* 4, no. 1 (1965): 45–61.

Morris, Robert D. *Composition with Pitch-Classes: A Theory of Compositional Design.* New Haven: Yale University Press, 1987.

Rahn, John. *Basic Atonal Theory.* New York and London: Longman, 1980.

Starr, Daniel. "Sets Invariance and Partitions." *Journal of Music Theory* 22, no. 1 (1978): 1–42.

Bitwise algorithms are described in the following sources:

Alphonce, Bo H. "The Invariance Matrix." Ph.D. dissertation, Yale University, 1974.

Harris, Craig R., and Alexander R. Brinkman. "An Integrated Software System for Set-Theoretic and Serial Analysis of Contemporary Music." *Journal of Computer-Based Instruction* 16, no. 2 (1989): 59–70.

Starr, Daniel. "Sets, Invariance and Partitions." *Journal of Music Theory* 22, no. 1 (1978): 1–42.

The first source below explores theory testing by computer. The second is based in part on extensive modeling of Perle's theories in computer programs:

Alphonce, Bo H. "Music Analysis by Computer—A Field for Theory Formation." *Computer Music Journal* 4, no. 2 (1980): 26–35.

———. Review of *Twelve-Tone Tonality*, by George Perle. *Journal of Music Theory* 26, no. 1 (1982): 179–205.

Exercises

1. In this chapter we have used bit vectors to indicate the pc content of a pc set. This representation can always be used to represent prime forms. Can it be used to store normal order? Why or why not?

2. Use the notion of bit vectors to prove that there are exactly 4095 distinct pc sets.

3. a) Use bit vectors to generate a list of each possible pc set.
   b) Have the program arrange the list in numeric order within cardinality classes.

4. Manually work through Forte's and Rahn's algorithms for the following sets:

   (a) 01378 (b) 12479A (c) 014689 (d) 0125679

   Explain the difference in the resulting prime form for the six set classes that differ. It will be helpful to write out the prime forms as bit vectors or compare the pattern of intervals between the prime forms.

5. Modify the procedures that implement Forte's prime-form algorithm (section 17.6.1) so that they calculate the correct prime form with only one call to *binsearch*, i.e., your algorithm must decide whether or not the set needs to be inverted.

6. Rahn defines the steps necessary to find a set's T*n*/T*n*I type (analogous to Forte's prime form) as follows:

   a) Find the normal form of the set.

   b) Transpose the normal form to begin on 0. This is the "representative form" of the set's T*n*-type.

   c) Perform T*n*I on the set and repeat steps (a) and (b). This yields the representative form of the set's T*n*I type.

   d) Compare the T*n*-type representative forms. The "most normal form" of the two is the representative form of the set's T*n*/T*n*I type.

   The "most normal form" is the set that is in the smallest span, and most packed to the left. Use the procedures for finding Rahn's normal form (section 17.6.3) to implement this algorithm. Your program should prompt the user for a pc set, read the set, and print out Rahn's T*n*/T*n*I-type representative.

7. Write a routine that uses matrix sorting (as in section 17.6.3) to implement Forte's prime-form algorithm. The primary difference will be the order in which the columns are sorted.

8. Write a program that calculates the numbers that could be used to implement Alphonce's algorithm as described in section 17.6.2.

9. Write a program that implements Alphonce's algorithm. This is easier than generating the data table.

10. Combine the program from exercise 7 with procedures implementing Starr's algorithm to write a program listing each possible set class and its set name. Arrange the list in numeric order by cardinality.

11. Write a function that calculates the number of elements in a pc set represented by its bit vector.

12. The binary representation of pc sets suggests an alternate method of calculating combinations. Suppose we store n elements in $A[i]$, $0 \leq i \leq n-1$. If we let each bit of a binary integer represent the order position (or subscript) of an element in the array, then binary numbers of magnitude 1 to $2^n - 1$ can be used to represent all possible combinations of size $1 - n$ of these elements. Review the algorithms given for bit vectors in the beginning of this chapter, and refine this algorithm. Then write a program that reads a set of n pcs into an array and then uses the binary numbers to generate all combinations within this set.

13. Modify the algorithm from exercise 12 so that you can specify the size of the combinations desired, i.e., n elements taken r at a time.

18| A Matrix-Searching Program

The program described in this chapter illustrates another application of bit vectors and places several other techniques that we have studied in the context of a larger program. Among these are the binary search tree and the multilinked data structure. In addition, two new topics are introduced: terminal control functions and bit maps.

18.1 Terminal Control Functions

Modern computer output devices have capabilities beyond simply displaying characters. A terminal may be able to display text in different character widths (80 and 132 characters per line are common) and in different formats (brighter, dimmer, blinking, reverse video, etc.). It is often possible to move the cursor directly to arbitrary screen positions, clear the screen, clear to the end of the current line, etc. These functions are controlled by special nonprinting characters (control characters), or by sequences of characters that have special meaning to the terminal or printer (control sequences). Control sequences frequently begin with the ASCII escape character, *chr*(27) in Pascal, which signals the device that the following characters are to be treated as a control sequence rather than as printing characters.

Control codes vary for different types of devices and for devices of the same type made by different makers. Inevitably, when a device becomes widely used, its functions and protocols are copied by other manufacturers, and some terminals and printers can emulate a number of different devices.[1] While this results in classes of terminals with identical characteristics, there is still no true standard, and programs that make use of features of a specific terminal will not operate properly with incompatible terminals. For this reason, procedures and functions that are hardware specific should be segregated and clearly identified to facilitate modification of the program for different terminals.

Table 18.1 shows some of the control sequences used by Digital Equipment Corporation's VT 100 and VT 200 terminals and compatibles. You can find the control codes available for your particular terminal in technical manuals provided by the manufacturer.

1. Examples of common emulations are the Xerox Diablo 630 printer and the Digital Equipment Corporation VT 100 and VT 200 series terminals. VT 100 and VT 200 are registered trademarks of Digital Equipment Corporation. Diablo is a registered trademark of Xerox Corporation.

Function	*Control Codes*
Move cursor to line *x* column *y*	ESC [*x* ; *y* H
Move cursor to line 1 col 1 (home)	ESC [; H
Erase from cursor to end of line	ESC [K
Erase from cursor to end of screen	ESC [J
Erase complete display	ESC [2 J
Begin to display negative (reverse) image	ESC [7 m
Begin to display characters underlined	ESC [4 m
Begin to display at increased intensity	ESC [1 m
Return to normal mode	ESC [0 m

Table 18.1. A Subset of the Control Sequences for DEC VT100/VT200 Terminals

Once you know the control characters for your terminal, you can design programs that make use of these special capabilities. The procedures shown below turn the highlight mode on and off for VT100/200 terminals. Function *ESC* returns the ASCII escape character. The control procedures write the appropriate character sequence to the output device. After procedure *reversevideo* is called, everything written to the terminal will be in highlight mode until procedure *normalvideo* is called.[2]

```
function ESC : char;
  begin
    ESC := chr(27)
  end;

procedure reversevideo;
  begin
    write(ESC, '[7m')
  end;

procedure normalvideo;
  begin
    write(ESC, '[m')
  end;
```

Procedure *moveto* is used for direct cursor addressing. For example, *moveto*(1, 1) moves the cursor from its current position directly to line one, column one of the screen. The next *write* statement will begin printing at this position. Other control functions for this terminal are discussed later in this chapter.

```
procedure moveto(line, col : integer);
  begin { place cursor on video screen }
    write(ESC, '[', line:1, ';', col:1, 'H')
  end;
```

2. Reverse video means that characters are printed on the screen in negative image, i.e., dark characters on a light background. Note that dark characters on a light background is standard on some CRTs, such as the screen on the Macintosh.

Pitch-Class Integers	*Bit Map*
A 9 0 B 3 4 1 2 6 5 8 7	1 1 1 1 0 0 0 0 0 0 0 0
B A 1 0 4 5 2 3 7 6 9 8	0 1 0 1 0 0 0 0 0 0 0 0
8 7 A 9 1 2 B 0 4 3 6 5	0 0 0 1 0 0 0 0 0 0 0 0
9 8 B A 2 3 0 1 5 4 7 6	0 0 0 1 0 0 0 0 0 0 0 0
5 4 7 6 A B 8 9 1 0 3 2	0 0 0 0 1 0 0 0 0 0 0 0
4 3 6 5 9 A 7 8 0 B 2 1	0 0 0 0 1 0 0 0 0 0 0 0
7 6 9 8 0 1 A B 3 2 5 4	0 0 0 0 1 0 0 0 0 0 0 0
6 5 8 7 B 0 9 A 2 1 4 3	0 0 0 0 1 1 1 1 0 0 0 0
2 1 4 3 7 8 5 6 A 9 0 B	0 0 0 0 0 0 0 0 1 1 1 1
3 2 5 4 8 9 6 7 B A 1 0	0 0 0 0 0 0 0 0 0 0 0 1
0 B 2 1 5 6 3 4 8 7 A 9	1 1 0 0 0 0 0 0 0 0 1 1
1 0 3 2 6 7 4 5 9 8 B A	0 1 0 0 0 0 0 0 0 0 0 1

Figure 18.1. A Twelve-Tone Matrix and Bit Map Showing Contiguous Instances of the Unordered Set A90B (''BACH'')

18.2 Bit Maps

Bit maps are arrangements of binary digits that show relationships in other data. For example, bit-mapped graphics use binary digits (bits) to indicate which pixels (picture elements) are to be ''turned on'' in order to display the desired pattern on the screen. The bit vectors described in the previous chapter are bit maps that indicate which pitch classes occur in a pc set. In this chapter we use a bit map to indicate the location of unordered sets in a twelve-tone matrix. Figure 18.1 illustrates this technique. The bit-map matrix on the right shows the locations of contiguous occurrences of the pitch classes (0, 9, 10, 11) in the matrix on the left.[3] Note that our definition of ''contiguous'' allows for ''wrap-around'' from the end of a row form to the beginning of the same row from.

Bit maps can be simulated in Pascal through several different methods. We can use actual binary integers (as in set numbers), boolean arrays (with *true* and *false* replacing 1 and 0), or sets. The best method depends on the function of the bit map and the operations that we need to perform on it. The binary integer model is ideal for bit vectors when we want to look up sets in a table or other data structure, because the numbers can be ordered to facilitate fast searching algorithms. We have also seen that the numeric value of this representation facilitates a fast prime-form algorithm. Boolean arrays and set types are convenient if we need to determine quickly if specific bits are set. For example, if *B* is a boolean matrix representing the bit map in figure 18.1, then simply referencing an array element in an **if** statement tests its value:

3. The matrix is derived from the row in Webern's String Quartet, Op. 28. The first tetrachord (B♭, A, C, B) spells ''BACH'' in the German system of naming notes. The second tetrachord is a transposed inversion of this figure, and the third is a transposition. In addition, the second hexachord is the retrograde inversion of the first.

if *B*[*i*, *j*]
  then the bit in row *i*, column *j* is on;

This has an advantage in speed; since the array element contains a boolean value, it does not need to be evaluated.

In this chapter we will create bit maps using Pascal's set type, declared as follows:

```
type
  checkrow = set of 0 .. 11;
  bitmap   = array[0..11] of checkrow;

var
  map : bitmap;
```

The map consists of an array of sets of integers in the range 0 through 11. The index of the array is the row number in the bit map, and the elements in the set are the numbers of the columns that are set (1) in that row. Thus the expression shown below is equivalent to the one shown above.

if *j* **in** *map*[*i*]
  then the bit in row *i*, column *j* is on;

Although the efficiency and space required for sets is implementation dependent, this representation takes less space than the boolean array in many Pascal implementations and should be efficient.[4]

18.3 A Matrix-Searching Program: Specifications

Function. The program is designed as an aid in twelve-tone serial analysis or composition. The user provides a twelve-tone row and the matrix is displayed on the screen, with transposition numbers printed across the top and down the left side, and order numbers printed to the right and below. Since theorists prefer matrices in different forms, the user will be given a choice of printing the matrix at the specified pitch level or transposing it to begin on 0. After the matrix is printed, the program loops, prompting the user for pitch collections he or she wants to locate in the matrix. For each pitch collection specified, the locations in which the pcs occur in the matrix in contiguous order positions are highlighted in reverse video. The user is then prompted for the next set. The positions of the previous set are rewritten in normal video, returning the matrix to its original appearance. Then the next set is displayed. If the elements of the pc set do not occur in contiguous order positions in the matrix, no action is taken other than to turn off the highlighting. Figure 18.2 approximates the appearance of the matrix for Webern's Op. 28 string quartet (transposed to 0)

4. Sets are often implemented internally as true bit maps, which are manipulated by bitwise operations. This is efficient in terms of both space and time, since the binary representation takes little space and bitwise operations translate directly into machine-level instructions. Of course, we could use a packed array of *boolean*, but the time required to reference each element would increase. (See the discussion of packed arrays in section 11.1.)

T	0	B	2	1	5	6	3	4	8	7	A	9	
0	**0**	**B**	2	1	5	6	3	4	8	7	**A**	**9**	0
1	1	**0**	3	2	6	7	4	5	9	8	B	**A**	1
A	**A**	**9**	**0**	**B**	3	4	1	2	6	5	8	7	2
B	B	**A**	1	0	4	5	2	3	7	6	9	8	3
7	7	6	9	8	0	1	**A**	B	3	2	5	4	4
6	6	5	8	7	**B**	**0**	**9**	**A**	2	1	4	3	5
9	9	8	B	A	2	3	**0**	1	5	4	7	6	6
8	8	7	A	9	1	2	**B**	0	4	3	6	5	7
4	4	3	6	5	9	A	7	8	0	**B**	2	1	8
5	5	4	7	6	A	B	8	9	1	**0**	3	2	9
2	2	1	4	3	7	8	5	6	**A**	**9**	**0**	**B**	A
3	3	2	5	4	8	9	6	7	B	A	1	**0**	B
	0	1	2	3	4	5	6	7	8	9	A	B	

Type set: **a90b**

Figure 18.2. Simulation of Search Request (transposed matrix)

T	0	B	2	1	5	6	3	4	8	7	A	9	
0	**A**	**9**	**0**	**B**	3	4	1	2	6	5	8	7	0
1	B	**A**	1	**0**	4	5	2	3	7	6	9	8	1
A	8	7	A	**9**	1	2	B	0	4	3	6	5	2
B	9	8	B	**A**	2	3	0	1	5	4	7	6	3
7	5	4	7	6	**A**	B	8	9	1	0	3	2	4
6	4	3	6	5	**9**	A	7	8	0	B	2	1	5
9	7	6	9	8	**0**	1	A	B	3	2	5	4	6
8	6	5	8	7	**B**	**0**	**9**	**A**	2	1	4	3	7
4	2	1	4	3	7	8	5	6	**A**	**9**	**0**	**B**	8
5	3	2	5	4	8	9	6	7	B	A	1	**0**	9
2	**0**	**B**	2	1	5	6	3	4	8	7	A	9	A
3	1	**0**	3	2	6	7	4	5	9	8	B	**A**	B
	0	1	2	3	4	5	6	7	8	9	A	B	

Type set: **a90b**

Figure 18.3. Simulation of Search Request (untransposed matrix)

Program Search - Synopsis:

To run:	search <return>
Prompt:	Type row:
Input:	12-tone row in pc notation as specified below, example: 1092837465ab <return>
Output:	matrix with transposition and order numbers
Prompt:	Type set:
Input:	pc sets in integer notation with a = 10, b = 11, blanks optional, terminate set with <return> Example: 014ab <return> enters 0 1 4 10 11 program removes duplicate pcs from input set subs for A and B: 't' = A; 'e' = B
Output:	location of set in matrix in reverse video
Commands:	? - print this synopsis
	h - " " "
	r - redraw matrix on screen
	* - reset special characters for 10 and 11
Messages:	error message and reprompt for bad input
Terminate:	Control-D, or <rubout>

Type return to continue

Figure 18.4. Simulated Instruction Screen

after the user requests locations of the pcs in the opening gesture (spelling "BACH"). Figure 18.3 shows the results of the same request with the matrix constructed at the original pitch level.[5]

Input. As in the previous chapter, both row and pitch collections are specified in hexadecimal notation, i.e., the digits 0123456789ab represent the integers 0 through 11. When reading pitch collections, the program will process all pcs on a single line and remove duplicates. The pitch collections may contain from 1 to 11 unique pcs. Appropriate error messages are printed for cardinalities less than 1 or greater than 11, or for erroneous input data. As in the last program, the user can specify and use substitute characters for 'a' and 'b'. The following special characters will be recognized when entered as the first character of an input line:

'?' or 'h'	—	print instruction summary
'*'	—	reset substitute characters for 10 and 11
'r'	—	redraw screen (useful if screen gets scrambled)

The final request ('r') redraws the matrix. This is useful, since it is possible to scramble the screen by typing the next set while the program is setting or unsetting

5. For technical reasons, the highlighted pitch classes are shown in boldface rather than reverse video in the simulations of the CRT screen.

highlighted pcs. The program is terminated by typing Control-D or <rubout> in response to the prompt 'Type set: '.

Output. It is impossible to show a complete program run in print. Figures 18.2 and 18.3 are a fair representation of the screen after one user request. In addition, when the user types 'help' or '?' in response to the 'Type set: ' prompt, the screen is cleared and the message shown in figure 18.4 is displayed. When the user types a carriage return, the screen is cleared again and the matrix and prompt are displayed once more.

18.4 Implementation

While it would be possible to search the matrix for locations of each input set, this approach would involve a great deal of redundant searching, and the time required to find the locations of each set would be relatively large. Instead, the matrix is scanned twice (for rows and columns), and each subset is stored with its location in a data structure designed for fast searching. This data structure is a multilinked structure consisting of a binary search tree with each node serving as the head node for a circular linked list (with pointer to the last node), as shown in figure 18.5.

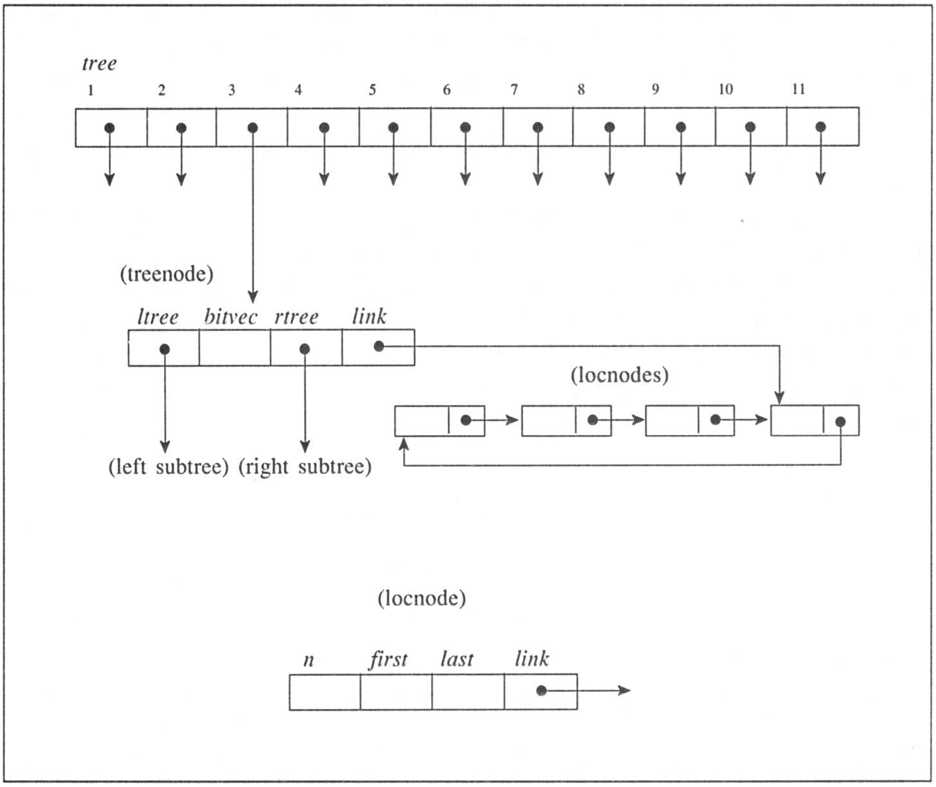

Figure 18.5. The Data Structure for Program *Search*

The *treenode* has four fields. *Ltree* and *rtree* point to the left and right subtrees (these are **nil** pointers in terminal nodes of the tree); *bitvec* is the bit vector representing the pc content of one or more segments of the matrix; and *link* points to the end of a circular linked list of *locnodes*. The list of *locnodes* is used to store all locations of each set of contiguous pcs in the matrix.

A *locnode* has four fields. *N* is the row or column in which the subset occurs. Since rows and columns are numbered from 0 to 11, 1 is added to the row or column number and the number is negated if it represents a column. The minus sign enables us to make a distinction between rows and columns. Adding 1 permits us to differentiate column 0 and row 0.[6]

The tree is constructed such that the left subtree contains smaller bit vectors and the right subtree contains larger bit vectors than the parent node. To minimize the size of the each tree, a different tree is used for each cardinality class. Trees for segments of cardinalities 1 through 11 are pointed to by an array of pointers called *tree*. *Tree*[*i*] points to the binary tree for sets of cardinality *i*.

This data structure has many advantages for fast searching. The unique bit vector representing a segment of the matrix occurs only once in the data structure. The circular list of *locnodes* hung on the *treenode* shows all locations of this set as contiguous order positions in the matrix. Each tree is ordered by bit vectors, which are inserted in the trees in approximately random order. The search tree is especially desirable because elements are placed in the correct position as the structure is built, and subsequent sorting is not required. While a tree is searched (or constructed), each time a left or right subtree is selected, half of the remaining list is eliminated. Thus the time required to find a single element is $O(\log_2 n)$, where n is the number of elements in the tree. The size of n is minimized by segregating the trees by cardinality.

In order to construct this data structure, it is necessary to calculate the bit vectors representing each matrix segment of cardinalities 1 through 11. To save time during this calculation, the matrix is copied to another temporary matrix, and each pitch class (*pc*) is replaced by the value 2^{pc}. Now the bit vector representing each contiguous segment can be calculated as the sum of these values for each of the imbricated subsets of the matrix. For example, if the first row of the original matrix contains the row

10 9 0 11 3 4 1 2 6 5 8 7

then the first row of the temporary matrix contains the values

1024 512 1 2048 8 16 2 4 64 32 256 128

The bit vectors for segments of cardinality n are calculated by adding the values of

6. It would be possible to use a separate "tag" field in the node to indicate derivation from a row or column; however, this would require an extra storage location for each node, and a large number of nodes will be required. Nodes *first* and *last* contain the beginning and ending positions of the set in the row or column. If the segment wraps around from the end to the beginning of a row, *last* is greater than 11. The actual location will be found later by using *last* modulo 12. *Link* points to the next node in the circular list, or to the current node if the list contains only one node.

pc:	10	9	0	11	3	4	1	2	6	5	8	7	
2^{pc}:	1024	512	1	2048	8	16	2	4	64	32	256	128	
sum:	1024 +	512 +	1						= 1577				(011000000001)
sum:		512 +	1 +	2048					= 2561				(101000000001)
sum:			1 +	2048 +	8				= 2057				(100000001001)
sum:				2048 +	8 +	16			= 2052				(100000011000)
sum:					8 +	16 +	2		= 26				(000000011010)
sum:						16 +	2 +	4	= 22				(000000010110)
							etc.						

Figure 18.6. Calculating Bit Vectors for Three-Note Segments of a Row

each set's *n* contiguous elements. Figure 18.6 illustrates the process for $n = 3$.

To save repetition of the nested loop structure that calculates these sets, the values for the column *i* are calculated at the same time as those for row *i*. In the following program segment, the temporary matrix (representing each *pc* as 2^{pc}) is called *p*.

```
for card := 1 to 11 do                          { set cardinality         }
  for i := 0 to 11 do                           { row number i            }
    for first := 0 to 11 do                     { position of first element }
      begin
        last := first + card - 1;               { position of last element  }
        bitvec1 := 0;                           { bitvec for rows           }
        bitvec2 := 0;                           { bitvec for columns        }

        for j := first to last do                        { calc bit vectors }
          begin { set bits }
            bitvec1 := bitvec1 + p[i, (j mod 12)];              { row    }
            bitvec2 := bitvec2 + p[(j mod 12), i]               { column }
          end; { set bits }

        getnode(t, i + 1, first, last);      { node for row bitvec      }
        treesort(bitvec1, t, list[card]);    { insert in tree           }
        getnode(t, -(i + 1), first, last);   { node for column bitvec   }
        treesort(bitvec2, t, list[card])     { insert in tree           }
      end;
```

As the program reads each pitch collection, it removes duplicate pcs and derives the bit vector and cardinality of the set. Then the binary tree for the appropriate cardinality is searched for the bit vector. If it is found, the circular list of *locnodes* is traversed, and a bit map of the matrix is constructed to represent the matching elements in the matrix. Then the bit map is scanned, and for each "on" element the appropriate element on the terminal screen is rewritten in reverse video. Before the next set is processed, the highlighted elements are turned off by again scanning the bit map and rewriting "on" elements in normal video mode.

Time is saved by using cursor addressing to rewrite only those elements that are to be (or have been) displayed in highlight mode. Cursor addressing is also used to place prompts and error messages on the screen. The entire matrix is drawn once after the imbricated segments have been calculated. Thereafter, it is necessary to redraw the matrix only after the user requests instructions, resets the substitute characters for 10 and 11, or explicitly requests that the screen be redrawn. The latter may become necessary if the user attempts to enter a new set while the screen is being updated (since the typed characters are printed wherever the cursor happens to be). This option could be obviated by sending control sequences that lock the keyboard while the screen is being updated.

18.5 The Program

Program *search* uses only the standard input and output files. Three constants are declared: *maxline*, the maximum number of characters on an input line, is used in declaring the buffer; *highlight* and *normal* are boolean flags that will indicate whether pcs in the matrix are to be displayed in reverse video or normal mode.

```
program search(input, output);
  const
    maxline   = 86;               { maximum line length + 1                 }
    highlight = true;             { flags for print functions               }
    normal    = false;            { used by procedure setrev                }
```

Type declarations include nodes and pointer types for the linked data structures. Variables of type *ptr1* point to *locnodes*. These will be used in circular linked lists containing the location of specific pc sets in the matrix. Variables of type *ptr2* point to *treenodes*, which are used to construct the binary search trees.

```
  type
    ptr1 = ↑locnode;
    locnode = record
                 n : integer;       { row or col # + 1; negative if column }
                 first : integer;   { beginning position in row or column  }
                 last  : integer;   { ending position in row or col        }
                 link  : ptr1       { link to next locnode in list         }
              end;

    ptr2 = ↑treenode;

    treenode = record
                  link   : ptr1;    { points to circular list of locnodes  }
                  bitvec : integer; { sigma 2**pcset[i], 1 <= i <= card    }
                  ltree  : ptr2;    { points to left  subtree              }
                  rtree  : ptr2     { points to right subtree              }
               end;
```

The bit map of the matrix is constructed as an array of sets containing integers 0 through 11. Each row is represented by a set of type *checkrow*, with elements in the set representing the columns of the row. The bit map is an array of twelve of these sets representing the twelve rows of the matrix.

```
checkrow = set of 0 .. 11;          { one row of bit map of matrix      }
bitmap   = array[0 .. 11] of checkrow;
```

Array types are used for an array of pointers to binary search trees, and the twelve-tone matrix. The transposition numbers for prime-form rows are stored in column –1, and for inversion forms in row –1 of the matrix. The rows and columns of the actual matrix are numbered 0 through 11 to facilitate modular arithmetic (for wrap-around from the end to the beginning of a row form). The input buffer is implemented as a record structure with an array and a position indicator.

```
matrix   = array[-1 .. 11, -1 .. 11] of integer;
twotable = array[0 .. 11] of integer;
treeptr  = array[1 .. 11] of ptr2;

buftype = record                    { implements the buffer             }
            B  : array[1 .. maxline] of char;
            bp : integer
          end;
```

The use of most of the global variables should be clear from the line comments and the discussion in the previous section. The boolean variable match will indicate whether or not the previous set was found in the matrix, and consequently whether the screen display and bit map need to be updated before the new set is processed. *Setnum*, *card*, and *code* will be passed to procedure *readset*, which will use them to return the set, its cardinality, and a return code indicating errors, requests for special action, or a successful read. *Asub* and *bsub* represent alternate characters that may be used to input pcs 'a' (10) and 'b' (11). These are initially set to 't' (ten) and 'e' (eleven) but can be reset by the user to customize the program to a degree. One possibility is to set them to special characters such as ',' and '.' so that all data can be entered from a numeric keypad.

```
var
  buffer : buftype;          { input buffer                              }
  m      : matrix;           { 12-tone matrix                            }
  map    : bitmap;           { for keeping track of matching pcs         }
  tree   : treeptr;          { pointers to binary trees                  }
  match  : boolean;          { true if last set occurred in matrix       }
  bitvec : integer;          { sum of 2**pcset[i], 1 <= i <= cardinality }
  card   : integer;          { cardinality of set                        }
  code   : integer;          { condition code returned by readset        }
  asub   : char;             { input substitute for a (10)               }
  bsub   : char;             { substitute for b (11)                     }
```

The following functions control special features of the computer terminal. The ones shown below are specific for DEC VT100 or VT200 terminals and compatibles made by other manufactures. If a different terminal is to be used, these functions must be rewritten to produce the required control sequences.

```
function ESC : char;                          { returns ASCII escape char }
  begin
    ESC := chr(27)
  end;

procedure reversevideo;                       { turns on highlight mode   }
  begin
    write(ESC, '[7m')
  end;

procedure normalvideo;                        { turns off highlight mode  }
  begin
    write(ESC, '[m')
  end;

procedure moveto(line, col : integer);        { direct cursor addressing  }
  begin
    write(ESC, '[', line:1, ';', col:1, 'H')
  end;

procedure clearline;                          { clear to eoln             }
  begin
    write(ESC, '[K')
  end;

procedure homecursor;                         { cursor to upper lh corner }
  begin
    write(ESC, '[;H')
  end;

procedure cleardisplay;                       { erase complete display    }
  begin
    write(ESC, '[2J')
  end;

procedure clearscreen;                        { clear to end of screen    }
  begin
    homecursor; cleardisplay
  end;
```

Procedure *instruct* is called when the user requests instructions by typing 'help' or '?' instead of a set. The procedure clears the screen and prints instructions. The *readln* at the end of the procedure forces the procedure to wait for the user to type a carriage return before terminating. Without this, the user would not have time to read these instructions.

```
procedure instruct;
  begin { instruct user }
    clearscreen;
    reversevideo;
    writeln('Program Search - Synopsis:');
```

```
    normalvideo;
    writeln('To run:     search <return>');
    writeln;
    writeln('Prompt:     Type row: ');
    writeln('Input:      12 tone row in pc notation as specified below');
    writeln('              Example: 1092837465ab <return>');
    writeln('Output:     matrix with transposition and order numbers');
    writeln;
    writeln('Prompt:     Type set:');
    writeln('Input:      pc sets in integer notation with a = 10, b = 11,');
    writeln('              blanks optional, terminate set with <cr>');
    writeln('              example: 014ab <return> enters 0 1 4 10 11');
    writeln('              program removes duplicate pcs from input');
    writeln('              sub for A and B: ''', asub, ''' = A; ''',
                                                   bsub, ''' = B');
    writeln('Output:     location of set in matrix in reverse video');
    writeln;
    writeln('Commands:   ? - print this synopsis');
    writeln('            h -    "       "      "');
    writeln('            r - redraw matrix on screen');
    writeln('            * - reset special characters for 10 and 11');
    writeln;
    writeln('Errors:     error message and reprompt for bad input');
    writeln('Terminate: Control-D, or <rubout>');
    reversevideo;                                  { enter highlight mode }
    write('Type return to continue ');
    normalvideo;                                   { leave highlight mode }
    readln                                         { wait for <cr>        }
  end; { instruct }
```

The following two functions return the tab and null characters. Both are used in the buffer procedures shown below.

```
function tab : char;
  begin
    tab := chr(9)
  end;

function null : char;
  begin
    null := chr(0)
  end;
```

Procedure *incr* adds one to its argument. It is called by various procedures in the program.

```
procedure incr(var x : integer);
  begin
    x := x + 1
  end;
```

Function *power* returns powers of two, which will be used in constructing bit vectors.

```
function power(x : integer) : integer;                   { powers of 2 }
  begin
    case x of
      0 : power :=    1;
      1 : power :=    2;
      2 : power :=    4;
      3 : power :=    8;
      4 : power :=   16;
      5 : power :=   32;
      6 : power :=   64;
      7 : power :=  128;
      8 : power :=  256;
      9 : power :=  512;
     10 : power := 1024;
     11 : power := 2048
    end { case }
  end;
```

The following procedures implement the internal buffer used to process input typed by the user. These procedures, which were listed in the previous chapter and in section 11.2, will be omitted here to save space.

```
procedure getline(var f : text; var buffer : buftype);          external;
function  eob(var buffer : buftype) : boolean;                   external;
function  nextchar(var buffer : buftype) : char;                 external;
procedure getchar(var buffer : buftype; var c : char);          external;
procedure skipbuf(var buffer : buftype);                          external;
function  affirmative(var buffer : buftype) : boolean;          external;
```

Procedure *init* initializes variables that will be used elsewhere in the program. Each element of the *tree* array is assigned a **nil** pointer. These elements will point to the binary search trees for sets of different cardinality. The boolean variable *match* will indicate whether the previous input set was found in the matrix. It is initialized to *false*. Finally, the variables representing substitutes for 'a' (10) and 'b' (11) are initialized to 't' and 'e', mnemonic for ten and eleven.

```
procedure init(var tree : treeptr; var match : boolean;
                                          var asub, bsub : char);
  var
    i : integer;
  begin
    for i := 1 to 11 do
      tree[i] := nil;
    match := false;
    asub := 't';
    bsub := 'e'
  end;
```

The following boolean functions are used to test characters in the input buffer while reading pitch collections. The purpose of each function should be obvious from its name.

```
function isdigit(ch : char): boolean;
  begin
    isdigit := ch in ['0' .. '9']
  end;

function isupper(ch : char) : boolean;
  begin
    isupper := ch in ['A' .. 'Z']
  end;

function islower(ch : char) : boolean;
  begin
    islower := ch in ['a' .. 'z']
  end;

function iscommand(ch : char) : boolean;
  begin
    iscommand := ch in ['r', 'R', 'h', 'H', '?', '*']
  end;

function ispc(ch : char) : boolean;
  begin
    ispc := isdigit(ch) or (ch in ['a', 'b', 'A', 'B', asub, bsub])
  end;
```

Procedure *getpc* reads a character from the buffer and returns the pitch-class integer (0 through 11) represented by that character. If the character is inappropriate, –1 is returned to signal an error.

```
procedure getpc(var buffer : buftype; var pc : integer);
  var
    t : char;
  begin
    skipbuf(buffer);
    t := nextchar(buffer);
    if ispc(t)
      then
        begin
          if isdigit(t)
            then pc := ord(t) - ord('0')
          else if islower(t)
            then pc := ord(t) - ord('a') + 10
          else if isupper(t)
            then pc := ord(t) - ord('A') + 10
          else if t = asub
            then pc := 10
          else if t = bsub
            then pc := 11;
          incr(buffer.bp)                          { advance buffer pointer }
        end
      else pc := -1                                { return error code      }
  end;
```

Procedure *readrow* uses *getpc* to read the twelve-tone row on which the matrix will be based. If the user types an illegal character, an error message is printed and the procedure is called recursively.

```
procedure readrow(var buffer : buftype; var m : matrix);
  var
    i   : integer;
    t   : integer;
    err : boolean;
  begin
    err := false;
    write('Type row: ');
    getline(input, buffer);
    i := 0;
    while (i <= 11) and not err do
      begin
        getpc(buffer, m[0, i]);                { get next pc in row      }
        err := m[0, i] = -1;
        t := m[0, i] - m[0,0];                 { and calc trans numbers }
        if t < 0
          then t := t + 12;
        m[-1, i] := t;                         { T for inversions        }
        m[i, -1] := 12 - t mod 12;             { T for prime forms       }
        incr(i)
      end;

    if err
      then
        begin
          moveto(3, 1);
          writeln('Error in input data');
          write('Do you need help? (y,n) :');
          if affirmative(buffer)
            then instruct;
          clearscreen;
          readrow(buffer, m)
        end
      else
        begin
          if m[0, 0] <> 0
            then
              begin
                write('Transpose matrix to begin on 0? (y/n): ');
                if affirmative(buffer)
                  then
                    for i := 0 to 11 do
                      m[0, i] := m[-1, i]
              end
        end
  end;  { readrow }
```

Procedure *fillmatrix* computes the rest of the values in the twelve-tone matrix.

```
procedure fillmatrix(var m : matrix);
  var
    i, j : integer;
    t    : integer;
```

```
begin
  for i := 1 to 11 do
    begin
      t := (12 - m[-1, i]);
      for j := 0 to 11 do
        m[i, j] := (m[0, j] + t) mod 12
    end
end;
```

Procedure *clear* clears the bit map by assigning the set representing each row a null set. This is equivalent to setting each bit to 0.

```
procedure clear(var map : bitmap);
  var
    i : integer;
  begin
    for i := 0 to 11 do
      map[i] := []                    { null set }
  end;
```

Procedure *insert* inserts the *locnode* pointed to by *y* at the end of the circular linked list pointed to by *x*. If *x* is **nil**, then link of *y* will point to *y*; thus the list is always circular if it is not empty.

```
procedure insert(var x : ptr1; var y : ptr1);
  begin { add node at end of circular list }
    if y = nil
      then
        begin { new list }
          y := x;
          y↑.link := y;
        end
      else
        begin { add to end of list }
          x↑.link := y↑.link;
          y↑.link := x;
          y := x
        end;
    x := nil
  end;
```

Getnode allocates a new *locnode* and sets the data fields. It returns a pointer *t* to the new node.

```
procedure getnode(var t : ptr1; i, first, last : integer);
  begin
    new(t);    { get new node of type x }
    t↑.n := i;
    t↑.first := first;
    t↑.last  := last
  end;
```

Procedure *getheadnode* allocates a new node for the binary search trees. The procedure is passed bit vector and a pointer to a *locnode*. After the head node is allocated, the bit vector is stored in the node, and the *locnode* is inserted into the circular linked list pointed to by link of *p*. The procedure returns *p*, a pointer to the new node.

```
procedure getheadnode(var p : ptr2; bitvec : integer; t : ptr1);
  begin { node in binary tree }
    new(p);
    p↑.bitvec := bitvec;
    p↑.ltree := nil;
    p↑.rtree := nil;
    p↑.link   := nil;
    insert(t, p↑.link)
  end;
```

Procedure *treesort* inserts a bit vector into a binary tree in the correct position. The procedure is passed the bit vector and a pointer *t* to a *locnode*. The tree is traversed recursively, always taking the left subtree if the bit vector is less than that in the current node or the right subtree if it is greater, until a matching bit vector is found or until a **nil** pointer is encountered. If a matching node is found, the *locnode* is inserted at the end of the circular list on that node. If a **nil** pointer is found, indicating that the bit vector does not yet occur in the tree, a new tree node is allocated and inserted as a terminal node. This method of sorting was described in chapter 16.

```
procedure treesort(bitvec : integer; var t : ptr1; var p : ptr2);
  begin
    if p = nil
      then getheadnode(p, bitvec, t)
    else if bitvec < p↑.bitvec
      then treesort(bitvec, t, p↑.ltree)
    else if bitvec > p↑.bitvec
      then treesort(bitvec, t, p↑.rtree)
    else insert(t, p↑.link)
  end;
```

Procedure *calc* calculates the bit vectors for each segment in the twelve-tone matrix and inserts the information into the data structure. The loop structure was described in section 18.4.

```
procedure calc(m : matrix; var tree : treeptr);
  var
    card, i, j, first, last, bitvec1, bitvec2 : integer;
    t  : ptr1;
    p  : matrix;

  begin { calc all subsets in matrix }
    p := m;                                 { copy matrix                 }
    for i := 0 to 11 do                     { convert to powers of 2      }
      for j := 0 to 11 do
        p[i, j] := power(p[i, j]);

                        { calculate bit vectors for ordered subsets }
    for card := 1 to 11 do                  { set cardinality             }
      for i := 0 to 11 do                   { row number i                }
        for first := 0 to 11 do             { position of first element   }
```

```
        begin
          last := first + card - 1;          { position of last element   }
          bitvec1 := 0;                      { bitvec for rows            }
          bitvec2 := 0;                      { bitvec for columns         }

          for j := first to last do
            begin { set bits }
              bitvec1 := bitvec1 + p[i, (j mod 12)];              { row }
              bitvec2 := bitvec2 + p[(j mod 12),i]                { col }
            end;  { set bits }

          getnode(t, i + 1, first, last);      { get node for row bitvec }
          treesort(bitvec1, t, tree[card]);  { insert in tree          }
          getnode(t, -(i + 1), first, last);{ node for row bitvec      }
          treesort(bitvec2, t, tree[card])   { insert in tree          }
        end
    end;  { calc }
```

Function *convert* returns the hexadecimal character representing each pitch-class integer. This is used for converting from the internal to the external form when printing data.

```
function convert(pc : integer) : char;
  begin
    pc := pc mod 12;
    case pc of
      0 : convert := '0';
      1 : convert := '1';
      2 : convert := '2';
      3 : convert := '3';
      4 : convert := '4';
      5 : convert := '5';
      6 : convert := '6';
      7 : convert := '7';
      8 : convert := '8';
      9 : convert := '9';
     10 : convert := 'A';
     11 : convert := 'B'
    end { case }
  end;
```

Procedure *setrev* is the key to the matrix display, since this is the procedure that turns on (or off) individual matrix elements in the display. The procedure is passed as an argument one of the constants *highlight* (*true*) or *normal* (*false*). If the highlight mode is on, *reversevideo* is called at the beginning of the procedure (turning on the highlight mode) and *normalvideo* is called at the end (turning it off). Then the bit map of the matrix is scanned, and for each "on" bit, the corresponding element of the twelve-tone matrix is printed at the correct position on the screen. This is accomplished by arithmetically mapping the matrix position into the *x* and *y* coordinates on the display, and using *moveto* to place the cursor in that position before printing each character. This procedure is called twice for each matching segment of the matrix—once to turn on the appropriate elements in the display and once to turn them off again.

```
procedure setrev(map : bitmap; highlight : boolean);
  var
    i, j : integer;
  begin { setrev }
    if highlight
      then reversevideo;                { turn highlighting on or off }
    for i := 0 to 11 do
      for j := 0 to 11 do
        if j in map[i]
          then
            begin
              moveto(i + 5, 3 * j + 5);
              write(convert(m[i, j]))
            end;
    if highlight
      then normalvideo                  { reset normal video            }
  end; { setrev }
```

Function *positive* returns *true* if its argument is greater than 0.

```
function positive(x : integer) : boolean;
  begin
    positive := x >= 0
  end;
```

Procedure *traverse* traverses the circular list of *locnodes* pointed to by *p*. The list contains the locations of a matching subset in the matrix. As each node is visited, the data in its fields are used to set appropriate bits in the bit map of the matrix. Recall that 1 has been added to each row or column number and that columns are indicated by negative numbers.

```
procedure traverse(p : ptr1);
  var
    t : ptr1;
    i : integer;
    n : integer;
  begin { traverse circular linked list }
    t := p↑.link;
    repeat
      if positive(t↑.n)
        then
          begin
            n := t↑.n - 1;
            for i := t↑.first to t↑.last do
              map[n] := map[n] + [i mod 12]
          end
        else
          begin
            n := ( t↑.n)    1;
            for i := t↑.first to t↑.last do
               map[i mod 12] := map[i mod 12] + [n]
          end;
      t := t↑.link
    until t = p↑.link;
    setrev(map, highlight)
  end;
```

Procedure *printmat* prints the entire matrix on the terminal screen. It is called in the beginning of the run, after other user requests have caused the screen to be cleared, and when the user explicitly requests that the matrix be redrawn.

```
procedure printmat(m : matrix);                    { print/reprint matrix }
  var
    i, j : integer;
  begin
    clearscreen;
    moveto(3, 1);
    write('T    ');                                 { top boarder    }
    for i := 0 to 11 do
      write(convert(m[-1, i]):1, '  ');
    writeln; writeln;
    for i := 0 to 11 do
      begin
        write(convert(m[i, -1]):1, '   ');          { left boarder   }
        for j := 0 to 11 do
          write(convert(m[i, j]):1, '  ');
        writeln(' ', convert(i))
      end;
    writeln;
    write('     ');                                 { bottom border  }
    for i := 0 to 11 do
      write(convert(i):1, '  ');
    writeln
  end;
```

Procedure *readset* uses variable parameters to return the bit vector representing the input set, the cardinality of the set, and a return code indicating a successful read, an error, or a request for other action.

```
procedure readset(var bitvec : integer; var n : integer;
                                                   var code : integer);

  type
    pcs = 0 .. 11;
    pset = set of pcs;
  var
    pc    : integer;
    check : pset;
  begin
    getline(input, buffer);
    check := [];                                   { null set             }
    n := 0;                                        { cardinality          }
    code := 0;                                     { signal OK            }
    bitvec := 0;
    skipbuf(buffer);
    if iscommand(nextchar(buffer))
      then
        begin
          case nextchar(buffer) of
            'r'         : code := 1;               { signal redraw screen }
            '?','h','H' : code := 4;               { request for help     }
            '*'         : code := 5;               { reset asub and bsub  }
          end { case }
        end;
```

```
    while not eob(buffer) and (code = 0) do
      begin
        getpc(buffer, pc);
        if pc >= 0
          then
            begin
              if not (pc in check)
                then
                  begin
                    incr(n);
                    bitvec := bitvec + power(pc);          { set bit }
                    check := check + [pc]
                  end;
              skipbuf(buffer)
            end
          else code := 2                     { signal illegal character }
      end;
    if code = 0                              { normal return code        }
      then if n = 0                          { but cardinality = 0       }
        then code := 3                       { signal null set           }
  end;
```

Function *search*, which attempts to locate a bit vector in a binary search tree, returns *true* if it succeeds or *false* if it fails. The tree is traversed recursively. At each node the left or right subtree is traversed, depending on whether the subject bit vector is less than or greater than that of the current node. If the number is found in the tree, procedure *traverse* is called to process the locations stored in the circular list of *locnodes* associated with the node, and *search* is assigned *true*, indicating that the search was successful.

```
function search(x : integer; p : ptr2) : boolean;
  begin
    search := false;
    if p <> nil
      then
        begin
          if x = p↑.bitvec
            then
              begin
                traverse(p↑.link);
                search := true
              end
          else if x < p↑.bitvec
            then search := search(x, p↑.ltree)
          else search := search(x, p↑.rtree)
        end
  end;
```

Procedure *prompt* prints the prompt 'Type set:' below the matrix in the display. It then clears the rest of the line, erasing the previous input set.

```
procedure prompt;
  begin
    moveto(20, 1);
    write('Type set: '); clearline
  end;
```

Procedure *setsub* resets characters the user may employ as an alternate means of entering pcs 10 and 11. The user is given an opportunity to make corrections after the variables are set, and then the matrix is redrawn on the terminal screen.

```
procedure setsub(var buffer : buftype; var asub, bsub : char);
  begin
    clearscreen;
    write('Type sub for 10: ');
    getline(input, buffer);                       { get line in buffer }
    skipbuf(buffer);                              { skip blanks        }
    getchar(buffer, asub);                        { read sub for 10    }
    write('Type sub for 11: ');
    getline(input, buffer);                       { get line in buffer }
    skipbuf(buffer);                              { skip blanks        }
    getchar(buffer, bsub);                        { read sub for 11    }
    writeln(asub, ' = A; ' , bsub,' = B');        { double check       }
    write('OK? (y/n): ');
    if not affirmative(buffer)
      then setsub(buffer, asub, bsub)
      else printmat(m)                            { redraw matrix      }
  end;
```

Procedure *error* is passed the code returned by *readset*. A **case** statement uses this key to print an appropriate error message or to call procedures that implement other user commands.

```
procedure error(var buffer : buftype; key : integer);
  begin
    case key of
      1 : printmat(m);                            { redraw matrix      }
      2 : begin                                   { input error        }
            moveto(22, 8);
            write('Error in input');
            moveto(23, 8);
            write('pc := 0|1|2|3|4|5|6|7|8|9|a|b,  blanks optional')
          end;
      3 : begin                                   { cardinality error  }
            moveto(22, 8);
            writeln('Error: cardinality > 11 or < 1)')
          end;
      4 : begin
            instruct;                             { give instructions  }
            printmat(m)                           { redraw matrix      }
          end;
      5 : setsub(buffer, asub, bsub)
    end { case }
  end;  { error }
```

After each successful match and before the next set is processed, the screen display must be updated to turn off highlighted characters, and the bit map must be reset to reflect no matching elements, i.e., all elements are turned off. These functions are performed by procedure *cleanup*.

```
procedure cleanup(var map : bitmap);
  begin
    setrev(map, normal);                 { redraw matched elements }
    clear(map)                           { clear map of matrix     }
  end;
```

The main procedure initializes the *power* and *tree* arrays, as well as variables *match*, *asub*, and *bsub*. Next it erases the screen and prints instructions if the user requests them. Then it reads the twelve-tone row, fills the matrix, calculates and stores the subsets and their locations, and prints the matrix on the terminal screen.

Now the user is asked to type a set. If this is not the first set and the previous set was found in the matrix, the display and bit map are updated. The set or command is read, and depending on the condition code, the set is processed, an error message is printed, or other appropriate action is taken. Note that *match* is assigned a boolean value indicating the success or failure of each search. This value will be used to determine whether the display and bit map need to be reset before the next request is processed. This loop is repeated until the user types end-of-file (Control-D). At this point the display is cleared and the program terminates.

```
begin { main }
  init(tree, match, asub, bsub);
  clearscreen;
  writeln('Do you need instructions (y/n)? ');
  if affirmative(buffer)
    then instruct;
  clearscreen;
  readrow(buffer, m);
  fillmatrix(m);
  calc(m, tree);                      { calculate and store subsets }
  printmat(m);
  prompt;
  while not eof do
    begin
      if match                        { if last set matched         }
        then cleanup(map);            { clean up                    }
      readset(bitvec, card, code);
      if code = 0
        then match := search(bitvec, tree[card])
        else error(buffer, code);
      prompt
    end;
  clearscreen
end.  { main }
```

It is impossible to illustrate accurately the input and output for this program on paper. Figures 18.2 through 18.4 simulate the appearance of the CRT screen after the user requests the location of a set or asks for instructions, although here bold fonts are used instead of a negative image. In an actual program run, the computer takes a few seconds to calculate the subsets and construct the data structure. After this, all requests are processed almost instantaneously.

The combined use of appropriate data representations, data structures, searching methods, and terminal control sequences results in an efficient and elegant program. It would be possible to design a simpler version that searches the matrix for each set as it is typed and prints the locations by row form and order number, e.g., $T_6I_{(2-7)}$. However, such a program would run more slowly and would not be as pleasant to use as the one described here.

References and Selected Reading

Study the following, or the technical manual for your terminal or personal computer system, to find out more about screen control on your system.

VT 220 Programmer Pocket Guide. 2d ed. Maynard, Mass.: Digital Equipment Corporation, 1984.

Many more matrix applications are described in the following:

Alphonce, Bo H. *The Invariance Matrix.* Ph.D. diss., Yale University, 1974. Ann Arbor: University Microfilms, 1975 [#75-15m280].

Morris, Robert D. *Composition with Pitch-Classes: A Theory of Compositional Design.* New Haven: Yale University Press, 1987.

Rogers, John E. "Some Properties of Non-Duplicating Rotational Arrays." *Perspectives of New Music* 7, no. 2 (1968): 80–102.

Other suggested reading:

Holtzmann, Stephen R. "A Generative Grammar Definition Language for Music." *Interface* 9 (1980): 1–47.

LaRue, Jan. "New Directions for Style Analysis." In *Musicology and the Computer*, edited by Barry S. Brook, 194–97. New York: City University of New York Press, 1970.

Lewin, David. "Forte's Interval Vector, My Interval Function, and Regener's Common-Note Function." *Journal of Music Theory* 21, no. 2 (1977): 194–237.

Stech, David A. "A Computer-Assisted Approach to Micro-Analysis of Melodic Lines." *Computers and the Humanities* 15 (1981): 211–21.

Exercises

1. Obtain the technical manual for an output device on your system and experiment with terminal control functions until you have some confidence in all facets of control.

2. Modify the control sequences for the program in this chapter so that it will work on your terminal. If you do not have a terminal with sufficient format control to use this program, modify the program to print output in a format appropriate for your terminal. This may be row forms and order numbers, or complete row forms with segments underlined.

3. Write a program that calculates invariance matrices[7] and displays the location of all pitch classes specified in the input.

7. See Bo Alphonce, *The Invariance Matrix* (Ann Arbor: University Microfilms, 1975).

4. A more challenging version of the invariance-matrix program could examine the diagonals for occurrences of the desired integer, and print out the relevant row forms with invariant segments highlighted. A further modification would be to find unordered invariant segments by searching for submatrices in which the required integer occurs in each row (or column).

5. Many extensions to the program shown in this chapter are possible. Any or all of the following would be useful exercises:

   a) Allow for rows of any reasonable length.

   b) Allow the option of using two different rows, and let the user specify the type of matrix (T matrix, I matrix, M matrix, MI matrix).

   c) Make it possible for the user to switch between matrix types while the program is running.

   d) Permit the user to specify that the program will match either contiguous elements or separate elements.

   e) Allow the user to change rows while the program is running.

19| Spelling Pitch Structures

In this chapter we will learn a number of new techniques: generating pseudo-random numbers; arithmetic manipulation of pitch in a form that gives correct results in pitch, spelling, and register; and modeling the structure of pitch collections. We will then use these techniques in a large CAI[1] program designed to provide drill and practice exercises for music students. Besides demonstrating the techniques discussed in the first part of the chapter, this program illustrates many techniques discussed in earlier chapters. It is a particularly good example of the use of Pascal's fixed records.

19.1 Generating Random Numbers

There are many uses for random numbers in programming. They are helpful in writing programs that simulate various processes, in generating input data for testing programs, and in making decisions or choices in a program. Random numbers have been used in ingenious solutions to many problems, such as finding the area under a curve by seeing how many random values fall below it.

Thus it is often useful to generate numbers that simulate a random series. This may be a series of m integers I_i, $0 \le I_i \le m - 1$, or a series of m real numbers R_i, $0 \le R_i \le 1$, that repeats after a given period. The goals are to make the period so long that the series does not repeat in typical situations, and to make the distribution of numbers uniform, i.e., each possible number equally probable.

The most common method of calculating this series is called the *linear congruential method.* This method uses a starting value S_0 (the *seed* value), a multiplier a, a constant increment c, and a modulus m. The sequence of random numbers (S_n) is calculated by the following formula:

$$S_{n+1} = (a\, S_n + c) \bmod m$$

$$\text{where} \quad \begin{aligned} n &\ge 0, \\ S_n &\ge 0, \\ a &\ge 2, \\ c &\ge 0, \\ m > S_n, &\quad m > a, \quad m > c. \end{aligned}$$

Since each number in the series is calculated from the previous number by this

1. Computer-Assisted Instruction.

formula, the numbers are not really random. While the theory behind the method is beyond the scope of this book, the choice of values is critical.[2] It is obvious from the use of modulo m that this formula produces a series of m integers with values between 0 and $m - 1$. The optimal values result in a period of length m, i.e., each integer between 0 and $m - 1$ occurs one time in the series. Knuth presents a proof that this is true only if the following conditions obtain:

1. c is relatively prime to m.
2. $a - 1$ is a multiple of p, for every prime p dividing m.
3. $a - 1$ is a multiple of 4, if m is a multiple of 4.[3]

We will use values $a = 25173$, $c = 13849$, and $m = 65536$.[4] A Pascal function for generating pseudo-random numbers using these values is shown below:[5]

```
function random(var seed : long) : integer;
  begin
    seed := ((25173 * seed) + 13849) mod 65536;
    random := seed
  end;
```

This function generates a uniform distribution of integers between 0 and 65535, with a period of 65536. Note that the function uses a variable parameter so that it can save the value of the new seed for generating the next number in the series. The function is used by declaring a global variable *seed*, and initializing it to any integer value before the function is called the first time. Since *seed* always has a value between 0 and 65535, the function can be modified to return a real value between 0 and 1 by returning the value (*seed* / 65536), as shown below:

```
function random(var seed : long) : real;
  begin
    seed := ((25173 * seed) + 13849) mod 65536
    random := seed / 65536
  end;
```

A random integer in a specified range can be obtained by several methods. Some authors have suggested using the **mod** operator to limit the range of integers. For example, an integer between 3 and 11 can be generated by

```
i := random(seed) mod 9 + 3
```

2. See the references at the end of this chapter for more information.

3. Donald E. Knuth, *The Art of Computer Programming*, vol. 2, *Seminumerical Algorithms*, (Reading Mass.: Addison-Wesley, 1969), 15–19.

4. These values are suggested by Peter Grogono (*Programming in Pascal*, 2d ed. [Reading, Mass.: Addison-Wesley, 1984]) and Doug Cooper and Michael Clancy (*Oh! Pascal!*, 2d ed. [New York: W.W. Norton, 1985]).

5. In these functions the nonstandard type *long* has been used to indicate that these procedures require 32-bit integers. If your computer uses 32-bit integers, these can be changed to *integer*. Later we will see a version of the function that does not require long integers.

This is generalized in the function shown below, which uses the integer version of function *random*:

```
function rand(low, high : integer) : integer;
  begin
    rand := random(seed) mod (high - low + 1) + low
  end;
```

However, random-number generators of this type can be affected in unpredictable ways by indiscriminate use of the **mod** operator (e.g., degenerating into shorter repeating patterns).

Another method is to use the *real* version of function *random* to scale the difference between the low and high values required. The result is added to *low* and rounded.

```
i := round(random(seed) * (high - low) + low)
```

Unfortunately, the probability of rounding to *low* or *high* is half that of any other integer between *low* and *high*. We correct for this in the following version of the function:

```
function irand(lo, hi : integer) : integer;
  begin
    irand := round(lo + random(seed) * (hi - lo + 1) - 0.5)
  end;
```

This is also useful when your are using a random-number generator provided by your computer system, since it is likely to return real numbers between 0 and 1.

The linear congruential method of calculating pseudo-random numbers will always generate the same number sequence from any given starting value. This is helpful for debugging a program, but it is not desirable in a real application. Many Pascal systems have a nonstandard function that returns an integer representing the time of day. Since the time includes hours, minutes, and seconds, it is useful for setting the *seed* value; however, this feature is not portable to systems that lack this function. An alternative is to create an external file that contains a single integer value. The *seed* is read from this file at the beginning of the program run and written back to it before termination. Thus each program run starts the sequence where the last run left off. The following procedures perform this function:

```
[  program test(input,output, rseed);

    var
      rseed : text;
      seed  : long;     ]

    procedure getseed(var f : text; var seed : long);
      begin
        reset(f);
        read(f, seed)
      end;
```

```
procedure saveseed(var f : text; seed : long);
  begin
    rewrite(f);
    write(f, seed)
  end;

begin { main }
  getseed(rseed, seed);
  ...
  saveseed(rseed, seed)
end.  { main }
```

Many computer systems include a random-number generator that has been tuned for optimum performance with the system. If one of these is available, you should use it. If not, the functions shown above work well on any system that uses 32-bit integers. The version shown below, with a period of 875, should work reasonably well on any system:

```
function random(var seed : integer) : real;
  begin
    seed := (36 * seed + 29) mod 875;
    random := seed / 875
  end;
```

If necessary, you can write variations of this function based on the examples shown above, or devise your own random-number generator using the guidelines specified above.

19.2 Manipulating cbrs

In chapter 6[6] we saw that pitch, spelling, and octave can be mapped into a single signed integer (cbr) in the form

$$\pm opcn$$

where	$\pm$	is an optional sign
	o	is the octave (0, 1, . . .),
	pc	is the pitch class (00, 01, . . ., 11), and
	n	is the name class (0, 1, . . ., 6)

The cbr is a single integer that represents pitches or intervals, as shown in table 19.1. Pitches are always positive; intervals may be signed to show direction. We suggested that a function that adds signed cbrs would enable us to calculate intervals or transpose cbrs, but we did not show the functions that would perform this task.

Calculations on signed cbrs are performed by converting the octave, name class, and pitch class to continuous pitch code (cpc) and continuous name code (cnc). The calculations are then done separately on the cpc and cnc codes. Since the octave depends on spelling rather than pitch, the octave of the result is derived from the cnc

6. The reader may wish to review section 6.2.

Pitch	*cbr*	*Interval*	*cbr*
C♯$_5$	5010	P1	0000
E𝄪$_3$	3062	M2	0021
G♭$_2$	2064	m2	0011
F♯$_2$	2063	m9	1011
C𝄫$_7$	7100	M3	0042
B$_4$	4116	M10	1042
B♯$_4$	4006	P12	1074
C♭$_5$	5110	d15	2110

Table 19.1. Examples of Continuous Binomial Representation

calculation. The following functions extract the necessary information from the cbr, and reconstruct the cbr from the component parts. Note that the octave, pc, and nc are extracted as positive numbers, as is the binomial integer br. The extra tests in function *cpc* are needed to calculate the correct value for C-flat <11,0>, B-sharp <0,6>, and other similar instances in which the difference between the pitch class for the natural note and that for the altered note would seem to indicate more than six sharps or flats. This is necessary because the cbr does not maintain a separate octave number for the name class and pitch class.

```
{ map octave, pc, and nc into cbr }
function cbr(octave, pc, nc : integer) : integer;
  begin
    if octave >= 0
      then cbr :=   octave * 1000 + pc * 10 + nc
      else cbr := -(abs(octave) * 1000 + pc * 10 + nc)
  end;


{ extract binomial representation (pc & nc) }
function br(cbr : integer) : integer;
  begin
    br := abs(cbr) mod 1000
  end;


{ extract octave from cbr }
function octave(cbr : integer) : integer;
  begin
    octave := abs(cbr) div 1000
  end;


{ extract pc from cbr }
function pitchclass(cbr : integer) : integer;
  begin
    pitchclass := br(cbr) div 10
  end;
```

```
{ extract nc from cbr }
function nameclass(cbr : integer) : integer;
  begin
    nameclass := br(cbr) mod 10
  end;


{ convert name class to natural pitch class }
function pitch(nc : integer) : integer;
  begin
    case nc of
      0 : pitch := 0;   { pc for c }
      1 : pitch := 2;   { pc for d }
      2 : pitch := 4;   { pc for e }
      3 : pitch := 5;   { pc for f }
      4 : pitch := 7;   { pc for g }
      5 : pitch := 9;   { pc for a }
      6 : pitch := 11   { pc for b }
    end { case }
  end; { pitch }


{ calculate continuous pitch code }
function cpc(cbr : integer) : integer;
  var
    o, p, n : integer;
    diff    : integer;
  begin
    o := octave(cbr);
    n := nameclass(cbr);
    p := pitchclass(cbr);
    diff := p - pitch(n);
    if diff > 6                    { adjust for more than six sharps }
      then o := o - 1
    else if diff < -6              { or for more than six flats      }
      then o := o + 1;
    if cbr < 0
       then cpc := -(12 * o + p)
       else cpc :=  (12 * o + p)
  end;


{ calculate continuous name code }
function cnc(cbr : integer) : integer;
  begin
    if cbr < 0
      then cnc := -(octave(cbr) * 7 + nameclass(cbr))
      else cnc :=   octave(cbr) * 7 + nameclass(cbr)
  end;
```

The following function adds two signed cbrs and returns the result in the same form. Since either cbr can be negative, the procedure can be used to subtract as well. In subtraction (adding a negative cbr to a positive cbr), the direction depends on the name class (spelling) rather than the pitch class, unless the two notes are spelled on the same letter name.

```
{ add or subtract two signed cbrs }
function add(cbr1, cbr2 : integer) : integer;
  var
    pitch, name, octave : integer;
    negative : boolean;
  begin
    pitch := abs(cpc(cbr1) + cpc(cbr2)) mod 12;
    name := cnc(cbr1) + cnc(cbr2);
    if name <> 0                          { base direction on cnc }
      then negative := name < 0           { unless ncs are equal  }
      else negative := (cpc(cbr1) + cpc(cbr2)) < 0;
           octave := abs(name) div 7;
    name := abs(name) mod 7;
    if negative
      then add := -cbr(octave, pitch, name)
      else add :=  cbr(octave, pitch, name)
  end; { add }
```

Since the cbrs can represent either pitches or intervals, this function is extremely useful. The interval between two encoded pitches *cbr1* and *cbr2* is calculated by subtracting the first from the second: *add(cbr2, –cbr1)* or *add(–cbr1, cbr2)*. The sign of the result indicates direction (descending intervals are negative), and compound intervals have an octave component greater than 0. If one *cbr* represents a pitch and the other an interval, the function transposes the pitch by an amount equal to the interval, which may be negative. As an added benefit, the *cbr* is not difficult to translate to and from more convenient external codes for input and output.

19.3 Representing Pitch Structures

Since each pitch in any collection of notes can be expressed as an interval above (or below) the first note, the binomial system can represent larger pitch structures. For example, the structure of any major triad can be expressed as a major third and a perfect fifth above the root. Thus the structure of a major triad can be represented by the br structure [000, 042, 074].[7] Each br represents an interval above the point of origin or root. In the same manner, the structure of any major scale can be represented as a series of intervals above the tonic.

Since all instances of a given structure are transpositionally equivalent, the correct spelling for any transposition can be calculated by adding the binomial representation of the desired root or tonic to each element of the structure.[8] Figure 19.1 illustrates the calculation of the notes in the G-flat major scale from the major-scale br structure.

If octave information is required, the same principle can be applied to cbr structures, with function *add* (from the previous section of this chapter) to do the calculations. Figure 19.2 shows the cbr structure of the major scale, transposed to begin on A_4.

7. The first two digits represent the pitch class; the last digit is the name class representing spelling.

8. Recall that the pc and nc components are added separately in mod 12 and mod 7, respectively.

The br structure of the major scale:

	00	21	42	53	74	95	116	00	

The G♭ Major scale is calculated by adding G♭ (64) to each element:

	00	21	42	53	74	95	116	00	
+	64	64	64	64	64	64	64	64	
	64	85	106	110	11	32	53	64	
(	G♭	A♭	B♭	C♭	D♭	E♭	F	G♭	)

Figure 19.1. Calculating the G♭ Major Scale from the BR structure

	0000	0021	0042	0053	0074	0095	0116	1000	
+	4095	4095	4095	4095	4095	4095	4095	4095	
	4095	4116	5010	5021	5042	5063	5084	5095	
(	A_4	B_4	$C\#_5$	D_4	E_5	$F\#_5$	$G\#_5$	A_5	)

Figure 19.2. Calculating the Major Scale on A_4 from the cbr Structure

(	G_4	A_4	B_4	C_5	D_5	E_5	$F\#_5$	G_5	)
	4074	4095	4116	5000	5021	5042	5063	5074	
−	4074	4074	4074	4074	4074	4074	4074	4074	
	0000	0021	0042	0053	0074	0095	0116	1000	

Figure 19.3. Calculating the CBR Structure of a Major Scale from a Model

Since we have already devised a method of calculating intervals from cbrs, we can calculate the structure from an example. The major-scale structure can be calculated from any major scale by subtracting the first pitch from each element, as shown in figure 19.3.

19.4 Program *Muspell*: Specifications

Program *muspell* was designed to meet the following specfications:

Function. The program will provide practice in spelling pitch structures (scales, chords, pitches, modes, altered chords, etc.). It will provide questions, read and check the user's answer, and give feedback in the form of verification that the response was correct, or appropriate messages if it is not. If the answer is incorrect, the user will be given a second chance to answer, and if the second try is also wrong, the correct answer will be printed and the question saved for later review. The program will be able to generate questions in many categories. The user will specify the categories from which questions will be chosen, the number of questions in each category, and the level of difficulty as a function of the number of accidentals in the root or tonic of the pitch structure. In addition, the user will be able to choose whether or not octave information is to be included in questions and answers, and beginners may specify "generic" questions and answers that are nonspecific with regard to accidentals. Generic questions may also include octave information if the user wishes. At the end of each set of questions, and at the end of the program run, the score will be printed as the percentage of correct answers, and the user will be given the opportunity to review questions missed. Scoring will be based on 1 point for each question answered correctly on the first try, 1/2 point for questions answered correctly on the second try, and 0 points for incorrect answers. The program will tabulate scores for review questions, but these will not affect the final score.

Input. Answers to questions will be given as strings of note names specified in the SCORE input format (see section 6.6). Each note is specified as the note name, optionally followed by any number of sharps or flats and the octave number. Sharps and flats are designated by the characters 's' (sharp) or 'f' (flat); double and triple accidentals are encoded by repeating the appropriate character. When octaves are specified, they are required for the first note, but need not be repeated except when the octave changes. Examples:

D F♯ A:	d fs a
C𝄪$_5$:	css5
F$_3$ A♭$_3$ C♭$_4$ E𝄫$_4$:	f3 af cf4 eff
F$_4$ F♭$_4$ F𝄫♭$_3$:	f4 ff fff3

Other information needed by the program is specified by numbers chosen from menus or questions requiring "yes" or "no" answers.

Output. The program prints instructions if required by the user. It then prints menus specifying categories of questions and prompts the user for other information (level of difficulty, use of octave numbers, number of questions in each category, etc.). The main menu allows the user to choose one of seven categories:

```
Problem Types:

  1.  Intervals
  2.  Scales
  3.  Scale Steps
  4.  Spelling Chords
  5.  Diatonic Chords
  6.  Altered Chords
  7.  I'll Try Anything

Type number:
```

Each choice, except for the last, results in a second menu with a number of sub-categories. After selecting the type of questions to be answered, the user provides other information, including the level of difficulty, whether or not register is to be included, and the number of questions required. Questions are chosen at random from the specified category.

The program provides messages confirming correct responses, or for incorrect ones it gives the correct answer in the same form as user input (see above). The percentage of correct answers is printed at the end of each problem set and again at the end of the program run. If there are syntatic errors in the user's input, the line is printed with a pointer to the error, and the user is prompted to reenter the response.

19.5 Implementation

Questions, and rules for constructing their answers, are stored in a data table. Each "rule" is a model that the program will use to compute the correct answer, which will then be compared to the student's answer. The primary and secondary categories of questions provided by the program are shown in table 19.2, as are the limits of each category in the table. Questions and model answers are read from an external data file. Each line of the file consists of a question terminated by a colon, followed by an answer model. For example, the entries for a major scale are as follows:

```
a major scale (one octave ascending) on:     c0 d e f g a b c1
a major scale (one octave descending) on:    c1 b0 a g f e d c
```

The table consists of an array of records, each of which contains a string (as a packed array of characters), an array for the elements of the answer, and the number of elements in the answer. As each line of data is read, the question is stored as a string, and the model of the answer is encoded as in continuous binomial representation. The cbr structure of the answer is then calculated by subtracting the first element from each other element (see section 19.3).

In the data file, some model answers are preceded by a plus or minus sign, as in the entries shown below:

```
a major seventh above:                       -c0 b
a major seventh below:                       -b0 c

o7/V in the major key of:                    +fs0 a c1 ef
o7/vi in the major key of:                   +gs0 b d1 f
```

The minus sign signals the program to omit the first element while calculating the cbr structure of the answer, so the user can specify a single note in response to questions such as

```
Spell a diminished twelfth above Bs2:
```

The plus sign indicates that the cbr representing the first pitch in the actual answer is to be added to each element of the structure, thus transposing the structure relative to some tonic (or root, as the case may be). This allows us to represent diatonic chord functions, applied (secondary) chord functions, etc.

Secondary Category	*Location in Table*	
1. Intervals		
1. Generic Simple Intervals (no sharps or flats)	251	263
2. Generic Compound Intervals	264	279
3. Fourths, Fifths, and Primes	1	6
4. Seconds and Thirds	7	14
5. Sixths and Sevenths	15	22
6. Review	1	22
7. Augmented and Diminished Intervals	23	50
8. Compound Intervals	51	74
9. Compound Intervals (aug. and dim.)	75	106
10. Review	23	106
2. Scales		
1. Generic	280	281
2. Major Scales	107	108
3. Minor Scales	109	114
4. Review	107	114
5. Diatonic Modes	115	128
6. Review	107	128
3. Scale Steps		
1. In Major	129	135
2. In Minor	136	144
3. Review	129	144
4. Altered Tones in Major and Minor	145	156
5. Review	129	156
4. Spelling Chords		
1. Generic Triads	282	282
2. Generic Seventh Chords	283	283
3. Spelling Triads	157	160
4. Spelling Seventh Chords	161	166
5. Review	157	166
5. Diatonic Chords		
1. Diatonic Triads in Major	167	173
2. Diatonic Triads in Minor	174	183
3. Review	167	183
4. Diatonic Seventh Chords in Major	184	190
5. Diatonic Seventh Chords in Minor	191	197
6. Review	167	197
6. Altered Chords		
1. Modal Mixture in Major and Minor	198	206
2. Applied Dominants in Major	207	216
3. Applied Dominants in Minor	217	226
4. Review	207	226
5. Applied vii^{o} and vii^{o7} in Major	227	236
6. Applied vii^{o} and vii^{o7} in Minor	237	246
7. Review	207	246
8. Augmented Sixths and Neapolitans	247	250
9. Review	198	250

Table 19.2. Program *Muspell* Question Categories

The program chooses each question by generating a random integer in the range corresponding to the desired question type in the data table:

```
qnum := irand(low, high);
```

The root or tonic is also generated using the random-number generator. The name class is obtained by generating an integer between 0 and 6. The pitch class for the natural note is obtained by table lookup, and then adjusted by adding a random number between limits set according to the desired level of difficulty. The octave is also chosen randomly. Finally, the components of the pitch are combined into a single integer in cbr format. For example, the following statements would generate a note with possible accidentals ranging from double flats to double sharps, somewhere in octaves 2 through 7.

```
nc := irand(0, 6);                    { get name class          }
pc := pitch(nc) + irand(-2, +2);      { get pitch class         }
pc := (pc + 12) mod 12;               { be sure range is 0-11   }
oct := irand(2, 7);                   { get octave              }
root := cbr(oct, pc, nc);             { convert to cbr          }
```

Suppose the generated root is E♭$_3$ (3032). Now the correct answer to the question is calculated by adding this value to each element of the cbr structure of the answer, and the user is asked the question, e.g.,

```
Spell a o7/V in the major key on Ef3

Type answer:
```

The user's answer is converted to cbr notation and compared to the answer calculated by the program. The function that compares the user's response and the computed answer uses a function passed as an argument to modify each element of the two arrays. Depending on the function used, the elements are compared as they are (with octave, pitch, and spelling components), or with various parts suppressed. For example, the octave can be suppressed, or if the question is generic, the pitch-class component is changed to 00, so it will always match.

The program's responses, whether to correct or incorrect answers, are also picked with the random-number generator, giving the session some variety. When questions are not answered correctly by the second attempt, the correct answer is printed on the user's screen, and the parameters for the question are saved in a queue. These values include the question number, level of difficulty, and flags indicating whether the question is generic or specific and whether or not octave numbers are to be included. At the end of each set of problems, the user is given an opportunity to review questions that were missed previously. For each review question, the appropriate values are removed from the queue. Each question uses the same values as in the original, but with a new randomly generated root or tonic. If the solution is missed, the user is given the correct answer and the question is placed in the queue again. Thus the question keeps returning in different guises until it is answered correctly.

At the end of each set of problems, any review problems that have not been answered are removed from the first queue and placed in a second queue. This mechanism allows the user to review incorrectly answered questions from each problem set, and to review all problems missed and not subsequently solved at the end of the program run.

At first glance it appears that this program does a fair amount of computation compared to a program that simply reads fixed questions and fixed answers. Is it worth the effort and computation time? With the methods described here, each problem is stored one time, along with the structure of the answer. For example, the question "Spell a major chord" is stored just once along with the cbr structure of the chord. This is a great improvement over storing every possible major chord, even without considering octave placement. The data table contains 283 questions with the structure of the answer for each. Within the range of all levels of difficulty, including natural notes, sharps, flats, double and triple sharps and flats, and generic questions, all with or without octave designations, the program chooses from over 87,000 possible variations of the questions and can calculate the correct answer to each in a few milliseconds.[9] Obviously, this level of diversity would be impossible if each question and its answer were stored separately, and you would not wish to create the list of questions even if you had enough computer memory and disk space to store them.

Why bother with double and triple accidentals? After all, the student will never encounter the key of B-triple-sharp major in the literature! But when exercises are pushed to these limits the student cannot rely on memorized answers. He or she must understand the structure of our tonal system in order to arrive at the correct answers. The higher levels of difficulty, once mastered, require mental gymnastics that make the usual spelling problems encountered in music seem trivial by comparison.

Figure 19.4 (below) shows the data file containing questions and model answers read by the program. The lines are numbered here so that you can compare them to the question categories listed in table 19.2. The line numbers are *not* part of the data.

```
 1. a perfect prime above:                    -c0 c
 2. a perfect prime below:                    -c0 c
 3. a perfect fourth above:                   -c0 f
 4. a perfect fourth below:                   -f0 c
 5. a perfect fifth above:                    -c0 g
 6. a perfect fifth below:                    -g0 c
 7. a major second above:                     -c0 d
 8. a major second below:                     -d0 c
 9. a major third above:                      -c0 e
10. a major third below:                      -e0 c
11. a minor second above:                     -c0 df
12. a minor second below:                     -df0 c
13. a minor third above:                      -c0 ef
```

9. There are 250 specific questions, each of which can be spelled on seven pitches, each of which may have any of seven accidentals, in any of six octaves or without octave information specified. The thirty-three generic questions can be transposed to seven pitches in any of six octaves or without octave information. Thus there are $250 \times 7^3 = 85{,}750$ variations of the specific questions and $33 \times 7^2 = 1{,}617$ variations of the generic questions, or a total of 87,367 possible variations of the 283 questions in the data base.

14. a minor third below:	-ef0 c
15. a major sixth above:	-c0 a
16. a major sixth below:	-a0 c
17. a major seventh above:	-c0 b
18. a major seventh below:	-b0 c
19. a minor sixth above:	-c0 af
20. a minor sixth below:	-af0 c
21. a minor seventh above:	-c0 bf
22. a minor seventh below:	-bf0 c
23. an augmented prime above:	-c0 cs
24. an augmented prime below:	-c0 cf
25. an augmented second above:	-c0 ds
26. an augmented second below:	-ds0 c
27. an augmented third above:	-c0 es
28. an augmented third below:	-es0 c
29. an augmented fourth above:	-c0 fs
30. an augmented fourth below:	-fs0 c
31. an augmented fifth above:	-c0 gs
32. an augmented fifth below:	-gs0 c
33. an augmented sixth above:	-c0 as
34. an augmented sixth below:	-as0 c
35. an augmented seventh above:	-c0 bs
36. an augmented seventh below:	-bs0 c
37. a diminished prime above:	-c0 cf
38. a diminished prime below:	-c0 cs
39. a diminished second above:	-c0 dff
40. a diminished second below:	-dff0 c
41. a diminished third above:	-c0 eff
42. a diminished third below:	-eff0 c
43. a diminished fourth above:	-c0 ff
44. a diminished fourth below:	-ff0 c
45. a diminished fifth above:	-c0 gf
46. a diminished fifth below:	-gf0 c
47. a diminished sixth above:	-c0 aff
48. a diminished sixth below:	-aff0 c
49. a diminished seventh above:	-c0 bff
50. a diminished seventh below:	-bff0 c
51. a perfect octave above:	-c0 c1
52. a perfect octave below:	-c1 c0
53. a perfect eleventh above:	-c0 f1
54. a perfect eleventh below:	-f1 c0
55. a perfect twelfth above:	-c0 g1
56. a perfect twelfth below:	-g1 c0
57. a perfect fifteenth above:	-c0 c2
58. a perfect fifteenth below:	-c2 c0
59. a major ninth above:	-c0 d1
60. a major ninth below:	-d1 c0
61. a major tenth above:	-c0 e1
62. a major tenth below:	-e1 c0
63. a major thirteenth above:	-c0 a1
64. a major thirteenth below:	-a1 c0
65. a major fourteenth above:	-c0 b1
66. a major fourteenth below:	-b1 c0
67. a minor ninth above:	-c0 df1
68. a minor ninth below:	-df1 c0
69. a minor tenth above:	-c0 ef1
70. a minor tenth below:	-ef1 c0

71. a minor thirteenth above:	-c0 af1
72. a minor thirteenth below:	-af1 c0
73. a minor fourteenth above:	-c0 bf1
74. a minor fourteenth below:	-bf1 c0
75. an augmented octave above:	-c0 cs1
76. an augmented octave below:	-cs1 c0
77. an augmented ninth above:	-c0 ds1
78. an augmented ninth below:	-ds1 c0
79. an augmented tenth above:	-c0 es1
80. an augmented tenth below:	-es1 c0
81. an augmented eleventh above:	-c0 fs1
82. an augmented eleventh below:	-fs1 c0
83. an augmented twelfth above:	-c0 gs1
84. an augmented twelfth below:	-gs1 c0
85. an augmented thirteenth above:	-c0 as1
86. an augmented thirteenth below:	-as1 c0
87. an augmented fourteenth above:	-c0 bs1
88. an augmented fourteenth below:	-bs1 c0
89. an augmented fifteenth above:	-c0 cs2
90. an augmented fifteenth below:	-cs2 c0
91. a diminished octave above:	-c0 cf1
92. a diminished octave below:	-cf1 c0
93. a diminished ninth above:	-c0 dff1
94. a diminished ninth below:	-dff1 c0
95. a diminished tenth above:	-c0 eff1
96. a diminished tenth below:	-eff1 c0
97. a diminished eleventh above:	-c0 ff1
98. a diminished eleventh below:	-ff1 c0
99. a diminished twelfth above:	-c0 gf1
100. a diminished twelfth below:	-gf1 c0
101. a diminished thirteenth above:	-c0 aff1
102. a diminished thirteenth below:	-aff1 c0
103. a diminished fourteenth above:	-c0 bff1
104. a diminished fourteenth below:	-bff1 c0
105. a diminished fifteenth above:	-c0 cf2
106. a diminished fifteenth below:	-cf2 c0
107. a major scale (one octave ascending) on:	c0 d e f g a b c1
108. a major scale (one octave descending) on:	c1 b0 a g f e d c
109. a natural minor scale (one octave ascending) on:	c0 d ef f g af bf c1
110. a natural minor scale (one octave descending) on:	c1 bf0 af g f ef d c
111. a harmonic minor scale (one octave ascending) on:	c0 d ef f g af b c1
112. a harmonic minor scale (one octave descending) on:	c1 b0 af g f ef d c
113. a melodic minor scale (one octave ascending) on:	c0 d ef f g a b c1
114. a melodic minor scale (one octave descending) on:	c1 bf0 af g f ef d c
115. an ionian mode (one octave ascending) on:	c0 d e f g a b c1
116. an ionian mode (one octave descending) on:	c1 b0 a g f e d c
117. a lydian mode (one octave ascending) on:	c0 d e fs g a b c1
118. a lydian mode (one octave descending) on:	c1 b0 a g fs e d c
119. a mixolydian mode (one octave ascending) on:	c0 d e f g a bf c1
120. a mixolydian mode (one octave descending) on:	c1 bf0 a g f e d c
121. an aeolian mode (one octave ascending) on:	c0 d ef f g af bf c1
122. an aeolian mode (one octave descending) on:	c1 bf0 af g f ef d c
123. a dorian mode (one octave ascending) on:	c0 d ef f g a bf c1
124. a dorian mode (one octave descending) on:	c1 bf0 a g f ef d c
125. a phrygian mode (one octave ascending) on:	c0 df ef f g af bf c1
126. a phrygian mode (one octave descending) on:	c1 bf0 af g f ef df c
127. a locrian mode (one octave ascending) on:	c0 df ef f gf af bf c1

128. a locrian mode (one octave descending) on:	c1 bf0 af gf f ef df c
129. the tonic pitch in the major key on:	-c0 c
130. the supertonic pitch in the major key on:	-c0 d
131. the mediant pitch in the major key on:	-c0 e
132. the subdominant pitch in the major key on:	-c0 f
133. the dominant pitch in the major key on:	-c0 g
134. the submediant pitch in the major key on:	-c0 a
135. the leading tone in the major key on:	-c0 b
136. the tonic pitch in the minor key on:	-c0 c
137. the supertonic pitch in the minor key on:	-c0 d
138. the mediant pitch in the minor key on:	-c0 ef
139. the subdominant pitch in the minor key on:	-c0 f
140. the dominant pitch in the minor key on:	-c0 g
141. the submediant pitch in the minor key on:	-c0 af
142. the raised submediant pitch in the minor key on:	-c0 a
143. the leading tone in the minor key on:	-c0 b
144. the subtonic pitch in the minor key on:	-c0 bf
145. the raised tonic pitch in the major key on:	-c0 cs
146. the raised supertonic pitch in the major key on:	-c0 ds
147. the raised subdominant pitch in the major key on:	-c0 fs
148. the raised dominant pitch in the major key on:	-c0 gs
149. the lowered submediant pitch in the major key on:	-c0 af
150. the lowered supertonic pitch in the major key on:	-c0 df
151. the lowered mediant pitch in the major key on:	-c0 ef
152. the raised tonic pitch in the minor key on:	-c0 cs
153. the lowered supertonic pitch in the minor key on:	-c0 df
154. the raised mediant pitch in the minor key on:	-c0 e
155. the raised subdominant pitch in the minor key on:	-c0 fs
156. the raised submediant pitch in the minor key on:	-c0 a
157. a major triad on:	c0 e g
158. a minor triad on:	c0 ef g
159. a diminished triad on:	c0 ef gf
160. an augmented triad on:	c0 e gs
161. a major-minor (dominant) seventh chord on:	c0 e g bf
162. a minor-minor seventh chord on:	c0 ef g bf
163. a major-major seventh chord on:	c0 e g b
164. a minor-major seventh chord on:	c0 ef g b
165. a half-diminished seventh chord on:	c0 ef gf bf
166. a diminished seventh chord on:	c0 ef gf bff
167. a tonic chord in the major key of:	+c0 e g
168. the supertonic chord in the major key of:	+d0 f a
169. the mediant chord in the major key of:	+e0 g b
170. the subdominant chord in the major key of:	+f0 a c1
171. the dominant chord in the major key of:	+g0 b d1
172. the submediant chord in the major key of:	+a0 c1 e
173. the leading-tone chord in the major key of:	+b0 d1 f
174. the tonic chord in the minor key of:	+c0 ef g
175. the supertonic chord in the minor key of:	+d0 f af
176. the mediant chord in the minor key of:	+ef0 g bf
177. the augmented mediant chord in the minor key of:	+ef0 g b
178. the subdominant chord in the minor key of:	+f0 af c1
179. the minor dominant chord in the minor key of:	+g0 bf d1
180. the major dominant chord in the minor key of:	+g0 b d1
181. the submediant chord in the minor key of:	+af0 c1 ef
182. the subtonic chord in the minor key of:	+bf0 d f
183. the leading-tone chord in the minor key of:	+b0 d f
184. the tonic seventh chord in the major key of:	+c0 e g b

```
185. the supertonic seventh chord in the major key of:   +d0 f a c1
186. the mediant seventh chord in the major key of:      +e0 g b d1
187. the subdominant seventh chord in the major key of:  +f0 a c1 e
188. the dominant seventh chord in the major key of:     +g0 b d1 f
189. the submediant seventh chord in the major key of:   +a0 c1 e g
190. the leading-tone seventh chord in the major key of: +b0 d1 f a
191. the tonic seventh chord in the minor key of:        +c0 ef g bf
192. the supertonic seventh chord in the minor key of:   +d0 g af c1
193. the mediant seventh chord in the minor key of:      +ef0 g bf d1
194. the subdominant seventh chord in the minor key of:  +f0 af c1 ef
195. the dominant seventh chord in the minor key of:     +g0 b d1 f
196. the submediant seventh chord in the minor key of:   +af0 c1 ef g
197. the leading-tone seventh chord in the minor key of: +b0 d1 f af
198. the minor tonic chord in the major key of:          +c0 ef g
199. the diminished supertonic chord in the major key of:+d0 f af
200. the major mediant chord in the major key of:        +ef0 g bf
201. the minor subdominant chord in the major key of:    +f0 af c1
202. the minor dominant chord in the major key of:       +g0 bf d1
203. the major submediant chord in the major key of:     +af0 c1 ef
204. the major subtonic chord in the major key of:       +bf0 d1 f
205. the major tonic chord in the minor key of:          +c0 e g
206. the major subdominant chord in the minor key of:    +f0 a c1
207. V/ii in the major key of:                           +a0 cs1 e
208. V7/ii in the major key of:                          +a0 cs1 e g
209. V/iii in the major key of:                          +b0 ds1 fs
210. V7/iii in the major key of:                         +b0 ds1 fs a
211. V/IV in the major key of:                           +c0 e g
212. V7/IV in the major key of:                          +c0 e g bf
213. V/V in the major key of:                            +d0 fs a
214. V7/V in the major key of:                           +d0 fs a c1
215. V/vi in the major key of:                           +e0 gs b
216. V7/vi in the major key of:                          +e0 gs b d1
217. V/III in the minor key of:                          +bf0 d1 f
218. V7/III in the minor key of:                         +bf0 d1 f af
219. V/iv in the minor key of:                           +c0 e g
220. V7/iv in the minor key of:                          +c0 e g bf
221. V/V (or V/v) in the minor key of:                   +d0 fs a
222. V7/V (or V7/v) in the minor key of:                 +d0 fs a c1
223. V/VI in the minor key of:                           +ef0 g bf
224. V7/VI in the minor key of:                          +ef0 g bf df1
225. V/VII in the minor key of:                          +f0 a c1
226. V7/VII in the minor key of:                         +f0 a c1 ef
227. o7/ii in the major key of:                          +cs0 e g bf
228. o7/iii in the major key of:                         +ds0 fs a c1
229. o7/IV in the major key of:                          +e0 g bf df1
230. o7/V in the major key of:                           +fs0 a c1 ef
231. o7/vi in the major key of:                          +gs0 b d1 f
232. viio/ii in the major key of:                        +cs0 e g
233. viio/iii in the major key of:                       +ds0 fs a
234. viio/IV in the major key of:                        +e0 g bf
235. viio/V in the major key of:                         +fs0 a c1
236. viio/vi in the major key of:                        +gs0 b d1
237. o7/III in the minor key of:                         +d0 f af cf1
238. o7/iv in the minor key of:                          +e0 g bf df1
239. o7/V (o7/v) in the minor key of:                    +fs0 a c1 ef
240. o7/VI in the minor key of:                          +g0 bf df1 ff
241. o7/VII in the minor key of:                         +a0 c1 ef gf
```

242. viio/III in the minor key of:	+d0 f af
243. viio/iv in the minor key of:	+e0 g bf
244. viio/V (viio/v) in the minor key of:	+fs0 a c1
245. viio/VI in the minor key of:	+g0 bf df1
246. viio/VII in the minor key of:	+a0 c1 ef
247. a Neapolitan chord in the key of:	+df0 f af
248. an Italian augmented sixth chord in the key of:	+af0 c1 fs
249. a German augmented sixth chord in the key of:	+af0 c1 ef fs
250. a French augmented sixth chord in the key of:	+af0 c1 d fs
251. a prime from:	-c0 c
252. a second above:	-c0 d0
253. a second below:	-d0 c0
254. a third above:	-c0 e0
255. a third below:	-e0 c0
256. a fourth above:	-c0 f0
257. a fourth below:	-f0 c0
258. a fifth above:	-c0 g0
259. a fifth below:	-g0 c0
260. a sixth above:	-c0 a0
261. a sixth below:	-a0 c0
262. a seventh above:	-c0 b0
263. a seventh below:	-b0 c0
264. an octave above:	-c0 c1
265. an octave below:	-c1 c0
266. a ninth above:	-c0 d1
267. a ninth below:	-d1 c0
268. a tenth above:	-c0 e1
269. a tenth below:	-e1 c0
270. an eleventh above:	-c0 f1
271. an eleventh below:	-f1 c0
272. a twelfth above:	-c0 g1
273. a twelfth below:	-g1 c0
274. a thirteenth above:	-c0 a1
275. a thirteenth below:	-a1 c0
276. a fourteenth above:	-c0 b1
277. a fourteenth below:	-b1 c0
278. a fifteenth above:	-c0 c2
279. a fifteenth below:	-c2 c0
280. a scale (one octave ascending) on:	c0 d e f g a b c1
281. a scale (one octave descending) on:	c1 b0 a g f e d c
282. a triad on:	c0 e g
283. a seventh chord on:	c0 e g b

Figure 19.4. The *Muspell* Data Base

19.6 The Program

In order to save space in the program listing below, some subroutines that have been discussed elsewhere in the text have been omitted. These routines are represented by the procedure or function heading with the directive *external*, and a page or section reference is given for the reader who wishes to see the actual code or reconstruct the entire program.

In addition to the standard files *input* and *output*, which are used for communicating with the user, program *muspell* uses two external files. The first (*data*) contains the question data base, and the second (*rseed*) the starting seed value for the random generator. The use of the constants should be obvious from the line comments.

```
program muspell(input, output, data, rseed);

  const
    tablesize   = 283;                   { length of data table          }
    maxline     =  90;                   { maxlength of buffer           }
    maxstring   =  55;                   { maximum lenght of strings     }
    maxtries    =   2;                   { maximum attemps to answer     }
    maxq        = 200;                   { size of queue for errors      }
                                         { set to 4x num of errors       }
    struclength =   8;                   { max length of problems        }
    sharp       = 's';                   { symbol for sharp              }
    flat        = 'f';                   { symbol for flat               }
```

The program uses a number of stuctured data types. *Buftype* will be used for the internal input buffer, and *qarray* for constructing the queues for review questions. Types *string*, *strucarray*, and *structype* are used for defining *entry*—the component type of the data table.

```
  type

    buftype     = record
                    B  : array[1 .. maxline] of char;
                    bp : integer
                  end;

    qarray      = array[0 .. maxq] of integer;
    string      = packed array[1 .. maxstring] of char;
    strucarray  = array[1 .. struclength] of integer;

    queue       = record                 { for implementing queues       }
                    front : integer;     {   index of front of queue     }
                    rear  : integer;     {   index of rear  of queue     }
                    list  : qarray       {   array for values            }
                  end;

    structype   = record
                    card  : integer;     { cardinality of structure      }
                    struc : strucarray   { cbr structure of item         }
                  end;

    entry       = record
                    name  : string;      { name of item                  }
                    rule  : structype    { construction rule of item     }
                  end;

    tabletype   = array[1 .. tablesize] of entry;
```

The functions of the global variables should be obvious from their names or line comments.

```
var
  buffer      : buftype;          { internal buffer for reading       }
  Q1, Q2      : queue;            { queues to store errors            }
  data        : text;             { external file for question data   }
  rseed       : text;             { file for last random number       }
  seed        : integer;          { the random-number seed            }
  table       : tabletype;        { a table of questions and models   }
  n           : integer;          { the number of entries in table    }
  total       : integer;          { total number of questions asked   }
  correct     : integer;          { number of correct responses       }
```

Next we declare utility routines that will be used throughout the program. Function *percent* will be used in reporting the user's success rate in answering questions.

```
procedure incr(var x : integer);
  begin
    x := x + 1
  end;

procedure decr(var x : integer);
  begin
    x := x - 1
  end;

function percent(x, total : integer) : real;
  begin
    percent := (x / total) * 100.0
  end;
```

The following routines implement the random-number generator, as explained in section 19.1. Here we use the 16-bit version; on a computer that uses 32-bit integers, the larger version should be substituted.

```
procedure getseed(var f : text; var seed : integer);
  begin
    reset(f);
    read(f, seed)
  end;

procedure saveseed(var f : text; var seed : integer);
  begin
    rewrite(f);
    write(f, seed)
  end;

function random(var seed : integer) : real;
  begin
    seed := ((36 * seed) + 29) mod 875;
    random := seed / 875
  end;

function irand(lo, hi : integer) : integer;
  begin
    irand := round(lo + random(seed) * (hi - lo + 1) - 0.5)
  end;
```

The following procedures implement two queues, using techniques described in section 10.7.2. Here we modify the procedures to use queues defined with records, so that the array and variables *front* and *rear*, used to define the queue, can be passed as one structured data item. This facilitates using the same procedures for multiple queues.

```
procedure init(var Q : queue);
  begin
    with Q do
      begin
        front := 0;
        rear  := 0
      end
  end;

function empty(var Q : queue) : boolean;
  begin
    with Q do
      empty := front = rear
  end;

function full(var Q : queue) : boolean;
  begin
    with Q do
      full := (rear + 1) mod (maxq + 1) = front
  end;

procedure insert(x : integer; var Q : queue);
  begin
    with Q do
      begin
        list[rear] := x;
        rear := (rear + 1) mod (maxq + 1)
      end
  end;

procedure remove(var x : integer; var Q : queue);
  begin
    with Q do
      begin
        x := list[front];
        front := (front + 1) mod (maxq + 1)
      end
  end;
```

The following boolean functions are named *isXXX*, where *XXX* is the type of value for which we are testing. In general, *isXXX* is *true* if its argument *c* is an *XXX*.

```
function isnote(c : char) : boolean;            { true if c is note name }
  begin
    isnote := c in ['a' .. 'g', 'A' .. 'G']
  end;
```

```
function issign(c : char): boolean;                 { true if c is a + or -   }
  begin
    issign := c in ['-', '+']
  end;

function isdigit(c : char): boolean;                { true if c is a digit    }
  begin
    isdigit := c in ['0' .. '9']
  end;

function isupper(c : char) : boolean;               { true if c is uppercase }
  begin
    isupper := c in ['A' .. 'Z']
  end;
```

The following functions convert from one data type to another; all are used in converting between the cbr pitch system and the external code used to communicate with the user.

```
{ convert note name to name class }
function tonc(c : char) : integer;
  begin
    case c of
      'c' : tonc := 0;
      'd' : tonc := 1;
      'e' : tonc := 2;
      'f' : tonc := 3;
      'g' : tonc := 4;
      'a' : tonc := 5;
      'b' : tonc := 6
     end { case }
  end; { tonc }

{ convert name class to integer }
function tochar(x : integer): char;
  begin
    case x of
      0 : tochar := 'C';
      1 : tochar := 'D';
      2 : tochar := 'E';
      3 : tochar := 'F';
      4 : tochar := 'G';
      5 : tochar := 'A';
      6 : tochar := 'B'
    end
  end;  { tochar }

{ convert name class to natural pitch class }
function pitch(nc : integer) : integer;
  begin
    case nc of
      0 : pitch := 0;   { pc for c }
      1 : pitch := 2;   { pc for d }
      2 : pitch := 4;   { pc for e }
      3 : pitch := 5;   { pc for f }
```

```
      4 : pitch := 7;   { pc for g }
      5 : pitch := 9;   { pc for a }
      6 : pitch := 11   { pc for b }
    end  { case }
  end;  { pitch }
```

The functions for calculating pitch using cbrs were discussed in section 19.2. They can be seen there or in the procedure library in appendix D.

```
function cbr(octave, pc, nc : integer) : integer;                  external;
function br(cbr : integer) : integer;                              external;
function octave(cbr : integer) : integer;                          external;
function pitchclass(cbr : integer) : integer;                      external;
function nameclass(cbr : integer) : integer;                       external;
function cpc(cbr : integer) : integer;                             external;
function cnc(cbr : integer) : integer;                             external;
function add(cbr1, cbr2 : integer) : integer;                      external;
```

The following subroutines implement an internal buffer (see section 11.2). The versions shown here, which are fully parameterized, can be seen in appendix D. The use of these procedures increases portability when programs are implemented under different Pascal compilers and operating systems. Note that the version of *nextchar* used in this program converts uppercase characters to lower case.

```
function  tab : char;                                              external;
function  null : char;                                             external;
function  toint(c : char) : integer;                               external;
procedure getline(var fi, fo : text; var buffer : buftype);        external;
function  eob(var buffer : buftype) : boolean;                     external;
function  tolower(c : char) : char;                                external;
function  nextchar(var buffer : buftype) : char;                   external;
procedure skipbuf(var buffer : buftype);                           external;
procedure printbuffer(var f : text; var buffer : buftype);         external;

procedure error(var f : text; var buffer : buftype; x : integer);
  begin
    printbuffer(f, buffer);
    writeln;
    case x of
      1 : writeln(f, 'Integer expected');
      2 : writeln(f, 'Syntax error in answer')
    end { case }
  end;

procedure getint(var fi, fo : text; var buffer : buftype;
                                         var x : integer);         external;
function  affirmative(var fin, fout : text) : boolean;             external;
```

The following procedure instructs new users in the use of the program. Since the instructions are too long to fit on just one screen of most CRTs, the procedure uses *readln* to wait for the user to type a carriage return. This device allows the user the time necessary to read the instructions.

```
procedure instruct;
  begin
    writeln;
    writeln('Welcome to Program Muspell, the program that can spell pitch');
    writeln('structures better and faster than most people, and can teach');
    writeln('you to do the same.');
    writeln;
    writeln('Program Muspell is designed to give you practice in spelling');
    writeln('pitch structures.  You will be asked to select question types');
    writeln('from menus, and will be able to specify level of difficulty,');
    writeln('the number of questions in each category, and whether or not');
    writeln('you wish to include octave information in the questions and');
    writeln('answers.  If you are a beginner, you may wish to do "generic"');
    writeln('questions at first.  These allow you to answer questions such');
    writeln('as "spell a fifth above B" without worrying about accidentals.');
    writeln('Higher levels of difficulty include notes, scales, functional');
    writeln('chords, etc., spelled with double and triple accidentals.  The');
    writeln('program can generate over 87000 different questions, but you');
    writeln('don''t have to answer them all at once.');
    writeln;
    write('Type <return> to continue: ');
    readln;
    writeln;
    writeln('Questions are asked and answered using notes specified as the');
    writeln('note name (A, B, C, ..., G) optionally followed by sharps and');
    writeln('flats and octave designations.  Note names may be typed in');
    writeln('upper or lower case.  A sharp or flat is typed as "s" or "f",');
    writeln('and may be repeated any number of times:  efff is E-triple-');
    writeln('flat, and bss is B-double-sharp.  When octaves are used, the');
    writeln('octave is specified by an integer following the note name.');
    writeln('We will use U.S.A. standard octave designations.  Each octave');
    writeln('runs from C to the B above it.  The octave beginning on middle');
    writeln('C is octave 4, the one below it is octave 3, the one above it');
    writeln('is octave 5, etc.  It is not necessary to specify the octave');
    writeln('number with each note, only the first one and then again');
    writeln('whenever the octave changes.  For example, the major scale on');
    writeln('G3 is spelled:');
    writeln;
    writeln('                 g3 a b c4 d e fs g');
    writeln;
    writeln('Enharmonic spellings are NOT acceptable, i.e., F-sharp is not the');
    writeln('same pitch as G-flat.  Remember that you must always type <return>');
    writeln('to enter your answer.  Before you do that, you can use the back-');
    writeln('space key to back up and change an answer.');
    writeln;
    write('Type <return> to continue:');
    readln;
    writeln;
    writeln('If you answer a question incorrectly you will be given a second');
    writeln('chance to answer.  If you miss again, the correct answer will');
    writeln('be printed, and the question will be saved for review.  You');
    writeln('will be given a chance to review missed questions at the end');
    writeln('of each set of problems and when you finish the program.  In');
    writeln('review sessions, questions will be repeated with variations, i.e,');
    writeln('the root or tonic and octave will probably not be the same as');
    writeln('in the original question.');
    writeln;
```

```
    writeln('At the end of each section of the drill, the program will let');
    writeln('you know how you are doing by printing the number of questions');
    writeln('answered and the percentage of correct answers.  You will');
    writeln('receive full credit for questions answered correctly the first');
    writeln('time and half credit if you get it right on the second try.');
    writeln('Review questions are not counted in your score.');
    writeln;
  end;  { instruct }
```

The following group of procedures processes input data, whether from the *data* file containing the question data base or the *input* file representing the student's answers to questions. Procedure *stringread* reads all of the characters in the buffer, up to a colon marking the end of the question. These characters are stored as a string in the question field of an *entry* record. Note that we cannot use *getchar*(*S*[*i*]), since most compilers do not permit single elements of packed arrays to be passed as variable parameters.

```
procedure stringread(var buffer : buftype; var S : string);
  var
    i : integer;
  begin
    i := 1;
    with buffer do
      begin
        while nextchar(buffer) <> ':' do
          begin
            S[i] := B[bp];
            incr(bp);
            incr(i)
          end;
        S[i + 1] := null;
        incr(bp)                      { skip : }
      end
  end;
```

The following procedures read data from the data table and process the user's answers to questions. Procedure *readnote* converts the notes in the SCORE input format to cbrs. The argument *x* is used to return the new note, or –1 signals an input error; *octave* is saved by using a variable parameter, so that the octave only needs to be typed for the first note and when it changes.

```
procedure readnote(var buffer : buftype; var x, octave : integer);
  var
    nc, pc : integer;
  begin
    if not isnote(nextchar(buffer))
      then x := -1  { signal error }
    else
      begin
        nc := tonc(nextchar(buffer));
        incr(buffer.bp);
        pc := pitch(nc);
```

```
        while nextchar(buffer) in [sharp, flat] do
          begin
            if nextchar(buffer) = sharp
              then incr(pc)
              else decr(pc);
            incr(buffer.bp)
          end;
        if pc < 0
          then pc := pc + 12
        else if pc > 11
          then pc := pc - 12;
        if isdigit(nextchar(buffer))
          then getint(input, output, buffer, octave);
        x :=  cbr(octave, pc, nc)
      end
  end;
```

Procedure *readstruc* uses procedure *readnote* to convert a string of notes in SCORE format to cbrs. The cbrs are stored in the array portion of *structype S*, and the number of elements in the *card* field of *S*. If there is an input error, the procedure prompts the user to reenter the line and calls itself recursively. This procedure is also used to read the model answers in the question file.

```
procedure readstruc(var buffer : buftype; var f : text; var S : structype);
  var
    err : boolean;
    octave : integer;
  begin
    err := false;
    octave := 0;     { default octave }
    S.card := 0;
    skipbuf(buffer);
    with S do
      while not eob(buffer) and not err do
        begin
          incr(card);
          readnote(buffer, struc[card], octave);
          err := struc[card] = -1;
          skipbuf(buffer)
        end;
    if err
      then
        begin
          error(output, buffer, 2);  { syntax error }
          write('Retype input: ');
          getline(f, output, buffer);
          readstruc(buffer, f, S)
        end
  end;
```

Procedure *getstruc* calculates the structure of a model answer. First it checks for the special cases for intervals and chord functions, i.e., the '–' and '+' signs. It then calls *readstruc* to convert the input to an array of cbrs, and calculates the cbr structure of the model by subtracting the first element from each element. If the first character was a minus sign, the first element is dropped. Finally, if the input began with '+', the structure is transposed to begin on the first note of the input string.

```
procedure transpose(var A : structype; interval : integer); forward;

procedure getstruc(var buffer : buftype; var f : text; var S : structype);
  var
    sample      : structype;
    first, p, i : integer;
    firstnote   : integer;
    dotrans     : boolean;
  begin
    skipbuf(buffer);
    dotrans := nextchar(buffer) = '+';
    if (nextchar(buffer) = '-')
      then first := 2
      else first := 1;
    if issign(nextchar(buffer))
      then incr(buffer.bp);
    readstruc(buffer, f, sample);            { read example              }
    firstnote := sample.struc[1];            { and save first note       }
                                             { now calculate intervals   }
    p := 1;                                  { next place to be filled   }
    for i := first to sample.card do
      begin                                  { calc and store interval   }
        S.struc[p] := add(sample.struc[i], -sample.struc[1]);
        incr(p)
      end;

    S.card := p - 1;                         { cardinality of structure }

    if dotrans                               { transpose structure       }
      then transpose(S, firstnote)
  end; { getstruc }
```

Procedure *readdata* reads the question data base, calling *stringread* and *getstruc* to convert the data to the proper format.

```
procedure readdata(var buffer : buftype; var f : text;
                              var table : tabletype; var n : integer);
  begin
    writeln(output, 'Reading data table');
    write(output, 'Please be patient, I''m working as fast as I can ... ');
    reset(f);
    n := 0;
    while not eof(f) do
      begin
        getline(f, output, buffer);
        incr(n);
        with table[n] do
          begin
            stringread(buffer, name);
            getstruc(buffer, f, rule)
          end
      end;
    writeln('Done')
  end;
```

The following output routines convert data from the internal form (cbrs) to the SCORE code used to communicate correct answers to the user. Procedure *writenote* performs the conversion and writes the note. First, the name class is extracted from the cbr, converted to the appropriate note name, and printed. Next, the pitch class is extracted and compared to the pitch class for the natural note. The difference indicates the number of accidentals; a positive difference indicates sharps, and a negative difference flats. If the absolute value of the difference is greater than 6, the mod 12 inverse is used and the sign changed. Thus 11 sharps become 1 flat, 7 flats become 5 sharps, etc. Now the appropriate number of sharp or flat symbols is printed. The calculation and printing of accidentals are omitted if generic intervals are specified. Finally, if octave information is indicated, the octave is extracted from the cbr and printed.

```
procedure writenote(var f : text; N : integer; useoct, generic : boolean);
  var
    pc, nc, dif, i : integer;
    sign   : char;
  begin
    nc := nameclass(N);
    write(f, tochar(nc));                          { print notename        }
    if not generic
      then
        begin
          pc := pitchclass(N);
          dif := pc - pitch(nc);                   { number of accidentals }
          if dif > 6
            then dif := dif - 12                   { convert to flats      }
          else if dif < -6
            then dif := dif + 12;                  { convert to sharps     }

          if dif < 0
            then sign := flat
            else sign := sharp;

          for i := 1 to abs(dif) do                { print accidentals     }
            write(f, sign)
        end;
    if useoct
      then write(octave(n):1);                     { print octave          }
    write(f, ' ')
  end;
```

Procedure *writesolution* calls *writenote* to print each note of the calculated solution.

```
procedure writesolution(var f : text; var solution : structype;
                                           useoctave, generic : boolean);

  var
    i : integer;
  begin
    with solution do
      for i := 1 to card do
        writenote(f, struc[i], useoctave, generic);
    writeln(f)
  end;
```

Procedure *writestring* prints a string terminated by a null character.

```
procedure writestring(var f : text; var S : string);
  var
    i : integer;
  begin
    i := 1;
    while S[i] <> null do
      begin
        write(f, S[i]);
        incr(i)
      end
  end;
```

The next group of routines implements the primary function of the program: generating questions, calculating answers, comparing the student's response to the calculated answer, etc. Procedure *transpose* transposes a cbr structure stored in *structype A* by adding the cbr stored in *interval* to each element.

```
procedure transpose(* var A : structype; interval : integer *);
  var
    i : integer;
  begin
    with A do
      for i := 1 to card do
        struc[i] := add(struc[i], interval)
  end;
```

Setlimits sets the maximum number of sharps and flats permitted with a root or tonic according to the level of difficulty. Note that at level 1 the accidentals depend in part on which note is being modified.

```
procedure setlimits(diflevel, nc : integer; var sharps, flats : integer);
  begin

    case diflevel of

      1 : begin
            sharps := 0;
            flats  := 0
          end;

      2 : case nc of

            0,3   : begin                         { C and E      }
                      flats  := 0;
                      sharps := 1
                    end;

            1,4,5 : begin                         { D, G, and A }
                      flats  := 1;
                      sharps := 1
                    end;
```

```
            2,6    : begin                         { E and B      }
                        flats   := 1;
                        sharps  := 0
                     end;

          end; { case }

     3 : begin
            sharps := 1;
            flats  := 1
          end;

     4 : begin
            sharps := 2;
            flats  := 2
          end;

     5 : begin
            sharps := 3;
            flats  := 3
          end
   end { case }
end;  { setlimits }
```

Procedure *getroot* uses the random-number generator to select a root or tonic for each question. The name class is randomly selected from the integers between 0 and 6, and the unmodified pitch class is obtained from function *pitch*. If the problem is not generic, the limits for the accidentals are set by *setlimits* according to the level of difficulty, and the pitch class is modified by a random number within these limits. Finally, the octave is generated, and the separate elements are combined into a cbr.

```
procedure getroot(var x : integer; diflevel : integer;
                                                  generic : boolean);
  var
    oc, pc, nc : integer;               { octave, name, and pitch class  }
    flats, sharps : integer;            { max number of flats and sharps }
  begin
    nc  := irand(0, 6);                           { get name class          }
    pc  := pitch(nc);                             { and pitch class         }
    if not generic                                { set sharps and flats    }
      then
        begin
          setlimits(diflevel, nc, flats, sharps);
          pc := pc + irand(-flats, sharps);       { add accidentals         }
          pc := (pc + 12) mod 12                  { adjust pitch class      }
        end;
    oc := irand(2, 7);                            { get octave              }
    x := cbr(oc, pc, nc)                          { return cbr              }
  end;
```

Function *ident* compares two cbr structures to see if they are to be considered "identical" according to the type of problem being solved. The variants are accomplished by passing function $f(x)$as an argument. If f is function *br*, octave information is omitted in the comparison.

```
function ident(var A, B : structype; function f(x : integer) : integer)
                                                              : boolean;
  var
    i : integer;
  begin
    if A.card <> B.card
      then ident := false
      else
        begin
          i := 1;
          while (f(A.struc[i]) = f(B.struc[i])) and (i < A.card) do
              incr(i);
          ident := f(A.struc[i]) = f(B.struc[i])
        end
  end;  { ident }
```

Other possible values for function *f* are *asis*, which returns *x* unmodified, function *nopc*, which replaces the pitch class with 0, and function *nameclass* (see above), which returns just the name class. The latter two functions are used for generic questions.

```
function asis(x : integer) : integer;          { returns argument      }
  begin
    asis := x
  end;

function nopc(x : integer) : integer;          { strip pitch class     }
  begin
    nopc := cbr(octave(x), 0, nameclass(x))
  end;
```

Function *goodanswer* calls *ident* with the appropriate function parameter, depending on the question type.

```
function goodanswer(answer, response : structype;
                       useoctave, generic : boolean) : boolean;
  begin
    if useoctave
      then if not generic
             then goodanswer := ident(answer, response, asis)
             else goodanswer := ident(answer, response, nopc)
      else if not generic
             then goodanswer := ident(answer, response, br)
             else goodanswer := ident(answer, response, nameclass)
  end;  { goodanswer }
```

Procedure *ask* articulates each question, using *writestring* to print the question, and *writenote* to print the root or tonic. It then elicits a response, which is processed by procedure *readstruc* and returned in the variable parameter *response*.

```
procedure ask(var buffer : buftype; var Q : entry; root : integer;
                var response : structype; useoctave, generic : boolean);
```

```
begin { ask }
  writeln(output);
  write(output, 'Spell ');
  writestring(output, Q.name); write(' ');
  writenote(output, root, useoctave, generic); writeln;
  writeln;
  write('Type answer: ');
  getline(input, output, buffer);
  readstruc(buffer, input, response)
end; { ask }
```

Procedure *message* prints messages to the user. The message, *n*, is chosen randomly within appropriate limits when the procedure is called.

```
procedure message(n : integer);
  begin
    case n of
      0 : writeln('Incorrect');                { incorrect response   }
      1 : writeln('Sorry');
      2 : writeln('That''s not right');
      3 : writeln('Oh, dear!');

      4 : writeln('Very good');                { correct response     }
      5 : writeln('Correct');
      6 : writeln('Very nice work');
      7 : writeln('Good!');

      8 : writeln('That''s much better');      { correct on 2d try    }
      9 : writeln('Correct');
     10 : writeln('Thanks, I needed that!');
     11 : writeln('I knew you could do it!');

     12 : writeln('You must be tired');        { still wrong 2d try   }
     13 : writeln('That is still incorrect');
     14 : writeln('This IS pretty difficult');
     15 : writeln('#%$*&^@!!!');
                                { ran program but didn't play the game }
     16 : writeln('Then why did you wake me up?');
     17 : writeln('Sorry about that');
     18 : writeln('Take two aspirin and call me in the morning');
     19 : writeln('See you later, transistor breath')
    end { case }
  end; { message }
```

Procedure *menu* prints the appropriate menu depending on the value of its argument.

```
procedure menu(n : integer);
  begin
    writeln;
    case n of
      0 : begin
            writeln('Problem Types:');
            writeln;
            writeln('  1.  Intervals');
            writeln('  2.  Scales');
```

```
        writeln('  3.  Scale Steps');
        writeln('  4.  Spelling Chords');
        writeln('  5.  Diatonic Chords');
        writeln('  6.  Altered Chords');
        writeln('  7.  I''ll Try Anything')
     end;

  1 : begin
        writeln('Interval Drills:');
        writeln;
        writeln('  1.  Generic Simple Intervals (no sharps or flats)');
        writeln('  2.  Generic Compound Intervals');
        writeln('  3.  Fourths, Fifths, and Primes');
        writeln('  4.  Seconds and Thirds');
        writeln('  5.  Sixths and Sevenths');
        writeln('  6.  Review');
        writeln('  7.  Augmented and Diminished Intervals');
        writeln('  8.  Compound Intervals');
        writeln('  9.  Compound Intervals (aug. and dim.)');
        writeln(' 10.  Review')
     end;

  2 : begin
        writeln('Scale Drills');
        writeln;
        writeln('  1.  Generic');
        writeln('  2.  Major Scales');
        writeln('  3.  Minor Scales');
        writeln('  4.  Review');
        writeln('  5.  Diatonic Modes');
        writeln('  6.  Review')
     end;

  3 : begin
        writeln('Scale Steps');
        writeln;
        writeln('  1.  In Major');
        writeln('  2.  In Minor');
        writeln('  3.  Review');
        writeln('  4.  Altered Tones in Major and Minor');
        writeln('  5.  Review')
     end;

  4 : begin
        writeln('Chord Drills');
        writeln;
        writeln('  1.  Generic Triads');
        writeln('  2.  Generic Seventh Chords');
        writeln('  3.  Spelling Triads');
        writeln('  4.  Spelling Seventh Chords');
        writeln('  5.  Review')
     end;

  5 : begin
        writeln('Diatonic Chord Drills');
        writeln;
        writeln('  1.  Diatonic Triads in Major');
```

```
          writeln('  2.  Diatonic Triads in Minor');
          writeln('  3.  Review');
          writeln('  4.  Diatonic Seventh Chords in Major');
          writeln('  5.  Diatonic Seventh Chords in Minor');
          writeln('  6.  Review')
        end;

    6 : begin
          writeln('Altered Chords');
          writeln;
          writeln('  1.  Modal Mixture in Major and Minor');
          writeln('  2.  Applied Dominants in Major');
          writeln('  3.  Applied Dominants in Minor');
          writeln('  4.  Review');
          writeln('  5.  Applied viio and viio7 in Major');
          writeln('  6.  Applied viio and viio7 in Minor');
          writeln('  7.  Review');
          writeln('  8.  Augmented Sixths and Neapolitans');
          writeln('  9.  Review')
        end;

    7 : begin
          writeln('Level of Difficulty (root or tonic):');
          writeln;
          writeln('  1.  No sharps or flats');
          writeln('  2.  Single sharp or flat (on some notes)');
          writeln('  3.  Single sharp or flat (on any note)');
          writeln('  4.  Double sharps or flats');
          writeln('  5.  Triple sharps or flats')
        end
  end; { case }
  writeln
end; { menu }
```

Randlimits sets *low*, *high*, and *generic* to reflect the location of problem categories in the question data base. The parameter *probtype* is generated by multiplying the major category number by 10 and adding the minor category number. Thus 11 is generic intervals, 12 is generic compound intervals, etc. (see table 19.2).

```
procedure randlimits(probtype : integer; var low, high : integer;
                                          var generic : boolean);
begin
  generic := (probtype = 11) or (probtype = 12)
         or (probtype = 21) or (probtype = 41) or (probtype = 42);

                                 (***************************)
                                 (*       INTERVALS         *)
  case probtype of               (***************************)
   11 : begin                    { generic (no sharp or flat) }
          low := 251;  high := 263
        end;

   12 : begin                    { generic compound           }
          low := 264;  high := 279
        end;
```

```
13 : begin                                { 4ths, 5ths, & primes          }
       low :=   1;  high :=   6
     end;

14 : begin                                { 2ds and 3rds                  }
       low :=   7;  high :=  14
     end;

15 : begin                                { 6ths and 7ths                 }
       low :=  15;  high :=  22
     end;

16 : begin                                { review                        }
       low :=   1;  high :=  22
     end;

17 : begin                                { augmented and diminished      }
       low :=  23;  high :=  50
     end;

18 : begin                                { compound                      }
       low :=  51;  high :=  74
     end;

19 : begin                                { compound aug and dim          }
       low :=  75;  high := 106
     end;

20 : begin                                { review                        }
       low :=  23;  high := 106
     end;
                                          (***************************)
                                          (*         SCALES          *)
                                          (***************************)
21 : begin                                { generic                       }
       low := 280;  high := 281
     end;

22 : begin                                { major scales                  }
       low := 107;  high := 108
     end;

23 : begin                                { minor scales                  }
       low := 109;  high := 114
     end;

24 : begin                                { review                        }
       low := 107;  high := 114
     end;

25 : begin                                { diatonic modes                }
       low := 115;  high := 128
     end;

26 : begin                                { review                        }
       low := 107;  high := 128
     end;
```

```
                                          (***************************)
                                          (*       SCALE STEPS       *)
                                          (***************************)
31 : begin                                { in major                  }
       low := 129;  high := 135
     end;

32 : begin                                { in minor                  }
       low := 136;  high := 144
     end;

33 : begin                                { review                    }
       low := 129;  high := 144
     end;

34 : begin                                { altered in major & minor  }
       low := 145;  high := 156
     end;

35 : begin                                { review                    }
       low := 129;  high := 156
     end;
                                          (***************************)
                                          (* CHORDS                  *)
                                          (***************************)
41 : begin                                { generic triads            }
       low := 282;  high := 282
     end;

42 : begin                                { generic 7th chords        }
       low := 283;  high := 283
     end;

43 : begin                                { triads                    }
       low := 157;  high := 160
     end;

44 : begin                                { 7th chords                }
       low := 161;  high := 166
     end;

45 : begin                                { review                    }
       low := 157;  high := 166
     end;
                                          (***************************)
                                          (* DIATONIC CHORDS         *)
                                          (***************************)
51 : begin                                { triads in major           }
       low := 167;  high := 173
     end;

52 : begin                                { triads in minor           }
       low := 174;  high := 183
     end;

53 : begin                                { review                    }
       low := 167;  high := 183
     end;
```

```
    54 : begin                                   { 7th chords in major          }
           low := 184;  high := 190
         end;

    55 : begin                                   { 7th chords in minor          }
           low := 191;  high := 197
         end;

    56 : begin                                   { review                       }
           low := 167;  high := 197
         end;
                                                 (****************************)
                                                 (*     ALTERED CHORDS       *)
                                                 (****************************)
    61 : begin                                   { mixture in major & minor     }
           low := 198;  high := 206
         end;

    62 : begin                                   { applied dom in major         }
           low := 207;  high := 216
         end;

    63 : begin                                   { applied dom in minor         }
           low := 217;  high := 226
         end;

    64 : begin                                   { review                       }
           low := 207;  high := 226
         end;

    65 : begin                                   { appl viio & viio7 in major }
           low := 227;  high := 236
         end;

    66 : begin                                   { appl viio & viio7 in minor }
           low := 237;  high := 246
         end;

    67 : begin                                   { review                       }
           low := 207;  high := 246
         end;

    68 : begin                                   { aug 6ths and Neapolitans     }
           low := 247;  high := 250
         end;

    69 : begin                                   { review                       }
           low := 198;  high := 250
         end;

    70 : begin                                   (****************************)
           low :=   1;  high := 250              (*        ANYTHING          *)
         end                                     (****************************)
  end  { case }
end;  { randlimits }
```

Procedure *testint* ensures that the user types an appropriate number in response to menus. It uses *x* to return the value, and *high* to check the limits.

```
procedure testint(var x : integer; high : integer);
  begin
    write('Type integer: ');
    getline(input, output, buffer);
    getint(input, output, buffer, x);
    if not (x in [1 .. high])
      then
        begin
          writeln('Answer must be 1 - ', high:1);
          testint(x, high)
        end
  end;
```

Setparms sets the parameters for each set of problems. The main menu is printed, and the user's choice noted. Depending on the primary category of question, a second menu is presented, and the secondary category is read. Now a key number, *probtype*, is calculated by multiplying the primary category by 10 and adding the secondary category. For example, a primary category of 3 with a secondary category of 4 results in a key of 34, and *randlimits* is called to set the value for *low*, *high*, and *generic*. Finally, the user is asked how many questions he or she wants to do and whether or not register is to be included, and the corresponding parameters are set.

```
procedure setparms(var buffer : buftype; var low, high, questions,
                   diflevel: integer; var useoctaves, generic : boolean);
  var
    p1, p2, probtype : integer;
  begin
    menu(0);                                  { print main menu        }
    testint(p1, 7);                           { read main category     }

    case p1 of                                { set secondary category }
      1   : begin
              menu(1); testint(p2, 10)
            end;

      2,5 : begin
              menu(p1); testint(p2, 6)
            end;

      3,4 : begin
              menu(p1); testint(p2, 5)
            end;

      6   : begin
              menu(6); testint(p2, 9)
            end;

      7   : p2 := 0
    end;  { case }
```

```
    probtype := (10 * p1) + p2;                { key for randlimits      }
    randlimits(probtype, low, high, generic);

    write('How many problems do you want? ');
    getline(input, output, buffer);
    getint(input, output, buffer, questions);

    if generic
      then diflevel := 1
      else
        begin
          menu(7);                             { get level of difficulty }
          testint(diflevel, 5)
        end;

    write('Do you want to include octave information? (y/n): ');
    useoctaves := affirmative(input, output)
  end;  { setparms }
```

Procedure *doproblem* presents a problem to the student and processes his answer. First, the root or tonic is obtained from procedure *getroot*, and the question is asked. Now the cbr structure of the answer is copied to variable *answer*, and *answer* is transposed to the new value of *root*. Then the user's response is compared to the calculated answer. If the values do not match, the user is given a second chance to answer correctly. The program's response depends on the user's performance. The procedure was designed so that it can be called from the primary problem-set generator, or from review procedures.

```
procedure doproblem(var buffer : buftype; var question : entry; qnum,
                    diflevel : integer; var right : integer; useoctaves,
                                    generic : boolean; var Q : queue);

  var
    response   : structype;              { to store user response       }
    answer     : structype;              { to store correct answer      }
    root       : integer;                { root or tonic as cbr         }
    attempt    : integer;                { attempt number               }
    retry      : boolean;                { true if user wants 2d chance }
    correct    : boolean;                { true if response is correct  }
    intoct     : integer;                { integer rep of useoctave     }
    intgen     : integer;                { integer rep of generic       }

  begin
    getroot(root, diflevel, generic);        { generate root or tonic    }
                                             { ask quest, get response   }
    ask(buffer, question, root, response, useoctave, generic);

                                             { calculate correct answer  }
    answer := question.rule;                 { copy structure to answer  }
                                             { transpose to root/tonic   }
    transpose(answer, root);
    attempt := 1;

    correct := goodanswer(answer, response, useoctave, generic);
```

```
    retry := true;
    while (attempt < maxtries) and (not correct) and (retry) do
      begin
        message(irand(0, 3));                    { write incorrect message   }
        write('Would you like to try it again? (y/n): ');
        if affirmative(input, output)
          then
            begin
              ask(buffer, question, root, response, useoctave, generic);
              correct := goodanswer(answer, response, useoctave, generic);
              incr(attempt)
            end
        else retry := false
      end;
    if (attempt = 1) and correct                 { got it first time         }
      then
        begin
          message(irand(4, 7));                  { write correct message     }
          right := right + 2
        end
    else if correct                              { second try                }
      then
        begin
          message(irand(8, 11));                 { that's better             }
          right := right + 1
        end
    else
      begin
        if retry
          then message(irand(12, 15));           { still not right           }
        if not full(Q)
          then
            begin
              if useoctaves                      { convert boolean flags     }
                then intoct := 1                 {    to integer             }
                else intoct := 0;
              if generic
                then intgen := 1
                else intgen := 0;
              insert(qnum, Q);                   { save question number      }
              insert(diflevel, Q);               { save diflevel             }
              insert(intoct, Q);                 { save useoctaves flag      }
              insert(intgen, Q)                  { save generic flag         }
            end
          else writeln('Queue full; cannot save question for review');
        write('The correct answer is: ');
        writesolution(output, answer, useoctave, generic)
      end
  end;  { doproblem }
```

Procedure *problemset* calls *setparms* to set the question parameters, and then uses a loop to generate the desired number of questions. Each question is chosen randomly from the correct segment of the question table, and *doproblem* is called to present the question and process the user's answer. After the set has been completed, the score is calculated and printed, and the number of questions and correct answers is added to the global totals. Finally, the user is given an opportunity to review any questions missed.

```
procedure review(var buffer : buftype; var table : tabletype;
                                       var Q : queue); forward;

procedure problemset(var buffer : buftype; var total, numright : integer;
                                var table : tabletype; var Q : queue);

  var
    qnum, i       : integer;         { question number and loop var }
    useoctave   : boolean;           { true if octaves are included }
                                     {   in questions and answers   }
    generic     : boolean;           { true if questions are generic}
                                     { i.e., no accidentals         }
    questions   : integer;           { number of questions in set   }
    right       : integer;           { number of correct answers    }
    diflevel    : integer;           { level of difficulty          }
    low, high   : integer;           { limits of choice in table    }

  begin
    right := 0;
    setparms(buffer, low, high, questions, diflevel, useoctaves, generic);

    for i := 1 to questions do
      begin
        qnum := irand(low, high);           { choose question randomly }
        doproblem(buffer, table[qnum], qnum, diflevel, right, useoctaves,
                                                      generic, Q)
      end;

    writeln;
    writeln('questions answered =', questions:4);
    writeln('correct responses  =', right / 2:6:1);
    writeln('score for this set =', percent(right, questions*2):6:1, '%');
    numright := numright + right;                { add to totals for }
    total    := total + questions;               {       program run }

    if not (right = questions * 2) and (not empty(Q))
      then
        begin
          writeln;
          write('Do you want to review questions missed? ');
          if affirmative(input, output)
            then review(buffer, table, Q)
        end
  end;    { problemset }
```

Getreview is called by the *review* procedure. This procedure removes the parameters for one question from the review queue.

```
procedure getreview(var qnum, diflevel : integer;
                          var useoctaves, generic : boolean; var Q : queue);
  var
    intoct, intgen : integer;
  begin                                 { get values from queue        }
    remove(qnum, Q);                    {    question number           }
    remove(diflevel, Q);                {    level of difficulty       }
    remove(intoct, Q);                  {    use octaves?              }
    remove(intgen, Q);                  {    generic?                  }
    useoctaves := intoct = 1;           { set boolean flags            }
    generic    := intgen = 1
  end;
```

Procedure *review* is very much like procedure *problemset*, except that the problems are taken from one of the review queues. The user is given the opportunity to terminate the review process after each question.

```
procedure review( var buffer : buftype; var table : tabletype;
                                                   var Q : queue );
  var
    qnum        : integer;                  { question number            }
    useoctave   : boolean;                  { true if octaves are included }
                                            {   in questions and answers  }
    generic     : boolean;                  { true if questions are generic}
                                            { i.e., no accidentals        }
    right       : integer;                  { number of correct answers   }
    questions   : integer;
    diflevel    : integer;                  { level of difficulty         }
    continue    : boolean;                  { flag to continue review     }
  begin
    right := 0;
    questions := 0;
    continue := true;
    while not empty(Q) and continue do
      begin
        incr(questions);
        getreview(qnum, diflevel, useoctaves, generic, Q);
        doproblem(buffer, table[qnum], qnum, diflevel,
                                   right, useoctaves, generic, Q);
        if not empty(Q)
          then
            begin
              write('Do you want to continue review? ');
              continue := affirmative(input, output)
            end
      end;
    writeln;
    writeln('review questions   =', questions:4);
    writeln('correct responses =', right / 2:6:1);
    writeln('score on review   =', percent(right, questions*2):6:1, '%')
  end;   { review }
```

Procedure *transfer* is called after each problem set to move any unsolved problems from the primary queue to the secondary queue. This ensures that the review session after each set of problems contains only problems from that session, while the final review will contain any unsolved questions from all sessions.

```
procedure transfer(var Q1, Q2 : queue);
  var
    x : integer;
  begin
    while not empty(Q1) and not full(Q2) do
      begin
        remove(x, Q1);                       { remove x from Q1          }
        insert(x, Q2)                        { and insert in Q2          }
      end;
    if not empty(Q1)                         { make sure that Q1 is empty }
      then init(Q1)
  end;  { transfer }
```

The main procedure initializes both queues, as well as global variables *total* and *correct*. It then reads the data file, converting each model answer to its cbr structure, reads the random-number seed from another external file, and prints directions for the new user. It then enters a loop that generates new sets of problems until the user indicates that he or she would like to stop. After each set, any unanswered review questions are moved to the secondary queue. When the user terminates the drill, he or she is given an opportunity to review any questions still in the review queue, and the final score for the drill is printed. Finally, the random-number seed is saved in an external file, so that the program will not generate the same set of questions the next time it is run.

```
begin { main }
  init(Q1);   init(Q2);                       { initialize queues          }
  total := 0; correct := 0;                   { initialize score vars      }
  readdata(buffer, data, table, n);           { read data table            }
  getseed(rseed, seed);                       { init random num generator  }
  write('Do you need instructions? (y/n): ');
  if affirmative(input, output)
    then instruct;
  write('Are you ready? (y/n): ');
  while affirmative(input, output) do
    begin
      problemset(buffer, total, correct, table, Q1);  { do problem set     }
      writeln;
      write('Would you like to do another set? (y/n): ');
      transfer(Q1, Q2)                        { move unanswered review     }
    end;                                      {    questions to Q2         }
  writeln;
  if total > 0
    then
      begin
        if not empty(Q2)
          then
            begin
              write('Do you want to review questions missed? (y,n):');
              if affirmative(input, output)
                then review(buffer, table, Q2)
            end;
        writeln;
        writeln('total score (does not include review questions)');
        writeln('total questions   =', total:4);
        writeln('correct responses =', correct / 2 :6:1);
        writeln('score,' ':13, '=', percent(correct, total * 2):6:1, '%')
      end
    else message(irand(16, 19));                    { so why did you call? }
  saveseed(rseed, seed)                             { save random number   }
end. { main }
```

A sample interactive session is shown below. While it is impossible to demonstrate all program functions and questions, we have attempted to illustrate a variety of problem types, levels of difficulty, and review strategies.

```
Reading data table
Please be patient, I'm working as fast as I can ... Done
Do you need instructions? (y/n) : no, thank you
Are you ready? (y/n): yes

Problem Types:

  1.  Intervals
  2.  Scales
  3.  Scale Steps
  4.  Spelling Chords
  5.  Diatonic Chords
  6.  Altered Chords
  7.  I'll Try Anything

Type integer: 1

Interval Drills:

  1.  Generic Simple Intervals (no sharps or flats)
  2.  Generic Compound Intervals
  3.  Fourths, Fifths, and Primes
  4.  Seconds and Thirds
  5.  Sixths and Sevenths
  6.  Review
  7.  Augmented and Diminished Intervals
  8.  Compound Intervals
  9.  Compound Intervals (aug. and dim.)
 10.  Review

Type integer: 1
How many problems do you want? 3
Do you want to include octave information? (y/n): n

Spell a sixth below C

Type answer: e
Correct

Spell a fifth above E

Type answer: b
Very good

Spell a third above E

Type answer: g
Good!

questions answered =   3
correct responses  =   3.0
score for this set = 100.0%

Would you like to do another set? (y/n): y
```

```
Problem Types:

  1.  Intervals
  2.  Scales
  3.  Scale Steps
  4.  Spelling Chords
  5.  Diatonic Chords
  6.  Altered Chords
  7.  I'll Try Anything

Type integer: 1

Interval Drills:

  1.  Generic Simple Intervals (no sharps or flats)
  2.  Generic Compound Intervals
  3.  Fourths, Fifths, and Primes
  4.  Seconds and Thirds
  5.  Sixths and Sevenths
  6.  Review
  7.  Augmented and Diminished Intervals
  8.  Compound Intervals
  9.  Compound Intervals (aug. and dim.)
 10.  Review

Type integer: 6
How many problems do you want? 3

Level of Difficulty (root or tonic):

  1.  No sharps or flats
  2.  Single sharp or flat (on some notes)
  3.  Single sharp or flat (on any note)
  4.  Double sharps or flats
  5.  Triple sharps or flats

Type integer: 1
Do you want to include octave information? (y/n): y

Spell a major second above D5

Type answer: ef5
Incorrect
Would you like to try it again? (y/n): y

Spell a major second above D5

Type answer: e5
Correct

Spell a perfect fifth above B4

Type answer: fs5
Very nice work

Spell a perfect fourth below G7
```

```
Type answer: d7
Good!

questions answered =   3
correct responses  =   2.5
score for this set =  83.3%

Would you like to do another set? (y/n): y

Problem Types:

  1.  Intervals
  2.  Scales
  3.  Scale Steps
  4.  Spelling Chords
  5.  Diatonic Chords
  6.  Altered Chords
  7.  I'll Try Anything

Type integer: 2

Scale Drills

  1.  Generic
  2.  Major Scales
  3.  Minor Scales
  4.  Review
  5.  Diatonic Modes
  6.  Review

Type integer: 4
How many problems do you want? 4

Level of Difficulty (root or tonic):

  1.  No sharps or flats
  2.  Single sharp or flat (on some notes)
  3.  Single sharp or flat (on any note)
  4.  Double sharps or flats
  5.  Triple sharps or flats

Type integer: 2
Do you want to include octave information? (y/n): n

Spell a major scale (one octave ascending) on E

Type answer: e fs gs a b cs ds e
Good!

Spell a major scale (one octave ascending) on Ds

Type answer: ds es fss gs as bs css ds
Very good

Spell a major scale (one octave ascending) on B

Type answer: b cs ds e fs gs a b
```

```
Sorry
Would you like to try it again? (y/n): y

Spell a major scale (one octave ascending) on B

Type answer: b cs ds e fs gs as b
That's much better

Spell a harmonic minor scale (one octave descending) on B

Type answer: b as gs fs e ds cs b
Incorrect
Would you like to try it again? (y/n): n
The correct answer is: B As G Fs E D Cs B

questions answered =   4
correct responses  =   2.5
score for this set =  62.5%

Do you want to review questions missed? n

Would you like to do another set? (y/n): y

Problem Types:

  1.  Intervals
  2.  Scales
  3.  Scale Steps
  4.  Spelling Chords
  5.  Diatonic Chords
  6.  Altered Chords
  7.  I'll Try Anything

Type integer: 4

Chord Drills

  1.  Generic Triads
  2.  Generic Seventh Chords
  3.  Spelling Triads
  4.  Spelling Seventh Chords
  5.  Review

Type integer: 5
How many problems do you want? 3

Level of Difficulty (root or tonic):

  1.  No sharps or flats
  2.  Single sharp or flat (on some notes)
  3.  Single sharp or flat (on any note)
  4.  Double sharps or flats
  5.  Triple sharps or flats

Type integer: 5
Do you want to include octave information? (y/n): y
```

```
Spell a major-minor (dominant) seventh chord on Fs5

Type answer: fs5 as cs5 e
Incorrect
Would you like to try it again? (y/n): y

Spell a major-minor (dominant) seventh chord on Fs5

Type answer: fs5 as cs6 e
That's much better

Spell a major triad on Css7

Type answer: css7 ess gss
Good!

Spell a major-major seventh chord on Esss7

Type answer: esss7 gssss bsss dsss8
Sorry
Would you like to try it again? (y/n): n
The correct answer is: Esss7 Gssss7 Bsss7 Dssss8

questions answered =   3
correct responses  =   1.5
score for this set =  50.0%

Do you want to review questions missed? y

Spell a major-major seventh chord on Dss2

Type answer: dss2 fsss ass csss3
Good!

review questions   =   1
correct responses =   1.0
score on review    = 100.0%

Would you like to do another set? (y/n): y

Problem Types:

  1.  Intervals
  2.  Scales
  3.  Scale Steps
  4.  Spelling Chords
  5.  Diatonic Chords
  6.  Altered Chords
  7.  I'll Try Anything

Type integer: 7
How many problems do you want? 6

Level of Difficulty (root or tonic):

  1.  No sharps or flats
  2.  Single sharp or flat (on some notes)
```

```
  3.  Single sharp or flat (on any note)
  4.  Double sharps or flats
  5.  Triple sharps or flats

Type integer: 3
Do you want to include octave information? (y/n): n

Spell the mediant pitch in the major key on Af

Type answer: c
Good!

Spell a minor thirteenth below E

Type answer: fs
That's not right
Would you like to try it again? (y/n): y

Spell a minor thirteenth below E

Type answer: gs
That's much better

Spell V7/V (or V7/v) in the minor key of B

Type answer: cs es gs b
Good!

Spell a melodic minor scale (one octave ascending) on Ds

Type answer: ds es fs gs as bs css ds
Very nice work

Spell a perfect fifth above Gs

Type answer: ds
Correct

Spell the raised supertonic pitch in the major key on Bf

Type answer: c
Incorrect
Would you like to try it again? (y/n): y

Spell the raised supertonic pitch in the major key on Bf

Type answer: cs
That's much better

questions answered =   6
correct responses  =   5.0
score for this set =  83.3%

Would you like to do another set? (y/n): y

Problem Types:
```

```
   1.  Intervals
   2.  Scales
   3.  Scale Steps
   4.  Spelling Chords
   5.  Diatonic Chords
   6.  Altered Chords
   7.  I'll Try Anything

Type integer: 7
How many problems do you want? 5

Level of Difficulty (root or tonic):

   1.  No sharps or flats
   2.  Single sharp or flat (on some notes)
   3.  Single sharp or flat (on any note)
   4.  Double sharps or flats
   5.  Triple sharps or flats

Type integer: 5
Do you want to include octave information? (y/n): y

Spell an augmented thirteenth below Es7

Type answer: g5
Very nice work

Spell the augmented mediant chord in the minor key of Fs5

Type answer: a c es
Sorry
Would you like to try it again? (y/n): n
The correct answer is: A5 Cs6 Es6

Spell a minor sixth above G4

Type answer: ef5
Good!

Spell a natural minor scale (one octave descending) on A3

Type answer: a3 g f e d c b2 a
Correct

Spell the minor subdominant chord in the major key of B7

Type answer: e g b
That's not right
Would you like to try it again? (y/n): n
The correct answer is: E8 G8 B8

questions answered =   5
correct responses  =   3.0
score for this set =  60.0%

Do you want to review questions missed? y
```

```
Spell the augmented mediant chord in the minor key of Dfff4

Type answer: ffff4 afff cff5
Very nice work
Do you want to continue review? n

review questions  =   1
correct responses =   1.0
score on review   = 100.0%

Would you like to do another set? (y/n): y

Problem Types:

  1.  Intervals
  2.  Scales
  3.  Scale Steps
  4.  Spelling Chords
  5.  Diatonic Chords
  6.  Altered Chords
  7.  I'll Try Anything

Type integer: 7
How many problems do you want? 3

Level of Difficulty (root or tonic):

  1.  No sharps or flats
  2.  Single sharp or flat (on some notes)
  3.  Single sharp or flat (on any note)
  4.  Double sharps or flats
  5.  Triple sharps or flats

Type integer: 5
Do you want to include octave information? (y/n): n

Spell the tonic pitch in the minor key on Ff

Type answer: ff
Correct

Spell an augmented third above B

Type answer: dss
Very good

Spell the mediant chord in the major key of Ds

Type answer: fss as css
Very good

questions answered =   3
correct responses  =   3.0
score for this set = 100.0%

Would you like to do another set? (y/n): n
```

```
Do you want to review questions missed? y

Spell a harmonic minor scale (one octave descending) on D

Type answer: d cs bf a g f e d
Correct
Do you want to continue review? y

Spell the minor subdominant chord in the major key of Ass7

Type answer: dss7 fss css
Oh, dear!
Would you like to try it again? (y/n): n
The correct answer is: Dss8 Fss8 Ass8
Do you want to continue review? y

Spell the minor subdominant chord in the major key of D4

Type answer: g4 bf df5
Sorry
Would you like to try it again? (y/n): y

Spell the minor subdominant chord in the major key of D4

Type answer: g4 bf d5
That's much better

review questions  =   3
correct responses =   1.5
score on review   =  50.0%

total score (does not include review questions)
total questions   =  27
correct responses =  20.5
score             =  75.9%
```

Program *Muspell.* Sample Run (Interactive)

References and Selected Readings

The linear congruential method of calculating random numbers was introduced in 1948 by Lehmer. The method is described in:

Lehmer, D. H. *Proceedings of the 2nd Symposium on Large-Scale Digital Computing Machinery.* Cambridge, Mass.: Harvard University Press, 1951.

For more information on generating and testing random numbers, see the following:

Knuth, Donald E. *The Art of Computer Programming.* Vol. 2, *Seminumerical Algorithms.* Reading, Mass.: Addison-Wesley, 1969.

Sedgewick, Robert. *Algorithms.* 2d ed. Reading Mass.: Addison-Wesley, 1988.

Algorithms for factoring integers into primes (necessary for designing random-number generators of the type described in this chapter) are presented in:

Knuth, Donald E. *The Art of Computer Programming.* Vol. 2, *Seminumerical Algorithms.* Reading, Mass.: Addison-Wesley, 1969.

Binomial structures were first introduced in the following source, as was the outline for a procedure for adding cbrs:

Brinkman, Alexander R. "A Binomial Representation of Pitch for Computer Processing of Musical Data." *Music Theory Spectrum* 8 (1986): 44–57.

The values for the 32-bit random-number generator given in section 19.1 were used in the following sources:

Cooper, Doug, and Michael Clancy. *Oh! Pascal!.* 2d ed. New York: W.W. Norton, 1985.

Grogono, Peter. *Programming in Pascal.* 2d ed. Reading Mass.: Addison-Wesley, 1984.

The following are a few of many sources that deal with computer-assisted instruction in music:

Killam, Rosemary N. "An Effective Computer-Assisted Learning Environment for Aural Skill Development." *Music Theory Spectrum* 6 (1984): 52–62.

Kolosick, Timothy. "A Machine-Independent Data Structure for the Representation of Musical Pitch Relationships: Computer-Generated Musical Examples for CBI." *Journal of Computer-Based Instruction* 13 (1986): 9–13.

Schaffer, John William. "Developing an Intelligent Music Tutorial: An Investigation of Expert Systems and Their Potential for Microcomputer-Based Instruction in Music Theory." Ph.D. dissertation, Indiana University, 1987.

Steinberg, Esther. *Teaching Computers to Teach.* Hillsdale, N.J.: Lawrence Erlbaum Associates, 1984.

Wittlich, Gary E. "Computer Applications: Pedagogy." *Music Theory Spectrum* 11, no. 1 (1989): 60-65.

Wittlich, Gary, E., John W. Schaffer and Larry R. Babb. *Microcomputers and Music.* Englewood Cliffs, N.J.: Prentice-Hall, 1986.

Exercises

1. Write a program that tests a random-integer generator, e.g., one of those presented in section 19.1, to see the length of the period. Your program should save the first number generated, and then count the number of integers generated until the first number appears again. Illustrate the cyclic nature of these generators by printing out the first twenty numbers at the beginning and again after the first value reappears.

2. Write a program that tests the distribution of integers generated by procedure *irand* (section 19.1). The program should generate a large number of integers (say 1,000) in the desired range, count the number of times each integer occurs, and print the results. Test the procedure with a variety of values for *low* and *high.*

3. Devise an algorithm for finding the prime factors of any given integer, and implement it as a Pascal procedure. You can get some help with this in references in the previous sections of this chapter.

4. Write a program that tests prospective values (supplied by the user) for the multiplier, increment, and modulus for linear congruential random-number generators. Print messages specifying which guidelines have been violated.

5. Write a program that generates values to be used in a random-number generator, using the criteria specified in section 19.1. A function for finding the greatest common divisor of two integers was presented in section 13.2.

You may wish to review chapter 14 before attempting the next two exercises.

6. One problem with the program presented in this chapter is that the table takes some time to read (especially if a Pascal interpreter is used instead of a compiler). If this program were to be used for drill in a classroom situation, it would be better to store the table in binary form so that no conversion or calculation would have to be done while reading. Write a program that reads this (as in the chapter) and then writes a second binary file containing elements of type *entry*. Then modify the declarations for the data file and procedure *readdata* in program *muspell*, so that it can read this table. Note that the binary file would not be portable from one Pascal system to another, i.e., the binary version of the table would have to be regenerated from the ASCII version of the data base presented in this chapter.

7. Modify program *muspell* so that it asks for the user's name and the date at the beginning of the program, and then keeps a log in the form of an external file containing users' names, dates, number of exercises of each category, level of difficulty, etc., and score for each problem set. The program should update the user log each time the program is run. You might then write another program that would print a report on any given user or on all users one at a time, based on the contents of the log file.

8. While program *muspell* provides a great deal of flexibility, the problems do tend to get difficult rather quickly after level 1. See if you can redesign the algorithm for levels of difficulty so that multiple accidentals will be introduced more gradually.

9. Consider additional problems that could be added to the question categories for program *muspell*, e.g., spelling chords up or down from the root, third, fifth, or seventh. Exactly how should the question and model answer be stated for each category?

10. Modify program *muspell* so that it can generate written examinations, using problem types and levels of difficulty specified by the instructor. The instructor should also be able to specify the number of different exams following the same format. Thus each student in the class could be given a unique exam using the same parameters. The program should also print answer sheets for each exam.

20| Score Processing

This chapter describes a system for computer processing of music scores that was developed and tested at the Eastman School of Music. This system consists of a program that interprets DARMS code, and a flexible linked data structure for representing the score within the computer memory. The score structure, which is easy to manipulate and is applicable to a broad spectrum of music-analytic activities, was designed to meet the following goals:

1. *Function.* The data structure should facilitate partitioning of the score by part (or voice) or by vertical simultaneity, but the path through the music should not be limited to these two. Segmentation by rests, articulations, slurs, instrumentation, register, dynamics, etc., must also be possible. The representation should permit examination of music detail and the context in which it occurs.
2. *Detail.* The representation of each music dimension should be easily manipulated by the programmer, yet accessible to the analyst. (a) The pitch representation must specify octave, pitch class, and spelling. (b) The system should provide for precise description and handling of rhythm of any complexity. (c) Other attributes that are often pertinent to analysis (dynamics, articulation, phrasing, etc.) should be adequately represented.
3. *Extensibility.* Although the initial implementation should be sufficient for many applications, the system must be extensible: it must be possible to add new features or information to the score representation as need arises.

The first task in meeting these goals was to develop a program that translates the DARMS encoding language into a format more accessible for analysis. The second was to design a flexible linked data structure for representing scores in the computer memory, and to write a procedure to implement this structure.[1]

The rest of this chapter is divided into three parts—a discussion of the DARMS interpreter, a description of the score structure and its construction, and some sample programs that use the system.

1. The orginal work on the DARMS interpreter and score structure design was begun in a doctoral-level seminar at Eastman in the spring of 1982. Although the programs have been substantially reworked and extended since that time, I would like to acknowledge the considerable contribution made by three members of the seminar: Dean Billmeyer, Jane Sawyer Brinkman, and Nola Reed Knouse.

20.1 The DARMS Interpreter

DARMS was chosen as the input language because of its economy, flexibility, and completeness. The DARMS subset processed by the current version of the translator was described in section 6.5.

Because it was designed for music printing, DARMS encodes the graphic symbols used to represent music, not their meaning. It "knows" what symbols are in the score and where they are, but not what they represent. In that sense, uninterpreted DARMS is about as useful to an analysis program as the printed score is to a person who cannot read music. We process DARMS code with a computer program called the DARMS interpreter. This program has two functions: to interpret the meaning of graphic symbols encoded in DARMS, and to calculate the temporal position of each event in the score.

One problem in interpreting DARMS in a computer program is that the code is characterized by the same dependence on context as the symbols it represents. For example, the pitch represented by a space code cannot be determined without knowledge of the clef, key signature, previous accidentals in the current measure, and even transposing characteristics of the instrument that will play the note. Similarly, the temporal position of the note is not encoded explicitly, but only implied by the total of the previous durations in the part. Vertical alignment between parts is usually only implicit. In addition, the encoder is allowed total freedom in deciding the order in which parts will be encoded, and many different arrangements are possible. The freedom of encoding order and the economy of code necessary to represent a passage of music make DARMS extremely attractive for encoding and storing music information, but the vertical and temporal relationship between symbols, as well as the meaning of the symbols themselves, must be resolved before analysis can begin.

Recall that DARMS syntax specifies that note attributes must be encoded in a specific order, and only attributes that occur in the score are encoded.[2] The structure of the program, shown in figure 20.1, reflects the order of encoding for notes. The portion of the program that deals with note attributes is designed as a chain of procedures, or coroutines, with each procedure calling the next. If an encoded note begins with a space code, the number is read and processed, then the next procedure checks for an accidental that would modify the pitch. The following procedures check, in order, for special note heads, duration codes, dots, ties, stems, etc. Procedure *subscan* is a secondary loop that processes those attributes for which the order is not prescribed—slurs, articulations marks, and various dictionary codes. Each procedure in the chain checks for its particular attribute, takes appropriate action if the attribute is encoded, and then calls the next procedure. At the end of the chain, the values for the current note are printed. The chain can be entered at several points, depending on the first encoded attribute of a note. For example, if the first encoded attribute is an accidental, it modifies the pitch of the previous note; if the first attribute is a duration code, the previous pitch is used. Thus the coroutines permit all

2. See table 6.7 on page 143.

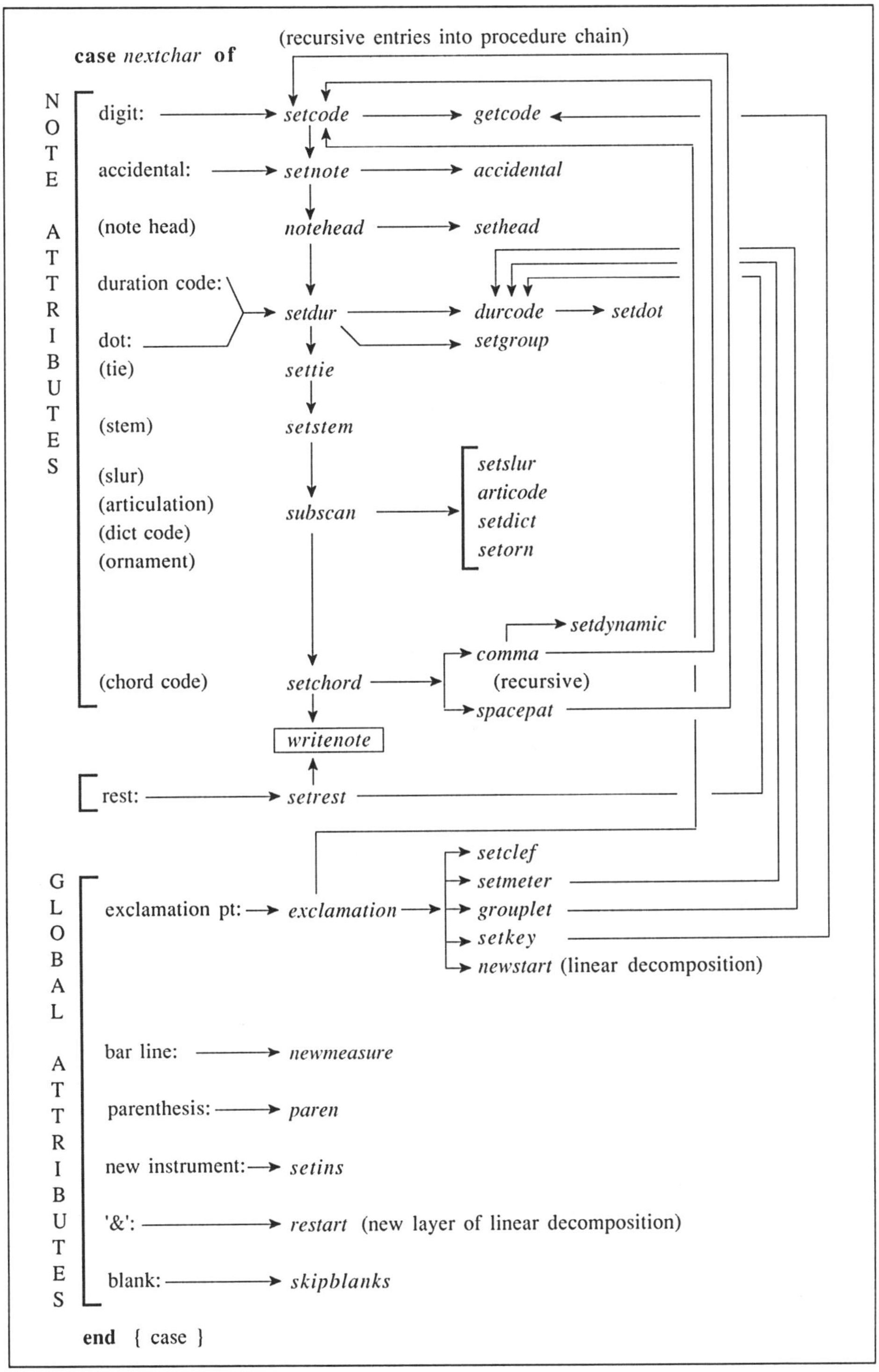

Figure 20.1. Program Structure for DARMS Interpreter

encoding shortcuts described in section 6.5. The chain can be entered recursively for simultaneous notes or chords.

If the next character in the buffer is not appropriate for note attributes, the other possibilities are checked. Most cases set or reset global attributes that affect calculation of note attributes. For example, if an exclamation point is found in the buffer, procedure *exclamation* is called. Since an exclamation point can signal many things in DARMS, this procedure looks ahead in the buffer and calls the appropriate routine to reset the clef, meter, or key signature, or to take other action.

The program keeps track of the current values for each part in an array of records, with fields to represent various attributes of notes, plus some local information for the part, such as the current meter, key signature, etc. The values of the fields are updated when necessary. Some attributes are "sticky," that is, once set they stay set until changed. Pitch, duration, dynamic level, and certain articulation and dictionary codes such as pizzicato and *Hauptstimme*, are treated in this manner. Other attributes, such as accents or staccato marks, apply to only one note and are canceled after the values for the note are printed. The processing for each part is independent of the other parts, permitting flexibility in encoding order. The analyst can choose how much of each part to encode in a stretch: the music can be encoded measure by measure, system by system, instrumental part by instrumental part, etc. The decoded data is printed in the order that it occurs in the DARMS code. The procedure that builds the linked structure will place everything where it belongs.

Some attributes that are not actually dealt with by the scanner are represented by dummy procedures. Examples are procedures that test for character literals, special note heads, and stem directions, which merely skip over the DARMS code representing these items. Also, although beaming information is used to calculate durations, the location of the beginnings and ends of beams is not maintained in the ouput at present. These and other procedures could be expanded easily if experience dictates that this information is needed in analytic procedures that deal with the score structure. Also, it is not difficult to write new procedures that add features of DARMS to the subset represented here.

The use of an array and procedures for implementing an internal buffer (described in section 11.2) enables us to examine not only the next character in the buffer, as with *input*↑, but to look ahead to the end of the current line of data. This makes it possible to interpret the code in a single pass, without first parsing the file into tokens. Error checking in the current version of the program is adequate but not elegant. Whenever an error is detected, the current line is printed with a marker indicating the current buffer position and an error message indicating the suspected error.[3]

The algorithms used in decoding DARMS pitch and rhythm codes were described elsewhere.[4] The treatment of other attributes is much simpler and will not be described here. The complete program is included in appendix C for study.

3. A future version of the interpreter will include more elaborate inline syntax checking using pattern-matching methods described in section 11.3.

4. Pitch algorithms are described in section 11.5; those for decoding rhythm are discussed in section 13.4.

The next two figures illustrate the result of the DARMS translation. Figure 20.2 shows the opening measures of Bartók's String Quartet No. 4, and one possible DARMS encoding of the same passage. Figure 20.3 is a portion of the output from the translation program, using the code in figure 20.2 as input data. The first letter of each line indicates what is to follow: *c* for comment, *b* for bar line, *m* for meter, *i* for note or rest, *p* for new part number, etc. Column numbers have been added above the first *i* line so that we can examine the results of the translation process. The number directly after the *i*, *b*, *m*, or *p* in column one is the numeric identifier for the current instrument. The number after the decimal point is the staff number for multiple-staff instruments (numbered from the top beginning with 0). The second and third columns are the starting and ending times for the note. All time is calculated with fractions implemented as records, as discussed in sections 13.2–13.3. Time is measured in whole-note units, starting with 0/1 at the beginning of the score. The fourth and fifth columns represent the position in measure time at the beginning and end of the note. When this is converted to a real number, the part before the decimal point indicates the measure, and the part after the decimal point is the fraction of a measure. The sixth column is pitch, with –1 indicating a rest. Pitch is represented as a four-digit number (cbr). The first digit is the octave, the middle two digits are the pitch class (0 through 11), and the last digit is a name class indicating the spelling, with integers 0 through 6 representing letter names C through B.[5] The seventh column is the fractional value of the duration. Column eight indicates ties: an odd digit signifies the beginning of a tie, and the following even digit the end. Column nine indicates articulations and dictionary codes in a format similar to that used in DARMS. Each mark is represented by a single character, and 0 indicates the absence of articulation marks. Column ten indicates slurs in a manner analogous to ties in column eight.

E = element	*ord(E)*	*Meaning*
trill	0	trill
mordent	1	mordent
turn	2	turn
flatN	3	flat above ornament
flatE	4	flat to right of ornament
flatS	5	flat below ornament
natN	6	natural above ornament
natE	7	natural to right of ornament
natS	8	natural below ornament
sharpN	9	sharp above ornament
sharpE	a	sharp to right of ornament
sharpS	b	sharp below ornament

Table 20.1. Encoding Ornaments

5. Mathematic operations on this pitch representation are described in chapter 19.

```
K***************************************************************************$
K Bartok String Quartet No. 4, measures 1–6.                                 $
K***************************************************************************$
I1 !G !M4:4,00@ALLEGRO, |QU| = 110$ RQ RE 9E_?V,VF 9#Q._ 7#E_ /
I2 !G !M4:4 1HJ,VF E 1–E_ 2QJ /
I3 !C !M4:4 RW / RW /
I4 !F !M4:4 RQ 17H_,VF 2Q_ /
I1 (8_ 7*L 6) (3L 1–) REQ /
I2 (2 1–_) 20–QL 18–E REQ /
I4 7#Q_ 27!C 8Q_ 33E_ REQ /
I1 19Q._ 18–E_ 19#H / (19*L5,V<1 20 21–L6,V<2) REH /
   RH ((2#L3 1#)) 20#Q.J / EL4 1Q_ 20#E_ 1Q._ 20E_ /
I2 RE 17E_ 18*HJ E (18–JL5 / 18–,V<1) 18*QL6,V<2 REH /
   RQE ((2L1 1)) 20HJ / EL2 Q. 19#E_ 20Q.J /
I3 RHE 3–E_,VF (4–_ 3*JL7,V<3) / 3Q 18EL8,V<4 REH /
   RE (7*L1 6# 5#J) HJ / EL2 5*EJ H 6–E_ 5EJ /
I4 RW / RHQE (9–L1 / 8 7J) H.J / EL2 6–Q.J E 7–_ 6QJ /
```

Figure 20.2. Bartók's String Quartet No. 4, first movement, mm. 1–6

```
p1  new instrument number
c Meter signature: 4 / 4  beats:    4; beatnote:  1 / 4
m1.0   0 /  1              1 /  1    1 /  1    1 /  4
c skipped literal: "@allegro, |qu| = 110$"
=========================================================================
  1      2        3        4        5       6     7       8  9 10 11  12 13
=========================================================================
i1.0   0 /  1   1 /  4   1 /  1   5 /  4    -1  1 /  4   0  0  0  x  -1  x
i1.0   1 /  4   3 /  8   5 /  4  11 /  8    -1  1 /  8   0  0  0  x  -1  x
i1.0   3 /  8   1 /  2  11 /  8   3 /  2  5053  1 /  8   0 _v  0  x  80  8
i1.0   1 /  2   7 /  8   3 /  2  15 /  8  5063  3 /  8   0  _  0  x  80  x
i1.0   7 /  8   1 /  1  15 /  8   2 /  1  5031  1 /  8   0  _  0  x  80  x
b1.0   1 /  1            2 /  1     0
p2  new instrument number
c Meter signature: 4 / 4  beats:    4; beatnote: 1 / 4
m2.0   0 /  1            1 /  1   1 /  1    1 / 4
i2.0   0 /  1   1 /  2   1 /  1   3 /  2  4042  1 /  2   1  0  0  x   80 8
i2.0   1 /  2   5 /  8   3 /  2  13 /  8  4042  1 /  8   2  0  0  x   80 x
i2.0   5 /  8   3 /  4  13 /  8   7 /  4  4032  1 /  8   0  _  0  x   80 x
i2.0   3 /  4   1 /  1   7 /  4   2 /  1  4053  1 /  4   1  0  0  x   80 x
b2.0   1 /  1            2 /  1     0
p3  new instrument number
c Meter signature: 4 / 4  beats:    4; beatnote: 1 / 4
m3.0   0 /  1            1 /  1   1 /  1    1 /  4
i3.0   0 /  1   1 /  1   1 /  1   2 /  1    -1  1 /  1   0  0  0  x   -1 x
b3.0   1 /  1            2 /  1     0
i3.0   1 /  1   2 /  1   2 /  1   3 /  1    -1  1 /  1   0  0  0  x   -1 x
b3.0   2 /  1            3 /  1     0
p4  new instrument number
c Meter signature: 4 / 4  beats:    4; beatnote: 1 / 4
m4.0   0 /  1            1 /  1   1 /  1    1 /  4
i4.0   0 /  1   1 /  4   1 /  1   5 /  4    -1  1 /  4   0  0  0  x   -1 x
i4.0   1 /  4   3 /  4   5 /  4   7 /  4  2000  1 /  2   0  _  0  x   80 8
i4.0   3 /  4   1 /  1   7 /  4   2 /  1  2095  1 /  4   0  _  0  x   80 x
b4.0   1 /  1            2 /  1     0
p1  new instrument number
i1.0   1 /  1   9 /  8   2 /  1  17 /  8  5042  1 /  8   0  _  0  x   80 x
i1.0   9 /  8   5 /  4  17 /  8   9 /  4  5021  1 /  8   0  0  1  x   80 x
i1.0   5 /  4  11 /  8   9 /  4  19 /  8  5000  1 /  8   0  0  2  x   80 x
i1.0  11 /  8   3 /  2  19 /  8   5 /  2  4074  1 /  8   0  0  1  x   80 x
i1.0   3 /  2  13 /  8   5 /  2  21 /  8  4032  1 /  8   0  0  2  x   80 x
i1.0  13 /  8   7 /  4  21 /  8  11 /  4    -1  1 /  8   0  0  0  x   80 x
i1.0   7 /  4   2 /  1  11 /  4   3 /  1    -1  1 /  4   0  0  0  x   80 x
b1.0   2 /  1            3 /  1     0
p2  new instrument number
i2.0   1 /  1   9 /  8   2 /  1  17 /  8  4053  1 /  8   2  0  0  x   80 x
i2.0   9 /  8   5 /  4  17 /  8   9 /  4  4032  1 /  8   0  _  0  x   80 x
i2.0   5 /  4   3 /  2   9 /  4   5 /  2  4011  1 /  4   0  0  1  x   80 x
i2.0   3 /  2  13 /  8   5 /  2  21 /  8  3106  1 /  8   0  0  2  x   80 x
i2.0  13 /  8   7 /  4  21 /  8  11 /  4    -1  1 /  8   0  0  0  x   80 x
i2.0   7 /  4   2 /  1  11 /  4   3 /  1    -1  1 /  4   0  0  0  x   80 x
b2.0   2 /  1            3 /  1     0
  etc. ...
```

Figure 20.3. Output from the DARMS Interpreter

Ornaments and dynamics are represented internally as sets of values from user-defined ordinal types, which can be extended easily if necessary. In column eleven, the digits 0 through b represent ornaments and associated accidentals, as shown in table 20.1. Each digit is the ordinal position of an element in the following enumerated type:

ornament = (*trill*, *mordent*, *turn*, *flatN*, *flatE*, *flatS*, *natN*, *natE*, *natS*, *sharpN*, *sharpE*, *sharpS*)

In the output from the interpreter, an ornament may be represented by a digit or a concatenation of digits. For example, 0b represents a trill symbol with a sharp to the right (east), and 238 represents a turn with a flat above and a natural below. An *x* represents the absence of an ornament.

Dynamics are represented in two ways. The numbers in column eleven represent the dynamic level as an integer: 70 = *mf*, 80 = *f*, 90 = *ff*, etc. At this point the dynamic level is undefined (–1) during crescendos and diminuendos. These values will be calculated by interpolation after the part is stored in a linked list. Column

E = *element*	*ord*(*E*)	*Meaning*
pppppp	0	(dynamic levels)
ppppp	1	
pppp	2	
ppp	3	
pp	4	
p	5	
mp	6	
mf	7	
f	8	
ff	9	
fff	a	
ffff	b	
fffff	c	
ffffff	d	
sfz	e	*sfz*, *ffp*, *fffmp*, *fz*, etc.
cresc	f	crescendo over single note
startcresc	g	start of crescendo over several notes
endcresc	h	end of crescendo over several notes
incresc	i	in crescendo
crescdim	j	<> over a single note
dim	k	diminuendo over single note
startdim	l	start of diminuendo over several notes
enddim	m	end of diminuendo over several notes
indem	n	within diminuendo
dimcresc	o	>< over a single note

Table 20.2. Encoding Dynamics

twelve indicates where dynamic marks actually occur in the score. The digits 0 through d represent the fourteen dynamic levels from *pppppp* to *ffffff*. Digits e through o represent other dynamic information (e.g., whether the note is the beginning or end of a crescendo or diminuendo), as shown in table 20.2. These digits are the ordinal positions of the elements of an enumerated type consisting of dynamic codes:

dynamic = (*pppppp*, *ppppp*, *pppp*, *ppp*, *pp*, *p*, *mp*, *mf*, *f*, *ff*, *fff*, *ffff*, *fffff*, *ffffff*,
sfz, *cresc*, *startcresc*, *endcresc*, *incresc*, *crescdim*,
dim, *startdim*, *enddim*, *indim*, *dimcresc*)

In the program output the digits may be concatenated. Thus 8g indicates a crescendo beginning at dynamic level forte, and 9h is the end of the crescendo at fortissimo. After the score structure is built, dynamics will be represented by the set type and by an integer between 0 (*pppppp*) and 130 (*ffffff*), with ten steps between each level to make gradations during crescendos and diminuendos.

In its current state, the scanner deals correctly with any type of key and meter signature, all clefs (movable), articulation codes (including several dictionary codes), basic ornaments, dynamics, ties, slurs, chords (in a number of different encoding schemes), multiple layers within parts, multiple-staff instruments, all duration codes and beamed notes, simple and nested grouplets, accidentals, rests, and various types of bar lines. The program was designed to be easily extended to other aspects of DARMS code as the need arises.

20.2 The Score Structure

One major problem in representing scores for computer processing is that the texture is often variable. While one part may have many notes, others may have few or none at all, and parts may divide and subdivide. Thus a score has much in common with a sparse matrix, i.e., a matrix in which a good majority of the storage locations are empty. Figure 20.4 shows an 11 by 12 matrix. The matrix is sparse, since out of 132 possible values only five actually occur in the matrix (an absent value is represented by 0). A linked representation of this matrix would store only the nonzero values and their locations.

Our data structure is based on circular, doubly linked lists with head nodes. This structure can be traversed in either direction with equal ease, with the head node marking the beginning and end of the list. Insertion is simplified, since there are no special cases: the same algorithm inserts nodes at the beginning, middle, or end of the list, even if the list is empty (see section 16.5.7).

The score representation is a multilinked ring structure consisting of many interlocking instances of the circular list described above. A simplified diagram of the links in the data structure is shown in figure 20.5. The spine of the data structure is a time line for the score, with each node containing the time when one or more events occur. Each spine node contains temporal information and link fields to connect it to notes in the part. Bidirectional horizontal links, shown at (b), enable us to traverse

0	0	2	0	0	0	0	0	0	0	0	0
0	0	0	0	0	0	0	0	0	0	0	0
0	0	0	0	0	0	0	0	40	0	0	0
0	0	0	0	0	0	0	0	0	0	0	0
0	0	0	0	0	19	0	0	0	0	0	0
0	0	0	0	0	0	0	0	0	0	0	0
0	0	0	0	0	0	0	0	0	0	0	0
0	0	0	7	0	0	0	0	0	0	0	0
0	0	0	0	0	0	0	0	0	0	0	0
0	0	0	0	0	0	0	0	0	0	0	0
0	0	0	0	0	0	99	0	0	0	0	0

Figure 20.4. A Sparse Matrix

the time line or any part or layer in either direction, moving forward or backward in the score at will. Start-time links, shown at (c), link together all events that begin at any given time. This list is also circular and doubly linked, with the spine node acting as the head node for the list. Stop-time links concatenate all events that terminate at any given time, as shown at (d). The start- and stop-time links allow us to examine vertical structure and to move either up or down in the score, crossing parts or traversing chordal structures in one voice. Nonnote events, such as bar lines, meter signatures, tempo indications, rehearsal marks, etc., are also linked to the spine, as shown at (e). Although the diagrams show each type of link separately, they exist simultaneously. Together, they allow an analysis program to move about in the score in any manner desired, looking back or ahead at will, combining horizontal and vertical motion in any manner required. This makes it possible for us to evaluate context to a degree that is difficult to achieve when dealing with one-dimensional representations such as strings.

Each *note* node has a pointer called *dlink* that points to a *data* node. Fields in the *data* node contain all other attributes of the note encoded as described above: pitch, duration, dynamic indications, articulations, ties, slurs and phrase marks, etc.

The data structure is built with variant records, facilitating pointers to many different node variants. The use of data nodes for notes helps to keep the variants approximately the same size. The *dlink* field of nonnote events is usually **nil**, but any node can be linked through this field to a *data* node. Thus special indicators, such as fermatas, can be linked to nonnote events, such as bar lines. The *data* nodes also

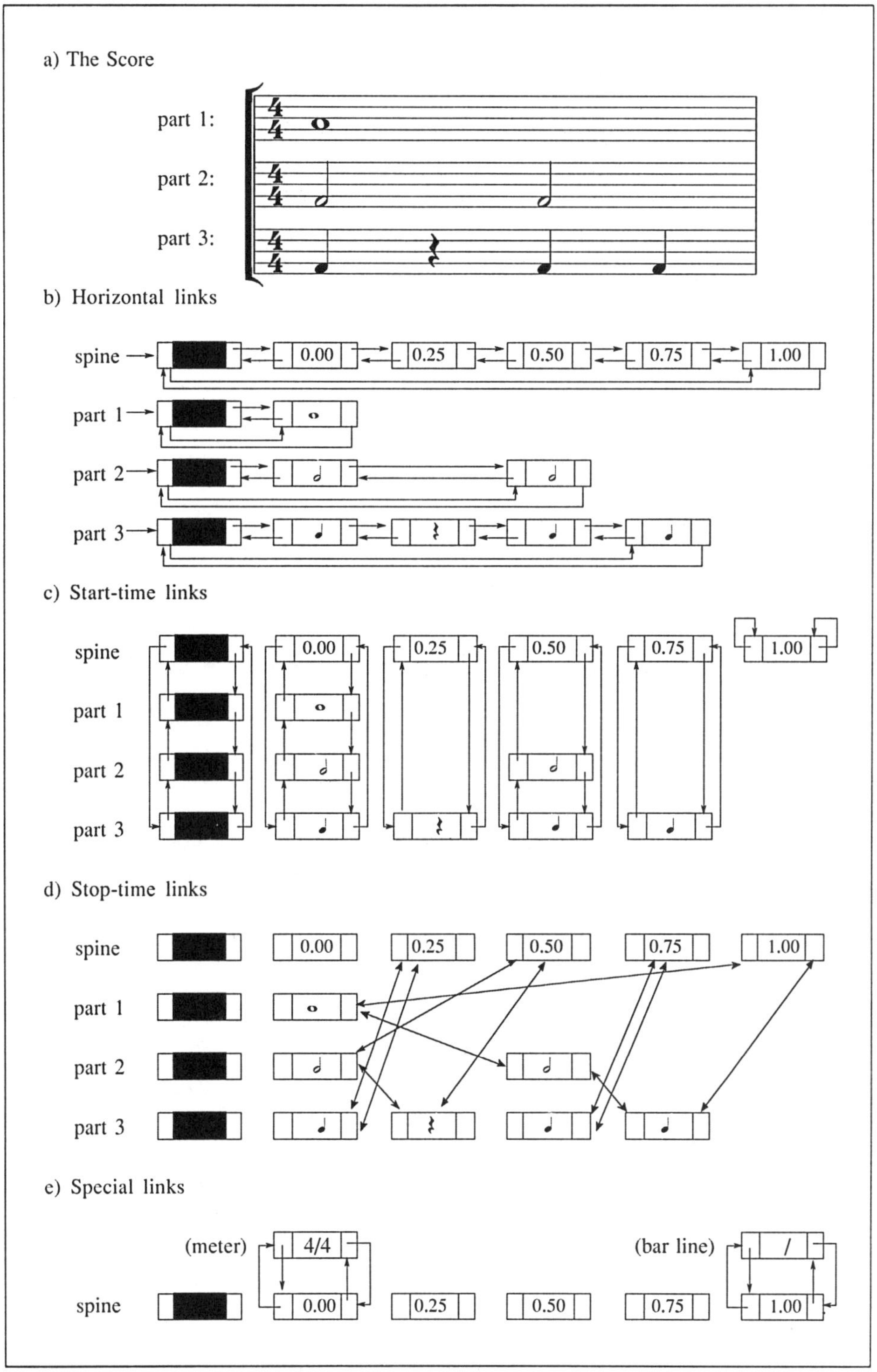

Figure 20.5. Links in the Score Structure

contain a *dlink* field. These could be used at a later date to implement freer "event lists" as described by Dannenberg.[6] The type definitions used to implement this node structure are stored in file *linkdefs.h*, below:

```
(***********************          Linkdefs.h        ***********************)
(* This file contains the type definitions used in the score structure.  *)
(*************************************************************************)
{ type }               { this keyword must occur in the calling program }

    buftype = record
                 B  : array[1 .. maxline] of char;     { array for buffer     }
                 bp : integer                          { position in buffer   }
              end;

    ornament = (trill, mordent, turn, flatN, flatE, flatS, natN,
                natE, natS, sharpN, sharpE, sharpS);

    orntype = set of ornament;

    articulation = (staccato, wedgeaccent, tenuto, accent, vaccent, fermata,
                    arco, pizz, snap, upbow, downbow,
                    hauptstimme, nebenstimme, terminator,
                    open, stopped);

    artictype  = set of articulation;

    dynamic = (pppppp, ppppp, pppp, ppp, pp, p, mp, mf, f, ff, fff, ffff,
               fffff, ffffff, sfz, cresc, startcresc, endcresc, incresc,
               crescdim, dim, startdim, enddim, indim, dimcresc);

    dynset = set of dynamic;

    fraction = record
                  num : integer;                      { numerator           }
                  den : integer                       { denominator         }
               end;

    intset = set of 1 .. 14;                          { set of integers     }

    dptr = ↑data;
    data = record
              pitch : integer;                        { pitch encoded as cbr }
              dur   : fraction;                       { duration as fraction }
              tie   : intset;                         { tie field            }
              artic : artictype;                      { articulation codes   }
              slur  : intset;                         { slur field           }
              orn   : orntype;                        { set of ornament codes}
              dyn1  : integer;                        { dynamics             }
              dyn2  : dynset                          { dynamics             }
           end;

    kind = (avail, head, spine, note, barline, metersig, trans, rest,
                                                      gracenote, keysig);
```

6. Roger Dannenberg, "A Structure for Representing, Displaying and Editing Music," in *Proceedings of the 1986 International Computer Music Conference* (San Francisco: Computer Music Association).

```
ptr = ↑node;
node =                       { all nodes contain the following fields }
  record
    tag   : kind;                         { type of record          }
    llink : ptr;                          { left link               }
    rlink : ptr;                          { right link              }
    dlink : dptr;                         { pointer to data node    }
    part  : real;                         { part.staff              }
    start : ptr;                          { for start times         }
    bstart: ptr;                          { backward start link     }
    stop  : ptr;                          { for stop times          }
    bstop : ptr;                          { backward stop link      }
    spec  : ptr;                          { for special events      }
    bspec : ptr;                          { backward spec link      }

                             { specific nodes contain in addition:   }
    case kind of
      avail : (link : ptr);            { for free list              }

      head     : ( );

      spine    : (time    : fraction;  { time as sum of durations   }
                  measure : fraction;  { integer part = measure     }
                                       { decimal = partmeasure      }
                  mlink   : ptr);      { pointer to meter sig node  }

      note,
      gracenote,
      rest     : ( );                  { dlink points to data node  }

      barline : (bartype : integer);

      metersig: (meter    : fraction;
                 beatnote : fraction);

      keysig:   (accidentals : integer;
                 sign        : char);

      trans    : (tlevel : integer);   { transposition level        }
                                       {    as signed cbr           }
  end;  { record }

part =
  record
    s : ptr;                           { pointer to spine           }
    p : ptr                            { pointer to part            }
  end;

partpointers = array[0 .. maxins] of part;{ ptrs into score structure }

partrange = 0 .. maxins;
partset = set of partrange;        { the set of "active" part numbers }

brset = array[1 .. 84] of integer; { set of binomial pcs             }
```

Figure 20.6. The Include File *linkdefs.h*

20.2.1 Building the Structure

Procedure *build* constructs the score data structure, using the output file from the DARMS interpreter (figure 20.3). Since the procedure takes notes and other symbols in any order and links them into the data structure in the correct position, the algorithm can be thought of as a two-dimensional sorting process that places each note in the vertical and horizontal dimensions.

Initially each part is constructed separately, with its own time line and its own linked list of note nodes. The data structure is accessed through an array of pointers called *instr* (see figure 20.7). *Instr* is an array of records, with two pointers for each part. For any part *i*, *instr* [*i*].*s* points to the spine (or time line), and *instr* [*i*].*p* points to the note nodes for the part. The array is initialized by obtaining two head nodes for each part and pointing the spine and part pointers to them. Since the lists are empty, the left and right link fields on each head node point back to the head node.

As each note is read, a note node is obtained from the storage allocation procedure, and the encoded attributes of the note are stored in appropriate fields. The time line in the spine is then examined to find where the note should be placed. If the start time of the new note does not occur in the list, a new spine node is allocated and linked into the spine. The note node is then linked vertically into the start-time list on the spine node, through use of the *start* and *bstart* fields, and horizontally into the part's note list, through use of *link* and *llink*. The note is also linked, through the *stop* and *bstop* fields, to a spine node at its termination time. This node may also have to be allocated and linked into the spine. Bar lines, meter signatures, etc., are linked into the spine but not into the note list. At this point each note is placed in the correct part in the correct temporal position, but the various parts are still not aligned vertically. Figure 20.8 shows the data structure at this stage, using the simple score from figure 20.5.

Finally, the spines are merged into a single time line, represented by the spine for part 0, *instr*[0].*s*. This process is illustrated in figure 20.9. At (a) the spine for part 1 has been merged with that for part 0, and the spine for part 2 is separate. To simplify the diagram the circular links are omitted, as are the stop-time links and specific time information. Spine nodes are identified by capital letters, note nodes are numbered, and special nodes are labeled with lowercase letters. For convenience, the nodes are drawn in temporal order, with time moving from left to right. Spine 2 will now be merged into spine 0. In the merging process, each node in spine 2 is compared to nodes in spine 0. If each spine has a node at the same time, spine 2's circular lists for start times, stop times, and special events are concatenated to the lists for spine 0, and the spine node from spine 2 is returned to the storage pool. This is the case in the first and fourth time slices, where nodes *D* and *F* duplicate action times in nodes *A* and *C* in the spine for part 0. If the time of the node in spine 2 does not occur in spine 0, the separate layer node is linked into spine 0 at the correct temporal position. When the merging process is complete there is only one time line, with one node for each action time in the score, and all notes that begin or end at the same time are linked together through the *start*/*bstart* and *stop*/*bstop* fields, as shown at (b).

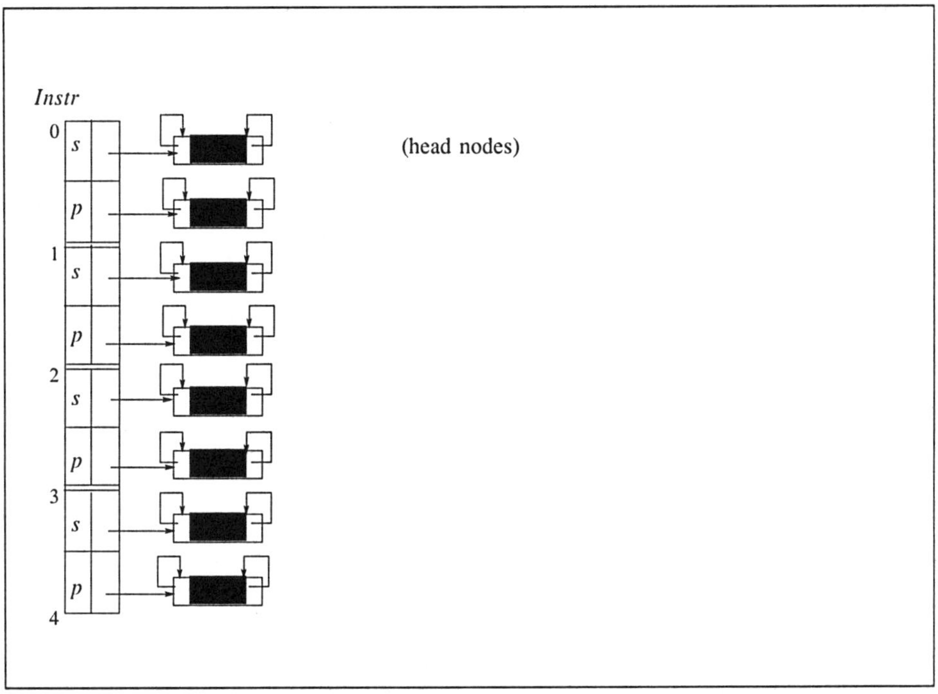

Figure 20.7. The Array *instr* after Initialization

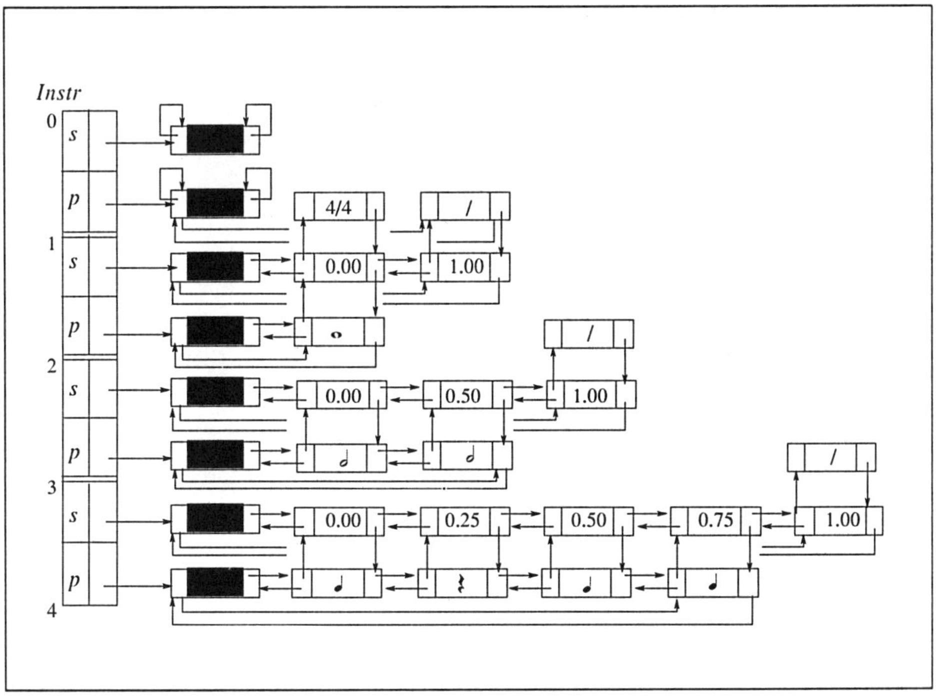

Figure 20.8. Partially Constructed Data Structure

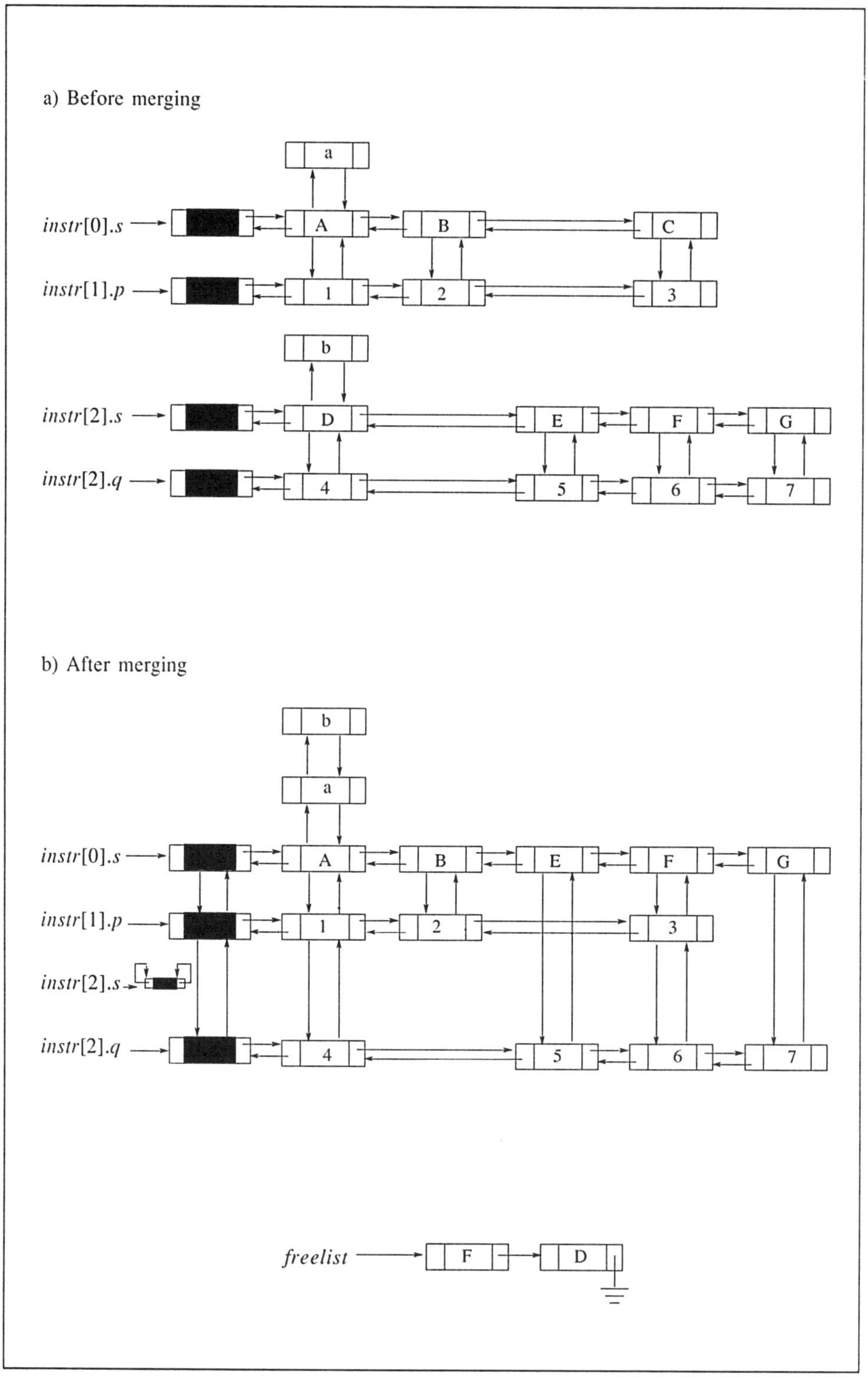

Figure 20.9. Merging Spines

Note that the head nodes for spine 0 and for each part are also linked in a doubly linked circular list through their *start* and *bstop* fields.

20.2.2 Special Cases

Several special cases are still to be discussed, with specific reference to figure 20.10. First, when the individual parts are constructed, it is possible to have two or more notes in one part with the same start time. This is the case when chords are encoded with any of several schemes available in DARMS. If a spine node already exists for a new note's starting time, the new note is not linked directly into the part list, but is linked into the start-time list of the spine node, and thus occurs conceptually just below the other note in the data structure. This situation is illustrated in figure 20.10 at (a). Chordal notes are not linked horizontally, i.e., *llink* and *rlink* of the node point to the node.

A second special case occurs when parts are encoded in layers with DARMS's linear decomposition mode. The solution here is to use a separate part and spine to link up the new layer, and then to merge these lists with the main ones for the part. In this case each layer is linked from left to right, as shown at (b). Chords can occur within layers, and many layers may exist in a part. Within the layered segment, note nodes are linked horizontally. However, *llink* of the first node in the layer and *rlink* of the last point to the note node. Thus the first and last nodes in a layer can be recognized.

For multiple-staff instruments, the top staff is linked as the primary part; additional staves are linked below it as separate parts, as shown at (c). The list representing each staff has a head node, which is linked vertically to the other head nodes, but which is not referenced directly by a pointer from the *instr* array. The part and staff for each node in the structure are stored in the *part* field of the node. This field contains a real number in the form *part.staff.* Staves are numbered from 0, representing the top (or only) staff in the part. For example, *part* number 1.0 represents the top staff in part 1, while 3.1 indicates the second staff of part 3.

Grace notes are linked to a note node in bidirectional circular lists through the *spec* and *bspec* fields, which are otherwise unused by notes; the note node serves as the head node of the list. Thus any number of grace notes may be linked to any note, and their order can be determined, even though the actual duration of grace notes is not specified.

Finally, it is useful to be able to locate quickly the current meter signature from any point in the score. For this purpose I have added a pointer, *mlink*, that points from each spine node to the previous meter note in the list of special nodes linked to the spine nodes. When the current meter is needed, it can be obtained by traversing the start-time list to the spine node and accessing the latest meter node through the *mlink* field. These links are shown at (b) of figure 20.10.

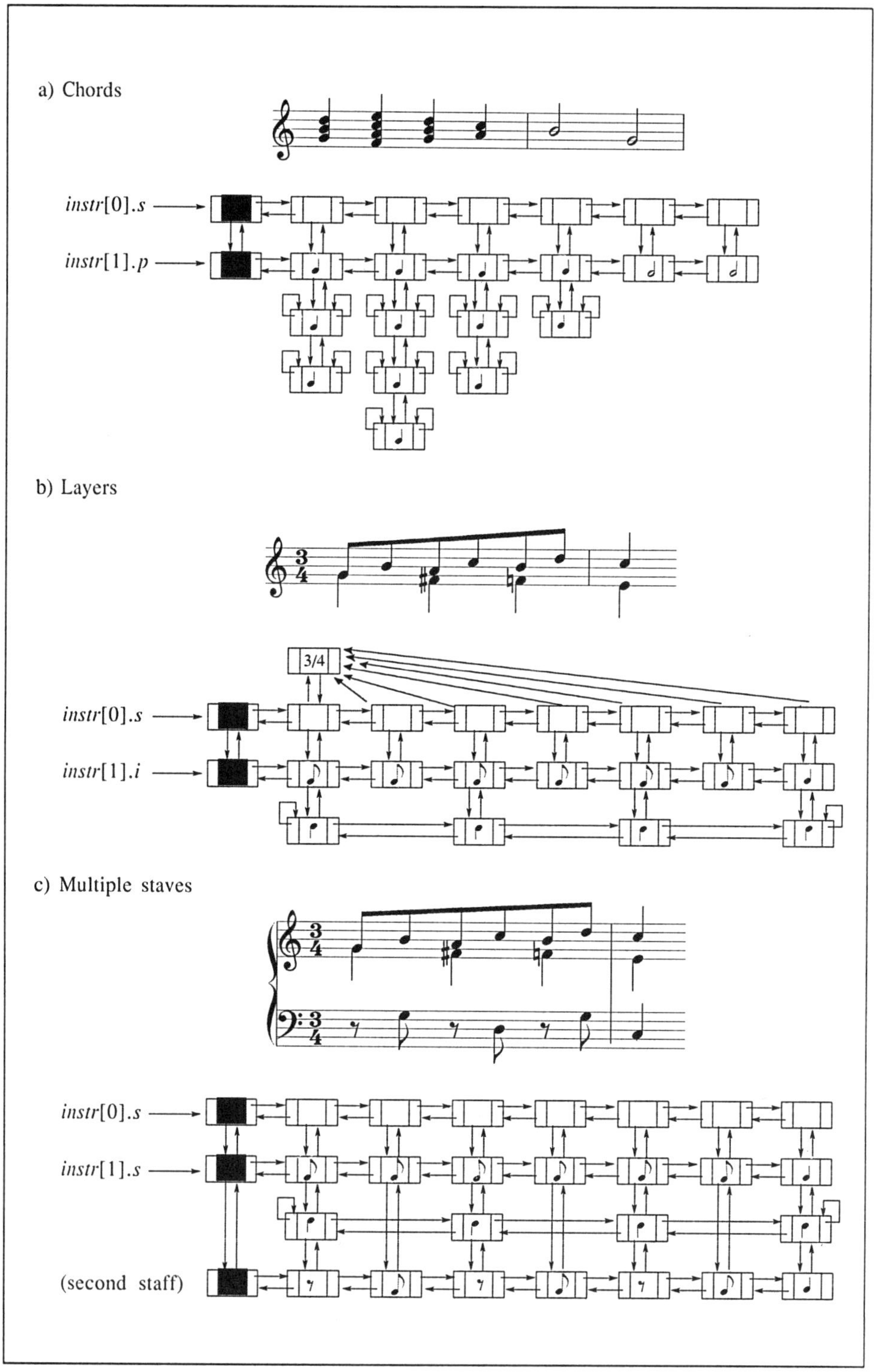

Figure 20.10. Links for Chordal Structures, Layers, and Multiple Staves

20.3 Using the Data Structure

Many of the functions and procedures used in dealing with the structure are included in the program library routines listed in appendix D. This toolbox approach, inspired by the UNIX operating system, has two advantages in this text. First, procedures in many systems can be compiled separately and stored in a program library or archive, which can be accessed by any Pascal program that requires them. Although separate compilation is an extension to standard Pascal, many systems do provide this facility. Second, by treating the procedures as external, we can avoid duplicating them in each of several programs that require their use. This saves a great deal of space, gives a better sense for the amount of new code required to solve each problem, and allows us to concentrate on process rather than detail. Individual library procedures are shown in appendix D; if external procedures are not supported by your system, the actual code can be placed in the program in place of the external procedure declaration.

In addition to the procedures in the library, the type definitions used in defining the data structures are declared in separate *include* files. These files omit the reserved word **type**, so they can be included in a program along with user-defined type definitions. In my UNIX system, this is accomplished by beginning the file with the symbol '#', and then using a directive to include the file in the program. For example, the types needed for the data structure, defined in a file called *linkdefs.h*, are included in the program, say *traverse*, as follows:[7]

```
#
program traverse(input, output, scoredata);
  const
    maxins = 15;                   { maximum number of parts          }
    maxline = 90;                  { length of internal line buffer   }

  type
#     include "linkdefs.h"

  var
    scoredata : text;              { external file for score          }
    instr     : partpointers;
      [ etc. ... ]
```

The first line begins with '#', signaling the compiler to preprocess the file. The line

```
#include "linkdefs.h"
```

tells the compiler to read the contents of the file *linkdefs.h* at this point in the program. This is followed by any other type definitions required by the program, in this case the definition of the score file (the output from the DARMS translator), the array of pointers (uninitialized) into the score structure, etc.

Following the type and variable definitions, a heading for each external procedure or function is provided with the directive *external*. These are followed by new pro-

7. A listing of file *linkdefs.h* was shown in figure 20.6.

cedures that are to be used by this program. The program is compiled along with the name of the library containing all of the separately compiled procedures, which are linked with the new procedures and main program after they are compiled.

The rest of this chapter discusses several simple programs that illustrate the use of the linked score structure and library discussed above. To save space and avoid repetition, many procedures are declared as external, and include files are used for two separate sets of declarations: those for the linked data structure, and those for a set-identifying procedure similar to that discussed in chapter 17. Listings and descriptions of the library procedures and include files can be found in appendix D.

The tag fields in each node identify the types of nodes, and are extremely useful in traversal of the various lists. For example, the spine (time line) is traversed by the following:

```
t := instr[0].s;                        { head node of spine }
t := t↑.rlink;                          { first spine node    }
while t↑.tag <> headnode do
  begin
    . . .

    t := t↑.rlink
  end;
```

If t points to a spine node, the list of notes and rests that start at that time can be traversed as follows:

```
t := t↑.start;                          { first note or rest }
while t↑.tag <> spine do
  begin
    . . .

    t := t↑.start
  end;
```

Since each note may be preceded by grace notes, a loop is nested in the above to examine them:

```
t := t↑.start;
while t↑.tag <> spine do
  begin
    t := t↑.spec;                       { get first grace note }
    while t↑.tag = gracenote do
      begin
        { visit grace note }
        t := t↑.tag
      end;
    { visit note or rest }
    t := t↑.start
  end;
```

Because each list is circular, the loop that traverses the list does nothing if the list is empty. For example, if there are no grace notes, then the statement t := t↑.*spec* points t to the current note node, and the grace-note loop does not execute. The entire data structure can be traversed by traversing the spine. As each spine node is visited, the list of special nodes is traversed, followed by the list of events that start at that time. Thus, if *t* points to the head node of the spine, the following algorithm scans the entire score structure:

```
t := t↑.rlink;                               { get first spine node     }
while t↑.tag <> headnode do
  begin { traverse spine }

    t := t↑.spec;                            { traverse special nodes }
    while t↑.tag <> spine do
      begin
        { visit special node }
        t := t↑.spec                         { get next special node    }
      end;

    t := t↑.start;                           { traverse notes/rests     }
    while t↑.tag <> spine do
      begin

        t := t↑.spec;                        { traverse grace notes     }
        while t↑.tag = gracenote do
          begin
            { visit grace note }
            t := t↑.spec                     { get next grace note      }
          end;

        { visit note or rest }

        t := t↑.start                        { get next note or rest    }
      end;

    t := t↑.rlink                            { get next spine node      }
  end; { traverse spine }
```

Since each part is linked horizontally through the *llink* and *rlink* fields, an alternate approach is to enter part *i* through the pointer *instr*[*i*], and to traverse the part instead of the spine.

Each note in a part is linked to the notes that precede it (through the *llink* field), to those that follow it (through *rlink*), and to the notes above it (through *bstart*) and below it (through *start*). Thus it is not difficult to determine the context in which a note occurs.

The starting time for any note or rest can be found by traversing the *start* fields up to the spine node, and reading the time (raw time or measure time). The stop time for any node can be found by traversing the *stop* fields up to the spine node that heads the stop-time list. For grace notes, one must first follow the *spec* pointers to the note node, and then traverse the start-time list.

The programs on the following pages utilize various ways of traversing the structure and interpreting the data contained in it. Each program makes use of procedures and functions from the program library listed in appendix D, and must declare an external data file for the output from the DARMS translator. Before beginning its specific task, the program calls procedure *build*, which constructs the score structure using the data from the translator, and returns the array of pointers into the spine and individual parts:

```
build(input, output, scoredata, instr, freelist); { build structure }
```

Build initializes the array of pointers, builds the structure, and calls a procedure that traverses the structure to interpolate dynamic levels during crescendos and diminuendos.

The programs are not meant to be perfect solutions to problems. They represent experiments in dealing with the data structure and exploring possible applications. Some of the programs are based in part on programs written under my guidance by graduate students at the Eastman School of Music. I have reworked all of the programs, in some cases to improve their function, in others to have them conform to a consistent format and user interface. The contributions of others to this work are noted in the discussions of individual programs.

20.3.1 Traversing the Data Structure

Program *proof* is designed for checking the score data, since the output is easier to read than DARMS code. The program illustrates the basic traversal discussed above, using separate procedures to traverse each simple list, and other refinements. In particular, the user specifies the exact measures and which parts he or she wants to examine. In this program, *visiting* each node consists of printing appropriate values stored in the fields of the record. This is facilitated by procedure *writenode*, which is implemented as a case statement keying on the tag field of the node. The values are printed to facilitate proofreading the code. The raw starting time and the measure number for each item are printed as real numbers rather than fractions. Pitches are identified with note names and standard octave numbers, e.g., C#$_4$, and some other fields are decoded as well. For example, articulation marks are printed using the DARMS symbols, and special dynamic codes such as crescendo or *ff* are listed in their mnemonic form rather than by single characters.

By maintaining a set of active instruments, we can extract data from any combination of instruments in the score. The user specifies these instruments by number (1 3 4) or "all." If only a single instrument is requested, the result is a listing from the beginning to end of all data pertaining to that instrument. If several instruments are specified, the values are printed by time slice, i.e., all values that occur at the beginning of the score are printed, followed by items from the second vertical slice, etc. The user specifies, by measure and beat, the portion of the score that is to be processed. The program sets pointers to the spine nodes at the beginning and end of the active "window," and the score is traversed between these points.

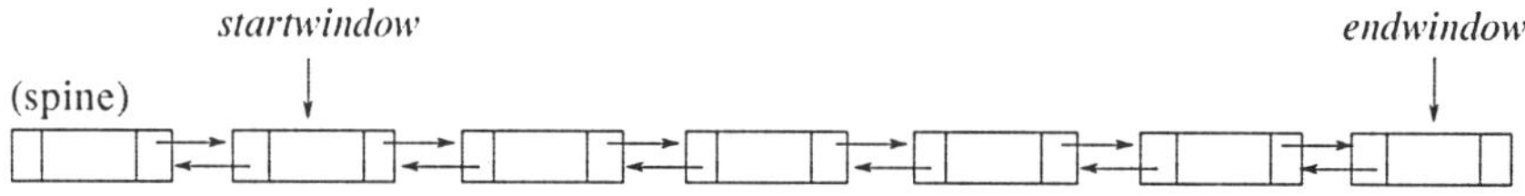

The main procedure is shown below. Procedure *build* constructs the data structure from the translated DARMS data. Procedure *setup* initializes the pointer variables *startwindow* and *endwindow* to point to the beginning and end of the spine, and initializes *parts*, a set of integers representing the various instruments, to include all parts. Within the **while not** *done* loop, the user is given the opportunity to change the size of the window and specify which instruments are to be examined. Then procedure *traverse* is invoked to traverse the score from the beginning to the end of the window, printing out the instruments included in the set of integers *parts*.[8]

```
begin { main }
  build(input, output, scoredata, instr, freelist);{ build structure     }
  setup(output, instr[0].s, parts, all,           { init window and     }
                     startwindow, endwindow);     {  active parts       }
  done := false;
  while not done do
    begin
      write('Reset target parts? (y/n): [n] ');
      if affirmative(input, output, no)
        then setins(input, output, parts, all);   { reset active parts }

      write('Reset window size? (y/n): [n] ');
      if affirmative(input, output, no)           { reset window size   }
        then setwindow(input, output,
                  instr[0].s, startwindow, endwindow); writeln;

      traverse(parts, startwindow, endwindow);    { traverse spine      }
      writeln;
      write('Do you want to continue? (y/n): [y] ');
      done := not affirmative(input, output, yes)
    end
end. { main }
```

The complete program (without external procedures and include files) is listed as program 20.1. This is followed by an abbreviated interactive work session, using the excerpt from the Bartók quartet shown in figure 20.2.

(see appendix E, page 891)

Program 20.1. *Proof*

In the program output, the first column is the instrument number; the next two are the temporal position as raw time and as measure; the fourth column is the pitch; and the fifth is the duration. Columns six through ten represent ties, articulation, slurs, ornaments, and dynamic level. The beginning of a tie or slur is indicated by an odd integer n, and terminated by the next even integer $n + 1$. The symbol x indicates

8. Most of the programs discussed in this chapter use the same user interface, i.e., the window and active parts are set automatically, and the user is given the opportunity to reset these parameters before each iteration of the loop. Procedures for handling these parameters are shown in appendix D.

absence of a tie, slur, or ornament. Articulation marks are shown using the DARMS code, or 0 if none is present. Dynamics are represented on a linear scale with 80 = *f*, 90 = *ff*, etc. The mnemonic value is printed where it appears in the score. For example, the first note is marked *f*, and the following notes have the same dynamic by default.

Note that function *affirmative* (see section 15.3.1) has been modified to provide a "default" value. When the program asks a question that requires a "yes" or "no" answer, the the most likely answer is provided in brackets, e.g.,

```
Reset target parts? (y/n): [n]
```

The user may indicate the bracketed answer, in this case "no," by pressing the carriage-return key. This saves typing when running the program. The new version of the function is listed in appendix D.

```
Building data structure ... Done

Defaults: measures =    1.000 to     7.000
          parts    =    1   2   3    4

Reset target parts? (y/n): [n]
Reset window size? (y/n): [n] y

Score segment from measure    1.000 to     7.000
Setting beginning of window ...
Type measure number: 1
Type beat: 1

Setting end of window ...
Type measure number: 3
Type beat: 1

 1.0    meter=  1/1     beat  =  1/4
 2.0    meter=  1/1     beat  =  1/4
 3.0    meter=  1/1     beat  =  1/4
 4.0    meter=  1/1     beat  =  1/4
 1.0    0.0000  1.0000  rest     1/4      x       0       x       x       -1
 2.0    0.0000  1.0000  E4       1/2      1       0       x       x       80 f
 3.0    0.0000  1.0000  rest     1/1      x       0       x       x       -1
 4.0    0.0000  1.0000  rest     1/4      x       0       x       x       -1

 1.0    0.2500  1.2500  rest     1/8      x       0       x       x       -1
 4.0    0.2500  1.2500  C2       1/2      x       _       x       x       80 f

 1.0    0.3750  1.3750  F5       1/8      x       _v      x       x       80 f

 1.0    0.5000  1.5000  F#5      3/8      x       _       x       x       80
 2.0    0.5000  1.5000  E4       1/8      2       0       x       x       80

 2.0    0.6250  1.6250  Eb4      1/8      x       _       x       x       80

 2.0    0.7500  1.7500  F4       1/4      1       0       x       x       80
 4.0    0.7500  1.7500  A2       1/4      x       _       x       x       80
```

```
1.0    0.8750  1.8750  D#5    1/8    x    _    x    x    80

1.0    /
2.0    /
3.0    /
4.0    /
1.0    1.0000  2.0000  E5     1/8    x    _    x    x    80
2.0    1.0000  2.0000  F4     1/8    2    0    x    x    80
3.0    1.0000  2.0000  rest   1/1    x    0    x    x    -1
4.0    1.0000  2.0000  F#3    1/4    x    _    x    x    80

1.0    1.1250  2.1250  D5     1/8    x    0    1    x    80
2.0    1.1250  2.1250  Eb4    1/8    x    _    x    x    80

1.0    1.2500  2.2500  C5     1/8    x    0    2    x    80
2.0    1.2500  2.2500  Db4    1/4    x    0    1    x    80
4.0    1.2500  2.2500  D4     1/4    x    _    x    x    80

1.0    1.3750  2.3750  G4     1/8    x    0    1    x    80

1.0    1.5000  2.5000  Eb4    1/8    x    0    2    x    80
2.0    1.5000  2.5000  Bb3    1/8    x    0    2    x    80
4.0    1.5000  2.5000  B4     1/8    x    _    x    x    80

1.0    1.6250  2.6250  rest   1/8    x    0    x    x    80
2.0    1.6250  2.6250  rest   1/8    x    0    x    x    80
4.0    1.6250  2.6250  rest   1/8    x    0    x    x    80

1.0    1.7500  2.7500  rest   1/4    x    0    x    x    80
2.0    1.7500  2.7500  rest   1/4    x    0    x    x    80
4.0    1.7500  2.7500  rest   1/4    x    0    x    x    80

1.0    /
2.0    /
3.0    /
4.0    /
1.0    2.0000  3.0000  C4     3/8    x    _    x    x    80
2.0    2.0000  3.0000  rest   1/8    x    0    x    x    80
3.0    2.0000  3.0000  rest   1/2    x    0    x    x    -1
4.0    2.0000  3.0000  rest   1/1    x    0    x    x    80

Do you want to continue? (y/n): [y]
Reset target parts? (y/n): [n] y
Available parts =    1   2   3   4
Type part numbers or all: 1 4
Reset window size? (y/n): [n] y

Score segment from measure   1.000 to    7.000
Setting beginning of window ...
Type measure number: 1
Type beat: 1

Setting end of window ...
Type measure number: 2
Type beat: 1
```

```
1.0    meter=  1/1      beat  =  1/4
4.0    meter=  1/1      beat  =  1/4
1.0    0.0000  1.0000   rest     1/4      x      0      x      x      -1
4.0    0.0000  1.0000   rest     1/4      x      0      x      x      -1

1.0    0.2500  1.2500   rest     1/8      x      0      x      x      -1
4.0    0.2500  1.2500   C2       1/2      x      _      x      x      80 f

1.0    0.3750  1.3750   F5       1/8      x      _v     x      x      80 f

1.0    0.5000  1.5000   F#5      3/8      x      _      x      x      80


4.0    0.7500  1.7500   A2       1/4      x      _      x      x      80

1.0    0.8750  1.8750   D#5      1/8      x      _      x      x      80

1.0    /
4.0    /
1.0    1.0000  2.0000   E5       1/8      x      _      x      x      80
4.0    1.0000  2.0000   F#3      1/4      x      _      x      x      80


Do you want to continue? (y/n): [y]
Reset target parts? (y/n): [n] y
Available parts =     1   2   3   4
Type part numbers or all: 2
Reset window size? (y/n): [n] y

Score segment from measure    1.000 to     7.000
Setting beginning of window ...
Type measure number: 1
Type beat: 1

Setting end of window ...
Type measure number: 4
Type beat: 3

2.0    meter=  1/1      beat  =  1/4
2.0    0.0000  1.0000   E4       1/2      1      0      x      x      80 f
2.0    0.5000  1.5000   E4       1/8      2      0      x      x      80
2.0    0.6250  1.6250   Eb4      1/8      x      _      x      x      80
2.0    0.7500  1.7500   F4       1/4      1      0      x      x      80
2.0    /
2.0    1.0000  2.0000   F4       1/8      2      0      x      x      80
2.0    1.1250  2.1250   Eb4      1/8      x      _      x      x      80
2.0    1.2500  2.2500   Db4      1/4      x      0      1      x      80
2.0    1.5000  2.5000   Bb3      1/8      x      0      2      x      80
2.0    1.6250  2.6250   rest     1/8      x      0      x      x      80
2.0    1.7500  2.7500   rest     1/4      x      0      x      x      80
2.0    /
2.0    2.0000  3.0000   rest     1/8      x      0      x      x      80
2.0    2.1250  3.1250   A3       1/8      x      _      x      x      80
2.0    2.2500  3.2500   B3       1/2      1      0      x      x      80
2.0    2.7500  3.7500   B3       1/8      2      0      x      x      80
2.0    2.8750  3.8750   Bb3      1/8      1      0      5      x      80 startcre
2.0    /
```

```
2.0    3.1250  4.1250  B3      1/4      x       0       6       x       90 endcresc
2.0    3.3750  4.3750  rest    1/8      x       0       x       x       90
2.0    3.5000  4.5000  rest    1/2      x       0       x       x       90

Do you want to continue? (y/n): [y] no thank you
```

Program 20.1. Sample Run (Interactive)

20.3.2 Matching Melodic Contours

The next program is based on an algorithm for finding melodic contours designed by Robert Fink.[9] In the present version of the program, the user is asked to enter a model of the desired contour using a subset of Leland Smith's SCORE Code (see section 6.6). The user enters pitches using the note names followed by any number of sharps or flats, encoded as *s* and *f*, respectively. Each note may be followed by an octave number, which defaults to octave 4, and remains in effect until it is changed. Thus the pitches C_4 $B\flat_3$ A_3 B_3 $C\sharp_4$ can be entered as

```
c    bf3    a    b    cs4
```

These pitches are converted to continuous binomial representation (see section 6.2) and stored in an array called *model*:

model

0	1	2	3	4	. . .
4000	3106	3095	3116	4010	

The intervals between these cbrs are calculated through use of the algorithm for adding (or subtracting) cbrs discussed in section 19.2. The function returns the difference between successive pitches as signed cbrs, which are stored in the *contour* array:

contour

1	2	3	4	. . .
–0021	–0011	+0021	+0021	

Another function converts this interval into the appropriate interval type. This is possible because the signed cbr includes the direction, the octave, the spelling, and the interval size in semitones. Thus the desired interval type is calculated by extracting the appropriate information from the cbr interval. For example, if the interval is a descending minor ninth (–1012), it can be represented in many forms, as shown in table 20.3. The intervals of the desired type are calculated and stored in *contour*[*i*],

9. Fink's contour algorithm was part of a music data-base program that used my score structure to store excerpts from the pieces in the data base. The original algorithm used either generic intervals or pc intervals and found only the first instance of a contour. I added several new contour types, extended the algorithm to find all instances of the contour, added the score window and target parts, and generalized the method of entering the model contour.

Interval Type	*Interval*	*Meaning*
Directed interval	–1	One semitone down
Compound directed interval	–13	Thirteen semitones down
Directed diatonic interval	–1	One diatonic step down
Compound directed diatonic	–8	Eight steps down
Directed specific interval	–012	Minor second down
Compound specific interval	–1012	Minor ninth down
Pitch class interval	11	Eleven semitones
Name class interval	6	Six diatonic steps
Direction only	1	Up (repeat = 0, down = –1)

Table 20.3. Different Representations of the CBR Interval –1012

$1 \leq i \leq icount$. The user may anchor the pattern by specifying that the contour must begin on a specific pitch. If no starting pitch is given, the pattern is unanchored and may begin on any pitch.

The score is searched part by part, including only the specified parts. For each part, the pseudo-code algorithm shown below is used to search for instances of the contour. The intervals in the part are calculated with the same type as target contour, i.e., the contour for which we are searching. The algorithm:

```
set found to false;
point q to first node in window, and attempt to advance to a note;
if q points to a note
  then
    repeat { move start of search through part }
      note1 is node q;
      obtain note2;                                   { next note in part }
      j := 0;                           { current position in interval array }
      set match flag to true;       { true until an interval fails to match }

      repeat { until match is false }
        if note1 and note2 are both notes
          then
            begin
              incr(j);                                     { current int no }
              calculate interval between note1 and note2;
              if pattern is anchored and this is the first interval
                then match := (note1 = startnote) and (interval = contour[j])
                else match := int = contour[j];
              assign note2 to note1;              { shift to next pair of notes }
              get new note2
            end
```

```
        else
          begin                                          { didn't get 2 good notes }
            match is false;
            incr(j)
          end
    until (whole contour has matched) or (part is exhausted) or (match is false)

    if all intervals in pattern have matched
      then
        begin
         found := true;
         write part and measure position
        end;
    assign q to next note in part and attempt to advance to note
  until (q is end-of-window) or (q is head node);

  if not found
    then report failure of search in this part
```

The program is shown below. See appendix D for external procedures.

(see appendix E, page 892)

Program 20.2. *Melpat*

The interactive work session shown below uses the Bartók excerpt shown earlier in this chapter (figure 20.2).

```
Building data structure ... Done

Defaults: measures =    1.000 to    7.000
          parts    =    1   2   3   4

Reset target parts? (y/n): [n]
Reset window size? (y/n): [n]

Interval types
  1. Directed intervals (+/- semitones)
  2. Directed intervals (compound)
  3. Directed diatonic (+/- diatonic step)
  4. Directed diatonic (compound)
  5. Directed br (with spelling)
  6. Directed cbr (compound)
```

```
  7. Direction only (up/down/repeat)
  8. Nondirected pc (int)
  9. Nondirected nc (nint)

Current type =  1
Type integer or <return>:

Type model in SCORE code or <return>: f5 fs ds e d c g4 ef

Type first note to anchor, or <return>:

Part:  1   1.375
Pattern not found in part  2
Pattern not found in part  3
Pattern not found in part  4

Do you want to continue? (y/n): [y]
Reset target parts? (y/n): [n]
Reset window size? (y/n): [n]

Interval types
  1. Directed intervals (+/- semitones)
  2. Directed intervals (compound)
  3. Directed diatonic (+/- diatonic step)
  4. Directed diatonic (compound)
  5. Directed br (with spelling)
  6. Directed cbr (compound)
  7. Direction only (up/down/repeat)
  8. Nondirected pc (int)
  9. Nondirected nc (nint)

Current type =  1
Type integer or <return>:

Type model in SCORE code or <return>: fs es ds

Type first note to anchor, or <return>:

Part:  1   5.500
Part:  2   5.375
Part:  3   5.125
Part:  4   4.875

Do you want to continue? (y/n): [y]
Reset target parts? (y/n): [n]
Reset window size? (y/n): [n]

Interval types
  1. Directed intervals (+/- semitones)
  2. Directed intervals (compound)
  3. Directed diatonic (+/- diatonic step)
  4. Directed diatonic (compound)
  5. Directed br (with spelling)
  6. Directed cbr (compound)
  7. Direction only (up/down/repeat)
  8. Nondirected pc (int)
  9. Nondirected nc (nint)
```

```
Current type =  1
Type integer or <return>: 3

Type model in SCORE code or <return>:

Type first note to anchor, or <return>:

Part:  1   2.000
Part:  1   5.500
Part:  2   1.750
Part:  2   5.375
Part:  3   5.125
Part:  4   4.875
Part:  4   5.000

Do you want to continue? (y/n): [y]
Reset target parts? (y/n): [n] y
Available parts =     1   2   3   4
Type part numbers or all: 1
Reset window size? (y/n): [n]

Interval types
  1. Directed intervals (+/- semitones)
  2. Directed intervals (compound)
  3. Directed diatonic (+/- diatonic step)
  4. Directed diatonic (compound)
  5. Directed br (with spelling)
  6. Directed cbr (compound)
  7. Direction only (up/down/repeat)
  8. Nondirected pc (int)
  9. Nondirected nc (nint)

Current type =  3
Type integer or <return>:

Type model in SCORE code or <return>:

Type first note to anchor, or <return>:

Part:  1   2.000
Part:  1   5.500

Do you want to continue? (y/n): [y]
Reset target parts? (y/n): [n] y
Available parts =     1   2   3   4
Type part numbers or all: all
Reset window size? (y/n): [n]

Interval types
  1. Directed intervals (+/- semitones)
  2. Directed intervals (compound)
  3. Directed diatonic (+/- diatonic step)
  4. Directed diatonic (compound)
  5. Directed br (with spelling)
  6. Directed cbr (compound)
  7. Direction only (up/down/repeat)
  8. Nondirected pc (int)
```

```
  9. Nondirected nc (nint)

Current type =  3
Type integer or <return>:

Type model in SCORE code or <return>:

Type first note to anchor, or <return>: e

Part:  1   2.000
Pattern not found in part  2
Part:  3   5.125
Pattern not found in part  4

Do you want to continue? (y/n): [y]
Reset target parts? (y/n): [n]
Reset window size? (y/n): [n]

Interval types
  1. Directed intervals (+/- semitones)
  2. Directed intervals (compound)
  3. Directed diatonic (+/- diatonic step)
  4. Directed diatonic (compound)
  5. Directed br (with spelling)
  6. Directed cbr (compound)
  7. Direction only (up/down/repeat)
  8. Nondirected pc (int)
  9. Nondirected nc (nint)

Current type =  3
Type integer or <return>: 7

Type model in SCORE code or <return>:

Type first note to anchor, or <return>:

Part:  1   2.000
Part:  1   2.125
Part:  1   2.250
Part:  1   2.375
Part:  1   2.500
Part:  1   5.500
Part:  2   1.750
Part:  2   2.125
Part:  2   2.250
Part:  2   5.375
Part:  3   3.750
Part:  3   5.125
Part:  3   5.250
Part:  4   2.500
Part:  4   4.875
Part:  4   5.000

Do you want to continue? (y/n): [y] n
```

Program 20.2. Sample Run (Interactive)

20.3.3 Vertical Segmentation of Scores

The next program does vertical segmentation of the score, i.e., it finds the set class represented by each vertical slice through the score. The user specifies the desired portion of the score and the parts to be examined. The program uses set-identifying procedures that are virtually identical to those described in chapter 17.

The pitch-extraction routine uses an array to tabulate the pitch classes in each vertical segment of the score. The array, *pcs*, is referenced by the pc integers 0 through 11. Each element *pcs*[*x*], $0 \le x \le 11$, contains the number of occurrences of pitch class *x* in the current vertical slice through the score. Each element of the array is initialized to 0, indicating that no pcs are active.

pcs

0	1	2	3	4	5	6	7	8	9	10	11
0	0	0	0	0	0	0	0	0	0	0	0

The spine, or time line, of the score is traversed from the beginning to the end of the active window. At each spine node, the program does the following:

1. The start-time list is traversed. For each note that begins at this time, the pitch class *x* is obtained and *pcs*[*x*] is incremented.
2. The stop-time list is traversed. For each note that ends at this time, the pitch class *x* is obtained and *pcs*[*x*] is decremented.
3. For each pitch class *x* that occurs more than once (i.e., *pc*[*x*] > 0), *x* is inserted into an array representing a set of pitch classes.
4. The array containing the set is passed to procedure *setcalc*, which calculates the prime form, normal order, interval vector, etc.
5. The required data is printed.

Only notes in parts specified as active by the user are tabulated; and as in the previous two programs, the user can reset the portion of the score and the active parts before each iteration of the main program loop.

The type definitions used in the set identification procedures are defined in the external file *setdefs.h*:

```
(***********************           setdefs.h          ***********************)
(* External type definitions needed by programs calling setid routines.    *)
(***************************************************************************)

{ type }

   ar100  = array[1 .. 12] of integer;
   row     = array[-1 .. 12] of integer;          { one row of matrix        }
   matrix  = array[ 0 .. 12] of row;              { matrix for calculations  }

   pftype  = (Forte, Rahn);                       { prime form type          }
```

```
pcint = 0 .. 11;
pcset = set of pcint;

fset =
  record                        { structure of record on set table      }
    z      : integer;           { number of z-related set, 0 if none    }
    mmi    : integer;           { set resulting from m5 or m7           }
    name   : integer;           { ordinal position in list              }
    setnum : integer            { sumation 2**pc[i] for i = 1 to card   }
  end;

ar300 = array[1 .. 229] of fset;

tabinfo =
  record
    start : integer;            { loc[n] = loc in table of beginning    }
    stop  : integer             { end of sublist for cardinality n      }
  end;

ar600 = array[1 .. 12] of tabinfo; { set-class locations in table       }

setinfo =                       { information record                    }
  record
    trans : integer;            { transposition level                   }
    form  : char;               { 'p' or 'i'                            }
    card  : integer;            { cardinality of set                    }
    z     : integer;            { z-related set or 0                    }
    name  : integer;            { ordinal number of set                 }
    mmi   : integer;            { set obtained by m5 or m7              }
    pcset : ar100;              { the given pitch class set             }
    prime : ar100;              { prime form of set                     }
    vector: ar100;              { interval vector for set               }
    symmetric : boolean         { true if inv = prime                   }
  end;
```

Figure 20.11. The Include File *setdefs.h*

Note that program 20.3 utilizes two include files, *setdefs.h* and *linkdefs.h*, and two external files—the first for the output from the DARMS interpreter, and the second for set tables.

(see appendix E, page 896)

Program 20.3. *Vert*

The following interactive program session again uses the short Bartók quartet segment shown in figure 20.2.

```
Building data structure ... Done
Reading set data ...Done

Setting prime-form type...
Type "Forte" or "Rahn": forte
Type = Forte

Defaults: measures =    1.000 to    7.000
          parts    =    1   2   3   4

Reset target parts? (y/n): [n]
Reset window size? (y/n): [n]

==================================================================
Measure        Normal Order   Set     Prime Form     IC Vector
=======        ============   ===     ==========     =========
  1.000        4              1-1     0                000000
  1.250        0,4            2-4     0,4              000100
  1.375        0,4,5          3-4     0,1,5            100110
  1.500        0,4,6          3-8     0,2,6            010101
  1.625        0,3,6          3-10    0,3,6            002001
  1.750        5,6,9          3-3     0,1,4            101100
  1.875        3,5,9          3-8     0,2,6            010101
  2.000        4,5,6          3-1     0,1,2            210000
  2.125        2,3,6          3-3     0,1,4            101100
  2.250        0,1,2          3-1     0,1,2            210000
  2.375        1,2,7          3-5     0,1,6            100011
  2.500        A,B,3          3-4     0,1,5            100110
  2.625        null           0-1     null             000000
  2.750        null           0-1     null             000000
  3.000        0              1-1     0                000000
  3.125        9,0            2-3     0,3              001000
  3.250        B,0            2-1     0,1              100000
  3.375        A,B            2-1     0,1              100000
  3.500        B,1            2-2     0,2              010000
  3.625        8,B,1          3-7     0,2,5            011010
  3.750        A,B,1          3-2     0,1,3            111000
  3.875        9,A,1          3-3     0,1,4            101100
  4.000        9,A,0          3-2     0,1,3            111000
  4.125        9,B,2          3-7     0,2,5            011010
  4.250        B,0,3          3-3     0,1,4            101100
  4.375        null           0-1     null             000000
  4.500        null           0-1     null             000000
  4.750        null           0-1     null             000000
  4.875        3              1-1     0                000000
  5.000        2              1-1     0                000000
  5.125        0,4            2-4     0,4              000100
  5.250        0,3            2-3     0,3              001000
  5.375        0,1,5          3-4     0,1,5            100110
  5.438        0,1,4          3-3     0,1,4            101100
  5.500        0,1,2,6        4-5     0,1,2,6          210111
  5.563        0,1,2,5        4-4     0,1,2,5          211110
  5.625        0,1,2,3        4-1     0,1,2,3          321000
  6.000        0,1,2,3        4-1     0,1,2,3          321000
```

```
  6.125          A,0,2,4         4-21    0,2,4,6           030201
  6.250          A,0,2,4         4-21    0,2,4,6           030201
  6.375          A,0,2,3         4-11    0,1,3,5           121110
  6.500          A,0,1,4         4-12    0,2,3,6           112101
  6.625          B,0,2,4         4-11    0,1,3,5           121110
  6.750          A,1,2,4         4-12    0,2,3,6           112101
  6.875          A,0,2,3         4-11    0,1,3,5           121110
  7.000          null            0-1     null              000000
=================================================================

Do you want to continue? (y/n): [y]
Reset target parts? (y/n): [n]
Reset window size? (y/n): [n] y

Score segment from measure   1.000 to    7.000
Setting beginning of window ...
Type measure number: 2
Type beat: 1

Setting end of window ...
Type measure number: 2
Type beat: 3.5

=================================================================
Measure         Normal Order   Set     Prime Form     IC Vector
=======         ============   ===     ==========     =========
  2.000         4,5,6          3-1     0,1,2            210000
  2.125         2,3,6          3-3     0,1,4            101100
  2.250         0,1,2          3-1     0,1,2            210000
  2.375         1,2,7          3-5     0,1,6            100011
  2.500         A,B,3          3-4     0,1,5            100110
  2.625         null           0-1     null             000000
=================================================================

Do you want to continue? (y/n): [y]
Reset target parts? (y/n): [n] y
Available parts =    1   2   3   4
Type part numbers or all: 1 2 4
Reset window size? (y/n): [n] y

Score segment from measure   1.000 to    7.000
Setting beginning of window ...
Type measure number: 6
Type beat: 1

Setting end of window ...
Type measure number: 7
Type beat: 1

=================================================================
Measure         Normal Order   Set     Prime Form     IC Vector
=======         ============   ===     ==========     =========
  6.000         0,2,3          3-2     0,1,3            111000
  6.125         A,2,4          3-8     0,2,6            010101
  6.250         A,2,4          3-8     0,2,6            010101
  6.375         A,2,3          3-4     0,1,5            100110
  6.500         A,1,4          3-10    0,3,6            002001
```

```
6.625         B,2,4        3-7    0,2,5        011010
6.750         A,2,4        3-8    0,2,6        010101
6.875         A,2,3        3-4    0,1,5        100110
7.000         null         0-1    null         000000
===============================================================

Do you want to continue? (y/n): [y] no thanks
```

Program 20.3. Sample Run (Interactive)

20.3.4 Some Other Segmentation Techniques

The program discussed in this section performs segmentation of the score using a variety of different criteria. In a computer system capable of running large programs with large data segments, this approach is ideal, since the data structure is built once, and the user can experiment with various techniques where they seem appropriate.[10]

After setting the active parts and portion of the score, the user chooses one of the following:

1. Linear collections set off by rests
2. Linear collections under slurs
3. General segmentation by part and temporal position
4. Vertical segments of the score set off by rests (chunks)
5. Segmentation by dynamic markings within chunks

Here, the term "general segmentation" refers to the process by which the analyst specifies the portion of the score by parts, measures, and beats, and no other criteria are used.[11]

In each of the procedures, n pitch classes are extracted from the specified score segment and stored in the array $pcl[i]$, $1 \leq i \leq n$. Although immediately repeated pcs are removed, the n pcs in the pitch collection may contain duplicates. The number of unique pitch classes in the array, c, represents the cardinality of the largest set in the array. Finally, each of the imbricated pitch-class sets of cardinality $card$, $3 \leq card \leq c$, is extracted from the pitch collection and identified by set name, prime form, and interval vector. For example, the pc sets extracted from the pc collection 0A1023 are shown below:

10. All of the programs in this chapter were written on a small UNIX system that permits only 64K per program, including program and data. This limitation influenced the approach used in these programs: implementing most processes as separate programs. This approach maximized the size of score segments that could be processed. In a 32-bit computer system with virtual memory capability, it would be desirable to combine many related procedures in one flexible program.

11. Program *segment* represents the combined work of three people: the algorithms for segmentation by rests and slurs and for calculating imbricated subsets were designed by Jane Sawyer Brinkman; the procedures for segmenting the score by dynamics or by "chunks" of notes set off by rests were designed by Rhonda Wright; and I added algorithms that print subsets aligned with the set from which they are derived and the general segmentation routine.

0A1023	*Name*	*Prime Form*	*Vector*
0A1 23	5-2	01235	332110
A1023	5-2	01235	332110
0A1 2	4-2	0124	221100
A102	4-2	0124	221100
1023	4-1	0123	321000
0A1	3-2	013	111000
A10	3-2	013	111000
102	3-1	012	210000
023	3-2	013	111000

The procedure used to extract the pc collection from the score segment varies. The general method used in each of the segmentation algorithms is described below.

Segmentation by Rests. For each specified part:

1. Locate the first node in the active window.
2. Skip all notes until a rest is found.
3. Skip the rests. The current node is the first node in a segment.
4. Skip notes to the next rest or the end of the window. This point represents the end of the segment.
5. Extract the pitch classes from notes in the segment and store them in an array.
6. Extract and identify imbricated pc sets in the pc collection in the array.
7. Repeat steps (3) through (6) until the end of the window is reached.

Segmentation by Slurs. For each specified part:

1. Locate the first node in the active window.
2. Skip notes until the beginning of a slur is found. The current node is the first node in a segment.
3. Skip notes until the end of the slur or the end of the window is located. This point represents the end of the segment.
4. Extract pitch classes from notes in the segment and store them in an array.
5. Extract and identify imbricated pc sets in the pitch collection in the array.
6. Repeat steps (2) through (5) until the end of the window is reached.

General Segmentation.

1. Find the first spine node in the window.
2. Traverse the start-time list from the current spine node; extract pitch classes from notes in specified parts and store them in an array.
3. Obtain the next spine node.
4. Repeat steps (2) through (3) until the end of the window is reached.
5. Extract and identify imbricated pc sets in the pitch collection.
6. Reset the window and active parts.
7. Repeat steps (1) through (6) until the user wishes to return to the main menu.

Segmentation by Vertical Chunks.

1. Find the first spine node in the window.
2. Traverse the start-time list at each spine node until a vertical slice containing only rests is found.
3. Traverse the start-time lists off of each spine node until a note is found. This vertical slice is the beginning of a segment.
4. Traverse the spine again until a vertical slice containing only rests, or the end of the window, is obtained. This point represents the end of the segment.
5. Traverse vertical slices within the segment through the start-time lists; extract the pc from each note in a designated part and store it in an array.
6. Repeat steps (2) through (3) until the end of the window is reached.
7. Extract and identify imbricated pc sets in the pitch collection in the array.
8. Repeat steps (3) through (7) until all segments in the window have been processed.

Segmentation by Dynamics within Vertical Chunks.

1. Find the first spine node in the window.
2. Traverse the start-time list from each spine node until a vertical slice containing only rests is found.
3. Traverse the start-time list from each spine node until a note is found. This vertical slice is the beginning of a segment.
4. Traverse the spine again until you find a vertical slice containing only rests or the end of the window. This point represents the end of the segment.
5. Traverse vertical slices within the segment through the start-time lists. For each note in a designated part, extract the pc and dynamic level and store them in an array.
6. From the array, extract all pcs of one dynamic level and store them in another array, which represents a pc collection.
7. Extract and identify imbricated pc sets in the pitch collection.
8. Repeat steps (6) through (7) until all dynamic levels represented in the segment have been processed.
9. Repeat steps (3) through (8) until all segments in the window have been processed.

The main procedure is a loop that allows the user to repeatedly specify the score window, the active parts, and the segmentation routine. The program is shown below, followed by a sample run using a Wolpe excerpt.

(see appendix E, page 898)

Program 20.4. *Segment*

♩= 92
1 Vln.
2 Vln.
Viola
Cello
pizz.
arco
f
pp
p
mf
pp
p

```
K***********************************************************************$
K Wolpe, String Quartet, mm. 1-8.                                       $
K***********************************************************************$
I1 !G !M4:4 RW / RQ RE.. 2T,VF 31QJ,V>3 E,V>4PP RE / RW / RHE
   31EL3,VMF (32- 38-L4) / RW /
I2 !G !M4:4 RW / RE 16EL3,VP<3 (18-L4 (2. (2J?Z,V<4F))) RH / RHQET
   (((31-?R,VF<3 32- 31*,V<4))) / (((32*_L3)) 30..J) 30QL4 RH /
   (30-L3,VMF 9) 3QL4 RH /
I3 !C !M4:4 1Q.,VP 2-EJ S RE.Q / RHE 30-E,VMF RQ / !G RQE (((9 30-
   31- 30*))) (((31*L3_)) 9..JL4) E RE / RW / !C RHQ 8Q,VMF /
I4 !F !M4:4 RE 1E?Z,VF 9Q?R (30-L3 2-L4) RQ / RW / RW / RW /
   RHE 8-Q,VMF 36-EL3 /
I1 !M7:4 RH (3L3,VMF<3 17-L4) 5-HJ_,V<4F E REQ /
I2 !M7:4 RE 6Q.J,VPP 6HJ 6E REQE 5EL3,VMF /
I3 !M7:4 RE 32EL3 4QJL4 HJ,VPP E REE 31-EL3,VMF<3 (36-L4,V<4 31*J) /
I4 !M7:4 35EL4 QJ,VPP HJ E RQH /
I1 !M6:4 RH 17+6+2Q?Z,VF RQE 5-E?RL3,VMF (31- 4J) / 4SL4,VPP RE.QH
   16+6+2Q,VF RQ /
I2 !M6:4 3QL4 (3L3,VF<3 17L4,V<4) 5H RH / RHQ (2L3,VF<3 16) 4H,V<4 /
I3 !M6:4 31Q RQHH / RWQQ /
I4 !M6:4 RE 9EJ?Z,VMF RQHH / (35-L3?R,VMF 34) 8QL4 (34L3,VP 8L4)
   RQH /
```

Figure 20.12. Stefan Wolpe: String Quartet, mm. 1–8.

The sample interactive work session shown below uses the first eight measures of the Wolpe String Quartet shown in figure 20.12 as input data. Note that the smallest sets analyzed are trichords, and that the dyads under slurs are not identified. This could be adjusted by changing the value of the program constant *smallset*.

```
==============================================================
This program partitions music into segments according to
various parameters.  Individual parts can be segmented by
rests or slurs.  Alternately, the program can extract "chunks"
of notes set off in the score by rests; can partition the
chunks by dynamic markings; or can segment the score by
specified beats and parts.  The latter is designated
"general" segmentation.  Imbricated subsets of the par-
titions are extracted and identified by set class and vector.
==============================================================

Building data structure ... Done
Reading set data ...Done

Setting prime-form type...
Type "Forte" or "Rahn": forte
Type = Forte

Defaults: measures =    1.000 to     9.000
          parts    =    1   2   3   4
```

```
Type one of the following:

        general
        rests
        slurs
        chunks
        dynamics

Enter your choice: slurs
Reset target parts? (y/n): [n]
Reset window size? (y/n): [n]

================================================================================
Part  Measures            Segment/Subset            Set     Prime Form      Vector
================================================================================
   1  4.625-4.875         9A8
                          9A8                       3-1     012             210000
--------------------------------------------------------------------------------
   1  7.750-8.000         A89
                          A89                       3-1     012             210000
--------------------------------------------------------------------------------
   2  5.000-5.250         657
                          657                       3-1     012             210000
--------------------------------------------------------------------------------
   4  8.000-8.167         657
                          657                       3-1     012             210000
--------------------------------------------------------------------------------
Do you want to continue? (y/n): [y]

Type one of the following:

        general
        rests
        slurs
        chunks
        dynamics

Enter your choice: rests
Reset target parts? (y/n): [n] y
Available parts =    1   2   3   4
Type part numbers or all: 1 2
Reset window size? (y/n): [n]

================================================================================
Part  Measures            Segment/Subset            Set     Prime Form      Vector
================================================================================
   1  4.625-5.000         9A8
                          9A8                       3-1     012             210000
--------------------------------------------------------------------------------
   1  6.286-6.786         78A
                          78A                       3-2     013             111000
--------------------------------------------------------------------------------
   1  7.333-7.500         B79
                          B79                       3-6     024             020100
--------------------------------------------------------------------------------
   1  7.750-8.042         A89
                          A89                       3-1     012             210000
```

```
-----------------------------------------------------------------------------
  1 8.667-8.833        957
                       957                      3-6     024            020100
-----------------------------------------------------------------------------
  2 2.125-2.500        7A5
                       7A5                      3-7     025            011010
-----------------------------------------------------------------------------
  2 3.906-4.500        8A9B7
                       8A9B7                    5-1     01234          432100
                       8A9B                     4-1     0123           321000
                        A9B7                    4-2     0124           221100
                       8A9                      3-1     012            210000
                        A9B                     3-1     012            210000
                         9B7                    3-6     024            020100
-----------------------------------------------------------------------------
  2 5.000-5.500        657
                       657                      3-1     012            210000
-----------------------------------------------------------------------------
  2 6.929-7.667        B79B
                       B79                      3-6     024            020100
                        79B                     3-6     024            020100
-----------------------------------------------------------------------------
  2 8.500-9.000        579
                       579                      3-6     024            020100
-----------------------------------------------------------------------------
Do you want to continue? (y/n): [y]

Type one of the following:

        general
        rests
        slurs
        chunks
        dynamics

Enter your choice: chunks
Reset target parts? (y/n): [n] y
Available parts =    1   2   3   4
Type part numbers or all: all
Reset window size? (y/n): [n] y

Score segment from measure   1.000 to    9.000
Setting beginning of window ...
Type measure number: 1
Type beat: 1

Setting end of window ...
Type measure number: 5
Type beat: 3

=============================================================================
Part  Measures         Segment/Subset           Set     Prime Form     Vector
=============================================================================
  0 1.000-1.750        5796A8
                       5796A8                   6-1     012345         543210
                       5796A                    5-3     01245          322210
                        796A8                   5-1     01234          432100
```

```
                          5796                      4-2     0124        221100
                           796A                     4-3     0134        212100
                            96A8                    4-2     0124        221100
                          579                       3-6     024         020100
                           796                      3-2     013         111000
                            96A                     3-3     014         101100
                             6A8                    3-6     024         020100
--------------------------------------------------------------------------------
 0  2.125-2.875           7A5989
                          7A598                     5-2     01235       332110
                          7A59                      4-11    0135        121110
                           A598                     4-4     0125        211110
                          7A5                       3-7     025         011010
                           A59                      3-4     015         100110
                            598                     3-3     014         101100
--------------------------------------------------------------------------------
 0  3.375-3.875           568795
                          56879                     5-1     01234       432100
                           68795                    5-1     01234       432100
                          5687                      4-1     0123        321000
                           6879                     4-1     0123        321000
                            8795                    4-2     0124        221100
                          568                       3-2     013         111000
                           687                      3-1     012         210000
                            879                     3-1     012         210000
                             795                    3-6     024         020100
--------------------------------------------------------------------------------
 0  3.906-4.500           8A9B7
                          8A9B7                     5-1     01234       432100
                          8A9B                      4-1     0123        321000
                           A9B7                     4-2     0124        221100
                          8A9                       3-1     012         210000
                           A9B                      3-1     012         210000
                            9B7                     3-6     024         020100
--------------------------------------------------------------------------------
 0  4.625-5.500           9A8657
                          9A8657                    6-1     012345      543210
                          9A865                     5-3     01245       322210
                           A8657                    5-2     01235       332110
                          9A86                      4-2     0124        221100
                           A865                     4-11    0135        121110
                            8657                    4-1     0123        321000
                          9A8                       3-1     012         210000
                           A86                      3-6     024         020100
                            865                     3-2     013         111000
                             657                    3-1     012         210000
--------------------------------------------------------------------------------
Do you want to continue? (y/n): [y]

Type one of the following:

        general
        rests
        slurs
        chunks
        dynamics
```

```
Enter your choice: dyn
Reset target parts? (y/n): [n]
Reset window size? (y/n): [n]

==========================================================================
Dyn   Measures          Segment/Subset          Set      Prime Form      Vector
==========================================================================
piano   m.  1           56
--------------------------------------------------------------------------
forte   m.  1           79A8
                        79A8                    4-1      0123            321000
                        79A                     3-2      013             111000
                         9A8                    3-1      012             210000
--------------------------------------------------------------------------
piano   m.  2           7
--------------------------------------------------------------------------
mp      m.  2           A
--------------------------------------------------------------------------
mf      m.  2           58
--------------------------------------------------------------------------
forte   m.  2           59
--------------------------------------------------------------------------
pp      m.  2           9
--------------------------------------------------------------------------
mf      m.  3           568795
                        56879                   5-1      01234           432100
                         68795                  5-1      01234           432100
                        5687                    4-1      0123            321000
                         6879                   4-1      0123            321000
                          8795                  4-2      0124            221100
                        568                     3-2      013             111000
                         687                    3-1      012             210000
                          879                   3-1      012             210000
                           795                  3-6      024             020100
--------------------------------------------------------------------------
forte   m.  3           8A
--------------------------------------------------------------------------
ff      m.  3 -  4      9B7
                        9B7                     3-6      024             020100
--------------------------------------------------------------------------
mf      m.  4 -  5      9A8657
                        9A8657                  6-1      012345          543210
                        9A865                   5-3      01245           322210
                         A8657                  5-2      01235           332110
                        9A86                    4-2      0124            221100
                         A865                   4-11     0135            121110
                          8657                  4-1      0123            321000
                        9A8                     3-1      012             210000
                         A86                    3-6      024             020100
                          865                   3-2      013             111000
                           657                  3-1      012             210000
--------------------------------------------------------------------------
Do you want to continue? (y/n): [y]

Type one of the following:

      general
```

```
        rests
        slurs
        chunks
        dynamics

Enter your choice: general
Reset target parts? (y/n): [n] y
Available parts =    1   2   3   4
Type part numbers or all: 2 3
Reset window size? (y/n): [n] 3
You must answer yes or no: y

Score segment from measure   1.000 to    9.000
Setting beginning of window ...
Type measure number: 3
Type beat: 1

Setting end of window ...
Type measure number: 4
Type beat: 2

===============================================================================
      Measures            Segment/Subset           Set     Prime Form      Vector
===============================================================================
   0  3.000-4.500         5687958A9B7
                          56879  A B               7-1     0123456         654321
                           68795 A B               7-1     0123456         654321
                          56879  A                 6-1     012345          543210
                           68795 A                 6-1     012345          543210
                            8795 A B               6-2     012346          443211
                             7958A B               6-2     012346          443211
                              958A B7              6-2     012346          443211
                               58A9B7              6-2     012346          443211
                          56879                    5-1     01234           432100
                           68795                   5-1     01234           432100
                            8795 A                 5-2     01235           332110
                             7958A                 5-2     01235           332110
                              958A B               5-4     01236           322111
                               58A9B               5-4     01236           322111
                                8A9B7              5-1     01234           432100
                          5687                     4-1     0123            321000
                           6879                    4-1     0123            321000
                            8795                   4-2     0124            221100
                             7958                  4-2     0124            221100
                              958A                 4-4     0125            211110
                               58A9                4-4     0125            211110
                                8A9B               4-1     0123            321000
                                 A9B7              4-2     0124            221100
                          568                      3-2     013             111000
                           687                     3-1     012             210000
                            879                    3-1     012             210000
                             795                   3-6     024             020100
                              958                  3-3     014             101100
                               58A                 3-7     025             011010
                                8A9                3-1     012             210000
                                 A9B               3-1     012             210000
                                  9B7              3-6     024             020100
-------------------------------------------------------------------------------
Continue with genseg? (y/n): [y]
```

```
Reset target parts? (y/n): [n] y
Available parts =    1   2   3   4
Type part numbers or all: all
Reset window size? (y/n): [n] y

Score segment from measure   1.000 to    9.000
Setting beginning of window ...
Type measure number: 2
Type beat: 2

Setting end of window ...
Type measure number: 2
Type beat: 4

==============================================================================
      Measures             Segment/Subset          Set     Prime Form     Vector
==============================================================================
  0  2.250-2.875           A5989
                           A598                    4-4     0125           211110
                           A59                     3-4     015            100110
                            598                    3-3     014            101100
------------------------------------------------------------------------------
Continue with genseg? (y/n): [y]

Reset target parts? (y/n): [n] y
Available parts =    1   2   3   4
Type part numbers or all: 2 3
Reset window size? (y/n): [n]

==============================================================================
      Measures             Segment/Subset          Set     Prime Form     Vector
==============================================================================
  0  2.250-2.875           A58
                           A58                     3-7     025            011010
------------------------------------------------------------------------------
Continue with genseg? (y/n): [y] n

Returning to main menu
Do you want to continue? (y/n): [y] n
```

Program 20.4. Sample Run (Interactive)

20.3.5 Locating Arbitrary Sets in the Score

The program discussed here is in some ways the most complex in this chapter.[12] The object of the program is to search a portion of the score for all instances of a pitch-class set specified by the user. As in other programs we have seen, the window into

12. The original program was written by Michael Votta, who used a recursive algorithm I suggested. This was the first program to utilize a "window" in the score structure, a feature that has been added to most of the other programs in this chapter. Although the program is substantially based on the original, I have added a number of features including the moving frame within the window, the option of entering sets as pitches rather than set names, the use of user-specified instruments, and the inclusion of normal order in the output data.

the score is defined by pointers to the spine. In order to limit the number of sets found, the program defines a smaller "frame," which is moved through the window as shown in figure 20.13.

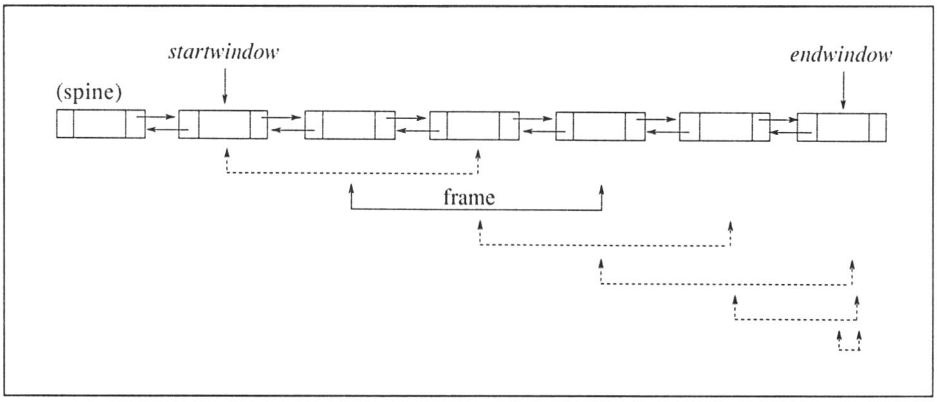

Figure 20.13. Moving a Frame through the Window

The user specifies the target set T, the window, the frame size, and the parts that are to be included in the search. As the frame is moved through the window, each set of pitch classes S within the frame and of the same cardinality as the target set T is checked to see if it is in the same set class as T, i.e., if S is related to T by transposition or by transposition after inversion.[13] The set-locating procedure eliminates superfluous matches by requiring that the first note in any matching set occur in the vertical slice at the beginning of the frame. This prevents locating the same group of notes several times in different frame positions. As each matching set is found, the location of the notes, the pcs, the note names, and the normal order of the resulting set are printed.

When matching sets are being sought, the notes within the frame are treated as a linear list, ordered from top to bottom within each vertical slice through the score:

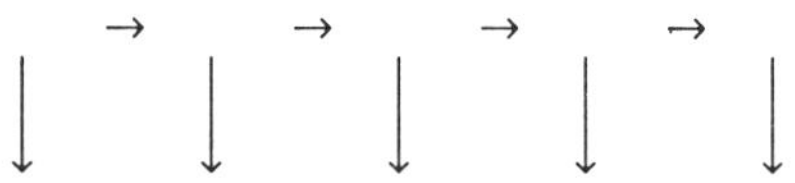

The object is to find each pc set S that is in the same set class as the target set T. The algorithm for searching the notes uses two procedures. The first, *traverse*, traverses the score structure within the frame. During the traversal, each note becomes the first pc in S, and procedure *next* is called to find the next pitch. The algorithm for *traverse* is shown below in pseudo code:

set pointer p to first spine node in window
set end-of-frame relative to p

13. Subset relations are determined with the procedures described in section 12.3.

```
repeat                                                { traverse spine }
  set p to first node in start-time list;
  while p is not a spine node do
    begin { traverse start-time list }
      if p points to a ''good'' note
        then
          begin
            extract pc of the note;
            add pc to set S;
            save values for note;
            invoke next to find next note in set;
            remove pc from set
          end;
      set p to next node in start-time list
    end; { traverse start-time list }
  set p to next spine node
until p is past end-of-frame                          { traverse spine }
if no matches were found
  then report failure of match
```

Procedure *next* follows essentially the same traversal as procedure *traverse*, except that it begins with the note just after the last note placed in set *S*. The procedure finds the next note that, combined with the pcs in set *S*, forms a subset of target set *T*. If the resulting set is of the same cardinality as *T*, the pertinent values for set *S* are printed, otherwise *next* is called recursively to get the next pc in the set.

```
repeat
  set p to next node in start-time list;
  while node p is not a spine node do
    begin { traverse start-time list }
      if p points to a ''good'' note
        then
          begin
            extract pc from note;
            add pc to set;
            save values for note;
            if cardinality of S = cardinality of T
              then print data for set S
              else invoke next recursively to find next note;
            remove pc from set
          end;
      set p to next start node
    end; { traverse start-time list }
  set p to next spine node
until p is past end-of-frame
```

The maximum depth of recursion is equal to the cardinality of the target set. Pointer *p* points to a "good" note if the following conditions are met:

1. The node is a note.
2. The note is in the specified parts.
3. If tied notes are to be excluded, the note is not tied to the previous note.
4. The pitch class of the note (*pc*) is not among those in the set.
5. The union of set *S* and *pc* is a subset of the target set *T*, i.e., $(S \cup pc) \subset T$.

The algorithm shown above locates each combination of notes within the frame that is in the same set class as the target set. When the frame is moved to the next vertical slice, a different set of T_n/T_nI related sets is found. Setting the frame size is critical. If it is too small, many important sets are missed; if it is too large, many sets will be insignificant due to the temporal distance between elements. For small sets, a frame size in vertical slices equal to the cardinality of the set works well, and this value is used unless the user specifies a different size. The definition of a "good" note is extensible and could be expanded to include more sophisticated criteria for segmentation.

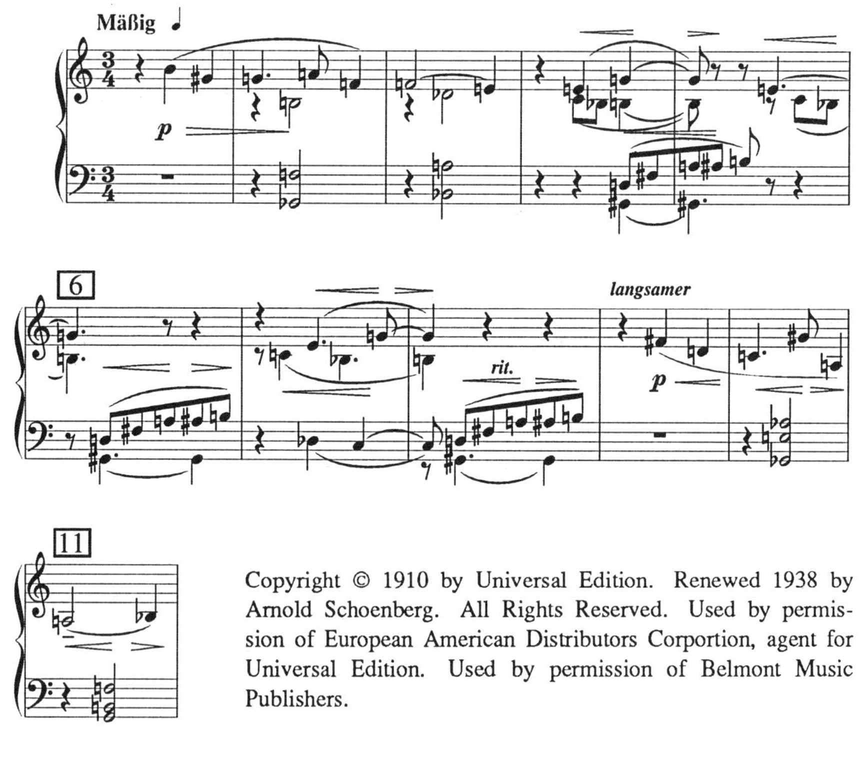

```
K***********************************************************************$
K Schoenberg, Op.11/1, mm. 1-11, encoded as four parts;                 $
K                  dynamics and phrasing omitted.                        $
K***********************************************************************$
I1 !G !M3:4 RQ 5Q 3# / 3*. 4*E 2*Q / 2*H 1*Q / RQ 1* 3*J / E REE
   1*Q.J / Q. REQ / RQ 1*Q. 3*EJ / Q RQQ / RQ 2#Q 0* / 19*Q. 3#E 17*Q
   / 17*H 18-Q /
I2 !G !M3:4 R1W / RQ 18*H / RQ 0-H / RQ (19 18-) 18*QJ / E REEE (19
   18-) / Q. REQ / RE 19*Q 18-. / *Q RQQ / R1W / RQ !F 9-H / RQ 7*H /
I3 !F !M3:4 R1W / RQ 7*H / RQ 9* / RQQ (5* 7# / 9* 9#) 30*E REQ / RE
   (5* 7# 9* 9# 30*) / RQ 5-Q 4J / E (5* 7# 9* 9# 30*) / R1W / RQ 6*H
   / RQ 3*H /
I4 !F !M3:4 R1W / RQ 1-H / RQ 3-H / RQQ 1#QJ / Q. REQ / RE 1#Q.J Q /
   R1W / RE 1#Q.J Q / R1W / RQ 1-H / RQ 1H /
```

Figure 20.14. Schoenberg: *Drei Klavierstücke*, Op. 11, No. 1, mm. 1–11.

Figure 20.14 is an excerpt from the first of Schoenberg's *Drei Kalavierstücke*, Op. 11, used for the sample run of program *setsearch*. Note that the encoding here is partial (pitch and duration only), and that our software does not support space codes to indicate nonstandard rest positions. Note also the use of *R1W* to indicate one measure of rest.

(see appendix E, page 906)

Program 20.5. *Setsearch*

```
Building data structure ... Done
Reading set data ...Done

Setting prime form type...
Type "Forte" or "Rahn": f
Type = Forte

Defaults: measures =   1.000 to   12.000
          parts    =   1   2   3   4

Reset target parts? (y/n): [n]
Reset window size? (y/n): [n] y

Score segment from measure   1.000 to   12.000
Setting beginning of window ...
Type measure number: 1
Type beat: 1
```

```
Setting end of window ...
Type measure number: 3
Type beat: 3
Do you wish to include tied notes? (y/n): [n]

Type set name or pcs: 3-3
Target set = 3-3/{014}

Reset frame size? (y,n): [n]

Searching:
====================================
Part  Measure  Beat  Note       PC
  1      1     2.00   B4         B
  1      1     3.00   G#4        8
  1      2     1.00   G4         7
normal order = {78B}
====================================
Part  Measure  Beat  Note       PC
  1      1     3.00   G#4        8
  1      2     1.00   G4         7
  2      2     2.00   B3         B
normal order = {78B}
====================================
Part  Measure  Beat  Note       PC
  3      2     2.00   F3         5
  4      2     2.00   Gb2        6
  1      2     2.50   A4         9
normal order = {569}
====================================
Part  Measure  Beat  Note       PC
  4      2     2.00   Gb2        6
  1      2     2.50   A4         9
  1      2     3.00   F4         5
normal order = {569}
====================================
Part  Measure  Beat  Note       PC
  1      3     1.00   F4         5
  2      3     2.00   Db4        1
  1      3     3.00   E4         4
normal order = {145}
====================================
Part  Measure  Beat  Note       PC
  2      3     2.00   Db4        1
  3      3     2.00   A3         9
  4      3     2.00   Bb2        A
normal order = {9A1}
====================================
Done

Continue? (y/n): [y]
Reset target parts? (y/n): [n]
Reset window size? (y/n): [n] y

Score segment from measure   1.000 to   12.000
Setting beginning of window ...
Type measure number: 9
Type beat: 1

Setting end of window ...
```

```
Type measure number: 12
Type beat: 1
Do you wish to include tied notes? (y/n): [n]

Type set name or pcs: 026
Target set = 3-8/{026}

Reset frame size? (y,n): [n]

Searching:
==================================
Part  Measure  Beat  Note      PC
  1       9    2.00   F#4       6
  1       9    3.00   D4        2
  1      10    1.00   C4        0
normal order = {026}
==================================
Part  Measure  Beat  Note      PC
  1       9    3.00   D4        2
  1      10    1.00   C4        0
  2      10    2.00   Ab3       8
normal order = {802}
==================================
Part  Measure  Beat  Note      PC
  1       9    3.00   D4        2
  1      10    1.00   C4        0
  4      10    2.00   Gb2       6
normal order = {026}
==================================
Part  Measure  Beat  Note      PC
  1       9    3.00   D4        2
  2      10    2.00   Ab3       8
  3      10    2.00   E3        4
normal order = {248}
==================================
Part  Measure  Beat  Note      PC
  1       9    3.00   D4        2
  2      10    2.00   Ab3       8
  4      10    2.00   Gb2       6
normal order = {268}
==================================
Part  Measure  Beat  Note      PC
  1      10    1.00   C4        0
  2      10    2.00   Ab3       8
  4      10    2.00   Gb2       6
normal order = {680}
==================================
Part  Measure  Beat  Note      PC
  1      10    1.00   C4        0
  3      10    2.00   E3        4
  4      10    2.00   Gb2       6
normal order = {046}
==================================
Part  Measure  Beat  Note      PC
  1      10    1.00   C4        0
  4      10    2.00   Gb2       6
  1      10    2.50   G#4       8
normal order = {680}
```

```
===================================
Part   Measure   Beat   Note       PC
  1       10     3.00    A3         9
  2       11     2.00    F3         5
  3       11     2.00    B2         B
normal order = {59B}
===================================
Part   Measure   Beat   Note       PC
  1       11     1.00    A3         9
  2       11     2.00    F3         5
  3       11     2.00    B2         B
normal order = {59B}
===================================
Part   Measure   Beat   Note       PC
  2       11     2.00    F3         5
  3       11     2.00    B2         B
  4       11     2.00    G2         7
normal order = {57B}
===================================
Done

Continue? (y/n): [y]
Reset target parts? (y/n): [n]
Reset window size? (y/n): [n]
Do you wish to include tied notes? (y/n): [n]

Type set name or pcs: 3-3
Target set = 3-3/{014}

Reset frame size? (y,n): [n]

Searching:
===================================
Part   Measure   Beat   Note       PC
  3       11     2.00    B2         B
  4       11     2.00    G2         7
  1       11     3.00    Bb3        A
normal order = {7AB}
===================================
Done

Continue? (y/n): [y]
Reset target parts? (y/n): [n]
Reset window size? (y/n): [n]
Do you wish to include tied notes? (y/n): [n]

Type set name or pcs: 3-3
Target set = 3-3/{014}

Reset frame size? (y,n): [n] y
The frame size in time slices is set relative to the
cardinality of the target set by adding a positive or
negative constant to the cardinality each time a new set
is specified.  The default constant is 0, indicating that
the frame size is equal to the set cardinality.
```

```
Enter constant or <return>: [0] +1

Searching:
===================================
Part  Measure   Beat   Note      PC
 1       10     1.00    C4        0
 2       10     2.00    Ab3       8
 1       10     3.00    A3        9
normal order = {890}
===================================
Part  Measure   Beat   Note      PC
 1       10     1.00    C4        0
 1       10     2.50    G#4       8
 1       10     3.00    A3        9
normal order = {890}
===================================
Part  Measure   Beat   Note      PC
 1       10     2.50    G#4       8
 1       10     3.00    A3        9
 2       11     2.00    F3        5
normal order = {589}
===================================
Part  Measure   Beat   Note      PC
 1       10     2.50    G#4       8
 1       11     1.00    A3        9
 2       11     2.00    F3        5
normal order = {589}
===================================
Part  Measure   Beat   Note      PC
 1       10     2.50    G#4       8
 3       11     2.00    B2        B
 4       11     2.00    G2        7
normal order = {78B}
===================================
Part  Measure   Beat   Note      PC
 3       11     2.00    B2        B
 4       11     2.00    G2        7
 1       11     3.00    Bb3       A
normal order = {7AB}
===================================
Done

Continue? (y/n): [y] n
```

Program 20.5. Sample Run (Interactive)

In the above program run, the initial frame size in vertical slices was equal to the cardinality of the set. The located instances of each set class increase considerably when the frame size is increased by even one slice, as illustrated by the last two searches.

20.3.6 Simple Harmonic Analysis

Two preliminary steps in the analysis of tonal music are the determination of the tonic key and the identification of other key areas that are tonicized. Program *cadid* was designed to find cadences in Bach chorales and to draw conclusions regarding their tonal implications.[14] The present program is intended to analyze pieces in major and minor keys; modal chorales would require further refining of the algorithm.

The program identifies chord types using a table of prime forms in binomial pitch representation (br), and an algorithm for finding prime forms and normal order in the system described in an earlier article.[15] In this implementation, the table models each common pitch structure by the following information: the cardinality of the set, the location of the prime form of the set, the location of the root in the prime-form array, an array containing the prime form of the set, a string naming the structure, and a numeric identifier associated with the sonority. This information is shown in table 20.4. Recall that the binomial representation of pitches is in the form *pcn*, where *pc* is the pitch class (0–11) and *n* is the name class (0–6) of the note.

This program extracts the pitches from each verticality in the score and stores them in an array, with duplicate pitches removed. Then the normal order of the set is calculated by procedure *brnorm*.[16] The algorithm for finding the chord inversion is as follows:[17]

1. The bass note, B is obtained from the score structure.
2. The transposition interval, T, (to prime form) is obtained by subtracting any element of the normal order from the corresponding element of the prime form.
3. The "prime" bass note, P, is found by adding B and T.
4. The location, L, of P in the prime form array is found.
5. The chord inversion, I, is calculated with the equation:

$$I = ((L + n - R) \bmod n)$$

where L is the position of the bass note in the prime array
n is the cardinality of the chord, and
R is the position of the root in the prime array

The resulting chord inversion code is: 0 = root position; 1 = first inversion; 2 = second inversion; and 3 = third inversion.

14. The program was written by Richard Elliot. I added mode identification and pointers from the "chord-line" structure to the corresponding spine nodes in the score structure. Other minor changes were necessary to adapt to changes in the data structure since the program was written.

15. See Alexander R. Brinkman, "A Binomial Representation of Pitch for Computer Processing of Musical Data," *Music Theory Spectrum* 8 (1986): 44–57. The normal-order algorithm is described on pages 53–54.

16. The Pascal procedure is included in the procedure library in appendix C.

17. From Richard Elliott, "Development of an Algorithm for Detection of Cadences," (unpublished paper written for Ph.D. seminar in music theory, Eastman School of Music, 1987), 3.

ID#	*Cardinality*	*Location of Root in Prime Form*	*Prime Form in BRs*	*Chord Type*
1	2	1	<**00**, 42>	major (5th omitted)
2	2	1	<**00**, 32>	minor (5th omitted)
3	3	1	<**00**, 42, 74>	major
4	3	1	<**00**, 32, 74>	minor
5	3	1	<**00**, 32, 64>	diminished
6	3	1	<**00**, 42, 84>	augmented
7	3	2	<00, **21**, 63>	dom. 7th (5th omitted)
8	4	2	<00, **11**, 53, 85>	major 7th
9	4	4	<00, 32, 64, **85**>	dom. 7th
10	4	3	<00, 32, **53**, 85>	minor 7th
11	4	2	<00, **21**, 53, 85>	1/2 dim. 7th
12	4	2	<00, **31**, 63, 95>	dim. 7th
13	3	3	<00, 22, **64**>	It. aug. 6th
14	4	4	<00, 32, **63**, 85>	Ger. aug. 6th
15	4	2	<00, **21**, 53, 85>	Fr. aug. 6th

Table 20.4. Prime Forms of Common Sets in Tonal Music

Before analyzing the harmonic progression, the program builds a data structure called the *chord line*, which contains the information on each vertical sonority. The chord line, which is implemented as an array of structures, contains the following information for each vertical sonority: the chord type and inversion; boolean values representing the presence or absence of a fermata and of the root in the soprano (for perfect cadences); the binomial representation of the root; and a pointer to the corresponding spine node in the score structure. The last element makes it possible to find the temporal position in the score, and also facilitates reexamination of the vertical sonority for context.

The program finds the tonic by examining the key signature and the final cadence of the piece. It then identifies cadences using the root movement, quality and inversion of both chords, soprano note (root, third, fifth, etc.), and the presence of fermatas. In music other than chorales, the test for fermatas might be replaced by a test for end-of-phrase marks, longer note values, rests, and the position of the chord in the measure.

This program represents an important first step in the analysis of tonal music. The techniques used could be combined with the examination of linear motion in more extensive higher-level analysis programs that are sensitive to context (harmonic prolongation, etc). Figure 20.15 shows a Bach chorale used for testing the program. The program output, using the encoded chorale as input, is shown below.

(see appendix E, page 909)

Program 20.6. *Cadid*

```
K**************************************************************************$
K J. S. Bach, Chorale: O Welt, ich muss dich lassen, St. Mat. Passion.      $
K**************************************************************************$
!A4:4,1–Q                                          K ANACRUSIS FLAG $
I1 !G !M4:4 !K1– 4Q / 2Q 3 (4 5) 6Q / 5H 4Q; (4 5) /
I2 !G !M4:4 !K1– 2Q / 0Q 1 (2 3) 4Q / 4 3 2; 2 /
I3 !F !M4:4 !K1– 31Q / 32Q (31 30) 9Q. 8E / 7Q 31 31; 31 /
I4 !F !M4:4 !K1– 7Q / 30Q (9 8) 7Q. 6E / 5Q 6 7; (7 8) /

I1 6Q 6 3 (4 3) / 2H 1Q; 19 / 2 3 (4 (5 6)) (5 4) / 3H.; 4Q /
I2 (2 1) (2 3) (1 0) 19Q / 19 18* 19; 1 / 0 19 19 0 / 1H.; 1Q /
I3 31 31 31 (31 30*) / (9 8) 7Q 8; 30– / 9 8 7 7 / 31H.; 9Q /
I4 9Q (2 3) 4Q 2 / 5H 4Q; 4 / 5 6 7 3 / 4H.; 4#Q /

I1 2 3 (4 5) 6Q / 5H 4Q; (4 5) / 6Q 6 3 (4 3) /
I2 0 19 19 0 / 0 3 2#; 2* / 2 2 (1 0) 19Q /
I3 9 8 (7 8) 9Q / (8 9) (30 31) 32Q; 32 / (31 30 31 32) 33Q 34 /
I4 5 6 7 7# / 8 1 5; 32 / (9 8 9 30) 31Q (7 6) /

I1 2H 1Q; 19 / 2 3 4 (3 (4 5)) / 4Q 3 2; //
I2 19 18* 19; 16 / 19 –18 (17 19) 2Q / 2 1 19; //
I3 (7 9) (8 7) 8Q; 6 / (7 31) (32 33) (34 31) (30 7) / 31Q. –30E 9Q; //
I4 (5 4) 5Q 4; –3 / 2 1 0 5 / (4 3) 4Q 0; //
```

Figure 20.15. Bach Chorale, "O Welt, ich muss dich lassen," *St. Matthew Passion*

```
Building data structure ... Done
Reading chord table ... Done

Building chord line ... Done

Tonic Key = F major

Cadences:

  Imperfect authentic cadence in I (F major) at m. 2.500

  IPA: vii6 > I in V (C major) at m. 4.500

  Half cadence in I (F major) at m. 6.000

  Half cadence in ii (G minor) at m. 8.500

  IPA: vii6 > I in V (C major) at m. 10.500

  Perfect authentic cadence in I (F major) at m. 12.500
```

Program 20.6. Output

20.3.7 A Graphic Representation of Scores

As a final example of data extraction from the score structure, we will examine a program that produces a graphic representation of the voice leading in the score. This is useful for visualizing many aspects of the music, including general registral ''shape,'' distribution of parts, rhythmic activity, etc.

The program output serves as input to the UNIX utility *graph*, which produces the graphic output. In the graphic output, pitch is represented on the vertical axis and time on the horizontal axis. Pitch is specified as continuous pitch code (cpc).[18] Time is represented as the ''raw'' time in the score, i.e., the sum of the fractional durations from the beginning of the segment, which is represented as 0/1. It would be nice to use measure as units on the horizontal axis; but this would result in a different scale for measures in different meters, e.g., a 2/4 measure would be stretched to take the same amount of space as a 3/4 or 4/4 measure.

The program traverses each part, printing pertinent information about each pitch. The data is specified as the <time, pitch> coordinates at the beginning and end of each line segment. Within each part, notes are connected until a rest is encountered, enabling us to see voice leading in the resulting graph.

The traversal in pseudo code follows:

18. See section 6.1.2.

```
set pointer t to the beginning of the window;
while t <> end-of-window do
  begin
    set t to the first node in start-time list;
    while t is not a spine node do
      begin
        if t points to a note in specified part
          then if t is first note in a part
               or t is the first note after a rest
               or t is a chord note
               or t is the first note in a layer
                 then plotnotes;
        set t to next node in start-time list
      end;
    set t to the next spine node
  end
```

Procedure *plotnotes* prints the values for the notes beginning with the current note and terminating when a rest or the end of a part is encountered, or when the end of a layer has been reached. The boolean variable *lastnote* is set to *true* when the latter condition has been met, i.e., when *rlink* of the node points to the node:

```
repeat
  write time at beginning of note;
  write continuous pitch code of note;
  write time at end of note;
  write continuous pitch code of note;
  lastnote := t↑.rlink = t;
  set t to next node in layer or part
until t is not a note or lastnote
write the string '" "' to break line in graph
```

(see appendix E, page 915)

Program 20.7. *Partplot*

The graph shown in figure 20.16 shows the voice leading in the first twenty-six measures of the Bartók's String Quartet No. 4, the first six bars of which were shown in figure 20.2. Since the meter is 4/4 and the piece does not begin with an anacrusis, the ticks on the horizontal axis correspond to bar lines. The ticks on the vertical axis represent each C, beginning with C_1 at the bottom of the graph.

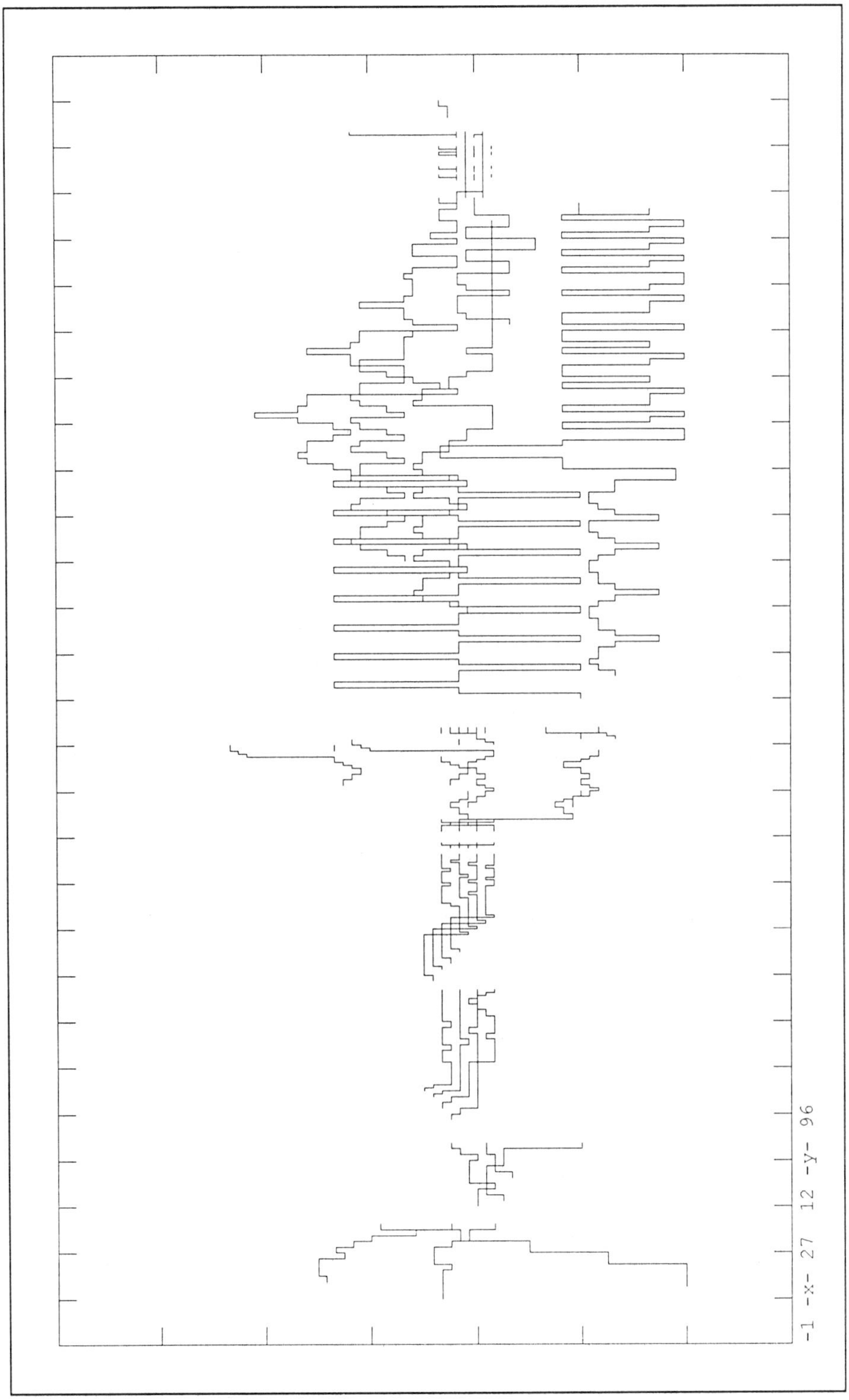

Figure 20.16. Voice-Leading Graph of Bartók's String Quartet No. 4, mm. 1–26

In this book I have presented many techniques that I and my students have found to be useful. However, it has been said that most of the important work in the field is yet to be done. In that sense, I trust that this represents not the end, but rather the beginning.

References and Selected Readings

Some of the material in the first part of this chapter was previously published in the following source, and is used with the permission of the publisher:

Brinkman, Alexander R. "Representing Musical Scores for Computer Analysis," *Journal of Music Theory* 30, no. 2 (1986): 225–75.

The following sources describe other linked score representations. Nerheim describes the data structure used in the MUSTRAN system at Indiana University. Wallraff describes the data structure used in the graphic score editor at the MIT Experimental Music Studio (MIT-EMS). Dannenberg's data structure is used for more recent work at Carnegie Mellon University. His structure uses a linked list of "events" attached to each time node. The event-list approach enables the programmer to define many different types of objects.

Dannenberg, Roger. "A Structure for Representing, Displaying and Editing Music." In *Proceedings of the 1986 International Computer Music Conference.* San Francisco: Computer Music Association, 153–60.

Nerheim, Rosalee. "Current Applications of a Music Representation and Processing System." In *Proceedings of the 1978 International Computer Music Conference.* San Francisco: Computer Music Association, 720–31.

Wallraff, Dean. "Nedit—A Graphical Editor for Musical Scores." In *Proceedings of the 1978 International Computer Music Conference.* San Francisco: Computer Music Association, 410–29.

Criteria for segmentation of atonal music are discussed in the following:

Hasty, Christopher. "Segmentation and Process in Post-Tonal Music." *Music Theory Spectrum* 3 (1981): 54–73.

The algorithm for calculating prime form and normal order in the binomial system is discussed in the following source:

Brinkman, Alexander R. "A Binomial Representation of Pitch for Computer Processing of Musical Data." *Music Theory Spectrum* 8 (1986): 44–57.

Program *cadid* is described in the following:

Elliott, Richard. "The Development of an Algorithm for Detection of Cadences." Unpublished paper written for Ph.D. seminar in music theory, Eastman School of Music, 1987.

Other suggested reading:

Aldwell, Edward, and Carl Schachter. *Harmony and Voice Leading.* 2d ed. San Diego: Harcourt Brace Jovanovich, 1989.

Bauer-Mengelberg, Stefan. "Computer-Implemented Music Analysis and the Copyright Law." *Computer and the Humanities* 14 (1980): 1–19.

Salzer, Felix, and Carl Schachter. *Counterpoint in Composition.* New York: McGraw-Hill, 1969.

Forte, Allen. "A Program for the Analytic Reading of Scores." *Journal of Music Theory* 10 (1966): 330–64.

Exercises

1. Review the record structures used in the score data structure and the descriptions given in sections 20.2 and 20.3.

   a) If *p* points to a note node, how do you reference each of the following:

      The part number?

      The pitch of the note?

      The pitch class?

      The name class?

      The octave?

      The duration (a fraction)?

      The dynamic (two forms)?

   b) How can you tell if the note is tied to the next note? To the previous note?

   c) How can you tell if the note is a chord tone, i.e., not in the primary line?

   d) How can you tell if the note is the first or last note in a layer?

   e) How can you tell if there are grace notes before the note?

   f) How do you find the note above it in the same time slice?

   g) How can you tell if there are no notes above the current one in the time slice?

   h) How does one find the note below it in the same time slice?

   i) How does one find other notes that terminate at the same time?

2. *Traversing the structure*:

   a) What is the fastest way to find the current meter signature?

   b) How can you find the measure number at the beginning of the note?

   c) How can you find the measure number at the end of the note?

   d) How can you find the raw time at the beginning of the note?

   e) How can you find the raw time at the end of the note?

   f) What is the tag field of the node pointed to by *part*[*i*].*p*? *part*[*i*].*s*?

   g) What is the part number of the time line (spine)?

   h) How does one get to the first spine node?

i) What is the fastest way to find the latest time in the score (as a fraction representing the measure number)?

j) When traversing the spine, how can you tell if the current node is the beginning of a measure?

k) How can one tell if part *i* is empty?

l) In a simple score (no chords or layers within parts), what is the easiest way to traverse an arbitrary part, say part *i*?

m) While traversing the primary line of a part, how can you tell if there are simultaneous notes at the same starting time in the same part?

n) Write a procedure that traverses the time line, printing out the starting time (as measure numbers) for each event.

o) If *t* points to a spine node, traverse the list of notes that begin at this node, printing out the pitch class of each note. Print any grace notes before the note.

p) If *t* points to a spine node, traverse the list of special nodes that begin at this time, printing out a list of node types.

Each of the following exercises should be implemented as a complete program. In addition, you should have many ideas in your own special areas of interest to pursue.

3. In a twentieth-century excerpt, find the point at which the aggregate is completed, i.e., when the last of the twelve pitch classes is introduced.

4. Extend the above program to find successive aggregates.

5. Write a program that counts the number of times each pitch class occurs in the piece, and calculates the frequency of occurrence of each pitch class as a percentage of the total. Do this twice, once using frequency of occurrence, and once using duration. Compare the two figures.

6. Develop a program that looks for pitches that are emphasized through various criteria, such as duration, articulation, repetition, register, and dynamics.

7. Write a program that prints a bar graph representing the tessitura of each part (see program assignment 1 in chapter 10).

8. Encode a Bach fugue, and write a program to find all entrances of the subject.

9. The melodic pattern-matching algorithm used in program 20.2 searches only the primary line for each part. Implement a more generalized algorithm that also looks in other "layers." Suggestion: Follow the basic traversal used in program 10.7 (graphics). Traverse the score through the start-time lists from each spine node and search all layers for the pattern beginning at each start time. You will have to watch for the ends of layers (or chord tones). (Since all lists are circular, you will match many repeated notes if you forget this!)

10. If your computer system has graphic capabilities, modify program 20.7 so that it works with your system. The techniques used in this program could be extended in many directions. One might develop a graphic representation of different parameters, e.g.,

dynamics, composite rhythm, aggregate turnover, or bandwidth and average frequency over time.

11. Encode some sixteenth-century counterpoint, say by Palestrina (omit the text). Write a program to locate and identify all nonharmonic tones.

12. Write a program that checks encoded species-counterpoint exercises for errors. Although some melodic characteristics apply to several species, you should deal with one species at a time.

13. Extend the harmonic-analysis program (program 20.6) to analyze the entire piece. A logical second step would be to identify nonchord tones.

14. It would be interesting to take a progressive approach to developing a harmonic-analysis program. I suggest following the learning sequence of Aldwell and Schachter, *Harmony and Voice Leading* (San Diego: Harcourt Brace Jovanovich, 1978). For example, first "teach" your program to identify simple I-V-I progressions, then add prolongations of the tonic through arpeggiation and passing chords, predominant harmonies, etc. It will be more difficult but more rewarding to use a context-sensitive approach than simply to label chords with Roman numerals.

15. Encode a twelve-tone piece and write a program that identifies all row forms used. Suggestions: (a) Review program 15.5 (maze threading); (b) You will do better using the intervals in the row than matching pitch classes. This is not too difficult for a simple piece. To generalize the process for any twelve-tone piece is nontrivial.

APPENDIX A

The ASCII Character Set

The ASCII (American Standard Code for Information Interchange) character set consists of 128 characters: 33 nonprinting control characters and 95 printing characters. In table A.1 below, the ordinal position of each character is found by adding the number to the left of the row with the number at the top of each column. For example, the character 'A' is 65 (60 + 5), the character '}' is 125 (120 + 5), and the blank character is 32 (30 + 2). For Pascal systems that use the ASCII set, these numbers correspond to the ordinal position of each character in the set, i.e., *ord*('a') is 97, and *chr*(97) is the character 'a'. Control characters can be generated using function *chr*, e.g., the null character is *chr*(0), and the tab character is *chr*(9). Table A.2 lists the special characters.

	0	1	2	3	4	5	6	7	8	9
0	NUL	SOH	STX	ETX	EOT	ENQ	ACK	BEL	BS	HT
10	LF	VT	FF	CR	SO	SI	DLE	DC1	DC2	DC3
20	DC4	NAK	SYN	ETB	CAN	EM	SUB	ESC	FS	GS
30	RS	US		!	"	#	$	%	&	'
40	(	)	*	+	,	-	.	/	0	1
50	2	3	4	5	6	7	8	9	:	;
60	<	=	>	?	@	A	B	C	D	E
70	F	G	H	I	J	K	L	M	N	O
80	P	Q	R	S	T	U	V	W	X	Y
90	Z	[	\	]	^	_	`	a	b	c
100	d	e	f	g	h	i	j	k	l	m
110	n	o	p	q	r	s	t	u	v	w
120	x	y	z	{	|	}	~	DEL		

Table A.1. The ASCII Character Set

ACK	Acknowledge	FF	Form Feed
BEL	Bell	FS	File Separator
BS	Backspace	GS	Group Separator
CAN	Cancel	HT	Horizontal Tab
CR	Carriage Return	LF	Line Feed
DC1	Device Control 1	NAK	Negative Acknowledge
DC2	Device Control 2	NUL	Null
DC3	Device Control 3	RS	Record Separator
DC4	Device Control 4	SI	Shift In
DEL	Delete	SO	Shift Out
DLE	Data Link Escape	SOH	Start of Heading
EM	End of Medium	STX	Start of Text
ENQ	Enquiry	SUB	Substitute
EOT	End of Transmission	SYN	Synnchronous Idle
ESC	Escape	US	Unit Separator
ETB	End of Transmission Block	VT	Vertical Tab
ETX	End of Text		

Table A.2. ASCII Control Characters

APPENDIX B

Type Compatibility and Operator Precedence

Type Compatibility

Two types are *compatible* if any one of the following conditions is true:

1. They are the same type.
2. One is a subrange of the other, or both are subranges of the same host type.
3. Both are set types, their base types are compatible, and either both are packed or neither is packed.
4. Both are string types with the same number of components.

A type is *assignable* if it neither is a file type nor contains a file type as a component of a structured type.

An expression, *E*, is *assignment-compatible* with a variable *V* if any one of the following is true:

1. *E* and *V* are the same assignable type (see above).
2. *V* is *real* and *E* is *integer*.
3. *V* and *E* are the same ordinal type or subranges of the same ordinal type, and the value of *E* is within the subrange defined by the type of *V*.
4. *V* and *E* are of the same set type (chapter 12), or are set types with base types that are the same or are subranges of the same ordinal type. Either both types or neither must be packed. The value of *E* must be a value of the type of *V*.
5. *V* and *E* are compatible string types.

Couper points out that Pascal does not strictly follow name type equivalence or structural type equivalence.[1] In the following example, types *fraction*, *ratio*, and *portion* are the same type, since they have been defined with the same type identifier:

```
type
   fractype = record
                 numerator   : integer;
                 denominator : integer
              end;

   fraction = fractype;
   ratio    = fractype;
   portion  = ratio;
```

Note, however, that two new type definitions are not identical even if their definitions are identical. Types *fraction* and *ratio*, as defined below, are not identical or even compatible types:

```
type
   fraction = record
                 numerator   : integer;
                 denominator : integer
              end;
```

1. Doug Couper, *Standard Pascal* (New York: W.W. Norton, 1983), 11.

```
ratio     = record
               numerator   : integer;
               denominator : integer
            end;
```

This is why predefined standard or user-defined types must be used when formal parameters are defined in subroutine headings.

Precedence of Operators

Table B.1 summarizes the rules of operator precedence used in evaluating expressions in Pascal. Note that precedence rules cross types. The operators for multiplication (*), real division (/), integer division (**div**), set intersection (*), and the boolean operator **and** all have the same level of precedence.

Parentheses can be used to circumvent the rules of operator precedence. Thus $4 - 2 * 6$ is equal to -8, but $(4 - 2) * 6$ is equal to 12. If parentheses are not present, a series of two or more operators of equal precedence is evaluated from left to right. Thus $7 + 3 - 2$ is evaluated as $(7 + 3) - 2$.

With dyadic operators (those with two operands), the order in which the operands are evaluated is implementation-dependent. The operands may be evaluated from left to right, right to left, simultaneously, or in some cases not at all. This last condition is possible in boolean expressions. For example, where B_1 and B_2 represent boolean expressions, the value of the expressions

$$B_1 \textbf{ or } B_2$$

and

$$B_1 \textbf{ and } B_2$$

may be determined after partial evaluation, in the first instance if either operand is *true*, and in the second if either is *false*. Although a particular compiler may take advantage of this fact, the guidelines listed above indicate that one cannot count on this. An expression such as $(x <> 0)$ **and** $(y / x > 1.0)$ may result in an error (divide by 0) during execution.

Operator	*Classification*
not	Boolean negation (highest precedence)
*, /, **div**, **mod**, **and**	Multiplying operators (next highest)
+, −, **or**	Adding operators (third highest)
=, <>, <, <=, >=, >, **in**	Relational operators (lowest precedence)

Table B.1. Precedence of Operators

APPENDIX C

A DARMS Interpreter

```
(************************   DARMS Interpreter   ************************)
(* This program translates a substantial subset of the DARMS music en-   *)
(* coding language (described in section 6.5) into an intermediate file  *)
(* that can be read by the score processing procedures described in      *)
(* Chapter 20.  The basic algorithms for decoding pitch and rhythm are   *)
(* described in sections 11.5 and 14.5, respectively.  The structure and *)
(* function of the program are described in section 20.1.                 *)
(*************************************************************************)
program DARMSinterpreter(input, output);
  const
    maxline  = 86;             { maximum line length + 1            }
    maxins   = 15;             { max no. of instruments             }
    maxgroup = 30;             { max no. of grouplet identifiers    }
    maxstaff =  3;             { max number of staves - 1           }
    sharp    = '#';            { DARMS symbol for sharp             }
    flat     = '-';            { DARMS symbol for flat              }
    natural  = '*';            { DARMS symbol for natural           }
    isrest   = true;           { flags to distinguish rest          }
    isnote   = false;          {   from note                        }

(*************************************************************************)
(*                          TYPE DEFINITIONS                              *)
(*************************************************************************)
  type
    buftype = record
                B  : array[1 .. maxline] of char;
                bp : integer
              end;

    fraction = record
                 num : integer;        { numerator   }
                 den : integer         { denominator }
               end;

    ornament = (trill, mordent, turn, flatN, flatE, flatS, natN,
                natE, natS, sharpN, sharpE, sharpS);

    orntype = set of ornament;

    articulation = (staccato, wedgeaccent, tenuto, accent, vaccent,
                    fermata, arco, pizz, snap, upbow, downbow,
                    hauptstimme, nebenstimme, terminator, open, stopped);

    artictype  = set of articulation;

    dynamic = (pppppp, ppppp, pppp, ppp, pp, p, mp, mf, f, ff, fff, ffff,
               fffff, ffffff, sfz, cresc, startcresc, endcresc, incresc,
               crescdim, dim, startdim, enddim, indim, dimcresc);

    dynset = set of dynamic;

    note = record
             dur    : fraction;    { fractional value of duration       }
             pitch  : integer;     { in continuous binomial rep         }
             tie    : integer;     { code for ties                      }
             artic  : artictype;   { articulation codes                 }
             sticky : artictype;   { "sticky" articulations             }
             orn    : orntype;     { ornament codes                     }
             slur   : integer;     { code for slurs                     }
             dyn1   : integer;     { dynamic level as integer           }
             dyn2   : dynset       { set of dynamic attributes          }
           end;

    pitchtable = array[0 .. 70] of integer;     { reference by cnc      }
    grouptable = array[1 .. 30] of fraction;    { grouplet constants    }

    chordtype  = (nochord, fullcode, basinc, spacpat);

    pdat = record                             { DATA for each part              }
             default     : fraction;          { current default dur. of note    }
             dot         : fraction;          { current value of dot            }
             time        : fraction;          { current time in part            }
             lastdot     : fraction;          { value of last dot               }
             restdot     : fraction;          { value of dot for rests          }
             beatnote    : fraction;          { value of beatnote               }
             lasttime    : fraction;          { latest time in layer            }
             lastmeas    : fraction;          { latest meas. time in layer      }
             tempbar     : fraction;          { saves time during linear decomp }
             measno      : fraction;          { measure postion                 }
             measure     : fraction;          { measure time for note           }
             meter       : fraction;          { number of beats per measure     }
             lrestdot    : fraction;          { value of dot of last rest       }
             start       : fraction;          { starting time, note or rest     }
             savestart   : fraction;          { starting time for lin. decomp   }
             savemeas    : fraction;          { starting mtime for lin decomp   }
             lastbar     : fraction;          { time at last barline            }

             chord       : chordtype;         { chord type                      }

             inum        : integer;           { instrument number               }
             clef        : integer;           { constant for current clef       }
             spacecode   : integer;           { current space code              }
             level       : integer;           { level of parenthesis (beams)    }
             savedyn     : integer;           { beginning value of crescendos   }
             stafftrans  : integer;           { stave transposition code        }
             trans       : integer;           { transposition value as cbr      }

             current     : note;              { values for current note         }
             restval     : note;              { values for current rest         }
             lastnote    : note;              { for restoring after parens      }
             lastrest    : note;              { value of last rest              }

             pushing     : boolean;           { true if current push code       }
             vol         : boolean;           { true if in cresc or dim         }
             dowrite     : boolean;           { writenote enable/disable        }
             slurcurrent : boolean;           { true if note has simple slur    }
             tiecurrent  : boolean;           { true if note has simple tie     }
             slurlast    : boolean;           { true if last note had slur      }
             tielast     : boolean;           { true if last note had tie       }

             keysig      : pitchtable;        { adjustment for keysignature     }
             adjust      : pitchtable         { keysig plus accidentals         }
           end;

    pdattab = array[0 .. maxins] of pdat;  { info for each instrument       }
```

```
(***************************************************************************)
(*                              GLOBAL VARIABLES                           *)
(***************************************************************************)
  var
    buffer      : buftype;          { stores one line of input            }
    inum        : integer;          { current instrument number           }
    group       : grouptable;       { grouplet definer constants          }
    partdata    : pdattab;
    lineno      : integer;          { current line number                 }

(***************************************************************************)
(*                              UTILITY ROUTINES                           *)
(***************************************************************************)

(************************             incr            ************************)
(* Adds one to its argument.                                               *)
(***************************************************************************)
  procedure incr(var x : integer);               { add one to argument      }
    begin
      x := x + 1
    end;

(************************             max             ************************)
(* Returns greater of x and y.                                             *)
(***************************************************************************)
  function max(x, y : integer) : integer;
    begin
      if x >= y
        then max := x
        else max := y
    end;

(************************            scale            ************************)
(* Returns pcs for natural scale, given name class.                        *)
(***************************************************************************)
  function scale(nc : integer) : integer;
    begin
      case nc of
        0 : scale :=  0;
        1 : scale :=  2;
        2 : scale :=  4;
        3 : scale :=  5;
        4 : scale :=  7;
        5 : scale :=  9;
        6 : scale := 11
      end { case }
    end; { scale }

(************************          normclef           ************************)
(* Returns space code for normal clef position.                            *)
(***************************************************************************)
  function normclef(clef : char) : integer;
    begin
      case clef of
        'c' : normclef := 25;
        'f' : normclef := 27;
        'g' : normclef := 23
      end { case }
    end; { normclef }

(************************            name             ************************)
(* Converts nc to note name.                                               *)
(***************************************************************************)
  function name(nc : integer) : char;
    begin
      case nc of
        0 : name := 'c';
        1 : name := 'd';
        2 : name := 'e';
        3 : name := 'f';
        4 : name := 'g';
        5 : name := 'a';
        6 : name := 'b'
      end { clef }
    end;  { name }

(************************           cartic            ************************)
(* Returns character representation of articulation code.                  *)
(***************************************************************************)
  function cartic(x : articulation) : char;
    begin
      case x of
        staccato     : cartic := '''';        { articulation codes         }
        wedgeaccent  : cartic := '"';
        tenuto       : cartic := '_';
        accent       : cartic := '>';
        vaccent      : cartic := '<';
        fermata      : cartic := ';';
        arco         : cartic := 'r';         { dictionary codes           }
        pizz         : cartic := 'z';
        snap         : cartic := 'q';
        upbow        : cartic := 'v';
        downbow      : cartic := 'd';
        hauptstimme  : cartic := 'h';
        nebenstimme  : cartic := 'n';
        terminator   : cartic := '¯';
        open         : cartic := 'o';
        stopped      : cartic := '+'
      end  { case }
    end;

(************************            imod             ************************)
(* Imod(x, m) = x mod m, but unlike many mod functions, it works prop-     *)
(* erly with negative x.                                                   *)
(***************************************************************************)
  function imod(a, b : integer) : integer;
    var
      r : integer;
    begin
      r := a - (a div b) * b;
      if r < 0
        then imod := r + b
        else imod := r
    end;
```

```
(***************************************************************************)
(*                            PITCH CODE ROUTINES                          *)
(*                         (Described in section 19.2)                     *)
(***************************************************************************)

(************************           cbr           ************************)
(* Maps octave, pc, and nc into continuous binomial representation.      *)
(***************************************************************************)
  function cbr(octave, pc, nc : integer) : integer;
    begin
      if octave >= 0
        then cbr :=   octave * 1000 + pc * 10 + nc
        else cbr := -(abs(octave) * 1000 + pc * 10 + nc)
    end;

(************************           br            ************************)
(* Extracts binomial representation from cbr.                             *)
(***************************************************************************)
  function br(cbr : integer) : integer;
    begin
      br := abs(cbr) mod 1000
    end;

(************************         octave          ************************)
(* Extracts octave from cbr.                                              *)
(***************************************************************************)
  function octave(cbr : integer) : integer;
    begin
      octave := abs(cbr) div 1000
    end;

(************************       pitchclass        ************************)
(* Extracts pitch class from cbr.                                         *)
(***************************************************************************)
  function pitchclass(cbr : integer) : integer;
    begin
      pitchclass := br(cbr) div 10
    end;

(************************        nameclass        ************************)
(* Extracts nameclass from cbr.                                           *)
(***************************************************************************)
  function nameclass(cbr : integer) : integer;
    begin
      nameclass := br(cbr) mod 10
    end;

(************************           cpc           ************************)
(* Calculates continuous pitch code from cbr.                             *)
(***************************************************************************)
  function cpc(cbr : integer) : integer;
    var
      o, p, n, diff : integer;
    begin
      o := octave(cbr);
      n := nameclass(cbr);
      p := pitchclass(cbr);
      diff := p - scale(n);
      if diff > 6
        then o := o - 1
      else if diff < -6
        then o := o + 1;
      if cbr < 0
        then cpc := -(12 * o + p)
        else cpc :=  (12 * o + p)
    end;

(************************           cnc           ************************)
(* Calculates continuous name code from cbr.                              *)
(***************************************************************************)
  function cnc(cbr : integer) : integer;
    begin
      if cbr < 0
        then cnc := -(octave(cbr) * 7 + nameclass(cbr))
        else cnc :=   octave(cbr) * 7 + nameclass(cbr)
    end;

(************************           add           ************************)
(* Adds two signed cbrs and returns result in same form.                  *)
(***************************************************************************)
  function add(cbr1, cbr2 : integer) : integer;
    var
      pitch, name, octave : integer;
      negative : boolean;
    begin
      pitch := abs(cpc(cbr1) + cpc(cbr2)) mod 12;
      name := cnc(cbr1) + cnc(cbr2);
      if name <> 0                                       { base direction on cnc }
        then negative := name < 0                        { unless ncs are equal  }
        else negative := (cpc(cbr1) + cpc(cbr2)) < 0;
      octave := abs(name) div 7;
      name := abs(name) mod 7;
      if negative
        then add := -cbr(octave, pitch, name)
        else add :=  cbr(octave, pitch, name)
    end;  { add }

(************************        tenscale         ************************)
(* Used for mapping two integers into one when the new value must be      *)
(* added as high order digits.  Returns the multiplication factor for     *)
(* the new integer before adding old.                                     *)
(***************************************************************************)
  function tenscale(x : integer) : integer;
    var
      t : integer;
    begin
      t := 1;
      while x > 0 do
        begin
          t := 10 * t;
          x := x div 10
        end;
      tenscale := t
    end;
```

```
(*************************************************************************)
(*                          BOOLEAN FUNCTIONS                            *)
(*************************************************************************)

(************************       isdigit          ************************)
(* Tests for numeric characters.                                         *)
(*************************************************************************)
 function isdigit(ch : char) : boolean;
   begin
     isdigit := ch in ['0' .. '9']
   end;

(************************       isacc            ************************)
(* Tests for accidental codes.                                           *)
(*************************************************************************)
 function isacc(ch : char) : boolean;
   begin
     isacc := ch in ['-', '#', '*']
   end;

(************************       isclef           ************************)
(* Tests for DARMS clef codes.                                           *)
(*************************************************************************)
 function isclef(ch : char) : boolean;
   begin
     isclef := ch in ['c', 'f', 'g']
   end;

(************************       isparen          ************************)
(* Tests for left or right parenthesis.                                  *)
(*************************************************************************)
 function isparen(ch : char) :  boolean;
   begin
     isparen := ch in ['(', ')']
   end;

(************************       isdur            ************************)
(* Tests for DARMS duration codes.                                       *)
(*************************************************************************)
 function isdur(ch : char) : boolean;
   begin
     isdur := ch in ['w', 'h', 'q', 'e', 's', 't', 'x', 'y', 'z', 'g']
   end;

(************************       isartic          ************************)
(* Tests for DARMS articulation codes.                                   *)
(*************************************************************************)
 function isartic(ch : char) : boolean;
   begin
     isartic := ch in ['''', '"', '_', '>', '<', ';']
   end;

(************************       isquest          ************************)
(* Tests for question mark (signals dictionary codes).                   *)
(*************************************************************************)
 function isquest(ch : char) : boolean;
   begin
     isquest := ch = '?'
   end;

(************************       isoh             ************************)
(* Tests for 'o', signalling ornament code.                              *)
(*************************************************************************)
 function isoh(ch :char) : boolean;
   begin
     isoh := ch = 'o'
   end;

(************************       isa              ************************)
(* Tests for 'a', signalling attach code.                                *)
(*************************************************************************)
 function isa(ch :char) : boolean;
   begin
     isa := ch = 'a'
   end;

(************************       isdict           ************************)
(* Tests for implemented dictionary codes.                               *)
(*************************************************************************)
 function isdict(ch : char) : boolean;
   begin
     isdict := ch in ['r', 'z', 'q', 'v', 'd', 'h', 'n', '-', 'o', '+']
   end;

(************************       isorn            ************************)
(* Tests for DARMS ornament codes.                                       *)
(*************************************************************************)
 function isorn(ch : char) : boolean;
   begin
     isorn := ch in ['t', ';', 'm', '?']
   end;

(************************       isslur           ************************)
(* Tests for DARMS slur codes.                                           *)
(*************************************************************************)
 function isslur(ch : char) : boolean;
   begin
     isslur := ch = '1'
   end;

(************************       isdynamic        ************************)
(* Tests for DARMS dynamic codes.                                        *)
(*************************************************************************)
 function isdynamic(ch: char) : boolean;
   begin
     isdynamic := ch in ['f', 'p', 'm', 's', 'z']
   end;

(************************       isstem           ************************)
(* Tests for DARMS stem-direction codes.                                 *)
(*************************************************************************)
 function isstem(ch : char) : boolean;
   begin
     isstem := ch in ['u', 'd']
   end;
```

```
(*************************          isbar           ************************)
(* Tests for DARMS bar line codes.                                          *)
(***************************************************************************)
  function isbar(ch : char) : boolean;
    begin
      isbar := ch in ['/', ':']
    end;

(*************************         isother          ************************)
(* Tests for other stuff.                                                   *)
(***************************************************************************)
  function isother(ch : char) : boolean;
    begin
      isother := ch in ['!', '/', '.', ' ', 'r', '&', 'i', '~', 'k',
                                                              '@', ',']
    end;

(*************************        goodtoken         ************************)
(* Tests for "legal" first char of token.                                   *)
(***************************************************************************)
  function goodtoken(ch : char) : boolean;
    begin
      goodtoken := isdigit(ch) or isdur(ch) or isacc(ch) { or isartic(ch)
               or isstem(ch) } or isparen(ch) or isbar(ch) or isother(ch)
    end;

(*************************          issign          ************************)
(* Tests for plus or minus sign.                                            *)
(***************************************************************************)
  function issign(c : char) : boolean;
    begin
      issign := c in ['-', '+']
    end;

(*************************         isupper          ************************)
(* Tests for upper case alphabetic characters.                              *)
(***************************************************************************)
  function isupper(c : char) : boolean;
    begin
      isupper := c in ['A' .. 'Z']
    end;


(***************************************************************************)
(*                            BUFFER ROUTINES                               *)
(* The following implement an internal buffer (section 11.2).  The        *)
(* version shown includes line numbers in getline and printbuffer.          *)
(***************************************************************************)


(*************************           tab            ************************)
(* Returns ASCII tab character.                                             *)
(***************************************************************************)
  function tab : char;
    begin
      tab := chr(9)
    end;

(*************************           null           ************************)
(* Returns ASCII null character.                                            *)
(***************************************************************************)
  function null : char;
    begin
      null := chr(10)
    end;

(*************************          toint           ************************)
(* Converts digit character to integer.                                     *)
(***************************************************************************)
  function toint(c : char) : integer;
    begin
      toint := ord(c) - ord('0')
    end;

(*************************         getline          ************************)
(* Reads one line into buffer and sets bp at beginning of buffer.           *)
(***************************************************************************)
  procedure getline(var fi, fo : text; var buffer : buftype;
                                         var lineno : integer);

    begin
      incr(lineno);
      with buffer do
        begin
          bp := 1;
          while not eoln(fi) and (bp < maxline) do
            begin
              read(fi, B[bp]);
              incr(bp)
            end;
          B[bp] := null;                              { mark end of line }
          if not eoln(fi)
            then writeln(fo, 'getline: warning, input line truncated');
          readln(fi);
          bp := 1                     { reset index at beginning of buffer }
        end
    end;

(*************************           eob            ************************)
(* True at end of buffer.                                                   *)
(***************************************************************************)
  function eob(var buffer : buftype) : boolean;
    begin
      with buffer do
        eob := B[bp] = null
    end;

(*************************         tolower          ************************)
(* Converts upper to lower case.                                            *)
(***************************************************************************)
  function tolower(c : char) : char;
    begin
      if isupper(c)
        then tolower := chr(ord(c) - ord('A') + ord('a'))
        else tolower := c
    end;
```

```
(************************          nextchar          ************************)
(* Returns next character in buffer.                                          *)
(******************************************************************************)
  function nextchar(var buffer : buftype) : char;    { next char in buffer }
    begin
      with buffer do
        if not eob(buffer)
          then nextchar := tolower(B[bp])
          else nextchar := ' '
    end;

(************************          skipbuf           ************************)
(* Skips to next nonblank char or end of buffer.                              *)
(******************************************************************************)
  procedure skipbuf(var buffer : buftype);
    begin
      with buffer do
        while (nextchar(buffer) in [' ', tab]) and not eob(buffer) do
          incr(bp)
    end;

(************************          getchar           ************************)
(* Reads next character in buffer.                                            *)
(******************************************************************************)
  procedure getchar(var buffer : buftype; var c : char);
    begin
      with buffer do
        begin
          c := B[bp];
          incr(bp)
        end
    end;

(************************        printbuffer         ************************)
(* Prints contents of buffer with pointer to current character.               *)
(******************************************************************************)
  procedure printbuffer(var f : text; var buffer : buftype;
                                                        lineno : integer);
    var
      i : integer;
    begin
      write(f, 'c ', lineno:5, ': ');            { line number in input file }
      i := 1;
      with buffer do
        begin
          while B[i] <> null do
            begin
              write(f, B[i]);
              incr(i)
            end;
          writeln(f);
          write(f, 'c error: ');
          for i := 1 to bp - 1 do
            write(f, '-');
          writeln(f, '↑');
        end
    end;  { printbuffer }

(************************           error            ************************)
(* Prints error message with buffer contents.                                 *)
(******************************************************************************)
  procedure error(var f : text; var buffer : buftype; errno : integer);
    begin { error }
      printbuffer(f, buffer, lineno);
      case errno of
        1: writeln(f, 'error 1: "', nextchar(buffer),
                                          '" not recognized by scanner.');
        2: writeln(f, 'error 2: "', nextchar(buffer), '" cannot follow !');
        3: writeln(f, 'error 3: "', nextchar(buffer),
                                               '" illegal accidental.');
        4: writeln(f, 'error 4: "', nextchar(buffer),
                                              '" is not a clef hanger');
        5: writeln(f, 'error 5: "', nextchar(buffer),
                                   '" : accidental, or digit expected');
        6: writeln(f, 'error 6: "', nextchar(buffer),
                                     '" is not an accidental code');
        7: writeln(f, 'error 7: "', nextchar(buffer),
                                           '" unbalanced parentheses');
        8: writeln(f, 'error 8: unbalanced parenthesis');
        9: writeln(f, 'error 9: "', nextchar(buffer),
                            '" cannot follow other duration codes');
       10: writeln(f, 'error 10: "', nextchar(buffer),
             '" cannot follow accidental in nonstandard key signatures');
       11: writeln(f, 'error 11: "', nextchar(buffer),
                                               '" is not a meter code');
       12: writeln(f, 'error 12: " ', nextchar(buffer),
                                                '" is not a rest code');
       13: writeln(f, 'error 13: " ', nextchar(buffer),
                                 '" : w expected for measures of rest');
       14: writeln(f, 'error 14: "', nextchar(buffer),
                                     '": too many articulation codes');
       15: writeln(f, 'error 15: instrument number must be >= 0');
       16: writeln(f, 'error 16: ',
                     'instrument number too big, maxins =', maxins:1);
       17: writeln(f, 'error 17: "', nextchar(buffer),
                                    '" : improper coding of barlines');
       18: writeln(f, 'error 18: improper dynamic code');
       19: writeln(f, 'error 19: "', nextchar(buffer),
                                  '" cannot follow m as dynamic mark');
       20: writeln(f, 'error 20: incorrect transposition level');
       21: writeln(f, 'error 21: "', nextchar(buffer),
                                       '" illegal after skip operator');
       22: writeln(f, 'calc: 22: ', nextchar(buffer),
                                                     ' is not defined');
       23: writeln(f, 'getint: integer expected');
       24: writeln(f, 'error 24: token delimiter expected');
       25: writeln(f, 'error 25: literal not terminated by $');
       26: writeln(f, 'error 26: ', nextchar(buffer),
                                                 ' bad dictionary code');
       27: writeln(f, 'error 27: compound ties must be numbered,',
                                                          ' e.g., j4j1');
       28: writeln(f, 'error 28: ', nextchar(buffer),
                                                   ' bad ornament code');
       29: writeln(f, 'error 29: ', nextchar(buffer), ' attach = N, E, S');
       30: writeln(f, 'error 30: ', nextchar(buffer),
```

```
                                           ' accidental required');
   31: writeln(f, 'error 31: space code too large; max. staves =',
                                                   maxstaff + 1:2);
   32: writeln(f, 'error 32: staff trans code must be multiple of 50');
   33: writeln(f, 'error 33: staff trans code greater than 100');
   34: writeln(f, 'getreal: number expected')
  end  { case }
end;   { error }

(************************          getint          ************************)
(* Reads integer from buffer.                                               *)
(****************************************************************************)
procedure getint(var f : text; var buffer : buftype; var x : integer);
  var
    negative : boolean;
  begin
    skipbuf(buffer);                              { skip blanks    }
    negative := nextchar(buffer) = '-';           { check for sign }
    if issign(nextchar(buffer))
      then incr(buffer.bp);                       { skip sign      }
    if not isdigit(nextchar(buffer))
      then error(f, buffer, 23)
      else
        begin { read number }
          x := 0;
          while isdigit(nextchar(buffer)) do
            begin
              x := 10 * x + toint(nextchar(buffer));
              incr(buffer.bp)
            end
        end;  { read number }
    if negative                                   { set sign       }
      then x := -x
  end;

(************************          getreal          ************************)
(* Reads real number from buffer.                                           *)
(****************************************************************************)
procedure getreal(var f : text; var buffer : buftype; var x : real);
  var
    scale : integer;
    negative : boolean;
  begin
    skipbuf(buffer);                              { skip blanks     }
    negative := nextchar(buffer) = '-';
    if issign(nextchar(buffer))
      then incr(buffer.bp);                       { skip sign       }
    x := 0;
    scale := 1;
    if not (isdigit(nextchar(buffer)) or (nextchar(buffer) = '.'))
      then error(f, buffer, 34)                   { number expected }
      else
        begin
          while isdigit(nextchar(buffer)) do
            begin
              x := 10 * x + toint(nextchar(buffer));
              incr(buffer.bp)                     { get next char   }
            end;
          if nextchar(buffer) = '.'
            then
              begin
                incr(buffer.bp);
                while isdigit(nextchar(buffer)) do
                  begin
                    x := 10 * x + toint(nextchar(buffer));
                    scale := scale * 10;
                    incr(buffer.bp)
                  end
              end;
          x := x / scale;
          if negative                             { set sign        }
            then x := -x
        end
  end;  { getreal }

(****************************************************************************)
(*                        RATIONAL ARITHMETIC ROUTINES                      *)
(*                         (Described in section 13.2)                      *)
(****************************************************************************)

(************************          swap          ************************)
(* Exchanges values of its arguments.                                       *)
(****************************************************************************)
procedure swap(var x, y : integer);
  var
    t : integer;
  begin
    t := x; x := y; y := t
  end;

(************************          gcd          ************************)
(* Returns the greatest common divisor of x and y.                          *)
(****************************************************************************)
function gcd(x, y : integer) : integer;
  var
    t : integer;
  begin
    x := abs(x);
    y := abs(y);
    if y > x
      then swap(x, y);
    while y <> 0 do
      begin
        t := x mod y;
        x := y;
        y := t
      end;
    gcd := x
  end;

(************************          fracadd          ************************)
(* Adds fractions a and b, returning result as c.                           *)
(****************************************************************************)
```

```
procedure fracadd(var c : fraction; a : fraction; b : fraction);
  var
    d1, d2, t : integer;
  begin
    d1 := gcd(a.den, b.den);
    if d1 = 1
      then
        begin
          c.num := a.num *  b.den + a.den * b.num;
          c.den := a.den * b.den
        end
      else
        begin
          t := a.num * (b.den div d1) + b.num * (a.den div d1);
          d2 := gcd(t, d1);
          c.num := t div d2;
          c.den := (a.den div d1) * (b.den div d2)
        end
  end;  { fracadd }

(************************          fracsub          ************************)
(* Subtracts fractions a and b, returning result as c.                      *)
(**************************************************************************)

 procedure fracsub(var c : fraction; a : fraction; b : fraction);
   begin
     b.num := -b.num;                              { negate second fraction }
     fracadd(c, a, b)                              { and then add           }
   end;  { fracsub }

(************************          fracmult          ************************)
(* Multiplies fractions a and b, returning result as c.                     *)
(**************************************************************************)
 procedure fracmult(var c : fraction; a : fraction; b : fraction);
   var
     d1, d2 : integer;
   begin
     d1 := gcd(a.num, b.den);
     d2 := gcd(a.den, b.num);
     c.num := (a.num div d1) * (b.num div d2);
     c.den := (a.den div d2) * (b.den div d1)
   end;  { fracmult }

(************************          fracdiv          ************************)
(* Divides fraction a by fraction b, returning result as c.                 *)
(**************************************************************************)
 procedure fracdiv(var c : fraction; a : fraction; b : fraction);
   begin
     swap(b.num, b.den);                          { invert second fraction }
     if b.den < 0                                 {    get the signs right }
       then
         begin { switch signs }
           b.num := -b.num;
           b.den := -b.den
         end;  { switch signs }
     fracmult(c, a, b)                            { and then multiply      }
   end;  { fracdiv }
```

```
(************************          fracwrite          ************************)
(* Writes fraction in standard format.                                      *)
(**************************************************************************)
 procedure fracwrite(var f : text; x : fraction);
   begin
     write(f, x.num:4, ' /', x.den:4 , ' ')
   end;

(************************          fracread          ************************)
(* Reads fraction from buffer.                                              *)
(**************************************************************************)
 procedure fracread(var f : text; var buffer : buftype; var x : fraction);
   begin
     getint(f, buffer, x.num);
     skipbuf(buffer);
     if nextchar(buffer) in ['/', ':']
       then incr(buffer.bp);
     getint(f, buffer, x.den)
   end;

(************************          reduce          ************************)
(* Reduces fraction.                                                        *)
(**************************************************************************)
 procedure reduce(var x : fraction);
   var
     t : integer;
   begin
     t := gcd(x.num, x.den);
     if t > 1
       then
         begin
           x.num := x.num div t;
           x.den := x.den div t
         end
   end;

(************************          equal          ************************)
(* Returns true if fractions x and y are equal.                             *)
(**************************************************************************)
 function equal(x, y : fraction) : boolean;
   begin
     equal := (x.num * y.den) = (y.num * x.den)
   end;

(************************          greater          ************************)
(* Returns true if fraction x is greater than fraction y.                   *)
(**************************************************************************)
 function greater(x, y : fraction) : boolean;
   begin
     greater := (x.num * y.den) > (y.num * x.den)
   end;

(************************          lessthan          ************************)
(* Returns true if fraction x is less than fraction y.                      *)
(**************************************************************************)
 function lessthan(x, y : fraction) : boolean;
   begin
```

```
      lessthan := (x.num * y.den) < (y.num * x.den)
    end;

(************************          init          ************************)
(* Initializes variables before beginning program run.                  *)
(************************************************************************)
  procedure init(var inum, lineno : integer; var group : grouptable;
                                             var partdata : pdattab);

    var
      i, j : integer;

    begin { init }
      inum := 1;                          { instrument number          }
      lineno := 0;                        { line number in input file  }

      for i := 0 to maxins do
        with partdata[i] do
          begin

            beatnote.num := 1;            { beatnote default = 1/4     }
            beatnote.den := 4;

            default.num := 1;             { default is 1/4 note        }
            default.den := 4;

            dot.num := 1;                 { dot = 1/8                  }
            dot.den := 8;

            lastbar.num := 0;             { default measure number 1   }
            lastbar.den := 1;

            measno.num := 1;              { default measure number 1   }
            measno.den := 1;

            measure.num := 1;             { measure at start of note   }
            measure.den := 1;

            meter.num := 4;               { meter default is 4/4       }
            meter.den := 4;

            restdot.num := 1;             { dot = 1/8                  }
            restdot.den := 8;

            start.num := 0;               { start time for note        }
            start.den := 1;

            time.num := 0;                { raw time begins at 0/1     }
            time.den := 1;

            chord := nochord;             { not in chord               }

            inum := i;
            clef := 9;                    { default is treble clef     }
            level := 0;                   { no parenthesis             }
            savedyn := 0;
            spacecode := 26;              { default space code         }

            stafftrans := 0;              { stave transposition code   }
            trans := 0;                   { no transposition (in C)    }

            with current do               { defaults for current note  }
              begin
                pitch    := 4000;         { pitch is C4                }
                dur.num  :=    1;         { duration is 1/4 note       }
                dur.den  :=    4;
                dyn1     :=   -1;         { dynamic is undefined       }
                dyn2     :=   [];
                tie      :=    0;         { tie field is not set       }
                slur     :=    0;         { slur field is not set      }
                artic    :=   [];         { no articulation            }
                sticky   :=   [];         { no "sticky" articulations  }
                orn      :=   []          { no ornaments               }
              end;

            with restval do               { defaults for rests         }
              begin
                pitch    := -1;           { pitch is undefined         }
                dur.num  :=  1;           { duration is quarter        }
                dur.den  :=  4;
                dyn1     := -1;           { dynamic is undefined       }
                dyn2     := [];
                tie      :=  0;           { no tie                     }
                slur     :=  0;           { or slur                    }
                artic    := []
              end;

            lastrest := restval;          { prev rest like current     }
            lastnote := current;          { prev note like current     }

            tielast := false;             { last note was not tied     }
            slurlast := false;            {   or slurred               }
            tiecurrent := false;          { current note is not tied   }
            slurcurrent := false;         {   or slurred               }
            vol := false;                 { not in cresc or dim        }
            pushing := false;             { push code not in effect    }

            for j := 0 to 70 do
              begin
                adjust[j] := 0;
                keysig[j] := 0
              end;
          end; { for i }

      for i := 1 to maxgroup do           { all grouplet constants set to 1/1 }
        begin
          group[i].num := 1;
          group[i].den := 1
        end
    end; { init }

(************************************************************************)
(*                      DARMS INTERPRETING ROUTINES                      *)
(************************************************************************)
```

```
(**********************************************************************)
(*                      KEY SIGNATURE ROUTINES                        *)
(**********************************************************************)

(*********************** standard      ***********************)
(* Called by procedure setkey whenever a standard key signature is en-  *)
(* countered.  Sets the "keysig" array to reflect the new key signature. *)
(**********************************************************************)
 procedure standard(var f : text;
                    var buffer : buftype;
                        inum, accidentals : integer;
                    var time, measno : fraction;
                    var keysig : pitchtable;
                    var sign : char);
    var
      nc, inc, acc, octave : integer;
      i                    : integer;

    begin
      writeln(f, 'c New key signature =', accidentals:3, ' ', sign);
      write(f, 'k', inum:1, ' ');
      fracwrite(f, time);
      write(f, '         ');
      fracwrite(f, measno);
      write(f, accidentals:4, ' ', sign); writeln;

      case sign of
        sharp : begin
                  nc := 3;                    { first sharp is f      }
                  inc := 4;                   { next is fifth above   }
                  acc := 1                    { adjustment is +1      }
                end;

        flat : begin
                  nc := 6;                    { first flat is B       }
                  inc := 3;                   { next is fourth above  }
                  acc := -1                   { adjustment is -1      }
                end;

        natural : accidentals := 0            { no accidentals        }
      end;  { case }

      for i := 1 to accidentals do            { set each accidental   }
        begin
          for octave := 0 to 9 do             { in each octave        }
            keysig[octave * 7 + nc] := acc;
          nc := (nc + inc) mod 7              { set next accidental   }
        end
    end;  { standard }

(*********************** nonstandard   ***********************)
(* Called by setkey whenever a nonstandard key signature is encountered. *)
(* Reads accidental signs and space codes and sets the "keysig" array    *)
(* accordingly.                                                          *)
(**********************************************************************)
 procedure getcode(var f : text; var buffer : buftype;
                                 var spacecode : integer); forward;

 procedure nonstandard(var f : text; var buffer : buftype;
                           clef : integer;
                       var time, measno : fraction;
                       var keysig : pitchtable ; sign : char);
   var
     octave, nc, acc : integer;
     spacecode       : integer;
   begin
     write(f, 'c non-standard key signature: ');
     repeat
       getcode(f, buffer, spacecode);
       nc := (spacecode + clef) mod 7;
       write(f, name(nc), sign, ' ');

       case sign of
         sharp   : acc := 1;
         flat    : acc := -1;
         natural : acc := 0
       end;  { case }

       for octave := 0 to 9 do
         keysig[octave * 7 + nc] := acc;

       if isacc(nextchar(buffer))
         then
           begin
             getchar(buffer, sign);
             if not isdigit(nextchar(buffer))
               then error(f, buffer, 10)
           end
     until not isdigit(nextchar(buffer));
     writeln
   end; { nonstandard }

(*********************** setkey        ***********************)
(* Handles nonstandard key signatures as well as traditional ones.  In  *)
(* DARMS code, nonstandard key signatures are encoded by following each *)
(* accidental with a space code representing the position of the acciden-*)
(* tal on the staff.  Setkey reads enough of the key signature to deter- *)
(* mine whether the key signature is standard or nonstandard, then calls *)
(* either standard or nonstandard. In either case the "keysig" array,   *)
(* indexed by continuous name codes, is set to reflect the new key signa-*)
(* ture.  This array will be copied to the array "adjust" whenever a    *)
(* barline is encountered.                                              *)
(**********************************************************************)
  procedure setkey(var f        : text; var buffer   : buftype;
                   var partdata : pdat);
    var
      accidentals : integer;
      sign        : char;
      i           : integer;

    begin { setkey }
      with partdata do
        begin
          for i := 0 to 70 do                  { initialize keysig array }
            keysig[i] := 0;
```

```
      incr(buffer.bp);                       { skip 'k'              }
      if isdigit(nextchar(buffer))
        then
          begin { standard key signature }
            getint(f, buffer, accidentals);
            if isacc(nextchar(buffer))
              then
                begin
                  getchar(buffer, sign);
                  standard(f, buffer, inum, accidentals,
                           time, measno, keysig, sign)
                end
              else error(f, buffer, 6)      { bad accidental code       }
          end   { standard key signature }
        else if isacc(nextchar(buffer))
          then
            begin   { nonstandard if sign is followed by a space code }
              getchar(buffer, sign);
              if isdigit(nextchar(buffer))
                then nonstandard(f, buffer, clef, time, measno,
                                                    keysig, sign)
                else standard(f, buffer, inum, 1 , time, measno,
                                                    keysig, sign)
            end
          else error(f, buffer, 5);      { expected accidental or digit }
      adjust := keysig
    end   { with partdata }
  end;  { setkey }


(************************************************************************)
(*                         LINEAR DECOMPOSITION                         *)
(************************************************************************)


(***********************          newstart        ***********************)
(* Called when the symbol pair '!&' is seen, indicating the beginning of *)
(* a section in linear decomposition mode.  The current values of the    *)
(* instrument's start and terminal times are saved so that they can be   *)
(* restored for the next layer.                                          *)
(************************************************************************)
  procedure newstart(var f : text; var buffer : buftype;
                                               var partdata : pdat);
    begin
      with partdata do
        begin
          incr(buffer.bp);                                { skip '&'  }
          savestart  := time;
          lasttime   := savestart;
          savemeas  := measno;
          lastmeas  := savemeas;
          tempbar   := lastbar;
          writeln(f, 'n', inum:1, ' begin linear decompostion')
        end   { with partdata }
    end;
```

```
(***********************          restart         ***********************)
(* Called when the symbol '&', indicating the beginning of a new layer,  *)
(* is encountered.  If the & is followed by a $ (end passage) the ter-   *)
(* minal time for the instrument is set to the end of the layer.  Other- *)
(* wise the start and terminal times are reset to the beginning of the   *)
(* layer.                                                                *)
(************************************************************************)
  procedure restart(var f         : text; var buffer    : buftype;
                                                var partdata : pdat);
    begin { restart }
      with partdata do
        begin
          incr(buffer.bp);                                  { skip '&' }
          if nextchar(buffer) = '$'
            then
              begin { endlayer }
                incr(buffer.bp);                            { skip '$' }
                if greater(lasttime, time)
                  then
                    begin
                      time := lasttime;
                      measno := lastmeas
                    end;
                writeln('$', inum:1, ' end linear decomposition')
              end   { endlayer }
            else
              begin { startlayer }
                if greater(time, lasttime)
                  then
                    begin
                      lasttime := time;
                      lastmeas := measno
                    end;
                time   := savestart;
                measno := savemeas;
                lastbar := tempbar;
                writeln('&', inum:1,' start layer of decomposition')
              end   { startlayer }
        end   { with partdata }
    end;  { restart }

(***********************         checklast        ***********************)
(* Checks and adjusts the tie and slur fields for simple tie or slur in *)
(* previous note.                                                        *)
(************************************************************************)
  procedure checklast(var x : note;
               var slurcurrent, slurlast, tiecurrent, tielast : boolean);
    begin
      if tielast
        then x.tie := tenscale(x.tie) * 2 + x.tie;
      tielast := tiecurrent;
      tiecurrent := false;
      if slurlast
        then x.slur := tenscale(x.slur) * 2 + x.slur;
      slurlast := slurcurrent;
      slurcurrent := false
    end;
```

```
(************************        dynadjust        ************************)
(* Adjusts dynamic after note is written; for special cases.               *)
(***************************************************************************)
  procedure dynadjust(var current, restval, lastnote, lastrest : note);
    begin
      if current.dyn2 <> []
        then    { set default level for next note }
          begin
            if (startcresc in current.dyn2) or (startdim in current.dyn2)
              then current.dyn1 := -1                { middle of cresc or dim }
            else if (dimcresc in current.dyn2)
                  or (crescdim in current.dyn2)
              then current.dyn1 := lastnote.dyn1;
            restval.dyn1 := current.dyn1;
            lastrest.dyn1 := restval.dyn1;
            current.dyn2 := [];
            restval.dyn2 := []
          end
    end;  { dynadjust }

(***************************************************************************)
(*                            OUTPUT ROUTINES                              *)
(***************************************************************************)

(************************        savelast         ************************)
(* Saves last dur and dot for rest or note when leaving beamed group.      *)
(***************************************************************************)
  procedure savelast(var partdata : pdat; rest : boolean);
    begin
      with partdata do
        if chord = nochord                         { not in chord            }
          then
            begin
              if not rest
                then
                  begin                            { save last note and dot }
                    lastdot  := dot;
                    lastnote := current
                  end
                else
                  begin                            { save last rest and dot }
                    lastrest := restval;
                    lrestdot := restdot
                  end;
                current.tie := 0;
                restval.tie := 0
            end
    end;  { savelast }

(************************        writeartic       ************************)
(* Prints articulation and dictionary codes.                               *)
(***************************************************************************)
  procedure writeartic(var f : text; x : artictype);
    var
      i    : articulation;
      n, j : integer;
    begin
      write(f, ' ');
      n := 0;
      if x = []
        then write(f, '0')
        else
          begin
            for i := staccato to stopped do
              if i in x
                then
                  begin
                    write(f, cartic(i));
                    incr(n)
                  end;
            for j := 1 to 3 - n do
              write(' ')
          end
    end;  { writeartic }

(************************         tochar          ************************)
(* Converts integers 0, 1, ... to characters '1'-'9', 'a', 'b', 'c', ... *)
(***************************************************************************)
  function tochar(x : integer) : char;
    begin
      if x < 10
        then tochar := chr(ord('0') + x)
        else tochar := chr(ord('a') + x - 10)
    end;

(************************         putdyn          ************************)
(* Prints ordinal position of each dynamic code.                           *)
(***************************************************************************)
  procedure putdyn(var fout : text; D : dynset);
    var
      i : dynamic;
    begin
      write(fout, ' ');
      if D = []
        then write(fout, 'x')
        else
          begin
            for i := pppppp to dimcresc do
              if i in D
                then write(fout, tochar(ord(i)))
          end
    end;

(************************         putorn          ************************)
(* Prints ordinal position of each ornament code.                          *)
(***************************************************************************)
  procedure putorn(var fout : text; O : orntype);
    var
      i : ornament;
    begin
      write(fout, ' ');
      if O = []
        then write(fout, 'x')
        else
```

```
        begin
          for i := trill to sharpS do
            if i in O
              then write(fout, tochar(ord(i)))
        end
    end;

(************************       writenote        ************************)
(* Prints the current data for a note or rest.                          *)
(************************************************************************)
 procedure writenote(var f        : text; var buffer : buftype;
                     var partdata : pdat;     rest   : boolean);
   var
     t : fraction;
     x : note;
     staff : integer;                        { current staff in part    }
   begin
     with partdata do
       begin
         if rest
           then x := restval
           else x := current;
         if chord = nochord     { not in chord }
           then
             begin
               start := time;                { start time for note      }
               fracadd(time, start, x.dur);  { terminal time for note   }
               fracdiv(t, x.dur, meter);     { dur as part of measure   }
               measure := measno;            { current measure number   }
               fracadd(measno, measno, t);   { new measure time         }
               checklast(x, slurcurrent, slurlast, tiecurrent, tielast);
                                        { adjust dynamic for next note }
               dynadjust(current, restval, lastnote, lastrest)
             end;
         if dowrite
           then
             begin
               write(f, 'i', inum:1, '.');   { instrument number        }
                         { the following catches rests after new staff }
               staff := max(spacecode div 50, stafftrans div 50);
               write(f, staff:1);            { staff number, normal 0   }
               fracwrite(f, start);          { start time               }
               fracwrite(f, time);           { terminal time            }
               fracwrite(f, measure);        { measure position         }
               fracwrite(f, measno);         { meano at end             }
               write(f, x.pitch:5, ' ');     { pitch code               }
               fracwrite(f, x.dur);          { duration as fraction     }
               write(f, x.tie:3);            { tie field                }
               writeartic(f, x.artic);       { articulation codes       }
               write(f, x.slur:3);           { slur codes               }
               putorn(f, x.orn);             { ornament codes           }
               write(f, x.dyn1:5);           { dynamic code             }
               putdyn(f, x.dyn2);            { dynamic codes            }
               writeln(f)
             end;

          if (not rest) or (rest and not isdur(nextchar(buffer)))
           then                              { check for token delimiter }
             if not (nextchar(buffer) in [' ', '(', ')'])
               then error(f, buffer,24);

                                             { save last note and dot   }
         savelast(partdata, rest)            { save pertinent values    }
       end   { with partdata }
   end;  { writenote }

(************************************************************************)
(*                          DYNAMIC ROUTINES                            *)
(************************************************************************)

(************************         assign         ************************)
(* Assigns set of values of the enumerated type dynamic (see global type *)
(* definitions) to the dynamic field of the note.  Also sets an integer *)
(* representation of dynamic level (f = 80, ff = 90, fff = 100, etc.)   *)
(************************************************************************)
 procedure assign(var fout : text; var buffer : buftype; var currentdyn,
                          lastdyn : integer; var d2 : dynset);
   var
     d : dynamic;
   begin  { assign dynamic code }
     case nextchar(buffer) of
       'p': begin
              d := p;
              incr(buffer.bp);               { skip first p             }
              while nextchar(buffer) = 'p' do
                begin                        { adjust for pp ... pppppp }
                  d := pred(d);
                  incr(buffer.bp)
                end
            end;
       'f': begin
              d := f;
              incr(buffer.bp);               { skip first f             }
              while nextchar(buffer) = 'f' do
                begin                        { adjust for ff ... ffffff }
                  d := succ(d);
                  incr(buffer.bp)
                end;
              if nextchar(buffer) = 'z'      { check for fz             }
                then
                  begin
                    currentdyn := lastdyn;
                    d := sfz
                  end
              else if isdynamic(nextchar(buffer))
                then
                  begin                      { check for fp, ffmp ...   }
                    assign(fout, buffer, currentdyn, lastdyn, d2);
                    d := sfz
                  end
            end;

       'm': begin
              incr(buffer.bp);               { skip m                   }
```

```
                    if nextchar(buffer) = 'p'
                      then d := mp
                    else if nextchar(buffer) = 'f'
                      then d := mf
                    else
                      begin
                        error(fout, buffer, 19);    { char cannot follow 'm'    }
                        incr(buffer.bp)
                      end
                  end;

            's' : begin
                    while nextchar(buffer) in ['s', 'f', 'z'] do
                      incr(buffer.bp);
                    if isdynamic(nextchar(buffer))
                      then assign(fout, buffer, currentdyn, lastdyn, d2)
                      else currentdyn := lastdyn;
                    d := sfz
                  end
          end; { case }

          if isdynamic(nextchar(buffer))
            then incr(buffer.bp);
          d2 := d2 + [d];                             { add dynamic to set        }
          if d in [pppppp .. ffffff]
            then currentdyn := ord(d) * 10
        end;

(************************         crescendo         ************************)
(* Handles all cases of crescendo or diminuendo, whether over a single    *)
(* note or several.                                                         *)
(***************************************************************************)
  procedure crescendo(var f : text; var buffer : buftype;
                                                  var partdata : pdat);
    var
      increase : boolean;
      i        : integer;                             { identifier no. }
    begin
      with partdata do
        begin
          increase := nextchar(buffer) = '<';
          incr(buffer.bp);                            { skip < or >     }
          if isdynamic(nextchar(buffer))
            then
              begin          { crescendo and diminuendo over a single note }
                assign(f, buffer, current.dyn1, lastnote.dyn1, current.dyn2);
                if increase
                  then current.dyn2 := current.dyn2 + [cresc]
                  else current.dyn2 := current.dyn2 + [dim];
                if nextchar(buffer) in ['<', '>']
                  then
                    begin
                      if increase and (nextchar(buffer) = '>')
                        then current.dyn2 := current.dyn2
                                                    - [cresc] + [crescdim]
                      else if nextchar(buffer) = '<'
                        then current.dyn2 := current.dyn2 - [dim] + [dimcresc]
                      else error(f, buffer, 18);
                      incr(buffer.bp)                 { skip last < or > }
                    end
              end
          else if nextchar(buffer) in ['<', '>']
            then
              begin     { cresc and dim over single note, no dynamic mark }
                if increase and (nextchar(buffer) = '>')
                  then
                    begin
                      current.dyn1 := lastnote.dyn1 + 10;
                      current.dyn2 := current.dyn2 + [crescdim]
                    end
                else if not increase and (nextchar(buffer) = '<')
                  then
                    begin
                      current.dyn1 := lastnote.dyn1 - 10;
                      current.dyn2 := current.dyn2 + [dimcresc]
                    end
                else error(f, buffer, 18);
                incr(buffer.bp)
              end
          else if nextchar(buffer) = ' '
            then
              begin                 { single note crescendo or diminuendo }
                if increase
                  then
                    begin
                      current.dyn1 := lastnote.dyn1 + 10;
                      current.dyn2 := current.dyn2 + [cresc]
                    end
                  else
                    begin
                      current.dyn1 := lastnote.dyn1 - 10;
                      current.dyn2 := current.dyn2 + [dim]
                    end
              end
          else if isdigit(nextchar(buffer))
            then
              begin             { cresc or dim over several notes         }
                getint(f, buffer, i);
                if odd(i)
                  then
                    begin       { beginning of cresc or dim               }
                      if increase
                        then    { beginning of crescendo                  }
                          begin
                            if vol
                              then current.dyn1 := current.dyn1
                              else current.dyn1 := lastnote.dyn1;
                            current.dyn2 := current.dyn2 + [startcresc]
                          end
                        else    { beginning of diminuendo                 }
                          begin
                            if not vol
                              then current.dyn1 := lastnote.dyn1;
                            current.dyn2 := current.dyn2 + [startdim]
```

```
                    end;
                  savedyn := current.dyn1          { save dynamic level }
                end
              else
                begin           { end of cresc or dim                       }
                  if isdynamic(nextchar(buffer))
                    then        { ending dynamic level given                }
                      assign(f, buffer, current.dyn1, lastnote.dyn1,
                                                          current.dyn2)
                    else    { no ending level given, calculate default }
                      if increase
                        then current.dyn1 := savedyn + 10   { end of < }
                        else current.dyn1 := savedyn - 10;  { end of > }
                  if increase
                    then current.dyn2 := current.dyn2 + [endcresc]
                    else current.dyn2 := current.dyn2 + [enddim]
                end;
            end
          else error(f, buffer, 18)
      end     { with partdata }
  end;  { crescendo }


(************************        setdynamic        ************************)
(* Sets the value of the dynamic field of a note.  Calls procedure        *)
(* assign to calculate the code for a standard dynamic marking (f, p, mf,*)
(* mp, sfz, etc.), and calls crescendo if a crescendo or diminuendo is   *)
(* in effect.                                                             *)
(**************************************************************************)
  procedure setdynamic(var f        : text;
                       var buffer   : buftype;
                       var partdata : pdat;
                           rest     : boolean);
    var
      xparen : boolean;                      { true if extra parenthesis }

    begin
      with partdata do
        begin
          incr(buffer.bp);                   { skip 'v'                  }
          xparen := nextchar(buffer) = '(';
          if xparen
            then incr(buffer.bp);            { skip parenthesis          }
          if isdynamic(nextchar(buffer))
            then
              begin
                assign(f, buffer, current.dyn1, lastnote.dyn1, current.dyn2);
                vol := true
              end;
          while nextchar(buffer) in ['<', '>']  { process cresc and dim  }
            do crescendo(f, buffer, partdata);
          if xparen and (nextchar(buffer) = ')')
            then incr(buffer.bp);            { skip parenthesis          }
          restval.dyn1 := current.dyn1;      { copy dynamic for rests    }
          restval.dyn2 := current.dyn2
        end    { with partdata }
    end;
```

```
(**************************************************************************)
(*                        PUSH AND SKIP OPERATORS                         *)
(**************************************************************************)

(************************        skipmeasure        ***********************)
(* Called by pushcode when ~nW is encoded. Advances position pointer for *)
(* part a duration equal to n full measures.                              *)
(**************************************************************************)
  procedure skipmeasures(var f : text; var buffer : buftype;
                         var measno, meter, time : fraction);
    var
      number : integer;                    { number of measures of rest }
      i      : integer;
    begin
      getint(f, buffer, number);
      if nextchar(buffer) = 'w'
        then
          begin
            incr(buffer.bp);               { skip 'w'                   }
            for i := 1 to number do
              begin
                measno.num := measno.num + 1;
                fracadd(time, time, meter)
              end
          end
        else error(f, buffer, 21)          { illegal skip operator      }
    end;

(************************        skipcode        **************************)
(* The skip operator ~ddd (where ddd is durations encoded as in rests)   *)
(* is used to advance the position pointer without recourse to rests and *)
(* empty measures.  If called immediately after a comma, the position    *)
(* pointer is reset to previous value after push is calculated.          *)
(**************************************************************************)
  procedure durcode(var f : text; var buffer : buftype;
                    var x , xdot : fraction; rest : boolean); forward;

  procedure skipcode(var f : text; var buffer : buftype;
                                                  var partdata : pdat);
    var
      t, tdot : fraction;                            { temp for durs   }
      partmeas : fraction;
    begin
      with partdata do
        begin
          incr(buffer.bp);                           { skip '~'        }
          if isdigit(nextchar(buffer))
            then skipmeasures(f, buffer, measno, meter, time)
          else if isdur(nextchar(buffer))
            then
              begin                       { advance position pointer }
                while isdur(nextchar(buffer)) do
                  begin
                    tdot.num := 1;                   { initialize dot  }
                    durcode(f, buffer, t, tdot, true); { get duration  }
                    fracadd(time, time, t);          { add to pointer  }
                    fracdiv(partmeas, t, meter);
```

```
                fracadd(measno, measno, partmeas)
              end
            end
          else error(f, buffer, 21)                 { illegal skip operator }
        end   { with partdata }
    end;

(***********************         pushcode         ***********************)
(* For push operator, time is saved before forward skip, then after next *)
(* item is correctly placed, the previous time is restored.             *)
(*************************************************************************)
  procedure setcode (var f         : text;
                     var buffer    : buftype;
                     var group     : grouptable;
                     var partdata  : pdat;
                         rest      : boolean); forward;

  procedure comma(var f         : text;
                  var buffer    : buftype;
                  var group     : grouptable;
                  var partdata  : pdat;
                      rest      : boolean);  forward;

  procedure pushcode(var f         : text;  var buffer : buftype;
                     var group     : grouptable;
                     var partdata  : pdat;  rest : boolean);
    var
      t1, t2 : fraction;
    begin { push operator }
      with partdata do
        begin
          pushing := true;                      { see comma              }
          t1 := time;                           { save terminal time     }
          writenote(f, buffer, partdata, rest);
          t2 := time;                           { save new terminal time }
          time := t1;                           { restore old time       }
          skipcode(f, buffer, partdata);        { push time ahead        }
          if nextchar(buffer) = ','
            then comma (f, buffer, group, partdata, rest);
          time := t2                            { restore previous time  }
        end   { with partdata }
    end;  { push operator }


(*************************************************************************)
(*                            CHORD ROUTINES                             *)
(*************************************************************************)

(***********************           comma          ***********************)
(* Skips commas (indicating simultaneities) and then calls setcode recur-*)
(* sively to interpret the next note.                                   *)
(*************************************************************************)
  procedure comma { var f         : text;
                    var buffer    : buftype;
                    var group     : grouptable;
                    var partdata  : pdat;
                        rest      : boolean };
    var
      t : note;
    begin { comma }
      while nextchar(buffer) = ',' do
        incr(buffer.bp);                       { skip commas                 }
      if nextchar(buffer) = 'v'
        then
          begin
            setdynamic(f, buffer, partdata, rest);
            writenote(f, buffer, partdata, rest)
          end
      else if nextchar(buffer) = '-'
        then pushcode(f, buffer, group, partdata, rest)
      else
        with partdata do
          begin { full encoded chord }
            t := current;                      { save previous values        }
            setcode(f,buffer, group, partdata, rest);
            chord := fullcode;                 { signal in-chord condition   }
            current := t;                      { restore note                }
            if not pushing
              then writenote(f, buffer, partdata, rest);
            pushing := false
          end
    end;  { comma }

(***********************         spacepat         ***********************)
(* Called when a vertical bar '|' is encountered indicating a chord in   *)
(* space pattern format.  Since the attributes for the whole chord are   *)
(* given after the final '|', a boolean variable dowrite is set to false.*)
(* This makes it possible to enter the default chain and traverse it to  *)
(* the end without writing a note.  Everything except writing is accom-  *)
(* plished, even setting the starting time for the chord.  Thus some     *)
(* attributes are set first, and remain in effect while others are reset *)
(* while falling out of recursion.  If the vertical bar is followed by a *)
(* space code, the procedure chain is reentered to set the specific      *)
(* values for this note that will override the defaults for the chord.   *)
(*************************************************************************)
  procedure setdur(var f         : text;
                   var buffer    : buftype;
                   var group     : grouptable;
                   var partdata  : pdat;
                       rest      : boolean); forward;

  procedure spacepat(var f         : text;
                     var buffer    : buftype;
                     var group     : grouptable;
                     var partdata  : pdat;
                         rest      : boolean);
    var
      t : note;

    begin
      with partdata do
        begin
          incr(buffer.bp);                            { skip '|'           }
          if not isdigit(nextchar(buffer))
```

```
        then
          begin                                  { set chordal defaults  }
            dowrite := false;                    { disable writenote     }
                                                 { enter chain at setdur }
            setdur(f, buffer, group, partdata, rest);
            chord := basinc;                     { signal space pattern  }
            dowrite := true                      { enable writenote      }
          end
        else
          begin                              { set values for this note  }
            t := current;
                                             { enter chain at space code }
            setcode(f, buffer, group, partdata, rest);
            if t.tie <> 0
              then current.tie := t.tie;
            current.pitch := t.pitch;        { set tie field             }
            chord := spacpat                 { signal space pat  chord   }
          end;
        writenote(f, buffer, partdata, rest)
      end
  end;  { spacepat }

(************************        setchord        ************************)
(* Checks for chords (full or space-pattern), and then calls writenote   *)
(*************************************************************************)
procedure setchord(var f        : text;
                   var buffer   : buftype;
                   var group    : grouptable;
                   var partdata : pdat;
                       rest     : boolean);
  begin { setchord }
    if nextchar(buffer) = ','
      then comma(f, buffer, group, partdata, rest)
    else if nextchar(buffer) = '|'
      then spacepat(f, buffer, group, partdata, rest)
    else writenote(f, buffer, partdata, rest)
  end;  { setchord }


(*************************************************************************)
(*                         OTHER NOTE ATTRIBUTES                         *)
(*************************************************************************)

(************************         setins         ************************)
(* Gets new instrument number.                                           *)
(*************************************************************************)
procedure setins(var f : text; var buffer : buftype; var inum : integer);
  var
    t : integer;
  begin { setins }
    incr(buffer.bp);                               { skip 'I'     }
    getint(f, buffer, t);
    if t < 0                                       { check range  }
      then error(f, buffer, 15)
    else if t > maxins
      then error(f, buffer, 16)
    else
      begin
        inum := t;
        writeln('p', t:1, '  new instrument number')
      end
  end;  { setins }

(************************         setslur        ************************)
(* Sets the slur field for the note being read.  For a two-note slur     *)
(* encoded only with an L, the slur field is set to 1.  When the second  *)
(* note of the two-note slur is read, procedure checklast will set its   *)
(* slur field to 2.  For all other slurs, which are encoded with an odd  *)
(* identifier number at the beginning and an even identifier number at   *)
(* the end, the id number is the value assigned to the slur field.       *)
(*************************************************************************)
procedure setslur(var f           : text;
                  var buffer      : buftype;
                  var x           : note;
                  var slurcurrent : boolean);

  var
    digit : integer;                        { identifier number        }
  begin  { set slur field }
    incr(buffer.bp);                        { skip 'L'                 }
    if isdigit(nextchar(buffer))
      then
        begin                               { read and store id number  }
          getint(f, buffer, digit);
          x.slur := x.slur * 10 + digit     { adjust for multiple slurs }
        end
      else
        begin                               { start of two-note slur    }
          x.slur := 1;
          slurcurrent := true
        end
  end;  { set slur field }

(************************       setornament      ************************)
(* Sets the ornament field of the note, using set of ornament.           *)
(*************************************************************************)
procedure setornament(var f : text; var buffer : buftype;
                                               var partdata : pdat);

  var
    x      : char;
    xparen : boolean;
  begin
    incr(buffer.bp);                               { skip 'O'           }
    with partdata, current do
      begin
        x := nextchar(buffer);
        if isorn(x)
          then
            case x of
          't', ';'  : orn := orn + [trill];
              'm'   : orn := orn + [mordent];
              '?'   : orn := orn + [turn];
            end  { case }
          else error(f, buffer, 28);               { bad ornament code  }
        incr(buffer.bp);                           { skip ornament code }
```

```
while isa(nextchar(buffer)) do
  begin { process attach code }
    incr(buffer.bp);          { skip A }
    x := nextchar(buffer);
    if x in ['n', 'e', 's']
      then
        case x of
          'n' : begin { north }
                  incr(buffer.bp);           { skip 'N'              }
                  xparen := nextchar(buffer) = '(';
                  if xparen
                    then incr(buffer.bp);  { skip parenthesis    }
                  x := nextchar(buffer);
                  if isacc(x)
                    then
                      case x of
                        '#' : orn := orn + [sharpN];
                        '-' : orn := orn + [flatN];
                        '*' : orn := orn + [natN]
                      end { case }
                    else error(f, buffer, 30); { bad accidental }
                  incr(buffer.bp);    { skip accidental }
                  if xparen and (nextchar(buffer) = ')')
                    then incr(buffer.bp)    { skip parenthesis    }
                end; { north }
          'e' : begin { east   }
                  incr(buffer.bp);           { skip 'E'              }
                  xparen := nextchar(buffer) = '(';
                  if xparen
                    then incr(buffer.bp);  { skip parenthesis    }
                  x := nextchar(buffer);
                  if isacc(x)
                    then
                      case x of
                        '#' : orn := orn + [sharpE];
                        '-' : orn := orn + [flatE];
                        '*' : orn := orn + [natE]
                      end { case }
                    else error(f, buffer, 30); { bad accidental }
                  incr(buffer.bp);    { skip accidental }
                  if xparen and (nextchar(buffer) = ')')
                    then incr(buffer.bp)    { skip parenthesis    }
                end; { east   }
          's' : begin { south }
                  incr(buffer.bp);           { skip 'S'              }
                  xparen := nextchar(buffer) = '(';
                  if xparen
                    then incr(buffer.bp);  { skip parenthesis    }
                  x := nextchar(buffer);
                  if isacc(x)
                    then
                      case x of
                        '#' : orn := orn + [sharpS];
                        '-' : orn := orn + [flatS];
                        '*' : orn := orn + [natS]
                      end { case }
                    else error(f, buffer, 30); { bad accidental }
                  incr(buffer.bp);    { skip accidental }
                  if xparen and (nextchar(buffer) = ')')
                    then incr(buffer.bp)    { skip parenthesis    }
                end   { south }
        end   { case }
      else error(f, buffer, 29)          { bad attach direction   }
  end   { process attach code }
    end { with partdata, current }
  end;  { setornament }

(************************             setdict           ************************)
(* Sets the articulation field of the note according to appropriate dic- *)
(* tionary codes.                                                          *)
(*****************************************************************************)
 procedure setdict(var f : text; var buffer : buftype;
                                                   var partdata : pdat);

   var
     x : char;
   begin
     incr(buffer.bp);                                        { skip '?'   }
     with partdata, current do
       begin
         x := nextchar(buffer);
         if isdict(x)
           then
             case x of
               'd'  : artic := artic + [downbow];
               'v'  : artic := artic + [upbow];
               'q'  : artic := artic + [snap];                { snap pizz }
               'r'  : begin
                        artic := artic + [arco];
                        artic := artic - [pizz];
                        sticky := sticky + [arco];
                        sticky := sticky - [pizz]
                      end;
               'z'  : begin
                        artic := artic + [pizz];
                        artic := artic - [arco];
                        sticky := sticky + [pizz];
                        sticky := sticky - [arco]
                      end;
               'o'  : begin
                        artic := artic + [open];
                        artic := artic - [stopped];
                        sticky := sticky - [stopped]
                      end;
               '+'  : begin
                        artic := artic + [stopped];
                        artic := artic - [open];
                        sticky := sticky + [stopped];
                      end;
               'h'  : begin
                        artic := artic + [hauptstimme];
                        artic := artic - [nebenstimme];
                        sticky := sticky - [nebenstimme];
                        sticky := sticky + [hauptstimme]
                      end;
```

```
              'n'   : begin
                        artic := artic + [nebenstimme];
                        artic := artic - [hauptstimme];
                        sticky := sticky + [nebenstimme];
                        sticky := sticky - [hauptstimme]
                      end;
              '~'   : begin
                        artic := artic + [terminator];
                        sticky := sticky - [hauptstimme, nebenstimme]
                      end
          end  { case }
        else error(f, buffer, 26);                  { bad dictionary code  }
        incr(buffer.bp)                             { skip dictionary code }
      end { with partdata, current }
  end;  { setdict }

(************************          setartic          ************************)
(* Sets the articulation field of the note being read.  For now, any      *)
(* integers following fermata codes are skipped.                           *)
(***************************************************************************)
 procedure setartic(var f : text; var buffer : buftype;
                    var partdata : pdat);
  var
    x : char;
  begin
    with partdata, current do
      begin
        x := nextchar(buffer);
        case x of
          '''' : artic := artic + [staccato];
          '"'  : artic := artic + [wedgeaccent];
          '_'  : artic := artic + [tenuto];
          '>'  : artic := artic + [accent];
          '<'  : artic := artic + [vaccent];
          ';'  : artic := artic + [fermata]
        end; { case }
        incr(buffer.bp);                          { skip articulation code }
        while isdigit(nextchar(buffer)) do
          incr(buffer.bp)                         { skip digits            }
      end { with partdata, current }
  end;  { setartic }

(************************          subscan           ************************)
(* Takes care of indeterminate portion of coding order: articulation,     *)
(* dictionary codes, slurs, and ornaments.  This is the place to add      *)
(* fingering codes if desired at a later date.                             *)
(***************************************************************************)
 procedure subscan(var f        : text;
                   var buffer   : buftype;
                   var group    : grouptable;
                   var partdata : pdat;
                       rest     : boolean);
  var
    x : char;
  begin
    with partdata, current do
      begin
        artic := sticky;                         { init articulation field }
        orn := [];                               { clear ornament field    }
        slur  := 0;                              { initialize slur field   }
        x := nextchar(buffer);
        while isartic(x) or isslur(x) or isquest(x) or isoh(x) do
          begin                                  { slur, art, or dict code }
            if isslur(x)
              then setslur(f, buffer, current, slurcurrent)
            else if isquest(x)                   { dictionary codes        }
              then setdict(f, buffer, partdata)
            else if isoh(x)                      { ornaments               }
              then setornament(f, buffer, partdata)
            else setartic(f, buffer, partdata);

            x := nextchar(buffer)
          end;

        restval.artic := current.artic;        { assign for rests also  }
        restval.slur  := current.slur;         { assign for rests also  }
        setchord(f, buffer, group, partdata, rest)
      end { with partdata }
  end;        { subscan }

(************************          setstem           ************************)
(* Dummy Procedure for now.                                                *)
(***************************************************************************)
 procedure setstem(var f        : text;
                   var buffer   : buftype;
                   var group    : grouptable;
                   var partdata : pdat;
                       rest     : boolean);
  begin { setstem }
    if isstem(nextchar(buffer))
      then incr(buffer.bp);         { skip stem code }
    subscan(f, buffer, group, partdata, rest)
  end;  { setstem }

(************************          settie            ************************)
(* Sets the tie field of the note to true if the note is tied to the      *)
(* next note.  It then calls setartic to check for articulations.         *)
(***************************************************************************)
 procedure settie(var f : text;
                  var buffer : buftype;
                  var group : grouptable;
                  var partdata : pdat;
                      rest : boolean);
  var
    x : integer;
  begin { settie }
    with partdata do
      begin
        if not (chord = basinc)                  { not base increment chord }
          then
            begin { set tie field }
              if nextchar(buffer) <> 'j'
```

```
          then
            begin { no tie }
              current.tie := 0;
              restval.tie := 0;
              tiecurrent := false
            end   { no tie }
          else if isdigit(buffer.B[buffer.bp+1])
            then
              while nextchar(buffer) = 'j' do
                begin                                { compound tie }
                  incr(buffer.bp);                   { skip 'j'     }
                  if isdigit(nextchar(buffer))
                    then
                      begin
                        getint(f, buffer, x);
                        current.tie := 10 * current.tie + x
                      end
                    else error(f, buffer, 27)        { no number    }
                end
              else
                begin                                { simple tie   }
                  incr(buffer.bp);                   { skip 'j'     }
                  current.tie := 1;
                  tiecurrent := true
                end;  { simple tie }
        restval.tie := current.tie
      end;  { set tie field }
    setstem(f, buffer, group, partdata, rest)
  end { with partdata }
end;   { settie }


(**********************************************************************)
(*                    RHYTHM AND DURATION ROUTINES                    *)
(**********************************************************************)

(***********************          paren         ***********************)
(* In DARMS, parentheses indicate beams (short form of encoding).  If a *)
(* left parenthesis is encountered, the level is incremented and the    *)
(* value of the default duration is halved.  For a right parenthesis,   *)
(* the level is decremented and the default note value is doubled.  If  *)
(* the level becomes less than 0, indicating unbalanced parentheses, an *)
(* error message is printed.  When the level is 0, the duration and dot *)
(* value at last note-time are restored, thus durations propagate to the *)
(* next note after a beam-group.                                         *)
(**********************************************************************)
procedure paren(var f : text; var buffer : buftype; var partdata : pdat);
  begin
    with partdata do
      begin
        if nextchar(buffer) = '('
          then
            begin                          { left parenthesis           }
              level := level + 1;
              default.den := default.den * 2
            end  { left parenthesis }
          else
            begin                          { right parenthesis          }
              level := level - 1;
              default.den := default.den div 2
            end;

        if level > 0
          then
            begin                          { reset duration and dot     }
              current.dur := default;
              restval.dur := default;
              dot.den := default.den * 2;
              restdot.den := default.den * 2
            end
        else if level = 0
          then
            begin                          { restore last duration and dot }
              dot := lastdot;
              restdot := lrestdot;
              current := lastnote;
              restval := lastrest
            end
        else if level < 0
          then error(f, buffer, 7);        { unbalanced parens          }
        incr(buffer.bp)
      end   { with partdata }
  end;  { paren }


(***********************        setgroup        ***********************)
(* Adjusts the duration code of a note in a grouplet by multiplying     *)
(* fractional duration by grouplet constant.                            *)
(**********************************************************************)
procedure setgroup(var f      : text;
                   var buffer : buftype;
                   var group  : grouptable;
                   var x      : note);
  var
    id : integer;                          { grouplet identifier number }
  begin { setgroup }
    getint(f, buffer, id);                 { read grouplet id number    }
    fracmult(x.dur, x.dur, group[id])      { multiply by grouplet const }
  end;  { setgroup }


(***********************         setdot         ***********************)
(* Processes dots in duration codes.                                    *)
(**********************************************************************)
procedure setdot(var buffer : buftype; var x, xdot : fraction);
  begin { setdot }
    while nextchar(buffer) = '.' do
      begin
        fracadd(x, x, xdot);
        xdot.den := xdot.den * 2;
        incr(buffer.bp)
      end
  end;  { setdot }
```

```
(************************        durcode          ************************)
(* Sets the duration of a note or rest according to the value of encoded *)
(* durations.  It also sets the value of dot to be half of the duration  *)
(* of the note.  It then calls setdot to adjust the duration and dot     *)
(* values for possible following dots.                                    *)
(*************************************************************************)
 procedure durcode( var f        : text;
                    var buffer   : buftype;
                    var x , xdot : fraction;
                    rest         : boolean );
   begin { set dur from durcode }
     if isdur(nextchar(buffer))
       then
         begin { set duration }
           x.num := 1;                         { set numerator            }
           xdot.num := 1;
           case nextchar(buffer) of
             'w': x.den :=   1;                { set denominator according }
             'h': x.den :=   2;                { to duration code          }
             'q': x.den :=   4;
             'e': x.den :=   8;
             's': x.den :=  16;
             't': x.den :=  32;
             'x': x.den :=  64;
             'y': x.den := 128;
             'z': x.den := 256;
             'g': begin { grace note }
                    x.num := 0;
                    x.den := 1
                  end   { grace note }
           end; { case }
           incr(buffer.bp);                    { skip duration code        }
           if nextchar(buffer) = 'w'           { breves,  longas, etc      }
             then
               while nextchar(buffer) = 'w' do
                 begin
                   x.num := x.num * 2;
                   incr(buffer.bp)
                 end
           else if nextchar(buffer) = 'z'      { dur shorter than 1/256    }
             then
               while nextchar(buffer) = 'z' do
                 begin
                   x.den := x.den * 2;
                   incr(buffer.bp)
                 end;
           if isdur(nextchar(buffer)) and (not rest)
             then
               begin
                 error(f, buffer, 9);
                 incr(buffer.bp)
               end;
           if x.num <> 0   { grace note }
             then xdot.den := x.den * 2
         end;  { set duration }
     setdot(buffer, x, xdot)                   { adjust for dots           }
   end;  { durcode }
```

```
(************************        setdur          ************************)
(* Calls durcode to set duration and dot values, then calls settie.     *)
(************************************************************************)
 procedure setdur( var f : text;
                   var buffer : buftype;
                   var group : grouptable;
                   var partdata : pdat;
                       rest : boolean );
  begin
    with partdata do
      begin
        if rest
          then
            begin { process rest }
              durcode(f, buffer, restval.dur, restdot, rest);
              if isdigit(nextchar(buffer))
                then setgroup(f, buffer, group, restval)
            end   { process rest }
          else
            begin { process note }
              durcode(f, buffer, current.dur, dot, rest);
              if isdigit(nextchar(buffer))
                then setgroup(f, buffer, group, current)
            end;  { process note }
        settie(f, buffer, group, partdata, rest)
      end   { with partdata }
  end;
```

```
(************************        grouplet          ************************)
(* Sets fractional value of constant for specified grouplet definer.     *)
(* This value will be used to adjust the fractional duration notes       *)
(* within grouplets.  The constant is stored as a fraction in the        *)
(* array "group" and is referenced by the grouplet's identifier number.  *)
(*************************************************************************)
 procedure grouplet(var f : text; var buffer : buftype;
                    var group : grouptable);
   var
     x, y      : fraction;
     dot       : fraction;
     num       : integer;
     id1, id2  : integer;                    { grouplet identifier numbers }
   begin
     getint(f, buffer, num);
     durcode(f,buffer, x, dot, false);            { calc fractional value   }
     x.num := x.num * num;                        { adjust numerator        }
     getint(f, buffer, id1);                      { read identifier number  }
     incr(buffer.bp);                             { skip colon              }
     if isdigit(nextchar(buffer))
       then getint(f, buffer, num)
       else num := 1;                             { default for numerator   }
     if isdur(nextchar(buffer))
       then durcode(f, buffer, y, dot, false)
       else
         begin
           y.den := x.den;                        { default for duration    }
           y.num := 1
         end;
```

```
      y.num := y.num * num;
      fracdiv(group[id1], y, x);                { calculate constant      }
      if isdigit(nextchar(buffer))
        then
          begin                                 { for nested grouplet     }
            getint(f, buffer, id2);
            fracmult(group[id1], group[id1], group[id2])
          end
    end;  { grouplet }


(************************        restmeasures        ************************)
(* Is called when a digit appears immediately after the rest indicator     *)
(* 'r', signifying a number of measures of whole rests.  For n bars of     *)
(* rests, the procedure prints n - 1 rests (equal to the duration of the   *)
(* current meter signature) followed by barlines, then prints a final      *)
(* rest, without the barline.  Thus 10 bars of rest followed by a meter    *)
(* change followed by 1 bar rest are encoded:                              *)
(*                   r10w / !m3/4 r1w /                                    *)
(* Note that a single bar rest is encoded r1w, not rw, so that the value   *)
(* of a measure will be output rather than that of a whole note.           *)
(***************************************************************************)
  procedure newmeasure(var f         : text;
                       var buffer    : buftype;
                       var partdata  : pdat;
                           key       : integer); forward;

  procedure restmeasures(var f         : text;
                         var buffer    : buftype;
                         var group     : grouptable;
                         var partdata  : pdat;
                             rest      : boolean);

    var
      number: integer;                        { number of measures of rest }
      i     : integer;

    begin { restmeasures }
      with partdata do
        begin
          getint(f, buffer, number);
          if nextchar(buffer) = 'w'
            then
              begin
                incr(buffer.bp);              { skip 'w'                  }
                restval.dur := meter;
                for i := 1 to number - 1 do
                  begin
                    writenote(f, buffer, partdata, isrest);
                    newmeasure(f, buffer, partdata, 0)
                  end;
                writenote(f, buffer, partdata, isrest)
              end
            else error(f, buffer, 13)
        end   { with partdata }
    end;

(************************         anacrusis          ************************)
(* Used to set the raw time, measure, and meter for segments that do not  *)
(* begin on beat one, bar one.                                            *)
(***************************************************************************)
  procedure anacrusis(var f : text; var buffer    : buftype;
                                    var partdata  : pdattab);
    var
      tempdur, tempdot, xmeasure   : fraction;
      tempbeat, tempmeter, pickup  : fraction;
      negative : boolean;
      i    : integer;
    begin
      incr(buffer.bp);                                        { skip !        }
      setmeter(f, buffer, partdata[0], false);
      tempbeat  := partdata[0].beatnote;
      tempmeter := partdata[0].meter;
      write(f, 'c: anacrusis: meter= ');
      fracwrite(f, tempmeter); writeln;
      if nextchar(buffer) = ','
        then incr(buffer.bp);
      xmeasure.num := 1;                                      { init measure }
      xmeasure.den := 1;
      getint(f, buffer, xmeasure.num);
      if nextchar(buffer) = ','
        then incr(buffer.bp);
      negative := nextchar(buffer) = '-';
      if issign(nextchar(buffer))
        then incr(buffer.bp);                                 { skip sign     }
      skipbuf(buffer);

      pickup.num := 0;                       { calc value of anacrusis     }
      pickup.den := 1;
      while isdur(nextchar(buffer)) do
        begin
          durcode(f, buffer, tempdur, tempdot, true);
          fracadd(pickup, pickup, tempdur)
        end;

      tempdur := pickup;                     { convert to part of measure }
      fracdiv(tempdur, tempdur, tempmeter);

      if negative                            { adjust measure position     }
        then fracsub(xmeasure, xmeasure, tempdur)
        else fracadd(xmeasure, xmeasure, tempdur);
             { set oldmeasure (off set for anacrusis)}

      if negative                            { init value for lastbar      }
        then fracsub(pickup, pickup, tempmeter)
        else pickup.num := -pickup.num;

      for i := 0 to maxins do
        with partdata[i] do
          begin
            measno   := xmeasure;            { set measure number          }
            meter    := tempmeter;           { set meter                   }
            beatnote := tempbeat;            { set beat note               }
            lastbar  := pickup               { fudge lastbar               }
          end;
```

```
      write(f, 'c   starting measure reset to ');
      fracwrite(f, xmeasure); writeln;
      if nextchar(buffer) = '['
        then
          begin
            incr(buffer.bp);
            getint(f, buffer, tempdur.num);
            skipbuf(buffer);
            if nextchar(buffer) = '/'
              then incr(buffer.bp);
            skipbuf(buffer);
            getint(f, buffer, tempdur.den);
            skipbuf(buffer);
            if nextchar(buffer) = ']'
              then incr(buffer.bp);

            for i := 0 to maxins do
              with partdata[i] do
                begin
                  time := tempdur;
                  fracadd(lastbar, lastbar, tempdur)
                end;
            write(f, 'c starttime set to fraction ');
            fracwrite(f, tempdur); writeln
          end { real time }
    end; { anacrusis }


(************************          setrest          ************************)
(* Calls setdur with the last parameter (rest) set to true.                 *)
(***************************************************************************)
  procedure setrest(var f        : text;
                    var buffer   : buftype;
                    var group    : grouptable;
                    var partdata : pdat;
                        rest     : boolean);
    begin { setrest }
      incr(buffer.bp);
      if isdigit(nextchar(buffer))
        then restmeasures(f, buffer, group, partdata, rest)
      else if nextchar(buffer) in [' ', '.', ')', '(']
        then setdur(f, buffer, group, partdata, rest)
      else if isdur(nextchar(buffer))
        then                             { allow for concatenated rests }
          while isdur(nextchar(buffer)) do
            setdur(f, buffer, group, partdata, rest)
      else error(f, buffer, 12)          { bad rest code                }
    end; { setrest }

(************************        getnotehead        ************************)
(* Returns note head (dummy procedure).                                     *)
(***************************************************************************)
  procedure getnotehead(var buffer : buftype);
    begin
      incr(buffer.bp);                                      { skip n    }
      incr(buffer.bp)                                       { skip code }
    end;

(************************          sethead          ************************)
(* Sets note head code.  (place holder for now)                             *)
(***************************************************************************)
  procedure sethead(var f        : text;
                    var buffer   : buftype;
                    var group    : grouptable;
                    var partdata : pdat;
                        rest     : boolean);
    begin
      if nextchar(buffer) = 'n'
        then getnotehead(buffer);
      setdur(f, buffer, group, partdata, rest)
    end;

(***************************************************************************)
(*                          DARMS PITCH ROUTINES                             *)
(***************************************************************************)

(************************        accidental        ************************)
(* Modifies the contents of the adjust array to reflect accidentals.        *)
(***************************************************************************)
  procedure accidental(var buffer : buftype; var adjust : pitchtable;
                                                 cnc    : integer);

    var
      t : integer;
    begin
      if isacc(nextchar(buffer))
        then
          begin
            t := 0;
            while isacc(nextchar(buffer)) do
              begin
                case nextchar(buffer) of
                  '#' : t := t + 1;
                  '-' : t := t - 1;
                  '*' : t := 0
                end;  { case }
                incr(buffer.bp)                       { skip accidental }
              end;
            adjust[cnc] := t
          end
    end;  { accidental }

(************************          setnote          ************************)
(* Is passed a space code, which it converts to continuous name code.      *)
(* The cnc is used to calculate the name class, pitch class, and octave.  *)
(* If an accidental is found "accidental" is called.  If the next charac-*)
(* ter is a '+', indicating a chord in base-incr format, the interval is *)
(* read and setnote is called recursively on (spacecode + int).           *)
(***************************************************************************)
  procedure setnote (var f        : text;
                     var buffer   : buftype;
                     var group    : grouptable;
                     var partdata : pdat;
                         rest     : boolean);
    var
      octave, nc, pc, cnc : integer;
```

```
    interval : integer;
    t        : integer;
  begin
    with partdata do
      begin
        cnc := spacecode mod 50 + clef;
        if isacc(nextchar(buffer))
          then accidental(buffer, adjust, cnc);
        if nextchar(buffer) = '+' then
          begin
            incr(buffer.bp);                        { skip '+'           }
            getint(f, buffer, interval);
            t := spacecode;                         { save space code    }
            spacecode := spacecode + interval;
            setnote(f, buffer, group, partdata, rest);
            spacecode := t;                         { restore space code }
            chord := basinc                         { base incr type     }
          end;
        nc     := cnc mod 7;
        octave := cnc div 7;
        pc     := imod(scale(nc) + adjust[cnc], 12);
        if not tielast or (ord(chord) > 0)
          then
            begin
              current.pitch := cbr(octave, pc, nc);   { set pitch code }
              if trans <> 0                 { and transpose if necessary }
                then current.pitch := add(current.pitch, trans)
            end;
        sethead(f, buffer, group, partdata, rest) { call note head proc }
      end
  end;  { setnote }

(**************************************************************************)
(*                          METER SIGNATURES                              *)
(**************************************************************************)

(************************           complex        ************************)
(* Processes meters of the form (2 + 3)/4.                                 *)
(**************************************************************************)
 procedure complex(var f : text; var buffer : buftype;
                                                var beats : fraction);
   var
     temp: fraction;
   begin
     temp.den := 1;
     incr(buffer.bp);  { skip + }
     getint(f, buffer, temp.num);
     fracadd(beats, beats, temp)
   end;

(************************           uneven         ************************)
(* Processes meters such as 3-1/2/4, i.e., 7/8.                            *)
(**************************************************************************)
 procedure uneven(var f : text; var buffer : buftype;
                                                var beats : fraction);
   var
     temp : fraction;
   begin
     incr(buffer.bp);                                         { skip '-' }
     getint(f, buffer, temp.num);
     incr(buffer.bp);                                         { skip '/' }
     getint(f, buffer, temp.den);
     fracadd(beats, beats, temp)
   end;

(************************          tempmeter       ************************)
(* Sets a temporary meter signature, meter, for each configuration such  *)
(* as x:y or x+y:z. The procedure is called by getbeats at the beginning *)
(* and then every time another such configuration occurs within the      *)
(* meter signature.                                                        *)
(**************************************************************************)
 procedure tempmeter(var f : text; var buffer: buftype;
                     var meter: fraction; var beatnote: fraction);
   var
     dot : fraction;
   begin
     getint(f, buffer, meter.num);
     while nextchar(buffer) = '+' do
       complex(f, buffer, meter);
     if nextchar(buffer) = '-'
       then uneven(f, buffer, meter);
     if (nextchar(buffer) = ':') or (nextchar(buffer) = '/')
       then
         begin
           incr(buffer.bp);
           if isdur(nextchar(buffer))        { allow for things like 3:h }
             then durcode(f, buffer, beatnote, dot, false)
             else getint(f, buffer, beatnote.den)
         end
       else error(f, buffer, 11)
   end;

(************************          getbeats        ************************)
(* Finds the number of beats in the measure, checking for meters such as *)
(* (3 + 4)/4 and (3-1/2)/4, also allowing for meters notated something   *)
(* like 2:4, 2/4, (2/4), and 3:h.                                          *)
(**************************************************************************)
 procedure getbeats(var f : text; var buffer: buftype;
                              var meter, beatnote : fraction);
   var
     meter2: fraction;
     beat2note: fraction;
   begin
     meter2.num := 1;
     meter2.den := 1;
     beat2note.num := 1;
     beat2note.den := 1;
     tempmeter(f, buffer, meter, beatnote);      { first given meter sig. }
     while nextchar(buffer) = '+' do
       begin
         incr(buffer.bp);
         tempmeter(f, buffer, meter2, beat2note);
         if beatnote.den <> beat2note.den        { different beat values  }
           then
```

```
          begin                              { convert to same        }
            if beat2note.den > beatnote.den
              then
                begin
                  meter.num := meter.num
                                 * (beat2note.den div beatnote.den);
                  beatnote.den := beat2note.den
                end
              else
                begin
                  meter2.num := meter2.num
                                 * (beatnote.den div beat2note.den);
                  beat2note.den := beatnote.den
                end
          end;
        fracadd(meter, meter, meter2)
      end
  end;


(************************       setmeter       ************************)
(* Reads a meter signature encoded in any of several fashions.  Converts *)
(* meter into beats (as a fraction to allow for non-integer values) and  *)
(* beatnote (also as a fraction to allow for compound meters such as 6/8,*)
(* where the beat note will be a 3/8 note).  Calls getbeats to compute   *)
(* the actual number of beats in the measure.  Later on it checks for a  *)
(* compound meter in the following fashion: If the number of beats is    *)
(* evenly divisible by 3 and is greater than 3, then it is a compound    *)
(* meter.  Then the number of beats is divided by 3, and the beatnote is *)
(* multiplied by 3.                                                      *)
(***********************************************************************)
 procedure setmeter(var f        : text; var buffer  : buftype;
                    var partdata : pdat;     print   : boolean);
  begin
    with partdata do
      begin
        meter.num := 4;                              { set defaults     }
        meter.den := 1;
        beatnote.num := 1;
        beatnote.den := 4;
        incr(buffer.bp);                             { skip 'M'         }
        if isdigit(nextchar(buffer))
          then getbeats(f, buffer, meter, beatnote)
        else if (nextchar(buffer) = '(') or (nextchar(buffer) = '<')
          then
            begin
              incr(buffer.bp);                       { skip '(' or '<' }
              getbeats(f, buffer, meter, beatnote);
              incr(buffer.bp)                        { skip ')' or '>' }
            end
        else if nextchar(buffer) = '$'
          then
            begin
              incr(buffer.bp);
              meter.num := 2;
              beatnote.den := 2
            end
        else if nextchar(buffer) = 'c'
          then
            begin
              incr(buffer.bp);
              meter.num := 4;
              beatnote.den := 4
            end
        else if nextchar(buffer) = 'o'
          then
            begin
              incr(buffer.bp);
              if nextchar(buffer) = '$'
                then
                  begin
                    incr(buffer.bp);
                    meter.num := 6;
                    beatnote.den := 8
                  end
                else
                  begin
                    meter.num := 9;
                    beatnote.den := 8
                  end
            end;

        if beatnote.num > 1
          then meter.num := meter.num * beatnote.num;

        if print
          then
            begin
              write(f, 'c Meter signature:',  meter.num : 2);
              if meter.den <> 1
                then write(f, ' /', meter.den * beatnote.den:2)
                else write(f, ' /', beatnote.den: 2)
            end;

        if (meter.num mod 3 = 0) and (meter.num div 3 >= 2)
          then
            begin
              if beatnote.num = 1
                 then beatnote.num := 3 * beatnote.num;
              meter.num := meter.num div 3
            end;

        if print
          then
            begin
              write(f, '  beats: ');
              if meter.den <> 1
                then
                  begin   { reduce to proper fraction }
                    write(f, (meter.num div meter.den):4, '-');
                    write(f, (meter.num mod meter.den):2, ' / ');
                    write(f, meter.den:2)
                  end
                else write(f, meter.num:4);
```

```
            writeln(f, '; beatnote: ', beatnote.num:2, ' /',
                                                 beatnote.den:2)
          end;
        fracmult(meter, meter, beatnote);    { meter as all one fraction }
        if print
          then
            begin
              write(f, 'm', inum:1, '.', stafftrans div 50:1, ' ');
              fracwrite(f, time); write('          ');
              fracwrite(f, measno); write(' ');
              fracwrite(f, meter);
              fracwrite(f, beatnote);
              writeln(f)
            end
      end
  end;  { setmeter }


(*************************************************************************)
(*                          CLEF ROUTINES                                *)
(*************************************************************************)

(************************          setclef          ************************)
(* Sets the constant "clef" to reflect the current clef.  This procedure *)
(* is called whenever a new clef code is encountered.  The clef constant *)
(* added  to the space code for a note yields the number of the note in  *)
(* the continuous name class scale.  The current version works properly  *)
(* for movable c, f, and  g clefs as well as for treble-tenor clef !KG-8.*)
(* The "normclef" array gives the normal space code position for each    *)
(* clef.  The normal position minus the actual position gives the offset *)
(* from the normal position for the clef.                                *)
(*************************************************************************)
 procedure setclef(var f : text; var buffer : buftype;
                               var clef : integer; spacecode : integer);
   var
     klef : integer;

   begin
     case nextchar(buffer) of
       'c': klef :=  3;
       'f': klef := -3;
       'g': klef :=  9
     end;  { case }
                                             { for movable clefs          }
     klef := klef + normclef(nextchar(buffer)) - spacecode;
     incr(buffer.bp);                        { skip clef code             }
     if  nextchar(buffer) = '-'
       then
         begin { treble-tenor klef }
           incr(buffer.bp); { skip - }
           if nextchar(buffer) = '8'
             then klef := klef - 7
             else error(f, buffer, 4)
         end;  { treble-tenor clef }
     clef := klef                            { assign clef for instrument }
   end;  { setclef }
```

```
(************************       gettranspose       ************************)
(* Reads a transposition interval, encoded as a quality, such as M, m,   *)
(* or P, and a size, such as 3 (third), 5 (fifth), etc.  Checks for an   *)
(* acceptable interval--no minor fifths or perfect thirds, please--and   *)
(* converts it to cbr notation.  An error message is printed if the      *)
(* interval is not acceptable.                                           *)
(* ***********************************************************************)

 procedure gettranspose(var f        : text;
                        var buffer   : buftype;
                        var partdata : pdat);

   var
     quality         : char;             { type of interval: M, m, or P   }
     down            : boolean;          { flag for transposition down M3 }
     octave, nc, pc  : integer;          { components of trans interval   }

   begin
     incr(buffer.bp);                    { skip 't'                       }
     octave := 0;
     skipbuf(buffer);

     down := nextchar(buffer) = '-';     { check direction                }
     if nextchar(buffer) in ['-', '+']
       then incr(buffer.bp);

     getchar(buffer, quality);           { and read interval              }
     getint(f, buffer, nc);
     nc := nc - 1;
     if nc >= 7
       then
         begin
           octave := nc div 7;
           nc := nc mod 7
         end;
     if ((quality in ['P', 'p']) and not (nc in [0, 3, 4]))
          or ((quality in ['M', 'm']) and (nc in [0, 3, 4]))
          or not (quality in ['M', 'm', 'P', 'p', 'a', 'A'])
       then error(f, buffer, 20)         { illegal interval type          }
       else
         begin
           pc := scale(nc);
           if quality = 'm'
             then pc := (pc + 11) mod 12
           else if quality in ['A', 'a']
             then pc := (pc + 1) mod 12;
           with partdata do
             begin
               trans := cbr(octave, pc, nc);
               if down
                 then trans := -trans;
               writeln('c new transposition level for part ', inum:1);
               write('t', inum:1, trans:8, '  ');
               fracwrite(f, time); writeln
             end
         end
   end;  { get transposition interval }
```

```
(************************          stc          ************************)
(* Sets staff transposition code.                                       *)
(**********************************************************************)
  procedure stc(var f : text; var buffer : buftype;
                                          var stafftrans : integer);
    begin
      getint(f, buffer, stafftrans);
      if stafftrans mod 50 <> 0
        then error(f, buffer, 32)                 { not a multiple of 50 }
      else if stafftrans div 50 > maxstaff
        then error(f, buffer, 33)                 { too many staves      }
      else writeln('!', stafftrans div 50:1,
                              ' new staff for instr ', inum:1)
    end;

(************************      exclamation      ************************)
(* Called when the scanner encounters an exclamation point.  Checks the *)
(* character after the exclamation point and calls the appropriate rou- *)
(* tine (keysig, clef, etc).  Thus exclamation serves as a junction box, *)
(* linking to several other procedures.                                 *)
(**********************************************************************)
  procedure exclamation(var f        : text;
                        var buffer   : buftype;
                        var partdata : pdat;
                            spcode : integer);
    begin
      incr(buffer.bp);                                 { skip '!'        }
      with partdata do
        if nextchar(buffer) = 'k'                      { key signature   }
          then setkey(f, buffer, partdata)
        else if isclef(nextchar(buffer))               { clef            }
          then
            begin
              if spcode mod 50 = 0
                then spcode := spcode + normclef(nextchar(buffer));
              setclef(f, buffer, clef, spcode)
            end
        else if nextchar(buffer) = 'm'                 { meter signature }
          then setmeter(f, buffer, partdata, true)
        else if isdigit(nextchar(buffer))              { grouplet definer }
          then grouplet(f, buffer, group)
        else if nextchar(buffer) = '&'          { new layer linear decomp }
          then newstart(f, buffer, partdata)
        else if nextchar(buffer) = '/'          { bar line                }
          then newmeasure(f, buffer, partdata, 2)
        else if nextchar(buffer) = 't'          { new transposition level }
          then gettranspose(f, buffer, partdata)
        else if nextchar(buffer) = '+'
          then stc(f, buffer, stafftrans)       { stave trans code        }
        else error(f, buffer, 2)
    end;

(************************        getcode        ************************)
(* Reads a space code and expands it if necessary.                      *)
(**********************************************************************)
  procedure getcode( var f : text; var buffer : buftype;
                                          var spacecode : integer );
  var
    lownote : boolean;
  begin
    lownote := false;
    if nextchar(buffer) = '0'
      then
        begin
          spacecode := 0;
          incr(buffer.bp);                                    { skip zero }
          lownote := isdigit(nextchar(buffer))
        end;
    if isdigit(nextchar(buffer))
      then getint(f, buffer, spacecode);
    if (not lownote) and (spacecode < 10)
      then spacecode := spacecode + 20
  end; { getcode }

(************************        literal        ************************)
(* Skips literals (performance directions etc.)                         *)
(**********************************************************************)
  procedure literal(var f : text; var buffer : buftype;
                                          spacecode : integer);
    begin
      write(f, 'c skipped literal: "');
      repeat
        write(f, nextchar(buffer));
        incr(buffer.bp)
      until (nextchar(buffer) = '$') or eob(buffer);
      writeln(nextchar(buffer), '"');

      if nextchar(buffer) = '$'
        then incr(buffer.bp)                            { skip terminator }
        else error(f, buffer, 25)
    end;

(************************        setcode        ************************)
(* Uses getcode(spacecode) to read a space code.  If the space code is  *)
(* followed by an exclamation point, exclamation is called to determine *)
(* next move.  Otherwise setnote, the next procedure in the chain, is   *)
(* called.  Getcode was separated from setcode so getcode could be      *)
(* called without entering the chain of defaults.                       *)
(**********************************************************************)
  procedure setcode( var f        : text;
                     var buffer   : buftype;
                     var group    : grouptable;
                     var partdata : pdat;
                         rest     : boolean } ;
    var
      t : integer;
    begin
      with partdata do
        begin
          t := spacecode;                           { save to restore later }
          if isdigit(nextchar(buffer))
            then getcode(f, buffer, spacecode);
          spacecode := spacecode + stafftrans;
          if ((spacecode div 50) > 2)
```

```
        then error(f, buffer, 31);           { too many staves        }
      if nextchar(buffer) = '!'
        then
          begin
            exclamation(f, buffer, partdata, spacecode);
            spacecode := t                  { restore space code     }
          end
      else if nextchar(buffer) = 'r'        { rest                   }
        then setrest(f, buffer, group, partdata, isrest)
      else if nextchar(buffer) = '@'
        then
          begin
            literal(f, buffer, spacecode);
            spacecode := t                  { restore space code     }
          end
      else setnote(f, buffer, group, partdata, rest)
    end
  end;   { setcode }

(************************           barcode          ************************)
(* Equipped to handle 10 varieties of bar lines (coded value specified): *)
(*                                                                        *)
(*                           /       0                                    *)
(*                           //      1                                    *)
(*                           /!/     4                                    *)
(*                           //:     5                                    *)
(*                           ://     6                                    *)
(*                           :/!/    8                                    *)
(*                           ://:    9                                    *)
(*                                                                        *)
(* The above currently constitute all codes beginning with either '/' or *)
(* ':', the two cases in which newmeasure is called directly from scan.  *)
(* Three types of barlines can begin with '!'. Procedure scan calls      *)
(* exclamation in this case and exclamation calls newmeasure.  In this   *)
(* event, a "key" of 2 is passed to newmeasure and on to barcode.  The   *)
(* key is added to the barline code, giving us the remaining three       *)
(* possibilities:                                                         *)
(*                           !/      2                                    *)
(*                           !//     3                                    *)
(*                           !//:    7                                    *)
(*                                                                        *)
(* An error is reported if a barline is incorrectly encoded; however,    *)
(* once enough information is obtained to determine a code, any remain- *)
(* ing code is skipped up to the next blank.                              *)
(**************************************************************************)
 procedure barcode(var f : text; var buffer : buftype;
                                     var code : integer; key : integer);
   begin       { determine barline code }
     if nextchar(buffer) = '/'
       then
         begin
           incr(buffer.bp);                          { skip '/'          }
           if nextchar(buffer) = ' '
             then code := 0
           else if nextchar(buffer) = '/'
             then
               begin
                 incr(buffer.bp);                    { skip '/'          }
                 if nextchar(buffer) = ' '
                   then code := 1
                 else if nextchar(buffer) = ':'
                   then code := 5
                 else error(f, buffer, 17)
               end
           else if nextchar(buffer) = '!'
             then code := 4
           else error(f, buffer, 17)
         end
     else if nextchar(buffer) = ':'
       then
         begin
           incr(buffer.bp); { skip : }
           if nextchar(buffer) = '/'                 { only legal case }
             then
               begin
                 incr(buffer.bp);    { skip / }
                 if nextchar(buffer) = '!'
                   then code := 8
                 else if nextchar(buffer) = '/'
                   then
                     begin
                       incr(buffer.bp);              { skip '/'          }
                       if nextchar(buffer) = ' '
                         then code := 6
                       else if nextchar(buffer) = ':'
                         then code := 9
                       else error(f, buffer, 17)
                     end
                 else error(f, buffer, 17)
               end
           else error(f, buffer, 17)
         end;
     code := code + key;
     while nextchar(buffer) <> ' ' do
       incr(buffer.bp)                          { skip extra DARMS code }
   end;         { barcode }

(************************         newmeasure         ************************)
(* Called when a barline is encountered by procedure scan.               *)
(**************************************************************************)
 procedure newmeasure( var f         : text;
                       var buffer    : buftype;
                       var partdata  : pdat;
                           key       : integer );
   var
     code : integer;                        { barline code             }
     bardur : fraction;                     { frac duration of bar     }

   begin { newmeasure }
     code := 0;                             { set default barline code }
     if nextchar(buffer) <> 'w'             { determine barline code   }
       then barcode(f, buffer, code, key);
                                            { check duration of measure }
```

```
      with partdata do
        begin
          fracsub(bardur, time, lastbar);
          fracsub(bardur, bardur, meter);     { calculate difference      }
          if bardur.num <> 0
            then
              begin                           { report duration error     }
                write(f, 'c error: instr. ', inum:1, '.',
                       stafftrans div 50:1, ' m. ',
                 (measno.num div measno.den) -1:1, ' beatcount off by: ');
                fracwrite(f, bardur);  writeln
              end;

          write(f, 'b', inum:1, '.', stafftrans div 50:1, ' ');
          fracwrite(f, time); write('          ');
          fracwrite(f, measno);
          write(code:6);
          writeln;
          lastbar := time;                    { save time for next test   }
          adjust := keysig                    { cancel accidentals        }
        end
    end;  { newmeasure }

(************************        skiptoken        ************************)
(* Skips over unused tokens (used to get past encoding errors).          *)
(*************************************************************************)
  procedure skiptoken(var buffer : buftype);
    begin
      while nextchar(buffer) <> ' ' do
        incr(buffer.bp)
    end;

(************************        badtoken         ************************)
(* Called by scanner if first character of token is not recognized.      *)
(*************************************************************************)
  procedure badtoken(var f : text; var buffer : buftype);
    begin
      error(f, buffer, 1);                             { report error   }
      incr(buffer.bp);                                 { skip bad char  }
      skiptoken(buffer)                                { skip token     }
    end;

(************************         reinit          ************************)
(* Reinitialize boolean variables.                                       *)
(*************************************************************************)
  procedure reinit(var partdata : pdattab);
    var
      i : integer;
    begin
      for i := 1 to inum do
        with partdata[i] do
          begin
            chord := nochord;
            dowrite := true;
            pushing := false
          end
    end;
```

```
(************************         comment         ************************)
(* Skips over comments.  Comment delimiters are 'k' ... '$'.  Comments   *)
(* may not contain newlines.                                             *)
(*************************************************************************)
procedure comment(var buffer : buftype);
  begin
    with buffer do
      begin
        incr(bp);                                     { skip 'k'       }
        while (B[bp] <> '$') and not eob(buffer) do   { skip comment   }
          incr(bp);
        if B[bp] = '$'
          then incr(bp)                               { skip '$'       }
      end
  end;  { comment }


(************************          scan           ************************)
(* The heart of the program, this procedure checks the first character   *)
(* of each new token and calls the appropriate routines to deal with     *)
(* each case.                                                            *)
(*************************************************************************)
  procedure scan(var f        : text;
                 var buffer   : buftype;
                 var inum     : integer;
                 var group    : grouptable;
                 var partdata : pdattab);
    begin
      while not eob(buffer) do
        begin
          if not goodtoken(nextchar(buffer))
            then badtoken(f, buffer)
            else
              begin
                reinit(partdata);
                if isdigit(nextchar(buffer))              { space code      }
                  then setcode(f, buffer, group, partdata[inum], isnote)

                else if isacc(nextchar(buffer))           { accidental      }
                  then setnote(f, buffer, group, partdata[inum], isnote)

                else if isdur(nextchar(buffer))           { duration code   }
                  then setdur(f,buffer, group, partdata[inum], isnote)

                else if nextchar(buffer) = '.'            { duration dot    }
                  then setdur(f, buffer, group, partdata[inum], isnote)

                else if nextchar(buffer) = 'r'            { rest            }
                  then setrest(f, buffer, group, partdata[inum], isrest)

                else if nextchar(buffer) = '!'            { exclamation pt  }
                  then
                    if buffer.B[buffer.bp+1] = 'a'        { anacrusis       }
                      then anacrusis(f, buffer, partdata)
                      else exclamation(f, buffer, partdata[inum], 0)
```

```
          else if isbar(nextchar(buffer))          { barlines       }
            then newmeasure(f, buffer, partdata[inum], 0)

          else if isparen(nextchar(buffer))        { parenthesis    }
            then paren(f, buffer, partdata[inum])

          else if nextchar(buffer) = 'i'           { instr number   }
            then setins(f, buffer, inum)

          else if nextchar(buffer) = '&'           { new layer, LDM }
            then restart(f, buffer, partdata[inum])

          else if nextchar(buffer) = '~'           { skipcode       }
            then skipcode(f, buffer, partdata[inum])

          else if nextchar(buffer) = 'k'           { comment        }
            then comment(buffer)

          else if nextchar(buffer) = '@'           { literal        }
            then literal(f, buffer, 0)

          else if nextchar(buffer) = ','           { comma          }
            then incr(buffer.bp)

          else if nextchar(buffer) = ' '           { blank          }
            then skipbuf(buffer)

        end   { scan code }
    end
  end;  { scan }


(************************         writelast         ************************)
(* Prints the last time in the score at end of segment.                    *)
(***************************************************************************)
  procedure writelast(var f : text; var partdata : pdattab);

    var
      temp : fraction;
      i    : integer;

    begin
      temp := partdata[1].time;

      for i := 2 to maxins do
        with partdata[i] do
          if greater(time, temp)
            then temp := time;

      write(f, 'c last fractional time =');
      fracwrite(f, temp);
      writeln(f)
    end;


(************************      main procedure      ************************)
(* Initializes global variables then passes one line at a time to pro-   *)
(* cedure scan.  It pays to learn to delegate responsibility!            *)
(**************************************************************************)
  begin { main }
    init(inum, lineno, group, partdata);

    while not eof do
      begin { process line }
        getline(input, output, buffer, lineno);        { read one line    }
        scan(output, buffer, inum, group, partdata)    { and interpret it }
      end;  { process line }

    for inum := 1 to maxins do                 { check for unbalanced parens  }
      with partdata[inum] do
      if level <> 0
        then writeln('c error: instrument', inum:3,
                     ' parenthesis level = ', level:2);

    writelast(output, partdata)                { print latest fractional time }
  end.  { main }
```

APPENDIX D

A Program Library

```
(***********************        linkdefs.h        ***********************)
(* This file contains the type definitions necessary for basic opera-    *)
(* tions in the linked score structure described in chapter 20.  The     *)
(* file can be included in any program that needs it by inserting the    *)
(* following line after the keyword type:                                *)
(*   #   include "linkdefs.h"                                            *)
(* where '#' is in the first column of a line.  On systems that do not   *)
(* permit include files, this file should be copied into the program at  *)
(* the appropriate location.                                             *)
(*************************************************************************)

{ type }
   buftype = record
                  B  : array[1..maxline] of char;     { array for buffer    }
                  bp : integer                        { position in buffer  }
                end;

   ornament = (trill, mordent, turn, flatN, flatE, flatS, natN,
               natE, natS, sharpN, sharpE, sharpS);

   orntype = set of ornament;

   articulation = (staccato, wedgeaccent, tenuto, accent, vaccent, fermata,
                   arco, pizz, snap, upbow, downbow,
                   hauptstimme, nebenstimme, terminator,
                   open, stopped);

   artictype  = set of articulation;

   dynamic = (pppppp, ppppp, pppp, ppp, pp, p, mp, mf, f, ff, fff, ffff,
              fffff, ffffff, sfz, cresc, startcresc, endcresc, incresc,
              crescdim, dim, startdim, enddim, indim, dimcresc);

   dynset = set of dynamic;

   fraction =
     record
       num : integer;                               { numerator           }
       den : integer                                { denominator         }
     end;

   intset = set of 1 .. 14;                         { set of integers     }

   dptr = ↑data;
   data = record
            pitch : integer;                        { pitch coded as cbr  }
            dur   : fraction;                       { duration as fraction }
            tie   : intset;                         { tie field           }
            artic : artictype;                      { articulation codes  }
            slur  : intset;                         { slur field          }
            orn   : orntype;                        { set of ornament codes}
            dyn1  : integer;                        { dynamics            }
            dyn2  : dynset                          { dynamics            }
          end;

   kind = (avail, head, spine, note, barline, metersig, trans, rest,
                                                  gracenote, keysig);

ptr = ↑node;
node =                         { all nodes contain the following fields }
  record
    tag   : kind;                                 { type of record        }
    llink : ptr;                                  { left link             }
    rlink : ptr;                                  { right link            }
    dlink : dptr;                                 { pointer to data node  }
    part  : real;                                 { part.staff            }
    start : ptr;                                  { for start times       }
    bstart: ptr;                                  { backward start link   }
    stop  : ptr;                                  { for stop times        }
    bstop : ptr;                                  { backward stop link    }
    spec  : ptr;                                  { for special events    }
    bspec : ptr;                                  { backward spec link    }

                               { specific nodes contain in addition:   }
    case kind of
      avail : (link : ptr);                  { for free list              }

      head    : ( );

      spine   : (time    : fraction;         { time as sum of durations   }
                 measure : fraction;         { integer part = measure,    }
                                             { decimal = partmeasure      }
                 mlink   : ptr);             { pointer to meter sig node  }

      note,
      gracenote,
      rest    : ( );                         { dlink points to data node  }

      barline : (bartype : integer);

      metersig: (meter    : fraction;
                 beatnote : fraction);

      keysig:   (accidentals : integer;
                 sign        : char);

      trans   : (tlevel : integer)           { transposition level        }
                                             { as signed cbr              }
  end;  { record }


part =
  record
    s : ptr;                                 { pointer to spine           }
    p : ptr                                  { pointer to part            }
  end;


partpointers = array[0 .. maxins] of part;{ ptrs into score structure }

partrange = 0 .. maxins;
partset = set of partrange;         { the set of "active" part numbers }

brset = array[1 .. 84] of integer; { set of binomial pcs              }
```

```
(************************          xtern.p          ************************)
(* This file contains the majority of the external procedures and func-   *)
(* tions used in the programs in chapter 20 and available for user-       *)
(* written programs.  In some Pascal systems this file can be compiled    *)
(* separately and linked with other compiled programs.  In systems that   *)
(* do not allow external procedures, the required procedures and func-    *)
(* tions can be copied into each program before compiling.  Prime-form    *)
(* routines and related procedures, are in file setcalc.p (page XXXff).   *)
(**************************************************************************)
  const
    maxins   = 15;
    maxline  = 90;
    maxstaff =  3;                                    { max staves - 1 }

  type
#   include "linkdefs.h"

        { the following are used locally in build and related procedures }
    temppointers = array[-1 .. maxins, 0 .. maxstaff] of part;
    checklayer = array[0 .. maxins, 0 .. maxstaff] of integer;
    listtype = array[0 .. maxins] of integer;


(**************************************************************************)
(*                           UTILITY ROUTINES                             *)
(**************************************************************************)

(************************          imod          ************************)
(* Imod(x,m) = x mod m, but unlike many mod functions, works properly   *)
(* with negative x.                                                      *)
(**************************************************************************)
  function imod(a, b : integer) : integer;
    var
      r : integer;
    begin
      r := a - (a div b) * b;
      if r < 0
        then imod := r + b
        else imod := r
    end;

(************************          frac          ************************)
(* Returns fractional part of real number.                               *)
(**************************************************************************)
function frac(x : real) : real;
  begin
    frac := x  - trunc(x)
  end;

(************************         skipln         ************************)
(* skip to next nonblank char or end of line in file f.                  *)
(**************************************************************************)
  procedure skipln(var f : text);
    begin
      while (f↑ = ' ') and not eoln(f) do
        get(f)
    end;

(************************          skipf          ************************)
(* skip to next nonblank char or end of file in file f.                   *)
(**************************************************************************)
  procedure skipf(var f : text);
    var
      done : boolean;
    begin
      done := false;
      repeat
        if eof(f)
          then done := true
        else if f↑ = ' '
          then get(f)
        else done := true
      until done
    end;

(************************          incr          ************************)
(* Add one to integer argument x.                                         *)
(**************************************************************************)
  procedure incr(var x : integer);
    begin
      x := x + 1
    end;

(************************          decr          ************************)
(* Subtract one from integer argument x.                                  *)
(**************************************************************************)
  procedure decr(var x : integer);
    begin
      x := x - 1
    end;



(**************************************************************************)
(*                           BUFFER ROUTINES                              *)
(**************************************************************************)


(************************         isdigit         ************************)
(* Tests for digit character.                                             *)
(**************************************************************************)
  function isdigit(ch : char) : boolean;
    begin
      isdigit := ch in ['0' .. '9']
    end;

(************************         issign          ************************)
(* Tests for plus or minus sign.                                          *)
(**************************************************************************)
  function issign(c : char) : boolean;
    begin
      issign := c in ['-', '+']
    end;
```

```
(************************           tab           ************************)
(* Returns ASCII tab character.                                             *)
(***************************************************************************)
  function tab : char;
    begin
      tab := chr(9)
    end;

(************************           null          ************************)
(* Returns ASCII null character, which marks the end of data in buffer.   *)
(***************************************************************************)
  function null : char;
    begin
      null := chr(0)
    end;

(************************           toint         ************************)
(* Converts digit to integer.                                               *)
(***************************************************************************)
  function toint(c : char) : integer;
    begin
      toint := ord(c) - ord('0')
    end;

(************************          getline        ************************)
(* Reads one line from input file into buffer.                             *)
(***************************************************************************)
  procedure getline(var fi, fo : text; var buffer : buftype);
    begin
      with buffer do
        begin

          bp := 1;
          while not eoln(fi) and (bp < maxline) do
            begin
              read(fi,B[bp]);
              incr(bp)
            end;

          B[bp] := null;                             { mark end of line }
          if not eoln(fi)
            then writeln(fo, 'Getline: warning, input line truncated');
          readln(fi);
          bp := 1                      { reset index at beginning of buffer }
        end
    end;

(************************           eob           ************************)
(* Tests for end of buffer.                                                 *)
(***************************************************************************)
  function eob(var buffer : buftype) : boolean;
    begin
      with buffer do
        eob := B[bp] = null
    end;

(************************          isupper        ************************)
(* Tests for uppercase alphabetic character.                                *)
(***************************************************************************)
  function isupper(c : char) : boolean;
    begin
      isupper := c in ['A' .. 'Z']
    end;

(************************          islower        ************************)
(* Tests for lowercase alphabetic character.                                *)
(***************************************************************************)
  function islower(c : char) : boolean;
    begin
      islower := c in ['a' .. 'z']
    end;

(************************           ispc          ************************)
(* Tests for pitch class digit (using duodecimal).                          *)
(***************************************************************************)
  function ispc(c : char) : boolean;
    begin
      ispc := c in ['0' .. '9', 'a', 'A', 'b', 'B']
    end;

(************************          tolower        ************************)
(* Converts uppercase to lowercase;  nonalphabetic chars unchanged.        *)
(***************************************************************************)
  function tolower(c : char) : char;
    begin
      if isupper(c)
        then tolower := chr(ord(c) - ord('A') + ord('a'))
        else tolower := c
    end;

(************************          nextchar       ************************)
(* Returns next character in buffer.                                        *)
(***************************************************************************)
  function nextchar(var buffer : buftype) : char;
    begin
      with buffer do
        if not eob(buffer)
          then nextchar := tolower(B[bp])
          else nextchar := ' '
    end;

(************************          skipbuf        ************************)
(* Skips blanks in buffer.                                                  *)
(***************************************************************************)
  procedure skipbuf(var buffer : buftype);
    begin
      with buffer do
        while (nextchar(buffer) in [' ',tab]) and not eob(buffer) do
          incr(bp)
    end;
```

```
(************************          getchar          ************************)
(* Reads next character in buffer.                                          *)
(****************************************************************************)
 procedure getchar(var buffer : buftype; var c : char);
   begin
     with buffer do
       begin
         c := B[bp];
         incr(bp)
       end
   end;

(************************        printbuffer        ************************)
(* Prints contents of buffer with pointer to current character.             *)
(****************************************************************************)
 procedure printbuffer(var f : text; var buffer : buftype);
   var
     i : integer;
   begin
     write(f, 'c buffer: ');
     i := 1;
     with buffer do
       begin
         while B[i] <> null do
           begin
             write(f, B[i]);
             incr(i)
           end;
         writeln(f);
         write(f, 'Error:    ');
         for i := 1 to bp - 1 do
           write(f, '-');
         writeln(f, '↑')
       end
   end;  { printbuffer }

(************************          getint           ************************)
(* Reads integer from buffer.                                               *)
(****************************************************************************)
 procedure getint(var fi, fo : text; var buffer : buftype; var x : integer);
   var
     negative : boolean;
   begin
     skipbuf(buffer);                                   { skip blanks    }
     negative := nextchar(buffer) = '-';                { check for sign }
     if issign(nextchar(buffer))
       then incr(buffer.bp);                            { skip sign      }
     if not isdigit(nextchar(buffer))
       then
         begin
           write(fo, 'you must type a number: ');
           getline(fi, fo, buffer);
           getint(fi, fo, buffer, x)
         end
       else
         begin { read number }
           x := 0;
           while isdigit(nextchar(buffer)) do
             begin
               x := 10 * x + toint(nextchar(buffer));
               incr(buffer.bp)
             end;
           if negative
             then x := -x                               { set sign       }
         end   { read number }
   end;

(************************          getreal          ************************)
(* Reads real number from buffer.                                           *)
(****************************************************************************)
 procedure getreal(var fi, fo : text; var buffer : buftype; var x : real);
   var
     scale    : integer;
     negative : boolean;
   begin
     skipbuf(buffer);                                   { skip blanks    }
     negative := nextchar(buffer) = '-';
     if issign(nextchar(buffer))
       then incr(buffer.bp);                            { skip sign      }
     x := 0;
     scale := 1;
     if not (isdigit(nextchar(buffer)) or (nextchar(buffer) = '.'))
       then
         begin { error }
           write(fo, 'you must type a number: ');
           getline(fi, fo, buffer);
           getreal(fi, fo, buffer, x)
         end
       else
         begin
           while isdigit(nextchar(buffer)) do
             begin
               x := 10 * x + toint(nextchar(buffer));
               incr(buffer.bp)
             end;

           if nextchar(buffer) = '.'
             then
               begin
                 incr(buffer.bp);
                 while isdigit(nextchar(buffer)) do
                   begin
                     x := 10 * x + toint(nextchar(buffer));
                     scale := scale * 10;
                     incr(buffer.bp)
                   end
               end;
           x := x / scale;
           if negative
             then x := -x                               { set sign       }
         end
   end;
```

```
(***************************************************************************)
(*                      RATIONAL ARITHMETIC ROUTINES                       *)
(***************************************************************************)


(************************          swap          ***************************)
(* Exchanges values of arguments.                                          *)
(***************************************************************************)
  procedure swap(var x, y : integer);
    var
      t : integer;
    begin
      t := x; x := y; y := t
    end;

(************************          gcd           ***************************)
(* Calculates greatest common divisor.                                     *)
(***************************************************************************)
  function gcd(x, y : integer) : integer;
    var
      t : integer;
    begin
      x := abs(x);
      y := abs(y);
      if y > x
        then swap(x,y);
      while y <> 0 do
        begin
          t := x mod y;
          x := y;
          y := t
        end;
      gcd := x
    end;

(************************         fracadd        ***************************)
(* Adds fractions a and b; returns result as c.                            *)
(***************************************************************************)
  procedure fracadd(var c : fraction; a : fraction; b : fraction);
    var
      d1,d2,t : integer;
    begin
      d1 := gcd(a.den, b.den);
      if d1 = 1
        then
          begin
            c.num := a.num *  b.den + a.den * b.num;
            c.den := a.den * b.den
          end
        else
          begin
            t := a.num * (b.den div d1) + b.num * (a.den div d1);
            d2 := gcd(t,d1);
            c.num := t div d2;
            c.den := (a.den div d1) * (b.den div d2)
          end
    end;  { fracadd }

(************************         fracsub        ***************************)
(* Subtracts fractions a and b; returns result as c.                       *)
(***************************************************************************)
  procedure fracsub(var c : fraction; a : fraction; b : fraction);
    begin
      b.num := -b.num;                          { negate second fraction }
      fracadd(c, a, b)                          { and then add           }
    end;  { fracsub }


(************************        fracmult        ***************************)
(* Multiplies fractions a and b; returns result as c.                      *)
(***************************************************************************)
  procedure fracmult(var c : fraction; a : fraction; b : fraction);
    var
      d1, d2 : integer;
    begin
      d1 := gcd(a.num, b.den);
      d2 := gcd(a.den, b.num);
      c.num := (a.num div d1) * (b.num div d2);
      c.den := (a.den div d2) * (b.den div d1)
    end;  { fracmult }


(************************         fracdiv        ***************************)
(* Divides fraction a by b; returns result as c.                           *)
(***************************************************************************)
  procedure fracdiv(var c : fraction; a : fraction; b : fraction);
    begin
      swap(b.num,b.den);                        { invert second fraction }
      if b.den < 0                              {    get the signs right }
        then
          begin                                 { switch signs           }
            b.num := -b.num;
            b.den := -b.den
          end;
      fracmult(c, a, b)                         { and then multiply      }
    end;  { fracdiv }


(************************         toreal         ***************************)
(* Converts fraction x to real number.                                     *)
(***************************************************************************)
  function toreal(x : fraction) : real;
    begin
      toreal := x.num / x.den
    end;


(************************        fracwrite       ***************************)
(* Writes fraction in fixed format.                                        *)
(***************************************************************************)
  procedure fracwrite(var f : text; x : fraction);
    begin
      write(f,x.num:4,' /', x.den:4, ' ')
    end;
```

```
(************************          fracread          ************************)
(* Reads fraction from buffer.                                                *)
(******************************************************************************)
  procedure fracread(var fin, fout : text; var buffer : buftype;
                                                          var x : fraction);
    begin { fracread }
      getint(fin, fout, buffer, x.num);
      skipbuf(buffer);
      if nextchar(buffer) in ['/',':']
        then incr(buffer.bp);
      getint(fin, fout, buffer, x.den)
    end;  { fracread }

(************************           reduce           ************************)
(* Reduces fraction.                                                          *)
(******************************************************************************)
  procedure reduce(var x : fraction);
    var
      t : integer;
    begin
      t := gcd(x.num,x.den);
      if t > 1
        then
          begin
            x.num := x.num div t;
            x.den := x.den div t
          end
    end;

(************************            equal           ************************)
(* Tests two fractions for equality.                                          *)
(******************************************************************************)
  function equal(x, y : fraction) : boolean;
    begin
      equal := (x.num * y.den) = (y.num * x.den)
    end;

(************************           greater          ************************)
(* True if fraction x is greater than fraction y.                             *)
(******************************************************************************)
  function greater(x, y : fraction) : boolean;
    begin
      greater := (x.num * y.den) > (y.num * x.den)
    end;

(************************           greater          ************************)
(* This version of greater is not as accurate as the above, but may          *)
(* prevent integer overflow on smaller systems.                               *)
(******************************************************************************)
{
  function greater(x, y : fraction) : boolean;
    begin
      greater := toreal(x) > toreal(y)
    end;
}
```

```
(************************          lessthan          ************************)
(* True if fraction x is less than fraction y.                                *)
(******************************************************************************)
  function lessthan(x, y : fraction) : boolean;
    begin
      lessthan := (x.num * y.den) < (y.num * x.den)
    end;

(******************************************************************************)
(*                        SCORE STRUCTURE ROUTINES                            *)
(* The following may be used with the linked score structure described       *)
(* in chapter 20.                                                             *)
(******************************************************************************)

(************************            empty           ************************)
(* Returns true if list x is empty.  Use for spine or part only.             *)
(******************************************************************************)
  function empty(x : ptr) : boolean;
    begin
      empty := x = x↑.rlink
    end;

(************************          starttime         ************************)
(* Returns the start time of a note.                                          *)
(******************************************************************************)
  function starttime(x : ptr) : real;
    var
      t : ptr;
    begin
      if x↑.tag = spine
        then starttime := toreal(x↑.time)
      else
        begin
          while x↑.tag = gracenote do
            x := x ↑.spec;
          if (x↑.tag = note) or (x↑.tag = rest)
            then
              begin { for note or rest }
                t := x↑.start;
                while t↑.tag <> spine do
                  t := t↑.start;
                starttime := toreal(t↑.time)
              end  { for note or rest }
          else if (x↑.tag = head) and not empty(x)
            then
              begin { for headnode }
                x := x↑.llink;
                t := x↑.stop;
                while t↑.tag <> spine do
                  t := t↑.stop;
                starttime := toreal(t↑.time)
              end  { for headnode }
            else starttime := -1.0
        end
    end;
```

```
(************************          stoptime          ************************)
(* Returns the stop time of a note.                                          *)
(****************************************************************************)
  function stoptime(x : ptr) : real;
    var
      t : ptr;
    begin { return stop time for note x }
      while x↑.tag = gracenote do
        x := x ↑.spec;
      t := x↑.stop;
      while t↑.tag <> spine do
        t := t↑.stop;
      stoptime := toreal(t↑.time)
    end;

(************************           measno           ************************)
(* Returns the measure number of an object in structure.                     *)
(****************************************************************************)
  function measno(x : ptr) : real;
    var
      t : ptr;
    begin
      if x↑.tag = spine
        then measno := toreal(x↑.measure)
      else
        begin
          while x↑.tag = gracenote do
            x := x ↑.spec;
          if (x↑.tag = note) or (x↑.tag = rest)
            then
              begin { for note or rest }
                t := x↑.start;
                while t↑.tag <> spine do
                  t := t↑.start;
                measno := toreal(t↑.measure)
              end  { for note or rest }
          else if (x↑.tag = head) and not empty(x)
            then
              begin { for headnode }
                x := x↑.llink;
                t := x↑.stop;
                while t↑.tag <> spine do
                  t := t↑.stop;
                measno := toreal(t↑.measure)
              end   { for headnode }
            else measno := -1.0
        end
    end;

(************************          tielast           ************************)
(* Tests to see if a note is tied to the previous note.  The tie field      *)
(* of a note contains a set of integers, with odd integers i, represent-   *)
(* ing beginning of tie, and even int i+1 the end.  Thus an even integer   *)
(* means that the note is tied to the previous note.  This is determined   *)
(* by removing all odd integers in set; if the result is not a null set,   *)
(* it must contain even integers (tie terminators).                        *)
(****************************************************************************)
  function tielast(p : ptr) : boolean;
    begin
      tielast := (p↑.dlink↑.tie - [1, 3, 5, 7, 9, 11, 13]) <> [ ]
    end;

(************************          tienext           ************************)
(* Tests to see if a note is tied to the next note.  Similar to tielast. *)
(****************************************************************************)
  function tienext(p : ptr) : boolean;
    begin
      tienext := (p↑.dlink↑.tie - [2, 4, 6, 8, 10, 12, 14]) <> [ ]
    end;

(****************************************************************************)
(*                          DYNAMIC ADJUSTMENT                              *)
(* These procedures interpolate the values representing dynamics during    *)
(* crescendos and diminuendos.  Procedure adjustdyne is called by pro-     *)
(* cedure build after the data structure is constructed.                   *)
(****************************************************************************)

(************************           xcresc           ************************)
(* Determines if at beginning of cresc or dim.                               *)
(****************************************************************************)
  function xcresc(x: dynset) : boolean;
    begin
      xcresc := (startcresc in x) or (startdim in x)
    end;

(************************         begincresc         ************************)
(* Finds beginning of crescendo or diminuendo.                               *)
(****************************************************************************)
  function begincresc(t : ptr) : ptr;
    var
      done : boolean;
    begin
      done := false;
      while not done do
        begin
          if t↑.tag = head
            then done := true
          else if xcresc(t↑.dlink↑.dyn2)
            then done := true
          else t := t↑.rlink
        end;
      if t↑.tag <> head
        then begincresc := t
        else begincresc := nil
    end;

(************************          endcresc          ************************)
(* Finds end of crescendo or diminuendo.                                     *)
(****************************************************************************)
  function endcres(t : ptr) : ptr;
    var
      done    : boolean;
      endflag : dynamic;          { code for end of crescendo or diminuendo }
    begin
```

```
        if t↑.tag <> head
          then
            begin
              if startcresc in t↑.dlink↑.dyn2
                then endflag := endcresc
                else endflag := enddim;
              done := false;
              repeat
                if t↑.tag = head
                  then done := true
                else if endflag in t↑.dlink↑.dyn2
                  then done := true
                else t := t↑.rlink
              until done
            end;
        endcres := t
      end;  { endcresc }

(************************         dyntraverse        ************************)
(* Traverses the notes within a crescendo or diminuendo.  It finds the    *)
(* dynamic range of the crescendo and then calculates the dynamic values *)
(* of each note by interpolation.                                          *)
(*************************************************************************)
  procedure dyntraverse(t, q : ptr);
    var
      startval   : integer;        { initial dynamic level              }
      endval     : integer;        { ending dynamic level               }
      range      : integer;        { dynamic range of cresc or dim      }
      durcresc   : real;           { total duration of cresc or dim     }
      time       : real;           { time at each point in the cresc    }
      tempstart  : real;           { starting time of note in cresc     }
      tempterm   : real;           { ending time of note in cresc       }
    begin
      durcresc := starttime(q) - starttime(t); { duration of cresc        }
      startval := t↑.dlink↑.dyn1;              { starting dynamic level   }
      if (q↑.tag <> head)
        then endval := q↑.dlink↑.dyn1
        else
          if startcresc in t↑.dlink↑.dyn2
            then endval := startval + 10
            else endval := startval - 10;
      range := endval - startval;
      tempstart := 0;                          { initialize starting time }
      tempterm := 0;                           { initialize ending time   }
      while t↑.rlink <> q do
        begin                                  { traverse crescendo       }
          tempterm := tempstart + toreal(t↑.dlink↑.dur);
          tempstart := tempterm;
          t := t↑.rlink;
          if (t↑.tag = note) or (t↑.tag = rest)
            then
              begin                            { calculate dynamic level  }
                time := tempstart / durcresc;
                t↑.dlink↑.dyn1 := round(time * range) + startval
              end
        end
    end;  { dyntraverse }
```

```
(************************         adjustdyn          ************************)
(* In each staff of part, finds beginnings and ends of crescendos and    *)
(* diminuendos and calls dyntraverse to interpolate values between them. *)
(*************************************************************************)
  procedure adjustdyn(temp : temppointers);
    var
      t, q  : ptr;
      inum  : integer;
      staff : integer;
    begin
      for inum := 1 to maxins do
        for staff := 0 to maxstaff do
          begin   { adjust each part }
            if not empty(temp[inum, staff].p)
              then
                begin
                  q := temp[inum, staff].p↑.rlink;  { point to first note }
                  while q <> nil do
                    begin                            { traverse part to    }
                      t := begincresc(q);            {  start of crescendo }
                      if t <> nil
                        then
                          begin
                            q := endcres(t);         { find end of cresc   }
                            dyntraverse(t,q)         { trav between them   }
                          end
                        else q := t
                    end
                end
          end
    end;

(*************************************************************************)
(*                     BUILDING THE SCORE STRUCTURE                        *)
(* The score structure and process of building it are described in sec-  *)
(* tion 20.1.                                                              *)
(*************************************************************************)

(************************          linkmeter         ************************)
(* Links each spine node to previous meter node through mlink field.      *)
(*************************************************************************)
  procedure linkmeter(spineptr : ptr);
    var
      p, t, m : ptr;
    begin
      m := nil;                               { pointer to last meter node }
      p := spineptr↑.rlink;                   { first spine node           }
      while p↑.tag <> head do
        begin
          t := p;
          repeat
            t := t↑.spec;
            if t↑.tag = metersig
              then m := t
          until (t↑.tag = spine) or (t↑.tag = metersig);
```

```
        p↑.mlink := m;
        p := p↑.rlink
      end
    end; { linkmeter }

(************************         getnode          ************************)
(* Gets a node from the free list.                                         *)
(***************************************************************************)
  procedure getnode(var p, freelist : ptr);
    begin
      if freelist = nil
        then new(p)
        else
          begin { pop stack }
            p := freelist;
            freelist := freelist↑.link
          end;
      p↑.start  := p;                          { set pointers, all circular }
      p↑.bstart := p;
      p↑.stop   := p;
      p↑.bstop  := p;
      p↑.spec   := p;
      p↑.bspec  := p;
      p↑.llink  := p;
      p↑.rlink  := p
    end;

(************************         release          ************************)
(* Return node to free list.                                               *)
(***************************************************************************)
  procedure release(var p, freelist : ptr);
    begin
      p↑.tag := avail;
      p↑.link := freelist;
      freelist := p;
      p := nil
    end;

(************************         dinsert          ************************)
(* Inserts node x after node p in doubly linked circular list.             *)
(***************************************************************************)
  procedure dinsert(x, p : ptr);
    begin
      x↑.rlink := p↑.rlink;
      x↑.llink := p;
      p↑.rlink↑.llink := x;
      p↑.rlink := x
    end;

(************************          remove          ************************)
(* Removes node x from circular doubly linked list.                        *)
(***************************************************************************)
  procedure remove(x : ptr);
    begin
      x↑.llink↑.rlink := x↑.rlink;
      x↑.rlink↑.llink := x↑.llink
    end;

(************************         instart          ************************)
(* Inserts node x after node p, linked through start/bstart fields.        *)
(***************************************************************************)
  procedure instart(x, p : ptr);
    begin
      x↑.bstart := p;
      x↑.start := p↑.start;
      x↑.start↑.bstart := x;
      p↑.start := x
    end;

(************************          instop          ************************)
(* Inserts node x after node p, linked through stop/bstop fields.          *)
(***************************************************************************)
  procedure instop(x, p : ptr);
    begin
      x↑.bstop := p;
      x↑.stop := p↑.stop;
      x↑.stop↑.bstop := x;
      p↑.stop := x
    end;

(************************          inspec          ************************)
(* Insert node x after node p, linked through spec/bspec fields.           *)
(***************************************************************************)
  procedure inspec(x, p : ptr);
    begin { insert at end of circular list }
      x↑.bspec := p;
      x↑.spec := p↑.spec;
      x↑.spec↑.bspec := x;
      p↑.spec := x
    end;

(************************         getspine         ************************)
(* Gets a spine node from the free list and inserts start and measure      *)
(* times.                                                                  *)
(***************************************************************************)
  procedure getspine(var q, freelist : ptr; start : fraction;
                                                measno : fraction);
    begin
      getnode(q,freelist);
      q↑.tag := spine;
      q↑.time := start;
      q↑.measure := measno
    end;

(************************         islayer          ************************)
(* True if first note in start field is in a layer rather than main part.*)
(***************************************************************************)
  function islayer(x : ptr) : boolean;
    begin
      if x = x↑.start
        then islayer := false
        else
          begin
            x := x↑.start;
            while (x↑.rlink <> x) and (x↑.tag <> head) do
```

```
          x := x↑.rlink;
        islayer := x↑.rlink = x
      end
  end;

(************************        predecessor        ************************)
(* Finds spine node for previous note in part.                              *)
(***************************************************************************)
 function predecessor(x : ptr) : ptr;
  begin
   while ((x = x↑.start) and (x↑.tag <> head)) or islayer(x) do
     x := x↑.llink;
   predecessor := x
  end;

(************************           link            ************************)
(* Links node x into spine through one of three fields determined by key:*)
(*                      1 = start/bstart fields                            *)
(*                      2 = stop/bstop fields                              *)
(*                      3 = spec/bspec fields                              *)
(***************************************************************************)
 procedure link(x,p : ptr; key : integer);
  begin
   case key of
     1 : instart(x,p↑.bstart);
     2 : instop(x,p↑.bstop);
     3 : inspec(x,p↑.bspec)
   end { case }
  end;

(************************          linkup           ************************)
(* Places node in linked data score structure.  Recall that each part,    *)
(* staff, or layer has its own spine at this point.                        *)
(***************************************************************************)
 procedure linkup(x, p, s : ptr; time, measno : fraction; key : integer;
                                                    var freelist : ptr);
  var
    t,q : ptr;

  begin
   if empty(s)                                     { if empty list         }
    then
     begin
       getspine(q, freelist, time, measno);        { get spine node        }
       dinsert(q, s);                              { insert it into spine  }
       link(x, q, key);                            { link note to spine    }
       if key = 1
        then dinsert(x, p)                         { link note to part     }
     end
   else if greater(time, s↑.llink↑.time)           { if time is latest     }
    then                                           {    insert at end      }
     begin
       getspine(q, freelist, time, measno);        { get spine node        }
       dinsert(q, s↑.llink);
       link(x, q, key);                            { link note to part     }
       if key = 1                                  { link note to spine    }
        then
         begin
           t := predecessor(q↑.llink);
           dinsert(x,t↑.start)                     { link note to part     }
         end
     end  { insert at end  }
   else
    if equal(time, s↑.llink↑.time)                 { if times are same     }
     then
      begin
        if (key = 1) and (s↑.llink↑.start = s↑.llink)
         then
          begin
            t := predecessor(s↑.llink);            { get penultimate node  }
            if t↑.tag = head                       { if it's a head node   }
             then dinsert(x,p)                     {   insert after it     }
             else dinsert(x,t↑.start)              { else use start field  }
          end;
        link(x, s↑.llink, key)                     { line x to spine       }
      end
   else if lessthan(time, s↑.rlink↑.time)          { note is before first  }
    then
     begin
       getspine(q, freelist, time, measno);        { get a spine node      }
       link(x, q, key);                            { link note to it       }
       dinsert(q, s);                              { insert spine node     }
       if key = 1
        then dinsert(x,p)                          { insert note in part   }
     end
   else
    begin
      t := s↑.rlink;                               { find correct location }
      while greater(time, t↑.rlink↑.time)
                     or equal(time, t↑.rlink↑.time) do
        t := t↑.rlink;
      if equal(time, t↑.time)                      { if times are same     }
       then
        begin
          if (key = 1) and (t = t↑.start)          { if link to start field}
           then                                    {    and it is empty    }
            begin
              q := predecessor(t);
              dinsert(x, q↑.start)
            end;
          link(x, t, key)
        end
      else
       begin                                       { insert after t        }
         getspine(q,freelist,time,measno);
         dinsert(q,t);
         link(x,q,key);
         if key = 1
          then
           begin
             t := predecessor(t);
             dinsert(x,t↑.start)
           end
       end
```

```
    end
  end; { linkup }

(************************           getheadnode          ************************)
(* Gets a headnode from the free list.                                             *)
(*********************************************************************************)
 procedure getheadnode(var p, freelist : ptr);
   begin
     getnode(p, freelist);
     p↑.tag := head
   end;

(************************              init              ************************)
(* Initializes empty score structure.                                              *)
(*********************************************************************************)
 procedure init(var temp : temppointers; var layer : checklayer;
                var freelist : ptr; var part : integer;
                                                  var staff : listtype);
   var
     i, j : integer;

   begin
     freelist := nil;
     part := 1;

     for i := 0 to maxins do
       staff[i] := 0;

     for i := -1 to maxins do
       for j := 0 to maxstaff do
         begin
           getheadnode(temp[i,j].p, freelist);
           getheadnode(temp[i,j].s, freelist)
         end;

     for i := 0 to maxins do
       for j := 0 to maxstaff do
         layer[i,j] := 0;

     part := 1
   end;

(************************            catstart            ************************)
(* Concatenates list y to end x, linked through start/bstart fields.              *)
(*********************************************************************************)
 procedure catstart(x, y : ptr);
   begin { concatenate list y to end of list x }
     if y↑.start <> y then
       begin
         x↑.bstart↑.start := y↑.start;       { end of x to begin of y }
         y↑.start↑.bstart := x↑.bstart;      { begin of y to end of x }
         x↑.bstart := y↑.bstart;             { head points to new end }
         y↑.bstart↑.start := x;              { point end to head node }
         y↑.start := y;                      { empty list y           }
         y↑.bstart := y
       end
   end;

(************************            catstop             ************************)
(* Concatenates list y to end x, linked through stop/bstop fields.                *)
(*********************************************************************************)
 procedure catstop(x, y : ptr);
   begin
     if y↑.stop <> y then
       begin
         x↑.bstop↑.stop := y↑.stop;          { end of x to begin of y }
         y↑.stop↑.bstop := x↑.bstop;         { begin of y to end of x }
         x↑.bstop := y↑.bstop;               { head points to new end }
         y↑.bstop↑.stop := x;                { point end to head node }
         y↑.stop := y;                       { empty list y           }
         y↑.bstop := y
       end
   end;

(************************            catspec             ************************)
(* Concatenates list y to end x, linked through spec/bspec fields.                *)
(*********************************************************************************)
 procedure catspec(x,y : ptr);
   begin
     if y↑.spec <> y then
       begin
         x↑.bspec↑.spec := y↑.spec;          { end of x to begin of y }
         y↑.spec↑.bspec := x↑.bspec;         { begin of y to end of x }
         x↑.bspec := y↑.bspec;               { head points to new end }
         y↑.bspec↑.spec := x;                { point end to head node }
         y↑.spec := y;                       { empty list y           }
         y↑.bspec := y
       end
   end;

(************************            sinsert             ************************)
(* Inserts node x after node p in doubly linked circular list, through           *)
(* the start/bstart fields.  Used by merge to link headnodes together.           *)
(*********************************************************************************)
 procedure sinsert(x, p : ptr);
   begin
     x↑.start := p↑.start;
     x↑.bstart := p;
     p↑.start↑.bstart := x;
     p↑.start := x
   end;

(************************             merge              ************************)
(* Merges spine y into spine x, leaving y empty.  Links z, the headnode          *)
(* for a part, into the end of the doubly linked circular list on x,             *)
(* through the start/bstart fields.  Z is nil when merge is called by           *)
(* procedure mergelayers.                                                         *)
(*********************************************************************************)
 procedure merge(x, y, z : ptr; var freelist : ptr);
   var
     t, q : ptr;
   begin
     if empty(x)                             { if x is empty          }
       then
```

```
        begin                                   {  transfer list y to x }
          y↑.rlink↑.llink := x;
          y↑.llink↑.rlink := x;
          x↑.rlink := y↑.rlink;
          x↑.llink := y↑.llink;
          y↑.llink := y;
          y↑.rlink := y
        end
      else                                      { otherwise merge lists }
        begin
          q := x↑.rlink;                        { get next node in x    }
          while not empty(y) do                 { while y is not empty  }
            begin
              t := y↑.rlink;                    { get next node in y    }
              if greater(t↑.time, x↑.llink↑.time) { if y later than     }
                then                            {    last node of x     }
                  begin                         {    concatenate lists  }
                    q↑.rlink := t;
                    t↑.llink := q;
                    y↑.llink↑.rlink := x;
                    x↑.llink := y↑.llink;
                    y↑.llink := y;
                    y↑.rlink := y
                  end
              else
                begin
                  remove(t);                    { remove node t and find}
                                                { correct location in x }
                  while greater(t↑.time, q↑.time) do
                    q := q↑.rlink;
                  if lessthan(t↑.time, q↑.time) { if t goes before q    }
                    then dinsert(t, q↑.llink)   {    insert t before q  }
                    else                        { otherwise concatenate }
                      begin                     {    vertical lists     }
                        catstart(q, t);
                        catstop(q, t);
                        catspec(q, t);
                        release(t, freelist)
                      end
                end
            end
        end; { merge lists }
    if z <> nil                         { if not a layer segment      }
      then                              {    merge head nodes         }
        begin
          sinsert(z, x↑.bstart);        { insert z at end of list x   }
          z↑.part := z↑.llink↑.part;    { set part number of headnode }
          x↑.part := 0.0                { redundant after first time  }
        end
  end;

(************************          build          ************************)
(* Builds the linked data structure, using the output from the DARMS in- *)
(* terpreter as input.                                                   *)
(*************************************************************************)
  procedure build(var fin, fout, scoredata : text;
                    var instr : partpointers; var freelist : ptr);

const
  tlayer = -1;                          { position in instr for layers     }

var
  buffer        : buftype;
  t, q          : ptr;
  start, stop   : fraction;
  measno        : fraction;
  measend       : fraction;
  inum, snum    : integer;
  temp          : temppointers;
  layer         : checklayer;
  part          : integer;
  staff         : listtype;

procedure readmeter(var buffer : buftype);
  begin                          { read meter signature from buffer }
    incr(buffer.bp); { skip m }
    getnode(t, freelist);
    t↑.tag := metersig;
    getreal(fin, fout, buffer, t↑.part);
    fracread(fin, fout, buffer, start);
    fracread(fin, fout, buffer, measno);
    fracread(fin, fout, buffer, t↑.meter);
    fracread(fin, fout, buffer, t↑.beatnote);
    linkup(t, temp[part, staff[part]].p, temp[part, staff[part]].s,
                                        start, measno, 3, freelist)
  end;

procedure readkey(var buffer : buftype);
  begin                            { read key signature from buffer }
    incr(buffer.bp); { skip k }
    getnode(t,freelist);
    t↑.tag := keysig;
    getreal(fin, fout, buffer, t↑.part);
    fracread(fin, fout, buffer, start);
    fracread(fin, fout, buffer, measno);

    getint(fin, fout, buffer, t↑.accidentals);
    skipbuf(buffer);
    getchar(buffer, t↑.sign);

    linkup(t, temp[part, staff[part]].p, temp[part, staff[part]].s,
                                        start, measno, 3, freelist)
  end;

function isartic(x : char) : boolean;
  begin                                 { test for legal artic code }
    isartic := x in [ '''', '"', '_', '>', '<', ';', 'd', 'v', 'q',
                      'r', 'z', 'o', '+', 'h', 'n', '~']
  end;

procedure readartic(var buffer : buftype; var artic : artictype);
  var
    x : char;
  begin                           { set articulation field of the note }
    artic := [];                                        { null set      }
    skipbuf(buffer);
```

```
        x := nextchar(buffer);                      { get next char   }
        if x = '0'
          then incr(buffer.bp)                      { skip 0s         }
          else
            while isartic(x) do
              begin
                case x of
                  '''' : artic := artic + [staccato];
                  '"'  : artic := artic + [wedgeaccent];
                  '_'  : artic := artic + [tenuto];
                  '>'  : artic := artic + [accent];
                  '<'  : artic := artic + [vaccent];
                  ';'  : artic := artic + [fermata];
                  'd'  : artic := artic + [downbow];
                  'v'  : artic := artic + [upbow];
                  'q'  : artic := artic + [snap];      { snap pizz       }
                  'r'  : artic := artic + [arco];
                  'z'  : artic := artic + [pizz];
                  'o'  : artic := artic + [open];
                  '+'  : artic := artic + [stopped];
                  'h'  : artic := artic + [hauptstimme];
                  'n'  : artic := artic + [nebenstimme];
                  '~'  : artic := artic + [terminator]
                end; { case }
                incr(buffer.bp);                       { skip artic code }
                while isdigit(nextchar(buffer)) do
                  incr(buffer.bp);                     { skip digits     }
                x := nextchar(buffer)
              end
      end; { readartic }

    procedure readintset(var buffer : buftype; var x : intset);
      var
        i : integer;
        c : char;
      begin                                       { read set of integers }
        x := [];                                  { start as empty set   }
        skipbuf(buffer);
        c := nextchar(buffer);
        if c = '0'
          then incr(buffer.bp)                    { skip zero            }
          else
            while c in ['1' .. '9', 'a' .. 'g'] do
              begin
                if isdigit(c)
                  then i := ord(c) - ord('0')
                  else i := ord(c) - ord('a');
                x := x + [i];                     { add i to set         }
                incr(buffer.bp);                  { skip character       }
                c := nextchar(buffer)             { get next char        }
              end
      end;

    function isdyn(c : char) : boolean;
      begin                               { test for legal dynamic code }
        isdyn := c in ['0' .. '9', 'a' .. 'o']
      end;

    procedure readdynset(var buffer : buftype; var D : dynset);
      begin                                 { set dynamic field of note }
        D := [];
        skipbuf(buffer);
        while isdyn(nextchar(buffer)) do
          begin
            case nextchar(buffer) of
              '0' : D := D + [pppppp];
              '1' : D := D + [ppppp];
              '2' : D := D + [pppp];
              '3' : D := D + [ppp];
              '4' : D := D + [pp];
              '5' : D := D + [p];
              '6' : D := D + [mp];
              '7' : D := D + [mf];
              '8' : D := D + [f];
              '9' : D := D + [ff];
              'a' : D := D + [fff];
              'b' : D := D + [ffff];
              'c' : D := D + [fffff];
              'd' : D := D + [ffffff];
              'e' : D := D + [sfz];
              'f' : D := D + [cresc];
              'g' : D := D + [startcresc];
              'h' : D := D + [endcresc];
              'i' : D := D + [incresc];
              'j' : D := D + [crescdim];
              'k' : D := D + [dim];
              'l' : D := D + [startdim];
              'm' : D := D + [enddim];
              'n' : D := D + [indim];
              'o' : D := D + [dimcresc]
            end; { case }
            incr(buffer.bp)
          end
      end; { readdynset }

    function isorn(c : char) : boolean;
      begin                               { test for legal ornament code }
        isorn := c in ['0' .. '9', 'a' .. 'b']
      end;

    procedure readornset(var buffer : buftype; var O : orntype);
      begin                                { set ornament field of note }
        O := [];
        skipbuf(buffer);
        if nextchar(buffer) = 'x'          { no ornaments               }
          then incr(buffer.bp)             {     skip x                 }
          else
            while isorn(nextchar(buffer)) do
              begin
                case nextchar(buffer) of
                  '0' : O := O + [trill];
                  '1' : O := O + [mordent];
                  '2' : O := O + [turn];
                  '3' : O := O + [flatN];
                  '4' : O := O + [flatE];
```

```
            '5' : O := O + [flatS];
            '6' : O := O + [natN];
            '7' : O := O + [natE];
            '8' : O := O + [natS];
            '9' : O := O + [sharpN];
            'a' : O := O + [sharpE];
            'b' : O := O + [sharpS]
          end;  { case }
          incr(buffer.bp)                                { skip code }
        end
  end;  { readornset }

procedure readnote(var buffer : buftype; q : ptr);
  var
    r : integer;
  begin
    incr(buffer.bp); { skip i }
    getnode(t,freelist);
    t↑.tag := note;                                 { set fields       }
    new(t↑.dlink);                                  { get data node    }
    getreal(fin, fout, buffer, t↑.part);            { part number      }
    part := trunc(t↑.part);
    staff[part] := round(frac(t↑.part) * 10);
    staff[part] := round(frac(t↑.part) * 10);       { staff number     }
    fracread(fin, fout, buffer, start);             { start time       }
    fracread(fin, fout, buffer, stop);              { stop  time       }
    fracread(fin, fout, buffer, measno);            { measure number   }
    fracread(fin, fout, buffer, measend);           { meas at note     }
    getint(fin, fout, buffer, t↑.dlink↑.pitch);     { part number      }
    fracread(fin, fout, buffer, t↑.dlink↑.dur);     { duration         }
    readintset(buffer, t↑.dlink↑.tie);              { tie field        }
    readartic(buffer, t↑.dlink↑.artic);             { artic marks      }
    readintset(buffer, t↑.dlink↑.slur);             { slur field       }
    readornset(buffer, t↑.dlink↑.orn);              { ornament codes   }
    getint(fin, fout, buffer, t↑.dlink↑.dyn1);      { dynamic integer  }
    readdynset(buffer, t↑.dlink↑.dyn2);             { spec dynamics    }

    if t↑.dlink↑.pitch < 0                          { it's a rest      }
      then t↑.tag := rest;
    if t↑.dlink↑.dur.num = 0                        { it's a gracenote }
      then
        begin { gracenote }
          t↑.tag := gracenote;                  { set tag          }
          inspec(t,q)                           { insert in list q }
        end   { gracenote }
      else
        begin { note or rest }
          catspec(t,q);                         { link gracenotes to t }
                                              { link into part & spine }
          inum := trunc(t↑.part);
          if layer[part, staff[part]] > 0
            then r := tlayer
            else r := part;
          linkup(t, temp[r, staff[part]].p, temp[r,  staff[part]].s,
                                        start, measno, 1, freelist);
          linkup(t, temp[r, staff[part]].p, temp[r, staff[part]].s,
                                        stop, measend, 2, freelist)
        end   { note or rest }
  end;  { readnote }

procedure readbar(var buffer : buftype);
  begin
    incr(buffer.bp); { skip b }
    getnode(t,freelist);
    t↑.tag := barline;
    getreal(fin, fout, buffer, t↑.part);
    fracread(fin, fout, buffer, start);
    fracread(fin, fout, buffer, measno);
    getint(fin, fout, buffer, t↑.bartype);
    linkup(t, temp[part, staff[part]].p, temp[part, staff[part]].s,
                                         start, measno,3, freelist)
  end;

procedure unlink(p : ptr);
  begin
    p↑.rlink↑.link := p↑.link;
    p↑.llink↑.link := p↑.llink;
    p↑.rlink := p;
    p↑.llink := p
  end;

procedure mergelayers;
  begin                                             { merge two layers }
    if not empty(temp[tlayer, staff[part]].s)
      then
        begin
          merge(temp[part, staff[part]].s, temp[tlayer, staff[part]].s,
                                                      nil, freelist);
          unlink(temp[tlayer, staff[part]].p)
        end
  end;

procedure startlayers(var layer : checklayer);
  begin                              { begin linear decomposition }
    if layer[part, staff[part]] > 0
      then writeln(fout, 'c Error: part', part:1,
                    ' already in linear decomposition mode')
  end;

procedure newlayer(var layer : checklayer);
  begin                              { new layer linear decomp }
    if layer[part, staff[part]] > 0
      then mergelayers;
    incr(layer[part, staff[part]])
  end;

procedure endlayers(var layer : checklayer);
  begin                              { end of linear decomp     }
    if layer[part, staff[part]] > 0
      then mergelayers;
    layer[part, staff[part]] := 0
  end;

procedure newins(var buffer : buftype);
```

```
    begin                                          { new instrument number    }
      incr(buffer.bp);                             { skip 'p'                 }
      getint(fin, fout, buffer, part)
    end;

  procedure newstaff(var buffer : buftype);
    begin                                          { begin new staff          }
      incr(buffer.bp);      { skip ! }
      getint(fin, fout, buffer, staff[part])
    end;

  begin { build }
    write(fout, 'Building data structure ... ');
    flush(output);                                 { empty buffer             }
    reset(scoredata);                              { open file for reading    }
    init(temp, layer, freelist, part, staff);      { setup headnodes          }
    getnode(q,freelist);                           { headnode for gracenotes  }

    while not eof(scoredata) do
      begin { read data }
        getline(scoredata, fout, buffer);
        if nextchar(buffer) = 'i'
          then readnote(buffer, q)
        else if nextchar(buffer) = 'b'
          then readbar(buffer)
        else if nextchar(buffer) = 'k'
          then readkey(buffer)
        else if nextchar(buffer) = 'm'
          then readmeter(buffer)
        else if nextchar(buffer) = 'n'
          then startlayers(layer)
        else if nextchar(buffer) = 'p'
          then newins(buffer)
        else if nextchar(buffer) = '&'
          then newlayer(layer)
        else if nextchar(buffer) = '$'
          then endlayers(layer)
        else if nextchar(buffer) = '!'
          then newstaff(buffer)
        { else skip for now }
      end;  { read data }

    adjustdyn(temp);                               { interpolate dynamics     }
    for inum := 1 to maxins do                     { merge spines }
      for snum := 0 to maxstaff do
        if not empty(temp[inum, snum].s)
          then merge(temp[0,0].s, temp[inum, snum].s,
                                      temp[inum, snum].p, freelist);

    for inum := 0 to maxins do                     { transfer ptrs to instr   }
      begin
        instr[inum].p := temp[inum,0].p;
        instr[inum].s := temp[inum,0].s
      end;

    linkmeter(instr[0].s);                         { link spine to meter nodes }
    writeln(fout, 'Done')
  end;  { build }
```

```
(***************************************************************************)
(*                         DATA CONVERSION ROUTINES                        *)
(***************************************************************************)

(***********************        convert          ***********************)
(* Returns character equivalent of pc integer.                             *)
(***************************************************************************)
  function convert(pc : integer) : char;
    begin
      case pc of
         0 : convert := '0';
         1 : convert := '1';
         2 : convert := '2';
         3 : convert := '3';
         4 : convert := '4';
         5 : convert := '5';
         6 : convert := '6';
         7 : convert := '7';
         8 : convert := '8';
         9 : convert := '9';
        10 : convert := 'A';
        11 : convert := 'B';
        12 : convert := 'C'                        { used for 12 in ic-vector }
      end   { case }
    end;

(***********************          tonc           ***********************)
(* Converts note name to name class.                                       *)
(***************************************************************************)
  function tonc(c : char) : integer;
    begin
      case c of
        'C', 'c' : tonc := 0;
        'D', 'd' : tonc := 1;
        'E', 'e' : tonc := 2;
        'F', 'f' : tonc := 3;
        'G', 'g' : tonc := 4;
        'A', 'a' : tonc := 5;
        'B', 'b' : tonc := 6
      end { case }
    end; { tonc }

(***********************         tochar          ***********************)
(* Converts name class to note name.                                       *)
(***************************************************************************)
  function tochar(x : integer): char;
    begin
      case x of
        0 : tochar := 'C';
        1 : tochar := 'D';
        2 : tochar := 'E';
        3 : tochar := 'F';
        4 : tochar := 'G';
        5 : tochar := 'A';
        6 : tochar := 'B'
      end
    end;  { tochar }
```

```
(************************          pitch          ************************)
(* Converts name class to natural pitch class.                            *)
(**************************************************************************)
  function pitch(nc : integer) : integer;
    begin
      case nc of
        0 : pitch := 0;                                          { pc for c }
        1 : pitch := 2;                                          { pc for d }
        2 : pitch := 4;                                          { pc for e }
        3 : pitch := 5;                                          { pc for f }
        4 : pitch := 7;                                          { pc for g }
        5 : pitch := 9;                                          { pc for a }
        6 : pitch := 11                                          { pc for b }
      end  { case }
    end;  { pitch }


(**************************************************************************)
(*                           MANIPULATING BRS                             *)
(**************************************************************************)


(************************         brdecode        ************************)
(* Returns pc and nc components of the binomial-pc br.                    *)
(**************************************************************************)
  procedure brdecode(br : integer; var pc, nc: integer);
    begin
      pc := br div 10;
      nc := br mod 10
    end;

(************************           tobr          ************************)
(* Returns single-number representation of the binomial pc <pc,nc>.       *)
(**************************************************************************)
  function tobr(pc, nc : integer) : integer;
    begin
      tobr := (10 * pc) + nc
    end;

(************************          bradd          ************************)
(* Returns the sum of br1 and br2.  The br1, br2 and sum are coded        *)
(* binomial pcs.                                                          *)
(**************************************************************************)
  function bradd(br1, br2 : integer) : integer;
    var
      pc1, nc1, pc2, nc2 : integer;

    begin
      brdecode(br1, pc1, nc1);
      brdecode(br2, pc2, nc2);
      bradd := tobr(imod(pc1 + pc2, 12), imod(nc1 + nc2, 7))
    end;

(************************        brsubtract       ************************)
(* Returns the difference br1 - br2, where br1 and br2 are binomial pcs. *)
(* The difference is a br encoded interval.                               *)
(**************************************************************************)
  function brsubtract(br1, br2 : integer) : integer;
    var
      pc1, nc1, pc2, nc2 : integer;

    begin
      brdecode(br1, pc1, nc1);
      brdecode(br2, pc2, nc2);
      brsubtract := tobr(imod(pc1 - pc2, 12), imod(nc1 - nc2, 7))
    end;

(************************          brnorm         ************************)
(* Finds the best normal order for binomial pcset of cardinality n.  The *)
(* normal form recognizes transpositional equivalence but not inversional*)
(* equivalence.  The procedure uses an array twice as long as pcset for  *)
(* workspace. The pcset is copied into the workspace twice.  This avoids *)
(* wrapping around for circular permutations.  The normal order is       *)
(* copied back into pcset for return.  Prime returns the prime form, and *)
(* pcset the normal order.                                                *)
(**************************************************************************)
  procedure brnorm(var pcset, prime : brset; var n : integer);
    var
      list : array[1 .. 168] of integer;                    { workspace }
      i, j, dif1, dif2, p, t1, t2 : integer;

    procedure sort(var list : brset; var m : integer);
      var
        i     : integer;
        have  : array[0 .. 126] of boolean;    { checks for duplicate brs }

      begin
        for i := 0 to 126 do
          have[i] := false;

        for i := 1 to m do
          have[list[i]] := true;

        m := 0;
        for i := 0 to 126 do
          if have[i]
            then
              begin
                incr(m);
                list[m] := i
              end
      end;

    procedure transpose(var pcset : brset; n : integer);
      var
        i : integer;
      begin
        for i := n downto 1 do
          pcset[i] := brsubtract(pcset[i],pcset[1])
      end;

    begin { brnorm }
      sort(pcset,n);
      for i := 1 to n do
```

```
      begin                                       { copy pcset into workspace }
        list[i] := pcset[i];
        list[i+n] := pcset[i]
      end;
                                                  { find largest interval     }
    dif1 := brsubtract(list[n+1],list[n]);
    p := 1;                                       { ptr to 1st br in norm ord }
    for i := 2 to n do
      begin
        dif2 := brsubtract(list[i],list[i-1]);
        if dif2 > dif1
          then
            begin
              p := i;
              dif1 := dif2
            end
          else if dif1 = dif2                     { if difs are equal then    }
            then
              begin                                     { make 2nd test       }
                j := 0; t1 := 0; t2 := 0;
                while (t1 = t2) and (j < n) do
                  begin
                    j := j + 1;
                    t1 := brsubtract(list[p + j], list[p]);
                    t2 := brsubtract(list[i + j], list[i])
                  end;
                if t2 < t1
                  then p := i;
              end
      end;
    for i := 1 to n do
      begin { copy back in normal order }
        pcset[i] := list[p];
        p := p + 1
      end;
    prime := pcset;                                     { make copy           }
    transpose(prime, n);                                { transpose to zero   }
    sort(prime, n)                                      { ensure proper order }
  end; { brnorm }


(***************************************************************************)
(*                          MANIPULATING CBRS                              *)
(***************************************************************************)


(************************             cbr            ***********************)
(* Maps octave, pc, and nc into continuous binomial representation.        *)
(***************************************************************************)
  function cbr(octave, pc, nc : integer) : integer;
    begin
      if octave >= 0
        then cbr :=   octave * 1000 + pc * 10 + nc
        else cbr := -(abs(octave) * 1000 + pc * 10 + nc)
    end;
```

```
(************************             br             ***********************)
(* Extracts binomial representation from cbr.                              *)
(***************************************************************************)
  function br(cbr : integer) : integer;
    begin
      br := abs(cbr) mod 1000
    end;

(************************           octave           ***********************)
(* Extracts octave from cbr.                                               *)
(***************************************************************************)
  function octave(cbr : integer) : integer;
    begin
      octave := abs(cbr) div 1000
    end;

(************************         pitchclass         ***********************)
(* Extracts pitch class from cbr.                                          *)
(***************************************************************************)
  function pitchclass(cbr : integer) : integer;
    begin
      pitchclass := br(cbr) div 10
    end;

(************************         nameclass          ***********************)
(* Extracts name class from cbr.                                           *)
(***************************************************************************)
  function nameclass(cbr : integer) : integer;
    begin
      nameclass := br(cbr) mod 10
    end;

(************************             cpc            ***********************)
(* Calculates continuous pitch code from cbr.                              *)
(***************************************************************************)
  function cpc(cbr : integer) : integer;
    var
      o, p, n : integer;
      diff    : integer;

    begin
      o := octave(cbr);
      n := nameclass(cbr);
      p := pitchclass(cbr);
      diff := p - pitch(n);
      if diff > 6
        then o := o - 1
      else if diff < -6
        then o := o + 1;
      if cbr < 0
        then cpc := -(12 * o + p)
        else cpc :=  (12 * o + p)
    end;

(************************             cnc            ***********************)
(* Calculates continuous name code from cbr.                               *)
(***************************************************************************)
```

```
function cnc(cbr : integer) : integer;
  begin
    if cbr < 0
      then cnc := -(octave(cbr) * 7 + nameclass(cbr))
      else cnc :=   octave(cbr) * 7 + nameclass(cbr)
  end;

(************************          add           ************************)
(* Adds two signed cbrs, returning result as signed cbr.  May be used to *)
(* subtract by making either parameter negative.                         *)
(*************************************************************************)
function add(cbr1, cbr2 : integer) : integer;
  var
    pitch, name, octave : integer;
    negative : boolean;
  begin
    pitch := abs(cpc(cbr1) + cpc(cbr2)) mod 12;
    name := cnc(cbr1) + cnc(cbr2);
    if name <> 0                   { base direction on cnc }
      then negative := name < 0    { unless nc's are equal }
      else negative := (cpc(cbr1) + cpc(cbr2)) < 0;
    octave := abs(name) div 7;
    name := abs(name) mod 7;
    if negative
      then add := -cbr(octave, pitch, name)
      else add :=  cbr(octave, pitch, name)
  end;  { add }


(*************************************************************************)
(*                          OUTPUT ROUTINES                               *)
(*************************************************************************)

(************************       writepitch       ************************)
(* Writes cbr in standard form: eg. 5106 = Bb5                           *)
(*************************************************************************)
procedure writepitch(var f : text; cbr : integer);
  var
    i             : integer;
    ncl, pcl, dif : integer;
    accidental    : char;
  begin
    ncl := nameclass(cbr);
    pcl := pitchclass(cbr);
    write(f, tochar(ncl));
    dif := pcl - pitch(ncl);
    if dif >= 6
      then dif := dif - 12                     { convert to flat(s)  }
    else if dif <= -6
      then dif := dif + 12;                    { convert to sharp(s) }
    if dif > 0
      then accidental := '#'
      else accidental := 'b';
    for i := 1 to abs(dif) do
      write(f, accidental);
    write(f, octave(cbr):1)
  end;

(************************         cartic         ************************)
{ Return character representation of articulation codes.                 *)
(*************************************************************************)
function cartic(x : articulation) : char;
  begin
    case x of
      staccato     : cartic := '''';           { articulation codes }
      wedgeaccent  : cartic := '"';
      tenuto       : cartic := '_';
      accent       : cartic := '>';
      vaccent      : cartic := '<';
      fermata      : cartic := ';';
      arco         : cartic := 'r';            { dictionary codes   }
      pizz         : cartic := 'z';
      snap         : cartic := 'q';
      upbow        : cartic := 'v';
      downbow      : cartic := 'd';
      hauptstimme  : cartic := 'h';
      nebenstimme  : cartic := 'n';
      terminator   : cartic := '¯';
      open         : cartic := 'o';
      stopped      : cartic := '+'
    end  { case }
  end;

(************************       writeartic       ************************)
(* Prints articulation and dictionary codes.                             *)
(*************************************************************************)
procedure writeartic(var f : text; x : artictype);
  var
    i : articulation;
  begin
    if x = []
      then write(f, '0')
      else
        begin
          for i := staccato to terminator do
            if i in x
              then write(f, cartic(i));
        end
  end;  { writeartic }

(************************        writedyn        ************************)
(* Prints dynamic codes as integer.                                      *)
(*************************************************************************)
procedure writedyn(var f : text; x : integer);
  begin
    write(f, x:1)
  end;

(************************       writefrac        ************************)
(* Prints fraction in standard format.                                   *)
(*************************************************************************)
procedure writefrac(var f : text; x : fraction);
  begin
    write(f, x.num:1, '/', x.den:1)
  end;
```

```
(************************          writeintset          ************************)
(* Prints set of integers in hexadecimal.  Null set represented by x.        *)
(******************************************************************************)
  procedure writeintset(var f : text; var x : intset);
    var
      i : integer;

      function tochar(i : integer) : char;          { convert int to char }
        begin
          if i < 10
            then tochar := chr(ord('0') + i)
            else tochar := chr(ord('a') + i - 10)
        end;

    begin
      if x = []
        then write(f, 'x')          { null set }
        else for i := 1 to 16 do
               if i in x
                 then write(f, tochar(i))
    end;  { writeintset }

(************************          printorn          ************************)
(* Prints ornament in mnemonic form.                                          *)
(******************************************************************************)
  procedure printorn(var fout : text; x : ornament);
    begin
      write(fout,' ');
      case x of
        trill       : write(fout, 'trill');
        mordent     : write(fout, 'mord');
        turn        : write(fout, 'turn');
        flatN       : write(fout, '-');
        flatE       : write(fout, '-');
        flatS       : write(fout, '-');
        natN        : write(fout, '*');
        natE        : write(fout, '*');
        natS        : write(fout, '*');
        sharpN      : write(fout, '#');
        sharpE      : write(fout, '#');
        sharpS      : write(fout, '#');
      end  { case }
    end;  { printorn }

(************************          putorn2          ************************)
(* Prints set of ornaments.                                                   *)
(******************************************************************************)
  procedure putorn2(var fout : text; O : orntype);
    var
      i : ornament;
    begin
      if O = []
        then write('x')
        else
          for i := trill to sharpS do
            if i in O
              then printorn(fout, i)
    end;

(************************          printdyn          ************************)
(* Prints dynamic in mnemonic form.                                           *)
(******************************************************************************)
  procedure printdyn(var fout : text; x : dynamic);
    begin
      write(fout,' ');
      case x of
        pppppp      : write(fout, 'pppppp');
        ppppp       : write(fout, 'ppppp');
        pppp        : write(fout, 'pppp');
        ppp         : write(fout, 'ppp');
        pp          : write(fout, 'pp');
        p           : write(fout, 'p');
        mp          : write(fout, 'mp');
        mf          : write(fout, 'mf');
        f           : write(fout, 'f');
        ff          : write(fout, 'ff');
        fff         : write(fout, 'fff');
        ffff        : write(fout, 'ffff');
        fffff       : write(fout, 'fffff');
        ffffff      : write(fout, 'ffffff');
        sfz         : write(fout, 'sfz');
        cresc       : write(fout, 'cresc' );
        startcresc  : write(fout, 'startcresc');
        endcresc    : write(fout, 'endcresc');
        incresc     : write(fout, 'incresc');
        crescdim    : write(fout, 'crescdim');
        dim         : write(fout, 'dim');
        startdim    : write(fout, 'startdim');
        enddim      : write(fout, 'enddim');
        indim       : write(fout, 'indim');
        dimcresc    : write(fout, 'dimcresc');
      end  { case }
    end;  { printdyn }

(************************          putdyn2          ************************)
(* Prints set of dynamics in mnemonic form.                                   *)
(******************************************************************************)
  procedure putdyn2(var fout : text; D : dynset);
    var
      i : dynamic;
    begin
      for i := pppppp to dimcresc do
        if i in D
          then printdyn(fout, i)
    end;

(************************          writenote          ************************)
(* Prints values for a note node.                                             *)
(******************************************************************************)
  procedure writenote(var f : text; t : ptr);
    begin
      if t↑.tag = note
        then
          begin
            write(f, t↑.part:4:1, tab, starttime(t):6:4, tab,
                                              measno(t):6:4, tab);
```

```
            writepitch(f, t↑.dlink↑.pitch); write(f, tab);
            writefrac(f, t↑.dlink↑.dur);  write(f, tab);
            writeintset(f, t↑.dlink↑.tie);  write(f, tab);
            writeartic(f, t↑.dlink↑.artic); write(f, tab);
            writeintset(f, t↑.dlink↑.slur); write(f, tab);
            putorn2(f, t↑.dlink↑.orn); write(f, tab);
            writedyn(f, t↑.dlink↑.dyn1);
            putdyn2(f, t↑.dlink↑.dyn2)
          end
      else if t↑.tag = rest
        then
          begin
            write(f, t↑.part:4:1, tab, starttime(t):6:4, tab,
                                                measno(t):6:4, tab);
            write(f, 'rest'); write(f, tab);
            writefrac(f, t↑.dlink↑.dur); write(f, tab);
            writeintset(f, t↑.dlink↑.tie);  write(f, tab);
            writeartic(f, t↑.dlink↑.artic); write(f, tab);
            writeintset(f, t↑.dlink↑.slur); write(f, tab);
            putorn2(f, t↑.dlink↑.orn); write(f, tab);
            writedyn(f, t↑.dlink↑.dyn1);
            putdyn2(f, t↑.dlink↑.dyn2)
          end
      else if t↑.tag = gracenote
        then
          begin
            write(f, t↑.part:4:1, tab, starttime(t):6:4, tab,
                                                measno(t):6:4, tab);
            writepitch(f, t↑.dlink↑.pitch); write(f, tab);
            write(f, 'gnote');  write(f, tab);
            writeintset(f, t↑.dlink↑.tie);  write(f, tab);
            writeartic(f, t↑.dlink↑.artic); write(f, tab);
            writeintset(f, t↑.dlink↑.slur); write(f, tab);
            putorn2(f, t↑.dlink↑.orn); write(f, tab);
            writedyn(f, t↑.dlink↑.dyn1);
            putdyn2(f, t↑.dlink↑.dyn2)
          end;
      writeln(f)
    end;

(************************          writebar          ************************)
(* Prints bar line code in mnemonic form.                                    *)
(****************************************************************************)
  procedure writebar(var f : text; t : ptr);
    begin
      write(f, t↑.part:4:1,tab);
      case t↑.bartype of
        0 : writeln(f, '/');
        1 : writeln(f, '//');
        2 : writeln(f, '!/');
        3 : writeln(f, '!//');
        4 : writeln(f, '/!/');
        5 : writeln(f, '//:');
        6 : writeln(f, '://');
        7 : writeln(f, '!//:');
        8 : writeln(f, ':/!/');
        9 : writeln(f, '://:')
      end { case }
    end;

(************************          writemeter          ************************)
(* Prints values for meter signature.                                        *)
(****************************************************************************)
  procedure writemeter(var f : text; p : ptr);
    begin
      write(f, p↑.part:4:1, tab, 'meter=', tab);
      writefrac(f, p↑.meter);  write(f, tab);
      write(f, 'beat =', tab);
      writefrac(f, p↑.beatnote);
      writeln(f)
    end;

(************************          writekey          ************************)
(* Prints key signature.                                                     *)
(****************************************************************************)
  procedure writekey(var f : text; p : ptr);
    begin
      write(f, p↑.part:1, tab, 'keysig=', tab, p↑.accidentals:1,
              p↑.sign:2);
      writeln(f)
    end;

(************************          writenode          ************************)
(* Calls appropriate procedures to print values for any node.                *)
(****************************************************************************)
  procedure writenode(var f : text; t : ptr);
    begin
      case t↑.tag of
        note,
        rest,
        gracenote  : writenote(f, t);
        metersig   : writemeter(f, t);
        keysig     : writekey(f, t);
        barline    : writebar(f, t)
      end  { case }
    end;

(************************          writeparts          ************************)
(* Prints part numbers for active parts in set.                              *)
(****************************************************************************)
  procedure writeparts(var f : text; x : partset);
    var
      t : integer;
    begin
      for t := 1 to maxins do
        if t in x
          then write(f, t:4);
      writeln(f)
    end;

(****************************************************************************)
(*                         INTERFACE ROUTINES                                *)
(* These routines are used in all of the score procedures in chapter 20.    *)
(****************************************************************************)
```

```
(************************          setins          ************************)
(* Sets target instruments.                                                *)
(***************************************************************************)
  procedure setins(var fin, fout : text; var parts, all : partset);
    var
      i      : integer;
      buffer : buftype;

    begin
      write(fout, 'Available parts = ');
      writeparts(fout, all);
      write(fout, 'Type part numbers or all: ');
      getline(fin, fout, buffer);
      skipbuf(buffer);
      if (nextchar(buffer) in ['a', 'A']) or eob(buffer)
        then parts := all
        else
          begin
            parts := [0];
            while not eob(buffer) do
              begin
                getint(fin, fout, buffer, i);
                parts := parts + [i];
                skipbuf(buffer)
              end
          end
    end;

(************************       affirmative       ************************)
(* Gets answer to y/n type question.                                       *)
(***************************************************************************)
  function affirmative(var fin, fout : text; default : boolean) : boolean;
    var
      buffer : buftype;

    begin
      getline(fin, fout, buffer);
      skipbuf(buffer);
      if eob(buffer)
        then affirmative := default
      else if nextchar(buffer) in ['y', 'Y']
        then affirmative := true
      else if nextchar(buffer) in ['n', 'N']
        then affirmative := false
      else
        begin
          write(fout, 'You must answer yes or no: ');
          affirmative := affirmative(fin, fout, default)
        end
    end;

(************************         getmeter        ************************)
(* Returns pointer to previous meter node or nil pointer.                  *)
(***************************************************************************)
  function getmeter(q : ptr) : ptr;
    begin
      if q↑.tag = head
        then q := q↑.llink;
      if q↑.tag = head                            { empty list               }
        then getmeter := nil
        else
          begin
            while q↑.tag <> spine do              { find spine node          }
              q := q↑.start;
            getmeter := q↑.mlink                  { return pointer to meternode }
          end
    end;  { getmeter }

(************************           setw          ************************)
(* Prompts user for beginning and end of score window.                     *)
(***************************************************************************)
  procedure setw(var fin, fout : text; S : ptr; var t : ptr;
                                                  var rmeasure : real);

    var
      measure  : integer;                                 { measure number }
      beat     : real;                                    { beat in bar    }
      meter    : real;                                    { beats per bar  }
      q        : ptr;                                     { temp pointer   }
      buffer   : buftype;

    begin
      write(fout, 'Type measure number: ');
      getline(fin, fout, buffer);
      getint(fin, fout, buffer, measure);
      t := S↑.rlink;
      while (toreal(t↑.measure) < measure) and (t↑.rlink↑.tag <> head) do
        t := t↑.rlink;

      q := getmeter(t);                                   { get meter node }
      if q <> nil
        then meter := (q↑.meter.num * q↑.beatnote.den) /
                      (q↑.meter.den * q↑.beatnote.num)
        else
          begin
            writeln(fout, 'Sorry, I Can''t find a meter node');
            write(fout, 'How many beats per bar? ');
            getline(fin, fout, buffer);
            getreal(fin, fout, buffer, meter);
            readln(fin, meter)
          end;

      write(fout, 'Type beat: ');
      getline(fin, fout, buffer);
      if eob(buffer)
        then beat := 1.0
        else getreal(fin, fout, buffer, beat);
      if (beat < 1.0)
        then
          begin
            writeln(fout, 'The first beat of a measure is beat 1');
            setw(fin, fout, S, t, rmeasure)
          end
```

```
      else
        begin
          rmeasure := measure + (beat - 1) / meter;
          while (toreal(t↑.measure) < rmeasure)
                                          and (t↑.rlink↑.tag <> head) do
            t := t↑.rlink
        end
  end;  { setw }


(************************          setwindow          ************************)
(* Sets pointers to beginning and end of window.                             *)
(*****************************************************************************)
  procedure setwindow(var fin, fout : text; spine : ptr;
                                 var startwindow, endwindow : ptr);
    var
      stime, etime : real;                      { starting and ending time }

    begin
      writeln(fout);
      writeln(fout, 'Score segment from measure',
                    toreal(spine↑.rlink↑.measure):8:3,
            ' to ', toreal(spine↑.llink↑.measure):8:3);
      writeln(fout, 'Setting beginning of window ...');
      setw(fin, fout, spine, startwindow, stime);     { set window         }
      writeln(fout);
      writeln(fout, 'Setting end of window ...');
      setw(fin, fout, spine, endwindow, etime);       { set end of window }
      if endwindow↑.tag <> head
        then endwindow := endwindow↑.rlink;           { get next node      }
      if stime > etime
        then
          begin
            writeln(fout, 'Start of window must precede end');
            setwindow(fin, fout, spine, startwindow, endwindow)
          end
    end;


(************************          allset          ************************)
(* Sets all to available parts in score.                                  *)
(**************************************************************************)
  procedure allset(spine : ptr; var all : partset);
    var
      t : ptr;

    begin
      all := [ ];
      t := spine;
      repeat
        all := all + [trunc(t↑.part)];
        t := t↑.start
      until t = spine
    end;


(************************          setup          ************************)
(* Initializes window and active parts.                                  *)
(*************************************************************************)
  procedure setup(var fout : text; spine : ptr; var parts, all : partset;
                                     var startwindow, endwindow : ptr);
    begin
      allset(spine, all);                         { all instruments      }
      parts := all;
      startwindow := spine↑.rlink;                { first node in spine }
      endwindow   := spine;                       { head node of spine  }
      writeln(fout);
      writeln(fout, 'Defaults: measures =',
                    toreal(spine↑.rlink↑.measure):8:3,
            ' to ', toreal(spine↑.llink↑.measure):8:3);
      write(fout, '            parts    =');
      writeparts(fout, parts);
      writeln(fout)
    end;  { initialize }


(************************          partcount          ************************)
(* Returns number of active parts in target set.                             *)
(*****************************************************************************)
  function partcount(var parts : partset) : integer;
    var
      i : integer;
      n : integer;

    begin
      n := 0;
      for i := 1 to maxins do
        if i in parts
          then incr(n);
      partcount := n
    end;
```

```
(************************          setdefs.h          ************************)
(* This file contains the additional type definitions needed by programs *)
(* calling pc set identification routines in file setcalc.p.  The file   *)
(* can be included in any program that needs it by inserting the follow- *)
(* ing line after the reserved word type:                                *)
(*      #   include "setdefs.h"                                          *)
(* where '#' is in the first column of a line.  On systems that do not   *)
(* permit include files, this file should be copied into the program at  *)
(* the appropriate location.                                             *)
(**************************************************************************)

{ type }

    ar100   = array[1 .. 12] of integer;
    row     = array[-1 .. 12] of integer;        { one row of matrix          }
    matrix  = array[ 0 .. 12] of row;            { matrix for calculating     }
                                                 {    Rahn's normal order     }

    pftype = (forte, rahn);                      { prime form type            }

    pcint = 0 .. 11;
    pcset = set of pcint;

    fset =
      record                          { structure of record on set table      }
        z      : integer;             { number of z-related set, 0 if none    }
        mmi    : integer;             { set resulting from m5 or m7           }
        name   : integer;             { ordinal position in list              }
        setnum : integer              { summation 2**pc[i] for i = 1 to card  }
      end;

    ar300 = array[1 .. 229] of fset;

    tabinfo =
      record
        start : integer;              { loc[n] = loc in table of beginning    }
        stop  : integer               { end of sublist for cardinality n      }
      end;

    ar600 = array[1 .. 12] of tabinfo; { set-class locations in table        }

    setinfo =                         { information record                    }
      record
        trans : integer;              { transposition level                   }
        form  : char;                 { 'p' or 'i'                            }
        card  : integer;              { cardinality of set                    }
        z     : integer;              { z-related set or 0                    }
        name  : integer;              { ordinal number of set                 }
        mmi   : integer;              { set obtained by m5 or m7              }
        pcset : ar100;                { the given pitch class set             }
        prime : ar100;                { prime form of set                     }
        vector: ar100;                { interval vector for set               }
        symmetric : boolean           { true if inv = prime                   }
      end;
```

```
(************************          setcalc.p          ************************)
(* This file contains external procedures for calculating pitch class    *)
(* set relations.  In some Pascal systems this file can be compiled sep- *)
(* arately, and linked with other compiled programs.  In systems that do *)
(* not allow external procedures, the required procedures and functions  *)
(* can be copied into each program before compiling.                     *)
(**************************************************************************)

  const
    maxins  = 15;
    maxline = 90;

  type
#   include "setdefs.h"
#   include "linkdefs.h"

(**************************************************************************)
(*                         EXTERNAL ROUTINES                              *)
(*                    (from file xtern.p, above)                          *)
(**************************************************************************)

    function  convert(pc : integer) : char;                        external;
    function  eob(var buffer : buftype) : boolean;                 external;
    function  isdigit(c : char) : boolean;                         external;
    function  islower(c : char) : boolean;                         external;
    function  ispc(c : char) : boolean;                            external;
    function  isupper(c : char) : boolean;                         external;
    function  nextchar(var buffer : buftype) : char;               external;

    procedure decr(var x : integer);                               external;
    procedure getint(var fi, fo : text; var buffer : buftype;
                                               var x : integer);   external;
    procedure getline(var fi,fo : text; var buffer : buftype);     external;
    procedure incr(var x : integer);                               external;
    procedure skipbuf(var buffer : buftype);                       external;

(**************************************************************************)
(*                          PC SET ROUTINES                               *)
(*                           (chapter 12.3)                               *)
(**************************************************************************)

(***********************           calc          ***********************)
(* Multiplies each element of set A by op, adds n (mod 12), and returns *)
(* the result as set B.  The procedure is called with op = 1 for iden-  *)
(* tity [B = Tn(A)], op = 11 for inversion [B = TnI(A)], op = 5 for M    *)
(* [B = TnM(A)], op = 7 for MI [B = TnMI(A)], where 0 <= n <= 11.        *)
(**************************************************************************)
  procedure calc(A : pcset; op, n : integer; var B : pcset);
    var
      pc : pcint;
    begin
      B := [];                                              { null set }
      for pc := 0 to 11 do
        if pc in A
          then B := B + [((pc * op) + n) mod 12]
    end;
```

```
(************************        transpose        ************************)
(* Performs Tn(A); returns result as B.                                   *)
(**************************************************************************)
 procedure transpose(A : pcset; n : integer; var B : pcset);
   var
     pc : pcint;
   begin
     B := [];                                               { null set }
     for pc := 0 to 11 do
       if pc in A
         then B := B + [(pc+n) mod 12]
   end;

(************************          invert         ************************)
(* Performs TnI(A); returns result as B.                                  *)
(**************************************************************************)
 procedure invert(A : pcset; n : integer; var B : pcset);
   var
     pc : pcint;
   begin
     B := [];                                               { null set }
     for pc := 0 to 11 do
       if pc in A
         then B := B + [(n + 12  - pc) mod 12]
   end;

(************************          subset         ************************)
(* Returns true if B is a subset of A.                                    *)
(**************************************************************************)
 function subset(A, B : pcset) : boolean;
   var
     t     : integer;
     C, D  : pcset;
     found : boolean;
   begin
     found := false;
     t := 0;
     while (t <= 11) and not found do
       begin
         transpose(B, t, C);
         invert(B, t, D);
         found := (C <= A) or (D <= A);
         t := t + 1
       end;
     subset := found
   end;


(**************************************************************************)
(*                          PRIME-FORM ROUTINES                           *)
(* Adapted from program setid (chapter 17) for use as external routines. *)
(**************************************************************************)


(************************         newtype         ************************)
(* Sets new prime form type (Forte, Rahn).                                *)
(**************************************************************************)
 procedure newtype(var fin, fout : text; var primetype : pftype);
   var
     buffer : buftype;
   begin
     writeln(fout);
     writeln(fout, 'Setting prime form type...');
     write(fout, 'Type "Forte" or "Rahn": ');
     getline(fin, fout, buffer);
     skipbuf(buffer);
     if nextchar(buffer) in ['f', 'F', 'r', 'R']
       then
         begin                                              { good response }
           if nextchar(buffer) in ['f', 'F']
             then
               begin
                 primetype := forte;
                 writeln(fout, 'Type = Forte')
               end
             else
               begin
                 primetype := rahn;
                 writeln(fout, 'Type = Rahn')
               end
         end
       else
         begin                                              { error         }
           writeln(fout, 'Illegal response');
           newtype(fin, fout, primetype)
         end
   end;  { newtype }

(************************        readtable        ************************)
(* Reads data from external set table.  Table is listed as figure 17.1   *)
(* in section 17.4.                                                       *)
(**************************************************************************)
 procedure readtable(var fout, data : text; var loc : ar600;
                                                    var table : ar300);
   var
     i : integer;

   begin { read external data into tables }
     write(fout, 'Reading set data ...');
     reset(data);
     for i := 1 to 12 do                                   { read loc table }
       with loc[i] do
         readln(data, start, stop);
     for i := 1 to 229 do                                  { read set table }
       with table[i] do
         readln(data, bitvec, name, z, mmi);
     writeln(fout, 'Done');
   end;

(************************          power          ************************)
(* Returns power of 2, i.e. 2 ** x                                        *)
(**************************************************************************)
 function power(x : integer) : integer;
   begin
```

```
    case x of
      0 : power :=    1;
      1 : power :=    2;
      2 : power :=    4;
      3 : power :=    8;
      4 : power :=   16;
      5 : power :=   32;
      6 : power :=   64;
      7 : power :=  128;
      8 : power :=  256;
      9 : power :=  512;
     10 : power := 1024;
     11 : power := 2048
    end { case }
  end;  { power }

(************************          pencode          ************************)
(* Returns bit vector representing n element set in pcset array.            *)
(***************************************************************************)
  function pencode(var pcset : ar100; n : integer) : integer;
    var
      t : integer;
      i : integer;
    begin
      t := 0;
      for i := 1 to n do
        t := t + power(pcset[i]);
      pencode := t
    end;

(************************          iencode          ************************)
(* Returns bit vector representing inverse of n element set stored in     *)
(* array pcset.                                                            *)
(***************************************************************************)
  function iencode(var pcset : ar100; n : integer) : integer;
    var
      t : integer;
      i : integer;
    begin
      t := 0;
      for i := 1 to n do
        t := t + power((12 - pcset[i]) mod 12);
      iencode := t
    end;

(************************          encode           ************************)
(* Encodes pcset in array as set of integers.                              *)
(***************************************************************************)
  procedure encode(var A : ar100; n : integer; var x : pcset);
    var
      i : integer;
    begin
      x := [];
      for i := 1 to n do
        x := x + [A[i]]                            { add to set using union }
    end;

(************************          decode2          ************************)
(* Decodes set number x into array a, and return cardinality n.            *)
(***************************************************************************)
  procedure decode2(x : pcset; var a : ar100; var n : integer);
    var
      pc : integer;
    begin
      n := 0;
      for pc := 0 to 11 do
        if pc in x
          then
            begin
              incr(n);
              a[n] := pc
            end
    end; { decode 2 }

(************************          decode3          ************************)
(* Decodes bit vector into target pcset.                                   *)
(***************************************************************************)
  procedure decode3(bitvec : integer; var target : pcset);
    var
      pc : integer;
    begin
      pc := 0;
      target := [];
      while bitvec > 0 do
        begin
          if odd(bitvec)
            then target := target + [pc];
          pc := pc + 1;
          bitvec := bitvec div 2
        end
    end;  { decode 3 }

(************************          decode           ************************)
(* Decodes bit vector x into array a, and returns cardinality n.           *)
(***************************************************************************)
  procedure decode(x : integer; var a : ar100; var n : integer);
    var
      pc : integer;
    begin
      n := 0;
      pc := 0;
      while x > 0 do
        begin
          if (x mod 2) = 1
            then
              begin
                incr(n);
                a[n] := pc
              end;
          incr(pc);
          x := x div 2
        end
    end;  { decode }
```

```
(************************          rotate          ************************)
(* Rotates bits in bit vector to left, bit thirteen rotates to position  *)
(* 1.  N.B. x * 2 = T1(x)                                                 *)
(**************************************************************************)
 procedure rotate(var x : integer);
   begin
     x := x * 2;
     if x > 4095
       then x := x - 4095
   end;


(************************          adjust          ************************)
(* Transforms Starr/Rahn/Morris bit vectors to Forte's. Also adjusts the *)
(* transposition level.                                                   *)
(**************************************************************************)
 procedure adjust(var bitvec, trans : integer);
   begin
     if bitvec = 355
       then begin
              bitvec := 395;
              trans := trans + 7
            end
     else if bitvec = 691
       then begin
              bitvec := 811;
              trans := trans + 8
            end
     else if bitvec = 717
       then begin
              bitvec := 843;
              trans := trans + 6
            end
     else if bitvec = 743
       then begin
              bitvec := 919;
              trans := trans + 7
            end
     else if bitvec = 755
       then begin
              bitvec := 815;
              trans := trans + 8
            end
     else if bitvec = 1467
       then begin
              bitvec := 1719;
              trans := trans + 9
            end
   end;  { adjust }


(************************        primeform         ************************)
(* Returns prime form as bit vector  PF is least value of all transposi-*)
(* tions of prime and inverted set as bit vectors.                        *)
(**************************************************************************)

function primeform(primetype : pftype;                    { forte or rahn   }
                   var pcset : ar100;                     { pc set          }
                           n : integer;                   { cardinality     }
                    var form : char;                      { p or i          }
                   var trans : integer;                   { n in Tn or TnI  }
               var symmetric : boolean;                   { true if p=i     }
                             : integer;                   { return type     }
  var
    p, i            : integer;             { set numbers for t0p and T0ip }
    plow, ilow      : integer;             { lowest p or i bit vectori    }
    ptrans, itrans  : integer;             { lowest value of tn or Tni    }
    j               : integer;             { transposition level          }

  begin { primeform }
    p := pencode(pcset, n);                { bit vector for prime form    }
    plow := p;
    i := iencode(pcset, n);                { bit vector for inversion     }
    ilow := i;
    ptrans := 0; itrans := 0;

    for j := 1 to 11 do                    { check other transp levels    }
      begin
        rotate(p);                         { transpose 1 semitone         }
        if p < plow
          then
            begin
              plow := p;
              ptrans := j
            end;
        rotate(i);                         { transpose 1 semitone         }
        if i < ilow
          then
            begin
              ilow := i;
              itrans :=  j
            end
      end;

    symmetric := (plow = ilow);            { check for symmetry           }
    if plow <= ilow
      then
        begin                              { Tn(plow)                     }
          if primetype = forte
            then adjust(plow, ptrans);     { change prime form            }
          primeform := plow;
          form := 'p';
          trans := (12 - ptrans) mod 12
        end
      else
        begin                              { TnI(plow)                    }
          if primetype = forte
            then adjust(ilow, itrans);     { change prime form            }
          primeform := ilow;
          form := 'i';
          trans := itrans mod 12
        end
  end;  { primeform }
```

```
(************************          ic          ************************)
(* Returns interval class of pc interval x.                              *)
(*************************************************************************)
 function ic(x : integer) : integer;
   begin
     if x > 6
       then ic := 12 - x
       else ic := x
   end;


(************************       makevector      ************************)
(* Calculates interval-class vector.                                     *)
(*************************************************************************)
 procedure makevector(var pcset : ar100; n : integer; var ivec : ar100);

   var
     i, j : integer;

   begin
     for i := 1 to 6 do
       ivec[i] := 0;
     for i := 1 to n - 1 do
       for j := i + 1 to n do
         incr(ivec[ic(abs(pcset[i] - pcset[j]))])
   end;  { calc interval vector }


(************************       binsearch       ************************)
(* Searches set table A, between indices lower and upper, for bit vector *)
(* x.  Returns zero if not found.                                        *)
(*************************************************************************)
 function binsearch(var A : ar300; lower, upper : integer;
                                            x : integer) : integer;

   var
     mid, answer : integer;

   begin
     answer := 0;
     while (upper >= lower) and (answer = 0) do
       begin
         mid := (lower + upper) div 2;
         if A[mid].bitvec = x
           then answer := mid
         else if x > A[mid].bitvec
           then lower := mid + 1
         else upper := mid - 1
       end;
       binsearch := answer
   end;  { binary search }
```

```
(*************************************************************************)
(*                         RAHN'S NORMAL ORDER                           *)
(* The following routines calculate Rahn's Normal Order.  Described in   *)
(* section 17.6.3.                                                       *)
(*************************************************************************)


(************************        setsort        ************************)
(* Sorts pc set in array A using Pascal's set type.                      *)
(*************************************************************************)
 procedure setsort(var A : ar100; n : integer);
   type
     pcset = set of 0 .. 11;

   var
     i, pc : integer;
     x     : pcset;

   begin
     x := [];
     for i := 1 to n do
       x := x + [A[i]];
     n := 0;                        { copy pcs into array in ascending order }
     for pc := 0 to 11 do
       if pc in x
         then
           begin
             incr(n);
             A[n] := pc
           end
   end;  { setsort }


(************************       swaparray       ************************)
(* Exchanges two arrays x and y; used by procedure sortmat.              *)
(*************************************************************************)
 procedure swaparray(var x, y : row);
   var
     t : row;

   begin
     t := x; x := y; y := t
   end;


(************************        sortmat        ************************)
(* Sorts n rows of matrix M on value in column key.                      *)
(*************************************************************************)
 procedure sortmat(var M : matrix; n, key : integer);
   var
     i, j, k : integer;

   begin
     for i := 0 to n - 1 do
       begin
         k := i;                              { get loc of smallest value  }
         for j := k + 1 to n do
```

```
          if M[j][key] < M[k][key]
            then k := j;
          swaparray(M[i], M[k])           { exchange with element i     }
        end
    end;  { sortmat }


(***********************          normal          ***********************)
(* Calculates Rahn's normal order.                                       *)
(*************************************************************************)
  procedure normal(var A : ar100; n : integer);
    var
      i, j      : integer;             { loop variables                  }
      c         : integer;             { n - 1                           }
      column    : integer;             { current column                  }
      dups      : integer;             { number of duplicate pcs in column }
      lastdups  : integer;             { number of dups in last column   }
      M         : matrix;              { matrix                          }

    begin
      setsort(A, n);                   { sort pc set                     }
      c := n - 1;                      { last column, numbered from zero }
      for i := 0 to c do               { copy set into matrix            }
        begin
          M[i, -1] := A[i+1];
          M[0, i] := A[i+1]
        end;

      for i := 1 to c do                       { do rotations            }
        for j := 0 to c do
          M[i,j] := M[0, (i+j) mod n];

      for i := 0 to c do                       { calculate intervals     }
        for j := 0 to c do
          M[i, j] := (M[i, j] + 12 - M[i, -1]) mod 12;

      sortmat(M, c, c);                        { sort matrix on last column }
      column := c;
      lastdups := c;
      repeat
        dups := 0;                             { how many duplicates?    }
        while (M[0, column] = M[dups + 1, column]) and (dups < lastdups) do
          incr(dups);
        if dups > 0
          then
            begin
              column := column - 1;
              if (dups < lastdups) or (column = -1)
                then sortmat(M, dups, column);
              lastdups := dups
            end
      until dups = 0;

      for i := 0 to c do              { copy normal order back to array A }
        A[i+1] := (M[0, i] + M[0, -1]) mod 12
    end;  { normal }

(***********************          setcalc          ***********************)
(* Calculates normal order, prime form, derivation, etc.                 *)
(*************************************************************************)
  procedure setcalc(var f : text; primetype : pftype; var dat : setinfo;
                              var loc : ar600; var table : ar300);
    var
      i    : integer;
      pos  : integer;                          { position in table       }
      test : integer;                          { for double checking     }
      x    : integer;                          { prime form as set number }

    begin { setcalc }
      with dat do
        begin
          test := pencode(pcset, card);
          x := primeform(primetype, pcset, card, form, trans, symmetric);
          decode(x, prime, card);              { store prime form in array }
          with loc[card] do
            pos := binsearch(table, start, stop, x);

          z     := table[pos].z;               { set other data fields   }
          mmi   := table[pos].mmi;
          name  := table[pos].name;
          makevector(prime, card, vector);

          if form = 'p'                        { store normal order      }
            then
              for i := 1 to card do
                pcset[i] := (prime[i] + trans) mod 12
            else
              for i := 1 to card do
                pcset[i] := (trans - prime[card - i + 1] + 12) mod 12;

          if test <> pencode(pcset, card)      { double check            }
            then writeln(f, 'Setcalc: prime form error');
          normal(pcset, card)                  { calc Rahn's normal order }
        end { with dat }
    end;  { setcalc }

(***********************          lineara          ***********************)
(* Does forward linear search of set table A, between indices lower and *)
(* upper, for bit vector x.  Returns location or 0.  N.B. the forward   *)
(* search finds the Rahn normal order.                                   *)
(*************************************************************************)
  function lineara(var A : ar300; lower, upper : integer; x : integer)
                                                                : integer;
    var
      i : integer;

    begin
      i := lower;
      while (i < upper) and (A[i].name <> x) do
        incr(i);
      if A[i].name = x
        then lineara := i
        else lineara := 0
    end;  { forward linear search }
```

```
(************************           linearb          ************************)
(* Does reverse linear search of set table A, between indices upper and    *)
(* lower, for bit vector x.  Returns location or 0.  Finds Forte prime    *)
(* form.                                                                   *)
(***************************************************************************)
 function linearb(var A : ar300; lower, upper : integer; x : integer)
                                                              : integer;

   var
     i : integer;

   begin
     i := upper;
     while (i > lower) and (A[i].name <> x) do
       decr(i);
     if A[i].name = x
       then linearb := i
       else linearb := 0
   end;  { backward linear search }



(************************          printset          ************************)
(* Prints pc set in hexadecimal.                                           *)
(***************************************************************************)
 procedure printset(var f : text; S : pcset);
   var
     i : integer;

   begin
     write(f, '{');
     for i := 0 to 11 do
       if i in S
         then write(f, convert(i));
     write(f, '}')
   end;



(************************           setname          ************************)
(* Pattern matching function, returns true if it matches a possible pcset*)
(* name in buffer.  N.B. bp is value parameter here, so it does not      *)
(* change in the rest of the program.                                    *)
(***************************************************************************)
 function setname(var buffer : buftype) : boolean;
   var
     temp : buftype;

   function digits : boolean;
     begin
       skipbuf(temp);
       with temp do
         begin
           digits := isdigit(B[bp]);
           while isdigit(B[bp]) do
             incr(bp)
         end
     end;

   function dash : boolean;
     begin
       skipbuf(temp);
       with temp do
         begin
           if B[bp] = '-'
             then
               begin
                 dash := true;
                 incr(bp)
               end
             else dash := false
         end
     end;

   begin { setname }
     temp := buffer;
     setname := false;
     if digits
       then if dash
       then setname := digits
   end;  { setname }

(************************           getname          ************************)
(* Returns cardinal and ordinal number of set name.  Reads from buffer.   *)
(***************************************************************************)
 procedure getname(var fin, fout : text; var buffer : buftype;
                                 var cardinal, ordinal : integer);
   begin
     getint(fin, fout, buffer, cardinal);
     skipbuf(buffer);
     incr(buffer.bp);                                      { skip dash }
     getint(fin, fout, buffer, ordinal)
   end;

(************************            getpc           ************************)
(* Reads a pc in hexadecimal notation from buffer.                         *)
(***************************************************************************)
 procedure getpc(var buffer : buftype; var pc : integer);
   var
     c : char;
   begin
     skipbuf(buffer);
     c := nextchar(buffer);
     if ispc(c)
       then
         begin
           if isdigit(c)
             then pc := ord(c) - ord('0')
           else if islower(c)
             then pc := ord(c) - ord('a') + 10
           else if isupper(c)
             then pc := ord(c) - ord('A') + 10;
           incr(buffer.bp)                        { advance buffer pointer }
         end
       else pc := -1                              { return error code      }
   end;
```

```
(************************          lookup          ************************)
(* Reads set name from buffer and finds set in set table.                    *)
(****************************************************************************)
  procedure lookup(var fin, fout : text;          { input and output files }
                   var buffer    : buftype;       { character buffer       }
                   var pcset     : ar100;         { array for set          }
                   var n         : integer;       { cardinality of set     }
                       primetype : pftype;        { prime form (forte/rahn }
                   var loc       : ar600;         { loc of cards in table  }
                   var table     : ar300;         { the set table          }
                   var code      : integer);      { return code            }

    var
      c, o : integer;                 { cardinal and ordinal part of name }
      x    : integer;                 { location of set c-o in table      }

    begin  { lookup }
      code := 0;                      { begin with good return code       }
      getname(fin, fout, buffer, c, o);
      if (c < 1) or (c > 12)                          { bad cardinality }
        then code := 1                                { = bad set name  }
        else
          begin                     { find set in table via linear search }
            if primetype = forte
              then x := linearb(table, loc[c].start, loc[c].stop, o)
              else x := lineara(table, loc[c].start, loc[c].stop, o);

            if x = 0                                  { didn't find it }
              then code := 1                          { bad set name   }
              else decode(table[x].bitvec, pcset,n)
          end
      end;  { lookup }



(************************          readset          ************************)
(* Prompts user for set name or pcs.  If a set name is specified, it       *)
(* calls lookup, otherwise it reads the set from the buffer.               *)
(****************************************************************************)
  procedure readset(var fin, fout : text;         { input and output files }
                    var pcset     : ar100;        { array for pc set       }
                    var n         : integer;      { cardinality of set     }
                        primetype : pftype;       { forte or rahn          }
                    var loc       : ar600;        { loc of cards in table  }
                    var table     : ar300);       { set table              }

    type
      pcs = 0 .. 11;
      pset = set of pcs;

    var
      pc     : integer;
      check  : pset;
      buffer : buftype;
      code   : integer;                          { return code            }
```

```
begin { readset }
  write(fout, 'Type set name or pcs: ');
  getline(fin, fout, buffer);
  if setname(buffer)                             { get set from table      }
    then
      lookup(fin, fout, buffer, pcset, n, primetype, loc, table, code)
    else
      begin
        check := [];                             { null set                }
        n := 0;                                  { cardinality             }
        code := 0;                               { signal OK               }

        while not eob(buffer) and (code = 0) do
          begin
            getpc(buffer, pc);
            if pc >= 0
              then
                begin
                  if not (pc in check)
                    then
                      begin
                        incr(n);
                        pcset[n] := pc;
                        check := check + [pc]
                      end;
                  skipbuf(buffer)
                end
              else code := 2                     { illegal character      }
          end;

        if code = 0                              { normal return code     }
          then if n = 0                          { but cardinality = 0    }
            then code := 3;                      { signal null set        }

        if code <> 0
          then
            begin  { error }
              case code of
                1 : writeln(fout, 'Bad set name');
                2 : writeln(fout, 'Bad input character');
                3 : writeln(fout, 'Null set')
              end;  { case }
              readset(fin, fout, pcset, n, primetype, loc, table)
            end     { error }
      end
end;  { readset }
```

APPENDIX E

Score Programs from Chapter 20

```
(***********************        PROGRAM PROOF       ***********************)
(* Traverses the score, printing values for each node (section 20.3.1).  *)
(*************************************************************************)

program proof(input, output, scoredata);
  const
    maxins    = 15;
    maxline   = 90;
    yes = true;
    no  = false;

  type
#   include "linkdefs.h"

  var
    instr       : partpointers;         { pointers into score structure  }
    freelist    : ptr;                  { pointer to stack of free nodes }
    scoredata   : text;                 { output from DARMS interpreter  }
    parts       : partset;              { set of active parts            }
    all         : partset;              { set of all possible parts      }
    startwindow : ptr;                  { pointers to beginning and end  }
    endwindow   : ptr;                  {  of active window in score     }
    done        : boolean;              { true when user wants to quit   }


(*************************************************************************)
(* External procedures and functions (see appendix D).                   *)
(*************************************************************************)

  procedure build(var fin, fout, scoredata : text;
                     var instr : partpointers; var free : ptr); external;
  procedure writenode(var f : text; t : ptr);                    external;
  procedure incr(var x : integer);                               external;
  procedure setins(var fin, fout : text; var parts,
                                         all : partset);         external;
  function  affirmative(var fin, fout : text;
                               default : boolean) : boolean;     external;
  procedure setwindow(var fin, fout : text; spine : ptr;
                     var startwindow, endwindow : ptr);          external;
  procedure setup(var fout : text; spine : ptr; var parts,
            all : partset; var startwindow, endwindow : ptr);    external;
  function  partcount(var parts : partset) : integer;            external;


(***********************         gtraverse         ***********************)
(* Traverses gracenote list through spec fields.                         *)
(*************************************************************************)
  procedure gtraverse(p : ptr);
    begin
      while p↑.tag = gracenote do
        begin
          writenode(output, p);
          p := p↑.spec
        end
    end;

(***********************        notetraverse       ***********************)
(* Traverses note list through start fields.                             *)
(*************************************************************************)
  procedure notetraverse(t : ptr; parts : partset);
    begin
      while t↑.tag <> spine do
        begin
          if trunc(t↑.part) in parts
            then
              begin
                gtraverse(t↑.spec);            { traverse gracenotes   }
                writenode(output, t)           { do current note       }
              end;
          t := t↑.start                        { get next note         }
        end
    end;


(***********************        spectraverse       ***********************)
(* Traverses list of "special" nodes through spec fields.                *)
(*************************************************************************)
  procedure spectraverse(p: ptr; parts : partset);
    begin
      while p↑.tag <> spine do
        begin
          if trunc(p↑.part) in parts           { is part number active }
            then writenode(output, p);
          p := p↑.spec                         { next spec node        }
        end
    end;


(***********************          traverse         ***********************)
(* Traverses spine from startwindow to endwindow.                        *)
(*************************************************************************)
  procedure traverse(parts : partset; startwindow, endwindow : ptr);
    var
      t : ptr;
      n : integer;

    begin { traverse spine }
      n := partcount(parts);                      { count active parts }
      t := startwindow;
      while (t <> endwindow) and (t↑.tag <> head) do
        begin
          spectraverse(t↑.spec, parts);           { special list       }
          notetraverse(t↑.start, parts);          { start list         }
          if n > 1
            then writeln;                         { separate slices    }
          t := t↑.rlink                           { next spine node    }
        end
    end; { traverse }
```

```
(************************     PROGRAM MELPAT      ************************)
(* Searches for contours in the linked score structure (section 20.3.2). *)
(*************************************************************************)
program melpat(input, output, scoredata);
  const
    maxins  = 15;             { maximum number of instrumental parts       }
    maxline = 90;             { maximum number of characters on input line }
    maxlen  = 100;            { maximum number of intervals in contour     }
    yes     = true;
    no      = false;

  type
#   include "linkdefs.h"

  array1 = array[0..100] of integer;   { for notes in model contour       }
  array2 = array[1..100] of integer;   { intervals between notes in model }

  var
    instr       : partpointers;        { pointers to score structure     }
    inum        : integer;             { current instrument number       }
    freelist    : ptr;                 { pointer to stack of free nodes  }
    scoredata   : text;                { output from DARMS interpreter   }
    model       : array1;              { to store model contour          }
    contour     : array2;              { to store intervals in contour   }
    icount      : integer;             { number of intervals in contour  }
    startnote   : integer;             { in binomial representation      }
    stype       : integer;             { search type                     }
    parts       : partset;             { set of active parts             }
    all         : partset;             { set of all possible parts       }
    startwindow : ptr;                 { pointers to beginning and end   }
    endwindow   : ptr;                 {  of active window in score      }
    done        : boolean;             { true when finished exploring    }

(*************************************************************************)
(* External procedures and functions (see appendix D).                   *)
(*************************************************************************)
  function  empty(x : ptr) : boolean;                              external;
  procedure build(var fin, fout, scoredata : text;
                  var instr : partpointers; var freelist : ptr);   external;
  function  starttime(x : ptr) : real;                             external;
  function  stoptime(x : ptr) : real;                              external;
  function  measno(x : ptr) : real;                                external;
  procedure incr(var x : integer);                                 external;
  procedure decr(var x : integer);                                 external;
  function  add(cbr1, cbr2 : integer) : integer;                   external;
  function  br(cbr : integer) : integer;                           external;
  function  cbr(octave, pc, nc : integer) : integer;               external;
  function  cnc(cbr : integer) : integer;                          external;
  function  cpc(cbr : integer) : integer;                          external;
  function  nameclass(cbr : integer) : integer;                    external;
  function  pitchclass(cbr : integer) : integer;                   external;
  function  octave(cbr : integer) : integer;                       external;
  function  isdigit(c : char) : boolean;                           external;
  function  pitch(nc : integer) : integer;                         external;
  function  tonc(note : char) : integer;                           external;
  procedure skipln(var f : text);                                  external;
  procedure writepitch(var fout : text; cbr : integer);            external;
```

```
(************************     main procedure      ************************)
(* Sets window and active instruments, then traverses score, printing    *)
(* nodes.  After each pass the user is given the opportunity to reset    *)
(* the active window and parts.                                          *)
(*************************************************************************)
  begin { main }
    build(input, output, scoredata, instr, freelist);{ build structure    }
    setup(output, instr[0].s, parts, all,             { init window and    }
                     startwindow, endwindow);         {  active parts      }
    done := false;
    while not done do
      begin
        write('Reset target parts? (y/n): [n] ');
        if affirmative(input, output, no)
          then setins(input, output, parts, all);     { reset active parts }

        write('Reset window size? (y/n): [n] ');
        if affirmative(input, output, no)             { reset window size  }
          then setwindow(input, output,
                 instr[0].s, startwindow, endwindow); writeln;

        traverse(parts, startwindow, endwindow);      { traverse spine     }
        writeln;
        write('Do you want to continue? (y/n): [y] ');
        done := not affirmative(input, output, yes)
      end
  end.  { main }
```

```
procedure setins(var fin, fout : text; var parts,
                                  all : partset);     external;
function  affirmative(var fin, fout : text;
                        default : boolean) : boolean;  external;
procedure setwindow(var fin, fout : text; spine : ptr;
                         var startwindow, endwindow : ptr);  external;
procedure setup(var fout : text; spine : ptr; var parts,
          all : partset; var startwindow, endwindow : ptr);     external;
function tielast(p : ptr) : boolean;                          external;

(************************          skiptonote       ************************)
(* Skips over any node that is not a note, or that is tied to previous   *)
(* note until a head node is reached.                                     *)
(*************************************************************************)
procedure skiptonote(var p : ptr);
  var
    done : boolean;
  begin
    done := false;
    repeat
      if p↑.tag = head                         { head node                  }
        then done := true
      else if p↑.tag <> note                   { not a note                 }
        then p := p↑.rlink
      else if p↑.tag = note                    { it's a note                }
        then if tielast(p)                     { if tied to previous note   }
               then p := p↑.rlink              {     skip it                }
               else done := true               { else use this one -        }
    until done                                 { have good note or headnode }
  end;  { skiptonote }

(************************            adjust         ************************)
(* Checks and adjusts bounds of pitch class.                             *)
(*************************************************************************)
procedure adjust(var nc, pc : integer);
  begin
    if pc < 0
      then pc := pc + 12;
    pc := pc mod 12;
    if nc < 0
      then nc := nc + 7;
    nc := nc mod 7
  end;

(************************           readnote        ************************)
(* Reads a note in SCORE code, returns cbr.                              *)
(*************************************************************************)
procedure readnote(var note : integer; var octave : integer);
  var
    c : char;                                  { for input                  }
    nc, pc : integer;                          { name class, pitch class    }

  begin
    skipln(input);
    read(c);
    nc := tonc(c);                             { lookup name class          }
    pc := pitch(nc);                           { lookup pitch class         }
    while input↑ in ['s', 'f'] do
      begin { process accidentals }
        read(c);
        if c = 's'
          then incr(pc)                                  { sharp }
          else decr(pc)                                  { flat  }
      end; { process accidentals }
    adjust(nc, pc);                                      { keep in range          }
    skipln(input);
    if isdigit(input↑)
      then read(octave);
    note := cbr(octave, pc, nc)
  end;

(************************           readtune        ************************)
(* Reads tune in Score Code, stores in model[i], 0 <= i <= n.            *)
(*************************************************************************)
procedure readtune(var model : array1; var n : integer);
  var
    octave : integer;
  begin
    octave := 4;
    skipln(input);
    if not eoln
      then
        begin
          n := -1;
          while not eoln(input) do
            begin
              incr(n);
              readnote(model[n], octave);
              skipln(input)
            end
        end;
    readln
  end;

(************************           interval        ************************)
(* Calculates interval between two cbrs, returns desired type.          *)
(*************************************************************************)
function interval(var x, y : integer; stype : integer) : integer;
  var
    i, t : integer;
  begin
    i := add(y, -x);
    case stype of
      1,8 : t := abs(pitchclass(i)); { dir semitone or int             }
      2   : t := abs(cpc(i));        { dir half w/ compound            }
      3,9 : t := abs(nameclass(i));  { dir diatonic step or dir int    }
      4   : t := abs(cnc(i));        { same w/ compound                }
      5   : t := abs(br(i)) ;        { directed binomial representation }
      6   : t := abs(i);             { continuous br                   }
      7   : if i = 0                 { direction only: up, down, repeat }
              then t := 0
              else t := 1
    end;  { case }
```

```
    if i < 0                          { get direction right              }
      then t := -t
      else t :=  t;
    if stype = 8      { ints }        { correct for int<a,b>             }
      then
        begin
          if t <= 0
            then t := t + 12
        end
    else if stype = 9 { nint }        { diatonic int<a,b>                }
      then
        if t < 0
          then t := t + 7;

    interval := t    { return interval }
  end;


(************************           calccontour         ************************)
(* Calculates intervals in model, using desired interval type.                *)
(******************************************************************************)
  procedure calccontour(var model : array1; var contour : array2;
       var n : integer; stype : integer);
    var
      i : integer;
    begin
      for i := 1 to n do
        contour[i] := interval(model[i-1], model[i], stype)
    end;


(************************            gettype            ************************)
(* Gets desired interval type from user.                                      *)
(******************************************************************************)
  procedure gettype(var stype : integer);
    begin
      writeln;
      writeln('Interval types ');
      writeln('   1. Directed intervals (+/- semitones)');
      writeln('   2. Directed intervals (compound)');
      writeln('   3. Directed diatonic (+/- diatonic step)');
      writeln('   4. Directed diatonic (compound)');
      writeln('   5. Directed br (with spelling)');
      writeln('   6. Directed cbr (compound)');
      writeln('   7. Direction only (up/down/repeat)');
      writeln('   8. Nondirected pc (int)');
      writeln('   9. Nondirected nc (nint)');
      writeln;
      writeln('Current type = ', stype:2);
      write('Type integer or <return>: ');
      skipln(input);
      if eoln(input)
        then readln
        else readln(stype);
      writeln
    end;
```

```
(************************           getcontour          ************************)
(* Reads and stores contour, type, and first note.                            *)
(******************************************************************************)
  procedure getcontour(var model : array1; var contour : array2;
             var n : integer; var startnote : integer; var stype : integer);
    var
      octave : integer;

    begin
      gettype(stype);
      writeln;
      write('Type model in SCORE code or <return>: ');
      readtune(model, n);
      writeln;
      calccontour(model, contour, n, stype);      { calculate contour    }

      write('Type first note to anchor, or <return>: ');
      skipln(input);
      if not eoln
        then
          begin
            octave := 4;
            readnote(startnote, octave);          { read startnote, if any }
            startnote := br(startnote)
          end
        else startnote := -1;                     { startnote undefined    }
      readln;
      writeln

    end; { getcontour }


(************************              wset             ************************)
(* Points q and endw to beginning and end of window in part.                  *)
(******************************************************************************)
  procedure wset(var q, endw : ptr; startwindow, endwindow : ptr);
    var
      time : real;
    begin
      if startwindow↑.tag = head           { startwindow may be end of part }
        then time := measno(startwindow↑.llink)
        else time := measno(startwindow);
                                           { set q to first node in window  }
      while (measno(q) < time) and (q↑.rlink↑.tag <> head) do
        q := q↑.rlink;
                                           { get time of end of window      }
      if endwindow↑.tag = head
        then time := measno(endwindow↑.llink)
        else time := measno(endwindow);

      if q↑.tag = head
        then endw := q↑.llink
        else endw := q;
                                           { find end of window             }
      while (measno(endw) < time) and (endw↑.rlink↑.tag <> head) do
        endw := endw↑.rlink
    end;  { findstart }
```

```
(*************************        partsearch        *************************)
(* Searches score for melodic pattern.                                       *)
(*****************************************************************************)
  procedure partsearch(var f : text; stype : integer; p : ptr;
                       part : integer; var contour : array2; icount : integer;
                          startnote : integer; startwindow, endwindow : ptr);

    var
      match        : boolean;            { flag for inner search loop   }
      found        : boolean;            { flag for outer search loops  }
      checkstart   : boolean;            { true = first note must match }
      j            : integer;            { looping                      }
      p1, p2       : integer;            { pitches which form interval  }
      int          : integer;
      q, endw      : ptr;                { pointers                     }
      note1, note2 : ptr;                { pointers                     }

    begin { partsearch }
      checkstart := startnote <> -1;     {  is startnote defined?       }
      found := false;
      q := p↑.rlink;                     { start of search in part i    }
      wset(q, endw, startwindow, endwindow);
      skiptonote(q);                     { get 1st good note            }
      if q↑.tag = note                   { success                      }
        then
          repeat                         { move starting point          }
            note1 := q; skiptoncte(note1); { set pointers               }
            note2 := note1↑.rlink; skiptonote(note2);
            j := 0;
            match := true;

            repeat { execute search until no match }
              if (note1↑.tag = note) and (note2↑.tag = note)    { 2 notes? }
                then
                  begin                                 { get interval     }
                    incr(j);                            { current int no.  }
                    p1 := note1↑.dlink↑.pitch;          { get pitches      }
                    p2 := note2↑.dlink↑.pitch;
                    int := interval(p1, p2, stype);     { calc interval    }
                    if checkstart and (j = 1)           { check 1st note?  }
                      then match := (br(p1) = startnote)
                                    and (int = contour[j])
                      else match := int = contour[j]; { check }
                    note1 := note2;                     { next two notes   }
                    note2 := note2↑.rlink; skiptonote(note2)
                  end
                else
                  begin                        { didn't get 2 good notes }
                    match := false;
                    incr(j)
                  end
            until (j > icount) or (note2↑.tag = head) or not match;

            if (j = icount + 1)
              then
                begin
                  found := true;
                  writeln(f, 'Part: ', part:2, measno(q):8:3)
                end;
            q := q↑.rlink;                                 { try next chunk   }
            skiptonote(q)
          until (q = endw) or (q↑.tag = head);            { end of window ? }
      if not found
        then writeln(f, 'Pattern not found in part ', part:2)
    end; { partsearch }


(************************       main procedure       ************************)
(* Builds score structure, sets defaults, and searches score.               *)
(****************************************************************************)
  begin { main }
    build(input, output, scoredata, instr, freelist);   { build structure }
    stype := 1;                           { search type: directed half steps }
    setup(output, instr[0].s, parts, all, startwindow, endwindow);

    done := false;
    while not done do
      begin
        write('Reset target parts? (y/n): [n] ');
        if affirmative(input, output, no)
          then setins(input, output, parts, all);      { reset active parts }

        write('Reset window size? (y/n): [n] ');
        if affirmative(input, output, no)              { reset window size  }
          then setwindow(input, output,
                   instr[0].s, startwindow, endwindow);
                                                       { get contour, etc.  }
        getcontour(model, contour, icount, startnote, stype);

        for inum := 1 to maxins do
          begin
            if inum in parts
              then
                if not empty(instr[inum].p)
                  then partsearch(output, stype, instr[inum].p, inum,
                         contour, icount, startnote, startwindow, endwindow)
          end;  { traverse part inum }
        writeln;
        write('Do you want to continue? (y/n): [y] ');
        done := not affirmative(input, output, yes)
      end
  end.  { main }
```

```
(************************       PROGRAM VERT        ************************)
(* Extracts pcs from each vertical slice through the score and identi-    *)
(* fies the pc sets (section 20.3.3).  File scoredata is output from the *)
(* DARMS interpreter; file setdata was listed on pages 631-633.           *)
(**************************************************************************)
program vert(input, output, scoredata, setdata);
  const
    maxins  =  15;                      { maximum number of instruments  }
    maxline = 90;                       { maximum input line length      }
    yes     = true;
    no      = false;

  type
#   include "linkdefs.h"
#   include "setdefs.h"
    pccounter = array[0 .. 11] of integer;               { to count pcs  }

  var
    instr       : partpointers;         { pointers into score structure  }
    freelist    : ptr;                  { pointer to stack of free nodes }
    setdata     : text;                 { pc set data file               }
    scoredata   : text;                 { output from DARMS interpreter  }
    loc         : ar600;                { locations of data in set table }
    table       : ar300;                { set table                      }
    dat         : setinfo;              { record for all pc-set info     }
    parts       : partset;              { set of active parts            }
    all         : partset;              { set of all possible parts      }
    startwindow : ptr;                  { pointers to beginning and end  }
    endwindow   : ptr;                  {  of active window in score     }
    done        : boolean;              { true when user wants to quit   }
    primetype   : pftype;               { forte or rahn                  }

(**************************************************************************)
(* External procedures and functions (see appendix D).                    *)
(**************************************************************************)
  procedure build(var fin, fout, scoredata : text;
                var instr : partpointers; var freelist : ptr);   external;
  function  measno(x : ptr) : real;                              external;
  procedure setcalc(var f : text; primetype : pftype;
        var dat : setinfo; var loc : ar600; var table : ar300);  external;
  procedure readtable(var fout, data : text; var loc : ar600;
                                      var table : ar300);        external;
  procedure incr(var x : integer);                               external;
  procedure decr(var x : integer);                               external;
  function  convert(pc : integer) : char;                        external;
  function  tab : char;                                          external;
  function  pitchclass(cbr : integer) : integer;                 external;
  procedure setins(var fin, fout : text; var parts,
                                        all : partset);          external;
  function  affirmative(var fin, fout : text;
                          default : boolean) : boolean;          external;
  procedure setwindow(var fin, fout : text; spine : ptr;
                          var startwindow, endwindow : ptr);     external;
  procedure setup(var fout : text; spine : ptr; var parts,
           all : partset; var startwindow, endwindow : ptr);     external;
  procedure newtype(var fin, fout : text;
                                      var primetype : pftype);   external;
```

```
(************************        gtraverse        ************************)
(* Traverses gracenote list through spec field. Procedure parameter inc  *)
(* either increments or decrements the appropriate element of pcs.       *)
(**************************************************************************)
  procedure gtraverse(t : ptr; var pcs : pccounter;
                                     procedure inc(var x : integer));
    begin
      while t↑.tag = gracenote do
        begin
          inc(pcs[pitchclass(t↑.dlink↑.pitch)]);
          t := t↑.spec
        end
    end;

(************************        atraverse        ************************)
(* Traverse start-time list, adding pcs that begin at given time.        *)
(**************************************************************************)
  procedure atraverse(t : ptr; parts : partset; var pcs : pccounter);
    begin
      while t↑.tag <> spine do
        begin
          if trunc(t↑.part) in parts                     { active part   }
            then
              if t↑.tag = note                           { and a note    }
                then
                  begin
                    gtraverse(t↑.spec, pcs, incr);       { gracenotes    }
                    incr(pcs[pitchclass(t↑.dlink↑.pitch)]) { current note }
                  end;
          t := t↑.start                     { get next note in time slice }
        end
    end;

(************************        btraverse        ************************)
(* Traverses stop-time list, subtracting  pcs that end at given time.    *)
(* Notes that started before the beginning of the window are ignored.    *)
(* X is measure number at beginning of window.                           *)
(**************************************************************************)
  procedure btraverse(t : ptr; parts : partset; var pcs : pccounter;
                                                             x : real);
    begin { traverse circular list through stop field }
      while t↑.tag <> spine do
        begin
          if trunc(t↑.part) in parts
            then
              if t↑.tag = note
                then
                  if measno(t) >= x         { did not start before window }
                    then
                      begin
                        gtraverse(t↑.spec, pcs, decr);   { remove grnotes }
                        decr(pcs[pitchclass(t↑.dlink↑.pitch)]) { & note  }
                      end;
          t := t↑.stop                                { get next note     }
        end
    end;
```

```
(************************          extract          ***********************)
(* Extracts pc set from counting array.  Pcset is used to return the psc,*)
(* n is the number of pcs returned.                                        *)
(***************************************************************************)
  procedure extract(var pcs : pccounter; var pcset : ar100; var n : integer);
    var
      pc : integer;
    begin { extract pcset }
      n := 0;
      for pc := 0 to 11 do
        if pcs[pc] > 0
          then
            begin
              incr(n);
              pcset[n] := pc
            end
    end;


(************************          clear          ***********************)
(* Clears pc-counting array.                                               *)
(***************************************************************************)
  procedure clear(var pcs : pccounter);
    var
      i : integer;

    begin { clear pcs array }
      for i := 0 to 11 do
        pcs[i] := 0
    end;  { clear pcs array }


(************************          printlist          ***********************)
(* Prints list of pcs in hexadecimal notation.                             *)
(***************************************************************************)
  procedure printlist(var A : ar100; n : integer);
    var
      i : integer;

    begin { print array }
      for i := 1 to n - 1 do
        write(convert(A[i]),',');
      write(convert(A[n]))
    end;  { print array }


(************************          printdata          ***********************)
(* Prints all data for one vertical time slice.                            *)
(***************************************************************************)
  procedure printdata(measure : real; var dat : setinfo);
    var
      i : integer;

    begin
      write(measure:7:3, tab, tab);                      { measure number    }
      if dat.card = 0                                     { null set          }
        then write('null', tab, tab, '0-1', tab, 'null',
                                                tab, tab, '  000000')
        else
          begin
            printlist(dat.pcset, dat.card);               { list normal order }
               write(tab, tab);
            write(dat.card:1, '-');                       { set name          }
            if dat.z <> 0                                 { print Z?          }
              then write('z');
            write(dat.name:1); write(tab);                { set name          }
            printlist(dat.prime,dat.card);                { prime form        }
            write(tab, tab, '  ');
            for i := 1 to 6 do                            { interval vector   }
              write(dat.vector[i]:1)
          end;
      writeln
    end;  { printdata }


(************************          vtraverse          ***********************)
(* Traverses score structure by vertical slices.                           *)
(***************************************************************************)
  procedure vtraverse(parts : partset; startwindow, endwindow : ptr;
                                                 primetype : pftype);
    var
      t : ptr;
      pcs : pccounter;                          { tally of pcs in vertical    }
      x : real;                                 { time at beginning of window }

    begin { traverse spine }
      writeln('===========================================================',
                                                           '=========');
      writeln('Measure', tab, tab, 'Normal Order', tab, 'Set', tab,
                                     'Prime Form', tab, 'IC Vector');
      writeln('=======', tab, tab, '============', tab, '===', tab,
                                      '==========', tab, '=========');
      clear(pcs);                                 { initialize pc array       }
      x := measno(startwindow);
      t := startwindow;                           { first spine node          }
      while t <> endwindow do
        begin { process vertical slice }
          atraverse(t↑.start, parts, pcs);        { traverse start-time list  }
          btraverse(t↑.stop, parts, pcs, x);      { traverse stop-time list   }
          extract(pcs, dat.pcset, dat.card);      { get set and cardinality   }
          if dat.card <> 0                        { identify set              }
            then setcalc(output, primetype, dat, loc, table);
          printdata(measno(t), dat);              { print data                }
          t := t↑.rlink                           { move to next slice        }
        end;  { process vertical slice }
      writeln('===========================================================',
                                                           '=========')
    end;  { vtraverse }
```

```
(***********************************************************************)
(*                           main procedure                            *)
(***********************************************************************)

 begin { main }
   build(input, output, scoredata, instr, freelist);{ build score struct }
   readtable(output, setdata, loc, table);        { read set table      }
   newtype(input, output, primetype);             { set primeform type  }
                                                  { init parts & window }
   setup(output, instr[0].s, parts, all, startwindow, endwindow);
   done := false;
   while not done do
     begin
       write('Reset target parts? (y/n): [n] ');
       if affirmative(input, output, no)
         then setins(input, output, parts, all); { reset active parts    }

       write('Reset window size? (y/n): [n] ');
       if affirmative(input, output, no)          { reset window size    }
         then setwindow(input, output,
                instr[0].s, startwindow, endwindow);

       writeln;                                   { traverse spine       }
       vtraverse(parts, startwindow, endwindow, primetype);
       writeln;
       write('Do you want to continue? (y/n): [y] ');
       done := not affirmative(input, output, yes)
     end
 end.  { main }
```

```
(************************   PROGRAM SEGMENT   ************************)
(* Designed to aid in the analysis of atonal music, this program par-  *)
(* titions the music into various segments, and analyzes the segments  *)
(* for pitch-class set contents.  Segmentation is based on several dif- *)
(* ferent criteria, as discussed in section 20.3.4.                   *)
(***********************************************************************)

program segment(input, output, scoredata, setdata);
  const
    maxins   = 15;              { maximum number of instruments          }
    maxline  = 90;              { maximum input line length              }
    smallset =  3;              { lowest cardinality of set desired      }
    maxpitch = 25;              { maximum no. of notes examined at once  }
    yes      = true;
    no       = false;

  type
#   include "linkdefs.h"
#   include "setdefs.h"

    storedyn = record
                 pc   : integer;      { pitch class    }
                 dyn  : integer;      { dynamic level  }
                 meas : integer       { measure number }
               end;

    ar6 = array[0 .. maxpitch] of integer;
    ar7 = array[0 .. 11] of boolean;
    ar8 = array[1 .. maxpitch] of storedyn;
    ar9 = array[0 .. maxpitch] of boolean;

  var
    startwindow : ptr;          { pointer to beginning of window in score }
    endwindow   : ptr;          { pointer to end of window in score       }
    freelist    : ptr;          { pointer to stack of free nodes          }
    instr       : partpointers; { array of ptrs to parts                  }
    loc         : ar600;        { set table locations by cardinality      }
    table       : ar300;        { the set table                           }
    scoredata   : text;         { file with output from DARMS interpreter }
    setdata     : text;         { pc-set data table                       }
    parts       : partset;      { "active" parts, i.e. deal with these    }
    all         : partset;      { set of all possible parts               }
    done        : boolean;      { true when user wants to quit            }
    primetype   : pftype;       { prime form type (forte, rahn)           }
    dat         : setinfo;      { record to contain all pc-set info       }
    inum        : integer;      { current instrument number               }
    key         : char;         { first letter of keyword                 }

(***********************************************************************)
(* Declarations for external Procedures and Functions (see appendix D). *)
(***********************************************************************)

  procedure build(var fin, fout, scoredata : text;
              var instr : partpointers; var freelist : ptr);      external;
  function  measno(x : ptr) : real;                                external;
  procedure setcalc(var f : text; primetype : pftype;
         var dat : setinfo; var loc : ar600; var table : ar300);  external;
```

```
procedure readtable(var fout, data : text; var loc : ar600;
                                       var table : ar300);   external;
procedure incr(var x : integer);                             external;
procedure decr(var x : integer);                             external;
function  convert(pc : integer) : char;                      external;
function  tab : char;                                        external;
function  pitchclass(cbr : integer) : integer;               external;
procedure setins(var fin, fout : text; var parts,
                                     all : partset);         external;
function  affirmative(var fin, fout : text;
                      default : boolean) : boolean;          external;
procedure setwindow(var fin, fout : text; spine : ptr;
                   var startwindow, endwindow : ptr);        external;
procedure setup(var fout : text; spine : ptr; var parts,
          all : partset; var startwindow, endwindow : ptr);  external;
procedure newtype(var fin, fout : text;
                              var primetype : pftype);       external;
function  empty(p : ptr) : boolean;                          external;

(************************          inform          ************************)
(* Gives general information to user.                                      *)
(***************************************************************************)
procedure inform;
  begin
    writeln;
    writeln('=============================',
                                  '================================');
    writeln('This program partitions music into segments according to');
    writeln('various parameters.  Individual parts can be segmented by');
    writeln('rests or slurs.  Alternately, the program can extract ',
                                                          '"chunks"');
    writeln('of notes set off in the score by rests; can partition the');
    writeln('chunks by dynamic markings; or can segment the score by');
    writeln('specified beats and parts.  The latter is designated');
    writeln('"general" segmentation.  Imbricated subsets of the par-');
    writeln('titions are extracted and identified by set class and ',
                                                          'vector.');
    writeln('=============================',
                                  '================================');
    writeln
  end;

(************************        printmenu         ************************)
(* Offers menu of segmentation types.                                      *)
(***************************************************************************)
procedure printmenu;
  begin
    writeln('Type one of the following:');
    writeln;
    writeln('        general');
    writeln('        rests');
    writeln('        slurs');
    writeln('        chunks');
    writeln('        dynamics');
    writeln
  end;

(************************        skiprests         ************************)
(* Skips consecutive rests in part.                                        *)
(***************************************************************************)
 procedure skiprests(var t: ptr);
   begin
     while (t↑.tag = rest) and (t↑.tag <> head) do
       t := t↑.rlink
   end;

(************************         nextrest         ************************)
(* Sets pointer to next rest or end of part.                               *)
(***************************************************************************)
 function nextrest(t: ptr): ptr;
   begin     { set pointer to next rest or end of part }
     t := t↑.rlink;
     while (t↑.tag <> rest) and (t↑.tag <> head) do
       t := t↑.rlink;
     nextrest := t
   end;

(************************          stslur          ************************)
(* Returns true if note is beginning of slur.                              *)
(***************************************************************************)
 function stslur(t : ptr) : boolean;
   begin
     stslur := false;
     if t↑.tag = note
       then stslur := ([1, 3, 5, 7, 9, 11, 13] * t↑.dlink↑.slur) <> []
   end;

(************************        beginslur         ************************)
(* Sets pointer to beginning of slur or end of part.                       *)
(***************************************************************************)
 function beginslur(t:ptr): ptr;
   begin
     while (not stslur(t)) and (t↑.tag <> head) do
       t := t↑.rlink;
     beginslur := t
   end;

(************************         getslur          ************************)
(* Returns odd integer representing end of slur.                           *)
(***************************************************************************)
 function getslur(t : ptr) : integer;
   var
     x    : integer;
   begin
     x := 1;
     if t↑.tag = note
       then
         while not (x in t↑.dlink↑.slur) do
           x := x + 2;
     getslur := x
   end;
```

```
(************************          endslur          ************************)
(* Return pointer to note ending slur beginning at note t, or end of part*)
(**************************************************************************)
  function endslur(t : ptr) : ptr;
    var
      id : integer;                         { id number of end of slur }
      gotit : boolean;
    begin
      id := getslur(t) + 1;
      gotit := false;
      if t↑.tag <> head
        then
          repeat
            t := t↑.rlink;
            if t↑.tag = note
              then gotit := id in t↑.dlink↑.slur
          until gotit or (t↑.tag = head);
      endslur := t
    end;

(************************          initpos          ************************)
(* Initializes position array to all false.                               *)
(**************************************************************************)
  procedure initpos(var position : ar9);
    var
      i : integer;
    begin
      for i := 0 to maxpitch do
        position[i] := false
    end;

(************************            copy            ************************)
(* Copies first c1-element pc set beginning with position p in n-element *)
(* collection pc1 into the array pc2.  C2 is cardinality of set pc2 and  *)
(* position array marks the location of each element extracted from pc1. *)
(**************************************************************************)
  procedure copy(var pc1 : ar6; n, p, c1 : integer;
                   var pc2 : ar100; var c2: integer; var position : ar9);
    var
      have : pcset;               { for weeding out duplicate pcs }
    begin
      c2 := 0;                    { cardinality of set in pc2              }
      have := [];                 { weeds out duplicates                   }
      initpos(position);          { keeps track of location of pcs from pc1 }
      repeat
        if not (pc1[p] in have)
          then
            begin
              incr(c2);
              pc2[c2] := pc1[p];
              position[p] := true;
              have := have + [pc1[p]];
              pc2[c2] := pc1[p]
            end;
        incr(p)                   { next position in array pc1             }
      until (c2 = c1) or (p = n + 1)
    end;
```

```
(************************          printlist          ************************)
(* Prints list of pcs in hexadecimal notation.                            *)
(**************************************************************************)
  procedure printlist(list : ar100; x,w : integer);
    var
      i : integer;
    begin
      for i := 1 to x do
        write(convert(list[i]):w)
    end;

(************************          writeinfo          ************************)
(* Prints set data from DAT record.                                       *)
(**************************************************************************)
  procedure writeinfo(dat : setinfo);
    begin
      write(tab);
      write(dat.card:1, '-');                             { set name        }
      if dat.z <> 0
        then write('z');
      write(dat.name:1,tab);
      printlist(dat.prime,dat.card,1);                    { prime form      }
      write(tab);
      if dat.card < 8
        then write(tab);
      printlist(dat.vector,6,1);                          { interval vector }
      writeln
    end;

(************************          fancyprint          ************************)
(* Prints elements from set aligned with corresponding elements in set.  *)
(**************************************************************************)
  procedure fancyprint(var pc1 : ar6; var position : ar9; n, w : integer);
    var
      i : integer;
    begin
      write(tab, tab, tab);
      for i := 1 to n do
        if position[i]
          then write(convert(pc1[i]):w)
          else write(' ':w);
      if n < 16
        then write(tab);
      if n < 8
        then write(tab)
    end;

(************************          imbricate          ************************)
(* Extracts and identifies imbricated subsets of pitch collection pc1.   *)
(**************************************************************************)
  procedure imbricate(var pc1 : ar6; n : integer);
    var
      position : ar9;             { location of pcs in pc1               }
      pc2      : ar100;           { specific sets to be analyzed         }
      largest  : integer;         { largest possible set from pc1        }
      first    : integer;         { location of first element in set     }
      c1, c2   : integer;         { cardinality of set in pc2            }
```

```
  begin { imbricate }
                        { find largest possible  pcset in collection pcl   }
    copy(pcl, n, 1, 12, pc2, largest, position);
    for cl := largest downto smallset do
      for first := 1 to (n + 1 - cl) do
        begin
          copy(pcl, n, first, cl, pc2, c2, position);
          if c2 = cl
            then
              begin   { do set identification }
                fancyprint(pcl, position, n, 1);       { print "on" pcs   }
                dat.pcset := pc2;
                dat.card := cl;
                setcalc(output, primetype, dat, loc, table);
                writeinfo(dat)
              end
        end;
    write('----------------------------------------');
    writeln('----------------------------------------')
                                                  { table separator }
  end;  { imbricate }


(************************        printdata        ***********************)
(* Prints instrument number, measures, and set, then imbricates set.     *)
(************************************************************************)
 procedure printdata(var pcl : ar6; n ,inum : integer;
                                              smeas, fmeas : real);
   var
     i : integer;
   begin
     write(inum:4, '  ', smeas:5:3, '-', fmeas:5:3, tab);
     for i := 1 to n do
       write(convert(pcl[i]):1);
     writeln;
     imbricate(pcl, n)
   end;


(************************        pcinsert         ***********************)
(* Inserts pc into array pcl.  Immediately repeated pcs are skipped.     *)
(************************************************************************)
 procedure pcinsert(pc : integer; var pcl : ar6; var n : integer);
   begin
     if n < maxpitch
       then if not (pcl[n] = pc)                   { skip repeated pcs      }
         then
           begin
             incr(n);
             if n <= maxpitch
               then pcl[n] := pc
           end
   end;


(************************        ctraverse        ***********************)
(* Traverses list through start field.  Stores pitches in array pcl.     *)
(* This takes care of chord structures.                                   *)
(************************************************************************)
 procedure ctraverse(t : ptr; inum : integer;
                                  var pcl : ar6; var n : integer);
   var
     p : integer;      { pitch class }

   begin
     while t↑.tag <> spine do
       begin
         if t↑.part = inum
           then
             begin
               if t↑.tag <> rest
                 then
                   begin
                     p := pitchclass(t↑.dlink↑.pitch);             { get pc }
                     pcinsert(p, pcl, n)
                   end
             end;
         t := t↑.start                              { get next node in list }
       end
   end;  { ctraverse }


(************************        traverse         ***********************)
(* Traverses score between nodes t and q.                                 *)
(************************************************************************)
 procedure traverse(t,q: ptr; inum : integer;
                                  var pcl : ar6; var n : integer);
   begin
     n := 0;
     while t <> q do
       begin
         ctraverse(t, inum, pcl, n);                { traverse start list }
         t := t↑.rlink                              { get next spine node }
       end
   end;


(************************          wset           ***********************)
(* Point q to first node in window.                                       *)
(************************************************************************)
 procedure wset(var q : ptr; startwindow : ptr);
   var
     x : real;

   begin
     x := measno(startwindow);
     q := q↑.rlink;                               { get first note in part }
     while (measno(q) < x) and (q↑.tag <> head) do
       q := q↑.rlink
   end;
```

```
(************************        restsegment        ************************)
(* Within window, segments part by rests.                                  *)
(***************************************************************************)
  procedure restsegment(q : ptr; inum : integer;
                              startwindow, endwindow : ptr);
    var
      t      : ptr;                    { first note in segment              }
      pcl    : ar6;                    { array to store pitch collection    }
      n      : integer;                { number of elements in collection   }
      endw   : real;                   { measno at end of window            }

    begin
      endw := measno(endwindow);       { measure no. at end of window       }
      wset(q, startwindow);            { point q to first node in window    }
      skiprests(q);                    { find first note in window          }
      while measno(q) < endw do
        begin
          t := q;                      { first note                         }
          q := nextrest(t);            { get next rest                      }
          traverse(t, q, inum, pcl, n);{ traverse segment                   }
          if n >= smallset             { throw it back if it's too small    }
            then printdata(pcl, n, inum, measno(t), measno(q));
          skiprests(q)                 { find first note in next segment    }
        end
    end;


(************************        slursegment        ************************)
(* Within window, finds segments under slurs.                              *)
(***************************************************************************)
  procedure slursegment(q : ptr; inum: integer;
                              startwindow, endwindow : ptr);
    var
      t      : ptr;                    { first note in segment              }
      pcl    : ar6;                    { array to store pitch collection    }
      n      : integer;                { number of elements in collection   }
      endw   : real;                   { measno at end of window            }

    begin
      wset(q, startwindow);            { point q to first node in window    }
      endw := measno(endwindow);
      while measno(q) < endw do        { process part in window             }
        begin
          t := beginslur(q);           { point t to beginning of slur       }
          q := endslur(t);             { point q to end of slur             }
          if q↑.tag <> head
            then
              begin                    { traverse notes under slur          }
                traverse(t,q↑.rlink, inum, pcl, n);
                if n >= smallset       { throw it back if it's too small    }
                  then printdata(pcl, n, inum, measno(t), measno(q));
              end
        end
    end;

(************************        dynwrite        ************************)
(*  Writes dynamic level as character literal.                          *)
(************************************************************************)
  procedure dynwrite(var x : integer);
    begin
      case x of
          0 : write('pppppp');
         10 : write('ppppp');
         20 : write('pppp');
         30 : write('ppp');
         40 : write('pp');
         50 : write('piano');
         60 : write('mp');
         70 : write('mf');
         80 : write('forte');
         90 : write('ff');
        100 : write('fff');
        110 : write('ffff');
        120 : write('fffff');
        130 : write('ffffff')
      end
    end;  { dynwrite }

(************************        findlast        ************************)
(* Finds last instance in array of dynamic level being sought.          *)
(************************************************************************)
  function findlast(var targdyn, b, a : integer; var dynar : ar8) : integer;
    begin
      while (dynar[b].dyn <> targdyn) and (b > a) do
        decr(b);
      findlast := b
    end;  { findlast }

(************************        dynprint        ************************)
(*  Prints data for dynamic segmentation.                               *)
(************************************************************************)
  procedure dynprint(var n : integer; var dynar : ar8; var pcl : ar6);
    var
      targdyn  : integer;                      { current level being printed }
      a,b,i,j  : integer;
      checkoff : intset;                       { for checking off dynamics   }
    begin
      checkoff := [];
      a := 1;
      while a <= n do
        begin
          j := 0;
          b := n;
          targdyn := dynar[a].dyn;             { find target dynamic         }
          dynwrite(targdyn);                   { print value of target dyn   }
          write(tab,'m. ', dynar[a].meas:2);{ print measure number           }
          b := findlast(targdyn,b,a, dynar);{ get last of target             }
          if dynar[b].meas <> dynar[a].meas { write ending measure           }
            then write(' - ',dynar[b].meas:2, tab)
            else write(tab, tab);
                        { copy pcs into pcl array, removing repeated pcs }
```

```
         for i := a to b do
           if (dynar[i].dyn = targdyn) and (pcl[j] <> dynar[i].pc)
             then
               begin
                 incr(j);
                 pcl[j] := dynar[i].pc;
                 write(convert(pcl[j]):1)
               end;
         writeln(tab);
         imbricate(pcl, j);                  { imbricate pitch collection  }
                                             { find next new dynamic       }
         checkoff := checkoff + [targdyn div 10];
         done := false;
         while not done do
           begin
             if a > n
               then done := true
             else if not((dynar[a].dyn div 10) in checkoff)
               then done := true
             else incr(a)
           end
       end
   end;         { dynprint }

(************************         checkit        ************************)
(* Adds pc to array pcl.  Immediately repeated notes are skipped.        *)
(************************************************************************)
 procedure checkit(p : integer; var n, count : integer; var pcl : ar6);
   begin { checkit }
     incr(count);                            { sound occurs in this slice }
     pcinsert(p, pcl, n)                     { insert pc p into array pcl }
   end; { checkit }

(************************         fixdyn         ************************)
(*  Converts dynamic level to standard levels from 0 up to 130.          *)
(************************************************************************)
 function fixdyn(var x : integer) : integer;
   begin          { fixdyn }
     fixdyn := x - (x mod 10)               { produces 70, 80, 90 etc. }
   end;           { fixdyn }

(************************          addyn         ************************)
(*  Inserts pc, dynamic level, and measure number in dynar array.        *)
(************************************************************************)
 procedure addyn(p : integer; var n, count : integer; t : ptr;
                                                   var dynar : ar8);
   begin
     incr(count);
     incr(n);
     if n <= maxpitch
       then
         begin
           dynar[n].pc := p;                        { store pitch class   }
           dynar[n].dyn := fixdyn(t↑.dlink↑.dynl);  { store dynamic level }
           dynar[n].meas := trunc(measno(t))        { meas no. as integer }
         end
   end;  { addyn }

(************************       dvtraverse       ************************)
(* Traverses a time slice for vertical chunking or dynamic segmentation. *)
(************************************************************************)
  procedure dvtraverse(var t : ptr; var n, count : integer;
                                 var pcl : ar6; var dynar : ar8);
    var
      p        : integer;        { pitch class                           }
      q        : ptr;            { looks backward to see if all parts rest }
      v        : ptr;            { finds stop time                       }
      holdover : boolean;        { check for held notes                  }

    begin   { dvtraverse }
      t := t↑.start;
      count := 0;
      while t↑.tag <> spine do
        begin
          if (t↑.tag <> rest) and (trunc(t↑.part) in parts )
            then
              begin
                p := pitchclass(t↑.dlink↑.pitch);
                if key = 'c'
                  then checkit(p, n, count, pcl)
                  else addyn(p, n, count, t, dynar)
              end;
          t := t↑.start
        end;
      if count = 0
        then
          begin
            holdover := false;
            q := t↑.llink↑.start;                 { back up one time slice }
            repeat
              v := q↑.stop;
              while v↑.tag <> spine do
                v := v↑.stop;
              if (measno(v) > measno(t)) and (trunc(q↑.part) in parts) and
                      (q↑.tag = note)
                then holdover := true;
              q := q↑.start
            until q↑.tag = spine;
            if holdover
              then incr(count)     { signal for no new notes, but one held }
          end
    end;  { dvtraverse }


(************************        nextchunk       ************************)
(* Finds the time for next chunk in vertical segments.                   *)
(************************************************************************)
 procedure nextchunk(var r,t : ptr; parts : partset);
   begin { nextchunk }
     t := t↑.start;
     while (t↑.tag = rest) or ((t↑.tag = note)
       and not (trunc(t↑.part) in parts)) do
         t := t↑.start;
     if (t↑.tag = spine)
       then
```

```
        begin
          t := t↑.rlink;
          nextchunk(r, t, parts)
        end
      else
        begin                               { reposition t at time value }
          repeat
            t := t↑.start
          until (t↑.tag = spine);
          r := t
        end
  end;  { nextchunk }

(***********************        chunkdynseg        ***********************)
(* Segments score according to vertical sections surrounded by rests.   *)
(************************************************************************)
 procedure chunkdynseg(startwindow, endwindow : ptr; parts : partset;
                                                         key : char);
   var
     r,t        : ptr;                { points to 1st and current time slice }
     firstmeas  : real;               { measure number at start of window    }
     lastmeas   : real;               { measure number at end   of window    }
     count      : integer;            { finds where all parts rest in chunk  }
     pcl        : ar6;                { stores pcs }
     dynar      : ar8;                { stores all info for dynamic segment  }
     n          : integer;            { number of elements in pcl or dynar   }
   begin { chunkdynseg }
     firstmeas := measno(startwindow);
     lastmeas  := measno(endwindow);
     t := instr[0].s↑.rlink;
     while measno(t) < firstmeas do
       t := t↑.rlink;
     n := 0;                              { no. of items in pcl              }
     nextchunk(r, t, parts);              { in case all parts rest at beg }
     while measno(t) < lastmeas do
       begin
         dvtraverse(t, n, count, pcl, dynar);
         if ((count = 0) and (n > 0))
           then
             begin
               if key = 'c'
                 then printdata(pcl, n, 0, measno(r), measno(t))
                 else dynprint(n, dynar, pcl);        { key = 'd'          }
               n := 0;
               if measno(t) < lastmeas
                 then t := t↑.rlink;                  { move to next slice }
               if measno(t) < lastmeas
                 then nextchunk(r, t, parts)          { skip over rests    }
             end;
         if (count <> 0)
           then t := t↑.rlink
       end;
     if (measno(t) >= lastmeas) and (count > 0) and (key = 'c')
       then printdata(pcl, n, 0, measno(r), lastmeas)
     else if (measno(t) >= lastmeas) and (count > 0) and (key = 'd')
       then  dynprint(n, dynar, pcl)
   end;  { chunkdynseg }
```

```
(***********************        printheading        ***********************)
(* Prints heading for table.  Version depends on segmentation type.      *)
(*************************************************************************)

 procedure printheading(key : char);
   begin
     writeln;
     writeln('=======================================',
                            '=======================================');
     case key of
    's','r','c' : writeln('Part  Measures', tab, tab, 'Segment/Subset',
                     tab, tab, 'Set', tab, 'Prime Form', tab, 'Vector');
        'g' : writeln('      Measures', tab, tab, 'Segment/Subset',
                     tab, tab, 'Set', tab, 'Prime Form', tab, 'Vector');
        'd' : writeln('Dyn   Measures', tab, tab, 'Segment/Subset',
                     tab, tab, 'Set', tab, 'Prime Form', tab, 'Vector');
     end;  { case }
     writeln('=======================================',
                            '=======================================')
   end;
```

```
(***********************        gtraverse        ***********************)
(* Traverses list through start field, picking up pitches in specified  *)
(* parts.                                                               *)
(************************************************************************)

 procedure gtraverse(t : ptr; parts : partset;
                                       var pcl : ar6; var n : integer);
   var
     p : integer;       { pitch class }

   begin
     while t↑.tag <> spine do
       begin
         if trunc(t↑.part) in parts
           then
             begin
               if t↑.tag <> rest
                 then
                   begin
                     p := pitchclass(t↑.dlink↑.pitch);          { get pc }
                     pcinsert(p, pcl, n)
                   end
             end;
         t := t↑.start                          { get next node in list }
       end
   end;  { ctraverse }
```

```
(************************          genseg          ************************)
(* Segments the score by user specified parts and beats alone.            *)
(**************************************************************************)
  procedure genseg(spine : ptr; var startwindow, endwindow : ptr;
                                                  var parts : partset);
    var
      done : boolean;                  { control looping in procedure     }
      t, q  : ptr;                     { pointers to spine                }
      pcl   : ar6;                     { array to store pitch collection  }
      n     : integer;                 { number of elements in collection }
    begin
      done := false;
      while not done do
        begin
          write('Reset target parts? (y/n): [n] ');
          if affirmative(input, output, no)
            then setins(input, output, parts, all); { reset active parts  }

          write('Reset window size? (y/n): [n] ');
          if affirmative(input, output, no)        { reset window size     }
            then setwindow(input, output,
                   spine, startwindow, endwindow);

          n := 0;
          t := startwindow;
          q := endwindow;
          while t <> q do
            begin
              gtraverse(t↑.start, parts, pcl, n);   { traverse start list }
              t := t↑.rlink
            end;
          if n >= smallset             { throw it back if it's too small  }
            then
              begin
                printheading('g');                { print table heading   }
                printdata(pcl, n, 0, measno(startwindow), measno(endwindow))
              end;

          write('Continue with genseg? (y/n): [y] ');
          done := not affirmative(input, output, yes);
          writeln
        end;
      writeln('Returning to main menu')
    end;  { genseg }

(************************       main procedure       ************************)
(* Build table, set window & parts, and then segment score interactively.*)
(**************************************************************************)
  begin  { main }
    inform;                        { give general information about program }
    build(input, output, scoredata, instr, freelist); { build structure    }
    readtable(output, setdata, loc, table);          { read set table      }
    newtype(input, output, primetype);               { set primeform type  }
                                                     { init parts & window }
    setup(output, instr[0].s, parts, all, startwindow, endwindow);
    done := false;
    while not done do
      begin
        printmenu;                                 { selection of commands }
        write('Enter your choice: ');
        readln(input,key);                         { read command          }

        if key in ['r', 's', 'c', 'd']
          then
            begin
              write('Reset target parts? (y/n): [n] ');
              if affirmative(input, output, no)    { reset active parts    }
                then setins(input, output, parts, all);

              write('Reset window size? (y/n): [n] ');
              if affirmative(input, output, no)    { reset window size     }
                then setwindow(input, output,
                       instr[0].s, startwindow, endwindow);
              printheading(key)                    { print table heading   }
            end;

        if key in ['d', 'c']                       { dynamics or chunk     }
          then chunkdynseg(startwindow, endwindow, parts, key)
        else if key = 'g'                          { general segmentation  }
          then genseg(instr[0].s, startwindow, endwindow, parts)
        else if key in ['r', 's']                  { rest or slur          }
          then
            begin { segmentation by parts }
              for inum := 1 to maxins do
                begin
                  if not empty(instr[inum].p) and (inum in parts)
                    then
                      case key of
                        'r': restsegment(instr[inum].p, inum, startwindow,
                                                              endwindow);
                        's': slursegment(instr[inum].p, inum, startwindow,
                                                              endwindow)
                      end
                end
            end { segmentation by parts }
        else writeln('Error in command');

        write('Do you want to continue? (y/n): [y] ');
        done := not affirmative(input, output, yes);
        writeln
      end
  end.  { main }
```

```
(***********************    PROGRAM SETSEARCH    ***********************)
(* Program setsearch finds all instances of a specified pc set within a  *)
(* "frame" that moves through the specified window in the score (section *)
(* 20.3.5).   File setdata was listed on pages 631-633.                   *)
(*************************************************************************)

program setsearch(input, output, scoredata, setdata);
  const
    maxins  = 15;                  { maximum number of parts in score    }
    maxline = 90;                  { max. number of characters on line   }
    yes     = true;
    no      = false;

  type

#   include "linkdefs.h"           { type definitions for link library   }
#   include "setdefs.h"            { type definitions for setid library  }

    infrec = record                { stores information on found notes   }
               part    : integer;  { part number in which note occurs    }
               measure : integer;  { measure in which note occurs        }
               beat    : real;     { the beat on which note begins       }
               pitch   : integer;  { pitch in continuous pitch code      }
               pc      : integer   { pitch class of note                 }
             end;

    inftype = array[1..12] of infrec;   { array of info on matching notes }

  var
    target      : pcset;        { set of pcs we're looking for               }
    startwindow : ptr;          { pointer to beginning of window in score    }
    endwindow   : ptr;          { pointer to end of window in score          }
    freelist    : ptr;          { pointer to stack of free nodes             }
    tcard       : integer;      { cardinality of target set                  }
    fconst      : integer;      { time slices per frame = tcard + fconst     }
    instr       : partpointers; { array of ptrs to parts                     }
    loc         : ar600;        { set table locations by cardinality         }
    table       : ar300;        { the set table                              }
    tie         : boolean;      { true if want to include ties               }
    scoredata   : text;         { file with output from DARMS interpreter    }
    setdata     : text;         { set-class data table                       }
    inf         : inftype;      { array of info on found notes               }
    parts       : partset;      { "active" parts, i.e. deal with these       }
    all         : partset;      { set of all possible parts                  }
    done        : boolean;      { true when user wants to quit               }
    primetype   : pftype;       { prime form type (forte, rahn)              }

(*************************************************************************)
(* External procedures and functions. (see appendix D).                  *)
(*************************************************************************)

  procedure build(var fin, fout, scoredata : text;
                    var instr : partpointers; var freelist : ptr); external;
  function  measno(x : ptr) : real;                                external;
  procedure readtable(var fout, data : text; var loc : ar600;
                                 var table : ar300);               external;
  procedure incr(var x : integer);                                 external;
  procedure decr(var x : integer);                                 external;
  function  convert(pc : integer) : char;                          external;
  function  tab : char;                                            external;
  function  pitchclass(cbr : integer) : integer;                   external;
  procedure setins(var fin, fout : text; var parts,
                                        all : partset);            external;
  function  affirmative(var fin, fout : text;
                            default : boolean) : boolean;          external;
  procedure setwindow(var fin, fout : text; spine : ptr;
                         var startwindow, endwindow : ptr);        external;
  procedure setup(var fout : text; spine : ptr; var parts,
           all : partset; var startwindow, endwindow : ptr);       external;
  procedure newtype(var fin, fout : text;
                                    var primetype : pftype);       external;
  procedure skipln(var f : text);                                  external;
  function  isdigit(c : char) : boolean;                           external;
  function  tielast(p : ptr) : boolean;                            external;
  function  subset(A, B : pcset) : boolean;                        external;
  procedure writepitch(var f : text; cbr : integer);               external;
  procedure decode2(x : pcset; var a : ar100; var n : integer);    external;
  procedure setcalc(var f : text; primetype : pftype;
       var dat : setinfo; var loc : ar600; var table : ar300);     external;
  procedure normal(var A : ar100; n : integer);                    external;
  procedure readset(var fin, fout : text; var pcset : ar100;
                  var n : integer; primetype : pftype;
                  var loc : ar600; var table : ar300);             external;
  procedure printset(var f : text; S : pcset);                     external;
  procedure encode(var A : ar100; n : integer; var x : pcset);     external;
  function  frac(x : real) : real;                                 external;
  procedure getline(var fi,fo : text; var buffer : buftype);       external;
  procedure getint(var fi, fo : text; var buffer : buftype;
                                       var x : integer);           external;
  function  eob(var buffer : buftype) : boolean;                   external;


(***********************          getset          ***********************)
(* Gets the target set (as pcs or set name), encodes it as a set of inte-*)
(* gers, calcs prime form, and prints target set.                        *)
(*************************************************************************)
  procedure getset(var fin, fout : text; primetype : pftype;
               var loc : ar600; var table : ar300; var target : pcset;
                                                   var card : integer);

    var
      dat : setinfo;
      pset : ar100;
    begin
      readset(fin, fout, pset, card, primetype, loc, table);
      dat.pcset := pset;
      dat.card := card;
      setcalc(fout, primetype, dat, loc, table);
      encode(dat.prime, card, target);
      write(fout, 'Target set = ');
      write(fout, dat.card:1, '-', dat.name:1,'/');
      printset(fout, target); writeln(fout)
    end;
```

```
(************************        getnform        ************************)
(* Decodes set and calculate normal form.                                *)
(*************************************************************************)
  procedure getnform(S : pcset; var nform : ar100);
    var
      card : integer;                    { cardinality of set       }
    begin
      decode2(S, nform, card);           { decode pcset into array  }
      normal(nform, card)                { and get normal order     }
    end;


(************************        printdata       ************************)
(* Prints data for notes in matching set.                                *)
(*************************************************************************)
  procedure printdata(inf : inftype; var match : boolean; S : pcset;
                                                  card : integer);

    var
      i     : pcint;
      nform : ar100;
    begin
      match := true;
      writeln('==================================');
      writeln('Part  Measure  Beat  Note       PC');
      for i := 1 to card do
        begin
          write(output, inf[i].part:3);               { part number     }
          write(output, inf[i].measure:8);            { measure         }
          write(output, inf[i].beat:8:2,'    ');      { beat            }
          writepitch(output, inf[i].pitch);           { note name       }
          writeln(output, tab, convert(inf[i].pc):2)  { pitch class     }
        end;
      getnform(S, nform);                             { get normal form }
      write(output, 'normal order = [');              { and print it    }
      for i := 1 to card do
        write(convert(nform[i]));
      writeln(']')
    end;


(************************       saveparams       ************************)
(* Saves values for matching note in inf array.                          *)
(*************************************************************************)
  procedure saveparams (note : ptr; var inf : inftype; card : integer);
    var
      mnum  : real;                                 { measure number }
      meter : real;                                 { beats per bar  }

    function barbeats(p : ptr) : real;     { find meter, return beats/bar }
      begin
        while p↑.tag <> spine do                    { get spine node }
          p := p↑.start;
        p := p↑.mlink;                              { and meter node }
        barbeats := (p↑.meter.num * p↑.beatnote.den) /
                    (p↑.meter.den * p↑.beatnote.num)
      end;

    begin
      mnum := measno(note);                              { measure (real)  }
      meter := barbeats(note);                           { beats per bar   }
      inf[card].part := trunc(note↑.part);               { part number     }
      inf[card].measure := trunc(mnum);                  { measure number  }
      inf[card].beat := (frac(mnum) * meter) + 1;        { beat number     }
      inf[card].pitch := note↑.dlink↑.pitch;             { pitch as cpc    }
      inf[card].pc := pitchclass(note↑.dlink↑.pitch)     { pitch class     }
    end;  { saveparams }


(************************        goodnote        ************************)
(* Called by procedure traverse.  A "good" note (a) does not duplicate a *)
(* pc already in set, (b) combines with previous notes to form a subset  *)
(* of target set, (c) it is not tied, unless we want tied notes, (d) it  *)
(* is in one of the parts we want to include.                            *)
(*************************************************************************)
  function goodnote(p : ptr; target : pcset; S : pcset; tie : boolean;
                                          parts : partset) : boolean;
    var
      x : integer;

    begin
      goodnote := false;
      if p↑.tag = note                                 { it's a note      }
        then if (trunc(p↑.part) in parts)              { in correct parts }
          then if tie or not tielast(p)                { tie is correct   }
            then
              begin
                x := pitchclass(p↑.dlink↑.pitch);      { get pc           }
                if not (x in S)                        { pc is unique     }
                  then  goodnote := subset(target, S + [x])
              end                                      { subset of target }
    end;  { goodnote }


(************************        moveframe       ************************)
(* Sets end of frame relative to current starting position in spine.    *)
(*************************************************************************)
  procedure moveframe(var endframe : ptr; endwindow : ptr; p : ptr;
                                              framesize : integer);
    var
      i : integer;

    begin
      endframe := p;
      i := 1;
      while (i < framesize) and (endframe <> endwindow) do
        begin
          endframe := endframe↑.rlink;
          incr(i)
        end
    end;
```

```
(************************          next          ************************)
(* Gets next note in linear succession, and then calls itself recursively*)
(* to get the note after that, etc.  Takes only 'good' notes (see above).*)
(* When a complete set is found, the location and values for each note   *)
(* are printed.                                                          *)
(*************************************************************************)
  procedure next(p, endframe : ptr; target : pcset; S : pcset;
                 card, tcard : integer; tie : boolean; parts : partset;
                                               var match : boolean);
    var
      pc : integer;                                { pitch class of note   }
    begin
      repeat                                       { traverse spine        }
        p := p↑.start;
        while p↑.tag <> spine do
          begin                                    { traverse time-slice   }
            if goodnote(p, target, S, tie, parts)
              then
                begin
                  pc := pitchclass(p↑.dlink↑.pitch);
                  S := S + [pc];                   { add to set            }
                  saveparams(p, inf, card);        { save parameters       }
                  if card = tcard                  { if set is complete    }
                    then printdata(inf, match, S, card)
                    else next(p, endframe, target, S,
                              card+1, tcard, tie, parts, match);
                  S := S - [pc]                    { remove pc from set    }
                end;
            p := p↑.start                          { get next note         }
          end;
        p := p↑.rlink                              { get next spine node   }
      until (p = endframe↑.rlink) or (p↑.tag = head)
    end;


(************************        traverse        ************************)
(* Traverses the score beginning at the beginning of specified window.   *)
(* When it finds a note, it calls next to find the next note in the set. *)
(* When all possibilities for first note have been exhausted recursively *)
(* by procedure next, traverse gets the new 'first' note.                *)
(*************************************************************************)
  procedure traverse(start, endwindow : ptr; target : pcset; card,
                     tcard, adjust : integer; tie : boolean; parts : partset);
    var
      p         : ptr;                  { pointer to first note          }
      pc        : integer;              { pitch class of note            }
      endframe  : ptr;                  { points to end of frame         }
      S         : pcset;                { set of "good" notes            }
      match     : boolean;              { false until a match is found   }
      framesize : integer;              { in time slices                 }

    begin
      match := false;                   { no matches found               }
      S := [];                          { null set of good notes         }
      framesize := tcard + adjust;      { set frame size                 }
      p := start;                       { first spine node in window     }
      repeat
        moveframe(endframe, endwindow, p, framesize);  { set end of frame }
        p := p↑.start;                           { next node in start list }
        while p↑.tag <> spine do                 { traverse time-slice     }
          begin
            if goodnote(p, target, S, tie, parts)
              then
                begin
                  pc := pitchclass(p↑.dlink↑.pitch);     { get pc           }
                  S := S + [pc];                 { mark it                  }
                  saveparams(p, inf, card);              { save values      }
                  if card = tcard                        { set is complete  }
                    then printdata(inf, match, S, card){ print vals      }
                    else                          { get next note in set }
                      next(p, endframe, target, S,
                                   card+1, tcard, tie, parts, match);
                  S := S - [pc]                          { unmark pc        }
                end;
            p := p↑.start                                { get next note    }
          end;
        p := p↑.rlink                                    { next spine node  }
      until (p = endframe↑.rlink) or (p↑.tag = head);

      if not match
        then                                       { no matches were found }
          begin
            writeln('===================================');
            writeln('set not found')
          end;
      writeln('===================================');
      writeln('Done');   writeln
    end;


(************************        setframe        ************************)
(* Sets the adjustment to the frame size.  The default frame size in     *)
(* time slices is equal to the cardinality of the target set.  The user  *)
(* can specify a positive or negative constant that is added to this size*)
(* each time the target is reset.  In the future it would  be nice to    *)
(* provide more flexibility, e.g., frame size in beats, measures, etc.   *)
(*************************************************************************)
  procedure setframe(var fconst : integer);
    var
      buffer : buftype;
    begin
      writeln('The frame size in time slices is set relative to the');
      writeln('cardinality of the target set by adding a positive or');
      writeln('negative constant to the cardinality each time a new set');
      writeln('is specified.  The default constant is 0, indicating that');
      writeln('the frame size is equal to the set cardinality.');
      writeln;
      write('Enter constant or <return>: [0] ');
      getline(input, output, buffer);
      if eob(buffer)
        then fconst := 0
        else getint(input, output, buffer, fconst)
    end;
```

```
(****************************************************************************)
(*                            main procedure                                *)
(****************************************************************************)
 begin { main }
   build(input, output, scoredata, instr, freelist);{build data structure}
   readtable(output, setdata, loc, table);          { read set table      }
   newtype(input, output, primetype);               { set prime form type }
   setup(output, instr[0].s, parts, all,            { init window, and    }
                       startwindow, endwindow);     { "active" parts      }

   done := false;                                   { not done yet        }
   fconst := 0;                                     { adjust to frame size}
   while not done do
     begin
       write('Reset target parts? (y/n): [n] ');    { reset parts?        }
       if affirmative(input, output, no)
         then setins(input, output, parts, all);

       write('Reset window size? (y/n): [n] ');    { reset window params? }
       if affirmative(input, output, no)
         then setwindow(input, output,
              instr[0].s, startwindow, endwindow);

       write('Do you wish to include tied notes? (y/n): [n] ');
       tie := affirmative(input, output, no);
       writeln;                                     { get target set      }
       getset(input, output, primetype, loc, table, target, tcard);
       writeln;
       write('Reset frame size? (y,n): [n] ');
       if affirmative(input, output, no)
         then setframe(fconst);
       writeln;

       writeln('Searching:');                       { search for set      }
       traverse(startwindow, endwindow, target, 1, tcard, fconst,
                                                          tie, parts);

       write('Continue? (y/n): [y] ');              { Are you finished?   }
       done := not affirmative(input, output, yes)
     end
 end. { main }
```

```
(***********************        PROGRAM CADID        ***********************)
(* Program Cadid identifies cadence type and local tonic at the end of    *)
(* each phrase of simple four-part tonal music, e.g., Bach chorales (sec-*)
(* tion 20.3.6).  Techniques in this program could be used as the first  *)
(* step in more comprehensive programs for the analysis of tonal music.  *)
(* File chorddata is listed at the end of the program.                   *)
(**************************************************************************)

program cadid(input, output, scoredata, chorddata);

  const
    sharp     = 's';                      { symbol for sharp                }
    flat      = 'f';                      { symbol for flat                 }
    maxchord  = 12;                       { max no. of chords in table      }
    maxins    = 15;                       { max instr in linked structure   }
    maxslice  = 60;                       { max no. of slices in piece      }
    maxstring = 76;                       { max stringlength + 1            }
    maxline   = 90;                       { maximum input line length       }

  type

#   include "linkdefs.h"

    keytype = (major, minor);             { mode of piece                   }

    string = packed array[1 .. maxstring] of char;
    entry = record
              card      : integer;        { cardinality of chord            }
              root      : integer;        { position of root in prime set   }
              chordcode : integer;        { integer representing chord type }
              primeset  : brset;          { primeform of br pcset           }
              chord     : string          { name of chord type              }
            end;

    chordtable = array[1 .. maxchord] of entry;  { lookup table             }

    slice = record
              cinfo     : integer;        { inversion and chord type        }
              sop       : boolean;        { true if root is in soprano      }
              rootnote  : integer;        { root of chord as BR             }
              fermat    : boolean;        { true if fermata in slice        }
              link      : ptr             { pointer to spine node           }
            end;

    chordline = array[1 .. maxslice] of slice;

  var                                     {        Global Variables         }
    chorddata : text;                     { external file for chordtable    }
    scoredata : text;                     { output from DARMS interpreter   }
    instr     : partpointers;             { linked data structure           }
    freelist  : ptr;                      { pointer to stack of free nodes  }
    T         : chordtable;               { table indexing chord types      }
    chordln   : chordline;                { array of chord slices in piece  }
    m         : integer;                  { no. of entries in chordline     }
    key       : integer;                  { key of piece in binomial rep    }
    mode      : keytype;                  { ordinal type (major, minor)     }
```

```
(************************** External Procedures **************************)
(* Declarations for external procedures (see appendix D).                *)
(*************************************************************************)
 function  br(cbr : integer) : integer;                            external;
 function  bradd(br1,br2 : integer) : integer;                     external;
 function  brsubtract(br1,br2 : integer) : integer;                external;
 procedure brnorm(var pcset, prime : brset; var n : integer);      external;
 procedure build(var fin, fout, scoredata : text;
                 var instr : partpointers; var freelist : ptr);    external;
 function  empty(x : ptr) : boolean;                               external;
 function  measno(x : ptr) : real;                                 external;
 function  nameclass(cbr : integer) : integer;                     external;
 function  pitchclass(cbr : integer) : integer;                    external;
 function  tochar(nc : integer) : char;                            external;
 function  pitch(pc : integer) : integer;                          external;
 procedure incr(var x : integer);                                  external;
 procedure decr(var x : integer);                                  external;
 procedure skipf(var f : text);                                    external;
 procedure skipln(var f : text);                                   external;

(***********************       readpset        ***********************)
(* Reads prime set of brs into array of table.                          *)
(*************************************************************************)
 procedure readpset(var f : text; var pset : brset; n : integer);
   var
     i : integer;
   begin
     skipf(f);
     for i := 1 to n do
       read(f, pset[i])
   end;

(***********************       readchord       ***********************)
(* Reads name of chord into packed array.                               *)
(*************************************************************************)
 procedure readchord(var f : text; var S : string);
   var
     i : integer;
   begin
     skipf(f);
     i := 1;
     while not eoln(f) do
       begin
         read(f,S[i]);
         incr(i)
       end;
     S[i] := chr(0)
   end;

(***********************       readtable       ***********************)
(* Reads external file containing chord table into array.               *)
(*************************************************************************)
 procedure readtable(var f : text; var T : chordtable);
   var
     i : integer;
   begin
     write('Reading chord table ...');
     reset(f);
     i := 1;
     while not eof(f) do
       begin
         skipf(f);
         read(f, T[i].card);
         skipf(f);
         read(f, T[i].root);
         skipf(f);
         read(f, T[i].chordcode);
         readpset(f, T[i].primeset, T[i].card);
         readchord(f, T[i].chord);
         skipf(f);
         incr(i)
       end;
     writeln('Done')
   end;

(***********************        getset         ***********************)
(* Returns cardinality of chord, weeds out rests.                       *)
(*************************************************************************)
 procedure getset(cbrs : brset; var pcset : brset; var n : integer);
   var
     i     : integer;
   begin
     n := 0;
     for i := 1 to 4 do
       if cbrs[i] <> -1
         then
           begin                                     { save br in pcset }
             incr(n);
             pcset[n] := cbrs[i]
           end
   end;

(***********************         ident         ***********************)
(* Checks set of brs against prime form.                                *)
(*************************************************************************)
 function ident(A, B : brset; n : integer) : boolean;
   var
     i : integer;
   begin
     i := 1;
     while (A[i] = B[i]) and (i < n) do
       incr(i);
     ident := A[i] = B[i]
   end;

(***********************       findchord       ***********************)
(* Finds chord in table matching prime form of chord at present slice.  *)
(*************************************************************************)
 procedure findchord(T : chordtable; prime : brset; n : integer;
                                              var loc : integer);
   var
     i    : integer;
     done : boolean;                          { true if chord is found }
```

```
  begin { findchord }
    i := 0;
    done := false;
    while (i < maxchord) and not done do
      begin
        incr(i);
        if n = T[i].card
          then done := ident(T[i].primeset,prime,n)
      end;
    if done
      then loc := i                          { chord found          }
      else loc := 0                          { chord not found      }
  end;  { findchord }

(************************         transint         ************************)
(* Returns the interval of transposition used in transposing normal     *)
(* order to prime form.                                                   *)
(**************************************************************************)
 function transint(pcset,prime : brset) : integer;
  begin
    transint := brsubtract(prime[1],pcset[1])
  end;

(************************         inversion        ************************)
(* Calculates inversion of chord.                                         *)
(**************************************************************************)
 function inversion(E : entry; cbrs : brset; trans, n, op : integer)
                                                              : integer;
  var
    bassnote : integer;
    pos      : integer;
  begin
    bassnote := bradd(cbrs[op],trans);
    pos := 0;
    repeat
      incr(pos)
    until E.primeset[pos] = bassnote;
    inversion := ((pos + n - E.root) mod n)
  end;

(************************         makeslice        ************************)
(* Constructs each slice in the chordline.                                *)
(**************************************************************************)
 procedure makeslice(var S : slice; inv : integer; sopr : boolean;
                     E : entry; croot : integer; ferm : boolean; p : ptr);
  begin
    S.cinfo := inv + (10 * E.chordcode);
    S.sop := sopr;
    S.rootnote := croot;
    S.fermat := ferm;
    S.link := p
  end;

(************************          xdecode         ************************)
(* Breaks the single integer "cinfo" into two separate integers repre-   *)
(* senting the chord type and the inversion.                              *)
(**************************************************************************)
 procedure xdecode(S : slice; var chord,inv : integer);
  begin
    chord := S.cinfo div 10;
    inv := S.cinfo mod 10
  end;

(************************          getcad          ************************)
(* Getcad is the principal procedure for finding cadences.  It checks    *)
(* first for root movement of either a descending 5th or an ascending    *)
(* minor 2nd (for vii6 - I progressions).  If such a root movement is    *)
(* found, the next check is for correct chord types, inversions, and the *)
(* presence of a fermata.  The check for a half cadence is at the moment *)
(* somewhat primitive, involving only the presence of a major root posi- *)
(* tion chord which does not fulfil the above root movement requirements *)
(* at the end of a phrase. Getcad returns an integer which represents    *)
(* the cadence type, or 0 if no cadence is found.                         *)
(**************************************************************************)
 procedure getcad(B : slice; rtprog,achord,ainv,bchord,binv : integer;
                                                  var cadtype : integer);
  var
    auth, half, perfect, vii : boolean;    { flags for cadences }
  begin
    auth := false;
    half := false;
    perfect := false;
    vii := false;
    if rtprog = 53
      then      { authentic cadence? }
        begin
          auth := (achord in [3, 7, 9]) and (binv = 0);
          perfect := B.sop;
          if auth and perfect and B.fermat
            then cadtype := 1                      { perfect authentic }
          else if auth and B.fermat
            then cadtype := 2                      {     authentic      }
        end
    else if rtprog = 11
      then                                         { vii6 - I cadence? }
        begin
          vii := (achord = 5) and (ainv = 1);
          if vii and B.fermat
            then cadtype := 3                      {       yes          }
        end
    else
      begin                                        { half cadence?      }
        half := (bchord in [1, 3]) and (binv = 0);
        if half and B.fermat
          then cadtype := 4                        {       yes          }
          else cadtype := 0                        { no cadence found   }
      end
  end;

(************************           roman          ************************)
(* Writes the roman numeral for scale degrees, given major or minor mode.*)
(**************************************************************************)
 procedure roman(n : integer; mode : keytype);
  begin
```

```
    n := nameclass(n);
    if mode = major
      then
        case n of
          0 : write('I');
          1 : write('ii');
          2 : write('iii');
          3 : write('IV');
          4 : write('V');
          5 : write('vi');
          6 : write('viio')
        end   { case }
      else
        case n of
          0 : write('i');
          1 : write('iio');
          2 : write('III');
          3 : write('iv');
          4 : write('v');
          5 : write('VI');
          6 : write('VII')
        end   { case }
  end;

(************************            name            ************************)
(* Prints note name in standard form.                                        *)
(****************************************************************************)
  procedure name(cbr : integer);
    var i : integer;
        nc, pc, dif : integer;
        accidental : char;
    begin
      nc := nameclass(cbr);
      pc := pitchclass(cbr);
      write(tochar(nc));
      dif := pc - pitch(nc);
      if dif >= 6
        then dif := dif - 12    { convert to flat(s) }
      else if dif <= -6
        then dif := dif + 12;   { convert to sharp(s) }
      if dif > 0
        then accidental := '#'
        else accidental := 'b';
      for i := 1 to abs(dif) do
        write(accidental)
    end;

(************************          printkey          ************************)
(* Prints key name with tonal center and mode.                               *)
(****************************************************************************)
  procedure printkey(key : integer; mode : keytype);
    begin
      name(key);
      if mode = major
        then write(' Major')
        else write(' minor')
    end;

(************************          writecad          ************************)
(* Prints the results of getcad in the form of cadence type, scale          *)
(* degree on which the final chord of the cadence occurs, and the           *)
(* measure no. at which it occurs.                                          *)
(****************************************************************************)
  procedure writecad(B : slice; newroot, key, cadtype : integer;
                                                       mode : keytype);
    const
      P4 = 53;                 { binomial representation for perfect fourth }

    var
      keyname : integer;
      lmode   : keytype;

    begin
      if cadtype > 0
        then
          begin
            case cadtype of
              1 : write('  Perfect authentic cadence in ');
              2 : write('  Imperfect authentic cadence in ');
              3 : write('  IPA: vii6 > I in ');
              4 : write('  Half cadence in ')
            end;   { case }

            newroot := brsubtract(newroot, key); { find scale degree       }
            if cadtype = 4
              then keyname := bradd(newroot, P4) { adjust for half cadence}
              else keyname := newroot;
            roman(keyname, mode);                { write scale degree      }
            if mode = major                      { set mode of new key     }
              then if nameclass(keyname) in [1, 2, 5]       { ii, iii, vi }
                     then lmode := minor
                     else lmode := major
              else if nameclass(keyname) in [0, 3, 4]       { i, iv, v    }
                     then lmode := minor
                     else lmode := major;
            keyname := bradd(keyname, key);      { actual tonicization     }
            write(' (');                         { write tonal center      }
            printkey(keyname, lmode);
            writeln(')', ' at m. ', measno(B.link):5:3);
            writeln
          end
  end;

(************************           getkey           ************************)
(* Calculates the major key associated with the key signature.              *)
(****************************************************************************)
  procedure getkey(p : ptr; var key : integer; var mode : keytype);
    var
      i, n : integer;

    begin
      mode := major;
      while (p↑.tag <> spine) and (p↑.tag <> keysig) do
        p := p↑.spec;
```

```
    if p↑.tag = keysig
      then
        begin
          n := p↑.accidentals;
          if p↑.sign = '-'
            then n := -n
        end
      else n := 0;  { No key signature }

    i := 0;
    key := 0;                                         { C Major         }
    if n >= 0                                         { sharps          }
      then while i < n do
        begin
          key := bradd(key,74);                       { go up by P5     }
          incr(i)
        end
      else while i > n do                             { flats           }
        begin
          key := brsubtract(key,74);                  { go down by P5   }
          decr(i)
        end
  end;

(***********************        checkkey        ***********************)
(* Checks the major key calculated by getkey against the final chord of  *)
(* the piece to see if it is actually in the major or else in relative   *)
(* minor.  At this point provision has not been made for modes.          *)
(*************************************************************************)
 procedure checkkey(var key : integer; root : integer; var mode : keytype);
  begin
    if (root = bradd(key, 95)) or (root = bradd(key, 42))
      then
        begin
          key := root;
          mode := minor
        end
  end;

(***********************        straverse       ***********************)
(* Traverses the chordline, checking each "slice" against its predecessor*)
(* to see if a cadence exists.  First the root progression is calculated,*)
(* next the chord information is decoded into chord type and inversion,  *)
(* and then this information is passed to getcad.  The results of getcad *)
(* are then printed by writecad.                                         *)
(*************************************************************************)
 procedure straverse(chordln : chordline; m, key : integer;
                                                    mode : keytype);
  var
    i : integer;
    oldroot, newroot : integer;
    rtprog : integer;                      { interval of root progression }
    A,B : slice;
    achord,bchord : integer;
    ainv,binv : integer;
    cadtype : integer;
  begin
    i := 1;
    A := chordln[i];
    oldroot := chordln[i].rootnote;
    while i < m do
      begin
        incr(i);
        B := chordln[i];
        newroot := chordln[i].rootnote;
        rtprog := brsubtract(newroot, oldroot);  { 53=5th,74=4th,11=2nd }
        xdecode(A, achord, ainv);
        xdecode(B, bchord, binv);
        getcad(B, rtprog, achord, ainv, bchord, binv, cadtype);
        writecad(B, newroot, key, cadtype, mode);
        A := B;
        oldroot := newroot
      end
  end;

(***********************        atraverse       ***********************)
(* Traverses the start field to pull out pertinent information for make- *)
(* slice, namely pitches, rests, and fermatas.                           *)
(*************************************************************************)
 procedure atraverse(p : ptr; var cbrs : brset; var ferm : boolean);
  begin
    while p↑.tag <> spine do
      begin
        if p↑.part <= 4
          then
            begin
              if p↑.tag = note
                then cbrs[trunc(p↑.part)] := br(p↑.dlink↑.pitch)
              else if p↑.tag = rest
                then cbrs[trunc(p↑.part)] := -1;
              if p↑.tag = note
                then ferm := fermata in p↑.dlink↑.artic
                else ferm := false
            end;
        p := p↑.start
      end
  end;

(***********************        vtraverse       ***********************)
(* Vtraverse is the backbone of the program.  Its primary functions are  *)
(* to find the key and traverse the spine of the linked data structure,  *)
(* constructing the chordline with procedure makeslice as it goes.       *)
(*************************************************************************)
 procedure vtraverse(s : ptr; T : chordtable; var m, key : integer;
                                                    var mode : keytype);
  var
    p     : ptr;
    ferm  : boolean;
    cbrs  : brset;
    prime : brset;
```

```
      pcset : brset;
      n     : integer;
      loc   : integer;
      inv   : integer;
      sop   : boolean;
      croot : integer;
      trans : integer;
    begin    { traverse spine }
      write('Building chordline...');
      m := 0;
      p := s↑.rlink;
      getkey(p↑.spec, key, mode);            { calculate key from keysig     }
      while p↑.tag <> head do
        begin { process node }
          ferm := false;                     { initialize fermata flag       }
          atraverse(p↑.start, cbrs, ferm);   { traverse start field          }
          getset(cbrs, pcset, n);            { find cardinality and pitches }
          brnorm(pcset, prime, n);           { get prime form                }
          findchord(T, prime, n, loc);       { find prime form in table      }
          if loc <> 0                        { if found                      }
            then
              begin
                incr(m);                             { pos in chordline     }
                trans := transint(pcset, prime);     { calc trans interval }
                                                     { calculate inversion }
                inv := inversion(T[loc], cbrs, trans, n, 4);
                                                     { is root in soprano? }
                sop := inversion(T[loc], cbrs, trans, n, 1) = 0;
                                                     { calc root            }
                croot := brsubtract(T[loc].primeset[T[loc].root], trans);
                                                     { add info to slice    }
                makeslice(chordln[m], inv, sop, T[loc], croot, ferm, p)
              end;
          p := p↑.rlink                              { get next time node   }
        end;  { process node }
      writeln('done');
      checkkey(key, croot, mode)                     { check for minor key }
    end;     { traverse spine }

(**************************************************************************)
(*                          main procedure                                *)
(**************************************************************************)
  begin    { main }
    build(input, output, scoredata, instr, freelist);{ build structure    }
    readtable(chorddata,T);                   { Read external chordtable  }
    writeln;
    vtraverse(instr[0].s, T, m, key, mode);   { Traverse spine, building  }
    writeln;                                  {    chordline              }
    write('Tonic = ');                        { report tonic key          }
    printkey(key, mode);
    writeln; writeln;
    writeln('Cadences:');
    writeln;
    straverse(chordln, m, key, mode);         { Analyze chordline         }
    writeln
  end.    { main }
```

```
(************************        file chorddata        ************************)
(* The following lists the file read by procedure readtable.                 *)
(******************************************************************************)

2  1   1  0  42  major (5th omitted)
2  1   2  0  32  minor (5th omitted)
3  1   3  0  42  74  major
3  1   4  0  32  74  minor
3  1   5  0  32  64  diminished
3  1   6  0  42  84  augmented
3  2   7  0  21  63  dom 7th (5th omitted)
4  2   8  0  11  53  85  major 7th
4  4   9  0  32  64  85  dom 7th
4  3  10  0  32  53  85  minor 7th
4  2  11  0  21  53  85  1/2 dim 7th
4  2  12  0  31  63  95  dim 7th
```

```
(************************        printgraph        ************************)
(* The following shell script was used to create the graph on page 811.  *)
(* Graph is a UNIX utility that creates graphs.  Plotfile is the output  *)
(* file from program partplot, using DARMS code for the first portion of *)
(* the Bartok String Quartet No. 4 as input; psplot is a program (Adobe, *)
(* Inc.) that translates UNIX plot files to PostScript; and lpr is the   *)
(* UNIX print spooler.  Thus the UNIX command line shown below runs pro- *)
(* gram graph (with a number of arguments specifying spacing, grid, etc.)*)
(* with plotfile as input; sends the output to program psplot; and sends *)
(* the output from psplot directly to a PostScript laser printer.        *)
(**************************************************************************)

graph -g 1 -w .96 -h .56 -x -1 27 1 -y 12 96 12 -b < plotfile | psplot | lpr
```

```
(************************     PROGRAM PARTPLOT     ************************)
(* Program partplot traverses a linked score structure printing pitch    *)
(* data in a format suitable for Unix's graph utility.  The notes in     *)
(* each part are connected until a rest occurs (section 20.3.7).         *)
(*************************************************************************)

program partplot(input, output, scoredata, plotfile);
  const
    maxins  = 15;
    maxline = 90;
    yes = true;
    no  = false;

  type
#   include "linkdefs.h"

  var
    instr       : partpointers;          { pointers into score structure  }
    freelist    : ptr;                   { pointer to stack of free nodes }
    scoredata   : text;                  { output from DARMS interpreter  }
    plotfile    : text;                  { output file for plot data      }
    parts       : partset;               { set of active parts            }
    all         : partset;               { set of all possible parts      }
    startwindow : ptr;                   { pointers to beginning and end  }
    endwindow   : ptr;                   {  of active window in score     }

(*************************************************************************)
(* External procedures and functions (see appendix D).                   *)
(*************************************************************************)

  procedure build(var fin, fout, scoredata : text;
                 var instr : partpointers; var freelist : ptr);    external;
  procedure setins(var fin, fout : text; var parts,
                                          all : partset);          external;
  function  affirmative(var fin, fout : text;
                         default : boolean) : boolean;             external;
  procedure setwindow(var fin, fout : text; spine : ptr;
                     var startwindow, endwindow : ptr);            external;
  procedure setup(var fout : text; spine : ptr; var parts,
                 all : partset; var startwindow, endwindow : ptr); external;
  function  starttime(x : ptr) : real;                             external;
  function  stoptime(x : ptr) : real;                              external;
  function  measno(x : ptr) : real;                                external;
  function  octave(cbr : integer) : integer;                       external;
  function  pitchclass(cbr : integer) : integer;                   external;
  function  nameclass(cbr : integer) : integer;                    external;
  function  cpc(cbr : integer) : integer;                          external;


(************************      plotnotes      ************************)
(* Prints plot data for segment beginning with note p to rest or end of *)
(* layer.                                                               *)
(*************************************************************************)
  procedure plotnotes(var f : text; t : ptr);

    var
      lastnote : boolean;

  begin { plotnotes }
    repeat
      write(f, starttime(t));               { raw time at beginning of note }
      write(f, cpc(t↑.dlink↑.pitch));       { cpc of note                   }
      write(f, stoptime(t));                { raw time at end of note       }
      writeln(f, cpc(t↑.dlink↑.pitch));     { cpc of note                   }
      lastnote := (t↑.rlink = t);           { chord note or last in layer   }
      t := t↑.rlink                         { next note in layer or part    }
    until (t↑.tag <> note) or (lastnote);
    writeln(f, ' " "')                      { breaks line in graph          }
  end;  { plotnotes }

(************************       traverse       ************************)
(* Traverses start-time lists off of spine. If note is first note in    *)
(* part, first note after a rest, a chord note, or first note in a layer,*)
(* then values in segment up to next rest are printed.                  *)
(*************************************************************************)
 procedure traverse(var f : text; startwindow, endwindow : ptr;
   var
     t : ptr;
   begin
     t := startwindow;                          { first node in window     }
     while t <> endwindow do
       begin
         t := t↑.start;                         { first node in startlist }
         while t↑.tag <> spine do
           begin
             if (t↑.tag = note) and (trunc(t↑.part) in parts)
               then if (t↑.llink↑.tag = head)   { first note in part       }
                    or (t↑.llink↑.tag = rest)   { first note after rest    }
                    or (t↑.llink = t)           { chord or first in layer }
                      then plotnotes(f, t);     { plot melodic segment     }
             t := t↑.start                      { next node in start list }
           end;
         t := t↑.rlink                          { next spine node          }
       end
   end;

(*************************************************************************)
(*                          main procedure                               *)
(*************************************************************************)
 begin { main }
   rewrite(plotfile);                               { open for printing  }
   build(input, output, scoredata, instr, freelist);{ build structure    }
   setup(output, instr[0].s, parts, all,            { init window and    }
                       startwindow, endwindow);     {  active parts      }
   write('Reset target parts? (y/n): [n] ');
   if affirmative(input, output, no)
     then setins(input, output, parts, all);        { reset active parts }
   write('Reset window size? (y/n): [n] ');
   if affirmative(input, output, no)                { reset window size  }
     then setwindow(input, output,
            instr[0].s, startwindow, endwindow);
   write('printing plot data in external file...');
   traverse(plotfile, startwindow, endwindow, parts);{ traverse spine    }
   writeln('Done')
 end.  { main }
```

Glossary

abstract data type A definition of a data structure in terms of its function and the operations defined for its use, without regard to the specific implementation. For example, the properties of a list, a stack, a queue, or a tree are the same whether the data type is implemented using an array or a linked data structure.

access To reference or alter the value of a variable.

actual parameter, argument A value passed to a procedure or function when it is called. See also *parameter*.

Ada A computer language designed for military embedded systems, i.e., real-time systems (computers and software) embedded within larger mechanical systems such as missiles or pilotless airplanes. In the 1970s the U. S. Department of Defence used several hundred different computer languages for this purpose. Ada is intended to replace these, thus simplifying software development an maintenance. The language was named after Augusta Ada Byrom, Countess of Lovelace and inventor of the stored program.

address The ordinal position of a storage location in the computer memory. Storage locations are numbered sequentially from 0 and are accessed through these numbers, or addresses.

ALGOL *ALGO*rithmic *L*anguage. The first computer language featuring structured design and modern data and control structures, ALGOL influenced many languages including Pascal, Modula-2, and Ada. ALGOL was designed by an international committee in Europe, and several versions were introduced between 1958 and 1968.

algorithm A detailed, unambiguous set of instructions for accomplishing a particular task.

allocate To assign memory locations for storing data within the computer. A Pascal system allocates memory for variables in the main program when the program is run, and for local variables in subroutines when the function or procedure is called. Memory can also be allocated on demand (see *dynamic allocation*).

ALU Arithmetic and Logic Unit. The ALU is the portion of the computer that performs arithmetic operations. It also has simple decision-making capabilities, i.e., it can test values resulting from computations and take specific actions as the result of these values.

analysis The first stage in designing an algorithm. Problem analysis includes specification of objectives, determination of special cases that must be dealt with, and exact specification of the input data and desired output.

anonymous type A data type that is not named. This occurs when the type of a structured variable is specified in the variable-definition part of a program rather than in the type-definition part, e.g.,

var
list : **array**[1 .. 100] **of** *integer*;

Variables declared in this way cannot be passed to subroutines as arguments.

application program A program designed to perform a specific task, usually for a user. Text editors, compilers, sorting programs, and music-analysis programs are examples of applications. Contrast to *operating system.*

argument A value passed to a subroutine. See *parameter.*

array A collection of data items stored in contiguous storage locations in memory. These memory locations are known by a common name and a subscript, or index number, indicating the position in the array, for example, *list* [1], *list* [2], . . ., *list* [*n*], where *list* is the name of the array, and the number in brackets is the subscript. The subscript may be a variable or expression; thus *list* [*i*], where *i* has an appropiate value, may refer to any element of *list.* Array elements may contain different types of values and may occupy more than one physical storage location in memory, although in most computer languages each element of an array must contain the same type of data.

array bounds The first and last values that may be used as subscripts of an array.

ASCII An acronym for *A*merican *S*tandard *C*ode for *I*nformation *I*nterchange.

assembly language A low-level programming language in which mnemonic instructions are used to represent machine-level instructions and memory locations. An assembler is a program that translates this code into numeric computer instructions.

assignment operator In Pascal, the compound symbol ':=', which is used in assignment statements.

assignment statement A Pascal construct, with the form

variable := *expression*;

which causes the value of a variable to be changed. When the statement is executed, the expression is evaluated and the resulting value is assigned to the variable. In a function, the value to be returned by the function is assigned to the function name.

base type The type of values that may be represented in a set type.

BASIC *B*eginner's *A*ll-Purpose *S*ymbolic *I*nstruction *C*ode. BASIC was designed at Dartmouth College in 1964 for teaching programming to novices. The language, which is usually implemented as an interpreter, emphasizes ease of use over the formulation of elegant solutions to problems.

batch Designed to run interaction with a user. Batch computer systems and batch programs are designed to be run in this manner. See also *interactive.*

bidirectional list A linked list in which each node contains a pointer to the previous node as well as to the next. Thus the list can be traversed in either direction.

See also *linked data structure.*

big-oh notation See *O-notation*

binary file A file in which values are stored using their internal (binary) representation rather than a character format. While binary files cannot normally be listed or printed using utility programs in the operating system, they can be written and read very quickly by a program, since no data conversion takes place.

binary search An efficient searching method that requires that the values be presorted in numeric order. The method is to test the value in the middle of the list. Either this is the required value or half of the list can be eliminated, since all values are either greater or less than the required value. The process is repeated until the value is found or it has been determined that the value does not occur in the list.

binary tree A tree in which each node has two possible branches. Binary trees, which are usually implemented as linked data structures, have many uses in computing, since they can be constructed and searched efficiently.

binomial representation (br) A pitch notation representing both the pitch class and name class (spelling) of a note or interval.

bit A binary digit. A bit can have one of two values, 0 or 1.

bit map A binary number or set of binary numbers in which the bits 0 and 1 are used to represent the presence of values in some other structure.

bit vector In this text, a twelve-bit binary number in which each bit represents the presence (1) or absence (0) of one pitch class in a pc set. Also the decimal representaton of this binary integer. For example, the pitch-class set [0, 1, 4] can be represented by binary 000000010011 or decimal 19. With this representaton, many operations can be performed on an entire set rather than on each element individually. In addition, the bit vector is useful in designing efficient data structures for storing and retrieving information about sets.

block A collection of data containing a fixed number of bytes, e.g., 512 or 1024.

boolean A Pascal ordinal data type that contains two values, *false* and *true.*

boolean operator In Pascal, the word symbols **not**, **and**, and **or**. Boolean operators take boolean values as operands.

bottom up A programming method characterized by writing and testing small pieces of a program before working out the overall structure. These program segments are usually implemented as functions and procedures, which are tested using a driver, i.e., a main program that tests the subroutine.

boundary condition The values at the first and last iterations of a loop. The term can also be applied to the initial and terminal conditions for recursive procedures or functions. Boundary conditions are also called the entry and exit condition.

br See *binomial representation.*

braces The special characters '{' and '}'. In Pascal braces are used to mark the beginning and end of comments.

brackets The special characters '[' and ']'. In Pascal brackets are used for array subscripts, e.g., $M[i, j]$ and for *set constructors.*

buffer An area in memory used to store data temporarily while it is being processed. In Pascal, the input buffer is an array of character data, with one character per array location, that is used to store data being read by a computer program. The value of the buffer variable *input*↑ is the next character to be read. Data is "buffered" because it is more efficient to transfer data between devices (terminals, disk drives, memory, and so forth) in *blocks* than one item at a time.

bug An error in a program. A bug may be syntactic or logical. A syntactic error prevents the program from compiling properly and is usually detected by the compiler. A logical bug is an error in the algorithm and is often more difficult to detect. See also *run-time error* and *compile-time error.*

byte A unit of computer memory, usually 7 or 8 bits. An alphabetic character stored in the computer occupies one byte.

C A programming language written by Brian Kernighan and Dennis Ritchie at Bell Telephone Laboratory circa 1972. C was designed for writing operating systems but has become widely used as a general-purpose language. It combines features of a high-level structured language with the capability for machine-level control of the computer. Most of the UNIX operating system was written in C.

cardinality The number of elements in a set.

case statement A control statement designed to select one of many possible branches in a program, depending on some value.

cbr See *continuous binomial representation.*

chaining See *nesting.*

character In Pascal, string of length one. Characters may be alphabetic ('a', 'b', 'c', 'A'), numeric ('0', '1', '9'), or "special" (';', '>', '?'). Some characters, known as *control characters*, have no representation in print.

circular list A linked list in which the last node has a pointer to the first node. If the list is *bidirectional*, the last node also has a pointer to the first.

cnc See *continuous name code.*

COBOL *CO*mmon *B*usiness *O*riented *L*anguage. Written during 1959–60 for business application, it became widely used on large computers.

combination A grouping of elements in which the order is not significant. The combinations of elements **a**, *b*, and *c* taken two at a time are (*a*, *b*), (*a*, *c*), and (*b*, *c*). Combinations with repetition also allow repeated elements, e.g., (*a*, *a*), (*b*, *b*), (*c*, *c*). See also *permutation.*

comment An annotation in a program added for clarification or explanation. Comments in Pascal are delimited by braces, { and }, or alternately by the combination of parentheses and asterisks, (* and *). Comments are intended for the human reader and are ignored by the compiler or interpreter.

compatible In Pascal, values are said to be "type compatible" if they represent elements of the same underlying type, even though they may have different subranges. The requirements for type compatibility are less rigorous than those for identical types.

compile To translate a program in a high-level language such as Pascal into machine language which is directly executable by the computer.

compiler A computer program designed to translate a program in a high-level language into machine-executable form.

compile-time error An error, usually in syntax, that can be detected while compiling a program. See also *run-time error.*

complement In set terminology, all possible elements that are not in a given set. For example, in a pitch-class set, within a 12-pc universe, the complement of (014) is (2356789AB). Here A and B represent 10 and 11.

component An element of a structured type. The type of values permitted is called the component type. For example, an array type declared as follows:

type
list = **array**[1..*max*] **of** *integer*;

can be used to store integers. The component type of a textfile is the character (type *char*). The flexibility of data types in Pascal derives from the fact that the component type may be another structured type. For example, the component of an array may be another array or a record.

compound statement A block of statements that can be treated as a single statement. In Pascal, compound statements are delimited by the reserved words **begin** and **end**.

computational method A procedure that has attributes of an algorithm but may not terminate under some conditions.

concatenate To join together as in a chain. The concatenation of the strings 'AB' and 'CDE' is the string 'ABCDE'.

conditional statement A general term used for statements that cause branching in a program. The term usually applies to the **if...then** and **if...then...else** constructions, although the **case** statement also belongs to this group.

constant An identifier representing a value that does not change during the course of a program. Constants may be defined by the user or may be predefined by the Pascal system. *Maxint*, the maximum value for integers, is an example of a predefined constant.

continuous binomial representation (*cbr*) A four-digit numeric pitch representation indicating the octave, pitch class, and name class (spelling) of a note or interval. The first digit is the octave, the next two digits are the pitch-class integer, and the final digit is the name class, indicating the spelling of the note. For example, 5063 represents $F\#_5$, i.e., octave 5, pitch class 6, name class 3 (F).

continuous name code (*cnc*) A numeric pitch representation in which the C-major diationic configuration of pitches is numbered successively from 0, which represents C_0. In this system there are seven diatonic steps in the octave. This system, which is reflected by the white keys on the piano, is used to model diatonic relationships.

continuous pitch code (*cpc*) A numeric pitch representation in which the chromatic tones are numbered successively from 0, which represents C_0. In this system there are twelve semitones in the octave.

control characters Special, nonprinting characters that are used internally by the computer system. One example is the newline character that marks the end of a line in a textfile. In Pascal, most control characters are specified by their ordinal position in the character set. For example, in the ASCII character set, *chr*(0) is the null character, and *chr*(9) is the tab character.

control statement A statement that alters the normal sequential flow of a computer program. Examples are loops (**while**, **repeat**, and **for**), conditionals (**if...then**, **if...then...else**), and the **goto**.

correct A program is said to be correct if it can be proven that it always works as expected. The process of proving the correctness of a program is called *verification.*

cpc See *continuous pitch code.*

CPU The *C*entral *P*rocessing *U*nit, which controls all parts of the computer.

crash To terminate abnormally. A program may crash as a result of a run-time error. A system crash results when an error in the operating system or hardware causes the computer to stop running (or hang) unexpectedly.

CRT *C*athode *R*ay *T*ube. The device used for the screen of a computer terminal.

curly braces See *braces.*

DARMS *D*igital *A*lternate *R*epresentation of *M*usic *S*cores. A system of encoding music for computer processing devised by Stefan Bauer-Mengelberg in 1963. DARMS is also known as Ford-Columbia Code because it originated at Columbia University under a Ford Foundation grant.

data structure A representation of data that defines the organization of the data and the means of accessing it. A given collection of data can often be represented in different data structures. For example, an ordered list of values could be stored in an array or a linked data structure. See also *abstract data type.*

data type The type of a unit of information in a computer language. Simple data types represent values that are usually treated as indivisible units, e.g., integers and characters. Structured data types allow one to group simple data items in meaningful ways, depending on relationships among the data. Arrays, records, and files are examples of structured data types in Pascal.

debugging The process of removing errors from a program.

decrement To subtract a fixed value, usually 1, from a value. To decrement a variable is to subtract 1 from it.

definition part The portion of a Pascal program, procedure, or function in which labels, constants, types, and variables are defined.

delimiter Special characters or combinations of characters that mark the limits of objects or data. In the English language, spaces and punctuation marks delimit words and phrases. In Pascal, comments are delimited by the special characters '{' and '}'. In encoded music, we might use the integer 0 or the special character '/' to represent bar lines, and thus to delimit measures.

device In computing, the term usually refers to equipment connected to the computer. Computer terminals, disk drives, and printers are examples of devices. The standard input and output files in Pascal are logically connected to specific devices. In most cases the standard input device is the keyboard and the standard output device is the CRT screen of the user's terminal.

dimension Refers to characteristics of an array. A one-dimensional array is sometimes called a vector; a two-dimensional array is usually called a *matrix*. See also *array bounds* and subscript.

direct access The property of a data structure or device that allows one to reference any element without accessing other elements. An array is a dircect access data structure since one can reference any element, say *A*[*i*], where *A* is the name of the array and *i* is a valid subscript. A disk drive is a direct-access storage device, since the operating system can go directly to any file. See also *sequential access.*

directive An identifier that takes the place of a program block in a function or procedure definition. The only directive defined in standard Pascal is *forward*, which means that the function or procedure will be defined later in the program. This is necessary in mutually recursive procedures, since a procedure must be defined before it is called in Pascal. Many Pascal implementatons define additional directives, e.g., *external*, for procedures that are not defined in the main program block. The *external* directive makes it possible to create libraries of routines that can be used in many programs.

documentation Aspects of a program that help to explain the program to the human reader. Documentation includes the use of mnemonic identifiers, block comments that explain procedures and functions, and line comments that help to clarify the purpose of program statements.

DOS *D*isk *O*perating *S*ystem. See *MS-DOS.*

down A computer system or device that is not running is said to be down. The system may have been halted in an orderly fashion by the operator, or it may have crashed as a result of a system error or hardware failure.

dynamic allocation The act of allocating memory while a program is running rather than when the program is compiled. In Pascal, memory can be allocated dynamically by calling the procedure *new.* Storage locations used for local variables and value parameters are allocated dynamically by the Pascal system when a subroutine is invoked.

efficiency A measure of how quickly an algorithm can perform its task. Efficiency is often specified through the use of big-oh notation.

elegance A desirable quality of a program or algorithm. A solution is said to be elegant if it performs its task in an efficient and intuitive way. Cooper and Clancy define elegance more precisely as the property that makes you say, "I wish I'd thought of that."[1] (An elegant definition.)

element See *array.*

empty statement In Pascal, a nonstatement. Since statements are separated by semicolons, an empty statement may result from using a semicolon without a statement where a statement is expected, or from inserting an extra semicolon.

1. Doug Cooper and Michael Clancy, *Oh! Pascal!*, 2nd ed. (New York: Norton, 1982), p. 569.

This may be intentional, e.g., in a **case** statement where a particular instance requires no action. More commonly empty statements are the result of inadvertently inserting a semicolon before the reserved word **end**, which marks the end of a compound statement. In most cases empty statements are benign; nontheless, they can cause problems. The semicolon after **do**, below, causes an infinite loop, since the empty statement will never cause the exit condition necessary to terminate the loop.

```
i := 1;
while i < 10 do;
   begin
      writeln(i);
      i := i + 1
   end;
```

entry condition The value of a controlling variable at the beginning of a loop or in the first call of a recursive procedure or function.

enumerated type A user-defined ordinal type in which the programmer specifies the elements of the type and their position relative to each other, e.g.,

```
type
   articulation = (tenuto, accent, staccato);
```

eof A boolean function that returns *true* when all elements of a file have been read.

eoln A boolean function that returns *true* when all characters on one line of a textfile have been read.

evaluate To calculate the value of an expression. If the expression is complex (consisting of more than one element), rules of precedence determine the order in which operators are applied. For example, in the assignment statement

$$i := a + b / c$$

the value of the expression $a + b / c$ is calculated and assigned to the variable i.

execute To cause some action. Statements, programs, and procedures are executed. As each statement in a program is executed, some action is performed.

exit condition The value of a controlling variable that will cause a loop to terminate, or that will terminate recursion in a procedure or function that invokes itself. If the exit condition is not met, the loop does not terminate.

expression A term or group of terms with operators, representing a value of some specific type. See *evaluate*.

extension A nonstandard feature of Pascal, i.e., one that is not specified by the ISO Pascal standard and thus cannot be expected in different compilers.

external file A file that exists apart from a program. An external file can be read or written by a program, but it remains in existence after the program terminates. See also *internal file*.

field See *record structure*.

field list The list of variable declarations naming the values and their types in a record declaration. The field list of the following record defines two fields:

```
type
  fraction =
    record
      numerator   : integer;
      denominator : integer
    end;
```

field width The number of spaces in which a value is to be printed. For example, if the integer 19 is printed using a field width of 8, the digits are preceded by six blank characters.

file In standard Pascal, a file is a sequential data type for storing similar components. An external file is useful for storing data between program runs; an internal file may be used for temporary storage while a program is running. Files containing data required by a program are often created with the use of a text editor.

file parameter The name of a file, used by the program to commmunicate with the outside world. Most Pascal program read data from the standard input file and write to the standard file output. Other file parameters may be used, with appropriate declarations, to declare additional files for reading and/or data.

fixed part See *record variant.*

fixed-point notation The standard representation of decimal numbers in which the position of the decimal point is fixed, i.e., placed after the whole part of the number and before the fractional part. Examples of real numbers in fixed-point notaton: 2.5, 785.892, 11000.123.

floating-point notation A representation of real numbers in which the decimal place always "floats" to a standard position, usually after the first digit. Floating-point notation uses a mantissa and an exponent that indicates the placement of the decimal-point in fixed-point notation. Floating-point notation, also known as "scientific notation," is useful for showing very large or very small numbers. A floating-point representation is used for real numbers within the computer.

flow diagram A graphic representation of an algorithm or process that utilizes differently shaped "boxes" connected by arrows. Usually rectangles are used for statements or processes, and diamonds are used to represent conditional statements that may result in different branches in the program.

flow of control The order in which statements (computer instructions) are executed in a computer program. Generally statements are executed sequentially, that is, one after the other. This order can be altered by various control structures that cause branching to other parts of a program, controlled repetition of a group of statements, etc. A procedure call causes a branch to a program segment that performs some specific task, followed by a return to the point from which the procedure was called.

for statement A looping construct in Pascal that causes a statement or compound statement to be executed a predetermined number of times.

forward declaration A directive indicating that the body of a procedure will occur later in the program. This is a necessary construct in standard Pascal for the implementation of mutually recursive procedures, since procedures must be declared before they are called.

function A subroutine that returns a value to the point from which it is called. Functions are called by using their names in expressions. The statement *y* := *sqr*(5) invokes the function *sqr* to calculate the value of its argument squared (5 × 5). Thus the statement assigns the value 25 to variable *y*.

function heading The first line of a function, consisting of the reserved word **function**, the function name, an optional parameter list, and a declaration of the type of value to be returned by the function.

garbage collection The process of returning allocated memory to the "storage pool" so that it can be reallocated.

GIGO An acronym for *G*arbage *I*n *G*arbage *O*ut, meaning that if the input data is incorrect the output will be useless.

global variable An identifier that is declared in the declaration part of the main program block and is known thoughout the whole program is said to be "global." See also *local.*

goto A Pascal construct that causes direct transfer to a statement identified with a statement label. **Goto**s are often used in earlier computer languages that do not have more modern control structures; they are usually avoided in a structured programming language like Pascal, since their indiscriminate use obscures program structure.

grouplet In this text, a generic term designating any irregular rhythmic grouping in music notation, e.g., triplets, quintuplets, septuplets, etc.

hardware The computer and peripherals. Contrast to *software.*

heading The first noncomment line of a program, function, or procedure. See *program heading*, *function heading*, *procedure heading*. See also *definition part* and *statement part* for the other parts of a program unit.

heap The area in computer memory used to dynamically allocate variables.

high-level language A computer language with constructs that are closer to natural language than those in assembly or machine language. A typical statement in a high-level language is compiled into many (low-level) machine instructions. High-level languages are frequently used for writing application programs, and are designed as "general purpose" languages, i.e., they can be used to solve many types of problems. One advantage of these languages is that compilers can be written for many different computer systems. Low-level languages tend to be designed for specific computers.

hybrid data structure A data structure that combines arrays and linked structures.

identical In Pascal, two variables have identical types only if they are defined using the same predefined data type. Thus anonymous types are never identical, even though their definitions may be the same.

identifier A name used to denote a constant, type, variable, procedure, or function.

if statement A decision construct that allows for program branching. Pascal provides two variants: **if...then** and **if...then...else**. The first executes a statement if its boolean expression is *true*, otherwise it does not execute it. The second form provides a means of choosing one of two statements, depending on the value of its boolean expression. The **if** statement is flexible, since the statement part may be any type of statement, including a compound statement, another **if** statement, or other structured control statements.

implement To bing to fruition. An algorithm is implemented as a computer program, compilers are implemented on different computer systems, etc. An *implementation* is the rendering of a program on a specific computer system. For example, the UNIX operating system has been implemented on, or ported to, many different computers from personal computers to mainframes.

in A Pascal construct used to test for inclusion in set types.

inclusion The state of being included. A specific element is said to be included in a set if it is a member of the set.

increment To increase a value, usually by 1. To increment a variable is to add 1 to it.

index Synonymous with *subscript* in an array. The term can also be used to indicate the ordinal position in any ordered type (file, linked list, etc.).

indirect access The use of a pointer variable to reference a value. The pointer's identifier is followed by an "up arrow" (↑). See *linked list*.

initialize To assign starting values to variables.

inorder traversal In a binary tree, a traversal in which each node is visited after its left subtree is traversed and before its right subtree is traversed.

input Data that is supplied to a program from some external source. In Pascal, *input* is the identifier used for the standard input file, i.e., the file that is used by default for input to the program.

input↑ See *buffer*.

input buffer See *buffer*.

input device Any device that can be used to enter external data into the computer. The keyboard on the the user's terminal is an input device, as is a punch-card reader.

instruction set The repertoire of instructions or operations that is built into a computer. Some computers that use a small number of instructions are called RISC, or *R*educed *I*nstruction *S*et *C*omputers. The older design is sometimes called CISC, for *C*omplex *I*nstruction *S*et *C*omputer.

integer A whole numbers (without a fractional part). In Pascal, the range of integers is limited by the number of binary digits used to represent them internally. The maximum size is implementation dependent, and is available through the standard identifier *maxint*.

interactive Designed to run with intervention by the user. On an interactive computer system, the user can communicate with the programs while they are running. An interactive program is one that is designed to run in this manner.

Interactive programs usually prompt the user when they require a response or instruction. See also *batch.*

internal file A file that is created by a program for temporary storage. The program can write to the file and reread data from the file, but it ceases to exist when the program terminates.

interpreter A computer-language processor that does not generate executable code (machine language) for the complete program. Typically, an interpreter interprets one program statement at a time, and generates the machine instructions to execute the statement. Interpreters are usually smaller than compilers and frequently do more error checking, but an interpreted program does not run as fast as one that is compiled. Contrast to *compiler.*

intersection The set of elements in common to two sets. The Pascal operator for calculating the intersection of two sets is '*'.

interval The distance between two pitches.

interval class In music theory, a pair of intervals that are related by inverse operation. Any pitch-class interval X has an inverse $\bar{X}$ that is equal to $(12 - X)$ mod 12. Thus the intervals 2 and 10 belong to the same interval class. The interval class is represented by the smaller of the two numbers. The inverse operator is equivalent to inverting an interval in tonal theory. Thus the inversion of a perfect fourth (5 semitones) is the perfect fifth (7 semitones), and vice versa.

invariance matrix A matrix devised for calculating invariant segments between two pitch class sets or between two forms of the same set.

invoke Used with procedures, a synonym for *call.* A procedure is invoked by using its identifier (name) as a program statement.

I/O Computer jargon for Input/Output. Pronounced "eye-oh."

iteration Repetition or looping. An iterative solution is one that uses a loop. See also *recursion.*

kludge An ad hoc solution, usually intended to correct an error in a program. It is often a poor substitute for designing the algorithm correctly in the first place. The term is also used for legitimate techniques that circumvent shortcommings in a programming language.

label In Pascal, a number, prefixed to a statement, that makes it possible to transfer control to that statement via a **goto** construct. Labels must be declared in the declaration part of a program or subroutine, and are used infrequently in structured programming.

lexicographic sorting Sorting text in alphabetic order. See also *sorting.*

library In programming, a group of subroutines that can be called by various programs. Many systems have special libraries for mathematical, statistical, or graphic applications, for example. The use of external procedures and functions (in libraries or archives) is an extension to standard Pascal, but is available in many Pascal systems.

linear decomposition A feature of DARMS music code that allows different "layers" of a score or part to be encoded conveniently.

linear search Searching a list one element at a time in sequential order.

link A pointer variable containing the address of a value. See *linked data structure.*

linked data structure A data structure made up of storage units, called nodes, which contain fields for data and pointers (or links) to other nodes. A pointer contains the address of another node in memory. A simple linked list is maintained with a pointer variable that contains the address of the first node in the list. Each node has a link field that contains the address of the next node. The link field of the last node is a **nil** pointer, that is, it does not point to anything.

linked list A linear list stored in a linked data structure.

LISP *LIS*t *P*rocessing Language (1959). A language used for processing lists of symbols of any type, including natural languages. Widely used in artificial-intelligence research.

list An ordered collection of values. A list may be stored in an array or a linked list.

literal In this text, a fixed value of any type, as contrasted to a *variable* or *constant,* which are represented by an identifier. A number may be represented by a numeric literal, e.g., 768 or 78.3. In Pascal, a string may be represented by a character literal enclosed in single quotation marks, e.g., 'This is a string'. See also *constant* and *variable.*

local variable A variable that is defined within a procedure or function, but is not known or recognized outside of that procedure or function. See also *global variable* and *scope.*

logarithm The power to which a base number must be raised in order to obtain a specific value.

lookup table An array used to store values related to their subscripts in a specific way. For example, the powers of 2 might be stored in an array called *power,* such that *power*[*i*] contains the value 2^i. This array can be used to obtain powers of 2 via table lookup. This process is more efficient than recalculating the values many times.

loop A program construct that causes a statement or group of statements to be repeated a fixed or variable number of times.

machine language The numeric language that runs a computer.

mainframe A large computer system designed to accommodate many users.

main memory The primary storage used for computer programs and data while a program is executing. External storage devices, such as tape and disk drives, are sometimes referred to as secondary memory. See also *RAM.*

main program The primary program block of a computer program. In a well-structured program, the main program usually calls separate procedures to perform various tasks.

matrix A two-dimensional array. A twelve-tone matrix could be stored in a twelve-row-by-twelve-column array. In the computer, the matrix is actually stored in contiguous memory locations, and an addressing algorithm is used to calculate the address of each element in the matrix. Matrices are referenced by the name of the matrix and two subscripts, or indices, representing the row and column number, for example, $M[i, j]$, where M is the name of the matrix, i is the row number, and *j* is the column number.

memory See *main memory.*

mnemonic Intended to assist memory. In most cases identifiers should be mnemonic, i.e., the name should suggest the purpose of the identifier. A variable that will represent a note should be called *note* rather than *x*.

Modula-2 A language designed by Niklaus Wirth during the middle to late 1970s, Modula-2 and its predecessor, Modula, are based on Pascal syntax with the addition of extensions for real-time programming, multiprocessing, and low-level machine access.

modularity A modular program is divided into subroutines (modules), each of which performs a well defined task, and has one point of entry and one exit point. Communication with other modules is through parameters, rather than through global variables. Modularity is generally considered a desirable characteristic, since modular programs are easier to understand, test, and extend programs which are not designed in this manner.

modulo With respect to a modulus of. The integers 3 and 15 are congruent *modulo* 12, since the remainder, 3, after dividing 15 by 12 is equal to the remainder after dividing 3 by 12.

MS-DOS *M*icro*S*oft *D*isk *O*perating *S*ystem. A popular operating system for personal computers designed and marketed by Microsoft Inc.

multilinked structure A data structure consisting of interconnected linked lists. For example each node of one list can contain pointers to other linked lists.

multitasking system An operating system that can execute two or more programs at the same time.

multiuser system A multitasking operating system that can support two or more users simultaneously.

MUSTRAN *M*usic *T*ranslator? A music coding language designed by Jerome Wenker at Indiana University.

name class (nc) The class of all pitches that are spelled with the same letter name, for example D, D-sharp, D-flat, D-double-flat, etc. The seven name classes C, D, E, F, G, A, B may be represented by the seven digits 0–6. Operations in this system are performed modulo 7.

nc See *name class.*

nesting Nesting, or chaining, refers to using one control structure within a similar structure, e.g., using a second **for** statement within the statement part of the first **for** loop. The following nested loops print the matrix *M*:

```
for i := 1 to rows do
  begin
    for j := 1 to columns do
      write(M[i, j];
    writeln
  end;
```

nil pointer A pointer variable that does not point at anything. In Pascal, this state is indicated by assigning a variable the reserved word **nil**, e.g., *p* := **nil**.

node An object in a linked data structure, including data and links to other nodes. See also *linked data structure.*

normal form A standard ordering for pitch-class sets defined by John Rahn.

normal order In this text, the specific ordering of a pitch-class set that maintains the original pitches but is either a transposition or a transposed inversion of the prime form.

null set An empty set, i.e., a set which contains no elements.

number crunching Any computing application that is heavily oriented toward numeric calculation. The term is often applied to scientific applications. In music applications, digital sound synthesis could be considered number crunching, since roughly 40000 numbers per second per channel must be calculated.

numeric pitch codes Various numeric representations of pitch.

O-notation A device used to specify the upper bounds on the running time of an algorithm. Informally, $O(n)$ means that the efficiency of the algorithm is proportional to the number of input values, n, and is thus linear. Some other common measures are $O(1)$ (constant time), $O(n^2)$ (exponential), $O(n^3)$ (quadratic), and $O(\log_2 n)$ (logarithmic).

object program A program that has been translated into machine language, and is thus ready to execute. Compare to *source program.*

oct.dec A pitch representation used in computer music-synthesis systems, consisting of a fixed-point number. The digits before the decimal place represent the octave; those after the decimal point represent a fraction of the octave. For example, 4.5 represents the pitch F#$_4$, which is half way between C_4 (4.0) and C_5 (5.0). Unlike **oct.pc** notation, *oct.dec* format can be used to represent any frequency.

oct.pc A pitch notation consisting of a floating-point number in which the whole part is the octave and the decimal part is the pitch class (00–11) representing a pitch within that octave. For example, 5.00 is C_5 and 4.03 is D#$_3$ or Eb$_3$.

operand, *operator* An operator is a symbol such as '+' or '–' that symbolizes an operator. Operands are the values affected by the operator. Operators that take two operands are said to be binary or dyadic. Operators that apply to one operand are unary. Operands and operators are combined to form expressions.

operating system A program that manages the resources of the computer and serves as an interface between the user and the hardware. Contrast with *application program.*

ordinal type A data type consisting of a fixed number of elements upon which the order is defined. In Pascal, integers are an ordinal type (ranging from *–maxint* to *maxint.* Real numbers are scaler but not ordinal, since the successor of a real number is indeterminate. In Pascal, the programmer can define ordinal types called enumerated types.

OS/2 A multitasking operating system developed by IBM.

output Data that is produced by a computer program. In Pascal output is the identifier used for the standard output file, i.e., the file that is used by default for output from the program. Compare to *input.*

output device A device (hardware) used to display output from a computer. The printer and the user's CRT screen are examples of output devices.

pack, unpack In Pascal, complex data types can be packed, i.e., stored in the least possible amount of memory space. For example, in a packed array of characters, two or four characters might be stored in each memory location. Using packed data structures minimizes memory requirements at the cost of execution speed, since the computer must unpack the data when it referenced. Pascal provides utilities for packing and unpacking arrays. A programmer can also pack information. For example, in this text we use a single integer (see *cbr*) to represent the octave, pitch class, and name class of a note.

parameter A symbolic name used to pass a value to a procedure or function. A distinction is made between the formal parameter (the symbolic name used in the procedure or function) and the actual parameter or argument (the value passed to the procedure and used in place of the formal parameter. In function *sqrt*(*x*), *x* is a formal parameter that may represent any positive real number. When the function is called, for example, *y* := *sqrt*(89.3), 89.3 is the actual parameter passed to the function and used in the calculation. Parameters can be of two types, called value and variable parameters. When a value parameter is used, a copy of the value of the actual parameter is passed to the subroutine (pass by value). When a variable parameter is used, the address of a variable is passed (pass by reference), thus the variable parameter can be used to return values to the calling procedure.

parameter list The part of a procedure or function heading in which formal parameters are defined.

Pascal A high-level, general-purpose programming language designed by Niklaus Wirth during the late 1960s and early 1970s.

pattern matching The process of looking for a predefined pattern in sequential data. The term refers to searching for words or patterns in character strings.

pc See *pitch class.*

peripheral Any hardware device that is attached to a computer.

permutation A grouping of elements in which the order is significant. The combinations of elements **a**, *b*, and *c* taken two at a time are (*a*, *b*), (*a*, *c*), (*b*, *a*), (*b*, *c*), (*c*, *a*), (*c*, *b*). See also *combination.*

pitch-class set A set of unique pitch classes, usually represented by pitch-class integers.

pitch class (pc) The class of pitches with membership defined by octave equivalence. For example, all D-flats and C-sharps in any octave belong to the same pitch class. Since there are twelve notes in an octave, there are twelve pitch classes. These are frequently represented by the pitch-class integers 0 through 11, with 0 = C, 1 = C# or Db, . . ., 11 = B. Operations on this system are performed modulo 12.

PL/I Programming Language I. Designed at IBM during the 1960s, incorporating features from FORTRAN, ALGOL, and COBOL, combined with many unique features, PL/I was intended to become *the* language for all applications. The language is huge and was first available primarily on IBM mainframes, but subsets have been implemented on microcomputers.

pointer A variable that contains the address of some data object, and thus "points" to that object. The data object is usually a record structure, but it may be a simple type as well.

pop An operation defined on the data type *stack*, which consists of taking the top value off of the stack.

port To implement an application program, operating system, etc., on a new computer. Also see *implement*. The term is also used to denote the part of a computer to which external devices are connected, e.g., terminal port, communications port.

postorder traversal In binary trees, a traversal in which each node is visited after its left and right subtrees have been traversed.

precedence Rules defining the order in which operands are applied in evaluating an expression. For example, division and multiplication are performed before addition and subtraction in arithmetic expressions. The order can be altered by using parentheses, e.g., (65 + 3) / 4.

precision The number of digits to the right of the decimal point when a real number is printed. Also the number of significant digits stored in the internal representation of a floating-point number.

preorder traversal In a binary tree, a traversal in which each node is visited before its left and right subtrees are traversed.

prime form A reference form of a pitch-class set; usually the normal order of a set or the inversion of this set, transposed to begin on 0. The prime form of a set is a set-class representative that stands for all pitch-class sets that are related by transposition or transposition after inversion. For example, the prime form 014 (C, C♯, E) represents all transpositions or transposed inversions of this set.

procedure A program unit that performs a specific task and can be called (or invoked) explicitly. The computer instructions comprising the definition of a procedure occur once in a program, but the program may cause these statements to be executed many times from different locations by "calling" the procedure. A procedure is called by invoking its name in a program statement. When this occurs, the program executes the statements in the procedure definition and then returns to the place in the program from which the procedure was called. In a recipe, the instruction "Add 1 cup of white sauce (see p. 453)" is analogous to a procedure call.

procedure call See *procedure*.

program An algorithm expressed in a language that can be executed by a computer.

program block In Pascal, consists of the *definition part* and *statement part* of a program, function, or procedure. The type and name of the block are stated in the heading. See *program heading*, *function heading*, and *procedure heading*.

program heading The first noncomment line of a program. The heading consists of the reserved word **program**, the identifier used to name the program, and a list of file parameters that the program will use for input and output from the program, e.g.,

program *HeadingDemo*(*input*, *output*);

PROLOG *PRO*gramming in *LOG*ic (1972). A language for logic programming, originally designed for theorem proving, that has emerged as an important tool in artificial-intelligence research.

prompt A line of text printed on the user's terminal to inform him that input is required. Used in interactive programs.

pseudo code A combination of Pascal control structures and English language often used to express algorithms. Pseudo code is particularly useful in the early stages of algorithm development or in giving an overview of an algorithm. Example:

```
if you are explaining an algorithm do
   use pseudo code
```

pseudo-random number A number in a series that simulates a random-number series. Most "random number" algorithms actually generate a series of pseudo-random numbers from a seed value. The series is not really random, since a given seed value always generates the same series.

push An operation defined on the data type *stack*, which consists of placing a value on the top of the stack.

queue A First In First Out (FIFO) data structure. The operations defined on queues are inserting a value at the rear of the queue, removing a value from the front of the queue, and testing for an empty or full queue. Queues can be implemented with arrays or linked structures.

radian A unit used to measure angles. 360 degrees is equal to 2π radians.

RAM *R*andom *A*ccess *M*emory. The primary memory in a computer.

random access The ability to directly reference any element in a data structure or storage device. A disk is a random-access device; an array is a random-access data structure. See also *sequential access*.

random number See *pseudo-random number*.

rational arithmetic Arithmetic using fractions rather than floating-point numbers. The advantage is that fractions can represent any value precisely, while floating-point numbers can only approximate some values. For example the fraction 1/3 can cannot be represented precisely in a computer using floating-point numbers. The precision is limited in implementaton: 0.3333333 . . . Fractions are represented exactly by defining a record structure with a numerator and denominator, and writing procedures that operate on these stuctures.

rational duration representation (rdr) A representation of music durations based on fractions, e.g., a quarter note is represented 1/4, a dotted quarter by 3/8, etc.

rdc See *reciprocal duration code*.

rdr See *rational duration representation*.

real In Pascal, the type *real* is used for storing floating-point numbers.

reciprocal duration code An encoding scheme in which durations are represented by the reciprocal of the fractional representation. For example, a quarter note is represented by the integer 4, a half note by 2, and a whole note by 1. A more advanced form uses periods to represent dots and commas to represent ties, e.g., a dotted quarter (4.), a doubly-dotted eighth (8..), a half note tied to a dotted quarter (2,4.).

record structure A structured data type in which a collection of related data of different types may be kept together under one name. The structure has "fields," which are names for specific items of information. It is possible to treat the record as a single item, or to access fields individually. Thus we may define a record structure of type *note* that has fields for pitch, duration, dynamics, and so forth. If *x* is a note, then *x.pitch* is its pitch, *x.dur* its duration, *x.link* the address of another note, and so forth. If *p* is a pointer to a record, the fields of that record are accessed as *p↑.pitch*, *p↑.dur*, *p↑.link*, and so forth.

record type A user-defined data type in which data objects may contain various related values of different types. In Pascal, we can define fixed records or variant records. A fixed record always has the same fields (subelements). A variant record contains some fixed fields, and other fields that may change depending on the variant in use. Variant records are defined with a tag field, the value of which indicates the current variant. Even though a variant record may have different fields, all variants of the same record are considered to be the same type, thus an array can be defined with a variant record as its component type.

record variant See *record type.*

recursion The capacity of a function or procedure to call itself. For example, *n!* (n factorial) can be defined for any positive *n*, as $n \times (n - 1)!$. Algorithms and data structures can be defined recursively. For example, a linked list can be defined thus: *A linked list is either empty or it consists of a pointer to a node that has a pointer to a linked list.* Although recursive definitions seem "circular," recursion is a powerful and elegant tool for developing many types of algorithms.

reference To access the value of a variable to obtain or set its value.

refinement See *stepwise refinement.*

register A storage location in the computer that has special properties. For example, the value in a register can often be incremented or tested without first being copied to the ALU. The exact properties and number of registers depend on the computer hardware and instruction set of a particular computer.

relational operators Pascal operators used for comparing values. The relational operators are < (less than), = (equal), > (greater than), <= (less than or equal), >= (greater than or equal), and <> (not equal). When relational operators are applied to appropriate operands, the result is a boolean value (*true* or *false*). For example, the expression $9 < 3$ evaluates to *false.*

repeat...until A loop construct in Pascal in which the condition that may terminate the loop is tested at the bottom of the loop. Thus the body of a **repeat...until** loop is always executed at least once.

reserved words Word symbols in Pascal that can only be used in a predefined way. For example, **begin** and **end** are used to mark the beginning and end of compound statements, and cannot be used as identifiers (names of variables, etc.).

robustness A program's ability to tolerate syntactic or value errors in the input data, thus difficult to crash.

root The element of a tree through which the tree is first accessed, usually drawn at the top of the tree. See *tree.*

run-time error An error that is detected while the program is running, often as a result of inappropriate data, e.g., dividing by 0. Run-time errors usually crash the program.

scientific notation See *floating-point notation.*

scope The portion of a program in which a given identifier (naming a variable, procedure, function, etc.) is recognized.

SCORE code A music encoding scheme designed by Leland Smith of Stanford University, and used primarily in music-synthesis and music-printing programs.

seed value A number used as a starting value in calculating a pseudo-random number series.

sequential access A data structure or device in which elements can only be referenced in a specific order. A linked list is a sequential data structure, and a tape drive is an example of a sequential storage device.

set constructor A device used in assigning values to a set type in Pascal, consisting of elements of the set enclosed in brackets. The empty set of any type is designated by [ ]. Other examples: ['0' .. '9'] (the set of numeric characters between '0' and '9'); [0, 1, 4] (a three-note set of integers).

set difference The set of elements in one set that are not elements of another set. The Pascal operator for calculating set difference is '–'.

set type A Pascal type used for representing unordered sets of values of the same ordinal type. Pascal provides operators for performing standard operations on sets: intersection; union; set difference; testing for inclusion, subset, or superset; etc.

side effect The byproduct of a subroutine occuring when a function or procedure changes the value of a global variable that is not passed as a parameter. This is not desirable. See also *modularity.*

simple type A data type in which each element is generally treated as a single, indivisible item. The predefined simple types in Pascal are *integer*, *char*, and *boolean.* In addition, the programmer can define enumerated types and pointer types.

SNOBOL4 *S*tri*N*g *O*riented Sym*BO*lic *L*anguage. An interpreted language designed during the late 1960s at Bell Telephone Laboratories for manipulating character strings and other nonnumeric data. SNOBOL4 and its predecessors have been used for many applications in music theory. The *SNOBOL3 Primer* was written by Allen Forte, a music theorist at Yale University.

software Programs; often subdivided into operating systems and applications.

sorting Ordering elements in a list according to some criteria, e.g., placing a list of integers in ascending or descending numeric order, or putting a list of words in alphabetic order.

source program A program in a high-level language such as Pascal or C. A compiler translates a high-level source program into object code.

sparse matrix A matrix in which a good majority of the elements may be empty. In computing, special techniques are used to represent these matrices in a minimum of space.

special symbols In Pascal, special characters or combinations of special characters that represent operators, for example, ':=' (the assignment operator), '+' (the addition or union operator), '<=' (less than or equal).

SPITBOL *SP*eedy *I*mplemen*T*ation of *S*no*BOL4*. A compiled version of SNOBOL.

square brackets See brackets.

stack A *F*irst *I*n *L*ast *O*ut (FILO) data structure. Generally, the operations defined on stacks are pushing a value onto the stack, popping a value off of the stack, and testing for a full or empty stack. Stacks can be implemented using arrays or linked data structures.

standard function A function that is required in conformant Pascal compilers by the ISO Pascal standard.

standard identifiers Predefined identifiers that are expected in standard Pascal. These include standard functions and procedures, and special identifiers like *maxint*.

standard input The standard input file in Pascal is called *input*. This identifier is usually connected logically to the keyboard on the user's terminal, although the specific device is implementation defined.

standard output The standard output file in Pascal is called *output*. This identifier is usually connected logically to the CRT screen on the user's terminal, although the specific device is implementation defined.

standard Pascal A Pascal implementation that conforms to the Pascal standard defined by the International Standards Organization (ISO). The standard is distributed in North America by American National Standards Institute (ANSI).

standard procedure A procedure required of conformant compilers in standard Pascal.

statement A basic unit of a computer program, e.g., a *read* statement, *write* statement, **if...then...else** statement, procedure call, etc.

statement label See *label*.

statement part The portion of a program, function, or procedure in which actions are specified by program statements. Structurally, the statement is delimited by the reserved words **begin** and **end**, and is thus equivalent to a compound statement. See also *heading* and *definition part*.

stepwise refinement A technique in structured programming that consists of developing an algorithm by subdividing each task into successively smaller and more precisely defined steps, until each step can be easily expressed in the computer language one is using. See also *top down*.

string In standard Pascal, a packed array of characters, or a character literal enclosed in single quotes. The packed array and the literal representation of a string are compatible types if they are the same length.

structured programming A programming technique that includes top-down design, stepwise refinement, and modularity, i.e., encoding the program in well-defined blocks. Structured programming techniques lead to clearer program structure. The resulting programs are generally easier to debug, maintain, and extend. Certain computer languages, such as Pascal, encourage structured programming.

structure type A data type in which each data object contains more than one element. Pascal allows the following structured types: arrays, records, sets, files, and linked data structures defined with pointers and records.

subprogram A generic name for a program block that can be invoked by name, i.e., a function or procedure.

subrange type A collection of contiguous values in a predefined or user-defined ordinal type. Subranges are specified by the first and last values separated by two periods, e.g., 0 .. 11 is the subrange of integers between 0 and 11, inclusive.

subscript A value in an ordinal type, enclosed in brackets, which references a specific element of an array. The specific value is often replaced by a variable with an appropriate value.

subset Any set whose elements are all members of another, larger set. Set A is said to be a subset of set B if each element of A is a member of B. A is a proper subset of B if the cardinality of A is less than that of B.

superset That set whose elements are selectively contained in a subset. Set A is a superset of set B if each element of B is an element of A. A is a proper superset of B if the cardinality of A is greater than that of B.

symbol table A table used in compilers that associates various identifiers (variables, labels, etc.) with specific memory locations in the computer memory.

syntax In a computer language, the way that word symbols, special symbols, identifiers, and operators can be combined to form legal program statements.

tag field A value in a variant record type that indicates which variant is currently in effect.

terminate To finish. A program loop terminates when the appropriate boolean condition is met. Programs are also said to terminate after the last statement has been executed and control returns to the operating system.

text editor An application program used for creating text in a form that can be saved on a storage medium, such as a floppy disk or a hard disk. This text may be a letter, a book, data, or a computer program.

textfile A file of characters, which may be divided into lines terminated by newline characters.

text processing The activity of creating, modifying, or formatting text. The text may be anything from computer data to programs to books.

top down A programming method in which the entire project is defined first in a general way in English, and then divided into separate logical processes. The programmer then works from the general to the specific, working out details and refining them until the solution is sufficiently detailed to be encoded in the intended computer language. The goal is to verify the correctness of the solution as far as possible at each successive stage. The top of the process is the general statement of the problem and the possible solution. The bottom, or end result, is the completed, verified program. See also *stepwise refinement.* Contrast with *bottom up.*

traversal The process of examining each value in a linked data structure (binary tree, linked list, etc.) in some specific order.

tree A heirarchical data structure in which each node can have zero or more subtrees, or branches. The initial entry point into the tree is called the root. Nodes without subtrees are called terminal nodes or leaves.

twelve-tone operator (TTO) Any of the standard operations performed on pitch-class sets in the twelve pc system. For any set X, the TTOs are $T_nP(X)$, $T_nI(X)$, $T_nM(X)$; and $T_nMI(X)$. In each case T_n implies transposition of the set by n semitones, $0 \leq n \leq 11$. Since the prime operator P indicates identity, the first operation is simple transposition. Sets are inverted by subtracting each element from 12. The M operator consists of multiplying each element in the set by 5, and MI consists of multiplication by 7. These operators convert minor seconds and major sevenths (interval class 1) into fourths and fifths (interval class 5), and vice versa. All other intervals either remain the same or remain in the same interval class. Identity and inversion can also be obtained by multiplication (by 1 and 11, respectively). Transposition is always applied after I, M, or MI. All operations are calculated modulo 12.

type clash An error that occurs when values used in assignment statements, expressions, or subroutine calls are incompatible, causing the program to crash.

type declaration The act of defining a user-defined data type. The data type may be an enumerated type or one of several varieties of structured types.

type declaration part The portion of a Pascal program in which user-defined data types are defined.

undefined variable A varible that has not been given a value explicitly. Although some Pascal systems initialize variables automatically, it is not good programming practice to count on this.

union operator In Pascal, the special symbol '+'. The union of two sets is the set of elements that occur in either set or both sets. Note that the same operator denotes addition when used with numbers.

UNIX A multiuser operating system developed at Bell Telephone Laboratories (AT&T) during the 1970s, and now available on many different types of computers from mainframes to personal computers.

user-defined ordinal type See *enumerated type.*

user-friendly A program, computer, or operating system that is easy to use (especially with little or no training) and tolerant of user errors.

value parameter See *parameter.*

variable A symbolic name for a storage location in the computer memory that can contain different values. Pascal is strongly typed: that is, variables can contain only one type of data, such as integers, real numbers, characters, or pointers, and attempts at implicit type conversion (for example, assigning a pointer value to an integer variable) usually result in program errors. Pascal also permits one to define variables that reference structured types, such as records.

variable declaration A statement that defines a variable by specifying the identifier that will be associated with it and the type of value that it will represent.

variable parameter See *parameter.*

variant record See *record type.*

verification The process of proving that an algorithm is correct.

visit A generic term that means to do something with the current node or value while traversing a linked data structure. Each node is visited during the traversal of a linked list. This may consist of printing the value of a field, counting the node, copying a value in the node into another list, etc.

while statement A loop construct in Pascal in which the condition that may terminate the loop is tested at the top of the loop. Thus the body of a **while** loop may not execute under certain conditions.

Index to Programs, Subprograms, and Algorithms

PART I Getting Started

General Index